THIRTEENTH EDITION

food for fifty

MARY MOLT, PH.D., R.D.

Assistant Director, Housing and Dining Services
Assistant Professor, Hospitality Management and Dietetics
Kansas State University

Prentice Hall

Boston Columbus Indianapolis New York San Francisco Upper Saddle River
Amsterdam Cape Town Dubai London Madrid Milan Munich Paris Montreal Toronto
Delhi Mexico City Sao Paulo Sydney Hong Kong Seoul Singapore Taipei Tokyo

Editor in Chief: Vernon Anthony
Acquisitions Editor: William Lawrensen
Developmental Editor: Sonya Kottcamp
Editorial Assistant: Lara Dimmick
Director of Marketing: David Gesell
Campaign Marketing Manager: Leigh Ann Sims
Curriculum Marketing Manager: Thomas Hayward
Senior Marketing Coordinator: Alicia Wozniak
Marketing Assistant: Les Roberts
Associate Managing Editor: Alexandrina Benedicto Wolf
AV Project Manager: Janet Portisch
Project Manager: Kris Roach
Senior Operations Supervisor: Pat Tonneman

Operations Specialist: Deidra Skahill
Senior Art Director: Diane Ernsberger
Manager, Rights and Permissions: Zina Arabia
Manager, Cover Visual Research and Permissions: Karen Sanatar
Text and Cover Designer: Ilze Lemesis
Color Insert Design: Wanda Espana
Cover Art: iStock
Lead Media Project Manager: Karen Bretz
Full-Service Project Management: Linda Zuk, WordCraft, LLC
Composition: S4Carlisle Publishing Services
Printer/Binder: Manufactured in the United States by RR Donnelley
Cover Printer: Coral Graphics
Text Font: New Baskerville

Credits and acknowledgments borrowed from other sources and reproduced, with permission, in this textbook appear on appropriate page within text.

Library of Congress Cataloging-in-Publication Data

Molt, Mary.
  Food for fifty / Mary Molt.—13th ed.
    p. cm.
  ISBN 0-13-613651-6 (978-0-13-613651-4) 1. Quantity cookery. 2.
Menus. I. Title.
  TX820.M57 2010
  641.5'7—dc22   2009047332

10   9   8   7

Prentice Hall
is an imprint of

www.pearsonhighered.com

ISBN-10:   0-13-613651-6
ISBN-13: 978-0-13-613651-4

To the many talented Kansas State University
Housing and Dining Services dietitians and
food service professionals that I have had
the privilege to learn from.
A special tribute to John Pence,
my boss, friend, and mentor,
whose support made this
thirteenth edition of *Food for Fifty* possible.
Thanks, John!

Contents

tables

Preface

For nearly 75 years, *Food for Fifty* has been used as a resource for students in quantity food production and food production management courses, and for people employed in foodservice management positions. The book is designed to provide foodservice professionals with quantity recipes that they can prepare, confident of quality outcomes and with information that will make their jobs easier. Since the book's origin, revisions have been made to keep abreast of the changing foodservice industry. In this thirteenth edition, many new recipes have been added that reflect current food preferences and modern eating styles, including meatless, vegan, and ethnic recipes and flavorful sauces, salsas, spice rubs, and accompaniments. This thirteenth edition of *Food for Fifty* has new and updated tables and charts, expanded guidelines for planning banquets and catered events, easier-to-use food production information, an enlarged section for healthful recipe adaptations, and expanded appendixes with menu-pricing methods and formulas for calculating yields. In addition, a longtime goal of *Food for Fifty* is to provide basic standardized recipes that can be adapted to produce foods similar to those shown in popular magazines, home-sized cookbooks, and trade publications. The basic recipes and straightforward production guides will assist production staff in making an endless variety of food products. This new edition has many features that will make recipe adaptations simple.

NEW TO THIS EDITION

The revision is intended to provide quantity recipes and food production resources that address the changing eating trends of today's customer. The new and updated recipes and updated food production information will provide students, faculty, and foodservice managers with the tools to produce a wide variety of quality food products that are on trend and popular with today's customer.

- Expanded sections on ways to make recipes more healthful and how to decrease fat, sodium, and sugar in recipes.
- Reordered text to make tables easier to locate and more usable.
- Updated food production tables include additional food items and new food items that have changed since the last edition.
- More than 100 new recipes and recipe revisions. The new recipes address eating preferences that have changed since the last edition. Many of the new recipes are no-meat (vegetarian), ethnic, or made using new and more flavorful ingredients, including sauces, marinades, rubs, and seasonings.

- Updated information for planning menus, special meals, and receptions. This new edition addresses planning responsibilities applicable for catering.
- New information explaining how recipes in *Food for Fifty* can be adapted, changed, combined, and renamed to produce upscale and trendy food products.
- New accompanying Workbook provides exercises for the students to apply the information to scale, convert, and cost.
- An Instructor's Manual that provides answers to the Workbook exercises is also available.

ORGANIZATION OF THE BOOK

Food for Fifty is divided into four major sections. Part I, "Serving Food in Quantity," offers guidelines and procedures for using *Food for Fifty* to produce contemporary menu items and for developing, constructing, and adjusting recipes. Directions for increasing recipe yields are helpful when adapting recipes given in this book to different yields and for increasing home-sized recipes for quantity production. Suggestions for reducing fat, sodium, and sugar in recipes are useful for modifying recipes. Guidelines are given for planning meals, with special consideration to different types of foodservices. Planning special foodservice events such as receptions, buffets, and banquets is discussed, and guidelines for planning are provided.

Part II, "Food Production Tables," provides references for planning and preparing food in quantity. This section provides a comprehensive table of amounts of food needed to serve 50 people and information for making food substitutions and weight and measure conversions.

Part III, "Foods and Food Production," includes a discussion of basic food products, general food science principles, and production fundamentals such as production and kitchen readiness; production scheduling; cooking guidelines, methods, and terms; cooking temperature tables; and quality food evaluation. This section has food safety guidelines that are useful for developing Hazard Analysis Critical Control Point (HACCP) plans and for ensuring food safety. Knife care and descriptions for basic knife cuts will be helpful for teaching inexperienced food production staff or students. A visual description of small equipment used in food production is included in this section.

Part IV, "Recipes," includes a wide variety of tested recipes given in yields of approximately 50 portions and many suggestions for variations of the basic recipes. Recipes are organized according to menu categories. Some recipe chapters begin with general timetables for preparing the recipes in that chapter.

At the back of the book is a list of menu-planning suggestions and garnishes (Appendix A), a list of trade and popular magazine resources (Appendix B), common pricing methods (Appendix C), and basic formulas for calculating yields and for purchasing food (Appendix D), as well as a glossary of menu and cooking terms.

DISTINCTIVE FEATURES OF THE BOOK

Food for Fifty has been recognized for nearly 75 years as a dependable resource for students and food production managers. Part II is considered by many to be an indispensable reference for food production information. The various tables are helpful for menu planning and purchasing and making food production assignments.

Dietitians, foodservice managers, and faculty members have, for many years, depended on the standardized recipes in *Food for Fifty*. Recipes are written in an easy-to-read format with standardized procedures that allow quality products to be prepared consistently. Suggested variations for many of the recipes increase the value of the recipe section. This new edition with many added ethnic and vegetarian dishes and entrée accompaniments increases *Food for Fifty*'s value as a resource for a broad variety of recipes. The nutrition information will be helpful in planning and preparing foods for clientele with different needs. Food production, service, and storage procedures will be useful for developing Hazard Analysis Critical Control Point (HACCP) plans.

Menu-planning information is given in concise terms in Part I. The discussion of planning procedures and the menu suggestion list in Appendix A are helpful to students and to foodservice managers whose responsibilities include menu planning. Many foodservices are called upon today to provide food for special events such as holiday meals, buffets, catered events, coffees, receptions, and teas. Part I offers suggestions for menus, organization, and service of these functions.

A REFERENCE BOOK AND TEACHING TEXT

Food for Fifty is written for many users. Students in quantity food production and foodservice management use the text as a resource for learning the standards, skills, and techniques inherent in quality food production. Instructors find beneficial the basic menu-planning and food production features that equip them with the tools necessary for designing teaching modules and supervising laboratories. The reliability of the recipes, tables, and charts in the book allows instructors to make assignments with confidence of a quality outcome. Additionally, the text provides a resource for instructing students on how to plan and serve special foodservice functions. Foodservice administrators, managers, and supervisors are also users of the text. *Food for Fifty* is a comprehensive resource for quantity recipes and technical food production information. The book serves as a foundation for the food production system.

ACKNOWLEDGMENTS

Kansas State University's residence hall dining program "make-it-from-scratch" culture and high quality standards have helped shape *Food for Fifty* for nearly 75 years. I would like to express sincere appreciation for the support and encouragement of John Pence, associate director of Housing and Dining Services, for continuing to value this endeavor. Special acknowledgment is given to John and his management staff for their support, advice, and creative ideas. I could not have completed this thirteenth edition of *Food for Fifty* without their help. Appreciation is extended also to the many colleagues, family, and friends who have, through the course of their association with the author, made this revision of *Food for Fifty* possible.

I would also like to thank the reviewers. They are: Carolyn Bednar, Texas Woman's College; Tracey Brigman, University of Georgia; Lois Cockerham, Southeast Community College; Gary Lee Frantz, South Dakota State University; Sandra M. Gross, West Chester University of Pennsylvania; Jim R. Haynes, Eastern Kentucky University; Robert M. Huff, Trident Technical College; William W. Leeder, Iowa Western Community College; Colette Leistner, Nicholls State University; Diana Manchester, Ohio University; Allen Powell, University of Arkansas at Fayettville; Richard F. Patterson, Western Kentucky University; Eljeana Quebedeaux, MS LDN RD, McNeese State University; Janet Shaffer, CWPC, Lake Washington Technical College; and Jane Francis Tilman, University of Texas at Austin.

About the Author

MARY MOLT, PH.D., R.D., L.D., is assistant director of Housing and Dining Services and assistant professor of Hospitality Management and Dietetics (HMD) at Kansas State University. She holds a bachelor's degree from the University of Nebraska—Kearney, a master's degree from Oklahoma State University, and a Ph.D. from Kansas State University. Dr. Molt has 35 years of professional experience at Kansas State University, with a joint appointment in academe and foodservice administration. Current responsibilities include team teaching food production management, assisting with supervised practice experiences for senior students in dietetics, and directing management activities for three residence hall dining centers serving more than 8,000 meals per day. Dr. Molt is active in the American Dietetic Association, the Kansas Dietetic Association, and the National Association of College and University Food Services (NACUFS). Twice she was recognized with the NACUFS Richard Lichtenfelt Award for outstanding service to the association. In 1995, Dr. Molt received the Theodore W. Minah Award, the highest honor given by NACUFS, for exceptional contribution to the foodservice industry. In 2008 a student scholarship in the NACUFS Midwest region was named the Mary Molt Student Excellence Award. The Award for Excellence in the Practice of Management was given to Dr. Molt in 1997 by the American Dietetic Association. She serves on several University committees, advises students in Kappa Omicron Nu, and holds membership in Kappa Omicron Nu, Phi Upsilon Omicron, and Phi Kappa Phi honor societies.

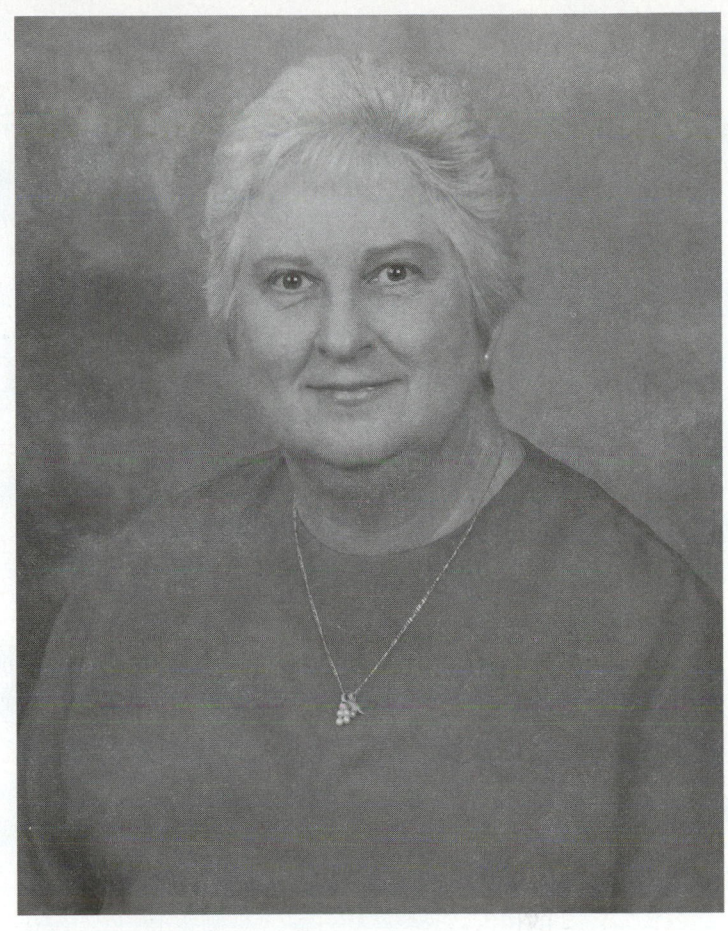

part I

Serving Food in Quantity

1

Introduction to the Foodservice Industry

The National Restaurant Association (NRA) defines the restaurant industry as that which encompasses all meals and snacks prepared away from home, including all take-out meals and beverages. The NRA reports that the industry encompasses 945,000 locations, employs more than 13 million people, and generates more than $560 billion in sales each year. This complex multibillion-dollar industry has a large impact on our nation's economy and on job opportunities for its citizens. The foodservice industry is an essential part of people's lives; on a typical day, 130 million people eat away from home. The NRA reports that 68 percent of adults say their favorite restaurant foods provide flavor and taste sensations that cannot easily be duplicated in their home kitchens. The increased demand for convenience, value, and socializing also makes eating away from home an attractive option. Creative menus, quality food, successful marketing strategies, and exceptional restaurant business practices help sustain the foodservice industry during times of economic downturn and reduced disposable incomes and provide the foundation for exceptional industry growth during more prosperous times. Regardless of the industry segment, their challenges are similar. Table 1.1 identifies some of the challenges foodservices are facing and some changes foodservices are making to address those challenges.

FOODSERVICE SEGMENTS

The foodservice industry can be categorized into a *commercial segment* and a *noncommercial* or *on-site segment*. The commercial segment includes establishments that are open to the public and operate for the explicit purpose of making a profit. Contract or managed service providers are generally included in the commercial segment even though they provide services to some of the same entities as self-operated, noncommercial providers. The difference is that they operate for profit. Noncommercial or on-site foodservices include business and industry, educational, governmental, and noncommercial organizations. Many on-site foodservices may be expected to make a profit, but it is not the primary goal for their activity. Rarely are noncommercial or on-site foodservice providers subsidized; facility use fees are often levied, and in most cases

funds must be generated for facility enhancements and equipment repair and replacement. These entities serve food principally to support the mission of the larger organization. For example, a university dining program may generate a profit, but its reason for operating is to provide foodservices to students, faculty, staff, and other college employees and to provide college catering services. Table 1.2 identifies categories of foodservice operations in both the commercial and noncommercial/on-site sectors of the foodservice industry.

HOW TO USE *FOOD FOR FIFTY*

Food for Fifty has many applications as a basic resource for students studying for professional careers in the foodservice industry and for foodservice operators needing a reliable food production resource. The book's value as a text for these basic functions is obvious. In this section many ways to use *Food for Fifty* will be identified.

A Basic Recipe Resource

- *Food for Fifty* recipes are written to provide step-by-step guidelines for producing standard-quality products. By adapting *Food for Fifty* recipes, combining two or more recipes, or changing plating presentations or garnishes, it is possible to produce dishes similar to the creative and attractive presentations seen in trade and popular magazines and cookbooks (Appendix C). Table 1.3 provides suggestions for using *Food for Fifty* recipes as the foundation for recipe development and menu planning activities. Adapting reliable quantity recipes will simplify recipe development and standardization efforts. Changes to *Food for Fifty* recipes in ways that may affect quality should be tested carefully before being used for quantity food production.
- There are few new foods, but there are unlimited ways to prepare and present foods in new and interesting ways. Dishes are modernized by changing flavor profiles, presentation styles, and cooking techniques, and by adding sauces, garnishes, and accompaniments. The wide variety of recipes in *Food for Fifty* provides a recipe development resource for changing menus to reflect the latest food trends.

TABLE 1.1 Foodservice industry challenges and changes being made in response to the challenges

Challenges

- The economy
- Less disposable income
- Slowdown in consumer spending
- Labor availability, hiring and retaining employees
- Availability of skilled employees
- Energy cost increases
- Fluctuations in food costs
- Increasing food costs
- Concerns regarding nutrition and food safety

- Competition
- Attracting new customers
- Increasing customer satisfaction
- Building repeat business
- Increasing sales volume
- Competition with grocery stores
- Obtaining credit or financing
- Equipment replacement/upgrade needs
- Renovation needs

Foodservice Changes Being Made in Response to Challenges

NUTRITION
- Healthy options for children's meals
- Healthy food choices
- Options for clientele with food allergies and intolerances
- Nutrition education materials for clientele

SERVICES
- Convenient meals-to-go options, meal replacement options
- Expanded children's menu and activities for children
- Customer participation in meal preparation
- Expanded technology options for customers

VALUE
- Enhanced focus on value, value pricing
- More food choices
- More dining venues
- More meal plan options
- More beverage choices (alcohol and nonalcohol)

FOOD
- More authentic ethnic options
- More highly flavored and creatively seasoned foods

DISCOUNTING
- Discounts for loyal customers
- Discounts for dining during slow times
- Discounts for bundled meals

PORTION SIZING
- Smaller portions for less cost

PROMOTIONS
- Food and drink specials, happy hours
- "Kids eat free" offers

SUSTAINABILITY/SOCIAL
- Locally sourced foods
- Organic foods
- Sustainable practices/green certified
- LEED certification for new and renovated spaces[a]

ATTENTION TO REVENUE AND EXPENSES
- Increasing menu prices
- Increasing energy efficiency
- Purchasing energy-saving equipment and energy control systems
- Evaluating purchasing practices and negotiating with suppliers
- Purchasing on the secondary market[b]
- Seeking special purchase offers
- Participating in buyer group programs
- Purchasing products with rebates
- Adding or expanding home and office delivery programs
- Expanding catering

[a]Leadership in Energy and Environmental Design (LEED) certification is a nationally accepted benchmark for the design, construction, and operation of high-performance green buildings.
[b]Foods available on the secondary market may be from overproduction of items from major manufacturers; oversupply of products produced for high-volume users such as chain restaurants; or availability of products not meeting exact specifications, such as French fry length, breading color, or flavor profiles. Many high-quality products can be purchased at a significant savings.
Table compiled using data from the *NRA 2009 Restaurant Industry Forecast* and other sources.

- Changing the name of a *Food for Fifty* recipe to reflect ingredient adaptations can update a recipe. For example, a simple grilled chicken breast can be renamed Jamaican Jerk Chicken when a Jamaican jerk spice rub, p. 729, is used to season the chicken in the Grilled Chicken Breast recipe, p. 480. A recipe for Gaucho Beef Steak with Chimichurri Sauce can be developed from two *Food for Fifty* recipes: Grilled Tampico Steak (cooking procedures only, without the Tampico seasonings), p. 435, and Chimichurri Sauce, p. 710.

Other examples describing similar adaptations of *Food for Fifty* recipes that reflect the flavor profiles and names of contemporary recipes are shown in Table 1.3.

The first step in adapting a *Food for Fifty* recipe to resemble a recipe from another source is to identify a recipe in *Food for Fifty* that is similar. Adaptations are easier, and less testing is needed, when the recipes are comparable in ingredients, preparation instructions, and cooking procedures. The next

TABLE 1.2 Commercial and noncommercial/on-site foodservice segments

Commercial Segment	Noncommercial/On-Site Segment[a]
EATING PLACES • Full-service restaurants (casual and fine dining) • Limited-service restaurants, limited menu (sometimes referred to as quick service or fast food) • Bars and taverns with food • Cafeterias, buffets • Snack and nonalcoholic beverage bars • Social caterers **CONTRACTED/MANAGED SERVICES**[a] • Industrial feeding, offices, hospitals, care facilities, colleges and universities, correctional facilities, in-transit services (airlines), recreation centers, etc. **LODGING** • Hotel restaurants and catering **RETAIL VENUES** • In-store restaurants, including delis and salad bars • Convenience stores **RECREATION AND SPORTS** • Theaters, bowling alleys, sports centers **MOBILE CATERERS** **VENDING**	• Hospitals • Elementary and secondary schools • Colleges and universities • Senior care: assisted living, congregate care, independent living, intermediate care, skilled nursing care • Other care facilities: homes for the mentally and physically disabled • Child care centers • Clubs, sporting and recreational camps • Community centers, senior centers, homeless shelters • Correctional facilities • Employee restaurant services • Military (troop feeding)[b] • Transportation

[a]Foodservices are categorized as commercial when they are managed by an outside contractor and categorized as noncommercial or on-site when self-operated. *Self-operated* means the foodservice is managed by an employee of the organization in which the foodservice is located. The foodservice administrator in a self-operated facility reports to someone within the organization. *Contracted or managed services* means a company has contracted with an organization to run their foodservice operation.
[b]The NRA categorizes military restaurant services in the United States (officers' and NCO clubs, military exchanges) as a third segment different from either commercial or noncommercial/on-site foodservices.
Table compiled using data from the *NRA 2009 Restaurant Industry Forecast* and other sources.

step is to rewrite the *Food for Fifty* recipe to incorporate the changes that will make the recipes more similar. For example, the rewritten recipe may include such changes to the *Food for Fifty* recipe as changing the flavor profile by using a different seasoning, adding or changing a sauce, altering a procedure, or changing ingredients. It is important to make only adaptations that are feasible and within the scope of the *Food for Fifty* recipe. Changes should not be made to use equipment that is not available, procedures that are unrealistic for the foodservice facility, or ingredients that are unavailable. Extensive changes to the *Food for Fifty* recipe will require more testing than when only simple changes are made.

A Resource for Standardizing Recipes

• Recipes should be carefully tested to ensure that a consistent product is produced each time the recipe is made in a specific food production facility. The term *standardized recipe* is often used to describe the recipes that produce these consistent results. *Food for Fifty* recipes and guidelines for recipe development, construction, and adjustment (p. 8) will be useful for formatting home-sized and other recipes and for beginning the recipe standardization process. Having examples of recipes formatted in a consistent manner will guide recipe developers and help them establish recipe formatting and content standards for their facilities' recipe files.

• The tables and charts in Chapter 4 will be useful when assigning weights to measures or measures to weights (Table 4.8) and for making other recipe calculations and ingredient substitutions. Edible portion/as purchased (EP/AP) conversion data for meats and produce and accurate count/weight information will be useful when standardizing recipes. For example, home-sized recipes usually specify count or volume measure for fresh produce such as diced carrots. Carrots by weight is a more accurate measure than volume or count and should be specified in a standardized recipe. Table 4.2 provides information on weight per cup of diced carrots.

TABLE 1.3 Examples of adaptations to *Food for Fifty* recipes

Contemporary Name	Adaptation Suggestions[a]
EGGS AND CHEESE	
Smoked Salmon and Goat Cheese Crepes	[Base recipe p. 255] Substitute smoked salmon and goat cheese for the chicken mixture.
California Omelet with Tomatillo Salsa	[Base recipes p. 386] Use fresh avocados and shredded Monterey Jack cheese in the filling. Ladle Tomatillo Sauce [p. 709] on the omelet.
FISH	
Grilled Salmon with Mustard Caper Butter	[Base recipe p. 404] Serve grilled salmon with 1 tsp Mustard-Caper Butter [p. 720] on top.
Grilled Salmon with Dill Mashed Potatoes	[Base recipes pp. 404, 798] Serve grilled salmon on top of mashed potatoes that have had fresh dill added to them. Garnish with fresh dill and lemon wedge. For potatoes with added tang, substitute buttermilk or sour cream for part of the milk.
MEATS	
Roast Pork Loin with Moroccan Charmoula Marinade	[Base recipe p. 462] Marinate Roast Pork Loin in Moroccan Charmoula Marinade [p. 711] before roasting.
Lamb Chops with Black Bean Pico de Gallo	[Base recipe p. 461] Serve lamb chops on top of Black Bean Pico de Gallo [p. 706].
Chicken Fajita Nachos	[Base recipe p. 203] Serve Nachos topped with Chicken Fajita meat [p. 673], fresh diced tomatoes, fresh sliced jalapeño peppers, and guacamole [p. 202].
Southwestern Beef Tenderloin with Chipotle Mashed Potatoes	[Timetable for direct grilling steak p. 427] Season beef with Southwest Steak Rub [p. 730]. Served cooked tenderloin leaned against a mound of Chipotle Sweet Potatoes [p. 808]. Garnish with one or two baked tomato halves [p. 815].
SALADS	
Frisée and Winter Pear Salad with Gorgonzola and Toasted Walnuts	[Base recipe p. 595] Substitute frisée for greens and thinly sliced winter pears for the fruit. Sprinkle with crumbled Gorgonzola and toasted walnuts [p. 609].
SANDWICHES	
Rustic Turkey Quesadillas	[Base recipe p. 672] Caramelize onions (procedure, p. 392) and use them in place of the corn-onion mixture. Substitute smoked Gouda for the cojack cheese and add shredded turkey to the quesadillas before grilling.
Tuscan Eggplant on Focaccia	[Base recipe p. 667] Placed grilled eggplant [p. 790] on Focaccia [p. 268] and top with Tomato, Olive, and Fennel Ragout [p. 707] or Tomato Pesto [p. 706].
Thinly Sliced Prime Rib of Beef on Sourdough with Blue Cheese Aioli	[Base recipe p. 430] Thinly slice prime rib and serve on Sourdough spread with Blue Cheese Mayo [p. 232].
VEGETABLES/OTHER	
Ginger-Roasted Parsnips	[Base recipe p. 823] Mix 1 Tbsp fresh minced ginger per pound of quartered parsnips before roasting.
Cauliflower Persillade	[Base recipe p. 786] Season cauliflower with Persillade [p. 712].
Orange-Scented Orzo	[Base recipe p. 509] Substitute grated orange zest and orange juice for the lemon zest and juice.
Ginger Barley and Edamame	[Base recipe p. 567] Substitute 4 lb steamed edamame for the green peas. Sauté 4 oz minced ginger root and 12 oz shiitake mushrooms along with the carrots. Reduce the salt and stir in soy sauce or another Asian condiment of choice.

[a]Adaptations are suggestions for how *Food for Fifty* recipes can be used to develop new recipes and menu items. The adaptations are not intended to be stand-alone recipes and may require testing and standardization.

A Resource for Menu Planning

- Menu planning implies that recipes are available to produce the food being planned. *Food for Fifty* is a valuable resource for the menu planner because of its comprehensive cache of recipes in all menu categories. The lists of recipes in the index and in Appendix A are also helpful to the menu planner because they provide lists of food options that are linked to a recipe. For example, a menu planner may go to Appendix A (p. 824) and choose from a list of options a specific soup to add to the menu.

- The recipes in *Food for Fifty* will help the menu writer incorporate the contemporary menu ideas shown in trade publications, popular magazines, and trendy cookbooks. See Table 1.3 on this page, for examples. *Food for Fifty* recipes can be adapted to easily produce new menu items (see p. 837, a basic recipe resource for new recipe development).

- Knowing the nutritional content of food items is increasingly important in menu planning. The recipes in *Food for Fifty* provide nutrition information helpful for writing menus that meet the nutritional requirements of the clientele whom they are serving. The guidelines for making healthful recipe changes will be useful for food production staff. For example, customers regularly ask for low-fat preparation methods to be used. Information on p. 13 identifies low-fat cooking methods and ways to decrease fat in entrées.

A Resource for Purchasing and Accurate Forecasting, Recipe Costing, and Pricing

- Calculating accurately the amount of food needed to produce recipes is critical to accurate costing, food quality, and customer satisfaction. *Food for Fifty* recipes and supporting tables in Chapter 4 provide accurate information for yields and portion sizes that are necessary for determining the amount of food to purchase.

- Documenting quality expectations and cost comparisons for convenience and value-added foods before purchasing may be necessary. Similar products made using *Food for Fifty* recipes can help identify the desired sensory characteristics useful for establishing purchasing specifications and quality standards for convenience and value-added foods. For example, *Food for Fifty*'s blueberry muffin recipe may be produced and analyzed before writing a specification for or an evaluation of frozen muffin batters. The amount of blueberries, the muffin size, muffin flavor, and cost are some comparison points.

- *Food for Fifty* recipe yields and portion sizes are accurately coordinated. Production staff can make recipes with confidence that recipes will yield correctly. Forecasting is easier when recipe yields are certain. Financial success is linked to knowing the menu item cost and being able to establish a correct selling price. *Food for Fifty* recipes provide the accuracy needed for these functions.

- The *Food for Fifty* recipes yield approximately 50 servings but can be adjusted easily for other yields by using the recipe extension procedures in Chapter 2.

A Resource for Planning Food Production and Foodservice Events

- Producing food in quantity requires an understanding of how food goes from its raw state to a finished product. The recipes in *Food for Fifty* are written to show clearly the production steps and can be a resource for food production managers to establish mise en place activities; write production worksheets; and assign tasks related to product storage, thawing time, prepreparation, preparation, assembly, and product holding.

- *Food for Fifty* can be used to plan special functions as receptions, brunches, and buffet meals. Chapter 3 includes information on menu planning, table and space arrangement, food presentation, and service. This information, along with the recipes, will be helpful when planning events for large and small numbers of diners.

A Resource for Education and Instruction on Quantity Food Production

- Recipes are at the center of all food production activities, and a well-written recipe that is organized correctly and written clearly can be useful for learning about food production principles. Well-written recipes help identify mise en place tasks (p. 143), provide information for accurate production scheduling (p. 144), identify efficient work procedures, and showcase correct cooking methods. They also help communicate the techniques necessary for producing a quality product.

- Efficient labor procedures were considered in writing *Food for Fifty* recipes. Recipes may serve as a model for making products using the minimum amount of labor. *Food for Fifty* can be used also for learning about knife skills, food safety procedures, and cooking methods appropriate for specific foods.

- Producing quality food requires a reference or goal for what the end-product attributes should be. *Food for Fifty* has information for writing quality standards and for evaluating food products. Because *Food for Fifty* recipes are written to consistently produce a quality product, they are useful for teaching food preparers what is required to achieve quality results. For example, *Food for Fifty* recipes identify many procedures that help ensure quality, such as preparation steps and procedures, cooking methods, and endpoint cooking temperatures.

- *Food for Fifty* recipes are written to be useful for planning food production, making staffing assignments, and organizing food production processes. Instructions for developing cooking methods, learning terminology, troubleshooting quality problems, and evaluating food quality can be developed using information in *Food for Fifty*.

RECIPE INFORMATION FOR RECIPES IN *FOOD FOR FIFTY*

Yield

The recipes in this book produce servings for 50 people unless otherwise stated. Factors that may affect yield include portioning, ingredient weighing error, mistakes in calculating increased or decreased quantities, abnormal handling loss, and variation in the edible portion (EP) and as purchased (AP) factors for food products such as fresh produce and meats.

A standard 12×20-inch counter pan has been indicated for many recipes. For baked desserts and some bread products, either a 12×18-inch or 18×26-inch pan is specified, as these are standard bakeware sizes. Weight of product per pan may need to be changed if pans other than those specified in the recipe are used. Care should be taken to scale products so that portion weight will be accurate and recipe yield remains correct. Tables 7.16 and 7.17 give capacities of baking and counter pans.

The number of servings per pan will depend on the portion size desired. Many standard-sized baking or counter pans will yield 24–32 servings per pan; when these size pans are indicated, the recipes generally are calculated for 48 or 64 servings. Yield adjustments may be made by cutting the servings into sizes that will yield the desired number of portions. Portion size is included in each recipe, and the yield is given in number of portions, volume produced, and/or number of pans. Some foodservices may wish to adjust the yield based on the clientele to be served.

Ingredients

In most cases, the type of ingredient used in testing the recipes has been specified—for example, granulated, brown, or powdered sugar and all-purpose or cake flour. Hydrogenated shortening was used in cake and pastry recipes; margarine or butter was used in cookies, some quick breads, and most sauce recipes. Solid fats such as margarine, butter, and hydrogenated fats were used interchangeably in recipes that specify "shortening." Canola, corn, soybean, or cottonseed oil was used in recipes that specify salad or vegetable oil. Sodium aluminum sulfate–type baking powder (double acting) and active dry yeast were used for leavening.

Fresh eggs, large size, weighing approximately 2 oz unshelled (¾ oz shelled) were used in the preparation of the recipes. Eggs are specified by both number and weight. In many foodservices, frozen eggs are used, in which case the eggs are weighed or measured. If the eggs are to be measured, the number and weight may easily be converted to volume by referring to Table 4.2.

Nonfat dry milk is indicated in some recipes, but in those specifying fluid milk, dry milk may be substituted. Table 4.5 gives a formula for conversion. In most cases, it is not necessary to rehydrate the dry milk because it is mixed with other dry ingredients, and water is added in place of the fluid milk. The amount of fat in the recipe may need to be increased slightly.

Nutritional values are identified for most *Food for Fifty* recipes. Unless stated otherwise, values are for the portion listed at the top of each recipe. Nutrient values for *Food for Fifty* recipes are approximate and are intended to be used as general guidelines. Values identified for recipes may vary from actual values if substitute ingredients are used. Differences may occur also if ingredient amounts are adjusted, portion sizes are different from those specified in the recipe, or production procedures are changed.

Weights and Measures

Quantities of dry ingredients weighing more than 1 oz are given by weight in ounces (oz) and pounds (lb). Weights are for foods as purchased (AP) unless otherwise stated. Liquid ingredients are indicated by measure: teaspoons (tsp), tablespoons (Tbsp), cups (cups), quarts (qt), and gallons (gal).

Accurate weighing and measuring of ingredients are essential for a satisfactory product. Weighing is more accurate than measuring and is recommended whenever possible, but reliable scales are essential. A table-model scale with a 15- to 20-lb capacity and ¼- to ½-ounce graduations (or an electronic digital readout scale with a 15- to 20-lb capacity) is suitable for weighing ingredients for 50 portions.

Standard measuring equipment should be used to ensure accuracy, and measurements should be level. Use the largest appropriate measure to reduce the possibility of error and to save time. For example, use a 1-gal measure once instead of a 1-qt measure four times. Flour is the exception: Use measures no larger than 1 qt for flour.

Cooking Time and Temperature

The cooking time given in each recipe is based on the size of pan and the amount of food in the pan. If a smaller or larger pan is used, an adjustment in cooking time may be necessary. The number of pans placed in the oven at one time also may affect the length of baking time; the larger the number of pans or the colder a product, the longer the cooking time. In convection ovens, the temperature as specified for a conventional oven should be reduced by 25–50°F and the total bake/roast time by 10 to 15 percent.

Critical Control Points

Monitoring cooking time and food temperature are important steps in the food production process because of their relationship to food contamination and food-borne illness. Time and temperatures are designated as critical control points (CCPs) in all Hazard Analysis Critical Control Point (HACCP) plans. Recipes in this book provide production, service, and storage procedures that can prevent or reduce food safety hazards of potentially hazardous foods. Standards for reducing food safety hazards may be found in Tables 7.1 and 7.9 (pp. 163, 168). Safe temperatures for cooked foods are shown in Table 7.6 (p. 165). Cooling procedures for hot foods are shown in Table 7.8 (p. 167). Examples of potentially hazardous foods can be found in Table 7.12 (p. 169). Recipes that contain potentially hazardous foods are identified in the recipe notes.

Abbreviations Used in Recipes

AP	as purchased
EP	edible portion
°F	degrees Fahrenheit
fl oz	fluid ounce
gal	gallon
g	gram
lb	pound
mg	milligram
oz	ounce
psi	pounds per square inch
pt	pint
qt	quart
tsp	teaspoon
Tbsp	tablespoon

Recipe Development, Construction, and Adjustment

RECIPE DEVELOPMENT AND CONSTRUCTION

Recipe files are a valuable resource for food production staff when general principles of recipe development and construction are used. Following are suggestions for writing quantity recipes.

A standard recipe format includes a **recipe title** that is simple and factual, describes the food, and indicates the main ingredients and general method of preparation. Products with names that are generally understood, such as chili, do not need additional descriptors. Recipe titles should provide the information necessary to locate a particular recipe in the file. **Indexing** recipes so they can be quickly retrieved is useful.

Names of **ingredients** should be consistent and listed in the order in which they are used in preparation. List first the ingredients that require pre-preparation for a later step so they will be ready when needed. Using a descriptive word before the ingredient tells what kind and form of food is purchased, or the cooking required before the food is used in the recipe; for example, *diced tomatoes* or *cooked chicken*. The descriptive words used after the ingredient indicate what preparation is necessary to make the food different from the form as purchased or pre-prepared; for example, *cooked chicken, diced*, or *diced tomatoes, drained*. For additional clarification, ingredients showing a weight gain or loss during preparation are often marked AP (as purchased) or EP (edible portion). For example, if a chili recipe specifies ground beef, 10 lb (AP), it will improve clarity to also specify the EP weight, 6 lb 8 oz (EP). The AP-to-EP conversion is variable because of product differences such as the amount of fat in the ground beef. Variance may also be caused by the different procedures followed when preparing products, such as the amount of waste in paring vegetables and fruits or the length of time a product is cooked (such as roast beef).

List **weights** when possible. **Measures** should be given in terms of standard measuring utensils such as cups, quarts, and gallons.

Portion size is the amount served to each customer, and **yield** is the total batch weight or number of servings the recipe will make. The portion size may be described in count, measure, or weight. Identifying serving utensils that are correctly sized for the portion size will aid in making yield predictions accurate. Overyielding or underyielding can often be explained by comparing the size of portion served with the portion size specified in the recipe.

Procedures are written in sequential order. Directions should be simple, easy to understand, and placed with the ingredients involved in the production step. The side-by-side format for ingredients and procedures as used in this book is easy for production staff to follow. Some recipe software packages are designed so the procedures follow the recipe ingredients at the bottom of the recipe. When possible, each production step should begin with an action verb such as **blend**, **add**, **mix**, or **stir**. Keep directions short. Descriptive terms should be used in the procedure steps only when needed for clarity. It is helpful if basic procedures and terminology are uniform for all recipes using similar products or similar production steps. For example, the procedures for making sweet roll dough and loaf bread dough are similar, so the procedures should be written in a similar way.

Timing information for such procedures as mixing, cooking, and marinating is important. Including **scaling** or **panning instructions** as a procedure step will improve recipe yield accuracy.

Food safety information (HACCP standards) such as end-point cooking temperatures, cold and hot holding temperatures, and safe handling procedures are important to include on each recipe. Highlighting recipe procedures that are critical control points (CCPs) reinforces food safety practices.

Writing **quality standards** on the recipe gives production staff a basis for evaluating the finished product. Quality standards are especially helpful to less experienced production staff and when recipes are either new or made infrequently. See p. 152 for examples of quality standards for selected products. For several recipes in this book, quality standards follow the recipe.

Equipment should be grouped in a way that simplifies gathering for production use. Identify oven temperatures for baked products.

RECIPE ADJUSTMENT

Recipes often need to be adjusted to meet the requirements of an individual foodservice. For example, the number of portions may need to be increased from 50 to the exact number to be served, or an adjustment in portion size may better reflect the policy of the dining facility or the requirements of the clientele. Portions for recipes in this book are average sized.

Enlarging home-sized recipes may require converting household measurements to weights and adjusting certain ingredient proportions as the recipes are expanded. These procedures, as well as directions for converting to metric weights and measures, are explained in the pages that follow.

Converting from U.S. Measurement to Metric

Two approaches are possible for converting recipes from U.S. to metric measures: soft conversion and hard conversion. **Soft conversion** translates weights and measures into their exact metric equivalents. An ounce would become 28.3 g; a quart would be 0.95 L. This method produces numbers that may be awkward to work with, and equipment may not be available to measure ingredients to the degree of accuracy required.

Hard conversion changes weights and measures to round metric sizes. For example, a 1-oz portion would convert to either 25 or 30 g, but not to 28.3 g; 1 qt would convert to 1 L. This method may be satisfactory for recipes that are not sensitive to formula adjustments, such as soups and beverages, but may not be suitable for cakes, breads, and other products in which accurate ingredient ratios are critical. Testing recipes to evaluate acceptability is recommended when using the hard conversion method. (Table 4.12 shows metric conversions.)

Converting from Weight to Measure

Quantities of most dry ingredients in recipes in this book are given by weight in ounces and pounds. If accurate scales are not available, however, or if scales do not have graduations for weighing small amounts, then the weights of ingredients may need to be converted to measures. A number of tables will be helpful:

- **Table 4.2**—Food Weights and Approximate Equivalents in Measure (p. 71)
- **Table 4.7**—Ounces and Decimal Equivalents of a Pound and Grams (Rounded) (p. 91)
- **Table 4.8**—Basic Equivalents in Measures and Weights (p. 91)
- **Table 4.9**—Guide for Rounding Off Weights and Measures (p. 92)
- **Table 4.10**—Weight (1–16 oz) and Approximate Measure Equivalents for Commonly Used Foods (p. 92)

The following example illustrates the procedure for converting ingredients in Baking Powder Biscuits (p. 231) from weight to measure.

- Change 5 lb flour to measure by multiplying by 4 cups. Turn to Table 4.2 (p. 71).
- The resulting 20 cups would be equivalent to 5 qt. See Table 4.8 (p. 91). For ingredients other than flour, a gallon measure

should be used. (Flour will pack down and weigh heavy when a large measure is used.)

- By referring to Table 4.10 (p. 92), you can quickly convert the 5 oz baking powder and 1 lb 4 oz shortening by finding the amount in the appropriate column or adding the columns together. The same information is included in the longer table (Table 4.2, p. 71), but for conversion of small amounts of commonly used foods, Table 4.10 is useful.

Increasing and Decreasing Recipe Yields

It may be necessary to change recipe yields in this book to meet the needs of individual situations. Recipes may need to be adjusted to produce batch sizes compatible with preparation equipment, such as mixers, ovens, and steam-jacketed kettles or consistent with pan sizes available. The availability of production staff may also necessitate changing recipe yields. See Tables 7.16, 7.17, and 7.20 (pp. 184, 185, and 186) for recommended equipment sizes and pan size capacities. Recipes may also need adjustment as portion sizes are increased or decreased or as purchase units for ingredients change. Three methods commonly used to adjust recipe yields are the **factor method**, the **percentage method**, and **direct-reading tables**.

Factor Method.   In the factor method, a conversion factor is determined and multiplied by each ingredient in the recipe. This process is explained in the following steps and in the Factor Method Table example.

Step 1a   When portion size remains the same.

Divide the desired yield by the known yield of the recipe being adjusted to determine the conversion factor. For example, to increase a 50-portion recipe to 125 portions, divide 125 by 50 for a factor of 2.5.

desired yield (125) ÷ known yield (50) =

conversion factor (2.5)

Step 1b   When portion size changes.

Recipe portion sizes may need to be changed for plate coverage reasons, because of the clientele being served, or to comply with the foodservice facility's objectives. To determine a conversion factor for a recipe that requires a different portion size from the original recipe, one must determine the yield of the original and the new recipe. Determine the yield of the existing recipe by multiplying the number of portions by the portion size. Determine the yield desired in the new recipe by multiplying the number of portions desired by the new portion size. To increase a 50-portion recipe with 3-oz portions to 125 portions each with 4 oz:

original recipe yield

(50 × 3-oz portion) = 150 oz

new recipe desired yield

(125 × 4-oz portions) = 500 oz

Determine the conversion factor by dividing the desired yield by the known yield of the recipe being adjusted.

$$\text{desired yield (500 oz)} \div \text{known yield}$$
$$\text{(150 oz)} = \text{conversion factor (3.3)}$$

Step 2 Whenever possible, convert ingredients to weight. Making this conversion will provide a number (weight) that is generally easier to use than volume measurement amounts that are not measurable using conventional volume measurement equipment (for example: $2\frac{1}{5}$ cups, $2\frac{1}{3}$ teaspoons). Any unit can be used, however, as long as the same unit is used in both the new and the old recipes. Some ingredients may be too small to convert to weight and should be left in measure.

Step 3 Multiply the amount of each ingredient in the original recipe by the factor. To work with decimal parts of a pound instead of ounces for this multiplication, Table 4.7 (p. 91) will be helpful.

Step 4 Add together the weights of all ingredients in the original recipe and multiply by the factor. Multiply the pounds and ounces separately.

Step 5 Add together the new weights of all ingredients for the adjusted recipe. If the answers in steps 4 and 5 are not the same, an error exists and the calculations should be checked. (A slight difference may exist because of rounding the figures.)

Step 6 Change weights of any ingredients that can be more easily measured than weighed.

Step 7 Check all amounts and use Table 4.9 (p. 92) for rounding off unnecessary fractions to simplify weights or measures as far as accuracy permits.

The Factor Method Table illustrates the procedure for adjusting Baking Powder Biscuits from 100 biscuits to 500, using the factor method of adjustment.

Percentage Method. The percentage method of recipe adjustment often is desirable, especially for large-volume production where batch sizes may vary greatly. For most large-volume foodservices, a computer software package with a recipe adjustment module has eliminated the need to hand-calculate recipe yields. Some computer systems use the percentage system for their method of adjustment.

The percentage method of adjustment requires that ingredient percentages be established only once; they remain the same for all future adjustments. Recipe increases and decreases are made by multiplying the percentage of each ingredient by the total weight desired. Checking ingredients for proper recipe balance is possible, because the percentage of each ingredient is available. The percentage method of adjustment is explained in the following steps:

Step 1 Convert all ingredients from measure or pounds and ounces to pounds and tenths of a pound (see Tables 4.2 and 4.7). Make desired equivalent ingredient substitutions such as frozen whole eggs for fresh eggs, or nonfat dry milk and water for liquid milk. Use edible portion (EP) weights when a difference exists between EP and as purchased (AP) weights (see Table 4.1). Individual meat items and other meats in entrée recipes that do not require the meat to be cooked before combining with other ingredients are calculated on AP weight. Examples are pork chops, meat loaf, and Salisbury steak.

Step 2 Total the weight of ingredients in the recipe, using EP weight where applicable.

Step 3 Calculate the percentage of each ingredient in relation to the total weight, using the following formula:

$$\frac{\text{individual ingredient weight}}{\text{total weight}} = \text{percentage of each ingredient}$$

The sum of the percentages must equal 100.

Step 4 Check the ratio of ingredients. Standards have been established for ingredient proportions of many items. The ingredients should be in proper balance before going further.

Step 5 Establish the weight needed to give the desired number of servings. The weight will be determined by portion size multiplied by the desired number of servings to be prepared. This weight may need to be adjusted because of pan sizes or equipment capacity (see Tables 7.16, 7.17, and 7.20).

Step 6 Handling loss must be added to the weight needed. It may vary from 1 to 10 percent, depending on the product. Similar items produce predictable losses, and with some experimentation these losses can be assigned accurately. The formula for incorporating handling loss is as follows:

$$\text{total weight needed} = \frac{\text{desired yield}}{100 \text{ percent} - \text{assigned handling loss percent}}$$

For example, cake has a handling loss of approximately 2 percent, and 72 lb of batter is needed to make nine $18 \times 26 \times 2$-inch pans. To determine the total amount of batter to be made, divide 72 lb by 98 percent (100 percent less 2 percent handling loss). Using this formula, as demonstrated in the Percentage Method Table, a recipe calculated for 73.47 lb of batter is needed.

Step 7 Multiply each ingredient percentage by the total weight to give the exact amount of each ingredient needed. The total weight of ingredients should equal

Factor Method Table

Step 1: Derive the factor	*Ingredients*	*Original recipe*	*Step 2: Convert to weight*	*Step 3: Multiply by factor*	*Steps 6 and 7: Change to measure and simplify*
$\dfrac{500 \text{ (new)}}{100 \text{ (original)}} = 5 \text{ (factor)}$	Flour, all-purpose	5 lb	5 lb	25 lb	25 lb
	Baking powder	5 oz	5 oz	25 oz	1 lb 9 oz
	Salt	2 Tbsp	1⅓ oz	6½ oz	6½ oz
	Shortening, hydrogenated	1 lb 4 oz	1 lb 4 oz	6 lb 4 oz	6 lb 4 oz
	Milk	1¾ qt	3 lb 8 oz	17 lb 8 oz	2 gal + ¾ qt
Steps 4 and 5: Total weight			10 lb 2 oz	50 lb 11 oz	

Percentage Method Table

Ingredients	*Original recipe*	*Step 1: Convert to decimal weights*	*Step 3: Calculate percentage*	*Step 7: Calculate weights*	*Step 8: Convert to pounds and ounces*
Flour, all-purpose	5 lb	5.0 lb	49.276	25.52 lb	25 lb 8 oz
Baking powder	5 oz	0.313 lb	3.085	1.60 lb	1 lb 10 oz
Salt	2 Tbsp	0.0839 lb	0.827	0.43 lb	6¾ oz
Shortening, hydrogenated	1 lb 4 oz	1.25 lb	12.319	6.38 lb	6 lb 6 oz
Milk	1¾ qt	3.5 lb	34.493	17.86 lb	2¼ gal
Step 2: Total weight		10.1469 lb	100.00	51.79 lb	

Step 4:
Check ratio of ingredients to see if they are within acceptable guidelines.

Step 5:

$$\text{Establish needed weight: } \frac{10.1469 \text{ (total weight of 100 biscuits)}}{100} = 0.1015 \text{ lb (weight per biscuit)}$$

$$500 \text{ (desired yield)} \times 0.1015 \text{ lb} = 50.75 \text{ lb of dough needed before handling loss}$$

Step 6:
Calculate handling loss. Estimated handling loss 2 percent:

$$\frac{50.75 \text{ lb (desired yield)}}{98 \text{ percent (100 percent} - 2 \text{ percent)}} = 51.79 \text{ lb total dough needed}$$

the weight needed as calculated in step 6. Once the percentages of a recipe have been established, any number of servings can be calculated, and the ratio of ingredients to the total will remain the same.

Step 8   Unless scales are calibrated to read in pounds and tenths of a pound, convert to pounds and ounces (Table 4.7, p. 91) or to measure (Table 4.2, p. 71). Use Table 4.9, p. 92, for rounding off unnecessary fractions. If volume measurements are required, Table 4.2 is helpful.

The example in the Percentage Method Table illustrates the procedure for adjusting Baking Powder Biscuits from 100 biscuits to 500, using the percentage method of adjustment.

Enlarging Home-Sized Recipes

Before enlarging a small-quantity recipe, be sure the recipe is appropriate for large-quantity production and that the same quality can be achieved in the larger amount. Appropriate equipment and pans also must be available. Quantity production procedures used in the particular foodservice may need to replace small-scale techniques.

Enlarging a small-quantity recipe in steps is more likely to be successful than increasing size too quickly. Following are suggestions for expanding home-sized recipes:

Step 1   Prepare the product in the amount of the original recipe, following the quantities and procedures

Step 2   Evaluate the product and decide whether it is acceptable for the foodservice. If adjustments are necessary, revise the recipe and make the product again. Prepare the small-quantity amount until the product is satisfactory.

Step 3   Double the recipe or expand it to an appropriate amount for the pan size that will be used, and prepare the product, making notations on the recipe of any changes you make. For example, additional cooking time may be needed for the larger amount. Use Table 2.3, p. 24, for increasing recipe size. Evaluate the product and record the yield, portion size, and acceptability.

Step 4   Double the recipe again, or if the product is to be baked, calculate the quantities needed to prepare one baking pan of the size that will be used in the foodservice. Use Table 2.3, p. 24, for increasing recipe size. If ingredients are to be weighed, home-sized measures should be converted to pounds and ounces or to pounds and tenths of a pound before proceeding further. Prepare and evaluate the product as before.

Step 5   If the product is satisfactory, continue to enlarge by increments of 25 portions or by pans until approximately 100 portions are prepared. Recipes with larger yields should be evaluated for acceptability and adjustment made each time the yield is increased significantly.

When increasing or decreasing recipe yields, it is important to evaluate whether changes are also needed in equipment or in the procedures that specify a time, such as mixing, baking, and boiling. Quality problems arise if the equipment used is too large or too small. It may become necessary to use equipment to mix an amount of product that could be hand-mixed in a smaller amount. Pie crust and muffins are examples of products that would likely require an equipment change when increasing a yield from a small amount to a high-volume amount.

Production time does not increase proportionately as yields increase. The cooking time and timing for various steps may, however, change as yields increase or decrease and as production equipment and pan sizes change.

Emphasizing Healthy Cooking

In order to help clientele meet nutritional needs and to support healthy eating initiatives, it is often necessary to make recipe ingredient and procedure changes. The information in this section will help food production staff produce flavorful, healthful, and nutritious food. Careful testing is advised when substituting ingredients or procedures in a recipe. Not all recipes will produce a quality product by simply making a substitution and may require additional changes.

Evaluation of flavor is closely correlated with customers' perception of how flavorful the food will be when eaten. Health-conscious choices are likely to be made when food looks, smells, feels, tastes, and sounds appetizing and delicious. The perception of flavor is *seen* through its color, visual texture and consistency, and freshness. Using colorful fresh fruit and vegetable accompaniments and paying strict attention to quality food and service standards will enhance the perception of good flavor and therefore garner customer acceptance without adding fat, salt, or sugar to the food. *Smelling* flavor adds favorably to the dining experience. Using aromatic herbs and spices instead of less-healthful ingredients to enhance the flavor experience is recommended. See Table 5.21, p. 134, for suggestions on using herbs and spices. Flavor can be *felt* through food's texture and mouthfeel. Cooking food correctly and serving it at its peak quality will enhance the flavor perception. Temperature impacts flavor and should be monitored closely throughout the serving period. Flavor perception can be *heard* by the sounds that come with preparation and eating: snap, crunch, and sizzle. Every attempt should be made to enhance the sound factor of the flavor experience. *Tasting* flavor is the most important factor in the flavor experience. Recipe adjustments can often be made to compensate for flavor when fat, sodium, and sugar are reduced. Adjustments can be made in recipes by techniques that build on the natural flavors of food such as caramelizing vegetables, adding "brightness" through citrus juices and vinegars, and deliberately building complementary flavors that awaken our taste receptors: bitter, salty, sour, sweet, and umami.

Cooking and serving food more healthfully can generally be accomplished by following a few basic guidelines, including the following:

- Serving smaller portions of foods high in fat, sodium, and complex carbohydrates. An easy-to-follow guideline is to visually divide the plate into thirds and serve one-third protein, one-third starchy vegetables including whole grains, and one-half nonstarchy vegetables.

- Increasing the amounts of fruit, vegetables, legumes, and whole grains.

- Emphasizing the use of lean meat, poultry, fish, and seafood.

- Reducing the amount of rich sauces and substituting instead flavorful herbs, spice rubs, salsas, vegetable and fruit purées, marinades, reduction glazes, and colorful fresh fruits and vegetables. Sauce amounts can be reduced by pooling a small amount of sauce under the food rather than on top.

- Cooking by methods other than frying. See the low-fat cooking methods described on p. 13.

- Using unsaturated fats whenever possible and discontinuing the use of trans fats. Use small amounts of flavorful vegetable oils such as olive oil and nut oils for seasoning.

- Using fresh, flavorful foods at their peak of flavor.

- Following proper processing, cooking, and serving procedures that preserve or enhance the freshness and quality of foods.

• Making healthy food appealing through color selection, food item pairings, cooking techniques, and attractive plate presentations.

Low-Fat Cooking Methods

Cooking methods that require adding fat will quickly increase calories. Fat absorption must be considered when calculating calories per serving. The following are some general guidelines for how much fat is absorbed during cooking:

Frying breaded meats	2 teaspoons for every 4-oz portion
Frying unbreaded meats	1 teaspoon for every 4-oz portion
Deep-fat fried potatoes	1¼ tablespoons for every 4-oz portion of potatoes
Sautéing, grilling, stir-frying	½ to ⅔ teaspoon per 4-oz serving of meat or vegetables

Selecting a cooking method that helps keep fat calories as low as possible is often an easy solution to reducing calories and making food more healthful.

Cooking Method	Healthful Attribute
Baking	Browning enhances the flavor of food.
Barbecuing	Food is cooked without adding additional fat. Meat drippings fall away. Dry rubs and spices used in barbecuing enhance flavor.
Braising and stewing	Food is cooked slowly in a flavorful liquid that can be defatted before serving.
Broiling	High heat and quick cooking retains vitamins and minerals. Food can be trimmed of visible fat and any fat remaining will drip from the food.
Dry-sautéing	The cooking pan using high heat with no additional fat can be deglazed with a flavorful liquid (stock or wine).
En papillote	Food, usually meat or fish and aromatic vegetables, is steamed without added fat.
Grilling	Food drippings are allowed to run through the open grate.
Oven-frying	Crispy surfaces can be achieved without using excess fat.
Pan-steaming	Food can be cooked in a small amount of liquid with no added fat.
Poaching	Food is cooked in a flavorful or aromatic liquid.
Roasting	High heat causes a Maillard reaction of browning and enhances the flavor without added fat.
Steaming	Food is cooked without added fat. Steaming reduces the amount of vitamin and mineral leaching that happens with the boiling of vegetables.
Stir-frying	Food is cooked over high heat with a small amount of fat.
Sweating	Vegetables cook in their own juices with only a little added fat.

Adapting recipes to be more healthful may require recipe testing and experimentation because appearance, taste, or quality may be impacted by changing cooking techniques or reducing, replacing, or adding ingredients. Following are suggestions for reducing fat, sodium, and sugar in recipes and for serving more healthful meals.

Decreasing fat in meat, fish, and poultry dishes

• Use lean cuts of meat with the visible fat trimmed.
• Use a lower grade of meat (usually less fat) for products where moist-heat cooking methods are used.
• Remove skin and excess fat from poultry. To retain moisture, poultry may be roasted with the skin on and removed before serving.
• Select white-meat poultry instead of legs and thighs and marinate before cooking.
• Substitute a more healthful cooking method for frying.
• Substitute ground poultry for part or all of the ground beef in casseroles.
• Use extra-lean ground beef in casseroles. Rinsing cooked ground beef will remove fat but is not generally recommended because of the flavor loss and also because of the fat added to the wastewater stream.
• Moisten meats with wine, stock, or citrus juice instead of high-fat drippings or gravies and season with herbs and spices.
• Pour fat from baking and roasting pans before deglazing or using the drippings for sauces and gravies.
• Add raw meat to stews and sauces without browning first with added fat.
• When appropriate, substitute vegetables for some of the meat in a recipe.
• Substitute turkey bacon and sausage for pork bacon and sausage.

Decreasing fat in egg and dairy products

• Replace some of the egg yolks with egg whites or egg substitutes. This may not be appropriate for all baked products. One should begin by replacing a small amount of egg yolk and increasing the amount replaced each time to determine a suitable limit.
• Substitute nonfat dairy products for foods such as cheese, cream cheese, ricotta cheese, milk, yogurt, and sour cream.
• Substitute evaporated low-fat milk for cream.

Decreasing fat in sauces and soups

• Reduce the amount of fat used to sauté vegetables. To prevent burning, cook over medium heat and stir often. Covering the pan may prevent burning, but the moisture that accumulates may reduce caramelization and flavor development.
• Substitute low-fat or nonfat milk or evaporated skim milk for whole milk or cream. To prevent curdling, add the milk late in the cooking process, heat the food slowly and gently, and hold as short a time as possible.

- Substitute low-fat cheese for whole-milk cheese.
- Substitute part or all plain low-fat or nonfat yogurt for sour cream. In cooked sauces, add 1 Tbsp cornstarch to each cup of yogurt before heating. Heat the food slowly and gently, do not boil, and add the yogurt as late as possible in the cooking process.
- When feasible, refrigerate soups, stews, and stocks until the fat congeals on top and skim it off. When it is not possible to refrigerate a product, use a ladle to skim as much fat as possible from the top.
- Thicken sauces with cornstarch, arrowroot, or flour paste slurry instead of a roux. For additional flavor, add wines, herbs, stock reductions, and concentrated bases. Puréed vegetables and starchy products such as potatoes, cooked legumes, barley, and rice may be used in place of roux to thicken some soups and sauces.
- Replace a traditional marinade or vinaigrette with one that has had up to half of the oil replaced with a starch-thickened liquid such as wine or fruit juice.
- Substitute fresh coulis, vegetable jus, salsas, or chutney for sauces made with fat.

Decreasing fat in salad dressings

- Substitute half of the oil with vinegar, infused vinegars, lemon juice, vegetable juice, fruit juice, or plain low-fat yogurt.
- Replace the oil in salad dressings with a reduced amount of intensely flavored oils such as nut oils, olive oils, or infused oils.
- Use low-fat or nonfat mayonnaise and cream cheese.

Decreasing fat in vegetables

- Instead of sautéing vegetables in fat, sweat them and season with a small amount of intensely flavored nut oil, olive oil, or infused oil.
- Substitute citrus juice and vinegars for fat. Add the juice or vinegar just before serving.
- Reduce the amount of fat used and roast vegetables in a hot oven to caramelize their natural sugars and bring out their natural flavor.

Decreasing fat in baking

- Use a silicone baking mat, silicone parchment paper, or a food-release cooking spray instead of greasing a pan.
- Use fruit purées such as applesauce, mashed bananas, and commercially sold prune purée to replace the fat in some quick-bread, bar cookie, and cake recipes. Begin by replacing a small amount of fat and increasing the amount replaced each time to determine a suitable limit.

Decreasing sodium

- Build a depth of flavor with herbs, spices, and acid items and reduce salt. See pp. 133–138 for suggestions. The most effective herbs and spices in replacing the taste of salt are basil, black pepper, chiles, cilantro, coriander, cumin, curry powder, dill seed, garlic, garlic powder, ginger, mint, onion, and parsley.
- Add acidic items to boost flavor: vinegar, flavored vinegars, wine.
- Dried fruit and toasted nuts and seeds add flavor without adding salt.
- Make stocks or use a reduced-salt commercial base.
- Purchase low- or reduced-sodium products. Make products from scratch rather than using convenience foods that often are higher in sodium.
- Rinse highly salted products.
- In some cases, salted products can be added to enhance flavor and provide some salt without adding salt directly. Examples of products that may be appropriate to use are anchovies, capers in brine (rinsed), mustard, olives, pickles, prosciutto, soy and fish sauce, and some cheeses such as Parmesan and Romano.
- Substitute cooked dry beans for canned beans.

Decreasing sugar

- Reduce the amount of sugar in recipes. The amount of sugar that can be replaced varies among recipes. Begin by eliminating a small amount of sugar and decreasing more each time to determine a suitable limit. Because sugar is important to the quality of baked products, it may not be possible to eliminate a large amount of sugar.
- Caramelize natural sugars in vegetables and fruits and reduce the added sugar for products that already have added sugar.
- Add spices that enhance sweet foods, and reduce the sugar. Spices and flavorings that enhance sweetness in foods include allspice, anise, cardamom, cinnamon, cloves, ginger, mace, nutmeg, and vanilla.
- Substituting honey, maple syrup, or molasses for part of the sugar in some products may provide enough flavor that the sugar can be reduced.
- When appropriate, reduce the amount of sugar in a sweet product and serve it warm or at room temperature (foods taste sweeter at warm temperatures).
- Whenever possible, substitute fruit and fruit juice for sugar.
- Use sugar substitutes following manufacturers' directions.

Direct-Reading Measurement Tables

Recipe adjustment may be made by using tables that have been developed for different numbers of portions. Using these charts requires minimal calculation. Table 2.1 can be used when the desired yields are divisible by 25 and the ingredients are given in **weights**. Table 2.2 is used when recipe ingredients are given in **volume measurements** and the yields can be divided by 25. Table 2.3 has yields that can be divided by 8 and is useful in enlarging home-sized recipes. Following are instructions for using direct-reading measurement tables.

Directions for Using Tables 2.1 and 2.2.

The choice of Table 2.1 or 2.2 depends on whether the recipe ingredients are given in weight (ounces and pounds) or in volume measurement (teaspoons, tablespoons, cups, quarts, or gallons). Table 2.1 is used for converting weighed ingredients using recipe yields that are divisible by 25. Table 2.2 is used for converting volume measures of ingredients using recipe yields that are divisible by 25. To adjust recipes, follow these steps:

1. Locate the column that corresponds to the original yield of the recipe to be adjusted. For example, assume the original recipe yields 100 portions. Locate the "100" column across the top of the chart on Table 2.1.

2. Go down this column to the amount of the ingredient required (or to the closest number to that figure) in the recipe to be adjusted. If the recipe for 100 portions requires 21 lb ground beef, for example, go down the column headed 100 to the figure "21."

3. Then go across the page, in line with that amount, to the column that is headed to correspond with the yield desired. For example, if only 75 portions are desired, begin with the 21 lb figure in the "100" column and slide across to the column headed "75" and read that figure. It indicates that 15 lb 12 oz ground beef would be required to make 75 portions with this recipe.

4. Record this figure as the amount of the ingredient required for the new yield of the recipe. Repeat steps 1, 2, and 3 for each ingredient in the original recipe to obtain the adjusted ingredient weight needed for the new yield. Follow the same procedure using Table 2.2 in adjusting ingredient amounts indicated in volume measures. Yields can be either increased or decreased in this manner.

5. If two columns need to be combined to obtain the desired yield, follow steps 1 through 4 and add the amounts given in the two columns to obtain the amount required for the adjusted yield. For example, to find the amount of ground beef for 225 portions of our hypothetical recipe, locate the figures in columns headed "200" and "25" and add them. In this example it would be 42 lb + 5 lb 4 oz, so the required total for ground beef would be 47 lb 4 oz.

6. The figures given in these tables are given in exact weights, including fractional ounces. After making yield adjustments for every ingredient, refer to Table 4.9 for rounding off fractional amounts that are not of sufficient proportion to change product quality.

Abbreviations used in the charts include the following:

oz = ounce

lb = pound

tsp = teaspoon

Tbsp = tablespoon

qt = quart

gal = gallon

(r) = slightly rounded

(s) = scant

The following equivalents are helpful in using the charts:

3 tsp = 1 Tbsp

4 Tbsp = ¼ cup

5 Tbsp + 1 tsp = ⅓ cup

8 Tbsp = ½ cup

10 Tbsp + 2 tsp = ⅔ cup

12 Tbsp = ¾ cup

16 Tbsp = 1 cup

4 cups = 1 qt

4 qt = 1 gal

TABLE 2.1 Direct-reading table for adjusting weight ingredients of recipes divisible by 25[a]

25	50	75	100	200	300	400	500
*[b]	*	*	¼ oz	½ oz	¾ oz	1 oz	1¼ oz
*	*	*	½ oz	1 oz	1½ oz	2 oz	2½ oz
*	*	*	¾ oz	1½ oz	2¼ oz	3 oz	3¾ oz
¼ oz	½ oz	¾ oz	1 oz	2 oz	3 oz	4 oz	5 oz
*	*	*	1¼ oz	2½ oz	3¾ oz	5 oz	6¼ oz
*	¾ oz	*	1½ oz	3 oz	4½ oz	6 oz	7½ oz
*	*	*	1¾ oz	3½ oz	5¼ oz	7 oz	8¾ oz
½ oz	1 oz	1½ oz	2 oz	4 oz	6 oz	8 oz	10 oz
*	*	1¾ oz	2¼ oz	4½ oz	6¾ oz	9 oz	11¼ oz
*	1¼ oz	2 oz	2½ oz	5 oz	7½ oz	10 oz	12½ oz
*	*	2 oz	2¾ oz	5½ oz	8¼ oz	11 oz	13¾ oz
¾ oz	1½ oz	2¼ oz	3 oz	6 oz	9 oz	12 oz	15 oz
*	*	2½ oz	3¼ oz	6½ oz	9¾ oz	13 oz	1 lb ¼ oz
*	1¾ oz	2¾ oz	3½ oz	7 oz	10½ oz	14 oz	1 lb 1½ oz
1 oz	2 oz	2¾ oz	3¾ oz	7½ oz	11¼ oz	15 oz	1 lb 2¾ oz
1 oz	2 oz	3 oz	4 oz	8 oz	12 oz	1 lb	1 lb 4 oz
1 oz	2¼ oz	3¼ oz	4¼ oz	8½ oz	12¾ oz	1 lb 1 oz	1 lb 5¼ oz
*	2½ oz	3½ oz	4½ oz	9 oz	13½ oz	1 lb 2 oz	1 lb 6½ oz
*	2½ oz	3½ oz	4¾ oz	9½ oz	14¼ oz	1 lb 3 oz	1 lb 7¾ oz
1¼ oz	2½ oz	3¾ oz	5 oz	10 oz	15 oz	1 lb 4 oz	1 lb 9 oz
*	2¾ oz	4¼ oz	5½ oz	11 oz	1 lb ½ oz	1 lb 6 oz	1 lb 11½ oz
1½ oz	3 oz	4½ oz	6 oz	12 oz	1 lb 2 oz	1 lb 8 oz	1 lb 14 oz
*	3¼ oz	4¾ oz	6½ oz	13 oz	1 lb 3½ oz	1 lb 10 oz	2 lb ½ oz
1¾ oz	3¾ oz	5¼ oz	7 oz	14 oz	1 lb 5 oz	1 lb 12 oz	2 lb 3 oz
2 oz	3¾ oz	5¾ oz	7½ oz	15 oz	1 lb 6½ oz	1 lb 14 oz	2 lb 5½ oz
2 oz	4 oz	6 oz	8 oz	1 lb	1 lb 8 oz	2 lb	2 lb 8 oz
2¼ oz	4¼ oz	6½ oz	8½ oz	1 lb 1 oz	1 lb 9½ oz	2 lb 2 oz	2 lb 10½ oz
2¼ oz	4½ oz	6¾ oz	9 oz	1 lb 2 oz	1 lb 11 oz	2 lb 4 oz	2 lb 13 oz
2½ oz	4¾ oz	7¼ oz	9½ oz	1 lb 3 oz	1 lb 12½ oz	2 lb 6 oz	2 lb 15½ oz
2½ oz	5 oz	7½ oz	10 oz	1 lb 4 oz	1 lb 14 oz	2 lb 8 oz	3 lb 2 oz
2¾ oz	5½ oz	8¼ oz	11 oz	1 lb 6 oz	2 lb 1 oz	2 lb 12 oz	3 lb 7 oz
3 oz	6 oz	9 oz	12 oz	1 lb 8 oz	2 lb 4 oz	3 lb	3 lb 12 oz
3¼ oz	6½ oz	9¾ oz	13 oz	1 lb 10 oz	2 lb 7 oz	3 lb 4 oz	4 lb 1 oz
3½ oz	7 oz	10½ oz	14 oz	1 lb 12 oz	2 lb 10 oz	3 lb 8 oz	4 lb 6 oz
3¾ oz	7½ oz	11¼ oz	15 oz	1 lb 14 oz	2 lb 13 oz	3 lb 12 oz	4 lb 11 oz
4 oz	8 oz	12 oz	1 lb	2 lb	3 lb	4 lb	5 lb
4½ oz	9 oz	13½ oz	1 lb 2 oz	2 lb 4 oz	3 lb 6 oz	4 lb 8 oz	5 lb 10 oz
5 oz	10 oz	15 oz	1 lb 4 oz	2 lb 8 oz	3 lb 12 oz	5 lb	6 lb 4 oz
5½ oz	11 oz	1 lb ½ oz	1 lb 6 oz	2 lb 12 oz	4 lb 2 oz	5 lb 8 oz	6 lb 14 oz
6 oz	12 oz	1 lb 2 oz	1 lb 8 oz	3 lb	4 lb 8 oz	6 lb	7 lb 8 oz
6½ oz	13 oz	1 lb 3½ oz	1 lb 10 oz	3 lb 4 oz	4 lb 14 oz	6 lb 8 oz	8 lb 2 oz
7 oz	14 oz	1 lb 5 oz	1 lb 12 oz	3 lb 8 oz	5 lb 4 oz	7 lb	8 lb 12 oz
7½ oz	15 oz	1 lb 6½ oz	1 lb 14 oz	3 lb 12 oz	5 lb 10 oz	7 lb 8 oz	9 lb 6 oz
8 oz	1 lb	1 lb 8 oz	2 lb	4 lb	6 lb	8 lb	10 lb
8½ oz	1 lb 1 oz	1 lb 9½ oz	2 lb 2 oz	4 lb 4 oz	6 lb 6 oz	8 lb 8 oz	10 lb 10 oz
9 oz	1 lb 2 oz	1 lb 11 oz	2 lb 4 oz	4 lb 8 oz	6 lb 12 oz	9 lb	11 lb 4 oz
9½ oz	1 lb 3 oz	1 lb 12½ oz	2 lb 6 oz	4 lb 12 oz	7 lb 2 oz	9 lb 8 oz	11 lb 14 oz
10 oz	1 lb 4 oz	1 lb 14 oz	2 lb 8 oz	5 lb	7 lb 8 oz	10 lb	12 lb 8 oz
11 oz	1 lb 6 oz	2 lb 1 oz	2 lb 12 oz	5 lb 8 oz	8 lb 4 oz	11 lb	13 lb 12 oz

TABLE 2.1	*Continued*						
25	**50**	**75**	**100**	**200**	**300**	**400**	**500**
12 oz	1 lb 8 oz	2 lb 4 oz	3 lb	6 lb	9 lb	12 lb	15 lb
13 oz	1 lb 10 oz	2 lb 7 oz	3 lb 4 oz	6 lb 8 oz	9 lb 12 oz	13 lb	16 lb 4 oz
14 oz	1 lb 12 oz	2 lb 10 oz	3 lb 8 oz	7 lb	10 lb 8 oz	14 lb	17 lb 8 oz
15 oz	1 lb 14 oz	2 lb 13 oz	3 lb 12 oz	7 lb 8 oz	11 lb 4 oz	15 lb	18 lb 12 oz
1 lb	2 lb	3 lb	4 lb	8 lb	12 lb	16 lb	20 lb
1 lb 1 oz	2 lb 2 oz	3 lb 3 oz	4 lb 4 oz	8 lb 8 oz	12 lb 12 oz	17 lb	21 lb 4 oz
1 lb 2 oz	2 lb 4 oz	3 lb 6 oz	4 lb 8 oz	9 lb	13 lb 8 oz	18 lb	22 lb 8 oz
1 lb 3 oz	2 lb 6 oz	3 lb 9 oz	4 lb 12 oz	9 lb 8 oz	14 lb 4 oz	19 lb	23 lb 12 oz
1 lb 4 oz	2 lb 8 oz	3 lb 12 oz	5 lb	10 lb	15 lb	20 lb	25 lb
1 lb 5 oz	2 lb 10 oz	3 lb 15 oz	5 lb 4 oz	10 lb 8 oz	15 lb 12 oz	21 lb	26 lb 4 oz
1 lb 6 oz	2 lb 12 oz	4 lb 2 oz	5 lb 8 oz	11 lb	16 lb 8 oz	22 lb	27 lb 8 oz
1 lb 7 oz	2 lb 14 oz	4 lb 5 oz	5 lb 12 oz	11 lb 8 oz	17 lb 4 oz	23 lb	28 lb 12 oz
1 lb 8 oz	3 lb	4 lb 8 oz	6 lb	12 lb	18 lb	24 lb	30 lb
1 lb 10 oz	3 lb 4 oz	4 lb 14 oz	6 lb 8 oz	13 lb	19 lb 8 oz	26 lb	32 lb 8 oz
1 lb 12 oz	3 lb 8 oz	5 lb 4 oz	7 lb	14 lb	21 lb	28 lb	35 lb
1 lb 14 oz	3 lb 12 oz	5 lb 10 oz	7 lb 8 oz	15 lb	22 lb 8 oz	30 lb	37 lb 8 oz
2 lb	4 lb	6 lb	8 lb	16 lb	24 lb	32 lb	40 lb
2 lb 2 oz	4 lb 4 oz	6 lb 6 oz	8 lb 8 oz	17 lb	25 lb 8 oz	34 lb	42 lb 8 oz
2 lb 4 oz	4 lb 8 oz	6 lb 12 oz	9 lb	18 lb	27 lb	36 lb	45 lb
2 lb 6 oz	4 lb 12 oz	7 lb 2 oz	9 lb 8 oz	19 lb	28 lb 8 oz	38 lb	47 lb 8 oz
2 lb 8 oz	5 lb	7 lb 8 oz	10 lb	20 lb	30 lb	40 lb	50 lb
2 lb 12 oz	5 lb 8 oz	8 lb 4 oz	11 lb	22 lb	33 lb	44 lb	55 lb
3 lb	6 lb	9 lb	12 lb	24 lb	36 lb	48 lb	60 lb
3 lb 4 oz	6 lb 8 oz	9 lb 12 oz	13 lb	26 lb	39 lb	52 lb	65 lb
3 lb 8 oz	7 lb	10 lb 8 oz	14 lb	28 lb	42 lb	56 lb	70 lb
3 lb 12 oz	7 lb 8 oz	11 lb 4 oz	15 lb	30 lb	45 lb	60 lb	75 lb
4 lb	8 lb	12 lb	16 lb	32 lb	48 lb	64 lb	80 lb
4 lb 4 oz	8 lb 8 oz	12 lb 12 oz	17 lb	34 lb	51 lb	68 lb	85 lb
4 lb 8 oz	9 lb	13 lb 8 oz	18 lb	36 lb	54 lb	72 lb	90 lb
4 lb 12 oz	9 lb 8 oz	14 lb 2 oz	19 lb	38 lb	57 lb	76 lb	95 lb
5 lb	10 lb	15 lb	20 lb	40 lb	60 lb	80 lb	100 lb
5 lb 4 oz	10 lb 8 oz	15 lb 12 oz	21 lb	42 lb	63 lb	84 lb	105 lb
5 lb 8 oz	11 lb	16 lb 8 oz	22 lb	44 lb	66 lb	88 lb	110 lb
5 lb 12 oz	11 lb 8 oz	17 lb 4 oz	23 lb	46 lb	69 lb	92 lb	115 lb
6 lb	12 lb	18 lb	24 lb	48 lb	72 lb	96 lb	120 lb
6 lb 4 oz	12 lb 8 oz	18 lb 12 oz	25 lb	50 lb	75 lb	100 lb	125 lb
7 lb 8 oz	15 lb	22 lb 8 oz	30 lb	60 lb	90 lb	120 lb	150 lb
8 lb 12 oz	17 lb 8 oz	26 lb 4 oz	35 lb	70 lb	105 lb	140 lb	175 lb
10 lb	20 lb	30 lb	40 lb	80 lb	120 lb	160 lb	200 lb
11 lb 4 oz	22 lb 8 oz	33 lb 12 oz	45 lb	90 lb	135 lb	180 lb	225 lb
12 lb 8 oz	25 lb	37 lb 8 oz	50 lb	100 lb	150 lb	200 lb	250 lb

[a] To be used with Table 2.2, which is similarly constructed for volume measures.
[b] An asterisk (*) means these amounts cannot be weighed accurately without introducing errors.
Source: Used with permission from *Quantity Food Preparation: Standardizing Recipes and Controlling Ingredients.* Copyright 1983 by the American Dietetic Association, Chicago.

TABLE 2.1   Direct-reading table for adjusting weight ingredients of recipes divisible by 25[a]

25	50	75	100
¼ tsp	½ tsp	¾ tsp	1 tsp
¼ tsp (r)	½ tsp (r)	1 tsp (s)	1¼ tsp
¼ tsp + ⅛ tsp	¾ tsp	1 tsp + ⅛ tsp	1½ tsp
½ tsp (s)	¾ tsp (r)	1¼ tsp (r)	1¾ tsp
½ tsp	1 tsp	1½ tsp	2 tsp
½ tsp (r)	1 tsp + ⅛ tsp	1¾ tsp(s)	2¼ tsp
½ tsp + ⅛ tsp	1¼ tsp	2 tsp (s)	2½ tsp
¾ tsp (s)	1¼ tsp + ⅛ tsp	2 tsp (r)	2¾ tsp
¾ tsp	1½ tsp	2¼ tsp	1 Tbsp
1 tsp + ⅛ tsp	2¼ tsp	1 Tbsp + ¼ tsp + ⅛ tsp	1½ Tbsp
1½ tsp	1 Tbsp	1½ Tbsp	2 Tbsp
1¾ tsp + ⅛ tsp	1 Tbsp + ¾ tsp	1 Tbsp + 2½ tsp + ⅛ tsp	2½ Tbsp
2¼ tsp	1½ Tbsp	2 Tbsp + ¾ tsp	3 Tbsp
2¼ tsp + ⅛ tsp	1 Tbsp + 2¼ tsp	2 Tbsp + 1⅛ tsp	3½ Tbsp
1 Tbsp	2 Tbsp	3 Tbsp	½ cup
1 Tbsp + 1 tsp	2 Tbsp + 2 tsp	¼ cup	⅓ cup
2 Tbsp	¼ cup	¼ cup + 2 Tbsp	½ cup
2 Tbsp + 2 tsp	⅓ cup	½ cup	⅔ cup
3 Tbsp	6 Tbsp	½ cup + 1 Tbsp	¾ cup
¼ cup	½ cup	¾ cup	1 cup
¼ cup + 1 Tbsp	½ cup + 2 Tbsp	¾ cup + 3 Tbsp	1¼ cups
⅓ cup	⅔ cup	1 cup	1⅓ cups
⅓ cup + 2 tsp	¾ cup	1 cup + 2 Tbsp	1½ cups
6 Tbsp + 2 tsp	¾ cup + 4 tsp	1¼ cups	1⅔ cups
¼ cup + 3 Tbsp	¾ cup + 2 Tbsp	1¼ cups + 1 Tbsp	1¾ cups
½ cup	1 cup	1½ cups	2 cups
½ cup + 1 Tbsp	1 cup + 2 Tbsp	1½ cups + 3 Tbsp	2¼ cups
½ cup + 4 tsp	1 cup + 2 Tbsp + 2 tsp	1¾ cups	2⅓ cups
½ cup + 2 Tbsp	1¼ cups	1¾ cups + 2 Tbsp	2½ cups
⅔ cup	1⅓ cups	2 cups	2⅔ cups
½ cup + 3 Tbsp	1¼ cups + 2 Tbsp	2 cups + 1 Tbsp	2¾ cups
¾ cup	1½ cups	2¼ cups	3 cups

TABLE 2.2   *Continued*

200	300	400	500
2 tsp	1 Tbsp	1 Tbsp + 1 tsp	1 Tbsp + 2 tsp
2½ tsp	1 Tbsp + ¾ tsp	1 Tbsp + 2 tsp	2 Tbsp + ¼ tsp
1 Tbsp	1½ Tbsp	2 Tbsp	2½ Tbsp
1 Tbsp + ½ tsp	1 Tbsp + 2¼ tsp	2 Tbsp + 1 tsp	2 Tbsp + 2¾ tsp
1 Tbsp + 1 tsp	2 Tbsp	2 Tbsp + 2 tsp	3 Tbsp + 1 tsp
1½ Tbsp	2 Tbsp + ¾ tsp	3 Tbsp	3 Tbsp + 2¼ tsp
1 Tbsp + 2 tsp	2½ Tbsp	3 Tbsp + 1 tsp	4 Tbsp + ½ tsp
1 Tbsp + 2½ tsp	2 Tbsp + 2¼ tsp	3 Tbsp + 2 tsp	4 Tbsp + 1¾ tsp
2 Tbsp	3 Tbsp	¼ cup	5 Tbsp
3 Tbsp	¼ cup + 1½ tsp	⅓ cup + 2 tsp	¼ cup + 3½ Tbsp
¼ cup	¼ cup + 2 Tbsp	½ cup	½ cup + 2 Tbsp
¼ cup + 1 Tbsp	¼ cup + 3½ Tbsp	½ cup + 2 Tbsp	¾ cup + ½ Tbsp
⅓ cup + 2 tsp	½ cup + 1 Tbsp	¾ cup	¾ cup + 3 Tbsp
¼ cup + 3 Tbsp	½ cup + 2½ Tbsp	¾ cup + 2 Tbsp	1 cup + 1½ Tbsp
½ cup	¾ cup	1 cup	1¼ cups
⅔ cup	1 cup	1⅓ cups	1⅔ cups
1 cup	1½ cups	2 cups	2½ cups
1⅓ cups	2 cups	2⅔ cups	3⅓ cups
1½ cups	2¼ cups	3 cups	3¾ cups
2 cups	3 cups	1 qt	1¼ qt
2½ cups	3¾ cups	1¼ qt	1½ qt + ¼ cup
2⅔ cups	1 qt	1¼ qt + ⅓ cup	1½ qt + ⅔ cup
3 cups	1 qt + ½ cup	1½ qt	1¾ qt + ½ cup
3⅓ cups	1¼ qt	1½ qt + ⅔ cup	2 qt + ⅓ cup
3½ cups	1¼ qt + ¼ cup	1¾ qt	2 qt + ¾ cup
1 qt	1½ qt	2 qt	2½ qt
1 qt + ½ cup	1½ qt + ¾ cup	2¼ qt	2¼ qt + ¼ cup
1 qt + ⅔ cup	1¾ qt	2¼ qt + ⅓ cup	2¾ qt + ⅔ cup
1¼ qt	1¾ qt + ½ cup	2½ qt	3 qt + ½ cups
1¼ qt + ⅓ cup	2 qt	2½ qt + ⅔ cup	3 qt + 1⅓ cups
1¼ qt + ½ cup	2 qt + ¼ cup	2¾ qt	3¼ qt + ¾ cup
1½ qt	2¼ qt	3 qt	3¾ qt

continued

TABLE 2.2   Direct-reading table for adjusting recipes with ingredient amounts given in volume measurement and divisible by 25[a]

TABLE 2.2 *Continued*

TABLE 2.2 Direct-reading table for adjusting recipes with ingredient amounts given in volume measurement and divisible by 25[a]

25	50	75	100
¾ cup + 1 Tbsp	1½ cups + 2 Tbsp	2¼ cups + 3 Tbsp	3¼ cups
¾ cup + 4 tsp	1⅔ cups	2½ cups	3⅓ cups
¾ cup + 2 Tbsp	1¾ cups	2½ cups + 2 Tbsp	3½ cups
¾ cup + 2 Tbsp + 2½ tsp	1¾ cups + 4 tsp	2¾ cups + ½ tsp	3⅔ cups
¾ cup + 3 Tbsp	1¾ cups + 2 Tbsp	2¾ cups + 1 Tbsp	3¾ cups
1 cup	2 cups	3 cups	1 qt
1¼ cups	2½ cups	3¾ cups	1¼ qt
1½ cups	3 cups	1 qt + ½ cup	1½ qt
1¾ cups	3½ cups	1¼ qt + ¼ cup	1¾ qt
2 cups	1 qt	1½ qt	2 qt
2¼ cups	1 qt + ½ cup	1½ qt + ¾ cup	2¼ qt
2½ cups	1¼ qt	1¾ qt + ½ cup	2½ qt
2¾ cups	1¼ qt + ½ cup	2 qt + ¼ cup	2¾ qt
3 cups	1½ qt	2¼ qt	3 qt
3¼ cups	1½ qt + ½ cup	2¼ qt + ¾ cup	3¼ qt
3½ cups	1¾ qt	2½ qt + ½ cup	3½ qt
3¾ cups	1¾ qt + ½ cup	2¾ qt + ¼ cup	3¾ qt
1 qt	2 qt	3 qt	1 gal
1¼ qt	2½ qt	3¾ qt	1¼ gal
1½ qt	3 qt	1 gal + 2 cups	1½ gal
1¾ qt	3½ qt	1¼ gal + 1 cup	1¾ gal
2 qt	1 gal	1½ gal	2 gal
2¼ qt	1 gal + 2 cups	1½ gal + 3 cups	2¼ gal
2½ qt	1¼ gal	1¾ gal + 2 cups	2½ gal
2¾ qt	1¼ gal + 2 cups	2 gal + 1 cup	2¾ gal
3 qt	1½ gal	2¼ gal	3 gal
3 qt + 1 cup	1½ gal + 2 cups	2¼ gal + 3 cups	3¼ gal
3½ qt	1¾ gal	2½ gal + 2 cups	3½ gal
3½ qt + 1 cup	1¾ gal + 2 cups	2¾ gal + 1 cup	3¾ gal
1 gal	2 gal	3 gal	4 gal
1 gal + 1 cup	2 gal + 2 cups	3 gal + 3 cups	4¼ gal
1 gal + 2 cups	2¼ gal	3¼ gal + 2 cups	4½ gal

TABLE 2.2   *Continued*

TABLE 2.2   Direct-reading table for adjusting recipes with ingredient amounts given in volume measurement and divisible by 25[a]

200	300	400	500
1½ qt + ½ cup	2¼ qt + ¾ cup	3¼ qt	1 gal + ¼ cup
1½ qt + ⅔ cup	2½ qt	3¼ qt + ⅓ cup	1 gal + ⅔ cup
1¾ qt	2½ qt + ½ cup	3½ qt	1 gal + 1½ cups
1¾ qt + ⅓ cup	2¾ qt	3½ qt + ⅔ cup	1 gal + 1⅔ cups
1¾ qt + ½ cup	2 qt + 3¼ cup	3 qt + 3 cups	1 gal + 2¾ cups
2 qt	3 qt	1 gal	1¼ gal
2½ qt	3¾ qt	1¼ gal	1½ gal + 1 cup
3 qt	1 gal + 2 cups	1½ gal	1¾ gal + 2 cups
3½ qt	1¼ gal + 1 cup	1¾ gal	2 gal + 3 cups
1 gal	1½ gal	2 gal	2½ gal
1 gal + 2 cups	1½ gal + 3 cups	2¼ gal	2¾ gal + 1 cup
1¼ gal	1¾ gal + 2 cups	2½ gal	3 gal + 2 cups
1¼ gal + 2 cups	2 gal + 1 cup	2¾ gal	3¼ gal + 3 cups
1½ gal	2¼ gal	3 gal	3¾ gal
1½ gal + 2 cups	3⅓ gal + 3 cups	3¼ gal	4 gal + 1 cup
1¾ gal	2½ gal + 2 cups	3½ gal	4¼ gal + 2 cups
1¾ gal + 2 cups	2¾ gal + 1 cup	3¾ gal	4½ gal + 3 cups
2 gal	3 gal	4 gal	5 gal
2½ gal	3¾ gal	5 gal	6¼ gal
3 gal	4½ gal	6 gal	7½ gal
3½ gal	5¼ gal	7 gal	8¾ gal
4 gal	6 gal	8 gal	10 gal
4½ gal	6¾ gal	9 gal	11¼ gal
5 gal	7½ gal	10 gal	12½ gal
5½ gal	8¼ gal	11 gal	13¾ gal
6 gal	9 gal	12 gal	15 gal
6½ gal	9¾ gal	13 gal	16¼ gal
7 gal	10½ gal	14 gal	17½ gal
7½ gal	11¼ gal	15 gal	18¾ gal
8 gal	12 gal	16 gal	20 gal
8½ gal	12¾ gal	17 gal	21¼ gal
9 gal	13½ gal	18 gal	22½ gal

continued

TABLE 2.2 *Continued*

25	50	75	100
1 gal + 3 cups	2¼ gal + 2 cups	3½ gal + 1 cup	4¾ gal
1¼ gal	2½ gal	3¾ gal	5 gal
1¼ gal + 1 cup	2½ gal + 2 cups	3¾ gal + 3 cups	5¼ gal
1¼ gal + 2 cups	2¾ gal	4 gal + 2 cups	5½ gal
1¼ gal + 3 cups	2¾ gal + 2 cups	4¼ gal + 1 cup	5¾ gal
1½ gal	3 gal	4½ gal	6 gal
1½ gal + 1 cup	3 gal + 2 cups	4½ gal + 3 cups	6¼ gal
1½ gal + 2 cups	3¼ gal	4¾ gal + 2 cups	6½ gal
1½ gal + 3 cups	3¼ gal + 2 cups	5 gal + 1 cup	6¾ gal
1¾ gal	3½ gal	5¼ gal	7 gal

Directions for Using Table 2.3. Many quantity recipes can be expanded from home-sized recipes. Table 2.3 is useful when enlarging small-quantity recipes. Instructions for using this table follow:

1. Locate the column that corresponds to the yield of the recipe to be increased. Example: If the recipe yields 8 portions, use the figures in the first column under the heading "8."

2. Locate the ingredient amount for each ingredient to be adjusted. Example: If the original recipe of 8 portions calls for 1 Tbsp sugar, find "1 Tbsp" in the column marked "8."

3. Locate the amount on the same line under the heading for the desired yield. Example: To increase the original recipe for 8 servings to 24, locate in the column marked "24" the number on the same line with "1 Tbsp" in the "8" column. In the case of 1 Tbsp sugar for 8 portions, the enlarged amount is 3 Tbsp.

4. Repeat this procedure for each ingredient in the recipe. Refer to Table 4.9 for rounding off awkward fractions and complicated measurements.

TABLE 2.2 *Continued*

200	300	400	500
9½ gal	14¼ gal	19 gal	23¾ gal
10 gal	15 gal	20 gal	25 gal
10½ gal	15¾ gal	21 gal	26¼ gal
11 gal	16½ gal	22 gal	27½ gal
11½ gal	17¼ gal	23 gal	28¾ gal
12 gal	18 gal	24 gal	30 gal
12½ gal	18¾ gal	25 gal	31¼ gal
13 gal	19½ gal	26 gal	32½ gal
13½ gal	20¼ gal	27 gal	33¾ gal
14 gal	21 gal	28 gal	35 gal

a To be used with Table 2.1, which is similarly constructed for weight measures.

Used with permission from *Quantity Food Preparation: Standardizing Recipes and Controlling Ingredients.* Copyright 1983 by the American Dietetic Association, Chicago.

Abbreviations in this table include the following:

tsp = teaspoon
Tbsp = tablespoon
qt = quart
gal = gallon
(b) = too small for accurate measure; use caution
(r) = slightly rounded
(s) = scant

Measuring spoon sizes are as follows:

1 Tbsp
1 tsp
½ tsp
¼ tsp
for ¾ tsp, combine ½ tsp + ¼ tsp
for ⅛ tsp, use half of ¼ tsp

Equivalents include the following:

3 tsp = 1 Tbsp
4 Tbsp = ¼ cup
5 Tbsp + 1 tsp = ⅓ cup
8 Tbsp = ½ cup
10 Tbsp + 2 tsp = ⅔ cup
12 Tbsp = ¾ cup
16 Tbsp = 1 cup
4 cups = 1 qt
4 qt = 1 gal

TABLE 2.3 Direct-reading table for increasing home-sized recipes with ingredient amounts given in volume measurement and divisible by 8

8	16	24	32
(b)	(b)	⅛ tsp	⅛ tsp (r)
(b)	⅛ tsp (r)	¼ tsp	¼ tsp (r)
¼ tsp (s)	¼ tsp (r)	½ tsp	¾ tsp (s)
¼ tsp	½ tsp	¾ tsp	1 tsp
¼ tsp (r)	¾ tsp (r)	1 tsp	1¼ tsp (r)
½ tsp (s)	¾ tsp (r)	1¼ tsp	1¾ tsp (s)
½ tsp	1 tsp	1½ tsp	2 tsp
½ tsp (r)	1¼ tsp (s)	1¾ tsp	2¼ tsp (r)
¾ tsp (s)	1¼ tsp (r)	2 tsp	2¾ tsp (r)
¾ tsp	1½ tsp	2¼ tsp	1 Tbsp
¾ tsp (r)	1¾ tsp (s)	2½ tsp	1 Tbsp + ¼ tsp (r)
1 tsp (s)	1¾ tsp (r)	2¾ tsp	1 Tbsp + ¾ tsp (s)
1 tsp	2 tsp	1 Tbsp	1 Tbsp + 1 tsp
1½ tsp	1 Tbsp	1½ Tbsp	2 Tbsp
2 tsp	1 Tbsp + 1 tsp	2 Tbsp	2 Tbsp + 2 tsp
2½ tsp	1 Tbsp + 2 tsp	2½ Tbsp	3 Tbsp + 1 tsp
1 Tbsp	2 Tbsp	3 Tbsp	¼ cup
1 Tbsp + ½ tsp	2 Tbsp + 1 tsp	3½ Tbsp	1¼ cup + 2 tsp
1 Tbsp + 1 tsp	2 Tbsp + 2 tsp	¼ cup	⅓ cup
1 Tbsp + 2¼ tsp	3 Tbsp + 2¾ tsp	⅓ cup	¼ cup + 3 Tbsp
2 Tbsp + 2 tsp	⅓ cup	½ cup	⅔ cup
3 Tbsp + 1¾ tsp	⅓ cup + 5 tsp	⅔ cup	¾ cup + 2 Tbsp
¼ cup	½ cup	¾ cup	1 cup
⅓ cup	⅔ cup	1 cup	1⅓ cups
⅓ cup + 4 tsp	¾ cup + 4 tsp	1¼ cups	1⅔ cups
⅓ cup + 5¼ tsp	⅔ cup + 3½ Tbsp	1⅓ cups	1¾ cups + 1¼ tsp
½ cup	1 cup	1½ cups	2 cups
½ cup + 2¼ tsp	1 cup + 5¼ tsp	1⅔ cups	2 cups + 3½ Tbsp
½ cup + 4 tsp	1 cup + 3 Tbsp	1¾ cups	2⅓ cups
⅔ cup	1 ⅓ cups	2 cups	2⅔ cups
¾ cup	1½ cups	2¼ cups	3 cups
¾ cup + 1¼ tsp	1½ cups + 2¾ tsp	2⅓ cups	3 cups + 2 Tbsp
¾ cup + 4 tsp	1⅔ cups	2½ cups	3⅓ cups
⅔ cup + 3½ Tbsp	1¾ cups + 1¼ tsp	2⅔ cups	3½ cups + 1 Tbsp
⅔ cup + ¼ cup	1¾ cups + 4 tsp	2¾ cups	3⅔ cups
1 cup	2 cups	3 cups	1 qt
1 cup + 4 tsp	2 cups + 2½ Tbsp	3¼ cups	1 qt + ⅓ cup
1 cup + 5¼ tsp	2 cups + 3½ Tbsp	3⅓ cups	4¼ cups + 3 Tbsp
1 cup + 2 Tbsp + 2 tsp	2¼ cups + 4 tsp	3½ cups	1 qt + ⅔ cup
1 cup + 3½ Tbsp	2¼ cups + 3 Tbsp	3⅔ cups	4¾ cups + 2 Tbsp
1¼ cups	2½ cups	3¾ cups	1¼ qt
1⅓ cups	2⅔ cups	1 qt	1¼ qt + ⅓ cup
1⅔ cups	3 ⅓ cups	1¼ qt	1½ qt + ⅔ cup
2 cups	1 qt	1½ qt	2 qt
2⅓ cups	1 qt + ⅔ cup	1¾ qt	2¼ qt + ⅓ cup
2⅔ cups	1¼ qt + ⅓ cup	2 qt	2½ qt + ⅔ cup
3 cups	1½ qt	2¼ qt	3 qt
3⅓ cups	1½ qt + ⅔ cup	2½ qt	3¼ qt + ⅓ cup
3⅔ cups	1¾ qt + ⅓ cup	2¾ qt	3½ qt + ⅔ cup
1 qt	2 qt	3 qt	1 gal

TABLE 2.3 Direct-reading table for increasing home-sized recipes with ingredient amounts given in volume measurement and divisible by 8

TABLE 2.3   *Continued*

48	64	96
¼ tsp	¼ tsp (r)	½ tsp
½ tsp	¾ tsp (s)	1 tsp
1 tsp	1¼ tsp (r)	2 tsp
1½ tsp	2 tsp	1 Tbsp
2 tsp	2¾ tsp (s)	1 Tbsp + 1 tsp
2½ tsp	1 Tbsp + ¼ tsp	1 Tbsp + 2 tsp
1 Tbsp	1 Tbsp + 1 tsp	2 Tbsp
1 Tbsp + ½ tsp	1 Tbsp + 1¾ tsp	2 Tbsp + 1 tsp
1 Tbsp + 1 tsp	1 Tbsp + 2¼ tsp	2 Tbsp + 2 tsp
1 Tbsp + 1½ tsp	2 Tbsp	3 Tbsp
1 Tbsp + 2 tsp	2 Tbsp + ¾ tsp	3 Tbsp + 1 tsp
1 Tbsp + 2½ tsp	2 Tbsp + 1¼ tsp	3 Tbsp + 2 tsp
2 Tbsp	2 Tbsp + 2 tsp	¼ cup
3 Tbsp	¼ cup	⅓ cup + 2 tsp
¼ cup	⅓ cup	½ cup
¼ cup + 1 Tbsp	⅓ cup + 4 tsp	½ cup + 2 Tbsp
⅓ cup + 2 tsp	½ cup	¾ cup
¼ cup + 3 Tbsp	½ cup + 4 tsp	¾ cup + 2 Tbsp
½ cup	⅔ cup	1 cup
⅔ cup	¾ cup + 2 Tbsp	1⅓ cups
1 cup	1⅓ cups	2 cups
1⅓ cups	1¾ cups	2⅔ cups
1½ cups	2 cups	3 cups
2 cups	2⅔ cups	1 qt
2½ cups	3⅓ cups	1¼ qt
2⅔ cups	3½ cups + 2½ tsp	1¼ qt + ⅓ cup
3 cups	1 qt	1½ qt
3⅓ cups	4¼ cups + 3 Tbsp	1½ qt + ⅔ cup
3½ cups	1 qt + ⅔ cups	1¾ qt
1 qt	1¼ qt + ⅓ cup	2 qt
1 qt + ½ cup	1½ qt	2¼ qt
1 qt + ⅔ cup	1½ qt + ¼ cup	2¼ qt + ⅓ cup
1¼ qt	1½ qt + ⅔ cup	2½ qt
1¼ qt + ⅓ cup	1¾ qt + 2 Tbsp	2½ qt + ⅔ cup
1¼ qt + ½ cup	1¾ qt + ⅓ cup	2¾ qt
1½ qt	2 qt	3 qt
1½ qt + ½ cup	2 qt + ⅔ cup	3¼ qt
1½ qt + ⅔ cup	2 qt + ¾ cup + 2 Tbsp	3¼ qt + ⅓ cup
1¾ qt	2¼ qt + ⅓ cup	3½ qt
1¾ qt + ⅓ cup	2¼ qt + ¾ cup	3 qt + 2⅔ cups
1¾ qt + ½ cup	2½ qt	3 qt + 3 cups
2 qt	2¾ qt + ⅓ cup	1 gal
2½ qt	3¼ qt + ⅓ cup	1¼ gal
3 qt	1 gal	1½ gal
3½ qt	1 gal + 2⅔ cups	1¾ gal
1 gal	1¼ gal + 1⅓ cups	2 gal
1 gal + 2 cups	1½ gal	2¼ gal
1¼ gal	1½ gal + 2⅔ cups	2½ gal
1¼ gal + 2 cups	1¾ gal + 1⅓ cups	2¾ gal
1½ gal	2 gal	3 gal

continued

TABLE 2.3   Direct-reading table for increasing home-sized recipes with ingredient amounts given in volume measurement and divisible by 8

TABLE 2.3   *Continued*

8	16	24	32
1 qt + ⅓ cup	2 qt + ⅔ cup	3¼ qt	1 gal + 1⅓ cups
1 qt + ⅔ cup	2¼ qt + ⅓ cup	3½ qt	1 gal + 2⅔ cup
1¼ qt	2½ qt	3¾ qt	1¼ gal
1¼ qt + ⅓ cup	2½ qt + ⅔ cup	1 gal	1¼ gal + 1⅓ cups
1½ qt + ⅔ cup	3¼ qt + ⅓ cup	1¼ gal	1½ gal + 2⅔ cups
2 qt	1 gal	1½ gal	2 gal

TABLE 2.3   *Continued*

48	64	96
1½ gal + 2 cups	2 gal + 2⅔ cups	3¼ gal
1¾ gal	2¼ gal + 1⅓ cups	3½ gal
1¾ gal + 2 cups	2½ gal	3¾ gal
2 gal	2½ gal + 2⅔ cups	4 gal
2½ gal	3¼ gal + 1⅓ cups	5 gal
3 gal	4 gal	6 gal

Planning Menus, Special Meals, and Receptions

Menu planning and serving special events are functions by which foodservice organizations are judged. The information in this chapter provides guidelines for planning menus, special meals, and receptions.

This chapter includes the following topics:

- Menu Planning: Types of Menus; Factors Affecting Menu Planning; Menu-Planning Procedures; Menu Planning for Different Types of Foodservice
- Planning Special Meals, Receptions, and Catered Events: Planning Responsibilities; Receptions and Teas; Coffees and Brunches; Buffet Meals; Banquet Service; Styles of Service; Wine and Bar Service

Menu Planning

Food eaten outside the home has become an integral part of the American lifestyle. Patrons expect to have food choices that are creative, exciting, and nutritious. Menu writers are challenged to plan innovative menus that support the goals of the organization and that cater to customers' preferences.

A well-planned menu is the cornerstone of a successful foodservice and the focal point from which many activities originate. An understanding of menu types, factors affecting menu planning, and planning procedures is important before menu writing can begin.

TYPES OF MENUS

The menu is an outline of food items to be included in each meal or, in the broader sense, a list of all food items offered by a foodservice. Types of menus used in foodservices may be classified as static or set, cycle, or single use. Menus may be further categorized according to the degree of choice as selective or nonselective and by the method of pricing.

Static or **set menus** include the same menu items every day, but with a variety of choices, the exact number depending on the type of foodservice. Static or set menus are appropriate when clientele change daily. Most commercial foodservices use this type of menu, and some hospitals have adopted this

static or restaurant-style menu pattern. Some restaurants change a few foods within a set menu to provide additional variety or to take advantage of special purchases and seasonal and locally grown foods.

A **cycle menu** is a carefully planned series of menus that offer different items from day to day for one week, two weeks, or some other time period, after which the menus are repeated. The length of the cycle depends on the type of foodservice. A short cycle is appropriate for foodservices having a frequent clientele turnover, such as hospitals. If a short cycle is used for patient meals, a longer cycle is necessary for the employees' and visitors' foodservice. In extended-care facilities, the cycle usually is 4–6 weeks. Using a cycle with numbers of days not divisible by seven ensures that the same menu is not served on the same day of the week. Dining establishments with frequent clientele turnover, such as restaurants, may prefer to use monthly or seasonal cycles or may use the same menu throughout the year. Many foodservices recognize seasonal changes by having spring, summer, autumn, and winter cycles.

Cycle menus save time for the planner and are effective tools for food and labor cost control, forecasting, and purchasing. Repetition of the same or nearly the same menu helps standardize preparation procedures and gives the employees an opportunity to become more efficient through repeated use of familiar recipes. Menus can become monotonous and repetitious, however, if not carefully planned. Regardless of the cycle length, menus should be constantly reviewed and updated. Each day's menu should be analyzed shortly after service, and any production problems or negative clientele feedback should be noted and corrections made before the next cycle. The menu planner must allow flexibility for changes due to holidays, special occasions, leftover food, availability of locally grown foods, and inability to obtain specific food items for production.

A **single-use menu** is one written for a special event, holiday meal, or catering function and is not repeated. Foodservices that use single-use menus regularly should keep a file of menus that can be adapted for various clientele or meal occasions.

Selective menus include two or more choices for each category of food offered: appetizers (to include soup), entrées, side dishes, breads, desserts, and beverages. A selective menu for a buffet or cafeteria-style service generally has more choices per category than for a served meal. Because of labor, clientele needs, or other reasons, some foodservices may plan a **semi-selective menu** with choices planned for some food categories, such as entrées, but not for all. Regardless of the number of choices, foods from which the individual patron may choose a well-balanced meal should be included.

Most commercial and noncommercial foodservices use a selective menu extensively. Selectivity in many colleges and universities, business and industry accounts, K–12 schools, and some hospital cafeterias is often achieved by a variety of stand-alone food concepts located close together in a food court or marketplace design. Venues may vary in the amount of individual menu selectivity, but the total menu items available from all venues collectively are usually abundant.

Nonselective menus have a single item in each menu category. To ensure nutritional adequacy, foods from each of the basic food groups should be included: grains, vegetables (lunch and dinner menus), fruits, milk, meat/beans. A nonselective menu may be modified to include a limited selection; for example, two entrées may be offered or a choice of two vegetables may be served. One entrée may be served with a choice of sides. A soup and salad may be offered as an alternative to an entrée and vegetable for those who prefer a lighter meal. When nonselective menus are served, a list of alternative items should be available for clientele who ask for a substitute item. Special attention should be given to having food items available on request that do not contain common allergens such as milk, eggs, peanuts, tree nuts, fish, shellfish, soy, and wheat.

Menus may also be classified by method of pricing. **Á la carte menus** price food items separately; the customer chooses menu items individually. **Table d'hôte menus** include the complete meal at a fixed price. It is common for foodservices that use a table d'hôte menu to offer more than one choice of complete menu. Banquet menus are examples of this strategy. **Prix fixe menus** are similar to table d'hôte menus in that the price for the meal is fixed. A prix fixe menu may offer choice within a menu category. **Du jour menus** or menus of the day are planned, written, and priced daily.

FACTORS AFFECTING MENU PLANNING

The production and service of food begin with the menu, which determines the foods to be purchased, the personnel needed and their work schedules, and the equipment necessary for production and service of the food. The menu is closely tied to financial management and marketing and, in a new foodservice, influences the design of the kitchen and selection of equipment. The menu, however, must be one that meets clientele expectations and that can be produced within facility constraints and demands. A number of factors must be considered when planning a menu.

Clientele

The menu planner must consider the makeup of the group to be served: age, gender, nutritional needs, food habits and customs, and individual preferences. This is especially important if the foodservice offers limited food choices, as in some extended-care facilities, child care centers, and retirement complexes. Menus in limited-choice foodservices are planned to meet the needs of most patrons, with enough flexibility to satisfy everyone. Planning menus for foodservices with a static population requires strict attention to the complete nutritional needs of the group. Such menus also must offer enough variety to minimize monotony and keep satisfaction high.

The *Dietary Guidelines for Americans* has been published jointly every 5 years since 1980 by the Department of Health and Human Services (HHS) and the Department of Agriculture (USDA). The guidelines provide information helpful to foodservice professionals for planning menus that will help clientele eat healthy. The guidelines also serve as the basis for federal food and nutrition education programs. The *Dietary Guidelines for Americans* (2005) is available at www.health.gov/dietaryguidelines. The guidelines encourage Americans to maintain a healthy lifestyle by:

- Consuming adequate nutrients within calorie needs
- Maintaining a healthy body weight
- Engaging in physical activity
- Increasing consumption of fruits, vegetables, whole grains, and fat-free or low-fat milk or milk products
- Reducing fat consumption and increasing consumption of foods low in trans fat, saturated fat, and cholesterol
- Choosing fiber-rich fruits, vegetables, and whole grains
- Consuming low-sodium and potassium-rich foods
- Consuming alcohol in moderation (if you drink alcohol)
- Avoiding food-borne illness by following food safety guidelines

USDA has released the MyPyramid food guidance system (www.mypyramid.gov) as an interactive tool designed to help consumers plan and assess food choices and to advise them on how to make smart choices from every food group, find balance between food and physical activity, get the most nutrition out of calories, and stay within daily calorie needs. MyPyramid (Figure 3.1) has been widely distributed and is often used by clientele for directing their food choices. The pyramid and serving guidelines (Tables 3.1 and 3.2) will be useful for planning healthful menus that support clientele eating according to the *Dietary Guidelines for Americans*.

Clients are increasingly more knowledgeable about flavorful foods and interesting food combinations and desire greater variety and an opportunity to select foods representing new culinary styles. Customers often request bold flavors represented in many ethnic flavor profiles. An increased emphasis has been seen in Asian, Latin American, and Mediterranean cuisines. See Table 5.22 (p. 138) for flavor profiles of foods from various countries and regions.

Meatless preferences are varied, and savvy menu planners consider the preferences of their vegetarian clientele. **Vegans** eat plant products only; **lacto-ovo-vegetarians** eat plant products,

FIGURE 3.1   MyPyramid.

reactions may be extremely serious for some people, and procedures should be established to protect against cross-contamination.

Planning acceptable menus requires the menu planner to be aware of food preferences and to periodically evaluate clientele acceptance of foods and food combinations. Plate waste analysis, customer preference surveys, food usage data, meal census information, and informational interactions with clients are a few ways to assess menu acceptability.

Popular food magazines, trade magazines, recently published cookbooks, television's food channel, culinary school publications, and new dining establishment themes help establish eating trends of consumers and can be used as menu-planning tools. Menu choices should include current dining trends, and adjustments to the flavor profiles, plating styles, and naming conventions of existing recipes will often satisfy clientele requirements for contemporary menu items. See the examples on page 5.

dairy, and eggs. **Pesco-vegetarians** eat fish and plant products and may or may not eat dairy and eggs. Religious customs are important in menu planning also. Table 3.3 identifies food practices of different religions.

Menu planners must consider the needs of customers with food allergies and have food choices available for them. The foods that account for most food-allergic reactions are egg, milk, tree nuts, peanuts, fish, shellfish, soy, and wheat. Allergic

Type of Foodservice

Menu plans cannot be generalized to a specific type of foodservice because of the wide variety of clientele most foodservice establishments serve. Many on-site foodservices (college and university, business and industry, hospitals, etc.) offer menu choices similar to those of commercial restaurants. Hospital menus for general-diet patients may be no different from those in any other

TABLE 3.1   Food Guide Pyramid daily recommendations

Ages	Grains[a]	Vegetables[b]	Fruits	Milk	Meat/beans	Oil (allowance)
Children 2–3	3 oz equivalents	1 cup	1 cup	2 cups	2 oz equivalents	3 tsp
Children 4–8	4–5 oz equivalents	1½ cups	1–1½ cups	2 cups	3–4 oz equivalents	4 tsp
Girls 9–13	5 oz equivalents	2 cups	1½ cups	3 cups	5 oz equivalents	5 tsp
Girls 14–18	6 oz equivalents	2½ cups	1½ cups	3 cups	5 oz equivalents	5 tsp
Boys 9–13	6 oz equivalents	2½ cups	1½ cups	3 cups	5 oz equivalents	5 tsp
Boys 14–18	7 oz equivalents	3 cups	2 cups	3 cups	6 oz equivalents	6 tsp
Women 19–30	6 oz equivalents	2½ cups	2 cups	3 cups	5 ½ oz equivalents	6 tsp
Women 31–50	6 oz equivalents	2½ cups	1½ cups	3 cups	5 oz equivalents	5 tsp
Women 51+	5 oz equivalents	2 cups	1½ cups	3 cups	5 oz equivalents	5 tsp
Men 19–30	8 oz equivalents	3 cups	2 cups	3 cups	6½ oz equivalents	7 tsp
Men 31–50	7 oz equivalents	3 cups	2 cups	3 cups	6 oz equivalents	6 tsp
Men 51+	6 oz equivalents	2½ cups	2 cups	3 cups	5½ oz equivalents	6 tsp

[a]At least half of all the grains eaten should be whole grains.
[b]Vegetables should include a variety of foods from all vegetable subgroups: dark green (broccoli, collard/mustard greens, kale, spinach, dark green leafy lettuce, endive, escarole); orange (carrots, pumpkin, sweet, potato, winter squash); dry beans and peas (black/garbanzo/ pinto/soy beans, black eyed/split peas, tofu); starchy (corn, green peas, white potatoes); other (cabbage, cauliflower, cucumbers, green/wax beans, iceberg lettuce, mushrooms, onions, tomatoes, mixed vegetable juice, summer squash).
Source: Adapted from U.S. Department of Agriculture, Center for Nutrition Policy and Promotion.
Note: Amounts are approximate for individuals who get less than 30 minutes per day of moderate physical activity, beyond normal daily activities. Those who are more physically active may be able to consume more while staying within calorie needs.

TABLE 3.2 Food amounts per cup or equivalent in the Food Guide Pyramid[a]

BREAD, CEREAL, RICE, PASTA GROUP

1 oz equivalent is equal to:
- 1 slice bread, 1 small muffin, ½ English muffin
- About 1 cup ready-to-eat cereal
- ½ cup cooked cereal, rice, or pasta

FRUIT GROUP

1 cup is equal to:
- 1 small apple, 1 medium banana, 1 pear, 3 medium plums, 1 large orange, 1 peach
- 32 seedless grapes, 8 large strawberries
- 1 cup sliced raw, cut-up, cooked fruit
- 1 cup 100% fruit juice
- ½ cup dried fruit

MEAT, POULTRY, FISH, DRY BEANS, EGGS, AND NUT GROUP

1 oz equivalent is equal to:
- 1 oz cooked lean beef, pork, ham, poultry (without skin), fish, shellfish
- 1 egg
- ½ oz nuts, seeds (12 almonds, 24 pistachios, 7 walnut halves)
- 1 Tbsp peanut butter
- ¼ cup cooked dry beans, peas
- ¼ cup baked beans, refried beans
- ¼ cup tofu
- 2 Tbsp hummus

MILK, YOGURT, CHEESE GROUP[b]

1 cup is equal to:
- 1 cup milk, yogurt
- ½ oz hard cheese (such as cheddar, mozzarella, Swiss, Parmesan)
- 2 oz processed cheese (American)
- ⅓ cup shredded cheese
- 1½ cups ice cream, 1 cup pudding made with milk

VEGETABLE GROUP

1 cup is equal to:
- 1 cup raw: bell pepper strips, broccoli florets, cauliflower florets, cucumber slices, tomatoes
- 2 medium carrots, 12 baby carrots, 2 large celery stalks, 1 large bell pepper
- 1 cup cooked vegetables
- 1 cup cooked greens
- 2 cups raw greens
- 1 cup whole or mashed beans and peas, cooked
- 1 cup tofu (about 8 oz)
- 1 cup tomato or mixed vegetable juice

[a]For a complete list of foods, see www.mypyramid.gov.
[b]Choose most often: fat-free milk and yogurt, low-fat cheeses, fat-free or low-fat milk-based desserts.
Source: Adapted from U.S. Department of Agriculture, Center for Nutrition Policy and Promotion.

TABLE 3.2 Food amounts per cup or equivalent in the Food Guide Pyramid

segment of the foodservice industry. Some retirement complexes offer a traditional three-meals-per-day pattern; others serve continuously throughout the day. Knowing the type of foodservice is less important when writing menus than understanding the needs of the clientele being served and the philosophy, mission, goals, and limitations of the foodservice.

Financial Limitations

Because financial goals are generally established for food and labor, the amount of money available to spend on food must be known before the menu is planned. In some foodservices a raw food cost allowance per meal or per day may be set. In these

TABLE 3.3 Food practices of different religions

TABLE 3.3 Food practices of different religions

BUDDHISM

Much variability exists between areas of the country and the sect. Generally Buddhists do not eat meat, especially beef as the cow is considered sacred. Dairy products, eggs, and some fish are usually eaten.

CHURCH OF JESUS CHRIST OF LATTER-DAY SAINTS (MORMONISM)

Mormons do not drink coffee, tea, or alcoholic beverages. Many Mormons refrain from drinking any beverage with caffeine.

EASTERN ORTHODOX

On fast days and periods of fast, meat, fish, and animal products are not eaten. Shellfish is allowed. Fast days include most Wednesdays and Fridays (except during the fast-free week following Christmas and Easter), the Eve of Theophany, the Beheading of John the Baptist, and the Elevation of the Holy Cross. Fast periods include Advent, Great Lent, the Fast of the Apostles, and the Feast of the Dormition of the Holy Theotokos.

HINDUISM

Most Hindus follow a vegetarian diet. If meat is eaten, beef and pork are forbidden. The cow is considered sacred.

JUDAISM

Orthodox and some conservative Jews follow Jewish dietary laws that define the use of animal products. Permitted are mammals that have cloven hooves and chew a cud (e.g., cattle, goats, sheep) and poultry with a crop and gizzard (e.g., chickens, ducks, geese, turkeys) and their eggs. Fish must have fins and scales. Meat and dairy products are not eaten together, and separate kitchen equipment is required for preparing meat and dairy products.

Jewish religious holidays with food elements include the following:
Rosh Hashanah—Challah (braided egg bread) and apples dipped in honey are common menu items.
Yom Kippur—A day of fasting. A light meal is served after sundown.
Hanukkah—Latkes (potato pancakes) are often served.
Passover—A Seder meal may be served. The foods for a Seder meal are specified.

ISLAM

Prohibited foods include pigs and any animal that catches food with its mouth or talons (birds of prey). Some Muslims eat only meat slaughtered according to a prescribed method. Some Muslims do not drink alcoholic beverages, coffee, or tea. During the month-long fasting period of Ramadan, Muslims over age 15 may eat only during the time before sunrise and after sunset.

PROTESTANTISM

Dietary customs vary among denominations.

ROMAN CATHOLICISM

Few dietary restrictions are stipulated. Catholics between ages 14 and 60 are required to abstain from eating meat on Ash Wednesday and Good Friday and during the Fridays of Lent. Some Catholics may abstain from eating meat on every Friday throughout the year.

SEVENTH-DAY ADVENTIST

Coffee, tea, alcoholic beverages, pork, and shellfish are not eaten. Milk and eggs are permitted. Many Seventh-Day Adventists do not eat meat or animal products. See the section on Judaism for animal products that are permitted.

foodservices daily food costs may fluctuate, but the cumulative average for a set period of time must stay within the established daily allowance. For menus in all-you-care-to-eat dining facilities, or for buffets, food cost can be controlled by serving high-cost items along with popular low-cost items. It is necessary to evaluate carefully the popularity of menu items in relation to cost. For example, adding low-cost items that are less popular than the more expensive items on the menu will not lower food costs significantly. A savvy menu writer will consider menu items that are high profit and popular, high profit and not popular, low profit and popular, and low profit and not popular when building menus that meet both customer satisfaction and financial goals.

Labor must be considered along with raw food cost. Some items with a low food cost may require a high amount of labor to prepare, and some items with a high food cost may require little labor. The menu should be planned so food production labor is used effectively.

In foodservices with à la carte pricing, the amount of money that can be spent on food is based on projected income from the sale of food. When the selling price must be within a predetermined range, the choice of menu items is especially important. The pricing methods described in Appendix C illustrate the relationship between menu item cost and selling price. Appendix D demonstrates the relationships between EP and AP cost per serving.

Food Availability

Although most foods are available year-round, there may be seasonal differences in quality and price. Peak seasons for fresh fruits and produce should be used when planning menus (Table 4.3, p. 82). Seasonal price differences occur also for nonproduce food products, such as fresh fish and poultry. Locally grown food products that are available at farmer's markets and elsewhere should be considered; they are usually fresh, of good quality, and reasonably priced. When buying locally grown produce, it is important to confirm that safe growing, handling, and delivery practices have been followed. Food contamination can be caused from such things as animal waste in water runoff or irrigation water supplied to crops, improper use of chemicals, poor pest control practices, unsanitized equipment used for crop harvesting and distribution, unsafe processing practices, lack of temperature control for products that have been harvested, and poor hand-washing and other sanitation practices of food handlers throughout the growing and distribution chain. The pack size of perishable products should be considered when planning menus so they can be used completely within their food safety time guidelines. For example, additional menu items should be planned to use the remainder of a container of plain yogurt when only a small amount was needed for another item. It is especially important to plan menus to use on-hand perishable products.

Production Capabilities

Available Equipment.   The type, size, and amount of food preparation, holding, and transporting equipment available are important factors in planning menus that can be produced. Special attention should be given to oven capacity, number of grills or fryers, refrigerator and freezer facilities, number and size of steam-jacketed kettles and steamers, and availability and capacity of mixers. Certain combinations of menu items often must be avoided because of lack of production equipment or serving pans and dishes.

Number and Experience of Employees.   The person-hours of labor available and the efficiency and skill of employees are important factors to consider when deciding on the variety and complexity of the menu. Understanding the relationship between menu and personnel will help the planner develop menus that can be prepared by the available staff.

Distribution of Work.   Menus should be planned to distribute the work evenly among the different areas of preparation. In determining a day's workload, the menu planner should consider not only one day's menu but also any preparation necessary for meals for the following day. Care should be

exercised so menus are not planned that create an excessive workload for employees one day and underutilize them the next. To introduce variety in the menu, a limited number of foods requiring time-consuming processes may be included if combined with other food items that require minimum preparation. Some foods require last-minute cooking to ensure high quality. To avoid confusion and delayed meal service, the menu should be planned to balance items that may be prepared early and those that must be cooked just before serving.

MENU-PLANNING PROCEDURES

Menu planning follows no absolute rules as long as clientele needs are satisfied and organization goals are met. It is suggested that menu planning be done without interruptions and that the following materials be available to the menu writer.

1. Menu forms as prescribed by type and needs of the foodservice.
2. Standardized recipe file.
3. Current trade periodicals and other foodservice publications.
4. Menu suggestions (Appendix A).
5. Previous menus.
6. Menu evaluation data to include customer and staff feedback.
7. *Dietary Guidelines for Americans* (full document available at www.health.gov/dietaryguidelines).

The following general guidelines should be considered when planning a menu.

Plan for Variety and Good Nutrition

1. Include a wide variety of foods from day to day to ensure adequate nutrients. Unless you provide a choice, avoid the same form of food on consecutive days, such as meat loaf on one day and spaghetti and meatballs the next.
2. Include foods that will allow clientele to meet the *Dietary Guidelines for Americans* as established by the U.S. Department of Agriculture and the U.S. Department of Health and Human Services (see p. 29 for guidelines).
3. Include food choices that will meet the needs of clientele with allergies and other health issues.
4. Include foods that will satisfy vegans, vegetarians, and clientele with religious-related preferences.
5. Avoid repeating the same food on the same day of the week. For this reason, a short cycle in which the days are divisible by seven is undesirable.
6. Avoid serving the same food too often or too close together on the menu.
7. Vary the method of preparation. For example, serve vegetables raw or cooked, seasoned, stir-fried, marinated, or with a sauce.
8. Introduce new foods regularly and, on a selective menu, pair a new food with a familiar well-liked food.

Plan for Eye Appeal

1. Try to visualize the appearance of the food on the plate.
2. Use at least one or two colorful foods on each menu.
3. Use colorful foods in combination with foods having little color.
4. When serving more than one vegetable, serve one green and one nongreen vegetable. Avoid serving vegetables that are the same color as the entrée.
5. Vary the shapes of food.

Plan for Contrast in Texture and Flavor

1. Offer crisp foods with soft foods.
2. Use strong- and mild-flavored foods together.
3. Balance light and heavy foods; for example, in a nonselective menu, pair light desserts with hearty entrées.
4. Avoid repeating foods with similar cooking methods.
5. Avoid using the same herbs and spices in foods served together on the same plate.
6. Avoid serving very strongly flavored foods with delicate or mild-flavored entrées.

Plan for Consumer Acceptance

1. Include food combinations most acceptable to the clientele.
2. The completed menu should, if possible, have a predominance of familiar and well-accepted menu items, with the introduction of new or less well-liked foods spaced throughout the menu period.
3. In nonselective menus, it is important that the less popular foods be accompanied by some that are well liked by most of the clientele.
4. Periodically assess the food preferences of the consumers.

Plan for Financial, Production, and Service Limitations

1. Include food combinations that can be prepared with available personnel and equipment.
2. Select menu items that will keep food costs within the budget allowance.

Plan for Minimizing Leftovers

1. Plan menu items so as much edible trim as possible can be incorporated into another menu item; for example, meat scraps in soup, stock, or other dishes, or raw meat trim in stew.
2. Plan menu item combinations so leftovers can be minimized; for example, include menu items that can be batch produced or cooked to order along with items requiring longer production times. Forecasting is easier, often resulting in fewer leftovers, when popular menu items are served along with less popular items.
3. Plan the menu to use leftover menu items in a different form; for example, roast turkey followed by turkey salad sandwich rather than the reverse order.

4. Carefully plan menus to use perishable ingredients that have an order quantity greater than the amount needed for a specific recipe. For example, if 5 lb of leeks are needed for a specific recipe but the order quantity is 10 lb, it is prudent to plan a menu to use the extra leeks.

Steps in Menu Planning

Determine a Time Period. Plan menus for at least a week at a time, preferably longer. If a cycle menu is being planned, decide on the length of the cycle. Decide on the meal pattern before beginning.

Proceed Systematically. Select menu items systematically. Entrées are selected first because they are the central focus of a meal and form the framework of the menu plan. Other foods are then chosen that complement the entrée.

Entrées. Select meat and other entrées for the entire cycle or length of time for which menus are being planned. When planning a week's menus only, choose entrées for a month or longer, then complete the menus as needed. In this way, an entrée cycle can be developed that would simplify planning each week's menus. Because entrées usually are the most expensive food on the menu, cost can be controlled to a great extent through careful planning at this point. A balance between high- and low-priced items will average out the cost over the week or period covered by the cycle.

On a selective menu, offer at least one meat and one meatless entrée, along with poultry and fish to complete the number of entrées required.

Be specific about method of preparation when recording the menu; for example, show pork chops as baked, stuffed, barbecued, breaded, or prepared using another method.

Soups and Sandwiches. Plan soups and sandwiches at the same time as entrées if they are to be offered as a main dish in lieu of meat or other entrées. On a selective menu, offer a cream soup and a stock soup. In a cafeteria, a variety of sandwiches may be offered that may not change from day to day.

Vegetables. Select vegetables that are compatible with the entrées. Potatoes, rice, or pasta may be included as one choice. On a selective menu, pair a popular vegetable with one that is less well liked.

Salads. If only one salad is to be offered, select one that complements or is a contrast in texture to the other menu items. On a selective menu, include a green salad and fruit, vegetable, and gelatin salads to complete the desired number. Certain salad items may be offered daily, such as tossed salad, cottage cheese, or cabbage slaw; or a salad bar may be a standard menu feature. See p. 593 for salad bar suggestions.

Breads.   Vary the kinds of breads offered or provide a choice of white or whole-grain bread and a hot bread.

Desserts.   If no choice is offered, plan a light dessert with a hearty meal and a rich dessert when the rest of the meal is not too heavy. On a selective menu, include a two-crust pie, a soft pie, cake, pudding, and a gelatin dessert. Ice cream, yogurt, baked custard, and fruit may be offered daily.

Breakfast Items.   Certain breakfast foods such as cooked and cold cereal, toast, and fruit juices may be standard. Variety may be introduced through a choice of entrées, hot breads, and fresh fruits.

Beverages.   A choice of beverages usually is provided. Coffee, decaffeinated coffee, tea, and milk, including low-fat milk, usually are offered. Lemonade, soft drinks, fruit punch, and a variety of juices may be included also.

Evaluate the Completed Menu.   After the menu has been planned, check carefully to see if it has met the established criteria. Evaluate the menu again after the meals have been served. Make notations of satisfactory menus and difficulties encountered in production and service of the meals. If the cycle is to be repeated, desired alterations should be noted.

The responsibility of the menu planner does not end with the writing of the menu. The task is completed only when the food has been prepared and served and the reaction of the consumer noted.

MENU PLANNING FOR DIFFERENT TYPES OF FOODSERVICE

Elementary and Secondary Schools

National School Lunch Program.   The National School Lunch Program (NSLP) is designed to provide nutritious, reasonably priced lunches to children in schools and residential child care centers, to contribute to a better understanding of good nutrition, and to foster good food habits. School foodservice is an integral part of the child's education.

The nutrition goals of the NSLP are designed to provide adequate calories and nutrients for specific age groups of children while reducing fat and saturated fat to recommended levels. The goals are based on the Recommended Dietary Allowances (RDAs) (one-fourth of the RDAs for breakfast, one-third of the RDAs for lunch), children's calorie (energy) requirements, and the *Dietary Guidelines for Americans* (p. 29). USDA nutrient standards for the NSLP set a one-third RDA requirement for calories, calcium, iron, protein, and vitamins A and C. Standards also specify that no more than 30 percent of calories come from fat and less than 10 percent of the fat calories come from saturated fat. States are required to establish their own nutrient standards for carbohydrates, cholesterol, fiber, and sodium.

Three menu-planning systems that meet federal guidelines are compared in Table 3.4. *Enhanced Food-Based Menu Planning* requires specific food group components in specific amounts for different established age/grade groups. *Nutrient Standard Menu Planning (NSMP)* uses computerized nutrient analysis of menus. This planning system uses a simplified menu pattern that requires that lunches include an entrée and milk. Other food items may be added to the menu. When averaged over a week, the menus must meet the nutrient standards and calorie requirements for specific age/grade groups. NSMP and *Assisted Nutrient Standard Menu Planning (Assisted NSMP)* are exactly alike except that for the latter, an outside consultant or other agency performs all functions of menu planning and nutrient analysis.

Not represented in Table 3.4 is the *Traditional Food-Based Menu Planning* system, used since the National School Lunch Program was established in 1946. Although the Traditional Food-Based Menu Planning system is still an option, it is used infrequently because of the difficulty in complying with the *Dietary Guidelines*. This system was designed to provide, over time, the RDA for key nutrients but without consideration for calorie needs or dietary fat.

To qualify for reimbursement, a school is required to use the framework specified in this table and to meet the minimum nutrition standard requirements described in Tables 3.5 and 3.6. Other foods may be added to improve acceptability and to satisfy students' appetites.

An "offer versus serve" provision allows students to choose fewer than all the food items offered. However, they must select a specified minimum amount of food in order for the lunch to be reimbursed. Schools are required to implement the "offer versus serve" provision for senior high school students. The implementation of this provision in middle, junior high, and elementary schools is left to the discretion of the local school food authorities.

The cycle menu is used to some extent in school foodservices, and many schools are using selective menus in which students may choose from two items of comparable nutritional value for part of the menu; for example, a student may have a choice of two vegetables and two fruits. Some schools offer multiple menus in which more than one complete menu that meets federal requirements is offered, such as a chef's salad or soup and sandwich meal. À la carte items are also provided in many schools. The more menu choices provided to students, the better their participation in the school foodservice programs.

Many foods in the Suggested Menu Items listed in Appendix A are suitable for school lunches. Keep in mind the nutrition requirements, cost, labor and equipment restraints, and food preferences of the age group served. Adding options such as salad bars, special-day celebrations, or ethnic and international food promotions allows the school foodservice operation to compete with commercial foodservices.

School Breakfast Program.   The importance of students eating a nutritious breakfast cannot be overemphasized. Breakfast furnishes fuel for the morning, when students do most of their learning. In 1975, Congress passed an amendment that made

TABLE 3.4 Comparison of school foodservice menu-planning systems

	Enhanced Food-Based Menu Planning	Assisted Nutrient Standard Menu Planning ("Assisted NuMenus")	Nutrient Standard Menu Planning ("NuMenus")
Meals are planned based on . . .	Enhanced Meal Pattern (must meet nutritional standards)	Required nutrient levels averaged over a school week	Required nutrient levels averaged over a school week
Reimbursable lunch requirements under "offer vs. serve"	Offer a minimum of 5 food items: • 1 meat/meat alt. • 2 vegetables/fruits • 1 grain/bread • 1 milk Senior high students must accept 3 food items. Students below senior high must accept 3 or 4 food items at the discretion of the school food authority.	• Schools must offer students at least 3 menu items: an entrée, fluid milk, and another menu item. • Students must select at least 2 of the 3 menu items; 1 of the 2 must be an entrée. • If more than 3 menu items are offered as a meal unit, students may decline no more than 2 menu items of the meal unit (entrée must be selected).	• Schools must offer students at least 3 menu items: an entrée, fluid milk, and another menu item. • Students must select at least 2 of the 3 menu items; 1 of the 2 must be an entrée. • If more than 3 menu items are offered as a meal unit, students may decline no more than 2 menu items of the meal unit (entrée must be selected).
Reimbursable breakfast requirements under "offer vs. serve"	Offer a minimum of 4 food items: • 1 milk • 1 vegetable/fruit/juice • 1 of the 3 following combinations: 1 meat/meat alt. AND 1 grain/bread OR 2 meat/meat alt. OR 2 grains/breads Students must accept 3 food items.	• Schools must offer fluid milk as a beverage or on cereal or both. Must offer at least 2 side dishes. • Students may decline a maximum of 1 menu item out of the 3 or more required menu items offered.	• Schools must offer fluid milk as a beverage or on cereal or both. Must offer at least 2 side dishes. • Students may decline a maximum of 1 menu item out of the 3 or more required menu items offered.
Menu items credited toward nutrient standard requirements	Only USDA-approved foods count toward meeting meal pattern.	All menu items count.	All menu items count.
Computer needs	Not required	Not required because nutrient analysis may be done by another school, a consultant, or a school food co-op.	Required—District must have computer hardware and USDA-approved nutrient analysis software.
Recordkeeping	• Production records document quantities planned and served. • CN (Child Nutrition) label or product analysis required for pre-prepared items. • Recipes and nutritional analysis of pre-prepared items.	• Production records document quantities planned and served. • Nutrient analysis required at school level.	• Production records document quantities planned and served. • Nutrient analysis required at school level.
Age/grade groupings (lunch)	Three grade groups are required: • Preschool • K–6 • 7–12 Four grade groups are optional: • Preschool • K–3 • 4–6 • 7–12 **Breakfast required** • Preschool • K–12 • 7–12 (optional)	Opt. 1—Grade Groups: • Preschool • K–6 (optional: K–3 and 4–6) • 7–12 Opt. 2—Age Groups: • 3–6 • 7–10 • 11–13 • 14 and older Opt. 3—Create custom groups **Breakfast required** • K–12 • 7–12 (optional)	Opt. 1—Grade Groups: • Preschool • K–6 (optional: K–3 and 4–6) • 7–12 Opt. 2—Age Groups: • 3–6 • 7–10 • 11–13 • 14 and older Opt. 3—Create custom groups **Breakfast required** • K–12 • 7–12 (optional)

continued

TABLE 3.4 Comparison of school foodservice menu-planning systems

TABLE 3.4 continued

	Enhanced Food-Based Menu Planning	Assisted Nutrient Standard Menu Planning ("Assisted NuMenus")	Nutrient Standard Menu Planning ("NuMenus")
Meeting *Dietary Guidelines*	• Schools must meet *Dietary Guidelines*. Nutrient analysis is optional. • State education agency will conduct nutrient analysis to determine whether *Dietary Guidelines* are met.	• Schools must meet *Dietary Guidelines* and are required to provide nutrient analysis at school level. Schools must document that they have served the recipes and menus used in the nutrient analysis. • State education agency will review nutrient analysis to determine whether *Dietary Guidelines* are met.	• Schools must meet *Dietary Guidelines* and are required to do nutrient analysis at school level. • State education agency will review nutrient analysis to determine whether *Dietary Guidelines* are met.
Advantages	Requires minimal training and change for local personnel.	Requires minimal training and change for local personnel. Menus will comply with the *Dietary Guidelines for Americans*.	Local district retains flexibility and control. Menus will comply with the *Dietary Guidelines for Americans*.
Disadvantages	School will not know whether it is meeting the *Dietary Guidelines* until it is reviewed by state education agency. Length of education agency review will increase substantially to allow time to perform nutrient analysis. Because of the length of time between reviews, problems could go uncorrected for long periods.	Costs may be incurred to have an outside party perform nutrient analysis. If a food vendor performs nutrient analysis, there may be financial implications. For example, schools may be required to use specified products. Schools will lose some control and flexibility.	Costs will be incurred for hardware and software. Personnel will need to spend time learning the software and setting up the system (i.e., entering local recipe and product data).

Notes:
- The Enhanced Food-Based Menu Planning Approach is a variation of the Traditional Menu Planning Approach. It is designed to increase calories from low-fat food sources in order to meet the *Dietary Guidelines*. The five food components are retained, but the component quantities for the weekly servings of vegetables and fruits and grains/breads are increased.
- Assisted Nutrient Standard Menu Planning (sometimes called "Assisted NuMenus") is a variation of Nutrient Standard Menu Planning. It is for schools that lack the technical resources to conduct nutrient analysis themselves. Instead, schools have an outside source, such as another school district, a state agency, or a consultant, plan and analyze a menu based on local needs and preferences. The outside source also provides schools with recipes and product specifications to support the menus. The menus and analyses are periodically updated to reflect any changes in the menu or student selection patterns.
- Nutrient Standard Menu Planning (sometimes called "NuMenus") is a computer-based menu-planning system that uses approved computer software to analyze the specific nutrient content of menu items automatically while menus are being planned. It is designed to help menu planners choose food items that create nutritious meals and meet the nutrient standards.
- Under the Traditional Food-Based Menu Planning Approach (not shown), schools must comply with specific component and quantity requirements by offering five food items from four food components. These components are meat/meat alternate, vegetables and/or fruits, grains/breads, and milk. Minimum portion sizes are established by ages and grade groups.
- The Alternate Menu Planning Approach (not shown) allows states and school districts to develop their own innovative approaches to menu planning, subject to the guidelines established in the regulations. These guidelines protect the nutritional and fiscal integrity of the program.

Source: From Kansas State Department of Education (KSDE) and USDA.

TABLE 3.4 Comparison of school foodservice menu-planning systems

TABLE 3.5 Age group nutrient standards for NuMenus and Assisted NuMenus[a]

Nutrients and energy allowances	Ages 3–6	Ages 7–10	Ages 11–13	Ages 14 and above
SCHOOL BREAKFAST				
Energy allowances/calories	419	500	588	625
Total fat (as a percentage of actual total food energy)	[b]	[b]	[b]	[b]
Saturated fat (as a percentage of actual total food energy)	[b]	[b]	[b]	[b]
Protein (g)	5.50	7.00	11.25	12.50
Calcium (mg)	200	200	300	300
Iron (mg)	2.5	2.5	3.4	3.4
Vitamin A (RE)	119	175	225	225
Vitamin C (mg)	11.00	11.25	12.50	14.40
SCHOOL LUNCH				
Energy allowance/calories	558	667	783	846
Total fat (as a percentage of actual total food energy)	[b]	[b]	[b]	[b]
Saturated fat (as a percentage of actual total food energy)	[b]	[b]	[b]	[b]
Protein (g)	7.3	9.3	15.0	16.7
Calcium (mg)	267	267	400	400
Iron (mg)	3.3	3.3	4.5	4.5
Vitamin A (RE)	158	233	300	300
Vitamin C (mg)	14.6	15.0	16.7	19.2

[a]School week averages for age groups.
[b]Fat should not exceed 30 percent of calories over a school week; saturated fat should be less than 10 percent of calories over a school week. In addition, be aware that for both total fat and saturated fat, fat grams will vary depending on calorie level.
Source: From U.S. Department of Agriculture.

TABLE 3.6 Grade group nutrient standards for NuMenus, Assisted NuMenus, and Enhanced Food-Based Menu Planning[a]

Nutrients and energy allowances

SCHOOL BREAKFAST	Preschool	Grades K–12	Grades 7–12 Option	
Energy allowances/calories	388	554	618	
Total fat (as a percentage of actual total food energy)	[b]	[b]	[b]	
Saturated fat (as a percentage of actual total food energy)	[b]	[b]	[b]	
Protein (g)	5	10	12	
Calcium (mg)	200	257	300	
Iron (mg)	2.5	3.0	3.4	
Vitamin A (RE)	113	197	225	
Vitamin C (mg)	11	13	14	
SCHOOL LUNCH	Preschool	Grades K–6	Grades 7–12	Grades K–3 Option
Energy allowance/calories	517	664	825	633
Total fat (as a percentage of actual total food energy)	[b]	[b]	[b]	[b]
Saturated fat (as a percentage of actual total food energy)	[b]	[b]	[b]	[b]
Protein (g)	7	10	16	9
Calcium (mg)	267	286	400	267
Iron (mg)	3.3	3.5	4.5	3.3
Vitamin A (RE)	150	224	300	200
Vitamin C (mg)	14	15	18	15

[a]School week averages for grade groups.
[b]Fat should not exceed 30 percent of calories over a school week; saturated fat should be less than 10 percent of calories over a school week. In addition, be aware that for both total fat and saturated fat, fat grams will vary depending on calorie level.
Source: From U.S. Department of Agriculture.

the School Breakfast Program (SBP) a permanent part of the Child Nutrition Act. All public and nonprofit private schools may participate in the SBP.

The school breakfast and lunch patterns for the various age groups is shown in Table 3.7. To qualify for reimbursement, a school is required to use this framework and to meet the minimum requirements, but other foods may be added to help improve acceptability and to satisfy students' appetites. "Offer versus serve" is also available to any school in the SBP, whereby students can refuse some items comprising a school breakfast.

Child and Adult Care Food Program

The Child and Adult Care Food Program (CACFP) was founded in 1968 to provide federal funds for meals and snacks to licensed public and nonprofit child care centers, and to family and group child care homes for preschool children. Funds are also provided for meals and snacks to eligible children and adults who are enrolled for care at participating child care centers, day care homes, after-school care programs, emergency shelters, and adult nonresidential day care centers. Both public and private nonprofit organizations are eligible to participate in CACFP.

To meet the nutritional needs of children and adults, specified meal patterns are followed. The required portion sizes for young children differ slightly between CACFP and school nutrition programs. CACFP Meal Pattern requirements are shown in Tables 3.8 and 3.9.

In planning food for children, their total daily food requirements should be considered. The combination of meals and snacks will vary according to the age group, their time of arrival at the center, and their length of stay. It is important that the planner consider the nutritional needs of the children, their food preferences, regional food habits, equipment, personnel, and other management functions.

Young children need nutritious foods at frequent intervals, but it is important to schedule the service of food to allow sufficient time between meals and supplements. Young children enjoy food they can handle easily. Finger food, snacks, and bite-size pieces are most popular. Banana slices, berries, dried fruit, fresh fruit wedges, carrot and celery sticks, broccoli and cauliflower florets, cheese cubes, and crackers are examples of finger foods.

Those responsible for foodservice in child care centers should provide the opportunity for children to learn about the foods they eat so they can begin to make wise, nutritious choices.

Colleges and Universities

College and university foodservice menus are representative of the marked change in the college foodservice industry over the last 20 years. The college customer on most campuses has several menu options: board plan cafeterias, à la carte dining facilities, specialty shops, multiconcept food courts, convenience stores, vending operations, cash cafeterias, and fine dining restaurants. Also commonplace are catering operations that support social, athletic, and university events both on and off campus.

More than one menu type may be appropriate for these varied functions because the menu must support many objectives. For example, a serving area may provide traditional board, cash meals, and carry-out food options from a single location. The success of these complex operations is closely linked to the menu design and the ability of the menu writer to satisfy both facility and customer objectives.

A selective menu pattern (p. 28) may be used for designing a traditional cycle menu. With today's campus diner, however, the most successful menus offer extensive variety. Menus must be exciting and creative and reflect choices that parallel student preferences. Basing menu decisions on accurate food trend data is necessary.

Consideration for good nutrition is important for all menu writers but offers a special challenge when the customer is generally from a healthy population and often between 18 and 28 years old. Customers of this age are more likely to make choices based on impulse preference than are clientele from a population with health and dietary concerns. The menu, to be successful, must allow for customer satisfaction and at the same time reflect the principles of sound nutrition and quality nutritious food. Customer input is necessary for designing menus that allow this to happen. See the *Dietary Guidelines for Americans* (p. 29).

The following section, "Commercial Foodservices," includes additional information appropriate to the college and university market.

Commercial Foodservices

Menu planning for commercial foodservices varies according to the type and size of operation, its goals, and the expected check average. Menus range from those suitable for fast-food concepts to formal seated-service restaurants.

The basic rules of menu planning apply to commercial foodservices. Type of foodservice must be determined, financial goals decided, production and service capabilities analyzed, and labor needs addressed. Assessing clientele wants is especially important and should be assessed accurately, using proven research procedures.

Commercial customers make choices daily about what and where to eat and the amount of money they will spend. It is often not enough for the menu planner to follow all the rules that make production and service possible without special consideration for the role the menu plays in making the commercial foodservice operation successful. The following are some guidelines that should be followed in designing the commercial menu:

- Decide what to serve and what to charge. Market research is necessary to assess accurately what customers will purchase.
- Design the presentation of the menu suitable to the operation. The layout and overall design should be readable and attractive and should support marketing goals.
- Determine the sequence of food items on the menu. A generally accepted sequence is appetizers or foods eaten first, then soups, entrées, and desserts. Within this order, salads,

TABLE 3.7 Food-based menu meal plans

	Minimum Quantities for Enhanced Food-Based Menus			
	Required			**Option**
	Ages 1–2	**Preschool**	**Grades K–12**	**Grades 7–12**
BREAKFAST				
MILK (FLUID)				
(As a beverage, on cereal, or both)	4 fl oz	6 fl oz	8 fl oz	8 fl oz
JUICE/FRUIT/VEGETABLE				
(Fruit and/or vegetable; or full-strength fruit juice or vegetable juice)	¼ cup	½ cup	½ cup	½ cup
Select *one* serving from each of the following components or *two* from one component:				
GRAINS/BREADS[a]				
One of the following or an equivalent combination:				
Whole-grain or enriched bread, whole-grain or enriched biscuit/roll, muffin, etc.	½ serving	½ serving	1 serving	1 serving
Whole-grain, enriched, or fortified cereal	¼ cup or ⅓ oz	⅓ cup or ½ oz	¾ cup or 1 oz	¾ cup or 1 oz
				Plus an additional serving of one of the grains/breads above
MEAT OR MEAT ALTERNATES				
Meat/poultry or fish	½ oz	½ oz	1 oz	1 oz
Cheese	½ oz	½ oz	1 oz	1 oz
Egg (large)	½	½	½	½
Peanut butter or other nut or seed butters	1 Tbsp	1 Tbsp	2 Tbsp	2 Tbsp
Cooked dry beans and peas	2 Tbsp	2 Tbsp	4 Tbsp	4 Tbsp
Nuts and/or seeds (as listed in program guidance)[b]	½ oz	½ oz	1 oz	1 oz
Yogurt (plain or flavored, sweetened or unsweetened)[c]	2 oz or ¼ cup	2 oz or ¼ cup	4 oz or ½ cup	4 oz or ½ cup

	Minimum Quantities for Enhanced Food-Based Menus				
	Required				**Option**
	Ages 1–2	**Preschool**	**Grades K–6**	**Grades 7–12**	**Grades K–3**
LUNCH					
MILK (AS A BEVERAGE)	6 fl oz	6 fl oz	8 fl oz	8 fl oz	8 fl oz
MEAT OR MEAT ALTERNATE (QUANTITY OF THE EDIBLE PORTION AS SERVED)					
Lean meat, poultry, or fish	1 oz	1½ oz	2 oz	2 oz	1½ oz
Cheese	1 oz	1½ oz	2 oz	2 oz	1½ oz
Large egg	½	¾	1	1	¾
Cooked dry beans or peas	¼ cup	⅜ cup	½ cup	½ cup	⅜ cup
Peanut butter or other nut or seed butters	2 Tbsp	3 Tbsp	4 Tbsp	4 Tbsp	3 Tbsp
Yogurt (plain or flavored, unsweetened or sweetened)	4 oz or ½ cup	6 oz or ¾ cup	8 oz or 1 cup	8 oz or 1 cup	8 oz or ¾ cup
The following may be used to meet no more than 50% of the requirement and must be used in combination with any of the above:					

continued

TABLE 3.7   continued

Peanuts, soynuts, tree nuts, or seeds, as listed in program guidance, or an equivalent quantity of any combination of the above meat/meat alternate (1 ounce of nuts/seeds = 1 ounce of cooked lean meat, poultry, or fish).	½ oz = 50%	¾ oz = 50%	1 oz = 50%	1 oz = 50%	¾ oz = 50%
VEGETABLES/FRUITS					
(2 or more servings of vegetables or fruits or both)	½ cup	½ cup	¾ cup plus extra ½ cup over a week[d]	1 cup	¾ cup
GRAINS/BREADS					
(Must be enriched or whole grain. A serving is a slice of bread or an equivalent serving of biscuits, rolls, etc., or ½ cup of cooked rice, macaroni, noodles, other pasta products, or cereal grains.)[a]	5 servings per week[d]	8 servings per week[d]	12 servings per week[d]	15 servings per week[d]	10 servings per week[d]
	Minimum of ½ per day[e]	Minimum of 1 per day[e]	Minimum of 1 per day[e]	Minimum of 1 per day[e]	Minimum of 1 per day[e]

[a]Grain/bread requirements are based on the weight of the enriched flour or whole grain in the product.
[b]No more than 1 oz of nuts and/or seeds may be served in any one meal.
[c]Frozen yogurt may not be counted.
[d]For the purposes of this chart, a week equals 5 days.
[e]Up to one grains/breads serving per day may be a dessert.
Note: The Enhanced Food-Based Menu Planning Approach uses the same meal pattern and age groups as the Traditional Food-Based Menu Planning Approach. For breakfast, the only difference is the addition of an optional age/grade group for grades 7–12 to better meet the needs of children in that crucial growth period by adding low-fat calories from additional servings of grains/breads. For lunch the enhanced approach is designed to increase calories from low-fat food sources in order to meet the *Dietary Guidelines*. The five food components are retained, but the component quantities for the weekly servings of vegetables and fruits and grains/breads are increased.
Source: From U.S. Department of Agriculture.

TABLE 3.7   Food-based menu meal plans

side orders, and beverages must be placed. Foods listed first within each category are selected most often, so consideration should be given to this placement.

- Write the menu names to describe the foods offered accurately and to merchandise the food item and the operation. The importance of the menu in creating atmosphere and serving as a marketing and advertising tool cannot be overemphasized.

Hospitals

Although hospital menus may be more complex, the principles of meal planning for health care facilities are the same as those for other types of foodservices. Foods must be provided for many kinds of diets, such as liquid, ground, soft, or regular; low-sodium, low-carbohydrate, or fat-restricted; and a wide range in caloric requirements. In addition, a foodservice venue generally is available for hospital personnel and visitors.

Like college and university foodservices, hospitals are adopting menus more characteristic of the commercial foodservice industry. An emphasis is placed on developing innovative menus and offering new and creative food items. Many

hospitals use catering and other food-related services as revenue centers.

Cycle menus are widely used in health care facilities. The length of patient stay is an important factor in determining the length of the cycle. In an acute-care hospital, where the average length of stay may be 3–5 days, a short cycle could be used. In an extended-care facility, a longer cycle would be more satisfactory. If a short cycle is used for patient meals, a longer cycle would be required for the employee cafeteria.

When developing a hospital meal pattern, the first step is to plan a regular or normal diet that will supply all food essentials necessary for good nutrition. This pattern then becomes the foundation for most diets required for therapeutic purposes and is the core of all meal planning in a hospital of any type or size. Patients requiring other than a normal diet will receive various modifications of the regular diet to fit their particular needs.

In planning a normal or regular diet, meals should be planned for each day as a unit. Each day's menu then can be checked to be sure that all essential foods have been included.

TABLE 3.8 Child care meal pattern requirements

Breakfast for Children

Select all three components for a reimbursable meal.

Food components	Ages 1–2	Ages 3–5	Ages 6–12[a]
1 MILK			
Fluid milk	½ cup	¾ cup	1 cup
1 FRUIT/VEGETABLE			
Juice,[b] fruit and/or vegetable	¼ cup	½ cup	½ cup
1 GRAINS/BREAD[c]			
Bread or	½ slice	½ slice	1 slice
Cornbread or biscuit or roll or muffin or	½ serving	½ serving	1 serving
Cold dry cereal or	¼ cup	⅓ cup	¾ cup
Hot cooked cereal or	¼ cup	¼ cup	½ cup
Pasta or noodles or grains	¼ cup	¼ cup	½ cup

Snack for Children

Select two of the four components for a reimbursable snack.

Food components	Ages 1–2	Ages 3–5	Ages 6–12[a]
1 MILK			
Fluid milk	½ cup	½ cup	1 cup
1 FRUIT/VEGETABLE			
Juice,[b] fruit and/or vegetable	½ cup	½ cup	¾ cup
1 GRAINS/BREAD[c]			
Bread or	½ slice	½ slice	1 slice
Cornbread or biscuit or roll or muffin or	½ serving	½ serving	1 serving
Cold dry cereal or	¼ cup	⅓ cup	¾ cup
Hot cooked cereal or	¼ cup	¼ cup	½ cup
Pasta or noodles or grains	¼ cup	¼ cup	½ cup
1 MEAT/MEAL ALTERNATE			
Meat or poultry or fish[d] or	½ oz	½ oz	1 oz
Alternate protein product or	½ oz	½ oz	1 oz
Cheese or	½ oz	½ oz	1 oz
Egg[e] or	½ egg	½ egg	½ egg
Cooked dry beans or peas or	⅛ cup	⅛ cup	¼ cup
Peanut or other nut or seed butters or	1 Tbsp	1 Tbsp	2 Tbsp
Nuts and/or seeds or	½ oz	½ oz	1 oz
Yogurt[f]	2 oz	2 oz	4 oz

continued

The selective menu adds much to the satisfaction of patients and also helps prevent waste. Choices that appeal to various patients usually can be made available with little extra work, if careful planning is used in pairing items on the menu. The main items on the selective menu are the same as those on the general menu. Some items, such as the choice of meat and vegetables, may be the same as foods prepared for one of the modified diets or for the cafeteria. Other choices may be soup or fruit juice, or fruit or ice cream in place of a prepared dessert. On the dinner menu, choices of light or heartier foods may do much to promote patient acceptance. Some hospitals have adopted a selective menu similar to the table d'hôte menu of the commercial sector. The same menu is offered daily but with a wide enough variety of choices that the patient can select a different meal each day. Patients may order any food item on the menu unless it is restricted on their diets.

TABLE 3.8 Child care meal pattern requirements

TABLE 3.8 continued

Lunch or Supper for Children

Select all four components for a reimbursable meal.

Food components	Ages 1–2	Ages 3–5	Ages 6–12[a]
1 MILK			
Fluid milk	½ cup	¾ cup	1 cup
1 FRUIT/VEGETABLE			
Juice,[b] fruit and/or vegetable	¼ cup	½ cup	¾ cup
1 GRAINS/BREAD[c]			
Bread or	½ slice	½ slice	1 slice
Cornbread or biscuit or roll or muffin or	½ serving	½ serving	1 serving
Cold dry cereal or	¼ cup	⅓ cup	¾ cup
Hot cooked cereal or	¼ cup	¼ cup	½ cup
Pasta or noodles or grains	¼ cup	¼ cup	½ cup
1 MEAT/MEAL ALTERNATE			
Meat or poultry or fish[d] or	1 oz	1½ oz	2 oz
Alternate protein product or	2 oz	1½ oz	2 oz
Cheese or	1 oz	1½ oz	2 oz
Egg[e] or	½	¾	1
Cooked dry beans or peas or	¼ cup	⅜ cup	½ cup
Peanut or other nut or seed butters or	2 Tbsp	3 Tbsp	4 Tbsp
Nuts and/or seeds or	½ oz	¾ oz	1 oz
Yogurt[f]	4 oz	6 oz	8 oz

[a]Children age 12 and older may be served larger portions based on their greater food needs. They may not be served less than the minimum quantities listed in this column.
[b]Fruit or vegetable juice must be full-strength. Juice cannot be served when milk is the only other snack component.
[c]Breads and grains must be made from whole-grain or enriched meal or flour. Cereal must be whole-grain or enriched or fortified.
[d]A serving consists of the edible portion of cooked lean meat or poultry or fish.
[e]One-half egg meets the required minimum amount (1 oz or less) of meat alternate.
[f]Yogurt may be plain or flavored, unsweetened or sweetened.
Source: From USDA Child and Adult Care Food Programs.

TABLE 3.8   Child care meal pattern requirements

Foodservices Serving Older Adults and People with Disabilities

Good menu planning is an important factor in meeting the nutritional needs as well as many social and psychological needs of older adults eating meals in extended-care facilities, retirement communities, or congregate dining sites, or in their homes via home-delivery programs. The menu-planning guidelines discussed earlier in this chapter will also be helpful when writing menus for older adult clientele and those with disabilities. When planning menus for older adults, it is especially important to get their input during the menu-writing process and their evaluation after the meals are served. Input mechanisms may include advisory councils, focus groups, suggestion boxes, or formal and informal surveys. Feedback may also be provided by production staff, service or support staff, and drivers who deliver meals in home-delivery programs.

Menu planners for older adults should be aware of the challenges unique to this age group. The habits and food preferences that have developed through the years may influence but should not determine entirely the meals planned for them. Healthy adults, regardless of age, need nutritious meals and, in planning the day's food, the basic pattern for the normal diet should be followed. Individual needs of the group members, such as difficulty in chewing, special dietary requirements, and limited mobility and activity, must also be considered.

In extended-care facilities and retirement communities, at least three well-planned meals should be served daily, with hot food at each meal. The menu pattern can follow a pattern similar to that of the regular hospital diet (pp. 28, 41), with adjustments in portions and some modification for residents with individual eating problems. If a nonselective menu is used, some system for choice will add to the residents' acceptance of the food. Choice may be provided by offering popular menu items daily in addition to a set menu, or through a choice of two items in each menu category for one meal a day. To improve satisfaction, long-term care facilities that offer a nonselective menu should consider using a 4- to 5-week cycle or longer and changing it seasonally. Holidays and special events are opportunities for adding menu variety to nonselective menus and should be planned within each cycle.

TABLE 3.9 Adult care meal pattern requirements

Breakfast for Adults

Select all three components for a reimbursable meal.

1 MILK	1 cup	Fluid milk
1 FRUIT/VEGETABLE	½ cup	Juice,[a] fruit and/or vegetable
1 GRAINS/BREAD[b]	2 slices	Bread or
	2 servings	Cornbread or biscuit or roll or muffin or
	1½ cups	Cold dry cereal or
	1 cup	Hot cooked cereal or
	1 cup	Pasta or noodles or grains

Lunch for Adults

Select all four components for a reimbursable meal.

1 MILK	1 cup	Fluid milk
2 FRUIT/VEGETABLE	1 cup	Juice,[a] fruit and/or vegetable
1 GRAINS/BREAD[b]	2 slices	Bread or
	2 servings	Cornbread or biscuit or roll or muffin or
	1½ cups	Cold dry cereal or
	1 cup	Hot cooked cereal or
	1 cup	Pasta or noodles or grains
1 MEAT/MEAT ALTERNATE	2 oz	Lean meat or poultry or fish[c] or
	2 oz	Alternate protein product or
	2 oz	Cheese or
	1	Egg or
	½ cup	Cooked dry beans or peas or
	4 Tbsp	Peanut or other nut or seed butter or
	1 oz	Nuts and/or seeds[d] or
	8 oz	Yogurt[e]

Supper for Adults

Select all three components for a reimbursable meal.

2 FRUIT/VEGETABLE	1 cup	Juice,[a] fruit and/or vegetable
1 GRAINS/BREAD[b]	2 slices	Bread or
	2 servings	Cornbread or biscuit or roll or muffin or
	1½ cups	Cold dry cereal or
	1 cup	Hot cooked cereal or
	1 cup	Pasta or noodles or grains
1 MEAT/MEAT ALTERNATE	2 oz	Lean meat or poultry or fish[c] or
	2 oz	Alternate protein product or
	2 oz	Cheese or
	1	Egg or
	½ cup	Cooked dry beans or peas or
	4 Tbsp	Peanut or other nut or seed butter or
	1 oz	Nuts and/or seeds[d] or
	8 oz	Yogurt[e]

continued

Foodservice programs producing food for the older adult population should plan menus that follow the *Dietary Guidelines for Americans*. (See Figure 3.1 and Tables 3.1 and 3.2.) The regulatory requirement for following the guidelines may vary among states.

USDA's Child and Adult Care Food Program (CACFP) is directed toward child and adult care food programs and was discussed on p. 39. Table 3.9 provides guidelines for adult care menu planning.

The Older Americans Act (OAA) provides for nutritional services for older adults and those with disabilities in either congregate settings or as home-delivered meals. The act requires that nutrition programs meet the most recent *Dietary Guidelines for Americans* published by the Secretaries of Health and Human Services and Agriculture. Meals must provide to each participating older individual (a) a minimum of 33⅓ percent of the dietary reference intakes established by the Food and Nutrition Board of the Institute of Medicine of the

TABLE 3.9   Adult care meal pattern requirements

TABLE 3.9 (rotated right margin) **Adult care meal pattern requirements**

TABLE 3.9 continued

Snacks for Adults

Select two of the four components for a reimbursable snack.

1 MILK	1 cup	Fluid milk
1 FRUIT/VEGETABLE	½ cup	Juice,[a] fruit and/or vegetable
1 GRAINS/BREAD[b]	1 slice	Bread or
	1 serving	Cornbread or biscuit or roll or muffin or
	¾ cup	Cold dry cereal or
	½ cup	Hot cooked cereal or
	½ cup	Pasta or noodles or grains
1 MEAT/MEAT ALTERNATE	1 oz	Lean meat or poultry or fish[c] or
	1 oz	Alternate protein product or
	1 oz	Cheese or
	½	Egg or
	¼ cup	Cooked dry beans or peas or
	2 Tbsp	Peanut or other nut or seed butter or
	1 oz	Nuts and/or seeds[d] or
	4 oz	Yogurt[e]

[a]Fruit or vegetable juice must be full-strength.

[b]Breads and grains must be made from whole-grain or enriched meal or flour. Cereal must be whole-grain or enriched or fortified.

[c]A serving consists of the edible portion of cooked lean meat or poultry or fish.

[d]Nuts and seeds may meet only half of the total meat/meat alternate serving and must be combined with another meat/meat alternate to fulfill the supper requirement.

[e]Yogurt may be plain or flavored, unsweetened or sweetened.

Source: From USDA Child and Adult Care Food Program.

National Academy of Sciences, if one meal per day is provided; (b) a minimum of 66 2/3 percent of the allowances if two meals per day are provided; (c) 100 percent of the allowances if three meals per day are provided; and (d) to the maximum extent practicable, meals must be adjusted to meet any special dietary needs of program participants.

Planning Special Meals, Receptions, and Catered Events

Planning special meals and receptions is a function of nearly every foodservice. The types of functions may include coffees, teas, receptions, brunches, buffets, banquets, and catered events. Regardless of the type of service provided, considerable planning is required to ensure a successful foodservice event.

PLANNING RESPONSIBILITIES

Careful planning is important to the success of any special event. The major responsibilities of the foodservice staff in charge of a special meal or other function are as follows:

- Confer with representatives of the group to be served to determine the type of function or theme; date, time, and place; number to be served; service desired; event's agenda; any special dietary needs of guests; budget range; and financial arrangements. Understanding the client expectations is important. For events off the premises, a site visit is recommended to clarify details such as electrical and water sources, guest access and traffic flow, catering access and staff parking, kitchen availability or staging area, storage for supplies, and travel time.

- Plan the menu with the client or client's representative. Provide creative ideas that harmonize with those of the client. Plan menus that can be produced with available resources. If the event is off the premises, food that can be prepared ahead of time and transported easily should be planned. Duplicate copies of the menu plans should be signed and kept by the client and the foodservice director. This procedure confirms the agreement and may prevent a misunderstanding of details and last-minute changes.

- Prepare a general outline with as complete a timeline as possible for the tasks to be accomplished. Include food and supply gathering, food preparation, travel time to and from the event and loading and unloading time (if off the premises), setup time, reheating and arranging food on serving dishes, serving time, and cleanup time.

- Determine food quantities and estimated cost of food to be served. Criteria to consider when planning food quantities for events include the age of the guests, gender, any pre- and postevent functions, length of the event, and type of service (buffet, sit-down, etc.). A general guideline is to prepare 20 percent more food for events with 20 guests, 15 percent more for 50 guests, and 10 percent more for 100 guests.

Events with more than 100 guests generally require preparing 5–10 percent more food than the guaranteed number.

- Place food orders. It is important that orders for foods not normally used be made early enough to ensure delivery.

- Prepare the dish and equipment list and arrange to obtain any additional items needed. A list including the amount and kind of linen, dishes, silverware, glassware, serving utensils, and tables and chairs required should be compiled by the manager and arrangements made for assembling these at least 1 day before they are to be used. Success of a special event is often evaluated by the creative use of different sizes and shapes of dishes and the methods used to present the food to guests.

- Prepare work schedules. A detailed work schedule includes preparation, cooking, serving, room setup, and cleanup assignments. If workers are inexperienced, the schedule should indicate a time for each task, detailed procedures, and other special instructions. For a seated-service luncheon or dinner, assign personnel to the serving counter from which plates will be filled. Assign and instruct servers for dining room service. See pp. 52–57 for directions for table setting and service.

- Supervise the setup of the room and the preparation and service of food. Complete the setup approximately 1 hour before guests arrive. Give last-minute attention to plate garnishes and food presentation.

- Supervise the dishwashing and cleanup of preparation and service areas.

- Prepare and keep on file a detailed report, including menu, number of guaranteed guests and actual attendance, quantity of food prepared and leftover amounts, temperature logs, income and expenses, and recommended changes and useful comments for service of similar events in the future. Record any unusual factors that may have affected consumption or attendance, such as weather, gender of guests, or any unusual circumstances regarding the event.

- Follow up with the client after the event to evaluate the success from the customer's point of view. Record information that can be used for future events.

RECEPTIONS AND TEAS

Receptions and teas may vary in degree of formality and may accommodate a few or many guests. The menu may be simple or elaborate and should be planned according to the type of event; the time of day; the number, age, and gender of guests to be served; and the money and labor available.

One or two beverages usually are offered—coffee and tea or coffee and punch. The menu may be limited to an attractive dessert, with nuts and mints, or it may include several sweet and savory selections such as sandwiches, cookies, or cakes. The following are suggested choices for a reception or tea:

Beverages:
Coffee, tea, hot spiced tea or cider, punch, wine

See Tables 3.10 and 3.11 for wine pairing quand purchasing guides. See p. 227 for nonalcoholic cocktail suggestions.

Breads:
Open-face sandwiches spread with a variety of fillings and decorated attractively

Rolled, ribbon, checkerboard, or pinwheel sandwiches

Thinly sliced baguette (toasted) with thinly sliced beef or pork tenderloin garnished with a fresh fruit salsa

Nut bread or fruit bread sandwiches with cream cheese or marmalade filling, cut in squares, triangles, circles, or oblong shapes

Cheese wafers or cheese straws

Miniature cream puffs filled with chicken or fish salad

Petite biscuits or savory muffins with sliced meat or salad filling

Dips:
Dips with a cheese, cream cheese, yogurt, or sour cream base served with crisp raw vegetables, fruits, and/or crackers and chips

Cakes, cookies, and tarts:
Petits fours or small decorated cupcakes

Meringue shells with whipped cream and fruit fillings

Small pecan or fruit tarts

Small tea cookies that offer a variety of shapes, flavors, and colors

Nuts and candies:
Salted, toasted, or spiced nuts

Candied orange or grapefruit peel

Mints in pastel colors

Fruit:
Fresh berries: raspberries, blackberries, strawberries; petite clusters of red, green, and/or champagne grapes

Figure 3.2 suggests a table arrangement for a reception or tea, using two lines of service and set up so that a guest may start by placing a beverage cup on a plate, then selecting food items. The silverware and napkin usually are last. Placing the cup on the plate first ensures adequate space for both food and beverage. If only one or two food selections are offered, beverages may be served last. Use Figure 3.2 as a guide, but start with plates and end with the beverage or beverages.

The table covering, centerpiece, tea service, silverware, and serving dishes should be attractive, and the food should be colorful and interestingly arranged. To prevent a crowded appearance, there should be a limited amount of silverware, china, napkins, and food on the table when the serving begins. A small serving table with extra china and silverware near the tea table is a convenience. Replacements of small dishes and appointments are brought on trays from the kitchen. If two beverages are served, they are placed at either end of the table. Cookies, sandwiches, and other foods should be arranged so they do not appear crowded. It is best to use small serving plates and replace them frequently so there is an assortment of food at all times. Arrangements should be made for people to pour the beverages, and employees or hostesses should be assigned to replenish the tea table and to take empty plates from guests.

COFFEES AND BRUNCHES

Coffees and brunches are easy and popular ways to entertain a few or many guests. An ample supply of hot, fresh coffee is necessary, and an alternate choice of tea and/or decaffeinated coffee may be offered. Flavored coffees and teas are popular beverage choices. One or more hot breads are served, and the menu may be expanded to include fresh fruit or juice. A fruit tray, with bite-size pieces of fresh fruit arranged on a silver or other appropriate tray, is an attractive centerpiece and an interesting addition to a coffee or brunch.

Brunch, a meal combining breakfast and lunch, usually includes a wider variety of food than does a coffee. The menu may consist of foods normally served at breakfast or may resemble a luncheon menu, depending partly on the hour of service. It may be quite simple, consisting of fruits, hot breads, and coffee; or it may be a more substantial meal that will replace lunch. The food usually is placed on a buffet table for self-service, but may be served to guests seated at tables. Brunch often starts with fruit juice or sparkling wines served to guests before they go to the buffet table. The main entrée may be one or several that are typical of breakfast, such as eggs in some form, bacon, ham, sausage, or a breakfast casserole; or a luncheon-type entrée of chicken, turkey, or fish. An assortment of breads usually is offered. A dessert may be served if the meal is scheduled late in the morning, but it should be light. Suggested foods for coffees and brunches are as follows:

Fruits and juices:
Orange, pineapple, or tomato juice

Fresh fruit cup or fresh berries

Melon wedges, fruit kebobs

Orange juice, champagne punch

Fruit trays:
Fresh pineapple chunks, orange sections, fresh strawberries, kiwi fruit, mangos, carambola (star fruit), fresh raspberries and blueberries

Apple slices, honeydew melon wedges, kiwi fruit, and frosted grapes

Plums or sweet cherries (bing), pear slices, cantaloupe wedges, green grapes, and cheese cubes

Entrées:
Canadian bacon, grilled ham, sausage patties on apple rings

Small biscuits or savory muffins with ham or turkey and sweet or savory spread

Scrambled eggs, egg and sausage casserole, omelets

Cheese and broccoli strata, quiche, cheese soufflé, crepes, broiled or grilled chicken breast on rice or pasta

Breads:
Small pecan or orange rolls, scones, kolaches, toasted

English muffins or bagels with marmalade and/or cream cheese

Coffee cake, Danish pastry

Small doughnuts or doughnut holes, cinnamon puffs

Small nut or fruit bread sandwiches

Desserts:
Fresh pineapple and berries, sherbet

Strawberry–sour cream crepes, fruit and cheese platters

Cookies or small cakes

BUFFET MEALS

Buffet meals provide a means of serving relatively large groups of people with a minimum of service personnel. The ability to offer a variety of foods makes buffets popular.

The steps to planning a buffet include theme development and menu planning, tables and space arrangement, food presentation, and service. The steps are not independent of each other and so must be considered together.

Menu Planning

The number of selections offered may depend on preparation time, space on the buffet table, and the equipment available for preparation and service. Client or guest expectations also must be considered. At a minimum, food selections on a buffet should be two or three entrées (beef, poultry, and a third choice such as fish, shellfish, or pork), one nonmeat entrée, one or two starches (potato, pasta, rice or other grain) one or two vegetables (green and nongreen), two or three salads, relishes, hot bread, dessert, and beverage. Guests generally try a little of everything, so keep portion sizes small, for the main entrée between 4 and 5 oz.

Plan a menu that is easy for guests to serve themselves. For example, avoid foods that are runny on the plate or hard to pick up. Foods that require extra silverware, such as butter spreaders and cocktail forks, usually are not served on a buffet.

Plan hot foods that hold well and serve easily. Rare sliced meat, delicate pasta, and French fries do not hold well on a buffet line, especially if they must remain in chafing pans for a period of time. Rare meat is best served from a carving station at generally the last stop at a buffet table. Select foods that will hold their quality when held hot, such as braised meat, meat with a glaze, carved meats, thick-walled pasta such as rigatoni, baked potatoes, and vegetable casseroles.

Choose foods that have different cooking methods, colors, temperatures, and textures. Grilled vegetables and pasta and grain salads made using vinaigrettes can be served from attractive serving dishes and not heated chafing pans. Plan foods that have color contrast in the pan, such as chicken served on top of a colorful rice, vegetable, or pasta base. Avoid serving creamed vegetables with sauced meat, strong-flavored vegetables with delicate entrées, or deep-fried potatoes with fried vegetables. Plan garnishes that are easy to use and will look good after being held on a buffet line.

Balancing expensive items with popular less-expensive items will help achieve financial goals. Placing the high-cost items last on the buffet line will help reduce costs. Goods appropriate for buffets may be selected from the Suggested Menu Items in Appendix A. Consider religious customs when planning the menu. (See Table 3.3.)

TABLE 3.10 Wine and food pairing guide

		Appetizers (light)	Cheese (mild)	Cheese (strong)	Pasta (light)
WHITE WINES (DRY)	Chablis (light bodied)	X	X		X
	Sauvignon Blanc (medium bodied)	X	X		X
	Fume Blanc (medium bodied)		X		X
	Pinot Blanc (medium bodied)		X		
	Pinot Gris (medium bodied)				X
	Chardonnay (full bodied)		X	X	
	Viognier (full bodied)		X		
WHITE WINES (SLIGHTLY SWEET)	Johannisberg Riesling (light bodied)	X			
	Gewürztraminer (light bodied)	X	X		
	Chenin Blanc (medium bodied)	X	X		X
	Ice Wines (medium bodied)			X	
WHITE WINES (SWEET)	Sauternes (medium bodied)			X	
RED WINES	Gamay-Beaujolais (light bodied)	X	X		X
	Pinot Noir (medium bodied)		X		
	Malbec (medium bodied)		X		
	Merlot (medium bodied)		X	X	
	Zinfandel (medium bodied)			X	
	Syrah/Shiraz (medium bodied)	X	X		
	Cabernet Sauvignon (full bodied)			X	
	Sangiovese/Chianti (light)	X	X		X
ROSÉ WINES	White Zinfandel and other "blush" wines (light bodied)	X	X		X
SPARKLING WINES AND CHAMPAGNE	Brut	X			
	Asti Spumante				
FORTIFIED DESSERT WINES	Port		X		
	Sherry	X (before dinner)			

continued

TABLE 3.10 Wine and food pairing guide

TABLE 3.10 continued

Pasta (robust)	Beef	Lamb	Pork/veal	Ham	Poultry	Seafood (heavy sauce)	Seafood (light or no sauce)	Tuna/salmon	Fruits/desserts
			X		X		X	X	
			X	X	X		X	X	
			X		X		X	X	
X			X	X	X	X	X	X	
X			X	X	X	X			
X		X	X		X	X			
X		X	X		X	X		X	
	X		X	X	X		X	X	X
					X			X	
			X	X	X		X		
									X (after dinner)
									X
	X		X	X	X		X	X	X
X	X	X	X	X	X	X		X	
	X		X						
	X		X						
X	X	X	X		X				
X	X	X	X	X	X			X	
	X								
X	X	X		X	X	X		X	
			X	X	X	X	X		X
				X	X	X	X	X	
									X (fruits)
									X
									X (after dinner)

Note: Serving temperatures: dry whites and rosés, 44–54°F; light-bodied reds, 50–55°F; medium-bodied to full-bodied reds, 55–65°F; sweet wines, 41–47°F; sweet fortified wines (port), room temperature; sparkling wines, 41–47°F.

TABLE 3.10 Wine and food pairing guide

TABLE 3.11 Wine purchasing guide

Size	Volume (ounces)	Servings per Container[a]	
		Dinner	Cocktail
187.5 milliliters (split)	6.35	1.5	2
375 milliliters (half)	12.7	3	4
750 milliliters (standard)	25.4	6	8
1 liter	33.8	8	11
1.5 liters (magnum)	50.7	12	17
3 liters	101.4	25	34
4 liters	135.2	34	45

[a]Number of servings per container is based on a 4-oz dinner portion size or 3-oz cocktail portion size. If larger or smaller glasses are used, an adjustment in the servings per container will need to be made.

Note: Hard liquor is generally 1½ oz per serving.

Table and Space Arrangement

Buffet tables and food items may be arranged in several ways. Figures 3.3 and 3.4 illustrate a buffet arrangement with one service line. A double line, as shown in Figures 3.5 and 3.6, will speed service but requires more space and duplicate serving dishes. Figure 3.7 illustrates a straight-line simple buffet arrangement, used when large groups serve themselves from both sides of the table. For a large group requiring a more elaborate buffet, it is advisable to set up several serving stations, each serving different food items. A typical four-station buffet for serving 200 people includes the following:

Salad station (round 72-inch table):
Salad plates, several salads, fresh fruit, bread and butters/ spreads, salad dressings, and crackers and cheeses

First entrée station (two serpentine tables arranged in an S shape):
Plates, display cooking station (stir-fry, perhaps), chafing pans for entrée accompaniments (pasta, rice, sauces), antipasto, breads, and butter/spreads

Second entrée station (see Figure 3.4 for table requirement):
Plates, carving station, chafing pans for entrée accompaniments (vegetables, potatoes/starches), sauces, breads, and butter/spreads

Dessert station (see Figure 3.6 for table requirement):
Plates, desserts and dessert sauces, cups and saucers, coffee/tea, and beverage condiments (sugar cubes, sweeteners, cream, whipped cream, citrus peel, cinnamon sticks, ground cinnamon, ground nutmeg, chocolate shavings)

All tables should include at least one centerpiece. Beverages other than coffee and tea should be served by the wait staff or at a separate table.

Moving people through a buffet line quickly is important. One buffet line per 125–150 people is adequate for casual events. Planning for 100 guests per line is recommended when the event is time sensitive, if guests arrive at one time, if the food offerings are extensive, or if the buffet line includes a carving station or action station. To reduce guests' wait time while standing in the buffet line, assign a staff member to release the tables to go through the buffet line a few at a time, beginning with the tables farthest from the buffet. Starting with the tables farthest from the buffet table will reduce the traffic near guests who are eating.

Food Presentation and Service

The success of a buffet meal depends not only on the quality of the food, but also on the attractiveness of the buffet table. Visual appeal may be increased by placing trays and chafing dishes at an angle to the table, raising trays on one or two corners so they slant toward guests, and displaying food trays and pans at different levels. Interesting colors may be introduced in the table covering, the serving dishes, the food, and the decorations.

The attractiveness of cold food plates and platters can be enhanced by carefully selecting the foods to include. Consider choosing items that are seasonal, practical, properly sized, and both traditional and nontraditional. The number of items on the platter should provide a full but not overcrowded display. Some open spaces heighten the display's attractiveness. **Flavor** enhances a platter when the foods selected are fresh and compatible. **Color** combinations that exhibit natural tones and vibrant colors provide attractive displays. **Texture** is achieved by varying the cooking methods and choosing foods with different textures. **Height** adds interest and visual appeal to food on a platter. Consider choosing foods with natural height differences. The **shape** of the food should be natural and not contrived. This can be accomplished by using a combination of cut, molded, loose, and whole food items.

Designing attractive cold platters requires applying some general principles. Buffet platters have three elements—a centerpiece or focal point, the main item, and a garnish.

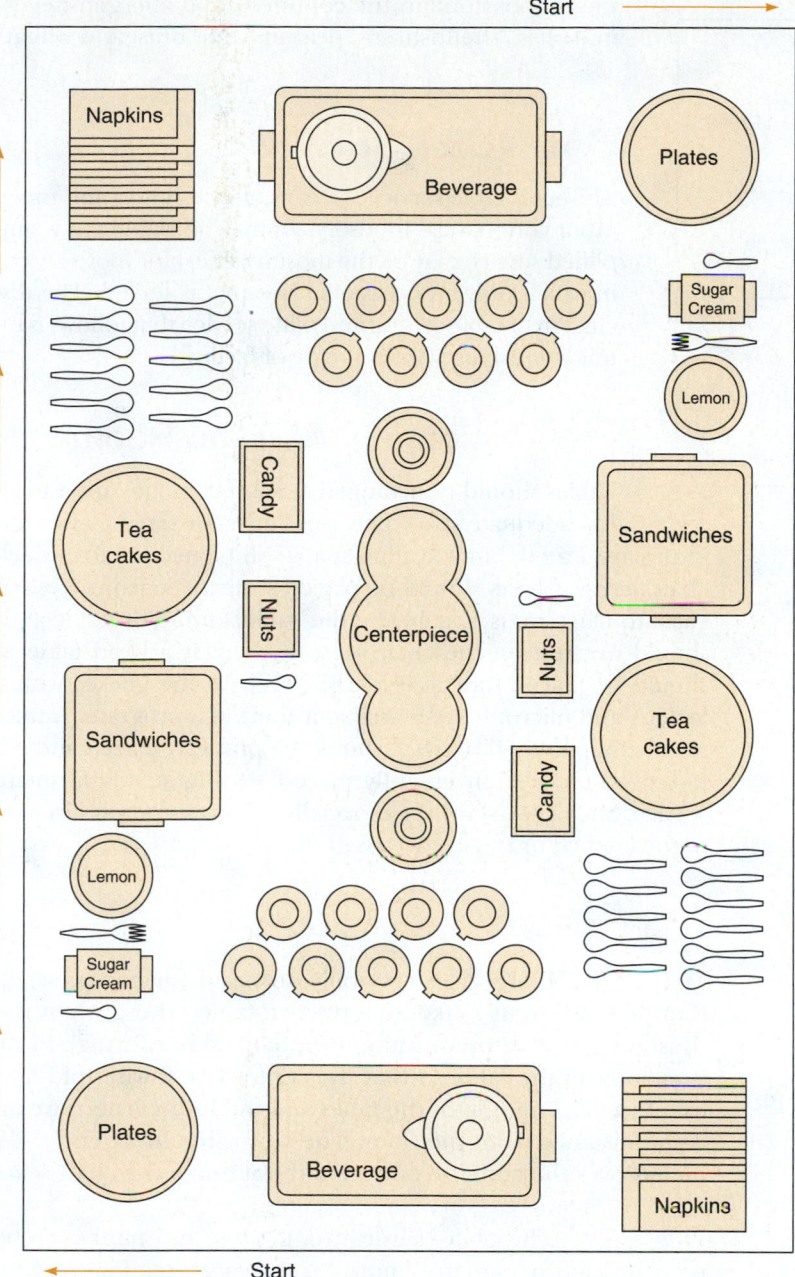

Start →

← Start

FIGURE 3.2   Table arrangement for a reception or tea.

The *garnish* serves the same function as for plated meals (p. 57) and should enhance and not overpower the platter. Platters with adequate color and texture may not need a garnish.

When arranging foods and other items on the buffet table, consider the **flow** of people through the line. The order of food should be logical. A generally accepted procedure is to arrange the food in the same order as if it were a served meal. Placing condiments and side dishes near the food they will accompany is suggested. Panning foods together that are intended to be served together is a presentation style that enhances food appeal and helps guests select food items more quickly. For example, chicken breasts, rice pilaf, and grilled vegetables could be placed together in the same chafing pan.

Using small serving dishes that hold less food and changing them throughout the event helps make the food look more attractive. Food items that are popular should have more servings per pan than low-volume items. It is recommended to not have more than 25 or 30 servings per pan for the highest-volume foods.

The plate size used on a self-service buffet and the amount of food in the serving pans and dishes will impact the amount of food guests take. Standard plate sizes are 11-inch, 10-inch, and 9-inch. The number of choices on a self-service buffet, the age and gender of the guests, and the budget should be considered when choosing plate size. If using a smaller plate, then consider placing salad plates alongside the salads. If dessert is served on the buffet table, then plates should be placed on the buffet table near the desserts. Desserts may be placed on a separate table from which guests will later serve themselves. An attractive dessert table will make a lasting impression on guests.

Make room between serving pans for ease of serving and for changing pans of food. Adequate spacing will be achieved when at least 1½ linear feet of space is allowed for each item on the buffet.

Buffets can become messy if foods are placed out of guests' **reach**. If possible, avoid placing food so guests must reach over other food items; however, when placing food behind other food is unavoidable, use care to put messy serving items to the front of the table. Elevating the food at the back of the table will help reduce drips and spills and also adds to the attractiveness of the food display. Elevation can be achieved by draping tablecloths or napkins over different-size cans or boxes.

Centerpieces and **decorations** add to the visual appeal of a buffet table and can be used to carry out a menu theme. Both should be sized appropriately for the space and not interfere with the service of the food.

Labeling food items that are unusual or not easily recognized is recommended. Because some people are allergic to nuts, it is advisable to identify products that contain nuts. In addition to labeling, service staff should be knowledgeable about

The *centerpiece* may be an uncut piece of the main item (a whole cheese, a small roast), an item related to the main item, a sauce or condiment for the main item, or a decorative-only item such as fresh flowers in a vegetable vase. Not all platters require a centerpiece, but all should have a focal point. The centerpiece should complement the main item and not dominate the platter.

The *main item* should be arranged artistically, keeping in mind that food should be easy for guests to self-serve. Another goal is to have the platters look nice throughout the serving period. Arranging foods in curves or with angled lines gives a sense of motion and adds to the design's artistry.

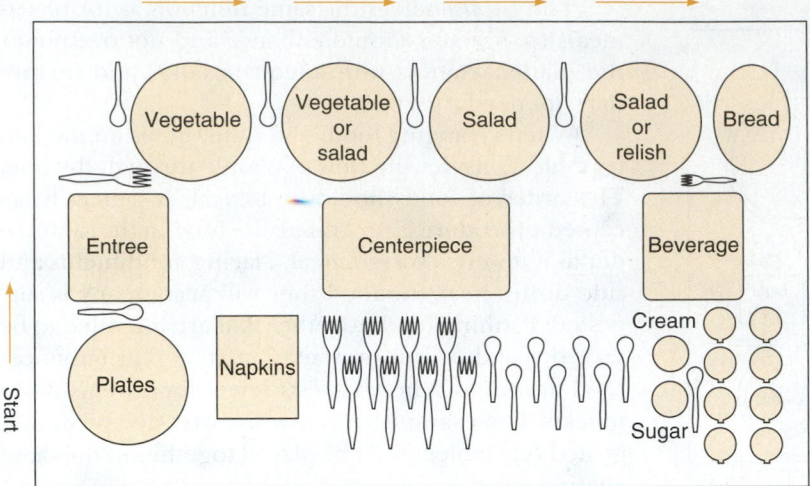

FIGURE 3.3 Table arrangement for buffet service, single line. Beverages may be served at tables. Desserts may be served from a dessert table or to guests at the individual tables. Suitable for serving very small numbers.

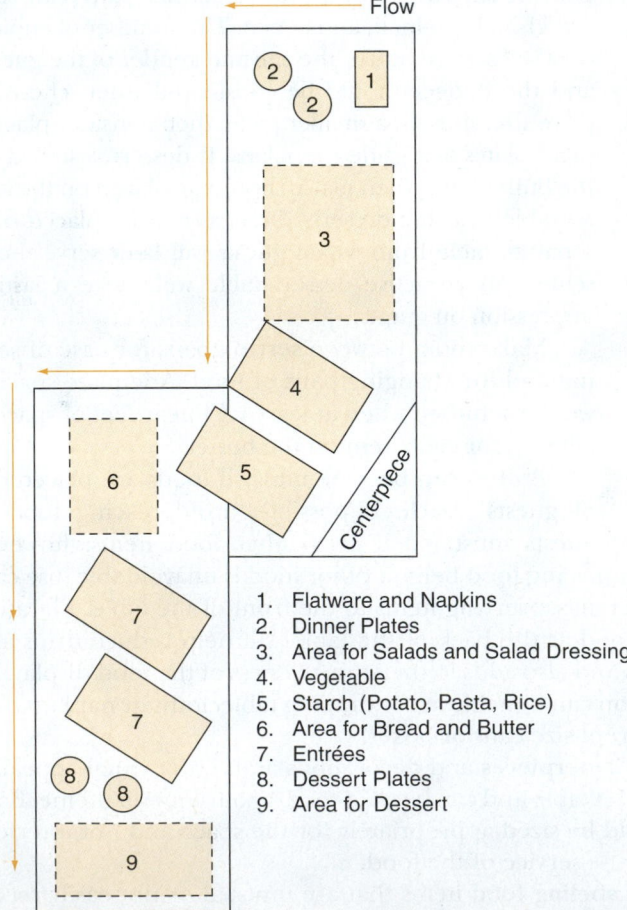

1. Flatware and Napkins
2. Dinner Plates
3. Area for Salads and Salad Dressings
4. Vegetable
5. Starch (Potato, Pasta, Rice)
6. Area for Bread and Butter
7. Entrées
8. Dessert Plates
9. Area for Dessert

FIGURE 3.4 Table arrangement for buffet service, single serving line using two 8 foot × 30 inch tables. Shorter tables may be used if desserts are served to guests or served from a separate table. This straight-line arrangement is suitable for serving 50 or fewer people.

what foods contain the common food allergens: eggs, milk, fish, shellfish, soy, peanuts, tree nuts, and wheat.

BANQUET SERVICE

Although table service for banquets in hotels and many other commercial foodservices may be elaborate, a simplified service may be the most practical for foodservices in which only an occasional banquet is served. The discussion of table setting and plate service that follows is intended primarily for this type of facility.

Preparation of the Dining Room

Tables should be arranged at least 48 inches apart to allow adequate space between tables for serving after the guests are seated. More seating space will be needed for wheelchair access. Chairs should be placed so that the front edge of each touches or is just below the tablecloth. The tablecloth should not rest on the chair seats. If there is a head table, it should be placed so that it is easily seen by the guests, with a lectern and microphone available if there is a program. Audiovisual equipment, if needed, should be properly placed and adjusted correctly. Conveniently placed serving stands facilitate service. Such provisions are especially important when distance to the kitchen or staging area is great.

Setting the Tables

Tablecloth   Tablecloths generally are used for banquets, although place mats make an attractive table setting when the finish of the tabletop permits and the meal is informal. Place the cloth on the table so that the center lengthwise fold falls exactly in the middle of the table and the four corners are an equal distance from the floor. The cloth should extend 6–12 inches over the tabletop and should not touch the chair seat.

The Cover   The plate, silverware, glasses, and napkin to be used by each person are known as the *cover* (see Figure 3.8). Consider 20 inches of table space as the smallest permissible allowance for each cover; 25–30 inches is better. Place all silverware and dishes required for one cover as close together as possible without crowding.

Silverware   Place knives, forks, and spoons about 1 inch from the edge of the table and in the order of their use (see Figure 3.8). Some prefer to place the salad or dessert fork next to the plate as the menu dictates. If the menu requires no knife, omit it from the cover. When cocktail forks are used, they are placed at the extreme right of the cover. If a butter spreader is used, lay it across the upper right side of the bread and butter plate with the cutting edge toward the center of the plate. It may be placed straight across the top of the plate or with the handle at a convenient angle. Dessert silverware often is not placed on the table when the cover is laid, except when the amount of silver required for the entire meal is small or

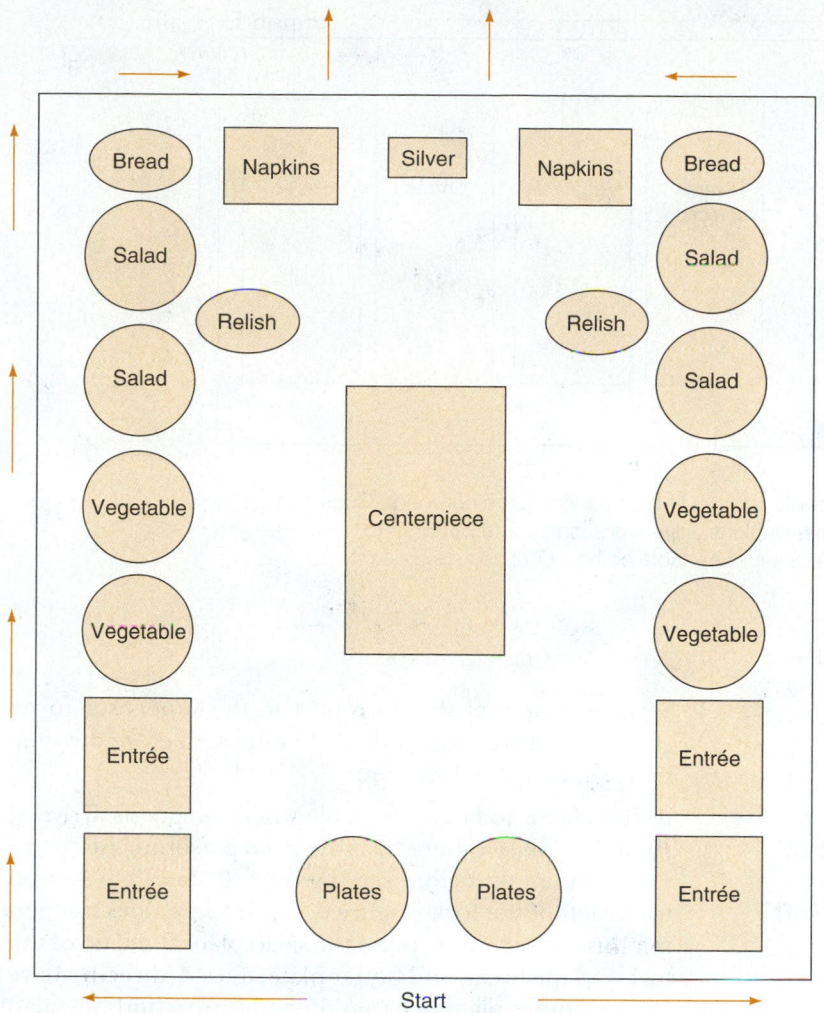

FIGURE 3.5   Table arrangement for buffet service, double line. Beverages may be served at tables. Desserts may be served from a dessert table or to guests at the individual tables. Suitable for serving small numbers.

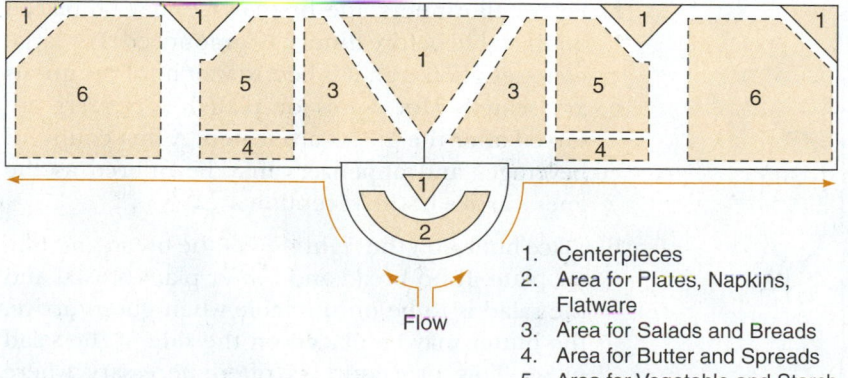

1. Centerpieces
2. Area for Plates, Napkins, Flatware
3. Area for Salads and Breads
4. Area for Butter and Spreads
5. Area for Vegetable and Starch (Potato, Pasta, Rice)
6. Area for Entrée and Accompaniments

FIGURE 3.6   Table arrangement for buffet service, double serving line using one side of two 8 foot × 30 inch tables and a small 30-inch-radius half-round table. Small tables may be added to each end if dessert is served. Arrangement is suitable for serving 150 people.

when it is necessary to simplify the service. If a dessert fork is used, it is sometimes placed in the area above the dinner plate so the guest will use it for the final course.

Napkin   Place the napkin at the left of the fork with the loose corner at the lower right and the open edges next to the edge of the table and the plate. It may be placed between the knife and fork if space is limited, and it may be folded into an accordion shape and placed upright. See Figure 3.9 for basic napkin folds.

Glasses   Place the water glass at the tip of the knife or slightly to the right. Goblets and footed tumblers often are preferred for luncheon or dinner and should be used for a formal dinner. Wineglasses are placed to the right of and slightly below the water glass.

Bread and Butter Plate   Place the bread and butter plate at the tip of the fork or slightly to the left.

Salt and Pepper   Salt and pepper shakers should be provided for every six covers. They should be placed parallel to the edge of the table and in line with sugar bowls and creamers.

Decorations   Some attractive decorations should be provided for the center of the table. A centerpiece should be low so the view across the table will not be obstructed. Candles should not be used in the daytime unless the lighting is inadequate or the day is dark. When used, they should be the sole source of light. Do not mix candlelight and daylight or candlelight and electric light. Tall candles in low holders should be high enough so that the flame is not on a level with the eyes of the guests. If place cards are used, they are set on the napkin or above the cover.

Seating Arrangement

The guest of honor, if a woman, usually is seated to the right of the host; if a man, to the right of the hostess. At banquets and public dinners, a man is seated to the left of his partner. Customs for seating guests may be different in countries other than the United States.

Service Counter Setup for Served Meals

Food should be served from hot counters or hot holding equipment. Some provision also must be made for keeping plates and cups hot. For serving 50 plates or less, the plan should provide one person to serve each food item. Such an arrangement for serving is termed a *setup*. For 60–100 people, two setups should be provided to hasten service. For more than 100 people, it is well to provide additional setups.

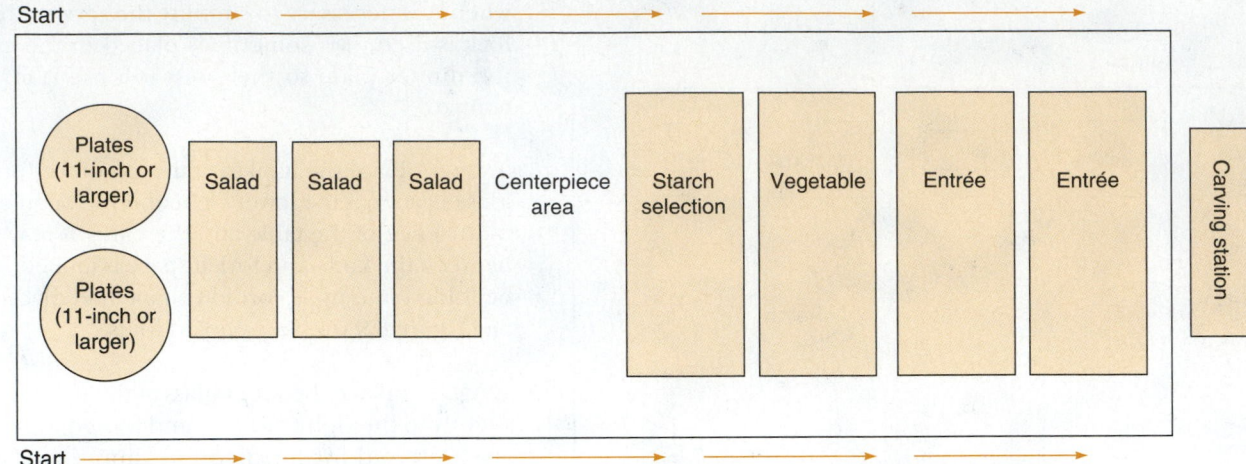

FIGURE 3.7 Table arrangement for buffet service, double straight line for serving large numbers. Guests serve themselves from either side of a single line of food items. Napkins, silverware, bread and butter, and beverages are usually placed at each table. Desserts may be served at a separate table or individually to each guest.

Food is placed on the hot counter in the following order: meat, potato or substitute, vegetables, sauces, and garnish. The supervisor should demonstrate the size of portions to be given and their arrangement on the plate. There should be a checker at the end of the line to remove with a damp cloth any food spots from the plate and to check the plate for completeness, arrangement, and uniformity of servings. The importance of standardized servings and food arrangement can hardly be overemphasized; these factors can determine the enjoyment of the guests and the financial success or failure of a meal.

FIGURE 3.8 Cover for a served meal: (1) bread and butter plate, with butter knife; (2) water glass; (3) wine glass; (4) napkin; (5) salad fork; (6) dinner fork; (7) knife; (8) teaspoon.

Table Service

1. Service personnel should report to the supervisor to receive final instructions at least 15 minutes before the time set for serving the banquet.

2. If the salad is to be on the table when the guests arrive, it should be placed there by the service personnel not more than 15 minutes before serving time. It should be placed to the left of the fork (Figure 3.10). If space does not permit this arrangement, place the salad plate at the tip of the fork and the bread and butter plate, if used, directly above the dinner plate between the water glass and the salad plate. If the salad is to be served as a separate course, it is placed between the knife and the fork, then removed before the main course is served.

3. Place creamer beside the sugar bowl.

4. Place relishes on the table, if desired.

5. For small dinners, the first course may be placed on the table before dinner is announced. For large banquets, however, it is best to wait until the guests are seated. Hot soups or plated appetizers are served after the guests are seated. A first course of beverages and appetizers may be offered as the guests arrive in the reception area.

6. Place butter on the right side of the bread and butter plate. If no bread and butter plate is used and the salad is to be on the table when guests arrive, the butter may be placed on the side of the salad plate. This procedure is often necessary where dishes and table space are limited. Butter may also be arranged on a serving plate and passed.

7. Place glasses filled with ice water on the table just before guests are seated.

8. When the guests are seated, service personnel line up in the kitchen for trays containing the first course. A general rule

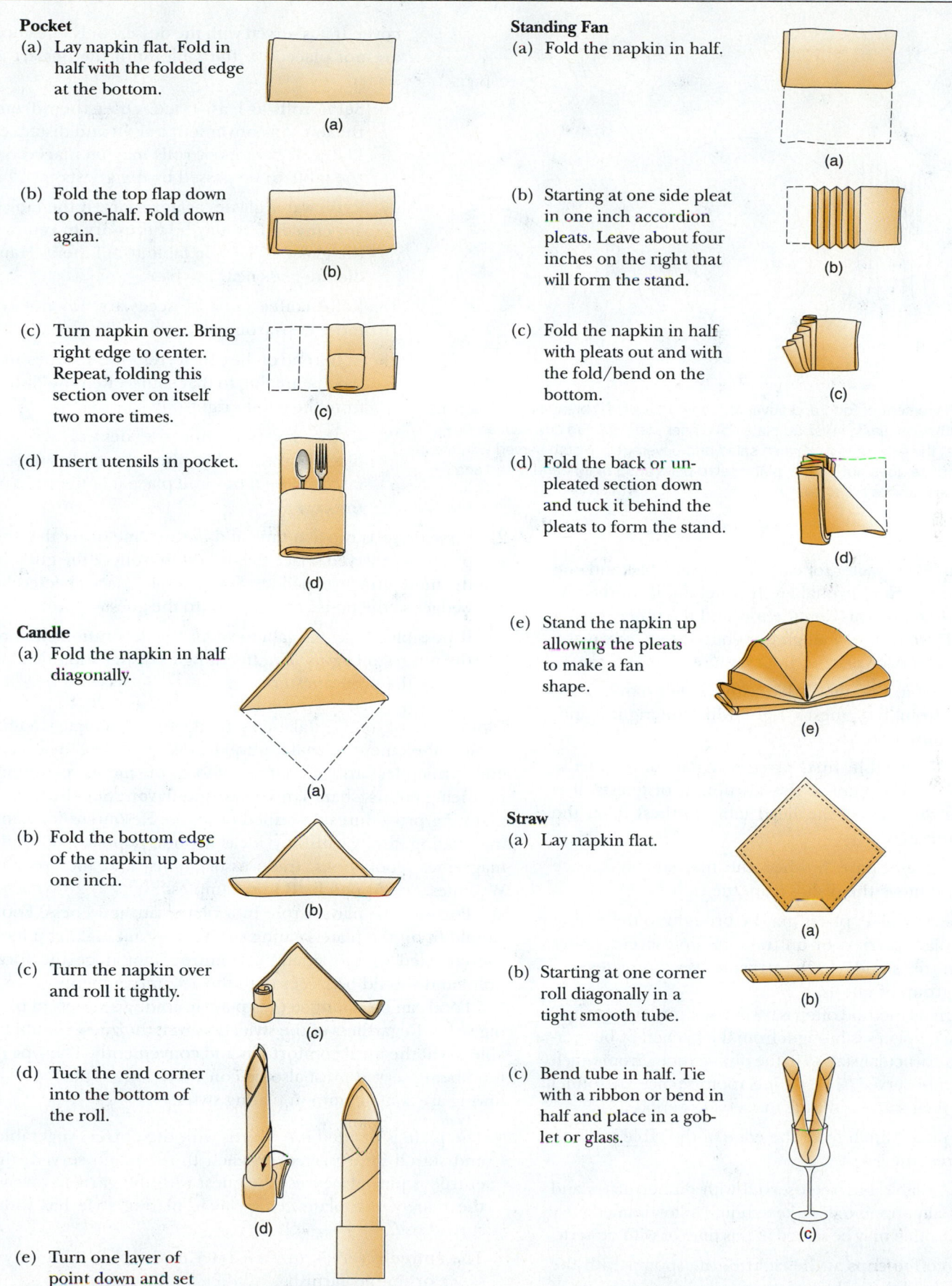

Pocket

(a) Lay napkin flat. Fold in half with the folded edge at the bottom.

(a)

(b) Fold the top flap down to one-half. Fold down again.

(b)

(c) Turn napkin over. Bring right edge to center. Repeat, folding this section over on itself two more times.

(c)

(d) Insert utensils in pocket.

(d)

Candle

(a) Fold the napkin in half diagonally.

(a)

(b) Fold the bottom edge of the napkin up about one inch.

(b)

(c) Turn the napkin over and roll it tightly.

(c)

(d) Tuck the end corner into the bottom of the roll.

(d)

(e) Turn one layer of point down and set on base.

(e)

Standing Fan

(a) Fold the napkin in half.

(a)

(b) Starting at one side pleat in one inch accordion pleats. Leave about four inches on the right that will form the stand.

(b)

(c) Fold the napkin in half with pleats out and with the fold/bend on the bottom.

(c)

(d) Fold the back or un-pleated section down and tuck it behind the pleats to form the stand.

(d)

(e) Stand the napkin up allowing the pleats to make a fan shape.

(e)

Straw

(a) Lay napkin flat.

(a)

(b) Starting at one corner roll diagonally in a tight smooth tube.

(b)

(c) Bend tube in half. Tie with a ribbon or bend in half and place in a goblet or glass.

(c)

FIGURE 3.9 Basic napkin folds.

FIGURE 3.10 Placement of food and cover for served meals: (1) bread and butter plate; (2) water glass; (3) wine glass; (4) salad plate; (5) dinner plate; (6) cup and saucer. The salad is placed at the left of the fork when salad and beverage are both served with the main course. If space does not permit, place salad plate at tip of fork and bread and butter plate, if used, above the dinner plate.

is to schedule one waiter for each one to two tables and one bus person for every two tables. It is helpful if two people work together, one carrying the tray and the other placing the food. Place the cocktail glasses, soup dishes, or canapé plates on the service plates, which are already on the table.

9. Serve food from the guest's left with the left hand. Serve beverages from the guest's right with the right hand. Proceed counterclockwise.

10. Serve the head table first, progressing in order to the other tables. To minimize the disruption of guests, it is preferable to position the head table farthest from the kitchen entrance.

11. When the guests have finished the first course, service personnel remove the dishes from the right.

12. For the main course, plates may be brought to the dining room on plate carriers or on trays holding several plates and set on tray stands. Each worker serves the plates to a specified group of guests.

   An alternate method often is used in serving large groups. A tray of filled plates is brought from the kitchen by bus personnel to a particular station in the dining room, from which the plates are served. The dining room service personnel remain at their stations during the serving period.

13. Place the plate 1 inch from the edge of the table with the meat nearest the guest.

14. As soon as a table has been served with dinner plates and salad, specially appointed workers should follow immediately with rolls. Coffee may be served at this time or with dessert.

15. Place the coffee cups at the right of the spoons with the handles toward the right at about the 5 o'clock position. If the coffee is served with the main course, the cup and saucer may be placed on the table with the rest of the

cover. If it is served with the dessert only, the cups are not placed on the table until the dessert is served.

16. Serve rolls at least twice. Offer them from the left at a convenient height and distance. Plates or baskets of rolls may be placed on the table to be passed by the guests.

17. Refill water glasses as necessary. If the tables are crowded, it may be necessary to remove the glasses from the table to fill them. Handle the glass near the base.

18. Refill coffee cups as necessary. Do not remove cups from table when filling.

19. At the end of the course, remove all dishes and food belonging to that course. Remove dishes from the guest's right.

20. If the silverware for the dessert was not placed on the table when the table was set, take it in on a tray and place it at the right of the cover.

21. Serve desserts two at a time and in the same order that the plates were served. Place the dessert in front of the guest in the most attractive manner. For example, place cheesecake wedges so the tip is pointing toward the guest.

22. If possible, clear the table except for decorations before the program begins. The handling of dishes should cease before the program starts.

Plate Presentation.   Balancing food items on a plate is a fundamental element in making food look appealing. The general principles are similar to those of menu planning: balancing colors, shapes, textures, and flavors. See the menu-planning procedures described on p. 33. Resources for naming, plating, and garnishing ideas include popular and trade magazines, cookbooks, trade associations, and food-related Web sites. See Appendix B for examples.

   Portion size plays a role in a plate's attractiveness. Food should fit on the plate's eating surface without making it look overcrowded or too small. The entrée should be the focal point and should be larger than the accompaniments.

   Food can be arranged on a plate following a variety of plating styles. Regardless of the style, however, the guest should be able to eat the meal comfortably and conveniently. The type of food being served must also be considered when plating. Following are some common plating styles:

- The plate is divided into thirds with the entrée, vegetable, and starch item placed on each third. When served, the entrée is placed nearest the guest with the garnish toward the rear of the plate. This classic plating style has widespread use.

- The entrée is served in the center of the plate with only a sauce or simple garnish.

- The entrée is served in the center of the plate with vegetables placed around it. The vegetables may be placed randomly or in an arranged pattern. Food that is randomly placed should be neat and orderly and not appear sloppy or haphazard.

- The entrée is leaned against a generous amount of vegetables or starch that has been placed in the center of the plate. Additional vegetables, sauce, and a garnish surround the entrée.
- The entrée is stacked on top of the starch or vegetable accompaniment. A sauce and garnish is added around the entrée.
- The vegetable or starch is in the center of the plate with the entrée placed neatly around it. A sauce under the vegetable or starch is common.
- Slices of the entrée are shingled on top of vegetables or a starch, and the garnish is placed to one side.

Regardless of the plating style, a few general guidelines will ensure the food's attractiveness.

1. Place the food on the plate's eating surface and not on the rim. The rim may be used for a simple garnish such as chopped fresh herbs.
2. Food should look balanced on the plate without the appearance of a heavy or a light side.
3. The food should be convenient to eat. Guests should not need to rearrange the food, dismantle an arranged or stacked display, or reorient the plate on the table before they begin eating.
4. Each food should maintain its own identity. This is accomplished by keeping space between items or by neatly placing foods close together. Sauces should not hide a food's color, flavor, or shape.
5. The entrée should serve as the focal point while working in harmony with the accompaniments so the plate has unity and cohesiveness. The accompaniments may serve as the garnish.
6. The garnish should contribute flavor, texture, and visual appeal to food. Garnishes should be appropriate for the food being served, and their placement should be carefully planned. Nonfunctional garnishes that add color but serve no other purpose and nonedible garnishes are not recommended. A garnish is not required or recommended if the plate is attractive without a garnish. Attractiveness can be achieved by using a plating style that complements the foods being served and by planning the accompaniments carefully.

STYLES OF SERVICE

The style of service will have an impact on the menu items and on the equipment and labor required to serve the meal. Following are some common styles of service.

American or Plate Service   Food items are placed on plates and delivered to guests. An attractive placement of food and garnish is important. Basic service rules for American service include the following:

- Serve food from the guest's left with the left hand (remember to *leave* on the *left*). Serve women first and proceed

counterclockwise. If the host or hostess is known, begin to his or her right. Staff one server per two tables (16–20 guests).

- Serve beverage from the guest's right with the right hand.
- Clear dishes from the guest's right (remember to *remove* on the *right*). Do not stack dishes or scrape plates in sight of guests.

Buffet   Food is prepared in the kitchen and arranged in serving pans for guests to serve themselves or to be served by service personnel. Appetizers, soups, and salads may be served at guests' tables before they go through the buffet. Staff one server per four tables and two buffet attendants per buffet line.

English   Platters of food are placed in front of the host or hostess, who places the food on individual plates. Whole pieces of food may be cut by the host or hostess. A waiter generally receives the filled plates and delivers them to the guests.

Family Service   Food is placed in bowls and platters on each table. Guests serve themselves.

French   Food is partially prepared in the kitchen and finished in the dining room in view of the guests. A variation of the French style is to carve or serve fully cooked food from a cart at table side. Staff one server per table (8–10 guests), or staff two people working together to serve food to two tables (16–20 guests).

Russian   Individual portions of food are transferred by a waiter from a platter to the guest's plate.

WINE AND BAR SERVICE

Alcoholic beverages are often a part of special-event menus. Following are some basic guidelines for pairing wine with food and for setting up a bar.

Wine and Food Pairings

No hard-and-fast rules exist for selecting wines to serve with various foods. Generally accepted practice and the personal taste and experience of the client should be considered when selecting wines. Table 3.10 provides guidelines for pairing food with some commonly requested wines. Table 3.11 gives the amount of wine in different-size bottles.

Bar Service

Bars should be stationed so guests see them on arrival. The location should be away from the dining area and buffet.

The number of bars and bartenders should be based on the number of guests. A general guideline is one bar per every 100 people with no more than two bartenders per bar. For

TABLE 3.12 Guidelines for stocking a bar

Item	Approximate stocking quantities for 50 people[a]	Item	Approximate stocking quantities for 50 people[a]
ALCOHOL		**MIXERS**	
Beer, regular	18 cans	Cola	12 cans
Beer, light	36 cans	Diet cola	12 cans
Beer, nonalcoholic	3 cans	Non-cola, clear	6 cans
Bourbon	½ bottle	Diet non-cola, clear	3 cans
Gin	1 bottle	Club soda	3 L
Rum	½ bottle	Ginger ale	3 L
Scotch	½ bottle	Tonic	6 L
Vermouth, dry	1 partial bottle	Bloody Mary mix[b]	2 qt
Vermouth, sweet	1 partial bottle	Orange juice	1 gal
Vodka[b]	½ bottle	Cranberry juice	1 qt
Whiskey	½ bottle	Grapefruit juice	1 qt
Wine, white (Chardonnay)	4 bottles (750 mL)	Pineapple juice	1 qt
Wine, blush (White Zinfandel)	3 bottles (750 mL)		
Wine, red (Cabernet Sauvignon or Merlot)	3 bottles (750 mL)	**GARNISHES**	
		Celery sticks	6 oz
		Cherries with stems	8 oz
		Lemons	5
		Limes	3
		Oranges	3
		Stuffed green olives	6 oz

[a]Quantities are generous. For bars located close to replenishment stock, the recommended quantity can be reduced.
[b]For morning events, increase the vodka and Bloody Mary mix and the orange juice. Champagne, sparkling wine, or fruit schnapps may be added for events such as receptions and weddings.
Note: For each guest estimate one mixed drink, one beer, or two glasses of wine per hour. For guests not drinking alcoholic beverages, have available three or four cans of soda or sparkling water. Plan 10 oz mixer, two to three glasses, and 1 lb ice per person. Plan for 50 percent of guests to drink wine, of which 35–40 percent will drink red wine.

50 people, one bartender is usually adequate. The volume expected and type of beverages served should be considered when deciding when to add additional bars or bartenders.

The kind of liquor and amount of bar stock depends on the type and length of function and the guests being served.

Table 3.12 provides general guidelines for stocking a bar. Glassware should be appropriate for the beverages being served.

State and local laws regarding alcohol service must be followed. Know the laws and educate employees about the laws before serving alcohol.

part II

Food Production Tables

Food Production Today

The information in this chapter is presented as a guide for ordering food, for adjusting and developing recipes, and for planning, preparing, and serving food. Quantities of food to prepare are based on 50 average-size portions, as are most of the recipes, but adjustments may need to be made to fit individual situations. Rarely is 50 the exact number to be served, and the portion size will vary according to the type of foodservice and the needs of the individuals in the group. Information is included in Chapter 2 that will assist with these recipe adjustments.

Most ingredients in the recipes are given in weights, but if volume measurements (teaspoons, tablespoons, cups, quarts, or gallons) are to be used, tables in this chapter will assist in converting from weights to measures. Metric measures are not used in the recipes, but charts for converting to metric are included in this chapter.

Guides for cooking temperatures and equipment capacity charts are given in Chapters 6 and 7. A glossary of cooking and menu terms appears at the end of the book.

TABLE INFORMATION

Table 4.1—Amounts of Food to Serve 50   This table suggests amounts of food to purchase and prepare for 50 people, based on the portion size listed in the table. If larger or smaller servings are needed or if the number of portions required is other than 50, an adjustment in the amount to prepare or purchase must be made. Because preparation losses must be considered in determining the amount to purchase for 50 portions, the ready-to-serve raw yield or the yield of cooked product is given for some products, with the amount as purchased (AP) to buy. The yields, which are given in decimal parts of a pound, can be converted to ounces by using Table 4.7. (p. 61)

Table 4.2—Food Weights and Approximate Equivalents in Measure   Information in this table is useful when converting recipe ingredients from weight to measure or vice versa and is helpful in adjusting or enlarging recipes and for recipe development. (p. 71)

Table 4.3—Yield, Availability, and Storage of Fresh Fruits and Vegetables   Information in this table gives yield percent, availability, and storage information for fresh fruits and vegetables. It is useful for calculating amounts to purchase and amount of edible product that can be expected after cleaning raw fruits and vegetables. Appendix C gives examples for how yields are used for purchasing and costing calculations. (p. 82)

Table 4.4—Equivalent Measure (Approximate) per Ounce for Dry Herbs or Spices and Fresh Herbs   Information in this table is useful for converting dry herbs and spices from measure to weight or weight to measure. (p. 86)

Table 4.5—Ingredient Substitutions (Approximate)   This table is useful when it is necessary to substitute one ingredient for another in a recipe. (p. 88)

Table 4.6—Ingredient Proportions   This table gives the relative proportion of ingredients in preparing certain types of foods. It is useful when evaluating recipes for the proper amount of leavening agents, seasonings, and thickening agents. (p. 90)

Table 4.7—Ounces and Decimal Equivalents of a Pound and Grams (Rounded)   This table is useful when increasing or decreasing recipes. The multiplication or division of pounds and ounces is simplified if the ounces are converted first to decimal parts of a pound. (p. 91)

Table 4.8—Basic Equivalents in Measures and Weights   This table is useful when converting measures (gallons, quarts, or cups) to smaller units such as cups, tablespoons, or teaspoons. Metric equivalents are given for commonly used weights and measures. (p. 91)

Table 4.9—Guide for Rounding Off Weights and Volume Measures   When enlarging home-sized recipes, the resulting quantities may be difficult to measure. This table aids in rounding fractions and complex measurements into amounts that are as simple as possible to weigh or measure while maintaining the accuracy needed for quality control. (p. 92)

Table 4.10—Weight (1–16 oz) and Approximate Measure Equivalents for Commonly Used Foods   In this table the equivalent measures (teaspoons, tablespoons, and cups) are given for selected ingredients, such as flour, salt, and sugar, that appear repeatedly in recipes. This information is the same as that given in Table 4.2 except that the equivalents are given for weights from 1 to 16 oz. (p. 92)

Table 4.11—Common Can Sizes Can sizes, with approximate weight or measure and number of portions, are included in this table as a purchasing guide. (p. 94)

Table 4.12—Metric Equivalents for Weight, Measure, and Temperature This table provides information that will be helpful in converting weights, measures, and temperatures as given in recipes to metric equivalents. (p. 94)

Amounts of Food to Serve, Yield, and Food Equivalent Information

TABLE 4.1 Amounts of food to serve 50[a]

Food	Serving portion	Amount for 50 portions	Miscellaneous information
BEVERAGES			
Cider	4 oz (½ cup)	2 gal	64 4-oz portions
Cocoa	6 oz (¾ cup)	2½ gal	50 6-oz portions
Unsweetened powder		8 oz	
Instant mix		2½ lb	
Coffee	6 oz (¾ cup)	2½ gal	
Regular or urn grind		1–1½ lb	1 lb = 5¾ cups ground
Freeze-dried		2–3 oz	
Instant		3 oz	
Lemonade	8 oz (1 cup)	3 gal	48 8-oz portions
Frozen concentrate		3 32-oz cans	dilute 1:4 parts water
Orange juice, see Juices			
Punch	4 oz (½ cup)	2–2½ gal	1 gal yields 32 4-oz portions
Tea			2½ gal yields 50 4-oz portions plus 30 refills
Hot	6 oz (¾ cup)	2½ gal	
Bulk		2 oz	Amount may vary with quality of tea
Iced	8 oz (1 cup)	3 gal	48 8-oz portions
1-oz bag		6 bags	6 1-oz bags make 3 gal
Instant		1–1½ oz	
Wine	See Tables 3.11 and 3.12		
BREAD AND CRACKERS			
Biscuits, baking powder	1 biscuit	4½ doz	
Dough ready for baking		5 lb	
Mix		2½ lb	
Bread			
1½-lb loaf	1 slice	2½ loaves	24 slices per loaf
2-lb pullman	1 slice	1½ loaves	36 slices per loaf
Breads, quick 5 × 9 × 2¾-inch loaves	1 slice	4 loaves	16 slices per loaf
Coffee cake, 12 × 18 × 2 inches	3 × 2¼ inches	2 pans	Cut 4 × 8
Batter, ready to bake		5–6 lb per pan	
Crackers			
Graham	2 crackers	1¾–2 lb	60–65 per lb
Saltines	4 crackers	1½ lb	150–160 per lb
Soda	2 crackers	1½–2 lb	65 per lb
Muffins	1 muffin	4½ doz	
Batter, ready to bake		5 lb	
Mix		3½ lb	
Pancakes	3½ oz	7 qt batter	2 4-inch cakes
Mix		6 lb	

continued

Beverages

Bread and Crackers

TABLE 4.1   continued

Bread and Crackers

Cereals

Dairy Products

Desserts

Food	Serving portion	Amount for 50 portions	Miscellaneous information
Rolls			
Breakfast, 3 oz	1 roll	4½ doz	
Dinner, 1½ oz	1 roll	4½ doz	
Frozen dough		10 lb	
Mix		5 lb	
Toast			
French	2 slices	7 lb bread	
Buttered or cinnamon	2 slices	7 lb bread	
Waffles	3 oz	6 qt batter	1 waffle
CEREALS			
Cooked cereal	⅔ cup	2 lb	2 gal cooked
Hominy grits	⅔ cup	2 lb	2 gal cooked
Cold cereal, flakes, crisp	1 oz (½–¾ cup)	3 lb	
Rice	½ cup	3–4 lb	6–8 qt cooked
See also Pasta			
DAIRY PRODUCTS			
Butter or margarine			
For sandwiches		1 lb	To butter 100 slices
For table	1–2 pats	1–1½ lb	
For vegetables	½–1 tsp	4–8 oz	
Cheese, cheddar,	1–1½ oz	3–5 lb	For sandwich or with cold cuts
Monterey Jack,			
Swiss, provolone			
Sandwich slices	1 oz	3¼ lb	
Cottage	2 oz (No. 20 dipper)	6½ lb	For salad or side dish
Cream	½ oz	2 lb	For salad or garnish
Dessert (cream, blue,	1 oz	3 lb	
Camembert)			
Cream			
Coffee		1–1½ qt	
Whipping	2 Tbsp	1½ pt	1½ qt whipped
Ice cream or sherbet, bulk	No. 12 dipper	2½ gal	Dish or sundae
	No. 16 dipper	1½ gal	With cake or cookie
	No. 20 dipper	1¼ gal	For à la mode
Milk			
Fluid	8 oz (1 cup)	3 gal	
Nonfat dry	8 oz (1 cup)	3 lb	3.5 oz (1⅓ cups) dry milk per qt of water. Volume may vary with brand.
Nondairy creamer	1 tsp	3 oz	
Sherbet			See Ice cream
Sour cream	1 oz (2 Tbsp)	3 lb	For baked potato
	1 tsp	8 oz	For garnish
Whipped topping mix			
Dry	2 Tbsp	5 oz	
Frozen	2 Tbsp	18 oz (1½ qt)	
Liquid	2 Tbsp	1½ pt	1½ qt whipped
Yogurt	8 oz (1 cup)	25 lb	
DESSERTS			
Cakes			
Angel food	1 oz	3–4 10-inch cakes	12–14 cuts per cake
Pound or loaf, 5 × 9 inches	3 oz	4 loaves	
Sheet, 12 × 18 × 2 inches	3 × 2¼ inches	2 pans	Cut 4 × 8
Batter, ready to bake		4–5 lb each	
Sheet, 18 × 26 × 2 inches	3 × 2½ inches	1 pan	Cut 6 × 10
Batter, ready to bake		8–10 lb	

TABLE 4.1	continued		
Food	**Serving portion**	**Amount for 50 portions**	**Miscellaneous information**
Cake mixes			
Angel food		4 lb	
Chocolate, white, yellow		5 lb	
Pies, 8 inch	⅙ pie	9 pies	Cut 6 pieces per pie
Filling			
Chiffon	3 cups per pie	6 qt	
Cream or custard	3 cups per pie	6 qt	
Fruit	3 cups (1 lb 8 oz) per pie	6 qt (10–12 lb)	
Meringue	4 oz per pie	2 lb	
Pastry			
1 crust	5 oz per pie	2 lb 8 oz	
2 crust	9 oz per pie	4 lb 8 oz	
Pies, 9 inch	⅛ pie	7 pies	Cut 8 pieces per pie
Filling			
Chiffon	3¾ cups per pie	6–7 qt	
Cream or custard	3¾ cups per pie	6–7 qt	
Fruit	3¾–4 cups (1 lb 14 oz)	6–7 qt (10–12 lb)	
Meringue	5–6 oz per pie	2–2¼ lb	
Pastry			
1 crust	9 oz per pie	4 lb	
2 crust	16 oz per pie	7 lb	
Puddings	½ cup (4 oz)	6¼ qt	No. 10 dipper
Toppings, sauce	2–3 Tbsp	2–3 qt	
EGGS			
Eggs			
In shell	1 egg	4½ doz	
Fresh or frozen, whole	1 egg	5 lb (2½ qt)	
FISH AND SHELLFISH			
Fish			
Fillets and steaks, 4 per lb	3 oz	14–16 lb	1 lb AP = 0.70 lb cooked fish
Whole, dressed	3 oz	40 lb	1 lb AP = 0.27 lb cooked fish
Lobster, meat only	4 oz	50 whole lobsters	1 lb lobster = approx. 4 oz meat 1½ lb lobster = 6–8 oz tail
Oysters, shucked	3–4 oz	1½–2 gal	1 lb AP = 0.38 lb cooked oysters
Scallops, frozen, to fry	3 oz	10–12 lb	
Shrimp			
Raw, in shell	2 oz	12½ lb	1 lb AP = 0.54 lb cooked shrimp
	3 oz	18–20 lb	
Raw, peeled and cleaned	3 oz	16 lb	1 lb peeled = 0.62 lb cooked shrimp
Cooked, peeled and cleaned	3 oz	10 lb	1 lb AP = 1.00 lb cooked shrimp
FRUITS[b]			
Canned			
For pies, see Desserts			
For salad or dessert	3–4 oz (½ cup)	2½–3 No. 10 cans	Most fruit yield 60–70 oz drained weight per No. 10 can. For fruits such as peach or pear halves and sliced pineapple, yield depends on count per can.

Desserts

Eggs

Fish and Shellfish

Fruits

continued

TABLE 4.1   continued

Fruits

Food	Serving portion	Amount for 50 portions	Miscellaneous information
Fresh			
Apples	1	½ box	Size 113
9 8-inch pies	⅙ pie	14–16 lb AP	1 lb AP = 0.91 lb ready to cook or serve raw with peels; 0.78 lb pared, cooked
7 9-inch pies	⅛ pie	16 lb AP	
Salad or dessert	3–3½ oz	15 lb AP	
Apricots	2	9 lb AP	Medium size 12 per lb
Avocados	½	25 avocados	Medium size 2 per lb
Salad	3 slices	12 avocados	1 lb AP = 0.60 lb ready to serve raw
Bananas	1	16 lb AP	Small, 5–6 inch
			1 lb AP = 0.65 lb ready to serve raw
Salad	3 oz	10 lb AP	Medium 7–8 inch, 3 per lb
Blueberries	4 oz	12–14 lb AP	1 lb AP = 0.95 lb ready to serve raw
Cherries, sweet	3 oz	10 lb AP	1 lb AP = 0.98 lb ready to serve with pits; 0.80 lb pitted
Cranberries, for sauce	¼ cup	4 lb AP	1 lb AP = 0.95 lb ready to cook
Fruit cup (mixed fruits)	3 oz (⅓ cup)	9 lb (6 qt)	
Grapefruit	½	25 fruit	64 to 80 size
Salad	5 sections	21 fruit	12 sections per fruit
			1 lb AP = 0.52 lb ready to serve raw
Grapes, seedless	4 oz	12–15 lb AP	1 lb AP = 0.94 lb ready to serve raw
With seeds			1 lb AP = 0.89 lb raw seeded
Kiwi	1 slice, as garnish	6–8 fruit	7–8 thin slices per fruit
Lemons			
For tea or fish	⅙	8–10 lemons	Medium, size 165
For lemonade	8-oz glass	3 doz	Medium, size 165
Limes			
Garnish	1 wedge	13 limes	4 wedges per lime
Limeade	8-oz glass	4½ doz	
Mangos, cubed or sliced	½ cup	20 lb AP	1 lb AP = 0.62 lb ready to serve raw
Melon			
Cantaloupe	½	25 melons (small)	
Fruit cup		5 melons	1 lb AP = 0.55 lb ready to serve raw
Salad slices		6 melons	
Casaba, honeydew	½	7 melons	1 lb AP = 0.55 lb or Persian ready to serve raw
Watermelon	12–16 oz	38–50 lb AP	1 lb AP = 0.57 lb fruit without rind
Nectarines	1 (5–6 oz)	16–19 lb AP	1 lb AP = 0.80 lb ready to serve raw, diced or sliced
Oranges	1	½ box	Size 113
Juice	4 oz (½ cup)	6¼ qt	16–18 doz size 113
Sections	5 sections	20 oranges	Size 150; 1 lb AP = 0.40 lb ready to serve, without membrane. 10–12 sections per orange.
Peaches	1 (5–6 oz)	16–19 lb AP	
Diced or sliced	½ cup	20 lb AP	1 lb AP = 0.76 lb ready to cook or serve raw
Pears	1 pear (5–6 oz)	17–19 lb AP	1 lb AP = 0.80 lb ready to cook or serve raw, unpared; 0.78 lb pared
Salad	3 slices	15–17 lb AP	8–10 slices per pear
Pineapple, cubed	½ cup	24 lb AP (6 pineapples)	1 lb AP = 0.50 lb ready to serve raw
Plums, Italian or purple	2	12½ lb AP	Medium size, 8 per lb
			1 lb AP = 0.85 lb ready to cook or serve raw
Rhubarb, 9 8-inch pies	⅙ pie	10–12 lb AP	1 lb AP = 0.86 lb ready to cook
7 9-inch pies	⅛ pie	12 lb AP	
Sauce	½ cup	14 lb AP	

TABLE 4.1 continued

Food	Serving portion	Amount for 50 portions	Miscellaneous information
Strawberries	4 oz	14 lb AP	1 lb AP = 0.88 lb ready to serve raw
Garnish	1 berry	1 qt AP	1 qt AP = about 1.32 lb ready to serve raw
			1 lb = 30–35 med. berries
Shortcake	¾ cup	8–9 qt AP	
Sundaes	½–¾ cup	6–8 qt AP	
Strawberries, frozen			
For pies, see Desserts			
For salad or dessert	4 oz (½ cup)	13–15 lb	
For topping	1½ oz	5 lb	
Ugli fruit	3 oz	12 lb	1 lb AP = 0.67 ready to serve

JUICES

Food	Serving portion	Amount for 50 portions	Miscellaneous information
Fruit or vegetable	4 oz (½ cup)	6¼ qt	
	6 oz (¾ cup)	9½ qt	
Canned	4 oz	4 46-oz cans	
	6 oz	7 46-oz cans	
Frozen	4 oz	4–5 12-oz cans	Dilute 1:3 parts water
		2 32-oz cans	Dilute 1:3 parts water
	6 oz	7 12-oz cans	Dilute 1:3 parts water
		3 32-oz cans	Dilute 1:3 parts water

MEAT

Beef

Food	Serving portion	Amount for 50 portions	Miscellaneous information
Brisket, corned, boneless	3 oz EP	25–30 lb AP	1 lb AP = 0.42 lb cooked lean meat
Brisket, fresh, boneless	3 oz EP	25–30 lb AP	1 lb AP = 0.46 lb cooked lean meat
Cubed, 1 inch, for stew	3 oz EP	12–15 lb AP	1 lb AP = 0.56 lb cooked lean meat
Ground			
80% lean	3 oz EP	11–13 lb AP	1 lb AP = 0.77 lb cooked meat
85% lean	3 oz EP	11–12 lb AP	1 lb AP = 0.80 lb cooked meat
Liver	3½ oz EP	16 lb AP	1 lb AP = 0.70 lb cooked liver
Roast			
Chuck, pot roast, boneless	3 oz EP	18 lb AP	1 lb AP = 0.70 lb lean cooked meat
With bone	3 oz EP	20–22 lb AP	1 lb AP = 0.45 lb cooked lean meat
Rib, standing	6 oz EP	45–50 lb AP	Bone in, oven prepared
Rib eye	3 oz EP	13–15 lb AP	1 lb AP = 0.73 lb lean cooked meat
Round, bottom boneless	3 oz EP	15–18 lb AP	1 lb AP = 0.70 lb cooked lean meat
Inside, boneless	3 oz EP	15–18 lb AP	1 lb AP = 0.70 lb cooked meat
Rump, boneless	3 oz EP	16–18 lb AP	1 lb AP = 0.62 lb cooked lean meat
Sirloin, boneless, trimmed	3 oz EP	16–18 lb AP	1 lb AP = 0.61 lb cooked lean meat
Short ribs, trimmed	3 oz EP	38–40 lb AP	1 lb AP = 0.25 lb cooked meat
Steaks			
Cubed, 4 per lb	3 oz EP	17 lb AP	
Flank, 4 per lb	3 oz EP	17 lb AP	1 lb AP = 0.67 lb cooked lean meat
Loin strip	8 oz AP	25 lb AP	Short cut, bone in
Round, boneless, 3 per lb	3½ oz EP	18–20 lb AP	1 lb AP = 0.59 lb cooked lean meat
Sirloin, boneless	3½ oz EP	14–16 lb AP	1 lb AP = 0.75 lb cooked lean meat
Tenderloin, trimmed	4 oz EP	14 lb AP	1 lb AP = 0.90 lb cooked lean meat
T-bone	8 oz AP	25 lb AP	
	12 oz AP	36–38 AP	

LAMB

Food	Serving portion	Amount for 50 portions	Miscellaneous information
Chops, rib, 4 per lb	2 each	25 lb AP	1 lb AP = 0.46 lb cooked lean meat
Roast, leg, boneless	3 oz EP	15 lb AP	1 lb AP = 0.61 lb cooked lean meat
With bone	3 oz EP	22 lb AP	1 lb AP = 0.45 lb cooked lean meat

continued

TABLE 4.1   continued

Food	Serving portion	Amount for 50 portions	Miscellaneous information
PORK, FRESH			
Chops, loin, with bone, 3 per lb	1 chop	17 lb AP	1 lb AP = 0.41 lb cooked lean meat
Cutlets, 3 or 4 per lb	3–3½ oz EP	12–15 lb AP	1 lb AP = 0.75 lb cooked meat
Ham, whole boneless	3 oz EP	18–20 lb AP	1 lb AP = 0.53 lb cooked lean meat
With bone	3 oz EP	20–22 lb AP	1 lb AP = 0.46 lb cooked lean meat
Shoulder, Boston butt, boneless	3 oz EP	18–20 lb AP	1 lb AP = 0.54 lb cooked lean meat
With bone	3 oz EP	19–21 lb AP	1 lb AP = 0.50 lb cooked lean meat
Shoulder, picnic, boneless	3 oz EP	20–22 lb AP	1 lb AP = 0.46 lb cooked lean meat
With bone	3 oz EP	25 lb AP	1 lb AP = 0.38 lb cooked lean meat
Roast, loin, boneless	3 oz EP	18–20 lb AP	1 lb AP = 0.54 lb cooked lean meat
With bone	3 oz EP	22–24 lb AP	1 lb AP = 0.41 lb cooked lean meat
Sausage, bulk	2-oz patty	12½–15 lb AP	1 lb AP = 0.47 lb cooked lean meat
Links, 12–16 per lb	2 links	7–8 lb AP	1 lb AP = 0.47 lb cooked lean meat
Spareribs	8–12 oz AP	25–40 lb AP	1 lb AP = 0.39 lb cooked meat
PORK, CURED			
Bacon, sliced			
Hotel pack	2 slices	4–5 lb	24 slices per lb
Sliced	2 slices	5–6 lb	17–20 slices per lb
Canadian	2 slices (2 oz)	10 lb	16 slices per lb
Ham, boneless	3 oz EP	15 lb AP	1 lb AP = 0.63 lb cooked lean meat
With bone	3 oz EP	18–20 lb AP	1 lb AP = 0.53 lb cooked lean meat
Fully cooked, ready to eat	3 oz EP	15 lb AP	
Pullman, canned	3 oz EP	12–15 lb AP	1 lb AP = 0.64 lb cooked lean meat
Shoulder, Boston butt, boneless	3 oz EP	16 lb AP	1 lb AP = 0.60 lb cooked lean meat
Shoulder, picnic, boneless	3 oz EP	18 lb AP	1 lb AP = 0.53 lb cooked lean meat
VARIETY AND LUNCHEON MEATS			
Braunschweiger	2 oz	7 lb	
Frankfurters			
8 per lb	2 franks	12½ lb	
10 per lb	2 franks	10 lb	
Knockwurst	3 oz	10 lb	
Sliced luncheon meat	1 oz	3¼ lb	16 slices per lb
VEAL			
Cubed, 1-inch, for stew	2 oz EP	12–15 lb AP	1 lb AP = 0.65 lb cooked lean meat
Cutlets, 3 or 4 per lb	3–3½ oz EP	12½–15 lb AP	1 lb AP = 0.80 lb cooked lean meat
Ground	3–4 oz EP	15–18 lb AP	1 lb AP = 0.73 lb cooked lean meat
Roast, leg, boneless	3 oz EP	15–18 lb AP	1 lb AP = 0.61 lb cooked lean meat
Shoulder, boneless	3 oz EP	18 lb AP	1 lb AP = 0.59 lb cooked lean meat
PASTA			
Macaroni, noodles, and spaghetti	4 oz	4½–5 lb dry	12 lb cooked
In casseroles	2 oz	2–3 lb dry	6–7 lb cooked
POULTRY			
Chicken			
Fryer parts			
½ breast (without back)	5 oz AP	15–16 lb AP	1 lb AP = 0.66 lb cooked chicken
1 drumstick and thigh	6 oz AP	19–20 lb AP	
1 drumstick	3 oz AP	10 lb AP	1 lb AP = 0.49 lb cooked chicken

Side tab labels: Pork, Fresh | Pork, Cured | Variety and Luncheon Meats | Veal | Pasta | Poultry

TABLE 4.1   continued

Food	Serving portion	Amount for 50 portions	Miscellaneous information
1 thigh	3 oz AP	10–11 lb AP	1 lb AP = 0.50 lb cooked chicken
2 wings	5 oz AP	15 lb AP	1 lb AP = 0.34 lb cooked chicken
Whole	¼ fryer	13 fryers	3½ lb each
	½ fryer	25 fryers	2–3 lb each
Whole, for stewing	3 oz cooked chicken without bone	26–28 lb AP	1 lb AP = 0.36 lb cooked chicken, not using neck and giblets; 0.41 lb using neck meat and giblets
Cooked, diced	2 oz	6 lb 4 oz	
Turkey, dressed, whole for roasting	3 oz EP (slices)	50 lb AP	1 lb AP = 0.53 lb cooked turkey with skin, without neck and giblets; without skin 0.47 lb
Boneless roll, raw	3–4 oz EP	16–18 lb AP	1 lb AP = 0.66 lb cooked turkey meat
Boneless roll, cooked	3–4 oz EP	12–15 lb AP	1 lb AP = 0.92 lb cooked turkey meat
Breasts, whole, raw	3 oz EP	19 lb AP	1 lb AP = 0.64 lb turkey meat with skin; 0.57 lb without skin
Leg quarters	3 oz EP	19 lb AP	1 lb AP = 0.53 lb cooked turkey; without skin 0.48 lb
Ground	3 oz EP	11–12 lb	1 lb AP = 0.85 lb cooked meat
Tenderloin (steaks)	4 oz	14–15 lb	1 lb AP = 0.90 lb cooked meat
Wings	3–4 oz EP	30 lb	1 lb AP = 0.32 lb cooked meat (without skin)
Turkey ham, cooked	1½ oz	5 lb	
Turkey, cooked, cubed	1½–2 oz	5–6 lb EP (18–20 lb AP)	3¾–4½ qt
Canned, see Chicken			

RELISHES

Food	Serving portion	Amount for 50 portions	Miscellaneous information
Catsup	1 oz	½ No. 10 can	1 No. 10 can = about 12 cups
	1 oz	4 14-oz bottles	
Mustard, prepared	½ tsp	½ cup	
Olives, green, whole	3	2 qt	88–90 per qt
Ripe, whole or pitted	3	1½ qt	120–150 per qt
Pickles, dill, whole	1 pickle	2½ qt	
Dill or sweet, sliced	1 oz	2¼ qt	
Pickle relish	1 oz	2 qt	1 gal = about 58 oz drained

SALADS AND SALAD DRESSINGS

Food	Serving portion	Amount for 50 portions	Miscellaneous information
Salads			
Bulky vegetable	1 cup	3 gal	
Fish or meat	½ cup	6–7 qt	
Fruit	⅓ cup	4¼ qt	
Gelatin	½ cup	1 12 × 20 × 2-inch pan	24-oz pkg flavored gelatin, 1 gal liquid
Potato	½ cup	6–7 qt	
Dressings			
Mixed in salad			
French, thin	1 Tbsp	3–4 cups	
Mayonnaise	1–2 Tbsp	1 qt	
Self-service			
Thousand Island, Roquefort, or Ranch	1–2 Tbsp	1½–2 qt	
French	1 Tbsp	1–1½ qt	

SAUCES

Food	Serving portion	Amount for 50 portions	Miscellaneous information
Gravy	3–4 Tbsp	3–4 qt	
Meat accompaniment	2 Tbsp	2 qt	
Pudding	2–3 Tbsp	2–3 qt	
Salsa	2–3 Tbsp	2–3 qt	Condiment for Mexican entrées
Vegetable	2–3 Tbsp	2–3 qt	

continued

TABLE 4.1   continued

Soups
Sugars, Jellies, Sweets, Nuts
Vegetables

Food	Serving portion	Amount for 50 portions	Miscellaneous information
SOUPS			
Soup			
First course	½–1 cup (4–8 oz)	2–3¼ gal	
Main course	1 cup (8 oz)	3¼ gal	
Soup			
Concentrated	1 cup (8 oz)	5 46-oz cans	
Soup base, paste		10 oz	For 2½ gal soup
SUGARS, JELLIES, SWEETS, NUTS			
Candies, small	2 each	1 lb	
Honey	2 Tbsp	5 lb (2 qt)	
Jam or jelly	1 Tbsp	2–3 lb	
Marshmallows	3	1–1½ lb	
Nuts, mixed	1½ Tbsp	1–1½ lb	
Sugar, cubes	1–2 cubes	1½ lb	
Granulated	1½ tsp	12 oz	
Syrup	¼ cup	3 qt	
Toppings for dessert	2 Tbsp	1½–2 qt	
VEGETABLES[b]			
Canned	2½ oz	2 No. 10 cans	Most vegetables yield 60–70 oz drained weight per No. 10 can
Dried			
Dehydrated potatoes			
Diced or sliced	3–4 oz	2–2½ lb AP	
Instant for mashing	4 oz	2–2¼ lb AP	
Dried beans	4 oz	5–6 lb AP	
Split peas or lentils	4 oz	4 lb AP	
Fresh			
Alfalfa sprouts	2 Tbsp	1 lb	1 lb AP = 0.95 ready to serve
Asparagus	3 oz	18–20 lb AP	1 lb AP = 0.60 lb ready to cook; 0.50 lb cooked
Beans, green or wax	3 oz	10–12 lb AP	1 lb AP = 0.88 lb ready to cook
Bean sprouts	2 Tbsp	12 oz	
Beets, topped	3 oz	12–14 lb AP	1 lb AP = 0.77 lb peeled; 0.73 lb cooked slices
Broccoli	3 oz	15–18 lb AP	1 lb AP = 0.63 lb ready to cook
Brussels sprouts	3 oz	12–14 lb AP	1 lb AP = 0.76 lb ready to cook
Cabbage			
Green	1 wedge or 3 oz shredded	12–14 lb AP	1 lb AP = 0.80 lb ready to cook or serve raw
Red, chopped or shredded	2 oz	10 lb AP	1 lb AP = 0.75 lb ready to cook or serve raw
Carrots, without tops	3 oz	14–16 lb AP	1 lb AP = 0.75 lb ready to cook or serve raw; 0.62 lb cooked
Strips for relish	3 strips, 4 × ½ inch	4–5 lb	
Cassava (manioc, tapioca)			
See Yucca			
Cauliflower	3 oz	16–18 lb AP	1 lb AP = 0.60 lb ready to cook or serve raw; 0.58 lb cooked
Salad pieces	¼ cup	8 lb AP	1 medium head = about 6 cups (50–75 florets)
Celery, sliced	3 oz	12–15 lb AP	1 lb AP = 0.70 lb ready to cook or serve raw; 0.62 lb cooked
Sticks for relishes	4 sticks, 4 × ½ inch	4–5 lb AP	
Celery cabbage	2 oz	9 lb AP	1 lb AP = 0.93 lb ready to serve raw
Corn, on cob	1 ear	5 doz (30–35 lb with husks)	1 lb AP = 0.40 lb EP cooked
Corn, popped	2 cups	6 gal	1 lb AP = 4½–5 gal popped
Cucumbers	1½ oz	5–6 lb AP	1 lb AP = 0.84 lb pared ready to serve raw

TABLE 4.1   continued

Food	Serving portion	Amount for 50 portions	Miscellaneous information
Edamame (soybeans), whole in shell	2 oz	10 lb AP	1 lb AP = 0.65 lb shelled
Eggplant	3 oz	12–15 lb AP	1 lb AP = 0.81 lb ready to cook
Endive, escarole	½ cup	8–10 lb AP	1 lb AP = 0.78 lb ready to serve
Lettuce			
Iceberg, wedges	⅙ head	8–10 heads	24 heads per crate
Broken, for salad	1 cup (2½ oz)	9½ lb AP	1 lb AP = 0.76 lb ready to serve
Garnish	1 leaf	4–5 lb AP	
Leaf, for garnish	1 leaf	3–4 lb AP	1 lb AP = 0.66 lb ready to serve
Bibb	2½ oz	9 lb	
Romaine, for salad	2½ oz	9 lb AP	1 lb AP = 0.64 lb ready to serve
Mushrooms, sliced	3 oz	12 lb AP	1 lb AP = 0.90 lb ready to serve raw or cook; 0.22 lb cooked
For sauce	1 oz	3–4 lb AP	
Onions			
Green, chopped for salad	¼ cup (with tops)	3½–4 lb AP	1 lb AP = 0.70 lb ready to serve raw with tops; 0.30 lb without tops
Green, whole for garnish	1 onion	1½ lb AP	1 lb AP = 30–40 onions
Mature	2 oz	7–8 lb AP	1 lb AP = 0.88 lb ready to serve raw or cook; 0.78 lb cooked
Whole, to bake	1 medium	12–15 lb AP	
Parsley (curly), for garnish or seasoning		1 lb AP	1 lb AP = 0.53 lb ready to serve raw without stems
Parsley (flat leaf, Italian) for seasoning			1 lb AP = 0.40 ready to use without stems
Parsnips	3 oz	12–15 lb AP	1 lb AP = 0.75 lb ready to cook
Peppers, green, red, and yellow strips	3 strips	4–5 lb AP	1 lb AP = 0.80 lb ready to cook or serve raw; 0.73 lb cooked
Chopped for salads	½ oz	1–2 AP	
Popcorn	2 cups	6 gal	1 lb AP = 5 gal popped
Potatoes, sweet, or yams to bake	1 potato (4½–5 oz)	18–20 lb AP	1 lb AP = 0.80 lb baked, without skins
Candied	4 oz	18 lb AP	1 lb AP = 0.80 lb peeled, ready to cook
Mashed	4 oz	18 lb AP	
Potatoes, white, baked	1 potato	17–25 lb AP	1 lb AP = 0.81 lb baked potato without skins
Mashed	4 oz (½ cup)	15 lb AP	1 lb AP = 0.81 lb ready to cook pared
Steamed	4 oz (1 potato)	16–17 lb AP	
French fried	4–5 oz	16–20 lb AP	1 lb AP = 0.81 lb ready to cook
Radishes, without tops, for relishes	2 oz	6 lb AP	1 lb AP = 0.94 lb ready to serve

continued

Vegetables

TABLE 4.1   continued

Food	Serving portion	Amount for 50 portions	Miscellaneous information
Salad greens	3 oz	10 lb	
Spinach	3 oz	12 lb AP	1 lb AP = 0.80 lb ready to cook or serve raw
For salad	1 oz	4–5 lb AP	
Squash, summer, yellow	3 oz	10 lb AP	1 lb AP = 0.95 lb ready to cook; 0.83 lb cooked
Zucchini	3 oz	10 lb AP	1 lb AP = 0.94 lb ready to cook; 0.86 lb cooked
Squash, winter, acorn	½ squash	20–25 lb AP	1 lb AP = 0.75 lb ready to cook in skin
Butternut	3 oz	12 lb AP	1 lb AP = 0.84 lb ready to cook pared
Hubbard, baked	2½-inch square	20–25 lb	
Mashed	3 oz	15 lb AP	1 lb AP = 0.70 lb ready to cook pared
Tomatoes	1 small	20 lb AP	
Sliced, salad	3 slices	15 lb AP	1 lb AP = 0.90 lb ready to cook or serve raw
Diced	½ cup	12–15 lb AP	1 lb AP = 0.75 lb peeled and seeded
Cherry, salad	1 oz	4 lb AP	1 lb AP = 0.97 lb stemmed
Turnips	3 oz	12–15 lb AP	1 lb AP = 0.79 lb ready to cook or serve raw; 0.78 lb cooked
Watercress	1 oz	7–10 lb AP	1 lb AP = 0.30 lb ready to serve raw
Yams, see Potatoes, sweet			
Yucca (Cassava, Manioc, Tapioca)	3 oz	12 AP	1 lb AP = 0.76 lb peeled cooked
Frozen			
Asparagus spears	3 oz	10 lb	
Beans, cut green or lima	3 oz	10 lb	
Broccoli	3 oz	10 lb	
Brussels sprouts	3 oz	10 lb	
Cauliflower	3 oz	10 lb	
Corn, whole kernel	3 oz	10 lb	
Peas	3 oz	10 lb	
Potatoes			
French fried	4 oz	12–13 lb	
Hashed brown	4 oz	12–13 lb	
Spinach	3 oz	10 lb	
MISCELLANEOUS			
Ice			
For water glasses	3–4 oz	10–12 lb	
For punch bowl		10 lb	
Potato chips	1 oz	3 lb	

[a]Abbreviations used: AP, as purchased; EP, edible portion.
[b]See Table 4.3 for yield information.

Vegetables

Miscellaneous

TABLE 4.2　Food weights and approximate equivalents in measure

Food	Weight	Approximate measure
Alfalfa sprouts	1 lb	8 cups
Allspice, ground	1 oz	4½ Tbsp
Almonds, blanched, slivered, chopped	1 lb	3½ cups
Almonds, whole	1 oz	24 nuts
Anchovies	1 oz	5–6 fillets
Apples, canned, pie pack	1 lb	2 cups
Apples, fresh, AP[a]	1 lb	3 medium (113)
Apples, fresh, pared and sliced	1 lb	2¾ cups
Apples, pared and diced, 1½-inch cubes	1 lb	3 cups
Applesauce	1 lb	2 cups
Apricots, canned halves, without juice	1 lb	2 cups 12–20 halves
Apricots, canned, pie pack	1 lb	2 cups
Apricots, dried, AP	1 lb	3 cups
Apricots, dried, cooked, without juice	1 lb	4½–5 cups
Apricots, fresh	1 lb	5–8 large 8–10 medium
Apricots, sliced	1 lb	3 cups
Asparagus, canned, cuts	1 lb	2½ cups
Asparagus, canned tips, drained	1 lb	16–20 stalks
Asparagus, fresh	1 lb	16–20 large spears 21–27 medium 27–35 thin
Avocado	1 lb	2 medium
Bacon bits	1 lb	3⅓ cups
Bacon, cooked	1 lb	85–95 slices
Bacon, uncooked	1 lb	14–25 slices
Bacon, uncooked, diced	1 lb	2¼ cups
Baking powder	1 oz	2⅓ Tbsp
	1 lb	2⅓ cups
Baking soda	1 oz	2⅓ Tbsp
	1 lb	2⅓ cups
Bananas, AP	1 lb	3 medium
Bananas, diced	1 lb	2½–3 cups
Bananas, mashed	1 lb	2 cups
Barbecue sauce	1 lb	2 cups
Barley, pearl	1 lb	2¼ cups 8 cups cooked
Basil, sweet, dried	1 oz	1⅓ cups
Basil leaves, fresh (loosely packed)	1 oz	¾ cup 40 medium leaves
Bay leaves, fresh	1 oz	½ cup
Bay leaves, dry, whole	1 oz	136 leaves
Beans, baked	1 lb	2 cups
Beans, fava	1 lb	3 cups
Beans, garbanzo, canned	1 lb	2½ cups
Beans, great northern, dried, AP	1 lb	2½ cups
Beans, green, cut, cooked	1 lb	3 cups

continued

TABLE 4.2   continued

Food	Weight	Approximate measure
Beans, green, cut, frozen	1 lb	3 cups
Beans, kidney, dried, AP	1 lb	2½ cups
Beans, kidney, dried, 1 lb AP, after cooking	2 lb 6 oz	6–7 cups
Beans, lima, dried, AP	1 lb	2½ cups
Beans, lima, dried, 1 lb AP, after cooking	2 lb 9 oz	6 cups
Beans, lima, fresh, canned, or frozen	1 lb	3 cups
Beans, navy or black turtle, dried, AP	1 lb	2¼ cups
Beans, navy, dried, 1 lb AP, after cooking	2 lb 3 oz	5½–6 cups
Beans, pinto, dried, AP	1 lb	2½ cups
Bean sprouts, canned, drained	1 lb	1 qt
Bean sprouts, fresh	1 lb	2 qt
Beef, cooked, diced	1 lb	3 cups
Beef, dried, solid pack	1 lb	3¾ cups
Beef, ground, raw	1 lb	2 cups
Beef base (paste)	1 lb	2½ cups
Beets, cooked, diced, or sliced	1 lb	2½–3 cups
Beets, fresh (without tops)	1 lb	3–4 medium 16–18 baby
Blackberries, fresh, frozen, IQF[b]	1 lb	3 cups
Blackberries or boysenberries, pie pack	1 lb	2½ cups
Black-eyed peas, dried	1 lb	2¾ cups
Blueberries, canned	1 lb	2 cups
Blueberries, fresh, frozen, IQF	1 lb	2½ cups
Bran, all bran	1 lb	2 qt
Bran flakes	1 lb	3 qt
Brazil nuts	1 oz	6–8 nuts
Bread, dry, broken	1 lb	8–9 cups
Bread, fresh	1 lb	8 oz dry crumbs
Bread, loaf	1 lb	16–18 slices, ½ inch each
Bread, sandwich	2 lb	36–40 slices, thin
Bread, soft, broken	1 lb	2½ qt
Bread crumbs, dry, ground	1 lb	4 cups (1 qt)
Bread crumbs, soft	1 lb	2 qt
Broccoli, florets	1 lb	4 cups
Broccoli, head	1 lb	1 medium
Brussels sprouts, AP	1 lb	1 qt
Buckwheat groats	1 lb	2½ cups 8–9½ cups cooked
Bulgur	1 lb	3 cups 8–9 cups cooked
Butter	1 lb	2 cups 4 4-oz sticks
Buttermilk, dry	1 oz	¼ cup
	1 lb	4 cups
Butterscotch chips	1 lb	2⅔ cups

TABLE 4.2   continued

Food	Weight	Approximate measure
Cabbage, raw, shredded	1 lb	1 qt lightly packed
Cabbage, AP, shredded, cooked	1 lb	1½ cups
Cake crumbs, soft	1 lb	6 cups
Cake mix	1 lb	4 cups
Cantaloupe	3 lb	1 melon, 6-inch diameter
Capers	1 lb	1¼ cups drained
Caraway seed	1 oz	4 Tbsp
Cardamom, ground	1 oz	5 Tbsp
Carrots, diced, cooked	1 lb	3 cups
Carrots, diced, raw	1 lb	3–3¼ cups
Carrots, fresh	1 lb	4–5 medium
Carrots, baby, fresh	1 lb	30–35 carrots
Carrots, ground, raw, EP[c]	1 lb	3 cups
Carrots, shredded	1 lb	4 cups
Carrots, sliced, frozen	1 lb	3½ cups
Cashew nuts	1 oz	18 nuts
Cashew nuts	1 lb	3¼ cups
		250 nuts
Catsup	1 lb	2 cups
Cauliflower, florets	1 lb	4 cups
Cauliflower, head	1 lb	1 medium
Cayenne pepper	1 oz	4⅓ Tbsp
Celery, chopped	1 lb	3 cups
Celery, diced	1 lb (1–2 bunches)	1 qt
Celery cabbage, shredded	1 lb	6 cups
Celery flakes, dried	1 oz	1⅓ cups
Celery salt	1 oz	2 Tbsp
Celery seed (whole)	1 oz	3⅔ Tbsp
Cheese, cheddar or Swiss, shredded	1 lb	4 cups
Cheese, cottage	1 lb	2 cups
Cheese, cream	1 lb	2 cups
Cheese, loaf, slices	1 lb	16–20 slices
Cheese, mozzarella, shredded	1 lb	3½ cups
Cheese, Parmesan or Romano, commercially grated	1 lb	3½ cups
Cheese, Parmesan or Romano, freshly grated	1 lb	7–8 cups
Cherries, glacé, candied	1 lb	96 cherries 2½ cups
Cherries, maraschino, drained	1 lb	50–60 cherries
Cherries, red, frozen	1 lb	2 cups
Cherries, red, pie pack, drained	1 lb	2½ cups
Cherries, Royal Anne, drained	1 lb	2½ cups
Cherries, sweet fresh	1 lb	45 cherries 2½ cups pitted
Chervil	1 oz	2½ cups
Chicken, cooked, cubed	1 lb	3 cups
Chicken, ready to cook	4–4½ lb	1 qt cooked, diced
Chicken base (paste)	1 lb	1¾ cups
Chili powder	1 oz	3⅔ Tbsp

continued

TABLE 4.2 continued

Food	Weight	Approximate measure
Chili sauce	1 lb	1⅓ cups
Chiles, green, diced	1 lb	2 cups
Chives, freeze-dried	1 oz	3⅓ cups
Chives, frozen	1 oz	⅓ cup
Chocolate, baking	1 lb	16 squares
Chocolate, grated	1 lb	3½ cups
Chocolate, melted	1 lb	2 cups (scant)
Chocolate chips	1 lb	2⅔ cups
Chocolate wafers	1 lb	4 cups crumbs
Cilantro, fresh	1 oz	¾ cup
Cilantro, dried leaf	1 oz	2 cups
Cinnamon, ground	1 oz	4 Tbsp
	1 lb	4 cups
Cinnamon sticks	1 oz	18 inches of sticks
Citron, dried, chopped	1 lb	2½ cups
Clear Jel	1 lb	3⅔ cups
	1 oz	3⅔ Tbsp
Clear Jel (instant)	1 lb	3½ cups
	1 oz	3½ Tbsp
Cloves, ground	1 oz	4½ Tbsp
Cloves, whole	1 oz	5 Tbsp
		500 cloves
Cocoa	1 lb	4½ cups
Coconut, flaked or shredded	1 lb	4¾ cups
Coffee, ground coarse	1 lb	5–5½ cups
Coffee, instant	1 oz	½ cup
Coffee, whole beans	1 lb	6–6½ cups
Coriander seed, ground	1 oz	5 Tbsp
Coriander seed, whole	1 oz	4 Tbsp
Corn, cream style, canned	1 lb	2 cups
Corn, whole, on the cob	1 lb	2 medium
Corn, whole kernel, canned, drained	1 lb	3 cups
Corn, whole kernel, frozen	1 lb	3 cups
Cornflake crumbs	1 lb	4½ cups
Cornflakes	1 lb	4 qt
Cornmeal, coarse	1 lb	3 cups
Cornmeal, 1 lb AP, dry, after cooking	6 lb	3 qt
Cornstarch	1 oz	3½ Tbsp
	1 lb	3½ cups
Corn syrup	1 lb	1½ cups
Couscous	1 lb	2¼ cups
Crab in shell	1 lb	½ cup cooked meat
Crabmeat, flaked	1 lb	3½ cups
Cracked wheat	1 lb	3½ cups
Cracker crumbs, medium fine	1 lb	5–6 cups
Crackers, 2⅝ × 2⅝ inch	1 lb	65 crackers
Crackers, graham	1 lb	60–65 crackers
Crackers, graham, crumbs	1 lb	4 cups
Crackers, saltines, 2 × 2 inch	1 lb	150–160 crackers
Cranberries, cooked	1 lb	1¾ cups
Cranberries, raw	1 lb	4 cups
Cranberry relish	1 lb	1¾ cups
Cranberry sauce, jellied	1 lb	2 cups

TABLE 4.2   continued

Food	Weight	Approximate measure
Cream of tartar	1 oz	3 Tbsp
Cream of Wheat or farina, quick, AP	1 lb	2⅔ cups
Cream of Wheat or farina, 1 lb AP, after cooking	8 lb	1 gal
Cream, sour	1 lb	2 cups
Cream, whipping	1 pt	1 qt whipped
Croutons	1 lb	2¼ qt
Cucumbers	1 lb	1½–2 medium
Cucumbers, diced, EP	1 lb	3 cups
Cucumbers, sliced	1 lb	50–60 slices
Cumin, ground	1 oz	4 Tbsp
Currants, dried	1 lb	3 cups
Curry powder	1 oz	4½ Tbsp
Dates, pitted	1 lb	2½ cups
Dill seed	1 oz	4 Tbsp
Dill weed	1 oz	9⅓ Tbsp
Eggplant	1 lb	8 slices, 4 × ½ inch 1 qt diced
Eggs, dried, whites	1 lb	5 cups
Eggs, dried, whole	1 lb	5⅓ cups
Eggs, dried, yolks	1 lb	5⅔ cups
Eggs, hard-cooked, chopped	1 lb	2⅔ cups
	1 doz	3½ cups
Eggs, shelled, fresh or frozen, whole	1 lb (approximately 1¾ oz per egg)	2 cups (8–10 eggs)
Eggs, shelled, fresh or frozen, whites	1 lb (approximately 1–1¼ oz per white)	2 cups (16–18 eggs)
Eggs, shelled, fresh or frozen, yolks	1 lb (approximately ½–¾ oz per yolk)	2 cups (22–26 eggs)
Eggs, whole, in shell[d]	1 lb	8–10 large eggs
Fennel seed	1 oz	3⅓ Tbsp
Figs, dry, cut fine	1 lb	2½ cups
Flour, all-purpose or bread	1 lb	4 cups
Flour, cake or pastry, unsifted	1 lb	3¾ cups
Flour, rye	1 lb	4 cups
Flour, whole wheat	1 lb	3¾–4 cups
Garlic, fresh	1 oz	6 large cloves
Garlic, fresh, minced	1 oz	3 Tbsp
Garlic powder	1 oz	3 Tbsp
Garlic salt	1 oz	2 Tbsp
Gelatin, granulated, flavored	1 lb	2¼ cups
Gelatin, granulated, unflavored	1 oz	3 Tbsp
	1 lb	3 cups
Ginger, candied, chopped	1 oz	2 Tbsp
Ginger, fresh, sliced	1 lb	3 cups
Ginger, ground	1 oz	4 Tbsp
	1 lb	4 cups
Graham cracker crumbs	1 lb	4 cups
Grapefruit, medium	1 lb	1 grapefruit 10–12 sections ⅔ cup juice

continued

TABLE 4.2   continued

Food	Weight	Approximate measure
Grapefruit sections	1 lb	2 cups
Grapes, cut, seeded, EP	1 lb	2¾ cups
Grapes, on stem	1 lb	1 qt
Grapes, seedless, fresh	1 lb	3 cups
Grits, hominy	1 lb	3 cups
Grits, hominy, 1 lb AP, after cooking	6½ lb	3¼ qt
Ham, cooked, diced	1 lb	3 cups
Ham, cooked, ground	1 lb	2½ cups
Hazelnuts (shelled)	1 lb	3½ cups
Hazelnuts (whole)	1 oz	20 nuts
Hominy, canned	1 lb	3 cups
Hominy grits, see Grits		
Honey	1 lb	1⅓ cups
Horseradish, prepared	1 oz	2 Tbsp
Ice cream	4½–6 lb	1 gal
Jam, jelly	1 lb	1⅓–1½ cups
Kasha	1 lb	2½ cups
		8½–10 cups cooked
Kiwi	1 lb	6 kiwi
Kumquats	1 lb	40 average
Lemon juice	1 lb	2 cups (8–10 lemons)
Lemon peel, dried	1 oz	4 Tbsp
Lemon peel (zest), fresh	1 oz	4 Tbsp
	1 lemon	2 Tbsp
Lemons, size 165	1 lb	4–5 lemons
		Yield ¾ cup juice
		3–4 Tbsp grated zest
Lentils, dried	1 lb	2¼ cups
		7 cups cooked
Lettuce, average head	2 lb	1 head
Lettuce, chopped or shredded	1 lb	6–8 cups
Lettuce, leaf	1 lb	25–30 salad garnishes
Limes, fresh	1 lb	5–6 limes
		15–20 thin slices, yield ¾ cup juice
		1–2 Tbsp grated zest
Macadamia nuts	1 oz	10–12 nuts
Macaroni, 1-inch pieces, dry	1 lb	4 cups
Macaroni, 1 lb AP, after cooking	3 lb	2–2¼ qt
Macaroni, cooked	1 lb	3 cups
Mace	1 oz	5 Tbsp
Mango	1 lb	1 large, 2 small
		1¾ cups
Margarine	1 lb	2 cups
Margarine, whipped	1 lb	2⅔ cups
Marjoram leaves, dried	1 oz	1 cup
Marshmallows (1¼ inch)	1 lb	80–90
Marshmallows, miniature (10 miniature = 1 regular)	1 lb	8 cups
	1 oz	52

TABLE 4.2   continued

Food	Weight	Approximate measure
Mayonnaise	1 lb	2 cups (scant)
Meat, cooked, chopped	1 lb	2 cups
Milk, evaporated	1 lb	1¾ cups
Milk, fluid, whole	1 lb	2 cups
Milk, nonfat, dry	1 lb	6 cups
	1 oz	6 Tbsp
Milk, sweetened, condensed	1 lb	1½ cups
Millet	1 lb	2¼ cups
		7 cups cooked
Mincemeat	1 lb	2 cups
Mint, whole leaf (dried)	1 oz	¾ cup
Molasses	1 lb	1⅓ cups
Monosodium glutamate	1 oz	2 Tbsp
Mushrooms, canned	1 lb	2 cups
Mushrooms, fresh, whole	1 lb	75 small
		40 medium
		20 large
Mushrooms, fresh, sliced	1 lb	5 cups raw
		1¾ cups cooked
Mustard, ground, dry	1 oz	4 Tbsp
	1 lb	5 cups
Mustard, prepared	1 oz	2 Tbsp
Mustard seed	1 oz	2⅓ Tbsp
Nectarine	1 lb	3 medium
Noodles, cooked	1 lb	2¾ cups
Noodles, 1 lb AP, after cooking	3 lb	2 qt
Nutmeats	1 lb	4 cups
Nutmeg, ground	1 oz	3⅔ Tbsp
Oats, rolled, quick, AP	1 lb	5⅓ cups
Oats, rolled, 1 lb AP, after cooking	2½ lb	4 qt
Oil, vegetable	1 lb	2–2⅛ cups
Okra	1 lb	2 cups sliced
Olives, AP	1 lb	⅔ cup chopped
Olives, green, small size, drained	1 lb	160 olives
Olives, green, stuffed	1 lb	2½ cups
Olives, ripe, sliced	1 lb	3⅓ cups
Olives, ripe, whole, drained	1 lb	140 small
		110 medium
		90 large
Onions, dehydrated	1 lb	8 lb raw (equivalent)
Onions, dehydrated, chopped	1 oz	5 Tbsp
	1 lb	5–6 cups
Onions, fresh, chopped	1 lb	2½–3 cups
Onions, green, sliced	1 lb	2½–3 cups
Onions, mature, AP	1 lb	2 medium
		3 small
Onion powder	1 oz	3 Tbsp
Onion salt	1 oz	2½ Tbsp
Onion soup mix	1 oz	2½ Tbsp
	1 lb	2⅔ cups
Orange juice, frozen	6 oz	3 cups reconstituted
	32 oz	4 qt reconstituted

continued

TABLE 4.2 continued

Food	Weight	Approximate measure
Orange peel, dried	1 oz	4 Tbsp
Orange peel, fresh	1 medium orange	3–4 Tbsp grated peel
Oranges	1 lb	2 cups bite-size pieces
Oranges, medium (size 113)	1 lb	3 oranges, unpeeled
		4 oranges, peeled
		10–11 sections each
		Yield 1 cup juice
Oregano, ground	1 oz	5 Tbsp
Oregano, leaf (dried)	1 oz	⅔ cup
Orzo	1 lb	2¼ cups
Oysters, shucked	1 lb	2 cups
Papaya	1 lb	1 medium
		1¼–1½ cups peeled and seeded
		¾–1 cup mashed
Paprika, ground	1 oz	4 Tbsp
Parsley (curly), coarsely chopped	1 oz	¾ cup
Parsley (flat leaf, Italian), coarsely chopped	1 oz	⅔ cup
Parsley flakes, dry	1 oz	1¼ cups
Parsnips, AP	1 lb	4–5 medium
Pasta	1 lb	see p. 507
Peaches, canned, sliced, drained	1 lb	2 cups
Peaches, fresh, AP	1 lb	3 medium
		2½ cups sliced
Peaches, sliced, frozen	1 lb	2 cups
Peanut butter	1 lb	2 cups
Peanuts, chopped, no skins	1 lb	3 cups
Peanuts, shelled	1 lb	3¼ cups
Pears, canned, drained, diced	1 lb	2½ cups
Pears, canned, large halves, drained	1 lb 14 oz	1 qt (9 halves)
Pears, fresh AP	1 lb	3 medium
		2¼ cups sliced
Peas, cooked, drained	1 lb	2¼ cups
Peas, dried, 1 lb AP, after cooking	2½ lb	5½ cups
Peas, split, dried, AP	1 lb	2⅓ cups
Pecans, chopped	1 lb	4 cups
Pecans, halves	1 oz	20 halves
Pecans, shelled, pieces	1 lb	4 cups
Pecans, whole in shell	1 lb	2⅓ cups shelled
Pepper, cayenne	1 oz	4⅓ Tbsp
Pepper, crushed, red	1 oz	6 Tbsp
Pepper, ground, black or white	1 oz	4 Tbsp
	1 lb	4 cups
Peppercorns	1 oz	6 Tbsp
Peppers, Anaheim	1 lb	3–4 large
Peppers, bell	1 lb	2–3 medium
Peppers, green, chopped	1 lb	3 cups
Peppers, green, dried flakes	1 oz	¾ cup
Peppers, jalapeño	1 lb	16 large
		24 medium

TABLE 4.2	continued	
Food	**Weight**	**Approximate measure**
Peppers, poblano	1 lb	5 medium
Peppers, serrano	1 lb	40 medium
Pickle relish	1 lb	2 cups
Pickles, chopped	1 lb	3 cups
Pickles, halves, 3 inch	1 lb	3 cups
		36 halves
Pimento, chopped	1 lb	2 cups
Pine nuts	1 oz	157 nuts
Pineapple, canned, crushed	1 lb	2 cups
Pineapple, canned, slices, drained	1 lb	8–12 slices
Pineapple, canned, tidbits	1 lb	2 cups
Pineapple, fresh	2–4 lb	1 pineapple
		2–4 cups, cubed
Pineapple, frozen, chunks	1 lb	2 cups
Pistachios	1 oz	48 nuts
Plantains	1 lb	2 large
		3 medium
		2 cups sliced
Plums	1 lb	6 medium
		2½ cups sliced
Pomegranates, whole	1 lb	2 large
		1¼ cup seeds
		¾–1 cup juice
Popcorn	1 oz	4–5 cups popped
Poppy seed	1 oz	3 Tbsp
Potato chips	1 lb	4–5 qt
Potato chips, crushed	1 lb	2 qt
Potatoes, dehydrated, diced	1 lb	5⅛ cups
Potatoes, dehydrated, flakes	1 lb	5 cups
Potatoes, dehydrated, granules	1 lb	2¼ cups
Potatoes, dehydrated, slices	1 lb	9⅔ cups
Potatoes, fresh, white, AP	1 lb	3 medium
Potatoes, fresh, white, cooked	1 lb	2½ cups
Potatoes, raw, new (small)	1 lb	10–12 potatoes
Potatoes, raw, white, cubed	1 lb	2⅔ cups
Potatoes, sweet	1 lb	3 medium
Potatoes, sweet, cooked	1 lb	2 cups
Poultry seasoning, ground	1 oz	7 Tbsp
Prunes, dried, size $^{30}/_{40}$, AP	1 lb	2½ cups
Prunes, dried, 1 lb AP, after cooking	2 lb	3–4 cups
Prunes, pitted, cooked	1 lb	3¼ cups
Pudding mix, dry, instant	1 lb	2½ cups
Pudding mix, dry, regular	1 lb	2¼ cups
Pumpkin, cooked	1 lb	2 cups
Quinoa, AP	1 lb	2¼ cups
Radishes, AP	1 lb	30–45 (without tops)
		16–20 (with tops)
Raisins, AP	1 lb	2½–3 cups
Raisins, 1 lb AP, after cooking	1 lb 12 oz	1 qt
Raisins, chopped	1 lb	2⅔ cups
Raspberries, fresh AP, or frozen IQF	1 lb	3 cups

continued

TABLE 4.2   continued

Food	Weight	Approximate measure
Raspberries, with syrup	1 lb	2 cups
Red hots	1 lb	2¼ cups
Rhubarb, raw, 1-inch pieces	1 lb	4 cups
Rhubarb, 1 lb EP, after cooking		2½ cups
Rice, Arborio	1 lb	2⅓ cups
Rice, brown, AP	1 lb	2½ cups
Rice, converted, AP	1 lb	2½ cups
Rice, cooked	1 lb	2¼ cups
Rice, 1 lb AP, after cooking	3½ lb	2 qt
Rice, precooked, AP	1 lb	4½ cups
Rice, regular, AP	1 lb	2⅓ cups
Rice, wild	1 lb	2⅔ cups
Rice, wild, 1 lb AP, after cooking	1 lb	5 cups
Rice cereal, crisp	1 lb	4 qt
Rosemary leaves (dried)	1 oz	7 Tbsp
Rutabagas, raw, cubed, EP	1 lb	3⅓ cups
Sage, finely ground	1 oz	9 Tbsp
Sage, rubbed	1 oz	¾ cup
Salad dressing, cooked	1 lb	2 cups
Salmon, canned	1 lb	2 cups
Salt (table)	1 oz	1½ Tbsp
	1 lb	1½ cups
Salt (kosher, Diamond Crystal)	1 lb	3 cups
Sauerkraut	1 lb	3 cups packed
Sausage, bulk, AP	1 lb	2 cups
Sausages, link, small	1 lb	16–17 links
Sesame seed	1 oz	3 Tbsp
Sherbet	6 lb	1 gal
Shortening, hydrogenated fat	1 lb	2¼ cups
Shrimp, cleaned, cooked, peeled	1 lb	3¼ cups
Soda, baking	1 oz	2⅓ Tbsp
Spaghetti, cooked	1 lb	2⅔ cups
Spaghetti, 1 lb AP, after cooking	3 lb	2 qt
Spinach, canned or frozen	1 lb	2 cups
Spinach, raw	1 lb	5 qt lightly packed
Spinach, raw, chopped	1 lb	3¼ qt
Spinach, 1 lb AP, after cooking	13 oz	2¾ cups
Split peas (dried)	1 lb	2⅓ cups / 4½ cups cooked
Squash, Hubbard, cooked	1 lb	2 cups
Squash, summer, fresh	1 lb	4 cups
Starch, waxy maize	1 oz	3 Tbsp
Strawberries, fresh or frozen, IQF	1 lb	2½–3 cups hulled and sliced
Strawberries, sliced, frozen, with syrup	1 lb	2 cups
Suet, ground	1 lb	3¾ cups
Sugar, brown, lightly packed	1 lb	3 cups
Sugar, brown, solid pack	1 lb	2 cups
Sugar, cubes	1 lb	96 cubes

TABLE 4.2   continued

Food	Weight	Approximate measure
Sugar, granulated	1 lb	2¼ cups
	1 oz	2¼ Tbsp
Sugar, powdered, unsifted	1 lb	3¼ cups
Sugar, powdered, XXXX sifted	1 lb	3¾ cups
Syrup, corn or maple	1 lb	1½ cups
Tapioca, quick cooking	1 lb	3 cups
Tapioca, 1 lb AP, after cooking		7½ cups
Tarragon, leaf	1 oz	1 cup
Tea, bulk	1 lb	6 cups
Tea, instant	1 oz	½ cup
Thyme, ground	1 oz	6 Tbsp
Thyme, leaves, dry	1 oz	9 Tbsp
Tomatillos	1 lb	10–12 medium
Tomatoes, canned	1 lb	2 cups
Tomatoes, fresh	1 lb	2–3 medium
		12 slices
Tomatoes, fresh, diced	1 lb	2¼ cups
Tomatoes, fresh plum	1 lb	6 medium
Tomato paste	1 lb	2 cups
Tortillas, corn, 8 inch	1 lb	16
Tortillas, flour, 8 inch	1 lb	12
Tortillas, flour, 10 inch	1 lb	9
Tuna, canned	1 lb	2 cups
Turkey, AP, dressed weight	14 lb	11–12 cups diced, cooked meat
Turmeric, ground	1 oz	4 Tbsp
Turnips, AP	1 lb	2–3
Vanilla and other extracts	1 oz	2 Tbsp
Vinegar	1 lb	2 cups
Walnuts, English, shelled	1 lb	4 cups
Wasabi powder	1 oz	6 Tbsp
Water	1 lb	2 cups
Watercress, EP	1 oz	½ cup
Watermelon	1 lb	1-inch slices, 6-inch diameter
Wheat germ	1 lb	5⅓ cups
Whipped topping, liquid	1 lb	2 cups
Wonton wrappers	1 lb	Approx. 60 wrappers
Yeast, compressed	1 oz	1 pkg
Yeast, dry	¼ oz	1 envelope
Yeast, dry, regular or instant	1 oz	3 Tbsp + 1 tsp
	1 lb	3⅓ cups
Yogurt	1 lb	2 cups
Zucchini, fresh, shredded	1 lb	3¼ cups

[a]AP denotes "as purchased," which refers to the status of the product before it is peeled, hulled, cored, or otherwise prepared for cooking.

[b]IQF denotes "individually quick frozen."

[c]EP denotes "edible portion," or the status of the product after it has been prepared for cooking or for serving raw.

[d]One case (30 doz) eggs weighs approximately 41–43 lb and yields approximately 35 lb liquid whole eggs.

TABLE 4.3 Yield, availability, and storage of fresh fruits and vegetables

Fruit/vegetable	Yield[*]	Availability	Storage (raw, before paring, cutting, or processing)	Ethylene
Apples	0.78	Some variety available year-round	35–40°F	Produces: Yes
		Peak: fall		Sensitive: Yes
Apricots	0.76	Available May–Aug	32–36°F	Produces: Yes
		Peak: Jun–Jul	Ripen at room temperature	Sensitive: Yes
Artichokes	0.25	Year-round	32–36°F	Produces: No
		Peak: Mar–May		Sensitive: No
Asparagus	0.60	Year-round	35–40°F	Produces: No
		Peak: Mar–Jun		Sensitive: Yes
Avocados	0.60	Hass variety available year-round	45–50°F unripe	Produces: Yes
		Peak: Dec–Apr	34–38°F ripe	Sensitive: Yes
Bananas (also see Plantains)	0.65	Year-round	60–65°F	Produces: Yes
			Do not refrigerate or store below 58°F	Sensitive: No (after ripening)
Beans, green or wax	0.88	Year-round	45–50°F	Produces: No
		Peak: May–Oct		Sensitive: Yes
Beets, without tops	0.77	Year-round	32–36°F	Produces: No
Beets, with tops	0.45	Peak: May–Oct		Sensitive: No
Belgian endive	0.85	Year-round	32–36°F	Produces: No
				Sensitive: Yes
Blackberries	0.95	Jun–Oct	32–36°F	Produces: Low
				Sensitive: No
Blueberries	0.95	Jun–Oct	32–36°F	Produces: Low
		Peak: late summer		Sensitive: No
Bok choy	0.75	Year-round	32–36°F	Produces: No
				Sensitive: Yes
Broccoli, whole stem	0.63	Year-round	32–36°F	Produces: No
				Sensitive: Yes
Brussels sprouts	0.76	Year-round	32–36°F	Produces: No
		Peak: Oct–Feb		Sensitive: Yes
Cabbage, green (head)	0.80	Year-round	32–36°F	Produces: No
				Sensitive: Yes
Cabbage, red (head)	0.75	Year-round	32–36°F	Produces: No
				Sensitive: Yes
Cabbage, Savoy	0.75	Year-round	32–36°F	Produces: No
		Peak: Aug–Apr		Sensitive: Yes
Cantaloupe, peeled	0.52	Peak: Jun–Nov	32–36°F	Produces: Yes
				Sensitive: No
Carambola (star fruit)	0.92	Jul–Feb	45–50°F	Produces: Low
				Sensitive: No
Carrots	0.75	Year-round	32–36°F	Produces: No
				Sensitive: Yes
Cauliflower	0.60	Year-round	32–36°F	Produces: No
		Peak: Oct–Feb		Sensitive: Yes
Celeriac (celery root)	0.60	Oct–Apr	32–36°F	Produces: No
				Sensitive: Yes
Celery	0.70	Year-round	32–36°F	Produces: No
				Sensitive: Yes
Chard, Swiss	0.92	Year-round	32–36°F	Produces: No
		Peak: Jul–Dec		Sensitive: Yes
Cherries (sweet), with pits	0.80	May–Aug	32–36°F	Produces: Low
				Sensitive: No
Chicory	0.78	Year-round	32–36°F	Produces: No
				Sensitive: Yes
Coconut		Year-round	32–36°F	Produces: No
				Sensitive: No

TABLE 4.3 continued

Fruit/vegetable	Yield*	Availability	Storage (raw, before paring, cutting, or processing)	Ethylene
Collards, leaves	0.65	Year-round	32–36°F	Produces: No
Collards, leaves and stems	0.74	Peak: Dec–Apr		Sensitive: Yes
Corn on cob, sweet	0.48	Year-round	32–36°F	Produces: No
		Peak: Jun–Sep		Sensitive: No
Cranberries	0.95	Sep–Jan	45–50°F	Produces: No
		Peak: Nov–Dec		Sensitive: No
Cucumbers, peeled	0.84	Year-round	45–50°F	Produces: Low
Cucumbers, peeled and seeded	0.55	Peak: Apr–Oct		Sensitive: Yes
Eggplant, unpeeled	0.90	Year-round	45–50°F	Produces: No
Eggplant, peeled	0.75	Peak: Jul–Sep	Do not store below 45°F	Sensitive: Yes
Endive (curly) and escarole	0.78	Year-round	32–36°F	Produces: No
				Sensitive: Yes
Endive, Belgian	0.85	Year-round	32–36°F	Produces: No
				Sensitive: Yes
Fennel (bulb)	0.45	Peak: Sep–May	32–36°F	
Figs	0.95	Jun–Oct	32–36°F	Produces: Yes
				Sensitive: No
Garlic cloves	0.85	Year-round	32–36°F	Produces: No
				Sensitive: No
Ginger root	0.75	Year-round	60–65°F	Produces: No
			Do not store below 55°F	Sensitive: No
Grapefruit (sections)	0.52	Year-round	45–50°F	Produces: Low
		Peak: Jan–Apr		Sensitive: Yes
Grapes			32–36°F	Produces: Low
Champagne	0.92	Late summer		Sensitive: Yes
Seedless, red and green	0.94	Year-round		
		Peak: Jun–Dec		
Herbs, fresh		Year-round	Basil: 45–50°F	Produces: No
Basil (leaves)	0.56		Others: 32–36°F	Sensitive: Yes
Chives (minced)	0.95			
Cilantro (leaves)	0.47			
Dill (weed)	0.44			
Marjoram	0.76			
Mint (leaves)	0.42			
Oregano (leaves)	0.78			
Parsley, curly (leaves)	0.53			
Parsley, Italian	0.40			
Rosemary (leaves)	0.80			
Sage	0.60			
Tarragon	0.80			
Thyme (leaves)	0.67			
Watercress	0.30			
Honeydew melon, peeled	0.66	Peak: May–Jan	60–65°F	Produces: Yes
				Sensitive: Yes
Jicama	0.80	Year-round	60–65°F	Produces: No
		Peak: Jan–May		Sensitive: No
Kale	0.65	Year-round	32–36°F	Produces: No
		Peak: Dec–Mar		Sensitive: No
Kiwi, peeled	0.80	Year-round	32–36°F	Produces: Yes
		Peak: Oct–May	Ripen at room temperature	Sensitive: Yes
Kohlrabi	0.55	Year-round	32–36°F	Produces: No
		Peak: Jun–Aug		Sensitive: No
Kumquat	0.98	Oct–Jun	45–50°F	Produces: No
		Peak: Jan–Mar	Do not store below 41°F	Sensitive: No

continued

TABLE 4.3 continued

Fruit/vegetable	Yield*	Availability	Storage (raw, before paring, cutting, or processing)	Ethylene
Leeks	0.45	Oct–Jun Peak: Oct–Dec	32–36°F	Produces: No Sensitive: Yes
Lettuce, head	0.76	Year-round	32–36°F	Produces: No Sensitive: Yes
Lettuce, leaf	0.66	Year-round	32–36°F	Produces: No Sensitive: Yes
Lettuce, romaine	0.64	Year-round	32–36°F	Produces: No Sensitive: Yes
Lemons/limes, sliced	0.78	Year-round	45–55°F	Produces: Yes Sensitive: Yes
Lemons/limes, wedges	0.90	Peak: Apr–Jul		
Mangos	0.62	Year-round Peak: May–Sep	60–65°F	Produces: Yes Sensitive: Yes
Melon (casaba, crenshaw, Juan Canary, Persian, Santa Claus)	0.55	Peak: Jun–Oct	60–65°F	Produces: Yes Sensitive: Yes
Mushrooms, trimmed	0.90	Year-round	32–36°F	Produces: No Sensitive: No
Napa cabbage	0.75	Year-round	32–36°F	Produces: No Sensitive: Yes
Nectarines	0.80	May–Sep Peak: Jul–Aug	51–77°F to ripen Chill damage to unripe fruit occurs between 36°F and 50°F. Store unripe fruit at 32–35°F.	Produces: Yes Sensitive: Yes
Okra	0.85	Year-round Peak: Jul–Oct	45–50°F	Produces: Low Sensitive: Yes
Onions, green (scallions)	0.70	Year-round Peak: Summer	32–36°F	Produces: No Sensitive: Yes
Onions, mature	0.88	Year-round Sweet peak: Apr–Aug	60–65°F	Produces: No Sensitive: No
Orange sections	0.40	Year-round Peak navels: Nov–May	45–50°F	Produces: Low Sensitive: Yes
Papaya	0.70	Year-round Peak: Feb–Apr	60–65°F	Produces: Yes Sensitive: Yes
Parsnips	0.75	Oct–Mar	32–36°F	Produces: No Sensitive: Yes
Peaches	0.76	May–Sep Peak: Jul–Sep	51–77°F to ripen Chill damage to unripe fruit occurs between 36°F and 50°F. Store unripe fruit at 32–35°F.	Produces: Yes Sensitive: Yes
Pears	0.80	Some varieties available year-round Peak: Anjou, Oct–May Bartlett, Aug–Dec Bosc, Sep–May Comice, Oct–Feb	60–70°F to ripen Store unripe fruit at 32°F	Produces: Yes Sensitive: Yes
Peas, green	0.38	Year-round Peak: Mar–Apr	32–36°F	Produces: No Sensitive: Yes
Peppers, chile	0.85	Year-round Peak: Jul–Sep	45–50°F	Produces: No Sensitive: Yes
Peppers, sweet bell	0.80	Year-round Peak: Jul–Nov	45–50°F	Produces: No Sensitive: No
Persimmon	0.75	Sep–Dec	60–65°F to ripen Store unripe fruit at 32–36°F	Produces: Yes Sensitive: Yes
Pineapple	0.50	Year-round Peak: Mar–Jun	45–50°F Do not store below 45°F	Produces: Low Sensitive: No

TABLE 4.3 continued

Fruit/vegetable	Yield*	Availability	Storage (raw, before paring, cutting, or processing)	Ethylene
Plantains	0.65	Year-round	60–65°F Do not store below 56°F	Produces: Yes Sensitive: Yes
Plums	0.85	May–Oct Peak: Aug–Sep	51–77°F to ripen Chill damage to unripe fruit occurs between 36°F and 50°F. Store unripe fruit at 32–35°F	Produces: Yes Sensitive: Yes
Pomegranates	0.50	Aug–Dec Peak: Oct–Dec	45°F Do not store below 41°F	Produces: No Sensitive: No
Potatoes, sweet	0.80	Year-round	60–65°F Do not store below 54°F	Produces: No Sensitive: Yes
Potatoes, white	0.81	Year-round	60–65°F Do not store below 42°F	Produces: No Sensitive: Yes
Radishes	0.94	Year-round	32–36°F	Produces: No Sensitive: Yes
Raspberries	0.95	Peak: Jun–Sep	32–36°F	Produces: Low Sensitive: No
Rhubarb	0.86	Year-round Peak: late spring, early summer	32–36°F	Produces: No Sensitive: No
Rutabagas	0.79	Year-round Peak: Jan–Mar	32–36°F	Produces: No Sensitive: Yes
Salsify (black or white)	0.65	Sep–May	32–36°F	Produces: No Sensitive: No
Spinach	0.80	Year-round	32–36°F	Produces: No Sensitive: Yes
Sprouts	0.95	Year-round	32–36°F	Produces: No Sensitive: Yes
Squash, acorn	0.75	Year-round Peak: Oct–Mar	60–65°F Do not store below 50°F	Produces: No Sensitive: Yes
Squash, butternut	0.84	Year-round Peak: Oct–Mar	60–65°F Do not store below 50°F	Produces: No Sensitive: Yes
Squash, Hubbard	0.70	Year-round	60–65°F	Produces: No
Squash, spaghetti	0.68	Year-round Peak: Apr–Sep Peak: Oct–Mar	45–50°F Do not store below 50°F	Produces: No Sensitive: Yes Sensitive: Yes
Squash, summer	0.95	Year-round Peak: Apr–Sep	45–50°F	Produces: No Sensitive: Yes
Squash, zucchini	0.94	Year-round Peak: Apr–Sep	45–50°F	Produces: No Sensitive: Yes
Strawberries	0.88	Year-round Peak: May–Jun	32–36°F	Produces: Low Sensitive: No
Tangerines/tangelos	0.60	Peak: Oct–May	45–50°F Do not store below 38°F	Produces: Low Sensitive: Yes
Tomatillos	0.75	Year-round Peak: Jul–Oct	45–50°F Do not store below 45°F	Produces: No Sensitive: No
Tomatoes	0.85	Year-round	60–65°F Do not store below 50°F	Produces: Yes Sensitive: Yes (when green)
Turnips	0.79	Year-round Peak: Apr–May; Sep–Oct	32–36°F	Produces: No Sensitive: Yes
Watermelon	0.57	Year-round Peak: Jun–Oct	45–50°F Do not store below 41°F	Produces: No Sensitive: No

* For percent yield, multiply the number by 100. For example: Apple yield = 78% (.78 × 100). Values in table represent the weight of ready-to-cook or ready-to-serve raw from 1 lb as purchased.

continued

P

R

S

T

W

TABLE 4.4 Equivalent measure (approximate) per ounce for dry herbs or spices and fresh herbs

Dry herb or spice	Equivalents (tsp per oz) (approx.)	Description
Allspice, ground	14	Flavor resembling blend of cloves, cinnamon, and nutmeg.
Anise seed	7	Warm licorice-like and mildly fennel-like taste.
Basil	40 (leaf) 15 (ground)	Anise, clove, and mint-like. Blends well with oregano, parsley, rosemary, thyme, sage, and saffron.
Bay leaf, crumbled, whole	47 136 (leaves)	Also known as *laurel*. Strong distinctive flavor.
Caraway seed, whole	8	Dill and anise-like flavor.
Cardamom, ground	15	Pungent, lemony flavor. Essential to Indian cookery.
Cayenne (red) pepper	13	Hot. Also known as *red pepper*.
Celery salt	6	Salt with a celery-like flavor.
Celery seed, ground	16 (ground) 11 (whole)	Slightly bitter with a celery-like flavor.
Chervil, leaf	40	Delicate flavor of parsley and mild anise.
Chili powder	11	Distinctive flavor in Mexican cookery.
Chinese five-spice	13	Warm, spicy, and sweet.
Chives, snipped (freeze-dried)	160	Mild onion and garlic flavor.
Cilantro, leaf	100	Assertive sage-citrus flavor. Use sparingly.
Cinnamon, ground	12	Distinctive flavor in baked goods. Essential ingredient in *curry* spice blends, *Chinese five-spice powder*.
Cloves	14 (ground) 16 (whole)	Strong aromatic spice. Commonly found in spice mixtures including *curry* and *bouquet garni*.
Coriander	16 (ground) 13 (whole)	Citrus-like aroma and mild mint flavor. An essential ingredient in *curry*, *garam masala*, and *pickling spice*.
Cumin	12 (ground) 8 (whole)	Potent spicy flavor that tends to dominate food. Used in Mexican, North African, and Indian dishes. Use sparingly.
Curry powder	14	Distinctive flavor in Indian cuisine.
Dill	11 (seed) 28 (weed)	Mild anise-parsley flavor.
Fennel seed	10	Mild licorice flavor. Common in Italian and Swedish cookery.
Fenugreek seed	7 (whole)	Powerful, aromatic and bittersweet, like burnt sugar, with a bitter aftertaste.
Ginger, ground	11	Spicy and pungent.
Mace	15	The lacy covering of the nutmeg seed. Flavor more delicate than nutmeg.
Marjoram	22 (ground) 52 (leaf)	Subtly minty and sweet, similar to oregano. Essential in Italian cooking.
Mint, whole leaf	39	Popular in Middle Eastern cooking.
Mustard	7 (seed) 13 (ground)	Pungent and slightly bitter.
Nutmeg, ground	11	Warm and spicy. Blends well with mace, cardamom, cinnamon, cloves, and ginger.
Oregano	16 (ground) 31 (leaf)	Minty and sweet.
Paprika	11	Sweet capsicum flavor.
Parsley flakes	65	Mild, sweet in flavor.
Pepper, black	13	

TABLE 4.4 continued

Dry herb or spice	Equivalents (tsp per oz) (approx.)	Description
Pepper, red	13 (ground) 18 (crushed)	Used to season Mexican dishes. Add in small quantities.
Pepper, white	11	Comes from the same pod as black pepper, but the outer shell is removed. Milder, more delicate flavor than black pepper.
Pickling spice	15	Spice mixture.
Poppy seed	9	Sweet-nut flavor. Best if toasted before use.
Poultry seasoning	23	Herb and spice mixture.
Pumpkin pie spice (mix)	16	Spice mixture.
Rosemary	19 (leaf) 17 (ground)	Spicy, strong, pine-like. Use sparingly.
Saffron, whole	40	Expensive spice used to impart a golden color and distinctive flavor to foods. Often used in Spanish rice dishes.
Sage	35 (leaves) 28 (ground) 34 (rubbed)	Strong flavored with a camphor-like taste. Blends well with rosemary, thyme, parsley, oregano, and bay leaf.
Savory, leaves	31	Slightly peppery, sharp and clove-like. Use sparingly.
Sesame seed	8	Distinctive flavor develops if toasted before use. Often used in Middle Eastern and Asian cooking.
Tarragon	18 (ground) 47 (leaf)	Spicy, aromatic, and sharp. Essential to French cooking.
Thyme	18 (ground) 26 (leaf)	Spicy and clove-like. Use sparingly.
Turmeric, ground	11	Used in small amounts to add a saffron-like color to foods. Used to flavor many African dishes.
Wasabi powder	18	Root vegetable grated and mixed with water to make a paste. Earthy with a strong hot flavor that dissipates soon after eating leaving a sweet taste.
Basil, sweet	0.75 cup/oz	
Bay leaves	0.50 cup/oz	
Cilantro, coarsely chopped	0.75 cup/oz	
Chives	0.66 cup/oz	
Dill weed	0.66 cup/oz	
Marjoram	1.00 cup/oz	
Mint	0.66 cup/oz	
Oregano	1.00 cup/oz	
Parsley, curly	0.75 cup/oz	
Parsley, flat leaf	0.62 cup/oz	
Rosemary	0.45 cup/oz	
Sage	0.75 cup/oz	
Tarragon	0.65 cup/oz	
Thyme	0.65 cup/oz	
Watercress	0.40 cup/oz	

Notes: • Spices should be stored in cool (68°F) and dry (humidity 60% or less) environment. Cool storage (32–45°F) is recommended for paprika, red pepper, chili powder, allspice, cloves, parsley flakes, dill, marjoram, and cumin. Generally, spices should not be held for longer than 3 months. All spices should be kept tightly closed and measured with dry utensils and away from steam.
  • Spices and herbs can be creatively combined to enhance the flavor of foods. The art of skillfully adding the right amount of seasonings is basic to successful cookery. Both low-sodium and low-calorie foods can be made more interesting by the addition of spices and herbs.

TABLE 4.4 Equivalent measure (approximate) per ounce for dry herbs or spices and fresh herbs

TABLE 4.5 Ingredient substitutions (approximate)

Recipe item	Amount	Substitute ingredient
Allspice	1 tsp	½ tsp cinnamon + ½ tsp ground cloves
Arrowroot (for thickening)	1 Tbsp	2 Tbsp flour
		1 Tbsp cornstarch
Baking powder	1 tsp	¼ tsp baking soda + ½ tsp cream of tartar
		¼ tsp baking soda + ½ cup buttermilk or sour milk (to replace ½ cup of the liquid)
Bread crumbs	1 cup dry	3 bread slices
Butter (salted) or margarine	1 lb	14 oz shortening + ½ tsp salt
		14 oz (1⅜ cups) oil + ½ tsp salt
Buttermilk	1 cup	1 Tbsp lemon juice or vinegar + enough whole milk to make 1 cup (let stand 5 min before using) or 1 cup unflavored yogurt
Celery, fresh	8 oz	½ cup dried flakes
Chocolate, unsweetened	1 oz (1 square)	3 Tbsp cocoa + 1 Tbsp (½ oz) butter or margarine
Cocoa	3 Tbsp	1 oz chocolate; reduce fat in recipe by 1 Tbsp
Corn syrup	1 cup	1 cup sugar + ¼ cup liquid
Cornstarch (thickening)	1 Tbsp	2 Tbsp flour, all-purpose
	1 oz	2 oz flour, all purpose
	1 Tbsp	2 tsp waxy maize starch
	1 oz	¾ oz waxy maize starch
Cracker crumbs	1 cup	1¼ cups dry bread crumbs
Cream		
Half and half	1 cup	¾ cup milk + 2–3 Tbsp butter or margarine
Whipping	1 cup	¾ cup milk + ⅓ cup butter or margarine (for cooking only)
Flour, all-purpose	1 cup (4 oz)	1½ cups bread flour
		1 cup + 2 Tbsp cake flour
		1 cup rye or whole wheat flour
		1 cup less 2 Tbsp cornmeal
		1 cup rolled oats
		1½ cups bread crumbs
Flour, all-purpose (thickening)	1 oz	1⅓ oz quick-cooking tapioca
		½ cup cornmeal
		⅔ oz cornstarch
		½ oz waxy maize starch, arrowroot
		¾ oz bread crumbs
Flour, cake	1 cup (4 oz)	1 cup less 2 Tbsp all-purpose flour
Garlic	1 medium clove	⅛ tsp garlic powder
		½ tsp garlic, minced, dry
		½ tsp garlic salt
Green peppers, fresh, chopped	8 oz EP	1 oz green pepper flakes, dry
Herbs, dried	1 tsp	1 Tbsp fresh, finely cut

TABLE 4.5 Ingredient substitutions (approximate)

TABLE 4.5   continued

Recipe item	Amount	Substitute ingredient
Herbs, fresh	1 Tbsp	1 tsp dried, whole ½ tsp ground
Honey	1 cup	1¼ cups granulated sugar + ¼ cup liquid
Milk, buttermilk or sour	1 cup	1 cup plain unsweetened yogurt 1 cup minus 1 Tbsp sweet milk + 1 Tbsp lemon juice or vinegar (allow to stand 5–10 minutes)
Milk, fluid, whole	1 cup	1 oz (⅓ cup) nonfat dry milk + water to make 1 cup + 1 Tbsp fat (optional) ½ cup evaporated milk + ½ cup water
	1 qt	4 oz nonfat dry milk + water to make 1 qt + 1¼ oz fat (optional)
Milk, sour[a]	1 cup	1 Tbsp vinegar or lemon juice + sweet milk to make 1 cup
Mushrooms, fresh	1 lb (6 cups)	3 oz dried 8 oz canned (drained weight)
Onions, fresh, chopped	8 oz EP	1 oz dehydrated onions, chopped or minced[b]
Orange peel, dried	1 Tbsp	2½ Tbsp grated fresh orange peel ½ tsp orange extract
Parsley, fresh, chopped	4 oz EP	1½ cups parsley flakes, dry
Sour cream	1 cup	1 cup yogurt
Stock, chicken or beef	1 gal	3 oz concentrated soup base + 1 gal water (commercial products may vary in strength; follow manufacturer's directions)
Sugar, brown	1 cup	1 cup granulated sugar + 2 Tbsp molasses
Sugar, granulated	1 cup (8 oz)	1⅓ cups brown sugar 1½ cups powdered sugar 1¼–1½ cups corn syrup less ¼–½ cup liquid in recipe
Tapioca, quick-cooking	1 Tbsp	1 Tbsp all-purpose flour (for thickening)
Vanilla bean	½ bean	1 Tbsp vanilla extract
Wine	1 cup	13 Tbsp water + 3 Tbsp lemon juice + 1 Tbsp sugar [Red] 1 cup cranberry juice [White] 1 cup apple or white grape juice
Yeast, active dry	¼ oz (1 pkg)	1 cake compressed
	1 oz	2 oz compressed
Yeast, instant		See manufacturer's directions for conversion from active dry or compressed
Yogurt, plain	1 cup	1 cup buttermilk 1 cup cottage cheese blended until smooth 1 cup sour cream

[a]To substitute buttermilk or sour milk for sweet milk, add ½ tsp baking soda and decrease baking powder by 2 tsp per cup of milk.
[b]Rehydrate onions unless they are to be used in a recipe in which there is a large volume of liquid. To rehydrate, cover onions with water, using the ratio of 1 oz dehydrated onions (½ cup) to ¾ cup of water. Let stand 20–30 minutes.

TABLE 4.5   Ingredient substitutions (approximate)

TABLE 4.6 Ingredient proportions

TABLE 4.6 Ingredient proportions

Function	Ingredient	Relative proportion
Leavening agents	Baking powder	1½–2 Tbsp to 1 lb flour
	Baking soda	2 tsp to 1 qt sour milk or molasses
	Yeast	½–1 envelope dry (⅛–¼ oz) to 1 lb flour (varies with ingredients and time allowed)
Seasonings	Salt	1–2 tsp to 1 lb flour
		1¼ tsp to 1 lb meat
		2 tsp to 1 qt water (for cereal)
		2½ tsp to 1 pt liquid (for rolls)
Thickening agents	Eggs	4–6 whole eggs to 1 qt milk
		8–12 egg yolks to 1 qt milk
		8–12 egg whites to 1 qt milk
	Flour	½ oz to 1 qt liquid—very thin sauce (cream soups, starchy vegetables)
		1 oz to 1 qt liquid—thin sauce (cream soups, nonstarchy vegetables)
		2 oz to 1 qt liquid—medium sauce (creamed foods, gravy)
		3–4 oz to 1 qt liquid—thick sauce (soufflés)
		4–5 oz to 1 qt liquid—very thick sauce (croquettes)
		1 lb to 1 qt liquid—pour batter (popovers)
		2 lb to 1 qt liquid—drop batter (cake muffins)
		3 lb to 1 qt liquid—soft dough (biscuits, rolls)
		4 lb to 1 qt liquid—stiff dough (pastry, cookies, noodles)
	Gelatin, granulated, unflavored	2 Tbsp to 1 qt liquid—plain gelatins (gelatin and fruit juices)
		2 Tbsp to 1 qt liquid—whips (gelatin and fruit juices whipped)
		3 Tbsp to 1 qt liquid—fruit gelatins (gelatin, fruit juices, and chopped fruit)
		3 Tbsp to 1 qt liquid—vegetable gelatins (gelatin, liquid, and chopped vegetables)
		3 Tbsp to 1 qt liquid—sponges (gelatin, fruit juice, and beaten egg whites)
		4 Tbsp to 1 qt liquid—Bavarian cream (gelatin, fruit juice, fruit pulp, and whipped cream)

Note: See Table 4.5 for ingredient substitutions.

TABLE 4.7 Ounces and decimal equivalents of a pound and grams (rounded)

Ounces	Decimal part of a pound	Grams (rounded)	Ounces	Decimal part of a pound	Grams (rounded)	Ounces	Decimal part of a pound	Grams (rounded)
¼	0.016		5¾	0.359		11¼	0.703	
½	0.031		6	0.375	170	11½	0.719	
¾	0.047		6¼	0.391		11¾	0.734	
1	0.063	28	6½	0.406		12	0.750	340
1¼	0.078		6¾	0.422		12¼	0.766	
1½	0.094		7	0.438	198	12½	0.781	
1¾	0.109		7¼	0.453		12¾	0.797	
2	0.125	57	7½	0.469		13	0.813	367
2¼	0.141		7¾	0.484		13¼	0.828	
2½	0.156		8	0.500	227	13½	0.844	
2¾	0.172		8¼	0.516		13¾	0.859	
3	0.188	85	8½	0.531		14	0.875	397
3¼	0.203		8¾	0.547		14¼	0.891	
3½	0.219		9	0.563	255	14½	0.906	
3¾	0.234		9¼	0.578		14¾	0.922	
4	0.250	113	9½	0.594		15	0.938	425
4¼	0.266		9¾	0.609		15¼	0.953	
4½	0.281		10	0.625	284	15½	0.969	
4¾	0.297		10¼	0.641		15¾	0.984	
5	0.313	142	10½	0.656		16	1.000	454
5¼	0.328		10¾	0.672				
5½	0.344		11	0.688	312			

Note: This table is useful when increasing or decreasing recipes. The multiplication or division of pounds and ounces is simplified if the ounces are converted to decimal parts of a pound. For example, when multiplying 1 lb 9 oz by 3, first change the 9 oz to 0.563 lb, using the table. Thus, the 1 lb 9 oz becomes 1.563 lb, which multiplied by 3 is 4.683 lb or 4 lb 11 oz.

TABLE 4.8   Basic equivalents in measures and weights

Equivalents	Abbreviations used in this book[a]	
1 Tbsp = 3 tsp, in liquids ½ fl oz	bu	bushel
⅛ cup = 2 Tbsp, in liquids 1 fl oz	fl oz	fluid ounce
¼ cup = 4 Tbsp, in liquids 2 fl oz	gal	gallon
⅓ cup = 5 Tbsp + 1 tsp	g	gram
½ cup = 8 Tbsp, in liquids 4 fl oz	kg	kilogram
⅔ cup = 10 Tbsp + 2 tsp	L	liter
¾ cup = 12 Tbsp, in liquids 6 fl oz	lb	pound
1 cup = 16 Tbsp = 48 tsp, in liquids 8 fl oz	mL	milliliter
1 pt = 2 cups, in liquids 16 fl oz	oz	ounce
1 qt = 2 pt = 4 cups, in liquids 32 oz	pk	peck
1 gal = 4 qt, in liquids 128 oz	pt	pint
1 lb = 16 oz	qt	quart
1 pk = 8 qt, approximately 12½ lb	Tbsp	Tablespoon
1 bu = 4 pk, approximately 50 lb	tsp	teaspoon

METRIC

1 g = 0.035 oz	1 tsp = 5 mL
1 kg = 2.2 lb (35 oz)	1 Tbsp = 15 mL
1 oz = 28 g	1 cup = 240 mL
1 lb = 454 g	1 qt = 0.95 L
1 mL = ⅓ tsp	1 gal = 3.8 L
1 L = 1.06 qt (34 fluid oz)	

[a]Periods are not necessary in abbreviations for quantity recipes.

TABLE 4.8   Basic equivalents in measures and weights

TABLE 4.9   Guide for rounding off weights and volume measures

If the total amount of an ingredient is:	Round it to:
WEIGHTS	
Less than 2 oz	Measure unless weight is ¼-, ½-, or ¾-oz amounts
2–10 oz	Closest ¼ oz or convert to measure
More than 10 oz but less than 2 lb 8 oz	Closest ½ oz
2 lb 8 oz–5 lb	Closest full ounce
More than 5 lb	Closest ¼ lb
MEASURES	
1 Tbsp or less	Closest ⅛ tsp
More than 1 Tbsp but less than 3 Tbsp	Closest ¼ tsp
3 Tbsp–½ cup	Closest ½ tsp or convert to weight
More than ½ cup but less than ¾ cup	Closest full tsp or convert to weight
More than ¾ cup but less than 2 cups	Closest full Tbsp or convert to weight
2 cups–2 qt	Nearest ¼ cup
More than 2 qt but less than 4 qt	Nearest ½ cup
1–2 gal	Nearest full cup or ¼ qt
More than 2 gal but less than 10 gal[a]	Nearest full quart
More than 10 gal but less than 20 gal[a]	Closest ½ gal
More than 20 gal[a]	Closest full gallon

[a]For baked goods or products in which accurate ratios are critical, always round to the nearest full cup or ¼ qt.
Note: This table is intended to aid in rounding fractions and complex measurements into amounts that are as simple as possible to weigh or measure while maintaining the accuracy needed for quality control.

TABLE 4.10 Weight (1–16 oz) and approximate measure equivalents for commonly used foods

Food item	1 oz	2 oz	3 oz	4 oz
Baking powder	2⅓ Tbsp	¼ cup + 1 tsp	⅓ cup + 2 Tbsp	½ cup + 1 Tbsp
Baking soda	2⅓ Tbsp	¼ cup + 1 tsp	⅓ cup + 2 Tbsp	½ cup + 1 Tbsp
Bread crumbs, dry	¼ cup	½ cup	¾ cup	1 cup
Butter or margarine	2 Tbsp	¼ cup	⅓ cup + 2 tsp	½ cup
Celery, chopped	¼ cup	½ cup	¾ cup	1 cup
Cornstarch	3½ Tbsp	⅓ cup + 2 Tbsp	⅔ cup	¾ cup + 2 Tbsp
Eggs, whole, whites or yolks, fresh or frozen	2 Tbsp	¼ cup	⅓ cup + 2 tsp	½ cup
Flour, all-purpose, unsifted	¼ cup	½ cup	¾ cup	1 cup
Flour, cake, unsifted	¼ cup	½ cup	½ cup + 3 Tbsp	¾ cup + 3 Tbsp
Milk, nonfat dry	⅓ cup	¾ cup	1 cup + 2 Tbsp	1½ cups
Nutmeats	¼ cup	½ cup	¾ cup	1 cup
Onion, chopped	3 Tbsp	⅓ cup + 2 tsp	½ cup + 1 Tbsp	¾ cup
Salt	1½ Tbsp	3 Tbsp	¼ cup + 1½ tsp	⅓ cup + 2 tsp
Shortening, hydrogenated fat	2 Tbsp + 1 tsp	¼ cup + 2 tsp	⅓ cup + 2 Tbsp	½ cup + 1 Tbsp
Sugar, brown, light pack	3 Tbsp	⅓ cup + 2 tsp	½ cup + 1 Tbsp	¾ cup
Sugar, granulated	2¼ Tbsp	¼ cup	¼ cup + 3 Tbsp	½ cup + 1 Tbsp
Sugar, powdered	3 Tbsp	⅓ cup + 2 tsp	½ cup + 1 tsp	¾ cup
Yeast, dry	3 Tbsp + 1 tsp	⅓ cup + 1 Tbsp	½ cup + 2 Tbsp	⅔ cup + 1 Tbsp

Food item	5 oz	6 oz	7 oz	8 oz
Baking powder	¾ cup	¾ cup + 2 Tbsp	1 cup + 1 tsp	1 cup + 3 Tbsp
Baking soda	¾ cup	¾ cup + 2 Tbsp	1 cup + 1 tsp	1 cup + 3 Tbsp
Bread crumbs, dry	1¼ cups	1½ cups	1¾ cups	2 cups
Butter or margarine	½ cup + 2 Tbsp	¾ cup	¾ cup + 2 Tbsp	1 cup
Celery, chopped	1¼ cups	1½ cups	1¾ cups	2 cups
Cornstarch	1 cup + 2 Tbsp	1¼ cups + 1 Tbsp	1½ cups + 1 Tbsp	1¾ cups
Eggs, whole, whites or yolks, fresh or frozen	½ cup + 2 Tbsp	¾ cup	¾ cup + 2 Tbsp	1 cup
Flour, all-purpose, unsifted	1¼ cups	1½ cups	1¾ cups	2 cups
Flour, cake, unsifted	1 cup + 3 Tbsp	1¼ cups + 3 Tbsp	1½ cups + 2 Tbsp	1¾ cups + 2 Tbsp
Milk, nonfat dry	1¾ cups + 2 Tbsp	2¼ cups	2½ cups + 2 Tbsp	3 cups
Nutmeats	1¼ cups	1½ cups	1¾ cups	2 cups
Onion, chopped	¾ cup + 3 Tbsp	1 cup + 2 Tbsp	1¼ cups + 1 Tbsp	1½ cups
Salt	⅓ cup + 2 Tbsp	½ cup + 1 Tbsp	⅔ cup	¾ cup
Shortening, hydrogenated fat	⅔ cup + 1 Tbsp	¾ cup + 2 Tbsp	1 cup	1 cup + 2 Tbsp
Sugar, brown, light pack	¾ cup + 3 Tbsp	1 cup + 2 Tbsp	1¼ cups + 1 Tbsp	1½ cups
Sugar, granulated	½ cup + 3 Tbsp	¾ cup + 2 Tbsp	1 cup	1 cup + 2 Tbsp
Sugar, powdered	¾ cup + 3 Tbsp	1 cup + 2 Tbsp	1¼ cups + 1 Tbsp	1½ cups
Yeast, dry	1 cup + 2 tsp	1¼ cups	1½ cups	1⅔ cups

TABLE 4.10 continued

Food item	9 oz	10 oz	11 oz	12 oz
Baking powder	1¼ cups + 1 Tbsp	1½ cups	1½ cups + 2 Tbsp	1¾ cups
Baking soda	1¼ cups + 1 Tbsp	1½ cups	1½ cups + 2 Tbsp	1¾ cups
Bread crumbs, dry	2¼ cups	2½ cups	2¾ cups	3 cups
Butter or margarine	1 cup + 2 Tbsp	1¼ cups	1⅓ cups + 1 Tbsp	1½ cups
Celery, chopped	2¼ cups	2½ cups	2¾ cups	3 cups
Cornstarch	2 cups	2 cups + 3 Tbsp	2⅓ cups + 2 Tbsp	2½ cups + 2 Tbsp
Eggs, whole, whites or yolks, fresh or frozen	1 cup + 2 Tbsp	1¼ cups	1⅓ cups + 1 Tbsp	1½ cups
Flour, all-purpose, unsifted	2¼ cups	2½ cups	2¾ cups	3 cups
Flour, cake, unsifted	2 cups + 2 Tbsp	2¼ cups + 2 Tbsp	2½ cups + 1 Tbsp	2¾ cups
Milk, nonfat dry	3¼ cups + 2 Tbsp	3¾ cups	4 cups + 2 Tbsp	4½ cups
Nutmeats	2¼ cups	2½ cups	2¾ cups	3 cups
Onion, chopped	1⅔ cups	1¾ cups + 2 Tbsp	2 cups + 1 Tbsp	2¼ cups
Salt	¾ cup + 2 Tbsp	¾ cup + 3 Tbsp	1 cup + 1 Tbsp	1 cup + 2 Tbsp
Shortening, hydrogenated fat	1¼ cups	1⅓ cups + 1 Tbsp	1½ cups + 1 Tbsp	1⅔ cups
Sugar, brown, light pack	1⅔ cups	1¾ cups + 2 Tbsp	2 cups + 1 Tbsp	2¼ cups
Sugar, granulated	1¼ cups	1¼ cups + 3 Tbsp	1½ cups + 1 Tbsp	1½ cups + 3 Tbsp
Sugar, powdered	1⅔ cups	1¾ cups + 2 Tbsp	2 cups + 1 Tbsp	2¼ cups
Yeast, dry	1¾ cups + 2 Tbsp	2 cups + 1 Tbsp	2¼ cups + 1 Tbsp	2½ cups

Food item	13 oz	14 oz	15 oz	16 oz
Baking powder	1¾ cups + 2 Tbsp	2 cups + 1 Tbsp	2 cups + 3 Tbsp	2⅓ cups
Baking soda	1¾ cups + 2 Tbsp	2 cups + 1 Tbsp	2 cups + 3 Tbsp	2⅓ cups
Bread crumbs, dry	3¼ cups	3½ cups	3¾ cups	4 cups
Butter or margarine	1½ cups + 2 Tbsp	1¾ cups	1¾ cups + 2 Tbsp	2 cups
Celery, chopped	3¼ cups	3½ cups	3¾ cups	4 cups
Cornstarch	2¾ cups + 2 Tbsp	3 cups + 1 Tbsp	3¼ cups + 1½ tsp	3½ cups
Eggs, whole, whites or yolks, fresh or frozen	1½ cups + 2 Tbsp	1¾ cups	1¾ cups + 2 Tbsp	2 cups
Flour, all-purpose, unsifted	3¼ cups	3½ cups	3¾ cups	4 cups
Flour, cake, unsifted	3 cups + 1 Tbsp	3¼ cups + 1 Tbsp	3½ cups	3¾ cups
Milk, nonfat dry	4¾ cups + 2 Tbsp	5¼ cups	5½ cups + 2 Tbsp	6 cups
Nutmeats	3¼ cups	3½ cups	3¾ cups	4 cups
Onion, chopped	2⅓ cups + 2 Tbsp	2½ cups + 2 Tbsp	2¾ cups + 1 Tbsp	3 cups
Salt	1¼ cups	1¼ cups + 1 Tbsp	1⅓ cups + 1 Tbsp	1½ cups
Shortening, hydrogenated fat	1¾ cups + 1 Tbsp	2 cups	2 cups + 2 Tbsp	2¼ cups
Sugar, brown, light pack	2⅓ cups + 2 Tbsp	2½ cups + 2 Tbsp	2¾ cups + 1 Tbsp	3 cups
Sugar, granulated	1¾ cups + 1 Tbsp	2 cups	2 cups + 2 Tbsp	2¼ cups
Sugar, powdered	2⅓ cups + 2 Tbsp	2½ cups + 2 Tbsp	2¾ cups + 1 Tbsp	3 cups
Yeast, dry	2⅔ cups + 1 Tbsp	2¾ cups + 3 Tbsp	3 cups + 2 Tbsp	3⅓ cups

TABLE 4.10 Weight (1–16 oz) and approximate measure equivalents for commonly used foods

TABLE 4.11 Common can sizes

TABLE 4.11 Common can sizes

Can size (industry term)	Approximate net weight or fluid measure	Approximate cups per can	Approximate number of 4-oz portions	Cans per case	Principal products
No. 10	6 lb/7 lb 5 oz	12–13	25	6	Institutional size for fruits, vegetables
No. 5 Squat	4–4¼ lb	8	16–20		Institutional size for canned fish, sweet potatoes
No. 3 Cyl	46 fl oz or 51 oz	5¾	10–12	12	Fruit and vegetable juices, condensed soups
No. 2½	26–30 oz	3½	5–7	24	Fruits, some vegetables
No. 2	18 fl oz or 20 oz	2½	5	24	Juices, fruits, ready-to-serve soups
No. 303	1 lb	2	4	24 or 36	Fruits, vegetables, ready-to-serve soups
No. 300	14–16 oz	1¾	3–4	24	Some fruits and meat products
No. 1 (Picnic)	10½–12 oz	1¼	2–3	48	Condensed soups
8 oz	8 oz	1	2	48 or 72	Ready-to-serve soups, fruits, vegetables

Note: When substituting one can for another size, one No. 10 can is approximately equivalent to 7 No. 303 (1 lb) cans; 5 No. 2 (1 lb 4 oz) cans; 4 No. 2½ (1 lb 13 oz) cans; or 2 No. 3 (46 to 50 oz) cans.

TABLE 4.12 Metric equivalents for weight, measure, and temperature

TABLE 4.12 Metric equivalents for weight, measure, and temperature

Weight		Measure		Temperature	
U.S.	Metric[a]	U.S.	Metric[b]	°F[c]	°C[d]
1 oz	28 g	1 tsp	5 mL	32	0
1½ oz	43 g	1 Tbsp	15 mL	100	38
2 oz	57 g	¼ cup (4 Tbsp)	60 mL	150	65
2½ oz	70 g	⅓ cup (5⅓ Tbsp)	80 mL	200	95
3 oz	85 g	½ cup (8 Tbsp)	120 mL	250	121
3½ oz	100 g	⅔ cup (10⅔ Tbsp)	160 mL	275	135
4 oz (¼ lb)	114 g	¾ cup (12 Tbsp)	180 mL	300	150
5 oz	142 g	1 cup (16 Tbsp)	240 mL	325	165
6 oz	170 g	2 cups (1 pint)	480 mL	350	175
7 oz	198 g	4 cups (1 qt)	0.95 L	375	190
8 oz (½ lb)	227 g	2 qt (½ gal)	1.89 L	400	205
9 oz	255 g	4 qt (1 gal)	3.79 L	425	220
10 oz	284 g			450	230
11 oz	312 g			475	245
12 oz (¾ lb)	340 g			500	260
13 oz	369 g				
14 oz	397 g				
15 oz	425 g				
1 lb (16 oz)	454 g				
2 lb	908 g				
2 lb 4 oz	1.02 kg				

[a]Basic formula used to calculate metric weights: 1 oz = 28.35 g. Resulting figures were rounded to nearest gram and to two decimal places for kilograms. Abbreviations used: oz = ounce; lb = pound; g = gram; kg = kilogram. To change grams to kilograms, move decimal three places to left: e.g., 28 g = 0.028 kg.

[b]Basic formulas used to calculate metric volume: 1 Tbsp = 14.8 mL, rounded to 15 mL; 1 cup = 237 mL, rounded to 240 mL; 1 qt = 0.95 L (4 × 237 ÷ 1000). Abbreviations used: tsp = teaspoon; Tbsp = tablespoon; pt = pint; qt = quart; gal = gallon; mL = milliliter; L = liter.

[c]To convert from °C to °F, the following formula is used: (°C × 9⁄5 + 32 = °F).

[d]To convert from °F to °C, the following formula is used: (°F − 32) × 5⁄9 = °C).

part III

Foods and Food Production

Food Product Information and Food Science

This chapter provides descriptive information and general purchasing and storage guidelines about the basic foods used as ingredients in *Food for Fifty* recipes. Cooking timetables and general food production techniques that are applicable to products in the basic food categories are presented in Chapter 6, p. 143.

The chapter includes the following topics:

- Dairy—Eggs, Cheese, Milk, and Milk Products (p. 96)
- Grains, Pasta, Flours, and Other Starches (p. 103)
- Meat (Beef, Lamb, Pork, Veal); Poultry; Fish and Shellfish (p. 108)
- Fresh Produce; Canned and Frozen Fruits and Vegetables; Tofu and Dried Beans, Lentils, and Peas (p. 113)
- Coffee and Tea; Condiments and Vinegars; Dried Herbs, Spices, and Seasonings; Nuts and Seeds (p. 131)

Dairy—Eggs, Cheese, Milk, and Milk Products

- General Information
- Purchasing and Storage
- Cooking and Recipes (see Chapter 12)

EGGS

Eggs are considered a staple in quantity food production kitchens because of their versatility and the number of functions they serve in the preparation of recipes. Eggs are used to make **emulsions** by aiding in the dispersion of one liquid within another with which it is usually not mixable. Hollandaise sauce is an example of a butter, liquid, and egg yolk emulsion. **Foams** for making food products such as angel food cakes, meringues, and soufflés are formed by incorporating air into egg whites.

Egg protein **coagulates** on heating to provide a soft, semisolid structure for food products such as omelets and custards,

and for meat and vegetable breading. The temperature at which egg protein coagulates and the time required for coagulation depends in part on the amount of egg in the mixture. Diluting egg protein with milk or adding sugar, as in baked egg custard, increases the temperature at which coagulation occurs. Undiluted egg white begins to coagulate and turn from a clear liquid to white at about 140°F. At about 149°F, the whites become opaque and firm. Egg yolk protein denatures and thickens at a slightly higher temperature than whites. Egg yolk begins to coagulate at about 149°F and loses its fluidity at 158°F. Egg protein heated at a high temperature becomes very firm and tough, as compared with the soft, tender texture obtained when heated at a lower temperature.

Soup stock can be **clarified** by adding egg whites and straining them out after they coagulate from being heated. The **flavor** of eggs alone, the flavor and **color** they add to other products, and their **nutritional** value also add to eggs' appeal for use in food products.

Chicken eggs are graded following standards established by the U.S. Department of Agriculture. The service is voluntary and is paid for by the egg packer. The USDA grade shield on the carton means the eggs were graded for quality and weight by a USDA grader. State agencies monitor compliance to quality and size standards for egg producers not using the USDA grading service. Cartons monitored by state agencies do not have a USDA shield. Quality characteristics for the different grades are identified in Table 5.1. Grade AA and A eggs are suitable for any use and especially when appearance is important. Because Grade B eggs are generally used for processed egg products, they are not usually available as shell eggs. All grades of eggs have the same nutritional values.

Total weight per dozen determines the size designation assigned to shell eggs. Size descriptions change at 3-ounces-per-dozen intervals. See Figure 5.1. The size of an egg is not related to the egg's quality grade.

Purchasing and Storage

Fresh Eggs.   Fresh eggs deteriorate rapidly at room temperatures. They should be shipped in refrigerated trucks and kept at 33–38°F or below. If kept under proper refrigeration, they

On Cooking: A Textbook of Culinary Fundamentals, fourth edition, provides an expanded discussion of food and purchasing information, cooking techniques, and equipment; that book was a source of information for *Food for Fifty.*

TABLE 5.1 Quality characteristics for chicken egg grades

Quality characteristics	Grade AA	Grade A	Grade B
Spread	Compact	Spreads slightly	Considerable spread
Egg white	Thick; firm	Reasonably firm	Thin
Egg yolk	Round; stands high; practically free from defects	Round; stands high; practically free from defects	Wide; flat
Shell	Clean; standard egg shape; unbroken	Clean; standard egg shape; unbroken	May be slightly stained; irregular shape permissible; unbroken

Source: USDA Fact Sheet, *Egg Products Preparation*

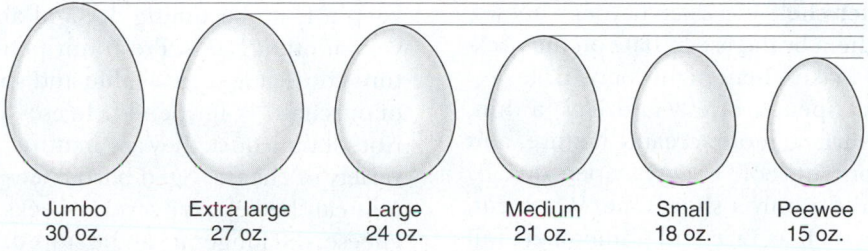

Jumbo	Extra large	Large	Medium	Small	Peewee
30 oz.	27 oz.	24 oz.	21 oz.	18 oz.	15 oz.

FIGURE 5.1   Chicken egg size designations and weight per dozen eggs.

Notes: • Table 4.2 provides additional information on weights for whole eggs, whites, and yolks.
• Because sizes of eggs may differ, recipes specifying the amount of egg by weight are more accurate than those specifying the number of eggs.

will retain their quality for 3–4 weeks. Eggs should be kept in their cartons or cases to prevent loss of moisture and, because the shell is porous, should be stored away from foods with strong odors. Eggs should not be washed before storage.

Processed Eggs.   Although fresh shell eggs are used extensively for table service, processed eggs are convenient to use in many food products. They eliminate the time-consuming task and the food safety risk of breaking eggs. Whole eggs, whites, and yolks are available in liquid, frozen, and dried forms. All eggs must be processed in sanitary facilities under USDA supervision and must bear the USDA inspection mark. They must be pasteurized and are routinely analyzed for bacterial contamination.

Frozen Eggs and Liquid Eggs   Because food safety regulations prohibit pooling eggs in quantity (breaking raw eggs into a container and storing them until needed), foodservice operations often choose to use frozen eggs or unfrozen liquid eggs in place of fresh eggs for many recipes. Eggs may be purchased as frozen or liquid whole eggs (combined yolks and whites), in the form of whites or yolks, and as blended egg products such as scrambled egg mix. High-quality eggs are used for liquid and frozen eggs, making them suitable for use in omelets, scrambled eggs, and baking. Because frozen egg yolks become viscous and gelatinous when thawed, they usually have added sugar, syrup, or salt and are generally used for baked products. Frozen liquid eggs are available in several container sizes. Because they are highly perishable, only sizes that can be used within 2–3 days after thawing should be purchased. The shelf life of liquid pasteurized eggs varies among processors, and their guidelines should be followed.

Frozen eggs should be kept frozen (shelf life 1 year) at 0°F or below and defrosted in the refrigerator, never at room temperature. Large 30-lb containers of egg products may take 2–3 days to defrost. Quart or half-gallon boxes will defrost in 24 hours or less. The maximum shelf life for liquid pasteurized eggs can be realized when stored in their original containers at 34–36°F.

Dried Eggs   Dried powdered whole eggs are used less frequently than frozen and fresh eggs—primarily for baking. Because dried eggs are very stable if kept tightly sealed, dry, and cool (preferably below 50°F), they are convenient when there is a lack of freezer and refrigerator space, such as on a ship, or when food is being prepared in a remote or isolated location. Dried eggs should be reconstituted only in the quantity that will be used immediately. In baking, dried eggs can be combined with the other dry ingredients in the recipe, and the amount of water needed to reconstitute can be added with the other liquid ingredients. Pasteurized dried egg white powder is readily available and, when reconstituted, it whips like fresh egg whites. It can be used safely in products that are not cooked.

CHEESE

Cheese is an excellent source of calcium and protein. It is a versatile food when used alone or as an ingredient in courses from appetizers to desserts. Understanding the characteristics of different cheeses is important for menu planning and for preparing quality food products that use cheese as an ingredient. See Exhibit 5 in the colored inserts for pictures of selected cheeses.

Natural Cheese

The type of milk used and the aging process will determine the flavor and texture of cheese. All **natural cheeses** are made in a similar way. The steps include the following:

• Promoting curd formation in milk by adding a starter of harmless lactic-acid–producing bacteria or a coagulating enzyme (often rennet, a natural enzyme extracted from cow stomachs)

- Draining the whey (liquid) from the curd
- Heating the curd to force additional whey from the curd
- Draining, salting, and pressing and shaping the curd
- Aging or ripening the curds (some cheeses are not ripened and some are inoculated with a specially selected mold before ripening)

Natural cheese can be classified according to the type of milk used (cow, goat, sheep) and its texture (fresh, soft, semisoft, firm, hard grating).

Fresh cheeses are unripened and do not have a rind. They range in consistency from creamy and smooth to curd mixtures. Fresh cheeses have a shorter shelf life than harder cheeses, making it important to use them by the use-by date on the package. High moisture content makes them highly perishable.

Soft cheeses have been ripened briefly and have a thin, velvety skin with desirable surface mold, creamy texture, and relatively high moisture content. Soft cheeses ripen quickly and after ripening are good for only a short time. When cut, some fully ripe soft cheeses such as Brie and Camembert will ooze slightly but will not run. Ripe soft cheese will feel spongy to the touch and have a nutty, aromatic smell.

Semisoft cheeses are ripened, have a moderate moisture content and hold their shape when sliced or cut. *Mild* and *smooth* characterize semisoft cheeses. They develop a more robust earthy flavor when aged.

Firm cheeses are low in moisture and often high in fat. They are aged for a longer time than softer cheeses, range in texture from crumbly to flexible, and flavor from sharp to mild, depending on the aging time.

Hard grating cheeses are aged for a long time until they have a dry, granular texture. They have a low moisture content and will keep for extended periods of time when kept tightly wrapped in a refrigerator. Grated cheese is at its best when served soon after grating.

Blue-veined cheeses range in texture from creamy to crumbly. A special mold is injected before ripening to give the cheeses a characteristic blue or blue-green vein and distinctive flavor. The moderate moisture content is similar to other semisoft cheeses.

Processed Cheese

Pasteurized **processed cheese** is made differently than natural cheeses. Processed cheese is made by mixing two or more natural cheeses using a heat process and adding emulsifiers, flavoring, and coloring. The cheese is poured into a mold and allowed to harden. Because pasteurization has killed all the live cultures, processed cheese will not ripen and has an extended shelf life. Flavor depends on the cheeses that were combined to make the product.

Pasteurized **processed cheese foods** and **cheese spreads** contain less cheese than processed cheese but are produced in the same way. Cream, milk (whole, skim, or nonfat solids), whey, and other foods, such as sun-dried tomatoes or chopped olives, may be added. Cheese food is milder and melts more quickly than processed cheese because of higher moisture content. Cheese spreads have the highest moisture content, are usually spreadable, and melt very easily.

Purchasing

Choosing cheeses for cooking or for eating requires knowledge of different cheeses and their unique characteristics. Table 5.2 provides a guide for selecting natural and processed cheeses.

Storage

Cheese should be refrigerated and packaged appropriately to keep it from becoming dry and absorbing the odors and flavors of other foods. Fresh unripened cheeses with high moisture content are perishable and should be used within 7 days of purchase. Soft ripened cheeses are good for only a short period of time once they are mature. Aging time depends on the variety of cheese. Aged hard cheeses with lower moisture content can be kept for several weeks or longer. The harder the cheese, the longer it can be stored. Some aged grating cheeses can be stored for a year or longer.

Some cheeses are made using special molds (blue, Brie, Camembert, Gorgonzola, Roquefort, and Stilton) and will have mold on the interior and exterior. The mold on these cheeses is safe to eat and is responsible for flavor and color. Molds that are not part of the manufacturing process (wild molds) are undesirable when growing on the surface of cheese. Mold on hard cheeses such as cheddar can be cut off and the cheese safely used. If cheese is soft or unripened, or if mold permeates deeply into the cheese, it should be discarded because the mold cannot be removed completely.

Freezing cheese may cause the texture to become dry, crumbly, and mealy. Hard cheeses are the most successfully frozen and should be thawed very slowly in the refrigerator to reduce the detrimental effects of freezing.

Cheese flavors are more pronounced if served at cool room but not cold temperatures. Taking cheese from the refrigerator approximately 30 minutes before serving is recommended. Fresh unripened cheeses such as cottage and cream cheese are exceptions and should be held and served below 41°F.

MILK

Milk is a food staple in every foodservice and is used both as a recipe ingredient and beverage. Strict processing and grading regulations ensure that quality standards are met throughout the production and distribution systems. Dairy products are very perishable and potentially hazardous; therefore, foodservices must follow procedures to keep it from souring and safe from bacteria growth and contamination.

All Grade A fluid milk and milk products purchased commercially for drinking and cooking are **pasteurized** or heated to a specified temperature for a designated period of time. Pasteurization ensures the destruction of disease-producing microorganisms that may be present in raw milk. It reduces the number of nonpathogenic bacteria and extends milk's shelf

TABLE 5.2   Guide for selecting natural and processed cheeses

FRESH CHEESE

Cheese type/milk used	Fat (approx.)	Characteristics	Purchasing notes	Mode of serving
Chèvre (general goat cheese)	6 g/oz	Mild, soft (when very fresh) to tangy, crumbly (when older)	Variety of shapes (cones, discs, logs); short shelf life	General cooking
Cottage (cow's)	1.2 g/oz (4% milkfat, creamed) 0.6 g/oz (2% milkfat)	Mild, slightly acid flavor; soft, texture with tender curds of varying size; white to creamy white	In cartons of varying sizes; short shelf life	As a side, mixed with fruit or vegetables, in dips
Cream (cow's plus cream)	10 g/oz	Delicate, slightly acid flavor; smooth texture; white	Block, loaf, whipped in tub	In salads, on sandwiches in dips, on crackers, on sweet breads, in desserts
Feta (sheep's, goat's, cow's)	6 g/oz (cow's) 7 g/oz (sheep's)	Salty; soft, flaky, similar to very dry high-acid cottage cheese; crumbly; becomes sharper with age; tangy; white	Block; stored in brine water for a 5- to 6-week shelf life	In salads, on pizza; melts easily
Mascarpone (cow's)	6 g/oz	Very mild, sweet, slightly tangy; soft, extremely smooth and creamy; pale yellow or ivory	Bulk or tubs; highly perishable	With fruit, spread on sweet bread, in desserts (tiramisu)
Mozzarella (cow's or less common in U.S. buffalo's)	5 g/oz (part skim milk) 6 g/oz (whole)	Delicate; mild, bland flavor; tender plastic-like texture, stringy; becomes elastic-like when heated; creamy white	Fresh in irregular balls or braided; best eaten soon after making; purchased shredded or sliced	Fresh in salads, sliced with olive oil, sliced on sandwiches, shredded on pizza, in/on casseroles
Neufchâtel (cow's)	6.5 g/oz	Mild, slightly acidic; soft and creamy, similar to cream cheese but lower in fat	Block; in loaf	In salads, in dips, on sandwiches, in desserts
Ricotta (cow's)	4 g/oz (whole) 2 g/oz (part skim)	Bland, slightly sweet; soft curds; moist to slightly dry, grainy; similar to cottage cheese but dry; white or ivory	In cartons of varying sizes; short shelf life	In salads, in cooked foods (ravioli, lasagna)

SOFT CHEESE

Cheese type/milk used	Fat (approx.)	Characteristics	Purchasing notes	Mode of serving
Bel Paese (cow's)	7.5 g/oz	Mild to moderately robust; soft to medium firm, smooth waxy body; creamy yellow interior	Small wheels, wedges	On crackers, with fruit, in sandwiches, dessert
Brie (cow's)	8 g/oz	Mild to pungent, depending on ripeness; soft, smooth; creamy yellow interior, edible thin white rind; ammonia smell when overripe	Round flat disk (2–4 lb each); over-ripens easily	Appetizer, sauces, with fruit, dessert
Camembert (cow's)	7 g/oz	Mild to tangy flavor depending on ripeness; smooth texture; creamy yellow interior; edible thin white rind; ammonia odor when overripe	Small, round oval disks; over-ripens easily	Dessert, with fruit
Limburger (cow's)	8 g/oz	Very strong flavor; pungent aroma; soft, smooth, and waxy; light yellow interior, brown exterior	Small cube, block	Appetizers, with crackers, dark breads, dessert

SEMISOFT CHEESE INCLUDING BLUE/BLEU-VEINED CHEESE

Cheese type/milk used	Fat (approx.)	Characteristics	Purchasing notes	Mode of serving
Blue (spelled *bleu* when imported) (cow's or goat's)	8 g/oz	Tangy, piquant, sharp; possibly crumbly; creamy white with blue veins and marbling	Cylindrical shape, wedges	Appetizers, salads, dips, salad dressings, sandwiches, with fruit, dessert
Brick (cow's)	8 g/oz	Mild to moderately sharp (depending on age); light yellow; semisoft to firm, elastic; creamy yellow	Loaf, brick, slices	Appetizers, sandwiches, snacks, dessert

continued

TABLE 5.2   Guide for selecting natural and processed cheeses

TABLE 5.2 Guide for selecting natural and processed cheeses

TABLE 5.2 continued

Cheese type/milk used	Fat (approx.)	Characteristics	Purchasing notes	Mode of serving
Danish Blue (cow's)	8 g/oz	Strong, sharp, salty; white with blue veins and marbling	Cylindrical shape, wedges, blocks	Appetizers, salads, dips, salad dressings, sandwiches, dessert
Fontina (cow's)	8 g/oz	Nutty; pungent aroma; medium yellow to pale gold; dense interior with small holes	Wheel	Added to sauces, sandwiches, dessert
Gorgonzola (cow's)	9 g/oz	Tangy, piquant; creamy white interior streaked with blue-green veins	Cylindrical shape, wedges, oblong	Appetizers, salads, dips, salad dressings, sandwiches, dessert
Maytag Blue (cow's) (made in Iowa)	8 g/oz	Strong, salty; crumbly, hard; creamy white or light yellow with blue veins and marbling	Cylindrical shape, wedges	Appetizers, dips, salads, salad dressing, with fruits (pears, apples), dessert
Havarti (cow's)	10 g/oz	Mild flavor; buttery, creamy texture, often with added dill, caraway seeds, peppers; pale yellow with small holes	Rounds, wheels, rectangular blocks, loaves	Appetizers, sandwiches
Monterey Jack (cow's)	9 g/oz	Semisoft to very hard (depending on age); mild to pungent; smooth texture, small openings throughout, creamy white to light yellow	Wheel, block	Sandwiches, in Mexican dishes
Muenster (cow's)	5 g/oz	Mild and mellow to pungent (depending on age); smooth, wax-like, small holes; creamy white to light yellow	Wheel, block	Appetizers, sandwiches, with fruit, dessert
Port du Salut (cow's)	7 g/oz	Smooth, buttery, rich; small openings; mellow to robust; creamy white or pale yellow interior, edible orange rind	Wheel, cylinder	Appetizers, with fruit, dessert
Roquefort (sheep's)	9 g/oz	Sharp, peppery, pungent flavor; slightly salty; semisoft, pasty, sometimes crumbly texture; white interior streaked with blue-green veins of mold (see Blue)	Cylindrical shape, wedges; imported only from France	Appetizers, salads, dips, salad dressings, sandwiches, dessert
Stilton (cow's)	10 g/oz	Pungent, tangy, rich; milder than Roquefort and Gorgonzola; crumbly, harder than Roquefort; medium yellow with blue-green marbling (see Blue)	Cylindrical shape, wedges; imported only from England	Appetizers, salads, dessert
FIRM CHEESE				
Cheddar (cow's)	10 g/oz	Mild to very sharp depending on age; hard and crumbly to soft depending on age; creamy white (not dyed) to medium yellow-orange	Wheel	Appetizers, sandwiches, sauces, grating, dessert
Colby (cow's)	9 g/oz	Mild to mellow flavor, similar to cheddar; softer body and more open texture than cheddar; light cream to orange	Block	In sandwiches, cooked foods
Edam (cow's)	7 g/oz	Mellow, nutlike, sometimes salty flavor; rather firm, rubbery texture, not too hard; creamy yellow or medium yellow-orange interior; surface coated with red wax	Loaf or sphere; may be coated with wax; usually shaped like a flattened ball	Appetizers, on crackers, with fresh fruit, dessert

continued

TABLE 5.2 continued

Cheese type/milk used	Fat (approx.)	Characteristics	Purchasing notes	Mode of serving
Emmenthaler/Swiss (cow's)	8 g/oz	Sweet, nutlike; shiny, smooth, hard, firm, slightly rubbery; large round gas holes or eyes; pale yellow	Wheel	Appetizers, in salads, sandwiches, fondue, with fruit and nuts
Gouda (cow's)	8 g/oz	Mellow, nutlike; smooth, hard; may have tiny holes; creamy yellow or medium yellow-orange interior	Wheel; red wax coating; usually shaped like a flattened ball	Appetizers, with fresh fruit, in cooked dishes
Gruyère (cow's)	9 g/oz	Sweet, nutlike; moist; highly flavored; small well-spaced holes; pale yellow	Wheel	Appetizers, in sauces, dessert
Jarlsberg (cow's)	9 g/oz	Mild, delicate sweet nutty flavor; large holes, hard; light yellow; similar to Emmenthaler	Wheel; coated with yellow wax	Sandwiches, cooked dishes
Provolone (cow's)	8 g/oz	Mild to sharp depending on age; hard, elastic; light yellow to golden brown	Various shapes (pear, sausage, round)	Sandwiches, cooked dishes, pasta dishes, pizza

HARD GRATING CHEESE

Cheese type/milk used	Fat (approx.)	Characteristics	Purchasing notes	Mode of serving
Asiago (cow's)	7 g/oz	Rich, nutty flavor; mild (young) sharp (aged); hard for grating after 2 years aging, crumbly after 1 year aging; melts easily; light yellow	Cylinder, flat block	Sliced with fruits (young), grated in pastas and sauces (aged)
Parmesan/Parmigiano-Reggiano (cow's)	7 g/oz	Sharp, complex, distinctive flavor; very hard, granular texture; light yellow	Cylinder, wheel; Parmigiano Reggiano imported only (France)	Grated, with pasta, in sauces, on salads and vegetables, on pizza, in lasagna, in cooking
Romano/pecorino (cow's, sheep's, goat's)	7.5 g/oz	Very sharp, piquant flavor, tangy; very hard, brittle, granular texture; yellowish white	Cylinder	Grated on salads, pasta, pizza

PROCESSED CHEESE

Cheese type/milk used	Fat (approx.)	Characteristics	Purchasing notes	Mode of serving
American (cow's)	7 g/oz	Mild flavor; semisoft to soft; smooth, plastic body; processed; creamy white or yellow-orange	Blocks, sliced or unsliced	In sandwiches, on crackers, for cooking (melts quickly and smoothly)

TABLE 5.2   Guide for selecting natural and processed cheeses

life. The term **ultra-pasteurization** refers to a process in which milk is heated and held at a higher temperature for a shorter length of time than in regular pasteurization. Milk stays fresh longer because almost all bacteria are destroyed during this process. Ultra-pasteurization is often used for whipping cream, half-and-half, and individual coffee creamers. **Ultra-high-temperature processing** is achieved by heating and holding milk at a sufficiently high temperature to kill all bacteria and packaging it in sterilized containers. Milk that has been ultra-high-temperature processed and packaged in sterilized containers is shelf stable and can be held without refrigeration for at least 3 months. Once opened, however, it must be refrigerated and used within a few days. Flavor changes can be noticed when milk is heated; ultra-high-temperature-processed milk has a slightly sweet, cooked milk taste. Chilling ultra-high-temperature processed milk before serving improves palatability.

Most milk available commercially has been **homogenized** by a process that divides and disperses milkfat globules so the fat and the liquid portions of the milk do not separate. The homogenization process causes milk to have a whiter color and a smooth, uniform texture.

Milkfat can be removed from milk to make a variety of fat-reduced products available. Table 5.3 identifies fluid milk products with varying amounts of milkfat.

A curdled appearance is the undesirable result of milk protein coagulation caused by heat, acid, salts, and phenolic compounds in fruits and vegetables. Curdling is usually caused by a combination of these factors and can be reduced by heating milk products at a low or moderate temperature for the shortest time possible. Milk-based products such as cream soups and sauces curdle easily when reheated. Reheat using low heat and serve at once.

TABLE 5.3 Types of milk and cream products

	% Milkfat	Description
FLUID MILK		
Milk	3.25	The term *milk* refers to *whole milk*. Contains 8.0 g total fat and 150 kcal per cup (240 mL). States may establish a minimum for milkfat in whole milk. Federal standards specify a minimum of 3.25%.
Reduced-fat	2	Synonymous terms are *low-fat 2%* and *less-fat milk*. Contains 4.7 g total fat and 122 kcal per cup (240 mL).
Low-fat	1	Synonymous term is *low-fat 1% milk*. Contains 2.6 g total fat and 102 kcal per cup (240 mL).
Skim	0.5	Synonymous terms are *fat-free*, *zero-fat*, *no-fat*, and *nonfat milk*. Less than 0.5 g total fat and 80 kcal per cup (240 mL).
CONCENTRATED FLUID MILK		
Evaporated	6.5 (whole)	Approximately 60% of the water removed.
Sweetened condensed	8 (whole)	Approximately 60% of the water removed. Sugar (usually sucrose) is added to whole or skim milk, which is concentrated to one-third its volume.
DRY MILK		
Nonfat		Made from pasteurized nonfat skim milk in a process that removes water. Disperses rapidly in cold water. $1\frac{1}{3}$ cups nonfat dry milk will make 1 qt fluid milk.
Whole or low-fat		Dry whole or low-fat milk has a shorter shelf life because of the fat content, and it disperses slowly in warm water.
Buttermilk		Processed the same as other dry milk and made from the liquid remaining after butter is produced from cream. Proportions may vary, but generally 1 cup dry buttermilk powder will make 1 qt fluid buttermilk. Dry buttermilk is usually mixed with the recipe's dry ingredients, and the water is added with the liquid ingredients.
CULTURED MILK		
Acidophilus milk		Cultured by adding *Lactobacillus acidophilus* bacteria to pasteurized skim or low-fat milk. Health benefit claims exist for drinking acidophilus milk and introducing *Lactobacillus acidophilus* bacteria into the intestine.
Buttermilk		Cultured by adding *Streptococcus lactis* or *Lactococcus lactis* bacteria to pasteurized whole, low-fat, or skim milk. Cultured buttermilk is thick and tart.
Yogurt		Cultured by adding lactic acid–producing bacteria to whole, low-fat, or skim milk. Flavorings, sweeteners, and solids such as fruit may be added. The resulting product is thick and tangy.
CREAM		
Half-and-half	10.5–17	A mixture of whole milk and cream. Used in place of light cream or coffee cream.
Light, coffee, or table cream	18–29	A lower-milkfat cream; not for whipping.
Cream	18 minimum	General name used when milkfat is 18% or more.
Light whipping cream or whipping cream	30–36	The minimum milkfat required for whipping.
Heavy whipping cream or heavy cream	36 minimum	Whips easily and holds its whipped shape longer than cream with less milkfat.
Crème fraîche	36 minimum	A high-milkfat cultured cream product, thinner than sour cream with a similar but less tart flavor and velvety texture. Because of its high fat content, it will not curdle easily when used in cooked products. When not available commercially, crème fraîche can be made. See Note.
Sour cream	18–22	Sweet cream cultured by adding *Streptococcus lactis* bacteria to light cream. Tangy, tart flavor.

Note: Crème fraîche can be made by mixing, in a stainless steel or glass bowl, regular pasteurized (preferably not ultra pasteurized) heavy cream heated to 100°F with an active culture fluid buttermilk using a ratio of 8 oz heavy cream to $1\frac{1}{2}$ Tbsp buttermilk. The mixture will thicken when covered loosely and placed in a warm place for 12–24 hours. Refrigerate after thickening and use within 5–7 days.

TABLE 5.3 Types of milk and cream products

Purchasing and Storage

Many types of milk are available for serving as a beverage or for cooking purposes. Table 5.3 describes a variety of milk products.

Fluid milk is a potentially hazardous food, and proper purchasing and storage procedures are important. When kept between 35°F and 40°F, fluid milk will keep for a week, and buttermilk will keep for 2–3 weeks. Shelf-stable milk (evaporated, condensed, and dry) will keep for 3–6 months unopened in cool 60–70°F temperature storage and for 3–5 days when reconstituted and held at 35–40°F. Most milk products are date stamped to facilitate rotation of stock. All milk products will absorb flavor from strong foods and refrigerator odors if not tightly covered. Freezing milk causes fat globules to coalesce, so frozen milk is not recommended for drinking. Frozen milk can, however, be used in baking and in other products where some fat separation will not be noticed.

CREAM

Cream is produced by separating milkfat from whole milk. The resulting products are used extensively in foodservice operations to give flavor, richness, and body to sauces, soups, and desserts. Table 5.3 identifies cream products with varying amounts of milkfat.

Cream with a high milkfat percentage is thicker than cream with low milkfat. Temperature also affects cream thickness because the fat globules firm up and become more viscous when cold. Both high milkfat content (at least 30 percent) and firm fat globules chilled to 35–40°F are required to successfully trap air into cream for whipped cream.

Purchasing and Storage

Cream is marketed in several forms, as identified in Table 5.3. Products with higher milkfat cost more than those with lower milkfat content. Cream will absorb flavors from strong foods or from the refrigerator if not tightly covered. It can be stored at 35–40°F for 3 weeks. Ultra-pasteurized cream will keep for 4 weeks. Most cream products are date stamped for keeping stock rotated. Cream may separate when frozen; freezing is not recommended.

BUTTER

Butter is produced by agitating cream until the liquid separates from the milkfat or butterfat. Butter contains 80 percent milkfat, not more than 16 percent water, and 2 to 4 percent milk solids. Butter is hard when chilled and soft at room temperature, and it melts at approximately 93°F. The smoke point of butter is lower than most other fats (see p. 142 for smoke points of selected fats).

Grading is not required, but because it provides consumers with assurance of quality, most manufacturers choose to have their product graded according to federal standards so they can use the USDA label. USDA Grades A and AA butters are used most often in foodservices. The USDA descriptors for AA grade butter are delicate, sweet flavor, with a fine, highly pleasing aroma. It is made from high quality fresh sweet cream, and it has a smooth, creamy texture with good spreadability. Grade A butter is described as fairly smooth in texture, pleasing in flavor, and made from fresh cream. Grade B butter may have a slightly acid flavor but is acceptable to consumers. Grade B butter is made from sour cream and is used most often by commercial food manufacturers.

Purchasing and Storage

Butter for foodservice use is generally marketed in quarter-pound cubes or sticks, four per pound box, and either salted or unsalted. If salt has been added, it should be only slightly detectable and not salty. Salt will increase the shelf life slightly and may mask subtle unpleasant flavors. Butter color will vary among manufacturers and will depend on the time of year, the breed of cow, and the food the cow eats. Unsalted butter is sometimes referred to as *sweet butter*; however, the designation indicates only that the butter was made from sweet cream and not sour cream.

European-style butter has a high milkfat content—usually between 82 and 86 percent—and is usually unsalted. It may be churned from cultured cream, which gives it a richer flavor and smoother texture. *Whipped butter* has air incorporated into it for easier spreading. *Clarified butter* or *drawn butter* has the water and milk solids removed. Butter can be clarified by melting and skimming off the white froth that forms on the top and removing the milk solids that settle to the bottom. Care should be taken to not overheat the butter and cause it to brown or burn. Yield after clarifying is approximately 75 percent.

Butter will easily absorb flavors from strong foods or refrigerator and freezer odors. When tightly covered and held between 32°F and 35°F, butter will keep for 4 weeks. At 0°F or below, it will keep for 6 months. Off flavors are more detectable in salted than in unsalted butter.

Grains, Pasta, Flours, and Other Starches

- General Information
- Purchasing and Storage
- Cooking and Recipes (see Chapter 16)

GRAINS

Grains are the edible seeds of a variety of grasses that are used extensively on menus because of their nutritional attributes and versatility. Grains are available whole or milled into various shapes and sizes. The milling process determines the characteristics of the end product and the uses for which it is suitable. Basic milling processes include cracking, grinding, hulling, and pearling or polishing. Cracking breaks open the grains, grinding reduces the grain to small particles of differing degrees of fineness, hulling removes the protective husk or covering, and pearling or polishing removes most or all of the hull, bran, and germ.

All grains have a similar structure. An outer layer of papery skin called **bran** covers the grain. Bran has very little flavor and is a good source of fiber. **Endosperm** is the starchy, central portion of the grain that contains most of the grain's starch and protein but very little fat or minerals. White flour is made primarily from the endosperm. The **germ** is the embryo of the plant and is rich in protein, fats, and minerals. The germ remains in whole-meal flour but is removed partially or entirely from white flour. Because of the high fat content, grain products that contain the germ portion will become rancid if exposed to air or stored for a long period of time.

Grain products are often enriched by adding back in the nutrients that were removed by the milling process. Enrichment standards for wheat flour include adding thiamin, riboflavin, niacin, iron, and folic acid to white flour. Some grain products are fortified with vitamins and minerals beyond the enrichment standards.

Grains are often used as thickening agents because the starch granules absorb water and swell when heated with liquid. Common grain thickening agents are cornstarch and wheat flour.

Purchasing and Storage

The most common cereal grains are barley, corn, oats, rice, rye, and wheat. Other less used grains are amaranth, buckwheat/kasha (which is considered with grains but is not a type of wheat or even a grain), millet, and quinoa. Table 5.4 and Exhibit 11 in the colored inserts identify cereal grains.

TABLE 5.4   Guide for selecting grains

Grain	Flavor/texture	General information[a]
Amaranth	Peppery flavor	• Gluten free. • Tiny seeds with high protein content. • Used in cereals and bread products (breads, muffins, pancakes) when mixed with wheat flour.
Barley	Nutty, sweet and earthy flavor with chewy, pasta-like texture	• Pearled barley (usual form used in cooking) has outer hull removed. • Used in soups and pilafs. • A softer texture will result from cooking in a large amount of liquid, as in a soup. • Requires a longer cooking time than rice.
Buckwheat/kasha	Nutty earthy flavor with a gritty sand-like texture	• Gluten free. • Not technically a plant seed but a fruit from a plant. • Whole buckwheat kernels are called *groats*. • Kasha is the roasted groats with a reddish-brown color. • Most often used as a side dish or in a salad. Also used in soba noodles. Raw buckwheat groats are ground into flour and used for griddle cakes and blinis and in pasta. Used with wheat flour for structure in bread products.
Bulgur	Nutty flavor and texture	• Wheat berries that have the bran removed are steam-cooked, dried, and ground into coarse, medium, or fine granules. • Cooks quickly, in about 10 minutes. • Not interchangeable for whole wheat in recipes. Used in side dishes, pilafs, and salads (traditionally in tabouli).
Corn	Sweet starchy flavor	• Gluten free. • Eaten as both a vegetable (sweet corn) and a dried grain product. Marketed as *cornmeal* when dried and ground into coarse or fine meal. White and yellow cornmeal are most common; blue cornmeal is available in some markets, especially in the Southwestern area of the United States. • Used in quick breads and flatbreads. Used with wheat flour for structure in bread products. Used in corn cakes, grits, polenta, tortillas, quick breads (muffins, bread).
Couscous	Mild flavor	• Small granules or pellets made from semolina flour (from the endosperm of a durum wheat berry). Small size *Moroccan couscous* is a little larger than cornmeal and cooks quickly. *Israeli couscous* is medium size, about the size of a peppercorn. *Lebanese couscous* is large, about the size of a small pea. • Most couscous is precooked (instant couscous) and needs only to be moistened with hot or boiling liquid and held for 5 minutes. The process for cooking couscous that has not been precooked requires fairly long periods of soaking and steaming.
Farro		• An ancient strain of wheat. Known also as *emmer* or *grano farro*. Sold as a gourmet specialty.
Kamut	Rich and buttery	• An heirloom wheat grain grown usually on organic farms.

continued

TABLE 5.4   Guide for selecting grains

TABLE 5.4	continued	
Grain	**Flavor/texture**	**General information[a]**
Hominy	Soft, chewy, starchy texture when cooked	• Gluten free. • Endosperm of the corn kernel that is removed from the bran and germ by drying and soaking process using lime or lye. • Dried hominy can be ground into grits (hominy grits) or into a flour (masa harina) and used often in Mexican and Southwestern food. • Cooked hominy is generally purchased canned. Also known as pozole.
Millet	Mild flavor	• Gluten free. • Purchased whole or as a flour. Whole millet is usually cooked like rice for a side dish or added in small amounts to bread dough for a crunchy texture. Millet flour can be used in flatbreads.
Oats	Slightly sweet flavor	• Not usually considered gluten free because of frequent contamination during growing or processing. • A whole-grain product used for hot cereal and in many baked products. *Rolled* or *old-fashioned oats* are made from oat groats (whole oat kernels without the husk) that have been steamed and rolled into flat flakes for faster cooking. *Quick oats* are rolled oats cut into smaller pieces to reduce the cooking time. *Instant oats* have been precooked and dried before rolling. They require no cooking and need only to be rehydrated in boiling water. *Steel cut* or *Irish* oats are oat groats that have been chopped into small pieces, have a much chewier texture, and require a longer cooking time than rolled or quick oats. Rolled and quick oats are interchangeable, with a slightly different texture resulting. Instant oats should not be substituted for rolled or quick oats.
Quinoa	Slightly bitter	• Gluten free. • Not a true grain but a tiny round seed of a South American plant similar to Swiss chard. • Used similar to rice. • Because they have a naturally bitter outer covering, they should be rinsed several times before cooking. Seeds become translucent when cooked and will absorb water at twice their volume.
Rice Brown rice Converted rice Basmati rice Arborio rice Wild rice	Mild, nutty, floral, earthy flavors depending on variety	• Gluten free. • The seed of a plant that grows in water. • *Long-grain rice* cooks up firm and fluffy with grains that are separate. Overcooking or excessive stirring while cooking will cause long-grain rice to become sticky. Retains its texture when held on a steam table or buffet line. Long-grain rice includes basmati, converted (parboiled), jasmine, and Texmati. • *Medium-grain rice* cooks up tender and moist, with grains that cling together. Becomes sticky when cool. Requires less water to prepare and has a higher starch content than long-grain rice. Used for making paella. • The small, short, plump, nearly round kernels of *short-grain rice* have a high starch content and become very tender and sticky when cooked. Chewy and springy. Risotto, sushi, and rice pudding are made with short-grain rice. Arborio is a short-grain rice.

Processed rice

• *Brown rice* is whole-grain rice with only the outer hull removed. It retains most of the bran layers that give it a light b[r]-, color, chewy slightly crunchy texture, and nut-like flavor. Available in short-, m[edium]-, or long-grain. Shelf life is shorter than that of white rice because of the oil co[ntent]. milled or polished to remove the outer husk and layers

• *Regular* or *white rice* h[a]d *polished rice*. of bran. Someti[m]e undergoes a steam-pressure process and is dried before milling.

• *Converted (parb*[oiled])[g]rains remain separate and plump. Has good holding quality after After cooki[ng] [nei]ther precooked nor instant and requires a longer cooking time than cooking[. Regular] white rice. Long-grain is most often used in foodservice. Both brown regul[ar r]ice can be processed into converted rice. an[d] *(instant) rice* has been milled, cooked, and dehydrated. It needs only to be [rehydr]ated to be ready to use. Does not hold up well after cooking; the grains quickly [lose] their shape and become soft and mushy.

[D]uring the milling process, white rice and converted rice are often *enriched* to replace the vitamins and minerals lost in the milling process when the bran and germ portion of the grain are removed. Vitamins and minerals are usually added to the outside of the kernel in the form of a white powdery substance. To retain the vitamins and minerals, white rice and converted rice should not be rinsed before or after cooking.

continued

TABLE 5.4   Guide for selecting grains

TABLE 5.4 continued

Grain	Flavor/texture	General information[a]

Varieties

- Aromatic or fragrant rices have subtle floral, nutty, or earthy nuances. *Basmati* cooks to a dry, fluffy texture with separate grains similar to regular long-grain rice. Basmati rice is extra long-grain. *Thai jasmine* or *jasmine* long-grain rice cooks up soft and tender. It is very fragrant with a more subtle flavor than basmati.
- *Italian short-grain rice* has polished white kernels that are a little longer than are wide.
- *Arborio rice,* used for risotto, is a common short-grain rice. It is very sticky with a white color.
- *Spanish rice* is similar to Italian short-grain rice but when cooked is a little lighter in texture. Spanish rice absorbs liquid evenly and retains an al dente mouthfeel.
- *Sticky* or *glutinous rice,* also called *sweet rice* and *sushi rice,* becomes extremely sticky when cooked. Used almost exclusively for Asian cooking and often for dessert dishes. Grains become bouncy and full when cooked. Has a high starch content and pearly white color.
- *Wild rice* is not a true rice but the large rice-looking seed of an aquatic reedlike grass. Native to the great lakes area of the U.S. Cultivated in other states. It has long unpolished kernels; nutty flavor; dark brown to black color; and firm chewy texture. Usually combined with other rices and ingredients for stuffing, salads, and side dishes. The longer grains are considered the best quality. Should be rinsed before using.

Rye
- A grain used primarily as a flour for making bread. It is available in three grades—light, medium, and dark—and either flaked or as a pearled grain.

Sorghum/milo
- Gluten free.
- A round seed that is usually ground into a flour.

Spelt — Mellow nutty flavor
- A variety of wheat.
- Can be used in place of common wheat in most recipes.

Teff
- Gluten free.
- Very small black ancient grain of the millet family. Principal grain in Ethiopian bread (injera), a soft, porous, thin pancake.

Triticale
- Hybrid cross of wheat and rye.

Wheat
- Contains large amounts of gluten.
- *Cracked wheat* and *whole wheat* are the whole kernel of wheat (wheat berry) without the bran removed. The wheat berry is either left whole or broken into varying degrees of coarseness without first cooking. To soften wheat berries, soak for 24 hours before being cooked in double their volume of water.
- *Wheat germ* is the part of the seed that will germinate to grow into a new plant. It contains the fat from the wheat kernel and is a good source of protein, fiber, vitamins B and E, and iron. Can be substituted for approximately 20 to 30 percent of the flour in bread. It can be purchased defatted for longer storage—up to 6 months.

[a]See Exhibit 11 in the colored inserts for pictures of selected grains.

TABLE 5.4 Guide for selecting grains

PASTA

Pasta is a generic name for a basic dough mixture of semolina or other high-protein hard wheat flour and durum. With the exception of noodles, which usually contain egg, various pasta products are made from the same basic dough. Flavor variations are many and include carrot, cracked black pepper, herb, garlic, lemon-pepper, tomato, and spinach.

Asian-style pastas are different from Italian pastas in that they may be made with rice, bean, and buckwheat flour as well as wheat flour. *Asian wheat noodles* are known as *somen noodles* when thin and delicate, similar to angel hair pasta, and *udon noodles* when thick, flat, and chewy. Curly, instant-cooking *ramen noodles* are also made with wheat. *Soba noodles* are made with wheat and buckwheat flour and are brownish-gray in color. Soba noodles are the thickness of spaghetti and slightly chewier in texture. *Asian egg noodles,* made with wheat, are called *lo mein* or *chow mein noodles.* Wonton and egg roll wrappers are egg noodles. *Rice noodles* can be wide similar to linguine or fettuccine, thin to very thin (*rice sticks*), or very thin (*rice vermicelli,* sold in nests). Thin *rice noodles* are often fried in hot fat and cook very quickly to a white, puffy, crunchy product. *Bean starch noodles,* also known as *bean threads, cellophane noodles, Chinese vermicelli,* and *glass noodles,* are thin translucent strands made from mung bean starch and can be fried in the same way as rice noodles.

Pu...

Pasta ...ing and Storage

(e.g., spa... ...be categorized into five basic groups: string shapes (e.g... ...are hundreds ...bbon (e.g., noodles), tubes (e.g., penne), foodservices app...), and mini pastas (e.g., acini). There ...apes. The shapes used most often in ...ure 5.2. Pasta may be purchased

Pasta	Shape	Pasta	Shape

Alphabets
Miniature pasta in letter shapes.
Used in soups.

Lasagna
Wide, long, flat noodles with wavy
    edges.
Baked layered with cheeses and sauces.

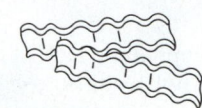

Bow ties, farfalle
Bow-shaped noodles.
Used with entrée sauces and also soups
    or salads.

Linguine
Thin narrow rods, slightly flattened.
Used with all sauces, especially cream
    sauces.

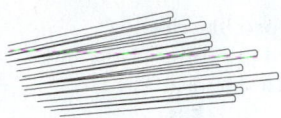

Capellini, angel hair
Delicate long thin threads.
Used with light sauces.

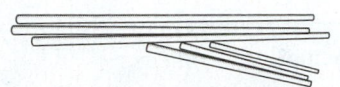

Elbow macaroni
Short tubes that are slightly curved.
Used in salads and casseroles.

Cavatappi
Spiral, ridged tubes (corkscrews).
Used in casseroles and with
    sauces.

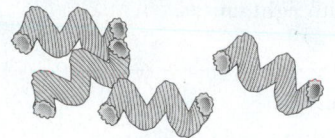

Macaroni
Long hollow round tubes,
    straight cut ends.
Baked in casseroles or
    with sauces.

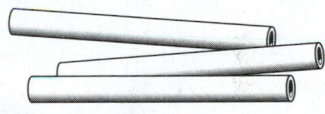

Conchiglie, shells
Shell shaped.
Used with sauces; larger shells stuffed,
    smaller shells used in salads.
Jumbo shells stuffed with cheese, meat,
    vegetables.

Manicotti
Giant pasta tubes.
Stuffed with cheese or
    meat fillings.

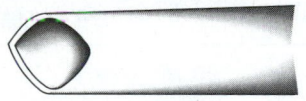

Dumplings
Flat, with rippled edges.
Used in soups and baked casseroles.

Mostaccioli
Medium-sized hollow tubes,
    ends cut diagonally.
Used in baked casseroles
    or with sauces.

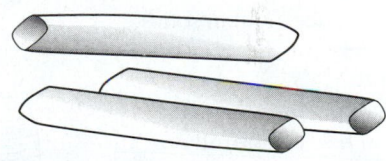

Fettuccine
Pasta shaped like ribbons, slightly thick.
Used with heavy creams or meat sauces.

Noodles
Narrow flat pasta; typically contains egg.
Used in a variety of casseroles, with
    sauces, and as a side dish.

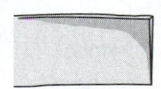

X-Wide Noodles

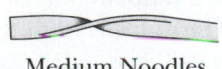

Wide Noodles

Medium Noodles

Fusilli
Long strands of spiraled spaghetti,
    corkscrew shaped.
Used with thick cream sauces or
    casseroles. Break into soups.

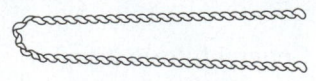

Kluski
Long narrow egg noodles, with
    homemade appearance.
Used for soups, baked casseroles,
    and with cream sauces.

Orecchiette
Ear shaped.
Used in casseroles, with sauces.

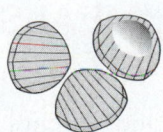

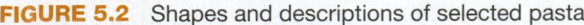

FIGURE 5.2   Shapes and descriptions of selected pasta.

Pasta	*Shape*

Pastina (tiny dough)

Ditalini

Used in soups and salads.
Very short hollow tube.

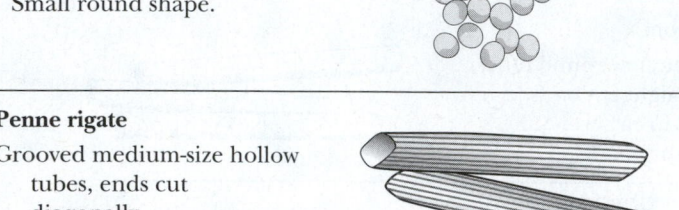

Orzo

Shaped like rice.
Used in soups, salads, and
as a side dish.

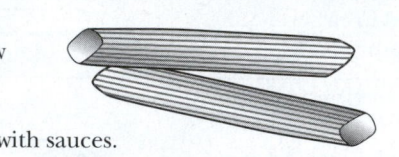

Stelline

Star shaped.

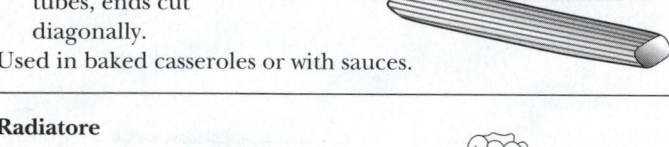

Acini

Small round shape.

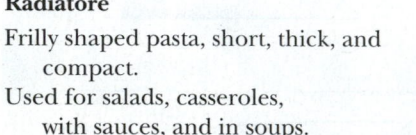

Penne rigate

Grooved medium-size hollow
tubes, ends cut
diagonally.
Used in baked casseroles or with sauces.

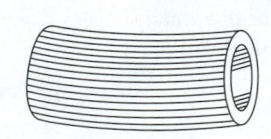

Radiatore

Frilly shaped pasta, short, thick, and
compact.
Used for salads, casseroles,
with sauces, and in soups.

Rigatoni

Large ribbed hollow tubes.
Used in baked casseroles or
with sauces.

Pasta	*Shape*

Rotini

Spiraled pasta.
Used in baked casseroles or
with salads.

Spaghetti

Long round rods.
Used with all sauces,
especially tomato.
Used in casseroles.

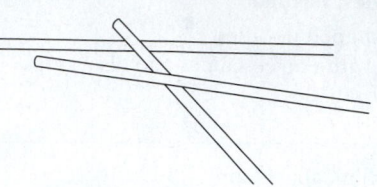

Spaghettini

Thin round rods.
Used like spaghetti, typically
with light sauces.

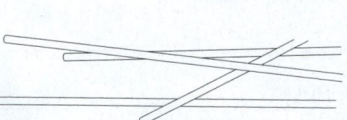

Vermicelli

Extra thin spaghetti-like rods.
Used with light delicate sauces.

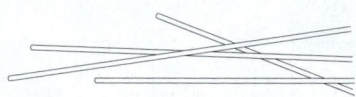

Wagon wheels

Die-cut shape resembling wheels.
Used with sauces, in salads
and soups.

Ziti

Short, hollow, round, medium-size tubes
with straight cut ends; resembles
large macaroni.
Used in baked casseroles or with sauces.

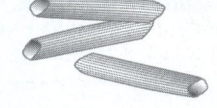

FIGURE 5.2   Continued

---

fresh, frozen, or dry. Precooked pasta is available in some markets.

Dry pasta will keep for several months when stored in a cool, dry, well-ventilated storage area. Fresh pasta is perishable and should be wrapped tightly and stored in a refrigerator and used within 2–3 days.

FLOURS, MEALS, AND OTHER STARCHES

Flours, meals, and starches are staples in food production kitchens. They are used for breads and baked sweet goods and for thickening fillings, soups, and sauces. Table 5.5 identifies flours, meals, and starches.

Meat—Beef, Lamb, Pork, Veal

- General Information
- Purchasing
- Storage
- Cooking Methods (see Chapter 6)
- Recipes (see Chapter 14)

The quality of cooked meat depends on the quality purchased, the storage and handling of the meat after delivery, and cooking methods. All meats marketed in interstate commerce in the United States must meet federal inspection standards for wholesomeness. Meat slaughtered, processed, and sold within a given state must be inspected using criteria at least equal to

TABLE 5.5   Flours and other starches

Flours/Meals/Starches

WHEAT FLOURS

All-purpose	Several flours blended to yield a flour with lower protein content than bread flour. For general foodservice use including breads, pastries, and basic cakes.
Bread	A high-protein white flour made from hard wheat. Used for bread products in which gluten development is desirable. Produces a bread with high volume.
Cake	A very low-protein white flour made from soft wheat. Used for delicate and fine-textured cakes where gluten development is undesirable.
Enriched	Enriched flour has iron and B vitamins added. Flour sold in interstate commerce must be enriched with iron, thiamin, riboflavin, niacin, and folic acid. Vitamin D and calcium are optional additions.
Instant	All-purpose flour that has been processed by moistening and re-drying to produce a product that flows freely without packing. Because it blends easily with liquids, it is used for thickening sauces and gravies. Instant flour is not interchangeable with other flours for baking.
Gluten	Wheat flour mixed with dried extracted gluten to increase the protein content. Used to adjust the protein levels of various yeast doughs.
Pasta	Flour made from hard durum wheat. Makes a sturdy dough desirable for pasta.
Pastry	A low-protein white flour usually made with soft wheat. Used for pastries, biscuits, and cookies where gluten development is undesirable.
Self-rising	A white flour that has leavening agents and salt added.
Whole wheat	Also called graham flour. Flour made by grinding the entire wheat kernel to different degrees of fineness. Higher in fiber than white flour because whole-wheat flour contains the bran.

OTHER FLOURS

Amaranth flour	Made by grinding amaranth seed. High content of the amino acid lysine. Added to wheat bread and other baked products for its nutritional contribution. Contains no gluten.
Buckwheat flour	Contains no gluten. Used primarily in pancakes and waffles.
Corn flour	Corn flour is a fine grind of cornmeal made from either white or yellow corn. Contains no gluten, so it must be added to wheat flour when used in yeast breads. Used primarily for quick breads.
Masa harina flour	Masa harina is a flour made from finely ground hominy. Used for making tortillas, tamales, and other Southwestern dishes.
Potato flour	Primarily potato starch.
Rice flour	Primarily rice starch.
Rye flour	Results from sifting rye meal. Contains a small amount of gluten but is usually combined with wheat flour in baking.
Soy flour	A flour made from soybeans. High in protein but contains no gluten and must be used with wheat flour in breads.
Triticale flour	Made from a grain that is a cross between wheat and rye. Some varieties contain enough gluten to make satisfactory yeast bread.

OTHER STARCHES

Arrowroot	A fine powder made from the root of a tropical plant. Used as a thickener.
Filé	A fine powder made from the leaves of sassafras trees. Used as a thickener, especially in gumbo.

TABLE 5.5   Flours and other starches

federal inspection standards. Government inspection of all meat is mandatory. Government grading is not required by law but, because it adds value, most meat is graded. Meat processors contract with the USDA Agriculture Marketing Service for meat to be graded by licensed federal graders.

Quality grading helps predict the expected eating characteristics (tenderness, juiciness, and flavor) of the cooked product. Beef grades are based on two primary factors: the amount of marbling present and the age of the animal. Texture, color, and firmness of the lean meat are also considered. Marbling is judged by the amount of inter- and intramuscular fat in the meat. USDA grades are based on nationally uniform federal standards of quality.

Yield grading is a system used for some meats that estimates the percentage of boneless and closely trimmed foodservice cuts that can be obtained from a carcass. These grades identify carcasses for differences in cutability or yield and are applied by the USDA grading service. Table 5.6 identifies quality and yield grades used for meat. Grade and yield stamps are shown in Figure 5.3.

The term *certified* implies that the USDA's Agriculture Marketing Service (AMS) has officially evaluated a beef product for class, grade, or other quality characteristics (as in the trademarked term *Certified Angus Beef*). When used under other circumstances, the term must be closely associated with the name of the organization responsible for the certification

TABLE 5.6 Quality and yield grades for meat

Beef[a]	Veal	Pork[b]	Lamb
QUALITY GRADES			
Prime	Prime	U.S. No. 1	Prime
Choice	Choice	U.S. No. 2	Choice
Select	Good	U.S. No. 3	Good
Standard	Standard	U.S. No. 4	Utility
YIELD GRADES[c]			
1	n/a	n/a	1
2	n/a	n/a	2
3	n/a	n/a	3
4	n/a	n/a	4
5	n/a	n/a	5

[a]Commercial, Utility, Cutter, and Canner (for beef) and Utility (for veal) are lower grades and not purchased for general foodservice use.
[b]Pork is not graded with USDA quality grades as it is generally produced from young animals that have been bred and fed to yield more uniformly tender meat. Backfat and muscle size are used to determine pork grades. No. 1 highest yield, No. 4 lowest yield.
[c]Number 1 represents the greatest yield (most lean); number 5 represents the smallest yield (least lean).

FIGURE 5.3   Quality grade and yield stamps for meat.

process (e.g., *XYZ Company's Certified Beef*). Standards for use of the terms *organic* and *natural* are not well established and may vary among producers or distributors. Meats marked with a special designation are often more expensive and should be marketed in a way that costs can be recouped.

Wet aging or **dry aging** may be used to improve the tenderness and flavor of beef. Pork, veal, and lamb are usually not aged because they are slaughtered at a relatively young age when the meat is most tender. Wet aging occurs in the vacuum package in which the meat is sealed. Dry aging is the process of holding meat, uncovered, in a sanitary environment, under strict temperature and humidity guidelines for 3–4 weeks. Meat is tenderized and undergoes a flavor change because natural enzymes and microorganisms begin to break down the meat tissue. Because of the more intense flavor and tenderness of dry-aged meat, it can be effectively merchandised on a menu and priced higher than wet-aged products. Weight loss during the dry-aging process reduces the yield and makes dry-aged meat more expensive than wet-aged meat.

Purchasing

Meat for foodservice use is available in primal (wholesale) cuts, subprimals, and portioned or retail cuts. The chuck, loin, rib, and round are the major wholesale cuts of beef, making

up 76 percent of the carcass. The primal cuts for beef, lamb, pork, and veal are shown in Exhibits 1–4 in the colored inserts.

Subprimals are produced by breaking down the primals into smaller cuts. *Portioned* or *retail cuts* are processed from subprimals into individual steaks, chops, and other products. For example, a strip loin (subprimal cut) is processed from the loin (primal cut) and may be further fabricated into a Kansas City strip steak (portioned or retail cut). Portioned cuts generally have the advantage of being more uniform, making costs more easily controlled. Their packaging often allows for safer, more efficient storage.

The National Association of Meat Purveyors (NAMP) publishes a *Meat Buyer's Guide* that identifies meat products and cuts. Because the guide is based on USDA's Institutional Meat Purchasing Specifications (IMPS) and is used universally in the foodservice industry, it is a useful communication tool for purchasing department personnel and vendors. Recipes and procedures may be standardized using specific IMPS/NAMP numbers. All purchasing offices should have a copy of the *Meat Buyer's Guide*.

Storage

Storing meat in a refrigerator at a cold temperature is necessary to retard bacterial growth and slow the action of muscle enzymes. Store fresh meat loosely covered with waxed paper at a temperature of 28–32°F with a relative humidity of 85–90 percent. Vacuum-packaged meat should remain in its sealed package until used. Fresh meat should be used as soon after purchase as possible, not more than 3–4 days later. Fresh meat stored in a vacuum package (seal unbroken) will keep for up to 21 days in the refrigerator. Once the vacuum seal is broken the meat should be used within 3–4 days.

Frozen meat requires a uniform holding temperature of 0°F or below. It should be well wrapped to exclude air and keep in moisture. When stored improperly, frozen meat may develop freezer burn, causing the surface to discolor and look dehydrated. Fresh beef may be kept frozen at −10°F for a year and 0°F for 6 months. Frozen meat should be kept wrapped while defrosting in a refrigerator at 30–35°F and should be cooked soon after defrosting. Once thawed, it should not be refrozen. Refreezing will result in some moisture loss and could pose a health risk if the total thawed time exceeds acceptable standards. Cooked meat may be frozen. For safety and quality reasons, it should be frozen soon after cooking and cooling.

Meat that is frozen using equipment that freezes it quickly (blast freezers) is superior to meat frozen in conventional freezers. For best quality, meat should be frozen quickly and thawed slowly. Quick freezing reduces the size of ice crystals, thereby lessening the number of ruptured muscle tissue cells and the amount of liquid lost during defrosting.

Cured meats and cured and smoked meats such as ham and bacon, sausages, and dried beef require refrigerator storage. Although ham, bacon, and other cured meats can be frozen, freezing should only be for short periods, because undesirable flavor changes occur because of their salt, spice, and fat content.

Poultry

- General Information
- Purchasing
- Storage and Safe Handling
- Cooking Methods (see Chapter 6, p. 143)
- Recipes (see Chapter 15, p. 475)

Poultry includes many different species of birds that are bred for eating. The popularity of poultry on menus results from its year-round availability, variety, relatively low cost, versatility, and customers' perceptions of a lower-fat entrée choice.

Inspection for wholesomeness is mandatory for poultry sold for human consumption. Grading for quality is voluntary. Because it adds value, poultry is almost always graded. Poultry processors contract grading services by licensed federal graders from the USDA Agriculture Marketing Service.

USDA grades (A, B, or C) are identified by a shield-shaped hang tag attached to the bird or printed on the package label. See Figure 5.4. Grade A poultry is sold almost exclusively in wholesale and retail outlets. Lower grades are used in products requiring further processing such as in commercially available soups and diced chicken entrées. Quality grades are not meant to grade tenderness but rather to grade overall quality related to bird conformation,

Grade Mark

FIGURE 5.4   USDA grade shield for poultry.

FIGURE 5.5   USDA inspection stamp for poultry.

thickness of flesh, fat covering, exposed flesh from skin tears, discolorations, feathers, and broken or disjointed bones.

Figure 5.5 illustrates a USDA inspection stamp for poultry that can be found on a hang tag attached to the bird or on the packaging label.

Purchasing

The variety of cooked and processed poultry products continues to increase, opening up opportunities for new and labor-saving menu options. Decisions about whether to purchase whole or cut-up birds or raw or cooked products must be based on the menu, the skills of employees to cut whole birds into pieces, the ability to use the bony pieces for stock, the amount of refrigerated storage space, the production equipment, the volume of poultry used, and both product and labor costs. Portioned cuts generally have the advantage of being more uniform, making costs easier to control, and their packaging often allows for safer storage with reduced opportunity for cross contamination.

Poultry is divided into six categories. Chicken, duck, goose, and turkey are the most commonly used, and guinea and pigeon are less common. The categories are subdivided into classes and are based primarily on age. Table 5.7 identifies the various categories and classes of poultry.

Storage

All poultry is highly perishable. Caution regarding cleanliness and temperature control should be exercised in storing poultry as well as throughout the pre-preparation and cooking processes. Fresh chilled poultry should be stored at a temperature of 28–32°F and used within 1–2 days. Fresh turkeys can be kept for up to 4 days at these temperatures. Frozen poultry can be kept hard-frozen at 0°F or lower for up to 6 months. Once thawed, poultry may be kept safely for 24 hours at 32°F before cooking. Poultry should never be refrozen.

Poultry is a potentially hazardous food and a potential carrier of illness-causing microorganisms, particularly salmonella bacteria, and should be handled carefully. Good practices for *handling poultry safely* include the following:

- Keep fresh poultry refrigerated in the coldest part of the refrigerator (28–32°F). Limit to 1 hour the amount of time during production that poultry is held outside refrigeration.
- Thaw poultry covered or wrapped on trays under refrigerated temperatures. (See Table 7.4 for approximate thawing times for poultry.) Arrange poultry on refrigerator shelves so that air can circulate.

TABLE 5.7   Categories and classes of poultry

TABLE 5.7   Categories and classes of poultry

	Weight	Description
CHICKEN CLASSES		
Cornish game hen	2 lb or less	(Or Rock Cornish game hen) Young or immature Cornish chicken or Cornish and White Rock chicken (5–6 weeks). Very tender and flavorful. Suitable for all cooking techniques. Often roasted and served whole.
Broiler or fryer	3½ lb or less	Young (under 13 weeks), soft, pliable, smooth-textured skin and flexible breastbone cartilage. Tender and flavorful. Most versatile, suitable for all cooking techniques.
Roaster	3½–5 lb	(Or roasting chicken) Young (3–5 months), soft, pliable, smooth-textured skin and somewhat less flexible breastbone cartilage than broiler or fryer. Tender and flavorful. Suitable for all cooking techniques.
Capon	6–10 lb	Surgically desexed male bird, under 8 months. Soft, pliable, smooth-textured skin. Tender and flavorful. Usually roasted.
Stewing hen	3½–8 lb	Mature female (more than 10 months). Flavorful and less tender than roaster with non-flexible breastbone tip. Generally stewed or braised.
DUCK CLASSES		
Broiler or fryer	2–4 lb	Young (8 weeks or less), very tender. Usually roasted at high temperature but suitable for all cooking techniques.
Roaster	4–6 lb	Young (16 weeks or less), tender, rich flavor, usually roasted.
Mature	4–6 lb	Older bird (6 months or older). Toughened flesh, usually braised.
GOOSE CLASSES		
Young goose	6–12 lb	Tender, usually roasted.
Mature goose	10–16 lb	Toughened flesh. Usually braised or stewed.
TURKEY CLASSES		
Fryer-roaster	4–9 lb	Immature bird (16 weeks or less); soft, pliable, smooth-textured skin and flexible breastbone cartilage. Tender and flavorful. Meat can be cut into scallops and sautéed or pan-fried.
Young	8–22 lb	Fully mature (8 months or less); soft, pliable smooth-textured skin, and somewhat flexible breastbone. Tender. Usually roasted. Sex designation is optional.
Yearling	10–30 lb	Fully mature (15 months or less). Reasonably smooth-textured skin. Reasonably tender. Roasted or stewed. Sex designation is optional.
Mature	10–30 lb	Older bird (over 15 months). Tough and usually ground or used as processed products.

Notes:
- Pigeon (mature bird), squab (immature pigeon that has not begun to fly), and guinea fowl (domestic descendant of a game bird and related to a pheasant) are less common poultry choices. The meat of squab (4 weeks old or less) and young guinea fowl (3 months) is tender but toughens and darkens with age. Pigeon and squab are often considered a game bird along with partridge, pheasant, and quail.
- Ratites are not considered a poultry class. They are flightless birds that include emu (native to Australia), ostrich (native to Africa), and rhea (native to South America). The meat is dark. Tenderness varies depending on where the meat is cut from the bird.

- Keep raw poultry and raw poultry juices away from other foods, particularly cooked foods, foods ready to eat, or any raw product with an endpoint cooking temperature below 165°F.
- Poultry should be completely thawed before cooking to ensure that all parts reach safe endpoint temperatures.
- Wash hands frequently and wash and sanitize countertops, cloths, cutting boards, knives, and other utensils used in preparing raw poultry before they come in contact with other raw or cooked foods.

- Cooking Methods (see Chapters 6 and 13)
- Recipes (see Chapter 13)

Fish and shellfish are available in most markets as (1) never frozen and sold as *fresh* or *chilled* or (2) quickly frozen within hours of being caught and sold as *flash-frozen* or *fresh-frozen*.

Fish and shellfish inspection by the U.S. Department of Commerce (USDC) is voluntary. Products inspected and certified under the USDC Seafood Inspection Program that meet all specified requirements can display one or more of the official marks or statements associated with the program. Figure 5.6 illustrates a "Packed Under Federal Inspection" (PUFI) mark. The mark or statement signifies that the product has been inspected in an approved facility and was found to be safe, wholesome, and properly labeled according to approved specifications or criteria.

Fish and Shellfish

- General Information
- Purchasing and Storage

FIGURE 5.6   Packed Under Federal Inspection (PUFI) mark for fish and shellfish.

FIGURE 5.7   Grade A stamp for fish and shellfish.

FIGURE 5.8   Product inspection stamp for fish and shellfish.

Figure 5.7 is the official U.S. Grade A mark signifying that a product has been processed under federal inspection in an approved facility and meets the established level of quality of an existing U.S. grade standard. The U.S. Grade A mark indicates that the product is of high quality, uniform in size, practically free from blemishes and defects, in excellent condition, and possessing good flavor and aroma. The USDC Lot Inspected mark, Figure 5.8, conveys that the products bearing the mark have been examined by the USDC Program.

Purchasing and Storage

Fish and shellfish are high-food-cost and very perishable items. Knowing product categories and market descriptions and understanding proper storage principles are important for foodservice managers. Tables 5.8–5.13 provide information useful for purchasing and storing fish and shellfish.

Fresh Produce; Canned and Frozen Fruits and Vegetables; Tofu and Dried Beans, Lentils, and Peas

- Fresh Produce—Grades, Yields, Availability, Storage
- Fresh Fruits, Vegetables, Herbs, and Edible Flowers—Pre-Preparation Guidelines and General Information
- Canned and Frozen Fruits and Vegetables
- Tofu and Dried Beans, Lentils, and Peas
- Cooking and Recipes (see Chapters 17 and 21)

FRESH PRODUCE

Fresh produce is used in every menu category and is a staple in all foodservice kitchens. Because of its various menu applications, seasonal nature, and perishable characteristics, food production staff must have sufficient information for purchasing, storing, preparing, and handling produce correctly. This chapter provides the general information necessary for using fresh fruits and vegetables while meeting the quality standards required in today's competitive marketplace. See Exhibits 6, 8, and 10 in the colored inserts for color pictures of fresh produce.

Fresh fruits and vegetables may be graded under the USDA voluntary grading program. Size, color, uniformity of shape, general appearance, maturity, and absence of defects are evaluated to assign grades to fresh produce. The USDA grades for fresh fruits and vegetables are U.S. Extra Fancy, U.S. Fancy, U.S. No. 1, U.S. No. 2, and U.S. No. 3. Not all grades are used for every fruit and vegetable classification, and not all fruits and vegetables are graded.

Several factors should be considered before specifying a grade when purchasing fruits and vegetables.

- Purchasing top-quality grades at the peak of harvest may not add the same value as during nonpeak times. Availability, price, quality, and appearance of fresh produce is best at peak harvest.
- Suppliers rarely sell all grades of produce. Communicating standards and product expectations to suppliers may achieve quality and value objectives.
- Suppliers may sell their products under a name or grade that is different from the USDA grade.
- For products in which exterior appearance is important (i.e., individual fruit sales), the top-quality grade, which usually has the highest cost, may be appropriate. If skin appearance is not important (i.e., apples for applesauce), a lower-quality grade with a lower cost should be specified.

TABLE 5.8 Categories of fish and shellfish

TABLE 5.8 Categories of fish and shellfish

CEPHALOPODS

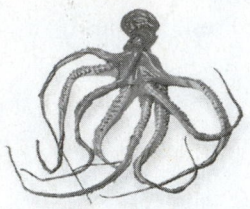
Octopus

Squid

- Tentacles attached directly to head.
- No hard outer shell, single internal shell called a cuttlebone.

CRUSTACEANS

Crayfish

Blue Crab

Maine Lobster

Shrimp

Stone Crab Claws

- Hard, joined outer shell.

FISH

- *Aberdeen cuts:* Rhombus-shaped cuts from a block of frozen fish. Usually breaded and battered. Also called *diamond cuts, French cuts.*
- *Bits or nuggets:* Small pieces of fish breaded or coated with batter. (See Note.) Round, square, or irregular shape. May be from solid fish or minced.
- *Boneless fillet:* Pin bones removed. U.S. federal grade standards allow for an occasional small bone in Grade A fillets.
- *Drawn fish:* Have entrails, gills, and scales removed.
- *Fillet:* Slice of fish of irregular size and shape. Cut made parallel to backbone. Weight varies, 2–12 oz.
- *Fingers:* Irregular pieces usually breaded or battered. Weight varies, 1–3 oz.
- *Fish sticks:* Rectangles cut from frozen block, usually 2 × 3 inches, 1–2 oz each, breaded or battered.
- *Headed and gutted:* Head, tails, fins, and viscera removed.
- *Portioned cuts:* Usually square or rectangular, cut from a block of frozen fish. Weights vary. Unbreaded or breaded.
- *Steaks:* Slices of dressed fish, ready for cooking. Usually from a large fish such as halibut, salmon, swordfish.
- *Whole or round fish:* Sold just as they come from the water. (See Note.)

MOLLUSKS

Abalone

Bluepoint Oysters

Cherrystones

Clams Mussels

Sea Scallops

- Soft-bodied shellfish covered by a shell.
- Univalves such as abalone, snails, and conch are single shelled.
- Bivalves are characterized by two shells joined by a hinge such as clams, mussels, scallops.

Notes: • Standard on breaded portions is 25% breading, 75% fish when raw; 35% breading, 65% fish when oven finished. Battered portions are typically 50% batter and 50% fish.
• Approximate yields: whole or round fish, 50%; headed and gutted fish, 70%; steaks, 90%; fillets and portions, 100%.

TABLE 5.9   Fish buying guide

Species	Fat or lean	Usual market forms	Characteristics
Bass, sea	Fat	Fillets, steaks, whole, pan-dressed	Flaky, white; rich flavor
Bluefish	Fat	Fillets	Dark, turning light when cooked; mild
Catfish	Lean	Whole, dressed, fillets	Firm flesh; abundant flavor (freshwater fish)
Cod	Lean	Fillets, steaks, breaded portions	Mild flavor; soft white meat, flakes easily
Dolphin (mahi-mahi)	Lean	Fillets	Firm, white meat, flaky; delicate flavor
Flounder	Lean	Whole, pan-dressed, fillets, breaded	Delicate flavor; white flesh
Grouper	Lean	Whole, steaks, fillets	Firm white flesh; mild
Haddock	Lean	Whole, steaks, fillets, breaded portions	Firm white flesh; mild
Halibut	Lean	Steaks, fillets	Fine texture, snow white; mild delicate flavor
Monkfish	Lean	Fillets, tail only	Very firm, white flesh; mild flavor
Orange roughy	Lean	Fillets	Snow-white flesh; delicate, almost bland flavor
Perch, lake	Lean	Dressed, fillets	Firm flesh; sweet flavor (freshwater fish)
Perch, ocean	Lean	Whole, fillets, breaded fillets and portions	Firm, white, flaky; mild flavor
Pike, walleye	Lean	Whole, fillets, round	Snowy white meat; sweet flavor (freshwater fish)
Pollock	Lean	Fillets, breaded, portions	Firm, white; mild flavor
Pompano	Fat	Whole, fillets	Firm, white; full flavor
Redfish	Lean	Whole, fillets	Light firm flesh; sweet flavor
Red snapper	Lean	Dressed, fillets, portions	Firm white flesh, flaky; mild, sweet flavor
Salmon, Atlantic	Fat	Dressed, steaks	Firm flesh, rich pink color; distinctive rich flavor
Salmon, coho (or Silver)	Fat	Drawn, dressed, steaks, fillets	Firm flesh, pinkish flesh; distinctive salmon flavor
Salmon, king (or chinook)	Fat	Drawn, dressed, steaks, fillets	Firm flesh, red-orange, flaky, distinctive rich flavor
Scrod (small cod or haddock)	Lean	Fillets, steaks, breaded portions	Firm, white flesh; mild
Shark	Fat	Steaks	Firm texture, white flesh; mild
Sole	Lean	Whole, fillets	Firm white flesh; delicate flavor
Swordfish	Fat	Steaks	Very firm texture, white when cooked; sweet
Tilapia	Lean	Whole, fillets	Firm texture, white; sweet flavor (farm raised only)
Trout, lake	Fat	Whole, drawn, fillets	Firm texture; rich flavor (freshwater fish)
Trout, rainbow	Lean	Whole, dressed, boned, fillets	Light delicate flesh; mild flavor (freshwater fish)
Tuna (ahi)	Fat	Steaks	Very firm, light gray when cooked; mild flavor
Turbot	Lean	Fillets	Firm, white; mild flavor
Whitefish	Fat	Whole, drawn, dressed, fillets	Tender white flesh; rich flavor (freshwater fish)
Whiting	Lean	Drawn, fillets, breaded portions	Firm texture, abundant flavor

Market forms—Following are the most common market forms of shellfish.

Clams—Clams are available alive in the shell; shucked, fresh or frozen; and canned, whole or chopped.

Crabs—Crabs may be purchased alive, but most are marketed cooked and frozen in the shell, as crab legs or claws, or as frozen or canned crab meat.

Lobsters—Northern lobsters are marketed alive in the shell or as cooked meat, fresh or frozen. Rock or spiny lobsters are marketed only as lobster tails, usually individually quick-frozen (IQF).

Oysters—Oysters are marketed alive in the shell; shucked, fresh or frozen; and canned. Eastern oysters are larger and more readily available than Pacific oysters. Sizes of Eastern and Gulf oysters are given in Table 5.10.

TABLE 5.10   Market sizes for oysters

EASTERN AND GULF OYSTERS

Size	Count per gallon	Pacific oyster sizes[a]
Counts or extra large	160 or less	Extra large
Extra selects or large	160–210	Large
Selects or medium (preferred for frying)	210–300	Medium
Standards or small	300–500	Small
Very small	Over 500	Extra small

[a]Pacific oysters generally do not require count-per-gallon sizing.
Based on information from the National Fisheries Institute, Washington, D.C.

TABLE 5.11 Count and descriptive names for raw shrimp (not peeled)

Name	Count per pound
Extra colossal	Less than 10
Colossal	10–15
Extra jumbo	16–20
Jumbo	21–25
Extra large	26–30
Large	31–35
Medium large	36–42
Medium	43–50
Small	51–60
Extra small	More than 60

Notes: • Count per pound is the most descriptive and accurate way to specify size.
• Shrimp are available raw or cooked, fresh or frozen, shelled or in the shell. Raw shrimp in the shell are called green shrimp. *Peeled and deveined* (P&D) shrimp have both the shell and sand vein removed. *Peeled, deveined, and cooked* (P&DC) shrimp have been cooked. Other terms used to specify the method of processing: *butterfly* (also called split or fantail), in which shrimp have been cut along the vein; *butterfly breaded*, split partway through on vein side, spread open, breaded; *whole breaded*, headless, usually deveined and with or without tail.
• *Prawn* is the name given to larger shrimp designated as jumbo or larger.

TABLE 5.12 Shellfish buying guide

Common name	Usual market forms	Characteristics
Abalone	Meat in shell	Tough flesh; delicate sweet flavor
Clams, quahog	Bushel, shucked	Large size, hard shell, chewy; not as sweet as other clams
Clams, littleneck	Bushel	Small; sweet
Clams, cherrystone	Bushel	Slightly larger than littleneck; sweet
Clams, soft-shell	Bushel, shucked	Tender; sweet
Conch	Bushel	Very firm, chewy texture; sweet flavor
Crabs, blue, hard-shell	Bushel, frozen meat	Tender; sweet
Crabs, blue, soft-shell	Dozen	Tender; sweet
Crabs, rock	Bushel	Firm texture; sweet claw meat
Crabs, Dungeness	Whole	Firm texture; very sweet white meat
Crabs, king	Legs only	Firm texture; sweet white meat
Lobsters	Whole	Firm texture; very sweet flavor
Lobsters, spiny	Tails only	Firm texture, stringy; sweet
Mussels	Bushel	Slightly tough texture; sweet
Oysters	Bushel/sack/gallon	Range from firm to tender; slightly salty
Scallops, ocean/bay	Gallon	Tender; sweet (see Note)
Shrimp	By count (see Table 5.11)	Firm texture; white sweet meat

Note: Large sea or ocean scallops are graded in sizes from 10–70 count per pound; bay scallops are smaller and graded in sizes from 70–120 per pound.

TABLE 5.13 Receiving and storing fresh fish and shellfish

Receiving	Storing
• Odor: Fresh, clean, sea smell, not strong and fishy. • Eyes: Clear and slightly bulged, not cloudy or sunken. • Gills: Bright red to maroon and moist, not slimy. • Flesh and texture: Shiny with no brownish or yellowish discoloration. Firm and elastic. • Fins, scales, skin: Fins and tails should be moist and flexible scales firmly attached. Fish without scales should be slick and moist. • Movement: Shellfish should be live. Lobster and crab should be active and move about. Mollusks should be tightly closed or snap shut when tapped.	• Stored between 30°F and 34°F. Fresh fish used within 2–3 days. • Place fresh fish in perforated pan placed inside a solid pan and pack with shaved or chipped ice. Drain and add ice as needed to keep fish surrounded in ice and away from water. • Mollusks should not be iced. Keep in same bags or boxes as delivered. Will stay alive for 5–7 days. • Crabs and lobster should be delivered wrapped in moist seaweed or damp paper. Refrigerate but do not ice. • Discard shellfish if they are not alive or if shells are cracked or broken. Live shellfish will close when tapped. Lobsters and crabs should move about.

Fresh-cut or precleaned produce is used in many food-service operations and is one of the fastest-growing segments of the produce industry. Because of the large demand and the production capabilities of large produce processors, the cost of some fresh-cut produce may be less than that of its uncut counterparts. When evaluating suppliers, it is important to ask questions about the reputation of the processors and to ask for documentation that they follow an approved HACCP plan. Assurance should be provided that safe raw produce is processed correctly in a clean, cold processing facility and distributed in a way that quality and product safety standards are met.

Table 4.3 provides yield, availability, and storage information for fresh fruits and vegetables. This table provides information for calculating the amount of AP (as purchased) fruits and vegetables needed to yield the EP (edible portion) weight specified in a recipe. The information may also be used to calculate the approximate EP yield from AP fruits and vegetables. Because fruits and vegetables vary in size and quality and because processing procedures and techniques differ, the EP yields in this table are approximate. The following example demonstrates EP and AP calculations.

When EP is known

- To calculate the amount of AP product needed to yield a specified amount of EP product, divide the desired EP weight by the figure given in the table.

For example, the recipe for Mashed Potatoes on p. 798 specifies 12 lb EP potatoes. To calculate the amount of potatoes to purchase (AP), divide 12 lb by the number associated with white potatoes in Table 4.3 ($12 \div 0.81 = 14.8$ lb). In this example, 15 lb potatoes would be purchased in order to yield the 12 lb peeled potatoes specified in the recipe. See Appendix D for more examples.

When AP is known

- To calculate the amount of EP product that AP product will yield, multiply the AP weight by the figure given in the table.

For example, to calculate the amount of peeled potatoes that a 15-lb bag of AP potatoes will yield, multiply the number associated with white potatoes by 15 lb ($15 \times 0.81 = 12.15$ lb). In this example, 15 lb potatoes will yield 12 lb peeled potatoes. See Appendix D for more examples.

Fresh Fruit—Pre-Preparation Guidelines and General Information

A variety of fresh fruits is available year-round to be used as ingredients in food products or as stand-alone menu items. Regardless of how fresh fruit is used, it must be handled and prepared in a way that retains its quality characteristics. The following information will help foodservice operators serve the highest quality fruit.

Apples

- Wash, pare, core, and remove bruises and spots. If the skins are tender and color appropriate, do not pare. See Exhibit 7 in the colored inserts.
- To dice, cut into rings and dice with a sectional cutter. Drop the diced pieces into salad dressing, lemon, pineapple, or other acid fruit juice to prevent discoloration. If diced apple is placed in fruit juice, drain before using in a salad.
- To section, cut into uniform pieces, with the widest part of the section not more than $\frac{1}{2}$ inch thick. Remove the core from each section. See Table 5.14 for varieties that are commonly available.

Apricots

- Wash before cutting by carefully and very quickly rinsing in cool water. Cut into halves or sections and remove the pit. Apricots are not usually peeled. They are most flavorful served at room temperature.

Avocados

- Wash before cutting. Peel as close to serving time as possible. To prevent browning, dip into dressing or lemon juice.
- To remove pit, cut the avocado in half and, while grasping both halves, carefully rotate the halves in opposite directions (the pit will remain in one half). Remove the pit from the avocado half by striking the pit sharply with the cutting edge of a chef's knife and rotating the knife and pit to loosen the pit. See Exhibit 9 in the colored inserts.
- Peel the leathery skin from the pulp. Serve avocados by the half or cut into cubes, slices, or other shape. If not served soon after cutting, dip avocado in lemon juice to keep it from turning brown. Avocados are botanically a fruit, but are usually served as a vegetable.

Bananas

- Wash before cutting or serving as whole fruit. As close to serving time as possible, remove skins and bruised or discolored parts.
- Cut into strips, sections, or slices. Dip each piece in pineapple juice or other acid fruit juice to prevent discoloration. (Also see Plantains.)

Berries

- Wash berries (except cranberries) by carefully and very quickly dipping into cool water and draining completely in a single layer. Wash just before using, as they soften quickly after washing. Do not let them soak in water. Cranberries are not fragile and should be thoroughly rinsed before using. See Table 5.14 for fruit varieties that are commonly available. See Exhibit 7 in the colored inserts for preparing strawberry fans.

TABLE 5.14 Varieties of common fruits

Fruit	Description
APPLES	
Braeburn	Red to red with greenish gold areas on the skin. Eating out of hand; salads.
Fuji	Red to yellow-green with red highlights. Sweet and spicy flavor. Eating out of hand; cooking.
Gala	Heart-shaped. Yellow-orange color with red stripes. Crisp and sweet. Eating out of hand; salads.
Golden Delicious	Yellow-green with freckling. Sweet and firm. All-purpose; eating out of hand; salads; cooking.
Granny Smith	Bright green with pink blush. Very crisp; tart. All-purpose; eating out of hand; salads; cooking.
Honeycrisp	Red mottled over a yellow background. Good holding qualities. Eating out of hand.
Jonathan	Bright red, firm, juicy, tart to acidic. Cooking; eating out of hand.
McIntosh	Mostly red with some green. Slightly tart to acidic. Cooking; eating out of hand; salads.
Northern Spy	Green and dark red. Firm, juicy, tart. Pies.
Pink Lady	Oblong, green fruit turns yellow at maturity, skin overlaid with pink or light red. Fine-grained, white flesh. Eating out of hand.
Red Delicious	Deep red, speckled with yellow. Mild, sweet juicy. Eating out of hand; salads.
Rome Beauty	Bright red, tart-sweet, firm. Baking; cooking.
Winesap	Bright red, tart-sweet, firm. All-purpose for baking; cooking.
BERRIES	
Blackberries	Deep purple to black; larger than raspberries. Loganberries, marionberries, and boysenberries are blackberry hybrids. Sweet to tart, depending on variety.
Blueberries	Dark blue or purple; dusty silver-blue bloom. Firm; range from pea to thumbnail size.
Cranberries	Shiny; round; firm; red to maroon in color. White flesh; distinct sour-tart flavor.
Currants	Tiny fruit; grows in grapelike clusters; black, red (most common), or white in color. Dried currants are made from a variety of grapes and not from currants.
Raspberries	Dime to small quarter size; very fine hairs on surface; red (most common) color; also golden and black. Cloudberries and dewberries are types of raspberries.
Strawberries	Shiny red, heart-shaped. Ranges in size from quarter to nearly egg size.
CITRUS	
Grapefruits	*White grapefruit* has light yellow flesh; *pink/red grapefruit* flesh varies from light rosy pink to ruby red. Softball sized; should be heavy for its size. Tart; pink grapefruit is usually sweeter than white.
Kumquats	Small; oblong-shaped; bright golden-orange. Sweet thin skin and tart flesh are both edible. Fresh whole or sliced for garnishing meats and fruit platters; also for preserves and marmalades.
Lemons	Oval-shaped fruit; bright yellow to yellow-green skin. Tart flavor; not generally eaten raw. *Meyer lemons* are sweeter than regular lemons; superior for delicate desserts.
Limes	Similar shape to a lemon but smaller. Skin ranges in color from dark to light green. *Key limes* are thin-skinned; light yellow-green color; sweet tart flavor. *Persian limes* are dark green; thin, smooth, shiny skin; sweet-tart flavor.
Oranges	Round fruit; orange skin or peel; orange flesh. *Navel oranges* are juicy and sweet; few seeds; have the thickest skin of all oranges; easy to peel. *Valencia oranges* are juicy and sweet with some seeds and thin skin. *Blood oranges* have a thin orange-red skin and dark maroon-red flesh that may look streaked. Blood oranges are smaller than other oranges.
Tangerines/tangelos/ mandarins	All have red-orange skin and resemble an orange. *Tangerine* skin is loosely attached and easy to peel. Sweet, mellow flavor; with seeds. *Tangelos* (a grapefruit-tangerine hybrid) are characterized by a knoblike formation at stem end; tart-sweet flavor; few seeds. *Mandarins* are rounder and larger than tangerines; peel easily; are tart or tart-sweet; may have some seeds. *Clementines* are the tiniest of the mandarins; small, very sweet, and usually seedless.
GRAPES	
Champagne	Very small, seedless, in tight clusters; easy to strip from tender stems; red to light purple. Often used on fruit and cheese platters or as a garnish.
Green/White Table	Thompson Seedless is a leading variety. Crisp texture and sweet flavor.
Red Table	Red Flame Seedless is a leading variety. Slightly tart flavor. Variegated color.
Purple/Black	Seed-in varieties include Concord, Red Emperor, and Ribier.
MELON	
Cantaloupe/Muskmelon	Round, cream-colored rind with netting or webbing; peach-colored flesh. When ripe, stem end is smooth and slightly depressed.
Casaba	Large, rounded, yellow, slightly ridged rind; creamy white flesh.

continued

TABLE 5.14 Varieties of common fruits

TABLE 5.14   continued

TABLE 5.14   Varieties of common fruits

Fruit	Description
Crenshaw	Large, rounded, slightly pointed stem end; smooth golden-green rind; golden-pink to creamy white flesh.
Honeydew	Large, rounded, smooth creamy yellow-green rind; light green flesh. Orange-fleshed honeydew flavor similar to cantaloupe.
Juan Canary	Oblong shaped, yellow rind; creamy white flesh.
Persian	Globe shaped; dark to light-green rind (turns lighter as it ripens) with light brown netting. Pink-orange flesh.
Santa Claus	Oblong shaped; mottled green and yellow rind. Light green flesh.
Watermelon	Large, round or oblong shaped; light to dark green rind. Most commonly has red flesh with black mature seeds. Also with yellow to bright orange flesh. Some seedless.

PEARS

Anjou	Egg shaped; thin light green skin that does not change color when ripe. Slightly sharp lemony flavor. Cream to ivory-colored flesh. Eating out of hand; with cheese; slicing in salads; poached.
Asian	Also called Chinese pear. Apple shape; yellow skin. Apple texture with pear flavor.
Bartlett	Bell shaped; thin green skin turning yellow when ripe. Juicy; sweet. Eating out of hand; with cheese; baking. Red variety available.
Bosc	Symmetrical rounded body with elongated neck; skin earthy brown with russeting. Good for eating out of hand, poaching, and baking.
Comice	Squat chubby shape with short neck and stem; skin greenish yellow, some red blush. Flesh ivory color; very soft and creamy texture; abundantly full of juice. Excellent for eating out of hand; with cheese; sliced into salads.

PLUMS

Black Frier	Dark purple with silvery bloom.
Damson	Small with light purple or reddish skin; green flesh. Good for pies.
Greengage	Green skin; yellow-green flesh.
Santa Rosa	Purple-crimson skin; light yellow or amber flesh.

Cherries

- Wash by submerging and swishing in cool water. After washing, drain completely, cut in half, and remove the pit or use a cherry pitter.

Citrus

- All citrus fruits should be washed before cutting or serving as whole fruit.

- Citrus fruits are characterized by juicy pulp and a rind, with only the *zest* (thin outer portion) having the fruit's characteristic color and oils that add flavor and aroma to foods. (See Exhibit 7 in the colored inserts.) The rind's *pith* (thick inner portion) is bitter and not used in recipes. See Table 5.14 for citrus fruit varieties that are commonly available.

- To section grapefruit, cut off a thick layer of skin from the top and bottom. Place the grapefruit on a cutting board, start at the top, and cut toward the board (Exhibit VII). Always cut with a downward stroke and deeply enough to remove the pith. Turn the grapefruit while cutting. When paring is completed and pulp is exposed, remove sections by cutting along the membrane of one section to the center of the fruit. Citrus fruit other than grapefruit may be sectioned, but generally the membrane between sections is not removed.

- Grapes should be washed thoroughly by submerging and swishing in cool water once or twice and draining completely.

Small clusters can be cut from the larger clusters by using a kitchen shears or sharp knife. Grapes may be seedless or with seeds. When fresh, grapes are firmly attached to the stem and have no browning where attached to the stem. See Table 5.14 for varieties that are commonly available.

Kiwi

- Wash before cutting by rinsing quickly in cool water. Remove the fuzzy skin with a very sharp paring knife. Slice, chop, dice, or cut into wedges. Kiwi may be cut in half cross-wise without peeling and served with a spoon to dip out the pulp.

Mango

- Wash before cutting by rinsing quickly in cool water. Cut in half by carefully sliding a sharp knife along both sides of the flat side of the seed. Scoop the flesh out of the shell. To cut into chunks, peel back the skin from each mango half and cut as desired. See Exhibit 7 in the colored inserts.

Melons

- Because melon grows directly on the ground and the rind can harbor disease-causing bacteria, thoroughly wash melons before cutting. Melons with a hollow cavity filled with seeds should be cut in half and the seeds scooped out. Cut in wedges (skin on or off), dice, cube, or make into balls using a melon ball cutter or spoon. Melon served with the rind on should not be stacked in a way that the rind comes in contact with the flesh that will be eaten. Store melon at 40°F or below. See Table 5.14 for melon varieties that are commonly available.

Nectarines

• Wash before cutting or serving as whole fruit by rinsing in cool water, being careful not to bruise. To remove the pit, cut the flesh in half completely to the pit. While grasping both halves, carefully rotate the halves in opposite directions to separate them. Remove the pit. Cut the flesh into wedges or slices. Drop into acid fruit juice to prevent discoloration. Nectarines are similar to peaches in shape, color, and flavor. They are smooth skinned and usually not peeled.

Papaya

• Wash before cutting. Cut papaya in half lengthwise and scoop out the seeds if desired, or leave them in as they are edible. For rings, carefully scoop out the seeds after cutting the papaya into circles.

Peaches

• Wash before cutting or serving as whole fruit by rinsing in cool water, being careful not to bruise. Remove the pit and smooth fuzzy skin just before serving. Dip pared fruit into acid fruit juice to prevent discoloration. Flesh ranges in color from white to creamy yellow to yellow-orange. When ripe, the fruit is soft, fragrant, and sweet to slightly tart, depending on variety. To remove the pit, cut the fruit in half and, while grasping both halves, carefully rotate the halves in opposite directions.

Pears

• Wash before cutting or serving as whole fruit by rinsing in cool water, being careful not to bruise. Peel and remove the core and seeds a short time before serving. Cut into halves, wedges, or slices. Dip the cut surface of the fruit into an acid fruit juice to prevent discoloration. See Table 5.14 for varieties that are commonly available.

Persimmons

• Wash before cutting. This round, squat-shaped fruit with a green leafy stem is the size of a small baseball and has pale orange to bright orange-red skin. The *fuyu* variety has a crunchy texture similar to that of an apple and can be eaten raw, sliced into salads, or puréed and used as an ingredient in baked goods. The pulp of the softer variety, *hachiya*, is astringent and best suited for use as an ingredient in baked goods.

Pineapple

• Wash before cutting. Pineapple is characterized by a dry, crisp shell and dark green leaves. Its color ranges from greenish-brown to golden-brown; the flesh is firm and light yellow with a sweet to sweet-acidic flavor. Pineapple does not continue to ripen once picked. See Exhibit 7 in the colored inserts for instructions on how to clean fresh pineapple.

Plantains

• Wash before cutting. Plantains are a banana-shaped fruit with thick greenish-yellow skin that darkens when ripe; it can be used at various stages of ripeness. In its green stage, the flesh is starchy similar to a potato or squash. When ripe, the plantain is sweet and starchy.

Plums

• Wash before cutting or serving as whole fruit by rinsing in cool water, being careful not to bruise. Plums range in shape from oblong to round and in flavor from sweet to tart. See Table 5.14 for varieties that are commonly available.

Pomegranates

• Remove the edible seeds by first cutting off the top of the pomegranate, then cutting the fruit into quarters. Work with one quarter at a time and submerge in a large bowl of water. Rub the seeds from the white pith. The seeds will sink to the bottom of the bowl. Remove and drain in a fine-hole colander or sieve. One large pomegranate will yield ⅔–¾ cup edible seeds.

Fresh Vegetables—Pre-Preparation Guidelines and General Information

Fresh vegetables add color, flavor, and texture to an array of menu items and must be prepared in a way to enhance their quality attributes. The following information will be useful for production staff when preparing fresh vegetables. Most fresh vegetables are pictured in Exhibits 8 and 10 in the colored inserts.

Artichokes

• Wash in cool water. Cut 1 inch off the top. Cut off the stem and bottom leaves. Trim the outer leaves, if necessary. With a melon ball cutter or spoon, remove and discard the fuzzy center core (choke). Immediately dip the cut flesh into lemon juice to prevent discoloration. The choke can also be removed after cooking.

Arugula

• Carefully trim tough stems from leaves (the leaves bruise easily). Wash the leaves by immersing in cool water. Repeat as necessary. Drain. See Table 5.15.

Asparagus

• Break or cut off the tough ends of stalks. Thoroughly wash the remaining portions in cool water. Remove lower scales if they harbor sand. The lower part of the stalks may be peeled. For blanched asparagus, immerse in boiling water

TABLE 5.15   Descriptions of greens for cooking, salad greens, and lettuces

GREENS FOR COOKING

Beet	Thin, deep red stems, flat green leaves, red ribs in leaves. Cook mature tops; use young, tender beet tops in salads.
Collard	Wide, flat, green leaves.
Dandelion	Thin white stems. Dark green, ragged-edged leaves.
Kale	A hardy dark-green curly leaf that may be cooked. More often used for decorative purposes as a salad bar garnish. Flowering kale makes a decorative salad bar garnish with its large, ruffle-edged leaves and attractive color varying from green to cream to violet.
Mustard	Long narrow stems. Large green curly leaves. Slightly bitter and spicy (hot).
Spinach	Dark-green, crinkled leaves with a bold flavor. More mature leaves are best when cooked.
Swiss chard (green and red)	Thick white (green chard) or red (red/ruby chard) stems; dark-green, large wrinkled leaves, with prominent white or bright red veins.
Turnip	Long, narrow green stems. Flat, green, and slightly fuzzy leaves.

SALAD GREENS AND LETTUCES

Arugula or rocket	Small, narrow, tender, smooth, notched leaves with a dark-green color and spicy peppery flavor. Small leaves are the mildest. Combines well with mild-flavored greens. May be considered an herb.
Bibb lettuce or limestone lettuce	Small cup-shaped lettuce with a deep rich green color that blends into whitish green near the core. Flavor is buttery and sweet. Texture delicate and tender. Similar to but smaller and more delicate than Boston lettuce.
Boston lettuce	Soft, pliable, fragile leaf. Delicate sweet flavor. Not as tender or sweet as Bibb lettuce. Deep green outside, blending to light yellow to nearly white near the core. Bruises easily and does not keep well.
Cabbage	*Green:* Pale green, tough, crisp leaves generally used in slaws. Round, compact head. *Napa (Chinese cabbage):* Pale green to white with tightly packed crinkled leaves. Mild flavor. *Red:* Purple, crisp leaves; may be used with other greens to add color. Round, compact head. Sweeter than green cabbage. *Savoy:* Light green, crinkly leaves with a delicate cabbage flavor. Loosely compact round head. Use sparingly in a tossed salad.
Endive (Belgian or French)	Characterized by an elongated stock of narrow, lightly packed leaves, resembling a spearhead (4–6 inches long). Off white or pale green in color. Turns greener when exposed to light. Mild, slightly bitter flavor and waxy texture. Served typically as a small, separate course salad or as a decorative component of an arranged salad.
Endive (curly) or chicory	A bunchy head with narrow, ragged-edged leaves. Mild center leaves, bitter outer leaves. Use sparingly in combination salads. Primarily used for garnishing or as a base.
Escarole	A variety of endive with broad leaves that do not curl at the tips. Texture is coarse and slightly tough, flavor somewhat bitter. Mix sparingly with other greens.
Frisée	Similar to curly endive. Feathery, thin, spiky leaves. Pale yellow interior leaves, green outer leaves. Less bitter than curly endive. Crisp, crunchy, and mildly peppery.
Iceberg (head lettuce)	Firm, round, compact head, bright to light green in color. Crisp leaves with a mild, delicate flavor. Stays crisp longer than most other lettuces. Mixes well with other greens; can be used for an underliner.
Leaf lettuce	Soft, fragile leaves, most with curly edges and crisp delicate texture. Bunched tightly. Red leaf or green leaf. Red leaf is tinged with red along the edges. Mixes well with other greens; used in sandwiches or as an underliner. Wilts easily and does not keep well.
Mâche	Small, round, spoon-shaped leaf with a sweet nutty flavor and delicate texture. Mix with other young tender greens.
Mesclun	Not a leaf but a mixture of tender, small lettuces. Available as a mixture in some markets.
Red oak leaf	Narrow leaves with deep scalloping. Resembles an oak leaf. Very tender with a nutty flavor. Green oak (lime green); red oak (dark red).
Radicchio	Small, round, compact head similar to iceberg lettuce. Maroon-red leaves with white ribs or veins and a bitter peppery taste. Combine sparingly with mild, tender greens.
Romaine or cos	Long, loaf-shaped head with long, narrow leaves. Coarse, dark-green outer leaves and greenish-yellow to light green inner ones. Very crisp texture, tender and sweet.
Spinach	Dark green, crinkled leaves with a bold flavor. Small, young tender leaves are best for salads. Tougher, more mature leaves can be cooked.
Watercress	Dark green, small, glossy leaves with a pungent, peppery flavor. Use as a garnish, in sandwiches, or mixed with tender leaf greens.

TABLE 5.15   Descriptions of greens for cooking, salad greens, and lettuces

for 2 minutes. Remove quickly and dip in ice-cold water. Drain. Use blanched asparagus on fresh vegetable platters.

Beans (any tender variety)

- Wash in cool water and trim the ends by cutting or snapping them off. Some varieties have tough strings that should be removed. For blanched beans, immerse in boiling water for $1\frac{1}{2}$–2 minutes. Remove quickly and dip in ice-cold water. Drain.

Beets

- Wash in cool water. Trim off the leaves, leaving 1 inch of stem and root remaining. Beets can be peeled before cooking but are most often peeled after cooking, when the peels slip off easily. Beet tops may be cooked as greens or, if small and tender, used in salads. The red variety is sweeter and more common than the golden variety. For beet greens, see Table 5.15.

Bok choy

- Cut off the stem end and separate the stalks. Wash in cool water. Trim off wilted or brown leaves. Bok choy has a bulb-like base with thick, tightly packed, celery-like stalks and large, dark-green leaves. It has a mild flavor, similar to cabbage, and is used for stir-fry, in soups, and as a main ingredient in Korean kimchi.

Broccoli

- Wash by immersing in cool water. Trim off blemished outer leaves and woody ends of stalks. For florets, separate florets from the stalk. Peel stalks if desired. Split or slice large stalks to help them cook evenly. See Exhibit 9 in the colored inserts.

Brussels sprouts

- Trim stem end, remove tough or dry outer leaves, and wash in cool water. Brussels sprouts have small, round heads with dark-green compact leaves. Slice for soups or cook whole. For even cooking, cut a cross in the stem end.

Cabbage

- Remove tough or dry outer leaves. Wash heads in cool water and cut into four to six pieces through the stem end. Remove the hard, white center core. Shred or cut as desired. Crisp in ice water for 15–30 minutes. Drain well. See Table 5.15.

Carrots

- Trim top and root end. Wash in cool water; peel off outer skin.

Cauliflower

- Remove all leaves and cut away dark spots. Wash in cool water. To separate florets, cut around the thick white core by using a paring knife to make a circular cut around the core.

Separate into florets, using your hands to break them apart. White is the predominant color; there are also green and purple varieties. See Exhibit 9 in the colored inserts.

Celery

- Trim any tough or dry portions from both ends of the stalks. Separate outer stalks from the heart. Use the outer stalks and leaves for stock, soup, and mirepoix. Wash in cool water, trim, and remove bruised or blemished parts. If desired, peel to remove strings. To *dice*, cut lengthwise. Several stalks can be cut at one time. Place on board and cut crosswise with a French knife. For celery *curls* or fans, cut celery into $2\frac{1}{2}$-inch lengths. Make lengthwise cuts $\frac{1}{8}$ inch apart about 1 inch long on one or both ends of celery strips. Place in ice water for about 2 hours before serving. For celery *rings*, cut celery into 2-inch lengths and then into pieces $\frac{1}{8}$ inch thick. Place in ice water for several hours. Each strip of celery will form a ring.

Celery root (celeriac)

- Wash in cool water and peel. Celery root is a bulb-shaped root that can be served raw in salads or cooked in soups, stews, and stir-fry. It has a crisp texture and celery-like flavor.

Chard, Swiss

- Use a chef's knife to cut (separate) leaves from the stems. Wash both stems and leaves by immersing in cool water. Repeat washing until all grit is gone. Trim any brown or blemished portions. See Table 5.15.

Collard greens

- Use a chef's knife to cut stems away from both sides of the leaves. Discard tough stems. Wash the leaves by immersing in cool water. Chop as desired. See Table 5.15.

Corn

- Remove the husk and stalk end. Rinse in cool water to remove the silklike fibers that surround the ear. Trim ends as required. Grilled corn may be cooked with the husk on.

Cress

- Separate the leaves for thorough washing. Wash in a spray of water or by immersing in cool water. Drain thoroughly. If gritty, repeat washing until grit is gone. Cress is a hot, peppery leaf that resembles radish leaves.

Cucumbers

- Wash in cool water. Peel or score lengthwise with a fork. Peel if cucumbers are waxed. If desired, cut in half lengthwise and scoop out seeds with a spoon. Dice or cut into slices, wedges, or spears. Crisp by placing sliced cucumbers in salted ice water for 30 minutes, drain, and rinse.

Daikon radish (Japanese or Oriental radish)

- Wash in cool water and peel. Daikon is a long, white, carrot-shaped root that can be served raw in salads or cooked in soups and stir-fries. It has a hot radish flavor.

Eggplant

- Wash in cool water and remove the stem and green cap. Eggplant can be served peeled or unpeeled. Slice lengthwise into strips or crosswise into rounds. Purple and white eggplants are spherical or egg-shaped and vary in size. Japanese eggplant is small and slender with a light to medium purple color. Good-quality eggplants are light in weight in relationship to size.

Endive, Belgian or French

- Trim and discard any decayed or wilted outer leaves. Wash by immersing in cool water very quickly. Drain thoroughly. If served fresh, cut out the tough core. See Table 5.15.

Endive, curly

- Separate the leaves for thorough washing. Discard any tough or wilted outer leaves and tough stems. Wash in a spray of water or by immersing in cool water. Drain thoroughly. If gritty, repeat washing until grit is gone. See Table 5.15.

Escarole

- Wash as for curly endive. See Table 5.15.

Fennel

- Trim stalks from the bulb and leaves; discard or use in stock. Wash by immersing in cool water. Drain thoroughly. Fennel has a distinctive aniselike flavor that becomes milder when cooked. The bulb is white and round with short celery-like stalks. It can be eaten raw or cooked (baked, grilled, steamed, sautéed). Peel and cut thin slices from the root end. Remove the core. Cut into thin wedges or long batons. The feathery leaves or fronds are used as an herb, and the seeds are used for flavoring.

Frisée

- Wash by immersing in cool water. Drain thoroughly. See Table 5.15.

Garlic

- Separate cloves from bulb. Trim root end and peel cloves. Remove and discard any sprouts from the inside of cloves.

Greens

- Greens should be clean, crisp, chilled, and well drained. It may be necessary to separate leaves for thorough washing. Discard brown or decayed leaves. Wash in a spray of water or by immersing in cool water. Repeat washing if necessary until all grit is gone. Shake off excess water, drain thoroughly, and refrigerate. Draining in a colander or on a rack placed on a baking sheet will keep the greens from standing in water while chilling. Cover with a clean damp cloth or plastic film to prevent dehydration. Table 5.15 describes common greens and lettuces.

Herbs

- Rinse in cool water. Discard brown or decayed leaves. Some recipes may require that the stems be removed from the leaves. See Table 5.18 for descriptions of commonly used herbs.

Jicama

- Peel and cut into strips, slices, cubes, or batons. Jicama are rounded in shape, with light brown skin, ivory flesh with a subtle sweet flavor, and a crisp, juicy texture. Serve raw (salads, relish tray) or cooked (stir-fry). Jicama can be substituted for water chestnuts.

Kale

- Separate leaves for thorough washing. Discard brown or decayed leaves. Wash in a spray of water or by immersing in tepid water. Drain thoroughly. For cooking, use a chef's knife to cut stems away from both sides of the leaves. Discard tough stems. Chop as desired. Kale is often used for decorative purposes as a salad bar garnish. Flowering kale makes a decorative salad bar garnish with its large, ruffle-edged leaves and attractive color varying from green to cream to violet.

Kohlrabi

- Trim and discard leaves and stalks. Peel the bulb. Wash in cool water. Cut into wedges or slice into very thin rounds. Kohlrabi is a globe-shaped root with green leaves attached by a thick stem. The bulb is similar in flavor to a turnip, and the leaves are similar to collard greens or kale. The bulb may be eaten raw; the leaves must be cooked.

Leeks

- Trim and discard the dark-green tops, tough outer leaves, and root end. Remove the root. Halve the leek lengthwise and wash thoroughly in running cool water. Leeks may need to be washed several times to remove trapped sand. If particularly sandy, let leeks soak in several changes of water. Leeks are characterized by a long thick stem and coarse drooping tops. They are a member of the green onion and shallot family and have a mild onion flavor. See Exhibit 9 in the color inserts.

Lettuce, leaf

- Trim stem and separate leaves for thorough washing. Discard brown or decayed leaves. Wash in a spray of water or by immersing in cool water (Figure 5.9). Drain thoroughly. See Table 5.15.

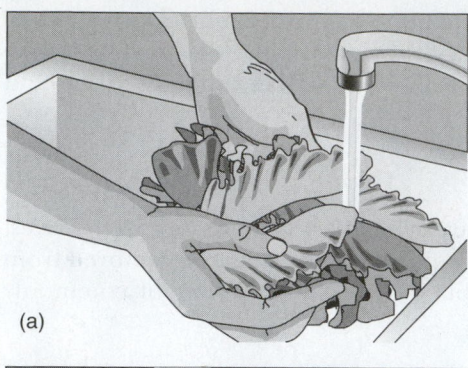
(a)

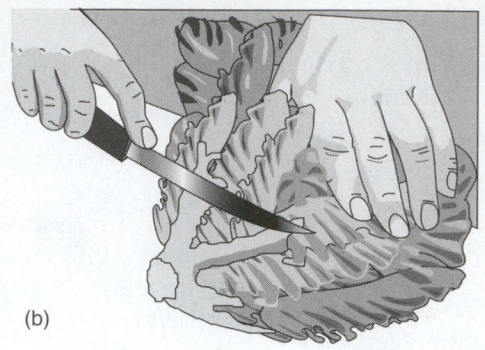
(b)

(c)

FIGURE 5.9 Preparing leaf lettuce. (a) Wash lettuce under cold running water. (b) Remove stem end by cutting with a sharp knife. (c) Place leaf end up in a perforated pan to drain. Chill 2 to 3 hours to crisp.

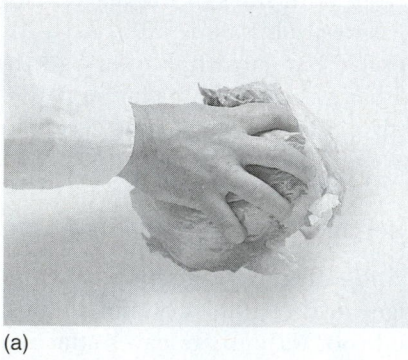
(a)

(b)

FIGURE 5.10 Coring head lettuce. (a) Hit stem end of lettuce sharply on flat surface. (b) Remove loosened core.

Lettuce, head

• Trim stem and remove any outside leaves that are wilted or brown. Immerse in cool water. Position to drain water from inside the head. To core iceberg lettuce, hit the stem end of the head sharply on a flat surface and remove the loosened core (see Figure 5.10). See Table 5.15.

Mushrooms

• Do not soak in water or scrub. Trim bottoms of stems. Wipe clean with a damp paper towel or rinse quickly in cold water just before serving or using in a recipe. Adding a small amount of acid to the water will help keep mushrooms from discoloring. See Table 5.16 and Exhibit 10 in the colored inserts for common types of mushrooms.

Napa (Chinese cabbage)

• Separate leaves for thorough washing. Wash in a spray of water or by immersing in cool water. Drain thoroughly. Napa

cabbage is oblong shaped with tightly packed, wrinkled leaves ranging in color from pale green to white. It has a mild cabbage flavor and tender crisp texture and may be eaten cooked or uncooked. See Table 5.15.

Okra

• Wash in cool water and trim the stem end. Leave whole or slice. Okra is a carrot-shaped pod ranging in length from 2 to 5 inches. It is medium to dark green in color with slight fuzz on the exterior.

Onions, green (scallions)

• Trim root end and green tops. Wash in cool water to remove dirt and sand.

Onions, mature

• Pour water over onions to cover. While they are submerged, remove the outer layer of the bulb, the firm root end, and all bruised or decayed parts. Peel without immersing in water by making a slit in the onion skin from stem end to root end and peeling away the outer layer. See Exhibit 9 in the colored inserts.

Parsnips

• Trim the tops and root tip. Wash in cool water; peel. If large and woody, split lengthwise and remove the core. Slice crosswise, dice, or cut in strips. Parsnips are a white smooth-skinned root with a carrotlike shape and range in length from 5 to 10 inches.

Peas

• Wash in cool water. Trim ends. To blanch sugar snap and snow peas, immerse in boiling water for 30 seconds or just until the peas brighten in color. Remove quickly and dip into ice water. Drain. Green peas must be shelled, and the pod is not edible. The edible pods of *sugar snap peas* are similar to but smaller than green peas. Sugar snap peas are not shelled and may be eaten raw or cooked. Strings should be removed from the pod. *Snow peas* are flat green edible pods with small immature peas inside. Pods can be eaten fresh or cooked. Snow peas open easily along the side and can be stuffed with a savory filling (leave hinged when opening). Removing the strings from the edge of the pod is optional. *Edamame* are fresh green soybeans. The pods are tough and not eaten. They may be served cold on a salad, stir-fried, or heated and served like other green peas or lima beans. Edamame resemble a small lima bean but are more rounded.

TABLE 5.16	Common types of mushrooms

AGARICUS

Description	This widely available variety of mushroom varies in color from creamy white to light brown and in size from small to jumbo. It is plump and dome shaped and is also referred to as a *button mushroom*.
Flavor/Texture	Pleasing mild woodsy flavor that intensifies when cooked. Those with open veils and darker caps are more mature and have a richer taste. Meatlike texture.
Handling	Refrigerate on arrival. Leave in shipping container until needed. Shelf life approximately 5–7 days.
Usage	Very versatile; may be used fresh or cooked. Before use, rinse quickly in cool water.

CRIMINI (ITALIAN BROWN, GOLDEN BROWN)

Description	Naturally dark cap that ranges in color from light tan to rich brown. Similar in appearance to Agaricus.
Flavor/Texture	Meatlike texture and earthy flavor is more intense than the Agaricus.
Handling	Refrigerate on arrival. Leave in shipping container until needed. Shelf life approximately 5–7 days.
Usage	Can be substituted in any recipe using white buttons when more full-bodied taste is preferred. Before use, rinse quickly in cold water.

ENOKI

Description	White in color with long stems and tiny white caps. Mushrooms are joined at the base and resemble bean sprouts.
Flavor/Texture	Light, mild sweet flavor with a crisp texture.
Handling	Refrigerate on arrival. Leave in shipping container until needed. Shelf life approximately 14 days.
Usage	Used for sandwiches, delicate salads, Asian dishes and soups, and garnishes. Trim base and separate stems. Before use, rinse quickly in cold water.

OYSTER

Description	Fluted cap resembles a fan or oyster shell. Colors range from a soft beige brown to gray.
Flavor/Texture	Delicate flavor and texture.
Handling	Carefully rotate stocks. Refrigerate in a bowl covered with slightly damp cloth. Shelf life approximately 5–7 days.
Usage	Sliced raw in salads or cooked in meat dishes. In preparations requiring extended cooking times, add mushrooms toward the end of the cooking period to preserve their delicate texture. Before use, rinse quickly in cool water.

PORTABELLA

Description	A mature crimini mushroom that is the largest of the commercially available mushrooms. May be 6 inches or more across. Large brown cap with dark brown gills.
Flavor/Texture	Meatlike, earthy flavor and meatlike texture.
Handling	Need circulating air to remain fresh. Shelf life 7–10 days.
Usage	Generally cooked. May be incorporated in a recipe or served as a center of the plate item in a meatlike fashion. Gills may be scraped out using a spoon (optional). Before use, rinse quickly in cool water.

SHIITAKE (BLACK FOREST OR GOLDEN OAK)

Description	Broad, umbrella-shaped caps, wide-open veils, and tan gills. Golden brown to dark brown in color.
Flavor/Texture	Rich, full-bodied, meaty, woodsy flavor with a spongy texture when cooked.
Handling	Refrigerate on arrival. Leave in shipping container until needed. Shelf life approximately 14 days.
Usage	Generally cooked. Tough stems should be chopped and used in stock or discarded. Before use, rinse quickly in cool water.

Note: Hundreds of varieties of edible mushrooms grow, but only a few are grown and sold commercially year-round. When in season, several wild varieties are sold locally at farmers' markets and some grocery stores. Because it is difficult to distinguish poisonous mushrooms from edible ones, fresh mushrooms should be purchased only from reputable purveyors. Some wild mushroom varieties include morels and chanterelles.

TABLE 5.16 Common types of mushrooms

Peppers, chile

- Wash. Cut off stem end. Halve the peppers from the stem end. Remove seeds and membrane (optional). **Capsaicin**, the chemical that causes the sensory reaction to hot chile peppers, is concentrated in the membrane or thin tissue that attaches the seeds to the soft, spongy, inside part of the pepper. When working with hot chiles, wear protective food-handling gloves and be careful not to touch eyes, lips, or nose. See Table 5.17 for descriptions of common peppers. See Exhibit 8 in the colored inserts.

Peppers, sweet bell

- Wash. Cut off the stem end and remove the core, seeds, and membrane. Cut into the desired shape. The most abundant colors are green, red, and yellow. To make *rings*, cut whole peppers into thin crosswise slices. To make *sticks*, cut peppers lengthwise into narrow strips. See Exhibit 9 in the colored inserts.

Potatoes

- Peel or, if peels are to be left on, scrub clean under cool running water. Remove eyes and blemishes from peeled

TABLE 5.17   **Chile pepper varieties**

Name	Description	Uses
Anaheim (also called mild green chile, green California)	Tapered, 6- to 7-inch-long pod. Deep green. Mild to medium hot. (500–1,500 SU[a])	Stuffed whole as for chile rellenos; chopped for salads and salsas; in tomato-based products.
Ancho	Dried poblano chile. Sweet flavor. Glossy mahogany red-brown in color. Heart shaped. (1,250–2,500 SU[a])	Sauces; moles; chile powders.
Banana (sweet)	Wide, blunt point. Pale yellow to orange red. (0–250 SU[a])	Chopped for salads and salsas; in tomato-based products.
Chipotle	Smoked-dried Jalapeño chile. Mottled light and dark brown. (5,000–10,000 SU[a])	Cooked Mexican products as in chili con carne; barbecue sauces; bean and cheese dishes.
Fresno	Small, tapered pod that is not too thin. Red or green. Very hot. (5,000–8,000 SU[a])	Chopped and generally used in cooked products. Can be used uncooked.
Guajillo	Long, thin, shiny brownish orange red. (2,000–4,500 SU[a])	Salsas; chile sauces; soups; stews
Habañero	Small, cherry-sized pepper, shaped like a miniature wrinkled bell pepper or lantern. Yellow, green, orange, or red. Extremely hot, use with caution. (100,000–500,000 SU[a])	Chopped in hot Mexican and Asian products.
Jalapeño	Small tapered pod, 2½–3½ inches long, ½–¾ inch wide. Bright green or greenish black. Very hot. (5,000–10,000 SU[a])	Chopped in cooked and uncooked products.
New Mexico	Long, wide, blunt-point pepper. Green or red. (500–1,500 SU[a])	Chopped in salads; as a garnish.
Piquin	Also *pequin*. Small, oval with a blunt point. Orange-red. Very hot. (50,000–100,000 SU[a])	Chopped in cooked and uncooked products.
Piri-piri	Small, wide, blunt point. Very hot. (30,000–60,000 SU[a])	Season soups, sauces, stews.
Poblano	Tapered bell pepper–like shape with a pointed end (3–5 inches long, 2–3 inches wide). Deep, dark green to almost black. Mild to slightly hot. (1,250–2,500 SU[a])	Stuffed whole; chopped in tomato-based products.
Scotch bonnet	Similar in shape to habañero. Extremely hot. Use with caution. (200,000–325,000 SU[a])	Chopped in hot Mexican, Caribbean, and Asian products.
Serrano	Tiny, very thin, tapering shape 1½–2 inches long, ½ inch wide. Dark green or red. Very hot. (10,000–25,000 SU[a])	Chopped in cooked and uncooked products.
Tepin	Round or oval. Red. (40,000–80,000 SU[a])	Chopped in cooked and uncooked products.
Thai	Tiny, extremely thin, tapered shape, ½–1 inch long, ¼ inch wide. Green or red. Extremely hot. (15,000–30,000 SU[a])	Season soups, sauces, and stews.

[a]Chile pepper heat is measured in *Scoville heat units (SU)*. Scoville heat units are approximate for reasons such as variation within a species, growing environment, water, and temperature. For comparison, the sweet bell pepper has an approximate Scoville rating of 0 units; pepperoncini are rated at 100–500 SU.

Note: Capsaicin, the chemical responsible for the sensory reaction to hot chile peppers, is released when the membrane or thin tissue that attaches the seeds to the soft, spongy, inside part of the pepper is ruptured. To minimize the release of capsaicin, make one cut to divide the chile and remove the ribs and seeds with a spoon. Rinse the chile in cool running water to wash away any capsaicin that spills onto the chile's flesh. Wear protective gloves and be careful not to touch eyes, face, or nose.

potatoes. Cut into cubes and cook; or wash, cook with skins on, peel, and dice. The oblong-shaped *Russet* potato is a widely used white potato variety. A high-starch, dry texture makes them a good choice for baking, roasting, mashing, and frying. Smooth-skinned *round red* and *round white* potatoes have a low-starch, waxy texture and are good for potato salads, roasting, boiling, and frying. The *long white* variety is oval-shaped with a thin tan-colored skin. Their medium-starch, waxy texture makes them a good all-purpose potato suitable for boiling, salads, soups, and roasting. Yellow-fleshed potatoes such as *Yukon Gold* and *Yellow Finn* have a buttery golden flesh and are suited for baking, mashing, and roasting. *Blue* and *purple* varieties have a flesh that ranges in color from dark blue or lavender to white and are characterized by a subtle nutty flavor. Color may dissipate some when cooked.

Radicchio

- Separate leaves for thorough washing. Discard brown or decayed leaves. Wash in a spray of water or by immersing in cool water. Drain thoroughly. See Table 5.15.

Radishes

- Trim off the root and stem end with a sharp knife. Wash. To make radish accordions, cut long radishes not quite through into 10–12 narrow slices. Place in ice water. Slices will fan out accordion style. To make roses, leave an inch or two of green stem. Cut four or five petal-shaped slices around the radish from the cut tip to the center. Place the radishes in ice water, and the petals will open.

Rutabaga

- Trim the root and stem end and peel off the thick skin. Cut into cubes for cooking. Rutabagas have a round shape similar to that of a turnip and a mild turniplike flavor with golden yellow flesh.

Salsify (oyster plant or vegetable oyster)

- Trim the ends and peel. To keep from discoloring, put the peeled root in acidulated water immediately after peeling. Salsify is a long, slender, parsnip-shaped root, either black skinned or white skinned. Black salsify is fleshier than white salsify and easier to peel. It has a mild artichoke-like flavor and crisp texture. Its flavor has also been compared to that of an oyster; thus the name *oyster plant.*

Shallots

- Trim off the root and tip. Make a slit in the papery skin from root to stem end. Peel off the light brown peppery skin. Shallots are a small onionlike bulb with a mild, sweet onion flavor and golden-purple flesh.

Spinach

- Separate leaves for thorough washing. Remove coarse stems and damaged leaves. Wash by immersing in cool water, lifting the spinach up and down to wash off grit. Lift the leaves from water. See Table 5.15.

Squash, winter (hard shell)

- Wash before cutting. Cut long squash in half lengthwise and round squash crosswise. Scoop out and discard the seeds and fibrous strings. Squash can be cooked with the peel on or off. If squash is baked before cutting, pierce the skin in several places to allow steam to escape. Squash should be heavy for their size. Most applicable baking methods: boiling (soup), braising, and roasting. Common winter squash include the following: *Acorn:* Dark-green color, sometimes with orange patches. Acorn shaped with yellow-orange flesh. Moderately sweet and sometimes fibrous. Small, 1–2 lb. *Banana:* Creamy yellow to pale orange rind. Large cylindrical shape with slightly pointed ends. *Buttercup:* Dark green and round with turban-shaped top. Orange sweet flesh; somewhat dry. Size varies, but most weigh about 3 lb. *Butternut:* Light tan or yellow-orange; thin, smooth skin that peels easily. Elongated pear shape with seeds in the bulbous end. Bright orange flesh cooks up creamy and smooth (never stringy). Size varies considerably but ranges from about 2 to 6 lb. *Hubbard:* Bluish-gray or dusty green, thick bumpy skin that is difficult to cut. Smooth, sweet, orange flesh. Old varieties weigh 10 lb or more; newer variety 3–5 lb. *Spaghetti:* Yellow, smooth, semihard skin. Oblong shaped. Pale golden flesh with stringy fibers that resemble spaghetti when separated (raked) with a fork. Size ranges from 3 to 5 lb. Spaghetti squash is cooked without cutting or peeling. *Sweet dumpling:* Cream colored with dark green stripes. Small, round, flattened on top. Whole squash can be stuffed with a grain mixture and served as an individual portion.

Squash, summer (soft shell)

- Trim the stem and blossom end. Wash to remove all soil that may have adhered to the squash. Summer squash is not usually peeled or seeded and can be eaten raw or cooked. Depending on the variety, summer squash can be cut in many shapes (diced, halves, ribbons, shredded, sticks, coins). Common summer squash include the following: *Pattypan:* Light green, yellow, or white skin. White flesh. Round, squat shape with scalloped edges. *Yellow crookneck:* Pale yellow skin. White flesh. Cylindrical in shape with a narrower curved neck. Has more seeds than zucchini. *Yellow zucchini:* Deep yellow skin with green at stem end. White flesh. Same cylinder shape as green zucchini. *Zucchini:* Dark-green, shiny rind with some light speckling. White flesh. Cylinder shaped, thinner when young.

Tomatillos

- Tomatillos, botanically a fruit but treated like a vegetable, are a small round fruit covered with a parchment-like, green husk; they have a tart citrusy flavor. Remove the husk and stem and rinse off the sticky coating before using. The fruit has a smooth, green skin resembling a green cherry tomato. The green flesh contains tiny edible seeds and a solid texture. Tomatillos have a lemony and acidic flavor. They are served in stews and casseroles or uncooked in salads and salsas.

Tomatoes

- Tomatoes are botanically a fruit but treated like a vegetable. Wash and remove the core, stem, and flower end. If peeling, place in wire basket and dip in boiling water for 10–20 seconds or until skins begin to loosen. Dip in ice water immediately and remove the skin and core.

Turnips

- Trim the root and stem end and peel off the thick skin. Cut small turnips into wedges or thin rounds; dice larger ones. Turnips have creamy white skin with pinkish-red at the stem end and white flesh. For turnip greens, see Table 5.15.

Watercress

- Remove thick stems from the leaves. Wash by immersing in cool water. Drain thoroughly. See Table 5.15.

Fresh Herbs and Flowers

Herbs are the leaves of aromatic plants that add aroma and a distinctive flavor to foods. Herbs may be used to enhance taste without added calories, fat, or sodium. Table 5.18 describes fresh herbs used in cooking and gives their flavor profile and common use. Most herbs can be purchased as dried leaves, seeds, or ground. The flavor profile may be different, however, between fresh and dried herbs. See Table 5.21 (p. 134) for herb and spice usage for different categories of food.

Edible flowers may be added to salads or used as a garnish to add color or flavor. See Exhibit 10 in the colored inserts. Flowers are perishable and should be held for only a few days. Store flowers in a small amount of water and dry with a paper towel before using. Table 5.19 provides a color and taste profile for commonly used flowers. When flowers are used as an ingredient rather than a garnish, sample the flowers first to make sure they complement the other foods used. Some flowers are poisonous and should be determined safe before using.

TABLE 5.18   Fresh herb descriptions, flavors, and usage

ARUGULA

Description	Small, narrow, tender, smooth, notched leaves with a dark green color. May also be considered a salad green. Also known as *rocket* and *roquette*.
Flavor	Spicy, peppery, and pungent. Small leaves are the mildest. Loses flavor when cooked. Add to cooked dishes just before serving.
Usage	Used in Mediterranean cuisine. Use small leaves in salads mixed with other mild-flavored greens. Seasoning for or complement to eggs, lamb, olives, pasta, poultry, salads, soufflés, soups, tomatoes.

BASIL

Description	Slightly crinkled, pointed leaves that range in color from medium or dark green to purple. Sweet basil is the most common variety, but other specialty varieties include cinnamon, lemon, and opal. Member of the mint family.
Flavor	Pungent, clovelike aroma and aniselike flavor. Aromatic, warm, and slightly peppery.
Usage	Widely used in Mediterranean cuisines and with poultry, tomato sauces, and many vegetables. Blends well with garlic, lemon, fennel, marjoram, oregano, thyme, and curry. Ingredient in pesto. Seasoning for or complement to eggs, fish, meat, pesto, pizza, poultry, rice, salads, spaghetti sauce, and vegetables, especially beans, cabbage, summer squash, tomatoes.

BAY LEAF (BAY LAUREL)

Description	Long, thick, aromatic, dull green leaves (½ inch wide, 1–2 inches long). Member of the laurel family.
Flavor	Peppery with hint of menthol when cooked. Flavor mellows when products cool.
Usage	Used to add flavor to meat, chicken, seafood dishes, and soups, stews, and casseroles. Usually discarded after cooking and before serving. Best if long simmered. Seasoning for or complement to fish, game, marinades, meats, poultry, sauces (especially tomato), soups, stews.

CHERVIL (SWEET CICELY)

Description	Small, fernlike leaves similar in appearance to parsley. Member of the parsley family.
Flavor	Delicate parsley flavor with a mild anise flavor and aroma.
Usage	One of the traditional fines herbes. Heat for a short time. Seasoning for or complement to breads, eggs, fish, poultry, salads, salad dressing, shellfish, soups, vegetables.

CHIVES

Description	Hollow, round, thin, sturdy stems that resemble young green onions. Bright green with round, purple flowers. Member of the onion family.
Flavor	Mild onion or garlic flavor.
Usage	One of the traditional fines herbes. Flavoring for any savory dish or as a garnish. Purple flowers can be used in salads. Heat for a short time. Seasoning for or complement to butters, cheese, eggs, fish, meat, potatoes, poultry, salads, sauces, soups, vegetables (especially beans, carrots, cauliflower, corn, mushrooms, peas, squash).

CILANTRO (CHINESE PARSLEY OR MEXICAN PARSLEY)

Description	The green leafy plant that produces coriander seeds. Resembles flat leaf parsley.
Flavor	Bold sage-citrus flavor that is sometimes characterized as bitter and astringent. Flavor is pronounced and unique.
Usage	Important herb in cooking Mexican and Southwestern fare and in Chinese, Indian, and Thai cuisines. Blends well with chiles, curry spices, and garlic. Best used raw or only slightly cooked. Use sparingly. Discard tough stems. Seasoning for or complement to cauliflower, chili, eggplant, fish, guacamole, meat, poultry, salads, salsa, tomatoes.

continued

TABLE 5.18   Fresh herb descriptions, flavors, and usage

TABLE 5.18   continued

DILL
Description	Feathery and delicate blue-green leaf. Dill seeds are flattened, oval, and brown.
Flavor	Leaves have an anise-parsley-celery flavor that is pungent and slightly bitter. Seeds have a caraway-like bitter flavor.
Usage	Common in European and Scandinavian cuisines. Flavor of the leaf diminishes with heat, and flavor of the seed increases. Seasoning for or complement to butters, dressings, eggs, fish, meat, potatoes, poultry, salads, sauces, seafood or chicken salads, soups, vegetables.

EPAZOTE
Description	Flat, thin green leaves. Grows wild and is also called wormseed or stinkweed.
Flavor	Strong, kerosene-like aroma and wild flavor.
Usage	Flavoring in Mexican and Southwestern cuisine. After drying, can be brewed. Seasoning for or complement to chiles, corn, pork, squash, tomatoes.

FENNEL
Description	Feathery leaf attached to a fennel bulb.
Flavor	Mild licorice flavor.
Usage	Chopped and sprinkled as a garnish. Seasoning for or complement to beans, lamb, omelets, pork, salads.

LAVENDER
Description	Thin leaves on long stems bearing a spiked purple flower.
Flavor	Aromatic herb. Flowers have a sweet, lemonlike flavor.
Usage	Used to flavor teas, tisanes, jams, and preserves.

LEMONGRASS (CITRONELLA GRASS)
Description	Strawlike stalk similar to green onions in appearance but with a woody texture.
Flavor	Strong aroma and lemon flavor.
Usage	Only the lower portion of the white stalk is used. Used in Southeast Asian cuisine. Seasoning for or complement to curries, fish, salsa, soups, vinaigrettes.

LOVAGE
Description	Tall, celery-like stalks with dark green, celery-like leaves.
Flavor	Celery-like flavor.
Usage	Leaves and stalks used in salads, stews, and as a garnish. Seeds used to flavor cooked savory dishes.

MARJORAM
Description	Tiny, rounded, bright green leaves similar to thyme. Member of the mint family.
Flavor	Aromatic, sweet-minty, slightly bitter. Similar to oregano but sweeter, milder, and less earthy.
Usage	Used in Greek, Italian, and Mexican dishes. Heat for a short time. Seasoning for or complement to fish, lamb, meat, omelets, pork, poultry, salads, soups, stews, vegetables (especially Brussels sprouts, zucchini, peas, potatoes).

MINT
Description	Pointed, textured leaf. Size depends on variety.
Flavor	Aromatic with a peppery, spicy flavor. Peppermint has a more pronounced menthol and less-sweet flavor than spearmint.
Usage	Used to flavor sweet and savory dishes. Used in Middle Eastern, Thai, and Vietnamese cuisine. Seasoning for or complement to cheeses, curries, fruit, lamb, potatoes, poultry, salads, soups, vegetables (especially green beans, beets, carrots, peas). Used to flavor teas and tisanes.

OREGANO
Description	Thin, woody stalks with small oval leaves that are larger than marjoram. Member of the mint family.
Flavor	Bold, bitter, earthy, clovelike flavor similar to marjoram and thyme.
Usage	Used to season Greek, Italian, Mexican, and Spanish dishes. Seasoning for or complement to beans, fish, lamb, meats, pizza, poultry, salad dressings, shellfish, tomato dishes and sauces, vegetables (especially avocado, broccoli, cabbage, eggplant, peppers, tomatoes).

PARSLEY (CURLY, ITALIAN, OR FLAT LEAF)
Description	Curly has small, curly, bright green leaves, and Italian has flat, darker green leaves.
Flavor	Grassy, peppery flavor. Curly is sweeter than Italian. Both have a distinctive clean, bitter flavor. Stems have stronger flavor than leaves.
Usage	Italian preferred for cooking. Used in savory dishes and as a garnish (curly). Component of fines herbes and of bouquet garni. Seasoning for or complement to fish, pasta, potatoes, poultry, rice, vegetables.

TABLE 5.18   Fresh herb descriptions, flavors, and usage

continued

TABLE 5.18   Fresh herb descriptions, flavors, and usage

TABLE 5.18   continued

ROSEMARY

Description	Leaves resemble short, spiky pine needles on a woody stalk. Member of the mint family.
Flavor	Fragrant, spicy, pinelike aroma and flavor.
Usage	Large branches can be soaked in water and used as skewers for grilled foods. Used in Middle Eastern dishes. Flavor is as intense when dried as when fresh. Cook for at least 10 minutes to release flavor. Seasoning for or complement to breads, lamb, meat, pizza, pork sausage, potatoes, soup, stews, veal, vegetables (especially cauliflower, eggplant, peas, potatoes).

SAGE

Description	Narrow, oval-shaped, elongated leaves with a gray-green color. Large leaves may be velvety. Member of the mint family.
Flavor	Assertive, slightly bitter, musty flavor.
Usage	May impart a "soapy" flavor when too much is used. Use sparingly. Seasoning for or complement to breads, pork, poultry, sausages, stuffings, vegetables (especially winter squash).

SAVORY (SUMMER SAVORY)

Description	Tiny, narrow green leaves. Member of the mint family. (Winter savory resembles rosemary and has a strong pine flavor.)
Flavor	Sharp, peppery, clovelike and slightly bitter. Subtle thyme flavor.
Usage	Use sparingly. Seasoning for or complement to chowders, eggs, fish, meat, pork, potatoes, poultry, soups, vegetables (especially asparagus, beans, Brussels sprouts, carrots, squash, tomatoes).

SORREL

Description	Pale green leaves that resemble spinach.
Flavor	Sharp, sour, lemony flavor.
Usage	Young leaves used as a salad green. Seasoning for or complement to eggs, fish, pork, poultry, salads, soufflés, sauces, and soups (especially cream-based).

TARRAGON

Description	Bushy with narrow, dark green leaves.
Flavor	Spicy and aromatic with a distinctive anise flavor.
Usage	Used in béarnaise sauce. Often used in French cuisine. A component of fines herbes. Use sparingly. Seasoning for or complement to cheese, eggs, fish, meat, poultry, shellfish, vegetables (especially artichokes, asparagus, beets, carrots, mushrooms, potatoes, squash), vinegars.

THYME

Description	Tiny, green-gray leaves on a small, bushy, woody stem. Member of the mint family.
Flavor	Aromatic, biting, spicy, mint or clovelike, lemony taste and aroma. Flavor varies with type of thyme.
Usage	An integral ingredient in bouquet garni. Important spice for Creole and Cajun dishes. Seasoning for or complement to eggplant, meat, peppers, poultry, seafood dishes, soups, sauces, tomatoes, vegetables (especially eggplant, onions, peppers, tomatoes).

Note: Fresh and dried herbs and spices are often combined and tied with twine in a bundle or tied in cheesecloth to provide flavorings, seasonings, and aromatics to sauces, stews, and soups. The spices are removed and discarded after the desired level of flavoring has been achieved. Classic combinations include the following: **bouquet garni** (1 bay leaf, 2 oz carrot sticks, 4 oz celery stalks and leaves, 1 fresh thyme sprig, 3 leek leaves, 4 parsley stems); **sachet d'épices** (1 bay leaf, 1 crushed garlic clove, ½ teaspoon dried thyme, 4 parsley stems, ½ teaspoon cracked peppercorns); and **oignon piqué** (1 whole onion studded with 12 cloves and 2 bay leaves that are slid into knife slits made in the onion). Often used to flavor liquids such as béchamel sauce.

For example, lily of the valley and daffodils should not be eaten. Call the local extension office for more information about flower varieties that are safe to eat. Buy flowers from a reputable foodservice distributor to make sure they are edible, free from harmful pesticides, and grown and handled in a safe manner.

CANNED AND FROZEN FRUITS AND VEGETABLES

The canning process changes the character of fruits and vegetables by softening their texture and often changing their color. Canned products are available in standard-sized cans (Table 4.11, p. 94). Vegetables may be water packed or packed with a variety of seasonings and sauces. Fruits also may be packed with water or in a sugar syrup (light, medium, or heavy). Solid-pack fruit without added water is available for products such as pies and fillings.

Canned fruits and vegetables will keep for an extended period of time in a cool storage area. Leaking or bulging cans should be discarded. Cans with deep dents or dented on a seam or around the lid should also be discarded.

Freezing is an effective method of preserving fruits and vegetables without causing as much color and texture change as canning. Individually quick-frozen (IQF) fruits and vegetables are easy to use and available in several carton sizes. Because they are frozen very quickly, ice crystals are small. Frozen products should be stored at a constant 0° to –10°F.

TABLE 5.19   Edible flowers

Flower	Flavor	Description
Bachelor's buttons	Bland	Pink, white, blue, and purple. 1-inch flowers.
Carnations, mini	Bland to bitter, peppery like cloves or nutmeg	Wide variety of colors.
Chive blossoms	Mild onion	Blue to lavender, ball shaped. 1-inch diameter.
Daisies	Bland, mild clover, mint	White or yellow petals with a yellow center. 1-inch diameter.
Dandelion	Bitter when old, slightly sweet when young	Yellow.
Daylily	Slightly sweet, bland	Various colors, variegated.
Lavender	Floral, herb, sweet citrus	Light to medium purple.
Lilac	Lemony	Light to medium purple, white.
Marigolds	Spicy, sometimes bitter	Saffron-like color. Yellow to deep rust color.
Nasturtiums	Radishlike, peppery	Orange, yellow, rust, or red flowers. 1-inch diameter.
Pansies	Bland, mildly grassy	Flat, multicolored flowers. 1- to 2-inch diameter.
Roses, mini	Sweet, fruity	Orange, red, pink, yellow.
Snapdragons	Slightly bitter	Yellow, pink, red, orange, white. Peanut shaped.
Squash blossoms	Mild, sweet, squashlike	Bright yellow.
Violas	Bland, wintergreen	Purple, yellow, white. Dime sized.
Violets	Slightly sweet, often peppery	Purple, yellow.

The USDA has established grades of quality for many canned and frozen vegetables and fruits. The grades are based on color, uniformity of size, shape, tenderness or degree of ripeness, and lack of blemishes. The label may designate U.S. Grade A (Fancy), U.S. Grade B (Extra-Select or Choice), and U.S. Grade C (Standard). The use of the USDA grades is voluntary and is paid for by the packer.

TOFU AND DRIED BEANS, LENTILS, AND PEAS

Tofu, a curd made from soybeans, is bland tasting and can be purchased in a range of textures. Because it absorbs the flavor of other foods, it is extremely versatile and used in a variety of sweet and savory products. *Silken tofu* is very soft and often puréed for sauces and dips. Because it falls apart easily, it should not be cooked for a long period of time. *Firm* and *extra-firm* tofu hold their shape better than silken or soft tofu and are best used in recipes specifying marinating or stir-frying. Tofu can be pressed to force out some of the water and make it firmer. Press tofu by placing it in a pan between several layers of clean cheesecloth and topping it with a counter pan. Put approximately 5 lb of weight in the pan above the tofu and, while under refrigeration, allow the weighted pan to press the tofu for several hours. Freezing makes tofu porous and gives it a tougher texture. Fresh tofu is usually packed in water and should be drained before using. Tofu is a potentially hazardous food and must be kept refrigerated.

Among the many kinds of dried legumes available are dried beans, lentils, and peas. High in protein and fiber, legumes are an important component in one's diet. Table 5.20 and Exhibit 10 in the colored inserts identify common varieties of dried beans, lentils, and peas.

Food Production and Service Staples

- Coffee and Tea
- Condiments and Vinegars
- Dried Herbs, Spices, and Seasonings
- Nuts and Seeds
- Extracts, Alcohol, and Sweeteners
- Fats

COFFEE AND TEA

Coffee beans or cherries are produced in more than 50 countries located in subtropical and equatorial regions. Arabica coffee beans, considered to be superior in flavor to robusta beans, are grown at the highest altitudes in the coolest climates. Beans are harvested—often picked by hand—then cleaned, fermented, and dried before being shipped as green coffee beans to coffee roasters around the world. Environmental conditions in the growing regions, soil chemistry, growing altitude, and harvesting and processing procedures all contribute to the flavor distinctions between coffees. The National Coffee Association of U.S.A., Inc. (www.ncausa.org) is a useful source for information about coffee.

High-altitude beans from Central and South America produce lively, light-bodied coffee with high concentrations of natural acids. Beans grown in Africa are robust, with fewer natural acids. Pacific beans feature moderate acidity and rich, mellow overtones.

Light/pale and *medium/city roast* are all-purpose roasts. *Brazilian* and *Viennese roasts* are also all-purpose roasts but are slightly darker than city roast. *French/dark* and *Italian/espresso*

TABLE 5.20 Common varieties of dried beans, lentils, and peas[a]

Name	Description
Appaloosa bean	Speckled red, or black and white. Long and thin.
Black bean/turtle bean	Dark black with a white line. Medium-sized and almost round.
Black-eyed pea	Ivory or beige in color with a black spot. Small kidney shapes.
Cannellini bean	White, smooth, long. Looks like and sometimes called a white kidney bean.
Chickpea/garbanzo bean	Beige. Rounded acorn shape with lumps.
Dry split peas	Green or yellow. Skin is removed and pea split in half.
Great northern bean	White. Large oval. Very common white bean.
Kidney bean	Reddish to dark brown. Kidney shaped.
Lentils	Small disk shape about the size of a split pea half. Brown, dark or light green, orange, and yellow.
Lima bean	Broad and flat shape. Ivory color.
Navy/pea bean	White. Small round. Very common white bean.
Pigeon pea	Small, nearly round, ivory-colored with orange-brown mottling.
Pinto bean	Medium-sized, kidney-shaped, mottled pink color.

[a]See Exhibit 10 in the color inserts for pictures of selected dry legumes.

Notes: • Generally beans are kidney shaped, lentils disk shaped, and peas round.
• Other varieties of beans are available. Flavor of beans varies slightly. Cooking times may vary slightly.

roasts are especially suited for after-dinner coffee and for serving with desserts and chocolate. Roast terminology may vary among geographic areas and among roasters.

Coffee is judged on four attributes: acidity, aroma, body, and flavor. Some *acidity* is a positive characteristic and refers to the tartness. The *aroma* provides the first hint as to the way the coffee will taste. Some coffees are more fragrant than others. *Body* refers to mouthfeel or how thick or heavy the coffee seems. Terms used to describe *flavor* include *mellow, harsh,* and *earthy.* Flavor is subjective and may be described differently by different tasters. The International Coffee Organization (www.ico.org) provides a vocabulary to describe the flavor of a coffee brew.

Specialty coffee refers to coffee made with flavored beans, espresso and espresso-based beverage, or coffee flavored with syrups, liquors, or other postbrew flavorings. Espresso-based drinks include the following:

Espresso—Espresso is made by forcing superheated water under pressure through a very dark-roasted, finely ground, packed coffee to make a strong, rich, smooth brew. A specially designed machine is necessary to make espresso. The process extracts more of the solids and flavor from the bean than conventional drip brewing. A single serving of espresso uses approximately 1/4 oz ground coffee to 1 1/2 oz water.

Americano—Made with one shot (1–1 1/2 oz) espresso and 6–8 oz hot water. Often served iced.

Cappuccino—Made by using one-third espresso, one-third steamed milk, and one-third foamed milk.

Caffé Latte—Made by using one-third espresso and two-thirds steamed milk.

Caffé Mocha—Made by using one-third espresso and two-thirds steamed milk and flavored with chocolate syrup. Usually served with whipped cream and shaved chocolate or cocoa powder.

Flavored syrups are added to individual servings in a proportion of approximately 1 oz per cup. Popular syrup flavorings include almond, caramel, chocolate, hazelnut, raspberry, strawberry, and vanilla. Shakers for dry flavorings such as allspice, chocolate, cinnamon, malt, nutmeg, and vanilla may be provided for self-service. Other condiments for coffee include brown or raw sugar, chocolate shavings, cinnamon sticks, citrus peel, and whipped cream.

Tea is made from the leaves of a shrublike evergreen that grows in warm, humid regions. Three main types of tea are available and are produced from the same plant by varying the processing.

Black tea derives its color from a special processing treatment that allows the leaves to ferment and oxidize. The process turns the leaves black and produces an amber-brown and rich-flavored brew. English Breakfast and orange pekoe are familiar black teas. Brew black tea at 212°F for 4–6 minutes.

Oolong tea is partially fermented and brews light in color. Brew oolong tea at 190–195°F for 5–8 minutes.

Green tea is made from leaves that are dried without fermenting. The brew is pale yellow-green in color. Green tea will be bitter if brewed with water that is too hot or if brewed for too long a time. Brew green tea at 160–165°F for 2–4 minutes.

White tea is unfermented and can be considered a subgroup of green tea. It produces a yellow-hued tea with a mellow flavor. Brew white tea at 180°F for 4–6 minutes.

CONDIMENTS AND VINEGARS

A condiment is added to a dish during or after cooking to introduce hot, piquant, sharp, spicy, or sweet flavors to foods. Some examples are fermented black bean sauce, fish sauce, hot pepper sauce, jam or jelly, ketchup, prepared mustard, and vinegar. Condiments may also be served on the side as an accompaniment. Accompaniment condiments include salsa and relishes.

Vinegar is used as an ingredient or is added to foods as a condiment to impart a clean, sharp flavor. The flavor of vinegar varies depending on the liquid used. White or distilled vinegar is neutral in flavor and only adds sharpness to foods. The degree of vinegar's tartness depends on the acidity or strength. Most vinegar is about 5 percent acidity, but some are as high as 8 percent. Strong vinegars may need to be diluted with water before using in a recipe. Types of vinegars include the following:

Balsamic—A sweet tart vinegar with a dark reddish-brown color and intense but mellow flavor. This red wine vinegar has been aged in wooden barrels. Long-aged vinegar is extremely expensive and used in very small quantities, often to flavor berries or delicate salad greens. The readily available and inexpensive balsamic vinegars are made using a quick caramelization and flavoring process instead of an aging process. Balsamic vinegar can be reduced (boiled to evaporate some of the water) to produce an intensely flavored sweet-sour "syrup."

Cider—A pale brown vinegar with mild acidity, fruity aroma, and slightly sweet apple flavor. Made from apple pulp or cider. Cider vinegar is an all-purpose vinegar.

Flavored—Another product is added to a vinegar (usually wine or distilled vinegar) to produce a product with the flavor and often the color of the added ingredients. Common products used to infuse vinegar to make a flavored vinegar include garlic, herbs (often tarragon), and fruit (often raspberries or figs).

Malt—A slightly sweet, mild-flavored vinegar made from malted barley. Often used as a condiment with fried foods, especially fish.

Rice—A clear, light, slightly sweet vinegar made from fermented rice. Often used to flavor rice used for sushi, pickled ginger, and other Asian dishes.

White or distilled—Sharp, strong, and vinegary with a neutral flavor. General-purpose vinegar.

Wine—A vinegar made from red or white wine, sherry, or champagne. The vinegar's color, flavor, and sharpness will depend on the characteristics of the wine used.

DRIED HERBS, SPICES, AND SEASONINGS

Dried herbs, spices, and seasonings are indispensable kitchen staples necessary for preparing and serving flavorful foods. Herbs are defined as the leaf, stem, and sometimes flower portion of an aromatic plant. Spices are defined as the dried bark, buds, flowers, fruits, roots, and seeds of aromatic plants. Seeds are sometimes classified separately. Table 5.24 describes some common seeds used in foods. Both spices and herbs are used to build flavor and add new flavor profiles to foods. Seasonings, such as salt, enhance natural flavors without causing a striking change in taste.

Herbs and Spices

Many spices and dried herbs can be purchased whole or ground. Ground products have relatively more surface area than whole products and lose their flavor more quickly. Most ground herbs and spices lose flavor when heated for a long period of time and should be added near the end of the cooking process. Whole spices can be added earlier in the cooking process without losing flavor.

Some flavor differences can be expected when dry herbs are substituted for fresh. A guideline for substituting dried herbs for fresh is to use $\frac{1}{3}$ the amount of fresh. For example, if a recipe specifies 1 Tbsp fresh herbs, the alternative would be to use 1 tsp dried. Table 4.4 (p. 86) provides the number of teaspoons per ounce for some commonly used dry herbs and spices.

For optimum flavor retention, dried herbs and spices should be stored in a cool (68°F), dry (humidity 60% or less) environment, out of direct sunlight. Very cool storage (32–45°F) is recommended for allspice, dill, chile powder, cloves, cumin, marjoram, parsley flakes, paprika, and red pepper. Generally dried herbs and spices should be held for no longer than 3 months in a tightly closed container. Whole spices have relatively less surface area than ground spices and retain their flavor for a longer time. Measure herbs and spices with a dry utensil away from cooking steam and moisture.

The same herbs and spices are used to flavor many different food products. Table 5.20 (p. 132) provides information about herb and spice usage for different categories of food.

Herbs and spices help define the ethnic flavors and cuisines of different cultures. Table 5.22 lists spices and herbs that provide the unique flavor profile associated with foods from various countries or geographic regions of the world.

Often spices and dried herbs are combined to make natural spice blends that are associated with different cuisines. Some common natural spice blends with ingredient measurements follow.

Natural Spice Blends

Bouquet Garni	Whole marjoram	4 Tbsp
	Whole thyme	3 Tbsp
	Parsley	2 Tbsp
	Ground bay leaf	$\frac{1}{4}$ tsp
Garam Masala	Ground coriander	7 Tbsp
	Ground cumin	10 Tbsp
	Ground cinnamon	4 tsp
	Ground cardamom	4 tsp
	Ground black pepper	2 tsp
	Ground cloves	2 tsp
	Ground mace	2 tsp
	Ground bay leaf	$\frac{1}{2}$ tsp
Quatre-Épices	Black pepper	7 Tbsp
	Ground nutmeg	8 tsp
	Ground cloves	4 tsp
	Ground ginger	4 tsp
Fines Herbes	Parsley	3 Tbsp
	Chives	3 Tbsp
	Chervil	1 Tbsp
	Tarragon	1 Tbsp
Herbes de Provence	Whole thyme	4 Tbsp
	Whole marjoram	8 tsp
	Basil leaves	8 tsp
	Fennel seed	4 tsp
	Rosemary	4 tsp
	Sage leaves	4 tsp

From McCormick Food Service Division.

TABLE 5.21 Herb and spice usage for different categories of food

Spice	Appetizers	Soups	Meat	Seafood	Poultry	Vegetables
ALLSPICE	Steamed shrimp, liver paté	Cream soups, split pea, oyster bisque	Ham, pork, gravy, marinade, spiced beef	Oyster stew, shellfish, poached fish	Quail, duck, goose, pheasant	Squash, sweet potatoes, carrots
ANISE	Oysters Rockefeller	Fish chowder, chicken soup	Veal, Hungarian goulash, beef marinade	Red snapper, lobster	Chicken, duck, quail	Cabbage, leeks
BASIL	Cheese, seafood	Minestrone, clam chowder	Beef stew, lamb, spareribs, beef marinade	Lobster, shrimp, squid, swordfish	Chicken, turkey stuffing, quiche	Sweet peppers, eggplant, potatoes, zucchini, tomatoes
BAY LEAF	Paté de foie gras	Onion, bean, vegetable, lobster bisque	Beef stew, broth, beef marinade	Seafood stew, poached fish, bouillabaisse	Chicken pot pie, gravy, marinade	Pickled vegetables, ratatouille, green beans
BLACK PEPPER	Paté	Gazpacho, lentil, minestrone	Steak, hamburger, gravy, pork, beef marinade	Poached fish, marinade, calamari	Fried chicken batter, duck	All vegetables
CARAWAY	Cheese spreads, Muenster cheese	Borscht, cream soups	Pork, meatloaf, sauerbraten	Shrimp, crab	Duck, goose	Cabbage, carrots, potatoes, French fries
CARDAMOM	Pickled herring	Chicken soup, fish soup	Lamb, meatloaf, hamburger	Trout, mussels	Roast chicken	Sweet potatoes, fried eggplant
CELERY SEED	Canapés, cheese dips, shrimp cocktail	Chicken, potato, vegetable, lentil, fish chowder	Beef stew, pot roast, ham, grilled beef	Tuna, shrimp, oyster stew	Eggs, omelets, stuffing	Potatoes, cauliflower, corn relish
CHIVES	Cream cheese, canapés, stuffed mushrooms	Chicken soup, vichyssoise	Pork, gravy, lamb	Salmon, oysters	Omelets, quiche	Cucumbers, baked potatoes, potato pancakes
CILANTRO	Ceviche, guacamole, salsa	Hot and sour soup	Chili con carne, beef stew	Poached fish, steamed fish	Chicken	Onion, tomatoes, chili peppers
CINNAMON	Fresh fruit	Lamb soup	Pork, ham, beef stew, lamb		Fruit stuffing for game	Sweet potatoes, carrots, squash
CLOVES	Spiced fruit	Beef noodle, beef vegetable, cream of tomato	Ham glaze, beef stew, gravy		Cornish hen, duck, gravy, stock	Boiled onions, sweet potatoes, carrots
CORIANDER	Corn pudding	Cream of chicken, hot and sour soup, consommé	Pork, ham, spareribs, marinade	Poached fish, steamed fish	Chicken, duck	Sweet potatoes, scalloped potatoes, braised celery
CUMIN	Nachos, cheese, salsa	Seafood gumbo, chili	Chili con carne, sausage, pork stew	Fried shrimp batter, deviled crab	Chicken stew, chicken croquettes	Sauerkraut, chile peppers, beans
DILL	Sour cream dips, deviled eggs, shrimp paté	Borscht, lobster bisque, tomato	Veal, grilled lamb, pork	All seafood	Chicken, omelets	Cucumbers, potatoes, green beans, braised cabbage
FENNEL	Shrimp cocktail, oysters Rockefeller	Creamed fish soup, fish chowder	Italian sausage, pork, meat loaf	All seafood (especially grilled)	Stuffing, chicken stew	Sautéed mushrooms, spinach, cabbage
GARLIC	Dips, escargot	Vegetable, oxtail	Beef, roast lamb, meatballs	All seafood, marinade	Chicken, quail, pheasant	Green beans, zucchini, potatoes
GINGER	Shrimp, cheese	Beef vegetable, beef noodle, hot and sour soup	Spareribs, pork, marinade	All seafood	Duck, poultry glaze	Sweet potatoes, carrots, stir-fry vegetables

TABLE 5.21 Herb and spice usage for different categories of food

TABLE 5.21   continued

Sauces	Salads	Dressings	Breads	Pastas and grains	Desserts	Beverages
Barbecue, sweet cream, creole	Fruit salad	Fruit dressing	Pancakes, waffles, muffins	Rice	Spice cake, angel food cake, pies	Mulled wine, tea, rum drinks
Tomato		Orange vinaigrette	Honey buns, sweet rolls, fritters		Spice cake, cookies, candy	Lemonade, cordials, espresso, hot milk punch
Barbecue, pesto, tomato	Vegetable salad, seafood salad, tomato salad	Italian, Russian, vinaigrette	Pesto bread, zucchini muffins	Rotini, rice, linguini, spaghetti		Carrot juice, tomato juice
Béchamel, creole, tomato, barbecue		Vinaigrette				
Tomato, barbecue, curry	Green salad	Vinaigrette, mayonnaise		Carbonara, fried rice, pasta		Tomato juice
Lemon, butter, cream	Coleslaw, potato salad	Mayonnaise, vinaigrette	Biscuits, rye bread, corn muffins	Risotto	Cookies, seed cakes	Kümmel
Curry, spiced yogurt	Fruit salad	Asian dressing		Risotto, rice pilaf	Ice cream, cakes, pastries, apple pie	Coffee, tea, glögg, spiced wine
Cream, creole, tomato	Tuna salad, potato salad, macaroni salad	Mayonnaise	Biscuits, breads, rolls	Pasta	Pastries	Tomato juice
Tomato, cream Hollandaise	Green salad Potato salad, macaroni salad	Green Goddess Thousand Island	Buttermilk bread Bread spreads, potato rolls	Pasta		
Yogurt sauce, tomato, curry		Mexican dressing	Herb bread	Lentils, Mexican green rice, Chinese noodles		
Custard sauce, yogurt sauce, sweet and sour	Fruit salad	Fruit dressing	Rolls, French toast, breads	Curried rice, risotto	Apple pie, chocolate cakes, cookies	Coffee, cider, mulled wine, hot chocolate
Béchamel, raisin sauce, curry		Fruit dressing	Cinnamon bread		Chocolate, gingerbread, mincemeat	Fruit punch, mulled wine
Curry, cream	Potato salad		Honey-wheat bread, corn bread	Orzo	Pastries, cookies, cakes	Pineapple juice, grapefruit juice
Barbecue, spiced yogurt	Bean salad	Spanish dressing	Jalapeño bread, corn bread	Rice		Kümmel
Mustard sauce, cream, cucumber sauce	Macaroni salad, potato salad, shrimp salad	Dill cream, mayonnaise, vinaigrette	Rye, pumpernickel, bread spreads	Rice, pasta		
Cream, curry	Potato salad, shrimp salad	Mayonnaise, vinaigrette, mustard	Cracker, rolls, bread sticks	Risotto rice	Apple pie, candy, pound cake	
Tomato, garlic butter	Green salad	Mayonnaise, vinaigrette, Italian	Garlic bread, bread spreads, focaccia	Linguini, spaghetti		
Curry, soy sauce, sweet and sour			Pastries	Couscous, rice	Gingerbread, pudding, apple pie	Mulled wine, tea, ginger beer

TABLE 5.21   Herb and spice usage for different categories of food

continued

TABLE 5.21   Herb and spice usage for different categories of food

TABLE 5.21   continued

Spice	Appetizers	Soups	Meat	Seafood	Poultry	Vegetables
MACE	Liver paté, cheese	Vichyssoise	Sausage	Potted shrimp, oyster stew	Creamed chicken, Cornish hens	Rutabaga, spinach, asparagus, sweet potatoes
MARJORAM	Fried cheese, paté, anchovies	Consommé, bean, corn, split pea	Lamb, hamburger, pork, veal	Baked fish, seafood breading	Chicken stuffing, eggs	Zucchini, tomato, carrots, peas, lima beans
MINT	Cucumber-yogurt dip	Fruit soup, split pea	Lamb stew, venison		Marinade	Peas, potatoes, cucumbers
MUSTARD	Deviled eggs, meatballs, ham spread	Creamed seafood	Ham glaze, beef, sausage, cold meat	Baked fish, crab		Baked-mashed potatoes, cabbage, sauerkraut
NUTMEG	Fruit	Mushroom soup	Pot roast, meatloaf, ham		Fried chicken batter, turkey stuffing	Spinach, carrots, sweet potatoes, braised cabbage
OREGANO	Fried cheese, paté, salsa, meatballs	Corn soup, vegetable soup, consommé	Pork, veal, lamb, hamburger	Seafood breading, baked fish	Chicken stuffing	Zucchini, tomatoes, carrots, green beans
PAPRIKA	Deviled eggs, nachos, potted cheese	Minestrone, seafood soup, chowder	Goulash, veal, sausage, meatloaf	Seafood breading, baked fish, shellfish	Chicken stuffing	Potatoes, cabbage, mushrooms, cucumbers
PARSLEY	Canapés, deviled eggs	Vegetable soup, chicken soup	Meatballs, hamburger, veal	Shellfish, baked fish	Chicken	Zucchini, potatoes, tomatoes, green beans
POPPY SEED	Cheese			Broiled fish, tuna casserole	Turkey stuffing	Green beans, onions, tomatoes
RED PEPPER	Deviled eggs	Hot and sour soup	Sausage	Crab cakes, shrimp	Omelets, chicken	
ROSEMARY		Consommé	Lamb, pork, venison, meat loaf, marinade	Baked fish, shrimp	Chicken, quail, pheasant, goose, Cornish hen	Eggplant, turnips, squash, potatoes
SAFFRON		Chicken soup, fish soup	Lamb	All seafood	Chicken stew, scrambled eggs	
SAGE	Cheese, country paté	Consommé, minestrone	Sausage, ham, lamb, veal, venison	Seafood stuffing, trout	Stuffing, quail, duck, goose, pheasant	Acorn squash
SAVORY	Goat cheese	Lentil, bean, split pea	Stuffing, veal, gravy, hamburger, meat loaf	Baked fish, sea bass	Stuffing, chicken, turkey, eggs	Onions, peas, green beans, navy beans
SESAME	Hummus dip		Beef, pork, hamburger, lamb	Baked fish, shrimp, scallops	Chicken	Vegetable stir-fry, green beans
TARRAGON	Mushroom caps	Turtle soup, fish chowder	Steak, beef stew, marinade	Lobster, shrimp	Cornish hens, marinade, chicken, eggs, omelets	Mushrooms, stuffed tomatoes
THYME		Oxtail, consommé	Sauerbraten, pork, lamb, marinade	Baked fish, seafood stuffing	Stuffing, chicken, fried chicken batter	Potatoes, tomatoes zucchini
TURMERIC	Deviled eggs	Chicken noodle, lentil		Shrimp, scallops	Chicken, eggs	
WHITE PEPPER	Veal paté	Consommé, vichyssoise		Baked fish	Chicken, turkey	Potatoes

TABLE 5.21   continued

Sauces	Salads	Dressings	Breads	Pastas and grains	Desserts	Beverages
Chicken cream, béchamel					Chocolate, vanilla pudding, gingerbread	Wassail, chocolate drinks
Barbecue, tomato, butter	Cucumber-yogurt salad	Oil and vinegar, French, Italian	Bread sticks, pizza, herb bread	Spaghetti, pasta, orzo		
Sweet sauce, yogurt sauce, mint sauce	Cucumber salad	Fruit dressing, yogurt dressing, cranberry dressing	Minted yogurt bread	Bulgur, orzo	Candy, chocolate	Iced tea, mint julep, hot chocolate
Cheese, sour cream, lemon-mustard yogurt sauce	Coleslaw	Vinaigrette, mayonnaise, rémoulade				
Cream mushroom sauce, béchamel		Creamy dressings	Cinnamon rolls	Tortellini, ravioli	Rice pudding, custard cakes, soufflés	Egg nog, brandy Alexander, punch
Barbecue, tomato, butter	Tomato and onion seafood salad	Oil and vinegar, French, Italian	Cheese bread, pizza, bread sticks	Pasta, rice, ravioli		
Barbecue Cream, yogurt		French, Russian	Garlic bread Muffins	Lasagna, rice Orzo		
Tartar sauce, béarnaise, tomato	Tuna or egg salad, macaroni salad, green salad	Mayonnaise, Italian, ranch, vinaigrette	Garlic bread	Pasta, orzo		
Curry, butter	Fruit salad	Oil and vinegar, blue cheese	Rolls, breads, crackers	Egg noodles, rice	Cakes, cookies, pastry filling, apple strudel	
Barbecue, tomato-anchovy		Mayonnaise, Thousand Island	Pizza, corn muffins	Rice, tabouli		Tomato juice, Bloody Mary
Tomato, cheese	Cold beef salad	Vinaigrette	Spoon bread, herb bread, pizza	Pasta, lentils		
Seafood saffron, vegetable cream, tomato			Rolls, biscuits, sweet breads	Rice, risotto, orzo	Cakes, rice pudding, cookies	
Tomato		Herb dressing	Sage bread, rolls	Risotto, fettuccine		
Tomato, horseradish			Savory rolls, herb bread	Lentils, egg noodles		
Hoisin sauce, peanut sauce	Green salad	Mayonnaise, tahini dressing	Buns, rolls, waffles, breads	Egg noodles, rice, bulgur	Cookies, pie, pastry, pecan pie	
Rémoulade, béarnaise, tartar, mustard sauce	Shrimp salad, tomato salad	Mayonnaise, vinaigrette, Green Goddess	Herb bread	Pasta, orzo	Rhubarb compote	
Tomato, thyme pesto		Vinaigrette	Bread spreads, herb rolls	Pasta, rice		Mulled wine
Cream, yogurt caper sauce, satay	Egg salad	Mayonnaise, creamy dressings	Breads	Rice, egg noodles		
Béchamel cream		Mayonnaise, vinaigrette		Rice, egg noodles		Vegetable juice

From McCormick Food Service Division.

TABLE 5.21   Herb and spice usage for different categories of food

TABLE 5.22	Regional flavorings
AFRICAN	Anise, cinnamon, coriander, cumin, mint, saffron
CHINESE	Anise, cinnamon, cloves, fennel, garlic, ginger, red pepper, sesame, soy sauce
FRENCH	Chives, fines herbes, garlic, marjoram, rosemary, shallots, tarragon, thyme
GERMAN	Caraway seed, dill seed, nutmeg, onion, paprika, rosemary
GREEK	Bay leaf, cinnamon, fennel, garlic, lemon, mint, oregano
HUNGARIAN	Caraway, cinnamon, dill, paprika, poppy seed
INDIAN	Anise, cardamom, celery seed, coriander, cumin, curry, garlic, ginger, nutmeg, red pepper
INDONESIAN	Caraway, cinnamon, cloves, curry, garlic, ginger, nutmeg, red pepper
ITALIAN	Basil, fennel, garlic, marjoram, oregano, pepper, sage
MEXICAN	Achiote, chile pepper, cilantro, coriander, cumin, garlic, lime, oregano, red pepper, sweet pepper
SPANISH	Anise, bay leaf, cinnamon, cumin, garlic, paprika, parsley, saffron
SWEDISH	Allspice, bay leaf, dill, cardamom, cinnamon, mustard, nutmeg
THAI	Chile pepper, citrus, coriander, dill, garlic, mint, turmeric

Many foodservice operators prefer to mix their own spice blends for signature menu items. See the recipes for dry seasoning blends on pp. 725–732. The following spice blends are available commercially.

Chinese five-spice—Equal parts of finely ground Szechuan pepper, star anise, cloves, cinnamon, and fennel seed.

Curry powder—There are many different curry mixtures, some sweet and others hot and pungent. Traditional curry mixtures contain many of the following spices: black pepper, cilantro, cinnamon, cloves, coriander, cumin, ginger, mace, red chiles, and turmeric.

Italian seasoning—Basil, marjoram, oregano, rosemary, sage, savory, and thyme are common spices used in an Italian seasoning blend.

Pickling spice—The blend of spice varies by manufacturer and will include black peppercorns and red chiles with some or all of the following: allspice berries, cinnamon stick, whole cloves, ginger, mustard seeds, coriander seeds, bay leaves, and dill seed.

The aroma and flavor of any whole spice or seed will be enhanced by toasting or dry-frying in a skillet or in the oven. See p. 732 for a procedure to toast spices.

Salt and Pepper

Salt is used in every food production kitchen throughout the world because of its ability to "round out" flavors in foods and provide a desirable flavor balance. Table 5.23 identifies and describes the salt and pepper seasonings used most often to enhance the natural flavors of food products.

Monosodium glutamate (MSG) resembles salt in appearance and enhances the natural flavor of food without imparting a distinct flavor of its own. MSG occurs naturally in some foods and is also manufactured commercially. The distinctive taste that MSG produces has been called *umami*. The umami taste is referred to as a "savory" taste, distinct from the four classical tastes of sweet, sour, salty, and bitter. MSG enhances the flavor of low-acid foods (fish, meats, poultry, and vegetables) but has little effect on high-acid foods (fruits) and milk products.

MSG has been designated as safe for consumption by the general population. However, it has been reported to cause a reaction in some people, and the FDA requires that it be listed as an ingredient when added to food. Foodservice operators should be aware of products that contain MSG so customers' inquiries about its use can be accurately answered.

NUTS AND SEEDS

Nuts and seeds are used to add both flavor and texture to foods. Nuts have a high fat content and will absorb odors or become rancid if held improperly or for too long a time. Nuts and seeds will retain their freshness for 3–6 months if stored tightly covered in a cool, dark, well ventilated area or up to 1 year in a freezer. The aroma and flavor of nuts and seeds will be enhanced by toasting or dry-frying in a skillet or in the oven. Toast nuts and seeds following the procedure on p. 732.

Common nuts and seeds used in the kitchen are described in Table 5.24.

EXTRACTS, ALCOHOL, AND SWEETENERS

Flavorings other than herbs and spices are important kitchen staples necessary for making flavorful dishes. Extracts and essential oils from aromatic plants, dissolved in alcohol, are com-

TABLE 5.23	**Salt and pepper seasonings**
Name	**Description**
SALT	
Curing	• A blend of salt and sodium nitrate. • Used for curing meats.
Kosher	• Purified rock salt without additives. • Lighter in weight and flakier than table salt. The lightness varies by brand. • Dissolves quickly and will not cloud clear food products. It is a cooking salt preferred by most foodservice professionals. • To achieve the same level of saltiness that table salt provides, the amount of kosher salt may need to be increased by 1½–2 times the volume. Saltiness differs among brands.
Rock	• Unrefined salt not used directly in food. • Used in some ice cream machines for freezing ice cream.
Table	• Commonly used for cooking and for adding to foods at the table. Dissolves slowly. • Has an additive to keep it free-flowing. Available both with and without added iodine.
Sea	• Well known are *fleur de sel* (French, "flower of the sea"), *sel gris* (French, "gray salt"), and Hawaiian. Sea salt is made from evaporating natural seawater and is available ground or in whole crystals. • Because of the presence of other minerals, sea salt has a more complex flavor and often a gray-brown color. The salt's flavor will vary depending on the geographic location of the seawater used. • Often used for finishing and as a condiment.
PEPPER	
Peppercorns	• *Black peppercorns* are the dried unripe berries of a climbing vine (*Piper nigrum*). • *White peppercorns* are from the dried ripened berry of same climbing vine as black peppercorns. • *Pink peppercorns* are similar to black and white peppercorns in size and shape but are not from the same plant. They are slightly bitter and not as spicy as black and white peppercorns. Used for color more than for flavor. • *Green peppercorns* are the immature fresh berries from the same vine as black and white peppercorns. They are either freeze-dried or put in a brine or vinegar to stay soft.
Other Peppers	• Cayenne, chile flakes, and paprika are sometimes used to season food. In addition to seasoning, these peppers are likely to impart their characteristic flavors.

Note: Salt and pepper may be mixed to simplify seasoning of meats and vegetables. A recommended mixture is four parts table salt to one part ground black pepper. Kosher and sea salt are less salty, and a higher salt ratio is recommended.

TABLE 5.23   Salt and pepper seasonings

monly used in baked products and sauces. Only small amounts of extracts are needed to flavor products and, if feasible, should be added toward the end of the cooking period. For products that are baked, the extracts should be incorporated into the fat to improve flavor retention. Keep alcohol-based extracts tightly closed and in a cool environment.

Liquors, liqueurs, distilled spirits, and wines add a flavor profile to foods that is distinctly different from other flavorings. The common selections for use in food production include ales, beers, brandies, cognacs, champagnes, liqueurs or cordials, red and white wines, ports, sauternes, sherry, and vermouth. Bourbon, rum, and whiskey are also used to flavor foods and beverages.

For flavoring purposes, it is not always necessary to purchase the highest quality of product available. For best results the products should, however, be a quality that is suitable for drinking. Table wines begin to lose their flavor after opening and should be used within a short amount of time. Keeping opened wines tightly closed and refrigerated will help preserve their flavor. Fortified wines (e.g., sherry, port), liqueurs or cordials (e.g., amaretto, crème de cacao, crème de cassis, kirsch, Kahlúa), and brandies (e.g., cognac) keep their quality longer than table wine. Room-temperature storage, away from heat and light, is acceptable. Refrigerator storage is recommended if space is available.

Sugars and syrups add flavor to foods when used as an ingredient in recipes or when added to food and beverages after cooking. Sugars and syrups used in kitchens are identified in Table 5.25.

FATS

Fat is the general term that describes a category of kitchen staples used for flavoring, as a cooking medium, and as an ingredient in many recipes. Generally fats can be categorized as solid or liquid. Solid fats include butter, lard, margarine, and shortening. **Butter** is the fat portion separated from cow's milk. **Lard** is the fat rendered from the fatty tissue of hogs. Because of lard's excellent shortening power, it makes flaky pie crusts. Because of the degree of saturation and health concerns, lard is used infrequently. **Margarine** or oleomargarine can be used in place of butter in most recipes. Some flavor differences may be noticed and some texture changes can be expected in baked products. Soybean and cottonseed are the primary oils used to make margarine. **Shortening** (vegetable) is a product made by hydrogenating vegetable oils into a more solid, plasticlike product. The degree of hydrogenation determines the hardness of the shortening. Partially hydrogenated vegetable oils

TABLE 5.24   Nuts and seeds

TABLE 5.24   Nuts and seeds

Name	Description
ALMOND	Teardrop shaped. Available whole, sliced, slivered, ground, and as paste. Blanched almonds have the brown skin removed. Pale brown woody shell.
BRAZIL NUT	Large, elongated oval shape and creamy white color. High oil content. Eaten raw and used for baking. Hard, dark brown, three-sided shell.
CASHEW	Kidney shaped with a distinct flavor. Eaten raw and used in cooking (especially in some Asian dishes) and baking. Always sold shelled.
CHESTNUT	Large brown teardrop-shaped nut always cooked before using. Distinctive flavor. High starch content. Used in stuffing, soups, sauces, and sweet dishes. Glossy dark-brown shell.
COCONUT	Large melon-sized nut with white, sweet, nutty-flavored meat and a crisp, chewy texture. Can be purchased in the shell or as processed shredded or flaked coconut (sweetened or unsweetened). *Coconut water* is the thin liquid from inside the raw coconut; it is usually discarded. *Coconut milk* is the liquid extracted after shredded coconut has been heated in boiling water. *Coconut cream* is similar to coconut milk but has less liquid and thus is more concentrated. *Cream of coconut* has added sugar and is not interchangeable with coconut cream.
HAZELNUT	Small round shape with a rich delicate flavor. When desired for some baked products, remove the outer brown skin by warming for 12–15 minutes in a 275°F oven. While nuts are still hot, carefully put them into a dry cloth and rub together. Shell is hard and shiny with a light colored top.
MACADAMIA	Small, round, white nut with a high fat content. Associated with Hawaiian cuisine. Used in cookies and sweet pastries. Sold shelled.
PEANUT	A legume that grows underground along the root of a plant. Available raw or roasted. Shell is light brown and breaks easily.
PECAN	Medium-brown nutmeat with a rich, maple-like flavor. Available in halves or various-size pieces. Used widely in breads, desserts, sweets. Shell is medium-brown, smooth, and glossy.
PINE NUT	Seeds of several species of pine trees. Also known as *piñon nuts* and *pignole*. Tiny, cream-colored, elongated kernel. High in fat and becomes rancid quickly. Used in breads, pastries, salads (toasted). Essential ingredient in pesto.
PISTACHIO	Green-colored nutmeat (red pistachios are dyed). Used in pastries and desserts. Hard, light-brown shell that opens at one end when mature.
POPPY SEED	Tiny, round, blue-black seeds, with a sweet nutty flavor and crunchy texture. Used in pastries, breads, salad dressings.
PUMPKIN SEED	Flat, oval, cream-colored seed with a mild nutty flavor. Semihard hull with soft oily interior. Eaten out of hand or used as garnish.
SESAME SEED	Small, flat ovals with a creamy-white or black color. Nutty, earthy flavor. Often ground into a paste (known as tahini) or served as a garnish (often toasted) in bread and meat dishes. Popular in Indian and Asian cuisines.
SUNFLOWER SEED	Small, flat, teardrop-shaped. Light tan in color with a nutty flavor. Used as a topping for salads, in cookies, or eaten out of hand. Shell is black and white.
WALNUT	Light brown in color with a mild, sweet flavor and tender texture. General all-purpose nut. Hard, light-brown, rounded shell.

TABLE 5.25   Sugars and syrups

Name	Description
SUGAR	
Brown	Refined sugar with some molasses that was extracted from the refining process added. Amount of added molasses determines if light or dark brown sugar.
Turbinado	A partially refined cane sugar with coarse crystals and a slight molasses flavor. May be used to flavor beverages.
Granulated	All-purpose sugar; also called table sugar. Can be made from sugar cane or sugar beets. Fine, uniformly shaped crystals.
Sanding	Large, coarse crystals that are slow to dissolve. Used primarily for adding sparkle to cookies and pastries.
Superfine	Also called castor sugar. Granulated sugar with very fine grains. Dissolves more quickly in cold liquids and when making products such as meringues.
Powdered	Also called confectioner's sugar. Made by mechanically grinding granulated sugar into a fine powder. Cornstarch is added to absorb moisture and prevent lumping. Sprinkled on cookies and pastries as a garnish and in icing, glazes, and for decorating.
SYRUP	
Flavored	A sugar or other syrup with added flavorings. Used to flavor beverages.
Honey	A distinctive sweetener made by honeybees from the flowers of a wide variety of plants. The color and flavor depend on the nectar collected by the bees and the season of the year. Most honey sold commercially is from the nectars of sweet clover and alfalfa.
Maple	Real maple syrup, made from the sap of maple trees. An artificial maple syrup is made by adding maple flavoring to corn syrup.
Molasses	A liquid by-product of the sugar refining process. The amount of refinement determines the color and flavor.

form trans fats when metabolized and are illegal to use in food-service establishments in some states because of the health risks associated with them. Newer trans-fat-free shortenings have vegetable oil mixed with very hard, fully hydrogenated oil to produce the desired softness. Vegetable shortening may be all-purpose or manufactured for a specific purpose, such as deep-fat frying or cake making. Shortening not designated as vegetable shortening may contain animal fat.

Oils are fats that are liquid at room temperature and are made by extracting oil from high-oil-content seeds, fruits (avocado), and vegetables. Because cost, flavor, and other attributes vary among oils, it is important to select the correct one for the intended use. Table 5.26 describes oils commonly used in cooking.

The temperature at which fat begins to break down and become unusable is called the *smoke point*. Cooking at high temperatures, such as for deep-fat frying or sautéing, requires a fat with a high smoke point. The smoke point can be low for oils used for flavoring purposes, as in salad dressings or for a condiment. Table 5.26 identifies the smoke point for commonly used frying fats.

TABLE 5.26   Oil descriptions and approximate smoke points of selected fats

Fat	Smoke point of selected fats	Description of selected oils
Butter	260°F	
Butter, clarified (ghee)	335–380°F/168–193°C	
Canola (rapeseed)	435–448°F/224–230°C	Light golden-colored oil processed from rapeseed. Flavorless, all-purpose oil for frying and general cooking. High in unsaturated fatty acids.
Coconut		Heavy oil extracted from coconuts. Used primarily in processed foods. High proportion of saturated fatty acids.
Corn	410°F/210°C	Medium-yellow oil. Mildly flavored. All-purpose oil.
Cottonseed	450°F/232°C	Pale-yellow oil processed from the cotton plant. Flavorless all-purpose oil, for frying.
Frying	Variable depending on oil used	Blend of oils that will remain stable when exposed repeatedly to high heat.
Grape seed	445°F/229°C	Light medium-yellow to pale green colored oil made from grape seeds. Aromatic oil with a delicate, mild flavor, it is often used for salad dressing.
Margarine	410–430°F/210–221°C	
Olive (virgin and extra virgin)	250°F/121°C	Virgin olive oil is from the first cold pressing and has the lowest acidity level and most flavor of any olive oil. Extra virgin designates a top grade of virgin olive oil. Varies from pale yellow to deep green depending on the processing procedures and the variety of olive used. Color is not a good indicator of flavor. Best for salads, sauces, and flavoring. May be used for light sautéing.
Olive (pure)	410°F/210°C	Made from the pulp remaining after the first pressing. Has the least flavor and is suitable for cooking. Heat and chemicals may be used to produce pure olive oil.
Peanut	450°F/232°C	Pale-yellow refined oil with a very subtle scent and flavor. Because of its high smoke point, often used in high-heat Asian cooking.
Safflower	450°F/232°C	Golden-colored oil with a light texture and neutral flavor. All-purpose oil.
Salad		Blend of oils, neutral or mild in flavor. All-purpose oil.
Sesame seed (untoasted)	410°F/210°C	Pronounced aroma and flavor. The light variety made from untoasted seeds is milder than the more intense darker variety made from toasted seeds. Flavoring for Asian dishes.
Soybean	450°F/232°C	Light-yellow, relatively heavy oil with a mild flavor. Frying oil.
Sunflower	390°F/200°C	Pale-yellow, light oil, neutral flavor and no aroma. Salad oil.
Vegetable		Made by blending several oils; it may be a heavy oil. Blended to have a mild taste and a high smoke point.
Walnut		Medium-yellow in color with a distinct nutty flavor and aroma. With a low smoke point, it is more suited for salads and flavoring than cooking. Other flavorful nut oils are almond and hazelnut.

Notes:
- Smoke point is the temperature at which a fat's chemical structure is altered, causing it to smoke. When this change occurs, it is often referred to as *breaking down*.
- Fats with a high smoke point should be used for high-heat cooking such as deep-fat frying and sautéing.
- The smoke point temperatures may vary for different brands of the same fat because of a slightly different chemical structure.
- Heating fats repeatedly can cause the smoke point to lower. Smoke points are lowered also by salt, water, overheating, food particles, and oxygen.
- Fryer fat should be changed when it becomes dark, smokes, foams, or develops off-flavors.

Quantity Food Production Fundamentals and Evaluating Food Quality

Organizing the production process and following basic food production principles is fundamental to producing quality food. This chapter describes how to develop a production schedule and carry out classic mise en place tasks. Basic cooking terms and methods will be explained.

Evaluating food quality at critical points throughout production is elementary to continuous improvement. The information and guides included in this chapter will make the evaluation task easier.

This chapter includes the following topics:

- Production and Kitchen Readiness
- Production Scheduling
- Cooking Methods and Terms
- Cooking Temperature Tables
- Evaluating Food Quality

PRODUCTION AND KITCHEN READINESS

Mise en place—a French term meaning "everything in its place"—describes a series of preliminary tasks that are essential for producing quality food in an efficient manner. The goal of these pre-preparation activities is to complete as much work as possible before the actual food production begins without detracting from the quality of the final products. The efficiencies achieved will help production staff apply their cooking skills effectively and will allow for greater attention to be given to preparing and serving quality food without the delays and interruptions that could jeopardize quality. A well-organized kitchen has the benefit of a more professional looking workplace and will likely be a more safe and sanitary environment.

The following guidelines represent the advance preparations, organization, and kitchen setup—designed to get "everything in its place"—that should be completed before food production begins. There is no specified order for completing mise en place tasks. Generally, however, it is recommended that the tasks requiring the most time, those involving

the most functional areas, and those that do not impact food quality be started first.

Assemble Tools and Equipment

The work space should be organized for convenience and efficiency before cooking begins. Store the equipment, tools, and supplies required to prepare the recipes and to hold and serve food conveniently where it will be needed. Equipment and supplies include mixing bowls, saucepans, cookware, thermometers, serving pans and plates, storage containers, measuring devices, tasting spoons and dishes, required hand tools, plastic film, aluminum foil, waxed paper, hot pads, gloves, cloths, and sanitizing solution. Preheat ovens and cooking surfaces and assemble equipment such as choppers and food processors. Set up work stations for sub-preparation steps such as breading and battering and assembly areas for products requiring last minute assembly such as salad plates. Plan the equipment for holding both hot and cold food throughout the various stages of production. Sharpen knives if needed, and store knives and cutting boards in a convenient location. See Chapter 7 for knife-sharpening instructions and information about basic tools and equipment used in food production.

Gather Ingredients

Assemble food products that will be needed and store them in a convenient location and at the correct temperatures if potentially hazardous. Wipe can lids, open packages and cans, wash fruits and vegetables, fill food bins, and so on.

Complete Pre-Preparation Steps and Prepare Subrecipes; Prepare Par Levels of Seasonings and Food Staples

Break down each recipe into its production stages and identify the sequence of steps to make the finished product. Prepare in advance any pre-preparation steps or subrecipes that will not jeopardize food quality. For example, clarify butter, toast nuts and spices, make seasoning mixes, make bread crumbs,

On Cooking: A Textbook of Culinary Fundamentals, fourth edition, provides an expanded discussion of food and purchasing information, cooking techniques, and equipment; that book was a source of information for *Food for Fifty.*

pare and cut fruits and vegetables, prepare garnishes, trim meats if needed, make mirepoix (see p. 737), drain fruit, blanch vegetables, and zest lemons. The goal is to have all ingredients ready to assemble so the final recipe preparation can be efficient and as close to service time as possible.

Prepare or assemble par levels of frequently used ingredients and products that are needed to produce the recipes. Examples of products that often have par level amounts established include seasoning bundles such as bouquet garni or sachet (pp. 133 and 402), marinades, pastes and rubs (pp. 720–732), spices, and fresh herb, fruit, and vegetable garnishes.

Weigh and Measure Ingredients

Whenever possible, weigh or measure the ingredients that are needed in the recipes. Assemble the ingredients close to the production area.

Clean the Workplace and Keep It Orderly

Work surfaces should be clean and sanitary before starting production and should be kept clean throughout the production period. Place sanitizing solution and clean wipe cloths in an easily accessed location away from food. Designate an area for soiled utensils, dishes, cloths, and trash receptacles.

PRODUCTION SCHEDULING

Production scheduling is a decision-making and communication process to establish the time sequence needed to transform raw food into quality menu items for a specific period of time or meal. It requires an understanding of production steps, timing requirements for production processes, food science and food safety principles, and quality standards. Knowledge about production staff's skills and talents and about how to use time, equipment, and space resources efficiently is also needed. Production scheduling is a control in the production process that minimizes production problems and delays and maximizes food quality. The production controls provided by a well-thought-out production schedule will help reduce the instances of both over- and underproduction. Producing too much or too little food may introduce food safety risks. In addition, it usually challenges food quality and often increases both food and labor costs.

Production scheduling includes developing a **production worksheet** (also called a *production sheet* or *production schedule*). A production worksheet is a written plan that communicates to production staff the work that is to be accomplished during a specific period of time. Items included on a production worksheet should be individualized to the needs of each organization. The following items are often included on production sheets and discussed at production meetings:

- Calendar date and meal or period of time the production schedule covers
- Menu items to be produced and recipe name if different from the menu item name
- Forecast amount and actual yield of recipes produced

- Names of production staff who are responsible for specific tasks
- Approximate starting and completion times for menu items (The production timing for a full menu must consider the production timing for each menu item, quality standards for each item, and available labor and equipment.)
- Batch cooking instructions and partial or just-in-time assembly expectations
- Substitutions or backup items
- Special instructions and comments
- Instructions for using preserved (leftover) foods (Instructions for safety and for making foods being served a second time look appealing and taste good; see also menu-planning guidelines for minimizing leftovers, p. 34)
- Instructions for handling anticipated leftover food
- Pre-preparation tasks and additional assignments
- Facilities may use the production worksheet to record end-point cooking temperatures and other HACCP information. When used for this purpose, a designated section should be established on the production worksheet so the information can be easily retrieved and reviewed.

COOKING METHODS AND TERMS

Food is cooked when heat is transferred from a heat source (usually gas or electric) to the food by one of three methods: conduction, convection, or radiation. **Conduction** is the transfer of heat via a food's direct contact with a metal pan, liquid, or air. Heat is also transferred when a cooler portion of a food conducts heat from a hotter area. **Convection** heat transfer is achieved by moving heated air, liquid, or steam around food. This can be from the natural movement of hot and cool liquids or gases, or from mechanical means such as fans that circulate air in an oven. **Radiation** heating occurs when waves of either microwave (light waves) or infrared energy (heat waves) are transmitted to the food. In most cooking methods, more than one means of heat transfer occurs. In all cases, heat is disseminated throughout the food by conduction. Table 6.1 identifies the primary method of heat transfer for the basic cooking methods.

Applying heat to food causes changes in color, texture, flavor, and shape. Understanding the effect of heat on protein, carbohydrates (starches and sugars), water, and fats will facilitate the control of the cooking processes to produce quality food.

Coagulation is the transformation of protein molecules from a soft to a firm state. Most proteins complete the coagulation process between 160°F and 185°F. Using excessive heat and cooking meat protein beyond the optimum coagulation point will cause excessive loss of moisture and toughening of the meat fibers.

When heated, starch granules absorb water and swell. This process, called **gelatinization**, is responsible for the thickening of liquids. The temperature at which starch granules gelatinize varies, depending on the specific starch and other ingredients in the product. Generally, however, swelling is usually complete at a temperature of 190–195°F. Proper starch gelatinization can be interrupted by such things as excessive and prolonged heat,

TABLE 6.1   Primary heat transfer for basic cooking methods

Cooking method	Convection	Conduction	Radiation
Barbecuing			X
Boiling	X		
Braising	X	X	
Broiling			X
Deep-fat frying	X	X	
Grilling			X
Oven-frying	X		
Pan-frying	X	X	
Poaching	X		
Roasting and baking	X		
Sautéing		X	
Simmering	X		
Steaming	X		
Stewing	X	X	
Stir-frying		X	

Note: All cooking methods cause a conduction heat transfer within the food once the food or its surface becomes heated. Some cooking methods use more than one method of transferring heat to the food. In this case, both methods are identified in the table. Table 7.21 identifies the large-equipment requirements for basic cooking methods.

insufficient heat, failure to disperse dry starch in melted fat or cold water, and excessive agitation after a gel is formed.

Browning and flavor changes occur when sugar is exposed to high heat and is allowed to **caramelize**. Caramelization starts at about 310°F. The sugars that caramelize may be common table sugar like that used in baked products or sugars that occur naturally in most foods. Excessive caramelization may give the food a burned flavor and an unappealing dark color.

Maillard reactions cause nonenzymatic browning similar to caramelization, except that they involve the interaction of sugars and proteins when heated at high temperatures. Maillard reactions are the causes for many desirable colors, aromas, and flavors in food. Maillard reactions begin at about 310°F.

Most food contains water that will turn to steam and **evaporate** when heated to the boiling point. If food is heated for too long a time or at too high a temperature, the excessive moisture loss will cause a dry product. Fat **melts** when heated and alters the texture and flavor of foods.

Foods are cooked by either dry or moist heat when they come in contact with hot air, fat, liquid, or steam. **Dry-heat methods** are those that use hot air or fat as the cooking medium or subject food to direct flame heat. **Moist-heat methods** cook by surrounding food with a hot liquid or steam. Because moist-heat cooking techniques used for meats and poultry (i.e., braising and stewing) inhibit browning, the meat or poultry is often browned first to develop flavor and color. The cooking process using both moist and dry heat methods is sometimes referred to as a **combination cooking method**.

Careful selection of the cooking medium and heat method is necessary to ensure that quality standards and the desired sensory characteristics are met. The following criteria should be considered when deciding on the cooking methods that are best suited for foods.

- **Texture of the food.** For example, firm, delicate, or dense. Foods must be able to withstand the handling required by the cooking method selected.
- **Amount of fat in meat or fish.** Foods with internal fat self-baste and stay moist without added moisture.
- **Amount of connective tissue in meat.** Moist-heat cooking methods soften connective tissue and have a tenderizing effect. Dry-heat methods do not.
- **Grade and location of the meat cut.** Grade and location of the cut on the animal determine the amount of internal fat and connective tissue.
- **Size, shape, and thickness of the food.** The way heat penetrates food varies among cooking methods making the food's physical characteristics an important consideration.
- **Sensory characteristics desired.** For example, color, flavor, texture. The cooking method used will have an impact on the food's color, flavor, and other sensory attributes.

Foods appropriate for the different cooking methods are identified in the following discussion of each method. Exhibits 1–4 in Chapter 5 provide suggested cooking methods for beef, pork, and lamb cuts. Timetables and specific food production information for various categories of food are identified at the beginning of each recipe chapter.

Dry-Heat Cooking Methods

Broiling, Griddle-Broiling/Pan-Broiling, Grilling, and Barbecuing.
Broiling, **griddle-broiling/pan-broiling**, and **grilling** techniques cook food using direct or radiant heat from a heat source either overhead or underneath. *Broiling* generally refers to heat from an overhead heat source; *grilling*, a heat

source underneath the food; *griddle-broiling* and *pan-broiling*, heat from a hot flat surface such as a griddle or heavy pan. Broiling and grilling temperatures are regulated by the food's distance from the heat source. **Barbecuing** and grilling differ only in that *barbecuing* generally means cooking food in an outdoor environment using wood, charcoal, or gas fuel.

Broiled and grilled foods have a browned, flavorful exterior and a moist interior. Broiling is suited for foods that are relatively thin and uniform in size, and with enough internal fat or added moisture to keep from becoming dry when subjected to high broiling or grilling temperatures. The following are examples of foods typically broiled and grilled:

Meat	*Poultry*	*Fish*	*Vegetables*	*Fruit*
Tender cuts, e.g., chops, steaks, patties; 1–2 inches thick.	Cook whole birds rotisserie style. Choose from half and quarter chicken pieces and boneless cuts. Brush with oil or marinate. See Table 15.1 for poultry cooking methods.	Oily fish, e.g., bass, salmon, swordfish, trout, tuna; 1–2 inches thick. Brush with oil before broiling or grilling.	Not usually broiled. Bell peppers, eggplant, mushrooms, onions, and squash are suitable for grilling if brushed with oil.	Bananas, grapefruit halves, pineapple.

Broiling and grilling procedures

1. Preheat broiler or grill. A preheated rack will provide the desired markings on the food.

2. Place food on the rack. Put the presentation side on the rack first. When grid marks are desired, halfway through cooking on the first side gently slide a spatula under the food and rotate a quarter turn. A distance of 3–5 inches from the heat source is recommended for beef and pork and 6–8 inches for poultry. The distance from the heat source should increase when broiling thick or very cold meat. Brushing lean cuts of meat and most poultry and fish with oil will keep them from sticking to the grate. Food to be broiled should be as dry as possible and at least 1 inch thick.

   Delicate or very tender foods that will be damaged by placing them directly on the broiler rack can be placed on a preheated heatproof pan and then placed under the broiler. Care should be taken to keep food from cooking in its own juices because if moisture accumulates, the method will change from dry heat to moist heat.

3. Broil or grill foods until the side closest to the heat source is attractively browned and cooked almost halfway through.

4. Turn food. Turn only once during cooking. To keep from piercing meat, use tongs or a long-handled spatula. Broil the second side to the desired doneness and season. See the tables in Chapters 14 and 15 (pp. 421, 475) for cooking timetables.

To keep thick cuts or meat cooked well done from becoming charred on the outside before reaching the desired internal temperature, move the meat farther from the heat source or finish it in the oven.

For high-volume production of beef steaks, it may be necessary to quickly mark the meat on a hot grill (only partially cooking), chill it quickly, and then place it on a sheet pan to finish cooking in the oven. Chilling the partially cooked steaks and finishing them at the same time is necessary when large numbers must be served. The chilling step can be skipped when it is not important to have all the steaks prepared at the same time.

Pan-broiling and griddle-broiling procedures

1. Place food on a preheated ungreased griddle or heavy frying pan. For more even cooking, remove meat, poultry, and fish from the refrigerator 30 minutes before cooking.

2. Cook slowly, turning as necessary. Because the food is in contact with the hot metal of the pan or griddle, turning more than once may be necessary for even cooking. If the piece of food is thick, reduce the temperature after browning.

3. Cook at a moderate temperature. To keep juices in, care should be taken not to puncture the food while cooking. Use long-handled tongs or a spatula for turning.

4. Do not add fat or water. Pour off or scrape away any excess fat or juices as they accumulate. If juices accumulate around the food, the method of cooking will change from dry heat to moist heat.

5. Cook food to the desired degree of doneness. Season. See the tables in Chapters 14 and 15 (pp. 421, 475) for approximate cooking times.

Barbecuing procedures

1. Ignite charcoal. When the coals are ash covered (in approximately 30 minutes), spread them into a single layer.

2. Place seasoned or unseasoned meat, fish, or poultry on the grill directly over the ash-colored, medium-hot coals. (Coals are medium-hot when a hand can be held at cooking height for 4 seconds before the heat forces it to be pulled away. Extreme care should be taken when measuring the temperature of the coals in this way.) For more even cooking, remove food from the refrigerator 30 minutes before cooking.

3. Grill the food item uncovered. See the tables in Chapters 14 and 15 (pp. 421, 475) for approximate cooking times. If using bamboo skewers, they should be soaked in water for at least 30 minutes to keep them from burning. If using a sauce or glaze, it should be brushed on several times during the last half of the cooking time. Turn the product as needed to keep it from burning. Season.

Roasting and Baking.   **Roasting** and **baking** refer to a cooking process using air heated in an oven. A dry cooking environment is maintained by putting the food in an open, low-sided pan without adding moisture. Food cooks when hot air is transferred by convection to the food's surface. The term *roasting* is generally used for meats and poultry and *baking* for fish, fruits, pastries, and vegetables. There are exceptions to the terms use, however, as in *baked ham* and *roasted red-skinned potatoes*. Roasting and baking methods are appropriate for a wide variety of foods that vary in size and shape.

Roasted and baked foods have a brown, rich-flavored, caramelized exterior and a moist interior. The degree of browning and caramelization depends on the cooking time, the oven temperature, and the nature of the product being cooked. Browning and tenderizing occurs when meat is roasted at a low, constant oven temperature. Less tender cuts with considerable connective tissue should be cooked at lower temperatures for a longer time than tender cuts. Moist-heat cooking methods will dissolve more connective tissue and are more appropriate than roasting for tough cuts of meat.

Meats may be frozen or partially or completely defrosted when the cooking process begins. Meat roasted from the frozen state will yield as much meat as roasts partially or completely thawed before cooking. However, when time is a factor, defrosting meat before cooking is the accepted method. The additional cooking time required for frozen roasts is from one-third to one-half again the amount of time recommended for cooking a similar cut from the chilled state. Oven temperature should not change.

Roasting and baking methods are appropriate for a variety of foods with varying sizes and shapes. The recipe sections of this book include information and procedures for baking breads (Chapter 10, p. 228) and desserts (Chapter 11, p. 282), and timetables for roasting fish (Chapter 13, p. 400), meats (Chapter 14, p. 421), and poultry (Chapter 15, p. 475).

The following are examples of foods typically roasted and baked:

Meat	*Poultry*	*Fish*	*Vegetables*	*Fruit*
Tender, relatively large or thick cuts (standing rib, filet, leg of lamb)	Whole, quartered, or half birds	Large and medium-sized whole fish or thick steaks or fillets	Most vegetables, especially root and starchy vegetables (carrots, beets, eggplant, parsnips, potatoes, turnips, winter squash)	Firm, large fruits (apples, peaches, pears)

Roasting and baking procedures for savory foods

1. Preheat the oven.
2. Prepare the foods to be roasted or baked. Brush with oil or butter, if appropriate (as for roasted potatoes and some lean meats, poultry, and fish). Add herbs and other seasonings. Prick whole potatoes to allow steam to escape. Salt does not penetrate far into a large piece of meat, so it makes little difference if a large beef roast is seasoned at the beginning or end of the roasting time. Salting the inside of whole birds will increase the salt flavor of the meat. Many whole turkeys and chickens and chicken pieces are injected with a brine solution. Little additional salt is needed to flavor many of these injected products.
3. Place the food in a shallow roasting pan so hot air can circulate around the product. When cooking meat, place the fat side up. As the fat melts and runs down over the meat, it bastes the roast. Basting adds flavor and keeps the surface from drying out. Place whole poultry in a shallow baking pan, breast side up. If the bird will not be carved for show, bake it breast side down so the fat from the back area will baste the dryer white meat. If the turkey is browning too quickly, tent with aluminum foil and remove foil toward the end of cooking so the bird browns.
4. Roast the food, uncovered, at the appropriate temperature until it reaches the desired doneness. Baste meat and poultry with the juices that collect in the pan or with a marinade as necessary to keep it from drying out and to add flavor. Vegetables and cut potatoes should be turned once or twice as they roast.

   Do not add water and do not cover meat. Adding water to the pan changes the cooking method from dry to moist heat.

   Roast at a constant oven temperature. High heat is used for small, very tender cuts of meat that cook quickly, such as beef tenderloin. Meats cooked at high temperatures will have more caramelization and greater shrinkage.
5. Toward the end of the roasting period, insert a meat thermometer so that the tip rests in the center of the roast without touching bone or fat. Vegetable and fruit doneness can be tested by inserting a fork to measure softness or tenderness.

   The length of the cooking period depends on several factors: oven temperature, size and shape of the food item, style of cut (bone-in or boneless), proportion of meat to bone, meat quality, oven load, and degree of doneness required. See the recipe chapters for timetables for roasting beef, lamb, pork, veal, and poultry (Chapters 14 and 15, pp. 421, 475).

   Meat and whole poultry should be removed from the oven and allowed to set in a warm place, generally tented with foil, for 15–30 minutes before being sliced or carved. Roasts will continue to cook during this period as the heat continues to penetrate to the center. Generally a 5–10°F rise or carryover can be expected. Small roasts lose surface heat rapidly and will have the lowest rise in temperature.

During this resting time, the meat will become more firm and easier to slice with minimal juice loss.

6. Season as appropriate.

Frying.   **Frying** is a dry-heat method of cooking and a term used to describe cooking in fat. The amount of fat distinguishes the methods of frying. **Deep-fat frying** uses a large amount of fat; **pan-frying** and **griddle-frying** (also called *griddling*) use a moderate amount of fat; **oven-frying** uses some fat; and **sautéing** and **stir-frying** use a small amount of fat.

Deep-fat frying heats food through conduction and convection by submerging it in hot fat. The high heat causes food to brown and cook quickly. Other frying methods cook foods through contact with fat but also through heat conducted from the pan or griddle. Pan-frying and griddle-frying are similar to pan and griddle-broiling except that both frying methods have fat added. Fat and drippings are not scraped away during griddle-frying as they are with griddle-broiling. The amount of added fat depends on the food being cooked.

Well-prepared deep-fat fried foods will have a crisp, golden-brown exterior, a minimum amount of fat absorption, and no off-flavors imparted by the frying fat. Most deep-fat fried foods have a coating of breading or batter to provide color, flavor, and crispness. The color and crispness of pan- and griddle-fried foods will depend on whether a coating or breading is used, the length of cooking time, and the nature of the product. Sautéed and stir-fried foods are cooked very quickly at a high temperature in a small amount of fat. They may or may not be browned, and crispness is not always an objective. Oven-fried foods are cooked at a high temperature in an oven after first being drizzled with fat. The food resulting from this production method is intended to resemble pan-fried and deep-fat fried foods in texture and exterior color. Following are examples of foods typically fried:

	Meat/poultry/eggs	*Fish*	*Vegetables/fruit*
Deep-fat fried	A variety of meat and poultry products, usually battered or breaded; bone-in or bone-out chicken pieces. Large pieces of meat or poultry are usually not deep-fat fried.	A variety of fish and shellfish, usually battered or breaded; shrimp.	A variety of vegetables, usually battered or breaded; mushrooms, okra, onions, potatoes.
Pan-fried	A variety of meat and poultry products. May be dredged in seasoned flour to form a crisp crust as for fried chicken. Chicken, turkey, veal scallops.	A variety of fish products. May be dredged in seasoned flour to form a crisp crust.	Eggplant, potatoes.
Griddle-fried	Boneless, thin meat and poultry products; fried eggs; scrambled eggs.	Thin fillets.	Hashed brown potatoes.
Oven-fried	Meat and poultry with some thickness; chicken pieces, quarters, or halves.	Thick fillets.	Not usually oven-fried.
Sautéed	Thin pieces of poultry and tender cuts of meat.	Thin fillets.	High-moisture vegetables: bell peppers, mushrooms, onions, summer and zucchini squash. Fruits: bananas, pineapple, apples, peaches.
Stir-fried	Small thin strips of poultry and tender cuts of meat.	Scallops, shrimp.	A variety of vegetables; beans, bell peppers, edamame, greens, mushrooms, onions, peas.

Deep-fat frying procedures

1. Prepare the food to be fried—cut, trim, bread, batter. Portioned prebreaded items can be cooked from a frozen state.

2. Heat the fat to approximately 360–375°F (or per recipe). Foods will absorb some fat during cooking. A cooking temperature that is too low will increase the amount of fat absorbed and cause the food to be excessively greasy. Adding 15 to 20 percent fresh fat or oil each day the fryer is in use will extend the life of the fat. Care should be taken not to damage fat. Fat is damaged by prolonged heating, overheating, moisture, salt, and food particles. Keeping fat clean by frequent filtering will extend its life considerably.

3. Submerge food in hot fat by either loading a wire basket with food to be fried and lowering it slowly into the fat or dropping the food directly into the hot fat. If food is crowded, it will not cook evenly and the fat temperature may be reduced too quickly, thereby increasing fat absorption and inhibiting browning. When filling a wire basket, do so away from the grease. Particles of food and ice crystals will damage the fat. Stacking an empty basket over a basket with food will help keep it submerged for even cooking.

4. Continue cooking until the outside of the product is browned and crisp and the meat reaches the desired doneness. Internal temperature is the most accurate indicator of doneness. A combination of sensory indicators is helpful in determining doneness: surface color, timing, and sampling for doneness. Cooking time depends on the

size of the food item, whether it is frozen or chilled, and whether the food has been precooked.

5. Remove meat or poultry from the fat and let it drain. Do not shake the basket over the fat if the product is coated; shaking will cause particles and crumbs to fall into the fat and damage it.

6. Transfer the food to a pan lined with a rack or absorbent paper. Season away from fat. Serve as soon as possible after frying. The crust on fried products softens quickly after cooking and should not be covered to trap moisture.

Pan- and griddle-frying procedures

1. Prepare the food to be fried—cut, flatten, bread with seasoned flour, crumbs, cornmeal, or similar coatings.

2. For pan-frying, heat (to approximately 325°F) enough fat in a heavy pan or skillet to cover the food to a depth of $\frac{1}{3}$ to $\frac{1}{2}$ inch. When using a griddle (solid cooking surface), put some fat where the food will be placed. For both pan-frying and griddle-frying, the amount of fat depends on the food being cooked.

3. Carefully place the food in the pan or on the griddle.

4. Cook slowly, uncovered, until the food is brown on one side. Turn and brown on the other side. Because the food is in contact with the hot metal of the pan or griddle, turning more than once may be necessary for even cooking. If meat is thick, reduce the temperature after browning. Pan- and griddle-fried meats may be browned and removed to a pan and finished in the oven. The pan should not be covered, and moisture should not be added.

5. Cook meat to the desired degree of doneness. Pan- and griddle-fried foods are usually done when browned on both sides. Drain on absorbent paper. Season. Pan-fried foods should be served as soon as possible after reaching their desired doneness.

Oven-frying procedures

1. Prepare the food to be oven-fried—dust or dredge with seasoned flour if desired, put on a greased baking pan, and drizzle food with oil or brush with melted fat. Season. Placing food on silicone paper will make cleanup easier.

2. Preheat the oven to 375–425°F. Place the food in the oven. Cook uncovered until the food is brown and cooked to the desired doneness.

3. Do not cover or add moisture.

Sautéing procedures

1. Prepare the food to be sautéed—flatten or cut to an even thickness, season food or dust in seasoned flour.

2. Heat a sauté pan and add a small amount of oil or fat (clarified butter, pure olive oil, frying oil) to cover the bottom of the pan. Both the pan and oil should be very hot when the food is added. The amount of oil depends on the food.

Meats with considerable internal marbling will require only a small amount of fat.

3. Place the food in the pan, presentation side down. To allow for proper color and flavor development, the food should not be crowded and the pieces should not overlap.

4. Fry the food on one side until browned. Using tongs, turn once and brown the other side. Thin meat used for sautéing is usually done when browned on both sides. When thicker meat is sautéed, the temperature should be lowered after some browning, or the food can be finished to the desired doneness in the oven.

5. Remove the food from the pan and make a sauce using the pan drippings if desired. All or some of the fat can be poured off before making a sauce using the pan drippings and the stuck-on bits that are removed in a **deglazing process** (adding a liquid such as broth, stock, water, or wine and scraping loose any stuck-on pieces of browned food). Reduce the liquid to sauce consistency.

6. Serve the food with the sauce or return the food to the sauce to quickly coat and rewarm if necessary. Meat should not cook in the sauce.

Stir-frying procedures

1. Prepare the food to be stir-fried—cut into small uniform pieces, cut meat into thin slices or strips. Partially freezing meat will facilitate slicing.

2. Heat a wok or other suitable pan and add a small amount of oil to the pan. Both the pan and the oil should be very hot when the food is added. Add oil-flavoring ingredients such as such as salt, garlic, ginger root, scallions, or chile peppers.

3. Add the main ingredient or meat and stir-fry quickly. Do not overcrowd the pan. Some browning is desirable, so delaying the stirring or tossing for a few minutes is advised. After slight browning has occurred, keep the food moving using a light tossing motion or stir with a spatula so it sears and cooks evenly. Stir and cook until the main ingredient is done, pushing it up the sides of the wok away from the most intense heat. If cooking meat, remove it from the pan and drain off any excess fat.

4. Add additional ingredients in sequence (those with the longest cooking time first), cooking and moving them up the sides of the wok. Cook until vegetables are tender-crisp.

5. Add thickening liquid and sauces (see p. 818 for cornstarch-and-water ratio). Cook just until the sauce thickens and the ingredients are lightly coated. Add the meat item back into the pan to reheat. Serve immediately.

Moist-Heat Cooking Methods

Moist-heat cooking methods transfer heat to food through liquid or steam. Food products cooked by moist-heat methods have a more subtle flavor, softer texture, and less browned appearance than those cooked with dry heat. Flavor and color differences are due in part to the absence of surface caramelization that occurs with dry heat.

Blanching and Parboiling. **Blanching** and **parboiling** describe the process of submerging food in a hot liquid for a brief time and then quickly chilling it in a cold liquid. The cooking time for parboiling food is longer than for blanching food. Boiling water is generally used to blanch and parboil fruits and vegetables. French fries may be blanched or parboiled in hot oil. Blanching and parboiling fruits and vegetables sets the color and loosens skins for easier peeling. Parboiling softens the food more than blanching and is appropriate for foods that will be finished by sautéing or stewing.

Blanching and parboiling procedures

1. Immerse fruits and vegetables in a large quantity of boiling water. The time depends on the amount of softening desired and the nature of the food. Blanching requires immersion for a few seconds to a minute. Parboiling may require several minutes, depending on the food and the degree of cooking desired.

2. After immersing for the desired amount of time, remove the food from the boiling water and plunge it immediately into ice water to stop the cooking process. The process of quickly chilling blanched or parcooked food is referred to as **shocking** or **refreshing.**

Braising. **Braising** is a cooking process that begins with dry heat and finishes with moist heat. Food is first browned using high heat and a small amount of fat and then liquid is added. The food is covered and cooked slowly over low heat. The braising liquid is served with the food as a sauce. *Fricasseeing* is a braising method in which food is simmered in a thickened liquid (gravy) rather than water or other nonthickened liquid. *Pot-roasting* also applies to this cooking method. Braised foods should have a deep color that is appropriate for the food being prepared and a robust flavor with a full-bodied sauce. Foods should retain their natural shape and be moist and *fork-tender*, which means a fork will slide out of the food easily after being inserted in the thickest part.

Portion-sized or larger pieces of meat and poultry are most often braised. The method is not used frequently for parboiled vegetables and whole fish.

Braising procedures

Using Thickened Liquid

1. Prepare the food to be braised—trim meat and poultry, season, and dredge in flour if desired. Dredging in flour increases browning and may be omitted.

2. Sear the food on all sides in a small amount of hot oil. Browning develops aroma, flavor, and color. Large pieces can be browned in a heavy pot on top of the stove, in the oven, or in a steam-jacketed kettle.

3. Remove the food from the pan and add mirepoix and any other ingredients. Cook until the desired color. For meats, the mirepoix is usually browned more than for poultry. One ounce of mirepoix for each pound of meat is a guideline. The standard mirepoix mix of vegetables is chopped onion or leeks (2 parts), chopped carrots (1 part), and chopped celery (1 part). For a white mirepoix, parsnips may be substituted for the carrots. Bacon or ham may be added to give flavor. The vegetables can be larger when the mirepoix will be cooked for an extended time. When a mirepoix is used for moisture and seasoning only, the vegetables can be left unpeeled, except for the onion. If the vegetables will become part of the dish, they should be peeled.

4. Add flour or a roux for thickening. Stir some liquid into the pan to deglaze and to combine with the flour or roux.

5. Return the food to the pan and add the cooking liquid. Liquids may be well-seasoned stock, tomato juice, wine, or appropriate jus. Add aromatics and seasonings as desired. Use enough liquid to cover approximately one-third of the food. For tough cuts of meat that will cook for an extended time and have considerable liquid evaporation, use enough liquid to cover up to half of the meat. If necessary to keep liquid on the product, add additional liquid during cooking.

6. Cover the pan with a tight-fitting lid or aluminum foil. Cook at a low oven temperature (275–300°F) until fork-tender or slowly on top of the stove. Simmer but do not boil. Steam that condenses on the lid and drops on the food will help keep the food moist. Exposed surfaces can be moistened with the braising liquid by turning the food occasionally.

7. Remove the food from the braising liquid when it is fork-tender and hold it in a warm place. If needed, adjust the sauce for seasoning and consistency. Serve meat with sauce. See the timetable for braising meat (Chapter 14, p. 428).

Using Unthickened Liquid

1. Omit step 4 for braising procedures using thickened liquids. Follow all other steps (1–3, 5–7).

2. Make a sauce from the braising liquid by reducing the liquid or thickening the liquid using arrowroot, cornstarch, or a roux. The liquid may be strained if desired, or the mirepoix puréed and returned to the liquid before thickening. Adjust for seasoning and consistency.

When vegetables are served with braised meat, they should be added to the liquid toward the end of the cooking period and cooked just long enough to be cooked through. Vegetables can be cooked separately and added to the liquid just before serving.

Boiling. **Boiling** refers to cooking food in a liquid that is bubbling rapidly. The water movement and high temperature cooks food quicker than poaching and simmering. Few foods are boiled; most are simmered. Boiling temperatures will toughen meat, fish, and egg protein and break up delicate foods. Rapid boiling is suited for cooking pasta, potatoes, and some root vegetables.

Boiling procedures

1. Bring liquid to a boil over high heat. Add seasonings if desired.

2. Add the food carefully to the rapidly boiling water. Adjust the temperature to maintain a boil. The higher the proportion of water to food, the faster the water will return to a boil.

3. Cook until the food reaches the desired doneness. See Chapter 14, p. 421, for timetables for cooking meat.

4. Remove the food from the boiling liquid and serve. Some foods, such as pasta, can be chilled quickly in cold water and reheated by submerging briefly in boiling water.

Poaching.   **Poaching** is a moist-heat cooking method that gently transfers heat from a cooking liquid to food that is completely submerged in the liquid. The poaching liquid can either cover the food entirely or, as in **shallow-poaching,** come halfway up the sides of the food. Poaching produces a product that is moist, plump, and tender. Foods are cooked within a temperature range of 160–180°F and only until they reach a safe internal temperature.

A flavorful cooking liquid that complements the food being poached should be used. Common poaching liquids and aromatics include broth, stock, court bouillon, wines, herbs, spices, and vegetables. Poached foods are often served with a flavorful sauce prepared separately.

Poaching procedure

1. Prepare the food to be poached—trim, wrap in cheesecloth, tie with string.

2. Bring the poaching liquid to the desired temperature. Some foods, such as eggs, are started in water that is close to the poaching temperature. Foods that are generally started in a cold liquid and gradually brought to the poaching temperature include dense fruits such as pears. Poaching liquid for fish may be acidulated water, court bouillon, bouquet garni liquid, fish stock, milk, or milk and water. See p. 402 for poaching liquids for fish.

3. Add the food to the poaching liquid. It is important to keep the food completely submerged in liquid or partially submerged for shallow poaching. Shallow poaching requires that the food be covered loosely to keep the food moist and bathed in liquid.

4. Poach food in the oven or on the stove top until just set or until the desired internal temperature is reached. Keep the poaching temperature between 160°F and 180°F. Skim as necessary to improve the appearance of the final product. When done, fish will flake easily when tested with a fork.

5. Remove the food carefully from the cooking liquid. Moisten hot food with some liquid to keep it from drying out. Foods cooled in the poaching liquid will continue to cook after being removed from the heat source and should be undercooked slightly. Food safety standards for chilling potentially hazardous foods must be followed.

Simmering.   **Simmering** is a term for cooking foods in a liquid that is held just below the boiling point (185–205°F.) Simmering is appropriate for meats such as corned beef and stew meat that need to be tenderized through long, slow, moist cooking. Simmered foods will be tender and will absorb flavor from a well-seasoned cooking liquid.

Simmering procedures

1. Prepare the food to be simmered.

2. Bring enough liquid to cover the food to a boil over high heat. Add mirepoix and seasonings as desired.

3. Add the food carefully to boiling water. Adjust the temperature to keep the liquid just below the boiling point (185–205°F).

4. Cook until the food reaches the desired doneness. Skim as necessary. See Chapter 14, p. 421, for a timetable for cooking meat in liquid.

5. Remove the food from the simmering liquid and serve or cool quickly in the cooking liquid following HACCP guidelines, p. 167.

Steaming, Cooking en Papillote, and Pan-Steaming. **Steaming, cooking en papillote,** and **pan-steaming** cook food by exposing it directly to steam. Steamed food will be moist, plump, flavorful, and visually appealing. Flavors may be added by wrapping food in aromatic leaves, stuffing it with flavorful ingredients, or marinating it. A wide variety of fish, meat, poultry, and vegetables can be steamed. Steaming keeps foods intact because it cooks without agitation. Good nutrient and color retention is achieved because there is minimal water to leach nutrients and pigment from the food.

Foods may be cooked using low-pressure, high-pressure, and zero-pressure steam equipment. Steaming is also achieved with smaller stove top pans and with small steamers such as rice cookers. Wrapping food tightly to allow steam to be formed by its own moisture is another steaming method.

Steaming procedures using commercial steam equipment

1. Place food to be steamed not more than 3–4 inches deep in stainless steel inset pans. Perforated pans provide the best circulation, but if cooking liquid needs to be retained, solid pans should be used.

2. Steam according to timetables for food items being cooked. See Chapter 21, p. 769, for vegetable timetables.

Steaming procedures using stove top methods

1. Bring a small amount of liquid to a gentle boil in a covered pan. Use enough liquid to last throughout the entire cooking time.

2. Add the food to be steamed in a single layer on a rack above the boiling liquid. Place the food so steam can circulate easily around the food.

3. Place a tight-fitting lid on top of the pan and allow steam to build up.

4. Steam the food until it reaches the desired doneness. Serve immediately with appropriate seasonings or sauce.

Steaming procedures using oven methods

1. Place frozen fish or chicken breast on greased aluminum foil. Season and flavor with lemon juice, spices, and thinly sliced vegetables.

2. Wrap securely. Place in shallow baking pan. Bake at 400°F for 20–25 minutes per inch of thickness.

Pan-steaming procedures

1. Follow the same procedures as for pan poaching, except cover the food with a tight-fitting lid. Keep water level as low as possible.

Cooking en papillote procedures

1. Cut parchment paper in a heart shape large enough so the food being encased will fit without being overcrowded. There should be enough room for the paper to expand during cooking. Butter or oil both sides of the paper to keep it from burning.

2. Place a bed of aromatics, vegetables, or sauce on half of the paper; then place the main item on top.

3. Fold the empty side of the paper over the filled side. Crimp the edges of the paper to form a tight seal.

4. Place the packet on a pan and into a very hot oven. Bake the encased food until it is puffy and browned and the main ingredient is just done. Using timing standards developed through experience is the best way of determining doneness. Controlling the size of the main ingredient and parcooking some foods are important to properly cooking foods en papillote.

Stewing. Stewing is a cooking method similar to braising, but the main item is cut into bite-sized pieces. Stews require enough liquid to just cover the meat. The main ingredient can be browned in a small amount of oil. Because stewed foods are cut smaller, the cooking time is less than for braising. See Chapter 14, p. 421, for a meat stewing timetable.

Stewing procedures

1. Follow braising procedures, except cut the main ingredient into smaller pieces and add enough liquid to just cover the main ingredients.

2. Garnishes and vegetables may be cooked separately and added to the stew toward the end of the stewing process.

COOKING TEMPERATURE TABLES

Timetables for specific food categories of foods are identified in the recipe chapters. This section includes basic time and temperature references for food production. Tables included in this section:

Table 6.2—Temperatures Used for Food Preparation This table identifies temperature guidelines for cooking food. (p. 153)

Table 6.3—Convection Oven Baking Times and Temperatures This table is useful when using convection ovens. Times and temperatures in recipes included in *Food for Fifty* have been tested using conventional ovens unless otherwise specified. (p. 154)

Table 6.4—Deep-Fat Frying Temperatures This table provides guidelines for deep-fat frying different types of menu items. (p. 155)

Table 6.5—Coatings for Deep-Fat Fried Foods Proportions of ingredients are given for typical coatings for deep-fat fried foods. (p. 156)

EVALUATING FOOD QUALITY

Quality control is achieved by continuous evaluation of food products in accordance with the standards established by the foodservice operation. By knowing the desired characteristics of the final product, checks can be established at critical points throughout production, holding, and service to ensure that quality is being achieved. Critical points in food production where quality can be compromised include ingredient weighing and measuring; preparation procedures and techniques; cooking times and temperatures; selection of tools, equipment, and utensils; sanitation; and the physical condition of the product throughout preparation. Holding and service functions share some of the same control points. Chapters 2–6 and general information in the recipe chapters provide information that is helpful for preparing quality food products that have good visual appeal and sensory characteristics and are safe from illness-causing microorganisms.

A quality food standard establishes the basis for judging a product's quality attributes. The quality standard should include sensory attributes such as color, consistency, crumb, crust, density, flavor, form, moistness or juiciness, shape, tenderness, texture, and volume. Descriptors may not be applicable to every product.

Production staff will find it helpful to have quality standards identified on the recipe so they can visualize what a quality product should represent. This is especially important for new menu items or for inexperienced cooks. Standards should be written for the actual recipes being used and should include terminology that considers the recipe's ingredients and food items. Following are examples of quality standards for selected food products.

TABLE 6.2   Temperatures used for food preparation

	°F	Notes
OVEN		
Extremely hot	500–525	Pocket flat breads (pita)
Very Hot	450–475	Pizza
Hot	400–425	Biscuits, pie pastry
Moderate	350–375	Cakes
Slow	300–325	Large roasts, poultry
DEEP-FAT FRYING		
Hot	395	French-fried potatoes
Moderate	375	Battered foods (vegetables)
Low	350	Chicken, fish
SUGAR COOKERY		
Caramelization	338	
Hard crack	310	Candy brittles
Soft crack	290	Taffy
Hard ball	266	Divinity
Firm ball	248	Caramels
Soft ball	239	Fudge
Very soft ball	234	Fondant
WATER TEMPERATURES		
Boiling	212	0 lb pressure at sea level (see Note)
Simmering	185–210	
Scalding	149	
Lukewarm	104	

Note: Boiling temperature varies slightly at higher altitudes.

TABLE 6.2   Temperatures used for food preparation

Bread

Banana Bread.   The top should be slightly rounded, pebbly, with a shallow crack down the middle section, and with a medium-brown tender crust. The bread should have an even grain, be free from tunnels, and have a light and tender texture with a moist, beige-colored crumb and dark-brown banana flecks. The flavor should be sweet and mild with a characteristic banana flavor.

Muffins.   The crust should be crisp, shiny, pebbly, and golden brown. The top should be rounded but not peaked. The volume should be large when compared with weight. The crumb should be moist, light, and tender with a slightly coarse, even grain and no tunnels. Flavor should be slightly sweet and characteristic of the nuts, fruit, spices, and other flavorings used.

French Bread.   The crust should be crisp, smooth, tender, and relatively thin with an even, golden brown color. The loaf should be symmetrically shaped. The grain should be fine and even with uniform thin cell walls. The crumb color should be creamy white and the texture moist, soft, elastic, and resilient with a nutlike flavor.

Desserts

White Cake.   The crust should be thin, soft, and a uniform golden brown. A slightly rounded top should be smooth and free from cracks. The grain should have small, uniform, evenly distributed thin-walled cells. The crumb should be resilient, soft, and velvety. The cake should be light, tender, and moist. The flavor should be delicately sweet and well blended.

Cherry Pie Crust.   Texture should be crisp, flaky, and tender. Both crusts should be rolled thin. The appearance of the top crust should be blistery with a soft luster. The color should be light and golden, with brown deepening slightly toward the edges. The flavor is pleasantly bland with a characteristic flavor, depending on the proportion of salt and the kind of fat used.

Cherry Pie Filling.   Cherries should be a rich, bright, shiny, red color in a transparent, smooth, thickened sauce. Whole cherries should be obvious. Fruit filling should ooze out gently from between the crusts when served. The pie should have a sweet-tart flavor, characteristic of red sour cherries.

Entrées

Beef Pot Pie.   The pastry top crust should be golden brown, crisp, and flaky. The vegetables should be bright and colorful and the meat a characteristic brown. Bite-size pieces of meat and vegetables should be tender but not mushy. The vegetables and meat should be evenly distributed in a smooth, medium-thick, beef-flavored sauce that flows slowly when spooned onto a plate. The beef and vegetable flavors should be characteristic and the seasonings balanced.

TABLE 6.3 Convection oven baking times and temperatures

Product	Oven temperature		Approximate baking time
	°F	°C	
MEATS			
Steamship round (50 lb, medium)	250–275	120–135	8–9 hr
Rolled beef roast (12–15 lb)	275	135	2½ hr
Standing rib, choice (20 lb, trimmed, rare)	250–300	120–150	2¾ hr
Lasagna	250–275	130	90 min
Hot dogs, 10 per lb (18 × 26-inch pan)	325	165	10–15 min
Baked stuffed pork chops	375	190	20–30 min
Bacon (on racks in 18 × 26-inch pans)	400	205	5–10 min
POULTRY			
Chicken breast and thigh	350	175	40 min
Chicken (2½ lb quartered)	350	175	30 min
Turkey, rolled (18-lb rolls)	310	155	3¾ hr
Turkey, whole (16–20 lb)	275–300	135–150	4–5 hr
FISH AND SHELLFISH			
Halibut steaks, codfish (frozen, 5 oz)	350	175	20 min
Lobster tails (frozen)	425	220	9 min
POTATOES			
Baked potatoes (120 count)	400	205	50 min
Oven-roasted potatoes (sliced or diced)	325	165	10 min
BAKED GOODS			
Frozen pie (22 oz)	400	205	30–35 min
Frozen pie (46 oz)	350	175	45–50 min
Fresh apple pie (20 oz)	350–375	175–190	25–30 min
Pumpkin pies	300	150	30–35 min
Fruit cobbler	300	150	30 min
Apple turnovers	350	175	15 min
Corn bread	335	170	20–25 min
Bread (24 1-lb loaves)	350	175	30 min
French bread	375	190	18–20 min
Yeast rolls	350	175	25 min
Croissant	325	165	15–18 min
Danish	335	170	12 min
Sheet cake (5 lb batter per pan)	325	165	25–35 min
Layer cake rounds	325	165	20–25 min
Fruit cakes	275	135	70 min
Brownies	325	165	20 min
Cookies	325–350	165–175	10–15 min
Cream puffs	350	175	20–25 min

Notes:
- Actual times and temperatures may vary from those shown. They are affected by weight of load, temperature of the product, recipe, and type of pan.
- For menu items not listed, use recommended time and temperature for conventional oven but reduce the temperature setting by 25–50°F and reduce the total bake/roast time by approximately 10 to 15 percent.
- The recipes in *Food for Fifty* were standardized using a conventional oven.

Chili. The color of the ground beef and beans should be a deep red-brown tomato color with the meat and beans mixed evenly throughout the mixture. The meat should be moist, not dry or crumbly, and the beans tender yet firm. The size of the meat pieces should be the same as the beans or a little smaller. The flavor should be distinct with meat, tomatoes, chile powder, and other seasonings well blended. The chili should have a thick sauce consistency that flows easily when ladled into a bowl.

Lasagna. The top should have a tomato-red color. The alternating layers of meat mixture, pasta, and cheese should be distinct. The noodles should be tender yet hold their shape. The spicy tomato-beef flavor of the meat mixture should blend

| TABLE 6.4 | Deep-fat frying temperatures |

Type of product	Preparation[a]	Temperature[b] °F	°C	Frying time[c] (minutes)
BREADS				
Doughnuts	See p. 257	375	190	3–5
French toast	See p. 259	360	180	3–4
Fritters	See p. 260	375	190	2–5
Sandwiches	Batter	350–375	175–190	3–4
FISH				
Fillets or pieces	Egg and crumb or batter	360–375	180–190	4–6
Oysters	Egg and crumb	375	190	2–4
Scallops	Egg and crumb	360–375	180–190	3–4
Shrimp	Batter or egg and crumb	360–375	180–190	3–5
FRUIT				
Bananas	Batter	375	190	1–3
POULTRY				
Chicken, pieces	Light coating or egg and crumb			
Fryers (1½–2 lb)		350	175	10–12
Fryers (2–2½ lb)		350	175	12–15
Chicken, half	Light coating or egg and crumb			
Fryers (1½–2 lb)		350	175	12–15
Turkey or chicken cutlets	Egg and crumb	325–350	165–175	5–8
VEGETABLES				
Cauliflower, precooked	See p. 794	370	185	3–5
Eggplant	See p. 794	370	185	5–7
Mushrooms	See p. 794	370	185	4–6
Onion rings	Batter	350	175	3–4
Potatoes, ½-inch strips	See p. 799			
Complete fry		365	182	6–8
Blanching		360	180	3–5
Browning		375	190	2–3
Frozen, fat blanched		375	190	2–3
Zucchini	See p. 794	370	185	4–6

[a] See Table 6.5 for light coating, egg and crumb, and batter.

[b] If food is frozen, use a lower temperature than listed and allow additional cooking time. At high altitudes, the lower boiling point of water in foods requires lowering of temperatures for deep-fat frying.

[c] The exact frying time will vary with the equipment used, size and temperature of the food pieces, and the amount of food placed in the fryer at one time. If the fryer is overloaded, foods may become grease-soaked.

Note: Use frying fat with a high smoking temperature (see p. 142). Filter fat regularly, at least daily or more often if fryer is in constant use. The breakdown of fat may be caused by using the fat for too long a period, cooking food at too high a temperature, failing to filter the fat regularly, or inadvertently getting salt into the fryer when salting food.

well with the cheeses and pasta. Lasagna servings should hold their shape, with the layers identifiable.

Soups

Beef Rice Soup.   The transparent brown beef broth stock should possess body and may have a slight sheen due to dispersed fat globules from the meat. The browned stew meat should be tender with a distinct beef flavor. The bite-size celery, finely chopped onions, and rice should be tender, yet firm enough to hold their shape. Flavor should be a blend of the characteristic flavors of the ingredients and seasonings.

Cream of Vegetable Soup.   The thin white-sauce base should be an off-white opaque color, with the characteristic color of the vegetables distributed throughout. The soup should be smooth, coating a spoon lightly. The vegetables should be finely chopped, retaining a slightly crisp but tender bite. The flavor should be mild with a blend of the characteristic flavors of the ingredients and seasonings.

Vegetables/Starches

Scalloped Potatoes.   The potato slices should be uniform in size, about 2 inches in diameter and 1/8 inch thick.

TABLE 6.5   Coatings for deep-fat fried foods

Ingredient	Light coating[d]	Egg and crumb[e]	Batter[f]
Egg[a]		3	6
Milk[b]	1 cup	1 cup	2 cups
Flour, all-purpose or whole wheat	1 lb	8 oz (optional)	12 oz
Salt[c]	2 tsp	1 tsp	2 tsp
Bread crumbs, fine		12 oz	
Baking powder			2 tsp
Shortening, melted, or vegetable oil			3 Tbsp
Seasonings		As desired	

[a] Cholesterol can be lowered by substituting egg whites for all or part of the eggs.
[b] Water may be substituted for milk, except in batter.
[c] Seasoned salt (p. 730) may be substituted.
[d] Dip prepared food in milk. Dredge with seasoned flour.
[e] Dip prepared food in flour (may omit), then in a mixture of beaten egg and milk. Drain. Roll in crumbs to cover (see Figure 15.2).
[f] Combine flour, salt, and baking powder. Add milk, beaten eggs, and shortening. Dip prepared foods in batter.

A creamy white sauce that contains tender, very finely chopped onions should cling to the tender yet firm, white, slightly opaque potatoes. The served product should form a barely rounded mass that spreads slightly. The mild potato flavor should be pleasant and blend with the delicate mild cooked flavor of the sauce. Seasonings should enhance the flavor of the potato-sauce mixture.

Harvard Beets.   The product should possess a deep-toned red color, with the beet slices having a tender yet firm texture, round shape, and smooth surface. The sauce should be a flowing, slightly gelatinous glaze with deep, red translucence. The beets should be evenly glazed and readily discernible. Flavor should be well blended and mildly sweet with a slightly sour sensation.

Tables 6.6–6.10 will help identify possible causes for inferior quality of quick and yeast breads, cakes, cookies, and pastry. Knowing the causes for inferior quality will be helpful for making adjustments to production procedures or recipe formulations that will improve quality. Information included in the recipe chapters will also be helpful in evaluating quality and identifying reasons for a deviation from the standards.

Evaluating food products regularly throughout preparation and service and making adjustments where necessary are important for ensuring good quality food and customer satisfaction. The forms in Tables 6.11, 6.12, and 6.13 will be helpful for evaluating the quality of food products.

TABLE 6.6   Quality standards for quick breads

Quality standards: Golden brown color, slightly rounded with pebbly top, well-proportioned shape; tender crust, even grain, with no tunnels; moist crumb, breaks easily without crumbling; light and tender; good flavor.

Deviation	Possible cause
Pale color	Overmixing, oven temperature too low
Rough surface	Undermixing, too much flour
Peaked shape	Wrong size pans, overmixing, incorrect liquid measurement, oven temperature too high
Undersized	Incorrect proportion of ingredients, inaccurate measurements, improper mixing, water too hot (leavening gone), oven temperature too low, too large a proportion of acidic ingredients (blueberries, oranges, etc.) or dough held too long before baking when using acidic ingredients, too much flour used when rolling biscuits
Texture coarse, tunneled	Incorrect proportion of ingredients, inaccurate measurements, overmixing
Dry	Too much flour or too little liquid, oven temperature too low, overbaking
Tough, elastic	Overmixing, too little liquid
Unpleasant flavor	Not enough salt, too much baking powder or soda, poor-quality fat or flavorings

TABLE 6.7   Quality standards for yeast breads

Quality standards: Symmetrical, uniform shape, rounded top, good volume; smooth, tender crust; golden brown color; fine, even grain, free from large air bubbles, thin cell walls; moist, silky, elastic crumb; nutlike flavor.

Deviation	Possible cause
Excessive volume	Too much yeast, too little salt, oven temperature too low, protein content of flour too high, overproofing
Poor volume	Protein content of flour too low, not enough yeast, over- or underdeveloped gluten, over- or underproofing, too much salt
Pale color	Not enough sugar, overfermented dough, oven temperature too low, crust formed before baking
Dark color	Excessive sugar or milk, oven temperature too high, baking time too long
Cracked	Overmixing, improper shaping, formation of dried crust before baking, cooling too fast
Coarse texture	Not enough flour, slack dough, underkneading, proofing period too long or at too high a temperature, oven temperature too low, temperature of dough out of mixer too high
Heavy texture	Yeast partially killed, not enough yeast, underkneading, poor distribution of ingredients, too-cool proofing temperature, too-short proofing period, excessive dough in pan, too much salt
Crumbly, dry	Too-stiff dough, oven temperature too low, underkneading
Poor flavor	Flat: too little salt
	Yeasty: too-long proofing period, proofing temperature too warm
	Sour: too-long proofing period, poor-quality ingredients

TABLE 6.8   Quality standards for cakes

Quality standards for butter cakes: Smooth surface, slightly rounded top, high volume; fine-grained, small, evenly distributed cell walls, light but not crumbly; soft texture, velvety, moist, light, tender crumb; delicate, sweet, well-blended flavor. Cakes other than chocolate should be a golden brown color.

Deviation	Possible cause
Peaked or cracked	Too much flour, too little liquid, overmixing, oven temperature too high
Flat top	Oven temperature too low (some cakes used for layering are formulated for a flat top)
Pale color	Too little sugar, too much liquid, wrong type of pan, underbaking, oven temperature too low
Too-dark color	Too much sugar, oven temperature too high, overbaking
Low volume	Too much shortening, too much liquid, insufficient leavening, undermixing, wrong size pan, too much standing time before baking or holding too long in a warm room, oven temperature too high
Large cells	Too little liquid, too much shortening, under- or overmixing, oven temperature too low
Compact texture	Overbeating
Crumbly texture	Too much shortening or sugar, too little liquid, insufficient mixing
Tunnels	Too much egg, too little sugar, overmixing, oven temperature too high, excessive bottom heat
Dry	Too little sugar, too much leavening, overbaking
Soggy	Too much shortening, undermixing, underbaking, improper cooling before covering
Tough	Too much shortening, protein content of flour too high, improper balance of ingredients, overmixing, overbaking, oven temperature too high
Unpleasant flavor	Flat, too little salt, rancid fat
Shrinkage	Oven temperature too low, overbaking

Quality standards for angel, sponge, or chiffon cakes: Thin, golden brown crust, rounded top, slightly split in the middle; fine texture, thin cell walls, light in weight in proportion to size; moist, tender crumb; delicate flavor.

Deviation	Possible cause
Thick, hard crust	Oven temperature too low, overbaked
Sticky crust	Too much sugar, insufficient baking
Large cracks	Mixture too stiff, overbeating eggs, oven temperature too high
Undersized, heavy	Grease on equipment or bowl, overbeating or underbeating egg whites, overmixing, improper balance of ingredients, oven temperature too high, cakes removed from pan too soon after baking, underbaking
Dry	Overbeating egg whites, too much flour, too little sugar, overbaking, oven temperature too low
Tough	Oven temperature too high, overmixing, sugar content too high, too much flour or wrong type used
Coarse	Overbeating egg whites, insufficient mixing, oven temperature too low

TABLE 6.8   Quality standards for cakes

TABLE 6.9 Quality standards for cookies

TABLE 6.9 Quality standards for cookies

Quality standards for drop cookies: Uniform shape and color; good flavor; crisp or chewy texture (true to type of cookie).

Deviation	Possible cause
Misshapen	Improper dropping of dough, oven temperature too high or too low, improper mixing
Excessive spreading	Too much liquid, too much fat and sugar, liquid fat substituted for solid fat, overcreaming, dough too warm, incorrect oven temperature, not peaked when dropped, cookies panned too close together
Dry, crumbly texture	Incorrect proportion of ingredients, inaccurate measuring, poor mixing or baking techniques, incorrect oven temperature

Quality standards for bar cookies: Uniform, well-cut shape; rich, moist eating quality; thin, delicate crust; appealing flavor.

Deviation	Possible cause
Crumbles when cut	Cut while too warm
Dry, crumbly texture	Overbaking, improper proportion of ingredients
Hard, crusty top	Overmixed, overbaked

Quality standards for rolled cookies: Retain shape of cutter; lightly browned surface; crisp or soft texture, depending on thickness.

Deviation	Possible cause
Tough	Excessive rerolling
Dry	Rolling in too much flour or rerolling

Quality standards for pressed and molded cookies: Well-defined pattern and shape; tender, crisp texture; rich, buttery flavor; delicately browned color.

Deviation	Possible cause
Misshapen	Improper use of cookie press or poor molding, dough too cold or too warm, dough placed on hot baking sheet, oven temperature too low
Crumbly, dry	Incorrect proportion of ingredients, insufficient shaping

Quality standards for refrigerator cookies: Uniform thin slices, lightly browned surface, crisp and crunchy texture, rich flavor.

Deviation	Possible cause
Irregular shape	Improper molding of dough roll, dough not chilled before slicing, improper slicing technique
Too soft	Cut too thick

TABLE 6.10 Quality standards for pastry

Quality standards: Golden brown color, blistery surface, uniform, attractive edges, fits pan well; flaky or mealy texture, cuts easily, pleasant bland flavor.

Deviation	Possible cause
Smooth surface	Overhandling, too much flour when rolling
Shrunken	Stretched crust when easing into pan, overmixing, protein content of flour too high, too much water
Tough	Too much water, overmixing, overhandling, protein content of flour too high
Not flaky	Temperature of dough too high, shortening too soft, overmixing
Too tender	Undermixing, not enough liquid, too much shortening
Soggy bottom crust	Baked too short a time, too much fat in crust, oven temperature too low or not enough bottom heat, using a filling that is too hot
Compact	Underbaking, too much liquid
Dry	Shortening cut in too finely, not enough liquid

TABLE 6.11   Evaluating food using sensory attributes

PRODUCT _____

Attribute	Score
VISUAL APPEARANCE Desirable characteristics: Comments:	EXCELLENT 1 - - - 2 - - - 3 - - - 4 - - - 5 - - - 6 - - - 7 POOR
AROMA Desirable characteristics: Comments:	EXCELLENT 1 - - - 2 - - - 3 - - - 4 - - - 5 - - - 6 - - - 7 POOR
FLAVOR Desirable characteristics: Comments:	EXCELLENT 1 - - - 2 - - - 3 - - - 4 - - - 5 - - - 6 - - - 7 POOR
TEXTURE Desirable characteristics: Comments:	EXCELLENT 1 - - - 2 - - - 3 - - - 4 - - - 5 - - - 6 - - - 7 POOR

TOTAL SCORE _____

Notes:
- Foods should be evaluated when they are at their ideal serving temperature.
- To improve objectivity when evaluating a food product, the desirable characteristics may be added to the score sheet in Table 6.11. For example, when evaluating muffins, the texture characteristics may be identified as a light tender crumb and slightly coarse, even grain. For meat, the descriptive words for texture would be in regard to tenderness; for French fries, crispness.
- Descriptive terminology to describe the desirable characteristics of food:

  Visual appearance may be described in terms of color, form/shape, lumpiness, size, smoothness, and uniformity, and whether the item is bright, fresh, natural, coarse, cracked, fine, flat, pale, pebbly, pointed, or rounded. Dullness, gloss, opaqueness, and transparency are also visual characteristics. Important also is appearance on the plate with attractive cuts and pleasing food arrangement.

  Aroma may be described in terms of characteristic aroma, pleasant, pungent, sour, and sweet.

  Flavor may be described in terms of acidic, balanced, bitter, distinct, full, mellow, mild, natural, pleasing, salty, sour, spicy, sweet, and unsweet.

  Texture (and mouthfeel, or the texture of food as perceived in the mouth) may be described in terms of coarse, crisp, crisp-tender, crumbly, elastic, firm, flaky, gritty, heavy, light, mealy, moist, smooth, soft, tender, tough. Consistency, viscosity, and grain may help describe desirable textures.

TABLE 6.11   Evaluating food using sensory attributes

TABLE 6.12 Evaluating food products during preparation and service

Evaluation points	Criteria to assess quality
Taste	a. Seasonings are balanced.
	b. Food production methods are appropriate for the product being prepared.
	c. Quality of ingredients used is appropriate for the product being prepared.
	d. Flavor profile of the finished product is characteristic of ingredients.
Proper production and holding	a. Food production procedures based on food science principles are followed; for example:
	• Meats, poultry, and fish are cooked just until the optimum endpoint temperature is reached.
	• Vegetables are brightly colored.
	• Starches are cooked just until done (al dente).
	• Sauces are smooth and have the correct consistency.
	b. Food is served at its optimum quality (generally within a very short time after preparation).
	c. HACCP principles are followed.
Presentation	a. Portion sizes are correct and uniform.
	b. Foods are presented or arranged in a manner that enhances their appeal.
	c. Foods being served together are complementary in color, consistency, form, and methods of preparation.
Serving temperature	a. Hot foods are served hot using warmed plates when possible.
	b. Cold foods are served cold using chilled plates/bowls when possible.

Note: Evaluating food products regularly throughout preparation and service and making adjustments where necessary are important for ensuring good quality food and customer satisfaction.

TABLE 6.13   Quality food evaluation form

FOOD PRODUCT _____

DATE AND MEAL SERVED _____

Overall Quality: <u>Excellent</u>   <u>Average</u>   <u>Poor</u>

TASTE   **LOW 1 - - 2 - - 3 - - 4 - - 5 - - 6 - - 7 HIGH**

[seasonings appropriate and balanced; appropriate food production methods followed; ingredient quality appropriate; flavor profile characteristic of ingredients]

Comments:

FOOD PRODUCTION PROCEDURES   **LOW 1 - - 2 - - 3 - - 4 - - 5 - - 6 - - 7 HIGH**

[food production procedures based on appropriate food science principles were followed]

Comments:

QUALITY DURING HOLDING/STAGING   **LOW 1 - - 2 - - 3 - - 4 - - 5 - - 6 - - 7 HIGH**

[food is served at its optimum quality including color, consistency, texture, and form]

Comments:

FOOD PRESENTATION   **LOW 1 - - 2 - - 3 - - 4 - - 5 - - 6 - - 7 HIGH**

[portion sizes are correct and uniform; foods are presented or arranged in a manner that enhances their appeal; foods are appealing in their color, form, textures, and method of preparation]

Comments:

SERVING TEMPERATURES   **LOW 1 - - 2 - - 3 - - 4 - - 5 - - 6 - - 7 HIGH**

[hot food served hot and with hot plates if appropriate; cold food served cold and with chilled plates if appropriate]

Comments:

Note: This scorecard is useful when evaluating food being served from a buffet line or hot counter, and for plated meals.

TABLE 6.13 Quality food evaluation form

CHAPTER 7

Food Safety, Knives, and Other Equipment

Food Safety

Preventing food-borne illness requires that correct procedures be established and followed for purchasing, storing, preparing, and serving food safely. The tables in this chapter identify general information and guidelines that will help reduce the risk of food-borne illness.

- *Table 7.1—Guidelines for Reducing the Risk of Food-Borne Illness* This table will be useful in developing food safety standards for food products, including purchasing, receiving, storing, food preparation, service, and leftover management. (p. 163)

- *Table 7.2—Instructions for Calibrating a Probe (Stem) Thermometer* (p. 164)

- *Table 7.3—Cold Food Storage Temperatures* This table identifies temperature and time guidelines for storing various categories of food. (p. 164)

- *Table 7.4—Refrigerator Defrosting Times for Meats, Seafood, and Poultry* This table provides time guidelines for safely defrosting meat, seafood, and poultry. (p. 165)

- *Table 7.5—Temperatures and Bacteria Growth* Bacteria activity related to temperatures is identified in this table. (p. 165)

- *Table 7.6—Safe Internal Temperatures for Cooked Foods* This table is useful for establishing endpoint cooking temperatures for potentially hazardous foods. (p. 165)

- *Table 7.7—Food Serving Temperatures and Holding Times* This table identifies serving temperatures and holding times for various categories of food products. Food quality versus food safety temperatures are contrasted in the Note section of this table. (p. 166)

- *Table 7.8—Food Cooling and Storage Procedures* This table identifies methods for safely cooling hot and cold foods. (p. 167)

- *Table 7.9—Time and Temperature Standards for Reducing Food Safety Hazards of Potentially Hazardous Foods* This table will be useful in developing time and temperature standards for reducing the risk of food-borne illness. (p. 168)

- *Table 7.10—Water Activity of Selected Foods* (p. 168)

- *Table 7.11—pH Values of Selected Foods* (p. 169)

- *Table 7.12—Potentially Hazardous Foods* (p. 169)

It is important to understand food safety terms when interpreting and applying food safety principles in a food production setting. Knowing basic food safety terms also gives food production employees a common language to use when communicating food safety concepts.

critical control point (CCP)—A step or procedure in the food-handling process where food safety hazards can be eliminated, prevented, or reduced to acceptable levels. CCPs are steps or procedures that, if not performed, may result in a hazard that would not be prevented in a later step. Food-handling procedures at a CCP should kill bacteria (cooking) or prevent or slow the growth of bacteria (cold storage or hot holding).

critical limit—A maximum or minimum value to which a hazard must be controlled at a CCP to minimize the risk of food-borne illness. Critical limits commonly established to eliminate hazards include standards related to time, temperature, pH, and water activity. All standards for CCPs must be as specific as possible and easily measured or monitored.

cross-contamination—The transfer of harmful substances (usually biological) from one food to another by means such as hands, equipment, utensils, or food to food contact.

control point (CP)—A step or procedure in the food-handling process where food safety hazards can be controlled. Loss of control at a control point does not lead to an unacceptable health risk because a step or procedure to eliminate, reduce, or limit food safety hazards will follow.

On Cooking: A Textbook of Culinary Fundamentals, fourth edition, provides an expanded discussion of food and purchasing information, cooking techniques, and equipment; that book was a source of information for *Food for Fifty.*

TABLE 7.1   Guidelines for reducing the risk of food-borne illness

PURCHASING/RECEIVING FOOD

- Purchase food products from reputable processors and distributors who apply HACCP principles.
- Upon delivery, visually inspect perishable food products for packaging defects (holes or tears) or for any sign of temperature abuse (for frozen products: ice crystals from product thawing and refreezing, refrozen liquid inside box or stained box from a defrosted product, partially defrosted or defrosted contents). Refrigerated foods should be received at 41°F or below, frozen foods at 0°F or below.
- Upon delivery, assess perishable food quality by odor, sight, and touch.
- Require distributors to include a "sell by" or "use by" date on perishable food items and a code for tracking the product.
- Record the delivery date for perishable food products. Save shellfish tags for 90 days.

STORING FOOD

- Upon delivery, store perishable food immediately in the freezer (0°F or below) or refrigerator (41°F or below).
- Prevent cross-contamination by storing cooked food above raw food and by storing raw meats on the lowest refrigerator shelf.
- Label and date foods that are removed from their original package.
- Store perishable food so the oldest food will be used first.

PREPARING FOOD

Food Preparation Procedures

- Wash hands before handling food, after handling raw food, and after touching anything that may contaminate hands.
- Process food in small batches, taking only small amounts of food out of the refrigerator at one time.
- Wash fruits and vegetables in cool running water before cutting, mixing with other foods, or serving whole.
- Keep juices from raw meat, poultry, and fish from contacting other foods. Raw poultry juices should not contact other raw meat or fish products because they have lower endpoint cooking requirements than poultry.
- Keep everything that touches food clean—utensils, pans, bowls, countertops, hands, gloves.
- Use tongs, disposable gloves on hands, or other methods to keep bare hands from touching ready-to-eat foods.
- Use separate cutting boards and utensils for cooked and uncooked meat, poultry, and fish and for raw and ready-to-eat foods.
- Avoid preparing raw and cooked foods in the same work area, and store raw and cooked foods in separate areas.
- Sanitize all utensils, pans, bowls, and food contact surfaces after being used for preparing potentially hazardous foods and before coming in contact with raw or ready-to-eat foods.

Cooking Procedures

- Batch-cook whenever possible and prepare food as close to service time as possible.
- Cook all meat to the required internal temperature to kill harmful organisms (see Table 7.6 on p. 165). Measure internal temperature in several places.
- Use an accurate thermometer or thermocouple to measure the internal temperature of potentially hazardous foods. Do not rely on color to determine whether meat, chicken, or fish has reached the correct endpoint temperature. See p. 164 for how to calibrate a stem or probe thermometer.
- Wash and sanitize thermometers after each use.

SERVING FOOD

- Keep potentially hazardous food either at or below 41°F or above 135°F. Take food temperatures every 30–45 minutes when being served from a hot serving counter or steam table or from a cold serving area such as a salad bar.
- When replenishing food on a buffet, do not mix fresh food with food that has been out for service. Do not mix raw food with cooked food.
- Use pans that are as small as feasible and replace pans of food often.
- Cover food whenever possible and protect with sneeze guards.
- Use tongs, disposable gloves on hands, or other method to keep bare hands from touching ready-to-eat foods.

LEFTOVER FOOD

- Freeze or refrigerate leftovers immediately. Follow established guidelines for cooling food quickly (p. 167). Reheat foods one time only to 165°F (within 2 hours).

TABLE 7.3 Cold food storage temperatures

TABLE 7.2 Instructions for calibrating a probe (stem) thermometer

1. Fill a medium-size glass with ice and add water to fill the glass.
2. Place the thermometer in the glass of ice water.
3. Wait 3 minutes. Stir the water occasionally.
4. After 3 minutes, the thermometer should read 32°F.

If the thermometer is out of calibration (does not read 32°F after 3 minutes):

1. Place the thermometer back in the ice water (add more ice if necessary for a high ratio of ice to water). Wait 2–3 minutes.
2. Using an adjustable wrench or pliers, turn the adjustable nut on the back side of the thermometer until the needle reads 32°F. (Always purchase adjustable stem thermometers.)
3. Add more ice to the glass if necessary and wait 3 minutes, stirring occasionally.
4. If the thermometer needle does not read 32°F, repeat the process.

Probe or stem thermometers can get out of calibration easily and must be handled with care. For accurate temperatures, calibrate probe thermometers each day, or more often if dropped or handled roughly.

TABLE 7.3 Cold food storage temperatures

Food	Refrigerator °F	Days	Freezer °F	Months
DAIRY/EGGS				
Ice cream			−10	3
Milk	32	7		
Eggs in shell	40	21		
Raw yolks/whites	40	2–4		
Liquid pasteurized (opened)	40	3		
FRESH MEATS				
Beef roast/steaks	32	3–5	0 to −20	6–12
Pork roast	32	3–5	0 to −20	3–6
Pork chops	32	3–5	0 to −20	3–4
Hamburger/ground pork/ground lamb	32	1–2	0 to −20	3–4
Beef cubes	32	1–2	0 to −20	3–4
Lamb roast/chops	32	2–3	0 to −20	6–9
Vacuum-packaged cuts	28–32	16–21	0 to −20	6–12
COOKED MEATS				
Browned meats	35	3–4	0 to −20	2–3
Bacon	35	7	0 to −20	1
Frankfurters				
Unopened package	32	14	0 to −20	1–2
Opened package	32	7	0 to −20	1–2
Lamb	32	3–4	0 to −20	2–3
Luncheon meats	32	3–5	0 to −20	1–2
FRESH POULTRY AND FISH				
Chicken/turkey				
Whole	32	1–2	0 to −20	12
Pieces	32	1–2	0 to −20	9
Fish	32	1	0 to −20	3
COOKED POULTRY				
With broth or gravy	35	1–2	0 to −20	6
Pieces, no gravy	35	3–4	0 to −20	4
Cooked dishes	35	3–4	0 to −20	4–6
Fried chicken	35	3–4	0 to −20	4

TABLE 7.4 Refrigerator defrosting times for meats, seafood, and poultry

Food	Approximate defrosting time (in refrigerator)
Large roast	4–7 hours per pound
Small roast	3–5 hours per pound
Chop or steak, 1 inch thick	12–14 total hours
Chicken[a], whole	1–2 days
Pieces	8–12 total hours
Turkey[a], whole, 8–12 lb	1–2 days
12–16 lb	2–3 days
16–20 lb	3–4 days
20–24 lb	4–5 days
Seafood, whole, steaks	12–24 total hours
Blocks, large whole	1–2 days

[a]Allow thawing time of 1–2 days for whole chickens and turkey roasts, and one day or less for cut-up chickens or small poultry pieces. Whole turkeys require approximately 5 hours thawing time for every pound of bird.

TABLE 7.5 Temperatures and bacteria growth

Temperature (°F)	Bacteria activity
212	Most bacteria destroyed
140 and above	Low survival rate, prevent bacteria growth
120–140	Survival and growth
60–120	Reproduce rapidly (99°F ideal for growth)
40–140	Survival and growth
32–40	Slow growth rate

TABLE 7.6 Safe internal temperatures for cooked foods

Food	Internal temperature
POULTRY[a]	
Boneless, ground, stuffed	165°F for 15 seconds
Bone-in pieces[b]	165°F for 15 seconds
Whole birds[b]	165°F for 15 seconds
GROUND/CHOPPED/TENDERIZED MEAT	
Beef, pork, sausage, lamb, fish	155°F for 15 seconds (see Notes)
PORK	
Pork, ham	145°F for 15 seconds
BEEF/VEAL/LAMB[c]	
Steaks, chops, roasts (see Notes)	145°F for 15 seconds
FISH	
Solid	145°F for 15 seconds
Stuffed	165°F
OTHER	
Reheated foods	165°F for 15 seconds (within 2 hr)
Stuffed pasta, stuffed meat	165°F for 15 seconds
Eggs	155°F for 15 seconds
Dairy, pasta, grains, rice	145°F for 15 seconds

[a]The FDA Food Code specifies that poultry must measure 165°F in all parts to be safe. Bone-in poultry is more difficult to cook to a consistent 165°F temperature. If using an ovenproof thermometer, place it in the whole chicken or turkey at the start of the cooking cycle. For turkey breasts, place the thermometer in the thickest part. For whole turkeys or whole chickens, place the thermometer in the thickest part of the inner thigh. Once the thigh has reached 165°F, check the wing and the thickest part of the breast to ensure that the chicken or turkey has reached a safe minimum internal temperature of 165°F throughout. Do not rely on pop-up thermometers that are often inserted in the breast of whole turkeys.

[b]Consumers may prefer whole-bird or bone-in poultry cooked to a slightly higher temperature (170–175°F). Poultry cooked to this higher temperature may be less moist.

[c]Whole beef and pork roasts are considered safe if cooked in a preheated oven and held for a specified length of time, as shown below:

continued

TABLE 7.6 Safe internal temperatures for cooked foods

TABLE 7.6   continued

Oven Type	Oven Temperature Based on Roast Weight	
	Less than 4.5 kg (10 lb)	4.5 kg (10 lb) or more
Still dry	177°C (350°F) or more	121°C (250°F) or more
Convection	163°C (325°F) or more	121°C (250°F) or more
High humidity[1]	121°C (250°F) or less	121°C (250°F) or less

[1]Relative humidity greater than 90% for at least 1 hour as measured in the cooking chamber or exit of the oven, or in a moisture-impermeable bag that provides 100% humidity.

Note: See Table 7.2, p. 164, for instructions for calibrating a probe (stem) thermometer.

Time and Temperature Requirements for Safe Food

Temperature °F (°C)	Time[1] in minutes	Temperature °F (°C)	Time[1] in minutes	Temperature °F (°C)	Time[1] in minutes
130 (54)	121	136 (58)	32	142 (61)	8
132 (56)	77	138 (59)	19	144 (62)	5
134 (57)	47	140 (60)	12	145 (63)	3

[1]Holding time may include post-oven heat rise.

Notes: • To obtain an even temperature throughout the product, foods cooked in a microwave oven must be stirred once or twice during the cooking process and held covered for 2 minutes after cooking. When using a microwave oven, endpoint temperature should reach 165°F in all parts of the food.
  • Current USDA regulations recommend cooking ground meat to 160°F, therefore removing the 15-second time requirement.

TABLE 7.7   Food serving temperatures and holding times

Food	Serving temp (°F)[a]	Approximate holding time
BEVERAGES		
Cold drinks—juices	40	30 minutes, if poured
Hot drinks	185	30–45 minutes
Coffee[b]	185	Hot plate, 20 minutes
		Insulated pot, 2 hours
DAIRY		
Ice cream	10	6–8 hours, dipped
Milk	34–38	
DESSERTS		
Pudding and refrigerator desserts	41 or less	
Pastries and cakes[c]	65–75	
ENTRÉES, SOUP		
Beef, roast[d]	150	10–15 minutes
Casseroles, stews	170–180	30–45 minutes
Chicken, baked	160	20–30 minutes
Eggs, scrambled	160	10–15 minutes
Ham, pork roast	160	10–15 minutes
Sandwiches, hot	160	10–15 minutes
Soup	170–180	45–60 minutes[e]

(margin) TABLE 7.6   Safe internal temperatures for cooked foods

(margin) TABLE 7.7   Food serving temperatures and holding times

TABLE 7.7   continued

Food	Serving temp (°F)[a]	Approximate holding time
SALADS		
All cold	41 or less	
SAUCES, VEGETABLES		
Hot sauces	145	30–60 minutes
Cold sauces	below 41	
Gravy	180	30–60 minutes
Vegetables in cream sauce	145–160	15–30 minutes
Vegetables unseasoned	160–170	15–20 minutes
Whipped potatoes	160–170	15–20 minutes

[a]See Table 7.2, p. 164, for instructions for calibrating a probe (stem) thermometer.

[b]Coffee brewing temperature is 195–200°F.

[c]Some pastries may be served warm (100°F). Hold potentially hazardous desserts such as pumpkin pie, pudding, and custards below 41°F.

[d]For whole meat roasts, the serving temperature will depend on the doneness of meat. Rare roast beef may be served at a temperature lower than 150°F when cooked following established time and temperature standards. See Table 7.6, p. 165.

[e]Cream soups may curdle if held at too high a temperature or held too long. Broth soups can be held for a longer time and at a higher temperature than cream soups.

Notes:
- Food temperatures can be retained by using heated or chilled plates, covering plates during delivery, or using a food delivery system designed to retain temperatures of food while being held and transported.
- With a few exceptions, food is at its peak quality when served as soon as possible after cooking or preparation.
- Serving temperatures may be different than endpoint cooking temperatures. For example, flour must be heated to a higher temperature to thicken gravy than the temperature recommended for holding gravy.
- *Quality food* temperatures are not synonymous with *food safety* temperatures. For example, a meat casserole may be safe when served at 135°F but would be a better quality product if served warmer (170–180°F).

TABLE 7.8   Food cooling and storage procedures

Standard: Cooked potentially hazardous foods (PHFs) must be cooled from 135°F to 70°F or less within 2 hours, and then to 41°F or less within an additional 4 hours. PHFs prepared from ingredients normally stored at room temperature, such as reconstituted foods and canned tuna, must be cooled to 41°F or less within 4 hours.

METHODS FOR COOLING HOT FOODS

Application	Procedure
Large roasts, whole poultry or fish	Cut large food items into smaller pieces.
Stews, chili, pasta casseroles, pudding	Pour hot, thick foods into clean, chilled, shallow, stainless steel pans, to no more than 2 inches deep.
Broth soups, thin sauces	Pour hot, thin foods into clean pans or pots, to no more than 3 inches deep.
Pourable thin or thick foods	Set pan of food in an ice water bath (set pan with hot food inside another pan filled with ice). Stir both the hot food and the ice. Replace ice as it melts.
Thick, pourable foods such as chili and pasta sauces that may be prepared, cooled, and heated for service at a later time	Delete part of the water in the recipe and add as ice in the cooling step. The weight of the ice should be equal to the water deleted from the recipe.

METHODS FOR CHILLING COLD FOODS

Chill ingredients thoroughly before combining (i.e., salad dressings, tuna, hard-cooked eggs, canned kidney beans).

Put dense products into clean, chilled, shallow, stainless steel pans to no more than 2 inches deep.

Notes:
- Hot foods will cool faster if loosely covered or uncovered. Protect uncovered food from contamination. Cover food tightly after chilling.
- Small amounts of food will cool more rapidly than large amounts. Whenever possible, divide food into small amounts.
- Allow air to circulate around pans. Do not stack pans.
- Chilling time can be shortened by stirring foods with a clean utensil once or twice during cooling.
- Rapid cooling equipment will provide the fastest chilling and is the recommended chilling method to reduce the risk of food-borne illness.

TABLE 7.9   **Time and temperature standards for reducing food safety hazards of potentially hazardous foods**

Step	Standard
Receiving	Frozen foods at 0°F or below
	Refrigerated foods at 41°F or below
Storage	Frozen foods at 0°F or below
	Refrigerated foods at 41°F or below for 7 calendar days or 45°F for 4 calendar days (the calendar day counting period begins as day 1 on the day the food is refrigerated)
Thawing	In refrigerator at 41°F or below
	Under potable, running cold water (70°F or less) for not more than 2 hours

FOOD PRODUCTION

Pre-preparation	Keep all PHFs at 41°F or below or at 135°F or above throughout pre-preparation time. Cool cooked products rapidly to 70°F within 2 hours and from 70°F to 41°F or below in 4 additional hours or less.
Preparation	*Cold foods:* Rapid cooling to 41°F or below
	Hot foods: Cook to internal temperatures specified in the recipe (reheated foods to 165°F). Maintain hot holding temperature at or above 135°F (see Notes).
Postproduction	Cool leftover food rapidly to 70°F within 2 hours and from 70°F to 41°F or less in 4 additional hours or less.
	Store cooked food in clean shallow pans or containers that are no more than 4 inches deep with a product depth of no more than 2 inches. If product is thick, stir frequently until cooled.
Serving	Maintain internal temperature at 135°F or more or 41°F or less (see Notes). Do not mix old product with freshly cooked product.
Cooling	Cool rapidly to 70°F within 2 hours and from 70°F to 41°F or less in 4 additional hours or less (see Postproduction).

Notes: • In some locations, regulatory agencies will permit time to be used as control rather than holding temperatures. For time to be used as a control, the following conditions must be met: (1) The product must be marked with the time it is removed from temperature control; and (2) the product must be cooked and served or discarded within 4 hours.
• Measure all temperatures with a cleaned and sanitized stem thermometer or thermocouple thermometer.

TABLE 7.10   **Water activity of selected foods**

Foods	Water activity (A_w)
Crackers	0.10
Fresh Fruits	0.91–1.00
MEATS	
Cured	0.87–0.95
Fresh	0.95–1.00
SWEETS	
Jam	0.75–0.80
Honey	0.54–0.75

Note: Salt and sugar solutions as well as drying reduce the water that is available for bacteria to grow. Most bacteria will not grow with a water activity below 0.85 A_w, yeast below 0.88 A_w, and molds below 0.82 A_w.

TABLE 7.11   pH values of selected foods

PROTEIN

Chicken	6.2–6.7
Fish	6.6–6.8
Ground beef	5.1–6.3
Ham	5.9–6.1

DAIRY

Buttermilk	4.5
Cheese	4.9–5.9
Milk	6.6–7.0
Yogurt	3.8–4.2

FRUITS AND VEGETABLES

Vegetables	4.2–6.5
Tomatoes, fresh	4.2–4.9
Fruits	2.0–6.7
Orange juice	4.0
Grapefruit	3.6

OTHER

Mayonnaise	3.0–4.1
Salad dressing	3.2–4.0

Note: Food's pH value has an effect on microbial growth. Most bacteria grow when food pH values are between 5.5 and 8.0. Disease-causing organisms grow very slowly in foods with a pH value below 4.6. Spoilage yeasts grow best when food pH values are between 4.0 and 6.5, and spoilage molds grow best between 4.5 and 6.8.

TABLE 7.12   Potentially hazardous foods

FOODS FROM RAW OR HEAT-TREATED ANIMAL SOURCES	Cheese (soft, unripened, and ripened hard cheeses that have been cut or opened) Eggs Fish, shellfish, crustaceans Meat Milk Poultry
FOODS FROM HEAT-TREATED PLANT SOURCES	Cooked beans Cooked pasta Cooked potatoes Cooked rice Soy products (i.e., tofu)
RAW PLANT SOURCE PRODUCTS	Melon (cut) Seed sprouts
OTHER	Fresh garlic in oil Rehydrated cooked and dried vegetables (onions)

Notes:
- A potentially hazardous food (PHF) is any food that can support rapid bacterial growth and cause food-borne illness. Foods that do not support bacterial growth are those with a pH 4.6 or below (acid foods) and those with a water activity (A_w) of 0.85 or less (dried, salted, sugared foods).
- Any PHF in a food renders it potentially hazardous (for example, bread dressing, casserole, creamed and broth soups, gravies, and cream filling).
- Bacteria live well in PHFs because they often are protein rich, moist, and neutral or low acid. PHFs are especially able to support bacteria growth when held in the temperature danger zone (41–140°F) for more than 4 hours (cumulative during the entire food-handling process).
- This table provides examples of PHFs and is not intended to be an all-inclusive list of specific foods and food products.

clean—Absence of visible soil, usually in reference to equipment, dishes, and flatware.

danger zone—The temperature at which potentially hazardous foods support rapid growth of harmful microorganisms, between 41°F and 135°F. Potentially hazardous foods (PHFs) should be heated or cooled so they pass through the temperature danger zone as quickly as possible.

HACCP—Hazard Analysis Critical Control Points; an evaluation system used to identify, monitor, and control food contamination risks in foodservice establishments. The seven steps in a HACCP system are (1) assessing hazards, (2) identifying CCPs, (3) establishing critical limits, (4) developing procedures to monitor CCPs, (5) taking corrective action (when deviations from the standard are identified), (6) setting up a record-keeping system, and (7) developing a HACCP verification plan.

hazards (in food)—Food contamination can be caused by biological, chemical, and physical hazards. Biological hazards include harmful bacteria, viruses, parasites, fungi, molds, and yeasts. Chemical hazards include toxins, pesticides, food additives, cleaning compounds, and heavy metals such as mercury. Physical hazards include foreign objects in food such as broken glass, metal shavings, staples, toothpicks/wood, and stones.

pH—A measure of a food product's acidity or alkalinity, expressed on a scale of 0 to 14. A pH of 7 is considered neutral. Microorganism growth is slowed when a product moves below or above the pH that is ideal for growth. At or below 4.6 pH (moderately acidic), disease-causing organisms grow very slowly.

potentially hazardous food (PHF)—Any food or food ingredient capable of supporting the growth of microorganisms. Potentially hazardous foods include foods of animal origin (raw or cooked) and foods of plant origin that have been heat-treated. Included also are raw seed sprouts, cut melon, and garlic and oil mixtures. See p. 169 for a more complete list of potentially hazardous foods.

sanitary—Describes a condition in which disease-causing microorganisms have been reduced to safe levels.

water activity—Bacteria require water activity (A_W) greater than 0.85 to grow. (Water has an A_W of 1.0.) Water activity explains why some dried foods such as beans or rice are not potentially hazardous but become so when rehydrated.

Knives and Other Equipment

Selecting and using the proper equipment are necessary to produce food in an efficient and effective manner. This section provides basic information about using and caring for knives and general information about identifying and using other equipment. This section includes the following topics:

- Knife Identification, Knife Care and Safety, and Knife Skills
- Hand Tools and Small Equipment

Tables in this chapter provide pan capacity guidelines, portioning information, and large-equipment requirements for food production.

- *Table 7.13—Knife Identification* This table is useful for selecting the correct knife to use for cutting food.
- *Table 7.14—Vegetable Cuts and Shapes* This table identifies basic cuts for vegetables.
- *Table 7.15—Basic Tools and Equipment* This table identifies basic categories of hand tools.
- *Table 7.16—Pan Capacities for Baked Products* This table is useful for calculating the number of pans and sizes needed for baked products and for accurately scaling batters and fillings (p. 184)
- *Table 7.17—Hotel/Counter Pan Capacities* This table provides information on counter pan sizes, scaling capacity, and number of portions per pan. (p. 185)
- *Table 7.18—Dipper Equivalents* This table identifies the approximate measure and weight for various dipper sizes. (p. 186)
- *Table 7.19—Ladle Equivalents* This table identifies the approximate measure and weight for various ladle sizes. (p. 186)
- *Table 7.20—Recommended Mixer Bowl and Steam-Jacketed Kettle Sizes for Selected Products* This table is helpful for selecting the appropriate size of mixer bowl and steam-jacketed kettle for the batch size being produced. (p. 186)
- *Table 7.21—Large-Equipment Requirements for Basic Cooking Methods* This table identifies cooking methods appropriate for the equipment generally found in a commercial kitchen. (p. 187)

KNIFE IDENTIFICATION, KNIFE CARE AND SAFETY, AND KNIFE SKILLS

Knife Identification

Choosing the correct style and shape of knife for a specific cutting task will save time and will provide the tool necessary to meet the quality standards for the product being produced. Safety is also improved when the knife selected fits its use. The types of knives identified in Table 7.13 do not represent all the knives that are available, but they are the basic ones required for general food production.

Knife Care and Safety

A set of good-quality knives is a costly investment, but if they are properly cared for, they will provide many years of safe and efficient service. A good knife-sharpening program is basic to proper knife care. A sharp knife is also more efficient and safer than a dull knife because less pressure is needed to cut foods. The edge of a sharp knife will cut with a minimum amount of pressure.

TABLE 7.13   Knife identification

BONING KNIFE (RIGID)
A thin blade especially suited for separating raw meat and poultry from the bone. A 5- to 7-inch-long blade. A filleting knife is similar but has a flexible blade.

BUTCHER KNIFE OR SCIMITAR
A large knife with a rigid 6- to 14-inch-long blade that curves upward at the tip. Designed for breaking down raw meat into smaller cuts.

CHEF'S OR FRENCH KNIFE
An all-purpose knife used for many chopping, dicing, mincing, and slicing tasks. A long, rigid blade in lengths from 8 to 14 inches. Blade is wide at the heel and tapers to a point at the tip.

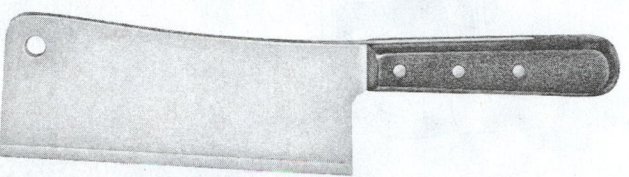

CLEAVER
A rectangular-shaped blade in various sizes that is usually heavy enough to cut through bones. Used for chopping.

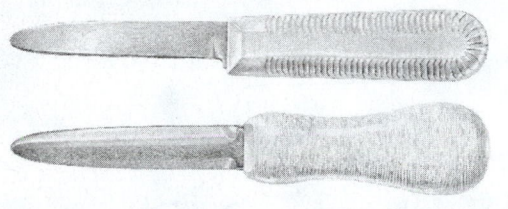

CLAM AND OYSTER KNIVES
Knives with short rigid blades used for opening clam and oyster shells. Clam knife has a sharp edge.

PARING KNIFE
A short knife with a 2- to 4-inch-long blade. Used for detail work and for trimming, peeling, and cutting fruits and vegetables.

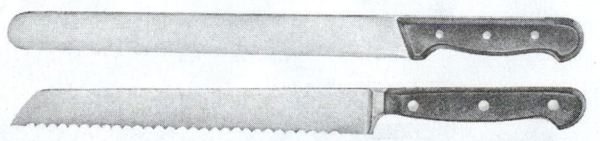

SLICER
A knife with a long, thin, flexible or rigid blade with either a pointed or a rounded tip. May be serrated. Used for slicing cooked meat, poultry, and breads.

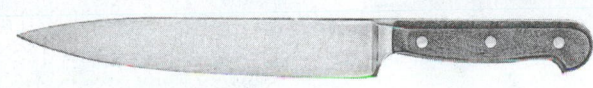

UTILITY KNIFE
An all-purpose knife used for light cutting or carving tasks. Smaller and lighter than a chef's knife with a blade from 5 to 7 inches long.

TABLE 7.13   Knife identification

Knife care and safety tips

1. *Keep knives sharp.*   A whetstone (or sharpening stone) or a good electric sharpener is used to return an edge to a dull knife. Knives that get considerable use should be checked daily and sharpened when needed. Knives can be easily damaged and should be sharpened only by trained staff. Many foodservices contract to have their knives sharpened professionally. See Figure 7.1 for instructions on how to sharpen a knife using a sharpening stone.

   A steel is not used to sharpen, but rather to smooth out nicks and irregularities in a knife's edge caused by normal use. Using a steel regularly keeps knives sharp longer and extends the time between sharpenings. See Figure 7.2 for instructions on how to hone a knife blade using a steel.

2. *Keep knives clean.*   Hand-wash, sanitize, and dry knives after finishing each task, or more often if necessary for food safety reasons. Soaking knives can damage wooden handles and is a safety hazard if knives are submerged in water and out of sight. Because hot dish-machine temperatures can damage knives, they should always be hand-washed and sanitized.

3. *Use a cutting surface that will protect the knife's edge.*   Glass, granite, marble, metal, and other hard surfaces will damage a knife. Wooden or composition cutting boards should always be used.

(a) Hold the knife at a 20-degree angle to a stone or steel when sharpening.

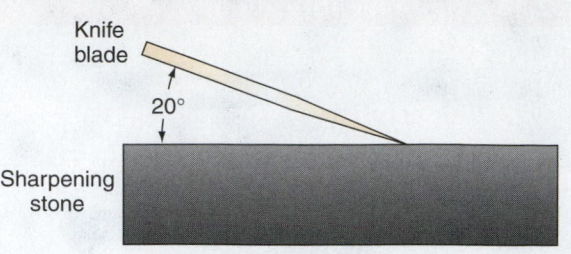

(b) Hold knife handle firmly with one hand and use the other hand to apply steady, even pressure and to guide the knife.

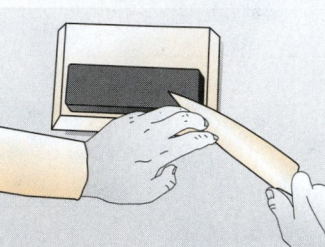

(c) Draw the knife over the stone while applying gentle, even, and light pressure on the blade. Sharpen only in one direction. Repeat on other side of the knife. Use the same number of strokes on each side of the knife.

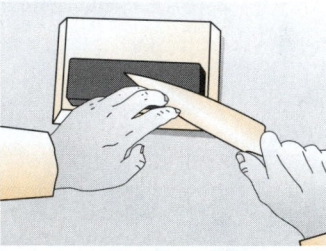

(d) Keep the motion smooth as the knife blade is drawn across the stone all the way to the heel of the knife. Finish by using a steel on the sharpened edge. (See Figure 7.2)

FIGURE 7.1   Sharpening a knife using a stone.

(a) Hold the knife at a constant 20-degree angle to a steel. See Figure 7.1.
Hold knife and steel away from you to prevent injury.
Position the knife so the heel of the blade is next to the steel.

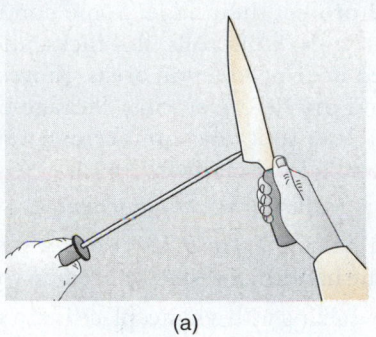

(a)

(b) Lightly and smoothly pass the knife blade along the steel in a
movement that makes an arc.

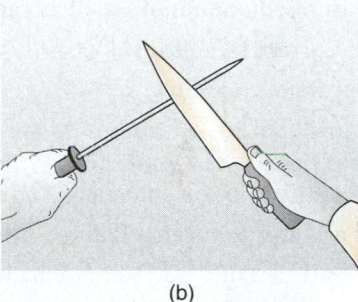

(b)

(c) Continue the stroke until the knife tip passes over the steel. Do not
strike the knife edge on the steel guard. Use only 5 or 6 strokes on
each side of the blade.

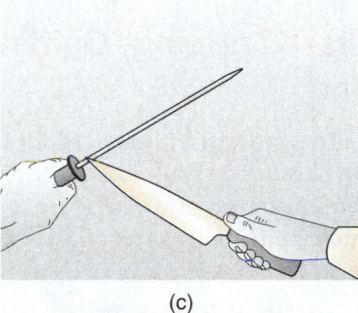

(c)

(d, e, f) Repeat the motion on the other side of the knife.

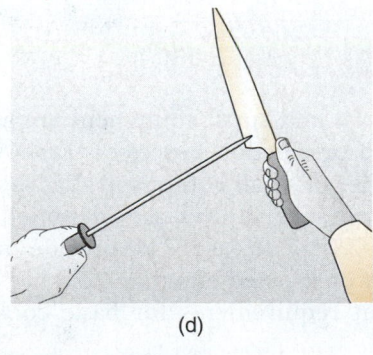

(d)

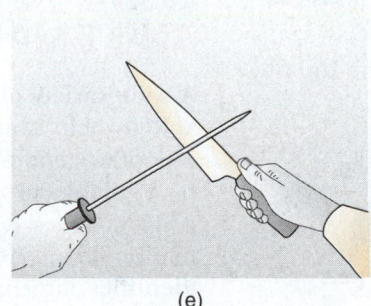

(e)

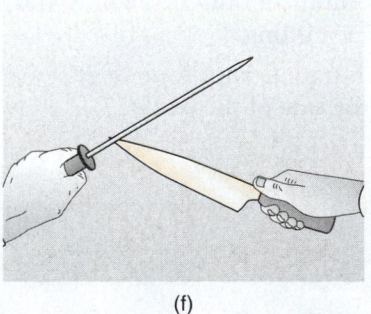

(f)

FIGURE 7.2 Honing a knife using a steel.

4. *Store knives properly.* There are many ways to store knives that will protect their edge. Some common methods are knife kit cases, knife rolls, slot racks, and magnet holders mounted near production areas. Knives should always be clean and dry before storing. Storage equipment should be kept clean so it does not become a source of contamination and a food safety hazard.

5. *Use safe procedures when handling knives.*

- When passing a knife, lay it down on the work surface with the handle closest to the person you are passing it to.

- When walking with a knife, place it in a sheath or hold it by the handle close to your leg, with the point facing down.

- Use a knife for its intended purpose only, and never use a knife to open containers such as cans or boxes.

- Use the correct knife for the task.

- Cut away from yourself.

- Keep knives sharp. Sharp knives are safer because less pressure is needed to make cuts. With less pressure, the chance of the knife or hand slipping is reduced.

- Do not attempt to catch a falling knife.

- Never leave a knife submerged in a sink of water or stored under a towel or similar covering.

- Never cut on a makeshift or unstable work surface.

Knife Skills—Gripping, Guiding, and Cutting

Gripping a knife properly is basic to skillfully and safely using a knife. A grip should be firm and controlling but not excessively tight. Following are two standard grips to use with a chef's or French knife. The parts of a chef's knife are identified in Figure 7.3.

1. Hold the handle with three fingers while gripping the blade between the thumb and index finger. This grip gives the maximum amount of stability and control and is useful for fine cutting.

2. Hold the handle with four fingers and place the thumb against the side of the blade.

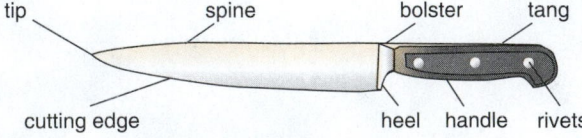

FIGURE 7.3 Idenfification of the parts of a chef's knife.

Guiding the knife with one hand while positioning and holding the food being cut with the other hand is a necessary skill for using a knife efficiently and effectively. Following are guidelines for guiding a chef's or French knife correctly:

1. Hold the food firmly with the fingertips and thumb curled under slightly, away from the cutting edge of the knife blade.

2. Allow the knife blade to sit against the knuckles with the fingertips tucked under.

3. The position of the hand holding the food (called the "guiding hand") controls the cut. As successive cuts are made, the fingertips should move back and control the width of each cut that is made.

Cutting food into uniform sized pieces adds to the visual attractiveness of products, helps convey quality standards, and shows production staff skills. Uniform sizes and shapes of ingredients also ensure that food will cook more evenly and thus enhances food quality. Descriptions of the basic vegetable cuts and shapes are given in Table 7.14.

Two cutting methods are commonly used. The methods differ in that in one method the tip of the knife never leaves the cutting board and in the other the tip is placed on the food being cut. *Method 1:* With the tip of the knife staying on the cutting board, lift the blade, and with a forward and down motion, cut the food. Finish the cut with the knife's cutting edge against the cutting board. For the second slice, lift the heel of the knife backward, just the opposite of the forward and down motion. The tip of the knife should not leave the cutting board. This method is efficient for chopping, slicing, and dicing foods that are small. *Method 2:* Start the cut with the knife's tip rested on top of the food being cut. Slice downward and forward. Repeat action. Medium sized food items are efficiently cut using this method.

HAND TOOLS AND SMALL EQUIPMENT

A wide variety of hand tools and small equipment are available to help simplify food production processes. Table 7.15 identifies general categories of small equipment that should be available to production staff. Knives are identified on p. 171. Tables 7.16, 7.17, 7.18, 7.19, and 7.20 provide information about the capacity of selected equipment. Table 7.21 identifies large-equipment requirements for basic cooking methods.

TABLE 7.14   **Vegetable cuts and shapes**

Dice	Processing method	Shape
Dicing is a cutting technique that produces a cube shape (six equal sides).	1. Cut a julienne or bâtonnet-shaped item with the dimension appropriate for the size of dice desired. For paysanne, use a ½ × ½-inch stick. 2. Gather the stick-shaped vegetables and cut through them crosswise at evenly spaced intervals. For paysanne, cut at ¼-inch or ⅛-inch intervals to make a tile-shaped item.	

Brunoise (broo-nwaz) (⅛ × ⅛ × ⅛ inch)
Fine brunoise (¹⁄₁₆ × ¹⁄₁₆ × ¹⁄₁₆ inch)

Small dice (¼ × ¼ × ¼ inch)

Medium dice (½ × ½ × ½ inch)

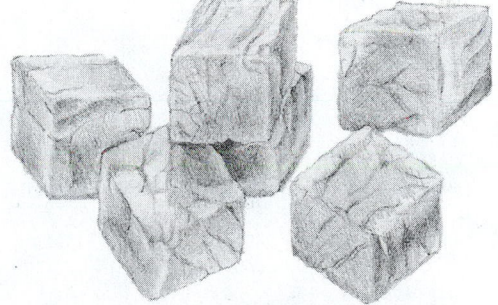

Large dice (¾ × ¾ × ¾ inch)

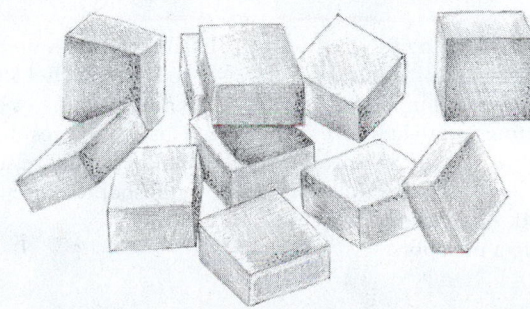

Paysanne (pahy-sahn) (tile shape) (½ × ½ × ¼ or ⅛ inch)

TABLE 7.14   Vegetable cuts and shapes

continued

TABLE 7.14 continued

TABLE 7.14 Vegetable cuts and shapes

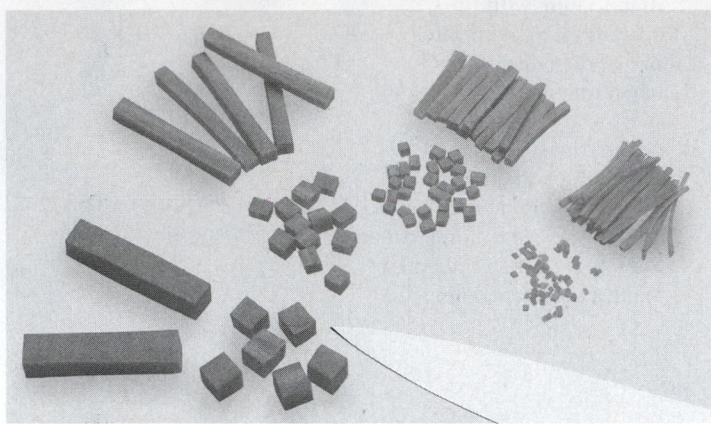

Chiffonade (chef-fon-nahd)	Processing method	Shape
A slicing technique that produces finely sliced or shredded leafy vegetables and herbs.	1. For tight heads such as Belgian endive and cabbage, core and, if large, cut in half. For herbs, remove stems. For loose leaves, roll large leaves into tight cigar-shaped cylinders. For small leaves, stack several leaves on top of one another and roll into cylinders. 2. Use a chef's or French knife to make very fine, parallel cuts. Hard heads such as cabbages or head lettuce can be shredded using a box grater or mandoline.	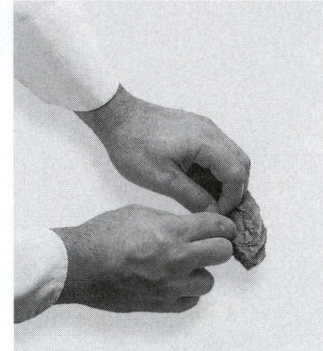 

Coarse chopping	Processing method	Shape
Slicing or chopping food without emphasizing uniform cuts. Generally used in dishes that are less refined in style where visual appearance is not important or in dishes that are strained or puréed. A technique used for making a mirepoix.	1. Chop according to guidelines for using a chef's or French knife, p. 174. 2. Cut into pieces that are not uniform but are similar in size and shape so they cook evenly.	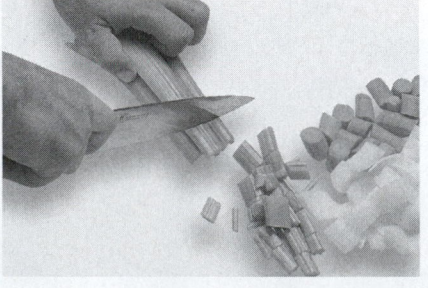

TABLE 7.14   continued

Julienne (ju-lee-en) and bâtonnet (bah-toh-nah)	Processing method	Shape
A cutting and dicing technique that produces a stick-shaped item. A julienne shape used for potatoes is often called an *allumette* (al-yoo-meht) cut.	1. Trim vegetables so that they have straight sides. 2. Slice the vegetable lengthwise into even slices that are the thickness desired (e.g., fine julienne, $\frac{1}{16}$ inch); julienne or allumette, $\frac{1}{8}$ inch; bâtonnet, $\frac{1}{4}$ inch). 3. Stack the slices, aligning the edges, and make parallel cuts of the same thickness as in step 2.	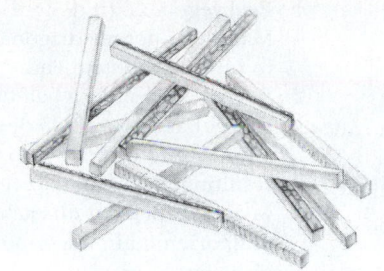

Mince	Processing method	Shape
Mincing is a technique for cutting items such as garlic, herbs, and shallots into very small, even pieces.	1. Pile the coarsely chopped item on a cutting board. 2. With the guiding hand, hold the tip of the knife on the cutting board and rapidly raise and lower the heel of the knife chopping through the vegetable. See method 1 under the guidelines for using a chef's or French knife, p. 174.	

continued

TABLE 7.14 Vegetable cuts and shapes

TABLE 7.14 Vegetable cuts and shapes

TABLE 7.14 continued

Oblique (oh-bleek)	Processing method	Shape
Also called a roll cut. A slicing technique used with long vegetables such as carrots, celery, and parsnips.	1. Peel vegetable (if desired). Make a 45-degree diagonal cut to remove the stem end. 2. Roll the vegetable a half-turn and cut at the same 45-degree angle as the first cut. The resulting piece will have a wedge-shaped cut on each end, oriented in the opposite direction. 3. Repeat the half-turn and cut pieces until the entire vegetable has been cut.	

Rondelles (ron-dellz)	Processing method	Shape
One of the simplest cuts for slicing vegetables such as carrots, cucumbers, and other cylindrical vegetables into disk-shaped or bias-cut disk-shaped pieces.	1. Peel vegetable (if desired). Make uniform slices perpendicular to the item being cut. 2. For diagonal or bias cuts, position the knife at the desired angle and cut into uniform slices. For half-moon cuts, cut slices in half.	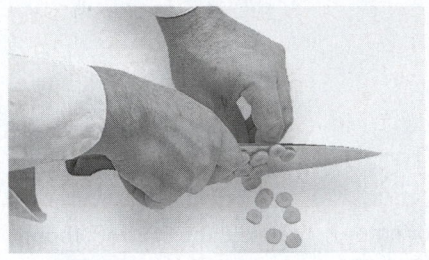 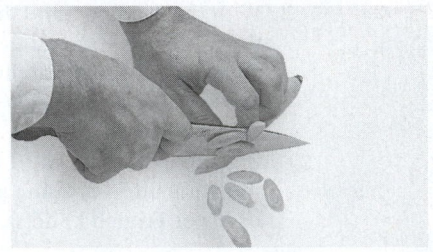

TABLE 7.14   continued

Tourné (toor-nay)	Processing method	Shape
A carving technique used for making football- or barrel-shaped vegetables with seven equal sides and flattened ends. A difficult cut requiring practice to carve equal sides. Used for large round or oval vegetables such as beets, large carrots, potatoes, turnips, rutabagas.	1. Peel vegetable (if desired). 2. For large vegetables, cut into smaller pieces approximately 2 inches thick. Cut large carrots into two sections. 3. Use a paring knife to carve seven smooth, even, curved sides with flattened ends. The resulting product should be thick at the center with tapered ends.	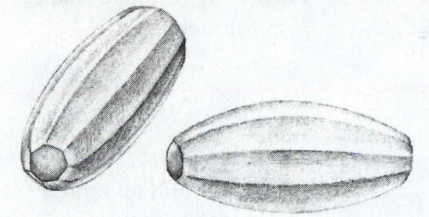 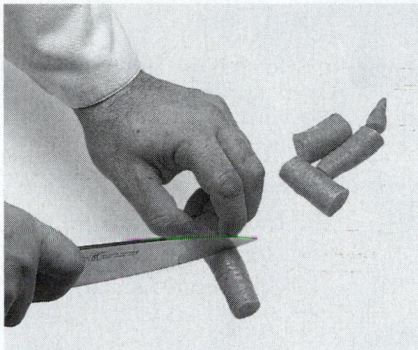 

TABLE 7.14 Vegetable cuts and shapes

TABLE 7.15   Basic tools and equipment

TABLE 7.15   Basic tools and equipment

BASIC HAND TOOLS (NONMECHANICAL)

Ball cutter

Portioning rounded shapes, as for melon balls

Meat mallet

General flattening, such as flattening meat before sautéing

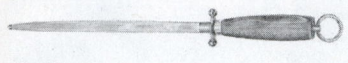

Chef's steel

Smoothing out irregularities on knife's edge between sharpening

Rubber spatula

General stirring and scraping

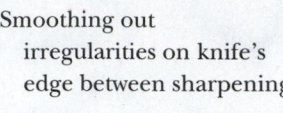

Chef's fork

General use and lifting meat from roasting pans

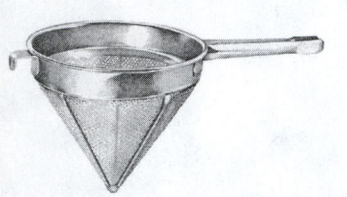

China cap

Straining and draining of food products (perforated metal)

Sieve

Removing particles or lumps from dry ingredients, often flour

Chinois (shee-nwah)

Straining stocks and sauces (fine mesh)

Sifter

Aerating and blending dry ingredients

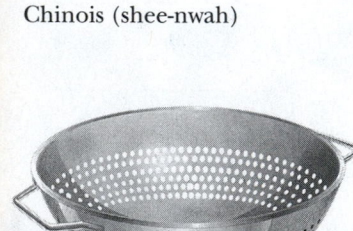

Colander

Draining food (perforated metal, large holes)

Skimmer

Removing food from a liquid (perforated disk)

Grill spatula

Turning food

TABLE 7.15   continued

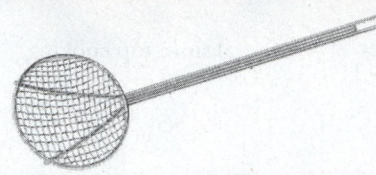

Spider

Removing food from a liquid, often fat (mesh disk)

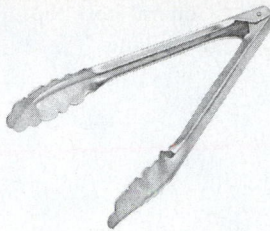

Tongs

General lifting, turning, and serving

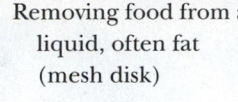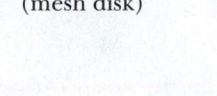

Spoons (perforated, plain, slotted)

General mixing and serving

Vegetable peeler

Paring vegetables

Straight spatula (cake spatula)

Spreading, such as for frosting

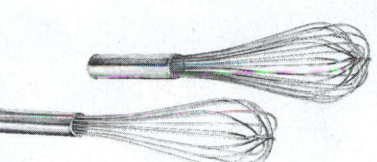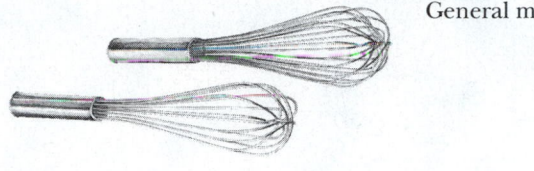

Whisks

General mixing

Strainer (round mesh)

Draining food

Zester

Removing zest from citrus

BASIC PANS

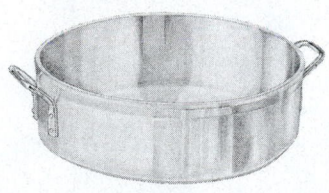

Brazier/rondeau (straight sides, double handles)

General food browning, long slow cooking

Saucepan

General heating

continued

TABLE 7.15   Basic tools and equipment

TABLE 7.15   continued

TABLE 7.15   Basic tools and equipment

Saucepot

General stove top
cooking

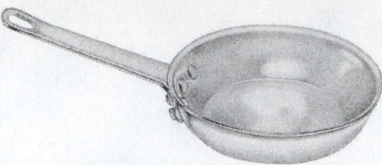

General stove top cooking

Sauteuse (sloped sides)

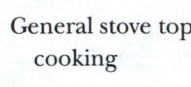

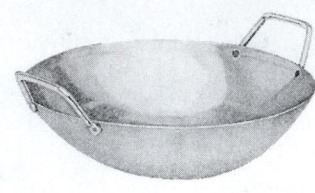

Wok

High-heat cooking,
stir-frying

General stove top
cooking

Sautoir (straight sides)

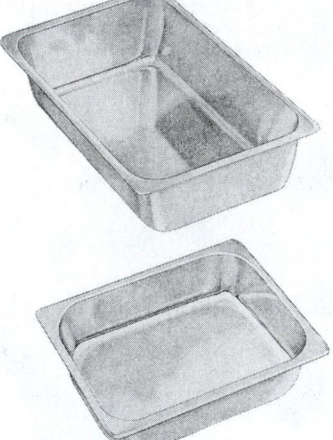

General baking

Hotel pans (counter pans,
steam-table pans)

TABLE 7.15   continued

MEASURING AND PORTIONING EQUIPMENT

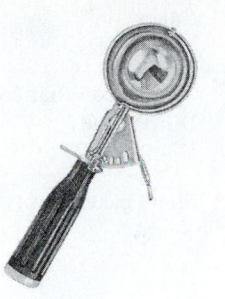

Dipper (scoop, disher)

Portioning (see Table 7.18 for sizes and weights)

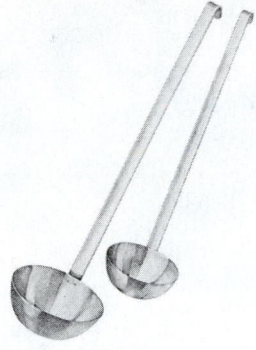

Ladles

Available in ¼-, ⅓-, ½-, and 1-cup units

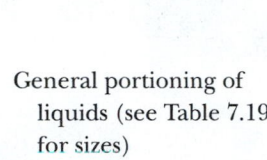

Volume measuring cups

General portioning of liquids (see Table 7.19 for sizes)

Liquid volume measure

Available in gallon/128-oz, half-gallon/64-oz, quart/32-oz, and pint/16-oz units

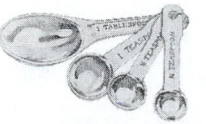

Measuring spoons

Usually sold in sets: ¼ tsp, ½ tsp, 1 tsp, 1 Tbsp

SMALL PROCESSING EQUIPMENT (MANUAL)

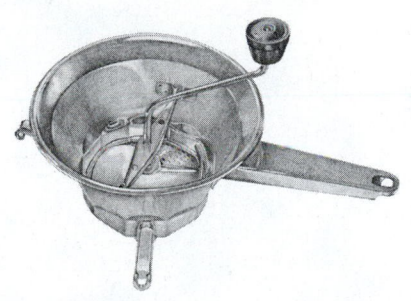

Food mill

Puréeing and straining food

Mandoline

General vegetable and fruit slicing

TABLE 7.15   Basic tools and equipment

TABLE 7.16 Pan capacities for baked products

Pan size/common name	Maximum capacity	Portion	Suggested use
18 × 26 × 2 inches (cake pan)	8–10 lb	Cut 6 × 10 (3 × 2½ inches)	Cakes
18 × 26 × 1 inch (full sheet pan)	4–6 lb	Cut 6 × 10 (3 × 2½ inches) Panned 8 × 12 Dropped 3 × 5	Sheet cakes, bar cookies Dinner rolls Cookies
13 × 18 × 1 inch (half sheet pan)	2–3 lb	Cut 5 × 6 (2½ × 3 inches)	Sheet cakes, bar cookies
12 × 18 × 2 inches	4–5 lb	Cut 5 × 6 (2½ × 3 inches)	Cakes
10-inch tube (tube pan)	2–2½ lb	Cut $\frac{1}{14}$	Chiffon cakes
9-inch round (cake pan)	1½ lb	Cut $\frac{1}{16}$	Layer cakes, corn bread
8-inch round (cake pan)	1¼ lb	Cut $\frac{1}{12}$–$\frac{1}{14}$	Layer cakes
9-inch round (pie pan)	1½ lb	Cut $\frac{1}{8}$	Pies
8-inch round (pie pan)	1 lb	Cut $\frac{1}{16}$	Pies
5 × 16 × 4 inches (loaf pan)	3–5 lb	Cut $\frac{1}{24}$–$\frac{1}{32}$ Cut $\frac{1}{24}$	Quick breads, yeast breads Cakes
5 × 8 × 4 inches (loaf pan)	1½–2½ lb	Cut $\frac{1}{12}$–$\frac{1}{16}$ Cut $\frac{1}{12}$	Quick breads, yeast breads Cakes
5 × 9 × 2¾ inches (loaf pan)	1½–2 lb	Cut $\frac{1}{16}$	Quick breads, yeast breads, cakes

Notes:
- The product volume/weight ratio will dictate the weight per pan.
- See recipes for specific instruction.
- A formula for determining scaling weight of cakes is given on p. 283.

TABLE 7.17   Hotel/counter pan capacities

Depth (in inches)	Maximum Capacity (approx.)		Nonspill Capacity (approx.)		Portions	Cut (inches)	Size
	qt	lb	qt	lb			
FULL (12 × 20)							
2½	8	16	6	12	48	4 × 12	3 × 1½ in
					32	4 × 8	3 × 2½ in
					24	4 × 6	3 × 3⅓ in
4	14	28	12	24			
6	21	42	18	36			
STANDARD HALF (12 × 10)							
2½	4	8	3	6	16	4 × 4	2¼ × 3 in
					12	3 × 4	3⅓ × 3 in
4	6½	13	6	12			
6	10	20	9	18			
LONG HALF (6.5 × 20)							
1¼	2	4	1½	3			
2½	3½	7	2½	5			
4	5½	11	4½	9			
6	8	16	7	14			
TWO-THIRDS (12 × 14)							
1¼	4	8	3	6			
2½	5½	11	4½	9			
4	9	18	8	16			
6	14	28	12	24			
THIRD (12 × 7)							
2½	2½	5	2	4			
4	4	8	3½	7			
6	6	12	5	11			
FOURTH (6 × 10)							
2½	1¾	3½	1½	3			
4	3	6	2½	5			
6	4½	9	3¾	7½			
SIXTH (6 × 7)							
2½	1¼	2½	1	2			
4	1¾	3½	1½	3			
6	2¾	5½	2½	5			
NINTH (4 × 7)							
2½	⅔	1⅓	½	1			
4	1½	3	1¼	2½			

TABLE 7.17   Hotel/counter pan capacities

TABLE 7.18　Dipper equivalents

TABLE 7.18　Dipper equivalents

Dipper number[a]	Approximate measure	Approximate weight	Suggested use
6	10 Tbsp (⅔ cup)	6 oz	Entrée salads
8	8 Tbsp (½ cup)	4–5 oz	Entrées
10	6 Tbsp (⅜ cup)	3–4 oz	Desserts, meat patties
12	5 Tbsp (⅓ cup)	2½–3 oz	Croquettes, vegetables, muffins, desserts, salads
16	4 Tbsp (¼ cup)	2–2¼ oz	Muffins, desserts, croquettes
20	3⅕ Tbsp	1¾–2 oz	Muffins, cupcakes, sauces, sandwich fillings
24	2⅔ Tbsp	1½–1¾ oz	Cream puffs
30	2⅕ Tbsp	1–1½ oz	Large drop cookies
40	1½ Tbsp	¾ oz	Drop cookies
60	1 Tbsp	½ oz	Small drop cookies, garnishes
100	Scant 2 tsp		Tea cookies

[a]Portions per quart.

Notes: • These measurements are based on food leveled off in the dipper. If food is left rounded in the dipper, the measure and weight are closer to those of the next-larger dipper. The number imprinted on the scraper blade identifies how many level scoops of that size are in one 32-fl-oz quart. For fluid ounces per dipper, divide 32 by the dipper size.

• *Scoop* and *disher* are terms often used synonymously with *dipper*.

TABLE 7.19　Ladle equivalents

Approximate weight	Approximate measure	Approximate portions per quart	Suggested use
1 oz	⅛ cup	32	Sauces, salad dressings
2 oz	¼ cup	16	Gravies, some sauces
4 oz	½ cup	8	Stews, creamed dishes
6 oz	¾ cup	5	Stews, creamed dishes, soup
8 oz	1 cup	4	Soup

Note: These measurements are based on food leveled off in the ladle. If food is left rounded in the ladle, the measure and weight are closer to those of the next-larger ladle.

TABLE 7.20 Recommended mixer bowl and steam-jacketed kettle sizes for selected products

	50 portions	100 portions	200 portions	500 portions
Breads, yeast	7 lb/12 qt MB[a]	14 lb/12 qt MB	28 lb/20 qt MB	70 lb/60 qt MB
Quick	10 lb/12 qt MB	20 lb/20 qt MB	40 lb/60 qt MB	100 lb/80 qt MB
Cakes, angel food	6 lb/12 qt MB	12 lb/30 qt MB	24 lb/60 qt MB	60 lb/2 batch sizes, 60 qt MB
Other	8 lb/12 qt MB	16 lb/20 qt MB	32 lb/30 qt MB	80 lb/80 qt MB
Cookies	5 lb/5 qt MB	10 lb/12 qt MB	20 lb/30 qt MB	50 lb/60 qt MB
Pastry	7 lb/12 qt MB	14 lb/20 qt MB	28 lb/30 qt MB	70 lb/80 qt MB
Pie fillings				
Fruit	12 lb/10 qt SJK 10 qt SP	24 lb/20 qt SJK 20 qt SP	48 lb/20 gal SJK	120 lb/20 gal SJK
Frozen/chiffon	12 lb/20 qt MB	24 lb/60 qt MB	48 lb/80 qt MB	120 lb/2 batch sizes, 80 qt MB
Puddings/pie fillings	12 lb/10 qt SJK 10 qt SP	24 lb/20 qt SJK 10 qt SP	48 lb/20 gal SJK	120 lb/20 gal SJK
Scrambled eggs	10 lb/12 qt MB	20 lb/20 qt MB	40 lb/60 qt MB	100 lb/2 batch sizes, 60 qt MB
Cheese soufflé	14 lb/30 qt MB	28 lb/60 qt MB	56 lb/2 batch sizes, 60 qt MB	140 lb/3 batch sizes, 80 qt MB
Meat loaf	12 lb/20 qt MB	24 lb/30 qt MB	48 lb/60 qt MB	120 lb/2 batch sizes, 80 qt MB
Spaghetti sauce	19 lb/20 qt SJK 15 qt SP	38 lb/20 gal SJK 20 qt SP	76 lb/20 gal SJK	190 lb/40 gal SJK
Pasta (and cooking water)	45 lb/20 gal SJK 25 qt SP	90 lb/20 gal SJK	180 lb/40 gal SJK	450 lb/80 gal SJK
Salad dressing	8 lb/12 qt MB	16 lb/20 qt MB	32 lb/60 qt MB	80 lb/80 qt MB
Soups/stews	25 lb/20 qt SJK 15 qt SP	50 lb/20 gal SJK 25 qt SP	100 lb/20 gal SJK	250 lb/40 gal SJK
Mashed potatoes	15 lb/20 qt MB	30 lb/30 qt MB	60 lb/80 qt MB	150 lb/3 batch sizes, 80 qt MB
Whipped cream or topping	1½ qt/5 qt MB	3 qt/12 qt MB	6 qt/30 qt MB	15 qt/60 qt MB

[a]Abbreviations used: MB = mixer bowl; SJK = steam-jacketed kettle; SP = stockpot.

TABLE 7.21 Large-equipment requirements for basic cooking methods

Cooking method	Equipment
Baking	Oven: deck, convection[a], conveyor, range
Blanching	Steam-jacketed kettle; range and stockpot or other pan
Boiling	Steam-jacketed kettle; range and stockpot or other pan
Braising	Tilting fry pan; steam-jacketed kettle; range and fry pan
Broiling	Broiler
Deep-fat frying	Deep-fat fryer; pressure fryer
Frying	Tilting fry pan; range and fry pan
Griddling	Griddle
Grilling	Grill
Oven-frying	Oven: deck, convection[a], conveyor, range
Pan-frying	Tilting fry pan; range and skillet
Poaching	Tilting fry pan; steamer; range and shallow pan
Roasting	Oven: deck, convection[a], conveyor, range
Sautéing	Tilting fry pan; range and sauté pan
Searing	Tilting fry pan; range and skillet
Simmering	Steam-jacketed kettle; range and stockpot or other pan
Steaming	Steamer: high pressure; low pressure; zero pressure; range
Stewing	Steam-jacketed kettle; tilting fry pan; range and stockpot
Stir-frying	Tilting fry pan; range and skillet; griddle; wok

[a]A convection oven cooks faster than a conventional oven. Reduce cooking time by 10 to 15 percent and the temperature by 25–50°F.

part IV

Recipes

Appetizers are foods served as a hot or cold first course before a meal and should complement the menu items that follow without duplicating flavors. Seafood cocktail (crab, lobster, oyster, shrimp), chunked fresh fruit cocktail, or soup is often served for an appetizer. **Hors d'oeuvres** may be served before a meal or may be the only food provided. They should be small (one or two bites), flavorful, and attractive. The style of service—whether buffet, served, or a combination of the two—will depend on the event and the expectations of the client or guest. Hors d'oeuvres and appetizers are similar, and the terms are often used interchangeably.

Cold hors d'oeuvres may be canapés, crudités, or dips. **Canapés** are tiny sandwiches made by spreading a well-seasoned mixture on a bread or vegetable base. Canapé bases include toasted or untoasted bread slices cut into various shapes, crackers, quick breads, melba toast, tiny biscuits, puff pastry rounds, and small shells made from pastry or savory dough. Vegetable bases may be slices of cucumber, summer squash, or other vegetables that will support the weight of the spread. Spreads are the primary flavor ingredient. Flavorful spreads include mixtures made from flavored butters or cream cheese. A salad mixture made from eggs, fish, cheese, or meat is often used for a canapé spread. All canapés should be artfully garnished. Some canapés are made by holding an attractive garnish in place with a small amount of spread. Making canapés close to serving time will help keep the bases from becoming soggy. **Crudités** are raw or slightly blanched vegetables, cut

into attractive shapes and artfully displayed and garnished. They are usually served with one or more dips. Presentation is important. Broad flat dishes, baskets, silver trays, and shallow decorative pans may be used for the container. Vegetables are arranged with consideration for shape, color, balance, and overall decorative appeal. **Dips** are accompaniments to chips, crackers, fruits, toasts, or vegetables. They should complement the foods being served with them. Dips may be served in attractive serving bowls or hollowed-out vegetables, such as cabbages or squash. Hot dips are often served in chafing pans.

Hot hors d'oeuvres are especially good for late-afternoon or evening events when a full meal is not served. Filled pastry or savory dough shells, skewered pieces of meat or vegetables, and chicken wings or small meatballs are popular hot hors d'oeuvres. Hot and cold hors d'oeuvres are usually served at the same event.

Table 8.1 is a general guideline for quantities of appetizers or hors d'oeuvres needed to serve 50 people. Table 8.2 suggests the number of appetizers or hors d'oeuvres needed per person during a reception or pre-dinner cocktail hour. Entrée and vegetable tray guidelines may be found in Table 8.3. The characteristics of the group being served, time of day, type and duration of event, and number of different items offered may require increasing or decreasing the amount of food recommended. Historical data from similar events will be useful in planning food quantities. Table 8.4 suggests names for hors d'oeuvres and appetizers.

TABLE 8.1   Suggestions for appetizers

Food item	Guide to serving quantities for 50
BEVERAGES	
Punch	2–2½ gal; recipes pp. 219–226
Wine	See Tables 3.11 and3.12, pp. 50–58
CANAPÉ SPREADS AND FILLINGS	
Chicken salad spread	Recipe p. 658 prepare ¼ recipe
Ham salad spread	Recipe p. 657 prepare ¼ recipe
Tuna salad spread	Recipe p. 658 prepare ¼ recipe
Miniature puffs	Recipe p. 373 prepare ¼ recipe
COCKTAILS	
Broiled grapefruit	25 fruit
Fruit cup	10 lb
Melon balls or cubes	10 lb
Punch	2 gal; recipes pp. 219–226
Shrimp cocktail	Recipe for sauce p. 694
DIPS	
Artichoke, hot	Recipe p. 194
Artichoke and crab, hot	Recipe p. 194
Baba ghanoush	Recipe p. 205
Basic, and variations	Recipe pp. 194–195
Garden dressing (dip)	Recipe p. 641
Guacamole	Recipe p. 202
Hummus	Recipe pp. 211–212
Layered Mexican	Recipe p. 201
Nacho	Recipe p. 203
Salsa	Recipe p. 702
Summer fruit	Recipe p. 195
Vegetable	Recipe p. 652
Yogurt	Recipes pp. 651–652
HORS D'OEUVRES	
Apple and cheese wedges	1½ lb cheese; 8 apples, cut in wedges
Carrot curls	3–4 lb
Celery sticks	3–4 lb
Cheese ball with crackers	Recipe p. 204; 125–150 crackers
Cheese balls, hot	Recipe p. 396; prepare ½ recipe, use No. 40 dipper
Cheese cubes	5 lb
Cheese olive puffs	Recipe p. 206
Cherry tomatoes	2 lb
Chicken wings	Recipe p. 207
Chips	5 lb
Cocktail sausages	3–5 lb
Crudités	12–15 lb assorted vegetables, p. 192
Deviled eggs	Recipe p. 395; prepare ½ recipe
Fruit chunks	8 lb
Marinated mushrooms	Recipe p. 602
Meatballs in barbecue sauce	Recipe p. 440; prepare ⅓ recipe, use No. 70 dipper
Mixed nuts	1–1½ lb
Party mix	3 lb
Pinwheels	Recipe p. 209
Quesadillas	Recipe p. 672
Sausage balls	100; recipe p. 206
Shrimp	Recipe p. 208
Shrimp, Caribbean	Recipe p. 417
Vegetable relishes	See p. 192 for ideas
Whole shrimp, with cocktail sauce	3–5 lb shrimp; recipe for sauce p. 694; prepare ½ recipe

TABLE 8.1   Suggestions for appetizers

TABLE 8.1   Suggestions for appetizers

TABLE 8.1   continued

SOUPS

Bouillon	Recipe p. 739; prepare ½ recipe for 4-oz portion
French onion	Recipe p. 755; prepare ½ recipe for 4-oz portion
Gazpacho	Recipe p. 767
Vichyssoise	Recipe p. 768; prepare ½ recipe for 4-oz portion

OTHER FINGER FOODS

Cheese ball and crackers	4 lb cheese, 40 oz crackers
Cheese block and crackers	4 lb cheese, 40 oz crackers
Fresh fruit platter	8–10 lb fruit
Fresh vegetables and dip	8–10 lb vegetables, 1 qt dip
Nut bread tea sandwiches	50–75 sandwiches
Tea sandwiches	40–60 tuna, ham, or chicken salad sandwiches
Petite rolls and cold cuts	40–60 petite rolls served with 5 lb assorted cold cuts and 2–3 lb cheese slices

Notes:
- The quantity of appetizers needed for 50 portions will depend on the group being served, the type of function, and the number of different items offered. If food items are served in combination with other foods, adjust the amounts to yield the approximate total weight or total number recommended. Example: Carrot curls, in combination with celery sticks, require a total weight of 3–4 lb.
- Preparing appetizers for an attractive buffet requires careful planning. Choosing foods that need last-minute preparation, along with those that can be produced in advance, is suggested. Following are useful guidelines for production planning:

  Canapés, spreads, and fillings: Highly perishable fillings should be made shortly before serving.

  Cocktails: Prepare fruit a day in advance. Cook and chill shrimp a day in advance. Make and chill beverages 1–3 days in advance.

  Dips: Prepare and chill 1–3 days in advance. Store in glass or other inert-material container.

  Hors d'oeuvres: Prepare vegetable relishes a day in advance; store in cold water. To freshen, cover with ice for 30 minutes before serving. Marinate vegetables a day in advance. Prepare cheese balls 1–5 days in advance; cover tightly. Cut cheese cubes no more than a day in advance; cover tightly.

  Soups: Prepare cold soups 1–2 days in advance, hot soups just before serving.

TABLE 8.2   Number of hors d'oeuvres and appetizers to prepare per person

	½ Hour Event		1 Hour Event		2–3 Hour Event	
	Hot	**Cold**	**Hot**	**Cold**	**Hot**	**Cold**
Men only	6	4	8	6	10	8
Women only	3	2	5	4	6	5

Notes:
- When serving shrimp, prepare five pieces per ½ hour event per person for cold shrimp and four pieces per ½ hour event per person for hot shrimp.
- If a dinner will follow, reduce by one-third the number of appetizers suggested.
- For hors d'oeuvres that do not come in piece servings, count 1 oz as one piece (dips, for example).
- Calculate 2 oz cheese per person.

TABLE 8.3   Meat, cheese, and vegetable trays

MEAT AND CHEESE TRAYS (APPROXIMATE AMOUNT TO SERVE 50)

Meat (shaved or thinly sliced)	Cheese (thinly sliced)	Bread (thinly sliced bread or buns)	Spreads/other
Choose 10 lb (total):	**Choose 3 lb (total):**	**Choose 125 small slices or 75 buns:**	**Use suggested amount:**
Cold cuts	American	Small buns	Margarine or butter, softened, 1 lb
Corned beef	Cheddar	Sliced bread	Mayonnaise or salad dressing, 1½ cups
Roast beef	Edam	Pumpernickel	Prepared mustard, 1 cup
Ham	Gouda	Rye	Horseradish, 1 cup
Pastrami	Monterey Jack	White	Leaf lettuce, 3 lb
Turkey	Muenster	Whole wheat	Alfalfa sprouts, 1 lb
	Provolone		Tomatoes, sliced, 7 lb
	Swiss		Onions, sliced, 2 lb
	See p. 99 for additional cheeses		

VEGETABLE TRAYS AND DIPS (APPROXIMATE AMOUNT TO SERVE 50; SEE NOTES)

Vegetables	Relishes	Dips
Choose 5 lb (total):	**Choose 3 lb (total):**	**Choose 1–1½ qt (total):**
Asparagus spears	Black or green olives	Hot artichoke
Beans, green or waxed	Dill pickle spears	Blue cheese
Belgian endive	Pickled beets	Creamy herb
Broccoli florets	Pickled eggs	Creamy onion
Baby carrots	Pickled vegetables	Dill
Carrot sticks or slices	Sweet pickles	Garden dressing
Cauliflower florets	Garnishes (p. 824)	(prepare ½ recipe)
Celery sticks	Chives	Italian
Cherry tomatoes	Flowers	Mayonnaise, flavored
Cucumber spears or circles	Herbs	(pp. 732–736)
Green beans	Scallions	Pesto
Green onions		Picante
Jicama		Seafood
Kohlrabi		Summer fruit
Mushrooms		Yogurt
Pea pods (sugar, snap, snow)		
Radishes, red and white		
Radish roses		
Red, green, or yellow bell peppers		
Zucchini spears		

Notes: • Meat and cheese may be rolled, folded, or stacked and garnished with leaf lettuce, parsley, and colorful vegetables. Vegetables look appealing when cut in creative shapes and garnished with crisp greens.
• Arranging food neatly so the tray will remain attractive is important. Including larger quantities of more-popular items will make food trays appear well supplied throughout the serving period. Color and flavor combinations also should be considerations for determining placement of food items.
• Crudité trays may require two or three times the amount of vegetables for an attractive display to be arranged and garnished.
• Blanching asparagus, broccoli, cauliflower, and green beans heightens their flavor and appearance (p. 150).

TABLE 8.4   Name suggestions for hors d'oeuvres and appetizers

CHEESE

Assorted domestic cheese and crackers
Assorted imported cheese and crackers
Cheese ball with crackers
Cheese block and crackers
Nacho dip and tortilla chips

FRUIT

Fresh fruit platter
Fresh fruit platter with domestic or
    imported cheese
Fresh berries and dip
Carved melon basket with summer fruits

Imported cheese and fruit tray with sweet
    crackers and hot fudge dip
Fresh seasonal melon

SEAFOOD

Shrimp peel with cocktail sauce
Iced peeled shrimp
Hot spiced shrimp peel
Smoked salmon with lavosh cracker bread
Whole poached salmon

VEGETABLES

Assorted fresh vegetables and dip
Fresh raw vegetable tray with dip
Open-faced vegetable canapés
Belgian endive with herbed cheese

MEAT/POULTRY

Chicken tenders with sauce
Prosciutto-wrapped melon
Sliced meat and cheese tray
Roast tenderloin of beef and cocktail rolls
Mini puffs with white chicken salad
Assorted decorated canapés
Stuffed pita pockets

Note: • *Food for Fifty* recipes will provide guidelines for making hors d'oeuvres and appetizer suggestions.

Appetizer Recipes

HOT ARTICHOKE DIP

Yield: 50 portions   *Portion:* 1½ oz
Oven: 350°F   *Bake:* 20–25 minutes

Ingredient	Amount	Procedure
Artichoke hearts, canned	2 lb 10 oz	Drain and chop artichoke hearts.
Garlic cloves, mashed	3	Stir remaining ingredients into artichoke hearts.
Mayonnaise	2 cups	
Worcestershire sauce	1½ tsp	
Parmesan cheese, grated	3 cups	
White pepper	¼ tsp	
		Pour into two 1-quart ovenproof bowls or pans. Bake at 350°F until mixture reaches 165°F (20–25 minutes). Serve warm (above 140°F) with chips or crackers.

Approximate nutritive values per portion

Calories	Carbohydrate	Protein	Fat	Cholesterol	Sodium	Fiber	Iron
92 kcal	5 g	2 g	7 g	4 mg	148 mg	1 g	0.5 mg

Note

- Potentially hazardous food. *Food Safety Standards:* Hold food for service at an internal temperature of 135°F or above. Do not mix old product with new. Cool leftover product quickly following time standards and cooling procedures on p. 167. Reheat leftover product quickly (within 2 hours) to 165°F or above. Reheat product only once; discard if not used.

Variation

- **Hot Crab and Artichoke Dip.** Add 1 lb chopped crabmeat before baking.

BASIC DIP

Yield: 50 portions

Ingredient	Amount	Procedure
Cream cheese	8 oz	Mix cream cheese until softened, using flat beater.
Sour cream	1 lb 8 oz	Add sour cream. Mix until smooth. Add ingredients for variations from following chart. Mix until evenly distributed. Chill quickly (within 4 hours) to below 41°F.

Note

- Dip may be thinned by adding a small quantity of buttermilk or milk.

VARIATIONS TO BASIC DIP RECIPE

Variation	Ingredients added to basic dip	Serve with
Avocado (guacamole) (see Notes)	(Delete cream cheese from Basic Dip; reduce sour cream to 8 oz) 1 lb 8 oz avocado pulp 1 Tbsp lemon juice 3 oz onion, finely chopped 2 Tbsp fresh cilantro, finely chopped ¼ tsp garlic powder 8 oz fresh tomatoes, diced	Tortilla chips Nacho chips
Blue Cheese	8 oz blue cheese, crumbled 1½ tsp lemon juice 1 Tbsp onion, finely chopped ½ cup buttermilk or milk	Crackers Fresh vegetables Chips
Creamy Herb	¼ cup fresh onion, finely chopped ¼ cup snipped fresh parsley ¼ cup fresh chives, chopped 1 Tbsp Worcestershire sauce ¼ tsp garlic powder	Fresh vegetables
Creamy Onion	2 oz dry onion soup mix ½ oz snipped fresh parsley or chives	Chips
Dill	1½ Tbsp chopped onion 1 Tbsp dill weed 1½ tsp Beau Monde seasoning	Fresh vegetables
Italian	1½ oz dry Italian salad dressing mix ½ oz snipped fresh parsley	Fresh vegetables
Picante	(Delete sour cream; increase cream cheese to 2 lb) 8 oz salsa (see Notes) ¼ cup fresh cilantro, chopped 1 oz stuffed olives, chopped	Tortilla chips Nacho chips Fresh vegetables Spread for canapés
Seafood	8 oz cooked shrimp, clam, or crab, finely chopped 1 oz dry onion soup mix 2 oz chile sauce 1½ Tbsp horseradish	Crackers Toasted party bread
Summer Fruit	(Delete cream cheese) 8 oz brown sugar or honey 1½ tsp vanilla	Fresh fruit
Yogurt, Vegetable Yogurt, Fruit	see p. 651 see p. 651	Fresh vegetables Fresh fruit

Note

- Chunky Avocado Dip may be made by deleting sour cream and using 2 lb cubed fresh avocados.
- More salsa may be added to Picante Dip for a thinner dip.

BRUSCHETTA

Yield: 50 portions   *Portion:* 2 slices

Ingredient	Amount	Procedure
French bread baguette (see Note)	100 slices	Slice baguette into ⅓- to ½-inch-thick diagonal slices.
Extra virgin olive oil	½ cup	Brush both sides lightly with extra virgin olive oil. Arrange on baking sheet.
Garlic cloves (optional)	4	Under a broiler, on a grill, or in a panini press, toast bread on both sides until golden brown.
		While still warm, gently rub one side of the toast with a garlic clove (optional).
		Top as desired. (See Variations.)

Note

- 1 lb baguette (approximately 2½ inch in diameter × 20 inches long) will yield approximately 40 ½-inch-thick slices or 60 ⅓-inch-thick slices.

Variations

- **Black Bean Pico de Gallo Bruschetta.** Topping recipe p. 706.
- **Garlic and Oil Bruschetta.** Rub warm toasted bread with garlic clove. Drizzle with extra virgin olive oil and sprinkle with kosher salt and black pepper. Serve immediately.
- **Mango Pico de Gallo Bruschetta.** Topping recipe p. 706.
- **Olive Tapenade Bruschetta.** Topping recipe p. 197.
- **Pork Tenderloin and Mango Bruschetta.** Roast 4 lb total of pork tenderloin (approximately 3 loins) (p. 462) and refrigerate. Slice cold pork tenderloins into thin medallions. Place one medallion on one slice of toasted bread. Top with ½ tsp Fruit Salsa (p. 704).
- **Roasted Tomato Salsa Bruschetta.** Topping recipe p. 709.
- **Tomato Arugula Bruschetta.** Gently mix 3 lb seeded and diced tomatoes with 2 small bunches arugula (tough stems removed, washed, dried, coarsely chopped). Drizzle with extra virgin olive oil and add salt and pepper. Toss gently only until juices of tomato mix with olive oil.
- **Tomato, Basil, and Mozzarella Bruschetta.** Slice Roma tomatoes and mozzarella cheese into thin slices. Layer on top of toasted bread: tomato slice, basil leaf, mozzarella cheese. Drizzle with extra virgin olive oil and add salt and pepper.
- **Tomato Basil Bruschetta.** Topping recipe p. 603 (drained).
- **Tomato–Serrano Salsa Bruschetta.** Topping recipe p. 708.

OLIVE TAPENADE

Yield: approximately 2 cups

Ingredient	Amount	Procedure
Green Olive Tapenade		
Pitted green olives with pimentos	1 lb	Combine all ingredients except oil in a food processor. Process until coarsely chopped and well blended. Continue to process while slowly adding olive oil.
Mayonnaise	2 Tbsp	
Lemon zest	2 tsp	
Lemon juice	2 Tbsp	
Flat leaf parsley	½ cup	
Yellow bell pepper	2 oz	Refrigerate in a covered container for up to 1 week.
Cracked black pepper	1 tsp	
Chive oil (see Note) or olive oil	½ cup	
Black Olive Tapenade		
Pitted Kalamata olives	1 lb	Combine all ingredients except oil in a food processor. Process until coarsely chopped and well blended. Continue to process while slowly adding olive oil.
Garlic cloves	3	
Capers, drained	¼ cup	
Flat leaf parsley	¼ cup	
Fresh thyme, leaves only	¼ cup	
Sun-dried tomatoes in oil	¼ cup	Refrigerate in a covered container for up to 1 week.
Ground red pepper	⅛ cup	
Olive oil	½ cup	
Olive and Sun-Dried Tomato Tapenade		
Green olives with pimentos	6 oz	Combine all ingredients except oil in a food processor. Process until coarsely chopped and well blended. Continue to process while slowly adding olive oil.
Pitted Kalamata olives	10 oz	
Anchovy fillets (optional)	2	
Sun-dried tomatoes in oil	4 oz	
Capers, drained	2 Tbsp	
Garlic cloves	2	
Fresh thyme, leaves only	1 Tbsp	
Flat leaf parsley	1 Tbsp	Refrigerate in a covered container for up to 1 week.
Extra virgin olive oil	½ cup	

Approximate nutritive values per teaspoon

Calories	Carbohydrate	Protein	Fat	Cholesterol	Sodium	Fiber	Iron
Green: 16 kcal	0.4 g	0 g	1.7 g	0 mg	44 mg	0.1 g	0.2 mg
Black: 16 kcal	0.5 g	0 g	1.7 g	0 mg	60 mg	0.2 g	0.21 mg
Sun-dried: 19 kcal	0.6 g	0 g	1.8 g	0 mg	75 mg	0.2 g	0.24 mg

Note

- **Chive Oil.** Combine 1 cup extra virgin olive oil with 1 oz fresh chives. Process in a food processor until bright green. Strain oil through a coffee filter or cheesecloth. Use for dressing pasta, in salad dressings, and as an infused oil. Use within 1 week.

STUFFED TINY POTATOES

Yield: 50 portions   *Portion:* 2 potatoes
Oven: 425°F/350°F

Ingredient	Amount	Procedure
Small round new potatoes, 1- to 1½-inch diameter, 1 oz each	7 lb	Wash potatoes, carefully keeping skin intact. Let air-dry completely. (See Note.)
Olive oil	2 Tbsp	Rub potatoes with olive oil. Roast in a 425°F oven until just tender (p. 823). (See Note.) Refrigerate until cold.
		Cut a ½-inch slice off each potato. Hollow out potatoes carefully, leaving sturdy walls. (Reserve the potato tops and flesh that was removed for another use.)
Filling	approx. 1 lb	Fill potato shells with approximately 1 tsp filling.
Warm Filling Suggestions Artichoke Dip, p. 194		Heat to 165°F (approximately 10 minutes) at 350°F. (For cold fillings, do not heat.)
Baba Ghanoush, p. 205 Taco meat filling, p. 676 Warm Tomato Olive and Fennel Ragout, p. 707 Tomato Pesto, p. 706		
Cold Filling Suggestion Guacamole, p. 202		

Notes

- Potentially hazardous food. *Food Safety Standards:* Hold food for service at an internal temperature of 135°F or above. Do not mix old product with new. Cool leftover product quickly following time standards and cooling procedures on p. 167. Reheat leftover product quickly (within 2 hours) to 165°F or above. Reheat product only once; discard if not used.
- Alternatively, cut raw potatoes in half and using a sturdy melon baller, scoop out the inside of the potato, leaving a thick wall. Toss potato shells with olive oil and add salt and pepper. Bake at 400°F until tender, about 15 minutes. Fill as desired. Alternately, do not toss with olive oil, and steam until just tender. Proceed according to recipe.

VIETNAMESE SPRING ROLLS

Yield: 50 rolls   *Portion:* 1 roll

Ingredient	Amount	Procedure
Rice vermicelli noodles	21 lb	Bring water to a boil in steam-jacketed or other large kettle. Stir rice vermicelli noodles into boiling water. Turn off heat and let set for approximately 1 minute until translucent. Stir to keep separated. Drain.
Water	2 gal	Immediately dip rice noodles in ice water to stop cooking. Drain well. (Expected yield of noodles is 5 lb.)
Carrots, fine julienne	12 oz	Using tongs, mix carrots, onion, lettuce, and ginger with drained noodles to make filling.
Green onion, finely sliced	3 oz	
Leaf lettuce, finely shredded	8 oz	
Fresh ginger, peeled and minced	2 oz	
Rice papers	50	Soak rice papers, one at a time, in hot water until soft, approximately 15–20 seconds. Remove from water and place on a flat work surface. Place 2 oz (approximately ⅔ cup) noodle-vegetable filling onto center of rice paper. Shape into a log shape across rice paper.
Sweet chile sauce (optional) (see Note)	3 cups	Spoon 1 Tbsp sweet chile sauce on top of filling (optional).
Basil or mint leaves (see Note)	2 oz	Carefully place 2 basil leaves, 2–3 cilantro leaves, and 2 shrimp halves (cut side down) on top of filling.
Cilantro leaves	2½ oz	Press filling down slightly to flatten. Fold in two sides and roll tightly, beginning with an open side. The shrimp and herbs should be visible through the rice paper wrapper and make a decorative roll.
Cooked shrimp, split (see Note)	50 shrimp	Lay seam side down. Serve with sweet chile sauce, hoisin peanut dipping sauce, or Asian Dipping Sauce (p. 701). (See Note.)

Approximate nutritive values per roll

Calories	Carbohydrate	Protein	Fat	Cholesterol	Sodium	Fiber	Iron
125 kcal	28 g	2 g	0.2 g	14 mg	85 mg	0.5 g	0.5 mg

Notes

- Potentially hazardous food. *Food Safety Standards:* Hold food for service at an internal temperature of 41°F or below. Do not mix old product with new. Keep leftover product chilled at 41°F or below. See p. 167 for cooling procedures.
- Sweet chile sauce is available from most broadline foodservice distributors. Make **Hoisin Peanut Dipping Sauce** by mixing together until smooth 4 cups hoisin sauce, 12 oz creamy peanut butter, 1 cup water, and ¼ cup rice vinegar.
- Use Vietnamese basil or Thai basil if available.
- Split shrimp lengthwise.

MARINATED CHEESE

Yield: 50 portions   *Portion:* 1 oz

Ingredient	Amount	Procedure
Extra virgin olive oil	1¾ cups	Stir together liquids, vegetables, herbs, and spices.
White vinegar	1¾ cups	
Diced pimento, drained	8 oz	
Fresh parsley, chopped	⅔ cup	
Green onion, minced	⅔ cup	
Garlic, minced	3 Tbsp	
Sugar, granulated	1½ oz	
Fresh basil, chopped	⅓ cup	
Salt	1½ tsp	
Black pepper	1½ tsp	
Yellow cheddar cheese	1 lb	Place cheese in a shallow pan. Pour marinade over cheese. Cover and refrigerate for 6 hours or longer.
White cheddar cheese	1 lb	To serve, arrange cheese cubes in a shallow serving dish. Spoon some marinade over the cheese.
Cream cheese	1 lb 8 oz	

Approximate nutritive values per oz cheese

Calories	Carbohydrate	Protein	Fat	Cholesterol	Sodium	Fiber	Iron
125 kcal	1 g	6 g	11 g	28 mg	182 mg	0 g	0.2 mg

Note

- Potentially hazardous food. *Food Safety Standards:* Hold food for service at an internal temperature of 41°F or below. Do not mix old product with new. Keep leftover product chilled at 41°F or below. See p. 167 for cooling procedures.

Variation

- **Marinated Cheese and Olives.** Substitute 12 oz drained and pitted green or black olives for 12 oz cheese.

LAYERED MEXICAN DIP

Yield: 50 portions or three 14-inch platters *Portion:* 4 oz

Ingredient	Amount	Procedure
Bean dip	4 lb (six 10½-oz cans)	
Avocado pulp	3 lb	Blend. Save for later step.
Lemon juice	6 Tbsp	
Salt	1 tsp	
Black pepper	1½ tsp	
Sour cream	1 lb 8 oz	Blend. Save for later step.
Mayonnaise	1½ cups	
Taco seasoning	3¾ oz	
Fresh tomatoes, diced	3 lb	
Green onions, sliced	9 oz	
Ripe olives, sliced	1 lb 4 oz	
Cheddar cheese, shredded	12 oz	

1. Spread 1 lb 5 oz bean dip on each of three 14-inch round platters.
2. Spread 1 lb avocado mixture over bean dip layer.
3. Spread 12 oz sour cream mixture over avocado layer.
4. Sprinkle remaining ingredients over each platter in the following order: tomatoes, green onions, olives, and cheese. Chill quickly to below 41°F. (See Note.)
5. Serve with tortilla or nacho chips.

Approximate nutritive values per portion

Calories	Carbohydrate	Protein	Fat	Cholesterol	Sodium	Fiber	Iron
212 kcal	8 g	5 g	18 g	14 mg	787 mg	4 g	1 mg

Notes

- Potentially hazardous food. *Food Safety Standards:* Hold food for service at an internal temperature of 41°F or below. Do not mix old product with new. Keep leftover product chilled at 41°F or below. See p. 167 for cooling procedures.
- Refried beans (½ recipe, p. 779) may be substituted for purchased bean dip.
- Salsa may be substituted for diced tomatoes, taco seasoning, and mayonnaise. Use 7½ cups salsa (2½ cups on each tray).

GUACAMOLE

Yield: 50 portions   *Portion:* 2 oz

Ingredient	Amount	Procedure
Avocado	12 (6 lb)	Peel, pit, and dice avocados.
Fresh lime juice	½ cup	Sprinkle lime juice on avocados. Stir lightly to mix.
Plain yogurt	1 cup	Mix yogurt and spices into avocado until well mixed.
Cumin, ground	1 tsp	
Hot pepper sauce	1 tsp	
Salt	½ tsp	
Black pepper	½ tsp	
Plum tomatoes, seeded and diced to ¼ inch	2 lb (EP)	Stir tomatoes, onion, and cilantro into avocado mixture.
Red onion, diced	6 oz (EP)	
Fresh cilantro, chopped	1 oz (EP)	
		Serve with tortilla chips or as a condiment.

Approximate nutritive values per portion

Calories	Carbohydrate	Protein	Fat	Cholesterol	Sodium	Fiber	Iron
100 kcal	6 g	1.5 g	8 g	0 mg	38 mg	3 g	1 mg

Note

- Potentially hazardous food. *Food Safety Standards:* Hold food for service at an internal temperature of 41°F or below. Do not mix old product with new. Keep leftover product chilled at 41°F or below. See p. 167 for cooling procedures.

NACHOS

Yield: 50 portions *Portion:* $3\frac{1}{2}$ oz sauce + 1 oz chips

Ingredient	Amount	Procedure
Shortening	1 oz	Sauté onion in shortening until tender.
Onion, chopped	3 oz	
Green chile peppers, chopped	6 oz	Add chiles and tomatoes to onion. Simmer for 15 minutes.
Diced tomatoes, canned	1 lb 8 oz	
Chicken Stock (p. 738)	2 qt	Add stock and seasonings. Bring to a boil. Reduce heat to medium.
Cumin, ground	1 Tbsp	
Garlic powder	2 tsp	
Processed cheese, shredded	6 lb 10 oz	Add cheese to hot mixture. Stir until melted.
Cornstarch	3 oz	Combine cornstarch and water to make a smooth paste. Add slowly to cheese mixture, stirring constantly.
Water	$\frac{1}{2}$ cup	Cook and stir until mixture thickens. Turn heat to low.
Nacho chips	4 lb	Place 12 nacho chips on dinner plate.
Jalapeño peppers, sliced	8 oz	Using a 4-oz ladle, pour $3\frac{1}{2}$ oz sauce over chips. Garnish with sliced jalapeño peppers.

Approximate nutritive values per portion

Calories	Carbohydrate	Protein	Fat	Cholesterol	Sodium	Fiber	Iron
424 kcal	26 g	16 g	29 g	58 mg	1138 mg	3 g	1 mg

Notes

- Potentially hazardous food. *Food Safety Standards:* Hold food for service at an internal temperature above 140°F. Do not mix old product with new. Cool leftover product quickly (within 4 hours) to below 41°F. See p. 167 for cooling procedures. Reheat leftover product quickly (within 2 hours) to 165°F. Reheat product only once; discard if not used.
- The sauce may be thinned with chicken broth.
- Canned cheese sauce may be substituted for scratch-prepared cheese sauce. Add green chile peppers and diced tomatoes if desired.

Variation

- **Quick Nacho Sauce.** In a steam-jacketed kettle combine 2 oz chopped onion, 4 oz canned green chiles (diced), $1\frac{1}{2}$ cups diced tomatoes, 1 qt water, 2 tsp ground cumin, 2 tsp garlic powder, and $\frac{1}{2}$ tsp dried cilantro. Bring to a boil, reduce heat, and simmer 15–20 min. Stir in 3 lb 12 oz shredded processed cheese. Stir until melted. Return temperature to 150°F.

CHEESE BALL

Yield: 50 portions   *Portion:* 1½ oz

Ingredient	Amount	Procedure
Cream cheese, softened	1 lb	Mix all ingredients until smooth, using flat beater. Shape into two balls, 2 lb 4 oz each. Chill quickly to below 41°F. (See Note.)
Blue cheese, crumbled	1 lb 8 oz	
Sharp cheddar cheese, shredded	2 lb	
Onion, finely minced	3 oz	
Worcestershire sauce	1 tsp	

Approximate nutritive values per portion

Calories	Carbohydrate	Protein	Fat	Cholesterol	Sodium	Fiber	Iron
154 kcal	1 g	8 g	13 g	39 mg	331 mg	0 g	0.5 mg

Notes

- Potentially hazardous food. *Food Safety Standards:* Hold food for service at an internal temperature of 41°F or below. Do not mix old product with new. Keep leftover product chilled at 41°F or below. See p. 167 for cooling procedures.
- Ball may be rolled in chopped pecans, snipped fresh parsley, or paprika.
- Cheese mixture may be shaped into a long roll. After chilling, slice and serve on crackers or other canapé base.

BABA GHANOUSH

Yield: 50 portions   *Portion:* 3 oz
Oven: 425°F

Ingredient	Amount	Procedure
Eggplant	10 lb	Cut eggplant in half. Place cut side down on greased or silicone-paper-lined bun sheet. Bake until soft. Cool, peel, chop, and mix until smooth.
Onions, chopped	12 oz EP	Add onions, parsley, and garlic to eggplant.
Fresh parsley, chopped	3 Tbsp EP	Mix well.
Garlic, minced	3 oz EP	
Fresh lemon juice	4 oz	Mix lemon juice, oil, tahini paste, and spices with vegetables.
Olive oil	2 oz	Hold for service at or below 41°F.
Tahini paste	3 oz	Serve as a dip with pita points or as a Middle Eastern spread.
Red pepper flakes	1¼ tsp	
Cumin, ground	1 Tbsp	
Salt	¼ tsp	

Approximate nutritive values per portion

Calories	Carbohydrate	Protein	Fat	Cholesterol	Sodium	Fiber	Iron
50 kcal	7 g	1.5 g	2.2 g	0 mg	18.3 mg	2.5 g	0.5 mg

Note

- Potentially hazardous food. *Food Safety Standards:* Hold food for service at an internal temperature of 41°F or below. Do not mix old product with new. Keep leftover product chilled at 41°F or below. See p. 167 for cooling procedures.

SAUSAGE BALLS

Yield: 50 portions   *Portion:* 2 balls
Oven: 350°F   *Bake:* 20–25 minutes, both steps

Ingredient	Amount	Procedure
Pork sausage, bulk	2 lb	Form sausage into 100 1-inch balls, using a No. 70 dipper. Place on baking sheet. Bake at 350°F for 15 minutes. Drain on paper towels.
Cheddar cheese, grated	1 lb	Combine cheese, margarine, flour, and seasonings in mixer bowl, using flat beater.
Margarine, softened	8 oz	
Flour, all-purpose	12 oz	
Salt	½ tsp	
Paprika	2 tsp	
		Wrap 2 Tbsp (No. 70 dipper) dough around each sausage ball. Place on ungreased baking sheet. Bake at 350°F for 8–10 minutes. Serve hot, above 140°F.

Approximate nutritive values per portion

Calories	Carbohydrate	Protein	Fat	Cholesterol	Sodium	Fiber	Iron
145 kcal	6 g	6 g	11 g	21 mg	296 mg	0.2 g	0.5 mg

Notes

- Potentially hazardous food. *Food Safety Standards:* Hold food for service at an internal temperature of 135°F or above. Do not mix old product with new. Cool leftover product quickly following time standards and cooling procedures on p. 167. Reheat leftover product quickly (within 2 hours) to 165°F or above. Reheat product only once; discard if not used.
- Balls may be frozen after wrapping with dough. Bake while still frozen at 400°F for 12–15 minutes.

Variation

- **Cheese Olive Puffs.** Wrap dough around large stuffed green olives. Bake same as for Sausage Balls.

HOT BARBECUED WINGS

Yield: 50 portions   *Portion:* 6 wing pieces
Oven: 400°F   *Bake:* 20–25 minutes

Ingredient	Amount	Procedure
Barbecue Sauce (pp. 688–689) Crushed red pepper	1¼ qt 1 tsp	Mix barbecue sauce and crushed red pepper.
Chicken wings, split, tip removed	20 lb	Pour barbecue sauce over chicken wings and stir to coat evenly. Place chicken wings on a lightly greased rack that is set inside a baking pan. (Wings should not touch.) Bake at 400°F for 10 minutes. Remove from oven and brush with barbecue sauce. Bake another 10–15 minutes until browned and internal temperature is 170°F. Remove from oven and serve. Additional heated barbecue sauce may be poured on wings before service. (Do not use the barbecue sauce that was used to sauce the raw wings.)

Approximate nutritive values per portion

Calories	Carbohydrate	Protein	Fat	Cholesterol	Sodium	Fiber	Iron
384 kcal	3 g	55 g	15 g	156 mg	316 mg	0.2 g	2 mg

Notes

- Always wash hands and wash and sanitize countertops, utensils, and containers between production steps when preparing raw poultry.
- Potentially hazardous food. *Food Safety Standards:* Hold food for service at an internal temperature of 135°F or above. Do not mix old product with new. Cool leftover product quickly following time standards and cooling procedures on p. 167. Reheat leftover product quickly (within 2 hours) to 165°F or above. Reheat product only once; discard if not used.

Variations

- **Cajun Wings.** Season chicken wings with Cajun Seasoning (p. 727). Serve with a Blue Cheese or Barbecue Sauce (pp. 688–689) or bottled hot pepper sauces.
- **Sweet and Sour Wings.** Substitute Sweet and Sour Sauce (p. 696) for Barbecue Sauce.

SHRIMP PEEL

Yield: 50 portions   *Portion:* 2 oz

Ingredient	Amount	Procedure
Water	3¾ qt	Bring water, lemon juice, lemons, and seasonings to a rolling boil in steam-jacketed or large kettle.
Lemon juice	½ cup	
Lemons, quartered	2	
Allspice, whole	1 Tbsp	
Bay leaves	8	
Cayenne pepper	2 tsp	
Cloves, whole	1 Tbsp	
Coriander, ground	1 tsp	
Dill weed	2 tsp	
Mustard seed	2 tsp	
Parsley, dried	3 Tbsp	
Salt	1 Tbsp	
Shrimp, medium to medium large, thawed	7 lb	Add shrimp and bring to a full rolling boil. Cook only until shrimp turn pink, approximately 3 minutes. Remove from heat and drain immediately. Chill quickly (4 hours or less) to below 41°F. (See p. 167 for cooling procedures.) To serve, arrange shrimp on top of shaved ice. Serve with Cocktail Sauce (p. 694). Garnish with lemon wedges and fresh herbs.

Approximate nutritive values per portion

Calories	Carbohydrate	Protein	Fat	Cholesterol	Sodium	Fiber	Iron
71 kcal	1 g	13 g	1 g	96 mg	225 mg	0 g	2 mg

Notes

- Potentially hazardous food. *Food Safety Standards:* Hold food for service at an internal temperature of 41°F or below. Do not mix old product with new. Keep leftover product chilled at 41°F or below. See p. 167 for cooling procedures.
- Frozen unthawed shrimp may be used. Stir after adding to boiling water.
- Shrimp may be served hot.
- A commercial shrimp boil may be substituted for spices.

TOMATO, BASIL, AND CHEESE PINWHEELS

Yield: 50 portions   *Portion:* 2 pinwheels

Ingredient	Amount	Procedure
Cream cheese	3 lb	Soften cream cheese to room temperature. Place in mixer bowl.
Fresh parsley, minced	4 oz	Add fresh herbs, garlic, tomatoes, pimento, and black olives to softened cream cheese.
Fresh basil, minced	2 oz	Mix until well blended.
Fresh thyme, minced	½ oz	
Fresh rosemary, finely minced	½ oz	
Garlic, minced	1 Tbsp	
Rehydrated dried tomatoes, minced	6 oz	
Pimento, diced, well drained	4 oz	
Black olives, coarsely chopped or thinly sliced, well drained	4 oz	
Flour tortillas, 12-inch	10	Place tortillas on work surface. Smooth 6 oz cream cheese mixture over tortillas. Roll very tightly (as for a jelly roll) to create a pinwheel effect. Cover and refrigerate until well chilled, 4–6 hours.
		Cut off ends of tortilla roll and discard. Portion remaining roll into 10 slices per roll.

Approximate nutritive values per portion

Calories	Carbohydrate	Protein	Fat	Cholesterol	Sodium	Fiber	Iron
150 kcal	10 g	3.6 g	11 g	30 mg	208 mg	1 g	1 mg

Note

- Potentially hazardous food. *Food Safety Standards:* Hold food for service at an internal temperature of 41°F or below. Do not mix old product with new. Keep leftover product chilled at 41°F or below. See p. 167 for cooling procedures.

FOCACCIA WITH HERB CHEESE SPREAD

Yield: 4 focaccia rounds with spread

Ingredient	Amount	Procedure
Focaccia	Recipe	Prepare focaccia.
Nonfat cream cheese, softened	2 cups	Combine cream cheese, sour cream, and mayonnaise in a mixer bowl. Beat on low speed until smooth.
Low-fat sour cream	1½ cups	
Low-fat mayonnaise	¼ cup	
Parmesan cheese, freshly grated	3 oz	Add cheese, herbs, and pepper. Mix until just combined.
Fresh basil, chopped	⅓ cup	
Fresh chives, minced	⅓ cup	
Garlic, minced	½ tsp	
Black pepper	½ tsp	
		Spread 6–8 oz spread on top of focaccia rounds and broil 6 inches from heat until spread melts (1–2 minutes). Cut into narrow strips or wedges. Serve warm.

Approximate nutritive values per recipe

Calories	Carbohydrate	Protein	Fat	Cholesterol	Sodium	Fiber	Iron
2158 kcal	242 g	61 g	100 g	50 mg	2759 mg	9 g	13 mg

Notes

- Potentially hazardous food. *Food Safety Standards:* Hold food for service at an internal temperature of 41°F or below. Do not mix old product with new. Keep leftover product chilled at 41°F or below. See p. 167 for cooling procedures.
- Serve as an appetizer or as an accompaniment to soup or salad.

RED PEPPER HUMMUS ON PITA POINTS

Yield: 50 portions   *Portion:* 3 oz hummus

Ingredient	Amount	Procedure
Garbanzo beans, canned, drained and rinsed	6 lb EP	Place garbanzo beans, garlic, tahini paste, and lime juice in food processor. Process until smooth.
Garlic, minced	7 oz	
Tahini paste	1 lb 5 oz	
Fresh lime juice	2⅔ cups	
Roasted red bell peppers p. 796	2 lb	Add seasonings to food processor. Process only until bell peppers are finely chopped.
Basil leaves, dried, crumbled	2¼ tsp	
Salt	3¾ tsp	
Crushed red pepper	1¼ tsp	
Black pepper	¼ tsp	
Pita or gyro bread	4 lb 8 oz	Cut pita or gyro bread into pie-shaped pieces.
Cucumbers, peeled, sliced	7 lb 8 oz	Serve hummus on bread points with slices of cucumber.

Approximate nutritive values per portion of hummus

Calories	Carbohydrate	Protein	Fat	Cholesterol	Sodium	Fiber	Iron
126 kcal	15.3 g	4.5 g	6 g	0 mg	307 mg	2.9 g	1 mg

Note

- Potentially hazardous food. *Food Safety Standards:* Hold food for service at an internal temperature of 41°F or below. Do not mix old product with new. Keep leftover product chilled at 41°F or below. See p. 167 for cooling procedures.

Variations

- **Greek Salad Plate with Red Pepper Hummus.** Combine in baker's bowl 5 lb tomato wedges, 2 lb 12 oz julienne-cut zucchini squash, 1 lb 8 oz peeled and sliced cucumbers, 1 lb whole pitted ripe olives, 3 lb 12 oz quartered artichoke hearts, 4 oz red onion rings, and 1 Tbsp cracked black pepper. Dress with 1 qt Italian dressing. Reserve for later step. *Plate assembly:* Place 3 oz fresh spinach on plate, leaving a bare spot for hummus. Top spinach with 5 oz reserved vegetable mixture. Sprinkle with 1 Tbsp crumbled feta cheese. Portion 2½ oz Red Pepper Hummus on plate sorrounded by 3 pita bread wedges. Total amount of spinach, 9 lb; feta cheese, 1 lb 4 oz; hummus, 7 lb 8 oz; pita bread, 25 7-inch rounds. Yield: 50 salad plates.

CILANTRO HUMMUS

Yield: 50 portions   *Portion:* 4 oz

Ingredient	Amount	Procedure
Cumin, ground	5 Tbsp	Spread spices in a thin even layer in a dry skillet. Heat until fragrant over medium heat 1–2 minutes, being careful not to burn. Shake pan throughout cooking to prevent burning. Cool.
Coriander, ground	2½ Tbsp	
Fennel seed	2½ tsp	
Garlic cloves	2 oz	Process in food processor until garlic and cilantro are coarsely chopped and liquids and spices are mixed.
Fresh cilantro	4 oz	
Olive oil	1½ cups	
Water	3½ cups	
Salt	1 Tbsp	
Ground red pepper	2 tsp	
Garbanzo beans, canned, drained	7 lb 4 oz	Add garbanzo beans, lemon juice, tahini paste, and toasted spices to food processor. Process until almost smooth. Refrigerate.
Fresh lemon juice	8 oz	
Tahini paste	8 oz	

Approximate nutritive values per portion

Calories	Carbohydrate	Protein	Fat	Cholesterol	Sodium	Fiber	Iron
176 kcal	17 g	4 g	11 g	0 mg	367 mg	3 g	1.7 mg

Note

- Potentially hazardous food. *Food Safety Standards:* Hold food for service at an internal temperature of 41°F or below. Do not mix old product with new. Keep leftover product chilled at 41°F or below. See p. 167 for cooling procedures.

Coffee

The type of coffee-making equipment used in a foodservice determines the method of preparation and the grind of coffee. Urns or modular brewers are used when large quantities of coffee are required, as on a rapidly moving cafeteria line or for a large catered function. Where the service is spread over a longer period, coffee may be prepared in small batches in a drip coffee maker, or for single servings in an espresso machine.

The equipment selected should make a clear, rich brew, hold the coffee at a consistent temperature, and provide the quantity needed at an appropriate speed with minimal labor. Regardless of the method used, certain guidelines should be observed:

1. Select a grind that is designed for the brewing equipment. Fine or vacuum grind is suitable for equipment that brews in 1–4 minutes (espresso machines), medium grind for drip makers that brew in 4–6 minutes, and coarse grind for urns that brew in 6–8 minutes.

2. Use fresh coffee. Coffee loses its strength and flavor rapidly after it is ground and exposed to air. Large amounts should not be stored. To maintain good coffee flavor, store ground coffee or whole beans in an airtight container at cool room temperature. Do not refrigerate. To keep unopened coffee for more than 2–3 weeks, store in the freezer in an airtight container. Do not refreeze.

3. Use a proportion of fresh, cold water to coffee that makes a brew of the strength preferred by the clientele. A proportion of 2½ gal water per pound of coffee (20 oz water to 1 oz coffee) makes a commonly accepted brew. See p. 215 for coffee recipes. For a stronger brew, use 1 lb coffee per 2 gal water.

4. Have the water cold, freshly drawn, accurately measured, and brought to a temperature of 195–205°F. Water that is too hot will extract bitter solids. Water that is too cold will not extract enough color or flavor. Bottled or filtered water may be used to brew coffee.

5. Hold brewed coffee at 185°F. Urn coffee can be held for up to 1 hour. Coffee brewed in small pots and kept warm by a heat source under the pot should be served within 20 minutes of brewing. Carafes that hold brewed coffee in an insulated serving decanter will hold the coffee for 2 hours or more. Reheating coffee results in a bitter brew.

6. Clean the coffee-making equipment after each use, following instructions that come with the equipment.

Specialty coffee refers to coffee made from flavored beans, espresso, and espresso-based drinks, or coffee flavored with syrups or other postbrew flavorings. See p. 132 for espresso-based drinks.

Tea

Tea is brewed by the process of infusion, in which boiling water is poured over tea leaves or bags. The following brewing guidelines should be followed.

- Start with fresh, high-quality tea.
- Start with fresh, cold water and bring it to a rolling boil. Do not boil the water for a long period of time.
- Use a stainless steel, earthenware, or porcelainlike pot that has been preheated with a small amount of hot water.
- Add tea bags or loose tea (in a strainer or infuser) to the pot. A generally acceptable brew is made by using 1 Tbsp loose tea or one tea bag per cup of water.
- The brewing time and water temperature vary among teas. Brew black tea at 212°F for 4–6 minutes; oolong tea at 195–205°F for 4–6 minutes; green tea at 160–165°F for 2–4 minutes; and white tea at 180°F for 4–6 minutes. Tea may become bitter if the tea bag or leaves are not removed from the water after the tea has steeped.

For iced tea, make the brew stronger than for hot tea to compensate for the ice that melts. Pour tea over ice just before serving.

A suggested selection of teas includes a black, green, and oolong variety, and a specialty or flavored tea such as black currant or raspberry. Caffeine-free and herbal tea selections also should be available. See p. 132 for descriptions of teas.

Punch

Punch may be made easily from frozen or canned juices in various combinations. Lemonade (p. 220) or Basic Fruit Punch (p. 219) makes a good base for many other fruit drinks when combined with fresh, frozen, canned, or powdered juices of the desired flavor.

The amount of sugar needed varies with the sugar concentration of the juices and individual preference. A recipe for Simple Syrup for sweetening punch is given on p. 220. If time does not allow making the syrup, the sugar may be added directly to the punch and stirred until the sugar is dissolved.

For punch that is to be served iced, the ingredients should be refrigerated. The chilled ingredients may be combined several hours in advance of service. If ginger ale or other carbonated beverage is to be used, however, it should be chilled and added just before serving. Hot punch should be served at 180°F. If wine or other liquor is an ingredient in hot punch recipes, the temperature should not exceed 180°F.

Punch may be served from a bowl and kept cold by adding ice cubes, or it may be poured over an ice mold (p. 219). It may also be served as a nonalcoholic cocktail in appropriate glassware and garnished. See p. 227 for a few suggestions for nonalcoholic cocktails that use recipes in this book. Hot punch may be served from a punch bowl or hot-holding equipment. Preheat a glass punch bowl with a small amount of hot water before filling with hot punch.

The amount of punch or iced beverage to prepare depends on the size of the punch cup or glass, the number of guests to be served, and whether second servings will be offered. Service from a punch bowl requires slightly more punch than if it is to be poured from a pitcher for individual service. It is always desirable to have extra chilled, unopened cans of the main punch ingredients to facilitate serving a larger crowd than anticipated.

Most recipes in this book were developed for 2–2½ gal punch. Each gallon will yield 32 half-cup portions. Punch cups vary in size from 3 to 6 oz, so it is important that the size be considered in determining the correct amount of punch to prepare.

Wine

Pairing wine with food is a matter of individual preference and usually requires some experimentation. Table 3.10 (p. 48) provides guidelines helpful for selecting wine. The amount of wine to serve depends on glass size and the type of meal or event. The volumes of different-size wine bottles are located in Table 3.11 (p. 50).

Beverage Recipes

COFFEE

Yield: 50 portions or 2½ gal   *Portion:* 6 oz (¾ cup)

Ingredient	Amount	Procedure
Coffee	1 lb	Use proper blend and grind for the coffee maker used.
Water, cold	2½ gal	Use method recommended by the manufacturer of the coffee maker.

Note

- The amount of water will vary with the brand of coffee and the strength preferred.

Variations

- **Iced Coffee.** Increase coffee to 2 lb. Pour over ice in glasses. Coffee may be cooled to room temperature but should not be refrigerated. Flavorings (e.g., vanilla or almond) may be added for variety.
- **Instant Coffee.** Use 3 oz instant coffee or 2 oz freeze-dried to 2½ gal boiling water. Dissolve the coffee in a small amount of boiling water and add to the remaining hot water. Keep hot just below the boiling point, 185–190°F.
- **Steeped Coffee.** Tie regular grind coffee loosely in a cloth bag. Immerse bag in cold water, which has been measured into a stainless steel kettle or stock pot. Heat to boiling point. Boil 3 minutes or until of desired strength. Remove coffee bag. Cover container and hold over low heat to keep at serving temperature.

HOT TEA

Yield: 50 portions or 2½ gal   *Portion:* 6 oz (¾ cup)

Ingredient	Amount	Procedure
Tea bags, 1 oz	2	Place tea bags in a stainless steel, enamel, or earthenware container.
Water, cold	2½ gal	Bring water to a boil; pour over tea. Steep for 3 minutes. Remove bags.

Notes

- If bulk tea is used, tie loosely in a bag.
- The amount of tea to be used will vary with the quality.
- Instant tea (¾–1 oz) may be used in place of the tea bags. The exact amount will vary according to the strength desired.

SPICED TEA

Yield: 48 portions or 1½ gal   *Portion:* 4 oz (½ cup)

Ingredient	Amount	Procedure
Water, boiling	1½ gal	Mix all ingredients except tea.
Sugar, granulated	1 lb 8 oz	Simmer for 20 minutes.
Lemon juice	¼ cup	Strain.
Lemon peel, grated	1 lemon	
Orange juice	1 cup	
Orange peel, grated	1 orange	
Cloves, whole	4 tsp	
Cinnamon sticks	1 oz	
Tea bag, 1 oz	1	Add tea bag to hot liquid. Steep for 5 minutes. Remove tea bag. Serve hot.

Approximate nutritive values per portion

Calories	Carbohydrate	Protein	Fat	Cholesterol	Sodium	Fiber	Iron
60 kcal	16 g	0.1 g	0 g	0 mg	7 mg	0 g	0 mg

Variation

- **Russian Tea.** Use only 1¼ gal water. Add 1 qt grape juice when adding other juice.

ICED TEA

Yield: 48 portions or 3 gal   *Portion:* 8 oz (1 cup)

Ingredient	Amount	Procedure
Tea bags, 1 oz	6	Place tea bags in a stainless steel, enamel, or earthenware container.
Water, boiling	1 gal	Pour boiling water over tea bags. Steep 4–6 minutes. Remove bags.
Water, cold	2 gal	Pour hot tea into cold water.
Ice, chipped or cubed	10–15 lb	Fill 12-oz glasses with ice. Pour tea over ice just before serving.

Notes

- Always pour the hot tea concentrate into the cold water. Do not refrigerate or ice the tea prior to service. Cloudiness develops in tea that has been refrigerated.
- Instant tea (1–1½ oz) may be used in place of the tea bags.
- Six to seven lemons, cut in eighths, may be served with the tea.
- Iced tea may be garnished with lemon or orange slices or mint leaves.

COCOA

Yield: 50 portions or 2½ gal   *Portion:* 6 oz (¾ cup)

Ingredient	Amount	Procedure
Sugar, granulated	1 lb 8 oz	Mix sugar, cocoa, and salt.
Cocoa	8 oz	
Salt	½ tsp	
Water	1 qt	Add water and mix until smooth.
		Boil for approximately 3 minutes or to form a thin syrup.
Milk	2½ gal	Heat milk to scalding. Stir in syrup.
Vanilla	1 tsp	Just before serving, add vanilla and stir until well mixed.

Approximate nutritive values per portion

Calories	Carbohydrate	Protein	Fat	Cholesterol	Sodium	Fiber	Iron
182 kcal	25 g	7 g	7 g	26 mg	121 mg	0 g	2 mg

Notes

- Potentially hazardous food. *Food Safety Standards:* Hold food for service at an internal temperature of 135°F or above. Do not mix old product with new. Cool leftover product quickly following time standards and cooling procedures on p. 167. Reheat leftover product quickly (within 2 hours) to 165°F or above. Reheat product only once; discard if not used.
- A marshmallow or 1 tsp whipped cream may be added to each cup if desired.
- Cocoa syrup may be made in amounts larger than this recipe and stored in the refrigerator for 3 or 4 days. To serve, add 1 qt cocoa syrup to each 2 gal hot milk.

Variations

- **Amaretto Cocoa.** Add ¾ cup amaretto along with the milk. Delete vanilla. For a nonalcoholic version, substitute 1½ Tbsp of almond extract for the amaretto.
- **Hot Chocolate.** Substitute 10 oz unsweetened baking chocolate for cocoa. Add to water and stir until melted.
- **Instant Hot Cocoa.** Dissolve 2½ lb instant cocoa powder in 2 gal boiling water.
- **Mexican Chocolate.** Follow hot chocolate recipe. Substitute 1 gal of hot coffee for 1 gal of milk. Add 1 oz (¼ cup) ground cinnamon.

FRENCH CHOCOLATE

Yield: 64 portions or 3 gal   *Portion:* 6 oz (¾ cup)

Ingredient	Amount	Procedure
Unsweetened chocolate	1 lb 2 oz	Combine chocolate and water. Cook over direct heat, stirring constantly, for 5 minutes or until chocolate is melted.
Water, cold	3 cups	Remove from heat. Beat with a wire whip until smooth.
Sugar, granulated	2 lb 8 oz	Add sugar and salt to chocolate mixture.
Salt	½ tsp	Return to heat. Cook over hot water 20–30 minutes or until thick. Chill.
Whipping cream	3½ cups	Whip cream. Fold into cold chocolate mixture.
Milk	2½ gal	Heat milk to scalding. To serve, place 1 Tbsp (rounded) chocolate mixture in each serving cup. Add hot milk to fill cup. Stir until well blended. Serve immediately.

Approximate nutritive values per portion

Calories	Carbohydrate	Protein	Fat	Cholesterol	Sodium	Fiber	Iron
247 kcal	28 g	6 g	14 g	38 mg	97 mg	1 g	0.5 mg

Notes

- Potentially hazardous food. *Food Safety Standards:* Hold food for service at an internal temperature of 135°F or above. Do not mix old product with new. Cool leftover product quickly following time standards and cooling procedures on p. 167. Reheat leftover product quickly (within 2 hours) to 165°F or above. Reheat product only once; discard if not used.
- The milk must be kept at 185°F during the serving period.
- The chocolate mixture may be stored for 24 hours in the refrigerator.
- To make in quantity, prepare chocolate syrup and add hot milk. Whip cream to soft peaks and fold into hot chocolate. Keep hot.

BASIC FRUIT PUNCH

Yield: 80 portions or 2½ gal   *Portion:* 4 oz (½ cup)

Ingredient	Amount	Procedure
Sugar, granulated	2 lb 8 oz	Mix sugar and water.
Water	1 qt	Bring to a boil. Cool.
Orange juice, frozen, undiluted	3 cups (two 12-oz cans)	Combine juices and water.
Lemon juice, frozen, undiluted	3 cups (two 12-oz cans)	Add sugar syrup and stir until mixed. Chill.
Water, cold	1½ gal	

Approximate nutritive values per portion

Calories	Carbohydrate	Protein	Fat	Cholesterol	Sodium	Fiber	Iron
74 kcal	19 g	0.3 g	0.1 g	0 mg	3 mg	0 g	0 mg

Notes

- If time does not allow making and cooling syrup, the sugar may be added to the cold punch and stirred until dissolved. Increase cold water to 1¾ gal.
- Ginger ale may be substituted for part or all of the water. Chill and add just before serving.

Variations

- **Ginger Ale Fruit Punch.** Use 1½ qt lemon juice, 1½ qt orange juice, 1 qt pineapple juice, and 1 gal water. Increase sugar to 3 lb. Add 2 qt ginger ale just before serving. Lime, orange, lemon, or raspberry sherbet may be added to punch just before serving.
- **Golden Punch.** Reduce orange and lemon juice to one 12-oz can each. Add two 46-oz cans pineapple juice.
- **Sparkling Grape Punch.** Reduce orange and lemon juice to one 12-oz can each. Add two 12-oz cans frozen grape juice. Just before serving, add two 20-oz bottles of ginger ale.

ICE MOLD

Yield: 1 mold

Ingredient	Amount	Procedure
Ice mold	1	Select mold that will fit in punch bowl.
Punch, juice, lemonade		Fill mold with liquid, half to two-thirds full. Freeze.
Garnishes	see Notes	Add garnishes and enough liquid to partially cover garnishes. Freeze.
		After thin layer of liquid and fruit are frozen, fill mold with liquid and freeze until firm.
		To unmold ice ring, dip the mold in warm water until the ice slips out easily. Place the ring in very cold punch, garnished side up. Replace mold as necessary.

Notes

- Some attractive garnishes include strawberries, cherries, pineapple, grapes, orange or lemon or lime slices, mint, ivy, and fresh flowers. (See p. 131 for flower garnishes.)
- If water is the liquid, use distilled or boiled tap water. Allow boiled water to sit and de-aerate for about 15 minutes.
- For a decorative ice mold, use two or three layers of garnish between layers of ice. Freeze the garnish in place before adding the layers of liquid.

SIMPLE SYRUP

Yield: 2 qt

Ingredient	Amount	Procedure
Sugar, granulated	2 lb	Mix sugar and water.
Water	1 qt	Boil for 3 minutes.
		Chill before using in punch.

Notes

- For a thicker syrup, increase sugar to 2 lb 8 oz and add 1 Tbsp corn syrup.
- May be stored in the refrigerator for use in beverages or where recipe specifies Simple Syrup.

LEMONADE

Yield: 48 portions or 3 gal   *Portion:* 8 oz (1 cup)

Ingredient	Amount	Procedure
Lemon juice	1¼ qt (approximately 30 lemons)	Mix lemon juice and sugar.
Sugar, granulated	2 lb 8 oz	
Water, cold	2¼ gal	Add water. Stir until sugar is dissolved. Chill.

Approximate nutritive values per portion

Calories	Carbohydrate	Protein	Fat	Cholesterol	Sodium	Fiber	Iron
97 kcal	25 g	0 g	0 g	0 mg	11 mg	0 g	0 mg

Notes

- Three 6-oz cans undiluted frozen lemon juice may be substituted for fresh lemon juice. Increase water to 2½ gal.
- Three 32-oz cans frozen lemonade concentrate, diluted 1:4 parts water, will yield 60 1-cup portions.
- Lemonade makes a good base for fruit punch.

BANANA PUNCH

Yield: 64 portions or 2 gal   *Portion:* 4 oz (½ cup)

Ingredient	Amount	Procedure
Sugar, granulated	2 lb	Mix sugar and water.
Water, hot	1½ qt	Boil for 3 minutes. Cool.
Orange juice, frozen, undiluted	1½ cups (one 12-oz can)	Combine juices, fruits, and water.
Lemon juice, frozen, undiluted	¾ cup (one 6-oz can)	Add cooled sugar syrup. Chill.
Water, cold	1 qt	
Crushed, pineapple	3 qt (one No. 10 can)	
Bananas, ripe, mashed	6 medium	
Ginger ale, chilled	1 qt	Add ginger ale just before serving.

Approximate nutritive values per portion

Calories	Carbohydrate	Protein	Fat	Cholesterol	Sodium	Fiber	Iron
105 kcal	27 g	1 g	0 g	0 mg	3 mg	1 g	0.5 mg

Notes

- Mixture may be frozen before ginger ale is added and held for use later.
- Two 46-oz cans of unsweetened pineapple juice and one 12-oz can lemonade may be substituted for the crushed pineapple and lemon juice.

Variation

- **Banana Slush Punch.** Mix and freeze juices, syrup, and mashed bananas. To serve, fill glass about half full of partially frozen slush and add chilled ginger ale.

CRANBERRY PUNCH

Yield: 80 portions or 2½ gal   *Portion:* 4 oz (½ cup)

Ingredient	Amount	Procedure
Cranberry juice	3 qt	Mix juices and water. Chill.
Pineapple juice	3 qt (two 46-oz cans)	
Lemonade, frozen, undiluted	1 qt (one 32-oz can)	
Water, cold	1 qt	
Ginger ale, chilled	three 28-oz bottles	Add ginger ale just before serving.

Approximate nutritive values per portion

Calories	Carbohydrate	Protein	Fat	Cholesterol	Sodium	Fiber	Iron
76 kcal	19 g	0 g	0 g	0 mg	5 mg	0.3 g	0.5 mg

SANGRIA SIPPER

Yield: 80 portions or 3¾ gal   *Portion:* 6 oz

Ingredient	Amount	Procedure
Grape juice, frozen, undiluted	three 12-oz cans	Combine juices and water. Stir well.
Orange juice, frozen, undiluted	three 12-oz cans	Refrigerate until time of service.
Lemonade, frozen, undiluted	three 12-oz cans	
Water	5 qt	
Club soda	7 qt	Just before service, combine juice mixture, club soda, and sliced fruit.
Oranges, thinly sliced	10	
Lemons, thinly sliced	9	
Limes, thinly sliced	6	
		Serve punch and sliced fruit in a stemmed goblet.

Approximate nutritive values per portion

Calories	Carbohydrate	Protein	Fat	Cholesterol	Sodium	Fiber	Iron
80 kcal	21 g	0.7 g	0 g	0 mg	21 mg	1 g	0.5 mg

Note

- May be garnished with skewered fruit.

WHITE WINE SANGRIA

Yield: 80 portions or 3¾ gal   *Portion:* 6 oz

Ingredient	Amount	Procedure
White wine	2 gal	Mix until sugar dissolves.
Orange juice	1½ qt	
Sugar	1 lb	
Oranges, thinly sliced	3 lb	Mix fruit with wine-juice mixture.
Peaches, peeled, thinly sliced (see Note)	4 lb	Let stand at room temperature for 3 hours, then refrigerate until cold.
Apples, thinly sliced	3 lb	
Limes, thinly sliced	1 lb	
		Pour 6 oz of sangria (liquid and fruit) over ice in a stemmed goblet.

Approximate nutritive values per portion

Calories	Carbohydrate	Protein	Fat	Cholesterol	Sodium	Fiber	Iron
95 kcal	8 g	0 g	0 g	0 mg	5 mg	0 g	0.5 mg

Note

- Mango and kiwi can be substituted for some or all of the peaches.

SPARKLING APRICOT–PINEAPPLE PUNCH

Yield: 80 portions or 2½ gal   *Portion:* 4 oz (½ cup)

Ingredient	Amount	Procedure
Apricot nectar	3 qt (two 46-oz cans)	Combine juices and water
Pineapple juice, unsweetened	3 qt (two 46-oz cans)	Chill.
Lemon or lime juice, frozen, undiluted	1½ cups	
Water, cold	2 qt	
Ginger ale, chilled	2 qt	Add ginger ale just before serving.

Approximate nutritive values per portion

Calories	Carbohydrate	Protein	Fat	Cholesterol	Sodium	Fiber	Iron
55 kcal	14 g	0.3 g	0 g	0 mg	4 mg	0.3 g	0.5 mg

MOCK PIÑA COLADA

Yield: 96 portions or 3 gal   *Portion:* 4 oz (½ cup)

Ingredient	Amount	Procedure
Vanilla ice cream mix, liquid, unfrozen	2 gal	Combine, using wire whip.
Milk	3 qt	Place in punch bowl.
Coconut extract	½ cup	
Rum extract	5 Tbsp	
Pineapple juice	1 qt	
Maraschino cherries, with stems	50	Serve in punch cup or stemmed glass. Garnish with maraschino cherry.

Approximate nutritive values per portion

Calories	Carbohydrate	Protein	Fat	Cholesterol	Sodium	Fiber	Iron
200 kcal	21 g	4 g	12 g	77 mg	64 mg	0 g	0.5 mg

Note

- Softened vanilla ice cream may be substituted for ice cream mix.

PINK CHAMPAGNE-STYLE PUNCH

Yield: 96 portions or 3 gal   *Portion:* 4 oz (½ cup)

Ingredient	Amount	Procedure
Water	2 qt	Heat water and sugar until sugar dissolves.
Sugar, granulated	1 lb 4 oz	Remove from heat and cool.
Red grapefruit juice, unsweetened	2 qt	Mix juices and grenadine syrup with water-sugar mixture.
Fresh lemon juice	½ cup	Refrigerate until ready to serve.
Grenadine syrup	1¼ cups	
Ginger ale	7 qt	Just before service, combine chilled juice mixture with chilled ginger ale.
		Ladle the punch into champagne glasses. Garnish with a strip of lemon peel.

Approximate nutritive values per portion

Calories	Carbohydrate	Protein	Fat	Cholesterol	Sodium	Fiber	Iron
65 kcal	17 g	0 g	0 g	0 mg	0 mg	0 g	0.5 mg

BLUSHING PINEAPPLE PUNCH

Yield: 50 portions or 1¾ gal   *Portion:* 4 oz (½ cup)

Ingredient	Amount	Procedure
Sugar, granulated	6 oz	Cook sugar, water, and cinnamon candies over low heat, stirring until candies are dissolved.
Water	1½ cups	
Cinnamon candies (red hots)	6 oz	
Pineapple juice	1 gal	Combine pineapple juice and cinnamon candy syrup.
Ginger ale	2 qt	Add ginger ale and ice just before serving.
Ice	8 oz	

Approximate nutritive values per portion

Calories	Carbohydrate	Protein	Fat	Cholesterol	Sodium	Fiber	Iron
84 kcal	21 g	0.3 g	0 g	0 mg	4 mg	0 g	0.5 mg

Variation

- **Red-Hot Tea.** Use following ingredients in place of those in recipe: 12 oz cinnamon candies dissolved in 5½ qt hot water. Add 16 oz concentrated orange juice and lemon juice to taste. Serve hot.

WASSAIL

Yield: 80 portions or 2½ gal   *Portion:* 4 oz (½ cup)

Ingredient	Amount	Procedure
Sugar, granulated	2 lb 8 oz	Mix sugar, water, and spices.
Water	2½ qt	Boil for 10 minutes.
Cloves, whole	1½ tsp	Cover and let stand for 1 hour in a warm place.
Cinnamon sticks	10 (1¼ oz)	Strain.
Allspice berries	10	
Crystallized ginger, chopped	2 oz	
Orange juice, strained	2 qt	When ready to serve, add juices and cider.
Lemon juice, strained	1¼ qt	Heat quickly to boiling point.
Apple cider	5 qt	
Crabapples or small oranges	6–10	To serve, pour hot mixture over fruit, studded with cloves, in a punch bowl.
Cloves, whole		If using a glass bowl, temper by filling with warm water to prevent cracking when hot punch is poured in.

Approximate nutritive values per portion

Calories	Carbohydrate	Protein	Fat	Cholesterol	Sodium	Fiber	Iron
105 kcal	27 g	0.4 g	0 g	0 mg	3 mg	0.5 g	0.5 mg

TOMATO JUICE COCKTAIL

Yield: 72 portions or 2¼ gal   *Portion:* 4 oz (½ cup)

Ingredient	Amount	Procedure
Tomato juice	8½ qt (six 46-oz cans)	Mix all ingredients. Chill.
Lemon juice	¾ cup	
Worcestershire sauce	3 Tbsp	
Hot pepper sauce	½ tsp	
Celery salt	3 Tbsp	

Approximate nutritive values per portion

Calories	Carbohydrate	Protein	Fat	Cholesterol	Sodium	Fiber	Iron
21 kcal	5 g	0.9 g	0 g	0 mg	644 mg	1 g	0.5 mg

SPICED CIDER

Yield: 80 portions or 2½ gal   *Portion:* 4 oz (½ cup)

Ingredient	Amount	Procedure
Cinnamon sticks	1¼ oz	Tie cinnamon, cloves, and allspice loosely in a clean white
Cloves, whole	2½ Tbsp	cloth to make a spice bag.
Allspice berries	2½ Tbsp	
Sugar, brown (see Note)	12 oz	Add spice bag, sugar, and mace to cider.
Mace	½ tsp	Bring slowly to the boiling point. Simmer for about 15 minutes.
Apple cider	2½ gal	Remove spices. Serve hot or chilled.

Approximate nutritive values per portion

Calories	Carbohydrate	Protein	Fat	Cholesterol	Sodium	Fiber	Iron
75 kcal	19 g	0 g	0 g	0 mg	5 mg	0.3 g	0.5 mg

Note

- If a very sweet cider is used, omit or reduce brown sugar.

Variations

- **Cider Punch.** Omit spices. Substitute 1 qt reconstituted frozen orange juice and 1 qt pineapple juice for an equal amount of cider. Garnish with thin slices of orange.
- **Hot Mulled Orange Cider.** Combine 2 gal apple cider, 1½ qt reconstituted frozen orange juice, and 1 cup reconstituted frozen lemon juice. Add 2 sticks cinnamon, 1½ tsp ground cinnamon, 1½ tsp whole cloves, and 10 oz sliced fresh orange peels that have been tied in a clean white cloth. Bring to a boil. Reduce heat and simmer for 15 minutes. Remove spice bag.
- **Spiced Cranberry Juice.** Substitute cranberry juice for apple cider. Reduce brown sugar to 4 oz.

SPICED ROSÉ WARMER

Yield: 80 portions or 2½ gal   *Portion:* 4 oz

Ingredient	Amount	Procedure
Apple juice	2 qt	Combine juices, lemon peel, water, sugar, and spices in a
Cranberry juice	2 qt	steam-jacketed or other kettle. Stir to dissolve sugar.
Lemon peel strips	2 lemons	Bring to a boil. Reduce heat and simmer for 10 minutes.
Water	2 qt	Remove and discard lemon peel.
Sugar, granulated	1 lb 12 oz	
Cinnamon sticks	12 inches	
Cloves, whole	½ tsp	
Rosé wine	1 gal	Add wine and lemon juice to juice mixture. Heat to 180°F.
Fresh lemon juice	1 cup	Garnish with lemon slices.

Approximate nutritive values per portion

Calories	Carbohydrate	Protein	Fat	Cholesterol	Sodium	Fiber	Iron
99 kcal	17 g	0 g	0 g	0 mg	0 mg	0 g	0.5 mg

Note

- Care should be taken when pouring hot liquid into a glass punch bowl. Heat punch bowl first with warm water, then pour hot beverage slowly into warm bowl.

RUBY WINE PUNCH

Yield: 80 portions or 2½ gal   *Portion:* 4 oz

Ingredient	Amount	Procedure
Water	1 qt	Combine water, sugar, and spices in a steam-jacketed or other kettle.
Sugar, granulated	1 lb 12 oz	Bring to a boil. Reduce heat and simmer for 10 minutes.
Cinnamon sticks	15 inches	Discard spices. (Chill water-sugar mixture if using for
Cloves, whole	1 Tbsp	cold punch.)
Cran-raspberry juice	1½ gal	Combine water-sugar mixture with juice and wine.
Burgundy wine	3 qt	Heat to 180°F.

Approximate nutritive values per portion

Calories	Carbohydrate	Protein	Fat	Cholesterol	Sodium	Fiber	Iron
106 kcal	21 g	0 g	0 g	0 mg	34 mg	0 g	0.5 mg

Notes

- For cold wine punch, heat water, sugar, and spices. Chill. Combine with cold juice and wine.
- Care should be taken when pouring hot liquid into a glass punch bowl. Heat punch bowl first with warm water, then pour hot beverage slowly into warm bowl.

NONALCOHOLIC COCKTAILS

Cocktail	Beverage to use	Garnish	Glassware
Apple Cooler	Spiced Cider, chilled (p. 226)	Apple on a skewer	Goblet
Citrus Spritzer	Ginger Ale Fruit Punch (p. 219)	Orange and lemon on skewer with maraschino cherry	Stemmed glass
Champale Punch	Pink Champagne-Style Punch (p. 224)	Lemon peel strip	Stemmed glass
Chocolate Mint Warmer	French Chocolate (p. 218)	Crème de menthe syrup Mint leaf	Cup or mug
Hot Apple Toddy	Spiced Cider, hot (p. 226)	Cinnamon stick	Mug
Piña Colada	Mock Piña Colada (p. 223)	Pineapple and maraschino cherry on skewer	Stemmed glass
Sangria Sipper	Sangria Sipper (p. 222)	Sliced fruit	Stemmed goblet
Tomato Juice Cocktail	Tomato Juice Cocktail (p. 225)	Celery stalk	Tumbler

Note

- Recipe yields may need to be adjusted, depending on the size of glassware used.

Quick Breads

Basic ingredients in all quick breads are flour, liquid, a leavening agent, and flavorings. Fat and eggs are usually included also. The type and quantity of each of these ingredients and their interaction affect the characteristics of the finished product. They may be classified, according to the proportion of flour to liquid, as:

- **Pour batter:** pancakes, waffles, popovers, crepes
- **Drop batter:** muffins, pan breads, drop biscuits
- **Soft dough:** rolled and cut biscuits

Quick breads are leavened by baking powder, baking soda, or steam, which act quickly, requiring them to be baked at once. If a double-acting baking powder is used, quick breads may be mixed, panned, refrigerated, and then baked as needed during the serving period, although they will have slightly decreased volume. A variety of sweet and savory quick breads may be made from basic biscuit and muffin recipes by adding fruits, nuts, and other flavorings.

Quick-bread mixes may be prepared by sifting together the dry ingredients, which generally include nonfat dry milk, and then cutting in the shortening. Such a mix may be made on days when the workload is light and stored for periods up to 6 weeks without refrigeration, or longer if refrigerated. Many foodservices use some type of commercial mix. The decision to purchase a mix or to prepare from scratch depends on the amount of time and skilled labor available, food inventories, and the cost and quality of the mix.

Pans for quick breads should be greased on the bottoms only. A coating mixture may be prepared and brushed on (p. 288), or the pans may be coated with a vegetable spray. Muffin pans with paper baking cups are often used. See p. 156 for quality standards for quick breads.

METHODS OF MIXING

Ingredients for most quick breads are combined by the muffin or biscuit method, although the conventional cake method, described on p. 282, is used for some loaf breads. Most quick-bread ingredients should be mixed only to blend, with as little handling as possible.

Muffin Method

The muffin method is used for muffins, pancakes, waffles, and popovers.

1. Mix the dry ingredients in a mixer bowl. If dry milk is used, add it to the other dry ingredients.
2. Combine beaten eggs, milk, and melted or liquid fat and add to the dry ingredients all at once.
3. Mix at low speed only enough to dampen the dry ingredients.

The mixture should be slightly lumpy and appear undermixed when put into the pan. Excess mixing causes gluten to develop and carbon dioxide to be lost, resulting in the formation of long "tunnels" in the baked product. Effects of overmixing are less evident in rich muffins and loaf breads that contain a high proportion of fat and sugar, or when the batter is made with cake or pastry flour. The batter should be dipped into pans carefully to avoid additional mixing.

Biscuit Method

The biscuit method is used mainly for baking powder biscuits.

1. Combine dry ingredients in a mixer bowl.
2. Cut fat into the flour with a flat beater or pastry knife.
3. Add liquid and mix to form a soft dough.
4. Knead dough on low speed for 15–30 seconds (or on a lightly floured board for 15–20 strokes) to develop the gluten. Kneading contributes to making a good-volume biscuit with a crumb that peels off in flakes. Overkneading or working in extra flour when kneading by hand may result in a biscuit that is compact and less tender. The volume can be affected also by the temperature of the liquid used and the amount of standing time before baking.

Conventional Cake Method

The conventional method, described on p. 282, may be used for coffee cakes, loaf breads, and rich muffins.

Yeast Breads

INGREDIENTS

An understanding of the functions of the main ingredients in yeast-raised doughs is essential to the production of good bread and rolls.

Flour

Flour used for baked products must contain enough protein to make an elastic framework of gluten that will stretch and hold the air bubbles of carbon dioxide gas formed as the dough ferments. *Bread flour* is made from hard wheat and contains more protein than other flour. It is used for making breads and pasta when strength and elasticity are required. *All-purpose flour* is milled from a blend of hard and soft wheat and contains enough protein to provide the gluten that is essential to making good rolls and yeast breads. An all-purpose flour, unless otherwise noted, was used in testing the recipes in this book. *Whole-wheat, rye*, and *specialty flours* add variety to breads. These flours should be combined with a high-protein flour because they do not have enough protein to effect proper gluten formation.

Yeast

Yeast is added to dough for its leavening effect, as well as to enhance the flavor and texture of the finished product. In the fermentation process, sugar in the dough is fermented, and carbon dioxide, ethanol, and other by-products such as lactic acid and acetic acid are released. Fermentation is controlled very carefully by monitoring time, temperature, and humidity throughout the mixing and rising process. When the yeast cells reach about 140°F, as they do soon after baking begins, the cells are destroyed and fermentation ceases. The continued rising is a result of heat expanding the gases trapped within the gluten structure.

The three types of yeast used for yeast bread doughs are compressed, active dry, and instant active dry. **Compressed yeast**, often referred to as fresh yeast, may be purchased in 1-lb cakes or 0.6-oz cubes. It is highly perishable and may be held under refrigeration (30–40°F) for 2–3 weeks. The longer the storage time, the more the yeast activity is lost. Compressed yeast is softened in lukewarm water (95°F) before it is added to the other ingredients.

Active dry yeast differs from compressed yeast in that the moisture is removed by dehydrating at a low temperature. The yeast does not require refrigeration and can be stored for several months in a cool, dry environment. It is recommended that yeast be stored for as short a time as possible because some yeast activity is lost during storage. Active dry yeast must be rehydrated before using in water that ranges in temperature between 105°F and 115°F. When substituting active dry yeast for compressed yeast, use 60 percent of the compressed yeast weight plus enough water to make up the difference.

Instant or **quick-rise dry yeast** differs from active dry yeast in its genetics and method of processing. Instant dry yeast is less sensitive to temperature extremes than active dry yeast and can be added to the dry ingredients without first reconstituting. Water at 125°F is recommended for hydrating the yeast and other dry ingredients. Water above about 138°F will destroy the living yeast organism. Instant dry yeast is vacuum packed and can be stored unopened for several months.

Liquid

The amount of liquid necessary to produce an optimum dough varies with the flour and generally is related to the flour's protein content. Flours with high protein values absorb more water than low-protein flour.

The liquid used for yeast breads generally is milk or water, although potato water or fruit juice may be used. Milk improves the browning and nutritive value of the bread and tends to delay staling. If fresh milk is used, it is scalded to stop enzyme action that may produce undesirable characteristics, then cooled to the appropriate temperature. Nonfat dry milk may be mixed with the dry ingredients or reconstituted and used in liquid form. The nutritive value of bread may be increased by the addition of extra quantities of dry milk.

The temperature of the liquid used has an effect on the endpoint dough temperature after mixing. When using high-speed mixers or making large quantities, it is necessary to calculate the water temperature based on factors such as friction heat generated by the equipment, flour temperature, and room temperature. For quantities used in this book, however, the following guidelines for water temperature are recommended: lukewarm (95°F) for compressed yeast, warm (105–115°F) for active dry yeast, and very warm (125°F) for instant active dry yeast that is mixed with flour and other ingredients.

Other Ingredients

Although used in small quantities, other ingredients influence the quality of the finished product. Salt is added for flavor and also helps control the rate of fermentation. Sugar, a ready source of food for the yeast, accelerates the action of the yeast. Although the addition of a small amount of sugar makes the dough rise faster, too much sugar inhibits yeast activity. Granulated sugar generally is used for bread making, but honey, corn syrup, brown sugar, and molasses are also used, especially in dark whole-grain bread, sweet rolls, or coffee cake. Fat is added to improve flavor, tenderness, browning, and keeping quality. Fat in large amounts, or fat added directly to the yeast, will slow its action. Eggs affect flavor, richness, tenderness, and color.

Bread Bases

Commercially available bread bases may include ingredients for dough conditioning, flavoring, and coloring, as well as flour, salt, eggs, and seeds or nuts. These bases generally require mixing with flour, yeast, and liquid. Mixing and proofing time and techniques may differ from standard procedures, so the manufacturer's instructions should be followed.

MIXING THE DOUGH

Mixing and kneading of dough has three important functions: to uniformly distribute the ingredients into a homogeneous mass, develop the gluten structure that will entrap the carbon dioxide gas, and develop the dough into a continuous gluten network that will have maximum gas-holding capacity. A repeated stretching-and-folding motion, performed always in the same direction, is the most effective way to produce quality bread with high volume; a soft, silky, uniform grain and texture; and good keeping quality. Dividing, rounding, sheeting, and shaping all have a beneficial effect on bread quality because they too contribute to the mixing functions.

The mixing speed and length of time will vary with the size of mixer and amount of dough. Overmixing and allowing the dough temperature to get too high will produce a product with a dense texture and low volume. Generally dough is mixed only until it leaves the sides and bottom of the bowl. When mixed adequately, a small piece of dough may be stretched, without tearing, to resemble a membrane (sometimes referred to as the *membrane test*).

Moisture content of the flour may vary, making it necessary to adjust slightly the amount of flour called for in the recipe. Reserving some of the flour specified and adding it as needed toward the end of the mixing process is suggested. Enough flour should be added to produce a soft—but not sticky—dough. Dough for rolls is usually softer than for loaf bread.

FERMENTATION OF DOUGH

The flavor and texture of the bread depend on the fermentation process. Fermentation begins when the dough is mixed and continues until the yeast is killed by the heat of the oven (approximately 140°F). After mixing is completed, the dough should be set in a warm place (80–85°F), with a relative humidity near 75 percent. The length of the fermentation period depends on the type of product, amount of yeast, strength of the flour, amount of sugar, and temperature of the dough and proofing area. Usually 1–1½ hours are required for the dough to double in bulk for the first time.

After the dough has doubled, air must be forced out and the dough returned to its original bulk. This may be done with a mixer using a dough arm or by hand for small amounts of dough. This process continues to decrease the size of the air bubbles and helps form a good grain and texture in the finished product. Dough at this stage may be retarded by chilling and held in a refrigerator for use at a later time. It is important to cover the dough tightly so that moisture is not lost and a dry, tough skin does not develop on the surface.

SHAPING, PROOFING, AND BAKING

After the dough has fermented until double and the air bubbles are forced out, the time has come to form it into the desired shape. A rest period of 10–15 minutes allows the gluten structure to relax and makes shaping easier (see p. 263 for recipes and directions for shaping). When panning rolls or bread, the distance between pieces will affect the shape, size, and amount of crust in the final product. Individual preference should be considered.

Panned bread or rolls should rise (proof) at 90–100°F and 80–85 percent humidity until double in bulk. A general test for assessing how long to proof is to press the dough lightly with a finger. When the dough has been proofed for the correct length of time, a slight indentation remains. When not proofed long enough, the dough will spring back, leaving no indentation. Overproofed dough will collapse when pressed with a finger. Too short a proofing period will produce a dense, undersized product with a tough crust; too long a proofing period will cause an open, crumbly, texture with low volume and unpleasant flavor.

Crust texture may be determined partly by the treatment applied both prior to baking and during the early stages in the oven. For a crisp crust, spray loaves or rolls with cold water before baking and again after about 10 minutes in the oven. An egg-white glaze (one slightly beaten egg white with 1 tsp water) also may be used to produce a crisp crust. For a shiny, golden crust, brush loaves or rolls with egg or egg-yolk glaze (one slightly beaten egg or egg yolk with 1 Tbsp water or milk) prior to baking. For a soft or tender crust, brush with melted butter or margarine immediately after baking; to give baked sweet rolls a shiny, glossy appearance, brush with simple syrup, then glaze as usual.

Most bread is baked at 375–400°F. Rich and sweet doughs may overbrown quickly and may need to be baked at a slightly lower temperature, 350°F. Generally, small rolls, spaced apart, are baked at a higher temperature than larger loaves so that they become browned in the short time it takes to bake them. For best volume and texture, preheat the oven before baking yeast breads. The final expansion of the dough, called "oven spring," occurs in the first 10–15 minutes of baking in a hot oven. The bread is usually done when tapping the crust produces a hollow sound and the sides, bottom, and top are golden brown, or when the internal temperature reaches 200–205°F. Remove bread from the pans immediately and place on a wire rack to prevent steaming and softening of the crust. Cool the loaves uncovered.

FREEZING YEAST DOUGHS AND BREADS

Yeast doughs can be frozen up to 6 weeks before or after shaping. Sugar and yeast are usually increased slightly. It is important that the dough be frozen quickly and covered tightly. Some quality loss can be expected when freezing dough using techniques available in most bakeries. Commercial processors are able to achieve better results.

To freeze baked bread and rolls, allow to cool to room temperature, then wrap and freeze. Frozen baked products should be allowed to return to room temperature before being warmed or used.

Quick-Bread Recipes

BAKING POWDER BISCUITS

Yield: 100 2½-inch biscuits or 130 2-inch biscuits
Oven: 425°F   *Bake:* 15 minutes

Ingredient	Amount	Procedure
Flour, all-purpose	5 lb	Combine flour, baking powder, and salt in mixer bowl.
Baking powder	5 oz	Mix on low speed until blended, approximately 10 seconds, using flat beater.
Salt	2 Tbsp	
Shortening, hydrogenated	1 lb 4 oz	Add shortening to flour mixture. Mix on low speed for 1 minute. Stop and scrape sides and bottom of bowl. Mix 1 minute longer. The mixture will be crumbly.
Milk	1¾ qt	Add milk. Mix on low speed to form a soft dough, about 30 seconds. Do not overmix. Dough should be as soft as can be handled.

1. Place half of dough on lightly floured board or table. Knead lightly 15–20 times.
2. Roll ¾ inch thick. Biscuits will approximately double in height during baking. Cut with a 2½-inch (or 2-inch) cutter; or cut into 2-inch squares with a knife. When using round hand cutters, cut straight down and do not twist to produce the best shape. Space the cuts close together to minimize scraps. Use of a roller cutter or cutting the dough into squares eliminates or reduces scraps. The scraps can be rerolled, but the biscuits may not be as tender.
3. Place on ungreased baking sheets ½ inch apart for crusty biscuits, just touching for softer biscuits. Repeat, using remaining dough.
4. Bake at 425°F for 15 minutes, or until golden brown.
5. Biscuits may be held 2–3 hours in the refrigerator until time to bake.

Approximate nutritive values per portion

Calories	Carbohydrate	Protein	Fat	Cholesterol	Sodium	Fiber	Iron
145 kcal	18 g	3 g	6 g	2 mg	278 mg	1 g	1 mg

Note

- 7 oz nonfat dry milk and 1¾ qt water may be substituted for fluid milk. Combine dry milk with other dry ingredients. Increase shortening to 1 lb 6 oz.

Variations

- **Buttermilk Biscuits.** Substitute cultured buttermilk (or 7 oz dry buttermilk and 1¾ qt water) for milk. Add 1 Tbsp baking soda to dry ingredients.
- **Butterscotch Biscuits.** Divide dough into eight parts. Roll each part into a rectangle ¼ inch thick. Spread with melted margarine or butter and brown sugar. Roll the dough as for jelly roll. Cut off slices ¾ inch thick. Bake at 375°F for 15 minutes.
- **Cheese Biscuits.** Reduce shortening to 1 lb and add 1 lb grated cheddar cheese.
- **Cinnamon Raisin Biscuits.** Substitute 2 lb 8 oz margarine for shortening. Combine 8 oz sugar and 2½ Tbsp cinnamon with dry ingredients. Add 1 lb 12 oz raisins to mixture after margarine has been mixed in. When baked, ice with Powdered Sugar Glaze (p. 316).
- **Drop Biscuits.** Increase milk to 2 qt. Drop by spoon or No. 30 dipper onto greased baking sheets.
- **Orange Biscuits.** Proceed as for Butterscotch Biscuits. Spread with orange marmalade.
- **Raisin Biscuits.** Reduce shortening to 14 oz and use ½ cup less milk; add 4 whole eggs, beaten, 3 Tbsp grated orange rind, 8 oz sugar, and 8 oz chopped raisins.
- **Scotch Scones.** Add 10 oz sugar and 7 oz currants to dry ingredients. Add 5 eggs, beaten, mixed with the milk. Cut dough in squares and then cut diagonally to form triangles. Brush lightly with milk before baking.
- **Shortcake.** Increase shortening to 1 lb 12 oz. Add 8 oz sugar.
- **Whole-Wheat Biscuits.** Substitute 2 lb whole-wheat flour for 2 lb all-purpose flour.

BASIC MUFFINS (CAKE METHOD)

Yield: 50 3-oz muffins or 70 2¼-oz muffins
Oven: 350°F   *Bake:* 18–20 minutes

Ingredient	Amount	Procedure
Sugar, granulated Shortening	1 lb 3 oz 14 oz	Cream sugar and shortening until fluffy, about 10 minutes, using flat beater.
Eggs	5 (9 oz)	Add eggs slowly to creamed mixture. Mix until blended. Scrape sides of bowl.
Flour, all-purpose Baking powder Salt	3 lb 3 oz 3 oz 1 Tbsp	Combine dry ingredients.
Milk Vanilla	1½ qt 1 Tbsp	Add milk and vanilla alternately with dry ingredients to creamed mixture. Do not overmix.
		Grease bottoms of muffin pans or line with paper baking cups. Portion batter into pans with No. 12 dipper for 3-oz muffins or No. 16 dipper for 2¼-oz muffins. Bake at 350°F for 18–20 minutes.

Approximate nutritive values per portion

Calories	Carbohydrate	Protein	Fat	Cholesterol	Sodium	Fiber	Iron
245 kcal	35 g	5 g	10 g	26 mg	320 mg	1 g	1 mg

Note

- 6 oz nonfat dry milk and 1½ qt water may be substituted for fluid milk. Combine dry milk with flour.

Variations

- **Chocolate Chip Muffins.** Add 1 lb chocolate chips to batter.
- **Coconut Muffins.** Add 1 lb flaked coconut to batter.
- **Honey Streusel Topping for Muffins.** Combine 8 oz brown sugar, 8 oz margarine or butter, 2 Tbsp honey, and ¼ tsp salt. Stir in 1 lb all-purpose flour. Sprinkle on top of muffins before baking.
- For other variations, see Basic Muffins (Muffin method), p. 233.

BASIC MUFFINS (MUFFIN METHOD)

Yield: 50 muffins   *Portion:* 2¼ oz
Oven: 400°F   *Bake:* 20–25 minutes

Ingredient	Amount	Procedure
Flour, all-purpose	2 lb 8 oz	Combine dry ingredients in mixer bowl.
Baking powder	2 oz	Blend on low speed for 10 seconds, using flat beater.
Salt	1 Tbsp	
Sugar, granulated	6 oz	
Eggs, beaten	4 (7 oz)	Combine eggs, milk, and oil.
Milk	1½ qt	Add to dry ingredients. Mix on low speed only long enough to blend, about 15 seconds.
Oil or melted shortening	8 oz (1 cup)	Batter will still be lumpy.
		Portion batter with No. 16 dipper into greased muffin pans, about ⅔ full. Batter should be dipped all at once with as little handling as possible. The dipped muffin batter may be refrigerated for up to 24 hours and baked as needed. See Notes. Bake at 400°F for 20–25 minutes, or until golden brown. Remove muffins from pans as soon as baked.

Approximate nutritive values per portion

Calories	Carbohydrate	Protein	Fat	Cholesterol	Sodium	Fiber	Iron
161 kcal	22 g	4 g	6 g	21 mg	261 mg	1 g	1 mg

Notes

- 6 oz nonfat dry milk and 1½ qt water may be substituted for fluid milk. Combine dry milk with other dry ingredients. Increase fat to 9 oz.
- No. 24 dipper yields 6½ dozen muffins.
- For best results, bake muffins immediately. If refrigerated, let come to room temperature before baking or they will have peaks or exploding tops.
- If adding acidic fruits, bake immediately. Acidic fruits will affect the leavening action.

Variations

- **Apple Muffins.** Add 1 lb chopped, peeled apples. Fold into batter.
- **Apricot Muffins.** Add 1 lb cooked apricots, drained and chopped. Fold into batter.
- **Blueberry Muffins.** Carefully fold 1 lb well-drained blueberries into the batter. Increase sugar to 10 oz. Bake immediately.
- **Cherry Muffins.** Add 1 lb well-drained, cooked cherries. Fold into batter.
- **Cornmeal Muffins.** Substitute 1 lb white cornmeal for 1 lb flour.
- **Cranberry Muffins.** Sprinkle 4 oz granulated sugar over 1 lb chopped raw cranberries. Fold into batter. Bake immediately.
- **Currant Muffins.** Add 8 oz chopped currants. Fold into batter.
- **Date Muffins.** Add 1 lb chopped dates. Fold into batter.
- **Jelly Muffins.** Drop ¼–½ tsp jelly on top of each muffin just before placing in the oven.
- **Nut Muffins.** Add 10 oz chopped nuts. Fold into batter.
- **Raisin Nut Muffins.** Add 6 oz chopped nuts and 6 oz chopped raisins. Fold into batter.
- **Spiced Muffins.** Add 1½ tsp cinnamon, 1 tsp ginger, and ½ tsp allspice to dry ingredients.
- **Whole-Wheat Muffins.** Substitute 12 oz whole-wheat flour for 12 oz white flour. Add ¼ cup molasses with liquid ingredients.

BANANA WHOLE-WHEAT MUFFINS

Yield: 50 muffins   *Portion:* 2¼ oz.
Oven: 350°F   *Bake:* 35–40 minutes

Ingredient	Amount	Procedure
Sugar, granulated	1 lb 9 oz	Cream sugar and shortening on medium speed until fluffy, using flat beater.
Shortening	13 oz	
Eggs	7 (12 oz)	Add eggs and vanilla to creamed mixture and mix thoroughly.
Vanilla	1 Tbsp	Scrape sides of bowl.
Bananas, mashed	2 lb 11 oz	Add bananas. Mix on medium speed for 10 minutes.
Flour, whole-wheat	10 oz	Combine dry ingredients.
Flour, all-purpose	1 lb 8 oz	Add to banana mixture.
Baking soda	3½ tsp	Mix on low speed only until blended. Scrape sides of bowl as needed.
Salt	1½ tsp	Portion batter into greased muffin pans with No. 16 dipper.
		Bake at 350°F for 35–40 minutes.

Approximate nutritive values per portion

Calories	Carbohydrate	Protein	Fat	Cholesterol	Sodium	Fiber	Iron
221 kcal	35 g	3 g	8 g	29 mg	161 mg	1 g	1 mg

Variation

- **Banana Muffins.** Delete whole-wheat flour. Increase all-purpose flour to 2 lb 2 oz.

OATMEAL MUFFINS

Yield: 50 muffins   *Portion:* 2¼ oz
Oven: 400°F   *Bake:* 15–20 minutes

Ingredient	Amount	Procedure
Rolled oats	14 oz	Combine rolled oats and buttermilk in mixer bowl. Let stand 1 hour.
Buttermilk	1¼ qt	
Eggs, beaten	5 (9 oz)	Combine eggs, sugar, and oil.
Sugar, brown	1 lb 4 oz	Add to rolled-oat mixture. Mix for 30 seconds.
Oil or melted shortening	1 lb	Scrape sides of bowl.
Flour, all-pupose	1 lb 4 oz	Combine dry ingredients.
Baking powder	5 tsp	Add to rolled-oat mixture. Mix on low speed only until dry ingredients are
Salt	2½ tsp	moistened, about 15 seconds.
Baking soda	2½ tsp	
		Portion batter with No. 16 dipper into greased muffin pans (⅔ full).
		Bake at 400°F for 15–20 minutes.
		Remove from pans as soon as baked.

Approximate nutritive values per portion

Calories	Carbohydrate	Protein	Fat	Cholesterol	Sodium	Fiber	Iron
213 kcal	26 g	4 g	10 g	23 mg	236 mg	0.3 g	1 mg

Notes

- 4 oz dry buttermilk and 1¼ qt water may be substituted for fluid buttermilk.
- Flavor may be varied by the addition of 1 tsp cinnamon to the dry ingredients.
- No. 24 dipper yields 7 dozen muffins.

Variation

- **Oatmeal Fruit Muffins.** Add 1 lb raisins, chopped dates, or other fruit. Fold into batter.

POPPY SEED–YOGURT MUFFINS

Yield: 50 muffins   *Portion:* 2¼ oz
Oven: 400°F   *Bake:* 18–22 minutes

Ingredient	Amount	Procedure
Flour, all-purpose	2 lb 8 oz	Blend. Set aside for later step.
Poppy seed	¼ cup	
Salt	2 tsp	
Baking soda	3½ tsp	
Sugar, granulated	1 lb 12 oz	Cream sugar and margarine on medium speed until light and fluffy, using flat beater.
Margarine	12 oz	
Eggs	9 (1 lb)	Combine and add gradually to creamed mixture. Mix until smooth.
Vanilla	4 tsp	
Lemon juice	1½ tsp	
Yogurt, plain	2 lb 3 oz	Add yogurt alternately with dry ingredients from first step, blending after each addition. Portion into prepared muffin pans using No. 16 dipper. Bake at 400°F for 18–22 minutes. Cool briefly before removing from pans.

Approximate nutritive values per portion

Calories	Carbohydrate	Protein	Fat	Cholesterol	Sodium	Fiber	Iron
222 kcal	35 g	5 g	7 g	38 mg	273 mg	1 g	1 mg

Variation

- **Glazed Poppy Seed–Yogurt Muffins.** Combine ¾ cup lemon juice and 2 Tbsp granulated sugar. Brush on baked muffins.

FRESH CRANBERRY SCONES

Yield: 50 portions   *Portion:* 1 scone
Oven: 400°F   *Bake:* 10–12 minutes

Ingredient	Amount	Procedure
Flour, all-purpose	3 lb 3 oz	Combine dry ingredients in mixer bowl.
Baking powder	3 oz	
Salt	1 Tbsp	
Butter very cold	1 lb 3 oz	Cut cold butter into small cubes. Add to dry ingredients. Cut butter into dry ingredients until mixture resembles coarse crumbs. Set aside.
Eggs	1 lb 6 oz	Mix eggs, honey, and cream until well blended.
Honey	10 oz	
Whipping cream	3 cups	
Fresh cranberries, coarsely chopped	12 oz	Add cranberries to egg-cream mixture. Add egg-cream mixture to dry ingredients. Mix on low speed only until dry ingredients are moistened. Do not overmix. Dough should be as soft as can be handled. Scale dough into 1-lb rounds onto floured table. Pat or roll dough into a circle ½ inch thick. Lightly dust tops with flour. Cut each circle using a floured knife into 6 wedges. Place wedges 4 × 6 onto greased or silicone-paper-lined 18 × 13 × 1-inch baking pan. Bake at 400°F for 10–12 minutes or until golden brown.
Orange marmalade or apricot jam	1 lb	Melt marmalade. Brush lightly over warm scones after removing from the oven. Serve scones warm with butter. Melt marmalade or jam.

Approximate nutritive values per portion

Calories	Carbohydrate	Protein	Fat	Cholesterol	Sodium	Fiber	Iron
290 kcal	34 g	5 g	15 g	88 mg	425 mg	1.1 g	2 mg

Note

• 6 oz sliced almonds can be folded into the dough along with the cranberries.

FRENCH BREAKFAST PUFFS

Yield: 50 puffs   *Portion:* 2¼ oz
Oven: 350°F   *Bake:* 20–25 minutes

Ingredient	Amount	Procedure
Margarine Sugar, granulated	1 lb 2 oz 1 lb 10 oz	Cream margarine and sugar on medium speed until light and fluffy, using flat beater.
Eggs	6 (10 oz)	Add eggs to creamed mixture. Blend on low speed, then beat on medium speed for 3–5 minutes.
Flour, all-purpose Baking powder Salt Nutmeg, ground Nonfat dry milk	2 lb 8 oz 2½ Tbsp 1 Tbsp 1½ tsp 3 oz	Combine dry ingredients.
Water	3⅓ cups	Add dry ingredients and water alternately, on low speed, to creamed mixture.
		Portion batter into greased muffin pans with No. 16 dipper. Bake at 350°F for 20–25 minutes.
Sugar, granulated Cinnamon, ground	1 lb 10 oz 2 Tbsp	Mix sugar and cinnamon.
Margarine, melted	1 lb 4 oz	When muffins are baked, remove from pans. Roll in melted margarine, then in sugar-cinnamon mixture.

Approximate nutritive values per portion

Calories	Carbohydrate	Protein	Fat	Cholesterol	Sodium	Fiber	Iron
368 kcal	48 g	4 g	18 g	24 mg	393 mg	1 g	1 mg

Notes

- 3½ cups fluid milk may be used in place of the nonfat dry milk and water.
- For small, tea-sized muffins, dip batter with No. 40 dipper into small (1½-inch) muffin pans.

Variations

- **Apple-Nut Muffins.** Add 1 lb chopped apples and 8 oz chopped nuts.
- **Plain Cake Muffins.** Delete nutmeg. Do not roll in sugar and cinnamon.

BISHOP'S BREAD

Yield: 64 portions or 2 pans, 12 × 18 × 2 inches   *Portion:* 3 × 2¼ inches
Oven: 365°F   *Bake:* 35–45 minutes

Ingredient	Amount	Procedure
Shortening Sugar, brown	1 lb 3 lb 2 oz	Cream shortening and sugar on medium speed for 5 minutes, using flat beater.
Flour, all-purpose Salt Cinnamon, ground	2 lb 14 oz 2 tsp 1 Tbsp	Combine flour, salt, and cinnamon. Add to creamed mixture and mix until well blended. Remove 1 lb 12 oz of the mixture to sprinkle on top later.
Flour, all-purpose Baking powder Baking soda	1 lb 2 oz 5 tsp 1½ tsp	Combine flour, baking powder, and soda.
Eggs, beaten Buttermilk	5 (9 oz) 1½ qt	Combine eggs and buttermilk. Add alternately with dry ingredients to creamed mixture. Scrape sides of bowl. Mix on low speed for about 30 seconds. (Batter will not be smooth.)
		Scale batter into two greased 12 × 18 × 2-inch baking pans, 5 lb per pan. Sprinkle 14 oz reserved topping over batter in each pan. Bake at 365°F for 35–45 minutes. Cut 4 × 8.

Approximate nutritive values per portion

Calories	Carbohydrate	Protein	Fat	Cholesterol	Sodium	Fiber	Iron
265 kcal	44 g	4 g	8 g	18 mg	157 mg	1 g	2 mg

Notes

- May be baked in one 18 × 26 × 2-inch pan. Cut 6 × 10 for 60 portions, 3 × 2½ inches.
- 4 oz dry buttermilk and 1 qt water may be substituted for fluid buttermilk.

BLUEBERRY COFFEE CAKE

Yield: 64 portions or 2 pans, 12 × 18 × 2 inches   *Portion:* 3 × 2¼ inches
Oven: 350°F   *Bake:* 45 minutes

Ingredient	Amount	Procedure
Sugar, brown	12 oz	Combine sugars, flour, cinnamon, and margarine.
Sugar, granulated	4 oz	Mix on low speed to a coarse crumb consistency, about 5 minutes, using flat beater.
Flour, all-purpose	4 oz	
Cinnamon, ground	2 tsp	Set aside for final step.
Margarine, soft	4 oz	
Shortening	14 oz	Cream shortening and sugar on medium speed for about 10 minutes.
Sugar, granulated	2 lb 10 oz	
Eggs	7 (12 oz)	Add eggs to creamed mixture and continue mixing, 3–5 minutes.
Flour, all-purpose	3 lb 6 oz	Combine flour, baking powder, and salt.
Baking powder	2 oz	
Salt	1 Tbsp	
Milk	3½ cups	Add dry ingredients and milk alternately to creamed mixture. Mix on low speed for 3 minutes. Scrape sides of bowl. Mix on medium speed for 10 seconds.
Blueberries, frozen or canned, well-drained and rinsed	2 lb	Carefully fold blueberries into batter. (Berries may be sprinkled on top of batter.)
		Scale batter into two greased 12 × 18 × 2-inch baking pans, 4 lb 12 oz per pan. Crumble topping mixture evenly over top of batter, 10 oz per pan. Bake at 350°F for 45 minutes. Cut 4 × 8.

Approximate nutritive values per portion

Calories	Carbohydrate	Protein	Fat	Cholesterol	Sodium	Fiber	Iron
220 kcal	31 g	4 g	9 g	24 mg	222 mg	1 g	1 mg

Notes

- May be baked in one 18 × 26 × 2-inch pan. Cut 6 × 10 for 60 portions, 3 × 2½ inches.
- 3 oz nonfat dry milk and 3½ cups water may be substituted for fluid milk. Add dry milk to other dry ingredients. Increase shortening to 15 oz.
- After cake is baked, thin Powdered Sugar Glaze (p. 316) may be drizzled in a fine stream over the top to form an irregular design.
- Recipe can be used for blueberry muffins. Sprinkle blueberries on top.

DUTCH APPLE COFFEE CAKE

Yield: 64 portions or 2 pans, 12 × 20 × 2 inches   *Portion:* 3 × 2½ inches
Oven: 365°F   *Bake:* 50–60 minutes

Ingredient	Amount	Procedure
Sugar, granulated	2 lb 8 oz	Cream sugar, shortening, and eggs on medium speed for 10 minutes, using flat beater.
Shortening	12 oz	
Eggs	8 (14 oz)	
Flour, all-purpose	2 lb 8 oz	Combine dry ingredients and mix until well blended.
Baking powder	2 oz	
Salt	2 tsp	
Milk	1 qt	Add milk and dry ingredients alternately to creamed mixture. Mix on low speed for 3 minutes. Scrape sides of bowl. Mix on medium speed for 10 seconds.
Apples, frozen or canned	2 lb 8 oz	Drain apples and chop. Combine with margarine, sugar, and cinnamon.
Margarine, melted	2 oz	
Sugar, granulated	1 lb 2 oz	
Cinnamon, ground	2 Tbsp	
		Scale batter into two greased 12 × 20 × 2-inch baking pans, 4 lb 6 oz per pan. Spread 1 lb 14 oz apple mixture over batter in each pan. Bake at 365°F for 50–60 minutes. Cut 4 × 8.

Approximate nutritive values per portion

Calories	Carbohydrate	Protein	Fat	Cholesterol	Sodium	Fiber	Iron
246 kcal	43 g	3 g	7 g	28 mg	180 mg	1 g	1 mg

Notes

- Cake batter may be mixed and panned the day before using. Refrigerate overnight, then add topping and bake.
- 4 oz nonfat dry milk and 1 qt water may be substituted for fluid milk.

COFFEE CAKE

Yield: 64 portions or 2 pans, 12 × 18 × 2 inches   *Portion:* 3 × 2¼ inches
Oven: 350°F   *Bake:* 25 minutes

Ingredient	Amount	Procedure
Margarine	10 oz	Place margarine, sugar, flour, cinnamon, and salt in mixer bowl.
Sugar, granulated	1 lb 4 oz	Mix on low speed until crumbly, using flat beater. Set aside, to be used later as
Flour, all-purpose	3 oz	topping.
Cinnamon, ground	1 oz	
Salt	1½ tsp	
Flour, all-purpose	3 lb 6 oz	Combine dry ingredients in mixer bowl.
Baking powder	2 oz	
Sugar, granulated	2 lb	
Salt	1⅔ Tbsp	
Eggs, beaten	6 (10 oz)	Combine eggs and milk.
Milk	1¼ qt	Add to dry ingredients.
		Mix on low speed until dry ingredients are just moistened.
Shortening, melted and cooled	1 lb 10 oz	Add shortening and mix on low speed for 1 minute.
		Scale dough into two greased 12 × 18 × 2-inch baking pans, 4 lb 2 oz per pan.
		Sprinkle with reserved topping mixture, 1 lb per pan.
		Bake at 350°F for 25 minutes or until done.
		Cut 4 × 8.

Approximate nutritive values per portion

Calories	Carbohydrate	Protein	Fat	Cholesterol	Sodium	Fiber	Iron
335 kcal	44 g	4 g	16 g	21 mg	363 mg	1 g	1 mg

Notes

- 5 oz nonfat dry milk and 1¼ qt water may be substituted for the fluid milk. Combine dry milk with other dry ingredients. Increase shortening to 1 lb 12 oz.
- May be baked in one 18 × 26 × 2-inch pan. Cut 6 × 10 for 60 portions 3 × 2½ inches.
- If used for breakfast, may be mixed and panned the day before. Refrigerate until morning, then bake. Allow 5–10 minutes extra time because batter will be cold.

WALNUT COFFEE CAKE

Yield: 4 cakes   *Portion:* 16 slices per cake
Oven: 350°F   *Bake:* 45–50 minutes

Ingredient	Amount	Procedure
Sugar, granulated	3 lb	Cream sugar and margarine on medium speed until light and fluffy, using
Margarine	1 lb	flat beater.
Eggs	16 (1 lb 12 oz)	Add eggs slowly to creamed mixture, beating well after each addition.
Vanilla	1 Tbsp	Add vanilla.
Flour, all-purpose	3 lb	Mix flour, baking powder, and salt together.
Baking powder	4 Tbsp	
Salt	2 tsp	
Milk	1 qt	Add milk alternately with dry ingredients to creamed mixture. Combine thoroughly after each addition.
Sugar, brown	2 lb	Combine brown sugar, margarine, flour, cinnamon, and walnuts for crumb mixture.
Margarine	4 oz	
Flour, all-purpose	2 oz	
Cinnamon, ground	1 Tbsp	
Walnuts, chopped	1 lb	
		Scale 1 lb 4 oz batter into each of four greased 10-inch tube pans.
		Sprinkle 6 oz crumb mixture over batter.
		Spread with 1 lb 4 oz batter.
		Top with 6 oz crumb mixture.
		Bake at 350°F for 45–50 minutes.
		Cool slightly. Remove from pans.
		Ice with Powdered Sugar Glaze (p. 316) if desired.
		Slice 16 servings per cake.

Approximate nutritive values per portion

Calories	Carbohydrate	Protein	Fat	Cholesterol	Sodium	Fiber	Iron
350 kcal	54 g	6 g	13 g	54 mg	193 mg	1 g	2 mg

Note

- 4 oz nonfat dry milk and 1 qt water may be substituted for the fluid milk.

CORN BREAD

Yield: 64 portions or 2 pans, 12 × 18 × 2 inches   *Portion:* 3 × 2¼ inches
Oven: 350°F   *Bake:* 35 minutes

Ingredient	Amount	Procedure
Yellow, cornmeal	2 lb	Combine dry ingredients in mixer bowl.
Flour, all-purpose	2 lb 2 oz	Blend on low speed for 1 minute, using flat beater.
Baking powder	3¾ oz	
Salt	2½ Tsp	
Sugar, granulated	10 oz	
Eggs	8 oz	Beat eggs. Combine with milk and oil.
Milk	1¾ qt	Add egg-milk mixture to dry ingredient all at once. Mix on low speed only until dry ingredients are moistened. Do not overmix; mixture will appear lumpy.
Vegetable oil	2 cups	
		Scale batter into two greased 12 × 18 × 2-inch baking pans, 5 lb per pan. Bake at 350°F for 35 minutes. Cut 4 × 8.

Approximate nutritive values per portion

Calories	Carbohydrate	Protein	Fat	Cholesterol	Sodium	Fiber	Iron
206 kcal	29 g	4 g	8 g	16 mg	288 mg	1.4 g	1.3 mg

Variations

- **Corn Bread Rounds.** Follow recipe for Corn Bread. Scale 2 lb of batter into each of five greased 9-inch round cake pans. Bake for 15–20 minutes. Cut each pan into 10 pie-shaped pieces. Serve warm.
- **Jalapeno Cheese Cornmeal Muffins.** Mix together 2 lb 4 oz flour, 4 tsp salt, 4 oz baking powder, 8 oz granulated sugar, and 1 lb cornmeal. Blend 12 oz eggs, 6¾ cups milk, and 1 lb 8 oz melted shortening. Add dry ingredients to flour mixture, mixing only until blended. Stir in 7 oz chopped green chiles (canned), 3 oz chopped jalapeños (canned), and 8 oz shredded cheddar cheese. Portion batter into prepared muffin cups with No. 12 dipper. Sprinkle very lightly with ancho chile powder. Bake at 350°F for 20–25 minutes, until golden brown.

SCALLION CORN CAKES

Yield: 50 cakes   *Portion:* 1 cake
Grill: 300°F

Ingredient	Amount	Procedure
Flour, all-purpose	1 lb	Combine dry ingredients in a mixer bowl and mix until blended.
Sugar, granulated	3 oz	
Nonfat dry milk	4 oz	
Cornmeal	1 lb	
Baking powder	2 oz	
Salt	2½ Tbsp	Combine liquids and onions. Add all at once to flour mixture.
Eggs	4 oz	Mix on low speed just until blended. Mixture may be lumpy.
Water	3½ cups	Drop with a No. 24 dipper onto a hot, oiled griddle. Cook for 2–3 minutes,
Oil	8 oz	until lightly browned. Turn and brown second side.
Green onions, finely chopped	3 oz	

Approximate nutritive values per cake

Calories	Carbohydrate	Protein	Fat	Cholesterol	Sodium	Fiber	Iron
131 kcal	18 g	3 g	5 g	10 mg	497 mg	1 g	1 mg

SPOON BREAD

Yield: 50 portions or 2 pans, 12 × 20 × 2 inches   *Portion:* 4 oz
Oven: 350°F   *Bake:* 45–60 minutes

Ingredient	Amount	Procedure
Milk	5¾ qt	Scald milk by heating to point just below boiling.
Cornmeal, yellow	1 lb 12 oz	Add cornmeal and salt to milk, stirring briskly with a wire whip.
Salt	1 oz (1½ Tbsp)	Cook 10 minutes, or until thick.
Eggs, beaten	25 (2 lb 12 oz)	Add eggs slowly to cornmeal mixture, while stirring.
Margarine, melted	6 oz	Add margarine and baking powder to cornmeal mixture. Stir to blend.
Baking powder	2 oz	
		Pour batter into two greased 12 × 20 × 2-inch baking pans, 8 lb per pan.
		Place in pans of hot water.
		Bake at 350°F for 45–60 minutes or until set.

Approximate nutritive values per portion

Calories	Carbohydrate	Protein	Fat	Cholesterol	Sodium	Fiber	Iron
190 kcal	18 g	8 g	10 g	122 mg	430 mg	2 g	1 mg

Notes

- Serve with crisp bacon, Creamed Chicken (p. 490), or Creamed Ham (p. 470).
- Potentially hazardous food. *Food Safety Standards:* Hold food for service at an internal temperature of 135°F or above. Do not mix old product with new. Cool leftover product quickly following time standards and cooling procedures on p. 167. Reheat leftover product quickly (within 2 hours) to 165°F or above. Reheat product only once; discard if not used.

BOSTON BROWN BREAD

Yield: 64 portions or 8 round loaves, 3¼ × 4½ inches   *Portion:* ½-inch slice
Steam pressure: 5 lb   *Steam:* 1¼–1½ hours

Ingredient	Amount	Procedure
Cornmeal, yellow	1 lb	Combine dry ingredients in mixer bowl.
Flour, whole-wheat	12 oz	Blend on low speed for 10 seconds, using flat beater.
Flour, all-purpose	12 oz	
Salt	1 oz (1½ Tbsp)	
Baking soda	1½ Tbsp	
Buttermilk	1½ qt	Blend buttermilk and molasses.
Molasses	2¼ cups	Add all at once to dry ingredients.
		Mix on low speed only until ingredients are blended.
		Fill eight greased 3¼ × 4½-inch cans ¾ full.
		Cover tightly with aluminum foil.
		Steam for 1¼–1½ hours.
		Cut 8 slices per loaf.

Approximate nutritive values per portion

Calories	Carbohydrate	Protein	Fat	Cholesterol	Sodium	Fiber	Iron
99 kcal	21 g	2 g	1 g	1 mg	275 mg	1 g	3 mg

Notes

- 12 oz raisins may be added.
- May be baked as loaves. Add 3 Tbsp melted fat. Scale into three 5 × 9-inch loaf pans, 2 lb 8 oz per pan. Bake at 375°F for 1 hour.

NUT BREAD

Yield: 80 portions or 5 loaves, 5 × 9 inches   *Portion:* ½-inch slice
Oven: 350°F   *Bake:* 50 minutes

Ingredient	Amount	Procedure
Flour, all-purpose	3 lb	Combine dry ingredients and nuts in mixer bowl.
Baking powder	1 oz	Mix on low speed until blended, using flat beater.
Salt	1 Tbsp	
Sugar, granulated	1 lb 8 oz	
Pecans or walnuts, chopped	1 lb	
Eggs, beaten	6 (10 oz)	Combine eggs, milk, and oil.
Milk	1½ qt	Add to dry ingredients.
Oil or melted shortening	4 oz	Mix on low speed only until blended.
		Scale batter into five greased 5 × 9 × 2¾-inch loaf pans, approximately 1 lb 14 oz per pan.
		Bake at 350°F for about 50 minutes. Cut 16 slices per loaf.

Approximate nutritive values per portion

Calories	Carbohydrate	Protein	Fat	Cholesterol	Sodium	Fiber	Iron
159 kcal	23 g	4 g	6 g	18 mg	129 mg	1 g	1 mg

Note

- 5 oz nonfat dry milk and 1½ qt water may be substituted for fluid milk. Combine dry milk with other dry ingredients. Increase shortening to 6 oz.

DATE NUT BREAD

Yield: 64 portions or 4 loaves, 5 × 9 inches   *Portion:* ½-inch slice
Oven: 350°F   *Bake:* 50 minutes

Ingredient	Amount	Procedure
Water, boiling Baking soda Dates, chopped	3¼ cups 1½ Tbsp 1 lb 8 oz	Add water and soda to dates. Let stand 20 minutes.
Shortening Sugar, granulated	3 oz 1 lb 12 oz	Cream shortening and sugar on medium speed for 5 minutes, using flat beater.
Eggs Vanilla	4 (7 oz) 1½ Tbsp	Add eggs and vanilla to creamed mixture. Mix on medium speed for 2 minutes.
Flour, all-purpose Salt Pecans or walnuts, chopped	2 lb 1½ tsp 8 oz	Combine flour, salt, and nuts. Add alternately with dates to creamed mixture. Scale batter into four greased 5 × 9 × 2¾-inch loaf pans, approximately 2 lb per pan. Bake at 350°F for about 50 minutes. Cut 16 slices per loaf.

Approximate nutritive values per portion

Calories	Carbohydrate	Protein	Fat	Cholesterol	Sodium	Fiber	Iron
168 kcal	32 g	3 g	4 g	13 mg	144 mg	1 g	1 mg

BANANA NUT BREAD

Yield: 64 portions or 4 loaves, 5 × 9 inches   *Portion:* ½-inch slice
Oven: 350°F   *Bake:* 50 minutes

Ingredient	Amount	Procedure
Margarine	10 oz	Cream margarine and sugar on medium speed for 5 minutes, using flat beater.
Sugar, granulated	1 lb 10 oz	
Eggs	5 (9 oz)	Add eggs to creamed mixture. Beat 2 minutes.
Bananas, mashed	1 lb 10 oz	Add bananas. Beat 1 minute.
Flour, all-purpose	2 lb	Combine dry ingredients and nuts.
Baking powder	4 Tbsp	
Salt	2 tsp	
Baking soda	½ tsp	
Pecans or walnuts, chopped	8 oz	
Milk	¾ cup	Add dry ingredients and milk to creamed mixture. Mix on low speed for 1 minute.

Scale batter into four greased 5 × 9 × 2¾-inch loaf pans, approximately 2 lb per pan. Bake at 350°F for 50 minutes. Cut 16 slices per loaf.

Approximate nutritive values per portion

Calories	Carbohydrate	Protein	Fat	Cholesterol	Sodium	Fiber	Iron
171 kcal	26 g	2 g	7 g	17 mg	175 mg	1 g	1 mg

CRANBERRY NUT BREAD

Yield: 80 portions or 5 loaves, 5 × 9 inches   *Portion:* ½-inch slice
Oven: 350°F   *Bake:* 50 minutes

Ingredient	Amount	Procedure
Fresh cranberries	1 lb 4 oz	Wash and sort cranberries.
Orange peel	7 oz	Coarsely grind cranberries and orange peel.
Flour, all-purpose	2 lb 8 oz	Combine dry ingredients in mixer bowl.
Sugar, granulated	2 lb 4 oz	Blend on low speed for 10 seconds or until mixed, using flat beater.
Baking powder	1 oz	
Salt	2 tsp	
Baking soda	2 tsp	
Eggs, beaten	5 (9 oz)	Combine and add to dry ingredients.
Orange juice	1½ cups	Mix on low speed, only until dry ingredients are moistened.
Water	3¾ cups	
Vegetable oil	½ cup	
Pecans or walnuts, chopped	1 lb	Add nuts and cranberry mixture to batter. Mix on low speed until blended. Batter may be lumpy.
		Scale batter into five greased 5 × 9 × 2¾-inch loaf pans, approximately 2 lb per pan. Bake at 350°F for about 50 minutes. Cut 16 slices per loaf.

Approximate nutritive values per portion

Calories	Carbohydrate	Protein	Fat	Cholesterol	Sodium	Fiber	Iron
164 kcal	27 g	2 g	6 g	14 mg	125 mg	1 g	1 mg

PUMPKIN BREAD

Yield: 80 portions or 5 loaves, 5 × 9 inches   *Portion:* ½-inch slice
Oven: 350°F   *Bake:* 50 minutes

Ingredient	Amount	Procedure
Sugar, granulated	2 lb 12 oz	Combine sugar, oil, pumpkin, and eggs in mixer bowl.
Vegetable oil	2 cups	Cream on medium speed for 10 minutes, using flat beater.
Pumpkin, canned	2 lb 6 oz	Scrape sides of bowl and beater.
Eggs	9 (15 oz)	
Flour, all-purpose	2 lb 2 oz	Combine dry ingredients.
Baking soda	4 tsp	
Baking powder	2 tsp	
Salt	1 Tbsp	
Cinnamon, ground	1 Tbsp	
Nutmeg, ground	1 tsp	
Water	1¼ cups	Add dry ingredients and water alternately to creamed mixture. Mix for 3 minutes on low speed. Scrape sides of bowl.
		Scale batter into five greased 5 × 9 × 2¾-inch loaf pans, approximately 1 lb 15 oz per pan. Bake at 350°F for 50 minutes or until done. Cool for 30 minutes before removing from pans. Cut 16 slices per loaf.

Approximate nutritive values per portion

Calories	Carbohydrate	Protein	Fat	Cholesterol	Sodium	Fiber	Iron
165 kcal	26 g	2 g	6 g	23 mg	158 mg	1 g	1 mg

Note

- 8 oz raisins or chopped nuts may be added.

PANCAKES

Yield: 7 qt batter or 100 cakes (50 portions)   *Portion:* two 4-inch cakes
Griddle: 350°F

Ingredient	Amount	Procedure
Flour, all-purpose	4 lb 8 oz	Place dry ingredients in mixer bowl.
Baking powder	4 oz	Mix on low speed until well blended, using flat beater.
Salt	2 Tbsp	
Sugar, granulated	12 oz	
Eggs	12 (1 lb 5 oz)	In another bowl, beat eggs until light.
Milk	3½ qt	Add milk and melted shortening to eggs.
Shortening, melted and cooled, or vegetable oil	12 oz	Add to dry ingredients. Mix on low speed for 30 seconds. If necessary, thin with milk. Refrigerate batter, removing small amounts from refrigerator as needed. Use No. 16 dipper to place batter on greased preheated griddle. Cook until surface of cake is full of bubbles and golden brown. Turn pancake and finish cooking.

Approximate nutritive values per portion

Calories	Carbohydrate	Protein	Fat	Cholesterol	Sodium	Fiber	Iron
297 kcal	42 g	8 g	11 g	60 mg	532 mg	1 g	2 mg

Notes

- Potentially hazardous food. *Food Safety Standards:* Hold food for service at an internal temperature of 41°F or below. Do not mix old product with new. Keep leftover product chilled at 41°F or below. See p. 167 for cooling procedures.
- 14 oz nonfat dry milk and 3½ qt water may be substituted for the fluid milk. Add dry milk to other dry ingredients. Increase shortening to 1 lb.

Variations

- **Apple Pancakes.** Add 1 lb chopped cooked apples and 1 tsp cinnamon or nutmeg.
- **Blueberry Pancakes.** Fold 1 lb individually quick-frozen (IQF) blueberries or well-drained and rinsed canned blueberries carefully into batter after cakes are mixed. Handle carefully to avoid mashing berries. If a large batch is being prepared, add berries to a small portion of the batter at one time. Serve with Blueberry Syrup, p. 719.
- **Buttermilk Pancakes.** Substitute buttermilk for milk. Add 1 Tbsp baking soda to dry ingredients; 14 oz dry buttermilk and 3½ qt water may be substituted for fluid buttermilk. Add dry buttermilk and soda to other dry ingredients. Increase shortening to 1 lb.
- **Pecan Pancakes.** Add 1 lb chopped pecans.
- **Silver Dollar Pancakes.** Portion 1–2 Tbsp batter onto hot griddle and cook as directed previously. Garnish with powdered sugar sprinkled on top of pancakes and fresh blueberries or raspberries.

WHOLE-WHEAT PANCAKES

Yield: 2½ gal batter or 100 cakes (50 portions)   *Portion:* 2 cakes
Griddle: 350°F

Ingredient	Amount	Procedure
Flour, whole-wheat	3 lb	Combine dry ingredients in mixer bowl. Mix, using flat beater, until blended.
Flour, all-purpose	2 lb 12 oz	
Sugar, granulated	8 oz	
Salt	2 oz (3 Tbsp)	
Baking powder	4 oz	
Baking soda	5½ tsp	
Nonfat dry milk	1 lb 2 oz	
Vegetable oil	3 cups	Add to dry ingredients, mixing just until large lumps disappear.
Water	1 gal + 2 cups	Refrigerate batter, removing small amounts from refrigerator as needed.
Eggs	2 lb (18 eggs)	Portion batter with No. 12 dipper onto greased preheated griddle.
		Bake until edges start to dry and bubbles appear on top surface.
		Flip and bake other side.

Approximate nutritive values per portion

Calories	Carbohydrate	Protein	Fat	Cholesterol	Sodium	Fiber	Iron
383 kcal	49 g	12 g	16 g	79 mg	832 mg	4 g	2 mg

Notes

- Potentially hazardous food. *Food Safety Standards:* Hold food for service at an internal temperature of 41°F or below. Do not mix old product with new. Keep leftover product chilled at 41°F or below. See p. 167 for cooling procedures.
- 1¼ gal fluid milk may be substituted for nonfat dry milk and water. Add fluid milk along with vegetable oil and eggs.

PANCAKE MIX

Yield: 12 lb mix

Ingredient	Amount	Procedure
Flour, all-purpose	9 lb	Combine ingredients in mixer bowl.
Baking powder	8 oz	Blend well, using flat beater or whip.
Salt	¼ cup	Store in covered container.
Sugar, granulated	1 lb 8 oz	
Nonfat dry milk	1 lb 8 oz	

Variation

- **Buttermilk Pancake Mix.** Substitute 1 lb 8 oz dry buttermilk for nonfat dry milk and add 2 Tbsp baking soda.

PANCAKES FROM MIX

Ingredient	30 cakes	50 cakes	100 cakes	200 cakes
Pancake mix	2 lb	3 lb	6 lb	12 lb
Eggs, beaten	4 (7 oz)	6 (10 oz)	12 (1 lb 5 oz)	24 (2 lb 10 oz)
Water	1 qt	1½ qt	3 qt	1½ gal
Oil or melted shortening	4 oz	6 oz	12 oz	1 lb 8 oz

To use mix:

1. Weigh appropriate amount of mix (p. 254) as given in the table.

2. Add beaten eggs, water, and cooled melted fat.

3. Stir only until mix is dampened.

4. Place on hot griddle with No. 16 dipper.

5. Cook until cake is full of bubbles. Turn and finish cooking.

WAFFLES

Yield: 6 qt batter or 50–60 waffles   *Portion:* 1 waffle

Ingredient	Amount	Procedure
Flour, all-purpose	3 lb	Combine dry ingredients in mixer bowl.
Baking powder	3 oz	Blend on low speed for 10 seconds, using flat beater.
Salt	2 Tbsp	
Sugar, granulated	4 oz	
Egg yolks	18 (11 oz)	Combine egg yolks, milk, and oil.
Milk	2¼ qt	Add to dry ingredients.
Oil or melted shortening	1 lb (2 cups)	Mix on low speed just enough to moisten dry ingredients.
Egg whites	18 (1 lb 5 oz)	Beat egg whites until stiff but not dry. Fold into batter.
		Refrigerate batter, removing from refrigerator small amounts as needed. Use No. 10 dipper to place batter on preheated waffle iron. Bake for about 4 minutes.

Approximate nutritive values per portion

Calories	Carbohydrate	Protein	Fat	Cholesterol	Sodium	Fiber	Iron
223 kcal	23 g	6 g	12 g	78 mg	428 mg	1 g	1 mg

Notes

- Potentially hazardous food. *Food Safety Standards:* Hold food for service at an internal tempoerature of 41°F or below. Do not mix old product with new. Keep leftover product chilled at 41°F or below. See p. 167 for cooling procedures.
- 9 oz nonfat dry milk and 2¼ qt water may be substituted for fluid milk. Mix dry milk with dry ingredients. Increase shortening to 1 lb 2 oz.

Variation

- **Pecan Waffles.** Add 6 oz chopped pecans.

CREPES

Yield: 50 portions or 5 qt batter   *Portion:* 2 crepes

Ingredient	Amount	Procedure
Flour, all-purpose Salt	2 lb 8 oz 1 oz (1½ Tbsp)	Combine flour and salt in mixer bowl.
Eggs	24 (2 lb 10 oz)	Beat eggs until fluffy.
Milk Margarine, melted	2¾ qt 6 oz	Add milk and margarine to eggs. Add to flour and mix until smooth. Batter will be thinner than pancake batter.
		Refrigerate batter, removing small amounts from refrigerator as needed. Portion batter with No. 20 dipper onto lightly greased hot griddle. Brown lightly on both sides. Crepes will roll best if they are not overbrowned. Stack, layered with waxed paper, until ready to use.

Approximate nutritive values per portion

Calories	Carbohydrate	Protein	Fat	Cholesterol	Sodium	Fiber	Iron
176 kcal	20 g	7 g	7 g	109 mg	281 mg	1 g	1 mg

Notes

- Potentially hazardous food. *Food Safety Standards:* Hold food for service at an internal tempoerature of 41°F or below. Do not mix old product with new. Keep leftover product chilled at 41°F or below. See p. 167 for cooling procedures.
- Crepes may be folded or rolled around desired filling. (See recipe for Chicken Crepes, p. 489.)
- If used for dessert crepes, add 3 Tbsp sugar to dry ingredients. Fill with fruit filling.

ZUCCHINI CORN CAKES

Yield: 50 portions   *Portion:* 3 pancakes

Ingredient	Amount	Procedure
Water	1 gal	Combine water and dry buttermilk in mixer bowl.
Dry buttermilk	1 lb 3 oz	
Eggs	2 lb 3 oz	Add eggs. Mix until combined, approximately 3 minutes.
Flour, all-purpose	6 lb	Combine dry ingredients in baker's bowl.
Salt	2½ Tbsp	Add dry ingredients to buttermilk mixture. Mix only until barely mixed.
Baking soda	1 tsp	(Overmixing will cause cakes to be tough.)
Baking powder	1 oz (2¼ Tbsp)	
Sugar, granulated	6 oz	
Black pepper	1½ Tbsp	
Vegetable oil	2 lb 3 oz	Add oil to flour mixture and mix lightly.
Zucchini squash, shredded	6 lb 3 oz EP	Fold zucchini squash and corn into batter just before cooking cakes.
Corn, whole-kernel, frozen, defrosted	3 lb 10 oz EP	Preheat grill to 325–350°F. Lightly grease grill.
		Using a No. 12 dipper, portion cakes onto hot grill.
		Flip cakes when browned and small bubbles appear on the top side. Brown second side of cakes.
		Remove from grill and shingle stack into 2-inch counter pans. Cover with waxed paper and serve soon after cooking.
		Serve with salsa and sour cream or other toppings.

Approximate nutritive values per portion

Calories	Carbohydrate	Protein	Fat	Cholesterol	Sodium	Fiber	Iron
450 kcal	51 g	12 g	23 g	79 mg	514 mg	1.5 g	3 mg

Note

- Potentially hazardous food. *Food Safety Standards:* Hold food for service at an internal temperature of 135°F or above. Do not mix old product with new. Cool leftover product quickly following time standards and cooling procedures on p. 167. Reheat leftover product quickly (within 2 hours) to 165°F or above. Reheat product only once; discard if not used.

CAKE DOUGHNUTS

Yield: 8 dozen doughnuts   *Portion:* 1 doughnut
Deep-fat fryer: 375°F   *Fry:* 3–4 minutes

Ingredient	Amount	Procedure
Eggs	6 (10 oz)	Beat eggs until light.
Sugar, granulated	1 lb 4 oz	Add sugar and oil to eggs.
Oil or melted shortening	3 oz	Mix on medium speed about 10 minutes.
Flour, all-purpose	3 lb 4 oz	Combine dry ingredients.
Baking powder	3 oz	
Salt	2½ tsp	
Nutmeg, ground	2 tsp	
Ginger, ground	¼ tsp	
Orange peel, grated	1 Tbsp	
Milk	1 qt	Add dry ingredients and milk alternately to egg mixture. Mix to form a soft dough. Add more flour if dough is too soft to handle. Chill.
		Roll dough ⅜ inch thick on floured board or table. Cut with floured 2½-inch doughnut cutter. Fry in deep fat for 3–4 minutes.
Sugar, granulated	8 oz	Sprinkle with sugar when partially cool.

Approximate nutritive values per portion (plus frying fat)

Calories	Carbohydrate	Protein	Fat	Cholesterol	Sodium	Fiber	Iron
176 kcal	21 g	2 g	2 g	14 mg	153 mg	0.4 g	1 mg

Note

- 4 oz nonfat dry milk and 1 qt water may be substituted for fluid milk. Mix dry milk with the dry ingredients. Increase shortening to 4 oz.

Variation

- **Chocolate doughnuts.** Substitute 2 oz cocoa for 2 oz flour.

DUMPLINGS

Yield: 50 portions   *Portion:* 2 dumplings
Steam pressure: 5 lb   *Steam:* 12–15 minutes

Ingredient	Amount	Procedure
Flour, all-purpose	2 lb 8 oz	Combine dry ingredients in mixer bowl.
Baking powder	3 oz (6 Tbsp)	Mix on low speed until blended, using flat beater.
Salt	2 Tbsp	
Eggs, beaten	6 (10 oz)	Combine eggs and milk.
Milk	5½ cups	Add to dry ingredients. Mix on low speed, only until blended.
		Portion batter with No. 24 dipper onto trays. Do not cover trays. Steam for 12–15 minutes.

Approximate nutritive values per portion

Calories	Carbohydrate	Protein	Fat	Cholesterol	Sodium	Fiber	Iron
109 kcal	19 g	4 g	2 g	28 mg	381 mg	1 g	1 mg

Notes

- 5 oz nonfat dry milk and 5½ cups water may be substituted for the fluid milk. Add dry milk to other dry ingredients.
- Serve with meat stew or stewed chicken. Mixture may be dropped onto hot meat mixture in counter pans and steamed.

Variation

- **Spaetzle (Egg Dumplings).** Use 1 lb 4 oz flour, 1 tsp baking powder, 1½ tsp salt, 6 eggs, and 3 cups milk. Mix as above. Drop small bits of dough or press through a colander or perforated pan into 3 gal simmering soup. Cook for approximately 5 minutes. Soup must be very hot to cook dumplings.

FRENCH TOAST

Yield: 50 slices   *Portion:* 1 slice

Ingredient	Amount	Procedure
Eggs	24 (2 lb 10 oz)	Beat eggs.
Milk Salt Sugar, granulated	1½ qt 1 Tbsp 4 oz	Add milk, salt, and sugar to eggs. Mix well. Refrigerate batter, removing small amounts from refrigerator as needed.
Bread slices, day-old	50	Dip bread into egg mixture. Do not let bread soak. (Care should be taken to avoid getting raw eggs on the cooked food.) Fry on a well-greased griddle or in deep fat at 360°F until golden brown. Serve sprinkled with powdered sugar.

Approximate nutritive values per portion (plus frying fat)

Calories	Carbohydrate	Protein	Fat	Cholesterol	Sodium	Fiber	Iron
124 kcal	15 g	6 g	4 g	105 mg	331 mg	3 g	1 mg

Note

- Potentially hazardous food. *Food Safety Standards:* Hold food for service at an internal temperature of 41°F or below. Do not mix old product with new. Keep leftover product chilled at 41°F or below. See p. 167 for cooling procedures.

Variations

- **Batter-Fried French Toast.** Use 1-inch-thick bread slices. Cut into triangles or leave whole. Dip in mixture made from 18 eggs (2 lb), 1¼ qt milk, ⅓ cup vegetable oil, 2 lb 8 oz all-purpose flour, 1 oz (1½ Tbsp) salt, and 1 oz (2⅓ Tbsp) baking powder. Fry in deep fat at 350–375°F until golden brown. Dredge in powdered sugar. Serve with warm maple syrup.
- **Cinnamon French Toast.** Add 1 tsp cinnamon to egg mixture.

FRITTERS

Yield: 50 portions   *Portion:* 2 fritters
Deep-fat fryer: 375°F   *Fry:* 4–6 minutes

Ingredient	Amount	Procedure
Flour, all-purpose	4 lb	Combine dry ingredients in mixer bowl.
Baking powder	4 oz	Mix on low speed for 10 seconds or until mixed, using flat beater.
Salt	1 Tbsp	
Sugar, granulated	2 oz	
Eggs, beaten	12 (1 lb 5 oz)	Combine eggs, milk, and oil.
Milk	2 qt	Add to dry ingredients. Mix only enough to moisten dry ingredients.
Oil or melted shortening	6 oz (¾ cup)	
		Portion batter with No. 30 dipper into hot deep fat. Fry at 375°F for 4–6 minutes. Serve with syrup.

Approximate nutritive values per portion (plus frying fat)

Calories	Carbohydrate	Protein	Fat	Cholesterol	Sodium	Fiber	Iron
211 kcal	31 g	7 g	6 g	56 mg	390 mg	1 g	2 mg

Notes

- Potentially hazardous food. *Food Safety Standards:* Hold food for service at an internal temperature of 41°F or below. Do not mix old product with new. Keep leftover product chilled at 41°F or below. See p. 167 for cooling procedures.
- 8 oz nonfat dry milk and 2 qt water may be substituted for fluid milk. Add dry milk to other dry ingredients.

Variations

- **Apple Fritters.** Add 3 lb tart raw apple, peeled and finely chopped, and 1 tsp cinnamon (optional).
- **Banana Fritters.** Add 3 lb bananas, mashed.
- **Corn Fritters.** Add 2 qt whole-kernel corn, drained.
- **Fruit Fritters.** Add 1 qt drained fruit: peach, pineapple, or other fruit.
- **Green Chile Fritters.** Add 2 lb 8 oz chopped green chiles, drained. Serve with nacho sauce (Nachos, p. 203). Make ¼ recipe.

CHEESE STRAWS

Yield: 6 dozen 4 × 1-inch straws
Oven: 350°F   *Bake:* 10–15 minutes

Ingredient	Amount	Procedure
Butter or margarine	6 oz	Cream butter on medium speed until soft.
Cheddar cheese, sharp, shredded	8 oz	Blend in cheese.
Flour, all-purpose	8 oz	Combine dry ingredients and add to cheese mixture on low speed.
Baking powder	2 tsp	
Salt	1 tsp	
Cayenne pepper	¼ tsp	
Eggs, beaten	3	Add eggs and water, combined.
Water	2 Tbsp	Mix on low speed to form a stiff dough. Chill.
		Roll ¼ inch thick and cut into strips 4 inches long and 1 inch wide. Place on ungreased baking sheet.
		Bake at 350°F for 10–15 minutes.

Approximate nutritive values per portion

Calories	Carbohydrate	Protein	Fat	Cholesterol	Sodium	Fiber	Iron
44 kcal	3 g	1 g	3 g	17 mg	71 mg	0 g	0.5 mg

Variation

• **Caraway Cheese Straws.** Add 2 tsp caraway seeds to flour before mixing.

Yeast Bread Recipes

WHITE BREAD

Yield: 16 1½-lb loaves
Oven: 400°F   *Bake:* 30–40 minutes

Ingredient	Amount	Procedure
Yeast, active dry	5 oz	Soften yeast in warm water.
Water, warm (110°F)	3 cups	Let stand 10 minutes.
Sugar, granulated	10 oz	Combine sugar, salt, dry milk, lukewarm water, and shortening.
Salt	5 oz	Add softened yeast.
Nonfat dry milk	14 oz	Mix on medium speed until blended, using dough arm.
Water, lukewarm	1 gal	
Shortening, melted	12 oz	
Flour, all-purpose	15 lb	Add flour. Mix on low speed for about 10 minutes or until dough is smooth and elastic and small blisters appear on the surface.

1. Let dough rise in a warm place (80°F) approximately 2 hours, or until double in bulk.
2. Punch down dough by pulling the dough up on all sides, folding it over the center, and pressing down, then turning over in the bowl. Shape into 16 loaves, 1 lb 8 oz each (Figure 10.1). Place in greased 5 × 9 × 2¾-inch loaf pans.
3. Let rise for approximately 1½ hours, or until double in bulk.
4. Bake at 400°F for 30–40 minutes or until loaves are golden brown and sound hollow when tapped.
5. Brush tops of loaves with melted margarine or butter.

Approximate nutritive values per loaf

Calories	Carbohydrate	Protein	Fat	Cholesterol	Sodium	Fiber	Iron
1918 kcal	359 g	56 g	26 g	4 mg	3586 mg	14 g	21 mg

Notes

- 1¼ gal fluid milk may be substituted for the water and dry milk. Scald milk and combine with sugar, salt, and shortening. Cool to lukewarm before adding to other ingredients.
- The dough temperature should be about 80°F when mixed.
- Mixing may be simplified by combining dry yeast with sugar, salt, dry milk, and 2 lb flour. Mix thoroughly. In mixer bowl, combine very warm water (120°F) and shortening. Blend on low speed. Add yeast-flour mixture while mixing on low speed. Add remaining flour gradually, mixing until a smooth, elastic dough is formed.
- Shortening may be increased to 1 lb and sugar to 12 oz if a richer dough is desired.
- A variety of shapes may be made from the dough.

Variations

- **Buffet Submarine Buns.** Scale dough into 1-lb portions. Shape into 18-inch-long loaves. (See Figure 10.1 for shaping instructions.) Use for Submarine Sandwiches (p. 662).
- **Cinnamon Bread.** After dough has been divided and scaled into loaves, roll each into a rectangular sheet. Brush with melted margarine or shortening; sprinkle generously with cinnamon and sugar. Roll as for jelly roll. Seal edge of dough and place in greased loaf pans, sealed edge down. Sprinkle top with cinnamon and sugar.
- **Raisin Bread.** Add 3 lb raisins to dough after mixing.
- **Sandwich Ring Bread.** Scale fermented dough into 11-oz balls and shape each ball into a 16-inch rope. Braid three ropes together and pinch ends to seal. Shape braided ropes into a 15-inch circle with a 5-inch center hole (work ends together to form a smooth ring). Proof ring in a warm place until double in bulk (30–40 minutes). Bake at 375°F until done (about 20 minutes).
- **Whole-Wheat Bread.** Substitute whole-wheat flour for half of the all-purpose flour.

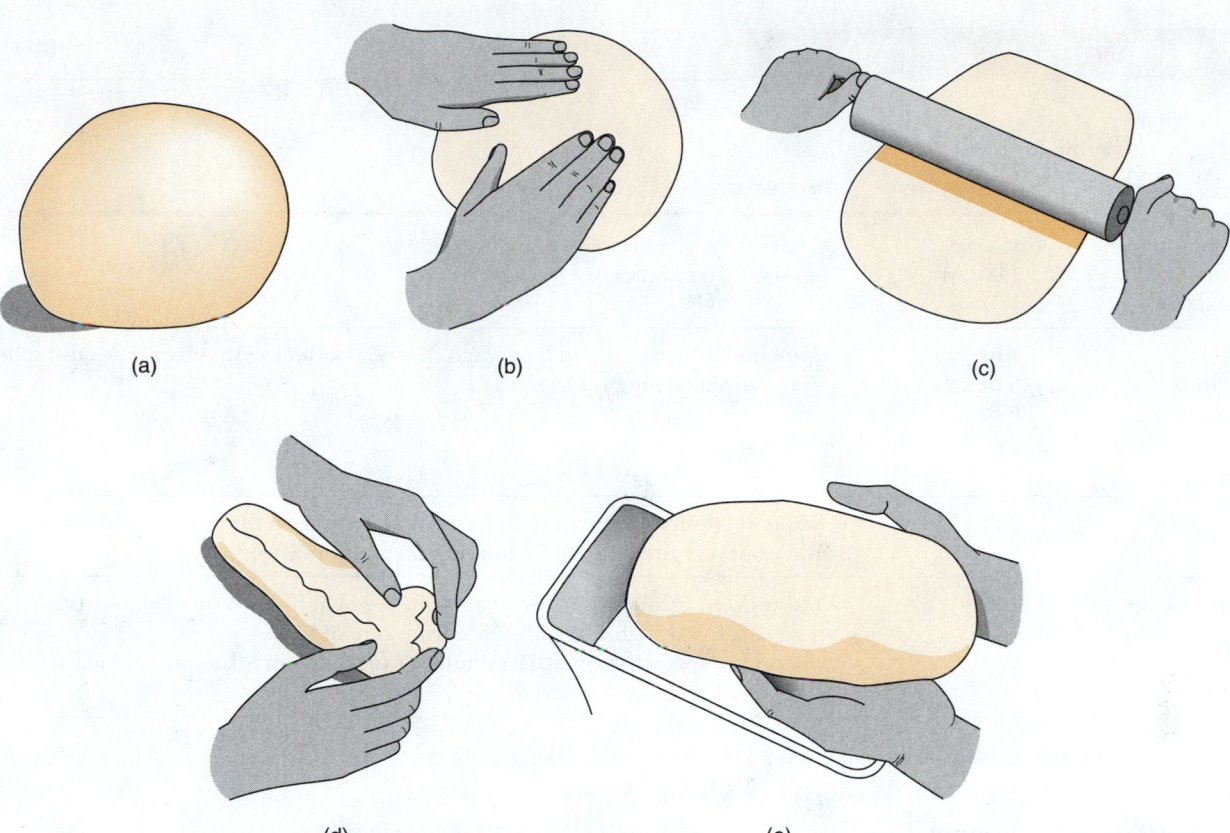

FIGURE 10.1   Shaping bread loaves: (a) Lightly flour the work surface. Divide the dough into smooth 1 lb 8 oz balls. (b) Press dough by hand to force out air bubbles. (c) Use a rolling pin to form a rectangle. (d) Begin at the short end of the rectangle and roll the dough tightly to make a loaf shape. Seal by pinching ends together. (e) Place dough, seam side down, in greased pan.

WHOLE-WHEAT BREAD

Yield: five 1½-lb loaves
Oven: 365°F   *Bake:* 30–35 minutes

Ingredient	Amount	Procedure
Yeast, active dry	1¼ oz	Combine yeast, warm water, and sugar.
Water, warm (110°F)	1¾ cups	Let stand 10 minutes.
Sugar, granulated	1 Tbsp	
Water, hot	1 qt	Combine hot water, dry milk, sugar, salt, and shortening in mixer bowl, using dough arm.
Nonfat dry milk	5 oz	Mix until shortening is softened.
Sugar, granulated	5 oz	
Salt	1½ oz	
Shortening	6 oz	
Flour, all-purpose	3 lb	Add enough flour to mixture in mixer bowl to make a thin, smooth batter.
		Add yeast mixture. Mix for 15 minutes on medium speed.
Flour, whole-wheat	1 lb	Add remaining all-purpose flour and whole-wheat flour in small amounts to make a soft dough that pulls itself from side of bowl.
		Mix on low speed for about 10 minutes or until dough is smooth and elastic and small blisters appear on the surface.

1. Let dough rise (proof) in warm place for about 2 hours or until double in bulk.
2. Punch down dough. Scale into five portions, 1 lb 8 oz each.
3. Shape into loaves. Place in greased 5 × 9 × 2¾-inch loaf pans. Let rise until double in size.
4. Bake at 365°F for 30–35 minutes.
5. Remove bread from oven. Brush with melted margarine.

Approximate nutritive values per loaf

Calories	Carbohydrate	Protein	Fat	Cholesterol	Sodium	Fiber	Iron
1539 kcal	256 g	41 g	37 g	5 mg	3466 mg	9 g	14 mg

Note

- Recipe may be used for Whole-Wheat Rolls. See p. 273 for procedure. Recipe makes approximately 100 1½-oz rolls. Bake at 375°F for 20–25 minutes.

Variations

- **Cornmeal Bread.** Delete whole-wheat flour. Add 1 lb cornmeal.
- **Egg Bread.** Delete whole-wheat flour. Increase all-purpose flour to 3 lb 12 oz. Add 5 eggs (8 oz), beaten.
- **Jalapeño Cheese Bread.** Delete whole-wheat flour. Increase all-purpose flour to 4 lb. Increase yeast to 1½ oz. Reduce nonfat dry milk to 1 oz. Add 3 oz seeded jalapeño peppers, finely chopped; 8 oz green chiles, chopped; 10 oz shredded cheddar cheese; and 8 oz shredded processed cheese.
- **White Loaves.** Delete whole-wheat flour. Increase all-purpose flour to 4 lb.

FRENCH BREAD

Yield: five 1 lb 12 oz loaves
Oven: 425°F   *Bake:* 25–30 minutes

Ingredient	Amount	Procedure
Yeast, active dry	1½ oz	Combine yeast, water, and sugar.
Water, warm (110°F)	2 cups	Stir to dissolve yeast. Let stand 10 minutes.
Sugar, granulated	2 oz	
Water, warm	3 cups	Add to yeast mixture. Mix until blended, using dough arm.
Shortening	3 oz	
Salt	1¾ oz	
Flour, all-purpose	5 lb	Add flour all at once. Mix on low speed to blend. Mix on medium speed for 7–10 minutes, or until sides of bowl are clean and dough makes a rhythmic slapping sound against side of bowl.

1. Let dough rise (proof) in a warm place for about 2 hours, or until double in bulk.
2. Punch down dough by pulling the dough up on all sides, folding it over the center and pressing down, then turning over in the bowl.
3. Divide into five portions, 1 lb 12 oz each. On lightly floured surface, roll or pat dough to a 12 × 6-inch rectangle.
4. Starting with longer side, roll up tightly, pressing dough into roll with each turn. Pinch edges and ends to seal.
5. Place on greased baking sheet sprinkled with cornmeal.
6. Proof until double in bulk.
7. With sharp knife, make two or three diagonal slashes across top of loaf.
8. Spray or brush with cold water.
9. Bake at 425°F for 25–30 minutes until golden brown. Spray or brush loaf with cold water several times during baking for a crisp crust.

Approximate nutritive values per loaf

Calories	Carbohydrate	Protein	Fat	Cholesterol	Sodium	Fiber	Iron
1875 kcal	360 g	50 g	22 g	0 mg	3864 mg	14 g	22 mg

Notes

- For a shiny, golden crust, brush loaves before baking with an egg glaze made from 1 slightly beaten egg and 1 Tbsp water or milk.
- After baking, leave uncovered at room temperature to keep the crust crisp.

DILLY BREAD

Yield: five 1½-lb loaves
Oven: 375°F   *Bake:* 30–35 minutes

Ingredient	Amount	Procedure
Yeast, active dry	1¼ oz	Combine yeast, water, and sugar.
Water, warm (110°F)	½ cup	Stir to dissolve yeast.
Sugar, granulated	3 oz	Let stand for later step.
Cottage cheese, cream style	1 lb 12 oz	Combine cottage cheese and water in mixer bowl.
Water, warm	1¼ cups	
Vegetable oil	¼ cup	Add oil, onion, dill weed, and eggs to cottage cheese mixture. Mix to blend, using dough arm.
Dehydrated chopped onion	½ oz	Add yeast mixture.
Dill weed	1 Tbsp	
Eggs	3 (6 oz)	
Flour, all-purpose	4 lb 2 oz	Combine dry ingredients. Add enough to cottage cheese mixture to make a smooth batter. Scrape sides of bowl occasionally.
Salt	1 Tbsp	Add remaining flour gradually until dough pulls itself from sides of bowl. Dough will be sticky.
Baking soda	½ tsp	Proof until double in bulk.
		Scale dough into five portions, 1 lb 8 oz each. Shape into loaves.
		Place in greased 5 × 9 × 2¾-inch loaf pans.
		Proof until double in size.
		Bake at 375°F for 30–35 minutes.
		Brush with melted margarine.

Approximate nutritive values per loaf

Calories	Carbohydrate	Protein	Fat	Cholesterol	Sodium	Fiber	Iron
1770 kcal	313 g	66 g	25 g	169 mg	2102 mg	13 g	19 mg

ENGLISH MUFFIN BREAD

Yield: five 1½-lb loaves
Oven: 375°F   *Bake:* 40–50 minutes

Ingredient	Amount	Procedure
Water, hot	2 cups	Combine hot water and oil in mixer bowl.
Vegetable oil	1½ cups	
Flour, all-purpose	2 lb	Add flour, sugar, salt, and eggs to water-oil mixture.
Sugar, granulated	6 oz	
Salt	2 oz	
Eggs, beaten	6 (10 oz)	
Yeast, active dry	1¼ oz	Dissolve yeast in warm water.
Water, warm (110°F)	1½ cups	Add to flour mixture. Mix on medium speed for 2 minutes, using dough arm.
Flour, all-purpose	2 lb	Add enough remaining flour to make a stiff batter. Cover and let rise until light and double in bulk. Punch down dough.
Cornmeal	2 oz	Grease five 5 × 9 × 2¾-inch loaf pans. Sprinkle with cornmeal. Scale 1 lb 8 oz dough per pan. Shape and place in pans. Sprinkle with cornmeal. Cover. Let rise until double in bulk. Bake at 375°F for 40–50 minutes or until loaf sounds hollow when tapped lightly.

Approximate nutritive values per loaf

Calories	Carbohydrate	Protein	Fat	Cholesterol	Sodium	Fiber	Iron
2176 kcal	323 g	49 g	75 g	242 mg	4483 mg	14 g	19 mg

FOCACCIA

Yield: 4 loaves
Oven: 450°F   *Bake:* 15–20 minutes

Ingredient	Amount	Procedure
Yeast, active dry	1 oz	Combine yeast, water, and sugar. Stir to dissolve yeast. Let stand for later step.
Water, warm (110°F)	2 cups	
Sugar, granulated	¼ tsp	
Olive oil	1½ cups	Add to yeast mixture. Mix until blended using dough arm.
Water, warm	2 cups	
Salt	1 Tbsp	
Flour, all-purpose	2 lb 10 oz	Add flour. Mix on low speed for about 10 minutes until dough is smooth and satiny.

1. Turn into lightly greased bowl, then turn over to grease top. Cover. Let rise in warm place (80°F) until double in bulk (30–40 minutes).
2. Shape with a rolling pin into four 1 lb 5 oz ovals, circles, or rectangles about ½–⅔ inch thick.
3. Make several very shallow parallel or fan-shaped cuts in center of bread, then gently pull the edges of the dough to slightly open the shallow cuts.
4. Put rounds on lightly greased pans.
5. Brush rounds with olive oil and sprinkle lightly with coarse sea salt and coarse ground pepper. Let rise for 20 minutes.
6. Bake at 450°F for approximately 15 minutes, until golden brown. Serve warm.

Approximate nutritive values per loaf

Calories	Carbohydrate	Protein	Fat	Cholesterol	Sodium	Fiber	Iron
1819 kcal	230 g	33 g	84 g	0 mg	1611 mg	9 g	13 mg

Note

- Focaccia may be split and filled with a sandwich filling or served unsplit as an accompaniment to soup or salad.

Variation

- **Focaccia with Onions.** Toss 1 lb thinly sliced onions with ¼ cup olive oil, ½ tsp salt, and ½ tsp pepper. Distribute approximately 4 oz onion mixture on focaccia after shaping. Let rise for 20–30 minutes and bake as directed.

OATMEAL BREAD

Yield: five 1½-lb loaves
Oven: 375°F   *Bake:* 30–35 minutes

Ingredient	Amount	Procedure
Yeast, active dry	1¼ oz	Combine yeast, warm water, and sugar.
Water, warm (110°F)	1 cup	Let stand for 10 minutes.
Sugar, granulated	2 tsp	
Water, hot	3 cups	Combine in mixer bowl, using dough arm.
Rolled oats	6 oz	
Molasses	1 cup	
Shortening	6 oz	
Salt	2 Tbsp	
Flour, all-purpose	3 lb 8 oz	Add enough flour to rolled-oats mixture to make a smooth, thin batter.
Eggs	4 (7 oz)	Add eggs and yeast mixture to batter. Mix for 15 minutes on medium speed.
		Add remaining flour in small amounts, on low speed, to make a soft dough. Let rest for 10 minutes.
		Knead on low speed for 10 minutes or until smooth and elastic, or until a small piece of dough can be stretched to resemble a thin membrane.
		Let rise until double in bulk.
Rolled oats	4 oz	Grease five 5 × 9 × 2¾-inch loaf pans.
		Coat each pan with ¼ cup rolled oats.
		Punch down dough. Scale 1 lb 8 oz dough for each pan and shape into a loaf.
		Place in prepared pans.
Egg whites	2 (2 oz)	Combine egg whites and water.
Water	1 Tbsp	Brush on loaves and sprinkle with rolled oats.
		Let rise until double in bulk.
		Bake at 375°F for 30–35 minutes.

Approximate nutritive values per loaf

Calories	Carbohydrate	Protein	Fat	Cholesterol	Sodium	Fiber	Iron
1926 kcal	327 g	51 g	45 g	169 mg	2650 mg	11 g	21 mg

Variation

- **Molasses Bran Bread.** Delete rolled oats and eggs. Increase water to 1 qt. Add 10 oz whole-wheat flour, 3 oz unprocessed bran, 1½ tsp ground ginger, and 4 oz nonfat dry milk.

POTATO BREAD

Yield: five 1½-lb loaves
Oven: 375°F   *Bake:* 30–35 minutes

Ingredient	Amount	Procedure
Water, boiling	2 cups	
Instant potatoes	5 oz	Pour boiling water over potatoes. Set aside for later step.
Yeast, active dry	1 oz	Combine yeast, warm water, and sugar. Let stand for 10 minutes.
Water, warm (110°F)	1 cup	
Sugar, granulated	1 tsp	
Water, hot	1½ cups	Combine hot water, dry milk, shortening, sugar, and salt in mixer bowl, using dough arm to mix and soften shortening.
Nonfat dry milk	4 oz	
Shortening	8 oz	Add potato mixture and mix until well blended.
Sugar, granulated	8 oz	
Salt	2 Tbsp	
Flour, all-purpose	3 lb 8 oz	Add enough flour to make a smooth batter. Add yeast mixture. Mix on medium speed for 15 minutes.
Eggs, beaten	5 (8 oz)	Add eggs and mix thoroughly. Add remaining flour in small amounts on low speed to make a soft dough. Proof until double in bulk.
		Punch down dough. Scale into five loaves, 1 lb 8 oz each. Place in greased 5 × 9 × 2¾-inch baking pans. Proof until double in size. Bake at 375°F for 30–35 minutes.

Approximate nutritive values per loaf

Calories	Carbohydrate	Protein	Fat	Cholesterol	Sodium	Fiber	Iron
2015 kcal	326 g	51 g	54 g	197 mg	3347 mg	10 g	17 mg

Note

- Dough may be shaped into rolls. Recipe makes approximately 100 1½-oz rolls. Bake at 375°F for 20–25 minutes.

Variation

- **Portuguese Sweet Bread.** Delete nonfat dry milk. Substitute 6 oz margarine for shortening. Increase sugar to 10 oz and eggs to 6 (10 oz).

SWEDISH RYE BREAD

Yield: five 1½-lb loaves
Oven: 375°F   *Bake:* 40–50 minutes

Ingredient	Amount	Procedure
Yeast, active dry Water, warm (110°F) Sugar, brown	2¼ oz 2 cups 1 oz	Combine yeast, warm water, and brown sugar. Let stand for 10 minutes.
Water, hot Salt Sugar, brown Molasses Shortening	3 cups 1 Tbsp 6 oz 6 oz (½ cup) 3 oz	Combine in mixer bowl. Mix thoroughly until shortening is softened.
Flour, all-purpose Flour, rye	3 lb 8 oz 12 oz	Combine flours. Add enough to mixture in mixer bowl to make a thin, smooth batter. Add yeast mixture. Mix on medium speed for 10 minutes, using dough arm. Reduce mixer speed. Add remaining flour in small amounts to make a soft dough that pulls itself from sides of bowl. Mix for about 10 minutes, until smooth and elastic, or until a small piece of dough can be stretched to resemble a thin membrane. Let rise until double in bulk.
		Punch down dough. Shape into five loaves, 1 lb 8 oz each. Place in five greased 5 × 9 × 2¾-inch loaf pans. Let rise until double in bulk. Bake at 375°F for 40–50 minutes or until bread sounds hollow when tapped lightly.

Approximate nutritive values per loaf

Calories	Carbohydrate	Protein	Fat	Cholesterol	Sodium	Fiber	Iron
1771 kcal	349 g	48 g	22 g	0 mg	29 mg	15 g	23 mg

Variations

- **Caraway Rye Bread.** Add 2 Tbsp caraway seeds to dough.
- **Limpa Rye Bread.** Decrease all-purpose flour to 2 lb and increase rye flour to 2 lb. Add 2 Tbsp fennel seed and 2 Tbsp grated orange peel.
- **Rye Rolls.** Shape into 1½-oz rolls. Yield: 7 dozen.

BASIC ROLL DOUGH

Yield: 8 dozen rolls   *Portion:* 1½ oz
Oven: 400°F   *Bake:* 15–25 minutes

Ingredient	Amount	Procedure
Sugar, granulated	1 tsp	Combine sugar and warm water. Add yeast.
Water, warm (110°F)	1 cup	Let stand 10 minutes.
Yeast, active dry	1½ oz	
Water, hot	1¼ qt	Place hot water, dry milk, sugar, salt, and shortening in
Nonfat dry milk	5 oz	mixer bowl.
Sugar, granulated	4 oz	Mix thoroughly, using dough arm, until shortening is
Salt	2 oz	softened.
Shortening	8 oz	
Eggs, beaten	4 (7 oz)	Add eggs and softened yeast.
Flour, all-purpose	4 lb 12 oz (variable)	Add flour to make a moderately soft dough. Mix on low speed for about 10 minutes until smooth and satiny, or until a small piece of dough can be stretched to resemble a thin membrane.

1. Turn into lightly greased bowl, then turn over to grease top. Cover. Let rise in warm place (80°F) until double in bulk.
2. Punch down. Divide into thirds for ease in handling. Shape into 1½-oz rolls or into desired shapes. (See Variations on p. 373.)
3. Let rise until double in bulk.
4. Bake at 400°F for 15–25 minutes or until golden brown.

Approximate nutritive values per portion

Calories	Carbohydrate	Protein	Fat	Cholesterol	Sodium	Fiber	Iron
117 kcal	19 g	3 g	3 g	9 mg	241 mg	1 g	1 mg

Notes

- 1¼ qt fluid milk may be used in place of nonfat dry milk and hot water. Scald milk, then add sugar, salt, and shortening, and cool to lukewarm.
- Mixing may be simplified by combining dry yeast with sugar, salt, dry milk, and 2 lb flour. Mix thoroughly. In mixer bowl combine 1¼ qt very warm water (120°F), shortening, and beaten eggs. Blend on low speed. Add remaining flour gradually, mixing until a smooth, elastic dough is formed.
- Allow 3–4 hours for mixing and rising. For a quicker-rising dough, increase yeast to 2 oz.

Variations

- **Bowknots.** Roll 1½-oz portions of dough into strips 9 inches long. Tie loosely into a single knot (see Figure 10.2).
- **Braids.** Roll dough ¼ inch thick and cut in strips 6 inches long and ½ inch wide. Braid three strips, fold under, and pinch to seal (see Figure 10.3).
- **Butterhorns.** Proceed as for Crescents, but do not form crescent shape.
- **Caramel Crowns.** Increase sugar in dough to 9 oz. Scale dough into balls, 1½ oz each. Drop into mixture of 1 lb 4 oz sugar and 3 Tbsp cinnamon to coat balls. Arrange 18 balls in each of five greased tube pans, into which 2 oz pecans, halves or coarsely chopped, have been placed. The pan should be about ⅓ full. Let rise until double in bulk. Bake at 350°F for 30 minutes. Immediately loosen from pan with a spatula. Invert pans to remove. Cool. Serve irregular side up to resemble a crown. Garnish with maraschino cherries.
- **Cloverleaf Rolls.** Pinch off 1-oz pieces of dough and roll into smooth balls. Fit into greased muffin pans, 3 balls per cup (see Figure 10.4).
- **Crescents.** Weigh dough into 12-oz portions. Roll each into a circle ⅛ inch thick and 8 inches in diameter. Cut into 12 triangles and brush top with melted margarine or butter. Beginning at base, roll each triangle, keeping point in middle of roll and bringing ends toward each other to form a crescent shape. Place on greased baking sheets 1½ inches apart (see Figure 10.5).
- **Dinner or Pan Rolls.** Shape dough into 1½-oz balls and place on well-greased baking sheets. Cover. Let rise until light. Brush with mixture made of egg yolk and milk—1 egg yolk to 1 Tbsp milk.

- **Fan Tan or Butterflake Rolls.** Weigh dough into 12-oz portions. Roll out into very thin rectangular sheet. Brush with melted margarine or butter. Cut in strips about 1 inch wide. Pile 6–7 strips together. Cut $1\frac{1}{2}$-inch pieces and place on end in greased muffin pans.
- **Gooey Buns.** Grease sides of one $18 \times 26 \times 2$-inch baking sheet. Combine in kettle or saucepan 8 oz margarine, 1 lb 8 oz brown sugar, and $\frac{3}{4}$ cup corn syrup. Cook until sugar is dissolved. Pour into prepared pan. Cool. If desired, sprinkle 1 lb pecans over mixture. Place $1\frac{1}{2}$-oz portions of dough 8×12 on sugar mixture. Let rise. Bake at 375°F for 20–25 minutes. Remove from oven and turn upside down onto $18 \times 26 \times 1$-inch baking sheet.
- **Half-and-Half Rolls.** Proceed as for Twin Rolls. Use one round plain dough and one round whole-wheat dough for each roll.
- **Hamburger Buns.** Divide dough into two portions. Roll each piece of dough into a strip $1\frac{1}{2}$ inches in diameter. Cut strips into pieces approximately $2\frac{1}{2}$ oz each. Round the pieces into balls. Place balls in rows on greased baking sheets $1\frac{1}{2}$–2 inches apart. Let stand for 10–15 minutes, then flatten to desired thickness with finger, rolling pin, or another baking sheet.
- **Hot Cross Buns.** Divide dough into thirds. Roll $\frac{1}{2}$ inch thick. Cut rounds 3 inches in diameter. Brush tops with beaten egg. Score top of bun to make a cross before baking, or make a cross on top with frosting after baking. (See p. 378 for variation.)
- **Hot Dog Buns.** Divide dough into two portions. Roll each piece of dough into a strip $1\frac{1}{2}$ inches in diameter. Cut strips of dough into pieces approximately $2\frac{1}{2}$ oz each. Round pieces of dough; roll into pieces approximately $4\frac{1}{2}$ inches long. Place in rows on greased baking sheets $\frac{1}{2}$ inch apart.
- **Parker House Rolls.** Divide dough into thirds. Roll dough to $\frac{1}{3}$ inch thick. Cut rounds 2–$2\frac{1}{2}$ inches in diameter with a biscuit cutter. Let dough rest a few minutes after cutting. Brush with melted butter or margarine. Crease the rolls across the center with the dull edge of a table knife. Fold over and press down on the folded edge (see Figure 10.6 and in the color insert).
- **Popcorn Rolls.** Shape dough into $1\frac{1}{2}$-oz balls. Place on greased baking sheets. Snip top of each ball twice with scissors.
- **Poppy Seed Rolls.** (a) Proceed as for Twists. Substitute poppy seed for sugar and cinnamon. (b) Proceed as for Cinnamon Rolls (pp. 279–280). Substitute poppy seed for sugar, cinnamon, and raisins.
- **Ribbon Rolls.** Scale dough into 12-oz pieces. Roll $\frac{1}{4}$ inch thick. Spread with melted margarine. Place on top of this a layer of whole wheat dough rolled to the same thickness. Repeat, using the contrasting dough until five layers thick. Cut with a $1\frac{1}{2}$-inch cutter. Place in greased muffin pans with cut surface down.
- **Rosettes.** Follow directions for Bowknots. After tying, bring one end through center and the other over the side.
- **Sesame Rolls.** Proceed as for Twin Rolls. Brush tops with melted margarine and sprinkle with sesame seeds.
- **Twin Rolls.** Scale dough into 12-oz pieces. Roll $\frac{5}{8}$ inch thick. Cut rounds 1 inch in diameter. Brush with melted margarine. Place on end in well-greased muffin pans, allowing two rounds for each roll.
- **Twists.** Scale dough into 12-oz pieces. Roll $\frac{1}{3}$ inch thick and spread with melted margarine, sugar, and cinnamon. Cut into strips $\frac{1}{3} \times 8$ inches, bring both ends together, and twist dough.
- **Whole-Wheat Rolls.** Substitute 2 lb 6 oz whole-wheat flour for 2 lb 6 oz all-purpose flour. Proceed as for Basic Roll Dough.

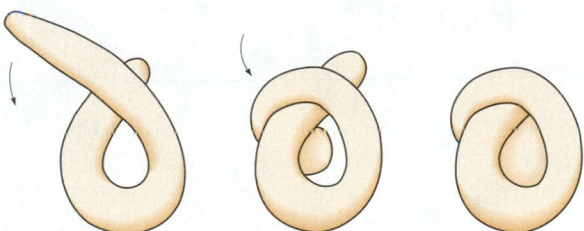

FIGURE 10.2   Shaping bowknot rolls

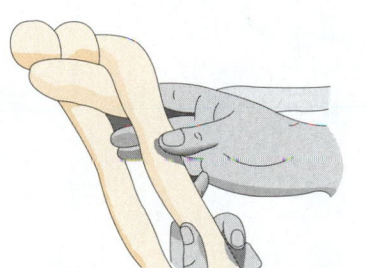 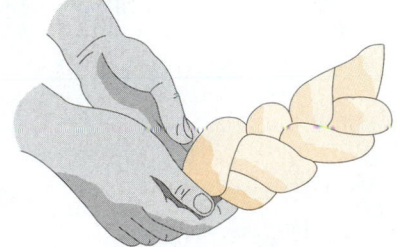

FIGURE 10.3   Braiding yeast dough

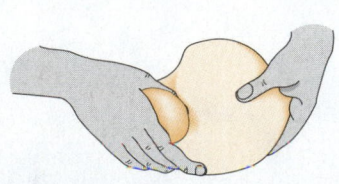 

FIGURE 10.4   Shaping and panning cloverleaf rolls

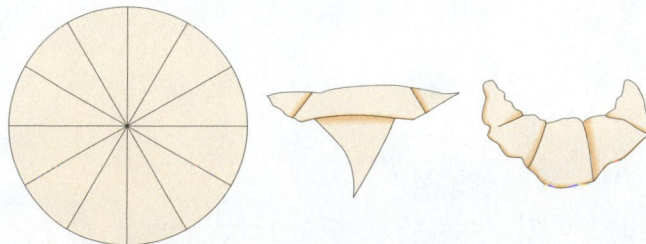

FIGURE 10.5   Shaping crescent rolls

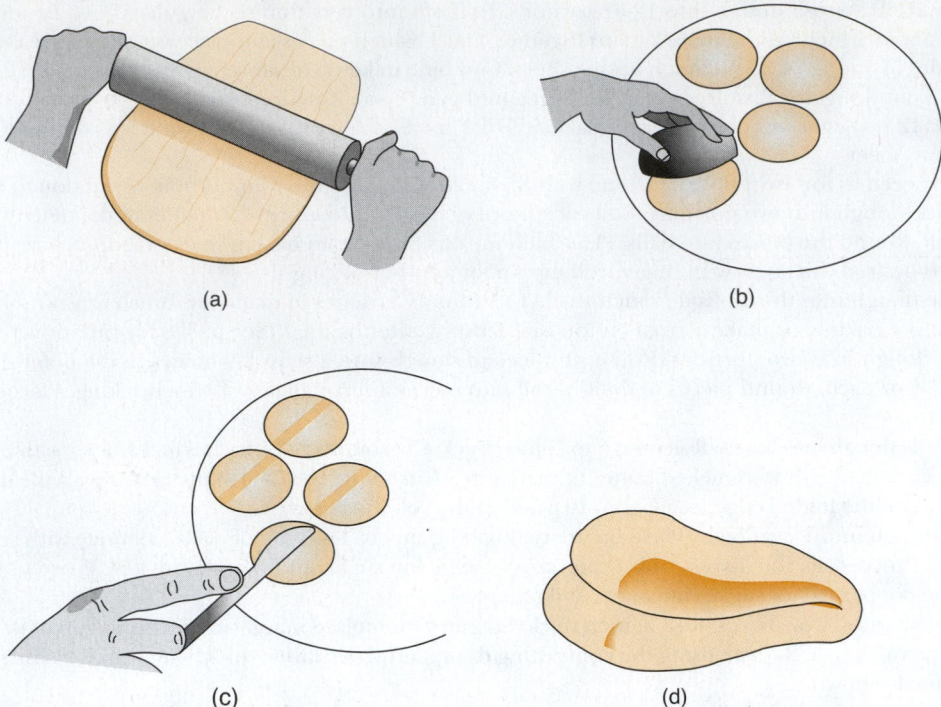

(a)

(b)

(c)

(d)

FIGURE 10.6 Shaping Parker House rolls. (a) Divide dough into thirds. Roll to $\frac{1}{3}$ inch thick and brush with melted margarine. (b) Cut into circles with cutter. (c) Crease rolls with back of a table knife. (d) Fold over and press down on folded edge.

BUTTER BUNS

Yield: 9–10 dozen buns   *Portion:* 1¾ oz
Oven: 400°F   *Bake:* 15–20 minutes

Ingredient	Amount	Procedure
Sugar, granulated	1 lb	Place sugar, salt, and margarine in mixer bowl.
Salt	1 oz	
Margarine or butter	1 lb 8 oz	
Milk	3 cups	Scald milk by heating to a point just below boiling. Add to ingredients in mixer bowl and mix. Cool to lukewarm.
Yeast, active dry	2 oz	Soften yeast in water.
Water, warm (110°F)	1 cup	
Eggs	12 (1 lb 5 oz)	Beat eggs and yolks.
Egg yolks	16 (10 oz)	Add eggs, lemon extract, and yeast to milk mixture. Mix until blended.
Lemon extract (optional)	4 tsp	
Flour, all-purpose	4 lb 8 oz	Add flour and mix thoroughly, using dough arm. Let dough rise until double in bulk. Portion with No. 30 dipper into greased muffin pans. Let rise for 1 hour. Bake at 400°F for 15–20 minutes.

Approximate nutritive values per portion

Calories	Carbohydrate	Protein	Fat	Cholesterol	Sodium	Fiber	Iron
146 kcal	18 g	4 g	6 g	55 mg	164 mg	1 g	1 mg

Note

• 3 oz nonfat dry milk and 3 cups water may be substituted for the fluid milk. Combine dry milk with flour. Increase margarine to 1 lb 9 oz.

RAISED MUFFINS

Yield: 8 dozen muffins   *Portion:* 2 oz
Oven: 350°F   *Bake:* 20 minutes

Ingredient	Amount	Procedure
Sugar, granulated Salt Shortening	12 oz 2 oz 9 oz	Place sugar, salt, and shortening in mixer bowl.
Milk	1½ qt	Scald milk by heating to a point just below boiling. Add to mixture in mixing bowl. Cool to lukewarm.
Yeast, active dry Water, warm (110°F)	1½ oz 1½ cups	Soften yeast in water.
Eggs, beaten	12 (1 lb 5 oz)	Add eggs and softened yeast to milk mixture.
Flour, all-purpose	2 lb	Add flour. Beat on medium speed for 10 minutes, using flat beater. Let rise in warm place for 1½ hours.
Flour, all-purpose	2 lb 12 oz (variable)	Add remaining flour. Beat until batter is smooth. Portion with No. 20 dipper into greased muffin pans. Let rise until double in bulk (about 1 hour). Bake at 350°F for 20 minutes.

Approximate nutritive values per portion

Calories	Carbohydrate	Protein	Fat	Cholesterol	Sodium	Fiber	Iron
139 kcal	22 g	4 g	4 g	28 mg	245 mg	1 g	1 mg

Note

• 6 oz nonfat dry milk and 1½ qt water may be substituted for the fluid milk. Combine dry milk with the first portion of flour.

BASIC SWEET ROLL DOUGH

Yield: 8 dozen rolls   *Portion:* 2 oz
Oven: 375°F   *Bake:* 20–25 minutes

Ingredient	Amount	Procedure
Yeast, active dry	2 oz	Soften yeast in warm water.
Water, warm (110°F)	1½ cups	
Water, hot	3 cups	Combine hot water, dry milk, sugar, shortening, and salt in mixer bowl.
Nonfat dry milk	3 oz	
Sugar, granulated	1 lb	Mix until shortening is softened, using dough arm. Cool to lukewarm.
Shortening	1 lb	
Salt	1¾ oz	
Eggs, beaten	9 (1 lb)	Add eggs and yeast to mixture in bowl. Blend.
Flour, all-purpose	5–6 lb (variable)	Add flour gradually on low speed. Mix on medium speed to a smooth dough, 5–6 minutes. Do not overmix. Dough should be moderately soft.

1. The dough temperature just after mixing should be 78–82°F.
2. Place dough in lightly greased bowl. Grease top of dough, cover, and let rise in warm place until double in bulk, about 2 hours.
3. Punch down and let rise again, about 1 hour.
4. Punch down and divide into portions for rolls. Let rest for 10 minutes.
5. Scale 2 oz per roll. Shape (see Variations) and let rise until rolls are almost double in bulk, about 45 minutes.
6. Bake at 375°F for 20–25 minutes.

Approximate nutritive values per portion

Calories	Carbohydrate	Protein	Fat	Cholesterol	Sodium	Fiber	Iron
167 kcal	25 g	4 g	5 g	20 mg	212 mg	1 g	1 mg

Notes

- Mixing may be simplified by combining dry yeast with sugar, salt, dry milk, and 2 lb flour. Mix thoroughly. Combine eggs, very warm water (120°F), and melted shortening. Add yeast-flour mixture on low speed. Add remaining flour gradually, mixing until a smooth, elastic dough is formed.
- 3 cups fluid milk may be used in place of nonfat dry milk and hot water. Scald milk, then add sugar, salt, and shortening, and cool to lukewarm.
- For a quicker-rising dough, increase yeast to 3 oz.

Variations

- **Cherry-Nut Rolls.** Add 1 tsp nutmeg, ½ tsp almond or lemon extract, 1 lb chopped glacé cherries, and 1 lb chopped pecans to dough. Shape into 1-oz balls. When baked, cover with glaze made of orange juice and powdered sugar.
- **Cinnamon Twists.** Combine 1 lb granulated sugar and 1 Tbsp cinnamon. Melt 4 oz margarine. Dip 2-oz portions of dough into melted margarine, then roll in sugar-cinnamon mixture. Elongate and twist dough portions into 3-inch-long rolls. Place side by side in two 13 × 18-inch baking pans. Bake at 375°F for 20–25 minutes.
- **Coffee Cake.** Scale 4 lb dough and roll out to size of 18 × 26 × 1-inch baking sheet. Cover top of dough with melted margarine or butter and topping (see p. 281). Fruit fillings may be used also.
- **Crullers.** Roll dough ⅓ inch thick. Cut into strips ½ × 8 inches. Bring two ends together and twist dough. Let rise, then fry in deep fat. Ice with Powdered Sugar Glaze (p. 316) or dip in fine granulated sugar.

(continued)

- **Danish Pastry.** Roll a 5-lb piece of dough into a rectangular shape about $\frac{1}{4}$ inch thick. Start at one edge and cover completely $\frac{2}{3}$ of the dough with small pieces of hard butter, margarine, or special Danish pastry shortening. The latter is stable at bakeshop temperature and is easier to use than butter or margarine. Use 2–5 oz per pound of dough. Fold the unbuttered $\frac{1}{3}$ portion of dough over an equal portion of buttered dough. Fold the remaining $\frac{1}{3}$ buttered dough over the top to make three layers of dough separated by a layer of fat. Roll out dough $\frac{1}{4}$ inch thick. This completes the first roll. Repeat folding and rolling two or more times. Do not allow the fat to become soft while working with the dough. Let dough rest for 45 minutes. Make into desired shapes.

- **Hot Cross Buns.** Add to dough 8 oz chopped glacé cherries, 8 oz raisins, 2 Tbsp cinnamon, $\frac{1}{4}$ tsp cloves, and $\frac{1}{4}$ tsp nutmeg. Shape into round buns, 1 oz per bun. When baked, make a cross on top with Powdered Sugar Glaze (p. 316).

- **Kolaches.** Add 2 Tbsp freshly grated lemon peel to dough. Shape dough into 1-oz balls. Place on lightly greased baking sheet. Let rise until light. Press down center to make cavity and fill with 1 tsp filling. Brush with melted margarine or butter and sprinkle with chopped nuts. Suggested fillings: chopped cooked prunes and dried apricots cooked with sugar and cinnamon; poppy seed mixed with sugar and milk; apricot or peach marmalade.

- **Long Johns.** Roll dough $\frac{1}{2}$ inch thick. Cut dough into rectangular pieces $\frac{1}{2} \times 4$ inches. Let rise until double in bulk. Fry in deep fat.

- **Swedish Braids.** Add to dough 1 lb chopped candied fruit, 8 oz pecans, and $\frac{1}{2}$ tsp cardamom seed. Weigh dough into $1\frac{3}{4}$-lb portions and braid. Place on greased $18 \times 26 \times 1$-inch baking sheets, four per pan. When baked, brush with Powdered Sugar Glaze (p. 316) made with milk in place of water.

FRUIT COFFEE RINGS

Yield: 8 rings
Oven: 350°F   *Bake:* 25–30 minutes

Ingredient	Amount	Procedure
Basic Roll Dough (p. 272) or Basic Sweet Roll Dough (p. 277)	10 lb (1 recipe)	Let dough rise until double in bulk. Divide dough into 1½-lb portions. Roll out each portion into a rectangular strip 9 × 14 × ⅓ inch.
Filling (see Suggested Fillings)	2 qt	Spread each strip with 1 cup filling. Roll as for Cinnamon Rolls. Arrange in ring mold or 10-inch tube pan. Cut slashes in dough with scissors about 1 inch apart. Let rise until double in bulk. Bake at 350°F for 25–30 minutes. Brush with Powdered Sugar Glaze (p. 316).

Suggested Fillings

• Use 2 qt Apricot Filling (p. 317) or apricot preserves, Fig Filling (p. 317), Prune-Date Filling (p. 317), orange marmalade, or a mixture of 1 lb margarine or butter and 1 lb honey whipped together until light and fluffy. Dough may be shaped in a twist.

CINNAMON ROLLS

Yield: 5 dozen rolls *Portion:* 3 oz
Oven: 375°F *Bake:* 20–25 minutes

Ingredient	Amount	Procedure
Basic Roll Dough (p. 272) or Basic Sweet Roll Dough (p. 277)	10 lb (1 recipe)	Let dough rise until double in bulk. Divide dough into eight portions, 1 lb 4 oz each. Roll each portion into a rectangular sheet, 9 × 14 × ⅛ inch.
Margarine or butter, melted	12 oz	Spread each sheet with melted margarine.
Sugar, granulated Cinnamon, ground	2 lb 1 oz (4 Tbsp)	Combine sugar and cinnamon. Sprinkle 6 oz over each sheet. Roll out following procedure in Figure 10.7. Cut into 1-inch slices. Place cut side down on greased baking sheets, in muffin pans, or in round pans. Let rise until double in bulk, about 45 minutes. Bake at 375°F for 20–25 minutes. After removing from oven, spread tops with Powdered Sugar Glaze (p. 316) made with milk in place of water, Peanut Butter Glaze (p. 315), or Chocolate Glaze (p. 315).

Approximate nutritive values per portion

Calories	Carbohydrate	Protein	Fat	Cholesterol	Sodium	Fiber	Iron
353 kcal	53 g	6 g	13 g	32 mg	393 mg	1 g	2 mg

Note

- 8 oz brown sugar may be substituted for part of the granulated sugar.

Variations

- **Butterfly Rolls.** Cut rolled dough into 2-inch slices. Press each roll across center parallel to the cut side with the back of a large knife handle. Press or flatten out the folds of each end. Place on greased baking sheets 1½ inches apart.
- **Butterscotch Rolls.** Use brown sugar and omit cinnamon, if desired. Cream 8 oz margarine or butter, 1 lb 8 oz brown sugar, and 1 tsp salt. Gradually add 1 cup water, blending thoroughly. Spread 10 oz of mixture over each of four greased 18 × 26 × 1-inch baking sheets or place 1 Tbsp mixture into each greased muffin pan cup. Place rolls cut side down in pans.
- **Caramel Pecan Rolls.** Melt 12 oz margarine. Add 1 lb chopped pecans, 2 lb 6 oz brown sugar, and 12 oz light corn syrup. Stir to mix. Scale 1 lb 10 oz into each 12 × 18 × 2-inch pan. Place rolls cut side down onto caramel mixture.
- **Cinnamon Raisin Rolls.** Use brown sugar in place of granulated sugar and add 8 oz raisins to filling.
- **Double Cinnamon Buns.** Proceed as for Butterfly Rolls. Roll sheet of dough from both sides to form a double roll.
- **Glazed Marmalade Rolls.** Omit cinnamon. Dip cut slices in additional melted margarine or butter and granulated sugar. When baked, glaze with orange marmalade mixed with powdered sugar until of a consistency to spread. Apricot marmalade, strawberry jam, or other preserves may be used for the glaze.
- **Honey Rolls.** Substitute honey filling for sugar and cinnamon. Whip 1 lb margarine or butter and 1 lb honey until light and fluffy.
- **Jumbo Cinnamon Rolls.** Use 24 lb dough, 3 lb granulated sugar mixed with 5 Tbsp cinnamon, and 1 lb margarine or butter. Divide dough into four 6-lb portions. Roll each portion into approximately a 26 × 26-inch square. Spread with 4 oz softened margarine and sprinkle with 1½ cups sugar-cinnamon mixture. Roll into a 26-inch-long roll. Cut into 12 slices 2 inches thick. Pan 2 × 4 in 12 × 18-inch baking pans. Proof until double in bulk. Bake at 350°F for 25 minutes or until done. Ice with Powdered Sugar Glaze (p. 316).
- **Orange Rolls.** Omit cinnamon. Spread with mixture of 1 lb 8 oz granulated sugar and 1 cup fresh grated orange peel. When baked, brush with a glaze made of powdered sugar and orange juice. If desired, use a filling made by creaming 1 lb margarine or butter, 2 Tbsp fresh grated orange peel, 2 lb granulated sugar, and ¾ cup undiluted frozen orange juice concentrate. Spread on dough.

- **Pecan Rolls.** Coarsely chop 1 lb 8 oz pecans. Sprinkle 8 oz over bottom of each of three 12 × 18 × 2-inch baking pans. Combine 2 lb margarine or butter, 2 Tbsp cinnamon, ⅓ cup corn syrup, ⅓ cup water, and 2 lb 8 oz brown sugar. Cook over medium heat until margarine melts. Pour over chopped nuts, 1 lb 12 oz per pan. Place rolls cut side down on mixture.
- **Sugared Snails.** Proceed as for Butterfly Rolls, rolling dough thinner before adding sugar filling. Cut rolled dough into slices ¾ inch thick. Dip cut surface of each roll in granulated sugar. Place on greased baking sheets ½ inch apart, with sugared side up. Allow to stand 10–15 minutes, then flatten before baking.

(a)   (b)   (c)

FIGURE 10.7   Preparing cinnamon rolls. (a) Roll dough into rectangular sheets, brush with melted margarine or butter, and sprinkle with sugar-cinnamon mixture. (b) Roll up as for jelly roll. (c) Cut into 1-inch slices and place in individual muffin cups or in a pan.

Fillings or Toppings for Coffee Cake and Sweet Rolls

1. *Almond Filling.*   Mix 1 lb almond paste, 1 lb granulated sugar, 12 oz margarine or butter, and 4 oz flour. Add 2 eggs and beat until smooth.

2. *Butter Cinnamon Topping.*   Cream 8 oz margarine or butter, 1 lb granulated sugar, 3 Tbsp cinnamon, and ½ tsp salt. Add 4 beaten eggs and 3 oz flour and blend.

3. *Butter Crunch Topping.*   Blend 1 lb granulated sugar, 1 lb margarine or butter, ½ tsp salt, 3 oz honey, and 2 lb flour together to form a crumbly mixture.

4. *Crumb Topping.*   Mix 8 oz margarine or butter, 12 oz granulated sugar, ½ tsp cinnamon, and 12 oz flour until crumbly. Add 4 oz chopped nuts if desired.

Desserts

Cakes and Icings

Cakes may be classified according to two major types: butter or shortened cakes and foam or sponge cakes. Butter cakes contain butter, margarine, or other shortening and usually are leavened with baking powder or with baking soda and an acid. True sponge cakes are leavened chiefly by air incorporated into beaten eggs, although modified sponge cakes may have baking powder added.

A properly balanced formula, correct temperature of ingredients, accurate measurements, controlled mixing of ingredients, proper relationship of batter to pan, and correct oven temperature and baking time are essential to good cake making. Cake flour yields better volume and finer texture than all-purpose flour and was used in testing recipes in this section, unless otherwise specified. If all-purpose flour is used, see Table 4.5 for substitution guidelines.

METHODS OF MIXING BUTTER OR SHORTENED CAKES

For all methods of mixing, weigh or measure ingredients accurately and have them at room temperature (75–80°F).

Conventional Method

1. Cream the shortening and sugar on medium speed, using a flat beater, for about 10 minutes or until light and fluffy.
2. Add the eggs and beat for 3–5 minutes on high speed. Stop the mixer and scrape the sides and bottom of the bowl and beater. Removing the beater to make sure the bottom of bowl is scraped is recommended.
3. Combine the flour, leavening, and other dry ingredients. Add alternately with the liquid to the creamed mixture.
4. Mix on low speed until thoroughly blended. Scrape the sides of the bowl and beater occasionally for even mixing.

Dough-Batter Method

1. Cream the flour, baking powder, and shortening on low speed for 2 minutes, using a flat beater. Scrape the sides of the bowl and beater. Mix for 3 minutes.
2. Add the sugar, salt, and half of the milk. Mix for 2 minutes. Scrape the bowl and beater. Mix for 3 minutes.
3. Combine the egg, flavoring, and the remaining milk. Add half to the flour mixture. Mix for 30 seconds. Scrape the bowl and beater. Mix for 1 minute.
4. Add the remaining egg mixture. Mix for 1 minute. Scrape the bowl and beater. Mix for 2½ minutes.

This method requires less time and fewer utensils than the conventional method and yields a good product. See p. 292 for White Cake made by the dough-batter method.

Dry Blending and Wetting Method

1. Blend dry ingredients in the mixer bowl and mix on low speed for 1 minute, using a flat beater.
2. Add 60 percent of the water to the dry ingredients. Mix slightly; the flour is not completely hydrated.
3. Add fat and mix on low speed for 1 minute, then on medium speed for 4 minutes.
4. Add 10 percent of the water. Mix for 1 minute on low speed, then for 3 minutes on medium speed.
5. Add the remaining water (30 percent), eggs, and flavoring. Mix for 3 minutes on low speed.

This method of mixing produces a cake with good volume and fine texture. Converting water from weight to liquid measurements may produce awkward numbers. A small adjustment of the three liquid additions may need to be made for easy measurement, but the total weight of water should be the same as the amount specified in the recipe. See p. 291 for White Cake made by the dry blending and wetting method of mixing.

Muffin Method

1. Mix the dry ingredients, including dry milk if used, in a mixer bowl.
2. Combine the liquids (beaten eggs, milk or water, and melted shortening or oil).
3. Add the liquids all at once to the dry ingredients. Mix at low speed only enough to combine ingredients.

This method is quick and most successful when the cake is used soon after baking.

METHODS OF MIXING FOAM OR SPONGE CAKES

Angel Food Cakes

1. Sift the flour with part of the sugar. This step helps the flour mix more evenly with the foam.

2. Beat the egg whites, using the whip attachment, until they form soft peaks. Egg whites should be at room temperature, and all utensils used for whipping must be dry and free from fat or grease. Salt and cream of tartar are added near the beginning of the beating process.

3. Gradually beat in the sugar that was not mixed with the flour. Continue to beat until the egg whites form stiff, glossy peaks. Do not overbeat.

4. Fold in the flour-sugar mixture carefully to minimize loss of air from the foam. Fold until it is absorbed, but no longer.

5. Place in ungreased tube, loaf, or sheet pans and bake immediately.

Sponge Cakes

All egg-foam cakes are similar in that they contain little or no shortening and depend for most or all of their leavening on the air trapped in beaten eggs. However, the whole-egg foams and egg-yolk foams are handled differently from those made with egg whites alone. In sponge cakes, the sugar and liquid are added to the eggs or egg yolks and beaten until light. Dry ingredients are folded in. Chiffon cakes contain baking powder, which is mixed with the flour, and a small amount of fat in the form of vegetable oil that is added to the egg yolks and liquid. The beaten egg whites are folded into the batter.

CAKE MIXES

Prepared cake mixes offer the foodservice a wide variety of products that can be produced with fewer and less-skilled employees than cakes prepared from scratch. However, care should be given to the selection of the mix, and the instructions for preparation should be followed carefully to ensure high-quality products. The formulas in commercial mixes are balanced, and deviations such as the substitution of milk for water or the addition of eggs may change the finished product.

SCALING BATTER

Pan Preparation

Prepare pans before mixing cake batters, so that cakes can be baked without delay as soon as they are mixed.

1. For butter cakes, grease pans and line with parchment cake liners or grease and dust with flour. For best results, use a solid shortening. Oil will cause the cake to stick to the pan. A commercial vegetable spray may be used, or a coating mixture may be prepared and brushed on the pans (p. 288). Sides of the pan should be left ungreased unless cakes are to be removed from the pan for layers.

2. For angel food cakes and other foam cakes, do not grease the pan. The batter must be able to cling to the sides to rise.

Scaling

Butter or other shortened cakes usually are baked as sheet cakes for ease of preparation and serving but may be baked in layers or as cupcakes. Layer cakes may be made by cutting 18×26-inch sheet cakes in half or layering two 13×18-inch sheet cakes. (See Figure 11.1 for layering and icing a sheet cake.)

The correct amount of cake batter per pan is important in producing a cake with consistently high quality and volume. Table 11.1 gives approximate weights of batter for selected pan sizes. The proper scaling weight for different batters, however, can be determined by actual baking tests and experimentation. Once it has been determined, scaling weights for all pan sizes using the same batter can be calculated mathematically. The formula follows.

Step 1   Experiment, using any pan, to determine the proper scaling weight.

Step 2   Determine the volume of the pan used, expressed as cubic inches.

$$\text{square or rectangular pan volume} =$$
$$\text{length} \times \text{width} \times \text{height}$$
$$\text{round pan volume} =$$
$$3.14 \times \text{radius squared} \times \text{height}$$

Step 3   Determine the cubic inches per ounce of batter (factor) by dividing the cubic inches (as found in Step 2) by the ounces of batter determined to be correct by experimentation in Step 1.

$$\text{factor} = \frac{\text{cubic inches in pan}}{\text{correct scaling weight per pan}}$$

Step 4   Find the proper scaling weight of the particular batter calculated for any pan by dividing the known factor into the pan volume.

$$\frac{\text{volume of cake pan to be used}}{\text{factor}} = \frac{\text{proper scaling}}{\text{weight of batter}}$$

The following example illustrates the procedure for calculating proper scaling weight for a cake. The proper scaling weight of a $6 \times 1\frac{1}{2}$-inch round chocolate cake was determined to be 8 ounces. What would be the scaling weight for the same batter in a $10 \times 1\frac{1}{2}$-inch round pan?

Step 1   Through experimentation, it was determined that 8 oz in a $6 \times 1\frac{1}{2}$-inch pan was correct.

Step 2   Volume $= 3.14 \times 3^2 \times 1.5 = 42$ cubic inches

Step 3   42 cubic inches ÷ 8 oz = 5.25 cubic inches per ounce
= factor

Step 4   10-inch pan volume = 3.14 × 5² × 1.5 = 118 cubic
inches. 118 cubic inches ÷ 5.25 (factor) = 22.5 oz
scaling weight

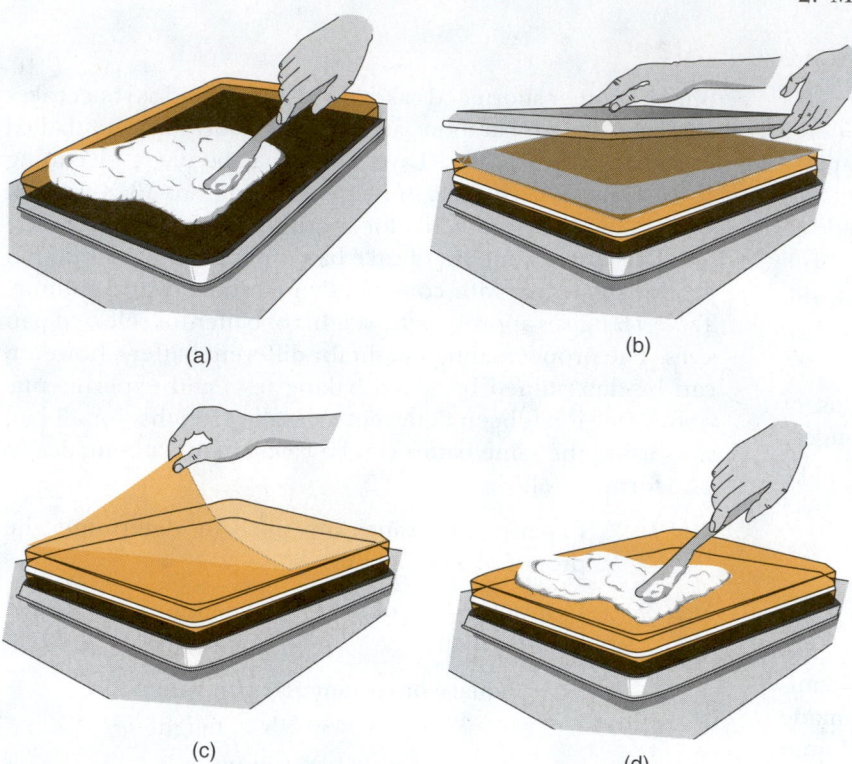

FIGURE 11.1   Layering and icing a sheet cake. (a) Remove sheet
cake from pan after loosening sides. Place top side down on inverted
baking sheet. Spread icing evenly over cake. (b) Carefully turn second
cake onto iced layer. (c) Remove cake liner if used. (d) Ice top and
sides of cake.

BAKING

Cake structure is fragile, so proper baking conditions are essential for quality products. The following are guidelines for producing quality cakes.

1. Preheat the oven.
2. Make sure the oven and shelves are level.
3. Make sure the batter is level in the pan and the pan is filled in the corners.
4. Do not let pans touch each other in the oven. If pans touch, air circulation is inhibited and the cakes rise unevenly.
5. Bake at the correct temperature. A too-high temperature can cause tunneling, a cracked top crust, or excessively high peaks. A too-low oven temperature can cause a pale top crust, a sticky top crust, or low volume.
6. Do not open ovens or disturb cakes until they have finished rising and are partially browned. In a convection oven, sheet cakes should be turned halfway through the baking time to ensure uniform baking and symmetry.
7. Test for doneness. Cakes are fully baked when the cake center springs back when touched lightly. A cake tester inserted near the center of the cake will come out clean. Shortened cakes will shrink away from the sides of the pan slightly.

Cooling and Removing from Pans

1. Cool butter layer cakes 10–15 minutes before removing from pans. Cool cakes completely before icing.
2. Sheet cakes may be left in the pans and iced when cool or removed from the pan and layered (Figure 11.1).

Pan size	Approximate weight per pan	Yield	Type of cake
12 × 18 × 2 inches	4–5 lb	30 portions (5 × 6)	Butter, sheet
		32 portions (4 × 8)	
13 × 18 × 1 inches (half-size baking sheet)	2–2½ lb	48 portions (6 × 8)	Butter, layer
18 × 26 × 2 inches	8–10 lb	60 portions (6 × 10)	Butter, sheet
		64 portions (8 × 8)	
8-inch round	16–20 oz per layer	16 portions (2 layers)	Butter, layer
9-inch round	20–24 oz per layer	16 portions (2 layers)	Butter, layer
10-inch tube	28–40 oz	14–16 portions	Foam, sponge
Cupcakes	1¾ oz each		Butter

TABLE 11.1   Approximate scaling weights and yields for cakes

Note   • See p. 285 for scaling weights for icings and fillings.

3. Invert pans of angel food cakes or sponge cakes and cool completely. Be sure the edges of the pan are supported so that the top of the cake does not rest on the table. When cool, loosen the cake from the sides of the pan with a spatula or knife and pull out carefully.

ICINGS AND FILLINGS

The presentation of cakes may be varied by the use of different icings and fillings. The amount to use will depend on the kind of cake to be iced and the individual preference of the patrons. Table 11.2 may serve as a guide. Sheet cakes usually are iced in their baking pans. Layered sheet cakes should be removed from the pans before icing (Figure 11.1). If possible, cakes should be iced as soon as they have cooled to help prevent drying. If un-iced cakes will not be used within a short time, they should be covered and kept in a closed cabinet or freezer. To freeze cakes, cover with plastic wrap or put in an airtight container. It is best to freeze cakes un-iced. Figure 11.2 suggests cutting configurations for cakes.

Cookies

Cookies are made in a variety of shapes, sizes, and textures. They may be crisp, soft, or chewy, depending on the proportion of ingredients, the method of mixing, and the baking time and temperature.

PROPORTION OF INGREDIENTS

Crisp cookies generally have a low proportion of liquid and a high sugar and fat content. Soft cookies have a high proportion of liquid and are lower in fat and sugar. Chewy cookies have high sugar and liquid content but are low in fat and have a high proportion of eggs. Some cookies are best when the dough spreads some during baking, while others must hold their shape. A high sugar or liquid content may increase cookie spread during baking.

METHODS OF MIXING

Most cookies are prepared by one of the following methods:

Creaming method—Cream shortening, sugar, and flavorings at low speed until blended. The amount of creaming can affect the texture of the cookies. A short creaming time is used for a chewy cookie; for a cookie with cakelike texture, the shortening and sugar are creamed until light and fluffy. The amount of creaming may also affect the spread of the cookie while it is baking. After the creaming is completed, blend in the eggs and liquid, then the flour and leavening. Mix the dough only until ingredients are combined.

TABLE 11.2	Approximate scaling weights for icings and fillings
Pan size	**Approximate weight per pan**
13 × 18 × 2 inch	1 lb 8 oz (3 cups)
18 × 26 × 2 inch	3 lb (1½ qt)
9-inch layer	1 lb (2 cups)
	⅔ cup in the middle
	1¼ cups top and sides
10-inch tube	12 oz (1¼ cups)

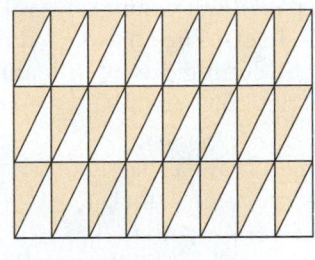

(a)   (b)

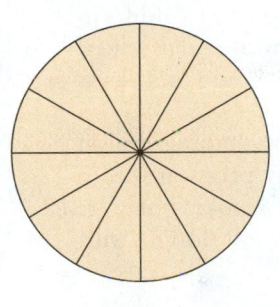
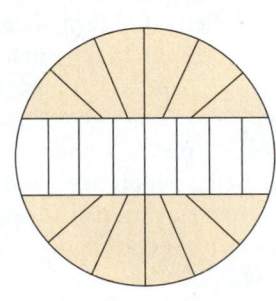

(c)   (d)

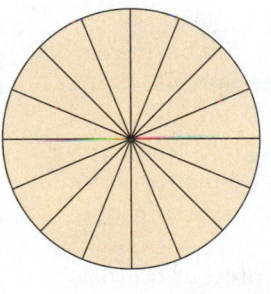
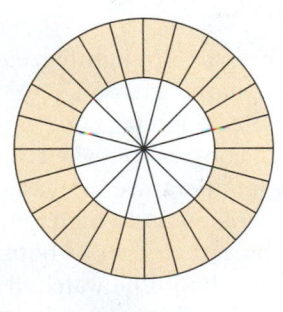

(e)   (f)

FIGURE 11.2   Suggested cutting configurations for cakes. (a) 18 × 26-inch baking sheet, 48 portions; (b) 18 × 26-inch baking sheet, 50 portions; (c) 8- to 12-inch round, 12 portions; (d) 10- to 12-inch round, 20 portions; (e) 8- to 12-inch round, 16 portions; (f) 10- to 12-inch round, 36 portions.

One-stage method—Place all ingredients in the mixer and mix at low speed until blended.

Sponge method—Beat eggs (whites, yolks, or whole) until light. Add the remaining ingredients and blend, being careful not to overmix or deflate the eggs.

SHAPING

Drop cookies are made from a soft dough, which is portioned onto prepared baking sheets with a dipper. A No. 40 dipper, which was used for most of the recipes in this book, makes a medium-size cookie, approximately 2½–3 inches in diameter and weighing about ¾ oz. Larger cookies may be made by using a No. 20 or No. 30 dipper, while Nos. 60 or 70 make tea cookies. If using the recipe for larger or smaller cookies, the yield may need to be adjusted by using the procedure on p. 8.

Bar cookies are made from a soft dough or batter that is spread evenly on prepared baking pans. Most recipes in this section suggest using two 13 × 18 × 1-inch pans (half baking sheet) or one 18 × 26 × 1-inch pan (baking sheet). The 13 × 18-inch pan will yield 30 2½ × 3-inch bars by cutting 5 × 6. An 18 × 26-inch pan may be cut 6 × 10 to yield 60 bars 3 × 2½ inches or 8 × 12 for 96 cookies.

Rolled cookies are made from a stiff dough that has been chilled thoroughly. The dough is rolled out to ⅛-inch thickness on a lightly floured board and cut with a cookie cutter.

Refrigerator cookies are made by shaping dough into rolls of uniform size (1–2 inches in diameter) and chilling, then cutting into slices. Using a slicing machine ensures uniform thickness. The dough may be made into rolls, wrapped in waxed or parchment paper, refrigerated or frozen, and baked as needed.

Molded or pressed cookies are made by shaping dough into small balls, which are then flattened by pressing with a mold or other flat utensil dipped in sugar. Cookies may be shaped also with a cookie press or, if using a soft dough, with a pastry bag.

BAKING

Pans are prepared by lightly greasing or lining with baking pan liners. A heavily greased pan increases the spread of the cookie. Some high-fat cookies can be baked on ungreased pans. Most cookies are baked at a relatively high temperature. A too-low temperature increases spreading and may produce dry, pale cookies. A too-high temperature decreases spreading and may burn the edges or bottoms.

Cookies should be watched carefully to prevent overbaking or burning. To test for doneness, touch the center of the cookie lightly with a finger. If almost no imprint remains and the cookie is browned, it is done. Fudge-type bars will be done when the top has a dull crust; cake like bars are done when a pick inserted in the center comes out clean. Soft cookies should be removed from the oven when they are still soft to the touch.

In most cases, to prevent sticking, the cookies should be removed from pans while they are still warm. If baking pan liners are used, the cookies may be left on the pan to cool. Very soft cookies, however, should not be removed until they are cool and firm enough to handle. Cookies should be completely cooled before storing.

STORING

Proper storage is important to maintain the quality and freshness of cookies. Crisp cookies may become soft if they absorb moisture, so they should be stored loosely covered away from moisture. Soft cookies should be stored tightly covered because they will become dry if allowed to lose moisture. All cookies are best if served soon after baking.

Pies

A good pie has a tender crust that cuts easily and a filling that will hold its shape when cut. Pie crust is an uncomplicated mixture, consisting of four ingredients: flour, shortening, water, and salt. The quality of the crust depends on the mixing technique as well as the type and proportion of ingredients.

INGREDIENTS

Tenderness depends largely on the kind of flour, the amount of fat and water used, and the amount of mixing. Choice of flour is important in pastry making. Gluten is developed from the protein present in wheat flours and gives structure and strength to baked goods. Pastry flour, which is made from soft wheat, has enough protein to produce the desired structure and flakiness, yet is low enough in protein to yield a tender product if handled properly. All-purpose flour, which is a blend of soft and hard wheats, contains enough protein to provide the gluten essential to make good pastry and is the type of flour used in recipes in this book.

Regular hydrogenated shortening is the fat used most often for pie crusts because it has the right plasticity to produce a flaky crust. It is firm and moldable enough to make a workable dough. The tenderness of pastry increases with the proportion of fat, but excess fat may cause the crust to be too tender to remove from the pan. Shortening should be cool when added to the flour. If it is warm, it blends too quickly with the flour.

Addition of a liquid, generally water, develops some gluten in the flour and gives structure and flakiness to the dough. Excess water gives a less tender product, but if not enough water is used, the crust will not hold together. The water should be cold (35–40°F) when added to the flour/fat mixture.

Salt, which is added mainly for flavor, is dissolved in the water before adding to the mix in order to ensure even distribution.

MIXING

Pastry is mixed by cutting the fat into the flour, then adding water and salt. The type of crust produced is partially determined by the method of combining the fat and flour. For a **flaky** crust, the fat and flour are mixed until small lumps are formed throughout the mixture. A **mealy** crust results when the fat and flour are thoroughly mixed until the mixture resembles cornmeal. Overmixing after the water has been added or using too much flour when rolling toughens pastry.

Pie dough should be kept cool during mixing and makeup. Chilling the dough for several hours, or until 50–60°F, allows the water to become distributed better throughout the dough and hardens the shortening so that it is less likely to soften during handling and shaping operations.

A pie crust mix, made by cutting the fat into the flour and salt mixture, may be stored in the refrigerator for 4–6 weeks and used as needed by adding water to make fresh pie crusts. If freezer storage is adequate, crusts may be made and frozen unbaked until needed.

Other Desserts

Although cakes, cookies, and pies remain popular, today's foodservices offer a wide variety of other desserts, such as fruit cobblers and crisps, cheesecake, frozen yogurt and ice cream, and fresh fruits in a variety of presentations. Recipes for many of these desserts are included in this section, as are the time-tested custards and other puddings, gelatin desserts, and refrigerator desserts used in many foodservices.

Basic custard consists of milk, sugar, eggs, and flavoring and may be of two types. Soft or stirred custard is cooked slowly over low heat, while stirring, until it is slightly thickened. It remains pourable when cooked. Baked custard, which is not stirred, is baked until it sets and becomes firm. Custards should be cooked to an internal temperature of 181–185°F. If heated beyond this point, the custard may curdle and become watery. Cooking baked custards in a water bath, in which the custard cups or baking pan are placed in a pan of hot water, helps prevent curdling.

Cream puddings contain starch thickeners and eggs, resulting in a thicker, more stable product. The thickener may be cornstarch, flour, tapioca, or a cereal product. These desserts require sweetening, usually sugar. Too much sugar interferes with the thickening of the eggs and the starch; therefore, a properly balanced formula is important. To make a cream pudding, the milk is added slowly to the combined dry ingredients, while stirring with a wire whip. The mixture is stirred occasionally and cooked until thickened in a steam-jacketed or other kettle over low heat to prevent scorching. The method of adding the eggs is also important to a smooth pudding. To avoid curdling when the eggs are added, a small amount of the hot mixture is first added to the beaten eggs, and then this mixture is stirred into the rest of the pudding. Cream puddings should be smooth and creamy.

Gelatin desserts, usually in the form of a fruit gelatin or Bavarian cream, are served as dessert choices in many institutions. A basic recipe for Fruit Gelatin Salad on p. 614 gives proportions for gelatin and fruit and instructions for preparing gelatin mixtures. Bavarian cream has whipped cream folded in.

Fruit offers a wide range of dessert possibilities and may be served fresh, poached, baked, as a sauce, or combined with other ingredients to make a baked dessert such as strawberry shortcake, fruit cobbler, or fruit crisp. A fresh-fruit and cheese plate, with in-season fresh fruit and cheese attractively displayed, is a popular dessert. Suggestions for a fruit and cheese dessert are given on p. 381.

Cake Recipes

COATING FOR BAKING PANS

Yield: 2 lb 12 oz

Ingredient	Amount	Procedure
Shortening	1 lb	Mix shortening until creamy.
Flour, all-purpose	12 oz	Add flour gradually, whipping until smooth. Start on low mixer speed, then move to medium.
Vegetable oil	2 cups	Add oil very slowly and whip until light and frothy. Store at room temperature in tightly closed containers. Apply to pans with pastry brush. Use to grease cake pans or cookie sheets.

ANGEL FOOD CAKE

Yield: 42 portions or three 10-inch cakes   *Portion:* 14 slices per cake
Oven: 350°F   *Bake:* 50–55 minutes

Ingredient	Amount	Procedure
Egg whites, fresh or frozen	2 lb 8 oz (5 cups)	Beat egg whites on high speed for 1 minute, using the whip attachment. Be sure utensils are free from grease.
Salt Cream of tartar	1 tsp 2 Tbsp	Add salt and cream of tartar. Continue beating until egg whites are just stiff enough to hold their shape.
Sugar, granulated	1 lb 8 oz	Add sugar slowly while beating on medium speed.
Vanilla Almond extract (optional)	1 Tbsp 1 tsp	Add flavorings. Continue beating on high speed for 2 minutes, or until mixture will stand in stiff peaks.
Sugar, granulated Flour, cake	12 oz 12 oz	Mix sugar and flour. Sift three times. Gradually add to egg whites on low speed. Continue folding for 2 minutes after last addition. Scale into three ungreased tube cake pans, 1 lb 12 oz per pan. Bake at 350°F for 50–55 minutes or at 400°F for 35 minutes. Invert cakes to cool. Cool completely before removing from pan. Run a long thin knife around edges and tube before removing cake from pan.

Approximate nutritive values per portion

Calories	Carbohydrate	Protein	Fat	Cholesterol	Sodium	Fiber	Iron
138 kcal	31 g	4 g	0 g	0 mg	96 mg	0 g	0.5 mg

Note

- To add sugar-flour mixture by hand, remove bowl from machine and fold mixture into meringue, using wire whip or spatula, adding 1 cup at a time. Mix about five strokes after each addition.

Variations

- **Chocolate Angel Food Cake.** Substitute 1½ oz cocoa for 1½ oz flour.
- **Frozen-Filled Angel Food Cake.** Cut each cake crosswise into three slices. Spread 1 pt softened strawberry ice cream on first layer and cover with cake slice. Spread second slice with 1 pt softened pistachio ice cream. Top with remaining slice. Frost top and sides with sweetened whipped cream (1 cup cream, 2 Tbsp powdered sugar, and ½ tsp vanilla per cake). Cover with toasted coconut. Freeze. Remove from freezer 1 hour before serving. Other ice cream or sherbet may be used.
- **Orange-Filled Angel Food Cake.** Cut each cake crosswise into three slices. Spread Orange Filling (p. 319) between layers, and ice top and sides with Orange Butter Icing (p. 313).

YELLOW ANGEL FOOD (SPONGE) CAKE

Yield: 42 portions or three 10-inch cakes   *Portion:* 14 slices per cake
Oven: 350°F   *Bake:* 30–45 minutes

Ingredient	Amount	Procedure
Egg yolks	1 lb 8 oz (3 cups)	Beat egg yolks on medium speed, using the whip attachment.
Water, boiling	2 cups	Add water to egg yolks. Beat on high speed until light, about 5 minutes.
Sugar, granulated	1 lb	Sift sugar. Add to egg mixture gradually, beating on high speed while adding.
Flour, cake Sugar, granulated	12 oz 12 oz	Combine flour and sugar. Add on low speed to egg mixture.
Flour, cake Baking powder Salt	10 oz $4\frac{1}{2}$ tsp 1 tsp	Mix flour, baking powder, and salt.
Fresh lemon juice Lemon peel, grated	3 Tbsp 1 Tbsp	On low speed, gradually add flour alternately with lemon juice and peel to egg mixture.
Vanilla Lemon extract	1 Tbsp $1\frac{1}{2}$ tsp	Add flavoring and continue mixing on low speed for 2 minutes.
		Scale into three ungreased tube cake pans, 1 lb 14 oz per pan. Bake at 350°F for 30–45 minutes. Immediately upon removal from oven, invert cakes to cool. Cool completely before removing from pan. Run a long thin knife around edges and tube before removing cake from pan.

Approximate nutritive values per portion

Calories	Carbohydrate	Protein	Fat	Cholesterol	Sodium	Fiber	Iron
186 kcal	31 g	4 g	5 g	208 mg	90 mg	0 g	2 mg

ORANGE CHIFFON CAKE

Yield: 42 portions or three 10-inch cakes   *Portion:* 14 slices per cake
Oven: 350°F   *Bake:* 45–50 minutes

Ingredient	Amount	Procedure
Flour, cake	1 lb 8 oz	Combine dry ingredients in mixer bowl. Mix on low speed for about 10 seconds, or until blended, using a flat beater.
Baking powder	1½ oz (3 Tbsp)	
Salt	2 tsp	
Sugar, granulated	1 lb 3 oz	
Egg yolks, beaten	1 lb (2 cups)	Combine egg yolks, oil, and water.
Vegetable oil	1½ cups	Add to dry ingredients. Mix on medium speed until smooth.
Water	1½ cups	
Fresh orange juice	1 cup	Add orange juice and peel gradually. Mix well after each addition, but avoid overmixing.
Orange peel, grated	2 Tbsp	
Egg whites	1 lb 4 oz (2½ cups)	Whip egg whites until foamy. Add cream of tartar and continue beating until egg whites form soft peaks.
Cream of tartar	2 tsp	
Sugar, granulated	1 lb 2 oz	Add sugar gradually and continue beating until very stiff. Fold gently into batter. Scale into three ungreased tube cake pans, 2 lb 12 oz per pan. Bake at 350°F for 45–50 minutes. Immediately on removal from oven, invert cakes to cool.
Orange Butter Icing (p. 313)	1½ qt	When cake has cooled, remove from pan and ice. Cool completely before removing from pan. Run a long thin knife around edges and tube before removing cake from pan.

Approximate nutritive values per portion

Calories	Carbohydrate	Protein	Fat	Cholesterol	Sodium	Fiber	Iron
418 kcal	66 g	5 g	16 g	139 mg	268 mg	0 g	2 mg

Variations

- **Cocoa Chiffon Cake.** Omit orange juice and peel. Add 5 oz cocoa to dry ingredients. Increase water to 2⅓ cups. Add 1 Tbsp vanilla.
- **Walnut Chiffon Cake.** Omit orange juice and peel. Increase water to 2⅓ cups. Add 2 Tbsp vanilla and 12 oz finely chopped walnuts. Ice with Burnt Butter Icing (p. 310).

WHITE CAKE (DRY BLENDING METHOD)

Yield: 60 portions or 2 pans, 12 × 18 × 2 inches   *Portion:* 2½ × 3 inches
Oven: 350°F   *Bake:* 25–30 minutes

Ingredient	Amount	Procedure
Flour, cake	1 lb 13 oz	Combine dry ingredients in mixer bowl. Mix on low speed for 1 minute.
Sugar, granulated	2 lb 5 oz	
Nonfat dry milk	3 oz	
Salt	4 tsp	
Baking powder	1¾ oz	
Water	1¾ cups	Add water. Mix slightly.
Shortening	1 lb	Add shortening. Mix for 1 minute on low speed. Mix for 4 minutes on medium speed.
Water	½ cup	Add water. Mix for 1 minute on low speed. Scrape bowl. Mix for 3 minutes on medium speed. Scrape bowl and beater.
Egg whites	1 lb	Add eggs, water, and vanilla. Mix for 3 minutes on low speed.
Eggs	3 oz	
Water	1 cup	
Vanilla	2 Tbsp	
		Scale batter into two greased 12 × 18 × 2-inch pans, 4 lb per pan. Bake at 350°F for 25–30 minutes. Cool and frost.

Approximate nutritive values per portion

Calories	Carbohydrate	Protein	Fat	Cholesterol	Sodium	Fiber	Iron
132 kcal	12 g	3 g	8 g	6 mg	248 mg	0 g	1 mg

Note
- May be baked in one 18 × 26 × 2-inch pan. Cut 6 × 10 for 60 portions.

Variation
- See p. 292.

WHITE CAKE (DOUGH-BATTER METHOD)

Yield: 60 portions or 2 pans, 12 × 18 × 2 inches   *Portion:* 2½ × 3 inches
Oven: 350°F   *Bake:* 35–40 minutes

Ingredient	Amount	Procedure
Flour, cake	2 lb 4 oz	Place flour, baking powder, and shortening in mixer bowl.
Baking powder	1½ oz	Mix on low speed for 2 minutes, using a flat beater.
Shortening, hydrogenated	1 lb 2 oz	Scrape sides of bowl. Mix for 3 minutes.
Sugar, granulated	2 lb 4 oz	Combine sugar, salt, and milk. Add to flour mixture.
Salt	1 Tbsp	Mix on low speed for 2 minutes.
Milk	2 cups	Scrape sides of bowl. Mix for 3 minutes.
Egg whites	12 (14 oz)	Combine egg whites, milk, and vanilla.
Milk	1⅓ cups	Add half to mixture in bowl. Mix on low speed for 30 seconds.
Vanilla	2 Tbsp	Scrape sides of bowl. Mix for 1 minute.
		Add remaining egg-milk mixture. Mix on low speed for 1 minute.
		Scrape sides of bowl. Mix for 2½ minutes.
		Scale batter into two greased 12 × 18 × 2-inch pans, 5 lb 7 oz per pan.
		Bake at 350°F for 35–40 minutes.
		Cool and ice. Cut 5 × 6.

Approximate nutritive values per portion

Calories	Carbohydrate	Protein	Fat	Cholesterol	Sodium	Fiber	Iron
216 kcal	31 g	3 g	9 g	2 mg	196 mg	0 g	1 mg

Notes

- 3 oz nonfat dry milk and 3⅓ cups water may be substituted for fluid milk. Increase shortening to 1 lb 3 oz. Mix dry milk with flour.
- May be baked in one 18 × 26 × 2-inch pan. Cut 6 × 10 for 60 portions.
- For six 9-inch layer pans, scale 1 lb 6 oz per pan.

Variations

- **Chocolate Chip Cake.** Add 12 oz chocolate chips to batter.
- **Coconut Lime Cake.** Scale into six 9-inch layer cake pans. When baked, cool, then spread Lime Filling (p. 319) between layers. Ice with Ice Cream Icing (p. 311). Sprinkle with toasted flaked coconut.
- **Cupcakes.** Portion batter with No. 20 dipper into muffin pans or paper baking cups. Yield: 7 dozen.
- **Lady Baltimore Cake.** Bake cake in layers. Prepare one recipe Ice Cream Icing (p. 311). To 1½ qt icing, add 1 tsp orange juice, 4 oz macaroon crumbs, 5 oz chopped almonds, and 6 oz chopped raisins. Spread on bottom layers; place second layers on top and spread with filling. Ice tops and sides with remaining frosting.
- **Poppy Seed Cake.** Add 6 oz poppy seeds that have been soaked in part of the milk. Ice with Chocolate Butter Cream Icing (p. 311).
- **Silver White Cake.** Scale batter into six 9-inch layer cake pans. When baked, cool and then spread Lemon Filling (p. 318) between layers. Ice with Ice Cream Icing (p. 311).
- **Starburst Cake.** Bake in two 12 × 18 × 2-inch pans. While cake is warm, perforate top with a meat fork every half inch. Prepare 2 qt flavored gelatin, and while still liquid slowly pour 1 qt over each cake. Cool and ice with Ice Cream Icing (p. 311) or other white icing.

CARROT CAKE

Yield: 60 portions or 2 pans, 12 × 18 × 2 inches   *Portion:* 2½ × 3 inches
Oven: 325°F   *Bake:* 40–45 minutes

Ingredient	Amount	Procedure
Sugar, granulated	2 lb 6 oz	Combine sugar, oil, and eggs.
Vegetable oil	2½ cups	Beat for 2 minutes on medium speed, using a flat beater.
Eggs	9 (1 lb)	
Flour, all-purpose	1 lb 12 oz	Combine dry ingredients.
Salt	1 oz (1½ Tbsp)	Add to oil mixture and beat for 1 minute.
Baking soda	⅔ oz (5 tsp)	
Cinnamon, ground	⅔ oz (3 Tbsp)	
Carrots, raw, grated	2 lb 8 oz	Add carrots and nuts. Mix until blended.
Nuts, chopped	1 lb	
		Scale batter into two greased 12 × 18 × 2-inch pans, 5 lb per pan.
		Bake at 325°F for 40–45 minutes.
		Ice with Cream Cheese Icing (p. 312).
		Cut 5 × 6.

Approximate nutritive values per portion

Calories	Carbohydrate	Protein	Fat	Cholesterol	Sodium	Fiber	Iron
263 kcal	32 g	4 g	14 g	32 mg	282 mg	2 g	1 mg

Note

- May be baked in one 18 × 26 × 2-inch pan cut 6 × 10 for 60 portions.

YELLOW CAKE

Yield: 60 portions or 2 pans, 12 × 18 × 2 inches   *Portion:* $2\frac{1}{2}$ × 3 inches
Oven: 350°F   *Bake:* 35–40 minutes

Ingredient	Amount	Procedure
Flour, cake	2 lb 5 oz	Place flour, baking powder, and shortening in mixer bowl.
Baking powder	$3\frac{3}{4}$ Tbsp	Mix on low speed for 2 minutes, using a flat beater.
Shortening, hydrogenated	1 lb	Scrape sides of bowl. Mix for 3 minutes.
Sugar, granulated	2 lb 13 oz	Combine sugar, salt, and milk. Add to flour mixture.
Salt	2 tsp	Mix on low speed for 2 minutes.
Milk	2 cups	Scrape sides of bowl. Mix for 3 minutes.
Eggs	8 (14 oz)	Combine eggs, milk, and vanilla.
Milk	$2\frac{1}{2}$ cups	Add half to flour mixture. Mix on low speed for 30 seconds.
Vanilla	2 Tbsp	Scrape sides of bowl. Mix for 1 minute.
		Add remaining egg mixture. Mix for 1 minute.
		Scrape sides of bowl. Mix for $2\frac{1}{2}$ minutes.
		Scale batter into two greased 12 × 18 × 2-inch baking pans, 4 lb 10 oz per pan. Bake at 350°F for 35–40 minutes. Cut 5 × 6.

Approximate nutritive values per portion

Calories	Carbohydrate	Protein	Fat	Cholesterol	Sodium	Fiber	Iron
232 kcal	36 g	3 g	9 g	29 mg	90 mg	0 g	1 mg

Notes

- 4 oz nonfat dry milk and $4\frac{1}{2}$ cups water may be substituted for fluid milk. Add dry milk to flour mixture. Divide water as stated in recipe.
- May be baked in one 18 × 26 × 2-inch pan. Cut 6 × 10 for 60 portions.
- For layer cakes, scale 1 lb 9 oz batter into each of six 9-inch layer cake pans.
- For cupcakes, portion with No. 30 dipper into muffin pan. Yield: $8\frac{1}{2}$ dozen.

Variations

- **Boston Cream Pie.** For two 12 × 18-inch pies, scale batter into four pans, 2 lb 5 oz each. When baked, spread Custard Filling (p. 318) on two cakes, 3 lb 3 oz each. Place other cakes on top. Cover with Chocolate Glaze (p. 315), 1 lb per cake. Cut 5 × 6.

  For two 18 × 26-inch pies, scale 4 lb 10 oz into each of two pans. Use 6 lb 6 oz Custard Filling and 2 lb Chocolate Glaze. Cut 6 × 10.

  For 9-inch layers, scale batter into eight pans, 1 lb 2 oz per pan. Use $\frac{1}{2}$ recipe Custard Filling. Spread $1\frac{1}{2}$ cups on each of four layers. Use $\frac{1}{2}$ recipe Chocolate Glaze, spreading $\frac{1}{2}$ cup on each pie.

  Powdered sugar sifted over top of pies may be substituted for Chocolate Glaze.
- **Cottage Pudding.** Cut cake into squares and serve with No. 20 dipper of fruit, lemon, nutmeg, or other sauce.
- **Dutch Apple Cake.** After the cake batter is poured into baking pans, arrange 2 lb 8 oz peeled sliced apples in rows over each pan. Sprinkle over top of each pan 4 oz granulated sugar and 1 tsp cinnamon, mixed.
- **Lazy Daisy Cake.** Mix 1 lb 2 oz melted margarine or butter, 2 lb brown sugar, 2 lb coconut, and $1\frac{1}{2}$ cups half-and-half, or enough to moisten to consistency for spreading. Spread over baked cake, 3 lb per pan, and brown under the broiler or in the oven.
- **Marble Cake.** Divide batter into two portions after mixing. To one portion add 3 Tbsp cocoa, 1 Tbsp cinnamon, and 1 tsp nutmeg. Place batters alternately in cake pans; swirl with knife.
- **Pineapple Upside-Down Cake.** Mix one No. 10 can drained crushed pineapple (or tidbits), 8 oz melted margarine or butter, 12 oz brown sugar, and 8 oz chopped nuts. Pour 4 lb 3 oz in each 12 × 18-inch baking pan. Pour cake batter over mixture. Apricots or peaches may be substituted for pineapple.
- **Praline Cake.** Substitute chopped pecans for coconut in Lazy Daisy Cake.

APPLESAUCE CAKE

Yield: 60 portions or 2 pans, 12 × 18 × 2 inches   *Portion:* 2½ × 3 inches
Oven: 350°F   *Bake:* 40–45 minutes

Ingredient	Amount	Procedure
Shortening, hydrogenated	1 lb	Cream shortening and sugar on medium speed for 10 minutes, using a flat beater.
Sugar, granulated	1 lb 14 oz	
Eggs	8 (14 oz)	Add eggs to creamed mixture. Mix on medium speed for 5 minutes.
Flour, cake	1 lb 12 oz	Combine dry ingredients.
Baking powder	2½ Tbsp	
Salt	1¾ tsp	
Baking soda	½ tsp	
Cinnamon, ground	2½ tsp	
Cloves, ground	1 tsp	
Nutmeg, ground	1 tsp	
Water	2½ cups	Add dry ingredients alternately with water on low speed to creamed mixture, ending with dry ingredients.
Applesauce	2½ cups	Add remaining ingredients.
Raisins	1 lb 4 oz	Mix on low speed only to blend.
Nuts, chopped	10 oz	
		Scale batter into two greased 12 × 18 × 2-inch baking pans, 5 lb per pan. Bake at 350°F for 40–45 minutes. Cool and ice. See Note for suggested icings. Cut 5 × 6.

Approximate nutritive values per portion

Calories	Carbohydrate	Protein	Fat	Cholesterol	Sodium	Fiber	Iron
245 kcal	35 g	3 g	11 g	28 mg	120 mg	1 g	1 mg

Notes

- May be baked in one 18 × 26 × 2-inch pan. Cut 6 × 10 for 60 portions.
- This cake is too tender to bake in layers.
- Suggested icings: Ice Cream Icing (p. 311) or Cream Cheese Icing (p. 312).

BANANA CAKE

Yield: 48 portions or three 2-layer cakes (9 inch)   *Portion:* 16 slices per cake
Oven: 350°F   *Bake:* 25–30 minutes

Ingredient	Amount	Procedure
Shortening, hydrogenated	1 lb	Cream shortening, sugar, and vanilla on medium speed for 10 minutes, using a flat beater.
Sugar, granulated	2 lb	
Vanilla	1 Tbsp	
Eggs	8 (14 oz)	Add eggs to creamed mixture and mix on medium speed for 3 minutes, then add bananas and mix for an additional 2 minutes.
Bananas, mashed	2 lb (4 cups)	
Flour, cake	2 lb	Combine dry ingredients.
Salt	1¼ tsp	
Baking powder	3⅓ Tbsp	
Baking soda	2 tsp	
Buttermilk	1 cup	Add dry ingredients alternately with buttermilk on low speed. Mix on medium speed for 2–3 minutes.
		Scale batter into six greased 9-inch layer cake pans, 1 lb 6 oz per pan. Bake at 350°F for 25–30 minutes. Cool. Remove from pans and ice. See Note for suggested icings.

Approximate nutritive values per portion

Calories	Carbohydrate	Protein	Fat	Cholesterol	Sodium	Fiber	Iron
254 kcal	39 g	3 g	11 g	35 mg	185 mg	1 g	1 mg

Notes

- May be baked in two 12 × 18 × 2-inch pans, scaled 4 lb 3 oz per pan. Cut 5 × 6 for 30 portions per pan.
- For sheet cake, bake in one 18 × 26 × 2-inch pan. Cut 6 × 10 for 60 portions.
- Suggested icings: Creamy Icing (p. 313) or Cream Cheese Icing (p. 312).

BURNT SUGAR CAKE

Yield: 60 portions or 2 pans, 12 × 18 × 2 inches   *Portion:* 2½ × 3 inches
Oven: 375°F   *Bake:* 35–40 minutes

Ingredient	Amount	Procedure
Sugar, granulated Shortening, hydrogenated	2 lb 11 oz 1 lb	Cream shortening and sugar on medium speed for 10 minutes, using a flat beater.
Egg yolks	8 (5 oz)	Add egg yolks to creamed mixture and mix on medium speed for 5 minutes.
Milk Water Burnt sugar syrup (see Note) Vanilla	2 cups 2 cups ⅔ cup 4 tsp	Combine liquids.
Flour, cake Baking powder Salt	2 lb 2 oz 2⅔ Tbsp 1¼ tsp	Combine dry ingredients. On low speed, add to creamed mixture alternately with liquids. Scrape sides of bowl. Mix for 2 minutes.
Egg whites	8 (9 oz)	Beat egg whites until they form soft peaks. Fold into batter on low speed.
		Scale batter into two greased 12 × 18 × 2-inch baking pans, 4 lb 8 oz per pan. Bake at 375°F for 35–40 minutes. Cool and ice. See Note for suggested icings. Cut 5 × 6.

Approximate nutritive values per portion

Calories	Carbohydrate	Protein	Fat	Cholesterol	Sodium	Fiber	Iron
232 kcal	36 g	2 g	9 g	31 mg	98 mg	0.4 g	1 mg

Notes

- **Burnt Sugar Syrup.** Place ⅓ cup granulated sugar in pan and melt slowly, stirring constantly. Cook until light brown (caramelized), being careful not to scorch. Add ⅓ cup boiling water. Cook slowly until a syrup is formed. For larger amounts, use 1 lb sugar and 2 cups boiling water.
- May be baked in one 18 × 26 × 2-inch pan cut 6 × 10; or in eight 9-inch layers, scaled 1 lb 2 oz per pan.
- Suggested icings: Burnt Butter Icing (p. 310), Creamy Icing (p. 313), Cream Cheese Icing (p. 312), or Ice Cream Icing (p. 311).

CHOCOLATE CAKE

Yield: 60 portions or 2 pans, 12 × 18 × 2 inches   *Portion:* 2½ × 3 inches
Oven: 350°F   *Bake:* 25–30 minutes

Ingredient	Amount	Procedure
Flour, cake	1 lb 8 oz	Combine dry ingredients in mixer bowl.
Cocoa	5 oz	Mix on low speed for 1 minute, using a flat beater.
Sugar, granulated	2 lb 5 oz	
Nonfat dry milk	2½ oz	
Salt	1 Tbsp	
Baking powder	1 oz	
Baking soda	3½ tsp	
Water	1½ cups	Add to dry ingredients.
Shortening	1 lb	Mix on low speed for 1 minute.
		Mix on medium speed for 3 minutes.
		Scrape sides of bowl and beater.
Water	1½ cups	Add and mix on low speed for 1 minute.
		Mix on medium speed for 2 minutes.
Eggs	10 (1 lb 2 oz)	Blend in eggs. Mix on low speed for 2 minutes.
Water	1 cup	
Vanilla	¼ cup	
		Scale batter into two greased 12 × 18 × 2-inch baking pans, 4 lb 2 oz per pan.
		Bake at 350°F for 25–30 minutes.
		Cool and ice. See Note for suggested icings.
		Cut 5 × 6.

Approximate nutritive values per portion

Calories	Carbohydrate	Protein	Fat	Cholesterol	Sodium	Fiber	Iron
200 kcal	29 g	3 g	9 g	36 mg	247 mg	0.3 g	2 mg

Notes

- Cake may be baked in one 18 × 26 × 2-inch pan. Cut 6 × 10 for 60 servings.
- Suggested icings: Chocolate Butter Cream Icing (p. 311), Mocha Icing (p. 315), or Ice Cream Icing (p. 311).

FUDGE CAKE

Yield: 48 portions or three 2-layer cakes (9 inch)   *Portion:* 16 slices per cake
Oven: 350°F   *Bake:* 25–30 minutes

Ingredient	Amount	Procedure
Shortening, hydrogenated	12 oz	Cream shortening, sugar, and vanilla on medium speed for 10 minutes, using a flat beater.
Sugar, granulated	2 lb	
Vanilla	1 Tbsp	
Eggs	6 (10 oz)	Add eggs and mix on medium speed for 5 minutes.
Cocoa	5 oz	Mix cocoa and hot water.
Water, hot	1½ cups	
Flour, cake	1 lb 12 oz	Combine flour, salt, and soda.
Salt	1 tsp	
Baking soda	1½ Tbsp	
Buttermilk	3 cups	Add dry ingredients alternately with buttermilk and cocoa to creamed mixture on low speed. Scrape sides of bowl and beater. Continue mixing until smooth and ingredients are mixed.
		Scale batter into six greased 9-inch layer cake pans, 1 lb 4 oz per pan. Bake at 350°F for 25–30 minutes. Cool. Remove from pans and ice. See Note for suggested icings.

Approximate nutritive values per portion

Calories	Carbohydrate	Protein	Fat	Cholesterol	Sodium	Fiber	Iron
217 kcal	34 g	3 g	8 g	26 mg	189 mg	0.4 g	2 mg

Notes

- For a 12 × 18-inch layer cake, scale into two 12 × 18 × 2-inch or two 13 × 18 × 1-inch pans, 3 lb 13 oz per pan. When baked and cooled, ice one cake, then remove cake from pan and place on top (see Figure 11.1). Ice top and sides.
- Suggested icings: Chocolate Butter Cream Icing (p. 311), Ice Cream Icing (p. 311), or Mocha Icing (p. 315).

Variations

- **Chocolate Cupcakes.** Portion with No. 20 dipper into muffin pans or paper liners. Yield: 5 dozen.
- **Chocolate Sheet Cake.** Bake in one 18 × 26 × 2-inch baking pan. Cut 6 × 10 for 60 portions.

GERMAN SWEET CHOCOLATE CAKE

Yield: 60 portions or 2 pans, 12 × 18 × 2 inches   *Portion:* 2½ × 3 inches
Oven: 350°F   *Bake:* 40–45 minutes

Ingredient	Amount	Procedure
German sweet chocolate	10 oz	Melt chocolate in water. Cool.
Water, boiling	1¼ cups	Add vanilla. Set aside.
Vanilla	2½ tsp	
Shortening, hydrogenated	1 lb 4 oz	Cream shortening and sugar on medium speed for 10 minutes, using a flat beater.
Sugar, granulated	2 lb 8 oz	
Egg yolks	10 (6 oz)	Add egg yolks one at a time. Beat well after each addition. Add chocolate mixture and blend.
Flour, cake	1 lb 9 oz	Combine flour, salt, and soda.
Salt	1¼ tsp	
Baking soda	2½ tsp	
Buttermilk	2½ cups	Add dry ingredients alternately with buttermilk to creamed mixture. Mix on low speed until smooth. Scrape sides of bowl.
Egg whites	10 (11 oz)	Beat egg whites until stiff peaks form. Fold into batter on low speed. Do not overmix. Scale batter into two greased 12 × 18 × 2-inch baking pans, 4 lb 7 oz per pan. Bake at 350°F for 40–45 minutes.
Coconut Pecan Icing (p. 312)	2 qt	When cool, ice with Coconut Pecan Icing. Cut 5 × 6.

Approximate nutritive values per portion

Calories	Carbohydrate	Protein	Fat	Cholesterol	Sodium	Fiber	Iron
378 kcal	43 g	4 g	22 g	63 mg	165 mg	1 g	1 mg

Notes

- May be baked in one 18 × 26 × 2-inch pan. Cut 6 × 10 for 60 portions.
- For four 2-layer cakes, scale into eight 9-inch layer cake pans, 1 lb 1 oz per pan. Cut 16 slices per cake for 64 portions.

PEANUT BUTTER CAKE

Yield: 60 portions or 1 pan, 18 × 26 × 2 inches　　　*Portion:* 2½ × 3 inches
Oven: 350°F　　*Bake:* 30–35 minutes

Ingredient	Amount	Procedure
Margarine	9 oz	Cream margarine, peanut butter, and sugar for 15 minutes, using a flat beater. Scrape bottom and sides of bowl after each 5 minutes.
Peanut butter, creamy	12 oz	
Sugar, granulated	2 lb 2 oz	
Eggs	5 (8 oz)	Add to creamed mixture.
Vanilla	2 Tbsp	
Flour, all-purpose	1 lb 12 oz	Combine flour, baking powder, and soda.
Baking powder	½ oz (3½ tsp)	
Baking soda	1 oz (2⅓ Tbsp)	
Buttermilk	4⅔ cups	Add dry ingredients and buttermilk alternately to creamed mixture. Scrape bottom and sides of bowl after each addition. Scale 8 lb batter into one 18 × 26 × 2-inch baking pan. Bake at 350°F for 30–35 minutes or until cake springs back when lightly depressed in the center.
Peanut Butter Icing (p. 314)	2 qt	Ice with Peanut Butter Icing.

Approximate nutritive values per portion

Calories	Carbohydrate	Protein	Fat	Cholesterol	Sodium	Fiber	Iron
333 kcal	52 g	4 g	13 g	17 mg	257 mg	1 g	1 mg

Notes

- ½ oz (1 Tbsp) caramel food color may be added for a darker color.
- May be baked in two 12 × 18 × 2-inch pans. Scale 4 lb batter per pan.

PINEAPPLE CASHEW CAKE

Yield: 48 portions or three 2-layer cakes (9 inch)   *Portion:* 16 slices per cake
Oven: 350°F   *Bake:* 25–30 minutes

Ingredient	Amount	Procedure
Margarine or butter	1 lb 2 oz	Cream margarine, sugar, and vanilla on medium speed for 10 minutes, using a flat beater.
Sugar, granulated	1 lb 14 oz	
Vanilla	1 Tbsp	
Egg yolks	10 (6 oz)	Add egg yolks in three portions, while creaming. Mix for 2 minutes.
Flour, cake	1 lb 14 oz	Combine flour, baking powder, and salt.
Baking powder	1½ oz	
Salt	1½ tsp	
Milk	2¼ cups	Add dry ingredients alternately with milk on low speed to creamed mixture.
Crushed pineapple, drained	1 lb	Add pineapple to batter. Mix on low speed only to blend.
Egg whites	10 (11 oz)	Beat egg whites on high speed until stiff but not dry. Fold into batter on low speed. Scale batter into six greased 9-inch layer cake pans, 1 lb 5 oz per pan. Bake at 350°F for 25–30 minutes.
Pineapple Icing (p. 314)	2 qt	When cool, remove cake from pans. Cover with Pineapple Icing and sprinkle with toasted cashews.
Cashew nuts, toasted, coarsely chopped	8 oz	

Approximate nutritive values per portion

Calories	Carbohydrate	Protein	Fat	Cholesterol	Sodium	Fiber	Iron
517 kcal	73 g	5 g	24 g	56 mg	450 mg	1 g	2 mg

Note

- May be baked in one 18 × 26 × 2-inch pan, cut 6 × 10 for 60 portions, or in two 12 × 18 × 2-inch pans, scaled 4 lb per pan, and cut 5 × 6 for 30 portions per pan.

GINGERBREAD

Yield: 60 portions or 2 pans, 12 × 18 × 2 inches   *Portion:* 2½ × 3 inches
Oven: 350°F   *Bake:* 40 minutes

Ingredient	Amount	Procedure
Shortening, hydrogenated	14 oz	Cream shortening and sugar on medium speed for 10 minutes, using a flat beater.
Sugar, granulated	14 oz	
Molasses	3½ cups	Add molasses and mix on low speed until blended.
Flour, cake	2 lb 4 oz	Combine dry ingredients.
Baking soda	2 Tbsp	
Salt	1½ tsp	
Cinnamon, ground	1 Tbsp	
Cloves, ground	1 Tbsp	
Ginger, ground	1 Tbsp	
Water, hot	3¾ cups	Add dry ingredients alternately with water to creamed mixture.
Eggs, beaten	7 (12 oz)	Add eggs and mix on low speed for 2 minutes. Scale batter into two greased 12 × 18 × 2-inch baking pans, 4 lb 3 oz per pan. Bake at 350°F for 40 minutes. Sprinkle with powdered sugar and serve warm or serve with Lemon Sauce (p. 716). Cut 5 × 6.

Approximate nutritive values per portion

Calories	Carbohydrate	Protein	Fat	Cholesterol	Sodium	Fiber	Iron
202 kcal	32 g	2 g	7 g	24 mg	190 mg	0.4 g	2 mg

Note

- May be baked in one 18 × 26 × 2-inch pan. Cut 6 × 10 for 60 portions.

Variations

- **Almond Meringue Gingerbread.** Cover baked Gingerbread with Meringue for pies (p. 344). Sprinkle with slivered or chopped almonds and brown in a 375°F oven.
- **Ginger Muffins.** Measure into greased muffin pans with No. 20 dipper. Yield: 7 dozen.
- **Praline Gingerbread.** Combine 1 lb melted margarine or butter, 2 lb brown sugar, 2 lb chopped pecans, and 1½–2 cups cream. Spread 2 lb 12 oz mixture over each pan. Brown under broiler, or return to oven and heat until topping is slightly browned.

POUND CAKE

Yield: 48 portions or 2 cakes (10-inch tube pans)   *Portion:* 24 slices per cake
Oven: 325°F   *Bake:* 1 hour 15 minutes–1 hour 25 minutes

Ingredient	Amount	Procedure
Flour, cake	1 lb 10 oz	Combine dry ingredients in mixer bowl.
Sugar, granulated	2 lb	Blend on low speed for 1 minute, using a flat beater.
Salt	1 Tbsp	
Baking powder	½ tsp	
Eggs	10 (1 lb 2 oz)	Add eggs to dry ingredients. Mix until ingredients are mixed evenly and lumps disappear. Batter will be stiff.
Shortening	1 lb 2 oz	Add shortening and milk to mixture in bowl. Cream on medium speed until very light, about 10 minutes.
Milk	¼ cup	
Milk	1½ cups	Add milk and extracts slowly. Mix on low speed for 2–3 minutes or just until blended.
Almond extract	1½ tsp	
Vanilla	1½ tsp	
		Scale batter into two greased 10-inch tube pans, 3 lb 6 oz per pan.
		Bake at 325°F for 1 hour 15 minutes to 1 hour 25 minutes, or until cake tests done.
		Drop bottom of cake pans onto counter from a distance of 2–3 inches as cakes are removed from oven to produce a compact texture.
		Cool. Remove from pans.
		Cut into 24 slices.

Approximate nutritive values per portion

Calories	Carbohydrate	Protein	Fat	Cholesterol	Sodium	Fiber	Iron
245 kcal	32 g	3 g	12 g	46 mg	155 mg	0.4 g	1 mg

Note

- May be baked in four loaf pans (5 × 9 × 2¾ inches), 1 lb 10 oz batter per pan. Cut in 12 slices.

PUMPKIN CAKE

Yield: 48 portions or 3 cakes (10-inch tube pans)   *Portion:* 16 slices per cake
Oven: 350°F   *Bake:* 60–70 minutes

Ingredient	Amount	Procedure
Eggs	12 (1 lb 4 oz)	Beat eggs on medium speed until blended.
Sugar, granulated	2 lb 10 oz	Add sugar to eggs gradually, beating on high speed until thick and lemon colored.
Vegetable oil	1 qt	Add oil very slowly on low speed.
Flour, all-purpose Baking powder Baking soda Salt Cinnamon, ground	2 lb 10 oz 2 Tbsp 2 Tbsp 1 Tbsp 3 Tbsp	Combine dry ingredients in a separate bowl.
Pumpkin, canned	3 lb	On low speed, add pumpkin alternately with dry ingredients, beginning and ending with dry ingredients.

Scale batter into three ungreased 10-inch tube pans, 3 lb 12 oz per pan.
Bake at 350°F for 60–70 minutes.
When cool, remove from pans and drizzle with Powdered Sugar Glaze (p. 316).

Approximate nutritive values per portion

Calories	Carbohydrate	Protein	Fat	Cholesterol	Sodium	Fiber	Iron
377 kcal	47 g	4 g	12 g	53 mg	220 mg	2 g	2 mg

CHOCOLATE ROLL

Yield: 48 portions or 4 pans, 12 × 18 × 2 inches   *Portion:* 1-inch slice
Oven: 325°F   *Bake:* 20 minutes

Ingredient	Amount	Procedure
Egg yolks	24 (14 oz)	Beat egg yolks on high speed, using a flat beater.
Sugar, granulated	2 lb 4 oz	Add sugar and continue beating until mixture is lemon colored, thick, and fluffy.
Unsweetened chocolate, melted	12 oz	Add chocolate and vanilla. Blend on low speed.
Vanilla	2 Tbsp	
Flour, cake	9 oz	Combine flour, baking powder, and salt. Add to creamed mixture on low speed.
Baking powder	1 Tbsp	
Salt	1½ tsp	
Egg whites	24 (1 lb 11 oz)	Beat egg whites on high speed until they form rounded peaks. Fold into cake mixture on low speed. Scale batter, 1 lb 7 oz per pan, into four greased 12 × 18 × 2-inch pans lined with baking liners. Bake at 325°F for 20 minutes.
		When baked, remove from pans and quickly remove baking liner. Trim edges if hard. Roll (Figure 11.3) and let stand a few minutes. Unroll and spread with one of the suggested fillings (see Note). Roll up securely. Cover with a thin layer of Chocolate Icing (p. 311).

Approximate nutritive values per portion

Calories	Carbohydrate	Protein	Fat	Cholesterol	Sodium	Fiber	Iron
159 kcal	28 g	4 g	5 g	35 mg	122 mg	0.6 g	1 mg

Note

- Suggested fillings: Custard Filling (p. 318) or whipped cream, plain or flavored with peppermint.

Variation

- **Ice Cream Roll.** Spread with a thick layer of softened vanilla ice cream. Roll up securely and wrap in waxed paper. Place in freezer for several hours before serving.

JELLY ROLL

Yield: 48 portions or 4 pans, 12 × 18 × 2 inches   *Portion:* 1-inch slice
Oven: 375°F   *Bake:* 12 minutes

Ingredient	Amount	Procedure
Eggs	27 (3 lb)	Beat eggs on high speed for 1–2 minutes, using a flat beater.
Sugar, granulated Vanilla	3 lb 1 Tbsp	Add sugar and vanilla to eggs. Beat for 10–15 minutes.
Flour, cake Cream of tartar Baking powder Salt	1 lb 8 oz 2 Tbsp 2 Tbsp 2 tsp	Mix dry ingredients. Fold on low speed into egg-sugar mixture.
		Scale batter, 1 lb 14 oz per pan, into four greased 12 × 18 × 2-inch baking pans lined with baking liners. Bake at 375°F for 12 minutes.
		When baked, turn onto a cloth or heavy paper covered with powdered sugar (Figure 11.3). Quickly remove baking liners and trim edges if hard. Immediately roll cakes tightly.
Jelly or Custard Filling (p. 318)	1 qt	When cooled but not cold, unroll, spread with jelly or Custard Filling, 1 cup per roll. Roll firmly and wrap with waxed paper.
Sugar, powdered	1 lb	Sprinkle top of each roll with 4 oz powdered sugar. Slice each roll into 12 portions.

Approximate nutritive values per portion

Calories	Carbohydrate	Protein	Fat	Cholesterol	Sodium	Fiber	Iron
311 kcal	67 g	5 g	3 g	121 mg	170 mg	0.3 g	2 mg

Note

- May be baked in two 18 × 26 × 1-inch pans, scaled 3 lb 12 oz per pan.

Variation

- **Apricot Roll.** Cover cakes with Apricot Filling (p. 317) and roll. Cover outside with sweetened whipped cream or whipped topping and toasted coconut.

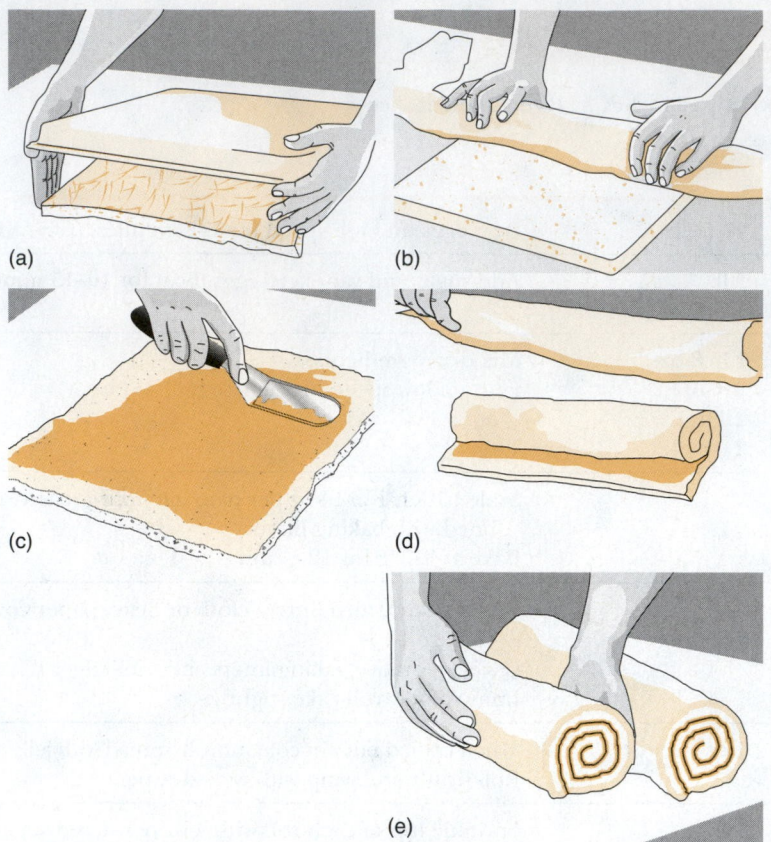

FIGURE 11.3 Rolling and filling a jelly roll. (a) Turn baked cake onto a cloth sprinkled with powdered sugar. Remove waxed or parchment paper. (b) While still warm, roll tightly. (c) When cooled but not cold, unroll and spread with filling. (d) Roll firmly. (e) Sprinkle finished jelly roll with powdered sugar.

PUMPKIN CAKE ROLL

Yield: 50 portions or 2 rolls   *Portion:* 25 slices per roll
Oven: 375°F   *Bake:* 15 minutes

Ingredient	Amount	Procedure
Eggs	18 (2 lb)	Whip eggs on high speed until thick and lemon colored, using a flat beater.
Sugar, granulated	2 lb 13 oz	Add sugar gradually while mixing on medium speed.
Pumpkin, canned Fresh lemon juice	2 lb 3 oz 2 Tbsp	Add pumpkin and lemon juice to egg mixture, mixing until blended.
Flour, all-purpose Baking powder Salt Cinnamon, ground Ginger, ground Nutmeg, ground	1 lb 2 oz 1 oz 1 Tbsp 1 oz 4 tsp 1 Tbsp	Combine dry ingredients in a bowl. Fold into pumpkin mixture. Scale batter, 4 lb per pan, into two greased 28 × 26 × 1-inch baking pans lined with baking liners. Bake at 375°F for 15 minutes or until cake tests done.
Sugar, powdered	6 oz	Sift powdered sugar generously onto a large white cloth. Loosen edges of cake and turn onto cloth. Remove paper (Figure 11.3). Roll cake and cloth up jelly-roll fashion. Cool.
Cream cheese, softened Margarine	2 lb 10 oz	Beat cream cheese and margarine until creamy, using flat beater.
Sugar, powdered Vanilla	1 lb 6 oz 1 Tbsp	Add sugar and vanilla to cream cheese mixture. Beat until smooth and creamy. Unroll cooled cake. Spread cream cheese filling over unrolled cakes, 2 lb per cake. Reroll cake.
Nuts, chopped	2 cups	Garnish with 1 cup nuts sprinkled over each roll. Chill. Cut each roll into 25 portions.

Approximate nutritive values per portion

Calories	Carbohydrate	Protein	Fat	Cholesterol	Sodium	Fiber	Iron
370 kcal	53 g	6 g	16 g	97 mg	318 mg	1 g	2 mg

Note
- If needed, sift additional powdered sugar over top of rolled cake.

Icing Recipes

BOILED ICING

Yield: 2 qt

Ingredient	Amount	Procedure
Sugar, granulated Water, hot	2 lb 1¼ cups	Combine sugar and water. Stir until sugar is dissolved. Boil without stirring to soft ball stage (238°F).
Egg whites	4 (4 oz)	Beat egg whites on high speed until stiff but not dry, using the wire whip attachment. Gradually pour syrup over egg whites while beating. Continue beating until icing is of consistency to spread.
Vanilla	1 Tbsp	Add vanilla. Spread on cake at once.

Approximate nutritive values per cup

Calories	Carbohydrate	Protein	Fat	Cholesterol	Sodium	Fiber	Iron
451 kcal	114 g	1 g	0 g	0 mg	26 mg	0 g	0 mg

Variation

- See variations of Ice Cream Icing (p. 311).

BURNT BUTTER ICING

Yield: 1¼ qt

Ingredient	Amount	Procedure
Butter or margarine	9 oz	Heat butter in saucepan until golden brown.
Sugar, powdered, sifted	1 lb 8 oz	Add sugar to butter and blend.
Vanilla Water, hot	1 Tbsp ½ cup	Add vanilla and water. Beat until of spreading consistency. Add more water if necessary.

Approximate nutritive values per cup

Calories	Carbohydrate	Protein	Fat	Cholesterol	Sodium	Fiber	Iron
899 kcal	137 g	1 g	41 g	0 mg	483 mg	0 g	0 mg

Note

- This amount will ice 8 dozen 1½-inch cookies. If used for cake, increase by one-fourth.

ICE CREAM ICING

Yield: 2½ qt

Ingredient	Amount	Procedure
Sugar, granulated Water, hot	1 lb 8 oz 1 cup	Combine sugar and water. Boil without stirring to soft ball stage (238°F).
Pasteurized egg whites	9 (10 oz)	Beat egg whites until frothy, using the wire whip attachment.
Sugar, powdered, sifted	3 oz	Add powdered sugar to egg whites and beat on high speed to consistency of meringue. Add hot syrup slowly and continue beating until mixture is thick and creamy.
Sugar, powdered, sifted Vanilla	8 oz 1 Tbsp	Add powdered sugar and vanilla. Beat until smooth. Add more sugar if necessary to make icing hold its shape when spread.

Approximate nutritive values per cup

Calories	Carbohydrate	Protein	Fat	Cholesterol	Sodium	Fiber	Iron
402 kcal	100 g	3 g	0 g	0 mg	49 mg	0 g	0 mg

Note

- This icing can be kept 2–3 days in a covered container in the refrigerator.

Variations

- **Bittersweet Icing.** Melt 8 oz unsweetened chocolate over hot water. Gradually stir in 1½ oz margarine or butter. When slightly cool, pour over white icing to form a design.
- **Candied Fruit Icing.** Add 8 oz chopped candied fruit.
- **Chocolate Icing.** Add 8 oz melted chocolate.
- **Coconut Icing.** Frost cake. Sprinkle with 4 oz dry shredded coconut.
- **Maple Nut Icing.** Delete vanilla. Flavor with 1½ tsp maple flavoring. Add 6 oz chopped nuts.
- **Maraschino Cherry Icing.** Delete vanilla. Add ½ tsp almond extract and 8 oz chopped maraschino cherries.
- **Peppermint Icing.** Add 8 oz finely crushed peppermint candy.

CHOCOLATE BUTTER CREAM ICING

Yield: 2 qt

Ingredient	Amount	Procedure
Margarine or butter	1 lb 8 oz	Cream margarine on medium speed until fluffy.
Evaporated milk	½ cup	Add milk and blend.
Sugar, powdered, sifted	1 lb 8 oz	Add sugar gradually. Mix on medium speed until smooth.
Unsweetened chocolate, melted Vanilla	6 oz 1 tsp	Add chocolate and vanilla. Beat on high speed until light and fluffy.

Approximate nutritive values per cup

Calories	Carbohydrate	Protein	Fat	Cholesterol	Sodium	Fiber	Iron
1067 kcal	94 g	4 g	81 g	5 mg	821 mg	1 g	2 mg

Note

- Milk may be substituted for evaporated milk.

COCONUT PECAN ICING

Yield: 2 qt

Ingredient	Amount	Procedure
Evaporated milk	2 cups	Combine milk, egg yolks, sugar, and margarine.
Egg yolks, beaten	6 (4 oz)	Cook in steam-jacketed kettle or over hot water until
Sugar, granulated	1 lb	thickened.
Margarine	8 oz	
Pecans, finely chopped	12 oz	Add pecans, coconut, and vanilla.
Coconut, flaked	12 oz	Cool, then beat well until thick enough to spread.
Vanilla	2 tsp	

Approximate nutritive values per cup

Calories	Carbohydrate	Protein	Fat	Cholesterol	Sodium	Fiber	Iron
1033 kcal	89 g	12 g	74 g	200 mg	350 mg	5 g	2 mg

CREAM CHEESE ICING

Yield: 1¾ qt

Ingredient	Amount	Procedure
Cream cheese, softened	12 oz	Blend cream cheese, margarine, and milk on medium speed
Margarine, softened	2 oz	until smooth.
Milk	¼ cup	
Sugar, powdered, sifted	2 lb 12 oz	Add sugar gradually to cheese-margarine mixture.
Vanilla	1 Tbsp	Add vanilla and beat until smooth and of spreading consistency.

Approximate nutritive values per cup

Calories	Carbohydrate	Protein	Fat	Cholesterol	Sodium	Fiber	Iron
927 kcal	181 g	4 g	24 g	55 mg	228 mg	0 g	1 mg

Variation

- **Orange Cheese Icing.** Substitute 1 Tbsp orange juice and 1 Tbsp grated orange peel for vanilla.

CREAMY ICING

Yield: 1½ qt

Ingredient	Amount	Procedure
Margarine	12 oz	Cream margarine on medium speed for 1 minute or until soft.
Evaporated milk Vanilla	½ cup 1 Tbsp	Add milk and vanilla. Mix until blended.
Sugar, powdered, sifted	2 lb	Add sugar gradually. Whip on medium speed until mixture is smooth and creamy.

Approximate nutritive values per cup

Calories	Carbohydrate	Protein	Fat	Cholesterol	Sodium	Fiber	Iron
1024 kcal	155 g	2 g	47 g	6 mg	558 mg	0 g	0.5 mg

Note

- Milk or cream may be substituted for evaporated milk.

Variations

- **Cocoa Icing.** Increase liquid to 1¼ cups. Add 6 oz cocoa sifted with the sugar.
- **Lemon Butter Icing.** Substitute ¼ cup lemon juice for an equal amount of milk, and 1½ Tbsp fresh grated lemon peel for the vanilla.
- **Orange Butter Icing.** Substitute ½ cup orange juice for an equal amount of milk, and 1 Tbsp fresh grated orange peel for the vanilla.

ORANGE ICING

Yield: 1½ qt

Ingredient	Amount	Procedure
Margarine	8 oz	Cream margarine until fluffy.
Sugar, powdered, sifted	2 lb 8 oz	Add sugar gradually on medium speed. Mix until creamy.
Vanilla Salt Fresh orange juice Fresh lemon juice Orange peel, grated	2 Tbsp ½ tsp ¼ cup ¼ cup 1 tsp	Add remaining ingredients. Blend until smooth.

Approximate nutritive values per cup

Calories	Carbohydrate	Protein	Fat	Cholesterol	Sodium	Fiber	Iron
1020 kcal	193 g	0 g	30 g	0 mg	538 mg	0 g	0.5 mg

PEANUT BUTTER ICING

Yield: 2 qt

Ingredient	Amount	Procedure
Sugar, powdered, sifted	3 lb	Cream powdered sugar and margarine for 5 minutes.
Margarine	10 oz	
Peanut butter, creamy	5 oz	Add to creamed mixture. Cream until fluffy. Spread on Peanut Butter Cake (p. 301).
Water, warm	¾ cup	
Vanilla	1 Tbsp	

Approximate nutritive values per cup

Calories	Carbohydrate	Protein	Fat	Cholesterol	Sodium	Fiber	Iron
1018 kcal	174 g	4 g	38 g	0 mg	469 mg	1 g	0.5 mg

Note

- ½ oz (1 Tbsp) caramel food color may be added for a darker color.

PINEAPPLE ICING (FOR PINEAPPLE CASHEW CAKE)

Yield: 2 qt

Ingredient	Amount	Procedure
Margarine	1 lb	Blend in mixer bowl, using a flat beater.
Sugar, powdered	1 lb 4 oz	
Salt	¼ tsp	
Pineapple juice	¾ cup	Add pineapple juice. Mix to blend.
Sugar, powdered	1 lb 6 oz	Add sugar in three additions. Beat on medium speed until light and of the desired consistency.

Approximate nutritive values per cup

Calories	Carbohydrate	Protein	Fat	Cholesterol	Sodium	Fiber	Iron
1048 kcal	167 g	1 g	46 g	0 mg	603 mg	0 g	0.5 mg

Note

- Crushed pineapple may be substituted for pineapple juice. Add additional juice in small quantities until icing is of spreading consistency.

MOCHA ICING

Yield: 2 qt

Ingredient	Amount	Procedure
Hot coffee, strong	1½ cups	Add coffee to margarine and cocoa.
Margarine, softened	3 oz	Mix on medium speed until blended.
Cocoa	4 oz	
Sugar, powdered, sifted	3 lb	Add sugar, salt, and vanilla. Mix until smooth.
Salt	¼ tsp	Add more sugar if necessary to make icing hold its shape when spread.
Vanilla	½ tsp	

Approximate nutritive values per cup

Calories	Carbohydrate	Protein	Fat	Cholesterol	Sodium	Fiber	Iron
761 kcal	179 g	3 g	10 g	0 mg	178 mg	0.2 g	5 mg

Note

- 2 Tbsp instant coffee, dissolved in 1½ cups hot water may be used in place of brewed coffee.

CHOCOLATE GLAZE

Yield: 1 qt

Ingredient	Amount	Procedure
Unsweetened chocolate	4 oz	Melt chocolate and margarine over low heat.
Margarine	3 oz	
Sugar, powdered, sifted	1 lb 5 oz	Add sugar, vanilla, and water gradually.
Vanilla	1 Tbsp	Beat until smooth. If needed, add boiling water, a few drops at a time, to make spreading consistency.
Water, boiling	½ cup	

Approximate nutritive values per cup

Calories	Carbohydrate	Protein	Fat	Cholesterol	Sodium	Fiber	Iron
877 kcal	159 g	3 g	32 g	0 mg	204 mg	2 g	2 mg

PEANUT BUTTER GLAZE

Yield: 5½ cups

Ingredient	Amount	Procedure
Margarine, melted	3 oz	Cream margarine and peanut butter.
Peanut butter, creamy	8 oz	
Sugar, powdered, sifted	1 lb 10 oz	Add sugar and milk alternately to make spreading consistency.
Milk	1 cup	Spread over rolls.

Approximate nutritive values per cup

Calories	Carbohydrate	Protein	Fat	Cholesterol	Sodium	Fiber	Iron
822 kcal	133 g	11 g	32 g	5 mg	336 mg	2 g	1 mg

POWDERED SUGAR GLAZE

Yield: 5 cups

Ingredient	Amount	Procedure
Sugar, powdered	2 lb	Mix until smooth, adding more water if necessary.
Corn syrup, white	½ cup	Cover tightly until needed. Stir before using.
Water, warm	¾ cup	
Vanilla	2 tsp	

Approximate nutritive values per cup

Calories	Carbohydrate	Protein	Fat	Cholesterol	Sodium	Fiber	Iron
791 kcal	206 g	0 g	0 g	0 mg	0 mg	0 g	0.5 mg

Notes

- Use for icing baked rolls or products requiring a thin icing.
- Thin, if necessary, to spread.

Filling Recipes

CHOCOLATE CREAM FILLING

Yield: 3 qt

Ingredient	Amount	Procedure
Chocolate chips	2 lb 4 oz (three 12-oz pkgs)	Combine chocolate chips, orange juice, and sugar.
Fresh orange juice or water	1 cup	Melt over hot water. Cool.
Sugar, granulated	8 oz	
Whipping cream	1½ qt	Whip cream until stiff.
		Fold into chocolate mixture.

Approximate nutritive values per cup

Calories	Carbohydrate	Protein	Fat	Cholesterol	Sodium	Fiber	Iron
827 kcal	81 g	7 g	61 g	133 mg	44 mg	0 g	2 mg

Note

- Use as filling for Orange Cream Puffs (p. 373).

Variation

- **Chocolate Mousse.** Whip 1½ cups (12 oz) pasteurized egg whites to soft peaks and fold into chocolate whipped cream mixture. Chill. May be frozen.

DATE FILLING

Yield: 1½ qt

Ingredient	Amount	Procedure
Dates, pitted, chopped	2 lb	Combine dates, water, and sugar.
Water	2¼ cups	Cook until mixture is thick. Cool.
Sugar, granulated	12 oz	

Approximate nutritive values per cup

Calories	Carbohydrate	Protein	Fat	Cholesterol	Sodium	Fiber	Iron
635 kcal	168 g	3 g	1 g	0 mg	8 mg	13 g	2 mg

Notes

- Use as cake or cookie filling.
- To add flavor, 6 oz jelly or ¼ cup orange juice may be used in place of ¼ cup water.

APRICOT FILLING

Yield: 2 qt

Ingredient	Amount	Procedure
Apricots, dried	2 lb	Cook apricots and water together until soft.
Water	2 cups	When cooked, chop apricots.
Sugar, granulated	1 lb	Add sugar, flour, salt, and lemon juice to apricots. Cook
Flour, all-purpose	4 oz	to a paste.
Salt	½ tsp	
Fresh lemon juice	½ cup	
Margarine	1 lb	Blend margarine into hot mixture.

Approximate nutritive values per cup

Calories	Carbohydrate	Protein	Fat	Cholesterol	Sodium	Fiber	Iron
951 kcal	139 g	6 g	46 g	0 mg	686 mg	9 g	6 mg

Variations

- **Fig Filling.** Substitute 2 lb dried figs, cooked and chopped, for the apricots. Increase lemon juice to 1 cup.
- **Prune-Date Filling.** Substitute 1 lb cooked, pitted, and chopped prunes and 1 lb chopped dates for the apricots.

CUSTARD FILLING

Yield: 4 qt

Ingredient	Amount	Procedure
Cornstarch	6 oz	Combine dry ingredients.
Sugar, granulated	1 lb	
Salt	½ tsp	
Milk, cold	2 cups	Add cold milk to dry ingredients and stir until smooth.
Milk, hot	2½ qt	Add cold mixture to hot milk, stirring constantly with wire whip. Cook over hot water until thick.
Eggs, beaten	10 (1 lb)	Add, while stirring, a small amount of hot mixture to the beaten eggs. Add to remainder of hot mixture, stirring constantly. Cook for 7 minutes.
Vanilla	2 tsp	Remove from heat. Add vanilla. Cool quickly to below 41°F. (See Note.)

Approximate nutritive values per cup

Calories	Carbohydrate	Protein	Fat	Cholesterol	Sodium	Fiber	Iron
307 kcal	47 g	10 g	9 g	146 mg	194 mg	0 g	0.5 mg

Notes

- Potentially hazardous food. *Food Safety Standards:* Hold food for service at an internal temperature of 41°F or below. Do not mix old product with new. Keep leftover product chilled at 41°F or below. See p. 167 for cooling procedures.
- Use as a filling for cakes, Cream Puffs (p. 373), Chocolate Roll (p. 305), and Eclairs (p. 373).
- To fill three 9-inch layer cakes, use ⅓ recipe.

LEMON FILLING

Yield: 1¾ qt

Ingredient	Amount	Procedure
Sugar, granulated	1 lb	Heat sugar and water to boiling point.
Water	3 cups	
Cornstarch	2½ oz	Blend cornstarch and cold water.
Water, cold	¾ cup	Gradually add to boiling sugar and water while stirring with a wire whip. Cook until thickened and clear, stirring constantly.
Egg yolks, beaten	4 (3 oz)	Stir a small amount of hot mixture into egg yolks, then blend egg yolks into hot mixture with the wire whip. Cook for 5–8 minutes while stirring.
Salt	¾ tsp	Add remaining ingredients. Stir to blend.
Fresh lemon juice	½ cup	Cool quickly to below 41°F. (See Note.)
Lemon peel, grated	2 tsp	
Margarine	1 oz (2 Tbsp)	

Approximate nutritive values per cup

Calories	Carbohydrate	Protein	Fat	Cholesterol	Sodium	Fiber	Iron
365 kcal	76 g	2 g	7 g	156 mg	281 mg	0.2 g	0.5 mg

Note

- Potentially hazardous food. *Food Safety Standards:* Hold food for service at an internal temperature of 41°F or below. Do not mix old product with new. Keep leftover product chilled at 41°F or below. See p. 167 for cooling procedures.

Variations

- **Lime Filling.** Substitute fresh lime juice and peel for the lemon juice and peel. Add a few drops green food coloring.
- **Orange Filling.** Substitute orange juice for the water and fresh orange peel for the lemon peel. Reduce lemon juice to 3 Tbsp.

MARMALADE NUT FILLING

Yield: 1 qt

Ingredient	Amount	Procedure
Margarine	2 oz	Melt margarine.
Walnuts, pieces	1 lb	Add nuts. Cook and stir until nuts are toasted.
Sugar, brown	6 oz	Add sugar and cinnamon. Cook until heated through.
Cinnamon, ground	1 tsp	
Orange marmalade	1 lb	Add marmalade. Mix well.

Approximate nutritive values per cup

Calories	Carbohydrate	Protein	Fat	Cholesterol	Sodium	Fiber	Iron
1052 kcal	79 g	30 g	76 g	0 mg	156 mg	4 g	5 mg

Notes

- Use for filling in fruit ring or sweet rolls.
- Apricot jam can be substituted for orange marmalade.

PRUNE FILLING

Yield: 1½ qt

Ingredient	Amount	Procedure
Sour cream	1 cup	
Margarine	2 oz	
Eggs, beaten	4 (7 oz)	
Prunes, pitted, cooked, and chopped	2 cups	Add cream, margarine, and eggs to prunes. Heat over hot water.
Sugar, granulated	1 lb	Mix dry ingredients. Add to prune mixture.
Salt	½ tsp	Cook and stir over hot water until thick. Cool.
Flour, all-purpose	1 oz (¼ cup)	

Approximate nutritive values per cup

Calories	Carbohydrate	Protein	Fat	Cholesterol	Sodium	Fiber	Iron
587 kcal	102 g	7 g	19 g	158 mg	332 mg	3 g	1 mg

Note

- 8 oz chopped nuts may be added.

Variation

- **Apricot Filling.** Substitute dried apricots for prunes.

Drop Cookie Recipes

BUTTERSCOTCH DROP COOKIES

Yield: 8 dozen cookies   *Portion:* ¾ oz per cookie
Oven: 375°F   *Bake:* 10–15 minutes

Ingredient	Amount	Procedure
Margarine	8 oz	Cream margarine and brown sugar on medium speed for 5 minutes, using a flat beater.
Sugar, brown	1 lb	
Eggs	4 (7 oz)	Add eggs and vanilla to creamed mixture. Mix on medium speed until well blended.
Vanilla	2 tsp	
Flour, all-purpose	1 lb 4 oz	Combine dry ingredients.
Baking powder	1 tsp	
Baking soda	2 tsp	
Salt	1 tsp	
Sour cream	1 lb	Add dry ingredients alternately with sour cream to dough. Mix on low speed until blended.
Walnuts, chopped	8 oz	Add nuts. Mix until blended. Chill dough until firm.
		Portion with No. 40 dipper 3 × 5 onto lightly greased or parchment-paper-lined 18 × 26-inch baking sheets. Bake at 375°F for 10–15 minutes. Cover with Burnt Butter Icing (p. 310) while cookies are still warm.

Approximate nutritive values per cookie

Calories	Carbohydrate	Protein	Fat	Cholesterol	Sodium	Fiber	Iron
84 kcal	10 g	2 g	4 g	11 mg	81 mg	0 g	0.5 mg

Variations

- **Butterscotch Squares.** Spread batter in 12 × 18 × 2-inch baking pan. Bake at 325°F for 25 minutes.
- **Chocolate Drop Cookies.** Add 4 oz unsweetened chocolate, melted, to creamed mixture.

COCONUT MACAROONS

Yield: 9 dozen cookies   *Portion:* ½ oz per cookie
Oven: 325°F   *Bake:* 15 minutes

Ingredient	Amount	Procedure
Egg whites Salt	8 (9 oz) ⅛ tsp	Beat egg whites and salt on high speed until frothy, using the whip attachment.
Sugar, granulated Sugar, powdered	12 oz 12 oz	Combine sugars and add gradually to egg whites.
Vanilla	2 tsp	Add vanilla. Continue beating on high speed until stiff.
Coconut, shredded	1 lb 6 oz	Carefully fold in coconut on low speed. Portion with No. 60 dipper 4 × 6 onto lightly greased or parchment-paper-lined 18 × 26-inch baking sheets. Bake at 325°F for 15 minutes.

Approximate nutritive values per cookie

Calories	Carbohydrate	Protein	Fat	Cholesterol	Sodium	Fiber	Iron
53 kcal	9 g	1 g	2 g	0 mg	24 mg	0 g	0 mg

CHOCOLATE CHIP COOKIES

Yield: 10 dozen cookies   *Portion:* ¾ oz per cookie
Oven: 375°F   *Bake:* 8–10 minutes

Ingredient	Amount	Procedure
Margarine Sugar, granulated Sugar, brown	12 oz 8 oz 8 oz	Cream margarine and sugars on medium speed for 5 minutes, using a flat beater.
Eggs Vanilla	4 (7 oz) 2 tsp	Add eggs and vanilla to creamed mixture and beat until light and fluffy.
Flour, all-purpose Salt Baking soda	1 lb 4 oz 1 tsp 2 tsp	Combine dry ingredients. Add on low speed to creamed mixture.
Nuts, coarsely chopped Chocolate chips	1 lb 1 lb 8 oz	Add nuts and chocolate chips. Mix until blended.
		Portion with No. 40 dipper 3 × 5 onto lightly greased or parchment-paper-lined 18 × 26-inch baking sheets. Bake at 375°F for 8–10 minutes.

Approximate nutritive values per cookie

Calories	Carbohydrate	Protein	Fat	Cholesterol	Sodium	Fiber	Iron
103 kcal	12 g	2 g	6 g	7 mg	69 mg	1 g	0.5 mg

Note

- For jumbo cookies, use No. 20 dipper. Bake at 365°F for 12–15 minutes.

BUTTERSCOTCH PECAN COOKIES

Yield: 10 dozen cookies   *Portion:* ¾ oz per cookie
Oven: 375°F   *Bake:* 10–12 minutes

Ingredient	Amount	Procedure
Margarine Sugar, brown	1 lb 2 lb	Cream margarine and sugar on medium speed for 5 minutes, using a flat beater.
Eggs Vanilla	4 (7 oz) 1 Tbsp	Add eggs and vanilla to creamed mixture. Mix on low speed until blended.
Flour, all-purpose Pecans, chopped	1 lb 8 oz 1 lb	Add flour and pecans. Mix on low speed until blended.
		Portion with No. 40 dipper 3 × 5 onto lightly greased or parchment-paper-lined 18 × 26-inch baking sheets. Bake at 375°F for 10–12 minutes.

Approximate nutritive values per cookie

Calories	Carbohydrate	Protein	Fat	Cholesterol	Sodium	Fiber	Iron
104 kcal	12 g	1 g	6 g	7 mg	41 mg	0.4 g	0.5 mg

OATMEAL COOKIES

Yield: 8 dozen cookies   *Portion:* ¾ oz per cookie
Oven: 375°F   *Bake:* 8–11 minutes

Ingredient	Amount	Procedure
Margarine	1 lb 4 oz	Cream margarine and sugars on medium speed for 5 minutes, using a flat beater.
Sugar, brown	8 oz	
Sugar, granulated	8 oz	
Eggs	2 (4 oz)	Add eggs and vanilla to creamed mixture. Continue to cream until well mixed.
Vanilla	2 tsp	
Flour, all-purpose	12 oz	Combine dry ingredients.
Salt	1 tsp	Add to creamed mixture.
Baking soda	2 tsp	
Rolled oats, uncooked	1 lb	Add oats. Mix on low speed until blended.
Raisins, softened	12 oz	Add raisins. Mix only to blend. Portion with No. 40 dipper 3 × 5 onto lightly greased or parchment-paper-lined 18 × 26-inch baking sheets. Flatten slightly. Bake at 375°F for 8–9 minutes for a chewy cookie, 10–11 minutes for a crisp cookie.

Approximate nutritive values per cookie

Calories	Carbohydrate	Protein	Fat	Cholesterol	Sodium	Fiber	Iron
104 kcal	14 g	1 g	5 g	5 mg	95 mg	0.3 g	0.5 mg

Notes

- For variety, add 8 oz chopped nuts, chocolate chips, or coconut.
- 2 tsp cinnamon may be added.

PEANUT BUTTER COOKIES

Yield: 9 dozen cookies   *Portion:* ¾ oz per cookie
Oven: 375°F   *Bake:* 8 minutes

Ingredient	Amount	Procedure
Margarine	1 lb	Cream margarine and sugars on medium speed for 5 minutes, using a flat beater.
Sugar, granulated	1 lb	
Sugar, brown	10 oz	
Eggs	4 (7 oz)	Add eggs and vanilla.
Vanilla	2 tsp	Continue beating until blended.
Peanut butter, creamy	1 lb 2 oz	Add peanut butter to creamed mixture. Blend on low speed.
Flour, all-purpose	l lb	Combine dry ingredients.
Baking soda	2 tsp	Add to creamed mixture. Mix on low speed until well blended.
Salt	1 tsp	
		Portion dough with No. 40 dipper 3 × 5 onto lightly greased or parchment-paper-lined 18 × 26-inch baking sheets. Flatten with tines of a fork. Bake at 375°F for 8 minutes.

Approximate nutritive values per cookie

Calories	Carbohydrate	Protein	Fat	Cholesterol	Sodium	Fiber	Iron
102 kcal	11 g	2 g	6 g	8 mg	109 mg	0.4 g	0.5 mg

Variations

- **Chocolate Chip Peanut Butter Cookies.** Add 1 lb chocolate chips.
- **Chunky Peanut Butter Cookies.** Use chunky peanut butter or add 12 oz chopped peanuts.

JUMBO CHUNK CHOCOLATE COOKIES

Yield: 5 dozen cookies   *Portion:* 3½ oz per cookie
Oven: 350°F   *Bake:* 10–12 minutes

Ingredient	Amount	Procedure
Sugar, brown	1 lb 8 oz	Cream sugars and shortening on medium speed for 5 minutes, using a flat beater.
Sugar, granulated	1 lb	
Shortening	2 lb	
Eggs, beaten	9 (1 lb)	Add eggs and vanilla to creamed mixture.
Vanilla	1½ Tbsp	
Flour, all-purpose	2 lb 8 oz	Combine dry ingredients and add to creamed mixture. Mix thoroughly.
Baking soda	4 tsp	
Salt	4 tsp	
Semisweet chocolate chunks	4 lb 12 oz	Add chocolate and nuts.
Nuts, chopped	1 lb	
		Portion with No. 20 dipper 3 × 4 onto lightly greased or parchment-paper-lined 18 × 26-inch baking sheets. Flatten slightly. Bake at 350°F for 10–12 minutes.

Approximate nutritive values per cookie

Calories	Carbohydrate	Protein	Fat	Cholesterol	Sodium	Fiber	Iron
502 kcal	56 g	7 g	31 g	32 mg	243 mg	4 g	3 mg

Note

- These cookies are best when served the same day they are baked.

DROP MOLASSES COOKIES

Yield: 8 dozen cookies   *Portion:* ¾ oz per cookie
Oven: 350°F   *Bake:* 8–10 minutes

Ingredient	Amount	Procedure
Flour, all-purpose	2 lb	Stir together flour, soda, and spices.
Baking soda	2⅔ Tbsp	Set aside.
Cinnamon, ground	¼ cup	
Cloves, ground	1 tsp	
Nutmeg, ground	1 tsp	
Ginger, ground	2 tsp	
Salt	2 tsp	
Oil or melted shortening	1 lb 8 oz	Combine oil and sugar in mixer bowl. Beat on medium speed for 5 minutes, using a flat beater.
Sugar, granulated	2 lb	
Eggs	4 (7 oz)	Add eggs, one at a time, beating well after each addition.
Molasses	1 cup	Add molasses gradually to egg mixture. Add dry ingredients gradually on low speed and mix well.
		Portion with No. 40 dipper 3 × 5 onto lightly greased or parchment-paper-lined 18 × 26-inch baking sheets. Bake at 350°F for 8–10 minutes.

Approximate nutritive values per cookie

Calories	Carbohydrate	Protein	Fat	Cholesterol	Sodium	Fiber	Iron
146 kcal	19 g	1 g	7 g	9 mg	153 mg	0.3 g	1 mg

Note

- Cookies will be soft in center.

GINGERSNAPS

Yield: 8 dozen cookies   *Portion:* $\frac{2}{3}$ oz per cookie
Oven: 375°F   *Bake:* 10–12 minutes

Ingredient	Amount	Procedure
Shortening	1 lb	Cream shortening and brown sugar until light and fluffy.
Sugar, brown	1 lb 4 oz	
Eggs	3 (5 oz)	Add eggs and molasses. Mix well.
Molasses	$\frac{2}{3}$ cup	
Flour, all-purpose	1 lb 6 oz	Combine dry ingredients. Add gradually to creamed mixture. Blend well.
Baking soda	$1\frac{2}{3}$ Tbsp	
Cinnamon, ground	$2\frac{1}{2}$ tsp	
Ginger, ground	$2\frac{1}{2}$ tsp	
Cloves, ground	$1\frac{1}{4}$ tsp	
Salt	$\frac{3}{4}$ tsp	
Sugar, granulated	8 oz	Portion with a No. 60 dipper. Roll dough in sugar and place 4 × 5 onto lightly greased or parchment-paper-lined 18 × 26-inch baking sheets. Bake at 375°F for 10–12 minutes.

Approximate nutritive values per cookie

Calories	Carbohydrate	Protein	Fat	Cholesterol	Sodium	Fiber	Iron
105 kcal	15 g	1 g	5 g	7 mg	87 mg	0.2 g	0.5 mg

PEANUT COOKIES

Yield: 9 dozen cookies   *Portion:* $\frac{3}{4}$ oz per cookie
Oven: 350°F   *Bake:* 10–12 minutes

Ingredient	Amount	Procedure
Margarine	12 oz	Cream margarine and sugars on medium speed for 5 minutes, using a flat beater.
Sugar, granulated	8 oz	
Sugar, brown	1 lb	
Eggs	4 (7 oz)	Add eggs and vanilla. Mix for 5 minutes.
Vanilla	2 tsp	
Flour, all-purpose	12 oz	Combine dry ingredients.
Baking soda	1 tsp	Add to creamed mixture.
Salt	1 tsp	
Rolled oats, quick, uncooked	10 oz	Add rolled oats and peanuts. Mix until blended.
Peanuts, salted	1 lb	
		Portion dough with No. 40 dipper 3 × 5 onto lightly greased or parchment-paper-lined 18 × 26-inch baking sheets. Bake at 350°F for 10–12 minutes.

Approximate nutritive values per cookie

Calories	Carbohydrate	Protein	Fat	Cholesterol	Sodium	Fiber	Iron
96 kcal	11 g	2 g	5 g	8 mg	66 mg	0.4 g	0.5 mg

PEANUT BUTTER CHOCOLATE CHIP COOKIES

Yield: 8 dozen cookies   *Portion:* ¾ oz per cookie
Oven: 350°F   *Bake:* 10–12 minutes

Ingredient	Amount	Procedure
Peanut butter, chunky	1 lb 8 oz	Cream peanut butter, sugar, and margarine on medium
Sugar, brown	1 lb 8 oz	speed for 5 minutes.
Margarine	12 oz	
Eggs	3 (5 oz)	Add eggs, honey, and vanilla.
Honey	¾ cup	Mix well.
Vanilla	1 Tbsp	
Flour, all-purpose	1 lb	Combine dry ingredients.
Rolled oats	3 oz	Add gradually to creamed mixture. Blend well.
Baking soda	1 Tbsp	
Salt	¾ tsp	
Semisweet chocolate chips	1 lb	Stir chocolate chips into batter. Refrigerate until dough is firm and not sticky.
		Portion dough with No. 40 dipper 3 × 5 onto lightly greased or parchment-paper-lined 18 × 26-inch baking sheets. Bake 350°F for 10–12 minutes.

Approximate nutritive values per cookie

Calories	Carbohydrate	Protein	Fat	Cholesterol	Sodium	Fiber	Iron
150 kcal	18 g	3 g	8 g	6.5 mg	130 mg	1 g	1 mg

SNICKERDOODLES

Yield: 8 dozen cookies   *Portion:* ¾ oz per cookie
Oven: 375°F   *Bake:* 8–10 minutes

Ingredient	Amount	Procedure
Margarine	1 lb	Cream margarine and sugar on medium speed for 5 minutes,
Sugar, granulated	1 lb 8 oz	using a flat beater.
Eggs	4 (7 oz)	Add eggs to creamed mixture. Mix thoroughly.
Flour, all-purpose	1 lb 6 oz	Mix dry ingredients. Add to creamed mixture.
Cream of tartar	4 tsp	Mix on low speed until well blended.
Baking soda	2 tsp	
Salt	½ tsp	
Sugar, granulated	8 oz	Combine sugar and cinnamon.
Cinnamon, ground	5 Tbsp	Portion dough with No. 40 dipper.
		Roll in sugar-cinnamon mixture.

Place 3 × 5 onto lightly greased or parchment-paper-lined 18 × 26-inch baking sheets. Bake at 375°F for 8–10 minutes or until lightly browned but still soft. These cookies puff up at first, then flatten out with crinkled tops.

Approximate nutritive values per cookie

Calories	Carbohydrate	Protein	Fat	Cholesterol	Sodium	Fiber	Iron
99 kcal	15 g	1 g	4 g	9 mg	86 mg	0 g	0.5 mg

DROP SUGAR COOKIES

Yield: 8 dozen cookies   *Portion:* ¾ oz per cookie
Oven: 375°F   *Bake:* 8–10 minutes

Ingredient	Amount	Procedure
Shortening	1 lb	Cream fats and sugar, starting on low speed, progressing to
Margarine or butter	1 lb 2 oz	medium, then high speed for 5 minutes, using a flat beater.
Sugar, granulated	2 lb	
Eggs	3 (5 oz)	Add eggs and vanilla to creamed mixture and mix thoroughly.
Vanilla	4 tsp	
Flour, all-purpose	1 lb 14 oz	Combine dry ingredients.
Cream of tartar	2 tsp	Add gradually to creamed mixture.
Baking soda	2½ tsp	Blend well.
Salt	½ tsp	

Portion with No. 40 dipper 3 × 5 onto lightly greased or parchment-paper-lined 18 × 26-inch baking sheets. Bake at 375°F for 8–10 minutes.

Approximate nutritive values per cookie

Calories	Carbohydrate	Protein	Fat	Cholesterol	Sodium	Fiber	Iron
152 kcal	16 g	1 g	9 g	6 mg	97 mg	0.2 g	0.5 mg

Notes
- Cookies will be soft in center.
- For jumbo cookies, use No. 20 dipper.

WHOLE-WHEAT SUGAR COOKIES

Yield: 8 dozen cookies   *Portion:* ¾ oz per cookie
Oven: 375°F   *Bake:* 8–10 minutes

Ingredient	Amount	Procedure
Margarine	1 lb	Cream margarine and sugar for 5 minutes or until light and
Sugar, granulated	2 lb	fluffy, using a flat beater.
Eggs	4 (7 oz)	Add eggs, vanilla, and milk. Mix well.
Vanilla	4 tsp	
Milk	½ cup	
Flour, whole-wheat	2 lb	Combine dry ingredients.
Baking powder	4 tsp	Add gradually to creamed mixture.
Baking soda	2 tsp	Blend well.
Salt	2 tsp	
Nutmeg, ground	2 tsp	
Orange peel, grated	4 Tbsp	
Sugar, granulated	4 oz	Combine sugar and cinnamon.
Cinnamon, ground	2 tsp	
		Portion with No. 40 dipper 3 × 5 onto lightly greased or parchment-paper-lined 18 × 26-inch baking sheets. Flatten slightly and sprinkle with sugar and cinnamon mixture. Bake at 375°F for 8–10 minutes.

Approximate nutritive values per cookie

Calories	Carbohydrate	Protein	Fat	Cholesterol	Sodium	Fiber	Iron
106 kcal	16 g	1 g	4 g	9 mg	131 mg	0 g	0.5 mg

Note

- Cookies will be soft in center.

FRUITCAKE COOKIES

Yield: 8 dozen cookies   *Portion:* 1 oz per cookie
Oven: 325°F   *Bake:* 12–15 minutes

Ingredient	Amount	Procedure
Dates, chopped	2 lb	Put dried fruits and nuts in a large bowl. Add flour and mix to coat dried fruits and nuts.
Dried apricots, chopped (see Notes)	1 lb	
Nuts, chopped (see Notes)	2 lb	
Flour, all-purpose	4 oz	Reserve for later step.
Butter, softened	8 oz	In a mixer bowl combine butter, sugar, eggs, vanilla, and dry ingredients. Mix to make a batter.
Sugar, brown, packed	12 oz	
Eggs	2	
Vanilla	1 tsp	Mix reserved fruit-nut mixture into batter. The mixture will be very stiff.
Cinnamon, ground	½ tsp	
Flour, all-purpose	6 oz	
Baking soda	1 tsp	
Salt	1 tsp	
		Portion dough with a No. 40 dipper onto lightly greased or parchment-paper-lined baking sheet. Flatten slightly if desired. (See Note.) Bake at 325°F for 12–15 minutes. Cookies do not spread.

Approximate nutritive values per cookie

Calories	Carbohydrate	Protein	Fat	Cholesterol	Sodium	Fiber	Iron
148 kcal	17 g	2 g	9 g	9 mg	34 mg	2 g	0.7 mg

Notes

- Other dried fruit, such as cherries, cranberries, or candied fruit, can be substituted for apricots.
- Select from walnuts, pecans, hazelnuts, or Brazil nuts. Nut pieces should be large.
- For a smaller cookie, use a No. 60 dipper (rounded). Yield: 12 dozen

Bar Cookie Recipes

BROWNIES

Yield: 60 portions or 2 pans, 12 × 18 × 1 inch   *Portion:* 2½ × 3 inches
Oven: 325°F   *Bake:* 20 minutes

Ingredient	Amount	Procedure
Eggs	15 (1 lb 10 oz)	Beat eggs on high speed for 5 minutes, using a flat beater.
Sugar, granulated Shortening, melted Margarine, melted Vanilla	2 lb 4 oz 10 oz 8 oz 2 Tbsp	Add sugar, fats, and vanilla to eggs. Mix on medium speed for 5 minutes.
Flour, cake Cocoa Baking powder Salt	14 oz 10 oz 2 tsp ½ tsp	Combine dry ingredients. Add to creamed mixture. Mix on low speed for about 5 minutes.
Nuts, chopped	12 oz	Add nuts to batter. Mix to blend.
		Scale batter into two lightly greased 12 × 18 × 1-inch baking pans, 3 lb 8 oz per pan. Bake at 325°F for 20 minutes. Do not overbake. Should be soft to touch when done. While warm, sprinkle with powdered sugar, or cool and cover with a thin layer of mocha or chocolate frosting if desired.

Approximate nutritive values per cookie

Calories	Carbohydrate	Protein	Fat	Cholesterol	Sodium	Fiber	Iron
221 kcal	26 g	4 g	12 g	52 mg	82 mg	0.7 g	2 mg

Notes

- 12 oz unsweetened chocolate may be substituted for the cocoa. Melt and add to the fat-sugar-egg mixture.
- 13 oz all-purpose flour may be substituted for cake flour.
- 2 lb chopped dates may be added.
- May be baked in one 18 × 26 × 1-inch baking pan.

FUDGE BROWNIES

Yield: 60 portions or 1 pan, 18 × 26 × 1 inch   *Portion:* 2½ × 3 inches
Oven: 325°F   *Bake:* 20–25 minutes

Ingredient	Amount	Procedure
Bitter chocolate	1 lb	Melt chocolate and shortening.
Shortening	1 lb 4 oz	
Flour, cake	10 oz	Combine dry ingredients in mixer bowl.
Flour, all-purpose	10 oz	
Baking powder	5½ tsp	
Salt	2¼ tsp	
Eggs	15 (1 lb 10 oz)	Combine eggs, sugar, and vanilla in mixer bowl. Beat well.
Sugar, granulated	3 lb	Blend chocolate mixture into egg-sugar mixture.
Vanilla	1 Tbsp	Add dry ingredients, beating only until blended.
		Scale 8 lb of batter into greased 18 × 26 × 2-inch pan. Smooth batter. Bake at 325°F for 20–25 minutes or until edges shrink slightly from edge of pan. Cool. Cut 6 × 10.

Approximate nutritive values per cookie

Calories	Carbohydrate	Protein	Fat	Cholesterol	Sodium	Fiber	Iron
260 kcal	32 g	3 g	15 g	52 mg	140 mg	1 g	1 mg

Variation

- **Fudge Nut Brownies.** Add 10 oz chopped walnuts to batter.

COCONUT PECAN BARS

Yield: 96 portions or 2 pans, 12 × 18 × 1 inch   *Portion:* 2 × 2¼ inches
Oven: 350°F   *Bake:* 15–20 minutes, first layer; 20–25 minutes, second layer

Ingredient	Amount	Procedure
Margarine	1 lb 8 oz	Blend margarine, brown sugar, and flour on low speed until mixture resembles coarse meal, using a flat beater.
Sugar, brown	12 oz	Press even layer of mixture into two 12 × 18 × 1-inch baking pans, 1 lb 12 oz per pan.
Flour, all-purpose	1 lb 4 oz	Bake at 350°F until light brown, 15–20 minutes.
Eggs, beaten	8 (14 oz)	Combine remaining ingredients to form topping.
Flour, all-purpose	4 oz	
Baking powder	1 Tbsp	
Salt	2 tsp	
Sugar, brown	2 lb 8 oz	
Vanilla	1 Tbsp	
Coconut, shredded or flaked	8 oz	
Pecans, chopped	12 oz	
		Spread topping over baked crust, 3 lb per pan. Bake 20–25 minutes. Ice with Orange Icing (p. 313) if desired. Cut 6 × 8.

Approximate nutritive values per cookie

Calories	Carbohydrate	Protein	Fat	Cholesterol	Sodium	Fiber	Iron
179 kcal	22 g	2 g	10 g	18 mg	137 mg	0.4 g	1 mg

Note

- May be baked in one 18 × 26 × 1-inch baking pan.

Variation

- **Dreamland Bars.** Reduce coconut to 4 oz. Increase pecans to 1 lb. Add 12 oz chopped maraschino cherries and 1 lb chopped dates. Combine 2 oz margarine or butter and 8 oz powdered sugar. Spread over top. Bake.

DATE BARS

Yield: 60 portions or 2 pans, 12 × 18 × 1 inch   *Portion:* 2½ × 3 inches
Oven: 350°F   *Bake:* 25–30 minutes

Ingredient	Amount	Procedure
Egg yolks	12 (7 oz)	Beat egg yolks on high speed until lemon colored, using a flat beater.
Sugar, granulated	2 lb	Add sugar to yolks gradually and continue beating after each addition.
Flour, all-purpose Baking powder Salt	1 lb 1½ Tbsp ½ tsp	Combine flour, baking powder, and salt.
Dates, chopped Nuts, chopped	3 lb 1 lb	Add dates and nuts to flour mixture. Combine with egg-sugar mixture.
Egg whites	12 (14 oz)	Beat egg whites on high speed until they form soft peaks, using the wire whip attachment. Fold into batter.
		Spread batter evenly into two lightly greased 12 × 18 × 1-inch baking pans, 4 lb 3 oz per pan. Bake at 350°F for 25–30 minutes.
Sugar, powdered	6 oz	Sift powdered sugar over top of warm baked bars. Cut 5 × 6.

Approximate nutritive values per cookie

Calories	Carbohydrate	Protein	Fat	Cholesterol	Sodium	Fiber	Iron
219 kcal	42 g	4 g	5 g	42 mg	54 mg	3 g	1 mg

Note

- May be baked in one 18 × 26 × 1-inch baking pan. Cut 6 × 10.

BUTTERSCOTCH SQUARES

Yield: 60 portions or 2 pans, 12 × 18 × 1 inch   *Portion:* 2½ × 3 inches
Oven: 325°F   *Bake:* 25 minutes

Ingredient	Amount	Procedure
Margarine Sugar, brown	1 lb 2 lb 8 oz	Cream margarine and sugar on medium speed for 5 minutes, using a flat beater.
Eggs Vanilla	10 (1 lb) 1 Tbsp	Add eggs, one at a time, and vanilla. Mix on low speed until blended.
Flour, all-purpose Baking powder Salt	1 lb 8 oz 2 Tbsp 1 tsp	Combine dry ingredients. Add to creamed mixture. Mix on low speed until blended.
Nuts, chopped (optional)	12 oz	Add nuts to batter. Mix to blend.
		Spread batter evenly in two lightly greased 12 × 18 × 1-inch baking pans, 3 lb 6 oz per pan. Bake at 325°F for 25 minutes. Cut 5 × 6.

Approximate nutritive values per cookie

Calories	Carbohydrate	Protein	Fat	Cholesterol	Sodium	Fiber	Iron
213 kcal	29 g	3 g	10 g	32 mg	154 mg	0.8 g	1 mg

Note

- May be baked in one 18 × 26 × 1-inch baking pan. Cut 6 × 10.

Variation

- **Butterscotch Chocolate Chip Brownies.** Add 1 lb chocolate chips.

OATMEAL DATE BARS

Yield: 96 portions or 2 pans, 12 × 18 × 1 inch   *Portion:* 2 × 2¼ inches
Oven: 325°F   *Bake:* 45 minutes

Ingredient	Amount	Procedure
Margarine Sugar, brown	1 lb 10 oz 2 lb 12 oz	Cream margarine and sugar on medium speed for 5 minutes, using a flat beater.
Flour, all-purpose Rolled oats, quick, uncooked Baking soda	2 lb 1 lb 8 oz 2⅔ Tbsp	Combine dry ingredients. Add to creamed mixture. Mix on low speed until crumbly. Spread 2 lb 10 oz prepared mixture into two 12 × 18 × 1-inch baking pans. Flatten to an even layer.
Date Filling (p. 317)	3 qt	Spread date filling over oatmeal mixture, 1½ qt per pan. Cover with remainder of dough, 1 lb 4 oz per pan. Bake at 325°F for 45 minutes. Cut 6 × 8 into bars.

Approximate nutritive values per cookie

Calories	Carbohydrate	Protein	Fat	Cholesterol	Sodium	Fiber	Iron
245 kcal	46 g	3 g	7 g	0 mg	184 mg	2 g	1 mg

Notes

- May be baked in one 18 × 26 × 1-inch baking pan. Cut 8 × 12.
- Crushed pineapple or cooked dried apricots may be used in place of dates in the filling.

MARSHMALLOW KRISPIE SQUARES

Yield: 60 portions or 2 pans, 12 × 18 × 1 inch   *Portion:* $2\frac{1}{2}$ × 3 inches

Ingredient	Amount	Procedure
Margarine	1 lb	Melt margarine. Add marshmallows and vanilla.
Marshmallows	4 lb	Stir until completely melted. Cook over low heat 3 minutes
Vanilla	1 Tbsp	longer, stirring constantly. Remove from heat.
Crisp rice cereal	2 lb 8 oz	Stir crisp rice cereal into marshmallow mixture until well-coated. Using buttered spatula, press mixture evenly into two lightly greased 12 × 18 × 1-inch baking pans, 3 lb per pan. Cut while warm, 5 × 6.

Approximate nutritive values per cookie

Calories	Carbohydrate	Protein	Fat	Cholesterol	Sodium	Fiber	Iron
225 kcal	41 g	2 g	6 g	0 mg	309 mg	0.4 g	2 mg

Note

- May be made in one 18 × 26 × 1-inch baking pan. Cut 6 × 10.

Variations

- **Chocolate Marshmallow Squares.** Cover squares with a thin, rich chocolate icing.
- **Peanut Butter Squares.** Add 1 lb 2 oz peanut butter to marshmallow mixture. Proceed as indicated. Frost with Chocolate Glaze (p. 315).

Pressed, Molded, and Rolled Cookie Recipes

BUTTER TEA COOKIES

Yield: 10 dozen cookies
Oven: 375°F   *Bake:* 10–12 minutes

Ingredient	Amount	Procedure
Butter	1 lb	Cream butter and sugar on medium speed for 5 minutes, using a flat beater.
Sugar, granulated	9 oz	
Egg yolks	6 (4 oz)	Add egg yolks and vanilla to creamed mixture. Mix on medium speed until blended.
Vanilla	1 tsp	
Flour, all-purpose	1 lb 4 oz	Add flour and mix on low speed. Chill dough.
		Shape with cookie press onto ungreased baking sheets. Bake at 375°F for 10–12 minutes.

Approximate nutritive values per cookie

Calories	Carbohydrate	Protein	Fat	Cholesterol	Sodium	Fiber	Iron
56 kcal	6 g	1 g	3 g	20 mg	32 mg	0 g	0.5 mg

Variation

- **Thimble Cookies.** Roll dough into 1-inch balls. Dip in egg white and roll in finely chopped pecans. Bake for 3 minutes at 325°F, then make indentation in center of cookies and fill with jelly. Bake for 10–12 minutes longer.

CHOCOLATE TEA COOKIES

Yield: 10 dozen cookies
Oven: 350°F   *Bake:* 6–10 minutes

Ingredient	Amount	Procedure
Margarine	1 lb	Cream margarine and sugar on medium speed for 5 minutes, using a flat beater.
Sugar, granulated	12 oz	
Eggs	2 (4 oz)	Add eggs and vanilla to creamed mixture. Blend on medium speed for 5 minutes.
Vanilla	1 Tbsp	
Flour, all-purpose	1 lb 2 oz	Combine dry ingredients.
Baking powder	1 tsp	Add to creamed mixture and mix on low speed until blended. Chill dough.
Salt	¼ tsp	Shape dough with cookie press onto ungreased baking sheets.
Cocoa	1 oz (¼ cup)	Bake at 350°F for 6–10 minutes.

Approximate nutritive values per cookie

Calories	Carbohydrate	Protein	Fat	Cholesterol	Sodium	Fiber	Iron
56 kcal	6 g	1 g	3 g	4 mg	44 mg	0 g	0.5 mg

SANDIES

Yield: 8 dozen cookies
Oven: 325°F   *Bake:* 20 minutes

Ingredient	Amount	Procedure
Margarine or butter Sugar, granulated Vanilla	12 oz 3 oz 1 tsp	Cream margarine, sugar, and vanilla on medium speed for 5 minutes, using a flat beater.
Flour, all-purpose Salt	1 lb 2 oz 1 tsp	Add flour and salt to creamed mixture. Mix on low speed until blended.
Water Pecans, finely chopped	1 Tbsp 8 oz	Add water and pecans and blend. Chill dough.
		Shape dough into small balls ¾ inch in diameter. If mixture crumbles so it will not stick together, add a small amount of melted margarine. Place on lightly greased or parchment-paper-lined baking sheets. Bake at 325°F until lightly browned, about 20 minutes.
Sugar, powdered, sifted	approx. 8 oz	Roll in powdered sugar while still hot.

Approximate nutritive values per cookie

Calories	Carbohydrate	Protein	Fat	Cholesterol	Sodium	Fiber	Iron
73 kcal	8 g	1 g	5 g	0 mg	56 mg	0.3 g	0.5 mg

Variation

- **Frosty Date Balls.** Add 1 lb chopped pitted dates.

BUTTERSCOTCH REFRIGERATOR COOKIES

Yield: 8 dozen cookies
Oven: 375°F   *Bake:* 8–10 minutes

Ingredient	Amount	Procedure
Margarine	8 oz	Cream fats and sugars on medium speed for 5 minutes, using a flat beater.
Shortening	8 oz	
Sugar, granulated	12 oz	
Sugar, brown	1 lb	
Eggs	4 (7 oz)	Add eggs and vanilla to creamed mixture. Mix on medium speed for 5 minutes.
Vanilla	2 tsp	
Flour, all-purpose	2 lb	Combine dry ingredients.
Cream of tartar	2 tsp	
Baking soda	2 tsp	
Dates, finely chopped	8 oz	Add dry ingredients, dates, and nuts to dough. Mix on low speed until well blended.
Nuts, chopped	8 oz	
		Form dough into three 2-lb rolls, 2 inches in diameter. Wrap in waxed paper. Chill several hours.
		Slice cookies ⅛ inch thick. Place on ungreased baking sheets.
		Bake at 375°F for 8–10 minutes.

Approximate nutritive values per cookie

Calories	Carbohydrate	Protein	Fat	Cholesterol	Sodium	Fiber	Iron
128 kcal	18 g	2 g	6 g	9 mg	54 mg	1 g	0.5 mg

CRISP GINGER COOKIES

Yield: 8 dozen cookies
Oven: 375°F   *Bake:* 8–10 minutes

Ingredient	Amount	Procedure
Molasses	1 cup	Combine molasses and sugar. Boil for 1 minute. Cool.
Sugar, granulated	8 oz	
Shortening	8 oz	Place shortening and molasses in mixer bowl. Blend on medium speed, using a flat beater.
Eggs	2 (4 oz)	Add eggs and mix thoroughly.
Flour, all-purpose	1 lb 12 oz (or more)	Combine dry ingredients. Add to molasses-egg mixture.
Salt	½ tsp	Mix on low speed until well blended.
Baking soda	1 tsp	
Ginger, ground	2 tsp	
		Form dough into two rolls 2 inches in diameter. Wrap in waxed paper. Chill thoroughly.
		Cut into ⅛-inch slices. Place on lightly greased baking sheets.
		Bake at 375°F for 8–10 minutes.

Approximate nutritive values per cookie

Calories	Carbohydrate	Protein	Fat	Cholesterol	Sodium	Fiber	Iron
70 kcal	11 g	1 g	3 g	5 mg	26 mg	0.2 g	0.5 mg

Note
- Dough may be rolled and cut with cookie cutter.

OATMEAL CRISPIES

Yield: 8 dozen cookies
Oven: 350°F   *Bake:* 12–15 minutes

Ingredient	Amount	Procedure
Flour, all-purpose	12 oz	Combine flour, salt, and soda in mixer bowl.
Salt	2 tsp	
Baking soda	2 tsp	
Shortening	1 lb	Add shortening, sugars, eggs, and vanilla to flour mixture.
Sugar, granulated	1 lb	Mix on low speed for about 5 minutes, using a flat beater.
Sugar, brown	1 lb	
Eggs	4 (7 oz)	
Vanilla	2 tsp	
Rolled oats, quick, uncooked	1 lb	Add rolled oats and nuts. Mix on low speed to blend.
Nuts, chopped	8 oz	Shape dough into three 2-lb rolls, 2 inches in diameter. Wrap in waxed paper and chill.
		Cut dough into slices ¼ inch thick. Place 2 inches apart on ungreased baking sheets. Bake at 350°F for 12–15 minutes.

Approximate nutritive values per cookie

Calories	Carbohydrate	Protein	Fat	Cholesterol	Sodium	Fiber	Iron
126 kcal	16 g	2 g	6 g	9 mg	76 mg	0.3 g	0.5 mg

Note

- For smaller cookies, form into four 1½-inch rolls and slice ⅛ inch thick. Yield: approximately 25 dozen.

Variation

- **Oatmeal Coconut Crispies.** Add 1 cup flaked coconut.

ROLLED SUGAR COOKIES

Yield: 10 dozen cookies   *Portion:* 2-inch cookie
Oven: 375°F   *Bake:* 7 minutes

Ingredient	Amount	Procedure
Margarine or butter	1 lb	Cream margarine and sugar on medium speed for 5 minutes, using a flat beater.
Sugar, granulated	1 lb	
Eggs	4 (7 oz)	Add eggs and vanilla to creamed mixture.
Vanilla	1 Tbsp	Blend on medium speed for 2 minutes.
Flour, all-purpose	1 lb 8 oz	Combine dry ingredients.
Salt	2 tsp	Add to creamed mixture. Mix on low speed until blended.
Baking powder	2 tsp	
Flour, all-purpose	4 oz	Mix flour and sugar.
Sugar, granulated	2 oz	Roll dough ⅛ inch thick on a surface that has been lightly dusted with flour-sugar mixture.
		Cut into desired shapes. Place on ungreased baking sheets.
		Bake at 375°F for 7 minutes or until lightly browned.

Approximate nutritive values per cookie

Calories	Carbohydrate	Protein	Fat	Cholesterol	Sodium	Fiber	Iron
71 kcal	9 g	1 g	3 g	7 mg	78 mg	0.2 g	0.5 mg

Variations

- **Christmas Wreath Cookies.** Cut rolled dough with doughnut cutter. Brush with beaten egg and sprinkle with chopped nuts. Decorate with candied cherry rings and pieces of citron arranged to represent holly.
- **Coconut Cookies.** Cut rolled dough with round cookie cutter. Brush with melted margarine or butter and sprinkle with shredded coconut, plain or tinted with food coloring.
- **Filled Cookies.** Cut dough with round cutter. Cover half with Fig or Date Filling (p. 317). Brush edges with milk and cover with remaining cookies. Press edges together with tines of fork.
- **Pinwheel Cookies.** Divide dough into two portions. Add 2 oz melted unsweetened chocolate to one portion. Roll each portion into the same size sheet, ⅛ inch thick. Place chocolate dough over the white dough and press together. Roll as for jelly roll. Chill thoroughly. Cut into thin slices.

Pie Recipes

PASTRY

Yield: 50 lb dough

Ingredient	Amount	Procedure
Flour, all-purpose	25 lb	Mix flour and shortening on low speed, using a flat beater.
Shortening, hydrogenated	18 lb	Mix until fat particles are the size of small peas for a flaky crust. For a mealy crust, mixture should resemble cornmeal.
Ice water	3¾ qt	Add water and salt to flour-fat mixture.
Salt	12 oz	Mix on low speed only until dough will hold together.

Approximate nutritive values per pound

Calories	Carbohydrate	Protein	Fat	Cholesterol	Sodium	Fiber	Iron
2268 kcal	173 g	23 g	166 g	0 mg	2643 mg	6 g	10 mg

Notes

- For seven 9-inch one-crust pies, use 4 lb; for seven 9-inch two-crust pies, use 7 lb. See pp. 341–343 for directions for preparation.
- For eight 8-inch one-crust pies, use 2 lb 8 oz; for eight 8-inch two-crust pies, use 4 lb 8 oz. See pp. 341–343 for directions for preparation.

PASTRY FOR ONE-CRUST PIES

Yield: 56 portions or 4 lb dough or seven 9-inch pies   *Portion:* 8 pieces per pie

Ingredient	Amount	Procedure

Flour, all-purpose
Shortening,
   hydrogenated
	2 lb
	1 lb 6 oz
		Mix flour and shortening on low speed for 1 minute, using a pastry knife
		  or flat beater.
		Scrape sides of bowl and continue mixing until shortening is evenly distributed,
		  1–2 minutes.

Ice water Salt	1–1¼ cups 1 oz (1½ Tbsp)	Dissolve salt in smaller amount of water (use reserved amount of water if needed). Add to flour mixture. Mix on low speed only until dough is formed, about 40 seconds. Portion into 9-oz balls for 9-inch pies. See Note for 8-inch pies.

TO MAKE A ONE-CRUST PIE:

1. Roll dough into a circle 2 inches larger than pie pan.

2. Fit pastry loosely into pan so there are no air spaces between the crust and pan (Figure 11.4).

3. Trim, allowing ½ inch extra to build up edge.

4. For custard-type pie, crimp edge, add filling, and bake according to the recipe.

5. For cream or chiffon pies, crimp edge (Figure 11.4) and prick crust with fork. Bake according to directions that follow.

6. Bake in a hot oven (425°F) for 10 minutes or until light brown. Cool. A second pan may be placed over the crust for the first part of baking, then removed and the crust allowed to brown. The second pan helps keep the crust in shape.

7. Fill baked crust with desired filling.

Approximate nutritive values per portion

Calories	Carbohydrate	Protein	Fat	Cholesterol	Sodium	Fiber	Iron
157 kcal	12 g	2 g	11 g	0 mg	172 mg	0.4 g	1 mg

Note

- For eight 8-inch pies, use 1 lb 3 oz flour, 13 oz shortening, 1 cup water, and 2½ tsp salt. Scale 5 oz for each crust. To serve, cut pies in six portions.

FIGURE 11.4 Preparing pastry for a baked pie shell. Holes are made in shells to keep them flat during baking.

PASTRY FOR TWO-CRUST PIES

Yield: 56 portions or 7 lb dough or seven 9-inch pies   *Portion:* 8 pieces per pie

Ingredient	Amount	Procedure
Flour, all-purpose	3 lb 6 oz	Mix flour and shortening on low speed for 1 minute, using a pastry knife or
Shortening, hydrogenated	2 lb 7 oz	flat beater. Scrape sides of bowl and continue mixing until shortening is evenly distributed, 1–2 minutes.
Ice water	1¾–2 cups	Dissolve salt in smaller amount of water (use reserved amount of water if needed).
Salt	1¾ oz (2½ Tbsp)	Add to flour mixture. Mix on low speed only until dough is formed, about 40 seconds. Portion into 9-oz balls for bottom crust and 7-oz for top crust. See Note for 8-inch pies.

TO MAKE A TWO-CRUST PIE:

1. Roll each ball of dough into a circle. Place pastry for bottom crust in pie pan, easing into pan without stretching the dough.

2. Trim off overhanging dough. If desired, leave ½ inch extra pastry around the edge and fold over to make a pocket of pastry to prevent fruit juices from running out.

3. Add desired filling.

4. Moisten edge of bottom crust with water (Figure 11.5).

5. Cover with top crust, in which slits or vents have been cut near the center to allow steam to escape.

6. Trim top pastry to extend ½ inch beyond edge of pan.

7. Fold edge of top pastry under edge of lower pastry, then seal by pressing the two crusts together and fluting with fingertips.

8. If desired, brush top crusts with milk and sprinkle with sugar.

9. Bake as directed in the recipe.

Approximate nutritive values per portion

Calories	Carbohydrate	Protein	Fat	Cholesterol	Sodium	Fiber	Iron
275 kcal	21 g	3 g	20 g	0 mg	286 mg	1 g	1 mg

Notes

- For eight 8-inch pies, use 2 lb flour, 1 lb 8 oz shortening, 1½–1¾ cups water, and 1 oz (1½ Tbsp) salt. Scale 5 oz for bottom crust and 4 oz for top crust. To serve, cut into six portions.
- Using scrap dough is often necessary. Using no more than 50 percent of scrap dough and restricting its use to bottom crusts is recommended. Care must be taken to handle the dough as little as possible.

Variation

- **Cheddar Cheese Pastry.** Use 2 lb 8 oz flour, 1 lb 13 oz shortening, 1 lb 14 oz shredded cheddar cheese, ¾ cup water, and 1½ oz salt. Add cheese after flour and shortening have been mixed.

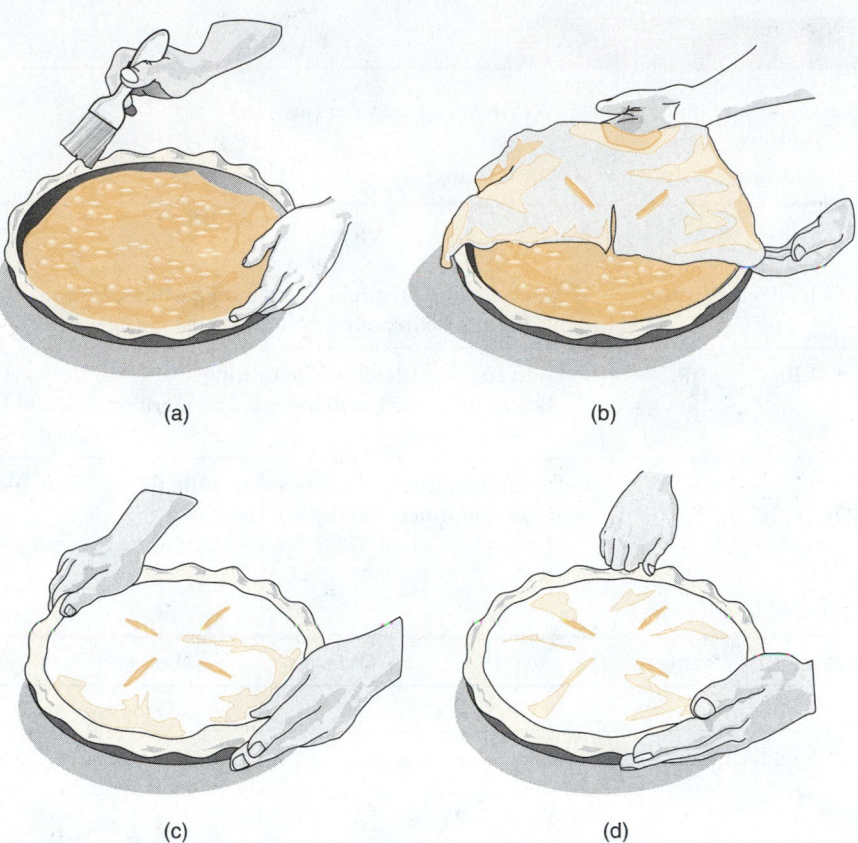

(a)   (b)

(c)   (d)

FIGURE 11.5   Preparing pastry for a two-crust pie. (a) Moistening edge of crust. (b) Placing top crust on filled pie. (c) Pressing top crust to seal tightly. (d) Fluting edge of pie.

GRAHAM CRACKER CRUST

Yield: 56 portions or seven 9-inch pies   *Portion:* 8 pieces per pie
Oven: 375°F   *Bake:* 5 minutes

Ingredient	Amount	Procedure
Graham cracker crumbs	2 lb	Mix all ingredients.
Sugar, granulated	15 oz	Pat 9 oz crumb mixture evenly into each pie pan. For 8-inch crusts, see Note.
Margarine, melted	15 oz	Bake at 375°F for about 5 minutes.

Approximate nutritive values per portion

Calories	Carbohydrate	Protein	Fat	Cholesterol	Sodium	Fiber	Iron
155 kcal	20 g	1 g	8 g	0 mg	169 mg	0 g	0.5 mg

Notes

- For eight 8-inch shells, use 1 lb 5 oz crumbs, 10 oz sugar, and 10 oz melted margarine. Portion 5 oz per shell.
- Vanilla wafer crumbs or chocolate cookie crumbs may be substituted for graham cracker crumbs.
- Crusts may be refrigerated several hours instead of baking.

Variation

- **Chocolate Crumb Crust.** Add 6 oz cocoa to graham cracker crumbs and sugar. Mix, then add melted margarine.

MERINGUE FOR PIES

Yield: 56 portions or meringue for seven 9-inch pies   *Portion:* 8 pieces per pie
Oven: 375°F   *Bake:* 10–12 minutes

Ingredient	Amount	Procedure
Salt	½ tsp	
Cream of tartar	½ tsp	
Pasteurized egg whites, room temperature	16 (2 cups/1 lb)	Add salt and cream of tartar to egg whites. Whip past frothy stage, on high speed, for approximately 1½ minutes, using the wire whip attachment.
Sugar, granulated	1 lb	Add sugar gradually while beating. Beat until sugar has dissolved. The meringue should be stiff enough to hold peaks but not dry.
		Spread meringue on filled pies while filling is hot, 5–6 oz per pie. The meringue should touch all edges of the crust. Brown in oven at 375°F for 10–12 minutes or until golden brown.

Approximate nutritive values per portion

Calories	Carbohydrate	Protein	Fat	Cholesterol	Sodium	Fiber	Iron
36 kcal	8 g	1 g	0 g	0 mg	33 mg	0 g	0 mg

Notes
- For 8-inch pies, use 4 oz per pie.
- For proper volume, egg whites must have no yolk mixed in them, and the beater and bowl must be free of any trace of fat. Even a small trace of fat will prevent the whites from foaming properly.
- Egg whites should be at room temperature before beating. The meringue will be higher and lighter.
- For food safety reasons, pasteurized egg whites are recommended.

MERINGUE SHELLS

Yield: 50 shells   *Portion:* 3 oz
Oven: 275°F   *Bake:* 1 hour

Ingredient	Amount	Procedure
Salt	1 tsp	
Cream of tartar	1 tsp	
Egg whites	28 (3 cups/1 lb 8 oz)	Add salt and cream of tartar to egg whites. Beat on high speed until frothy, using the wire whip attachment.
Sugar, granulated	3 lb	Add sugar ½ cup at a time, beating on high speed after each addition, until sugar is dissolved and mixture will hold its shape, 20–30 minutes.
		Place mixture on greased and floured baking sheets with No. 10 dipper and shape into nests with spoon, or place on pans with pastry tube. Bake at 275°F for about 1 hour. Watch carefully the last 15–20 minutes to avoid overcooking. Meringues should be white, not brown. If overcooked, they are too brittle. Serve ice cream or fruit in the center.

Approximate nutritive values per portion

Calories	Carbohydrate	Protein	Fat	Cholesterol	Sodium	Fiber	Iron
112 kcal	27 g	1 g	0 g	0 mg	65 mg	0 g	0 mg

Variations

- **Angel Pie.** Place meringue in well-greased and floured pie pans, about $1\frac{1}{4}$ qt per pan. Use spoon to build up sides. After baking, fill each shell with 3 cups Cream Pie filling (p. 352), Lemon Pie filling (p. 354), or Chocolate Cream Pie filling (p. 352). Then top with a thin layer of whipped cream.
- **Meringue Sticks.** Force mixture through pastry tube to form sticks. Sprinkle with chopped nuts. Bake.

PIES MADE WITH CANNED FRUIT

Yield: 56 portions or seven 9-inch pies   *Portion:* 8 pieces per pie
Oven: 400°F   *Bake:* 30 minutes

Ingredient	Amount	Procedure
Pastry for Two-Crust Pies (p. 342)	7 lb	Make pastry. Divide into 9-oz balls for bottom crusts and 7-oz balls for top crusts. Roll and place bottom crusts in seven 9-inch pie pans. For 8-inch pies, see Note.
Fruit, pie pack	2 No. 10 cans	Drain fruit. Measure liquid and add water to make 2 qt. Bring $1\frac{1}{2}$ qt liquid to boiling point.
Cornstarch	8 oz	Mix remaining liquid with cornstarch and add gradually to hot liquid, while stirring with a wire whip. Cook until thick and clear.
Sugar, granulated Salt	3 lb 8 oz 2 tsp	While still hot, add sugar and salt. Mix thoroughly and bring to boiling point. Add drained fruit and mix carefully to avoid breaking or mashing fruit. Cool slightly.
		Scale 1 lb 12 oz–2 lb ($3\frac{1}{2}$–4 cups) filling into each unbaked pie shell. Moisten edge of bottom crust with water. Cover with top crust. Seal edge, trim, and flute edges (Figure 11.5). Bake at 400°F for 30 minutes or until crust is browned.

Notes

- For eight 8-inch pies, make 4 lb 8 oz dough for crusts and portion into 5 oz for bottom crust and 4 oz for top crust. For filling, use $1\frac{1}{2}$ No. 10 cans fruit, 3 lb sugar (variable), 6 oz cornstarch, and $1\frac{1}{2}$ tsp salt. Drain liquid from fruit and add water to make $1\frac{1}{2}$ qt liquid. Scale 1 lb–1 lb 8 oz (approximately 3 cups) filling per pie.
- Suggested fillings: apple, apricot, blackberry, cherry, gooseberry, or peach.
- Other thickening agents may be used, such as waxy maize (6 oz total for 9-inch or $4\frac{1}{2}$ oz total for 8-inch pies) or tapioca (9 oz total for 9-inch or $7\frac{1}{2}$ oz total for 8-inch pies).

PIES MADE WITH FROZEN FRUIT

Yield: 56 portions or seven 9-inch pies   *Portion:* 8 pieces per pie
Oven: 400°F   *Bake:* 30–40 minutes

Ingredient	Amount	Procedure
Pastry for Two-Crust Pies (p. 342)	7 lb	Make pastry. Divide into 9-oz balls for bottom crusts, 7-oz balls for top crusts. Roll and place bottom crusts in seven 9-inch pie pans. For 8-inch pies, see Note.
Fruit, frozen	10 lb	Thaw fruit. Measure juice. If necessary, add water to bring total liquid to 1½–2 qt according to consistency desired.
Sugar, granulated	See Table 11.3	Combine sugar and starch.
Cornstarch or waxy maize (see Note)	See Table 11.3	Add to hot liquid, stirring with a wire whip.
Seasonings	See Table 11.3	Add seasonings to thickened liquid and pour over fruit. Mix carefully to avoid breaking or mashing fruit.
		Scale 1 lb 12 oz–2 lb (3½–4 cups) filling into each unbaked pie shell. Moisten edge of bottom crust with water. Cover with top crust in which slits have been made for steam to escape. Seal edge, trim, and flute edges (see Figure 11.5). Bake at 400°F for 30–40 minutes or until fruit is done and crust is golden brown.

Notes

- Allow 2–3 oz cornstarch or 2–2½ oz waxy maize per qt of liquid. Use of waxy maize or other waxy starch products results in a translucent soft gel through which the fruit shows clearly. The color is brighter and the gel is less opaque and less rigid, making it ideal for thickening fruit fillings. It is important to use a waxy starch if the pies are to be frozen.
- For eight 8-inch pies, use 4 lb 8 oz pastry, portioned 5 oz for bottom crust and 4 oz for top crust. Portion 1 lb–1 lb 8 oz (approximately 3 cups) filling per pie.

TABLE 11.3   Guide for using frozen fruit in pies or cobblers (seven 9-inch pies)

Fruit (10 lb)	Sugar*	Thickening Cornstarch*	Thickening Waxy maize*	Seasonings
Apples	1 lb 8 oz	3 oz	2½ oz	Salt, 1 tsp; nutmeg, 1 tsp; cinnamon, 1 Tbsp; butter, 2 oz
Apricots	2 lb	5½ oz	4 oz	Cinnamon, 2 tsp
Berries	2¾–3½ lb	6½ oz	5 oz	Lemon juice, 2 Tbsp; salt, 1 tsp
Blueberries	3 lb	8 oz	6 oz	Salt, 1 tsp; butter, 2 oz; lemon juice, 1½ cups; cinnamon, 1 tsp
Blue plums	2–2½ lb	5½ oz	4 oz	Salt, 1 tsp; butter, 2 oz
Cherries	1 lb 12 oz	7 oz	5 oz	Salt, 1 tsp
Gooseberries	6 lb	14 oz	10 oz	Salt, ½ tsp
Peaches	1 lb 6 oz	5½ oz	4 oz	Butter, 1 oz; salt, 1 tsp; almond extract, ¼ tsp; cinnamon, 1 tsp; nutmeg, 1 tsp
Pineapple	2 lb	5½ oz	4 oz	Salt, 1 tsp
Rhubarb	5 lb	7 oz	5 oz	Salt, 1 tsp
Strawberries	2 lb	12 oz	8½ oz	Lemon juice, ¾ cup; red color, ¾ tsp

*The amount of sugar and cornstarch or waxy maize added to the fruit will vary according to the pack of the fruit and individual preferences of flavor and consistency. Frozen fruits packed without the addition of sugar are known as *dry pack*. When sugar is added during the freezing process, the ratio is usually 3, 4, or 5 parts by weight of fruit to 1 part by weight of sugar. Use less thickening for cobblers. Some fruits are available individually quick-frozen (IQF) without added sugar.

FRESH APPLE PIE

Yield: 56 portions or seven 9-inch pies   *Portion:* 8 pieces per pie
Oven: 400°F   *Bake:* 45 minutes

Ingredient	Amount	Procedure
Pastry for Two-Crust Pies (p. 342)	7 lb	Make pastry. Divide into 9-oz balls for bottom crusts, 7-oz balls for top crusts. Roll and place bottom crusts in seven 9-inch pie pans. For 8-inch pies, see Note.
Apples, tart, fresh	12 lb EP 15 lb AP	Peel, core, and slice apples.
Sugar, granulated Flour, all-purpose Cinnamon, ground	3 lb 4 oz 1 Tbsp	Combine sugar, flour, and cinnamon. Add to apples and mix carefully.
Margarine	8 oz	Portion 2 lb 4 oz filling into each unbaked crust. Add 1 oz margarine to each pie. Moisten edge of bottom crust. Cover with perforated top crust. Seal edge, trim excess dough, and flute edges (see Figure 11.5). Bake at 400°F for 45 minutes or until apples are tender.

Approximate nutritive values per portion

Calories	Carbohydrate	Protein	Fat	Cholesterol	Sodium	Fiber	Iron
462 kcal	62 g	3 g	24 g	0 mg	326 mg	3 g	1 mg

Notes
- For eight 8-inch pies, use 4 lb 8 oz dough for crust and portion 5 oz for bottom crust and 4 oz for top crust. Portion filling, 2 lb per pie.
- Suggested apples are Jonathan, Granny Smith, and Winesap. Frozen (IQF) apples may be substituted for fresh apples.

Variation
- **Apple Crumb Pie.** Omit top crust. Sprinkle apples with **Streusel Topping:** Mix 1 lb flour, 1 lb 10 oz sugar, 2 oz nonfat dry milk, and 1 tsp salt. Cut in 10 oz margarine or butter and add 6 oz chopped pecans. Use 1 cup per pie. Bake until apples are tender and topping is brown.

SOUR CREAM APPLE NUT PIE

Yield: 56 portions or seven 9-inch pies   *Portion:* 8 pieces per pie
Oven: 450°F, 350°F   *Bake:* 10 minutes, 55 minutes

Ingredient	Amount	Procedure
Pastry for One-Crust Pies (p. 341)	4 lb	Make pastry. Line seven 9-inch pie pans, 9 oz per pan. For 8-inch pies, see Note.
Sour cream	3 lb	Combine and mix until thoroughly blended.
Sugar, granulated	8 oz	
Flour, all-purpose	6 oz	
Eggs	4 (6 oz)	
Vanilla	2 Tbsp	
Salt	1 tsp	
Frozen sliced apples	8 lb 8 oz	Combine apples and sour cream mixture, being careful not to break apples.
		Scale 1 lb 12 oz filling into each unbaked crust. Bake at 450°F for 10 minutes. Reduce temperature to 350°F and continue baking until filling is slightly puffed and golden brown, about 40 minutes.

TOPPING

Ingredient	Amount	Procedure
Flour, all-purpose	5 oz	Combine flour, sugars, and cinnamon.
Sugar, brown	4 oz	
Sugar, granulated	5 oz	
Cinnamon, ground	2 Tbsp	
Margarine	5 oz	Add margarine to dry ingredients. Mix until crumbly.
Walnuts, coarsely chopped	8 oz	Add nuts. Mix in. Scale 3½ oz topping over each pie and bake for 15 minutes.

Approximate nutritive values per portion

Calories	Carbohydrate	Protein	Fat	Cholesterol	Sodium	Fiber	Iron
345 kcal	36 g	5 g	21 g	24 mg	254 mg	2 g	1 mg

Note

- For eight 8-inch pies, use 2 lb 8 oz dough portioned 5 oz per pie. For filling, scale apple mixture 1 lb 8 oz per pie and topping 3 oz per pie.

RAISIN PIE

Yield: 56 portions or seven 9-inch pies   *Portion:* 8 pieces per pie
Oven: 400°F   *Bake:* 30 minutes

Ingredient	Amount	Procedure
Pastry for Two-Crust Pies (p. 342)	7 lb	Make pastry. Divide into 9-oz balls for bottom crusts, 7-oz balls for top crusts. Roll and place bottom crusts in seven 9-inch pie pans. For 8-inch pies, see Note.
Raisins Water, hot	4 lb 4½ qt	Simmer raisins in water until plump. Cool slightly.
Sugar, granulated Cornstarch Salt	2 lb 4 oz 6 oz 2 tsp	Combine sugar, cornstarch, and salt. Add to raisins and cook until thickened. Remove from heat.
Fresh lemon juice Margarine	6 Tbsp 3 oz	Add lemon juice and margarine to raisin mixture. Cool slightly.
		Portion 2 lb 4 oz (3½–4 cups) filling into each unbaked crust. Moisten edge of bottom crust. Cover with perforated top crust. Seal edge, trim excess dough, and flute edges (see Figure 11.5). Bake at 400°F for 30 minutes or until crust is golden brown.

Approximate nutritive values per portion

Calories	Carbohydrate	Protein	Fat	Cholesterol	Sodium	Fiber	Iron
465 kcal	68 g	4 g	21 g	0 mg	384 mg	2 g	2 mg

Note

- For eight 8-inch pies, use 4 lb 8 oz dough, portioned 5 oz for bottom crust and 4 oz for top crust. For filling, portion 1 lb 14 oz (3–3½ cups) filling per pie.

Variation

- **Dried Apricot Pie.** Use 5 lb dried apricots. Cover with hot water; let stand 1 hour. Cook slowly without stirring until tender. Combine 4 lb granulated sugar and 2½ oz cornstarch. Mix with ½ cup cold water. Add to fruit a few minutes before it is done. Continue cooking until juice is clear. Proceed as for Raisin Pie.

RHUBARB PIE

Yield: 56 portions or seven 9-inch pies   *Portion:* 8 pieces per pie
Oven: 400°F   *Bake:* 35 minutes

Ingredient	Amount	Procedure
Rhubarb, fresh or frozen	10 lb EP	If fresh rhubarb is used, wash and trim. Do not peel. Cut in 1-inch pieces.
Sugar, granulated	5 lb 8 oz	Combine and stir into rhubarb. Let stand 30 minutes.
Tapioca, quick-cooking	6 oz	
Salt	2 tsp	
Orange peel, grated	3 Tbsp	
Pastry for Two-Crust Pies (p. 342)	7 lb	Make pastry. Divide into 9-oz balls for bottom crusts, 7-oz balls for top crusts. Roll and place bottom crusts in seven 9-inch pie pans, 9 oz per pan. For 8-inch pies, see Note.
Margarine, melted	5 oz	Portion 2 lb 4 oz filling into each unbaked crust. Distribute margarine over filling in each pie. Moisten edges with cold water. Cover with top crust or pastry strips. Press edges together. Bake at 400°F for 35 minutes or until crust is golden brown and fruit is tender.

Approximate nutritive values per portion

Calories	Carbohydrate	Protein	Fat	Cholesterol	Sodium	Fiber	Iron
494 kcal	72 g	4 g	22 g	0 mg	391 mg	2 g	1 mg

Notes

- For eight 8-inch pies, use 4 lb 8 oz dough portioned 5 oz for bottom crust and 4 oz for top crust. Scale 1 lb 14 oz filling per pie.
- 8 oz cornstarch or 5 oz waxy maize starch may be substituted for the tapioca.

CRANBERRY RASPBERRY PIE

Yield: 56 portions or seven 9-inch pies   *Portion:* 8 or 10 pieces per pie
Oven: 400°F   *Bake:* 50–60 minutes

Ingredient	Amount	Procedure
Pastry for Two-Crust Pies (p. 342)	7 lb	Make pastry. Divide into 9-oz balls for bottom crusts, 7-oz balls for top crusts. Roll and place bottom crusts in seven 9-inch pie pans.
Sugar, granulated	5 lb	Combine in mixing bowl using a wire whip. Reserve for later step.
Salt	1¾ tsp	
Tapioca	6 oz	
Frozen raspberries (IQF)	3 lb 12 oz	Do not thaw IQF raspberries. Scale 8 oz raspberries and 11 oz cranberries into each pie shell.
Fresh cranberries, washed and picked over	4 lb 12 oz	Sprinkle with 12 oz sugar-tapioca mixture reserved from earlier step.
Butter, melted	4 oz	Drizzle 1 Tbsp melted butter over each pie. Roll top crusts and place on filling. Seal edges.
		Bake at 400°F in a conventional oven until juices are bubbling and crusts are golden brown, about 50–60 minutes. Cool before cutting. Cut each pie into 8 or 10 wedges.

Approximate nutritive values per ⅛ pie

Calories	Carbohydrate	Protein	Fat	Cholesterol	Sodium	Fiber	Iron
497 kcal	72 g	4 g	23 g	0 mg	460 mg	5 g	1 mg

Approximate nutritive values per ⅒ pie

Calories	Carbohydrate	Protein	Fat	Cholesterol	Sodium	Fiber	Iron
398 kcal	58 g	3 g	18 g	0 mg	369 mg	4 g	1 mg

RHUBARB CUSTARD PIE

Yield: 56 portions or seven 9-inch pies 　　*Portion:* 8 pieces per pie
Oven: 375°F 　　*Bake:* 45–50 minutes

Ingredient	Amount	Procedure
Pastry for One-Crust Pies (p. 341)	4 lb	Make pastry. Line seven 9-inch pie pans, 9 oz per pan. Flute edges. For 8-inch pies, see Note.
Rhubarb, fresh or frozen	8 lb EP	If fresh rhubarb is used, wash and trim. Do not peel. Cut into ¼-inch pieces.
Eggs, beaten	12 (1 lb 5 oz)	Add eggs to rhubarb.
Sugar, granulated	4 lb 8 oz	Mix dry ingredients. Add to rhubarb mixture. Scale 2 lb (4½ cups) filling into each unbaked crust.
Flour, all-purpose	9 oz	
Salt	1 tsp	Bake at 375°F for 45–50 minutes or until custard is set.
Lemon peel, grated	1 tsp	Cool. Refrigerate if not served within 4 hours.

Approximate nutritive values per portion

Calories	Carbohydrate	Protein	Fat	Cholesterol	Sodium	Fiber	Iron
345 kcal	55 g	4 g	13 g	45 mg	227 mg	2 g	1mg

Notes

- Potentially hazardous food. Store at temperature below 41°F.
- For eight 8-inch pies, use 2 lb 8 oz dough, portioned 5 oz per pie. Use 1 lb 12 oz filling per pie.
- May be topped with Meringue (p. 344).
- Unbaked pie may be covered with a top crust or a latticed top made of pastry strips ⅛-inch thick.

CREAM PIE

Yield: 56 portions or seven 9-inch pies   *Portion:* 8 pieces per pie
Oven: 425°F for pastry, 375°F for meringue   *Bake:* 10 minutes, 10–12 minutes

Ingredient	Amount	Procedure
Pastry for One-Crust Pies (p. 341)	4 lb	Make pastry. Line seven 9-inch pie pans, 9 oz per pan. For 8-inch pies, see Note. Flute edges and prick crust with fork (Figure 11.4). Bake at 425°F for 10 minutes or until light brown. Cool.
Milk	3¾ qt	Heat milk to boiling point in a steam-jacketed or other large kettle.
Sugar, granulated	2 lb 12 oz	Mix sugar, cornstarch, and salt.
Cornstarch	13 oz	Add cold milk and stir until smooth.
Salt	2½ tsp	Add to hot milk gradually, stirring briskly with a wire whip.
Milk, cold	1¼ qt	Cook until smooth and thick, approximately 10 minutes.
Egg yolks, beaten	20 (13 oz)	Add, while stirring, a small amount of hot mixture to the egg yolks. Add to remaining hot mixture, stirring constantly. Stir slowly and cook for 5–10 minutes. Remove from heat.
Margarine	5 oz	Stir in margarine and vanilla.
Vanilla	2½ Tbsp	Pour 2 lb (4 cups) filling into each baked pie shell.
Egg whites	20 (1 lb 6 oz)	Prepare Meringue (p. 344).
Salt	½ tsp	Cover each filled pie with 5 oz meringue.
Sugar, granulated	1 lb 4 oz	Bake at 375°F for 10–12 minutes or until meringue is golden brown.
Cream of tartar	½ tsp	Cool quickly (within 4 hours) to below 41°F. Refrigerate until served.

Approximate nutritive values per portion

Calories	Carbohydrate	Protein	Fat	Cholesterol	Sodium	Fiber	Iron
397 kcal	55 g	7 g	17 g	40 mg	380 mg	0.5 g	1 mg

Notes

- Potentially hazardous food. Store at temperature below 41°F.
- For eight 8-inch pies, use 2 lb 8 oz dough, portioned 5 oz per pie. Use 1 lb 12 oz (3½ cups) filling per pie.

Variations

- **Banana Cream Pie.** Slice 1 large banana into each pie shell before adding cream filling.
- **Chocolate Cream Pie.** Add 6 oz cocoa or 8 oz unsweetened chocolate. Increase sugar to 3 lb. If using cocoa, mix with cornstarch and sugar. If using chocolate, melt and add to hot milk.
- **Coconut Cream Pie.** Add 10 oz toasted coconut to filling and sprinkle 2 oz coconut over meringue.
- **Date Cream Pie.** Add 3 lb chopped, pitted dates to cooked filling.
- **Fruit Glazed Pie.** Use frozen blueberries, strawberries, or cherries. Thaw 6 lb frozen fruit and drain. Measure 1 qt fruit syrup, adding water if needed to make that amount. Add slowly to a mixture of 6 oz sugar, 4 oz cornstarch, and ¾ cup lemon juice if using blueberries, strawberries or sweet cherries or ¾ cup additional water if using sour cherries. Cook until thick and clear. Cool slightly. Add drained fruit. Spread over cream pies.
- **Nut Cream Pie.** Add ½ cup chopped pecans or other nuts.
- **Pineapple Cream Pie.** Add 3½ cups crushed pineapple, drained, to cooked filling.

BUTTERSCOTCH CREAM PIE

Yield: 56 portions or seven 9-inch pies   *Portion:* 8 pieces per pie
Oven: 425°F for pastry, 375°F for meringue   *Bake:* 10 minutes, 10–12 minutes

Ingredient	Amount	Procedure
Pastry for One-Crust Pies (p. 341)	4 lb	Make pastry. Line seven 9-inch pie pans, 9 oz per pan. For 8-inch pies, see Note. Flute edges and prick crust with fork (Figure 11.4). Bake at 425°F for 10 minutes or until light brown.
Margarine	1 lb	Melt margarine. Stir in sugar.
Sugar, brown	2 lb 8 oz	Cook over low heat to 220°F, stirring occasionally.
Milk	3 qt	Add milk slowly to margarine-sugar mixture while stirring with a wire whip. Stir until all sugar is dissolved. Heat mixture to boiling.
Cornstarch	6 oz	Combine cornstarch, flour, and salt.
Flour, all-purpose	6 oz	
Salt	1 Tbsp	
Milk, warm	1 qt	Combine milk and eggs. Add to cornstarch and flour mixture and mix.
Eggs	5 (9 oz)	Add to the hot mixture while stirring. Cook until thick.
Egg yolks	10 (6 oz)	Remove from heat.
Margarine	4 oz	Add margarine and vanilla. Cool partially.
Vanilla	2 Tbsp	Fill baked pie shells, 1 lb 12 oz (3½ cups) per pie.
Egg whites	16 (1 lb 2 oz)	Prepare Meringue (p. 344).
Salt	½ tsp	Cover each filled pie with 5 oz meringue.
Sugar, granulated	1 lb	Bake at 375°F for 10–12 minutes, or until meringue is golden brown.
Cream of tartar	½ tsp	Cool quickly (within 4 hours) to temperature below 41°F. Refrigerate until served.

Approximate nutritive values per portion

Calories	Carbohydrate	Protein	Fat	Cholesterol	Sodium	Fiber	Iron
427 kcal	49 g	6 g	23 g	68 mg	465 mg	0.5 g	1 mg

Notes

- Potentially hazardous food. Store at temperature below 41°F.
- For eight 8-inch pies, use 2 lb 8 oz dough portioned 5 oz per pie. Use 1 lb 8 oz (3 cups) filling per pie.

LEMON PIE

Yield: 56 portions or seven 9-inch pies   *Portion:* 8 pieces per pie

Oven: 425°F pastry, 375°F meringue   *Bake:* 10 minutes, 10–12 minutes

Ingredient	Amount	Procedure
Pastry for One-Crust Pies (p. 341)	4 lb	Make pastry. Line seven 9-inch pie pans, 9 oz per pan. For 8-inch pies, see Note. Flute edges and prick bottom and sides of crust with fork. Bake at 425°F for 10 minutes or until light brown.
Water Salt Lemon zest, grated	2¼ qt 2 tsp 3 lemons	Heat water, salt, and lemon zest to boiling point.
Sugar, granulated Cornstarch Water, cold	3 lb 8 oz 12 oz 3 cups	Mix sugar and cornstarch. Add cold water and stir until mixed. Add slowly to boiling water, stirring constantly with a wire whip. Cook until thickened and clear. Remove from heat.
Egg yolks, beaten	16 (1½ cups)	Add, while stirring, a small amount of hot mixture to egg yolks. Add to remaining hot mixture, stirring constantly. Return to heat and cook for about 5 minutes. Remove from heat.
Margarine Fresh lemon juice	3 oz 1½ cups	Add margarine and lemon juice. Blend. Scale into baked pie shells, 1 lb 10 oz (3½ cups) per pie.
Egg whites Salt Sugar, granulated Cream of tartar	16 (1 lb 2 oz) ½ tsp 1 lb ½ tsp	Prepare Meringue (p. 344). Cover each pie with 5 oz meringue. Bake at 375°F for 10–12 minutes, or until meringue is golden brown. Cool quickly (within 4 hours) to temperature below 41°F. Refrigerate until served.

Approximate nutritive values per portion

Calories	Carbohydrate	Protein	Fat	Cholesterol	Sodium	Fiber	Iron
355 kcal	55 g	3 g	14 g	61 mg	302 mg	0.5 g	1 mg

Notes

- Potentially hazardous food. Store at temperature below 41°F.
- For eight 8-inch pies, use 2 lb 8 oz dough portioned 5 oz per pie. Use 3 cups filling per pie.

CUSTARD PIE

Yield: 56 portions or seven 9-inch pies   *Portion:* 8 pieces per pie
Oven: 450°F, 350°F   *Bake:* 15 minutes, 20 minutes

Ingredient	Amount	Procedure
Pastry for One-Crust Pies (p. 341)	4 lb	Make pastry. Line seven 9-inch pie pans, 9 oz per pan. For 8-inch pies, see Note. Flute edges.
Eggs Sugar, granulated Salt Vanilla	30 (3 lb 4 oz) 1 lb 14 oz 1¼ tsp 2½ Tbsp	Beat eggs slightly. Add sugar, salt, and vanilla. Mix.
Milk, scalded	1¼ gal	Add hot milk, slowly at first, then more rapidly. Pour into unbaked pie shells, 1 qt per pie.
Nutmeg, ground	2 tsp	Sprinkle nutmeg over top of pies. Bake at 450°F for 15 minutes. Reduce heat to 350°F and bake for 20 minutes, or until a knife inserted halfway between the edge and center comes out clean. Cool quickly (within 4 hours) to below 41°F. Refrigerate until served.

Approximate nutritive values per portion

Calories	Carbohydrate	Protein	Fat	Cholesterol	Sodium	Fiber	Iron
312 kcal	32 g	8 g	17 g	124 mg	296 mg	0.4 g	1 mg

Notes

- Potentially hazardous food. Store at temperature below 41°F.
- For eight 8-inch pies, use 2 lb 8 oz dough portioned 5 oz per pie. For filling, use 24 (2 lb 8 oz) eggs, 1 lb 8 oz sugar, 1 tsp salt, 2 Tbsp vanilla, and 1 gal milk, portioned 3 cups per pie.

Variation

- **Coconut Custard Pie.** Add 1 lb flaked coconut. Omit nutmeg.

PUMPKIN PIE

Yield: 56 portions or seven 9-inch pies   *Portion:* 8 pieces per pie
Oven: 450°F, 350°F   *Bake:* 15 minutes, 30 minutes

Ingredient	Amount	Procedure
Pastry for One-Crust Pies (p. 341)	4 lb	Make pastry. Line seven 9-inch pie pans, 9 oz per pan. For 8-inch pies, see Note. Flute edges.
Eggs, beaten Pumpkin	14 (1 lb 8 oz) 2½ qt (3 No. 2½ cans)	Combine eggs and pumpkin in mixer bowl.
Sugar, granulated Sugar, brown Ginger, ground Cinnamon, ground Salt	1 lb 12 oz 10 oz 1½ tsp 1½ Tbsp 1 Tbsp	Combine sugars and seasonings. Add to pumpkin mixture.
Milk, hot	2¾ qt	Add milk to pumpkin mixture. Mix. Pour into unbaked pie shells, 1 qt per pie. Bake at 450°F for 15 minutes. Reduce heat to 350°F and bake for 30 minutes, or until a knife inserted halfway between the edge and center comes out clean. Cool quickly (within 4 hours) to below 41°F. Refrigerate until served.

Approximate nutritive values per portion

Calories	Carbohydrate	Protein	Fat	Cholesterol	Sodium	Fiber	Iron
295 kcal	38 g	5 g	14 g	58 mg	329 mg	2 g	2 mg

Notes

- Potentially hazardous food. Store at temperature below 41°F.
- For eight 8-inch pies, use 2 lb 8 oz pastry portioned 5 oz per pie. Use 3½ cups filling per pie.
- Undiluted evaporated milk may be substituted for fresh milk.
- One pound chopped pecans may be sprinkled over tops of pies after 15 minutes of baking. Continue baking.

Variation

- **Praline Pumpkin Pie.** Mix 12 oz finely chopped pecans, 14 oz brown sugar, and 8 oz margarine or butter. Pat 4 oz of the mixture into each unbaked pie shell before pouring in filling.

PECAN PIE

Yield: 56 portions or seven 9-inch pies   *Portion:* 8 pieces per pie
Oven: 350°F   *Bake:* 40 minutes

Ingredient	Amount	Procedure
Pastry for One-Crust Pies (p. 341)	4 lb	Make pastry. Line seven 9-inch pie pans, 9 oz per pan. For 8-inch pies, see Note. Flute edges.
Sugar, granulated Margarine Salt	5 lb 5 oz 1 Tbsp	Cream sugar, margarine, and salt on medium speed until fluffy, using a flat beater.
Eggs, beaten	30 (3 lb 4 oz)	Add eggs to creamed mixture and mix well.
Corn syrup, white Vanilla	1¼ qt 3 Tbsp	Add corn syrup and vanilla. Blend thoroughly.
Pecan halves or pieces	2 lb	Place 4½ oz pecans in each unbaked pie shell. Pour 1 lb 8 oz (3 cups) egg-sugar mixture over pecans. Bake at 350°F for 40 minutes, or until filling is set.

Approximate nutritive values per portion

Calories	Carbohydrate	Protein	Fat	Cholesterol	Sodium	Fiber	Iron
568 kcal	78 g	6 g	27 g	112 mg	365 mg	1.5 g	3 mg

Note
- For eight 8-inch pies, use 2 lb 8 oz pastry portioned 5 oz per pie. Use 2½ cups filling and 4 oz pecans per pie.

PECAN CREAM CHEESE PIE

Yield: 56 portions or seven 9-inch pies   *Portion:* 8 pieces per pie
Oven: 375°F, 350°F   *Bake:* 10 minutes, 40–45 minutes

Ingredient	Amount	Procedure
Pastry for One-Crust Pies (p. 341)	4 lb	Make pastry. Line seven 9-inch pie pans, 5 oz per pan. For 8-inch pies, see Note. Flute edges and prick crust with fork (Figure 11.4). Bake at 375°F for 10 minutes or until set. Cool.
Cream cheese, softened Sugar, granulated	3 lb 12 oz 1 lb	Combine cream cheese and sugar in mixer bowl. Beat on medium until smooth, using a flat beater.
Eggs Salt Vanilla	7 (12 oz) 1 tsp 2 Tbsp	Add eggs, salt, and vanilla to creamed mixture. Beat until smooth. Spread 12 oz filling into each pie shell.
Pecan pieces	2 lb 3 oz	Sprinkle 5 oz pecans over cream cheese layer.
Eggs Sugar, brown Corn syrup Vanilla	11 (1 lb 4 oz) 8 oz 2 lb 8 oz 1 Tbsp	Combine eggs, sugar, corn syrup, and vanilla in mixer bowl. Mix until blended. Scale 10 oz (approximately 1 cup) over pecans. Bake at 350°F for 40–45 minutes. Cool. Refrigerate for 6–8 hours before serving.

Approximate nutritive values per portion

Calories	Carbohydrate	Protein	Fat	Cholesterol	Sodium	Fiber	Iron
514 kcal	43 g	7 g	36 g	103 mg	337 mg	2 g	3 mg

Notes

- Potentially hazardous food. Store at temperature below 41°F.
- For eight 8-inch pies, use 2 lb 8 oz pastry portioned 5 oz per pie. For the filling, portion 11 oz cream cheese filling, 8 oz (1 cup) syrup mixture, and 4 oz pecans per pie.

CHOCOLATE CHIFFON PIE

Yield: 56 portions or seven 9-inch pies   *Portion:* 8 pieces per pie
Oven: 425°F (pastry)   *Bake:* 10 minutes

Ingredient	Amount	Procedure
Pastry for One-Crust Pies (p. 341)	4 lb	Make pastry. Line seven 9-inch pie pans, 9 oz per pan. For 8-inch pies, see Note. Flute edges and prick crust with a fork (Figure 11.4). Bake at 425°F for 10 minutes or until light brown.
Gelatin, unflavored Water, cold	1½ oz 1½ cups	Sprinkle gelatin over water. Let stand for 10 minutes.
Unsweetened chocolate Water, boiling	8 oz 3 cups	Melt chocolate. Add hot water slowly. Stir until mixed. Add gelatin and stir until dissolved.
Egg yolks, beaten Sugar, granulated Salt	24 (1 lb) 1 lb 8 oz 1½ tsp	Combine egg yolks, sugar, and salt. Cook until mixture begins to thicken.
Vanilla	2 Tbsp	Add vanilla and chocolate to egg mixture. Chill until mixture begins to congeal.
Pasteurized egg whites Sugar, granulated	24 (1 lb 12 oz) 1 lb 8 oz	Beat egg whites until frothy. Gradually add sugar and beat at high speed until meringue can be formed into soft peaks. Fold into chocolate mixture. Scale into baked pie shells, 1 lb (4 cups) per pie. Cool quickly (within 4 hours) to below 41°F. Refrigerate until served.
Cream, whipping Sugar, granulated	1 qt ¼ cup	Just before serving, whip cream. Add sugar. Spread 1 cup whipped cream over each pie.

Approximate nutritive values per portion

Calories	Carbohydrate	Protein	Fat	Cholesterol	Sodium	Fiber	Iron
365 kcal	40 g	6 g	21 g	123 mg	263 mg	1 g	1 mg

Notes

- Potentially hazardous food. Store at temperature below 41°F.
- For eight 8-inch pies, use 2 lb 8 oz pastry portioned 5 oz per pie. For filling, use 12 oz (3 cups) per pie.
- Graham Cracker Crust (p. 343) may be used in place of pastry.

Variations

- **Chocolate Peppermint Chiffon Pie.** Cover pie with whipped cream to which 1 lb crushed peppermint candy sticks has been added.
- **Chocolate Refrigerator Dessert.** Use ⅔ recipe Chocolate Chiffon Pie. Spread 12 oz vanilla wafer crumbs over bottom of 12 × 20 × 2-inch pan. Pour in chocolate chiffon mixture and cover with 1 lb 12 oz crumbs.
- **Frozen Chocolate Chiffon Pie.** Fold in 3 cups whipped cream. Pile into pastry or graham cracker crust. Spread over tops of pies 1½ cups whipped cream sweetened with 3 Tbsp sugar. Freeze. Serve frozen.

STRAWBERRY CHIFFON PIE

Yield: 56 portions or seven 9-inch pies   *Portion:* 8 pieces per pie
Oven: 425°F (pastry)   *Bake:* 10 minutes

Ingredient	Amount	Procedure
Pastry for One-Crust Pies (p. 341)	4 lb	Make pastry. Line seven 9-inch pie pans, 9 oz per pan. For 8 inch pies, see Note. Flute edges and prick crust with fork (Figure 11.4). Bake at 425°F for 10 minutes or until light brown.
Strawberries, sliced, frozen	3 lb 12 oz	Drain strawberries. Reserve juice.
Strawberry gelatin Water, boiling	1 lb 4 oz 1¼ qt	Dissolve gelatin in boiling water.
Strawberry juice drained from berries Fresh lemon juice	2 lb (1 qt) ⅔ cup	Add enough water to reserved juice to make 1 qt. Combine lemon and strawberry juices. Add to gelatin mixture. Chill until partially set. Stir occasionally.
Whipped topping	3 cups	Whip topping stiff but not dry. Whip gelatin mixture until soft peaks form. Fold in whipped topping.
Salt Pasteurized egg whites Sugar, granulated	1 tsp 10 (12 oz) 12 oz	Gradually add sugar. Beat until stiff peaks form. Add salt to egg whites. Beat until soft peaks form. Fold in gelatin mixture. Fold strawberries into mixture. Portion 1 lb 4 oz filling into each baked pie shell. Cool quickly (within 4 hours) to below 41°F. Refrigerate until served.

Approximate nutritive values per portion

Calories	Carbohydrate	Protein	Fat	Cholesterol	Sodium	Fiber	Iron
295 kcal	29 g	7 g	15 g	14 mg	472 mg	1.3 g	1 mg

Notes

- Potentially hazardous food. Store at internal temperature below 41°F.
- For eight 8-inch pies, use 2 lb 8 oz pastry portioned 5 oz per pie. For the filling, use 1 lb per pie.

LEMON CHIFFON PIE

Yield: 56 portions or seven 9-inch pies   *Portion:* 8 pieces per pie
Oven: 425°F (pastry)   *Bake:* 10 minutes

Ingredient	Amount	Procedure
Pastry for One-Crust Pies (p. 341)	4 lb	Make pastry. Line seven 9-inch pie pans, 9 oz per pan. For 8-inch pies, see Note. Flute edges and prick crust with fork (Figure 11.4). Bake at 425°F for 10 minutes or until light brown.
Gelatin, unflavored Water, cold	1½ oz 1¾ cups	Sprinkle gelatin over water. Let stand for 10 minutes.
Sugar, granulated Salt Fresh lemon juice Egg yolks, beaten	1 lb 8 oz 2 tsp 2½ cups 21 (13 oz)	Cook in steam-jacketed kettle or over hot water until consistency of custard. Remove from heat. Add softened gelatin. Stir until dissolved. Add sugar, salt, and lemon juice to egg yolks.
Lemon peel, grated	2 Tbsp	Add lemon peel. Chill until mixture begins to congeal.
Pasteurized egg whites Sugar, granulated	21 (1 lb 8 oz) 1 lb 2 oz	Beat egg whites until frothy. Gradually add sugar and beat until meringue forms soft peaks. Fold into lemon mixture. Scale into baked pie shells, 1 lb (4 cups) per pie. Cool quickly (within 4 hours) to below 41°F. Refrigerate until served.
Cream, whipping Sugar, granulated	1 qt ½ cup	Just before serving, whip cream. Spread 1 cup cream over each pie.

Approximate nutritive values per portion

Calories	Carbohydrate	Protein	Fat	Cholesterol	Sodium	Fiber	Iron
331 kcal	37 g	5 g	19 g	103 mg	280 mg	0.5 g	1 mg

Notes

- Potentially hazardous food. Store at temperature below 41°F.
- For eight 8-inch pies, use 2 lb 8 oz pastry portioned 5 oz per pie. For the filling, use 12 oz (3 cups) per pie.
- Graham Cracker Crust (p. 343) may be used in place of pastry.

Variations

- **Frozen Lemon Pie.** Increase sugar in custard to 2 lb. Delete sugar from meringue. Beat egg whites and fold into 2 qt whipped cream. Fold into chilled lemon mixture. Pour into Graham Cracker Crust (p. 343). Freeze. Serve frozen.
- **Lemon Refrigerator Dessert.** Crush 3 lb 8 oz vanilla wafers. Spread half of crumbs in bottom of 12 × 20 × 2-inch pan. Pour chiffon pie mixture over crumbs and cover with remaining crumbs.
- **Orange Chiffon Pie.** Substitute 2 cups orange juice for 2 cups lemon juice. Substitute grated orange peel for lemon peel.

ICE CREAM PIE

Yield: 56 portions or seven 9-inch pies   *Portion:* 8 pieces per pie
Oven: 500°F   *Bake:* 2–3 minutes

Ingredient	Amount	Procedure
Graham Cracker Crust (p. 343)	1 recipe	Prepare seven 9-inch crusts. For 8-inch pies, see Note.
Vanilla ice cream	2 gal	Soften ice cream. Dip into prepared crusts, using 4½ cups per pie. Freeze for several hours.
Salt Pasteurized egg whites Sugar, granulated Vanilla	¾ tsp 24 (2 lb 10 oz) 1 lb 8 oz 1½ tsp	Add salt to egg whites. Beat until frothy, using the wire whip attachment. Add sugar gradually, beating at high speed until sugar has dissolved. Add vanilla. Cover pies with meringue, 9 oz per pie. Brown quickly (2–3 minutes) in oven at 500°F. Return to freezer if not served immediately.
Chocolate Sauce (p. 714)	1½ qt	Serve with chocolate sauce or fresh strawberries.

Approximate nutritive values per portion

Calories	Carbohydrate	Protein	Fat	Cholesterol	Sodium	Fiber	Iron
467 kcal	64 g	7 g	22 g	35 mg	339 mg	0.3 g	1 mg

Notes

- For eight 8-inch pies, portion 1 qt ice cream per pie. Cover with 8 oz meringue.
- Pastry crust, baked, may be used in place of graham cracker crust.
- Other flavors of ice cream may be used.

Variation

- **Raspberry Alaska Pie.** Thicken three 40-oz packages frozen red raspberries with 2 oz cornstarch. Make thin layers of thickened berries and ice cream in graham cracker crusts, using about half of the berries. Proceed as for Ice Cream Pie. Spoon remaining berries over individual servings of pie.

FROZEN MOCHA ALMOND PIE

Yield: 56 portions or seven 9-inch pies   *Portion:* 8 pieces per pie

Ingredient	Amount	Procedure
Graham Cracker Crust (p. 343)	1 recipe	Prepare seven 9-inch crusts. For 8-inch pies, see Note.
Gelatin, unflavored Water, cold	1½ oz 1 cup	Sprinkle gelatin over water. Let stand for 10 minutes.
Sugar, granulated Salt Coffee, hot Egg yolks, beaten	1 lb 8 oz 1 Tbsp 2 qt 18 (11 oz)	Add sugar, salt, and coffee to egg yolks. Cook in steam-jacketed kettle or over hot water until mixture coats spoon. Remove from heat. Add softened gelatin. Stir until dissolved. Chill until mixture is consistency of unbeaten egg whites.
Cream of tartar Pasteurized egg whites Sugar, granulated	1½ tsp 18 (1 lb 5 oz) 1 lb 8 oz	Add cream of tartar to egg whites. Beat until frothy. Add sugar gradually and beat on high speed until consistency of meringue. Fold into gelatin mixture.
Whipping cream Sugar, granulated	1 qt ¼ cup	Whip cream. Add sugar to one-third of the whipped cream. Save for topping.
Almonds, toasted Vanilla	1 lb 2 Tbsp	Add almonds and vanilla to remaining whipped cream. Fold into gelatin mixture. Pour into prepared crusts. Spread remaining whipped cream over pies and freeze. Remove from freezer 15–20 minutes before serving.

Approximate nutritive values per portion

Calories	Carbohydrate	Protein	Fat	Cholesterol	Sodium	Fiber	Iron
378 kcal	48 g	6 g	19 g	90 mg	312 mg	0.7 g	1 mg

Notes

- For eight 8-inch pies, use 2 lb 8 oz pastry, portioned 5 oz per pie. Portion filling 3 cups per pie.

Other Dessert Recipes

BUTTERSCOTCH PUDDING

Yield: 50 portions or 6 qt   *Portion:* ½ cup

Ingredient	Amount	Procedure
Margarine Sugar, brown	10 oz 3 lb 4 oz	Cook margarine and sugar in steam-jacketed kettle until sugar starts to dissolve.
Water, warm	1 qt	Add water slowly, while stirring. Turn off heat.
Milk	2½ qt	Add milk to warm mixture.
Cornstarch Flour, all-purpose Salt Milk	6 oz 2½ oz ½ tsp 3 cups	Combine dry ingredients in mixer bowl. Add milk to make a smooth paste. Slowly add to warm sugar-milk mixture, stirring constantly. Cook until mixture thickens. Turn off heat.
Eggs	8 (14 oz)	Beat eggs on medium speed for 3 minutes. Add some of the hot mixture to the beaten eggs while still beating. Gradually add egg mixture to hot mixture. Turn on heat. Cook to 185°F.
Vanilla	2 Tbsp	Stir in vanilla. Cool quickly to temperature below 41°F. (See Note.) Cover with plastic wrap or waxed paper while cooling to prevent formation of film. Serve cold with No. 10 dipper (rounded).

Approximate nutritive values per portion

Calories	Carbohydrate	Protein	Fat	Cholesterol	Sodium	Fiber	Iron
222 kcal	36 g	3 g	7 g	42 mg	128 mg	0 g	1 mg

Note

- Potentially hazardous food. *Food Safety Standards:* Hold food for service at an internal temperature of 41°F or below. Do not mix old product with new. Keep leftover product chilled at 41°F or below. See p. 167 for cooling procedures.

CHOCOLATE PUDDING

Yield: 50 portions or 6 qt   *Portion:* ½ cup

Ingredient	Amount	Procedure
Sugar, granulated	2 lb 6 oz	Combine dry ingredients.
Flour, all-purpose	6 oz	
Cornstarch	3 oz	
Salt	1 tsp	
Cocoa	8 oz	
Milk	1 gal	Pour milk into steam-jacketed kettle or stockpot.
		Gradually add dry ingredients while stirring briskly with a wire whip.
		Heat to boiling point, then cook until thickened, about 20 minutes. Stir occasionally.
		Remove from heat.
Margarine	8 oz	Add margarine and vanilla. Blend.
Vanilla	2 Tbsp	Cool quickly to temperature below 41°F. (See Note)
		Cover with plastic wrap or waxed paper while cooling to prevent formation of film.
		Serve cold with No. 10 dipper (rounded).

Approximate nutritive values per portion

Calories	Carbohydrate	Protein	Fat	Cholesterol	Sodium	Fiber	Iron
193 kcal	32 g	4 g	7 g	11 mg	127 mg	0 g	2 mg

Note

- Potentially hazardous food. *Food Safety Standards:* Hold food for service at an internal temperature of 41°F or below. Do not mix old product with new. Keep leftover product chilled at 41°F or below. See p. 167 for cooling procedures.

Variations

- **Chocolate Banana Pudding.** Slice 12 bananas into cooled pudding.
- **Chocolate Pudding with Chips.** Stir 8 oz peanut butter, butterscotch, or chocolate chips into cooled pudding.

TAPIOCA CREAM PUDDING

Yield: 50 portions or 6 qt   *Portion:* ½ cup

Ingredient	Amount	Procedure
Milk	1 gal	Heat milk to boiling point in a steam-jacketed kettle or stock pot.
Tapioca, quick-cooking	9 oz	Add tapioca gradually while stirring with a wire whip. Cook until clear, stirring frequently.
Egg yolks, beaten Sugar, granulated Salt	10 (6 oz) 1 lb 2 tsp	Mix egg yolks, sugar, and salt. Add slowly to hot mixture while stirring. Cook for about 10 minutes. Remove from heat.
Egg whites (see Note) Sugar, granulated	10 (12 oz) 4 oz	Beat egg whites until frothy. Add sugar and beat on high speed to form a meringue.
Vanilla	2 Tbsp	Fold egg whites and vanilla into hot tapioca mixture. Cool quickly to temperature below 41°F (see Note). Serve cold with No. 10 dipper (rounded).

Approximate nutritive values per portion

Calories	Carbohydrate	Protein	Fat	Cholesterol	Sodium	Fiber	Iron
129 kcal	20 g	4 g	4 g	54 mg	137 mg	0 g	0.5 mg

Notes

- Use of pasteurized egg whites is recommended.
- Potentially hazardous food. *Food Safety Standards:* Hold food for service at an internal temperature of 41°F or below. Do not mix old product with new. Keep leftover product chilled at 41°F or below. See p. 167 for cooling procedures.

Variation

- **Fruit Tapioca Cream.** Add 1 qt chopped canned peaches or crushed pineapple, drained. Add ½ tsp almond extract for peach tapioca.

VANILLA CREAM PUDDING

Yield: 50 portions or 6 qt   *Portion:* ½ cup

Ingredient	Amount	Procedure
Milk Sugar, granulated	3 qt 1 lb	Heat milk and sugar in steam-jacketed kettle.
Sugar, granulated Cornstarch Salt Milk, cold	1 lb 4 oz 6 oz 1½ tsp 2¼ qt	Combine dry ingredients with cold milk in mixer bowl. Whip until smooth. Add to hot milk mixture slowly, stirring constantly with a wire whip. Cook mixture until it is thickened and there is no starch taste, approximately 10 minutes.
Egg yolks, beaten	20 (12 oz)	Add, while stirring, a small amount of hot mixture to the beaten eggs. Add to remainder of hot mixture in kettle, stirring constantly. Stir slowly and cook for about 2 minutes. Remove from heat.
Margarine Vanilla	4 oz 2 Tbsp	Stir in margarine and vanilla. Cool quickly to temperature below 41°F. (See Note) Cover with waxed paper while cooling to prevent formation of film. Serve cold with No. 10 dipper (rounded).

Approximate nutritive values per portion

Calories	Carbohydrate	Protein	Fat	Cholesterol	Sodium	Fiber	Iron
197 kcal	29 g	5 g	7 g	101 mg	139 mg	0 g	0.5 mg

Note

- Potentially hazardous food. *Food Safety Standards:* Hold food for service at an internal temperature of 41°F or below. Do not mix old product with new. Keep leftover product chilled at 41°F or below. See p. 167 for cooling procedures.

Variations

- **Banana Cream Pudding.** Add 12 bananas, sliced, to cooled pudding.
- **Chocolate Cream Pudding.** Add 6 oz sugar and 8 oz cocoa.
- **Coconut Cream Pudding.** Add 8 oz shredded coconut just before serving.
- **Pineapple Cream Pudding.** Add 1 qt crushed pineapple, well drained.

BAKED DATE PUDDING

Yield: 54 portions or 1 pan, 12 × 20 × 2 inches   *Portion:* 3 oz
Oven: 350°F   *Bake:* 45 minutes

Ingredient	Amount	Procedure
Water, hot	2½ cups	Pour hot water over dates in mixer bowl. Cover and let dates
Dates	2 lb 4 oz	steam for 15 minutes.
		Mix on low speed and then on medium speed until dates are broken into small pieces.
Sugar, granulated	1 lb	Combine dry ingredients in bowl and stir until blended.
Flour, all-purpose	1 lb	Add to date mixture. Mix on low speed only until blended.
Baking powder	1½ oz	Scale into well-greased 12 × 20 × 2-inch baking pan.
Nonfat dry milk	2 oz	
Salt	1½ tsp	
Walnuts, coarsely chopped	12 oz	
Sugar, brown	1 lb 4 oz	Mix sugar, margarine, and water. Heat to boiling point.
Margarine	2 oz	Pour hot sauce over batter in pan. Do not stir.
Water, boiling	1½ qt	Bake at 350°F for 45 minutes. Cool.
		Cut 6 × 9 for 54 portions or 6 × 8 for 48 portions. Serve with whipped cream or whipped topping.

Approximate nutritive values per portion

Calories	Carbohydrate	Protein	Fat	Cholesterol	Sodium	Fiber	Iron
205 kcal	40 g	3 g	5 g	0 mg	160 mg	2 g	1 mg

LEMON CAKE PUDDING

Yield: 60 portions or 2 pans, 12 × 20 × 2 inches   *Portion:* 2½ × 3 inches
Oven: 350°F   *Bake:* 1 hour

Ingredient	Amount	Procedure
Egg yolks	35 (1 lb 6 oz)	Beat egg yolks, lemon juice, and margarine together until
Fresh lemon juice	5 cups	lemon colored.
Margarine, softened	3 oz	
Sugar, granulated	6 lb	Combine sugar, flour, and salt.
Flour, all-purpose	1 lb 3 oz	
Salt	1 oz (1½ Tbsp)	
Milk	3 qt	Add dry ingredients and milk alternately to egg mixture on low speed, ending with dry ingredients.
Pasteurized egg whites	27 (2 lb)	Beat egg whites on high speed, until stiff, using the wire whip attachment. Blend into egg mixture on low speed.
		Pour pudding into two 12 × 20 × 2-inch counter pans, 9 lb 8 oz per pan. Set filled pans in two other counter pans that have been filled half full with boiling water. Bake at 350°F for 1 hour. Cut 5 × 6.

Approximate nutritive values per portion

Calories	Carbohydrate	Protein	Fat	Cholesterol	Sodium	Fiber	Iron
297 kcal	56 g	6 g	6 g	140 mg	232 mg	0.3 g	1 mg

Note

- Potentially hazardous food. Store at internal temperature below 41°F.

CHEESECAKE

Yield: 48 portions or six 8-inch cakes   *Portion:* 8 pieces per cake
Oven: 350°F   *Bake:* 40–45 minutes

Ingredient	Amount	Procedure
Graham cracker crumbs	1 lb 8 oz	Combine crumbs, sugar, and margarine.
Sugar, granulated	12 oz	Place 1 cup crumb mixture into each of six 8-inch pie pans or six 6 × 6-inch square cake pans.
Margarine, melted	12 oz	Press crumbs to sides and bottom of pans.
Cream cheese	4 lb 8 oz	Let cheese stand until it reaches room temperature. Cream until smooth, using a flat beater.
Eggs	11 (1 lb 3 oz)	Add eggs slowly to cream cheese while beating.
Sugar, granulated	1 lb 2 oz	Add sugar and vanilla to cheese mixture. Beat on high speed for about 5 minutes.
Vanilla	2 Tbsp	Place about 3 cups filling in each shell. Bake at 350°F for 30–35 minutes or until set. Do not overbake.
Sour cream	1¼ qt	Mix sour cream, sugar, and vanilla.
Sugar, granulated	4 oz	Spread 1 cup topping on each cake.
Vanilla	1½ tsp	
Graham cracker crumbs	4 oz	Sprinkle with a few graham cracker crumbs. Bake for 10 minutes.

Approximate nutritive values per portion

Calories	Carbohydrate	Protein	Fat	Cholesterol	Sodium	Fiber	Iron
420 kcal	35 g	7 g	28 g	106 mg	321 mg	0 g	1 mg

Note

- Potentially hazardous food. Store below 41°F.

Variation

- **Cheesecake with Fruit Glaze.** Cover baked cheesecake with the following glaze: Thaw and drain 6 lb frozen strawberries, raspberries, or cherries. Measure 1 qt fruit syrup, adding water if needed to make that amount. Add slowly to mixture of 4 oz cornstarch, 6 oz granulated sugar, and ¾ cup lemon juice if using berries or sweet cherries or ¾ cup additional water if using sour cherries. Cook until thick and clear. Cool slightly. Add drained fruit. Spread over cheesecakes. Canned fruit pie fillings may be used for the glaze.

BAKED CUSTARD

Yield: 50 custards   *Portion:* 4 oz
Oven: 325°F   *Bake:* 40–45 minutes

Ingredient	Amount	Procedure
Eggs	20 (2 lb 3 oz)	Beat eggs slightly, using the wire whip attachment.
Sugar, granulated	1 lb 4 oz	Add sugar, salt, cold milk, and vanilla.
Salt	½ tsp	Mix on low speed only until blended.
Milk, cold	1 qt	
Vanilla	2 Tbsp	
Milk	1 gal	Scald milk by bringing to point just below boiling. Add to egg mixture and blend.
Nutmeg, ground	2 tsp	Pour mixture into custard cups that have been arranged in baking pans. Sprinkle nutmeg over tops. Pour hot water around cups. Bake at 325°F for 40–45 minutes or until a knife inserted in custard comes out clean (180°F). Cool quickly (within 4 hours) to below 41°F.

Approximate nutritive values per portion

Calories	Carbohydrate	Protein	Fat	Cholesterol	Sodium	Fiber	Iron
136 kcal	16 g	6 g	5 g	98 mg	95 mg	0 g	0.5 mg

Notes

- Potentially hazardous food. Store at internal temperature below 41°F.
- Custard may be baked in a 12 × 20 × 2-inch pan set in a pan of hot water. Cut 5 × 8 for 40 portions.

Variations

- **Bread Pudding.** Pour liquid mixture over 1 lb dry bread cubes and let stand until bread is softened. Add 1 lb raisins if desired. Bake. Day-old sweet rolls may be substituted for bread.
- **Caramel Custard.** Add 1 cup Burnt Sugar Syrup (p. 297) slowly to scalded milk and stir carefully until melted.
- **Rice Custard.** Use ½ Baked Custard recipe, adding 1 lb AP cooked rice, 1 lb raisins, and 3 oz melted margarine or butter.

FLOATING ISLAND

Yield: 50 portions or 6 qt   *Portion:* ½ cup (4 oz)

Ingredient	Amount	Procedure
Milk	4½ qt	Heat milk to boiling point.
Sugar, granulated Cornstarch Salt	1 lb 4 oz ½ tsp	Combine sugar, cornstarch, and salt. Add gradually to hot milk, stirring briskly with a wire whip. Cook over hot water or in steam-jacketed kettle until slightly thickened.
Egg yolks, beaten Vanilla	27 (1 lb 2 oz) 2 Tbsp	Gradually stir egg yolks and vanilla into hot mixture. Continue cooking until thickened, about 5 minutes.

Egg whites
Sugar, granulated
	27 (1 lb 14 oz)
	12 oz
		Beat egg whites on high speed past the frothy stage,
		    approximately 1½ minutes, using the wire whip attachment.
		Add sugar gradually, while beating. Beat until sugar has dissolved
		    and mixture resembles meringue.
		Drop by spoonfuls onto hot water and bake at 375°F until set.

		Cool custard slightly and pour into sherbet dishes, or dip, using a No. 10 dipper. Lift meringues from water with a fork and place on top of portioned custards. Add dash of nutmeg. Chill quickly before serving (below 41°F within 4 hours).

Approximate nutritive values per portion

Calories	Carbohydrate	Protein	Fat	Cholesterol	Sodium	Fiber	Iron
164 kcal	23 g	6 g	6 g	121 mg	95 mg	0 g	0.5 mg

Notes

- Potentially hazardous food. Store at an internal temperature below 41°F.
- See p. 167 for recommended cooling procedures.

Variation

- **Creamy Custard Sauce with Fruit.** Ladle 3 oz custard over fresh fruit. Suggested combinations are sliced bananas, blueberries, and sliced peaches; or cubed pineapple, raspberries, and sliced peaches.

CHRISTMAS PUDDING

Yield: 48 portions   *Portion:* 3 oz
Steam pressure: 5–6 lb   *Steam:* 40–45 minutes

Ingredient	Amount	Procedure
Carrots, raw, peeled	1 lb 4 oz EP	Grate carrots and potatoes.
Potatoes, raw, peeled	1 lb 11 oz EP	
Sugar, granulated	2 lb	Cream sugar and margarine on medium speed, using a flat
Margarine	1 lb	beater.
Raisins	1 lb 4 oz	Add raisins, dates, and nuts to creamed mixture.
Dates, chopped	1 lb 4 oz	Add carrots and potatoes.
Nuts, chopped	12 oz	Mix on low speed until blended.
Flour, all-purpose	1 lb	Combine dry ingredients.
Baking soda	4 tsp	Add to fruit mixture. Mix on low speed until blended.
Cinnamon, ground	1 Tbsp	
Cloves, ground	1 Tbsp	
Nutmeg, ground	1 Tbsp	
Salt	¼ tsp	
		Portion mixture with No. 16 dipper into greased muffin pans.
		Cover each filled pan with an inverted empty muffin pan.
		Steam for 40–45 minutes.
		Serve warm with Vanilla Sauce (p. 716), Hard Sauce (p. 717), or Nutmeg Sauce (p. 716).
		Garnish with holly leaf and whole cranberries for Christmas.

Approximate nutritive values per portion

Calories	Carbohydrate	Protein	Fat	Cholesterol	Sodium	Fiber	Iron
304 kcal	50 g	3 g	12 g	0 mg	213 mg	3 g	1 mg

Variation

- **Flaming Pudding.** Dip sugar cube in lemon extract. Place on hot pudding and light just before serving.

CREAM PUFFS

Yield: 50 portions
Oven: 425°F, 325°F

Portion: 1 puff
Bake: 15 minutes, 30 minutes

Ingredient	Amount	Procedure
Margarine or butter Water, boiling	1 lb 1 qt	Melt margarine in boiling water.
Flour, all-purpose Salt	1 lb 3 oz 1 tsp	Add flour and salt all at once to boiling mixture. Beat vigorously. Remove from heat as soon as mixture leaves sides of pan. Transfer to mixer bowl. Cool slightly.
Eggs	16 (1 lb 12 oz)	Add eggs one at a time, beating on high speed after each addition.
		Drop batter with No. 24 dipper onto greased baking sheets. Bake at 425°F for 15 minutes. Reduce heat to 325°F and bake for 30 minutes longer.
		When ready to use, make a cut in top of each puff with a sharp knife. Fill with Custard Filling (p. 318), using a No. 16 dipper. Top with Chocolate Sauce (p. 714) if desired.

Approximate nutritive values per portion plus filling

Calories	Carbohydrate	Protein	Fat	Cholesterol	Sodium	Fiber	Iron
128 kcal	9 g	3 g	9 g	68 mg	149 mg	0.3 g	1 mg

Note

- Potentially hazardous food. Hold for service at below 41°F internal temperature when filled.

Variations

- **Butterscotch Cream Puffs.** Fill cream puffs with Butterscotch Pudding (p. 364). Top with Butterscotch Sauce (p. 713) if desired.
- **Eclairs.** Shape cream puff mixture by piping with a pastry tube, ¾ inch wide and 4 inches long. Bake. Split lengthwise. Proceed as for Cream Puffs. When filled, ice with Chocolate Glaze (p. 315).
- **Ice Cream Puffs.** Fill puffs with vanilla ice cream and serve with Chocolate Sauce (p. 714).
- **Orange Cream Puffs with Chocolate Filling.** Add ½ cup grated orange peel and 10 oz chopped almonds to cream puff mixture. Bake. Fill with Chocolate Cream Filling (p. 316) or Chocolate Pudding (p. 365).
- **Puff Shells.** Make bite-size shells with pastry tube or No. 100 dipper. Bake. Fill with chicken, fish, or ham salad. Yield: approximately 200 puffs.

PINEAPPLE BAVARIAN CREAM

Yield: 60 portions or 2 pans, 12 × 20 × 2 inches   *Portion:* 2½ × 3 inches

Ingredient	Amount	Procedure
Gelatin, unflavored Water, cold	3 oz 1 qt	Sprinkle gelatin over water. Let stand for 10 minutes.
Crushed pineapple Sugar, granulated	1 No. 10 can 1 lb 12 oz	Heat pineapple and sugar to boiling point.
Fresh lemon juice	¼ cup	Add gelatin to pineapple mixture. Stir until dissolved. Add lemon juice. Chill until mixture begins to congeal.
Whipping cream	1 qt	Whip cream and fold into pineapple mixture. Pour into 50 individual molds or two 12 × 20 × 2-inch pans. Cut 5 × 6.

Approximate nutritive values per portion

Calories	Carbohydrate	Protein	Fat	Cholesterol	Sodium	Fiber	Iron
129 kcal	20 g	2 g	5 g	18 mg	9 mg	0.4 g	0.5 mg

Note

- May be used for pie filling.

Variations

- **Apricot Bavarian Cream.** Substitute 3 lb cooked dried apricots or 6 lb sieved canned apricots for the crushed pineapple.
- **Strawberry Bavarian Cream.** Substitute 6 lb fresh or frozen sliced strawberries for pineapple.

RUSSIAN CREAM

Yield: 50 portions or 5 qt   *Portion:* 4 oz

Ingredient	Amount	Procedure
Gelatin, unflavored Water, cold	1½ oz 1¼ qt	Sprinkle gelatin over cold water. Let stand for 10 minutes.
Light cream (half- and-half) Sugar, granulated	1½ qt 2 lb	Combine half-and-half and sugar. Heat until warm in steam-jacketed kettle or over hot water. Stir in softened gelatin. Heat until gelatin and sugar are dissolved but do not boil. Cool.

Sour cream
Vanilla
	2 lb 8 oz
	2½ Tbsp
		When mixture begins to thicken, fold in sour cream and
		   vanilla, which have been beaten until smooth. Cool quickly
		   (within 4 hours) to below 41°F.

Raspberries, frozen	5 lb	Dip pudding with No. 12 dipper. Serve with No. 30 dipper of partially defrosted raspberries.

Approximate nutritive values per portion

Calories	Carbohydrate	Protein	Fat	Cholesterol	Sodium	Fiber	Iron
209 kcal	32 g	3 g	8 g	21 mg	26 mg	2 g	0.5 mg

Notes

- Potentially hazardous food. Store at internal temperature below 41°F.
- See p. 167 for recommended cooling procedures.

APPLE CRISP

Yield: 64 portions or 2 pans, 12 × 20 × 2 inches *Portion:* 3 × 2½ inches
Oven: 350°F *Bake:* 45–50 minutes

Ingredient	Amount	Procedure
Sugar, granulated	12 oz	Mix sugar and lemon juice with apples.
Fresh lemon juice	⅓ cup	Arrange in two greased 12 × 20 × 2-inch baking pans,
Apples, sliced	15 lb EP	8 lb per pan.
Margarine, soft	1 lb 4 oz	Combine remaining ingredients and mix until crumbly.
Flour, all-purpose	12 oz	Spread evenly over apples, 2 lb 4 oz per pan.
Rolled oats, quick-cooking, uncooked	12 oz	Bake at 350°F for 45–50 minutes
Sugar, brown	2 lb	Serve with whipped cream, ice cream, or cheese.
		Cut 4 × 8.

Approximate nutritive values per portion

Calories	Carbohydrate	Protein	Fat	Cholesterol	Sodium	Fiber	Iron
240 kcal	43 g	2 g	8 g	19 mg	80 mg	2 g	1 mg

Notes

- Fresh, frozen, or canned apples may be used.
- 1 tsp cinnamon or nutmeg may be added to the topping.
- 8 oz finely chopped pecans may be added to the topping.

Variations

- **Cheese Apple Crisp.** Add 8 oz grated cheese to topping mixture.
- **Cherry Crisp.** Substitute frozen pie cherries for apples. Increase granulated sugar to 1 lb. Add ½ tsp almond extract.
- **Fresh Fruit Crisp.** Combine 3 lb granulated sugar, 12 oz flour, 1 Tbsp nutmeg, and 1 Tbsp cinnamon. Add to 15 lb fresh fruit, peeled and sliced. Top with mixture of 2 lb 6 oz margarine, 2 lb 8 oz brown sugar, and 2 lb 6 oz flour. Cream margarine, add brown sugar and flour, and mix until of dough consistency. Spread over fruit. Bake. Serve warm with cream.
- **Peach Crisp.** Substitute sliced peaches for apples.

BAKED APPLES

Yield: 50 portions *Portion:* 1 apple
Oven: 375°F *Bake:* 45 minutes

Ingredient	Amount	Procedure
Apples	50	Wash and core apples.
		Peel down about one-fourth of the way from the top.
		Place in baking pans, peeled-side up.
Sugar, granulated	3 lb	Mix sugar, water, salt, and cinnamon. Pour over apples.
Water, hot	3 cups	Bake at 375°F until tender, about 45 minutes, basting
Salt	1 tsp	occasionally while cooking to glaze.
Cinnamon, ground	1 Tbsp	Test for doneness with a pointed knife inserted in the apple.

Approximate nutritive values per portion

Calories	Carbohydrate	Protein	Fat	Cholesterol	Sodium	Fiber	Iron
187 kcal	48 g	0 g	0 g	0 mg	45 mg	3 g	0.5 mg

Notes

- Use apples of uniform size, suitable for baking, such as Rome Beauty or Jonathan.
- Amount of sugar will vary with tartness of apples.
- ½ cup red cinnamon candies may be substituted for cinnamon.
- Apple centers may be filled with chopped dates, raisins, nuts, or mincemeat.
- 3 oz margarine or butter may be added to the syrup for flavor.

APPLE DUMPLINGS

Yield: 50 dumplings *portion:* 1 dumpling
Oven: 350°F *Bake:* 25–30 minutes

Ingredient	Amount	Procedure
Pastry for Two-Crust Pies (p. 342)	7 lb	Make pastry. Scale into 10-oz balls. Chill for 10 minutes or more.
Flour, all-purpose Sugar, granulated Salt Cinnamon, ground	10 oz 6 lb 1 Tbsp 1 Tbsp	Make sauce. Combine flour, sugar, salt, and cinnamon.
Water, hot	1½ gal	Add dry ingredients to water while stirring with a wire whip. Cook until thickened.
Margarine	1 lb	Add margarine and stir until margarine is melted. Remove from heat.
Vanilla	2 Tbsp	Add vanilla.
Apples, medium	50	Wash, core, and peel apples.
Margarine	1 lb 8 oz	Roll pastry ⅛ inch thick. Position apple on dough and cut a circle approximately 7 inches in diameter around it. Insert 1 Tbsp margarine into center of each apple. Push toward center of apple.
Sugar, granulated Cinnamon, ground Nutmeg, ground	1 lb 5 oz 1½ Tbsp 2 tsp	Combine sugar, cinnamon, and nutmeg. Use mixture to fill centers of apples. Enclose the apple in the cut dough, pinching to seal the edges. Turn the apple over so that the bottom is the top and make three slashes in the top of the apple. Place in lightly greased baking pans. Bake for 15 minutes at 350°F. Baste dumplings with half of the sauce and bake for 10–15 minutes longer or until golden brown. Serve dumplings with additional warm sauce as desired.

Approximate nutritive values per portion

Calories	Carbohydrate	Protein	Fat	Cholesterol	Sodium	Fiber	Iron
831 kcal	116 g	4 g	41 g	0 mg	668 mg	4 g	2 mg

Notes

- Apples may be wrapped with dough and frozen for later use. To serve, make sauce and bake as directed but allow 15–20 minutes longer baking time.
- Sliced apples, frozen or fresh, may be used in place of whole apples. Cut pastry into 6-inch squares. Place No. 10 dipper of fruit in the center and sprinkle with sugar-cinnamon mixture. Fold corners of pastry to the center and on top of fruit and seal edges together. Bake as directed for Apple Dumplings.

APPLESAUCE

Yield: 50 portions   *Portion:* ½ cup (4 oz)

Ingredient	Amount	Procedure
Apples, tart	15 lb AP	Wash, peel, and core apples. Cut into quarters.
Water	1 qt	Add water to apples. Cook slowly until soft.
Sugar, granulated	3 lb	Add sugar and stir until dissolved. Serve with No. 10 dipper (rounded).

Approximate nutritive values per portion

Calories	Carbohydrate	Protein	Fat	Cholesterol	Sodium	Fiber	Iron
185 kcal	48 g	0 g	0 g	0 mg	2 mg	3 g	0.5 mg

Notes

- Thin slices of lemon, lemon juice, or 1 tsp cinnamon may be added.
- Peaches or pears may be substituted for apples.
- Apples may be cooked unpeeled.
- Amount of sugar will vary with tartness of apples.

Variation

- **Apple Compote.** Combine sugar and water and heat to boiling point. Add apples and cook until transparent.

FRUIT COBBLER

Yield: 64 portions or 2 pans, 12 × 20 × 2 inches   *Portion:* 3 × 2½ inches
Oven: 425°F   *Bake:* 30 minutes

Ingredient	Amount	Procedure
Fruit, frozen	10 lb	Drain fruit. Reserve juice.
Juice drained from fruit, plus water to make total amount needed	2 qt	Heat juice and water to boiling point.
Sugar, granulated	1–2 lb (see Table 11.3, p. 346)	Mix sugar, cornstarch, and seasonings, if any.
Cornstarch	6 oz	
Seasonings	See Table 11.3, p. 346	
Water, cold	2 cups	Add cold water to dry ingredients and stir until smooth. Add to hot juice while stirring briskly with a wire whip. Cook until thickened.
		Add cooked, drained fruit to thickened juice. Mix carefully to prevent breaking or mashing fruit. Cool. Pour into two 12 × 20 × 2-inch baking pans, 9 lb 6 oz per pan.
Pastry (p. 340) or Biscuit Topping for Fruit Cobbler (p. 379)	3 lb	Roll pastry or topping to fit pans. Place on top of fruit. Seal edges to sides of pan. Perforate top. Bake at 425°F for 30 minutes or until top is browned. Cut 4 × 8.

Approximate nutritive values per portion

Calories	Carbohydrate	Protein	Fat	Cholesterol	Sodium	Fiber	Iron
193 kcal	32 g	1.4 g	3.7 g	5 mg	80 mg	1.6 g	1 mg

Notes

- Use cherries, berries, peaches, apricots, apples, plums, or other fruits.
- The amount of sugar will vary with the tartness of the fruit.
- For canned fruit, see p. 345.

Variations

- **Fruit Slices.** Use 2 lb 12 oz pastry. Line an 18 × 26 × 2-inch baking pan with 1 lb 8 oz of the pastry. Add fruit filling prepared as for cobbler. Moisten edges of dough and cover with crust made of remaining pastry. Trim and seal edges and perforate top. Bake at 400°F for 1–1¼ hours.
- **Peach Cobbler with Hard Sauce.** Use 10 lb frozen sliced peaches, thawed, and mixed with 1 lb sugar, 1 tsp nutmeg, 4 oz flour, and 6 oz margarine, melted. Top with pastry crust and bake. Serve warm with Hard Sauce (p. 717) or ice cream.

BISCUIT TOPPING FOR FRUIT COBBLER

Yield: topping for two 12 × 20-inch pans or 64 portions

Ingredient	Amount	Procedure
Flour, all-purpose	1 lb 6 oz	Blend dry ingredients in mixer bowl.
Baking powder	1 oz	
Salt	1 tsp	
Sugar, granulated	3 oz	
Nonfat dry milk	2 tsp	
Shortening	8 oz	Cut shortening into dry ingredients on low speed until it appears as coarse as cornmeal.
Eggs	2 (4 oz)	Beat eggs. Add water and blend.
Water	1¼ cups	Add to flour-shortening mixture.
		Blend on low speed until a soft dough is formed.
		Scale 1 lb 8 oz dough per pan. Roll to fit 12 × 20-inch pan.
		Roll onto rolling pin. Place over filling in pan, allowing dough to extend up edge of pan, about 1 inch all around (to allow for shrinkage).
		Cut several slits in dough.
Milk	¼ cup	Brush top of each pan with 2 Tbsp milk and 2 Tbsp sugar.
Sugar, granulated	2 oz	

Approximate nutritive values per portion

Calories	Carbohydrate	Protein	Fat	Cholesterol	Sodium	Fiber	Iron
79 kcal	10 g	1 g	4 g	8 mg	81 mg	0.3 g	0.5 mg

OLD-FASHIONED STRAWBERRY SHORTCAKE

Yield: 50 individual shortcakes   *Portion:* 1 shortcake + ¾ cup (6 oz) strawberries
Oven: 375°F   *Bake:* 12–15 minutes

Ingredient	Amount	Procedure
Fresh strawberries	9 qt	Wash, drain, and stem strawberries.
Sugar, granulated	2 lb (variable)	Slice and sweeten. Adjust sugar according to sweetness of berries.
Flour, all-purpose	4 lb	Mix dry ingredients in mixer bowl.
Baking powder	5 oz	
Salt	1 Tbsp	
Sugar, granulated	1 lb 5 oz	
Margarine or butter	2 lb	Cut margarine into dry ingredients, using a pastry blender or flat beater. Mixture should have coarse, mealy consistency.
Milk	1½ qt	Stir milk quickly into flour mixture. Mix just enough to moisten.
		Portion dough with No. 20 dipper onto ungreased baking sheets. Place about 2 inches apart to allow for spreading. Bake at 375°F for 12–15 minutes or until golden brown.
Half-and-half or whipping cream	1½ qt (3 qt if whipped)	To serve, dip ¾ cup (6 oz) strawberries over shortcake. Serve with half-and-half or top with whipped cream.

Approximate nutritive values per portion

Calories	Carbohydrate	Protein	Fat	Cholesterol	Sodium	Fiber	Iron
470 kcal	69 g	6 g	20 g	15 mg	611 mg	3 g	2 mg

Note

- For frozen strawberries, use 12 lb. Portion ½ cup over shortcake.

FRUIT AND CHEESE DESSERT

Yield: 50 portions   *Portion:* 2⅓–3 oz

Ingredient	Amount	Procedure

Fruit—choose from:
Apples, cut in
   wedges
Bananas, cut in
   chunks
Kiwifruit, cut in
   wedges
Pears, quartered
Pineapple spears
Strawberries
	5–6 lb	Select fruit in season that offers contrast in color and texture.
		Arrange attractively on a platter or tray.

Dessert cheese—
   choose from:
Blue
Brie
Camembert
Gruyère
Port du Salut
	3–4 lb	Place cheese on the platter with the fruit or alongside.
		Cut cheese into serving pieces or provide knife or cheese server so guests
		   may serve themselves.
		Garnish. Seasonal garnishes are appropriate.

Dessert crackers or wafers	2–2½ lb	Serve fruit and cheese with dessert crackers or wafers.

Approximate nutritive values per portion

Calories	Carbohydrate	Protein	Fat	Cholesterol	Sodium	Fiber	Iron
242 kcal	26 g	11 g	12 g	32 mg	435 mg	5 g	1 mg

Note

• See p. 48 for wine accompaniments.

CHAPTER 12

Eggs and Cheese

Egg, Cheese, and Milk Cookery

Eggs, cheese, and milk are basic ingredients in many quantity recipes, and their cookery requires carefully controlled temperatures and cooking times.

EGG COOKERY

Important rules in egg cooking are to use low temperatures and short cooking times. Eggs should be cooked until the white is completely coagulated (set) and the yolk begins to thicken. It is not necessary to cook eggs until hard or rubbery to kill bacteria that may be present. Egg white coagulates between 140°F and 149°F. Whole eggs cooked until the white is set (completely coagulated and firm) and the yolk is beginning to thicken (no longer runny but not hard) are considered to have met necessary time and temperature requirements for safety.

Poached, soft- or hard-cooked, and scrambled eggs should be prepared as close to service as possible by batch cooking or cooking to order. If eggs must be held on a hot counter, they should be undercooked slightly to compensate for the additional heating that will occur. Directions for cooking eggs are given beginning on p. 384.

CHEESE COOKERY

Cheese used in cooking should be appropriate in flavor and texture to the item being prepared and should blend well with other ingredients. Aged natural cheese or processed cheese blends more readily than green or unripened cheese. Processed cheese is a blend of fresh and aged natural cheeses that have been melted, pasteurized, and mixed with an emulsifier. It has no rind or waste, is easy to slice, and melts readily. During processing, however, it loses some of the characteristic flavor of natural cheese. For this reason, a natural cheese with a more pronounced flavor may be preferred for cheese sauce and as an addition to other cooked foods where a distinctive cheese flavor is desired.

Cheese to be combined with other ingredients usually is ground, shredded, or diced to expedite melting and blending.

Cheese melts in a 300–325°F oven, so baked dishes containing cheese should be cooked at a temperature no higher than 350°F. Excessive temperature and prolonged cooking cause cheese to toughen and become stringy and the fat to separate. When making cheese sauce, the cheese should be added after the white sauce is completely cooked and the mixture heated only enough to melt the cheese. When cheese is used as a topping, a thin layer of buttered bread crumbs will protect it from the heat and from becoming stringy.

Because it is available in many forms, cheddar cheese is commonly used in quantity food preparation and ranges in flavor from mild to very sharp. Cheese may be used for appetizers, sandwiches, and salads, or with crackers and fruit for dessert (see p. 381 for dessert suggestions). Table 5.2, p. 99, lists some of the most common cheeses.

MILK COOKERY

Milk should be heated or cooked at a low temperature. At high temperatures, the protein in milk coagulates, leaving a film on the surface and a coating on the sides of the kettle. This coating tends to scorch when milk is heated over direct heat. To prevent formation of this coating, milk should be heated over water, in a steamer, or in a steam-jacketed kettle. Whipping the milk to form a foam or tightly covering the pan and heating the milk to below boiling temperature help prevent formation of a surface film.

Curdling may be caused by holding the milk at high temperature or by adding foods containing acids and tannins. For example, the tannins in potatoes often cause curdling of the milk used in scalloped potatoes. Milk in combination with ham or certain vegetables, such as asparagus, green beans, carrots, peas, or tomatoes, may curdle. Curdling may be lessened by limiting the salt used, adding the milk in the form of a white sauce, keeping the temperature below boiling, and shortening the cooking time. Danger of curdling in tomato soup may be lessened by adding the tomato to the milk, by having both milk and tomato hot when they are combined, or by thickening the milk or tomato juice before they are combined.

Dry milk is substituted often for fluid milk in quantity cooking, because dry milk is comparatively lower in cost and easy to handle and store. It is available as whole milk, nonfat milk, and buttermilk. Nonfat dry milk is pure, fresh milk from which the fat and water have been removed. It has better keeping qualities than whole dry milk, although both should be kept dry and cool. Once reconstituted, dry milk should be refrigerated.

When dry milk is used in recipes that contain a large proportion of dry ingredients, such as bread, biscuits, and cakes, the only change in method would be to mix the unsifted dry milk with the other dry ingredients and use water in place of fluid milk. For best results, dry milk should be weighed, not measured. Package directions for reconstituting dry milk solids should be followed. A general guide is to use 3.5 oz, by weight, of instant or regular spray process nonfat dry milk plus 3¾ cups water to make 1 qt liquid milk; or 1 lb plus 3¾ qt water to make 1 gal. The same proportion is used for dry buttermilk. For some foods, additional fat (1.2 oz per quart of liquid) should be added. Additional amounts of nonfat dry milk may be added to some foods to supplement their nutritional value, although excessive amounts that affect palatability should not be used.

Egg and Cheese Recipes

PROCEDURE FOR COOKING EGGS

Method	Equipment and procedure

Hard or soft cooked (in shell)	**Kettle:**
	1. Place eggs in wire baskets and lower into kettle of boiling water. Simmer (do not boil), timing as follows:
	
	    Soft cooked *Hard cooked*
	    5–7 minutes 10–15 minutes
	
	2. Immerse hard-cooked eggs in cold water or serve immediately. Serve soft-cooked eggs immediately after cooking.
	Steamer:
	1. Place eggs in perforated counter pans, 3 dozen per 12 × 20 × 2-inch pan.
	2. Place in steamer and time as follows:
	
	Pressure *Soft cooked* *Hard cooked*
	5 lb 5–7 minutes 8–10 minutes
	15 lb 4–6 minutes 7–9 minutes
	0 lb 6–8 minutes 9–10 minutes
	
	3. Immerse in cold water or serve immediately.

Hard cooked (out of shell)	**Steamer:** 1. Crack eggs into a 12 × 20 × 2-inch solid, greased counter pan. Eggs should be thick enough in pans so whites come up to level of yolks (4 dozen per pan). 2. Place in steamer and time as follows: *Pressure* *Hard cooked* 5 lb 6–8 minutes 15 lb 5–7 minutes 0 lb 6–8 minutes 3. Remove from steamer and drain off any accumulated condensate. Chop and cool quickly (within 4 hours) to below 41°F.
Poached	**Fry pan or kettle:** 1. Break eggs into individual dishes. Carefully slide eggs into simmering water in fry pan or other shallow pan. The addition of 1 Tbsp salt or 2 tsp vinegar to the water increases the speed of coagulation and helps maintain shape. 2. Keep water at simmering (not boiling) temperature. Cook for 5 minutes. 3. Remove eggs with slotted spoon. **Steamer:** 1. Break eggs into water in 12 × 10 × 2-inch counter pans. 2. Place eggs into steamer and time as follows: *Pressure* *Soft poached* 5 lb 3–4 minutes 15 lb 2–3 minutes 0 lb 3–5 minutes 3. To serve, lift out of water into a warmed pan.
Fried	**Skillet or griddle:** 1. Break eggs into individual dishes. Slide carefully into hot fat in skillet or on griddle. 2. Cook over low heat until of desired hardness, 5–7 minutes: *Sunny side up:* 7 minutes at a cooking surface temperature of 250°F. *Over easy:* 3 minutes at a cooking surface temperature of 250°F on one side, then turn the egg and fry for another 2 minutes on the other side.
Scrambled	See recipe, p. 385

Notes

- Hard-cooked eggs will peel easier if the raw eggs have been held in the refrigerator for 24 hours before cooking. A greenish color may appear on the yolks of hard-cooked eggs when the eggs have been overcooked or allowed to cool slowly in the cooking water. Cooking the eggs for the minimum length of time required to make them solid and cooling them in cold running water or ice water help prevent this color formation.
- Cook scrambled eggs in small batches (no larger than 3 qt) until no visible liquid egg remains. Do not combine raw egg mixture with cooked scrambled eggs. Keep scrambled egg mixture below 41°F.
- Do not combine eggs that have been held in a steam table pan with a fresh batch of eggs. Always use a fresh steam table pan.
- The practice of breaking large quantities of eggs together and holding for a period of time greatly increases the risk of bacterial contamination.
- Never leave eggs or egg-containing products at temperatures between 41°F and 140°F (room temperature) for more than 1 hour (including preparation and service).
- Hold cold egg dishes below 41°F.
- Hold hot egg dishes above 140°F. Do not hold hot foods on buffet line for longer than 30 minutes.
- When refrigerating a large quantity of a hot egg-rich dish or leftover, divide into several shallow containers so it will cool quickly. See p. 167 for recommended cooling procedures.

SCRAMBLED EGGS

Yield: 50 portions   *Portion:* 4 oz

Ingredient	Amount	Procedure
Eggs (see Note)	100 (11 lb)	Break eggs into mixer bowl. If using frozen eggs, defrost. Beat slightly on medium speed using a wire whip.
Milk Salt	2 qt 2⅔ Tbsp	Add milk and salt to eggs. Beat until blended. Refrigerate mixture, removing small amounts as needed.
Margarine	10 oz	Melt margarine in fry pan, griddle, or steam-jacketed kettle. Pour in egg mixture (see Note). Cook over low heat, stirring occasionally, until of desired consistency. Eggs should be glossy and 165°F. Serve with a spoon or No. 10 dipper (rounded).

Approximate nutritive values per portion

Calories	Carbohydrate	Protein	Fat	Cholesterol	Sodium	Fiber	Iron
162 kcal	2 g	10 g	12 g	320 mg	407 mg	0 g	1 mg

Notes

- Potentially hazardous food. *Food Safety Standards:* Hold food for service at an internal temperature of 41°F or below. Do not mix old product with new. Keep leftover product chilled at 41°F or below. See p. 167 for cooling procedures.
- Breaking and pooling large quantities of shell eggs is not recommended.
- Recommend using pasteurized eggs when scrambled egg mixture must be held longer than 2 hours. See Variations for scrambled eggs using refrigerated pasteurized eggs.
- The type of equipment used will determine batch size. Eggs should be cooked in small batches and held for a minimum amount of time before serving.
- **Steamer Method.** Melt 4 oz margarine in each of two steamer or counter pans. Pour egg mixture into pans. Steam for 6–8 minutes at 5 lb pressure until desired degree of hardness is reached.
- **Oven Method.** Melt 4 oz margarine in each of two counter or baking pans. Pour egg mixture into pans. Bake for approximately 20 minutes at 350°F, stirring once after 10 minutes of baking.
- Egg whites may be substituted for half of the whole eggs.

Variations

- **Scrambled Eggs and Cheese.** Add 1 lb 4 oz grated cheddar cheese.
- **Scrambled Eggs and Chipped Beef.** Add 1 lb 4 oz chopped chipped beef. Reduce salt to 1 Tbsp or less.
- **Scrambled Eggs and Ham.** Add 1 lb 4 oz chopped cooked ham. Reduce salt to 1 Tbsp or less.
- **Scrambled Eggs Using Refrigerated Pasteurized Eggs.** Whip 2 lb 12 oz (5½ cups) thawed egg whites until frothy. To egg whites, add and mix in 9 lb 12 oz (1¼ gal) whole liquid eggs, 2 cups milk, 3½ tsp salt, and 1 Tbsp black pepper. Yield: 50 4-oz servings.

CREAMED EGGS

Yield: 50 portions   *Portion:* 5 oz

Ingredient	Amount	Procedure
Eggs, hard cooked (p. 384)	75	Peel eggs. Set aside for later step. Refrigerate if not using immediately.
Margarine Flour, all-purpose Salt White pepper	1 lb 8 oz 1 oz (1½ Tbsp) ¼ tsp	Melt margarine. Add flour, salt, and pepper. Stir until smooth. Cook for 5 minutes.
Milk	1 gal	Add milk gradually, stirring constantly with wire whip. Cook until thickened.
		Slice or quarter hard-cooked eggs. Refrigerate if not using immediately. When ready to serve, pour hot sauce over eggs. Mix carefully. Reheat if necessary to 165°F.

Approximate nutritive values per portion

Calories	Carbohydrate	Protein	Fat	Cholesterol	Sodium	Fiber	Iron
242 kcal	8 g	13 g	17 g	330 mg	410 mg	0 g	1 mg

Note

- Potentially hazardous food. *Food Safety Standards:* Hold food for service at an internal temperature of 135°F or above. Do not mix old product with new. Cool leftover product quickly following time standards and cooling procedures on p. 167. Reheat leftover product quickly (within 2 hours) to 165°F or above. Reheat product only once; discard if not used.

Variations

- **Curried Eggs.** Substitute chicken broth for 2 qt milk. Add 2 Tbsp curry powder. May be served with steamed rice or chow mein noodles.
- **Eggs à la King.** Substitute Chicken Stock for 2 qt milk. Add 1 lb sautéed mushrooms, 12 oz chopped green bell peppers, and 8 oz chopped pimiento.
- **Goldenrod Eggs.** Mash or rice egg yolks. Add sliced whites to sauce. Serve on toast. Sprinkle mashed yolks over the top.
- **Scotch Woodcock.** Add 1 lb sharp cheddar cheese to sauce. Cut eggs in half lengthwise and place in pans. Pour sauce over eggs. Cover with buttered crumbs. Bake until heated through and crumbs are brown.

OMELET MIXTURE WITH OMELET VARIATIONS (GRILLED)

Yield: 9 lb 8 oz (50 portions)   *Portion:* 3 oz

Ingredient	Amount	Procedure
Egg whites	2 lb 2 oz	Whip egg whites until frothy.
Eggs Salt White pepper	7 lb 8 oz 1 Tbsp 1 Tbsp	Add eggs, salt, and pepper to egg whites. Mix until combined, 45–60 seconds.
		Hold egg mixture in refrigerator. Take out only the amount that will be used within 15 minutes. Portion 3 oz egg mixture onto lightly greased preheated grill. Cook until eggs are barely set and do not appear wet. Portion filling over half of each omelet. (See Variations.) Fold or roll omelet over filling. Heat through. Hold hot in a single layer in a 12 × 20 × 2-inch pan. Serve soon after preparation, within 10 minutes.

Notes

- Potentially hazardous food. *Food Safety Standards:* Hold food for service at an internal temperature of 41°F or below. Do not mix old product with new. Keep leftover product chilled at 41°F or below. See p. 167 for cooling procedures.
- Recipe tested using frozen egg whites and refrigerated liquid whole eggs. Thaw egg whites completely in refrigerator before whipping.

Variations

- **Cheese and Bacon Omelet.** Portion 1 oz shredded processed cheese and ½ oz crumbled cooked bacon over each omelet before folding. Total amount of cheese, 3 lb; total amount of cooked bacon, 1½ lb.
- **Cheese Omelet.** Portion 1½ oz shredded processed cheese over each omelet before folding. Total amount of cheese, 4 lb 12 oz.
- **Denver Omelet.** Sauté 12 oz chopped onions, 8 oz diced green bell pepper, and 8 oz diced red bell pepper until soft. Drain. Add 2 lb chopped ham and heat through. Portion 1 oz sauteéd mixture and ½ oz shredded cheese over each omelet before folding.
- **Jelly Omelet.** Portion 1 oz tart jelly over each omelet before folding.
- **Potato and Cheese Omelet.** Portion 2 oz cooked hash brown potatoes and ½ oz cheese over each omelet before folding. Total amount of potatoes, 6 lb 4 oz. Total amount of cheese, 1 lb 8 oz.
- **Western Omelet with Bacon and Onions.** Cook, drain, and crumble 2 lb bacon. Sauté 1 lb chopped onions. Mix crumbled bacon with onions. Portion 1½ oz bacon-onion mixture over each omelet before folding.

BAKED OMELET

Yield: 48 portions or 2 pans, 12 × 20 × 2 inches   *Portion:* 3 oz
Oven: 325°F   *Bake:* 45 minutes

Ingredient	Amount	Procedure
Margarine	12 oz	Melt margarine. Add flour and seasonings. Stir until smooth.
Flour, all-purpose	8 oz	Cook 5 minutes.
Salt	2 Tbsp	
White pepper	½ tsp	
Milk	3 qt	Add milk gradually, stirring constantly with a wire whip. Cook until thick.
Egg yolks, beaten	24 (15 oz)	Add egg yolks and mix well with wire whip.
Egg whites	24 (1 lb 12 oz)	Beat egg whites until they form rounded peaks. Fold into egg yolk mixture.
		Pour mixture into two greased 12 × 20 × 2-inch baking pans, 5 lb per pan. Set pans in counter pans with 3 cups hot water in each. Bake at 325°F for approximately 45 minutes or until set, 180°F internal endpoint temperature. Cut 4 × 6.

Approximate nutritive values per portion

Calories	Carbohydrate	Protein	Fat	Cholesterol	Sodium	Fiber	Iron
146 kcal	7 g	6 g	11 g	122 mg	394 mg	0 g	0.5 mg

Note

- Potentially hazardous food. *Food Safety Standards:* Hold food for service at an internal temperature of 41°F or below. Do not mix old product with new. Keep leftover product chilled at 41°F or below. See p. 167 for cooling procedures.

Variations

- **Bacon Omelet.** Fry 1 lb 8 oz diced bacon; substitute bacon fat for margarine in white sauce. Add diced bacon to egg mixture.
- **Baked Cheese Omelet.** Add 12 oz grated cheese before placing pans in ovens.
- **Ham Omelet.** Add 3 lb finely diced cooked ham. Reduce salt to 1 Tbsp or less.
- **Mushroom and Cheese Omelet.** Add 8 oz grated cheese and 6 oz sliced mushrooms.
- **Spanish Omelet.** Add 8 oz chopped green chiles to egg mixture. Serve with Salsa (p. 702).

POTATO OMELET (BAKED)

Yield: 56 portions or 2 pans, 12 × 20 × 2 inches   *Portion:* 6 oz
Oven: 325°F   *Bake:* 1 hour

Ingredient	Amount	Procedure
Bacon slices	50	Arrange bacon, slightly overlapping, in baking pans. Cook in oven at 400°F until crisp. Remove from pans. Place on paper towels to absorb fat.
Potatoes, cooked, diced	9 lb (EP)	Brown potatoes slightly in bacon fat. Remove to two greased 12 × 20 × 2-inch baking pans, 4 lb 8 oz per pan.
Eggs, beaten Milk, hot Salt White pepper Cayenne pepper	36 (3 lb 15 oz) 3 qt 2 oz 1 tsp few grains	Combine eggs, milk, and seasonings. Pour over potatoes.
		Bake at 325°F for approximately 1 hour, or until set, 180°F internal endpoint temperature. Serve as soon as removed from oven. Cut 4 × 7. Place a slice of crisp bacon on top of each serving.

Approximate nutritive values per portion

Calories	Carbohydrate	Protein	Fat	Cholesterol	Sodium	Fiber	Iron
180 kcal	19 g	9 g	8 g	148 mg	552 mg	2 g	1 mg

Notes

- Potentially hazardous food. *Food Safety Standards:* Hold food for service at an internal temperature of 41°F or below. Do not mix old product with new. Keep leftover product chilled at 41°F or below. See p. 167 for cooling procedures.
- 4 oz chopped green bell pepper and 4 oz chopped onion may be added.

Variation

- **Potato-Ham Omelet.** Omit bacon. Add 4 lb diced cooked ham to potatoes. Reduce salt to 1 Tbsp.

CHINESE OMELET (BAKED)

Yield: 48 portions or 2 pans, 12 × 20 × 2 inches   *Portion:* 4 oz
Oven: 325°F   *Bake:* 45 minutes

Ingredient	Amount	Procedure
Rice, long-grain	2 lb (AP)	Cook rice according to directions on p. 542.
Water	2½ qt	
Salt	1 Tbsp	
Margarine or vegetable oil	1 Tbsp	
Margarine	4 oz	Melt margarine. Add flour and salt. Stir until smooth.
Flour, all-purpose	2 oz	Cook for 5 minutes.
Salt	1 tsp	
Milk	1 qt	Add milk gradually, stirring constantly with wire whip. Cook until thickened.
Cheddar cheese, sharp, shredded	1 lb	Add cheese to white sauce. Stir until cheese is melted.
Egg yolks	24 (15 oz)	Beat egg yolks until light and fluffy. Add seasonings.
Dry mustard	1 tsp	Add to cheese sauce. Stir until smooth.
Salt	2 Tbsp	Add rice and mix to blend.
Paprika	1 tsp	
Egg whites	24 (1 lb 12 oz)	Beat egg whites until they form soft peaks.
		Fold into rice mixture.
		Pour into two greased 12 × 20 × 2-inch pans, 7 lb per pan.
		Bake at 325°F for approximately 45 minutes or until set, 180°F internal endpoint temperature.
		Cut 4 × 6.
		Serve with Cheese Sauce (p. 683), Italian Tomato Sauce (p. 691), or Mushroom Sauce (p. 687).

Approximate nutritive values per portion

Calories	Carbohydrate	Protein	Fat	Cholesterol	Sodium	Fiber	Iron
185 kcal	18 g	8 g	9 g	126 mg	614 mg	0.4 g	1 mg

Note

- Potentially hazardous food. *Food Safety Standards:* Hold food for service at an internal temperature of 135°F or above. Do not mix old product with new. Cool leftover product quickly following time standards and cooling procedures on p. 167. Reheat leftover product quickly (within 2 hours) to 165°F or above. Reheat product only once; discard if not used.

ASIAN OMELET

Yield: 50 portions   *Portion:* 1 omelet

Ingredient	Amount	Procedure
Egg whites	1 lb	Whip egg whites until frothy.
Eggs Salt Black pepper	3 lb 4 oz 2 tsp 1¼ tsp	Add eggs, salt, and pepper to egg whites. Mix on low speed only until mixed, 45–60 seconds.
Sugar snap peas, thawed Water chestnuts, sliced	12 oz 1 lb 6 oz	Coarsely chop peas and chestnuts. Add to egg mixture.
Bean sprouts, canned, drained Green onions, sliced	1 lb 6 oz 2 oz	Stir bean sprouts and onions into eggs.
		Heat flat-top griddle to 275°F. Oil generously. Portion 2½ oz omelet mixture onto hot grill. Turn omelet when lightly browned. Do not fold. Cook second side until lightly browned. Serve as an entrée with Asian Mirin Sauce.

Approximate nutritive values per omelet

Calories	Carbohydrate	Protein	Fat	Cholesterol	Sodium	Fiber	Iron
59 kcal	3 g	5 g	3 g	126 mg	161 mg	1 g	1 mg

Note

- Potentially hazardous food. *Food Safety Standards:* Hold food for service at an internal temperature of 135°F or above. Do not mix old product with new. Cool leftover product quickly following time standards and cooling procedures on p. 167. Reheat leftover product quickly (within 2 hours) to 165°F or above. Reheat product only once; discard if not used.

EGG AND SAUSAGE BAKE

Yield: 48 portions or 2 pans, 12 × 20 × 2 inches   *Portion:* 6 oz
Oven: 325°F   *Bake:* 1 hour

Ingredient	Amount	Procedure
Bread, sliced	2 lb 8 oz	Cut bread in cubes. Cover bottoms of two greased 12 × 20 × 2-inch baking pans with bread cubes. Pans should be well covered.
Sausage, bulk	9 lb	Brown sausage. Drain well.
Cheddar cheese, shredded	2 lb 8 oz	Spread cheese and sausage over bread cubes.
Eggs, beaten Milk Dry mustard	42 (4 lb 8 oz) 3 qt 1½ Tbsp	Combine eggs, milk, and mustard. Pour over mixture in pans, 2½ qt per pan. May be mixed, covered, and refrigerated overnight.
		Bake uncovered at 325°F for approximately 1 hour or until set, 180°F internal endpoint temperature. If browning too fast, cover with foil. Cut 4 × 6.

Approximate nutritive values per portion

Calories	Carbohydrate	Protein	Fat	Cholesterol	Sodium	Fiber	Iron
568 kcal	15 g	32 g	42 g	286 mg	1483 mg	3 g	3 mg

Notes

- Potentially hazardous food. *Food Safety Standards:* Hold food for service at an internal temperature of 135°F or above. Do not mix old product with new. Cool leftover product quickly following time standards and cooling procedures on p. 167. Reheat leftover product quickly (within 2 hours) to 165°F or above. Reheat product only once; discard if not used.
- Chopped ham or bacon may be substituted for sausage.

Variations

- **Sausage-Potato Bake.** Substitute frozen hashed brown potatoes for bread cubes.
- **Egg-Potato Bake.** Delete sausage. Substitute frozen hashed brown potatoes for bread cubes.

ROASTED PEPPER AND BASIL FRITTATA

Yield: 48 portions   *Portion:* 4½ oz (1 wedge)
Oven: 350°F   *Bake:* 17–20 minutes

Ingredient	Amount	Procedure
Onions, thinly sliced Olive oil	12 lb (EP) 2½ cups	Using a covered pan, fry onions in oil on low heat, 200°F, until reduced in bulk. Uncover and continue cooking on very low heat until onions are browned and dry (12 lb fresh sliced onions will yield approximately 4 lb after cooking).
Roasted red bell peppers, diced (p. 796) (see Note) Salt	1 lb (EP) 1 oz	Stir peppers and salt into cooked onion.
Eggs	60 (6 lb 12 oz)	Break eggs into bowl. Beat until blended.
Parmesan cheese, shredded Black pepper	6 oz 2 tsp	Add onion mixture, cheese, and pepper to eggs. Stir to mix.
Fresh basil, torn into small pieces	4 oz	Add basil to egg mixture. Mix lightly.
Butter, melted	12 oz	Pour 2 oz butter into six 13-inch round 1-inch-deep pizza pans. Scale 2 lb 4 oz of egg mixture into each pan. (Stir often while scaling in pans to keep the vegetables evenly distributed.) Bake at 350°F for approximately 20 minutes, or until eggs are set and top has some brown speckling beginning to occur. Cut into eight wedges.

Approximate nutritive values per portion

Calories	Carbohydrate	Protein	Fat	Cholesterol	Sodium	Fiber	Iron
250 kcal	11 g	10 g	19 g	270 mg	350 mg	2.3 g	1 mg

Notes

- Potentially hazardous food. *Food Safety Standards:* Hold food for service at an internal temperature of 135°F or above. Do not mix old product with new. Cool leftover product quickly following time standards and cooling procedures on p. 167. Reheat leftover product quickly (within 2 hours) to 165°F or above. Reheat product only once; discard if not used.
- Use freshly shredded Parmesan cheese.
- Frozen roasted peppers may be substituted for freshly roasted peppers. When using frozen roasted peppers, place in a single layer on a baking sheet and heat in a 375°F oven until heated through (discard liquid that accumulates).
- 6 oz reconstituted sun-dried tomatoes can be substituted for 6 oz roasted red peppers.
- Frittata can be cooked in an ovenproof 10-inch sauté pan. Melt 2 Tbsp butter in pan. When butter begins to foam, pour 1 lb 3 oz egg mixture into pan. Turn heat to very low and cook until eggs are set on the bottom and only slightly runny on the surface. Put pan under broiler until eggs become set but not browned. Cut into four wedges.

QUICHE

Yield: 48 portions or twelve 8-inch quiches   *Portion:* ¼ quiche
Oven: 375°F   *Bake:* 25–30 minutes

Ingredient	Amount	Procedure
Flour, all-purpose	1 lb 13 oz	Make pastry according to directions on p. 340.
Salt	1 Tbsp	Line twelve 8-inch pie pans with pastry, 5 oz per pan.
Shortening	1 lb 4 oz	Partially bake shells at 375°F for about 10 minutes.
Water, cold	1¼ cups	
Eggs	30 (3 lb 4 oz)	Beat eggs. Add cream, milk, and seasonings.
Cream or half-and-half	2 qt	
Milk	2 qt	
Salt	1½ tsp	
White pepper	½ tsp	
Swiss cheese, grated	3 lb	Sprinkle partially baked shells with Swiss cheese, 4 oz per pie, and bacon or ham,
Bacon, chopped, cooked, and drained, or ham, finely diced	1 lb	2 oz per pie. Pour egg mixture into shells, 15 oz (approximately 2 cups) per pie.
Parmesan cheese, grated	8 oz	Sprinkle with Parmesan cheese, 2 Tbsp per pie. Bake until custard is set and lightly browned, 180°F internal endpoint temperature.

Approximate nutritive values per portion

Calories	Carbohydrate	Protein	Fat	Cholesterol	Sodium	Fiber	Iron
473 kcal	18 g	21 g	35 g	189 mg	589 mg	0.5 g	1 mg

Note

- Potentially hazardous food. *Food Safety Standards:* Hold food for service at an internal temperature of 135°F or above. Do not mix old product with new. Cool leftover product quickly following time standards and cooling procedures on p. 167. Reheat leftover product quickly (within 2 hours) to 165°F or above. Reheat product only once; discard if not used.

Variations

- **Mushroom Quiche.** Delete bacon and Parmesan cheese. Sprinkle 3 lb sliced fresh mushrooms and 8 oz finely chopped onions sautéed in 4 oz margarine over bottoms of shells, approximately 4 oz per pie.
- **Sausage Quiche.** Substitute 1 lb cooked, drained sausage (1 lb 12 oz AP) for bacon or ham.
- **Seafood Quiche.** In place of bacon, use 3 lb flaked crab meat, shrimp pieces, or other seafood; 1 lb sliced fresh mushrooms; and 12 oz finely chopped onions sautéed in 4 oz margarine. Scale approximately 5 oz per pie. Delete Parmesan cheese.
- **Swiss Spinach Quiche.** Delete bacon and Parmesan cheese. Increase Swiss cheese to 6 lb. Add 3 lb 8 oz chopped spinach, well drained. Add 1 tsp nutmeg.

LEEK AND ROASTED PEPPER QUICHE

Yield: 50 portions or ten 9-inch quiches   *Portion:* ⅕ quiche
Oven: 325°F   *Bake:* 60 minutes

Ingredient	Amount	Procedure
Flour, all-purpose	3 lb	Make pastry according to directions (p. 340).
Shortening	2 lb	Line ten 9-inch pie shells.
Salt	1½ oz	Partially bake shells at 375°F for about 10 minutes.
Water, cold	1½–1¾ cups	
Mushrooms, coarsely chopped	5 lb (AP)	Sauté mushrooms in butter until softened and liquid has evaporated. Weight after sautéing should equal 2 lb.
Butter	8 oz	Reserve for later step.
Onions, coarsely chopped	12 oz (EP)	Sauté onions in butter until tender and slightly browned.
Butter	8 oz	Add leeks and continue cooking until wilted.
Leeks, thinly sliced	2 lb 12 oz (EP)	
Roasted red bell peppers, coarsely chopped (p. 796)	1 lb 4 oz	Add mushrooms reserved from earlier step and roasted peppers to sautéed onions. Scale 10 oz vegetable mixture in each quiche shell.
Swiss cheese, shredded	3 lb 12 oz	Toss cheese with flour.
Flour, all-purpose	4 oz	Sprinkle 6 oz cheese over vegetables in each pan.
Egg whites	12 oz	Whip egg whites until frothy. Add eggs and blend until just mixed.
Eggs, beaten slightly	2 lb 12 oz	
Milk	1¾ qt	Combine eggs, milk, and spices.
White pepper	¾ tsp	Scale 11 oz of egg-milk mixture over cheese in each pan (approximately 1½ cups).
Crushed red pepper	¾ tsp	Set pans on 18 × 26 × 1-inch pan. Bake at 325°F until quiche reaches 180°F, about 1 hour.

Approximate nutritive values per portion

Calories	Carbohydrate	Protein	Fat	Cholesterol	Sodium	Fiber	Iron
550 kcal	32 g	19 g	40 g	160 mg	940 mg	2 g	3 mg

Notes

- Potentially hazardous food. *Food Safety Standards:* Hold food for service at an internal temperature of 135°F or above. Do not mix old product with new. Cool leftover product quickly following time standards and cooling procedures on p. 167. Reheat leftover product quickly (within 2 hours) to 165°F or above. Reheat product only once; discard if not used.
- Vegetable base can be substituted for chicken base. Adjust salt as necessary.

Variation

- **Vegetable Quiche.** Thaw 1 lb frozen broccoli cuts in a colander. Drain. Steam 1 lb finely chopped carrots. Drain. Mix vegetables together. Combine 4 lb 12 oz shredded processed Swiss cheese and 5½ oz flour. In each quiche shell, scale 8 oz cheese, then 3 oz drained vegetables. Prepare the liquid by whipping 1 lb egg whites until frothy and mixing with 3 lb 12 oz slightly beaten eggs. Add 5 lb 10 oz milk, 1 tsp nutmeg, and 2 tsp white pepper. Proceed according to recipe.

DEVILED EGGS

Yield: 50 portions   *Portion:* 2 halves

Ingredient	Amount	Procedure
Eggs, hard cooked (p. 384)	50	Peel eggs. Cut in half lengthwise. Remove yolks to mixer bowl. Arrange whites in rows on a tray.
Milk	½ cup	Mash yolks, using flat beater. Add milk and mix until blended.
Mayonnaise or salad dressing	1½ cups	Add remaining ingredients to yolks and mix until smooth. Refill whites with mashed yolks, approximately 1½ Tbsp for each half egg white. Sprinkle with paprika (optional). Chill quickly to below 41°F.
Salt	1 Tbsp	
Dry mustard	2 tsp	
Sugar, granulated	1 tsp	
Cider vinegar	½ cup	

Approximate nutritive values per portion

Calories	Carbohydrate	Protein	Fat	Cholesterol	Sodium	Fiber	Iron
105 kcal	3 g	6 g	7 g	215 mg	242 mg	0 g	1 mg

Notes

- Potentially hazardous food. *Food Safety Standards:* Hold food for service at an internal temperature of 41°F or below. Do not mix old product with new. Keep leftover product chilled at 41°F or below. See p. 167 for cooling procedures.
- Pastry bag may be used to fill egg whites. Yolk mixture should be smooth and creamy. Use plain or rose tip.
- 6 oz finely chopped pimentos may be added to yolk mixture.

Variations

- **Dilled Eggs.** Combine 1¾ qt vinegar, 1¼ qt water, 1 Tbsp dill weed, 1 tsp white pepper, 1 oz (1½ Tbsp) salt, ¼ tsp dry mustard, 1 Tbsp onion juice, and 3 garlic cloves. Pour over peeled hard-cooked eggs. Cover tightly and refrigerate overnight.
- **Hot Stuffed Eggs.** To mash egg yolks, add 3 oz melted margarine or butter, 2 tsp salt, ⅛ tsp cayenne pepper, 1 Tbsp prepared mustard, and 1 lb minced ham. Arrange stuffed eggs in two 12 × 20 × 2-inch baking pans. Cover with 1 gal white sauce (p. 683), 2 qt per pan. Bake at 325°F for 30 minutes. Sprinkle with chopped parsley. Ham may be added to the white sauce instead of to egg yolks.
- **Pickled Eggs.** Combine 3½ cups beet juice, 3½ cups vinegar, 12 oz granulated sugar, and ¼ tsp salt. Stir until sugar is dissolved. Pour over peeled hard-cooked eggs. Cover tightly and refrigerate overnight.
- **Smoked Eggs.** Combine ½ cup soy sauce, 1 Tbsp salad oil, 1 tsp liquid smoke, 5 tsp granulated sugar, and 1¼ cups water. Pour over peeled hard-cooked eggs. Marinate for 2–3 hours. Stir eggs occasionally to keep them moistened with marinade.

CHEESE BALLS

Yield: 50 portions or 150 balls   *Portion:* 3 balls
Deep-fat fryer: 360°F   *Fry:* 2–3 minutes

Ingredient	Amount	Procedure
Cheddar cheese, shredded	9 lb	Mix cheese, flour, and seasonings.
Flour, all-purpose	8 oz	
Salt	2 Tbsp	
Cayenne pepper	few grains	
Egg whites	48 (3 lb 8 oz)	Beat egg whites until stiff. Fold into cheese mixture.
		Shape into balls 1–1¼ inches in diameter or dip with No. 30 dipper onto trays or baking sheets.
		Chill.
Eggs, beaten	6 (10 oz)	Combine eggs and milk.
Milk	2 cups	Dip cheese balls in egg mixture, then roll in crumbs.
Bread crumbs	1 lb 8 oz	Chill for several hours.
		Fry in deep fat for 2–3 minutes. Serve immediately.

Approximate nutritive values per portion

Calories	Carbohydrate	Protein	Fat	Cholesterol	Sodium	Fiber	Iron
429 kcal	15 g	27 g	29 g	112 mg	927 mg	0.6 g	1 mg

Notes

- Potentially hazardous food. *Food Safety Standards:* Hold food for service at an internal temperature of 41°F or below. Do not mix old product with new. Keep leftover product chilled at 41°F or below. See p. 167 for cooling procedures.
- Serve cheese balls in center of hot buttered pineapple rings, three per serving.
- For serving as first-course accompaniment, use half the recipe and shape into balls ½–¾ inch in diameter. Yield: 150 balls.
- For two cheese balls per portion, use No. 24 dipper. Yield: 40 portions.

CHEESE SOUFFLÉ

Yield: 48 portions or 2 pans, 12 × 20 × 2 inches   *Portion:* 4 oz
Oven: 300°F   *Bake:* 55–60 minutes

Ingredient	Amount	Procedure
Margarine	1 lb 4 oz	Melt margarine. Add flour and salt. Stir until smooth.
Flour, all-purpose	10 oz	Cook for 5 minutes.
Salt	1 tsp	
Milk	3 qt	Add milk gradually, stirring constantly with wire whip. Cook until thick.
Egg yolks, beaten	38 (1 lb 8 oz)	Add egg yolks to white sauce, stirring constantly. Cook for 2 minutes.
Cheddar cheese, shredded	1 lb 8 oz	Add cheese to sauce and stir until cheese is melted. Remove from heat.
Cream of tartar	2 tsp	Add cream of tartar to egg whites. Beat until stiff, but not dry.
Egg whites	38 (2 lb 12 oz)	
		Fold into cheese mixture.
		Scale mixture into two 12 × 20 × 2-inch baking pans, greased only on the bottoms, 6 lb 12 oz per pan.
		Bake at 300°F for 55–60 minutes or until set.
		Cut 4 × 6.

Approximate nutritive values per portion

Calories	Carbohydrate	Protein	Fat	Cholesterol	Sodium	Fiber	Iron
265 kcal	8 g	11 g	21 g	205 mg	323 mg	0.2 g	1 mg

Notes

- Potentially hazardous food. *Food Safety Standards:* Hold food for service at an internal temperature of 135°F or above. Do not mix old product with new. Cool leftover product quickly following time standards and cooling procedures on p. 167. Reheat leftover product quickly (within 2 hours) to 165°F or above. Reheat product only once; discard if not used.
- Serve with Cheese Sauce (p. 683), Fresh Mushroom Sauce (p. 687), or Shrimp Sauce (p. 683).

Variation

- **Mushroom Soufflé.** Add 1 lb chopped mushrooms and 5 oz chopped green bell peppers to uncooked mixture. Serve with Béchamel Sauce (p. 684).

CHEESE AND BROCCOLI STRATA

Yield: 56 portions or 2 pans, 12 × 20 × 2 inches   *Portion:* 8 oz
Oven: 325°F   *Bake:* 1–1½ hours

Ingredient	Amount	Procedure
Bread slices, dry	2 lb	Cut bread into 1½-inch cubes. Set aside.
Broccoli cuts, frozen	5 lb	Cook broccoli until tender crisp.
Cheddar cheese, shredded	2 lb	Layer as follows in each pan: 　　8 oz bread cubes 　　2 lb 8 oz broccoli 　　1 lb cheese 　　8 oz bread cubes
Eggs, beaten Milk Salt Prepared mustard Hot pepper sauce	9 dozen (12 lb) 1 gal 2 oz 3 oz (6 Tbsp) 1½ tsp	Combine eggs, milk, and seasonings. Pour 1¼ gal into each pan. Smooth down evenly.
Paprika	½ tsp	Sprinkle with paprika, ¼ tsp per pan. Set each pan in another counter pan containing 3 cups hot water. Baked uncovered at 325°F until custard sets, approximately 1–1½ hours, 180°F internal endpoint temperature. Cut 4 × 7.

Approximate nutritive values per portion

Calories	Carbohydrate	Protein	Fat	Cholesterol	Sodium	Fiber	Iron
307 kcal	14 g	21 g	18 g	441 mg	784 mg	2 g	2 mg

Notes

- Potentially hazardous food. *Food Safety Standards:* Hold food for service at an internal temperature of 135°F or above. Do not mix old product with new. Cool leftover product quickly following time standards and cooling procedures on p. 167. Reheat leftover product quickly (within 2 hours) to 165°F or above. Reheat product only once; discard if not used.
- Baking time may be reduced if milk mixture is warmed to 140°F before baking.
- May be served with 1 oz Cheese Sauce (p. 683).

Variation

- **Asparagus Cheese Strata.** Substitute asparagus for broccoli. Frozen asparagus cuts (thawed and drained) may be used. Serve with Cheese Sauce (p. 683).

WELSH RAREBIT

Yield: 50 portions or 6½ qt   *Portion:* ½ cup (4 oz)

Ingredient	Amount	Procedure
Margarine	10 oz	Melt margarine. Add flour and salt. Stir until smooth.
Flour, all-purpose	8 oz	Cook for 5 minutes.
Salt	1 oz (1½ Tbsp)	
Milk	1 gal	Add milk gradually, stirring constantly with wire whip. Cook until thickened.
Cheddar cheese, shredded	5 lb	Add cheese and seasonings to sauce.
Dry mustard	2 Tbsp	Cook over hot water until cheese is melted.
Worcestershire sauce	2 Tbsp	Serve on toast or toasted buns.
White pepper	½ tsp	

Approximate nutritive values per portion

Calories	Carbohydrate	Protein	Fat	Cholesterol	Sodium	Fiber	Iron
290 kcal	8 g	14 g	22 g	58 mg	571 mg	0 g	0.5 mg

Note

- Potentially hazardous food. *Food Safety Standards:* Hold food for service at an internal temperature of 135°F or above. Do not mix old product with new. Cool leftover product quickly following time standards and cooling procedures on p. 167. Reheat leftover product quickly (within 2 hours) to 165°F or above. Reheat product only once; discard if not used.

Variation

- **Welsh Rarebit with Bacon.** Serve rarebit over toast, with 2 slices cooked bacon and 2 slices fresh tomato.

Time and Temperature Timetables and Guidelines

Fish by nature is tender and free of tough fibers that need to be softened by cooking; it should be cooked only until the fish flakes easily when tested with a fork. Fish may be cooked in many ways, but the best method is determined by size, fat content, and flavor. Baking and broiling are suitable for fat fish. If lean fish is baked or broiled, fat is added to prevent dryness, and it often is baked in a sauce. Fish cooked in moist heat requires very little cooking time and usually is served with a sauce. Frying is suitable for all types, but those with firm flesh that will not break apart easily are best for deep-fat frying. Table 13.1 suggests cooking methods for specific types of fish. Table 13.2 lists cooking times and temperatures.

TABLE 13.1	Fin fish cooking guide
Species	**Cooking methods**
Bass, sea	Fry, broil, bake
Bluefish	Bake, poach
Catfish	Fry
Cod	Bake, fry, broil
Dolphin (mahimahi)	Broil, sauté, bake
Flounder	Fry, bake, broil
Grouper	Fry, bake, poach
Haddock	Broil, bake, fry, poach
Halibut	Broil, bake, fry, poach
Monkfish	Broil, sauté
Orange roughy	Sauté, broil
Perch, ocean	Pan-fry, bake, deep-fat fry
Pike, walleye	Pan-fry
Pollock	Fry, broil, bake
Pompano	Sauté, broil
Redfish	Pan-fry, blackened
Red snapper	Bake, fry, broil
Salmon	Bake, poach, broil, pan-fry
Shark	Grill, broil
Sole	Bake, fry, broil, poach
Swordfish	Broil, bake, poach
Trout, lake	Bake, poach, pan-fry
Trout, rainbow	Pan-fry, oven-fry, broil, bake
Tuna (ahi)	Bake, broil, sauté
Turbot	Fry, bake, broil
Whitefish	Bake, broil, poach
Whiting	Deep-fat fry, broil, sauté

Whole Fish for Buffet Display. Rinse and dry fish, then salt inside and out. Bake at 325°F until fish flakes easily, about 2 hours for a 12-lb fish and approximately 3 hours for a 20–24-lb fish. When done, gently remove skin, then garnish, being careful to arrange garnish so that fish can be cut and served easily. See p. 410 for Baked Whole Salmon.

TABLE 13.2   Methods of cooking fin fish and shellfish

Type	Baking Temperature (°F)	Baking Time (minutes)	Broiling (3–4 inches from heat) Time (minutes)	Deep-fat frying (350–375°F) Time (minutes)	Pan-frying (moderate heat) Time (minutes)
Fin fish					
Dressed, 3–4 lb	350–400	40–60			
Pan-dressed, ½–1 lb	350–400	25–30	5–15	4–5	15–20
Steaks, ½–1¼ inch	350–400	25–35	5–15	4–5	15–25
Fillets	350–400	25–35	5–15	4–5	8–10
Portions, 1–6 oz	350–400	30–40		4–5	8–10
Sticks, ¾–1¼ oz	400	15–20		3–5	
Shellfish					
Clams, live, shucked	450	12–15	5–8	2–3	4–5
Crabs, live, soft shell			8–10	2–4	
Lobsters, live, ¾–1 lb	400	15–20	12–15	2–4	8–10
Spiny lobster tails, frozen, ¼–½ lb	450	20–30	8–12	3–5	8–10
Oysters, live, shucked	450	12–15	5–8	2–3	4–5
Scallops, ocean	350	15–20	6–8	2–3	4–6
Shrimp, headless, raw, peeled	350	15–20	5–8	2–3	8–10

Source: Adapted from *How to Eye and Buy Seafood,* National Marine Fisheries Service, U.S. Department of Commerce; *Seafood, Foodservice Training,* U.S. Department of Commerce; and *Seafood, Foodservice Training Manual,* National Fisheries Institute.

Notes:
- A basic guide is to bake or pan-fry fish for 20–25 minutes (350–400°F) per inch of thickness for frozen fish; 10–15 minutes per inch of thickness for thawed or fresh fish.
- For steaming fish or shellfish, see Table 13.3.
- Endpoint internal temperature must be 145°F.

TABLE 13.2   Methods of cooking fin fish and shellfish

TABLE 13.3   Timetable for steaming fish and shellfish

TABLE 13.3   Timetable for steaming fish and shellfish

Type	Amount per pan	Pan size	Procedure	5 PSI	15 PSI	Pressureless
				Time (minutes)		
Clams, soft shell	8–10 servings	12 × 20 × 2½ inches, perforated	Place washed clams in a 2½-inch perforated pan inside a 4-inch solid pan with 2–3 qt water.	6–8	4–6	6–8
Clams, hard shell	12 each, 3 lb	12 × 20 × 2½ inches	As above.	6–8	4–6	6–8
Crabs	10–16 each	12 × 20 × 2½ inches, perforated	Put live crabs in perforated pan. Steam cook.	16–18	14–16	16–18
Fish fillets (haddock, sole, cod)	5 lb	12 × 20 × 2½ inches	Place preportioned fresh or defrosted fish in pan, skin side down. Season as desired. Time depends on thickness of fish.	4–12	2–8	4–12
Fish steaks	5 lb	12 × 20 × 2½ inches	Place steaks, fresh or defrosted, in shallow pan. Season as desired. Time depends on thickness of fish.	6–12	4–8	6–12
Lobster (1–1½ lb each)	4–5 each	12 × 20 × 2½ inches, perforated	Put lobsters in perforated pan. Steam cook.	6–8	4½–6	6–8
Lobster (1½–2 lb each)	4 each	12 × 20 × 2½ inches, perforated	Put lobsters in perforated pan. Steam cook.	8–10	7–9	8–10
Oysters	12 each, 3 lb	12 × 20 × 2½ inches, perforated	Put oysters in perforated pan. Steam cook.	4–6	3–4	5–7
Shrimp, cooked and deveined (12–15), frozen	5 lb	12 × 20 × 2½ inches	Place shrimp in solid pan. Add 1 qt water and seasonings if desired.	4–8	3–6	4–8
Shrimp, raw	10 lb	12 × 20 × 2½ inches, perforated	Place shrimp in perforated pans, being careful not to overcrowd. Steam cook.	7–9	4–5	8–11

Acidulated Water. Use 1 Tbsp salt and 3 Tbsp lemon juice or vinegar for each quart of water.
Court Bouillon. Add to 1 gal water ¾ cup each chopped carrots, chopped onion, and chopped celery; 3 Tbsp salt; ½ cup vinegar; 2 or 3 bay leaves; 6 peppercorns; 9 cloves; and 3 Tbsp margarine or butter. Boil gently for 20–30 minutes. Strain to remove spices and vegetables.
Bouquet Garni. Place in cheesecloth tied into a bag: 6 parsley sprigs, 2 celery tops, 3 bay leaves, 1 tsp dried thyme, and 1 tsp peppercorns. Makes enough to season 1 gal liquid.

Fish and Shellfish Recipes

BAKED FISH FILLETS

Yield: 50 portions   *Portion:* 5 oz
Oven: 375°F   *Bake:* 25–35 minutes

Ingredient	Amount	Procedure
Fish fillets, 5 oz	50	Dip fish in margarine.
Margarine, melted	1 lb	
Bread crumbs	1 lb 12 oz	Combine bread crumbs, flour, and seasonings.
Flour, all-purpose	12 oz	
Salt	1 Tbsp	
Paprika	1½ Tbsp	
Seasoned salt	1 Tbsp	
Marjoram	1 tsp	
Lemon peel, grated	1 tsp	
		Dredge fish with crumb mixture and place on greased baking pans. Bake at 375°F for approximately 10 minutes for each inch of thickness, or until fish flakes easily when tested with a fork at thickest part and internal temperature is 145°F.

Approximate nutritive values per portion

Calories	Carbohydrate	Protein	Fat	Cholesterol	Sodium	Fiber	Iron
281 kcal	25 g	17g	13 g	49 mg	832 mg	1 g	1 mg

Notes

- Potentially hazardous food. *Food Safety Standards:* Hold food for service at an internal temperature of 41°F or below. Do not mix old product with new. Keep leftover product chilled at 41°F or below. See p. 167 for cooling procedures.
- Double the cooking time for frozen fish that has not been defrosted.
- Fish portions or steaks may be substituted for fish fillets.
- Refrigerate all fish not currently being prepared or cooked.

Variation

- **Herbed Marinated Fish Steak.** Make Fish Marinade (p. 222). Marinate steaks for 3 hours. Grill or broil according to Table 13.2.

HALIBUT FILLET OR SALMON FILLET

Yield: 50 portions   *Portion:* 6 oz
Oven: 400°F *Griddle:* 350°F

Ingredient	Amount	Procedure
Halibut or salmon fillets or steaks, 6 oz Seasoning rub or marinade or salt and cracked black pepper	50 each pp. 722, 728, 729	**Baked** Season fish. Place fish on oiled silicone-lined baking pan. Bake at 400°F to an internal temperature of 140°F, approximately 10 minutes for each inch of thickness. **Grilled** Season fish. Place on oiled hot griddle. Brown on both sides, turning once. Cook to an internal temperature of 140°F, approximately 10 minutes for each inch of thickness. **Poached** See procedures on p. 151

Approximate nutritive values per portion without seasoning or marinade (halibut, baked)

Calories	Carbohydrate	Protein	Fat	Cholesterol	Sodium	Fiber	Iron
167 kcal	0 g	32 g	3.5 g	49 mg	82 mg	0 g	1 mg

Note

- Potentially hazardous food. *Food Safety Standards:* Hold food for service at an internal temperature of 135°F or above. Do not mix old product with new. Cool leftover product quickly following time standards and cooling procedures on p. 167. Reheat leftover product quickly (within 2 hours) to 165°F or above. Reheat product only once; discard if not used.

Variations

- **Baked Cod in Charmoula Sauce.** Pour Moroccan Charmoula, p. 711, on cod before baking.
- **Grilled Swordfish with Moroccan Charmoula.** Rub swordfish with Moroccan Charmoula, p. 711, before grilling.

BAJA FISH TACO

Yield: 50 portions   *Portion:* 1 taco

Ingredient	Amount	Procedure
Tortillas, 8-inch	50	Warm to soften.
Roasted Corn and Black Bean Slaw (p. 600)	6 lb 8 oz	Prepare recipe.
Fresh Anaheim Salsa Rojo (p. 703)	3 1b	Prepare recipe.
Breaded fish pieces, 2–3 oz	8 lb	Deep-fat fry fish until golden brown and cooked through.
Lemon wedges	50	To serve: 1. Place warm tortilla on plate. 2. Place one piece of fish off center of tortilla. 3. Place 2 oz slaw over fish. 4. Ladle 1 oz (2 Tbsp) salsa over slaw. 5. Close tortilla over filling. 6. Garnish with 1 lemon wedge.

Approximate nutritive values per taco

Calories	Carbohydrate	Protein	Fat	Cholesterol	Sodium	Fiber	Iron
397 kcal	37 g	13 g	22 g	22 mg	640 mg	6 g	0.6 mg

Note

- Potentially hazardous food. *Food Safety Standards:* Hold food for service at an internal temperature of 135°F or above. Do not mix old product with new. Cool leftover product quickly following time standards and cooling procedures on p. 167. Reheat leftover product quickly (within 2 hours) to 165°F or above. Reheat product only once; discard if not used.

FAJITA-SPICED TROUT

Yield: 50 portions   *Portion:* 6 oz fillet

Ingredient	Amount	Procedure
Boneless trout fillet, 6 oz	50 fillets	Pat trout fillets dry.
Potato flakes, dry	1 lb 8 oz	Mix potato flakes, cornstarch, flour, and seasonings to make a breading.
Cornstarch	10 oz	Coat each fillet with breading mixture.
Flour, all-purpose	4 oz	
Fajita seasoning	10 oz	
Salt	4 oz	
Vegetable oil	4 cups	Heat oil in fry pan. Place breaded trout into hot oil, presentation side down. Cook until browned. Turn and cook other side. Remove from skillet and drain. If necessary, continue cooking in a 350°F oven until done.

Approximate nutritive values per portion

Calories	Carbohydrate	Protein	Fat	Cholesterol	Sodium	Fiber	Iron
350 kcal	22 g	37 g	11 g	100 mg	1331 mg	1 g	1 mg

Note

- Potentially hazardous food. *Food Safety Standards:* Hold food for service at an internal temperature of 135°F or above. Do not mix old product with new. Cool leftover product quickly following time standards and cooling procedures on p. 167. Reheat leftover product quickly (within 2 hours) to 165°F or above. Reheat product only once; discard if not used.

Variation

- **Fajita-Spiced Catfish with Asian Rice and Chile-Cilantro Dipping Sauce.** Substitute U.S farm-raised catfish for trout. To serve: Portion 2 cups Asian Fried Rice (p. 546) in large deep bowl. Lay prepared catfish fillet over top of rice and ladle ⅓ cup Chile Cilantro Sauce (p. 700) over top. Garnish with leaves of fresh herbs. Note: increase rice recipe on p. 542 to yield a 2-cup serving.

LEMON BAKED FISH

Yield: 50 portions   *Portion:* 5 oz
Oven: 375°F   *Bake:* 25–35 minutes

Ingredient	Amount	Procedure
Fish fillets, 5 oz	50	Thaw fish (if frozen) and bake, using either Method 1 or Method 2.

METHOD 1

Ingredient	Amount	Procedure
Margarine	1 lb 8 oz	Place 16 thawed fillets onto each 18 × 26-inch sheet pan.
Fresh lemon juice	⅓ cup	Melt margarine. Mix with lemon juice and seasonings.
Salt	1 oz (1½ Tbsp)	Brush generously on each piece of fish.
Paprika	3 Tbsp	Bake at 375°F for approximately 10 minutes for each inch of thickness or until fish flakes easily with a fork when tested at the thickest part and internal temperature is 145°F. Transfer to 12 × 10 × 2-inch pans.

METHOD 2

Ingredient	Amount	Procedure
Shortening, melted	l lb	Mix shortening, salt, pepper, and lemon juice.
Salt	1 Tbsp	Dip each piece of fish into seasoned fat.
White pepper	1 tsp	
Fresh lemon juice	½ cup	
Flour, all-purpose	1 lb	Dredge fish with flour. Place close together in single layer in greased baking pans.
Margarine, melted	2 oz	Mix margarine and milk and drizzle over fish.
Milk	¾ cup	Bake at 375°F for approximately 10 minutes for each inch of thickness or until fish flakes easily when tested with a fork at thickest part and internal temperature is 145°F. Sprinkle with chopped parsley before serving.

Approximate nutritive values per portion—Method 1

Calories	Carbohydrate	Protein	Fat	Cholesterol	Sodium	Fiber	Iron
228 kcal	0 g	27 g	13 g	75 mg	464 mg	0 g	0.5 mg

Approximate nutritive values per portion—Method 2

Calories	Carbohydrate	Protein	Fat	Cholesterol	Sodium	Fiber	Iron
253 kcal	7 g	28 g	12 g	75 mg	257 mg	0.3 g	1 mg

Notes

- Potentially hazardous food. *Food Safety Standards:* Hold food for service at an internal temperature of 135°F or above. Do not mix old product with new. Cool leftover product quickly following time standards and cooling procedures on p. 167. Reheat leftover product quickly (within 2 hours) to 165°F or above. Reheat product only once; discard if not used.
- Double the cooking time for frozen fish that has not been defrosted.
- Refrigerate all fish not in the preparation process or being cooked.

Variation

- **Creole Baked Fish.** Make spice mixture of 1 cup dried parsley flakes, ½ cup crushed red pepper, ½ cup black pepper, ½ cup paprika, ¼ cup crushed thyme leaves, ¼ cup crumbled rosemary, 2 Tbsp crumbled oregano, and 2 Tbsp crumbled basil. Brush fish fillets with melted margarine. Sprinkle generously with spice mixture. Follow baking directions for Lemon Baked Fish—Method 1.

BREADED FISH FILLETS

Yield: 50 portions *Portion:* 5 oz
Deep-fat fryer: 360°F *Fry:* 4–5 minutes

Ingredient	Amount	Procedure
Frozen fish fillets, 5 oz	50	Dredge fish in mixture of flour, salt, and pepper.
Flour, all-purpose	8 oz	
Salt	1 Tbsp	
White pepper	1 tsp	
Eggs, beaten	6 (11 oz)	Combine eggs and milk.
Milk	2 cups	
Bread crumbs	1 lb 4 oz	Dip fish in egg mixture, then in crumbs.
		Fry in deep fat at 360°F for 4–5 minutes or until fish is golden brown and internal temperature is 145°F.
		Serve at once or place for a short time in uncovered counter pans in 250°F oven until service.

Approximate nutritive values per portion

Calories	Carbohydrate	Protein	Fat	Cholesterol	Sodium	Fiber	Iron
205 kcal	12 g	30 g	3 g	103 mg	340 mg	1 g	1 mg

Notes

- Potentially hazardous food. *Food Safety Standards:* Hold food for service at an internal temperature of 135°F or above. Do not mix old product with new. Cool leftover product quickly following time standards and cooling procedures on p. 167. Reheat leftover product quickly (within 2 hours) to 165°F or above. Reheat product only once; discard if not used.
- Keep refrigerated all fish not being prepared or cooked.
- Suggested fish: flounder, sole, haddock, perch, grouper.

Variation

- **Cornmeal-Breaded Fish Fillets.** Delete eggs, milk, and bread crumbs. Increase flour to 1 lb. Mix flour, 2 lb 8 oz cornmeal, salt, and pepper. Dip fish fillets into cornmeal-flour mixture, thoroughly coating each piece. Fry according to directions.

FILLET OF SOLE AMANDINE

Yield: 50 portions   *Portion:* 5 oz
Oven: 375°F   *Bake:* 15–20 minutes

Ingredient	Amount	Procedure
Fillet of sole, 3 per lb	17 lb	Dredge fish in mixture of flour, salt, and pepper.
Flour, all-purpose	8 oz	Place in greased counter pans in single layers.
Salt	1 Tbsp	
White pepper	1 tsp	
Onion, finely chopped	4 oz	Sauté onion and garlic in margarine.
Garlic clove, minced	1	
Margarine	1 lb 8 oz	
Water	2 cups	Combine water, lemon juice, and seasonings. Add onion and garlic.
Fresh lemon juice	1½ cups	Heat, but do not boil.
Salt	1 Tbsp	Just before baking, pour sauce over fish, 1 cup per pan.
White pepper	1 tsp	
Almonds, slivered	8 oz	Sprinkle almonds over fish.
		Bake at 375°F for approximately 10 minutes for each inch of thickness or until fish flakes easily when tested with a fork at thickest part and internal temperature is 145°F.

Approximate nutritive values per portion

Calories	Carbohydrate	Protein	Fat	Cholesterol	Sodium	Fiber	Iron
324 kcal	5 g	39 g	16 g	104 mg	548 mg	1 g	1 mg

Notes

- Potentially hazardous food. *Food Safety Standards:* Hold food for service at an internal temperature of 135°F or above. Do not mix old product with new. Cool leftover product quickly following time standards and cooling procedures on p. 167. Reheat leftover product quickly (within 2 hours) to 165°F or above. Reheat product only once; discard if not used.
- Keep refrigerated all fish not being prepared or cooked.
- Other white fish, such as halibut, haddock, cod, or flounder, may be used. Baking time on thicker fillets or steaks will be 25–35 minutes.

BROILED TUNA WITH WHITE BEANS AND TOMATO SAUCE

Yield: 50 portions   *Portion:* 6 oz tuna, 3 oz sauce
Broiler: 400°F   *Broil:* 10 minutes

Ingredient	Amount	Procedure
Red wine vinegar	¾ cup	Combine vinegar, oil, and seasonings.
Olive oil	½ cup	
Black pepper	1½ tsp	
Salt	2 tsp	
Tuna steaks, 6 oz (approximately 1 inch thick)	50	Brush oil mixture evenly over both sides of tuna steaks. Arrange tuna on oiled sheet pans. Place pans in preheated 400°F broiler. Cook for approximately 5 minutes on each side, until fish flakes easily and reaches 145°F.
White Bean and Tomato Sauce	recipe p. 704	Serve tuna over a 3-oz bed of White Bean and Tomato Sauce. Garnish plate with fresh basil or thyme.

Approximate nutritive values per portion

Calories	Carbohydrate	Protein	Fat	Cholesterol	Sodium	Fiber	Iron
401 kcal	33 g	51 g	7 g	74 mg	245 mg	1 g	7 mg

Note

- Potentially hazardous food. *Food Safety Standards:* Hold food for service at an internal temperature of 135°F or above. Do not mix old product with new. Cool leftover product quickly following time standards and cooling procedures on p. 167. Reheat leftover product quickly (within 2 hours) to 165°F or above. Reheat product only once; discard if not used.

Variation

- **Broiled Halibut with Black Bean Sauce.** Substitute halibut steaks for tuna. Substitute Black Bean and Tomato Sauce (p. 705) for White Bean and Tomato Sauce.

LEMON RICE–STUFFED COD

Yield: 50 portions   *Portion:* 6 oz cod, 2¼ oz rice
Oven: 350°F   *Bake:* 25–30 minutes

Ingredient	Amount	Procedure
Cod fillets, 6 oz	50	Cut cod portions to open like a wallet, hinged in center.
Celery, diced Onion, chopped Margarine	12 oz 6 oz 4 oz	Sauté celery and onion in margarine in steam-jacketed kettle or other large pan.
Water, hot Salt Thyme, dried	1½ qt 1 Tbsp 1 tsp	Add water and seasonings to vegetable mixture.
Rice, uncooked	1 lb 4 oz	Stir in raw rice. Cover and simmer until rice is tender and liquid is absorbed, approximately 15 minutes.
Yogurt, plain Lemon, peeled and diced	1 lb 4 oz	Stir in yogurt and lemon.
		Place No. 16 dipper (2¼ oz) of rice mixture on one side of fish fillet. Fold other half over top to close like a wallet. Place on greased baking sheets or 12 × 20-inch counter pans. Bake uncovered at 350°F for approximately 25–30 minutes or until fish flakes easily when tested with a fork at thickest part and internal temperature reaches 145°F. Serve garnished with a slice of lemon.

Approximate nutritive values per portion

Calories	Carbohydrate	Protein	Fat	Cholesterol	Sodium	Fiber	Iron
207 kcal	10 g	31 g	3 g	75 mg	253 mg	0.2 g	1 mg

Notes

- Potentially hazardous food. *Food Safety Standards:* Hold food for service at an internal temperature of 135°F or above. Do not mix old product with new. Cool leftover product quickly following time standards and cooling procedures on p. 167. Reheat leftover product quickly (within 2 hours) to 165°F or above. Reheat product only once; discard if not used.
- Keep refrigerated all fish not being prepared or cooked.
- Brown rice or a brown and wild rice mixture may be substituted for white rice.
- Any firm fish may be substituted for cod: orange roughy, perch, pollock.

BAKED WHOLE SALMON, CHILLED

Yield: 1 salmon or 50 portions
Oven: 350°F   *Bake:* 2 hours

Ingredient	Amount	Procedure
Whole salmon, thawed	1 (approx. 10 lb)	Thoroughly wash fish. Rub inside and outside of fish while running cool, clear water over. Place fish on 12 × 20-inch sheet pan that has been sprayed with vegetable spray or lined with parchment paper. Bake at 350°F for approximately 1 hour.
		Remove from oven and skin fish. Cut skin behind head, down the length of back and halfway down across belly. Remove cut skin. Leave head, fins, and tail on.
Margarine or butter, melted	4 oz	Combine melted margarine and lemon juice. Use to baste fish. Return fish to oven and bake approximately 1 hour or until fish flakes easily when tested with a fork at thickest part and internal temperature reaches 145°F.
Fresh lemon juice	½ cup (4 oz)	
		Remove fish from oven. Cool quickly to below 41°F following cooling procedures on p. 167. Fish should be cooked 1 day in advance to be served on cold buffet.

TO SERVE WHOLE BAKED SALMON:

1. Place fish on attractive tray.
2. Garnish with orange, lemon, and cucumber slices; carrot curls, ripe olives, and shredded cabbage. If mouth is large and open, a fluted orange can be inserted.

Approximate nutritive values per portion

Calories	Carbohydrate	Protein	Fat	Cholesterol	Sodium	Fiber	Iron
148 kcal	0 g	19 g	7 g	35 mg	64 mg	0 g	0.5 mg

Notes

- Potentially hazardous food. *Food Safety Standards:* Hold food for service at an internal temperature of 41°F or below. Do not mix old product with new. Keep leftover product chilled at 41°F or below. See p. 167 for cooling procedures.
- Thaw fish in refrigerator for 1–2 days.

POACHED SALMON

Yield: 50 portions   *Portion:* 5 oz
Oven: 350°F   *Bake:* 10–15 minutes

Ingredient	Amount	Procedure
Onion, coarsely chopped	4 oz	Put vegetables, seasonings, and lemon into a cheesecloth bag.
Parsley sprigs	2 oz	
Celery tops, coarsely chopped	4 oz	
Bay leaves	8	
Thyme, dried	4 tsp	
Peppercorns, black	2 tsp	
Salt	4 tsp	
Lemons, thickly sliced	2	
Water	2 gal	Combine water and wine. Cover and simmer seasoning bag with liquid for 15 minutes.
White wine	1 qt	Discard seasoning bag.
Salmon fillets, 5 oz (fresh or thawed)	50	Lightly grease four 12 × 20 × 4-inch pans. Divide salmon evenly into pans. Carefully pour approximately 2 qt of simmering hot liquid over salmon. (Fish should be just covered with liquid.) Bake uncovered at 350°F for 10–15 minutes or until fish flakes easily and reaches a temperature of 145°F. Remove salmon carefully from liquid. Serve with Horseradish Caper Sauce (p. 694) or Fruit Salsa (p. 704).

Approximate nutritive values per portion

Calories	Carbohydrate	Protein	Fat	Cholesterol	Sodium	Fiber	Iron
190 kcal	4 g	16 g	11 g	0 mg	179 mg	0 g	0.5 mg

Notes

- Potentially hazardous food. *Food Safety Standards:* Hold food for service at an internal temperature of 135°F or above. Do not mix old product with new. Cool leftover product quickly following time standards and cooling procedures on p. 167. Reheat leftover product quickly (within 2 hours) to 165°F or above. Reheat product only once; discard if not used.
- The thermometer or thermocouple probe must be inserted in the fish without first passing through the poaching liquid.
- Salmon may be served hot or cold. If served cold, chill quickly (within 4 hours) to 41°F or below.
- For alternative poaching liquids, see Table 13.3, p. 402.

SALMON LOAF

Yield: 50 portions or 5 loaves, 5 × 9 inches   *Portion:* 4½ oz
Oven: 325°F   *Bake:* 1–1½ hours

Ingredient	Amount	Procedure
Milk, scalded	3¾ cups	Mix milk and bread cubes.
Bread cubes, soft	1 lb 4 oz	
Eggs, beaten	18 (2 lb)	Add eggs to milk and bread mixture.
Salmon, flaked	10 lb	Add salmon and other ingredients.
Salt	1 oz (1½ Tbsp)	Mix lightly.
Paprika	1 tsp	Scale salmon mixture into five greased 5 × 9-inch loaf pans, 2 lb 14 oz per pan.
White pepper	1 tsp	Bake at 325°F for 1–1½ hours or until internal temperature reaches 180°F.
Onion, chopped	3 oz	
Fresh lemon juice	½ cup	

Approximate nutritive values per portion

Calories	Carbohydrate	Protein	Fat	Cholesterol	Sodium	Fiber	Iron
196 kcal	7 g	22 g	8 g	130 mg	785 mg	0.3 g	1 mg

Notes

- Potentially hazardous food. *Food Safety Standards:* Hold food for service at an internal temperature of 135°F or above. Do not mix old product with new. Cool leftover product quickly following time standards and cooling procedures on p. 167. Reheat leftover product quickly (within 2 hours) to 165°F or above. Reheat product only once; discard if not used.
- For a lighter textured product, beat egg whites separately and fold into salmon mixture.

Variation

- **Tuna Loaf.** Substitute drained tuna for salmon.

TUNA AND NOODLES

Yield: 48 portions or 2 pans, 12 × 20 × 2 inches   *Portion:* 8 oz
Oven: 350°F   *Bake:* 30–45 minutes

Ingredient	Amount	Procedure
Noodles	3 lb AP	Cook noodles according to directions on p. 507.
Water, boiling	3 gal	Drain. (Should yield 9 lb cooked.)
Salt	2 oz (3 Tbsp)	
Vegetable oil	2 Tbsp	
Tuna	5 lb 8 oz	Flake tuna and add to noodles.
Margarine	8 oz	Melt margarine in steam-jacketed or other kettle. Add onion and celery.
Onion, chopped	1 lb 8 oz	Sauté until tender.
Celery, chopped	1 lb 8 oz	
Flour, all-purpose	6 oz	Add flour and pepper to onion mixture. Stir until blended.
Black pepper	½ tsp	Cook for 5–10 minutes.
Chicken base	3 oz	Stir in chicken base.
Water	1 gal	Add water gradually, stirring constantly with a wire whip. Cook until thickened.
		Add tuna and noodles to sauce.
		Stir gently until well blended.
Processed cheese, shredded	8 oz	Scale noodle mixture into two greased 12 × 20 × 2-inch baking pans, 13 lb per pan.
Paprika	½ tsp	Sprinkle with cheese, 4 oz per pan.
		Sprinkle lightly with paprika.
		Bake at 350°F until mixture is heated to 180°F and cheese is melted, 30–45 minutes.

Approximate nutritive values per portion

Calories	Carbohydrate	Protein	Fat	Cholesterol	Sodium	Fiber	Iron
251 kcal	25 g	19 g	8 g	47 mg	1044 mg	1 g	2 mg

Notes

- Potentially hazardous food. *Food Safety Standards:* Hold food for service at an internal temperature of 135°F or above. Do not mix old product with new. Cool leftover product quickly following time standards and cooling procedures on p. 167. Reheat leftover product quickly (within 2 hours) to 165°F or above. Reheat product only once; discard if not used.
- Two 46-oz cans cream of mushroom or cream of celery soup and 1 qt milk may be substituted for the sauce made from margarine, flour, chicken base, and water.

Variations

- **Tuna Macaroni Casserole.** Substitute macaroni for noodles.
- **Tuna and Rice.** Substitute 1 lb 8 oz rice for the noodles. Cook rice according to directions on p. 542.

CREAMED TUNA

Yield: 50 portions or 7½ qt   *Portion:* 4 oz

Ingredient	Amount	Procedure
Eggs, hard cooked (p. 384)	9	Peel eggs and chop coarsely; reserve for later step.
Margarine	12 oz	Melt margarine in steam-jacketed or other kettle.
Flour, all-purpose	6 oz	Add flour and salt. Stir until smooth.
Salt	1 Tbsp	Cook for 5 minutes.
Milk	1 gal	Add milk gradually, stirring constantly with a wire whip. Cook until thickened.
Green bell pepper, chopped	6 oz	Add bell pepper, pimento, and seasonings to sauce.
Pimento, chopped	6 oz	
Worcestershire sauce (optional)	6 Tbsp	
Cayenne pepper	¼ tsp	
Tuna, flaked	5 lb	Add tuna and eggs to sauce. Heat to 180°F. Serve with 4-oz ladle on toast, biscuits, or corn bread.

Approximate nutritive values per portion

Calories	Carbohydrate	Protein	Fat	Cholesterol	Sodium	Fiber	Iron
179 kcal	7 g	16 g	9 g	62 mg	413 mg	0.2 g	1 mg

Notes

- Potentially hazardous food. *Food Safety Standards:* Hold food for service at an internal temperature of 135°F or above. Do not mix old product with new. Cool leftover product quickly following time standards and cooling procedures on p. 167. Reheat leftover product quickly (within 2 hours) to 165°F or above. Reheat product only once; discard if not used.
- Other cooked fish may be substituted for tuna.

Variations

- **Creamed Salmon.** Substitute salmon for tuna.
- **Creamed Tuna and Celery.** Delete hard-cooked eggs and green bell pepper. Add 1 lb diced cooked celery, 3 oz chopped onion sautéed in margarine, and 3 oz chopped pimento.
- **Creamed Tuna and Peas.** Delete hard-cooked eggs and green bell pepper. Add 3 lb frozen peas, cooked until just tender and drained.
- **Tuna Rarebit.** Delete hard-cooked eggs. Add 1 lb 8 oz shredded cheddar cheese.

DEVILED CRAB

Yield: 50 portions   *Portion:* 3 oz
Oven: 400°F   *Bake:* 15 minutes

Ingredient	Amount	Procedure
Crabmeat	6 lb	Separate crabmeat into flakes.
Eggs, beaten	5 (9 oz)	Combine eggs, lemon juice, and seasonings.
Fresh lemon juice	¼ cup	Add to crabmeat. Mix lightly.
Salt	1 oz (1½ Tbsp)	
Black pepper	2 tsp	
Cayenne pepper	few grains	
Worcestershire sauce	1 Tbsp	
Onion juice (optional)	2 Tbsp	
Margarine	12 oz	Melt margarine in steam-jacketed or other kettle.
Flour, all-purpose	8 oz	Add flour and stir until smooth.
		Cook for 5 minutes.
Milk	2 qt	Add milk gradually to flour mixture, stirring constantly with a wire whip.
		Cook until thick.
Prepared mustard	1½ tsp	Add mustard to sauce. Combine with crab mixture. Mix lightly.
		Fill individual casseroles or shells.
Bread crumbs	8 oz	Combine crumbs and margarine.
Margarine, melted	4 oz	Sprinkle over crab.
		Bake at 400°F for approximately 15 minutes or until internal temperature reaches 180°F.

Approximate nutritive values per portion

Calories	Carbohydrate	Protein	Fat	Cholesterol	Sodium	Fiber	Iron
186 kcal	9 g	13 g	11 g	81 mg	614 mg	0.3 g	1 mg

Notes

- Potentially hazardous food. *Food Safety Standards:* Hold food for service at an internal temperature of 135°F or above. Do not mix old product with new. Cool leftover product quickly following time standards and cooling procedures on p. 167. Reheat leftover product quickly (within 2 hours) to 165°F or above. Reheat product only once; discard if not used.
- Lobster, shrimp, or imitation crab may be substituted for crabmeat.

SCALLOPED OYSTERS

Yield: 50 portions or 2 pans, 12 × 20 × 2 inches   *Portion:* 5 oz
Oven: 400°F   *Bake:* 30 minutes

Ingredient	Amount	Procedure
Oysters	6 qt	Drain oysters, saving liquor.
Cracker crumbs	3 qt	Mix crumbs, margarine, and seasonings.
Margarine, melted	1 lb	Spread a third of the crumbs over bottoms of two greased
Salt	1 oz (1½ Tbsp)	12 × 20 × 2-inch baking pans.
Paprika	½ tsp	Cover with half of the oysters; repeat with crumbs and oysters.
White pepper	½ tsp	
Milk	1 qt	Mix milk and oyster liquor. Pour over top of oysters.
Oyster liquor or milk	3 cups	Cover with remaining crumbs.
		Bake at 400°F for approximately 30 minutes until internal temperature reaches 165°F.

Approximate nutritive values per portion

Calories	Carbohydrate	Protein	Fat	Cholesterol	Sodium	Fiber	Iron
164 kcal	14 g	3 g	11 g	5 mg	585 mg	0 g	1 mg

Notes

- Potentially hazardous food. *Food Safety Standards:* Hold food for service at an internal temperature of 135°F or above. Do not mix old product with new. Cool leftover product quickly following time standards and cooling procedures on p. 167. Reheat leftover product quickly (within 2 hours) to 165°F or above. Reheat product only once; discard if not used.
- 2 cups finely chopped, partially cooked celery may be added.

CARIBBEAN SHRIMP

Yield: 50   *Portion:* 4 oz

Ingredient	Amount	Procedure
Large shrimp, peeled and deveined, tails left on	15 lb AP	Combine shrimp, oil, and seasonings. Marinate shrimp in refrigerator for 1 hour.
Olive oil	1½ cups	
Garlic, finely minced	4 oz EP	
Thyme, dried, whole	4 Tbsp	
Rosemary, dried, whole	4 Tbsp	
Black pepper	1 Tbsp	
Crushed red pepper	1 Tbsp	
Salt	2 tsp	
		Drain. Discard excess marinade. Over medium-high heat, cook shrimp in a single layer on a lightly oiled griddle or skillet. Cook until shrimp turn pink and are done (145°F, 4–8 minutes). Turn halfway through cooking time.
Fresh limes (optional)	8	Garnish with lime wedges.

Approximate nutritive values per portion

Calories	Carbohydrate	Protein	Fat	Cholesterol	Sodium	Fiber	Iron
175 kcal	1 g	27 g	6.5 g	0 mg	240 mg	0.2 g	1 mg

Notes

- Potentially hazardous food. *Food Safety Standards:* Hold food for service at an internal temperature of 135°F or above. Do not mix old product with new. Cool leftover product quickly following time standards and cooling procedures on p. 167. Reheat leftover product quickly (within 2 hours) to 165°F or above. Reheat product only once; discard if not used.
- Shrimp can be skewered and served for a hot or cold appetizer or as an entrée on a bed of seasoned rice or pasta.

CREOLE SHRIMP WITH RICE

Yield: 50 portions   *Portion:* 4 oz creole shrimp + 4 oz rice

Ingredient	Amount	Procedure
Onion, finely chopped	10 oz	Cook onion, celery, and garlic in shortening until almost
Celery, finely chopped	12 oz	tender but not brown.
Garlic, minced	1 tsp	
Shortening	8 oz	
Flour, all-purpose	6 oz	Add flour and seasonings. Stir until smooth.
Salt	1 oz (1½ Tbsp)	Cook for 5 minutes.
Cayenne pepper	¾ tsp	
Tomato juice	2 cups	Add tomato juice, tomatoes, and sugar. Cook for 10 minutes.
Tomatoes, canned	2½ qt	
Sugar, granulated	1 Tbsp	
Shrimp, cooked, peeled, and deveined	6 lb EP	Add shrimp and pepper to sauce. Heat to 165°F.
Green bell pepper, chopped	8 oz	
Rice, converted	3 lb 8 oz	Cook rice according to directions on p. 542.
Water, boiling	4¼ qt	Serve shrimp with 4-oz ladle over No. 10 dipper of rice.
Salt	2 Tbsp	
Margarine or vegetable oil	2 Tbsp	

Approximate nutritive values per portion

Calories	Carbohydrate	Protein	Fat	Cholesterol	Sodium	Fiber	Iron
233 kcal	32 g	12 g	6 g	84 mg	667 mg	1 g	3 mg

Notes

- Potentially hazardous food. *Food Safety Standards:* Hold food for service at an internal temperature of 135°F or above. Do not mix old product with new. Cool leftover product quickly following time standards and cooling procedures on p. 167. Reheat leftover product quickly (within 2 hours) to 165°F or above. Reheat product only once; discard if not used.
- If raw shrimp are used, purchase 12–14 lb. Cook as directed on p. 402.

Beef Made Easy

EXHIBIT 1

Retail Beef Cuts and Recommended Cooking Methods

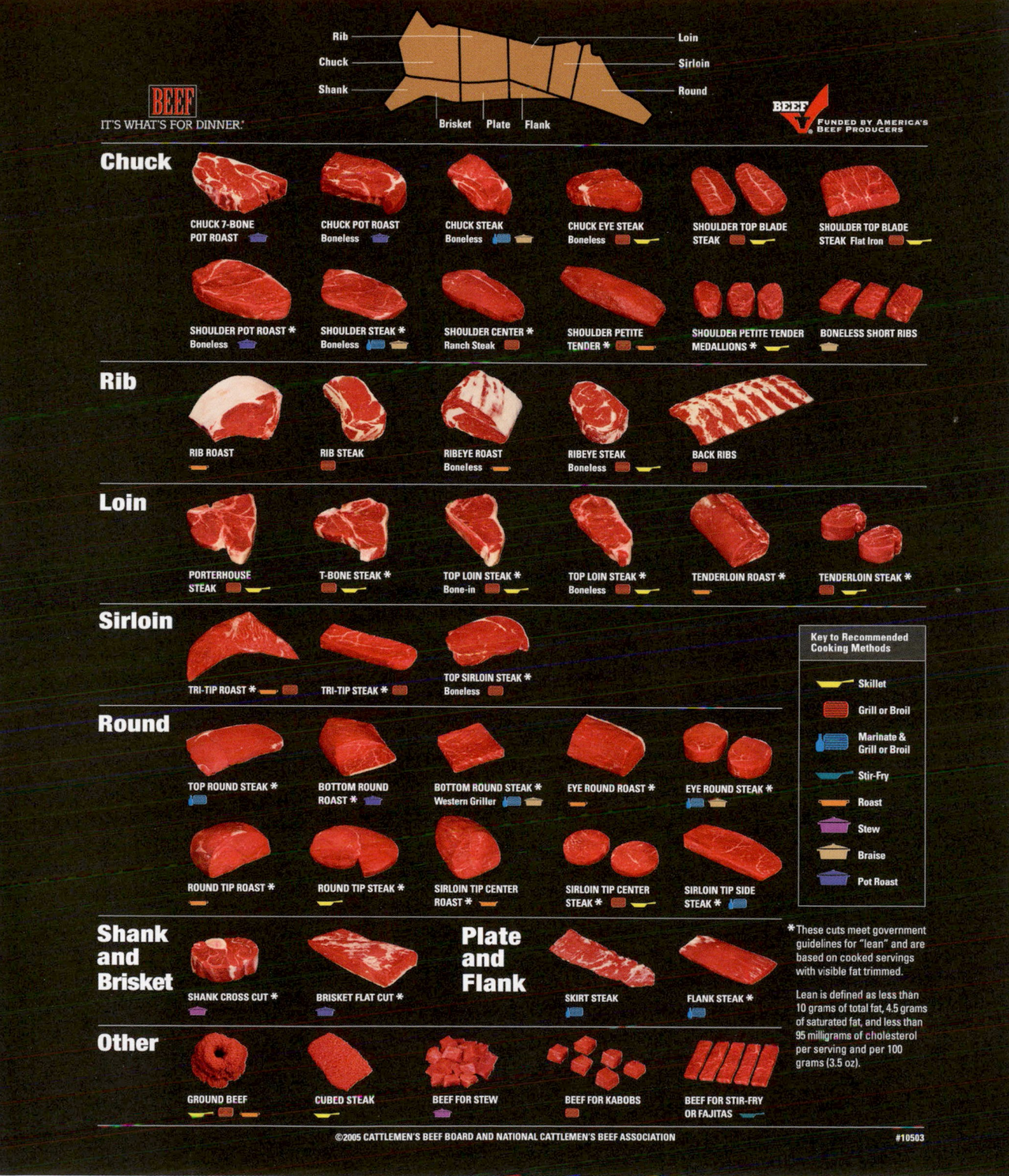

BEEF
IT'S WHAT'S FOR DINNER.®

Rib · Chuck · Shank · Brisket · Plate · Flank · Loin · Sirloin · Round

BEEF FUNDED BY AMERICA'S BEEF PRODUCERS

Chuck
- CHUCK 7-BONE POT ROAST
- CHUCK POT ROAST Boneless
- CHUCK STEAK Boneless
- CHUCK EYE STEAK Boneless
- SHOULDER TOP BLADE STEAK
- SHOULDER TOP BLADE STEAK Flat Iron
- SHOULDER POT ROAST * Boneless
- SHOULDER STEAK * Boneless
- SHOULDER CENTER * Ranch Steak
- SHOULDER PETITE TENDER *
- SHOULDER PETITE TENDER MEDALLIONS *
- BONELESS SHORT RIBS

Rib
- RIB ROAST
- RIB STEAK
- RIBEYE ROAST Boneless
- RIBEYE STEAK Boneless
- BACK RIBS

Loin
- PORTERHOUSE STEAK
- T-BONE STEAK *
- TOP LOIN STEAK * Bone-in
- TOP LOIN STEAK * Boneless
- TENDERLOIN ROAST *
- TENDERLOIN STEAK *

Sirloin
- TRI-TIP ROAST *
- TRI-TIP STEAK *
- TOP SIRLOIN STEAK * Boneless

Round
- TOP ROUND STEAK *
- BOTTOM ROUND ROAST *
- BOTTOM ROUND STEAK * Western Griller
- EYE ROUND ROAST *
- EYE ROUND STEAK *
- ROUND TIP ROAST *
- ROUND TIP STEAK *
- SIRLOIN TIP CENTER ROAST *
- SIRLOIN TIP CENTER STEAK *
- SIRLOIN TIP SIDE STEAK *

Shank and Brisket
- SHANK CROSS CUT *
- BRISKET FLAT CUT *

Plate and Flank
- SKIRT STEAK
- FLANK STEAK *

Other
- GROUND BEEF
- CUBED STEAK
- BEEF FOR STEW
- BEEF FOR KABOBS
- BEEF FOR STIR-FRY OR FAJITAS

Key to Recommended Cooking Methods
- Skillet
- Grill or Broil
- Marinate & Grill or Broil
- Stir-Fry
- Roast
- Stew
- Braise
- Pot Roast

*These cuts meet government guidelines for "lean" and are based on cooked servings with visible fat trimmed.

Lean is defined as less than 10 grams of total fat, 4.5 grams of saturated fat, and less than 95 milligrams of cholesterol per serving and per 100 grams (3.5 oz).

©2005 CATTLEMEN'S BEEF BOARD AND NATIONAL CATTLEMEN'S BEEF ASSOCIATION · #10503

Courtesy of The Beef Checkoff

EXHIBIT

2

American Lamb
Cuts and How to Cook Them

Leg

Whole Leg
(Roast)

Short Cut Leg, Sirloin Off
(Roast)

Shank Portion Roast
(Roast)

Center Leg Roast
(Roast)

Center Slice
(Broil, Grill, Panbroil, Panfry)

American-Style Roast
(Roast)

Frenched-Style Leg Roast
(Roast)

Boneless Leg Roast (BRT)
(Roast)

Frenched Hindshank
(Braise)

Sirloin Chop
(Braise, Broil, Grill, Panbroil, Panfry)

Boneless Sirloin Roast
(Roast)

Top Round
(Roast)

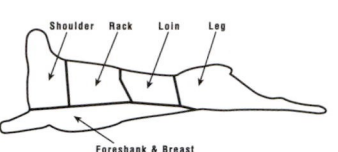

Shoulder   Rack   Loin   Leg

Foreshank & Breast

Loin

Loin Roast
(Roast)

Boneless Loin Strip (BRT)
(Roast)

Loin Chop
(Broil, Grill, Panbroil, Panfry)

Double Loin Chop
(Broil, Grill, Panbroil, Panfry)

Tenderloin
(Roast)

Foreshank & Breast

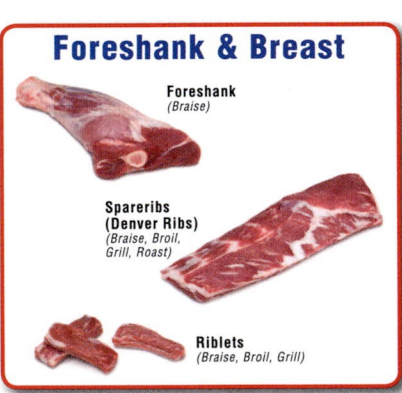

Foreshank
(Braise)

Spareribs (Denver Ribs)
(Braise, Broil, Grill, Roast)

Riblets
(Braise, Broil, Grill)

AMERICAN LAMB BOARD

www.americanlamb.com

Rack

Crown Roast
(Roast)

Rib Roast
(Broil, Grill, Roast)

Rib Chop
(Broil, Grill, Panbroil, Panfry, Roast)

Frenched Rib Chop
(Broil, Grill, Panbroil, Panfry, Roast)

Shoulder

Square Cut Shoulder Whole
(Braise, Roast)

Saratoga Roast
(Braise, Roast)

Boneless Shoulder Roast (BRT)
(Braise, Roast)

Blade Chop
(Braise, Broil, Grill, Panbroil, Panfry)

Arm Chop
(Braise, Broil, Grill, Panbroil, Panfry)

Other Cuts

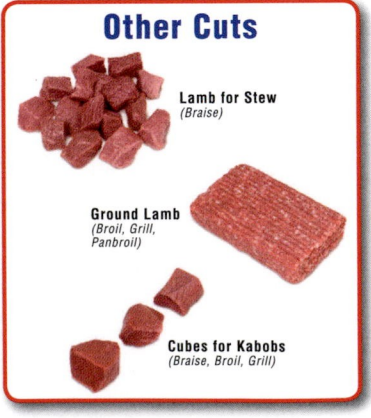

Lamb for Stew
(Braise)

Ground Lamb
(Broil, Grill, Panbroil)

Cubes for Kabobs
(Braise, Broil, Grill)

Courtesy of The American Lamb Board

EXHIBIT

3

Pork Basics

Upper row (l-r):
Bone-in Blade Roast,
Boneless Blade Roast
Lower row (l-r):
Ground Pork (The Other Burger®),
Sausage, Blade Steak

Cooking Methods
*Blade Roast/Boston butt –
roast, indirect heat on grill,
braise, slow cooker*
*Blade Steak –
braise, broil, grill*
*Ground Pork –
broil, grill, roast (bake)*

Shoulder Butt

Upper row (l-r):
Smoked Picnic,
Arm Picnic Roast
Lower row:
Smoked Hocks

Cooking Methods
*Smoked Picnic Roast –
roast, braise*
*Arm Picnic Roast –
roast, braise, slow cooker*
*Smoked Hocks –
braise, stew*

Picnic Shoulder

Top:
Spareribs
Bottom:
Slab Bacon, Sliced Bacon

Cooking Methods
*Spareribs –
roast, indirect heat on
grill, braise, slow cooker*
*Bacon –
broil, roast (bake),
microwave*

Side

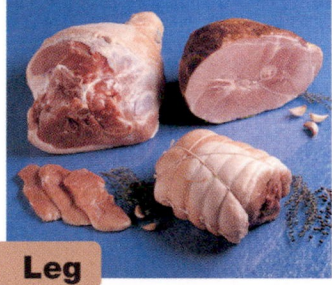

Upper row (l-r):
Bone-in Fresh Ham,
Smoked Ham
Lower row (l-r):
Leg Cutlets,
Fresh Boneless Ham Roast

Cooking Methods
*Fresh Leg of Pork –
roast, indirect heat on grill,
slow cooker*
*Smoked Ham –
roast, indirect heat on grill*
*Ham Steak –
broil, roast*

Leg

Loin

Chops

Upper row (l-r):
Sirloin Chop, Rib Chop, Loin Chop
Lower row (l-r):
Boneless Rib End Chop, Chef's Prime Filet™ –
Boneless Center Loin Chop, America's Cut™ –
Butterfly Chop

Cooking Methods
Cutlets (⅛ to ⅜ inch) – sauté
Thin (½ to ¾ inch thick) – grill, broil,
Thick (1¼ to 1½ inch thick) – grill, broil, roast

Roasts

Upper row (l-r):
Center Rib Roast (Rack of Pork),
Bone-in Sirloin Roast
Middle:
Boneless Center Loin Roast
Lower row (l-r):
Boneless Rib End Roast,
Chef's Prime™ – Boneless Sirloin Roast

Cooking Methods
roast, indirect heat on grill, slow cooker

Tenderloin & Canadian-Style Bacon

Left: Tenderloin **Right:** Canadian-Style Bacon

Cooking Methods
Tenderloin – roast, grill, pan broil
Canadian-Style bacon – roast, broil, sauté

Ribs

Left: Country-Style Ribs **Right:** Back Ribs

Cooking Methods
roast, indirect heat on grill, braise, slow cooker

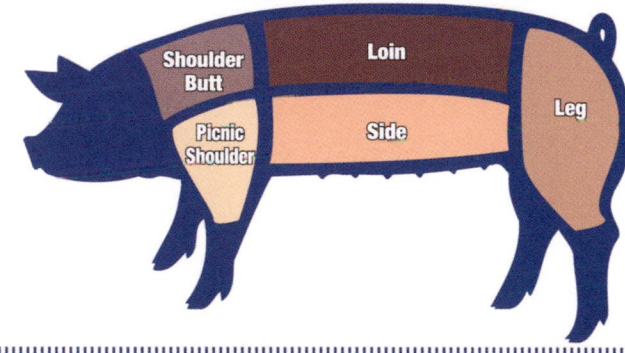

Shoulder Butt — Loin — Leg
Picnic Shoulder — Side

Roasts
No-fuss family dinner or holiday favorite

THE MANY SHAPES OF PORK

Cut Loose!

When shopping for pork,
consider cutting traditional
roasts into a variety of
different shapes

Chops
Dinner, backyard
barbecue or
gourmet entree

Cubes
Great for kabobs,
stew and chili
*grill, stew, braise,
broil*

Strips
Super stir fry,
fajitas and salads
grill, sauté, stir fry

Cutlets
Delicious breakfast
chops and
quick sandwiches
*1/8 to 3/8 inch thick –
sauté, grill*

www.TheOtherWhiteMeat.com

Courtesy of the National Pork Board

EXHIBIT

4

Veal Cuts

Leg (Round)

Veal Leg Rump Roast Boneless
Dry Heat

Veal Leg Cutlet
Dry Heat

Loin

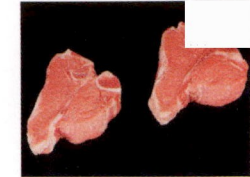

Veal Loin Chops
Dry Heat

Rib

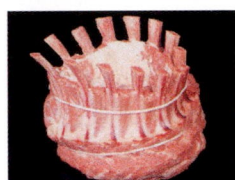

Veal Rib Rump Roast
Dry Heat

Veal Rib Chops
Dry Heat

Dry heat cooking: broiling, grilling, pan-broiling, pan-frying (sautéing), roasting, stir-frying.

Moist heat cooking: braising, stewing, pot roasting, cooking in liquid

Shoulder

Veal Shoulder Arm Steak
Moist Heat

Veal Shoulder Blade Steak
Moist Heat

Veal Shoulder Arm Roast Boneless
Moist Heat

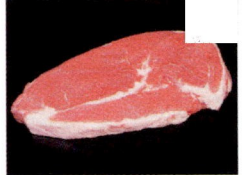

Veal Shoulder Arm Steak Boneless
Moist Heat

Breast

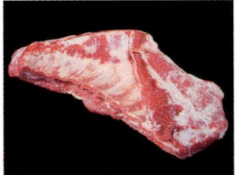

Veal Breast
Moist Heat

Veal Breast Boneless
Moist Heat

Veal Breast Riblets Boneless
Moist Heat

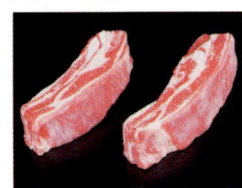

Veal Breast Riblets
Moist Heat

Shank   ## Other Cuts

Veal Shank Cross Cuts
Moist Heat

Ground Veal
Dry Heat

Veal Cubed Steak
Dry Heat

Veal for Stew
Moist Heat

Courtesy of The Beef Checkoff

Brie

Boursin

Gorgonzola

Havarti

Monterey Jack

Roquefort

Stilton

Cheddar

Emmenthaler (Swiss)

Gruyére

Asiago

Provolone

Parmigiano–Reggiano (Parmesan)

EXHIBIT

6

Fruits

Apple - Gala

Apple - Golden Delicious

Apple - Granny Smith

Apple - McIntosh

Apple - Red Delicious

Apple - Rome

Apricots

Common Yellow Bananas

Bing Cherries

Rainier Cherries

Blackberries

Blueberries

Cranberries

White Currants

Red Currants

Raspberries

Strawberries

Citrus - White Grapefruits

Citrus - Red Grapefruits

Citrus - Kumquats

Citrus - Lemons

Citrus - Limes

Citrus - Key Limes

Citrus - Tangerines

Citrus - Blood Oranges

Citrus - Valencia Oranges

Citrus - Navel Oranges

Concord Grapes

Red Flame Grapes

Thompson Seedless Grapes

Fruits

(continued)

Kiwis

Mangos

Medjool Dates

Melon - Cantaloupes

Melon - Green Honeydews

Melon - Casaba

Melon - Santa Claus

Melon - Gold Honeydews

Melon - Crenshaw

Melon - Gold Watermelon

Melon - Watermelon

Fruits

(continued)

Nectarines

Papayas

Red Papayas

Peaches

Pear - Anjou

Pear - Red d'Anjou

Pear - Asian

Pear - Bartlett

Pear - Bosc

Damson Plums

Santa Rosa Plums

Persimmons

Pineapples

Pomegranates

Plantains

Rhubarb

Star Fruits
(Carambola)

EXHIBIT

7

Procedures for Preparing Selected Fruits

Coring Apples

Method #1: Use apple corer by inserting at stem end and pushing core and seeds out through the blossom end.

Method #2: Cut apple into quarters. Use paring knife to cut away core and seeds.

Making Citrus Supremes

1. Cut peel and white pith from citrus.

2. Remove individual segments by gently cutting alongside each membrane.

Making Lemon and Lime Zest

Use a zester to remove paper-thin strips of the colored rind. Do not use the bitter white pith.

Making Citrus Zest Strips

Using a peeler or sharp knife, remove colored rind. Cut rind into thin strips.

Cutting Mangos

1. Note flattened shape. Cut along each side of flat pit to remove two sections.

2. Cube each section by making crosswise cuts through flesh just to skin. Press up on skin side of mango half to expose cubes.

3. Cut cubes off to use in salads or other dishes.

Peeling and Slicing Pineapple

1. Slice off top and stem end. Stand pineapple on end and cut off peel in vertical strips. Use a sharp tip paring knife to remove eyes.

2. Cut fruit into quarters. Cut the woody core away from the flesh.

3. Cut cubes off to use in salads or other dishes.

Making Strawberry Fans

Cut thin slices of strawberry without cutting through the stem. Lightly press to fan out the berry and expose the cut slices.

EXHIBIT

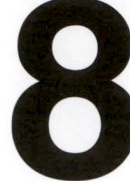

8 Vegetables

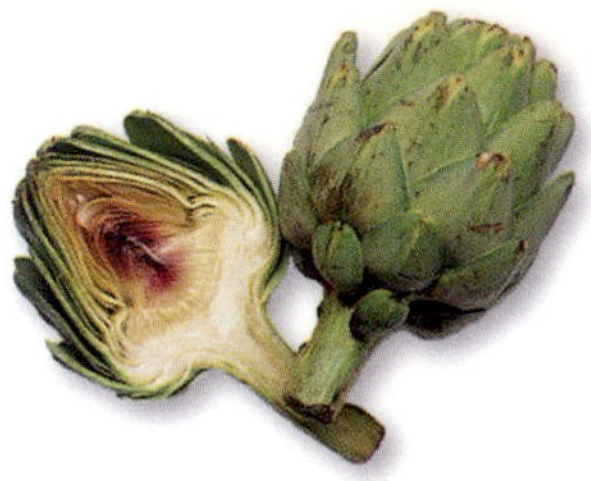
Artichokes

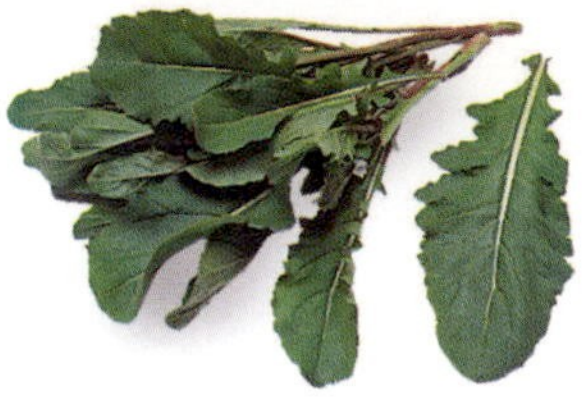
Arugula

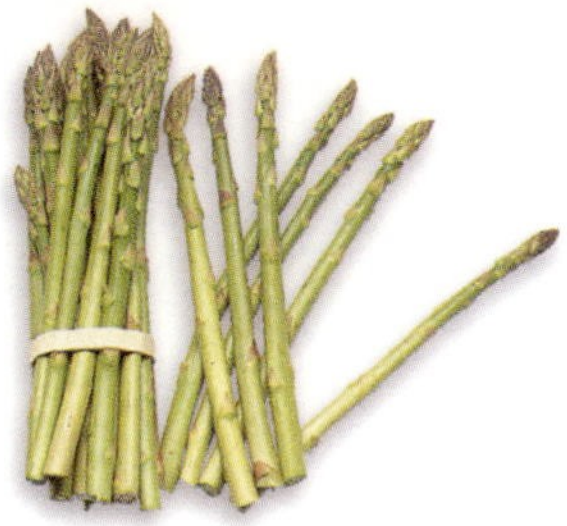
Asparagus

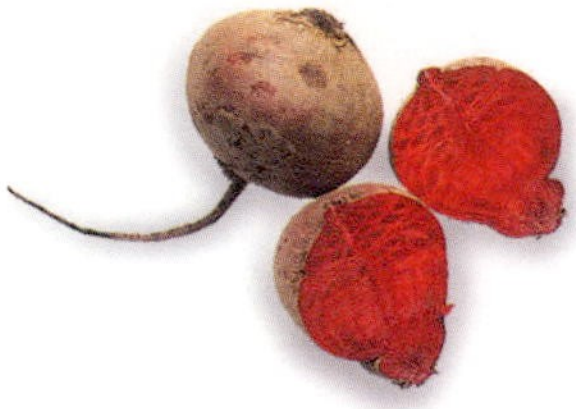
Beets

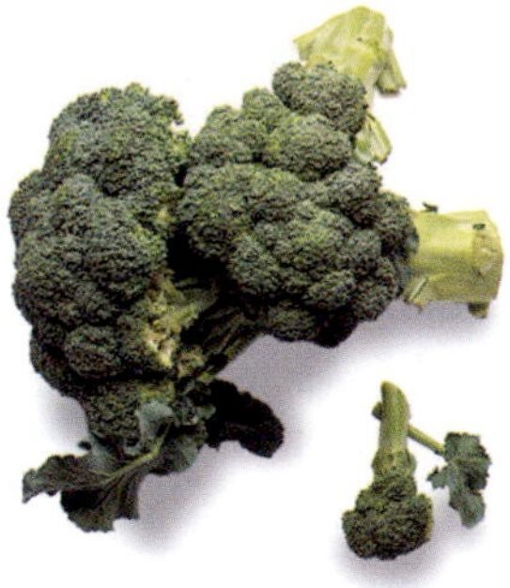
Broccoli

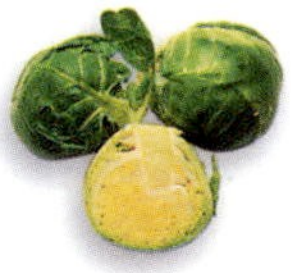
Brussels Sprouts

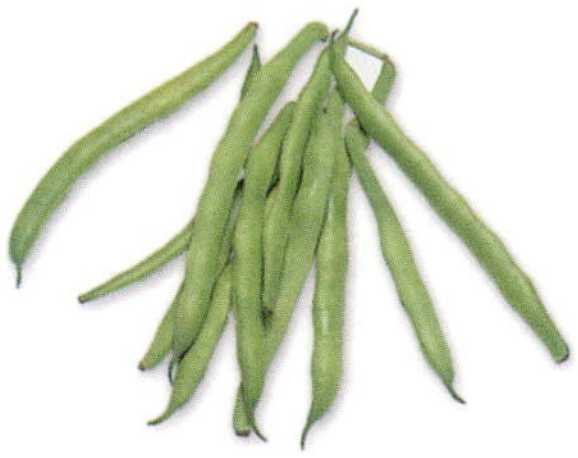
Green Beans

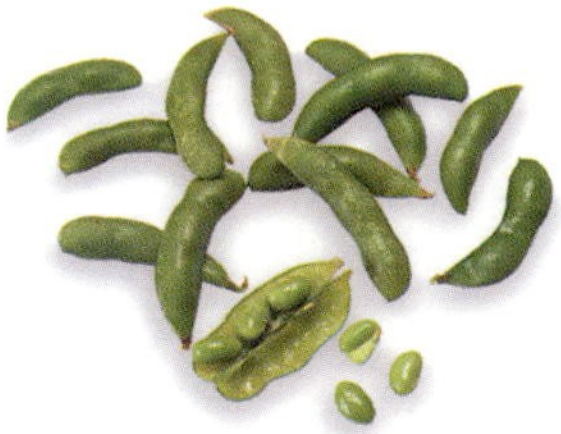
Soy Beans (Edamame)

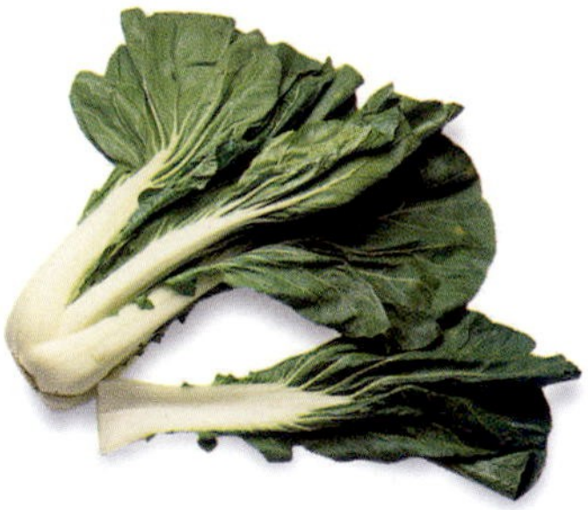
Bok Choy

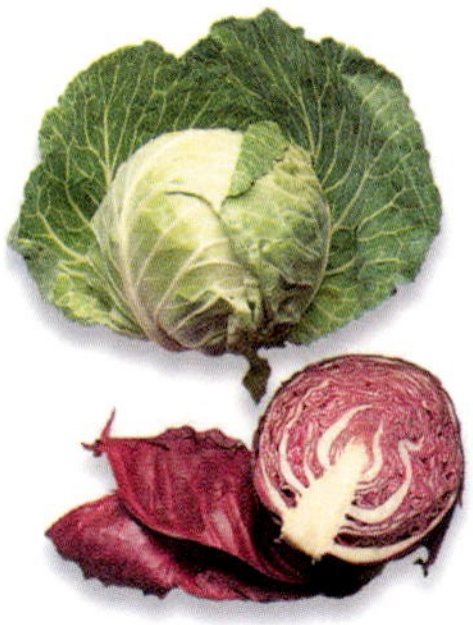
Green and Red Cabbages

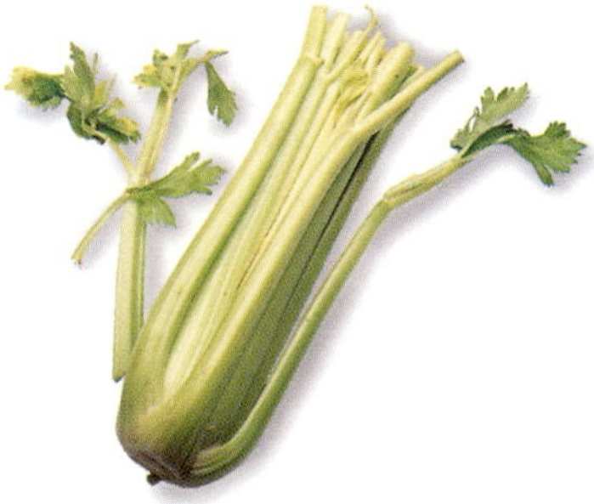
Celery

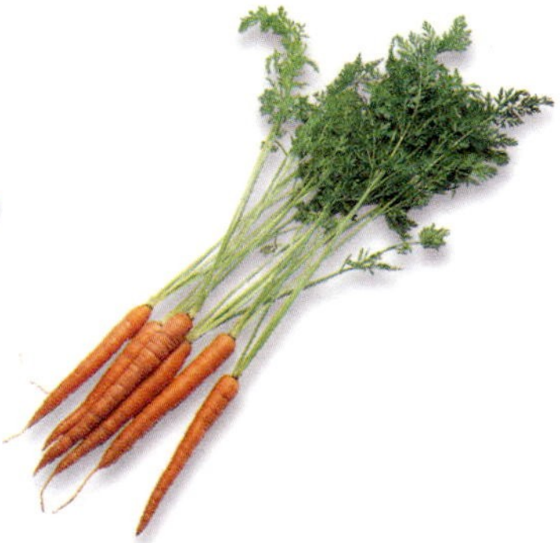
Carrots

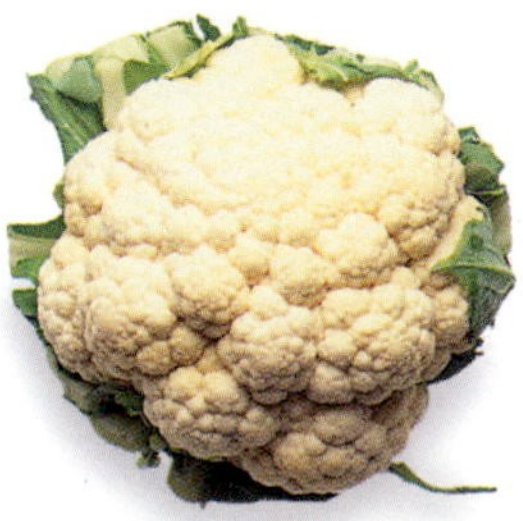
Cauliflower

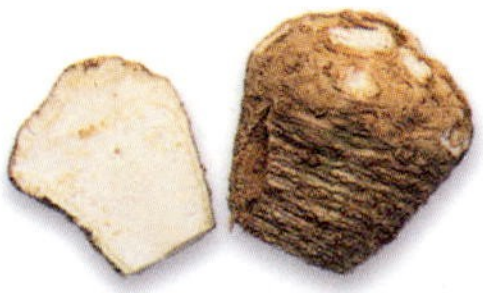
Celery Root

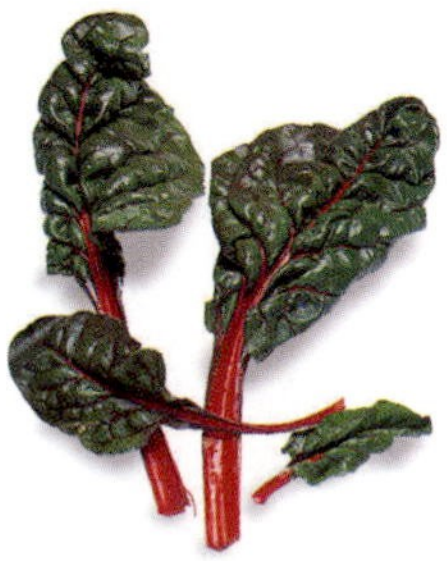
Swiss Chard

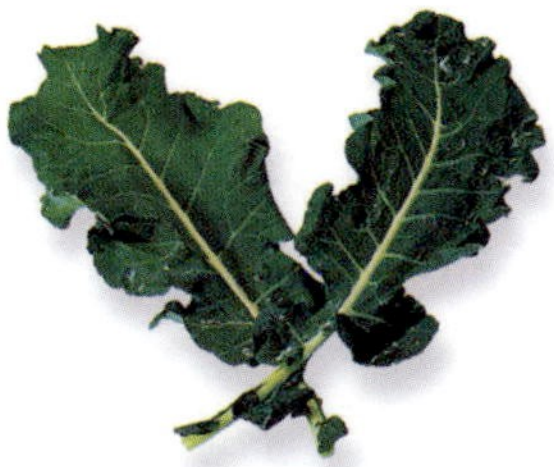
Collard Greens

Cucumbers

Yellow and White Corn

Western Eggplant

Japanese Eggplant

Belgian Endive

Curly Endive

Escarole

Fennel

Garlic

Dandelion

Mustard

Sorrel

Turnip Greens

Jicama

Kale

Ornamental Kale

EXHIBIT

8

Vegetables

(continued)

Kohlrabi

Leeks

Red and Green
Leaf Lettuce

Boston

Baby Red Oak Leaf

Romaine

Mache

Napa Cabbage

Iceberg

Savoy

Okra

Red Onion

Yellow Onion

Pearl Onions

Scallions

White Onions

Parsnips

Fresh Shelling Peas

Snow Peas

Yellow Hot

Poblano

Green and
Red Jalapeno

Red and Green
Serrano

Anaheim

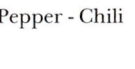

Pepper - Chili

Pepper - Habanera

Pepper - Green Bell

Pepper - Dried Chiles

Pepper - Red and Yellow Bell

Vegetables

(continued)

Potato - Fingerling

Potato - Purple

Potato - Red

Potato - Russet

Potato - White

Potato - Yukon Gold

Potato - Sweet

Rutabagas

Radicchio

Red Radishes

Shallots

Spinach

Squash - Acorn

Squash - Banana

Squash - Butternut

Squash - Spaghetti

Squash - Yellow Crookneck

Squash - Zucchini

Tomatillos

Tomatoes

Turnips

Watercress

Procedure for Preparing Selected Vegetables

Dicing Onions

1. Remove the stem end and trim the root end, leaving root core intact. Peel away any damaged or non-edible outer skin.

2. Cut in half through stem and root.

3. Cut parallel slices from stem end to root end. Do not cut completely through root end.

4. Make one to two horizontal cuts being careful to not cut through the root end.

5. Cut slices to produce diced onion.

Chopping and Mincing Garlic

1. Lightly crush individual garlic cloves to separate garlic flesh from papery skin.

2. Using a rocking motion with knife tip on cutting board, chop cloves until desired size.

3. Make garlic paste by first finely chopping garlic and then dragging the knife along the board, mashing the garlic.

Cutting Broccoli and Cauliflower Florets

1. Cut off stem end and leaves.

2. Cut florets off of the core.

3. Cut off woody portion of stalk. Cut florets and spears.

Washing Leeks

1. Trim the root end.

2. Discard dark tops and slice the white portion in half lengthwise.

3. Rinse leeks thoroughly under running water to remove all traces of sand and grit.

Cutting Romaine Lettuce

1. Trim the outer leaves and tips. Split the head lengthwise.

2. Cut along the length of the head. Wash and drain well before using.

3. Alternatively: Trim away the outer and damaged leaves. Peel leaves from core. Cut rib from each leaf and cut leaf to desired size. Wash and drain well before using.

Procedure for Preparing Selected Vegetables

(continued)

Making Julienne Peppers

1. Trim ends from peppers. Take out seeds and core.

2. Remove light colored ribs.

3. Slice the peppers in julienne strips.

Coring Jalapeño Peppers

Cut pepper in half lengthwise. Using your thumb, force the seeds and stem from the pod. Wear gloves to keep capsaicin away from hands.

Peeling and Pitting an Avocado

1. Cut in half lengthwise. Separate halves using a twisting motion.

2. Strike the pit with a knife to imbed the blade. Twist the blade to remove pit.

3. Using a large spoon, scoop the flesh from the skin.

Edible Flowers

Nasturtiums

Calendulas

Pansies

Herbs

Basil

Opal Basil

Bay Leaves

Chervil

Chives

Cilantro

Dill

Epazote

Lavender

Lemongrass

EXHIBIT

10

Flowers, Herbs, Mushrooms, Legumes

(continued)

Marjoram

Peppermint

Spearmint

Oregano

Parsley

Italian Parsley

Rosemary

Sage

Savory

Sorrel

Tarragon

Thyme

Flowers, Herbs, Mushrooms, Legumes

(continued)

EXHIBIT

10

Mushrooms

White Mushrooms

Enokidake Mushrooms

Oyster Mushrooms

Portabella Mushrooms

Morel Mushrooms

Shiitake Mushrooms

Dry Legumes

Black Beans

Red Kidney Beans

Lentils

Black-Eyed Peas

Great Northern Beans

Pinto Beans

EXHIBIT

11

Grains

Cornmeal

Grits

Hominy (corn)

Barley

Buckwheat/Kasha

Bulgur

Couscous

Millet

Arborio Rice

Basmati Rice

Brown Rice

Converted Rice

Wild Rice

Oats

Quinoa

ORIENTAL SHRIMP AND PASTA

Yield: 50 portions   *Portion:* 6 oz shrimp and sauce + 4 oz pasta

Ingredient	Amount	Procedure
Sugar, granulated	1 oz	Combine in steam-jacketed or other kettle. Blend with a wire whip.
Cornstarch	10 oz	
White pepper	½ tsp	
Ginger, ground	1½ Tbsp	
Garlic powder	¾ tsp	
Cayenne pepper	few grains	
Water	1½ gal	Stir into dry ingredients.
Soy sauce	1 cup	Cook and stir with a wire whip until thickened and clear.
Soup base, clam	5 oz	
Sliced bamboo shoots, canned	1 lb	Rinse bamboo shoots and water chestnuts. Drain. Add to sauce.
Sliced water chestnuts, canned	1 lb	
Broccoli stalks, sliced	1 lb 12 oz	Cook vegetables (p. 770) until tender-crisp. Drain.
Carrots, julienne	12 oz	Add to sauce.
Green onions, cut into ½-inch pieces	8 oz	Add onions and shrimp to sauce. Heat to 165°F.
Shrimp, cooked	2 lb 8 oz	
Fettuccine	5 lb	Cook according to directions on p. 507. Drain.
Water	5 gal	Serve 6 oz shrimp over 4 oz cooked pasta.
Salt	5 oz	
Vegetable oil	3 Tbsp	

Approximate nutritive values per portion

Calories	Carbohydrate	Protein	Fat	Cholesterol	Sodium	Fiber	Iron
165 kcal	16 g	9 g	7 g	45 mg	2412 mg	0.2 g	1 mg

Note

- Potentially hazardous food. *Food Safety Standards:* Hold food for service at an internal temperature of 135°F or above. Do not mix old product with new. Cool leftover product quickly following time standards and cooling procedures on p. 167. Reheat leftover product quickly (within 2 hours) to 165°F or above. Reheat product only once; discard if not used.

BROILED SEA SCALLOP GRATIN

Yield: 50 portions   *Portion:* 4 oz (4–5 scallops)
Broiler: 400°F   *Broil:* 10 minutes

Ingredient	Amount	Procedure
Sea scallops, large	13 lb	
Fresh lime juice	2¼ cups	Combine juice, parsley, pepper, onions, oil, and salt.
Fresh parsley, minced	2 oz (1½ cups)	Carefully mix scallops with marinade and refrigerate for 30 minutes.
Red bell pepper, minced	8 oz	Place scallops on an oiled sheet pan. Distribute liquid evenly over scallops.
		Place pan in a preheated 400°F broiler and cook for 5 minutes. Remove from broiler and turn scallops.
Green onions, minced	8 oz	Return to broiler and cook until scallops are firm, approximately
Southwest-flavored oil	1 cup	4–5 additional minutes (internal temperature 145°F).
Salt	1½ tsp	Serve with a little liquid spooned over the top of scallops.
		Garnish with cilantro sprigs.

Approximate nutritive values per portion

Calories	Carbohydrate	Protein	Fat	Cholesterol	Sodium	Fiber	Iron
189 kcal	7 g	28 g	6 g	63 mg	384 mg	1 g	2 mg

Notes

- Potentially hazardous food. *Food Safety Standards:* Hold food for service at an internal temperature of 135°F or above. Do not mix old product with new. Cool leftover product quickly following time standards and cooling procedures on p. 167. Reheat leftover product quickly (within 2 hours) to 165°F or above. Reheat product only once; discard if not used.
- Four to five scallops may be put in a gratin dish and broiled as needed for service. Keep scallops not being prepared in the refrigerator and remove as needed for production.
- Southwest-flavored oil is available commercially. Olive oil and ¼ tsp crushed red pepper may be substituted for commercially prepared oil.
- Other flavored oils may be substituted for Southwest-flavored oil.
- Scallops may be baked at 350°F for 15–20 minutes.

CHAPTER 14

Time and Temperature Timetables and Guidelines

Cooking meat to the correct doneness requires that cooking times and temperatures be followed carefully. The timetables in this chapter (Tables 14.1 through 14.9) will be helpful for producing quality meat products. Meat cooking methods are described in Chapter 6.

Degree of Doneness

Proper cooking is one of the most effective ways to kill harmful bacteria and maintain quality standards. The time required to reach the optimum degree of doneness will vary depending on such things as the equipment, product temperature, product size, and quantity being cooked at one time. For steaks that are broiled, pan-broiled, or grilled, the easiest way to determine doneness is by cutting a small slit and checking the color of the meat near the bone, or near the center of a boneless cut. Ground beef should always be cooked to 155°F or above for 15 seconds. Cooking to 160°F, which is often recommended, provides a safety factor because the time variable is removed.

Color is not always an accurate predictor for end temperature, because of the meat pH or the interaction of beef with other ingredients. End temperatures should be verified with a sanitized thermometer or thermocouple.

TABLE 14.1 Timetable for roasting beef

TABLE 14.1 Timetable for roasting beef

Cut	Oven temperature (°F, preheated)	Approximate weight (pounds)	Approximate total cooking time (based on meat removed directly from refrigerator)	Remove roast from oven when internal temperature reaches (°F):
Rib eye roast, small end	350	3–4	Medium rare: 1½–1¾ hr Medium: 1¾–2 hr	135 150
		4–6	Medium rare: 1¾–2 hr Medium: 2–2½ hr	135 150
		6–8	Medium rare: 2–2¼ hr Medium: 2½–2¾ hr	135 150
	325	8*–10*	Medium rare: 2½–3¼ hr Medium: 3–3¾ hr	135 145
Rib eye roast, large end	350	3–4	Medium rare: 1¾–2¼ hr Medium: 2–2½ hr	135 150
		4–6	Medium rare: 2–2½ hr Medium: 2½–3 hr	135 150
		6–8	Medium rare: 2¼–2½ hr Medium: 2¾–3 hr	135 150
Rib roast, chine bone removed	350	4–6 (2 ribs)	Medium rare: 1¾–2¼ hr Medium: 2¼–2¾ hr	135 150
		6–8 (2–4 ribs)	Medium rare: 2¼–2½ hr Medium: 2¾–3 hr	135 150
		8–10 (4–5 ribs)	Medium rare: 2½–3 hr Medium: 3–3½ hr	135 150
Tenderloin roast, well trimmed	425	2–3 (center cut)	Medium rare: 35–40 min Medium: 45–50 min	135 150
		4–5 (whole)	Medium rare: 50–60 min Medium: 60–70 min	135 150
Round tip roast, cap off	325	3–4	Medium rare: 1¾–2 hr Medium: 2¼–2½ hr	140 155
		4–6	Medium rare: 2–2½ hr Medium: 2½–3 hr	140 155
		6–8	Medium rare: 2½–3 hr Medium: 3–3½ hr	140 155
		8*–10*	Medium rare: 3–3¾ hr Medium: 3¾–4½ hr	135 150
Top round roast	325	6*–8*	Medium rare: 2½–3 hr	135
		8*–10*	Medium rare: 3–3¾ hr	135
Eye round roast	325	2–3	Medium rare: 1½–1¾ hr	135
Tri-tip roast	425	1½–2	Medium rare: 30–40 min Medium: 40–45 min	135 150

*Tent loosely with aluminum foil halfway through roasting time.

Notes: Medium rare doneness = 145°F final internal temperature after 15–20 minutes standing time.

Medium doneness = 160°F final internal temperature after 15–20 minutes standing time.

Well done = 170°F final internal temperature after 15–20 minutes standing time.

Information based on consumer roasting data. Cooking times and temperatures for quantity production may vary depending on the roast size, number of roasts in the oven, temperature of roast before cooking, and equipment.

During the required standing time, temperature will rise 5–10°F.

Source: From the National Cattlemen's Beef Association.

TABLE 14.2   Timetable for roasting veal

TABLE 14.2   **Timetable for roasting veal**

Cut	Approximate weight (pounds)	Oven temperature (°F)	Interior temperature of roast when removed from oven (°F)*	Minutes per pound based on one roast	Approximate total cooking time (hours)
VEAL					
Loin roast	3–4	300–325	155 (medium)	34–36	1¾–2⅓
			165 (well)	38–40	2–2⅔
Loin roast, boneless	2–3	300–325	155 (medium)	18–20	¾–1
			165 (well)	22–24	¾–1¼
Rib roast	4–5	300–325	155 (medium)	25–27	1⅔–2¼
			165 (well)	29–31	2–2½
Crown roast (12–14 ribs)	7½–9½	300–325	155 (medium)	19–21	2¼–3¼
			165 (well)	21–23	2½–3½
Rib eye roast	2–3	300–325	155 (medium)	26–28	1–1½
			165 (well)	30–33	1–1⅔
Rump roast, boneless	2–3	300–325	155 (medium)	33–35	1–1¾
			165 (well)	37–40	1¼–2
Shoulder roast, boneless	2¼–3	300–325	155 (medium)	31–34	1¼–1½
			165 (well)	34–37	1¼–1¾

*For safety, lamb and veal must reach a temperature of 145°F or above for 15 seconds. During the required 15–20 minute standing time, temperature will rise 5°F.

Source: Compiled from materials by the National Cattlemen's Beef Association, Veal Committee.

TABLE 14.3   **Timetable for roasting lamb**

Cut	Size	Cooking method	Cooking time	Internal temp.*
Lamb leg, bone in	5–7 lb	Roast 325°F	20–25 min/lb	Medium rare 145°F
			25–30 min/lb	Medium 160°F
			30–35 min/lb	Well done 170°F
Lamb leg, bone in	7–9 lb	Roast 325°F	15–20 min/lb	Medium rare 145°F
			20–25 min/lb	Medium 160°F
			25–30 min/lb	Well done 170°F
Lamb leg, boneless, rolled	4–7 lb	Roast 325°F	25–30 min/lb	Medium rare 145°F
			30–35 min/lb	Medium 160°F
			35–40 min/lb	Well done 170°F
Shoulder roast or shank leg half	3–4 lb	Roast 325°F	30–35 min/lb	Medium rare 145°F
			40–45 min/lb	Medium 160°F
			45–50 min/lb	Well done 170°F
Cubes, for kebobs	1–1½ inches	Broil/grill	8–12 min	Medium 160°F
Ground lamb patties	2 inches thick	Broil/grill	7–11 min	Medium 160°F
			15–19 min	
Chops, rib or loin	1–1½ inches	Broil/grill	7–11 min	Medium rare 145°F
			15–19 min	
Leg steaks	½ inch thich	Broil/grill 4 inches from heat	14–18 min	Medium rare 145°F
Stew meat, pieces	1–1½ inches	Cover with liquid, simmer	1½–2 hours	Medium rare 145°F
				Medium 160°F
Shanks	8 oz–1 lb	Cover with liquid, simmer	1½–2 hours	Medium 160°F

*For safety, lamb must reach a temperature of 145°F or above for 15 seconds. During the required 10–15 minute standing time, temperature will rise 5–10°F.

Source: Compiled from materials by the American Lamb Board.

TABLE 14.3   Timetable for roasting lamb

TABLE 14.4 Timetable for roasting pork in conventional oven

Cut	Weight	Oven temperature (°F)	Food product internal temperature (°F)*	Minutes per pound*	Approximate total cooking time
Loin, boneless	8–12 lb	325	150–155	17–20	2½–3½ hr
Fresh ham, boneless, tied	10–14 lb	325	150–155	20–25	3½–4½ hr
Whole tenderloin	¾–1 lb	425–450	155–160	—	20–30 min
Spareribs (panned flat)	Up to 3 lb	325	Well done	—	1½ hr
Loin, back ribs (shingled)	1¾–2½ lb	325	Well done	—	1½ hr
Bacon, flat pack	18–22 slices/lb	400	—	—	6–8 min
Sausage	1-oz patties/links	400	Well done	—	15–20 min
Boneless cured ham, fully cooked	10–12 lb	325	140	15–18	2½–3½ hr
Boneless pork chop	4 oz	425	160	—	18–20 min
	5 oz	425	160	—	22–24 min
	6 oz	425	160	—	24–26 min
	8 oz	425	160	—	25–27 min
Bone-in pork chop	4 oz	425	160	—	10–12 min
	5 oz	425	160	—	12–14 min
	6 oz	425	160	—	15–17 min
	8 oz	425	160	—	25–30 min

*Smaller roasts require more minutes per pound than larger roasts. During the required 10–15 minute standing time, temperature will rise 5–10°F.
Source: Compiled from materials by National Pork Board and other sources.

TABLE 14.5 Timetable for roasting pork in convection oven

Cut	Weight	Oven temperature (°F)	Food product internal temperature (°F)*	Minutes per pound*	Approximate total cooking time
Loin, boneless, tied	8–12 lb	275	150–155	12–15	2–2½ hr
Fresh ham, boneless, tied	10–14 lb	275	150–155	13–16	3–3½ hr
Whole tenderloin	¾–1 lb	425	155–160	—	20–25 min
Spareribs (panned flat)	Up to 3 lb	275	Well done	—	60–70 min
Loin, back ribs (shingled)	1¾–2½ lb	275	Well done	—	60–70 min
Bacon, flat pack	18–22 slices/lb	325	—	—	4–6 min
Sausage	1-oz patties/links	325	Well done	—	10–12 min
Boneless cured ham, fully cooked	10–12 lb	275	140	10–12	2–2½ hr
Boneless pork chop	4 oz	425	160	—	6–8 min
	5 oz	425	160	—	8–10 min
	6 oz	425	160	—	13–15 min
	8 oz	425	160	—	15–17 min
Bone-in pork chop	4 oz	425	160	—	8–10 min
	5 oz	425	160	—	11–13 min
	6 oz	425	160	—	13–15 min
	8 oz	425	160	—	20–22 min

*Smaller roasts require more minutes per pound than larger roasts. During the 10–15 minute standing time, temperature will rise 5–10°F.
Source: Compiled from materials by the National Pork Board and other sources.

TABLE 14.6 Timetable for broiling meat

Meat	Cut	Approximate thickness or weight	Distance from heat (inches)	Approximate Total Cooking Time (Minutes)		
				Medium rare (145°F)	Medium (160°F)	Well done[c] (170°F)
BEEF	Porterhouse/T-bone steaks	¾ inch	2–3	10	13	
		1 inch	3–4	15	20	
		1½ inches	3–4	27	32	
	Rib steaks	¾ inch	2–3	9	12	
		1 inch	3–4	13	17	
		1½ inches	3–4	24	31	
	Rib eye steaks	¾ inch	2–3	8	10	
		1 inch	3–4	14	18	
		1½ inches	3–4	21	27	
	Top sirloin steak, boneless	¾ inch	2–3	9	12	
		1 inch	3–4	16	21	
		2 inches	3–4	34	39	
	Sirloin cubes	1–1¼ inches	3–4	8	10	
	Tenderloin steak	1 inch	2–3	13	16	
		1½ inches	3–4	18	22	
	Top loin steak, boneless	¾ inch	2–3	9	11	
		1 inch	3–4	13	17	
	Tri-tip roast (bottom sirloin)	1½–2 lb	4–5	20	30	
	Chuck shoulder steak, boneless[a]	1 inch	3–4	16	21	
	Eye round steak	1 inch	2–3	9		
	Top round steak[a]	1 inch	2–3	17–18		
	Flank steak[a]	1½–2 lb	2–3	13	18	
	Ground beef patties[b]	½ × 4 inches (4/lb)	3–4		8–10	10–12
		¾ × 4 inches (3/lb)	3–4		12–14	
PORK	Loin/rib chop (bone-in or boneless)	¾ inch	3		8–10	
		1½ inches	5		12–16	
	Kebobs	1-inch piece	3–5		10–15	
	Tenderloin	½–1 lb	5		15–25	
	Ground pork patties[b]	½ inch	3–5		8–10	10–12
	Butterflied single loin roast (boneless)	3 lb	5		22–24	
LAMB	Shoulder, rib, loin, and sirloin chops	1–1½ inches	3–4	7–11	(150°F) 12–15	
	Center leg chops	1 inch	4	14–18	(150°F) 20	
	Ground lamb patties	1 (4 oz) (2 inches)	3–4	7–11	15	

[a] Marinate beef cuts 6–8 hours if desired.

[b] The FDA Food Code requires ground meat be cooked to 155°F or above for 15 seconds. USDA recommends cooking ground meat patties to 160°F.

[c] National Cattlemen's Beef Association does not recommend broiling beef to 170°. National Pork Board recommends cooking pork to 160°F. Meat cooked to 170°F will not be pink and will be less juicy than if cooked to 160°F or less.

Source: Compiled from materials by the National Cattlemen's Beef Association, National Pork Board, American Lamb Council, and other sources.

TABLE 14.6 Timetable for broiling meat

TABLE 14.7 Timetable for griddle-broiling meat (surface 400–450°F)

Meat	Cut	Approximate thickness or weight	Approximate Total Cooking Time (minutes)		
			Medium rare (145°F)	Medium (160°F)	Well done (170°F)
BEEF	Top loin steak (boneless)	¾ inch	10	12	
		1 inch	12	15	
	Rib eye steak	¾ inch	8	10	
		1 inch	12	15	
	Top round steak (marinate)	¾ inch	11–12	not recommended	
		1 inch	15–16	not recommended	
	Top sirloin (boneless) steak	¾ inch	10	13	
		1 inch	15	20	
	Tenderloin steak	½ inch	3½	5½	
		¾ inch	7	9	
		1 inch	10	13	
	Ground beef patties*	½ × 4 inch (4/lb)	10	12	
		¾ × 4 inch (3/lb)		12–15	
LAMB	Chops	1–1½ inches	8–12	12–15	
	Ground lamb patties*	1 (4 oz) (2 inches)		10–15	12–15
PORK	Smoked ham slice	½ inch			6–10
	Bacon				2–3
	Pork chop (bone-in or boneless)	½ inch		8–10	
		1 inch		12–15	

*The FDA Food Code requires ground meat to be cooked to 155°F or above for 15 seconds. USDA recommends cooking ground meat patties to 160°F.

Source: Compiled from materials by the National Cattlemen's Beef Association, American Lamb Council, and National Pork Producers Council.

TABLE 14.8 Timetable for direct-grilling steak

Steak	Approximate thickness or weight	Approximate Total Cooking Time (Minutes)	
		Medium rare (145°F)	Medium (160°F)
Chuck top blade	1 inch	18	22
Chuck shoulder	¾ inch	14	17
	1 inch	16	20
Flank	1½–2 lb	17	21
Ground beef patties	½ × 4 (4/lb)		11–13*
Boneless top loin	¾ inch	10	12
	1 inch	15	18
Porterhouse/T-bone	¾ inch	10	12
	1 inch	14	16
	1½ inches	20 (covered)	24 (covered)
Rib	¾ inch	6	8
	1 inch	9	12
	1½ inches	22 (covered)	27 (covered)
Rib eye	¾ inch	6	8
	1 inch	11	14
	1½ inches	17 (covered)	22 (covered)
Top round	¾ inch	8–9	not recommended
	1 inch	16–18	not recommended
	1½ inches	25–28 (covered)	not recommended
Top sirloin (boneless)	¾ inch	13	16
	1 inch	17	21
	1½ inches	22 (covered)	26 (covered)
	2 inches	28 (covered)	33 (covered)
Tenderloin	1 inch	13	15
	1½ inches	14 (covered)	16 (covered)

*The FDA 1999 Food Code requires ground beef to be cooked to 155°F or above for 15 seconds. USDA recommends cooking ground beef patties to 160°F.

Note: All cook times are based on beef removed directly from the refrigerator.

Source: Compiled from materials by the National Cattlemen's Beef Association.

TABLE 14.9   Timetable for braising meat

Meat	Cut	Average thickness or weight	Approximate total cooking time
BEEF	Pot roast	4–6 lb	3–4 hr
	Round steak	1–2½ inches	1½–3 hr
	Short ribs	2 × 2 × 4 inches	1½–2½ hr
LAMB	Shanks	½ lb	1–1½ hr
	Riblets	¾ × 2½ × 3 inches	1½–2 hr
PORK	Loin/rib chop (bone-in or boneless)	¾ inch	30 min
		1½ inch	45 min
	Spareribs/back ribs		1½ hr
	Country-style ribs		1½–2 hr
	Shoulder steaks	¼ inch	40–50 min
	Cubes	1–1¼ inches	45–60 min
	Boston blade (boneless)	2½–3½ lb	2–2½ hr
	Boston blade (bone-in)	3–4 lb	2¼–2¾ hr
	Sirloin (boneless)	2½–3½ lb	1¾–2¼ hr
VEAL	Cutlets	½ × 3 × 5½ inches	¾–1 hr
	Steaks or chops	½–¾ inch	¾–1 hr

Source: Compiled from materials by the National Cattlemen's Beef Association, Veal Committee, National Pork Producers Council, and American Lamb Council.

TABLE 14.10   Timetable for cooking meat in liquid (large cuts and stews)

Cut	Average size or weight	Approximate Total Cooking Time	
		Minutes per pound	Total hours
Fresh beef	4–8 lb	40–50	3–4
Corned beef	6–8 lb	40–50	4–6
Beef shank crosscuts	1–1½ inches		2–3
Lamb or veal for stew	1-inch cubes		1¼–1½
Beef for stew	1–1½ inch cubes		1¾–2¼
Spareribs			2–2½
Country-style ribs			2–2½
Cubes	1–1¼ inch cubes		¾–1

Source: Compiled from materials by the National Cattlemen's Beef Association, National Pork Producers Council, and American Lamb Council.

Beef Recipes

POT ROAST OF BEEF

Yield: 50 portions   *Portion:* 3 oz
Oven: 450°F, 300°F   *Bake:* 30 minutes, 3 hours

Ingredient	Amount	Procedure
Beef, boneless, inside round	18 lb	Season meat with salt and pepper. Place in roasting pan and brown at 450°F for about 30 minutes.
Salt	1 oz (1½ Tbsp)	
Black pepper	½ tsp	
Water	2 qt	When meat is browned, add water. Reduce heat to 300°F. Cover and cook slowly until tender (3 hours). Add water as necessary. When meat is done (160–170°F), remove from pan. Let stand ½ hour before slicing.
Flour, all-purpose	6 oz	Mix flour and cold water, stirring with a wire whip until smooth.
Water, cold	1½ cups	Add to drippings in pan.
Water (additional)	as necessary	Remove excess fat if necessary and add water to make 1 gal liquid.
Salt	1 oz (1½ Tbsp)	Add salt and pepper. Cook until thickened.
Black pepper	½ tsp	

Approximate nutritive values per portion

Calories	Carbohydrate	Protein	Fat	Cholesterol	Sodium	Fiber	Iron
208 kcal	3 g	31 g	7 g	92 mg	490 mg	0 g	3 mg

Notes

- Potentially hazardous food. *Food Safety Standards:* Hold food for service at an internal temperature of 135°F or above. Do not mix old product with new. Cool leftover product quickly following time standards and cooling procedures on p. 167. Reheat leftover product quickly (within 2 hours) to 165°F or above. Reheat product only once; discard if not used.
- Beef chuck may be used. Increase to 20 lb AP.
- Meat may be cooked in a steam-jacketed kettle. Brown in a small amount of fat. Add water, salt, and pepper. Cover kettle and cook until tender. Add water as necessary.
- 2 lb carrots, 2 lb celery, and 12 oz onion, cut into chunks, may be added for flavoring during the last hour of cooking. See Table 4.2 for amount to use if serving vegetables as an accompaniment.

Variations

- **Savory Pot Roast or Brisket.** Place meat in baking pan. Sprinkle with 5 oz dry onion soup mix. Cover tightly with aluminum foil. Bake at 300°F for 5–6 hours. Remove foil and bake ½ hour longer. Use juice for gravy. If brisket is used, increase to 25 lb. Cooked Barbecue Sauce (p. 688) may be added for the last half hour of cooking.
- **Smoked Beef Brisket.** Use 25 lb well-trimmed beef brisket. Combine ⅔ cup liquid smoke, 2 Tbsp salt, 2 Tbsp onion salt, ¼ cup celery salt, ¼ cup garlic salt, ½ cup Worcestershire sauce, and 1 oz black pepper. Spread on brisket. Cover with aluminum foil. Seal. Refrigerate overnight. Bake at 275°F for 4 hours, covered. Uncover and spread with Barbecue Sauce (pp. 688, 689). Bake for 1 hour longer. To serve, slice in thin slices across the grain of the meat.
- **Yankee Pot Roast.** Add 1½ qt tomato puree and one bay leaf to the cooking water.

ROAST BEEF STRIP LOIN OR PRIME RIB OF BEEF

Yield: 50 portions *Portion:* 6 oz
Oven: 325°F

Ingredient	Amount	Procedure
Boneless beef strip loin or boneless beef prime rib	25 lb	Place roasts in a 12 × 20 × 2-inch counter pan (one roast per pan), fat side up.
Seasoning rub or kosher salt and cracked black pepper	pp. 725–732	If using a rub, coat the entire surface of the meat, using approximately 4 oz rub mixture per 12–15 lb roast. If not using a rub, liberally add salt and pepper to the meat.
		Roast in a conventional oven at 325°F to an internal temperature of 135°F. (See Note.) Remove from oven, tent with foil, and let stand for 15–20 minutes before slicing. Internal temperature will increase 5–10°F during standing time.

Approximate nutritive values per meat portion without seasonings or acccompaniments

Calories	Carbohydrate	Protein	Fat	Cholesterol	Sodium	Fiber	Iron
314 kcal	1 g	55 g	8 g	144 mg	655 mg	0.4 g	4 mg

Notes

- Potentially hazardous food. *Food Safety Standards:* Hold food for service at an internal temperature of 135°F or above. Do not mix old product with new. Cool leftover product quickly following time standards and cooling procedures on p. 167. Reheat leftover product quickly (within 2 hours) to 165°F or above. Reheat product only once; discard if not used.
- See p. 422 for roasting timetable.

SAUERBRATEN

Yield: 50 portions   *Portion:* 4 oz
Oven: 350°F   *Bake:* 2–2½ hours

Ingredient	Amount	Procedure
Red wine	3 cups	Heat to boiling point. Do not boil.
Red wine vinegar	2½ cups	Cool to room temperature.
Water	2½ cups	
Bay leaves	5	
Juniper berries, whole	14	
Peppercorns, black	18	
Beef, boneless, inside round	20 lb	Rub beef with salt and pepper.
Salt	4 oz	
Black pepper	2 Tbsp	
Onions, sliced	4 lb EP	Place meat and onions in deep pans.
		Pour marinade over beef. Turn beef to moisten all sides with marinade. Cover tightly.
		Refrigerate for 2–3 days, turning the meat twice a day if meat is not covered with marinade.
		Strain marinade and reserve to pour over beef.
		Place meat in roasting pan. Pour strained marinade over meat. Cover tightly.
		Roast at 350°F until internal temperature reaches 145°F.
		Remove meat from liquid.
		Reserve liquid for gingersnap sauce.
		Slice beef. Place in two 2-inch counter pans.

Gingersnap Sauce

Ingredient	Amount	Procedure
Liquid from roast	3½ qt	Measure liquid from roast. Add water if needed.
Gingersnaps, crushed	1 lb	Add gingersnaps. Bring to a boil, stirring constantly until mixture thickens.
		Ladle gingersnap sauce over beef. Additional sauce may be served with meat.

Approximate nutritive values per portion

Calories	Carbohydrate	Protein	Fat	Cholesterol	Sodium	Fiber	Iron
252 kcal	5 g	34 g	8 g	102 mg	936 mg	1 g	4 mg

Note

- Potentially hazardous food. *Food Safety Standards:* Hold food for service at an internal temperature of 135°F or above. Do not mix old product with new. Cool leftover product quickly following time standards and cooling procedures on p. 167. Reheat leftover product quickly (within 2 hours) to 165°F or above. Reheat product only once; discard if not used.

PEPPER STEAK

Yield: 50 portions   *Portion:* 6 oz meat + 4 oz rice

Ingredient	Amount	Procedure
Beef round or sirloin, cut into thin strips	13 lb	Cook meat in shortening in kettle or deep fry pan until lightly browned, about 10 minutes.
Shortening	8 oz	
Beef Stock (p. 738)	2 qt	Add stock, tomatoes, onions, and seasonings to meat.
Diced tomatoes, canned	1 No. 10 can	Simmer until tender, 1–1½ hours, stirring occasionally.
Onions, chopped	1 lb	
Garlic cloves	3, cut in half	
Salt	2 Tbsp	
Green bell peppers, thinly sliced in rings	12	Add peppers and cook until tender but firm and brightly colored.
Cornstarch	3 oz	Combine cornstarch, water, and soy sauce into a smooth paste.
Water, cold	2½ cups	Add to meat-vegetable mixture. Cook until thickened (approximately 5 minutes).
Soy sauce	⅔ cup	
Rice, converted	3 lb 8 oz	Cook rice according to directions on p. 542.
Water, boiling	4¼ qt	Serve 6 oz meat mixture over 4 oz rice.
Salt	2 Tbsp	
Margarine or vegetable oil	2 Tbsp	

Approximate nutritive values per portion

Calories	Carbohydrate	Protein	Fat	Cholesterol	Sodium	Fiber	Iron
401 kcal	32 g	42 g	11 g	68 mg	1021 mg	1 g	4 mg

Note

- Potentially hazardous food. *Food Safety Standards:* Hold food for service at an internal temperature of 135°F or above. Do not mix old product with new. Cool leftover product quickly following time standards and cooling procedures on p. 167. Reheat leftover product quickly (within 2 hours) to 165°F or above. Reheat product only once; discard if not used.

GINGER ORANGE BEEF

Yield: 50 portions   *Portion:* 4 oz

Ingredient	Amount	Procedure
Beef strips (see Note)	8 lb AP	Place raw beef strips in baker's bowl.
Soy sauce	2 cups	Mix liquids and seasonings. Pour over beef strips and stir to coat beef.
Fresh orange juice	3½ cups	Cover beef with marinade and refrigerate at below 41°F for 8–10 hours or overnight.
Vegetable oil	6¾ cups	or overnight.
Rice wine vinegar	1¾ cups	Before cooking, drain marinade from beef strips. Discard marinade.
Mirin (cooking sake)	1½ cups	
Cinnamon, ground	2¼ Tbsp	
Ginger, ground	3½ Tbsp	
Sugar, granulated	6 oz	
Vegetable oil	¼ cup	Coat bottom of a tilting fry pan with oil. Heat to 350°F. Place drained beef strips in hot skillet. Sauté just until browned.
Sliced water chestnuts, canned, drained	1 lb 5 oz EP	Add chestnuts and peas and cook until chestnuts are heated through and peas are barely cooked (170°F).
Snow peas, fresh or frozen	1 lb 8 oz EP	Turn off heat.
Carrots, fine julienne	1 lb 12 oz EP	Add vegetables. Cook just until warmed through. Chill.
Green bell peppers, batonnet cut	1 lb 6 oz EP	
Green onions, thinly sliced	12 oz EP	Use Ginger Orange Beef in wraps, salad plates, or rice bowls.

Approximate nutritive values per portion

Calories	Carbohydrate	Protein	Fat	Cholesterol	Sodium	Fiber	Iron
460 kcal	16 g	9.5 g	51 g	51 mg	1150 mg	1.6 g	2 mg

Notes

- Potentially hazardous food. *Food Safety Standards:* Hold food for service at an internal temperature of 135°F or above. Do not mix old product with new. Cool leftover product quickly following time standards and cooling procedures on p. 167. Reheat leftover product quickly (within 2 hours) to 165°F or above. Reheat product only once; discard if not used.
- Beef strips should be from a tender cut of beef.

SWISS STEAK

Yield: 50 portions *Portion:* 5 oz
Oven: 350°F *Bake:* 1½–2 hours

Ingredient	Amount	Procedure
Beef round, sliced, ¾ inch thick	17 lb	Cut meat into portions, 3 per lb.
Flour, all-purpose	1 lb	Mix flour, salt, and pepper. Pound into meat with mallet or cleaver.
Salt	3 oz	
Black pepper	2 tsp	
Shortening, hot	1 lb 8 oz	Brown meat in shortening. Place, slightly overlapping, in two 12 × 20 × 2-inch counter pans.
Fat (meat drippings), hot	6 oz	Make gravy according to directions on p. 685.
Flour, all-purpose	6 oz	Add 1½ qt gravy to each pan of meat.
Salt	2 tsp	Cover tightly with aluminum foil.
Black pepper	¾ tsp	Bake at 350°F for 1½–2 hours.
Water or beef stock	3 qt	

Approximate nutritive values per portion

Calories	Carbohydrate	Protein	Fat	Cholesterol	Sodium	Fiber	Iron
363 kcal	10 g	33 g	21 g	87 mg	819 mg	0.4 g	5 mg

Notes

- Potentially hazardous food. *Food Safety Standards:* Hold food for service at an internal temperature of 135°F or above. Do not mix old product with new. Cool leftover product quickly following time standards and cooling procedures on p. 167. Reheat leftover product quickly (within 2 hours) to 165°F or above. Reheat product only once; discard if not used.
- Portioned steaks, cut 3 per pound, may be substituted for beef round. Reduce cooking time to 1½ hours.

Variations

- **Baked Steak Teriyaki.** Combine 2 cups pineapple juice, drained from canned sliced pineapple, 1 qt water, 1½ cups soy sauce, ½ tsp garlic powder, ¼ tsp ginger, and ¼ cup honey. Bring to a boil. Thicken with 1½ cups cold water and ½ cup cornstarch, mixed. Pour 2 lb 8 oz mixture over each pan of browned steaks. Cover tightly. Bake at 325°F for 1–1½ hours or until tender. Garnish with green bell pepper rings and pineapple slices.
- **Chicken-Fried Steak.** Dip portioned steaks or beef cutlets into mixture of 6 eggs and 3 cups milk, then into crumb mixture (1 lb 4 oz bread crumbs, 12 oz flour, 3 oz salt, and 2 Tbsp pepper). Brown steaks in hot shortening. Arrange slightly overlapping in lined counter pans. Cover with aluminum foil. Bake at 325°F for 30–45 minutes or until tender.
- **Country-Fried Steak.** Use beef round cut ⅜ inch thick. Proceed as for Swiss Steak but do not add gravy. Place steaks on racks in roaster or counter pans. Cover bottom of pan with water, 2 cups per pan. Cover with aluminum foil and bake. Make Cream Gravy (p. 685) to serve with the steaks.
- **Spanish Steak.** Substitute Spanish Tomato Sauce (p. 692) for gravy.
- **Steak Smothered with Onions.** Proceed as for Swiss Steak. Add 3 lb sliced onions, slightly browned.
- **Swiss Steak with Tomatoes.** Substitute 1 No. 10 can tomatoes for the gravy. Add 8 oz chopped onions.

TAMPICO GRILLED STEAK

Yield: 50 portions   *Portion:* 1 steak
Griddle: 350°F

Ingredient	Amount	Procedure
Sirloin steaks, 5 oz	50	Bring steaks to room temperature in batches.
Ancho flavor concentrate (see Note)	11 oz	Stir flavorings together until blended. Brush approximately 2 tsp over both sides of steak.
Chipotle flavor concentrate	2 oz	
Olive oil	10 oz	
Fresh lime juice	⅔ cup	
Fresh cilantro, chopped	¾ cup	
Garlic, minced	2 Tbsp	
Salt	1½ Tbsp	
Lime wedge (optional)	1 lb 4 oz	Heat griddle to 350°F. Oil lightly. Place steaks on hot griddle and cook for 3–4 minutes. Turn over and cook for another 2–3 minutes. Turn once only. Cook to an internal temperature of 145°F for medium rare, 160°F for medium. Hold for service at or above 135°F. Garnish with lime wedge (optional).

Approximate nutritive values per steak

Calories	Carbohydrate	Protein	Fat	Cholesterol	Sodium	Fiber	Iron
305 kcal	4 g	31 g	18 g	77 mg	484 mg	1 g	2 mg

Notes

- Potentially hazardous food. *Food Safety Standards:* Hold food for service at an internal temperature of 135°F or above. Do not mix old product with new. Cool leftover product quickly following time standards and cooling procedures on p. 167. Reheat leftover product quickly (within 2 hours) to 165°F or above. Reheat product only once; discard if not used.
- Minor's Ancho flavor concentrate (made from ancho peppers and sautéed onions) and Minor's Chipotle Flavor Concentrate (a blend of red, chipotle, and jalapeño peppers with onion, garlic, and spice) are available from most broadline foodservice distributors.

Variations

- **Grilled Sirloin with Fried Tomato Chile Sauce.** Prepare **Skillet Fried Tomato Chile Sauce** using following recipe. In a food processor (in batches), purée 4½ qt chopped tomatoes, 3 Tbsp sliced jalapeño peppers, 4 Tbsp minced garlic, 1½ tsp cinnamon, and 1½ tsp allspice. Tomatoes should be slightly chunky. Heat 1½ Tbsp oil in skillet. Add tomato mixture. Cook until flavors are blended and the sauce is slightly reduced, about 15 minutes. Stir in 1½ Tbsp dried oregano leaves. Grill sirloin steak as for Tampico Grilled Steak. Portion 1 oz tomato sauce to the side of or on top of the steak at time of service.
- **Grilled Sirloin with Herb Steak Butter.** Prepare 1 lb 10 oz **Steak Butter** by mixing the following ingredients together in a mixing bowl until smooth: 1 lb 8 oz softened butter, 1 tsp finely minced garlic, 6 Tbsp fresh lemon juice, 1½ Tbsp dried chives, 2 Tbsp dried basil leaves, 1 Tbsp mesquite-flavored seasoning, 1 Tbsp paprika, 1 tsp salt, ¼ tsp black pepper, and ¼ tsp crushed red pepper. Grill sirloin steak as for Tampico Grilled Steak. Portion ½ oz (1 Tbsp) Steak Butter over hot steak at time of service.
- **Smokehouse BBQ Sirloin.** Grill sirloin steak as for Tampico Grilled Steak. Portion 1 oz smoky BBQ sauce over steak at time of service.

SIRLOIN STEAK MILANO

Yield: 50 portions   *Portion:* 1 steak + 4 oz sauce
Griddle: 350°F

Ingredient	Amount	Procedure
Sirloin steaks, 5 oz	50	Bring steaks to room temperature in batches.
Salt Cracked black pepper Oil	2½ oz 5 Tbsp 8 oz	Blend spices together in baker's bowl. Rub spice mixture onto both sides of steak.
		Heat griddle to 350°F. Oil lightly. Place steaks on hot griddle and cook for 4–5 minutes. Turn over and cook for another 2–3 minutes. Turn over once only. Cook to an internal temperature of 145°F.
Milano sauce (p. 692)	8 qt	Scale 2 lb hot Milano sauce per 12 × 10 × 2-inch pan. Place 6 steaks in a single layer over sauce.
Shredded mozzarella cheese	1 lb 4 oz	Top each steak with cheese. Cover pan to melt cheese.

Approximate nutritive values per portion

Calories	Carbohydrate	Protein	Fat	Cholesterol	Sodium	Fiber	Iron
334 kcal	6 g	36 g	19 g	83 mg	736 mg	1 g	3 mg

Notes

- Potentially hazardous food. *Food Safety Standards:* Hold food for service at an internal temperature of 135°F or above. Do not mix old product with new. Cool leftover product quickly following time standards and cooling procedures on p. 167. Reheat leftover product quickly (within 2 hours) to 165°F or above. Reheat product only once; discard if not used.
- Serve the steak and sauce with a pasta accompaniment.

SALISBURY STEAK

Yield: 50 portions   *Portion:* 5 oz cooked
Oven: 325°F   *Bake:* 40 minutes

Ingredient	Amount	Procedure
Ground beef	16 lb	Combine all ingredients and mix on low speed until blended. *Do not overmix.*
Bread crumbs	2 lb	
Eggs	2 lb	
Onions, chopped	10 oz	
Salt	3 oz	
Black pepper	2 tsp	
Milk	1½ qt	
		Portion meat with No. 8 dipper (mounded) onto lightly greased baking sheets (7 oz per steak).
		Flatten slightly into football shape.
		Bake at 325°F for approximately 40 minutes or until internal temperature reaches 170°F.
		Pour off grease.
Brown Gravy (p. 685)	1 gal	Serve with Brown Gravy.

Approximate nutritive values per portion

Calories	Carbohydrate	Protein	Fat	Cholesterol	Sodium	Fiber	Iron
400 kcal	15 g	29 g	24 g	157 mg	1149 mg	1 g	3 mg

Notes

- Potentially hazardous food. *Food Safety Standards:* Hold food for service at an internal temperature of 135°F or above. Do not mix old product with new. Cool leftover product quickly following time standards and cooling procedures on p. 167. Reheat leftover product quickly (within 2 hours) to 165°F or above. Reheat product only once; discard if not used.
- Steaks may be browned on a grill.
- 1 oz (½ cup) dehydrated onions, rehydrated in ¾ cup water, may be substituted for fresh onions.

Variation

- **Bacon-Wrapped Beef.** To 15 lb ground beef, add 4 oz chopped green bell pepper, 8 oz chopped onion, 2½ cups catsup, 2 Tbsp salt, and 1 Tbsp black pepper. Shape as for Salisbury Steak and wrap one slice bacon around each portion. Place on baking sheet. Bake at 350°F for 40–45 minutes. Internal temperature must reach 155–160°F for 15 seconds.

STIR-FRIED BEEF WITH SUGAR SNAP PEAS

Yield: 50 portions   *Portion:* 7 oz beef and sauce + 4 oz rice

Ingredient	Amount	Procedure
Sugar, granulated	2 Tbsp	Combine sugar, pepper, and cornstarch in steam-jacketed or
White pepper	¾ tsp	other kettle.
Cornstarch	8 oz	
Water, cold	1¼ gal	Add gradually to dry ingredients, stirring constantly with wire whip.
Beef soup base	4 oz	Cook and stir until mixture thickens and looks clear.
Molasses	4 oz	Reduce heat. Cover and keep warm for use in final step.
Soy sauce	8 oz	
Vegetable oil	¼ cup	Pour enough vegetable oil into a large or tilting fry pan just to cover bottom of pan. Heat to 375°F.
Tender beef strips	5 lb	Add beef strips. Stir-fry until done, 155°F.
Garlic, minced	1½ oz	Add to beef and stir-fry until peas are tender-crisp.
Sugar snap peas	4 lb	
Sliced water chestnuts, canned, drained	3 lb	
		Stir in sauce reserved from earlier step. Serve immediately.
Rice, converted	3 lb 8 oz	Cook rice according to directions on p. 542.
Water	4¼ qt	Serve 7 oz beef mixture over 4 oz cooked rice.
Salt	2 Tbsp	
Margarine	2 Tbsp	

Approximate nutritive values per portion

Calories	Carbohydrate	Protein	Fat	Cholesterol	Sodium	Fiber	Iron
270 kcal	39 g	12 g	7 g	24 mg	1095 mg	1 g	3 mg

Notes
- Potentially hazardous food. *Food Safety Standards:* Hold food for service at an internal temperature above 140°F. Do not mix old product with new. Cool leftover product quickly (within 4 hours) to below 41°F. See p. 167 for cooling procedures. Reheat leftover product quickly (within 2 hours) to 165°F. Reheat product only once; discard if not used.
- Snow peas may be substituted for sugar snap peas.
- Caramel color may be used to darken sauce.

KEBOBS

Yield: 50 portions *Portion:* 1 kebob
Oven: 400°F *Bake:* 15–20 minutes

Ingredient	Amount	Procedure
Beef (tender), cut in 1½-inch cubes	20 lb	Place beef in stainless steel baker's bowl.
Salad oil	2 lb	Combine oil and seasonings.
Soy sauce	2½ cups	Pour over beef cubes to cover completely.
Fresh lemon juice	2 cups	Refrigerate for 24–36 hours.
Worcestershire sauce	1 cup	Drain well. Discard marinade.
Prepared mustard	1 cup	
Garlic, minced	½ oz	
Black pepper	1 oz (4 Tbsp)	
Green bell peppers	1 lb 6 oz	Cut peppers into ¾-inch squares.
Onions, small whole, canned	4 lb	Thread beef cubes (5 oz), peppers, onions, and pineapple alternately on skewer. Do not crowd.
Pineapple, fresh or fresh-frozen chunks	2 lb	Place on oiled 18 × 26 × 1-inch baking sheets. Bake at 400°F for approximately 8–10 minutes.
Skewers, bamboo, soaked in water for 30 minutes or more	50	Turn. Continue baking for 5–10 minutes more; total 15–20 minutes, depending on degree of doneness desired (must reach at least 140°F).
Cherry tomatoes	1 lb 10 oz	Place a cherry tomato on tip of each skewer. Place in 12 × 20 × 2-inch pans with liners. Keep hot.

Approximate nutritive values per portion

Calories	Carbohydrate	Protein	Fat	Cholesterol	Sodium	Fiber	Iron
484 kcal	7 g	44 g	30 g	91 mg	1056 mg	0.4 g	5 mg

Notes

- Potentially hazardous food. *Food Safety Standards:* Hold food for service at an internal temperature of 135°F or above. Do not mix old product with new. Cool leftover product quickly following time standards and cooling procedures on p. 167. Reheat leftover product quickly (within 2 hours) to 165°F or above. Reheat product only once; discard if not used.
- Other garnishes may be substituted for those listed in recipe: tomato quarters, mandarin orange sections, carrot chunks (slightly cooked), stuffed olives, or button mushrooms. Poultry or shellfish may be substituted for the beef. Marinate only 12–24 hours.

MEAT LOAF

Yield: 50 portions or 5 loaves, 5 × 9 inches   *Portion:* 4 oz
Oven: 325°F   *Bake:* 1½ hours

Ingredient	Amount	Procedure
Ground beef	10 lb	Mix all ingredients on low speed until blended, using a flat beater. Do not overmix.
Ground pork	2 lb	Press meat mixture into five 5 × 9-inch pans, 3 lb 4 oz per pan.
Bread crumbs, soft	12 oz	Bake at 325°F for approximately 1½ hours, or until internal temperature reaches 180°F.
Milk	1 qt	Meat loaf may also be made in a 12 × 20 × 4-inch counter pan.
Eggs	12 (1 lb 5 oz)	Press mixture into pan. Divide into two loaves (Figure 14.1).
Onion, finely chopped	4 oz	Increase baking time to 2 hours.
Salt	2 Tbsp	
Black pepper	1 tsp	
Cayenne pepper	few grains	

Approximate nutritive values per portion

Calories	Carbohydrate	Protein	Fat	Cholesterol	Sodium	Fiber	Iron
276 kcal	6 g	21 g	18 g	120 mg	376 mg	0.3 g	3 mg

Notes

- Potentially hazardous food. *Food Safety Standards:* Hold food for service at an internal temperature of 135°F or above. Do not mix old product with new. Cool leftover product quickly following time standards and cooling procedures on p. 167. Reheat leftover product quickly (within 2 hours) to 165°F or above. Reheat product only once; discard if not used.
- Ground pork may be omitted. Increase ground beef to 12 lb.
- Topping of 8 oz brown sugar, 2 Tbsp dry mustard, 1¼ cups catsup, and 1 Tbsp nutmeg may be spread over loaves the last ½ hour of cooking.
- ½ oz (¼ cup) dehydrated onion, rehydrated in ½ cup water, may be substituted for fresh onion.

Variations

- **Barbecued Meatballs.** Measure with No. 8 dipper and shape into balls. Cover with 1 gal Barbecue Sauce (pp. 688, 689).
- **Italian Meatballs.** Omit cayenne pepper. Increase onion to 8 oz. Add ¼ cup minced garlic, 1 cup grated Parmesan cheese, 1 cup grated Romano cheese, 1½ cups chopped fresh parsley, and 4 tsp dried oregano leaves. Proceed as for Swedish Meatballs (p. 443). If adding to Italian Tomato Sauce, cook until partially done. Add to sauce and continue cooking until done.
- **Meatballs.** Measure with No. 8 dipper and shape into balls. Proceed as for Swedish Meatballs (p. 443) or Spaghetti with Meatballs (p. 536).
- **Vegetable Meat Loaf.** Add 2 cups catsup; 8 oz each raw carrots, onions, and celery; and 4 oz green bell peppers. Grind vegetables. Pour a small amount of tomato juice over loaves before baking.

FIGURE 14.1 Shaping meat loaf. (a) Press mixture into counter pans, then smooth top. (b) Form into two loaves.

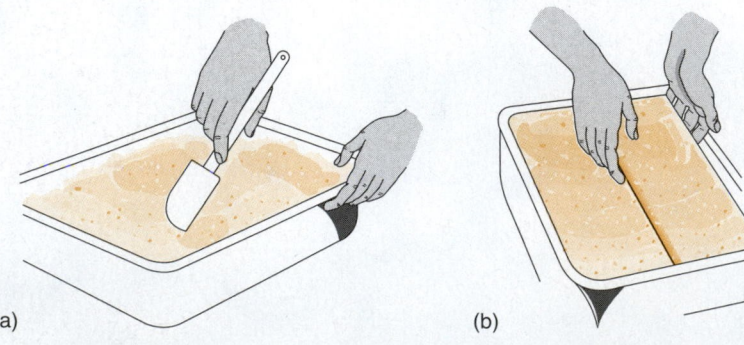

(a)   (b)

SPANISH MEATBALLS

Yield: 50 portions   *Portion:* Two 3-oz meatballs
Oven: 325°F   *Bake:* 1½ hours

Ingredient	Amount	Procedure
Rice, converted	1 lb 2 oz	Cook rice (p. 542) until slightly underdone.
Water	1¼ qt	Drain off excess liquid.
Salt	1 tsp	
Ground beef	12 lb	Place ground beef in mixer bowl.
Eggs	12 (1 lb 5 oz)	Add cooked rice and other ingredients.
Potatoes, cooked and mashed	1 lb	Mix until blended, using a flat beater. Do not overmix.
Onion, grated	4 oz	
Green bell peppers, chopped	4 oz	
Salt	2 oz (3 Tbsp)	
Black pepper	1½ Tbsp	
		Form meatballs, using a No. 12 dipper. Place in a single layer on two 12 × 20 × 2-inch baking pans.
		Bake at 325°F for 1½ hours, or until internal temperature of meatballs reaches 180°F.
		Drain off fat.
Chile sauce	3 qt	Mix chile sauce and water.
Water	2 qt	Pour over meatballs.
		Cover tightly and bake an additional 30 minutes. Add more liquid if necessary.

Approximate nutritive values per portion

Calories	Carbohydrate	Protein	Fat	Cholesterol	Sodium	Fiber	Iron
348 kcal	25 g	22 g	18 g	117 mg	1344 mg	0.4 g	3 mg

Notes

- Potentially hazardous food. *Food Safety Standards:* Hold food for service at an internal temperature of 135°F or above. Do not mix old product with new. Cool leftover product quickly following time standards and cooling procedures on p. 167. Reheat leftover product quickly (within 2 hours) to 165°F or above. Reheat product only once; discard if not used.
- Spanish Tomato Sauce (p. 492) or tomato puree may be substituted for chile sauce.
- ½ oz (¼ cup) dehydrated onion, rehydrated in ½ cup water, may be substituted for fresh onion.

HOMESTYLE BEEF MEATBALLS WITH CHIPOTLE SAUCE

Yield: 50 portions   *Portion:* 2 meatballs
Oven: 350°F   *Bake:* 30–40 minutes

Ingredient	Amount	Procedure
White bread	1 lb 4 oz	Break bread into pieces. Put in mixer bowl.
Milk	1 qt	Add milk, eggs, vegetables, and seasonings to bread. Mix until well blended.
Eggs	2 lb 8 oz	
Onion, finely chopped	10 oz	
Celery, finely chopped	10 oz	
Garlic, minced	1 Tbsp	
Catsup	½ cup	
Worcestershire sauce	¼ cup	
Salt	2 oz	
Black pepper	2 tsp	
Red pepper flakes	¼ tsp	
Ground beef	20 lb	Add thawed ground beef to bread mixture. Continue to mix on low speed to combine. Do not overmix. Using a No. 12 dipper (rounding slightly), portion meatballs into a baking pan. Bake at 350°F for 30–40 minutes. Drain meatballs and transfer to serving pan.
Chipotle Sauce (p. 686)	10 lb	Prepare Chipotle Sauce. Serve 4–5 oz sauce over two meatballs.

Approximate nutritive values per portion

Calories	Carbohydrate	Protein	Fat	Cholesterol	Sodium	Fiber	Iron
483 kcal	15 g	35 g	31 g	202 mg	891 mg	1 g	4 mg

Note

- Potentially hazardous food. *Food Safety Standards:* Hold food for service at an internal temperature of 135°F or above. Do not mix old product with new. Cool leftover product quickly following time standards and cooling procedures on p. 167. Reheat leftover product quickly (within 2 hours) to 165°F or above. Reheat product only once; discard if not used.

Variations

- **Lamb Patties.** Soak 1 lb 10 oz soft bread crumbs in 1 qt whole milk in a mixer bowl. Mix in 1 lb 10 oz whole fresh eggs (beaten slightly), 8 oz finely chopped onion, 3 oz salt, and 1 tsp black pepper. Add 14 lb ground lamb and mix on low speed only until blended. Portion into 6-oz patties. Place 5 × 7 on a silicone paper-lined bun sheet and flatten slightly. Bake at 325°F for approximately 25 minutes until 165°F. Drain well after cooking. Serve with Tomatillo Mint Salsa, p. 708.
- **Meatball Grinder.** Prepare Homestyle Beef Meatballs and scale into 1½-oz balls. Cook meatballs in oven until 165°F. Drain and transfer to 12 × 10 × 2-inch pans. Prepare ¼ recipe Marinara Sauce (p. 690). Ladle 2 lb marinara sauce over each full pan of meatballs. Stir gently to coat meatballs with sauce. Cover and heat to 165°F. Using a spoon so some sauce is served, place 5–6 meatballs with sauce on a French bread bun. Sprinkle with 1 Tbsp shredded Parmesan cheese.
- **Meatballs in Sofrito Sauce.** Prepare Homestyle Beef Meatballs and scale into 1½-oz balls. Cook meatballs in oven until 165°F. Drain. Put meatballs in **Sofrito Sauce** and simmer for 10–15 minutes until sauce thickens slightly. Transfer to serving pan and sprinkle with gremolata (optional). **Sofrito Sauce:** In a tilting fry pan or other heavy-bottomed pan, sauté until tender 1 lb chopped onion, 1 lb chopped red or green bell peppers, 1 Tbsp ground cumin, and 6 minced garlic cloves in ⅓ cup extra virgin olive oil. Cool slightly and transfer to a food processor. Add 2 lb 12 oz canned diced tomatoes (undrained), 1½ cups water, 1 cup cilantro leaves, 3 medium jalapeño peppers, 1 tsp black pepper, and 1½ tsp salt. Process until smooth.
- **Savory Meatballs with Chipotle Chile Sauce.** In a mixer, break up 20 lb ground beef. Mix together 1 lb 5 oz soft bread crumbs, 1 qt milk, 2½ lb whole eggs, 2 oz salt, 1 Tbsp black pepper, ½ cup catsup, 10 oz chopped onion, and 10 oz chopped celery. Add ground beef to the egg-milk mixture and mix on low speed until just mixed. Do not overmix. Portion with No. 12 dipper, rounding slightly, into baking pan. (Each meatball should weigh 4 oz.) Bake meatballs at 350°F for 30–40 minutes or until internal temperature is 175°F. Drain meatballs after baking. One serving is two meatballs. Prepare Chipotle Chile Sauce, p. 686. Ladle 3 oz sauce over two meatballs.

SWEDISH MEATBALLS

Yield: 50 portions   *Portion:* Two 2½-oz meatballs
Oven: 300°F   *Bake:* 45–60 minutes

Ingredient	Amount	Procedure
Bread, cubed	2 lb 8 oz	Soak bread in milk for 1 hour.
Milk	1½ qt	
Ground beef	5 lb	Combine meat, potatoes, onions, and seasonings in mixer bowl.
Ground pork	3 lb	Add bread. Mix to blend, using a flat beater. Do not overmix.
Potatoes, raw, grated	1 lb 4 oz	
Onions, minced	12 oz	
Salt	2 oz	
Black pepper	2 tsp	
		Form meatballs, using a No. 16 dipper. Place in a single layer on baking pans.
		Brown in hot oven (400°F).
		Transfer to two 12 × 20 × 2-inch counter pans.
Flour, all-purpose	6 oz	Add flour and seasonings to meat drippings and blend.
Salt	2 tsp	Add milk gradually, stirring constantly with a wire whip.
Black pepper	¾ tsp	Cook until smooth and thickened.
Meat drippings	6 oz	Pour over meatballs.
Milk	3 qt	Bake at 300°F for 45–60 minutes, or until internal temperature of meatballs reaches 180°F.

Approximate nutritive values per portion

Calories	Carbohydrate	Protein	Fat	Cholesterol	Sodium	Fiber	Iron
292 kcal	20 g	20 g	15 g	56 mg	768 mg	3 g	3 mg

Notes

- Potentially hazardous food. *Food Safety Standards:* Hold food for service at an internal temperature of 135°F or above. Do not mix old product with new. Cool leftover product quickly following time standards and cooling procedures on p. 167. Reheat leftover product quickly (within 2 hours) to 165°F or above. Reheat product only once; discard if not used.
- Veal or ground turkey may be substituted for part of the beef.
- 1½ oz (¾ cup) dehydrated onions, rehydrated in 1 cup water, may be substituted for fresh onions.

BEEF STEW

Yield: 50 portions   *Portion:* 7 oz

Ingredient	Amount	Procedure
Beef, 1-inch cubes	15 lb AP (10 lb EP)	Brown beef in kettle or oven.
Water Salt Black pepper Worcestershire sauce	2 qt 2 oz (3 Tbsp) 2 tsp ¾ cup	Add water and seasonings to meat. Cover and simmer for 2 hours. Add more water as necessary.
Potatoes, cubed Carrots, sliced or cubed Onions, cubed Celery, diced	4 lb 3 lb 1 lb 12 oz	Cook vegetables in steamer or in small amount of water in kettle or oven.
Flour, all-purpose Water	12 oz 1 qt	Mix flour and water until smooth. Add to meat and cook until thickened. Add vegetables and, if necessary, return heat to 180°F.

Approximate nutritive values per portion

Calories	Carbohydrate	Protein	Fat	Cholesterol	Sodium	Fiber	Iron
236 kcal	16 g	27 g	6 g	77 mg	543 mg	1 g	4 mg

Notes

- Potentially hazardous food. *Food Safety Standards:* Hold food for service at an internal temperature of 135°F or above. Do not mix old product with new. Cool leftover product quickly following time standards and cooling procedures on p. 167. Reheat leftover product quickly (within 2 hours) to 165°F or above. Reheat product only once; discard if not used.
- One 40-oz package of frozen green peas may be added just before serving. Reheat to serving temperature.

Variations

- **Beef Pot Pie.** Add one 40-oz package frozen peas. Place cooked stew in two 12 × 20 × 2-inch counter pans, 13 lb per pan. Make Pastry for One-Crust Pies (p. 341). Roll out 2 lb per pan and place on stew. Bake at 425°F for 20–25 minutes.
- **Beef Stew with Biscuits.** Place hot stew in two 12 × 20 × 2-inch counter pans. Prepare ½ recipe of Baking Powder Biscuits (p. 231). Cut into 48 2½-inch biscuits. Place on hot stew, 24 per pan. Bake at 425°F for 15–20 minutes.
- **Beef Stew with Dumplings.** Drop Dumplings (p. 258) on meat mixture and steam for 15–18 minutes.
- **Beef Stew with Tomatoes.** Delete carrots and celery. Add 4 lb canned diced tomatoes and 1 lb 8 oz green bell pepper strips in the last 5 minutes of cooking.

GREEN CHILE STEW AND CORN BREAD

Yield: 50 portions   *Portion:* 8 oz

Ingredient	Amount	Procedure
Beef, strips or cubes	5 lb	Brown beef in steam-jacketed or other large kettle.
Water	1 gal	Add water. Cover and simmer until tender.
Green chile peppers, canned	5 lb	Add vegetables and spices. Cover and simmer until onion is cooked (approximately 30 minutes).
Pinto beans, canned, drained	3 lb 8 oz	
Diced tomatoes, canned	2 qt	
Onions, chopped	2 lb	
Garlic, minced	1 oz	
Salt	2½ Tbsp	
Cumin	1 Tbsp	
Oregano leaves, dried	1 Tbsp	
Corn Bread (p. 244)	1 recipe	Serve 8 oz stew in a bowl with a wedge of Corn Bread alongside.

Approximate nutritive values per portion

Calories	Carbohydrate	Protein	Fat	Cholesterol	Sodium	Fiber	Iron
323 kcal	41 g	18 g	10 g	56 mg	1014 mg	5 g	3 mg

Note

- Potentially hazardous food. *Food Safety Standards:* Hold food for service at an internal temperature of 135°F or above. Do not mix old product with new. Cool leftover product quickly following time standards and cooling procedures on p. 167. Reheat leftover product quickly (within 2 hours) to 165°F or above. Reheat product only once; discard if not used.

BEEF STROGANOFF

Yield: 50 portions or 2 gal   *Portion:* 6 oz stroganoff + 4 oz noodles

Ingredient	Amount	Procedure
Beef round, cut in ¼-inch strips	12 lb	Brown meat in shortening.
Shortening	8 oz	Add onion and seasonings.
Onion, chopped	1 lb 4 oz	
Salt	1 Tbsp	
Black pepper	1 tsp	
Beef Stock (p. 738)	2½ qt	Add stock to meat and simmer for 35–40 minutes or until meat is tender.
Flour, all-purpose	8 oz	Mix flour, water, and Worcestershire sauce and stir until smooth.
Water, cold	2 cups	Add to meat while stirring and cook until thickened.
Worcestershire sauce	¾ cup	
Mushrooms, fresh, sliced	2 lb 8 oz	Sauté mushrooms in margarine.
Margarine, melted	4 oz	
Sour cream	1 qt	Add sour cream to meat mixture, stirring constantly. Add mushrooms. Heat to 180°F.
Noodles	4 lb 8 oz	Cook noodles according to directions on p. 507.
Water	4½ gal	Serve 6 oz stroganoff over 4 oz noodles.
Salt	2 oz	
Vegetable oil	3 Tbsp	

Approximate nutritive values per portion

Calories	Carbohydrate	Protein	Fat	Cholesterol	Sodium	Fiber	Iron
597 kcal	50 g	61 g	17 g	92 mg	1180 mg	3 g	5 mg

Notes

- Potentially hazardous food. *Food Safety Standards:* Hold food for service at an internal temperature of 135°F or above. Do not mix old product with new. Cool leftover product quickly following time standards and cooling procedures on p. 167. Reheat leftover product quickly (within 2 hours) to 165°F or above. Reheat product only once; discard if not used.
- May be served over rice. Cook 3 lb 8 oz rice in 4¼ qt water, 2 Tbsp salt, and 2 Tbsp oil. See p. 542.

Variation

- **Ground-Beef Stroganoff.** Substitute ground beef for beef round. Add 1 lb 8 oz chopped celery, ¼ cup paprika, ¼ cup Worcestershire sauce, and 2 tsp dry mustard.

BEEF LO MEIN

Yield: 50 portions   *Portion:* 4 oz beef + 4 oz pasta

Ingredient	Amount	Procedure
Sugar	1½ Tbsp	Combine sugar, pepper, and clear Jel in a steam-jacketed or large kettle.
White pepper	½ tsp	
Clear Jel (see Note)	4 oz	
Water	3¾ qt	Add liquids, beef base, garlic, and ginger to dry ingredients while stirring constantly with a wire whisk.
Molasses	3½ Tbsp	
Soy sauce	½ cup	Cook and stir until mixture thickens and looks clear, 190°F. Reduce heat and keep sauce warm.
Beef base	3 oz	
Garlic, minced	1 tsp	Reserve sauce for later step. Expected yield is 3½ qt.
Fresh ginger, minced	1 tsp	
Sirloin beef tips	7 lb	Cook beef tips and garlic in a steam-jacketed kettle until the meat is browned.
Garlic, minced	3 oz	
Water	3½ qt	Add water to kettle to cover beef. Simmer until meat is tender.
Soy sauce	1 cup	Measure sauce reserved from earlier step. Add water if necessary to make 7 lb 3 oz of sauce (3½ qt).
Green onions, cut in 1-inch lengths	6 oz	
Ground red pepper	1½ tsp	Stir sauces, onions, and pepper into meat.
Bamboo shoots, canned, drained	1 lb	Rinse bamboo shoots and add to meat mixture.
Broccoli florets, fresh	1 lb 8 oz	Add broccoli and peppers to meat. Heat to 180–190°F until the broccoli is tender-crisp.
Roasted red bell peppers, julienne sliced		
Fettuccine	12 lb 8oz	Prepare pasta according to directions on p. 507. Portion a 4-oz ladle of beef over 4 oz pasta.

Approximate nutritive values per portion

Calories	Carbohydrate	Protein	Fat	Cholesterol	Sodium	Fiber	Iron
306 kcal	43 g	21 g	5 g	32 mg	1061 mg	2 g	2 mg

Notes

- Potentially hazardous food. *Food Safety Standards:* Hold food for service at an internal temperature of 135°F or above. Do not mix old product with new. Cool leftover product quickly following time standards and cooling procedures on p. 167. Reheat leftover product quickly (within 2 hours) to 165°F or above. Reheat product only once; discard if not used.
- Alternatively, substitute ⅓ less cornstarch (2½ oz) for Clear Jel. Clear Jel is available from most broadline foodservice distributors.

KOREAN BBQ BEEF

Yield: 50 portions   *Portion:* 4 oz beef + 4 oz rice

Ingredient	Amount	Procedure
Oil	2 Tbsp	Heat oil in the bottom of a steam-jacketed or other pan. Add garlic, ginger, and pepper. Cook for 2–5 minutes until garlic and ginger are fragrant.
Garlic, minced	1 Tbsp	
Fresh ginger, minced	1 Tbsp	
Red pepper flakes	1 tsp	
Soy sauce	7 oz	Blend liquids, sugar, and cornstarch in baker's bowl. Add to garlic mixture.
Rice wine vinegar	8 oz	
Water	14 oz	
Sugar, granulated	1 cup	Cook and stir until thickened and clear.
Cornstarch	4½ Tbsp	
Sesame seed oil	2 tsp	Stir sesame oil into sauce. Reserve sauce for later step. Should yield 2 lb 4 oz sauce.
Oil	2 Tbsp	Lightly coat bottom of tilting fry pan or other heavy-bottomed pan with oil. Add beef tips and cook until just done. Do not overcook.
Beef sirloin tips	8 lb	
Teriyaki sauce (low sodium)	1 qt	Mix teriyaki sauce with 2 lb 4 oz of sauce reserved from earlier step. Stir sauce into beef and stir to coat. Transfer to pans.
Green onions	1 lb	Cut green onions into 1-inch lengths. Sprinkle over beef.
Rice	3 lb 8 oz	Cook rice according to directions on p. 542. Serve 4 oz meat over 4 oz rice.
Water	4¼ qt	
Salt	2 Tbsp	
Margarine or vegetable oil	2 Tbsp	

Approximate nutritive values per portion

Calories	Carbohydrate	Protein	Fat	Cholesterol	Sodium	Fiber	Iron
279 kcal	39 g	19 g	5 g	35 mg	1591 mg	0 g	3 mg

Note

- Potentially hazardous food. *Food Safety Standards:* Hold food for service at an internal temperature of 135°F or above. Do not mix old product with new. Cool leftover product quickly following time standards and cooling procedures on p. 167. Reheat leftover product quickly (within 2 hours) to 165°F or above. Reheat product only once; discard if not used.

CHOP SUEY

Yield: 50 portions   *Portion:* 5 oz chop suey + 4 oz rice

Ingredient	Amount	Procedure
Beef, julienne strips	5 lb	Brown meat in steam-jacketed or other kettle.
Pork, julienne strips	2 lb	
Water	2 qt	Add water and salt to meat.
Salt	2 tsp	Simmer until tender.
Cornstarch	8 oz	Make a smooth paste of cornstarch and water.
Water, cold	1¼ cups	Pour slowly into meat and broth, stirring constantly while pouring. Cook until thickened.
Soy sauce	1 cup	Add soy sauce and Worcestershire sauce. Stir to blend.
Worcestershire sauce	1 cup	
Green bell peppers, sliced	4 oz	Steam vegetables until tender-crisp.
Onions, sliced	1 lb	
Celery, diagonally sliced	2 lb	
Bean sprouts, canned, undrained	3 lb	Add bean sprouts and vegetables to meat mixture just before serving.
Rice, converted	3 lb 8 oz	Cook rice according to directions on p. 542.
Water	4¼ qt	Serve 5 oz chop suey over 4 oz rice.
Salt	2 Tbsp	
Margarine or vegetable oil	2 Tbsp	

Approximate nutritive values per portion

Calories	Carbohydrate	Protein	Fat	Cholesterol	Sodium	Fiber	Iron
247 kcal	34 g	16 g	5 g	34 mg	746 mg	1 g	3 mg

Notes

- Potentially hazardous food. *Food Safety Standards:* Hold food for service at an internal temperature of 135°F or above. Do not mix old product with new. Cool leftover product quickly following time standards and cooling procedures on p. 167. Reheat leftover product quickly (within 2 hours) to 165°F or above. Reheat product only once; discard if not used.
- 8 oz water chestnuts may be added.
- May be served over 2 oz chow mein noodles (6 lb) instead of rice.

Variation

- **Chicken Chow Mein.** Substitute cubed, cooked chicken or turkey for beef and pork; chicken stock for water. Delete green bell peppers and add 1 lb sliced mushrooms. Serve over rice or chow mein noodles.

VEGETABLE CHOW MEIN

Yield: 50 portions   *Portion:* 6 oz chow mein + 2 oz noodles

Ingredient	Amount	Procedure
Water	5¼ qt	Combine in steam-jacketed kettle.
Sugar, granulated	2 oz	Heat to a simmer.
Salt	2¼ tsp	
White pepper	1 tsp	
Ginger, ground	1 tsp	
Garlic powder	1 tsp	
Soy sauce	1¼ cups	
Cornstarch	10 oz	Blend cornstarch, water, and soup base to a smooth paste.
Water	2¼ cups	Add slowly to broth, stirring constantly.
Chicken soup base	¾ oz	Cook until thickened and clear.
Bamboo shoots, canned	12 oz	Drain vegetables. Rinse and drain again.
Bean sprouts, canned	1 lb 4 oz	Add to mixture in kettle.
Sliced water chestnuts, canned	1 lb	
Celery	12 oz	Cut celery into diagonal slices.
Onions	8 oz	Dice onions into ½-inch cubes.
Carrots	1 lb 4 oz	Cut carrots into matchsticks.
		Steam vegetables until tender-crisp.
		Add to mixture.
Pimento, canned, chopped, drained	4 oz	Add to mixture.
Mushrooms, canned, drained	1 lb	
Broccoli, fresh	1 lb 8 oz	Divide broccoli tops into florets. Cut stalks into ¼-inch slices.
Green bell peppers	4 oz	Cut peppers into ½-inch squares.
		Steam until tender-crisp.
		Scale sauce into two 12 × 10 × 6-inch pans, approximately 9 lb per pan. Stir 12 oz broccoli and 2 oz peppers into each pan.
Chow mein noodles	6 lb	Ladle 6 oz chow mein over 2 oz chow mein noodles.

Approximate nutritive values per portion

Calories	Carbohydrate	Protein	Fat	Cholesterol	Sodium	Fiber	Iron
346 kcal	43 g	7 g	17 g	0 mg	883 mg	3 g	3 mg

Notes

- Potentially hazardous food. *Food Safety Standards:* Hold food for service at an internal temperature of 135°F or above. Do not mix old product with new. Cool leftover product quickly following time standards and cooling procedures on p. 167. Reheat leftover product quickly (within 2 hours) to 165°F or above. Reheat product only once; discard if not used.
- May be served over rice instead of chow mein noodles. Cook 3 lb 8 oz rice according to directions on p. 542.

THIN AND CRISPY PIZZA

Yield: 50 portions   *Portion:* 1 wedge
Oven: 490°F conveyor; 400°F conventional

Ingredient	Amount	Procedure
Water	2¾ cups	Warm water to 120–130°F. Pour into mixer bowl.
Flour, all-purpose Salt Shortening Instant yeast	2 lb 7 oz 2¼ tsp 4 oz ¾ oz	Add flour, salt, shortening, and yeast to water. Stir with dough hook on #1 (low) speed to blend. Knead until smooth and elastic on #2 (medium) speed. Scale into 12-oz balls. Oil the top of the balls. Cover tightly with plastic bag. Refrigerate overnight.
Olive oil Cornmeal	2 oz 2 oz	Brush olive oil over pizza pan. Sprinkle cornmeal over pan. Sheet dough rounds to fit 12- or 14-inch pans. Place dough on pans and ease to fit. Brush each crust with 1 Tbsp olive oil.
Pizza sauce Shredded Parmesan cheese Toppings (see Note) Shredded mozzarella cheese	1 lb 1 lb 10 oz 1 lb	**Topping Procedure** 1. Smooth 3 oz pizza sauce over dough, leaving ½-inch border. 2. Sprinkle 3 oz shredded Parmesan cheese over sauce. 3. Place 2 oz toppings on cheese. 4. Sprinkle 3 oz mozzarella cheese on top. Bake at 400°F in a conventional oven, or at 490°F in an conveyor oven.

Approximate nutritive values per wedge

Calories	Carbohydrate	Protein	Fat	Cholesterol	Sodium	Fiber	Iron
204 kcal	19 g	9 g	10 g	16 mg	384 mg	1 g	1.4 mg

Notes

- Potentially hazardous food. *Food Safety Standards:* Hold food for service at an internal temperature of 135°F or above. Do not mix old product with new. Cool leftover product quickly following time standards and cooling procedures on p. 167. Reheat leftover product quickly (within 2 hours) to 165°F or above. Reheat product only once; discard if not used.
- Topping suggestions: pepperoni, ground beef, sausage, spicy chicken, mushrooms, olives, onions.

PIZZA

Yield: 48 portions or 3 pans, 18 × 26 × 1 inches, or 6 round 14-inch pans   *Portion:* 7 oz
Oven: Baking sheet, 475°F for 10–12 minutes; round, 500°F for 5–8 minutes

Ingredient	Amount	Procedure
DOUGH		
Flour, all-purpose	5 lb	Place flour, salt, sugar, and dry milk in mixer bowl. Mix on low speed, using
Salt	1½ oz	a dough hook.
Sugar, granulated	4 oz	
Nonfat dry milk	2 oz	
Yeast, active dry (see Note)	1½ oz	Soften yeast in warm water.
Water, warm (110°F)	1½ qt	
Shortening	4 oz	Add softened yeast and shortening to dry ingredients.
		Mix on low speed to form dough.
		Continue kneading until smooth and elastic.
		Cover and let rise until double in bulk, about 2 hours.
		Punch down dough according to directions on p. 263 and let rest for 45 minutes.
PIZZA SAUCE		
Onions, chopped	12 oz	Cook onions in shortening until transparent.
Shortening or oil	1 oz	Add tomatoes, sugar, and seasonings.
Tomato juice	2 qt	Heat to boiling. Reduce heat and simmer for 30–45 minutes. Cool.
Tomato paste	1 qt	Remove bay leaves.
Sugar, granulated	2 oz	Spread sauce over dough, 1 qt per 18 × 26-inch pan or 1–1¼ cups per
		14-inch round pan. (See Table 14.11 for portioning guidelines.)
Oregano, dried, crumbled	1 Tbsp	
Basil, dried, crumbled	2 Tbsp	
Garlic powder	1 tsp	
Black pepper	1 tsp	
Bay leaves	3	
SEASONED BEEF		
Ground beef	9 lb	Brown beef in steam-jacketed kettle or pan until internal temperature
Salt	1 Tbsp	reads 155°F for 15 seconds. Drain well.
Fennel seed	1 tsp	Add seasonings, stirring to distribute.
Paprika	1 tsp	Sprinkle evenly over tomato sauce, approximately 1 lb 8 oz per
Cayenne pepper	½ tsp	18 × 26 × 1-inch pan, 8 oz per 14-inch round pan.
Oregano, dried, crumbled	1 tsp	
Basil, dried, crumbled	1 Tbsp	

Approximate nutritive values per portion

Calories	Carbohydrate	Protein	Fat	Cholesterol	Sodium	Fiber	Iron
502 kcal	50 g	28 g	21 g	72 mg	958 mg	4 g	5 mg

TABLE 14.11 Portioning guidelines for pizza

Size (round) (in)	Sauce (oz)	Cheese (oz)	Dough (oz)
7	1½	2	4–6
10	3	3½	12–14
12	4	6	16–20
14	6	8	16–22
16	8	12	26

Amount of dough will vary depending on whether a thin, medium, or thick crust is desired.

Notes

- Active dry yeast may be mixed with dry ingredients. See p. 229 for procedure.
- Sausage (4 lb 8 oz) may be substituted for 4 lb 8 oz ground beef. Omit fennel, paprika, cayenne pepper, and garlic.
- Dough may be mixed and refrigerated for use up to 24 hours later. Remove dough from refrigerator and let sit at room temperature for 1–1½ hours before shaping. Shape into dough rounds and let rise for 1 hour before topping.
- Bake within 30 minutes after topping to prevent a doughy layer. Once the doughy layer has formed, it cannot be reversed.

Variations for Making 14″ Round Pizzas

- **Ground Beef and Mushroom Pizza.** Layer in the following order: 10 oz sauce; 8 oz shredded mozzarella cheese; 8 oz seasoned ground beef; 3 oz canned sliced mushrooms, drained; and 3 oz shredded mozzarella cheese.
- **Ground-Beef Pizza Supreme.** Layer in the following order: 10 oz sauce; 8 oz shredded mozzarella cheese; 8 oz seasoned beef; 1 oz each diced onions, chopped green bell peppers, and sliced ripe olives; and 3 oz shredded mozzarella cheese.
- **Pepperoni Pizza.** Layer in the following order: 10 oz sauce, 8 oz shredded mozzarella cheese, 2 oz sliced pepperoni (arranged evenly over the top), and 3 oz mozzarella cheese.
- **Triple Cheese Pizza.** Layer in the following order: 10 oz sauce, 8 oz shredded mozzarella cheese, 4 oz shredded Monterey Jack cheese, and 4 oz shredded cheddar cheese.
- **Garden Pizza.** Layer in the following order: 10 oz sauce; 6 oz shredded mozzarella cheese; 2 oz shredded cheddar cheese; 1 oz each diced green bell peppers, canned sliced mushrooms, diced onion, and sliced ripe olives.

ASSEMBLY AND BAKING

If using 18 × 26 × 1-inch baking sheet:

1. Divide dough into three portions, 2 lb 8 oz each. Roll out very thin, stretching to fit three 18 × 26 × 1-inch baking sheets. Allow 1¼ inches to extend up sides of pan.
2. Spread 1 qt sauce over dough.
3. Sprinkle 1 lb 8 oz seasoned beef over sauce.
4. Top each pan with 1 lb 4 oz mozzarella cheese.
5. Bake at 475°F for 10–12 minutes in a conventional oven.
6. Cut each pan 2 × 4 and then each of the 8 pieces diagonally, yielding 16 pie-shaped portions per pan (48 slices).

If using 14-inch round pans:

1. Prepare six 14-inch pans by spraying lightly with vegetable spray.
2. Press 1 lb 6 oz dough into pans, allowing 1 inch to extend up sides.
3. Perforate dough with fork or dough docker.
4. Choose pizza topping from Variations and layer in the order given.
5. Bake until crust is browned, sauce is bubbly, and cheese is melted. (See Table 14.12 for time and temperature guidelines.)
6. Cut each pizza into 8 slices, yielding 8 portions per pan (48 slices).

TABLE 14.12   Approximate temperatures and times for cooking pizza

Oven type	Temp. (°F)	6–8 inches (minutes)	10–12 inches (minutes)	14–17 inches (minutes)
Convection	325	10–12	12–15	16–20
Conveyor (Impinger)	500	5–7	5–7	5–7
Conventional	450	13–15	15–18	18–22
Deck	450	13–15	15–18	18–22
Pizza deck	500	8–10	10–12	10–14

TACO SALAD CASSEROLE

Yield: 48 portions or 3 pans, 12 × 20 × 2 inches   *Portion:* 8 oz

Ingredient	Amount	Procedure
Corn chips	2 lb 8 oz	Spread corn chips in bottoms of three 12 × 20 × 2-inch counter pans, 14 oz per pan.
Ground beef	8 lb AP	Brown meat in steam-jacketed kettle until internal temperature reaches 155°F for 15 seconds. Drain off fat.
Onions, minced Garlic cloves, minced	8 oz 3	Add onions and garlic to meat. Cook until tender.
Flour, all-purpose Tomato juice	3 oz 1¼ qt	Combine flour and tomato juice and add to meat mixture.
Vinegar, cider Catsup Chile sauce Sugar, granulated Salt Black pepper Chile powder Cayenne pepper Hot pepper sauce Worcestershire sauce Red beans, canned	2 Tbsp 1½ cups 1 cup 2 Tbsp 2 Tbsp ½ tsp 2 tsp ¼ tsp ¾ tsp 1 tsp 3 lb 12 oz	Add to meat mixture. Blend. Heat until very hot. Scale 4 lb 5 oz meat sauce over each pan of chips. Keep warm and serve soon after vegetables are layered on top. (See Note for an alternate assembly method.)
Lettuce, chopped Green bell peppers, chopped Onions, finely chopped Tomatoes, fresh, diced	4 lb 12 oz 12 oz 2 lb 10 oz	Combine vegetables. Mix gently. Sprinkle over hot meat mixture, 2 lb 8 oz per pan.
Processed cheese, shredded	2 lb 10 oz	Sprinkle 14 oz cheese over each pan. Cut 4 × 4. Serve immediately.

Approximate nutritive values per portion

Calories	Carbohydrate	Protein	Fat	Cholesterol	Sodium	Fiber	Iron
422 kcal	30 g	22 g	24 g	60 mg	1183 mg	5 g	3 mg

Notes

- Potentially hazardous food. *Food Safety Standards:* Hold food for service at an internal temperature of 135°F or above. Do not mix old product with new. Cool leftover product quickly following time standards and cooling procedures on p. 167. Reheat leftover product quickly (within 2 hours) to 165°F or above. Reheat product only once; discard if not used.
- Chips will become soggy if held for very long. Spread meat on chips only as needed.
- Casserole may be assembled on each plate individually. Place ¾ oz taco chips on plate. Ladle 4 oz hot meat mixture over chips and top with 2½ oz salad mixture and ¾ oz shredded cheese.
- Serve with Salsa (p. 702) or commercial salsa.
- 1 oz (½ cup) dehydrated onions, rehydrated in ¾ cup water, may be substituted for the fresh onions that are added to the ground beef.

SHREDDED BEEF BURROS

Yield: 50 portions   *Portion:* 1 Burro
Oven: 325°F

Ingredient	Amount	Procedure
Beef roast (inside round)	12 lb	Roast beef in a 325°F oven until medium. Shred beef coarsely. Hold for later step.
Onions, chopped	1 lb 8 oz	Sauté onions in margarine until tender-crisp.
Margarine	3 oz	Add green chiles and heat through.
Diced green chiles, canned	1 lb	
Flour, all-purpose	3 oz	Add flour and spices to onions and chiles.
Garlic powder	1¾ tsp	Cook for 10–15 minutes, stirring often.
Cumin ground	2 Tbsp	
Chile powder	¼ cup	
Picante sauce	1¼ qt	Add sauce, water, and soup base. Cook until thickened.
Water	2¾ cups	Add shredded roast beef reserved from earlier step. Heat to 170°F, stirring often.
Beef soup base (paste style)	2 oz	Transfer to 12 × 10 × 4-inch pans.
Flour tortillas, 8-inch	50	Warm tortillas in an oven or microwave until pliable. Keep covered.
Lettuce, shredded	2 lb	Lay tortilla flat and portion a No. 12 dipper of meat filling on bottom third.
Cheese, shredded	2 lb	Distribute approximately ½ oz each of shredded lettuce, shredded cheese, and diced tomato on top of meat. Do not overfill.
Tomatoes, diced	2 lb	To roll: 1. Fold two sides of wrap 1 inch over filling. 2. Roll tightly as for jelly roll, starting to roll from side that is not over filling. Serve with picante sauce if desired.

Approximate nutritive values per portion

Calories	Carbohydrate	Protein	Fat	Cholesterol	Sodium	Fiber	Iron
259 kcal	26 g	25 g	5 g	51 mg	774 mg	4 g	2 mg

Note

- Potentially hazardous food. *Food Safety Standards:* Hold food for service at an internal temperature of 135°F or above. Do not mix old product with new. Cool leftover product quickly following time standards and cooling procedures on p. 167. Reheat leftover product quickly (within 2 hours) to 165°F or above. Reheat product only once; discard if not used.

Variation

- **Beef Chimichangas.** Prepare shredded beef as for Shredded Beef Burros. Warm 50 12-inch tortillas until pliable. Work with one tortilla at a time. Brush edge of tortillas with water. Place No. 12 dipper of filling (4 oz) slightly below center of tortillas. Shape meat into a log that extends to 1 inch on each side of wraps. Fold bottom edge over filling. Fold sides in, then roll into a cylinder. Place seam side down on silicone paper-lined pan until ready to deep-fat fry. Fry at 325°F until golden brown and crisp. Internal temperature should be at least 165°F. Serve toppings as for Shredded Beef Burros.

SPANISH RICE

Yield: 50 portions or 2 pans, 12 × 20 × 2 inches *Portion:* 8 oz
Oven: 350°F *Bake:* 1 hour

Ingredient	Amount	Procedure
Rice, converted	2 lb 8 oz	Cook rice according to directions on p. 542.
Water, boiling	3 qt	
Salt	1 oz (1½ Tbsp)	
Vegetable oil	2 Tbsp	
Ground beef	7 lb	Cook beef until internal temperature reaches 155°F.
Onions, chopped	1 lb 8 oz	Add onions, peppers, and celery to meat.
Green bell peppers, chopped	8 oz	Cook for about 10 minutes.
Celery, chopped	8 oz	
Diced tomatoes, canned	1 No. 10 can	Add remaining ingredients to meat mixture.
Chile sauce	3 cups	Combine with cooked rice.
Tomato paste	3 cups	Scale into two 12 × 20 × 2-inch pans, 15 lb per pan.
Salt	2 oz (3 Tbsp)	Bake at 350°F for 1 hour.
Black pepper	¼ tsp	
Cayenne pepper	few grains	
Sugar, granulated	2 Tbsp	
Water	2 cups	

Approximate nutritive values per portion

Calories	Carbohydrate	Protein	Fat	Cholesterol	Sodium	Fiber	Iron
260 kcal	30 g	14 g	10 g	38 mg	1115 mg	2 g	3 mg

Notes

- Potentially hazardous food. *Food Safety Standards:* Hold food for service at an internal temperature of 135°F or above. Do not mix old product with new. Cool leftover product quickly following time standards and cooling procedures on p. 167. Reheat leftover product quickly (within 2 hours) to 165°F or above. Reheat product only once; discard if not used.
- 3 lb bacon, diced and cooked, may be substituted for the ground beef.
- 3 oz (1½ cups) dehydrated onions, rehydrated in 2 cups water, may be substituted for fresh onions.

Variations

- **Spanish Rice and Black Beans.** Heat ¾ cup olive oil in tilting fry pan. Sauté 1 oz minced garlic, 10 oz chopped onions, 1 lb 4 oz green bell pepper, and 2 lb 4 oz raw white rice until vegetables are translucent and rice begins to brown. Add 1 qt water, 2¼ qt tomato juice, 3 Tbsp ancho flavor concentrate (see Note), 2 tsp chipotle flavor concentrate, 1½ tsp cumin, 3/4 tsp crushed red pepper, and 1 tsp dried oregano leaves. Bring to a boil. Reduce heat and simmer until rice cooks, about 20 minutes. Stir in 1 lb rinsed and drained black beans and 6 oz whole kernel corn. Cook until liquid is absorbed and beans and corn are hot. (Note: Minor's Ancho Flavor Concentrate and Minor's Chipotle Flavor Concentrate are available from most broadline foodservice distributors.)
- **Stuffed Peppers.** Wash 25 large green bell peppers and remove stem end. Cut peppers in half lengthwise. Remove seeds and tough white portion. Place in baking pans and steam or parboil for 3–5 minutes. Place No. 8 dipper of Spanish Rice in each pepper half. Combine two 50-oz cans tomato soup and 2 qt tomato sauce. Ladle 2 oz over each pepper. Bake at 350°F for 45–60 minutes. Ladle extra sauce over peppers during baking.

CHEESEBURGER PIE

Yield: 48 portions or 2 pans, 12 × 20 × 2 inches   *Portion:* 8 oz (6 oz meat)
Oven: 400°F   *Bake:* 30–35 minutes

Ingredient	Amount	Procedure
Ground beef	12 lb AP (8 lb EP)	Brown beef in steam-jacketed or other kettle until internal temperature reaches 155°F. Drain off fat.
Onions, chopped	1 lb 4 oz	Add onions and peppers to meat. Cook until vegetables are tender.
Green bell peppers, chopped	1 lb 4 oz	
Garlic powder	1 tsp	Add seasonings and tomatoes.
Salt	1 oz (1½ Tbsp)	Simmer for 30 minutes or until thick.
Chile powder	3 oz	Scale meat mixture into two 12 × 20 × 2-inch pans, 9 lb per pan.
Cumin, ground	1 tsp	
Cayenne pepper	¼ tsp	
Sugar, brown	1 oz	
Diced tomatoes, canned	7 lb 12 oz	

CHEESE BISCUIT TOPPING

Ingredient	Amount	Procedure
Flour, all-purpose	2 lb 14 oz	Combine dry ingredients in mixer bowl on low speed for 1 minute, using a flat beater.
Baking powder	2¾ oz (6 Tbsp)	
Salt	2 Tbsp	
Dry mustard	1 tsp	
Nonfat dry milk	7 oz	
Shortening	12 oz	Cut shortening and cheese into flour on low speed for 1–1½ minutes.
Processed cheese, shredded	10 oz	
Water	1½ qt	Add water to make a thick batter. Mix only until flour is moistened.
		With No. 20 dipper, place topping 4 × 6 over meat mixture just before baking. Bake at 400°F for 30–35 minutes. Cut 4 × 6.

Approximate nutritive values per portion

Calories	Carbohydrate	Protein	Fat	Cholesterol	Sodium	Fiber	Iron
432 kcal	30 g	25 g	24 g	65 mg	892 mg	2 g	4 mg

Notes

- Potentially hazardous food. *Food Safety Standards:* Hold food for service at an internal temperature of 135°F or above. Do not mix old product with new. Cool leftover product quickly following time standards and cooling procedures on p. 167. Reheat leftover product quickly (within 2 hours) to 165°F or above. Reheat product only once; discard if not used.
- 2½ oz (1¼ cups) dehydrated onions, rehydrated in 2 cups water, may be substituted for fresh onions.

Veal Recipes

VEAL BIRDS

Yield: 50 portions   *Portion:* 4 oz
Oven: 300°F   *Bake:* 2 hours

Ingredient	Amount	Procedure
Onions, finely chopped	8 oz	Sauté onions and celery in margarine.
Celery, finely chopped	8 oz	
Margarine	8 oz	
Beef base	1½ oz	Combine soup base, seasonings, and water. Add to sautéed vegetables.
Salt	1 tsp (see Note)	
Black pepper	1½ tsp	
Sage, ground	1 Tbsp	
Water	2 qt	
Bread, dry, cubed	2 lb	Add bread gradually to vegetable mixture, tossing lightly until thoroughly mixed.
Veal cutlets, 4 oz	50	Place No. 16 dipper of bread mixture on each piece of meat. Roll and fasten with a pick.
Flour, all-purpose	8 oz	Combine flour and salt.
Salt	2 oz	Roll each "bird" in flour and brown in hot shortening.
Shortening	1 lb 8 oz	Place in two 12 × 20 × 2-inch counter pans.
Water	1 qt	Add 2 cups water to each pan. Cover with aluminum foil. Bake at 300°F for 1½–2 hours. (Internal temperature 165°F.)

Approximate nutritive values per portion

Calories	Carbohydrate	Protein	Fat	Cholesterol	Sodium	Fiber	Iron
414 kcal	17 g	42 g	19 g	128 mg	759 mg	1 g	2 mg

Notes

- Potentially hazardous food. *Food Safety Standards:* Hold food for service at an internal temperature of 135°F or above. Do not mix old product with new. Cool leftover product quickly following time standards and cooling procedures on p. 167. Reheat leftover product quickly (within 2 hours) to 165°F or above. Reheat product only once; discard if not used.
- Veal round, ¼ inch thick, cut into 4-oz pieces, may be substituted for the cutlets.
- 1 oz (½ cup) dehydrated onions, rehydrated in ¾ cup water, may be substituted for fresh onions.
- If beef base is highly salted, reduce or delete salt in recipe.

Variations

- **Beef Birds.** Make with beef cubed steaks or flank steaks.
- **Pork Birds.** Make with pork cutlets.
- **Veal Birds with Sausage Stuffing.** Reduce bread to 2 lb 8 oz. Reduce salt to 1 tsp and sage to 1 Tbsp. Add 2 lb 8 oz sausage, cooked and drained.

BREADED VEAL CUTLETS

Yield: 50 portions   *Portion:* 4 oz
Oven: 325°F   *Bake:* 45–60 minutes

Ingredient	Amount	Procedure
Veal cutlets, 4 oz	12 lb 8 oz	Dredge cutlets with seasoned flour.
Flour, all-purpose	8 oz	
Salt	1 oz (1½ Tbsp)	
Black pepper	¼ tsp	
Eggs, beaten	7 (12 oz)	Combine eggs and milk.
Milk	1½ cups	Dip cutlets in egg mixture, then roll in crumbs.
Bread crumbs, fine	1 lb	
Shortening	1 lb 8 oz	Brown meat in hot fat. Place, slightly overlapping, in two 12 × 20 × 2-inch counter pans. Add 2 cups water to each pan. Cover with aluminum foil. Bake at 325°F for 45–60 minutes.

Approximate nutritive values per portion

Calories	Carbohydrate	Protein	Fat	Cholesterol	Sodium	Fiber	Iron
378 kcal	11 g	41 g	18 g	159 mg	363 mg	0.5 g	2 mg

Notes

- Potentially hazardous food. *Food Safety Standards:* Hold food for service at an internal temperature of 135°F or above. Do not mix old product with new. Cool leftover product quickly following time standards and cooling procedures on p. 167. Reheat leftover product quickly (within 2 hours) to 165°F or above. Reheat product only once; discard if not used.
- Veal round, sliced ¼ inch thick and cut into 5-oz portions, may be used.

Variations

- **Veal Cacciatore.** Dredge cutlets with flour. Brown in fat and place in baking pans. Pour over sauce made of 1 lb chopped bell peppers, 1 lb chopped onions, and ⅛ tsp minced garlic, simmered in margarine or butter for 10 minutes; 1 lb 8 oz sautéed sliced mushrooms; 1½ qt canned tomatoes; ¼ cup vinegar; 2 qt Chicken Stock (p. 738); 1 oz salt; and 1 tsp black pepper. Bake for 45 minutes.
- **Veal New Orleans.** To 2 qt medium White Sauce (p. 683), add 8 oz chopped onions, 12 oz sliced mushrooms, 2 Tbsp Worcestershire sauce, ¼ tsp salt, ¼ tsp black pepper, ¼ tsp paprika, and 3½ cups tomato soup. Arrange browned breaded cutlets in two 12 × 20 × 2-inch counter pans. Pour 1¾ qt sauce over each pan. Cover with aluminum foil and bake at 325°F for 1 hour.
- **Veal Parmesan.** Add 8 oz grated Parmesan cheese to bread crumbs. After cutlets are browned and arranged in baking pans, pour 2 qt Italian Tomato Sauce (p. 691) over them. Top with 1 lb 8 oz grated mozzarella cheese. Bake at 325°F for 1 hour.
- **Veal Piccata.** Flour cutlets and brown in hot shortening. Arrange in two 12 × 20 × 2-inch counter pans. Sauté 1 lb sliced mushrooms and 2 garlic cloves, minced, in 2 Tbsp margarine. Add 2½ cups Beef Stock (p. 738) and 2 Tbsp lemon juice. Bring to a boil. Pour 2 cups over each pan. Sprinkle ¼ cup Parmesan cheese over each pan. Cover with aluminum foil. Bake at 325°F for 1 hour.
- **Veal Scallopini.** Dredge cutlets with seasoned flour and sauté in hot shortening. Arrange in baking pans. Sauté 3 lb fresh sliced mushrooms and 1 lb chopped onion in 8 oz margarine. Add 2 qt Chicken Stock (p. 738), 1½ cups lemon juice or vinegar, and 1 tsp each dried parsley, rosemary, and oregano or marjoram. Pour over cutlets. Bake at 325°F for 1 hour.

Lamb Recipes

ROASTED RACK OF LAMB

Yield: 50 portions *Portion:* 8 oz with bone
Oven: 375°F

Ingredient	Amount	Procedure
Racks of lamb (each 8 bone racks, approx. 2 lb each)	13	Place roasts in a 12 × 20 × 2-inch counter pan (one roast per pan), fat side up.
Seasoning rub or salt and black pepper	p. 720	If using a rub, coat the entire surface of the meat, using approximately 1 oz rub mixture per 3 lb roast. If not using a rub, add salt and pepper to the meat. Roast in a conventional oven at 375°F to desired doneness (145°F for medium rare, 155°F medium). Remove from oven, tent with foil, and let stand for 15 minutes before slicing. Internal temperature will increase 5–10°F during standing time. One serving is one double bone portion or two single bone portions (4 servings per 8-bone rib roast).

Approximate nutritive values per portion without seasoning

Calories	Carbohydrate	Protein	Fat	Cholesterol	Sodium	Fiber	Iron
249 kcal	0 g	29 g	14 g	97 mg	90 mg	0 g	2.3 mg

Note

- Potentially hazardous food. *Food Safety Standards:* Hold food for service at an internal temperature of 135°F or above. Do not mix old product with new. Cool leftover product quickly following time standards and cooling procedures on p. 167. Reheat leftover product quickly (within 2 hours) to 165°F or above. Reheat product only once; discard if not used.

GRILLED LAMB CHOPS

Yield: 50 portions   *Portion:* 1 chop
Griddle: 400°F

Ingredient	Amount	Procedure
Lamb loin chops, 6 oz	50	Heat griddle to 400°F. Oil generously.
Olive or vegetable oil	¼ cup	Brush lamb chops with olive oil and season with salt and pepper.
Salt	1 oz	Place lamb chops on hot griddle and cook for 2–3 minutes. Turn over and
Cracked black pepper	1½ Tbsp	cook for another 2–3 minutes. Turn over once only. Cook to an internal
(See Variations.)		temperature of 145°F for medium rare, 160°F for medium.
		Hold for service at or above 135°F.

Approximate nutritive values per chop

Calories	Carbohydrate	Protein	Fat	Cholesterol	Sodium	Fiber	Iron
190 kcal	0 g	23 g	10 g	80 mg	303 mg	0 g	2 mg

Notes

- Potentially hazardous food. *Food Safety Standards:* Hold food for service at an internal temperature of 135°F or above. Do not mix old product with new. Cool leftover product quickly following time standards and cooling procedures on p. 167. Reheat leftover product quickly (within 2 hours) to 165°F or above. Reheat product only once; discard if not used.
- Rib chops can be substituted for loin chops.

Variations

- **Grilled Charmoula Lamb Chops.** Marinate chops in Moroccan Charmoula, p. 711, before grilling.
- **Grilled Lamb Chops with Tomatillo Mint Chutney.** Serve lamb chops with 2 Tbsp Tomatillo Mint Chutney, p. 709.

Pork Recipes

ROAST PORK LOIN

Yield: 50 portions   *Portion:* 4 oz
Oven: 350°F

Ingredient	Amount	Procedure
Boneless pork loin	20 lb	Place roasts in a 12 × 20 × 2-inch counter pan (one roast per pan), rib side down.
Seasoning rub or marinade or salt and cracked black pepper (See Variations.)	p. 720	If using a rub, coat the entire surface of the meat, using approximately 2 oz rub mixture per 6–7 lb roast. If not using a rub, add salt and pepper to the meat.
		Roast in a conventional oven at 350°F to an internal temperature of 150°F. Remove from oven, tent with foil, and let stand for 15 minutes before slicing. Internal temperature will increase 5–10°F during standing time.

Approximate nutritive values per meat portion without added seasonings or accompaniments

Calories	Carbohydrate	Protein	Fat	Cholesterol	Sodium	Fiber	Iron
213 kcal	0 g	23 g	11 g	106 mg	49 mg	0 g	1 mg

Note

- Potentially hazardous food. *Food Safety Standards:* Hold food for service at an internal temperature of 135°F or above. Do not mix old product with new. Cool leftover product quickly following time standards and cooling procedures on p. 167. Reheat leftover product quickly (within 2 hours) to 165°F or above. Reheat product only once; discard if not used.

Variations

- **Caribbean Citrus Marinated Pork Loin.** Prepare **Citrus Marinade** by mixing 12 oz white vinegar, 1 lb 4 oz fresh lime juice, 8 oz fresh grapefruit juice, 8 oz fresh orange juice, 2 Tbsp dried oregano leaves, 1½ Tbsp black pepper, and 3 Tbsp Adobo Seasoning, p. 725. Pour marinade over pork (coating entire surface with marinade) and refrigerate for 24 hours. Place pork and marinade in 12 × 20 × 4-inch pans. Roast at 375°F until meat reaches 145°F, about 75 minutes. Tent with foil and let stand for 10 minutes before slicing.
- **Garlic Peppercorn Pork Loin.** Brush pork loins with olive oil. Cover with approximately 1 cup crushed peppercorns and approximately ¾ cup minced garlic. Roast as for Roast Pork Loin.
- **Herbed Pork Loin.** Combine 1½ oz salt, 2 Tbsp dried whole rosemary, 2 Tbsp dried whole thyme, 3 Tbsp black pepper, ½ cup minced garlic, ¾ cup fresh lemon juice, and ¾ cup vegetable oil. Rub paste over roasts. Refrigerate for several hours or overnight. Roast as for Roast Pork Loin.
- **Honey-Cumin Pork Loin with Caramelized Onions.** Blend together 10 oz honey, 5 Tbsp fresh lime juice, 4 Tbsp ground cumin, 1½ Tbsp kosher salt, and 1 tsp ground red pepper. Divide honey-spice mixture in half. Rub pork roasts with half of the honey-spice mixture, approximately 2 Tbsp per roast. Toss 4 lb 8 oz onions with the reserved honey-spice mixture. Place onions in pan around pork roast. Roast as for Roast Pork Loin.
- **Jeweled Pork Loin.** Rub 1 Tbsp black pepper over all sides of each loin. Cut vertical slits 1 inch deep along top of roasts. Cut 8 oz dried pitted prunes and 8 oz dried apricots into medium-size pieces. Push fruit into the slits on top of the loin. Roast as for Roast Pork Loin.
- **Rosemary Pork Loin.** Combine ¼ cup dried whole rosemary, 2 tsp garlic powder, 2 tsp cumin, and 2 tsp salt. Sprinkle over pork before roasting. Roast as for Roast Pork Loin.
- **Southwest Seasoned Pork Loin.** Rub pork loin roasts with **Southwest Blend**, p. 730 (approximately 1 Tbsp per roast), before roasting. Roast as for Roast Pork Loin.
- **Teriyaki-Glazed Pork Loin.** Make marinade by combining 2 cups soy sauce, 1 cup cooking sherry, ¼ cup granulated sugar, 3 Tbsp black pepper, ¼ cup minced garlic, and 1½ cups oil. Pour over roasts. Turn to cover all sides. Marinate in refrigerator for a minimum of 8 hours or overnight. Drain and discard marinade. Roast as for Roast Pork Loin.

RACK OF PORK

Yield: 50 portions　　　*Portion:* 8 oz
Oven: 350°F

Ingredient	Amount	Procedure
Bone-in pork loin	40 lb	Place roasts in a 12 × 20 × 2-inch counter pan (one roast per pan), rib side down.
Seasoning rub or salt and cracked black pepper	p. 725	If using a rub, coat the entire surface of the meat, using approximately 2 oz rub mixture per 6–7 lb roast. If not using a rub, add salt and pepper to the meat. Roast in a conventional oven at 350°F to an internal temperature of 150°F. Remove from oven, tent with foil, and let stand for 15 minutes before slicing. Internal temperature will increase 5–10°F during standing time. Serve portions with the bone attached.

Approximate nutritive values per meat portion without added seasonings or accompaniments

Calories	Carbohydrate	Protein	Fat	Cholesterol	Sodium	Fiber	Iron
679 kcal	0.4 g	39 g	58 g	195 mg	181 mg	0.1 g	2.3 mg

Note

- Potentially hazardous food. *Food Safety Standards:* Hold food for service at an internal temperature of 135°F or above. Do not mix old product with new. Cool leftover product quickly following time standards and cooling procedures on p. 167. Reheat leftover product quickly (within 2 hours) to 165°F or above. Reheat product only once; discard if not used.

BREADED PORK CHOPS

Yield: 50 chops   *Portion:* 5 oz
Oven: 400°F, 325°F   *Bake:* 10 minutes, 1 hour

Ingredient	Amount	Procedure
Pork chops, cut 3 per lb	17 lb	Dredge chops with seasoned flour.
Flour, all-purpose	12 oz	
Salt	3 oz	
Black pepper	2 Tbsp	
Eggs, beaten	6 (10 oz)	Combine eggs and milk.
Milk	3½ cups	Dip chops in egg mixture, then roll in crumbs.
Bread crumbs	1 lb 4 oz	Place in single layer on greased sheet pans.
		Bake at 400°F until browned, about 10 minutes.
Water	1 qt	Remove chops from oven and arrange in partially overlapping rows in two 12 × 20 × 2-inch counter pans.
		Add 2 cups water to each pan. Cover pans.
		Bake at 325°F for approximately 1 hour, until internal temperature reaches 160°F.

Approximate nutritive values per portion

Calories	Carbohydrate	Protein	Fat	Cholesterol	Sodium	Fiber	Iron
239 kcal	15 g	20 g	11 g	81 mg	810 mg	1 g	2 mg

Note

• Potentially hazardous food. *Food Safety Standards:* Hold food for service at an internal temperature of 135°F or above. Do not mix old product with new. Cool leftover product quickly following time standards and cooling procedures on p. 167. Reheat leftover product quickly (within 2 hours) to 165°F or above. Reheat product only once; discard if not used.

Variations

• **Baked Pork Chops.** Dredge chops with 1 lb flour, ¼ cup vegetable oil, 2 oz salt, and 1 tsp black pepper, mixed. Place on well-greased sheet pans. Bake at 350°F until thoroughly cooked and browned, approximately 1¼ hours.

• **Baked Pork Chops and Apples.** Brown chops as for Breaded Pork Chops. Place in two greased 12 × 20 × 2-inch baking pans. Pour over 1 qt apple juice, 2 cups per pan. Bake at 350°F for 1 hour. Serve with Buttered Apples (p. 637).

• **Pork Chops and Dressing.** Serve chops with No. 16 dipper of Bread Dressing (p. 604) and ladle of gravy dipped over.

• **Stuffed Pork Chops.** Use 6-oz pork chops and cut a pocket in each chop. Fill with Bread Dressing (use ¼ recipe, p. 604) or Apple Stuffing (p. 604, ½ recipe). Brown chops and place in baking pans. Pour 2 cups water or chicken broth in each pan. Cover and bake at 350°F for 1½ hours. Internal temperature must reach 165°F for 15 seconds.

DEVILED PORK CHOPS

Yield: 50 chops   *Portion:* 5 oz
Oven: 350°F   *Bake:* 1–1½ hours

Ingredient	Amount	Procedure
Chile sauce	1½ qt	Combine into a sauce.
Water	3 cups	
Dry mustard	1 tsp	
Worcestershire sauce	3 Tbsp	
Fresh lemon juice	3 Tbsp	
Onion, grated	2 tsp	
Pork chops, cut 3 per lb	17 lb	Dip each chop in sauce. Place in single layer on greased sheet pans. Bake at 350°F for 1–1½ hours, or until internal temperature reaches 160°F.

Approximate nutritive values per portion

Calories	Carbohydrate	Protein	Fat	Cholesterol	Sodium	Fiber	Iron
182 kcal	7 g	17 g	9 g	54 mg	446 mg	0 g	1 mg

Note

- Potentially hazardous food. *Food Safety Standards:* Hold food for service at an internal temperature of 135°F or above. Do not mix old product with new. Cool leftover product quickly following time standards and cooling procedures on p. 167. Reheat leftover product quickly (within 2 hours) to 165°F or above. Reheat product only once; discard if not used.

Variations

- **Barbecued Pork Chops.** Place chops on greased baking sheets. Brush with melted fat. Sprinkle with salt. Brown chops in 450°F oven for 12–15 minutes. Transfer to counter pans. Pour Barbecue Sauce (pp. 688, 689) over chops. Bake at 325°F for 1½ hours or until chops are tender.
- **Chile-Seasoned Pork Chops.** Prepare a spice blend by combining 6 Tbsp chile powder, 2 Tbsp ground cumin, 2 tsp garlic powder, 1 Tbsp onion powder, 1 tsp salt, and 2 tsp black pepper. Mix 1 Tbsp of the spice mixture with 1 cup vegetable oil. Cover and store for several hours to blend seasonings with oil. Save the remaining dry spice mixture to sprinkle on top of the chops. To cook chops, oil griddle with seasoned oil and heat to 350°F. Place chops on griddle and cook until browned; turn and brown other side. Sprinkle remaining seasonings lightly over chops. Place in 12 × 10 × 2-inch counter pans. Cover with foil and bake at 350°F for 1 hour.
- **Honey-Glazed Pork Chops.** Marinate pork chops for 4 hours in a mixture of 2 cups soy sauce, 6 oz honey, 1 cup applesauce, 1 oz salt, and 4 oz granulated sugar. Place in single layer on greased baking sheets. Bake at 350°F for 1 hour. Turn and brush with marinade as needed.
- **Pork Chops Supreme.** Arrange chops in single layer in baking pans. Sprinkle with salt. Combine 1 lb brown sugar, 3 cups catsup, and 1 cup fresh lemon juice. Place about 2 Tbsp (No. 30 dipper) on each chop. Cut 4 medium onions into thin slices. Place 1 slice on top of each chop. Cover and bake at 350°F for 45 minutes. Uncover and bake for 30 minutes longer.

BARBECUED SPARERIBS

Yield: 50 portions   *Portion:* 8 oz
Oven: 350°F   *Bake:* 2½ hours

Ingredient	Amount	Procedure
Pork spareribs or loin back ribs	25 lb	Separate ribs into 8-oz portions. Place in roasting pans. Brown uncovered in oven at 350°F until browned lightly, about 30 minutes. Pour off fat.
Barbecue Sauce (pp. 688, 689)	3 qt	Pour sauce over ribs. Cover with aluminum foil. Bake at 350°F until meat is tender, about 1½ hours. Uncover and bake for an additional 20–30 minutes.

Approximate nutritive values per portion

Calories	Carbohydrate	Protein	Fat	Cholesterol	Sodium	Fiber	Iron
590 kcal	8 g	66 g	31 g	206 mg	644 mg	1 g	3 mg

Notes

- Potentially hazardous food. *Food Safety Standards:* Hold food for service at an internal temperature of 135°F or above. Do not mix old product with new. Cool leftover product quickly following time standards and cooling procedures on p. 167. Reheat leftover product quickly (within 2 hours) to 165°F or above. Reheat product only once; discard if not used.
- For larger portions, use 40 lb spareribs and 1 gal Barbecue Sauce.

Variations

- **Baked Spareribs with Dressing.** Brown ribs as for Barbecued Spareribs. Pour off fat. Spread with mixture of 2 oz salt, 2 tsp pepper, 1½ tsp ground sage, 1 lb chopped apples, 2 tsp caraway seeds, 1 tsp ground cloves, and 12 oz brown sugar. Bake for 1½ hours until tender. Baste to keep moist. Serve with Bread Dressing (p. 504).
- **Baked Spareribs with Sauerkraut.** Sprinkle ribs with 2 oz seasoned salt. Brown lightly. Pour off fat. Remove ribs from pan. Add 2 No. 10 cans sauerkraut to baking pan and place ribs on top. Bake for 1 hour.
- **Barbecued Short Ribs.** Substitute beef short ribs for spareribs.
- **Sweet-Sour Spareribs.** Brown spareribs for 30 minutes in 400°F oven, or simmer in water for 1 hour. Drain and cover with Sweet-Sour Sauce (p. 696). Bake at 350°F until meat is done. Serve with Steamed Rice (p. 542) or Fried Rice with Almonds (p. 542).

SWEET-SOUR PORK

Yield: 50 portions   *Portion:* 5 oz pork + 4 oz rice

Ingredient	Amount	Procedure
Pork strips, julienne	10 lb AP (7 lb EP)	Brown pork in steam-jacketed kettle.
Water	2 qt	Add water to pork and simmer until meat is tender.
Vinegar	1¼ qt	Combine and add to pork.
Soy sauce	1½ cups	Simmer until sugar is dissolved and pineapple is hot, 10–15 minutes.
Catsup	1½ cups	
Sugar, granulated	2 lb	
Pineapple juice	1 qt	
Pineapple chunks	1 lb	
Cornstarch	8 oz	Combine to make a smooth paste.
Water	2 cups	Pour slowly into pork mixture, stirring constantly.
Ginger, ground	1½ tsp	Cook until thickened and clear.
Garlic powder	½ tsp	
Carrots, fresh, sliced	1 lb 12 oz	Steam carrots until tender-crisp.
		Add to mixture.
Snow peas	1 lb	Stir in just before serving.
Rice, converted	3 lb 8 oz	Cook rice according to directions on p. 542.
Water, boiling	4¼ qt	Serve 5 oz pork over 4 oz rice.
Salt	2 Tbsp	
Margarine or vegetable oil	2 Tbsp	

Approximate nutritive values per portion

Calories	Carbohydrate	Protein	Fat	Cholesterol	Sodium	Fiber	Iron
350 kcal	59 g	17 g	6 g	40 mg	862 mg	1 g	2 mg

Note

- Potentially hazardous food. *Food Safety Standards:* Hold food for service at an internal temperature of 135°F or above. Do not mix old product with new. Cool leftover product quickly following time standards and cooling procedures on p. 167. Reheat leftover product quickly (within 2 hours) to 165°F or above. Reheat product only once; discard if not used.

Variations

- **Sweet-Sour Beef.** Substitute beef strips for pork.
- **Sweet-Sour Chicken.** Substitute cooked chicken or turkey for the pork. Do not brown.

GLAZED BAKED HAM

Yield: 50 portions   *Portion:* 4 oz
Oven: 325°F   *Bake:* 1½–2 hours

Ingredient	Amount	Procedure
Boneless hams, fully cooked	14 lb	Place ham fat side up on a rack in roasting pan. Do not cover. Bake at 325°F for approximately 1½ hours, or until internal temperature reaches approximately 130°F. Remove ham from the oven and drain off drippings. Score ham ¼ inch deep in diamond pattern. Stud with whole cloves if desired.
Glaze (see Glaze Variations)		Brush or pour glaze on ham (approximately ½ cup per ham). Return ham to the oven and heat until browned and the internal temperature reaches 140°F. Reglaze two or three times during baking to deepen the color.

Approximate nutritive values per meat portion without glaze

Calories	Carbohydrate	Protein	Fat	Cholesterol	Sodium	Fiber	Iron
119 kcal	6 g	18 g	3 g	60 mg	1211 mg	0 g	0 mg

Notes

- Potentially hazardous food. *Food Safety Standards:* Hold food for service at an internal temperature of 135°F or above. Do not mix old product with new. Cool leftover product quickly following time standards and cooling procedures on p. 167. Reheat leftover product quickly (within 2 hours) to 165°F or above. Reheat product only once; discard if not used.
- If using a whole cured raw ham, not precooked, increase cooking time to 4–4½ hours, or simmer for 3–4 hours in a kettle, then trim, glaze, and complete cooking in the oven. Cook raw ham to an internal temperature of 160°F.

Glaze Variations

- **Apricot Glaze.** Melt 1 cup apricot preserves with ¼ cup fruit juice. Brush on ham.
- **Basic Ham Glaze.** Combine 8 oz brown sugar, 2 Tbsp cornstarch, ¼ cup corn syrup, and 2 Tbsp pineapple juice. Spoon over ham.
- **Brown Sugar Glaze.** Combine 6 oz brown sugar, 1½ tsp dry mustard, and ¼ cup cider vinegar. Brush on ham.
- **Cranberry Glaze.** Brush strained cranberry sauce on ham, approximately ½ cup per ham.
- **Honey Mustard Glaze.** Combine 1 cup honey, ½ cup Dijon mustard, ¼ cup fresh orange juice, 1 tsp dried tarragon leaves, 4 tsp balsamic vinegar, 2 tsp Worcestershire sauce, and ¼ tsp onion powder. Brush on ham or pork chops.
- **Orange Glaze.** Combine 1 cup orange marmalade and ¼ cup of fresh orange juice. Brush on ham.

HAM LOAF

Yield: 50 portions or 5 pans, 5 × 9 inches   *Portion:* 4 oz
Oven: 350°F   *Bake:* 1–1½ hours

Ingredient	Amount	Procedure
Ground cured ham	7 lb	Combine all ingredients in mixer bowl. Mix on low speed, using a flat beater, only until ingredients are blended. *Do not overmix.*
Ground fresh lean pork	7 lb	
Onion, finely chopped	4 oz	
Milk	1 qt	
Eggs, beaten	14 (1 lb 8 oz)	
Black pepper	1 tsp	
Bread crumbs	1 lb	
		Press meat mixture into five 5 × 9-inch loaf pans, 3 lb 8 oz per pan. Bake at 350°F for 1–1½ hours, or until internal temperature reaches 180°F. If desired, cover tops of loaves with glaze (see Variations) during last 30 minutes of cooking. Cut 10 slices per pan.

Approximate nutritive values per portion

Calories	Carbohydrate	Protein	Fat	Cholesterol	Sodium	Fiber	Iron
208 kcal	13 g	27 g	10 g	124 mg	1019 mg	0.3 g	2 mg

Notes

- Potentially hazardous food. *Food Safety Standards:* Hold food for service at an internal temperature of 135°F or above. Do not mix old product with new. Cool leftover product quickly following time standards and cooling procedures on p. 167. Reheat leftover product quickly (within 2 hours) to 165°F or above. Reheat product only once; discard if not used.
- Meat may be baked in 12 × 20 × 4-inch baking or counter pan. Press mixture into pan and divide into 2 loaves. Increase baking time to 1½–2 hours.
- 4 lb ground beef may be substituted for 4 lb fresh pork.
- ½ oz (¼ cup) dehydrated onion, rehydrated in ½ cup water, may be substituted for fresh onion.

Variations

- **Glazed Ham Balls.** Measure with No. 8 dipper and shape into balls. Place on baking sheets. Brush with glaze (following) and bake for 1 hour.
- **Glazed Ham Loaf.** Cover tops of loaves with a mixture of 1 lb 8 oz brown sugar, 1 cup vinegar, and 1½ Tbsp dry mustard.
- **Ham Patties with Cranberries.** Measure with No. 8 dipper and shape into patties. Spread pan with Cranberry Sauce (p. 638). Place ham patties on sauce and bake for 1 hour.
- **Ham Patties with Pineapple.** Measure with No. 8 dipper and shape into patties. Top each with slice of pineapple and a clove. Pour pineapple juice over patties and bake for 1 hour.

CREAMED HAM

Yield: 50 portions or 6¼ qt   *Portion:* 4 oz (½ cup)

Ingredient	Amount	Procedure
Margarine	1 lb	Melt margarine. Add flour and stir until smooth.
Flour, all-purpose	6 oz	Cook for 5 minutes.
Milk	1 gal	Add milk gradually, stirring constantly with a wire whip. Cook until thickened.
Ham, cooked	6 lb	Cut ham in cubes or grind coarsely.
Salt	to taste	Add to sauce and heat slowly for about 20 minutes, or until internal temperature
White pepper	½ tsp	reaches serving temperature (170–180°F). Add salt, if needed, and pepper. Serve 4 oz ham over biscuits, toast, spoon bread, corn bread, or baked potato.

Approximate nutritive values per portion

Calories	Carbohydrate	Protein	Fat	Cholesterol	Sodium	Fiber	Iron
180 kcal	11 g	12 g	14 g	33 mg	938 mg	0 g	0.5 mg

Notes

- Potentially hazardous food. *Food Safety Standards:* Hold food for service at an internal temperature of 135°F or above. Do not mix old product with new. Cool leftover product quickly following time standards and cooling procedures on p. 167. Reheat leftover product quickly (within 2 hours) to 165°F or above. Reheat product only once; discard if not used.
- 1 lb chopped celery or sliced mushrooms or 1 dozen chopped hard-cooked eggs may be added. Reduce ham to 5 lb.

Variation

- **Plantation Shortcake.** Substitute 3 lb cooked turkey for 3 lb cooked ham. Substitute Chicken Stock (p. 738) for half of milk in sauce. Add 1 lb grated cheddar cheese. Serve over hot corn bread.

OVEN-FRIED BACON

Yield: 50 portions   *Portion:* 2 slices
Oven: 400°F; convection, 325°F   *Bake:* 6–10 minutes; convection 4–6 minutes

Ingredient	Amount	Procedure
Bacon, 17–20 slices per lb	100 slices (5–6 lb)	Arrange bacon slices on baking sheets. Bake at 400°F, without turning, until crisp, about 6–10 minutes. In convection oven, cook at 325°F for 4–6 minutes. Pour off accumulating fat as necessary. Drain on paper towels or place in perforated pans for serving.

Approximate nutritive values per portion

Calories	Carbohydrate	Protein	Fat	Cholesterol	Sodium	Fiber	Iron
73 kcal	0 g	4 g	6 g	11 mg	202 mg	0 g	0.5 mg

Note

- Bacon may be purchased separated and arranged on parchment paper, ready to be placed on baking sheets and baked.

Variation

- **Oven-Fried Sausage.** Arrange 1-oz sausage patties or links on baking sheets. In conventional oven, bake at 400°F for 15–20 minutes. In convection oven, bake at 325°F for 10–12 minutes.

BREAKFAST POLENTA

Yield: 50 portions   *Portion:* 2 triangles
Griddle: 325°F

Ingredient	Amount	Procedure
Pork sausage	10 lb	Brown sausage over medium heat. Stir to prevent large pieces from forming. Drain well. Reserve for later step.
Water Salt	2½ gal 1½ oz (2½ Tbsp)	Bring water and salt to a boil.
Cornmeal	3 lb 14 oz	Add cornmeal gradually to boiling water, stirring constantly with a wire whip. Reduce heat to medium. Cook for 15 minutes, stirring often. Mixture should be stiff and will follow the whip around the kettle. Turn off heat.
Margarine Black pepper	2 oz 1 Tbsp	Stir margarine and pepper into cornmeal mixture. Add cooked sausage reserved from earlier step. Stir well to distribute the sausage evenly. Scale into oiled or food-release-sprayed 18 × 13 × 1-inch pans, 4½ lb each. Smooth with spatula. Cover with film to prevent formation of a crust. Refrigerate for at least 8 hours until set.
		Cut cold polenta 3 × 3. Then cut each square into two triangles to yield 18 triangles per pan. Grill triangles on lightly greased flat top griddle preheated to 325°F or tilting fry pan until browned.
Maple syrup	3¼ qt	Serve 2 triangles with 2 oz maple syrup.

Approximate nutritive values per portion

Calories	Carbohydrate	Protein	Fat	Cholesterol	Sodium	Fiber	Iron
492 kcal	68 g	14 g	18 g	49 mg	493 mg	3 g	2 mg

Notes

- Potentially hazardous food. *Food Safety Standards:* Hold food for service at an internal temperature of 135°F or above. Do not mix old product with new. Cool leftover product quickly following time standards and cooling procedures on p. 167. Reheat leftover product quickly (within 2 hours) to 165°F or above. Reheat product only once; discard if not used.
- Alternatively, scale into 5 × 9-inch loaf pans, 4 lb 5 oz each. Chill thoroughly before slicing into ½-inch slices. Grill as for Breakfast Polenta.

Variation

- **Fried Cornmeal Mush.** Add 2 oz salt to 2 gal water. Bring to a boil. Mix 4 lb cornmeal with 2½ qt cold water. Pour cornmeal water mixture gradually into boiling water, stirring constantly. Cook until very thick, 10–15 minutes. Scale into five greased 5 × 9-inch loaf pans, 4 lb 5 oz per pan. Cover with waxed paper to prevent formation of crust. Chill for 24 hours. Cut into ½-inch slices. Cook on greased grill preheated to 350°F. Grill until browned and crisp on both sides. Serve with warm maple syrup.

CHEESE-STUFFED HOT DOGS

Yield: 50 portions   *Portion:* 2 frankfurters
Oven: 350°F   *Bake:* 30 minutes

Ingredient	Amount	Procedure
Hot dogs, 10 per lb	10 lb	Split hot dogs lengthwise, but do not cut completely through.
Cheddar cheese	3 lb	Cut cheese into strips about 3½ inches long.
Pickle relish	1 qt	Place a strip of cheese and ½ Tbsp relish in each hot dog .
Bacon, 24–26 slices per lb	100 slices (4–5 lb)	Wrap a slice of bacon around each hot dog. Secure with a pick. Place on greased baking sheets. Bake at 350°F for 30 minutes.

Approximate nutritive values per portion

Calories	Carbohydrate	Protein	Fat	Cholesterol	Sodium	Fiber	Iron
497 kcal	9 g	21 g	42 g	86 mg	1543 mg	0 g	2 mg

Notes

- Potentially hazardous food. *Food Safety Standards:* Hold food for service at an internal temperature of 135°F or above. Do not mix old product with new. Cool leftover product quickly following time standards and cooling procedures on p. 167. Reheat leftover product quickly (within 2 hours) to 165°F or above. Reheat product only once; discard if not used.
- The names *wieners, hot dogs,* and *frankfurters* are often used interchangeably. Beef, pork, or poultry wieners are available.

Variations

- **Barbecued Hot Dogs.** Place hot dogs in counter pans. Cover with Barbecue Sauce (pp. 688, 689). Bake at 400°F for about 30 minutes. Add more sauce if necessary.
- **Chili Dog.** Serve 2 oz Chili con Carne (p. 744) over a hot dog in a hot dog bun. Chili may be made with or without beans.
- **Hot Dog and Sauerkraut.** Steam hot dogs or cook in boiling water. Serve with sauerkraut (2 No. 10 cans) that has been heated.
- **Nacho Dog.** Serve 2 oz Nacho Sauce (p. 203) over a hot dog in a hot dog bun. Sprinkle over the top one or more of the following: chopped green chiles or jalapeño peppers, chopped tomatoes, chopped black olives, or chopped onion.

CREAMED SAUSAGE AND BISCUITS

Yield: 50 portions   *Portion:* 4 oz gravy over 2 biscuits

Ingredient	Amount	Procedure
Baking Powder Biscuits (p. 231)	100	Prepare biscuits according to recipe.
Ground sausage	7 lb 8 oz AP (5 lb EP)	Cook raw sausage in tilting or large fry pan until browned and 155°F. Weight after browning should be 5 lb. Drain well. Reserve sausage for later step.
Margarine Flour	1 lb 1 lb 6 oz	Mix margarine and flour in a steam-jacketed or other large kettle. Stir with a wire whip. Cook for 10–15 minutes, stirring often.
Milk	1¾ gal	Stir milk into margarine-flour mixture, stirring constantly with a wire whip. Cook until mixture thickens.
Salt Black pepper	2 tsp 1 tsp	Add salt and pepper to creamed mixture. Stir in cooked sausage reserved from earlier step. Heat to 180–190°F.
		Serve 2 biscuits split in half with 4 oz gravy.

Approximate nutritive values per portion

Calories	Carbohydrate	Protein	Fat	Cholesterol	Sodium	Fiber	Iron
425 kcal	17 g	14 g	31 g	57 mg	586 mg	0.4 g	1 mg

Notes

- Potentially hazardous food. *Food Safety Standards:* Hold food for sercice at an internal temperature of 135°F or above. Do not mix old product with new. Cool leftover product quickly following time standards and cooling procedures on p. 167. Reheat leftover product quickly (within 2 hours) to 165°F or above. Reheat product only once; discard if not used.
- Also called Biscuits and Gravy.

SAUSAGE ROLLS

Yield: 50 rolls   *Portion:* 1 roll + 2 oz gravy
Oven: 400°F   *Bake:* 20 minutes

Ingredient	Amount	Procedure
Sausages, link	12 lb 8 oz	Partially cook sausages. Remove from fat.
Flour, all-purpose	3 lb	Make into biscuit dough, according to directions on p. 231.
Baking powder	3 oz	
Salt	3½ tsp	
Shortening	12 oz	
Milk	1 qt	
		Divide biscuit dough into two portions.
		Roll each portion ½ inch thick and cut into 3 × 4-inch rectangles.
		Place two sausages in the center of each piece of dough and fold over.
		Place seam side down on greased baking sheets.
		Bake at 400°F for 20 minutes, until bread is browned and sausage temperature is at least 170°F.
Margarine	6 oz	Melt margarine, add flour, and blend. Add salt and pepper. Cook for 5 minutes.
Flour, all-purpose	6 oz	Add water gradually, stirring constantly. Cook until smooth and thickened.
Salt	2 tsp	Ladle 2 oz gravy over each sausage roll.
Black pepper	½ tsp	
Water or chicken broth	3 qt	

Approximate nutritive values per portion

Calories	Carbohydrate	Protein	Fat	Cholesterol	Sodium	Fiber	Iron
478 kcal	26 g	18 g	33 g	64 mg	1360 mg	1 g	3 mg

Note

- Potentially hazardous food. *Food Safety Standards:* Hold food for service at an internal temperature of 135°F or above. Do not mix old product with new. Cool leftover product quickly following time standards and cooling procedures on p. 167. Reheat leftover product quickly (within 2 hours) to 165°F or above. Reheat product only once; discard if not used.

Variations

- **Italian Sausage Sandwich.** Grill fifty 5- to 6-inch-long Italian sausages. Serve one sausage in a long bun with 1 oz Sandwich Tomato Sauce (p. 527) ladled on top. Serve with sautéed green bell peppers and onions. May be sprinkled with 1 oz shredded mozzarella cheese.
- **Pigs in Blankets.** Substitute 50 wieners for link sausages. Place each wiener diagonally on dough portion and roll up. Delete gravy. May serve with Cheese Sandwich Sauce (p. 683).
- **Pigs in Blankets with Cheese.** Wrap 1 oz cheese around each wiener. Proceed as for Pigs in Blankets.

Handling Poultry Safely

Poultry is perishable and a potential carrier of illness-causing microorganisms. It should be handled with care to ensure food safety. Good handling practices include the following:

- Keeping fresh poultry refrigerated in the coldest part of the refrigerator (28–32°F). Limit the time during production that poultry is at room temperature to 30 minutes to 1 hour.

- Thawing poultry in the refrigerator. (See Table 7.4 for approximate thawing times for poultry.)

- Keeping raw poultry and raw poultry juices separate from other foods.

- Washing hands frequently and washing and sanitizing countertops, cutting boards, knives, and other utensils used in preparing raw poultry before they come in contact with other raw or cooked foods.

Time and Temperature Timetables and Guidelines

TABLE 15.1   Cooking methods for poultry

Kind of poultry	Class	Average ready-to-cook weight (pounds)	Cookery method	Per-person allowance, ready-to-cook weight (ounces)
Chicken	Broiler-fryer	3–4½	Fry, broil, grill, roast	¼–½ bird
	Roaster	5–8	Roast	12–16
	Breast, boneless		Grill, broil	5–6
Turkey	Whole	8–24	Roast	12–16
	Roast, boned and tied	12	Roast	5–6
	Roll, ready to cook	3–6	Roast	5–6
	Cutlet		Grill, broil	
	Steaks	¼–½	Grill, broil	
	Tenderloin		Grill, broil	
	Wings		Roast, broil	
	Drumsticks		Roast, broil	
Duck		3–7	Roast	12–16
Goose		6–12	Roast	12–16

Notes • For cooked yields for chicken and turkey, see pp. 66–67.
  • For additional information on amounts of poultry to purchase, see Table 4.1.
  • For roasting times, see Table 15.2. For broiling and grilling times, see Broiling or Grilling, p. 146.

TABLE 15.2   Roasting guide for poultry (defrosted)

Kind of poultry	Ready-to-cook weight (pounds)	Approximate total roasting time at 325°F	Internal temperature of poultry when done (°F)
Chicken, whole roasters	$2\frac{1}{2}$–4	$1\frac{1}{2}$ hr	170–175°F
Ducks	3–7	1–2 hr	170–175°F
Geese	6–8	$2\frac{1}{2}$–$3\frac{1}{2}$ hr	170–175°F
	8–12	$3\frac{1}{2}$–$4\frac{1}{2}$ hr	170–175°F
Turkeys, whole, thawed	7–12	$2\frac{1}{2}$–3 hr	170–175°F
	12–16	3–$3\frac{1}{2}$ hr	170–175°F
	16–20	$3\frac{1}{2}$–4 hr	170–175°F
	20–24	4–$4\frac{1}{2}$ hr	170–175°F
	24–30	$4\frac{1}{2}$–5 hr	170–175°F
Turkey, breast and breast portions	4–6	$1\frac{1}{2}$–$2\frac{1}{4}$ hr	170
	6–8	$2\frac{1}{4}$–$3\frac{1}{4}$ hr	170
Turkey roast, boneless	3–10	35–45 min per pound	170
Turkey tenderloin		18–30 min at 400°F	170
Turkey wings, drumsticks, wing drummettes, thighs		1–$1\frac{3}{4}$ hr	170–175°F

Notes • Thermometer is inserted in thigh muscle of whole turkeys and in center of turkey roasts. The thermometer should not touch bone.
• The FDA Food Code specifies that poultry must measure 165°F in all parts to be safe. Bone-in poultry is more difficult to cook to a consistent 165°F temperature. If using an ovenproof thermometer, place it in the whole poultry at the start of the cooking cycle. For turkey breasts, place thermometer in the thickest part. For whole turkeys or whole chickens, place in the thickest part of the inner thigh. Once the thigh has reached 165°F, check the wing and the thickest part of the breast to ensure that the chicken or turkey has reached a safe minimum internal temperature of 165°F throughout. Do not rely on pop-up thermometers that are often inserted in the breast of whole turkeys.
• Consumers may prefer whole bird or bone-in poultry cooked to a slightly higher temperature (170–175°F). Poultry cooked to this higher temperature may be less moist.

1. Place chicken, breast side up, on cutting board. Cut skin between thigh and body, near the thigh joint.
2. Bend legs backward until bones break at hip joints. Remove leg-thigh from carcass by cutting between the joints.
3. Separate thighs and drumsticks. Locate knee joint by bending thigh and leg together. With skin side down, cut through joints of each leg.
4. With chicken on back, remove wings by cutting inside of wing just over joint. Pull wing away from body and cut top down through joint.
5. Separate breast and back by placing chicken on its breast and cutting along backbone from bird's tail to head. (Pictures (5) and (6) show splitting a chicken with wings and legs intact. Remove legs and wings as described in steps above when cutting a chicken in pieces. Leave wings and legs on when splitting a chicken in half.)
6. Lay bird flat and remove backbone by cutting through ribs connecting it to breast. May also separate breast and back by placing chicken on back and cutting (toward board) through joints along each side of rib cage.
7. Split the breast by putting skin side down and cutting in half. May cut wishbone from the breast.

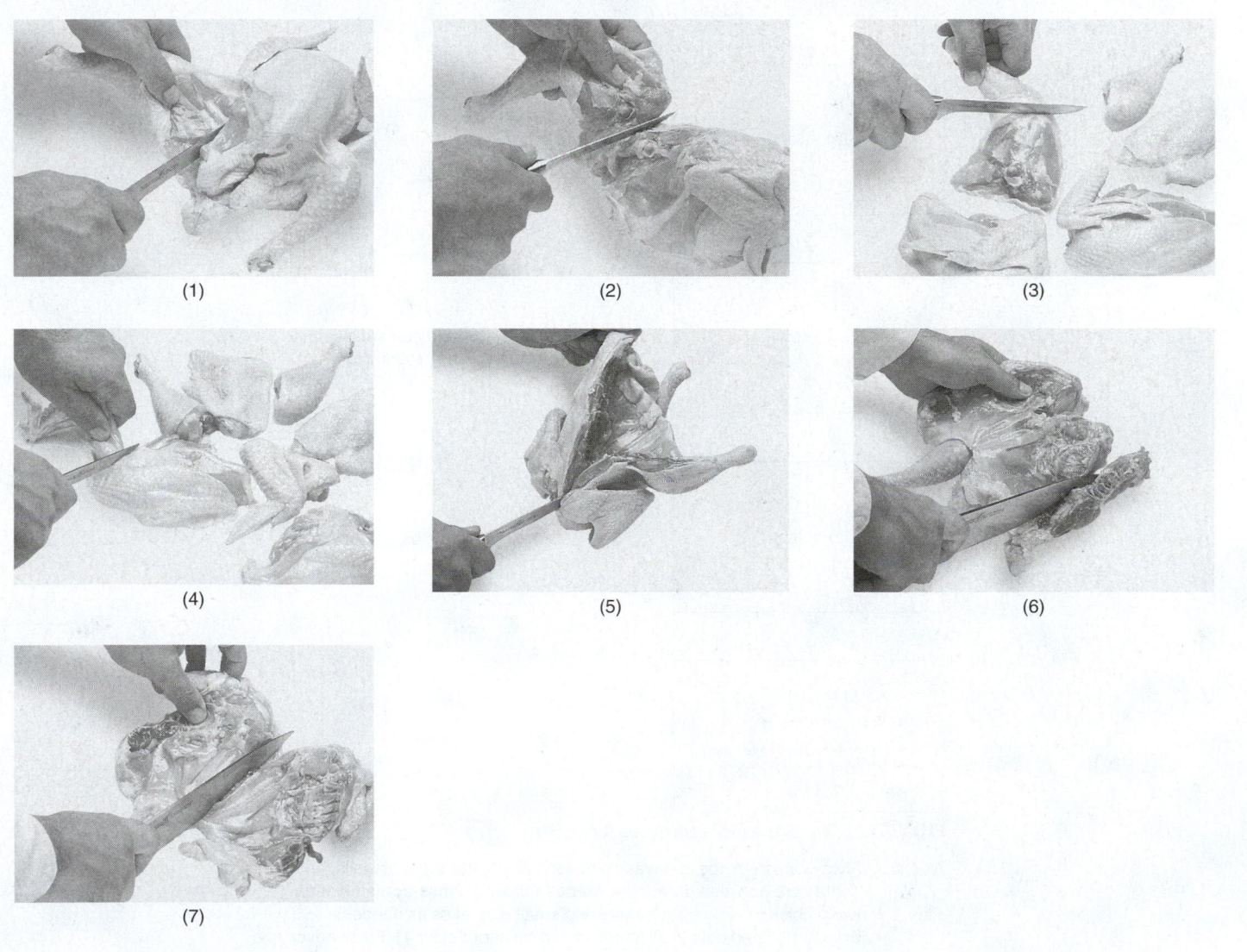

(1)   (2)   (3)

(4)   (5)   (6)

(7)

FIGURE 15.1   Cutting up a whole chicken.

Arrange work station in the order shown in the diagram.

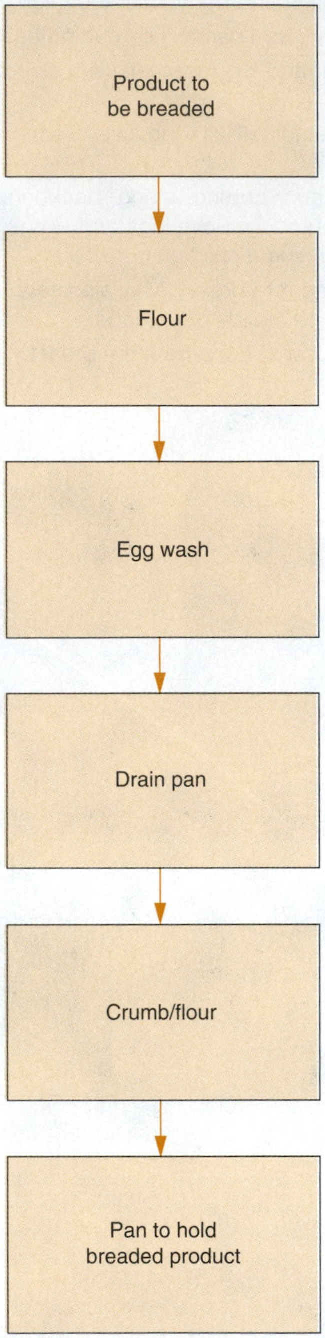

Product to be breaded	1. Thaw chicken pieces.
Flour	2. Dredge chicken with seasoned flour. See Table 6.5 for amounts of breading ingredients.
Egg wash	3. Dip in egg-milk mixture.
Drain pan	4. Drain. A perforated pan set inside a solid counter pan is satisfactory.
Crumb/flour	5. Roll chicken in crumbs.
Pan to hold breaded product	6. Place on baking sheet.

FIGURE 15.2   Breading techniques for poultry.

Notes: • Always wash hands and wash and sanitize countertops, utensils, and containers between production steps to prevent cross-contamination.
• Keep chicken refrigerated, removing small quantities as needed.
• Breading ingredients in all steps should be kept below 41°F whenever possible and discarded after being held above 41°F for 2 hours.

Poultry Recipes

FRICASSEE OF CHICKEN

Yield: 50 portions   *Portion:* 3 oz cooked meat
Oven: 325°F   *Bake:* 1½–2 hours

Ingredient	Amount	Procedure
Chicken legs, thighs, breasts	40 lb AP	Mix flour and seasonings. Dredge chicken pieces with seasoned flour.
Flour, all-purpose	12 oz	
Salt	2 Tbsp	
White pepper	1 tsp	
Shortening	1 lb	Brown chicken in hot shortening. Remove to roasting pan and just cover with boiling water. Bake at 325°F, adding more water if necessary, until chicken is tender, 1½–2 hours.
Margarine	10 oz	When tender, remove chicken from stock.
Flour, all-purpose	6 oz	Make gravy, using liquid in which chicken was cooked
Chicken broth	3½ qt	(see p. 738). Serve over chicken.

Approximate nutritive values per portion

Calories	Carbohydrate	Protein	Fat	Cholesterol	Sodium	Fiber	Iron
618 kcal	8 g	75 g	31 g	279 mg	1108 mg	0.4 g	10 mg

Notes

- Potentially hazardous food. *Food Safety Standards:* Hold food for service at an internal temperature of 135°F or above. Do not mix old product with new. Cool leftover product quickly following time standards and cooling procedures on p. 167. Reheat leftover product quickly (within 2 hours) to 165°F or above. Reheat product only once; discard if not used.
- Always wash hands and wash and sanitize countertops, utensils, and containers between production steps when preparing raw poultry.

Variation

- **Chicken Tahitian.** Use chicken quarters. Melt 12 oz shortening in baking pans. Arrange chicken in pans in single layer. Brown in 425°F oven for 30 minutes. Brush chicken with mixture of two 12-oz cans undiluted frozen orange juice, 1 lb melted margarine, 2 Tbsp ground ginger, and 2 Tbsp soy sauce. Bake at 325°F for 30–40 minutes, basting as needed until chicken is glazed. Serve with Steamed Rice (p. 542) and garnish with slivered almonds and avocado wedges.

GRILLED CHICKEN BREAST

Yield: 50 portions   *Portion:* 6 oz
Griddle: 325°F

Ingredient	Amount	Procedure
Chicken breasts, boneless, skinless	19 lb	Heat griddle to 325°F. Oil generously.
Seasoning rub or marinade or salt and black pepper (see Variations)	p. 720	Season chicken. Place chicken breasts on hot griddle. Brown on both sides, turning once. Cook to an internal temperature of 165°F. Hold for service at or above 140°F.

Approximate nutritive values per chicken portion without added seasonings or accompaniments

Calories	Carbohydrate	Protein	Fat	Cholesterol	Sodium	Fiber	Iron
233 kcal	0 g	26 g	14 g	57 mg	67 mg	0 g	1 mg

Notes

- Potentially hazardous food. *Food Safety Standards:* Hold food for service at an internal temperature of 135°F or above. Do not mix old product with new. Cool leftover product quickly following time standards and cooling procedures on p. 167. Reheat leftover product quickly (within 2 hours) to 165°F or above. Reheat product only once; discard if not used.
- Always wash hands and wash and sanitize countertops, utensils, and containers between production steps when preparing raw poultry.

Variations

- **Blackened Chicken.** Rub chicken with Cajun Seasoning (p. 727) before grilling.
- **Chicken Breast Dijon.** In baker's bowl, mix 2⅔ cups honey, 2 cups Dijon mustard, 1½ cups fresh or reconstituted frozen lemon juice, 1½ tsp dried tarragon leaves, and ¾ cup Worcestershire sauce. Brush glaze over chicken breasts during last few minutes of grilling.
- **Chicken Breast with Grilled Tomato Sauce.** Sauté 2 Tbsp minced garlic in 1½ cups vegetable oil until fragrant but not browned. Add 5 lb 12 oz firm tomatoes, diced, and 1½ Tbsp granulated sugar. Sauté 2 minutes until heated. Add ⅓ cup red wine vinegar, 1½ Tbsp salt, 2 Tbsp black pepper, and ½ cup snipped fresh parsley. Toss lightly. Ladle 2 oz sauce over cooked chicken breast.
- **Curried Chicken Breast.** In baker's bowl, blend 1 qt vegetable oil, 2⅔ cups fresh or reconstituted frozen lemon juice, 6 oz curry powder, 3 oz minced garlic, ½ tsp cayenne, and ½ tsp ground cumin. Place chicken breasts in marinade and turn so all surfaces are covered. Cover and refrigerate for several hours or overnight. Drain. Grill as for Grilled Chicken Breast.
- **Herb-Marinated Chicken Breast.** In baker's bowl, mix 2½ cups red wine vinegar, 2 tsp dried rosemary leaves, ¼ tsp ground thyme, 3 Tbsp minced garlic, 2 Tbsp salt, and 1 qt vegetable oil. Place chicken breasts in marinade and turn so all surfaces are covered. Cover and refrigerate for several hours or overnight. Drain. Grill as for Grilled Chicken Breast.
- **Sesame Mustard Chicken.** Prepare sauce by combining in steam-jacketed kettle or saucepan 1½ qt water, 2¾ cups cider vinegar, ¼ cup cooking sherry, 1 lb 4 oz granulated sugar, ¾ cup soy sauce, 2 oz dry mustard, 1 tsp turmeric, 1 oz toasted sesame seeds, 2 oz cornstarch, and 5 tsp sesame oil. Heat to boiling, stirring constantly, until thickened. Ladle 2 oz sauce over cooked chicken breast.
- **Tarragon Chicken.** Follow recipe for Lime Tarragon Turkey Steaks, p. 501. Substitute chicken breasts for turkey. Grill as for Grilled Chicken Breast.

CHICKEN CACCIATORE

Yield: 50 portions   *Portion:* 1 chicken breast with sauce
Oven: 325°F   *Bake:* 50–60 minutes

Ingredient	Amount	Procedure
Onion powder	2 Tbsp	Mix seasonings. Divide into two bowls, one with ¼ of the amount and one with ¾ of the amount.
Garlic, granulated	2 Tbsp	
Oregano, dried	2 Tbsp	Reserve both bowls for later steps.
Basil, dried	2 Tbsp	
Salt	2 Tbsp	
Black pepper	2 Tbsp	
Olive oil	¾ cup	Heat olive oil in steam-jacketed or other large kettle. Add vegetables and cook until vegetables are tender.
Onion, chopped	4 oz	
Diced bell peppers (combination of green, red, and yellow)	6 lb 4 oz	Stir in the ¼ portion of the seasonings reserved from earlier step.
Fresh mushrooms, sliced	3 lb 4 oz	
Chopped tomatoes, canned	1¾ gal	Stir tomatoes, tomato paste, vinegar, and cooking wine into the vegetables.
Tomato paste	3 lb	
Balsamic vinegar	4 oz	
White cooking wine	3 cups	Reserve sauce for later step.
Chicken breasts, boneless, skinless, 6 oz	50	Sprinkle chicken breasts with the reserved ¾ portion of the seasoning. Heat oil to 350°F in a tilting or other fry pan. Brown chicken breasts. When browned, shingle two rows of 8–9 breasts into three 12 × 20 × 2-inch pans.
Salad oil	1½ cups	Scale 9 lb of sauce reserved from earlier step over each pan of chicken. Cover and bake at 325°F for 50–60 minutes, until chicken reaches 165°F.

Approximate nutritive values per portion

Calories	Carbohydrate	Protein	Fat	Cholesterol	Sodium	Fiber	Iron
359 kcal	18 g	38 g	14 g	94 mg	833 mg	4 g	3.5 mg

Notes

- Potentially hazardous food. *Food Safety Standards:* Hold food for service at an internal temperature of 135°F or above. Do not mix old product with new. Cool leftover product quickly following time standards and cooling procedures on p. 167. Reheat leftover product quickly (within 2 hours) to 165°F or above. Reheat product only once; discard if not used.
- Always wash hands and wash and sterilize countertops, utensils, and containers between production steps when preparing raw poultry.

CHEESE-STUFFED CHICKEN BREAST

Yield: 50 portions   *Portion:* 5–7 oz
Oven: 375°F   *Bake:* 15 minutes, 30 minutes

Ingredient	Amount	Procedure
Chicken breasts, boneless, skinless 4–6 oz	50	Flatten chicken breasts and sprinkle with salt and pepper. (Keep chicken refrigerated, removing small quantities as needed for production.)
Salt	2 Tbsp	
Black pepper	2 Tbsp	
Butter or margarine, softened	1 lb 8 oz	Mix together butter and seasonings. Spread each chicken breast with 1 tsp seasoned butter (save remaining seasoned butter for later step).
Oregano, dried, crumbled	2½ tsp	
Marjoram, dried, crumbled	1 Tbsp	
Fresh parsley, chopped	½ oz	
Swiss cheese	1 lb 8 oz	Cut cheese into ½-oz strips and roll inside each piece of chicken.
Flour, all-purpose	1 lb	Roll each chicken breast in flour, then egg, then crumbs.
Eggs, beaten	12 (1 lb 4 oz)	Place in 12 × 20 × 2-inch pans.
Bread crumbs, dry	2 lb	Bake at 375°F for 15 minutes until internal temperature reaches 165°F.
Dry white wine	3 cups	Heat wine with seasoned butter reserved from earlier step. Pour over chicken and bake for 30 minutes. Baste occasionally.

Approximate nutritive values per portion

Calories	Carbohydrate	Protein	Fat	Cholesterol	Sodium	Fiber	Iron
403 kcal	16 g	31 g	22 g	146 mg	571 mg	1 g	2 mg

Notes

- Potentially hazardous food. *Food Safety Standards:* Hold food for service at an internal temperature of 135°F or above. Do not mix old product with new. Cool leftover product quickly following time standards and cooling procedures on p. 167. Reheat leftover product quickly (within 2 hours) to 165°F or above. Reheat product only once; discard if not used.
- Always wash hands and wash and sanitize countertops, utensils, and containers between production steps when preparing raw poultry.
- Monterey Jack cheese may be substituted for Swiss.

Variation

- **Cheese-Stuffed Chicken with Tomato Basil Sauce.** Sauté 8 oz chopped onion and 3 Tbsp minced garlic in ½ cup olive oil. Add 2 cups white wine and cook to reduce, approximately 5 minutes. Add 8 lb EP fresh tomatoes that have been peeled, seeded, and diced, along with 4 oz chopped fresh green onion, 1½ oz chopped fresh basil, and ½ tsp salt. Stir gently and briefly, 2–3 minutes. A mixture of chopped fresh herbs may be used. Choose from basil, marjoram, tarragon, thyme, and fennel. Serve 3 oz sauce over cooked chicken breast. Chicken and sauce may be served with pasta, rice, or couscous. A good-quality marinara sauce can be substituted for the Tomato Basil Sauce.

PAN-FRIED CHICKEN

Yield: 50 portions   *Portion:* 8–12 oz AP

Ingredient	Amount	Procedure
Chicken legs, thighs, breasts, bone-in	40 lb	Keep chicken refrigerated, removing small quantities as needed for preparation.
Flour, all-purpose Salt Paprika or poultry seasoning Black pepper	1 lb 2 Tbsp 1 Tbsp 1 tsp	Mix flour and seasonings. Dredge chicken pieces with seasoned flour.
Shortening	1 lb	Brown chicken in hot shortening, ½ inch deep in pan. Reduce heat and cook slowly until tender, 45–60 minutes or until internal temperature reaches 170°F. Turn for even browning.

Approximate nutritive values per portion

Calories	Carbohydrate	Protein	Fat	Cholesterol	Sodium	Fiber	Iron
644 kcal	13 g	64 g	36 g	192 mg	432 mg	0.3 g	3 mg

Notes

- Potentially hazardous food. *Food Safety Standards:* Hold food for service at an internal temperature of 135°F or above. Do not mix old product with new. Cool leftover product quickly following time standards and cooling procedures on p. 167. Reheat leftover product quickly (within 2 hours) to 165°F or above. Reheat product only once; discard if not used.
- Always wash hands and wash and sanitize countertops, utensils, and containers between production steps when preparing raw poultry.
- Chicken may be browned in a skillet, then placed in counter pans or baking pan, skin side up, and finished in the oven at 325°F for 20–30 minutes.

Variations

- **Chicken Cacciatore.** Brown chicken as above. Arrange in two 12 × 20 × 4-inch counter pans. Sauté 1 lb 8 oz coarsely diced onions and 2 minced garlic cloves in 5 oz margarine. Add 1 lb 8 oz green bell peppers cut into strips, 2 lb sliced mushrooms, 1 No. 10 can diced tomatoes with juice, ½ tsp oregano, ½ tsp thyme, and 1 qt Chicken Stock (p. 738). Thicken with 4 oz flour mixed with 2 cups cold water. Pour over chicken, 3½ qt per pan. Cover with aluminum foil. Bake at 325°F for 1 hour.
- **Chicken Cantonese.** Flour chicken and brown as above. Place in 12 × 20 × 2-inch counter pans. Cover with aluminum foil. Bake at 350°F for approximately 1 hour. Before serving, cover with sauce made of 3 qt pineapple juice, 3 qt orange juice, 12 oz flour, 3 lb pineapple cubes, 12 oranges peeled and diced, 1 lb 4 oz almonds slivered and browned, 2 tsp nutmeg, and 2 tsp salt. Combine juice and flour; cook until thickened. Add seasonings, fruit, and almonds. Pour over chicken. Bake uncovered for about 10 minutes. Serve with cooked rice.
- **Deep-Fat Fried Chicken.** Use 1¾–2 lb broiler-fryers, cut in serving pieces, or chicken quarters. Dredge in seasoned flour as for Pan-Fried Chicken; or dredge in flour, dip in egg and milk mixture (3 eggs to 1 cup milk), and roll in crumbs (12 oz); or dip in batter (p. 156). Fry in deep fat at 325°F for 12–15 minutes or until golden brown and cooked through. For larger fryers, brown in deep fat, drain, then place in baking pans and finish in the oven at 325°F for 20–30 minutes.
- **Southern Fried Chicken.** Dip chicken pieces in buttermilk, then dredge in flour seasoned with salt and pepper. Refrigerate chicken for 30 minutes. Dredge chicken in flour again and pan-fry as for Pan-Fried Chicken.

OVEN-FRIED CHICKEN

Yield: 50 portions   *Portion:* 1 chicken quarter or 2 pieces
Oven: 350°F   *Bake:* 1 hour

Ingredient	Amount	Procedure
Flour, all-purpose	1 lb	Mix flour and seasonings.
Nonfat dry milk	8 oz	Dredge chicken with seasoned flour.
Salt	2 Tbsp	Place in single layer on greased or parchment-lined baking sheets.
Paprika	1 Tbsp	
Black pepper	1 tsp	
Chicken quarters or chicken	50	
breasts and thighs	100	
Margarine, melted	1 lb	Brush chicken with melted margarine. Bake at 350°F for 1 hour or until chicken is browned and tender and internal temperature reaches 170°F.

Approximate nutritive values per portion

Calories	Carbohydrate	Protein	Fat	Cholesterol	Sodium	Fiber	Iron
500 kcal	9 g	61 g	23 g	167 mg	504 mg	0 g	3 mg

Notes

- Potentially hazardous food. *Food Safety Standards:* Hold food for service at an internal temperature of 135°F or above. Do not mix old product with new. Cool leftover product quickly following time standards and cooling procedures on p. 167. Reheat leftover product quickly (within 2 hours) to 165°F or above. Reheat product only once; discard if not used.
- Always wash hands and wash and sanitize countertops, utensils, and containers between production steps when preparing raw poultry.
- Chicken may be breaded. See Table 6.5 for coatings and Figure 15.2 for procedures.

Variations

- **Barbecued Chicken.** Brown chicken at 425°F for 20–30 minutes. Reduce heat to 325°F. Pour 1½ gal Cooked Barbecue Sauce (p. 688) over chicken. Bake for 40–45 minutes.
- **Chicken Parmesan.** Combine 1 lb flour, 1 oz salt, ½ tsp black pepper, and ¾ cup Parmesan cheese. Dredge chicken pieces in flour mixture, then dip in mixture of 12 (1 lb 5 oz) eggs and 1 qt milk, then back into flour mixture. Arrange chicken on greased or parchment-paper-lined baking sheets. Drizzle lemon butter (8 oz melted butter or margarine and ¼ cup fresh lemon or lime juice) over chicken. Bake at 325°F for 1 hour. Use drippings from baking sheets for gravy.
- **Chicken Teriyaki.** Marinate chicken overnight in a marinade of 3 cups soy sauce, 10 oz brown sugar, 1½ Tbsp garlic powder, and 1½ Tbsp ground ginger. Arrange chicken pieces in single layer on greased or parchment-paper-lined baking sheets. Bake at 350°F for 30 minutes. Remove from oven. Brush chicken with remaining marinade and bake until tender, about 30 minutes. 1 cup orange juice or pineapple juice may be added to the marinade.
- **Herb Baked Chicken.** Combine 1 lb 8 oz dry bread crumbs, 8 oz flour, 1½ oz salt, 1 Tbsp paprika, 1½ tsp onion salt, 1 tsp garlic salt, 1 Tbsp rosemary, and ¾ cup vegetable oil. Dredge chicken with crumb mixture. Place on parchment-paper-lined 18 × 26 × 1-inch baking sheets. Bake at 350°F for 1 hour.
- **Italian Baked Chicken.** Melt 3 lb butter. Dip chicken in melted margarine, then roll in coating mixture of 3 lb dry bread crumbs, 1 cup chopped fresh parsley, 2 Tbsp paprika, 1 Tbsp salt, 3 Tbsp garlic salt, 2 Tbsp crumbled dried oregano, 1½ tsp crumbled dried basil, 1 tsp black pepper, and 12 oz grated Parmesan cheese. Place in shallow baking pans with skin side up. Bake at 350°F for 1 hour.

CHICKEN BREAST PARMESAN

Yield: 50   *Portion:* 6 oz
Oven: 350°F   *Bake:* 30 minutes

Ingredient	Amount	Procedure
Oil	2 cups	Mix oil with mustard in a baker's bowl.
Grey Poupon mustard	4 oz	
Dry bread crumbs	2 lb	Blend bread crumbs, cheese, parsley, and basil in a second baker's bowl.
Shredded Parmesan cheese	1 lb 10 oz	
Parsley, dried	⅔ cup	
Basil, dried	2 Tbsp	
Chicken breasts, boneless, skinless	19 lb	Coat chicken breasts lightly in mustard mixture. Dredge in bread crumb mixture. Place 24 breasts on a lightly oiled 18 × 26 × 1-inch pan. Bake at 350°F for 30 minutes or until the internal temperature reaches 165°F.

Approximate nutritive values per portion

Calories	Carbohydrate	Protein	Fat	Cholesterol	Sodium	Fiber	Iron
389 kcal	8 g	31 g	26 g	66 mg	419 mg	0.4 g	1.6 mg

Note

- Potentially hazardous food. *Food Safety Standards:* Hold food for service at an internal temperature of 135°F or above. Do not mix old product with new. Cool leftover product quickly following time standards and cooling procedures on p. 167. Reheat leftover product quickly (within 2 hours) to 165°F or above. Reheat product only once; discard if not used.

Variation

- **Chicken Parmesan with Marinara Sauce.** Ladle 2 oz marinara sauce on chicken before serving.

ORANGE-GLAZED CORNISH GAME HENS

Yield: 50   *Portion:* 16 oz (1 hen)
Oven: 325°F   *Bake:* 1½–1¾ hours

Ingredient	Amount	Procedure
Cornish game hens	50	Wash hens inside and out. Remove packaged giblets. Place 4 × 4 in 18 × 26 × 2-inch pans.
Butter or margarine, melted	1 lb 8 oz	Brush hens with melted butter. Bake at 325°F for 1½–1¾ hours or until internal temperature reaches 180°F; follow glazing instructions that follow.
Orange juice, frozen, undiluted	2 cups	Blend together juice concentrate, syrup, and marmalade. Brush over poultry 30 minutes before end of roasting time and again 15 minutes before end of roasting time.
Corn syrup, light	2¼ cups	
Orange marmalade	12 oz	

Approximate nutritive values per portion

Calories	Carbohydrate	Protein	Fat	Cholesterol	Sodium	Fiber	Iron
559 kcal	19 g	59 g	26 g	211 mg	298 mg	0 g	3 mg

Notes

- Potentially hazardous food. *Food Safety Standards:* Hold food for service at an internal temperature of 135°F or above. Do not mix old product with new. Cool leftover product quickly following time standards and cooling procedures on p. 167. Reheat leftover product quickly (within 2 hours) to 165°F or above. Reheat product only once; discard if not used.
- Always wash hands and wash and sanitize countertops, utensils, and containers between production steps when preparing raw poultry.
- Other glazes may be substituted for orange glaze. See p. 468 for apricot, brown sugar, and honey glazes.

WHOLE ROASTED TURKEY

Yield: 50 servings   *Portion:* 6 oz
Oven: 325°F (see Note)

Ingredient	Amount	Procedure
Whole turkeys, thawed	40 lb	Remove giblets and neck from body and neck cavities of turkeys (see Note). Rinse inside and outside of turkeys with cold water. Pat dry. Sprinkle salt and pepper inside cavity. Tuck wing tips under shoulders of turkeys if desired. Place 2 turkeys, breast side up, in each 18 × 26 × 2-inch pan (see Note).
Oil	2 oz	Brush turkey breasts with oil. Roast at 325°F. Tent loosely with aluminum foil if browning too quickly. Safe when cooked to an internal temperature of 165°F when checked with a food thermometer in the innermost part of the thigh and thickest part of the breast. For reasons of customer preference, turkeys may be cooked to a temperature higher than 165°F but not more than 180°F. (See Note for roasting timetable.) Remove from oven, tent with foil, and let stand for 15 minutes before carving.

Approximate nutritive values per portion (½ white and ½ dark meat)

Calories	Carbohydrate	Protein	Fat	Cholesterol	Sodium	Fiber	Iron
312 kcal	0 g	33 g	11 g	186 mg	114 mg	0 g	3 mg

Notes

- Potentially hazardous food. *Food Safety Standards:* Hold food for service at an internal temperature of 135°F or above. Do not mix old product with new. Cool leftover product quickly following time standards and cooling procedures on p. 167. Reheat leftover product quickly (within 2 hours) to 165°F or above. Reheat product only once; discard if not used.
- Thaw turkey in the refrigerator (40°F or below). Allow approximately 24 hours for every 5 lb. Thaw turkey in its original wrapper and on a tray or pan to catch any juices.
- Pop-up thermometers inserted in the breast of some turkeys by the processor may be unreliable.
- Cooking turkey breast side down adds moistness to the breast but yields a less attractive whole bird.
- Giblets and neck may be simmered in water to make stock for gravy or dressing. Chop giblets and add to gravy for Giblet Gravy.
- Cook stuffing outside the turkey. For food safety reasons, cooking stuffing inside the turkey is not recommended.
- Whole turkey roasting timetable (325°F)

4½–7 lb	2–2½ hr	18–22 lb	3½–4 hr
7–9 lb	2½–3 hr	22–24 lb	4–4½ hr
9–18 lb	3–3½ hr	24–30 lb	4½–5 hr

CHICKEN AND BROCCOLI STIR-FRY

Yield: 50 portions   *Portion:* 4 oz chicken and broccoli + 4 oz rice

Ingredient	Amount	Procedure
Water, cold	4½ qt	Prepare sauce by blending together the liquids, spices, and cornstarch.
Soy sauce	2⅔ cup	Stir with a wire whip until well blended.
Chicken base	1½ oz	Cook over medium heat until thick and translucent. Stir often during cooking.
Ginger, ground	1 Tbsp	
Garlic, minced	2 oz	Keep hot (above 165°F). Save for later step.
Crushed red pepper	¼ tsp	
Sesame oil	4 oz	
Cornstarch	7 oz	
Fresh ginger, thinly sliced,	1 tsp	Sauté ginger and garlic in hot oil for 2–3 minutes, until softened.
Garlic, minced	1 tsp	Add chicken and cook until done, 165°F, stirring often during cooking.
Vegetable oil	½ cup	
Chicken, raw, cut in strips	6 lb	
Sliced water chestnuts, canned, drained	2 lb EP	Add water chestnuts and mushrooms to the cooked chicken. Stir-fry until mushrooms are softened.
Fresh mushrooms, sliced	1 lb EP	Add Chinese cabbage, broccoli, and onions. Stir-fry for an
Chinese cabbage, 1-inch slices	2 lb EP	additional 2–3 minutes, until vegetables are barely tender.
Broccoli florets	1 lb 8 oz EP	Pour hot sauce reserved from earlier step over chicken-vegetable mixture.
Green onions, 1-inch slices	6 oz EP	
Rice, converted	3 lb 8 oz	Cook rice according to directions on p. 542.
Water, boiling	4¼ qt	Serve 4 oz chicken-vegetable mixture over 4 oz rice.
Salt	2 Tbsp	
Vegetable oil	2 Tbsp	

Approximate nutritive values per portion

Calories	Carbohydrate	Protein	Fat	Cholesterol	Sodium	Fiber	Iron
275 kcal	35 g	16 g	7 g	38 mg	1300 mg	2 g	2 mg

Notes

- Potentially hazardous food. *Food Safety Standards:* Hold food for service at an internal temperature above 135°F. Do not mix old product with new. Cool leftover product quickly, following time standards and cooling procedures on page 167. Reheat leftover product quickly (within 2 hours) to 165°F. Reheat product only once; discard if not used.
- Always wash hands and wash and sanitize countertops, utensils, and containers between production steps when preparing raw poultry.

Variations

- **Beef and Broccoli Stir-Fry.** Substitute beef strips for chicken, and beef base for chicken base. Reduce water chestnuts to 1 lb 8 oz and Chinese cabbage to 1 lb 6 oz. Increase broccoli to 3 lb and mushrooms to 1 lb.
- **Chicken and Vegetable Stir-Fry.** Follow recipe for Chicken and Broccoli Stir-Fry. Use a total of 7 lb assorted vegetables. Select from broccoli florets, carrots, Chinese cabbage, mushrooms, water chestnuts, onions (green or mature), snow peas, or sugar snap peas.
- **Pork Stir-Fry.** Substitute pork loin strips for chicken.
- **Tofu Stir-Fry.** Delete chicken. Just before serving, gently stir in 3 lb diced (¼-inch) tofu. Substitute vegetable base for chicken base if desired.
- **Vegetable Stir-Fry.** Delete chicken. Increase vegetables to 12 lb. Select from bell peppers (any color), broccoli florets, carrots, cauliflower florets, Chinese cabbage, mushrooms, water chestnuts, onions (green or mature), snow peas, sugar snap peas, summer squash, or zucchini.

CHICKEN AND SNOW PEAS OVER RICE

Yield: 50 portions   *Portion:* 4 oz sauce + 4 oz rice

Ingredient	Amount	Procedure
Sugar, granulated	2 Tbsp	Combine in steam-jacketed kettle or saucepan.
Cornstarch	8 oz	
Black pepper	1¼ tsp	
Ginger, ground	1¼ tsp	
Garlic powder	¼ tsp	
Water	1¼ gal	Stir in water, soy sauce, and chicken base.
Soy sauce	¾ cup	Cook until clear and thickened.
Chicken base	4 oz	Turn off heat. Cover and keep warm.
Chicken strips or cubes, raw	12 lb 8 oz	Stir-fry chicken in hot oil until lightly browned and cooked through to an internal temperature of 165°F. Drain off any liquid.
Green onions, sliced	6 oz	Add chicken and vegetables to reserved sauce.
Mushrooms, canned, drained	1 lb 10 oz	Cook for about 1 minute until snow peas are hot.
Snow peas, frozen	2 lb 12 oz	
Rice, converted	3 lb 8 oz	Cook rice according to directions on p. 542.
Water	4¼ qt	Serve 4 oz sauce over 4 oz cooked rice.
Salt	2 Tbsp	
Margarine	2 Tbsp	

Approximate nutritive values per portion

Calories	Carbohydrate	Protein	Fat	Cholesterol	Sodium	Fiber	Iron
311 kcal	37 g	24 g	7 g	55 mg	1047 mg	1 g	2 mg

Notes

- Potentially hazardous food. *Food Safety Standards:* Hold food for service at an internal temperature of 135°F or above. Do not mix old product with new. Cool leftover product quickly following time standards and cooling procedures on p. 167. Reheat leftover product quickly (within 2 hours) to 165°F or above. Reheat product only once; discard if not used.
- Always wash hands and wash and sanitize countertops, utensils, and containers between production steps when preparing raw poultry.

SZECHWAN CHICKEN WITH CASHEWS

Yield: 50 portions   *Portion:* 6 oz chicken + 4 oz rice

Ingredient	Amount	Procedure
Vegetable oil	1 cup	Heat oil in steam-jacketed kettle. Add ginger and garlic and cook until
Fresh ginger, sliced	3 oz EP	translucent. Remove ginger and discard.
Garlic, minced	3 oz EP	
Chicken strips, raw (unbreaded)	6 lb	Add chicken to hot oil. Stir-fry to 165°F.
Green onions, 1-inch lengths	1 lb 8 oz EP	Add onions and peppers to chicken. Stir-fry for 1–2 minutes.
Green bell peppers, 1-inch dice	3 lb 8 oz EP	
Mushrooms, canned, drained (reserve juice)	3 lb 8 oz EP	Drain mushrooms and water chestnuts. (Reserve mushroom liquid.) Add mushrooms and water chestnuts to chicken-vegetable mixture.
Sliced water chestnuts, canned, drained	12 oz EP	Stir-fry until hot, 1–2 minutes. Reserve for later step (keep hot, above 140°F).
Mushroom liquid plus water	2 qt	Combine liquids, chicken base, cornstarch, and pepper. Mix until smooth.
Soy sauce	¼ cup	Cook sauce until thickened and clear.
Chicken base	1 oz	
Cornstarch	6 oz	
Cayenne pepper	1 tsp	
Cashews	1 lb	Stir chicken mixture (reserved from earlier step), cashews,
Pimento, chopped	2 oz	and pimento into sauce.
Rice, converted	3 lb 8 oz	Cook rice according to directions on p. 542.
Water, boiling	4¼ qt	Serve 6 oz chicken over 4 oz rice.
Salt	2 Tbsp	
Margarine or vegetable oil	2 Tbsp	

Approximate nutritive values per portion

Calories	Carbohydrate	Protein	Fat	Cholesterol	Sodium	Fiber	Iron
320 kcal	39 g	17 g	11 g	38 mg	632 mg	3 g	2 mg

Notes

- Potentially hazardous food. *Food Safety Standards:* Hold food for service at an internal temperature of 135°F or above. Do not mix old product with new. Cool leftover product quickly following time standards and cooling procedures on p. 167. Reheat leftover product quickly (within 2 hours) to 165°F or above. Reheat product only once; discard if not used.
- Always wash hands and wash and sanitize countertops, utensils, and containers between production steps when preparing raw poultry.

CHICKEN CREPES

Yield: 50 portions   *Portion:* 2 crepes
Oven: 325°F   *Bake:* 10 minutes

Ingredient	Amount	Procedure
Margarine	1 lb 8 oz	Melt margarine in steam-jacketed or other large kettle.
Flour, all-purpose	12 oz	Add flour and salt. Blend and cook for 5 minutes.
Salt	1 oz (1½ Tbsp)	
Chicken Stock (p. 738)	1½ gal	Gradually add stock, stirring constantly with a wire whip.
or milk		Cook until thickened.
Cooked chicken, diced	10 lb	Combine chicken, mushrooms, and seasonings.
Mushrooms, chopped	two 8-oz cans	Add enough sauce to hold chicken together (1–2 qt).
Worcestershire sauce	2 Tbsp	Reserve remaining sauce to ladle over crepes.
Curry powder	2 Tbsp	
Salt	to taste	
Crepes (p. 255)	1 recipe	Make batter. Fry on lightly greased griddle, using No. 20 dipper (1¾ oz) of batter.
		Brown lightly on one side.
		Turn and cook to set batter.
		Place crepes on trays, with waxed paper between layers. Hold for next step.
		Portion No. 20 dipper of chicken mixture onto each crepe; roll and place on baking sheets.
		Heat in 325°F oven for 10 minutes, or until internal temperature reaches 165°F.
		Serve with remaining sauce, ladled on top.

Approximate nutritive values per portion

Calories	Carbohydrate	Protein	Fat	Cholesterol	Sodium	Fiber	Iron
411 kcal	27 g	37 g	21 g	155 mg	1055 mg	1 g	3 mg

Notes

- Potentially hazardous food. *Food Safety Standards:* Hold food for service at an internal temperature of 135°F or above. Do not mix old product with new. Cool leftover product quickly following time standards and cooling procedures on p. 167. Reheat leftover product quickly (within 2 hours) to 165°F or above. Reheat product only once; discard if not used.
- 1 lb sautéed mushrooms may be added to sauce that is ladled over crepes.

Variations

- **Fruit Cheese Crepes.** Fill crepes (recipe on p. 255) with 1½ Tbsp of the following mixture: 2 lb cream cheese, whipped and combined with 2 cups sour cream. Serve with frozen strawberries or raspberries, thickened slightly, or with prepared fruit pie filling, heated.
- **Spinach Crepes.** Omit chicken and sauce. Fill crepes with cooked Spinach Soufflé (p. 811). Serve with Cheese Sauce (p. 683) or Swiss Cheese and Mushroom Sauce (p. 687).

CHICKEN À LA KING

Yield: 50 portions   *Portion:* 6 oz (¾ cup)

Ingredient	Amount	Procedure
Cooked chicken	6 lb	Dice chicken.
Margarine Onion, minced	1 lb 12 oz 4 oz	Melt margarine in steam-jacketed or other large kettle. Add onion and sauté until tender.
Flour, all-purpose Salt White pepper	1 lb 4 oz 1 oz (1½ Tbsp) 1 tsp	Add flour and seasonings to onion. Stir and cook for 5 minutes.
Chicken Stock (p. 738) Milk	3 qt 2¼ qt	Add stock and milk, stirring constantly with a wire whip. Cook until thickened.
Green bell pepper, chopped Pimento, shredded Mushrooms, sliced, sautéed	4 oz 4 oz 1 lb	Add to sauce.
		Fold chicken gently into sauce. Check seasoning. Heat to 170°F. Serve over biscuits, toast points, or rice.

Approximate nutritive values per portion

Calories	Carbohydrate	Protein	Fat	Cholesterol	Sodium	Fiber	Iron
289 kcal	16 g	9 g	21 g	43 mg	586 mg	1 g	8 mg

Notes

- Potentially hazardous food. *Food Safety Standards:* Hold food for service at an internal temperature of 135°F or above. Do not mix old product with new. Cool leftover product quickly following time standards and cooling procedures on p. 167. Reheat leftover product quickly (within 2 hours) to 165°F or above. Reheat product only once; discard if not used.
- 18–20 lb AP chicken will yield approximately 6 lb cooked meat.
- ½ oz (¼ cup) dehydrated onion, rehydrated in ½ cup water, may be substituted for fresh onion.

Variations

- **Creamed Chicken.** Delete green bell pepper, pimento, and mushrooms.
- **Tuna à la King.** Substitute tuna for chicken. Stir carefully to avoid breaking up tuna pieces.
- **Turkey à la King.** Substitute turkey for chicken.

HOT CHICKEN SALAD

Yield: 56 portions or 2 pans, 12 × 20 × 2 inches, or 50 individual casseroles   *Portion:* 5 oz
Oven: 350°F   *Bake:* 25–30 minutes

Ingredient	Amount	Procedure
Cooked chicken breasts	6 lb	Dice chicken.
Celery, diced	4 lb	Combine and add to chicken. Mix lightly.
Onion, chopped	3 oz	Scale mixture into two 12 × 20 × 2-inch counter pans, 7 lb per pan.
Almonds, browned and chopped coarsely	1 lb	If using individual casseroles, portion with No. 8 dipper.
Fresh lemon juice	½ cup	
Lemon peel, grated	3 Tbsp	
White pepper	1 tsp	
Salt	1 Tbsp	
Mayonnaise	1½ qt	
Cheddar cheese, shredded	3 lb	Sprinkle cheese over top of salad mixture.
Potato chips, crushed	12 oz	Distribute potato chips uniformly over cheese. Bake at 350°F for 25–30 minutes, or until bubbly. Cut 4 × 7 or serve with No. 8 dipper.

Approximate nutritive values per portion

Calories	Carbohydrate	Protein	Fat	Cholesterol	Sodium	Fiber	Iron
440 kcal	7 g	22 g	37 g	80 mg	491 mg	1 g	1 mg

Notes

- Potentially hazardous food. *Food Safety Standards:* Hold food for service at an internal temperature of 135°F or above. Do not mix old product with new. Cool leftover product quickly following time standards and cooling procedures on p. 167. Reheat leftover product quickly (within 2 hours) to 165°F or above. Reheat product only once; discard if not used.
- Swiss cheese may be substituted for cheddar cheese.
- 2 lb of the cheese may be added to the chicken mixture and 1 lb sprinkled on top.
- Salad should be served as soon as possible after preparation.

Variation

- **Hot Turkey Salad.** Substitute turkey for chicken. A 16- to 18-lb turkey (AP) will yield approximately 6 lb cooked meat.

SCALLOPED CHICKEN

Yield: 48 portions or 2 pans, 12 × 20 × 2 inches   *Portion:* 8 oz
Oven: 350°F   *Bake:* 30–40 minutes

Ingredient	Amount	Procedure
Cooked chicken	6 lb	Cut chicken into ½-inch pieces. Save for layering step.
Margarine Flour, all-purpose Chicken base	1 lb 8 oz 3 oz	Melt margarine in steam-jacketed or other kettle. Stir in flour and chicken base. Cook for 5 minutes.
Water	1 gal	Add water to roux while stirring with a wire whip. Cook until thickened.
Eggs, beaten	12 (1 lb 5 oz)	When sauce is thick, add small amount of hot mixture to eggs, then stir into remainder of sauce. Save for layering step.
Dry bread, cubed Salt Black pepper Sage, ground, or poultry seasoning	2 lb 6 oz 1 tsp 2 tsp 1½ tsp	Add seasonings to bread. Mix to distribute seasonings.
Margarine Celery, chopped Onion, chopped Chicken base	10 oz 8 oz 8 oz 2 oz	Sauté celery and onion in melted margarine. Stir in chicken base. Add to bread.
Water	2½ qt	Add water to bread. Toss lightly. Do not overmix.
		Place dressing, sauce, and chicken in two greased 12 × 20 × 2-inch counter pans, layered in each pan as follows: a. 4 lb 8 oz dressing c. 3 lb chicken b. 1¼ qt sauce d. 1¼ qt sauce
Cracker crumbs, coarse Margarine, melted	6 oz 3 oz	Mix crumbs and margarine and sprinkle on mixture, 4 oz per pan. Bake at 350°F for 30–40 minutes, internal temperature 180°F. Cut 4 × 6.

Approximate nutritive values per portion

Calories	Carbohydrate	Protein	Fat	Cholesterol	Sodium	Fiber	Iron
334 kcal	18 g	21 g	20 g	99 mg	1005 mg	3 g	2 mg

Notes

- Potentially hazardous food. *Food Safety Standards:* Hold food for service at an internal temperature of 135°F or above. Do not mix old product with new. Cool leftover product quickly following time standards and cooling procedures on p. 167. Reheat leftover product quickly (within 2 hours) to 165°F or above. Reheat product only once; discard if not used.
- Scalloped Chicken may be made by preparing one recipe of Bread Dressing (p. 504) and scaling it in the following manner in each of two 12 × 20 × 2-inch pans. Scale 4 lb dressing into pans and spread evenly. Arrange 3 lb cooked chicken over dressing. Scale 4 lb dressing over chicken, spreading evenly. Bake at 325°F for 1 hour 15 minutes. Serve with chicken gravy (p. 685).
- 1 oz (½ cup) dehydrated onion, rehydrated in ¾ cup water, may be substituted for fresh onion.

Variation

- **Scalloped Turkey.** Substitute turkey for chicken.

BRUNSWICK STEW

Yield: 50 portions or 3 gal   *Portion:* 8 oz (1 cup)

Ingredient	Amount	Procedure
Cubed fresh pork	2 lb AP	Brown pork. Drain off fat.
Cooked chicken	7 lb 8 oz	Cube chicken.
Celery, diced	1 lb 8 oz	Cook vegetables until partially done.
Carrots, diced	2 lb 4 oz	
Potatoes, diced	2 lb	
Onions, finely chopped	10 oz	
Margarine	8 oz	Melt margarine in steam-jacketed or other large kettle.
Flour, all-purpose	8 oz	Add flour and stir until smooth.
Chicken Stock (p. 738)	1 gal	Add stock gradually, stirring constantly with a wire whip. Add salt and pepper.
Salt	1 Tbsp	Add chicken, pork, and vegetables. Simmer until vegetables are tender.
White pepper	1½ tsp	Do not overcook.
Green peas, frozen	1 lb	Add peas. Cook for an additional 5 minutes. Stew should be fairly thick. Serve in soup bowls or deep plates.

Approximate nutritive values per portion

Calories	Carbohydrate	Protein	Fat	Cholesterol	Sodium	Fiber	Iron
246 kcal	12 g	25 g	10 g	65 mg	493 mg	1 g	2 mg

Note

- Potentially hazardous food. *Food Safety Standards:* Hold food for service at an internal temperature of 135°F or above. Do not mix old product with new. Cool leftover product quickly following time standards and cooling procedures on p. 167. Reheat leftover product quickly (within 2 hours) to 165°F or above. Reheat product only once; discard if not used.

Variations

- **Brunswick Chicken Pasta.** Prepare as for Brunswick Pork and Chicken Pasta. Substitute chicken thigh meat for cubed pork.
- **Brunswick Pork and Chicken Pasta.** Using a small amount of oil, brown 2 lb pork cut into 1-inch cubes and 10 lb chicken thigh meat, cut if necessary into ½-inch pieces. (Expected meat yield after cooking is 6 lb 12 oz.) Reserve meat for later step. Steam and do not drain 1 lb 6 oz sliced celery, 2 lb carrot coins, and 10 oz chopped onion. Reserve vegetables and liquid for later step. Cook and drain 1 lb 12 oz rotini (3 lb 6 oz cooked). Reserve for later step. Melt 12 oz margarine in steam-jacketed kettle. Stir in 12 oz flour, 1 Tbsp white pepper, and 1½ Tbsp poultry seasoning. Cook, stirring often, for 20 minutes or until medium brown in color. Turn off heat and stir in 5 oz chicken base. Using a whisk, gradually add 1¼ gal water, stirring until completely mixed with flour mixture. Cook to 190°F until thickened, stirring often. Stir in 12 oz frozen green peas, reserved pork, chicken, and pasta. Heat to at least 165°F. Transfer to 12 × 20 × 2-inch pans (6 lb per pan).

CHICKEN POT PIE

Yield: 50 portions or 2 pans, 12 × 20 × 2 inches   *Portion:* 8 oz
Oven: 400°F   *Bake:* 20–25 minutes

Ingredient	Amount	Procedure
Onions, chopped	14 oz	Sauté onions in margarine in steam-jacketed or other large kettle.
Margarine	12 oz	
Flour, all-purpose	1 lb 6 oz	Add flour and pepper to onions. Stir until blended.
Black pepper	1 tsp	Cook for 30 minutes.
Chicken Stock (p. 738)	1¼ gal	Add stock, stirring constantly with a wire whip. Cook until thickened, stirring often. Check for seasoning. Add salt if necessary.
Cooked chicken	6 lb	Cut chicken into ½- to ¾-inch pieces. Add to sauce.
Celery, sliced	1 lb 8 oz	Cook celery and carrots until partially done.
Carrots, sliced	2 lb	Drain. Fold into sauce.
Green peas, frozen	2 lb	Add peas (uncooked) to chicken mixture. Mix carefully. Scale chicken into two 12 × 20 × 2-inch counter pans, 12 lb per pan.
Pastry (p. 340)	3 lb	Roll out 1 lb 8 oz pastry to fit each pan. Place on chicken mixture and seal edges to pan. Bake at 400°F for 20–25 minutes or until crust is browned and internal temperature is 180°F.

Approximate nutritive values per portion

Calories	Carbohydrate	Protein	Fat	Cholesterol	Sodium	Fiber	Iron
370 kcal	26 g	21 g	20 g	46 mg	590 mg	2 g	2 mg

Notes

- Potentially hazardous food. *Food Safety Standards:* Hold food for service at an internal temperature of 135°F or above. Do not mix old product with new. Cool leftover product quickly following time standards and cooling procedures on p. 167. Reheat leftover product quickly (within 2 hours) to 165°F or above. Reheat product only once; discard if not used.
- Chicken mixture may be topped with Baking Powder Biscuits (p. 231).
- 1¾ oz (¾ cup) dehydrated onion, rehydrated in 1¼ cups water, may be substituted for fresh onion.

Variations

- **Individual Chicken Pot Pie.** Prepare 50 pastry rounds (p. 340). Cut pastry in circles to fit tops of individual casserole dishes. Scale 8 oz pot pie mixture into casserole dish. Top pot pies with pastry and bake at 350°F for 30–45 minutes, until brown.
- **Turkey Pie.** Substitute turkey for chicken.

VEGETABLE POT PIE

Yield: 50 portions   *Portion:* 1 pot pie
Oven: 350°F   *Bake:* 30–45 minutes

Ingredient	Amount	Procedure
Margarine	12 oz	Melt margarine. Stir in flour and pepper.
Flour	1 lb 8 oz	Cook roux until light tan, approximately 20 minutes, stirring often.
Black pepper	½ tsp	
Water	3¾ qt	Dissolve vegetable base in water. Pour water mixture and milk into roux, stirring constantly with a wire whip. Cook sauce until thickened.
Vegetable base	4 oz	
Milk	7 cups	
Brown mustard	4 oz	Stir mustard and parsley into sauce. Taste for salt and adjust as needed.
Parsley, dried	2 Tbsp	
Baby carrots	2 lb 12 oz	Steam carrots until tender, 1–2 minutes. Drain. Add to sauce.
Cubed potatoes	5 lb 4 oz	Steam potatoes until tender, 3–5 minutes. Drain. Add to sauce.
Onions, diced	1 lb 8 oz	Steam onions and celery until tender-crisp. Drain. Add to sauce.
Celery, sliced	8 oz	
Mushrooms, canned, drained	1 lb	Add mushrooms, peppers, corn, and peas to sauce.
Green bell peppers, diced	8 oz	Scale 8 oz into each individual casserole dish.
Red bell peppers, diced	8 oz	
Corn	8 oz	
Green peas	1 lb	
Pastry circles (p. 340)	50	Cut pastry in circles to fit tops of individual casserole dishes. Top pot pies with pastry and bake at 350°F until brown, 30–45 minutes.

Approximate nutritive values per pot pie

Calories	Carbohydrate	Protein	Fat	Cholesterol	Sodium	Fiber	Iron
563 kcal	55 g	9 g	34 g	3 mg	926 mg	4 g	3 mg

Note

- Potentially hazardous food. *Food Safety Standards:* Hold food for service at an internal temperature of 135°F or above. Do not mix old product with new. Cool leftover product quickly following time standards and cooling procedures on p. 167. Reheat leftover product quickly (within 2 hours) to 165°F or above. Reheat product only once; discard if not used.

CHICKEN AND NOODLES

Yield: 50 portions or 2 pans, 12 × 20 × 2 inches   *Portion:* 8 oz
Oven: 350°F   *Bake:* 30 minutes

Ingredient	Amount	Procedure
Cooked chicken	7 lb 8 oz	Cut chicken into ½-inch pieces.
Noodles Water, boiling Salt Vegetable oil	3 lb 3 gal 3 oz 1 Tbsp	Cook noodles according to directions on p. 507. Drain.
Margarine Onion, chopped	12 oz 2 oz	Melt margarine in a steam-jacketed or other large kettle. Add onion and sauté until tender.
Flour, all-purpose Salt	7 oz 1 Tbsp	Add flour and salt to onion. Stir until blended. Cook for 5 minutes.
Milk or chicken stock (p. 738)	3½ qt	Add milk gradually, stirring constantly with a wire whip. Cook until thickened. Combine chicken, cooked noodles, and sauce. Scale into two 12 × 20 × 2-inch counter pans, 11 lb 12 oz per pan. Bake at 350°F for 30 minutes or until internal temperature reaches 180°F.

Approximate nutritive values per portion

Calories	Carbohydrate	Protein	Fat	Cholesterol	Sodium	Fiber	Iron
331 kcal	26 g	25 g	14 g	91 mg	414 mg	0.1 g	2 mg

Notes

- Potentially hazardous food. *Food Safety Standards:* Hold food for service at an internal temperature of 135°F or above. Do not mix old product with new. Cool leftover product quickly following time standards and cooling procedures on p. 167. Reheat leftover product quickly (within 2 hours) to 165°F or above. Reheat product only once; discard if not used.
- 20–22 lb AP chicken will yield approximately 7 lb 8 oz cooked meat.
- ¼ oz (2 Tbsp) dehydrated onion, rehydrated in ¼ cup water, may be substituted for fresh onion.

Variations

- **Chicken and Noodles with Mushrooms.** Add 2 lb sliced mushrooms, sautéed with the onion.
- **Pork and Noodle Casserole.** Substitute 10 lb pork, diced and cooked, for chicken.
- **Turkey and Noodle Casserole.** Substitute cooked turkey for chicken (cook 18- to 20-lb turkey).

CHICKEN WITH NOODLES ON WHIPPED POTATOES

Yield: 50 portions   *Portion:* 5 oz chicken and noodles + 4 oz potatoes

Ingredient	Amount	Procedure
Water	5½ qt	Mix water and chicken base in a steam-jacketed kettle.
Chicken base (see Note)	3 oz	
Onion, chopped	8 oz	Add vegetables and seasonings. Bring to a rolling boil.
Celery, chopped	8 oz	
Black pepper	¾ tsp	
Rubbed sage	½ tsp	
Rosemary, dried	½ tsp	
Parsley flakes, dried	1 Tbsp	
Egg noodles, ¼-inch (frozen)	2 lb	Stir noodles into boiling liquid mixture. Reduce heat and simmer for 35–45 minutes. Stir often to keep noodles separated.
Cooked chicken, diced	2 lb 12 oz	Add chicken to noodle mixture. Stir carefully to prevent breaking up chicken.
Water, cold	1 lb 8 oz	In a separate bowl, blend cold water and flour together using a wire whip.
Flour	1½ oz	Add water-flour slurry to the broth, pouring through a strainer if not smooth. Stir constantly but gently while adding to prevent lumps from forming. Simmer until mixture reaches 200°F and sauce thickens.
Whipped Potatoes (p. 798)	13 lb	Prepare Whipped Potatoes according to recipe. Serve 5 oz of chicken and noodles over 4 oz whipped potatoes.

Approximate nutritive values per portion

Calories	Carbohydrate	Protein	Fat	Cholesterol	Sodium	Fiber	Iron
266 kcal	33 g	18 g	7 g	56 mg	1243 mg	2.5 g	2 mg

Notes

- Potentially hazardous food. *Food Safety Standards:* Hold food for service at an internal temperature of 135°F or above. Do not mix old product with new. Cool leftover product quickly following time standards and cooling procedures on p. 167. Reheat leftover product quickly (within 2 hours) to 165°F or above. Reheat product only once; discard if not used.
- Use a high-quality chicken base. The salt concentration of bases varies by brand. Check for salt and adjust as necessary.

CHICKEN AND RICE CASSEROLE

Yield: 50 portions or 2 pans, 12 × 20 × 2 inches   *Portion:* 8 oz
Oven: 350°F   *Bake:* 1 hour

Ingredient	Amount	Procedure
Cooked chicken	6 lb	Dice chicken.
Rice, converted	2 lb 8 oz	Cook rice according to directions on p. 542.
Water, boiling	2 qt	
Salt	2 Tbsp	
Margarine or vegetable oil	2 Tbsp	
Margarine, melted	6 oz	Sauté onion, celery, and mushrooms in margarine.
Onion, chopped	3 oz	
Celery, chopped	8 oz	
Mushrooms, sliced	1 lb	
Flour, all-purpose	8 oz	Add flour to vegetables and stir to blend.
Milk	1½ qt	Add milk and stock, stirring constantly with a wire whip.
Chicken Stock (p. 738)	2 qt	Cook until thickened.
White pepper	¼ tsp	Add pepper. Add salt if needed.
Almonds, slivered	6 oz	Add almonds, pimento, and chicken to sauce. Combine carefully.
Pimento, chopped	3 oz	Scale into two lightly greased 12 × 20 × 2-inch baking pans, 10 lb 8 oz per pan.
Bread crumbs	9 oz	Combine bread crumbs, margarine, and cheese.
Margarine, melted	3 oz	Sprinkle over mixture in pans, 9 oz per pan.
Cheddar cheese, shredded	6 oz	Bake at 350°F for 1 hour or until internal temperature reaches 180°F.

Approximate nutritive values per portion

Calories	Carbohydrate	Protein	Fat	Cholesterol	Sodium	Fiber	Iron
320 kcal	29 g	21 g	13 g	53 mg	585 mg	1 g	2 mg

Notes

- Potentially hazardous food. *Food Safety Standards:* Hold food for service at an internal temperature of 135°F or above. Do not mix old product with new. Cool leftover product quickly following time standards and cooling procedures on p. 167. Reheat leftover product quickly (within 2 hours) to 165°F or above. Reheat product only once; discard if not used.
- Sliced water chestnuts may be substituted for almonds.
- Chopped parsley may be sprinkled over the baked product just before serving.
- ¼ oz (2 Tbsp) dehydrated onion, rehydrated in ¼ cup water, may be substituted for fresh onion.

SINGAPORE CURRY

Yield: 50 portions   *Portion:* 8 oz curry + 6 oz rice

Ingredient	Amount	Procedure
Cooked chicken	15 lb	Cut chicken into ¾-inch pieces. Reserve for later step.
Margarine	1 lb	Melt margarine in steam-jacketed or other large kettle.
Flour, all-purpose	1 lb 4 oz	Add flour and stir until smooth. Cook for 5 minutes.
Chicken Stock (p. 738)	5 qt	Add stock gradually, stirring constantly with a wire whip. Cook until thickened.
Salt	1 tsp	
White pepper	½ tsp	Add salt, pepper, and curry powder.
Curry powder	2 oz	Add chicken and stir gently to prevent breaking of chicken pieces. Return temperature to 170°F. Taste and add more seasonings as the chicken takes up the curry flavor. It should be quite yellow and have a distinct curry flavor.
Rice, converted	5 lb	Cook rice according to directions on p. 542.
Salt	3 oz	This amount of rice will allow generous servings, 6 oz.
Water, boiling	6¼ qt	
Margarine or vegetable oil	3 Tbsp	
French-fried onion rings	50 servings	Serve curried chicken over rice, with accompaniments. See Note for directions for serving.
Fresh tomatoes, sliced	10 lb	
Bananas, cut in thick slices or chunks	10 lb	
Pineapple chunks, drained	1 No. 10 can	
Coconut, shredded or flaked	1 lb 8 oz	
Salted peanuts	1 lb	
Chutney	three 1-lb jars	

Approximate nutritive values per portion

Calories	Carbohydrate	Protein	Fat	Cholesterol	Sodium	Fiber	Iron
869 kcal	103 g	47 g	31 g	113 mg	1047 mg	7 g	6 mg

Notes

- Potentially hazardous food. *Food Safety Standards:* Hold food for service at an internal temperature of 135°F or above. Do not mix old product with new. Cool leftover product quickly following time standards and cooling procedures on p. 167. Reheat leftover product quickly (within 2 hours) to 165°F or above. Reheat product only once; discard if not used.
- Shrimp, veal, lamb, or a combination of chicken and pork may be used, allowing 6 oz cooked meat per person.
- For a Singapore Curry buffet, arrange foods on a buffet table in the following order: rice, curried chicken or other meat, and accompaniments in the order listed in the recipe. Each guest serves rice in the center of the plate, dips a generous serving of curried meat over the rice, and then adds accompaniments as desired.

TURKEY AND DUMPLINGS

Yield: 48 portions or 2 pans, 12 × 20 × 2 inches   *Portion:* 8 oz

Ingredient	Amount	Procedure
Margarine	14 oz	Melt margarine in steam-jacketed or other kettle. Sauté onions until tender.
Onions, chopped	1 lb	
Flour, all-purpose	1 lb 8 oz	Stir flour and pepper into onions. Cook for 5–10 minutes, stirring often.
Black pepper	1½ tsp	
Water	1½ gal	Add water and chicken base to mixture in kettle. Cook until thickened, stirring often.
Chicken base	6 oz	
Cooked turkey	6 lb 10 oz	Cut turkey into ½-inch cubes. Add to sauce.
Celery, chopped	1 lb 10 oz	Steam celery and carrots until tender-crisp.
Carrots, sliced	2 lb 4 oz	Fold into turkey mixture. Scale into two 12 × 20 × 2-inch pans, 13 lb per pan.

STEAMED DUMPLINGS

Ingredient	Amount	Procedure
Flour, all-purpose	2 lb 4 oz	Combine flour, baking powder, and salt in mixer bowl. Mix until blended.
Baking powder	3 oz	
Salt	2 Tbsp	
Eggs, beaten	5 (9 oz)	Combine eggs, milk, and seasonings.
Milk	1½ qt	Add to dry ingredients and mix only until blended.
Fresh parsley, chopped	1 oz	Portion 4 × 6 with No. 24 dipper onto turkey and gravy.
Poultry seasoning	2 tsp	Steam until dumplings are done, approximately 20 minutes.

Approximate nutritive values per portion

Calories	Carbohydrate	Protein	Fat	Cholesterol	Sodium	Fiber	Iron
336 kcal	35 g	18 g	14 g	62 mg	1593 mg	2 g	3 mg

Notes

- Potentially hazardous food. *Food Safety Standards:* Hold food for service at an internal temperature of 135°F or above. Do not mix old product with new. Cool leftover product quickly following time standards and cooling procedures on p. 167. Reheat leftover product quickly (within 2 hours) to 165°F or above. Reheat product only once; discard if not used.
- Steam as soon as dumplings are portioned onto gravy. Product holds well after cooking.
- 2 oz (1 cup) dehydrated onion, rehydrated in 1½ cups water, may be substituted for fresh onion.

LIME TARRAGON TURKEY STEAK

Yield: 50 steaks   *Portion:* 6 oz
Grill: 350°F   *Grill:* 4–7 minutes per side

Ingredient	Amount	Procedure
Turkey steaks, 6 oz	50	
Vegetable oil	3½ cups	Combine oil, liquids, and spices in stainless steel container.
Lime juice, frozen, reconstituted	1 qt	Pour over turkey steaks and refrigerate for several hours or overnight. Turn if necessary to make sure both sides of turkey are coated.
Cooking sherry	2 cups	
Garlic, minced	4 oz	
Fresh chives, chopped	3 oz	
Tarragon, dried	½ cup	
Salt	2½ oz	
Black pepper	5 tsp	
Dry mustard	1 tsp	
Worcestershire sauce	¼ cup	
Water	2 cups	
		Drain marinade from turkey steaks.
		Preheat grill to 350°F.
		Grill steaks for approximately 4–7 minutes per side until internal temperature reaches 165°F.

Approximate nutritive values per portion

Calories	Carbohydrate	Protein	Fat	Cholesterol	Sodium	Fiber	Iron
240 kcal	3 g	30 g	11 g	66 mg	630 mg	0 g	2 mg

Notes

- Potentially hazardous food. *Food Safety Standards:* Hold food for service at an internal temperature of 135°F or above. Do not mix old product with new. Cool leftover product quickly following time standards and cooling procedures on p. 167. Reheat leftover product quickly (within 2 hours) to 165°F or above. Reheat product only once; discard if not used.
- Always wash hands and wash and sanitize countertops, utensils, and containers between production steps when preparing raw poultry.

Variations

- **Creole Turkey Steaks.** Prepare Creole Spice Mixture, p. 406 (Creole Baked Fish). Dip turkey steaks in melted margarine, then sprinkle generously with spice mixture. Grill steaks until done, 4–7 minutes per side.
- **Lime Tarragon Chicken Breast.** Substitute chicken breast for turkey steak.

CORN BREAD DRESSING

Yield: 50 portions or 1 pan, 12 × 20 × 2 inches   *Portion:* 4 oz
Oven: 375°F   *Bake:* 20–30 minutes

Ingredient	Amount	Procedure
Corn Bread (p. 244), ⅓ recipe	3 lb 10 oz	Prepare Corn Bread. Crumble.
Bread, cubed or torn	1 lb 12 oz	Crumble bread. Add to Corn Bread.
Margarine Onions, chopped Celery, chopped	4 oz 1 lb 1 lb 8 oz	Melt margarine in steam-jacketed or other kettle. Add onions and celery. Sauté until vegetables are tender. Add bread.
Chicken base Water, hot Salt (see Note) Poultry seasoning Black pepper	2 oz 3 qt 1 tsp 1 Tbsp 1 tsp	Combine chicken base, water, and seasonings. Pour over bread mixture. Stir lightly to moisten.
		Scale mixture (12 lb) into lightly greased 12 × 20 × 2-inch pan. Bake at 375°F for 20–30 minutes or until 180°F. Serve with No. 12 dipper.

Approximate nutritive values per portion

Calories	Carbohydrate	Protein	Fat	Cholesterol	Sodium	Fiber	Iron
157 kcal	23 g	4 g	6 g	15 mg	546 mg	2 g	1 mg

Notes

- Potentially hazardous food. *Food Safety Standards:* Hold food for service at an internal temperature of 135°F or above. Do not mix old product with new. Cool leftover product quickly following time standards and cooling procedures on p. 167. Reheat leftover product quickly (within 2 hours) to 165°F or above. Reheat product only once; discard if not used.
- If chicken base is highly salted, reduce or delete salt in recipe.

BREAD DRESSING (OR STUFFING)

Yield: 50 portions or 1 pan, 12 × 20 × 2 inches   *Portion:* 4½ oz
Oven: 325°F   *Bake:* 1 hour 15 minutes

Ingredient	Amount	Procedure
Onion, chopped	1 lb	Sauté onion and celery in margarine until lightly browned.
Celery, chopped	1 lb	
Margarine	1 lb	
Water (see Note)	1 gal	Add water, chicken base, and seasonings to sautéed vegetables. Heat until hot.
Chicken base	3 oz	
Salt (see Note)	1 Tbsp	
Black pepper	1 Tbsp	
Poultry seasoning (see Note)	1 Tbsp	
Thyme, ground	1 Tbsp	
Dry bread, cubed	3 lb 12 oz	Add bread gradually to vegetable mixture, tossing lightly until thoroughly mixed. Avoid overmixing, which causes dressing to be soggy and compact.
		Scale dressing (15 lb) into lightly greased 12 × 20 × 2-inch pan. Bake at 325°F for approximately 1 hour 15 minutes, internal temperature 180°F. Serve with No. 10 dipper.

Approximate nutritive values per portion

Calories	Carbohydrate	Protein	Fat	Cholesterol	Sodium	Fiber	Iron
159 kcal	17 g	4 g	9 g	0 mg	757 mg	4 g	1 mg

Notes

- Potentially hazardous food. *Food Safety Standards:* Hold food for service at an internal temperature of 135°F or above. Do not mix old product with new. Cool leftover product quickly following time standards and cooling procedures on p. 167. Reheat leftover product quickly (within 2 hours) to 165°F or above. Reheat product only once; discard if not used.
- The amount of liquid will depend on the dryness of the bread.
- If chicken base is highly salted, reduce or delete salt in recipe.
- Sage may be used for part or all of the poultry seasoning.

Variations

- **Apple Stuffing.** Add 1 lb finely chopped apples. Reduce bread cubes to 3 lb 4 oz.
- **Chestnut Stuffing.** Add 1 lb 4 oz cooked chestnuts, chopped. Reduce bread to 3 lb 8 oz. Substitute 2 qt milk for 2 qt water.
- **Mushroom Stuffing.** Reduce celery and onion to 8 oz each. Sauté 2 lb fresh mushrooms with the vegetables.
- **Nut Stuffing.** Add 2 cups chopped almonds or pecans that have been browned lightly in 4 oz melted margarine. Substitute 1 qt milk for 1 qt water.
- **Oyster Stuffing.** Add 1 lb 8 oz oysters.
- **Raisin Stuffing.** Add 1 lb seedless raisins.
- **Sausage Stuffing.** Reduce bread cubes to 3 lb 4 oz. Add 2 lb sausage, cooked and drained, and 1 lb tart apples, peeled and chopped.

Pasta, Rice, Cereals, and Foods with Grains, Beans, and Tofu

The cooking of pasta, rice, cereals, and grains is similar. Water is added, heat is applied, and cooking is continued until the starch granules gelatinize. Dry beans are cooked in a liquid (generally water or stock) until softened. Tofu (bean curd) does not need to be cooked before being incorporated in a recipe.

Pasta

Most dry pasta will approximately double in **volume** after cooking (egg noodle volume remains about the same). Thickness varies among pasta shapes, and the volume increase is directly related to this variation. Certain shapes such as ziti, lasagna, and rigatoni have more fluctuation in their volume increase than do spaghetti and macaroni. The **weight** of dry pasta increases, but the amount depends on the type of pasta. See p. 507 for the weight increase of selected pastas.

Pasta is best if cooked uncovered at a fast boil, using plenty of water. A general rule is to allow 1 gal water, 1 oz (1½ Tbsp) salt, and 1½ tsp cooking oil for every pound of pasta. Directions for cooking are given on p. 507. Pasta should be cooked until it is tender but firm (**al dente**), then drained to stop the cooking. Overcooking produces a soft, pasty product that breaks easily when combined with sauces or other ingredients.

Rice

Long-grain rice is cooked until all water is absorbed, so the key to properly cooked rice is the proportion of rice to water and the correct cooking time. Converted (parboiled) long-grain white rice requires slightly more water and a longer cooking time than regular long-grain or medium-grain rice. Table 16.1 gives basic proportions and yields for converted rice. The cooking time for brown rice is almost double that of white rice. Rice may be cooked in a kettle, steamer, or oven. See p. 542 for cooking directions. Cooked rice is a potentially hazardous food and should be stored outside the temperature danger zone.

Cereals

Cereals may be whole, cracked, flaked or rolled, or granular. The amount of water used for cooking determines the volume of the finished product. Cereal swells until all water has been absorbed or until the limit of the grain is reached. As a rule, granular cereals absorb more water than whole or flaked. The fineness of grind of the cereal and the amount of bran or cellulose are factors that determine the length of time a cereal needs to be cooked. Cereals cooked in quantity usually are prepared in a steam-jacketed kettle or steamer but may be cooked in a heavy kettle on top of the range. Directions for cooking breakfast cereals are given on p. 562.

Beans

Many varieties of dry beans are available. Some commonly used ones are described on p. 132.

Most dry beans will double to triple in bulk during cooking. Because sorting machines may mistake rocks or other debris for dry beans, it is recommended that beans be sorted before rinsing and cooking.

Some general cooking guidelines:

1. Place beans in a large pot or steam-jacketed kettle and cover with water. Bring the water to a boil and skim foam if necessary. Cover loosely and reduce heat so beans simmer slowly.

2. Cook until beans are slightly tender. Stir very carefully as the beans become tender so they are not broken and do not become mushy.

3. Season as desired. A general rule is to add 2 tsp salt to 1 lb beans. Other seasonings may be added.

4. Cook, stirring very carefully, until the beans are tender. Add additional water if necessary. Drain and serve or store in refrigerator until needed. Cooked beans are a potentially hazardous food. Follow cooling guidelines on p. 167.

Soaking beans before cooking will reduce the cooking time by about 25 percent.

TABLE 16.1 Basic proportions and yields for converted rice

Rice	Water*	Salt	Approximate volume yield	Approximate number of 4-oz servings
1 lb	$1\frac{1}{4}$ qt	1 Tbsp	2 qt	16
2 lb	$2\frac{1}{2}$ qt	2 Tbsp	1 gal	32
3 lb	$3\frac{3}{4}$ qt	3 Tbsp (2 oz)	$6\frac{1}{4}$ qt	50
4 lb	5 qt	$\frac{1}{4}$ cup ($2\frac{1}{2}$ oz)	$8\frac{1}{2}$ qt	68
5 lb	$6\frac{1}{4}$ qt	$\frac{1}{3}$ cup ($3\frac{1}{2}$ oz)	11 qt	88
8 lb	10 qt	$\frac{1}{2}$ cup (5 oz)	$18\frac{1}{2}$ qt	148
10 lb	$12\frac{1}{2}$ qt	$\frac{3}{4}$ cup (8 oz)	24 qt	192

* Liquids other than water that can be used are chicken, beef, or vegetable stock or base; tomato or vegetable juice; and diluted orange or apple juice.

Pasta Recipes

COOKING PASTA

Yield: 50 portions   *Portion:* 4 oz

Ingredient	Amount	Procedure
Water	5 gal	Bring water to a rapid boil. Add salt and oil.
Salt	5 oz	Add pasta gradually while stirring.
Vegetable oil (optional)	3 Tbsp	Return to boiling. Cook uncovered at a fast boil until tender but firm (***al dente***),
Pasta	5 lb	5–10 minutes (see Cooking Times table). Stir occasionally to prevent sticking. Test for doneness. Drain.

Notes

- Weight of cooked pasta will vary, depending on length of time cooked.
- Addition of oil is optional. It helps prevent foaming and sticking.
- If pasta is to be used as an ingredient in a recipe requiring further cooking, undercook slightly.
- If product is not to be served immediately, drain and rinse quickly with cold water. To keep pasta from becoming sticky or drying out, toss lightly with a little vegetable oil. Cover tightly and store in the refrigerator. To reheat, put pasta in a colander and immerse in rapidly boiling water just long enough to heat through. *Do not continue to cook.* Or, reheat in a microwave oven.
- Pasta can be covered tightly and refrigerated or frozen. Reheat to serving temperature.

Approximate Yield and Cooking Times for Selected Pastas

Type of pasta	*Approximate cooking time (al dente) (min)*	*Yield of cooked pasta from 1 lb dry pasta*
Acini di pepe	8	3 lb 4 oz
Bow ties	11	2 lb
Fettuccine	8	2 lb 12 oz
Kluski	15	2 lb 12 oz
Lasagna noodles	15	2 lb
Linguine	10	2 lb 8 oz
Elbow macaroni	6	2 lb 12 oz
Mostaccioli	10	2 lb 4 oz
Noodles	6	2 lb 12 oz
Orzo	6	2 lb 8 oz
Rigatoni	10	2 lb
Rotini	8	2 lb
Shells	9	2 lb 8 oz
Spaghetti	10	2 lb 8 oz
Vermicelli	7	2 lb 8 oz
Wheels	11	2 lb
Ziti	10	2 lb 4 oz

ORZO PILAF

Yield: 50 portions   *Portion:* 4 oz

Ingredient	Amount	Procedure
Orzo	3 lb 8 oz	Cook orzo according to directions on p. 507. Do not overcook.
Water, boiling	3½ gal	Drain and keep hot. Save for later step.
Salt	2 Tbsp	
Vegetable oil	2 Tbsp	
Green onions, thinly sliced	1 lb 4 oz	Sauté onions, garlic, mushrooms, and almonds in oil until onions
Garlic, minced	2 oz	and mushrooms are just tender.
Fresh mushrooms, sliced	1 lb 12 oz	
Almonds	12 oz	
Olive oil	1 cup	
Fresh parsley, minced	3 oz	Stir parsley, juice, and seasonings into vegetable mixture.
Fresh lemon juice	2 Tbsp	Mix with cooked orzo.
Rosemary, dried	2 Tbsp	Heat if necessary to 165°F. Serve immediately.
Black pepper	1 tsp	
Salt	1 tsp	

Approximate nutritive values per portion

Calories	Carbohydrate	Protein	Fat	Cholesterol	Sodium	Fiber	Iron
208 kcal	28 g	6 g	9 g	0 mg	311 mg	1 g	2 mg

Note

- Potentially hazardous food. *Food Safety Standards:* Hold food for service at an internal temperature of 135°F or above. Do not mix old product with new. Cool leftover product quickly following time standards and cooling procedures on p. 167. Reheat leftover product quickly (within 2 hours) to 165°F or above. Reheat product only once; discard if not used.

Variations

- **Orzo and Feta.** Delete 1 tsp salt (not the salt from the pasta cooking water). Stir in 1 lb 10 oz crumbled feta cheese along with the parsley, juice, and rosemary.
- **Rosemary Orzo Amandine.** Soak 2 oz sundried tomatoes in 8 oz hot water for 2 hours or more. Drain and coarsely chop tomatoes. Toast slivered almonds (see toasting instructions that follow). Reduce mushrooms to 8 oz. Stir in 12 oz sliced ripe olives and the rehydrated tomatoes. (To toast almonds: Spread in single layer on half-sized bun sheet. Toast in oven at 300°F for 15–20 minutes or until nuts turn golden and become fragrant. Turn two or three times during toasting to prevent burning.)

LEMON ORZO

Yield: 50 portions *Portion:* 4 oz

Ingredient	Amount	Procedure
Orzo	5 lb	Cook according to directions on p. 507.
Water	5 gal	Drain.
Salt	5 oz	
Fresh chives, finely sliced	3 oz EP	Combine chives, lemon, pepper, and oil.
Lemon peel, grated	1 Tbsp	Stir into pasta. Serve hot, above 140°F.
Fresh lemon juice	1 cup	
Black pepper	1 tsp	
Olive oil	2 cups	

Approximate nutritive values per portion

Calories	Carbohydrate	Protein	Fat	Cholesterol	Sodium	Fiber	Iron
250 kcal	34 g	6 g	9 g	0 mg	290 mg	1 g	2 mg

Notes

- Potentially hazardous food. *Food Safety Standards:* Hold food for service at an internal temperature of 135°F or above. Do not mix old product with new. Cool leftover product quickly following time standards and cooling procedures on p. 167. Reheat leftover product quickly (within 2 hours) to 165°F or above. Reheat product only once; discard if not used.
- Other pasta shapes may be substituted for the orzo.

MACARONI AND CHEESE

Yield: 48 portions or 2 pans, 12 × 20 × 2 inches   *Portion:* 8 oz
Oven: 350°F   *Bake:* 20 minutes

Ingredient	Amount	Procedure
Macaroni	3 lb 8 oz	Cook macaroni according to directions on p. 507.
Water, boiling	3½ gal	Drain.
Salt	2 Tbsp	
Vegetable oil	2 Tbsp	
Margarine	12 oz	Melt margarine. Stir in flour and seasonings.
Flour, all-purpose	8 oz	Cook for 5–10 minutes.
Salt	2 Tbsp	
Dry mustard	1 Tbsp	
Worcestershire sauce	¼ cup	
Milk	1 gal	Add milk gradually, stirring constantly with a wire whip.
		Cook until thickened.
Cheddar cheese, sharp, shredded	4 lb	Add cheese to sauce. Stir until cheese melts.
		Pour over macaroni and mix carefully.
		Scale into two greased 12 × 20 × 2-inch baking pans, 12 lb per pan.
Bread crumbs	1 lb	Mix crumbs and melted margarine.
Margarine, melted	6 oz	Sprinkle over macaroni and cheese, 8 oz per pan.
		Bake at 350°F for about 20 minutes, until 180°F.

Approximate nutritive values per portion

Calories	Carbohydrate	Protein	Fat	Cholesterol	Sodium	Fiber	Iron
456 kcal	40 g	18 g	25 g	51 mg	790 mg	2 g	2 mg

Notes

- Potentially hazardous food. *Food Safety Standards:* Hold food for service at an internal temperature of 135°F or above. Do not mix old product with new. Cool leftover product quickly following time standards and cooling procedures on p. 167. Reheat leftover product quickly (within 2 hours) to 165°F or above. Reheat product only once; discard if not used.
- For variety, use rotini, shells, or other shapes of pasta.
- A combination of Swiss and mozzarella cheeses may be substituted for some or all of the cheddar cheese.

Variation

- **Macaroni, Cheese, and Ham.** Add 3 lb chopped ham, 1 lb 8 oz per pan. Reduce salt to 1 Tbsp.

HERBED FETTUCCINE

Yield: 50 portions   *Portion:* 4 oz

Ingredient	Amount	Procedure
Margarine	1 lb 10 oz	Melt margarine in steam-jacketed or other kettle.
Garlic cloves, minced	6	Add garlic and cook until golden. Save for later step.
Cream cheese, softened	3 lb 4 oz	Mix cream cheese on medium speed until fluffy, using a flat paddle.
Fresh parsley, minced	½ cup	Blend into cream cheese.
Basil, dried, crumbled	2 Tbsp	
Black pepper	1 tsp	
Salt	2 tsp	
Water, boiling	1 qt	Add water gradually to cream cheese mixture. Mix until smooth. Add margarine and garlic. Mix until smooth.
Fettuccine	1 lb 12 oz AP	Cook fettuccine according to directions on p. 507.
Water, boiling	2 gal	Drain.
Salt	1½ oz	
Vegetable oil	2 Tbsp	
		Scale cooked fettuccine into two 12 × 10 × 4-inch counter pans, 2 lb 12 oz each. Stir 3 lb 6 oz cream cheese sauce into each pan of hot pasta. Cover. Keep hot, approximately 180°F. Sprinkle with Parmesan cheese and snipped fresh parsley just before serving.

Approximate nutritive values per portion

Calories	Carbohydrate	Protein	Fat	Cholesterol	Sodium	Fiber	Iron
272 kcal	12 g	5 g	23 g	48 mg	364 mg	0.4 g	1 mg

Notes

- Potentially hazardous food. *Food Safety Standards:* Hold food for service at an internal temperature of 135°F or above. Do not mix old product with new. Cool leftover product quickly following time standards and cooling procedures on p. 167. Reheat leftover product quickly (within 2 hours) to 165°F or above. Reheat product only once; discard if not used.
- Other fresh herbs may be substituted for parsley.

NOODLES ROMANOFF

Yield: 50 portions or 2 pans, 12 × 20 × 2 inches   *Portion:* 5 oz
Oven: 350°F   *Bake:* 30 minutes

Ingredient	Amount	Procedure
Noodles	3 lb	Cook noodles according to directions on p. 507.
Water, boiling	3 gal	Drain.
Salt	3 oz	
Vegetable oil (optional)	1 Tbsp	
Onions, chopped	6 oz	Sauté onions in margarine until tender.
Margarine	10 oz	
Flour, all-purpose	4 oz	Add flour and seasonings to onions, stirring constantly.
Salt	1 oz (1½ Tbsp)	Cook for 5–10 minutes.
Garlic powder	¼ tsp	
Milk	1¼ qt	Add milk gradually to flour mixture, stirring constantly. Cook until thickened.
Parmesan cheese, grated	4 oz	Add cheeses, sour cream, and paprika to sauce.
Cottage cheese	2 lb 8 oz	Combine hot noodles and sauce.
Sour cream	2½ cups	
Paprika	1 Tbsp	
Cheddar cheese, shredded	8 oz	Scale pasta mixture into two 12 × 10 × 2-inch counter pans, 8 lb per pan. Sprinkle with cheese, 4 oz per pan. Bake at 350°F for approximately 30 minutes or until heated to 180°F.

Approximate nutritive values per portion

Calories	Carbohydrate	Protein	Fat	Cholesterol	Sodium	Fiber	Iron
247 kcal	24 g	10 g	12 g	44 mg	502 mg	1 g	2 mg

Notes

- Potentially hazardous food. *Food Safety Standards:* Hold food for service at an internal temperature of 135°F or above. Do not mix old product with new. Cool leftover product quickly following time standards and cooling procedures on p. 167. Reheat leftover product quickly (within 2 hours) to 165°F or above. Reheat product only once; discard if not used.
- Linguine or other pasta may be substituted for the noodles.

PASTA WITH CLAM SAUCE

Yield: 50 portions   *Portion:* 6 oz sauce + 4 oz pasta

Ingredient	Amount	Procedure
Margarine	1 lb 8 oz	Melt margarine in a large kettle.
Flour, all-purpose	1 lb	Stir in flour and cook for 5–10 minutes.
Milk, hot	6½ qt	Add milk and seasonings to flour-margarine mixture, while stirring.
Salt	2 oz	Heat to boiling.
Nutmeg, ground	½ tsp	
Half-and-half	1½ qt	Reduce heat. Add half-and-half slowly and continue to cook until thickened.
Minced clams	2 lb	Stir clams into sauce. Keep hot, 180°F.
Pasta	5 lb	Cook pasta according to directions on p. 507.
Water, boiling	5 gal	Serve 6 oz sauce over 4 oz pasta.
Salt	5 oz	
Vegetable oil (optional)	3 Tbsp	

Approximate nutritive values per portion

Calories	Carbohydrate	Protein	Fat	Cholesterol	Sodium	Fiber	Iron
435 kcal	47 g	15 g	21 g	77 mg	893 mg	1 g	6 mg

Notes

- Potentially hazardous food. *Food Safety Standards:* Hold food for service at an internal temperature of 135°F or above. Do not mix old product with new. Cool leftover product quickly following time standards and cooling procedures on p. 167. Reheat leftover product quickly (within 2 hours) to 165°F or above. Reheat product only once; discard if not used.
- Clam sauce is excellent served on whole-wheat pasta.
- 2 oz chopped green onion tops, 2 oz chopped chives, or 6 oz sliced mushrooms may be added for variety and color.
- Reduce fat by substituting milk for the light cream.

Variations

- **Pasta with Cheese Sauce.** Delete salt, nutmeg, and clams. Reduce margarine to 1 lb, flour to 12 oz, milk to 5 qt, and cream to 1 qt. Stir in 4 oz chicken base. Add 2 oz Parmesan cheese, 8 oz provolone cheese, and 4 oz shredded Swiss cheese, and stir until melted. Thin with hot milk if sauce becomes too thick.
- **Pasta with Shrimp Sauce.** Substitute 4 lb cooked salad shrimp for the clams.

PASTA PRIMAVERA

Yield: 50 portions   *Portion:* 5 oz sauce + 4 oz pasta

Ingredient	Amount	Procedure
Fresh carrots	1 lb	Cut carrots into thin julienne strips $1\frac{1}{2}$ inches long. Steam until tender-crisp. Drain. Save for later step.
Broccoli cuts	1 lb	Steam broccoli until tender-crisp. Drain. Save for later step.
Onion, chopped	4 oz	Add onion and garlic to melted margarine.
Garlic cloves, minced	4	Cook until onion is tender.
Margarine, melted	12 oz	
Flour, all-purpose	12 oz	Add flour. Stir with a wire whip until flour is mixed in. Cook for 5 minutes, stirring often.
Water	$2\frac{3}{4}$ qt	Combine water, milk, and chicken base and gradually add to roux, stirring with a wire whip.
Milk	$2\frac{1}{2}$ qt	
Chicken base	4 oz	Cook, stirring often, until thickened and no starchy flavor remains.
Fresh parsley, snipped	$2\frac{1}{2}$ cups	Add to hot sauce.
Basil, dried, crumbled	$\frac{1}{2}$ cup	Add carrots and broccoli cuts. Keep hot, 180°F. Thin as needed with hot milk or chicken stock.
Ham, $\frac{1}{2}$-inch diced	1 lb 8 oz	
Frozen peas	10 oz	
Mushrooms, sliced	8 oz	
Pasta	5 lb	Cook pasta according to directions on p. 507.
Water, boiling	5 gal	Drain.
Salt	5 oz	Serve 5 oz sauce over 4 oz pasta, accompanied by Parmesan cheese.
Vegetable oil	3 Tbsp	

Approximate nutritive values per portion

Calories	Carbohydrate	Protein	Fat	Cholesterol	Sodium	Fiber	Iron
337 kcal	43 g	13 g	12 g	59 mg	683 mg	2 g	4 mg

Notes

- Potentially hazardous food. *Food Safety Standards:* Hold food for service at an internal temperature of 135°F or above. Do not mix old product with new. Cool leftover product quickly following time standards and cooling procedures on p. 167. Reheat leftover product quickly (within 2 hours) to 165°F or above. Reheat product only once; discard if not used.
- Vegetable base may be substituted for chicken base.
- $\frac{1}{2}$ oz ($\frac{1}{4}$ cup) dehydrated onion, rehydrated in $\frac{1}{2}$ cup water, may be substituted for fresh onion.

SWISS BROCCOLI PASTA

Yield: 50 portions   *Portion:* 4 oz sauce + 4 oz pasta

Ingredient	Amount	Procedure
Broccoli cuts	1 lb 12 oz	Steam broccoli until tender-crisp. (Do not overcook.) Drain. Save for later step.
Margarine, melted	8 oz	Combine melted margarine and flour in steam-jacketed or other kettle.
Flour, all-purpose	8 oz	Stir and cook until smooth (5–10 minutes).
Milk	3¼ qt	Add milk gradually. Cook over low heat, stirring constantly, until thick. Do not boil. Turn off heat.
Swiss cheese, shredded	3 lb 4 oz	Add cheese to hot sauce and stir until melted.
Nutmeg, ground	¼ tsp	Stir in nutmeg.
Sliced mushrooms, canned, drained	1 lb	Stir in mushrooms and broccoli. Keep hot, 180°F.
Pasta	5 lb	Cook pasta according to directions on p. 507.
Water, boiling	5 gal	Drain.
Salt	5 oz	Serve 4 oz sauce over 4 oz pasta.
Vegetable oil	3 Tbsp	Thin sauce as necessary with hot milk.

Approximate nutritive values per portion

Calories	Carbohydrate	Protein	Fat	Cholesterol	Sodium	Fiber	Iron
381 kcal	41 g	18 g	16 g	79 mg	1312 mg	2 g	3 mg

Note

- Potentially hazardous food. *Food Safety Standards:* Hold food for service at an internal temperature of 135°F or above. Do not mix old product with new. Cool Leftover product quickly following time standards and cooling procedures on p. 167. Reheat leftover product quickly (within 2 hours) to 165°F or above. Reheat product only once; discard if not used.

Variation

- **Ham and Swiss Broccoli Pasta.** Omit nutmeg. Reduce cheese to 2 lb 8 oz, broccoli to 1 lb, and mushrooms to 8 oz. Add 2 lb diced ham and 8 oz diced green bell pepper.

LASAGNA FLORENTINE (WITH FROZEN LASAGNA NOODLE SHEETS)

Yield: 48 portions   *Portion:* 10 oz
Oven: 350°F   *Bake:* 1–1½ hours

Ingredient	Amount	Procedure
Chopped spinach, thawed	3 lb 8 oz AP (3 lb EP)	Steam spinach until just cooked. Drain well. Check weight after steaming. Need 3 lb chopped spinach for a later step.
Vegetable oil Onions, chopped Green bell peppers, chopped Garlic, minced	½ cup 1 lb 4 oz EP 12 oz EP 2 oz EP	Heat oil to 350°F in steam-jacketed or other large kettle. Sauté vegetables until tender.
Chopped tomatoes, canned Tomato juice Tomato paste Sugar, granulated Fresh parsley, minced Oregano, dried Bay leaves Basil, dried	6 lb 2¼ qt 1 qt 2 Tbsp 1¾ oz 2 tsp 4 2 tsp	Stir tomato products, sugar, and herbs into sautéed vegetables. Bring to a boil. Reduce heat and simmer uncovered for 25 minutes.
Cottage cheese, cream style Parmesan cheese, grated Eggs Salt Black pepper	5 lb 4 oz 1 lb 9 oz 1 Tbsp 1 Tbsp	Combine cheeses, eggs, and seasonings. Mix with spinach reserved from earlier step. Mix well.
Frozen lasagna sheets Mozzarella cheese, shredded Parmesan cheese, grated	6 lb 2 lb 14 oz 4 oz	Layer into two 12 × 20 × 2-inch pans according to following directions for each pan: 1. Tomato sauce: 1 qt + ½ cup 2. Lasagna sheets: 1 lb 8 oz (6 sheets) 3. Spinach mixture: 2 lb 5 oz 4. Mozzarella cheese: 11 oz 5. Repeat steps 1 through 4 6. Tomato sauce: 1 qt 7. Parmesan cheese: 2 oz
		Bake at 350°F for 1–1½ hours. Cover with foil if browning too quickly. Endpoint temperature should be 180–190°F. Let set for 10–15 minutes after removing from the oven. Do not cover. Cut 4 × 6.

Approximate nutritive values per portion

Calories	Carbohydrate	Protein	Fat	Cholesterol	Sodium	Fiber	Iron
390 kcal	36 g	25 g	16 g	63 mg	1065 mg	3.5 g	2 mg

Note

- *Potentially hazardous food. Food Safety Standards:* Hold food for service at an internal temperature of 135°F or above. Do not mix old product with new. Cool leftover product quickly following time standards and cooling procedures on p. 167. Reheat leftover product quickly (within 2 hours) to 165°F or above. Reheat product only once; discard if not used.

SPINACH LASAGNA (DEEP DISH)

Yield: 64 portions or 2 pans, 12 × 20 × 2 inches   *Portion:* 10 oz
Oven: 350°F   *Bake:* 1½–2 hours

Ingredient	Amount	Procedure
Onions, chopped	1 lb 8 oz	Sauté vegetables in hot oil.
Green bell pepper, chopped	12 oz	
Garlic, minced	2 oz	
Vegetable oil	½ cup	
Diced tomatoes, canned	8 lb	Stir tomato products and seasonings into sautéed vegetables. Simmer uncovered for about 20 minutes.
Tomato juice	3 qt	Remove bay leaves. Use sauce in layering steps.
Tomato paste	2 lb 8 oz	
Fresh parsley, chopped	3 oz	
Oregano, dried, crumbled	1 Tbsp	
Basil, dried, crumbled	1 Tbsp	
Bay leaves	2	
Spinach, chopped	3 lb	Cook spinach. Drain.
Cottage cheese	5 lb	Mix. Add to spinach.
Parmesan cheese, grated	1 lb	
Eggs, beaten	5 (8 oz)	
Salt	1 Tbsp	
Black pepper	2 tsp	
Lasagna noodles, dry	5 lb	See the following directions for layering.
Mozzarella cheese, shredded	3 lb 12 oz	

Layer ingredients in each of two 12 × 20 × 4-inch pans as follows:
1. Tomato sauce, 3 lb 4 oz
2. Dry noodles, 13 oz
3. Spinach-cheese mixture, 2 lb 5 oz
4. Mozzarella cheese, 11 oz
5. Repeat layers 1 through 4
6. Dry noodles, 13 oz
7. Tomato sauce, 3 lb 4 oz
8. Mozzarella cheese, 8 oz

Bake at 350°F covered with aluminum foil for approximately 1 hour, or until internal temperature reaches 180°F. Remove foil and bake for an additional 30–60 minutes or until hot and bubbly. If browning too fast, cover again with foil. Let set for 15–20 minutes before cutting. Cut 4 × 8.

Approximate nutritive values per portion

Calories	Carbohydrate	Protein	Fat	Cholesterol	Sodium	Fiber	Iron
346 kcal	37 g	20 g	13 g	80 mg	902 mg	4 g	4 mg

Notes

- Potentially hazardous food. *Food Safety Standards:* Hold food for service at an internal temperature of 135°F or above. Do not mix old product with new. Cool leftover product quickly following time standards and cooling procedures on p. 167. Reheat leftover product quickly (within 2 hours) to 165°F or above. Reheat product only once; discard if not used.
- Frozen lasagna noodle sheets may be used. Reduce diced tomatoes to 5 lb 8 oz, tomato juice to 2¼ qt, and tomato paste to 2 lb. Replace dry noodles with 6 lb frozen lasagna sheets, using 3 lb per pan.
- 3¾ oz (1¾ cups) dehydrated onions, rehydrated in 3 cups water, may be substituted for fresh onions.

LASAGNA

Yield: 48 portions or 2 pans, 12 × 20 × 2 inches   *Portion:* 6 oz
Oven: 350°F   *Bake:* 45–60 minutes

Ingredient	Amount	Procedure
Ground beef	5 lb AP	Cook beef, onions, and garlic until meat reaches an internal temperature of 155°F.
Onions, finely chopped	12 oz	
Garlic cloves, minced	2	Drain off fat.
Tomato sauce	3 qt	Add tomato products and seasonings to meat.
Tomato paste	1 qt	Simmer for about 30 minutes, stirring occasionally.
Black pepper	1 tsp	
Basil, dried, crumbled	1 tsp	
Oregano, dried, crumbled	1 Tbsp	
Lasagna noodles, dry	2 lb 8 oz	Cook noodles according to directions on p. 507.
Water, boiling	2 gal	Store in cold water to keep noodles from sticking.
Salt	2 oz	Drain when ready to use.
Vegetable oil	2 Tbsp	
Mozzarella cheese, shredded	2 lb 8 oz	Combine cheeses.
Parmesan cheese, grated	6 oz	Arrange in two greased 12 × 20 × 2-inch counter pans in layers in the following order:
Ricotta cheese or cottage cheese, dry or drained	2 lb 8 oz	Meat sauce, 1 qt Noodles, overlapping, 1 lb 12 oz Cheeses, 1 lb 4 oz
		Repeat sauce, noodles, and cheese.
		Spoon remainder of meat sauce on top.
		Bake at 350°F for 45–60 minutes.
		Let stand for 15–20 minutes before cutting. Cut 4 × 6.

Approximate nutritive values per portion

Calories	Carbohydrate	Protein	Fat	Cholesterol	Sodium	Fiber	Iron
329 kcal	26 g	20 g	16 g	77 mg	1205 mg	2 g	3 mg

Notes

- Potentially hazardous food. *Food Safety Standards:* Hold food for service at an internal temperature of 135°F or above. Do not mix old product with new. Cool leftover product quickly following time standards and cooling procedures on p. 167. Reheat leftover product quickly (within 2 hours) to 165°F or above. Reheat product only once; discard if not used.
- 1½ oz (¾ cup) dehydrated onions, rehydrated in 1 cup water, may be substituted for fresh onions.

LASAGNA (WITH FROZEN LASAGNA NOODLE SHEETS)

Yield: 48 portions   *Portion:* 8 oz
Oven: 350°F   *Bake:* 1–1½ hours

Ingredient	Amount	Procedure
Ground beef	5 lb AP (3 lb EP)	Cook beef, onions, and garlic until meat reaches an internal temperature of 155°F.
Onions, finely chopped	2 lb 12 oz EP	
Garlic, minced	1 oz EP	
Chopped tomatoes, canned	3 qt	Add tomato products and seasonings to ground beef mixture. Simmer uncovered for 45 minutes.
Tomato purée	3 cups	
Tomato paste	4½ cups	
Salt	2 oz	
Black pepper	1 tsp	
Oregano, dried	3 Tbsp	
Basil, dried	3 Tbsp	
Fresh parsley, chopped	1½ oz	
Frozen lasagna sheets	3 lb	Layer into two 12 × 20 × 2-inch pans according to the following directions for each pan:
Mozzarella cheese, shredded	4 lb	1. Meat sauce: 2 lb
Cottage cheese, cream style	5 lb 8 oz	2. Lasagna sheets: 12 oz (3 sheets)
		3. Cottage cheese: 1 lb 5 oz
Parmesan cheese, grated	10 oz	4. Parmesan cheese: 2½ oz
		5. Mozzarella cheese: 12 oz
		6. Meat sauce: 2 lb 8 oz
		7. Repeat steps 2–6
		8. Mozzarella cheese: 8 oz
		Cover with foil. Bake at 350°F for 1–1½ hours. Uncover for the last 20–30 minutes.
		Before cutting, let set for 10–15 minutes after removing from the oven. Do not cover. Cut 4 × 6.

Approximate nutritive values per portion

Calories	Carbohydrate	Protein	Fat	Cholesterol	Sodium	Fiber	Iron
440 kcal	37 g	33 g	18 g	70 mg	1100 mg	3.4 g	3 mg

Note

- Potentially hazardous food. *Food Safety Standards:* Hold food for service at an internal temperature of 135°F or above. Do not mix old product with new. Cool leftover product quickly following time standards and cooling procedures on p. 167. Reheat leftover product quickly (within 2 hours) to 165°F or above. Reheat product only once; discard if not used.

BASIL AND PARMESAN BOWS WITH SUGAR SNAP PEAS

Yield: 50 entrées or 100 accompaniment portions   *Portion:* 8 oz (entrée) or 4 oz (accompaniment)

Ingredient	Amount	Procedure
Pasta, bow tie shape	11 lb	Cook pasta according to directions on p. 507.
Water, boiling	11 gal	Drain.
Salt	11 oz	Save for later step.
Vegetable oil	⅓ cup	
Olive oil	1½ cup	Heat oil to 350°F in tilting fry pan or steam-jacketed kettle.
Crushed red pepper	¼ tsp	Add pepper.
Sugar snap peas, fresh or frozen	4 lb 8 oz EP	Sauté sugar snap peas and garlic in hot oil just until peas are tender-crisp.
Garlic, minced	2 oz EP	Add peas to pasta. Stir carefully to mix.
		Transfer into four 12 × 20 × 4-inch pans.
Parmesan cheese, freshly shredded	2 lb	Sprinkle 8 oz cheese and approximately ½ cup fresh basil on each pan. Toss to blend.
Fresh basil, chopped	2 oz	

Approximate nutritive values per portion (Entrée Portion)

Calories	Carbohydrate	Protein	Fat	Cholesterol	Sodium	Fiber	Iron
270 kcal	28 g	11 g	13 g	38 mg	242 mg	3.4 g	2 mg

Notes

- Potentially hazardous food. *Food Safety Standards:* Hold food for service at an internal temperature of 135°F or above. Do not mix old product with new. Cool leftover product quickly following time standards and cooling procedures on p. 167. Reheat leftover product quickly (within 2 hours) to 165°F or above. Reheat product only once; discard if not used.
- Basil oil can be substituted for olive oil. Basil oil can be purchased or made by combining ½ cup olive oil, 1 cup vegetable oil, and 1 tsp dried basil leaves. Store covered in refrigerator for 24 hours before using.

GARLIC AND RED PEPPER PENNE

Yield: 50 entrées or 100 accompaniment portions   *Portion:* 8 oz (entrée) or 4 oz (accompaniment)

Ingredient	Amount	Procedure
Penne	12 lb	Cook according to directions on p. 507. Drain.
Water, boiling	12 gal	
Salt	12 oz	
Crushed red pepper	1 Tbsp	Sauté pepper, garlic, and basil in oil.
Garlic cloves, minced	12 oz EP	Mix with drained pasta.
Basil, dried	¼ cup	
Olive oil	2 cups	
Fresh parsley, chopped	6 oz	Add parsley and salt to pasta. Toss to mix.
Salt	2 tsp	Keep warm, 160°F.

Approximate nutritive values per portion (Entrée Portion)

Calories	Carbohydrate	Protein	Fat	Cholesterol	Sodium	Fiber	Iron
225 kcal	30 g	5.4 g	8.7 g	0 mg	123 mg	1.6 g	2 mg

Note

- Potentially hazardous food. *Food Safety Standards:* Hold food for service at an internal temperature of 135°F or above. Do not mix old product with new. Cool leftover product quickly following time standards and cooling procedures on p. 167. Reheat leftover product quickly (within 2 hours) to 165°F or above. Reheat product only once; discard if not used.

Variation

- **Lemon and Herb Penne.** Mix together 1 cup fresh lemon juice, 1 lb fresh minced parsley, 5 Tbsp dried basil, and 1 Tbsp black pepper. Toss herb-lemon mixture with 12 lb cooked penne. Drizzle 2 cups olive oil over pasta and mix. Stir in 2 lb freshly grated Parmesan cheese.

PEPPER AND GARLIC PASTA SHELLS

Yield: 50 entrées or 100 accompaniment portions   *Portion:* 8 oz (entrée) or 4 oz (accompaniment)

Ingredient	Amount	Procedure
Large shell pasta	6 lb	Cook according to directions on p. 507.
Water	3 gal	Drain and reserve for later step. Expected yield is 14 lb 8 oz.
Salt	2 oz	
Olive oil	3 cups	Heat olive oil in steam-jacketed or other large kettle. Add onions, garlic, and pepper.
Onions, chopped	2 lb	Sauté until onions are beginning to soften.
Garlic, minced	4 oz	
Crushed red pepper	1 tsp	
Bell peppers (combination of green, yellow, and red)	3 lb 12 oz	Add the peppers, carrots, and mushrooms. Sauté until tender-crisp.
Carrot sticks, matchstick	1 lb	
Mushrooms, sliced	1 lb 4 oz	
Water	2½ cups	Blend water and vegetable base. Pour over vegetables.
Vegetable base	1 Tbsp	
Flat leaf parsley, chopped	1 oz	Stir in parsley, cheese, and pepper. Scale 6 lb per 12 × 10 × 2-inch pan.
Parmesan cheese, shredded	1 lb	
Black pepper	1 Tbsp	
Parmesan cheese, shredded	8 oz	Sprinkle 2 oz cheese, over the top of each pan of pasta.

Approximate nutritive values per portion (Entrée Portion)

Calories	Carbohydrate	Protein	Fat	Cholesterol	Sodium	Fiber	Iron
450 kcal	44 g	14 g	22 g	14 mg	750 mg	4 g	1.5 mg

Note

- Potentially hazardous food. *Food Safety Standards:* Hold food for service at an internal temperature of 135°F or above. Do not mix old product with new. Cool leftover product quickly following time standards and cooling procedures on p. 167. Reheat leftover product quickly (within 2 hours) to 165°F or above. Reheat product only once; discard if not used.

ROASTED EGGPLANT AND CHICKPEA RAGOUT ON PENNE

Yield: 50 portions   *Portion:* 6 oz sauce + 4 oz penne
Oven: 400°F

Ingredient	Amount	Procedure
Eggplant, unpeeled, ¾-inch cubes	5 lb EP	Gently mix eggplant with 1½ Tbsp salt. Let drain in colander for 30 minutes. Rinse eggplant well, two or three times. Dry on paper towel.
Olive oil	2 oz	Place eggplant in bowl. Pour oil over eggplant and mix to coat. Place eggplant in a single layer on a baking sheet. Roast at 400°F for 10–12 minutes, turning once halfway through. Reserve for later step.
Olive oil	2 oz	Heat oil to 350°F in tilting or other large fry pan.
Red bell peppers, ½-inch dice	12 oz EP	Add vegetables, turmeric, and pepper to oil.
Yellow bell peppers, ½-inch dice	8 oz EP	Sauté vegetables for 5 minutes.
Green bell peppers, ½-inch dice	12 oz EP	
Onions, ½-inch dice	2 lb 4 oz EP	
Garlic, minced	2 oz EP	
Turmeric	1 tsp	
Crushed red pepper	¼ tsp	
Tomato paste	5 oz	Add tomato paste and water to vegetables.
Water	8 oz	Cook and stir until most of the liquid has been absorbed.
Diced tomatoes, canned	2 lb 4 oz	Add tomatoes and beans to vegetable mixture.
Garbanzo beans, canned, drained	3 lb 10 oz EP	Stir in eggplant reserved from earlier step.
Thyme, dried	2½ tsp	Add seasonings and water to eggplant mixture.
Salt	1 oz	Simmer, stirring occasionally, until mixture has thickened and vegetables are tender (15–20 minutes).
Parsley, dried	6 Tbsp	Transfer into serving pans and cover.
Basil, dried	1 Tbsp	
Water	1¾ qt	
Penne	6 lb	Cook penne according to directions on page 507. Drain.
Water	6 gal	Serve 6 oz ragout over 4 oz pasta.
Salt	6 oz	
Vegetable oil (optional)	3 Tbsp	

Approximate nutritive values per portion

Calories	Carbohydrate	Protein	Fat	Cholesterol	Sodium	Fiber	Iron
250 kcal	43 g	9 g	5 g	53 mg	431 mg	4.7 g	3 mg

Notes

- Potentially hazardous food. *Food Safety Standards:* Hold food for service at an internal temperature of 135°F or above. Do not mix old product with new. Cool leftover product quickly following time standards and cooling procedures on p. 167. Reheat leftover product quickly (within 2 hours) to 165°F or above. Reheat product only once; discard if not used.
- A frozen bell pepper blend can be substituted for the green, red, and yellow bell peppers.

RIGATONI AND SPINACH

Yield: 50 entrées or 100 accompaniment portions   *Portion:* 8 oz (entrée) or 4 oz (accompaniment)

Ingredient	Amount	Procedure
Rigatoni	8 lb	Cook pasta according to directions on p. 507.
Water	8 gal	Drain.
Salt	8 oz	Reserve pasta for later step.
Vegetable oil (optional)	¼ cup	
Basil oil (see Note)	1½ cups	Heat oil to 350°F in steam-jacketed or other large kettle.
Onion, chopped	8 oz EP	Sauté onion and garlic until tender.
Garlic, minced	8 oz EP	Stir in pepper.
Crushed red pepper	5 tsp	
Vegetable base	1 oz	Dissolve vegetable base in water. Add liquid, spinach, and oil to garlic-onion mixture. Cook only until spinach is wilted.
Water	2 cups	
Fresh spinach, coarsely chopped	3 lb 4 oz EP	Stir spinach mixture into pasta reserved from earlier step.
Vegetable oil	¼ cup	
Parmesan cheese, grated	2 lb	Stir 1 lb Parmesan cheese into pasta. Serve the remainder of the cheese as a condiment.

Approximate nutritive values per portion (Entrée Portion)

Calories	Carbohydrate	Protein	Fat	Cholesterol	Sodium	Fiber	Iron
255 kcal	22 g	12 g	13 g	14 mg	457 mg	1.8 g	2 mg

Notes

- Potentially hazardous food. *Food Safety Standards:* Hold food for service at an internal temperature of 135°F or above. Do not mix old product with new. Cool leftover product quickly following time standards and cooling procedures on p. 167. Reheat leftover product quickly (within 2 hours) to 165°F or above. Reheat product only once; discard if not used.
- Basil oil can be purchased or made by combining ½ cup olive oil, 1 cup vegetable oil, and ½ tsp dried basil leaves. Store covered in refrigerator for 24 hours before using.

BAKED ZITI WITH FOUR CHEESES

Yield: 48 portions or 2 pans, 12 × 20 × 4 inches   *Portion:* 8 oz
Oven: 350°F   *Bake:* 20–25 minutes

Ingredient	Amount	Procedure
Crushed tomatoes, canned	5½ qt	Combine tomato products and seasonings in steam-jacketed kettle.
Tomato purée	1 qt	Cover and simmer for about 10 minutes.
Onion, finely chopped	3 oz	Turn off heat.
Basil, dried, crumbled	1 Tbsp	
Oregano, dried, crumbled	2 tsp	
Fresh parsley, minced	4 oz	
Black pepper	½ tsp	
Salt	1 oz (1½ Tbsp)	
Ziti	3 lb	Cook according to directions on p. 507. Drain.
Water	3 gal	Cooked yield should be about 6 lb 6 oz.
Salt	3 oz	
Vegetable oil (optional)	2 Tbsp	
Cottage cheese	3 lb	Layer as follows into two 12 × 20 × 4-inch pans:
Mozzarella cheese, shredded	1 lb 8 oz	1. 2 lb sauce
Swiss cheese, shredded	1 lb 8 oz	2. 1 lb 10 oz cooked ziti
		3. 12 oz cottage cheese
		4. 6 oz mozzarella cheese
		5. 6 oz Swiss cheese
		Repeat steps 1–5.
		Smooth 2 lb sauce over top.
Fresh parsley, minced	4 oz	Sprinkle 2 oz parsley over sauce.
Provolone cheese, shredded	1 lb	Sprinkle 8 oz provolone cheese over parsley.
		Cover. Bake at 350°F for 20–25 minutes or until 180°F and
		cheese melts.

Approximate nutritive values per portion

Calories	Carbohydrate	Protein	Fat	Cholesterol	Sodium	Fiber	Iron
302 kcal	29 g	18 g	13 g	62 mg	1372 mg	2 g	3 mg

Note

- Potentially hazardous food. *Food Safety Standards:* Hold food for service at an internal temperature of 135°F or above. Do not mix old product with new. Cool leftover product quickly following time standards and cooling procedures on p. 167. Reheat leftover product quickly (within 2 hours) to 165°F or above. Reheat product only once; discard if not used.

SOUTHWEST ZITI

Yield: 50 portions   *Portion:* 8 oz

Ingredient	Amount	Procedure
Basil oil (see Note)	1 cup	Heat oil in steam-jacketed kettle.
Onions, chopped	1 lb 3 oz EP	Add onions to hot oil and sauté until fragrant.
Green bell peppers, coarsely chopped	8 oz EP	Add peppers and garlic. Sauté for 2–3 minutes longer.
Garlic, minced	5 Tbsp EP	
Diced tomatoes, canned (see Note)	9 lb 8 oz EP	Add to sautéed vegetables. Mix well. Simmer until slightly thickened.
Red wine vinegar	2⅓ cup	
Basil, dried (see Note)	2 Tbsp	
Cilantro, dried (see Note)	1½ Tbsp	
Salt	1½ tsp	
Black pepper	2 Tbsp	
Ziti	5 lb	Cook pasta according to directions on p. 507. Drain.
Water	5 gal	Scale 3 lb pasta into 12 × 10 × 2-inch pans.
Salt	5 oz	Lightly drizzle olive oil or basil oil over pasta. Stir to coat. Scale 3 lb sauce over each pan of pasta. Toss lightly.
Parmesan cheese, grated	2 lb	Serve sprinkled with Parmesan cheese.

Approximate nutritive values per portion

Calories	Carbohydrate	Protein	Fat	Cholesterol	Sodium	Fiber	Iron
335 kcal	2.5 g	11 g	21 g	52 mg	1170 mg	1.6 g	2 mg

Notes

- Potentially hazardous food. *Food Safety Standards:* Hold food for service at an internal temperature of 135°F or above. Do not mix old product with new. Cool leftover product quickly following time standards and cooling procedures on p. 167. Reheat leftover product quickly (within 2 hours) to 165°F or above. Reheat product only once; discard if not used.
- Olive oil may be substituted for basil oil. Basil oil can be purchased or made by combining ½ cup olive oil, 1 cup vegetable oil, and ½ tsp dried basil leaves. Store covered in refrigerator for 24 hours before using.
- Diced fresh tomatoes can be substituted for canned tomatoes.
- ⅓ cup fresh basil, chopped, and ⅓ cup fresh cilantro, chopped, may be substituted for dried basil and cilantro. When using fresh herbs, add for only the last few minutes of the sauce cooking period.

PASTA WITH VEGETABLE SAUCE

Yield: 50 portions or 2½ gal sauce   *Portion:* 6 oz sauce + 4 oz pasta

Ingredient	Amount	Procedure
Onions, chopped	2 lb	Sauté onions in oil until tender, using a steam-jacketed or
Olive oil	1 cup	other large kettle.
Green bell peppers, cut in 1-inch squares	1 lb	Add peppers, carrots, and seasonings to onions. Mix well.
Carrot coins	1 lb	
Oregano, dried, crumbled	2 Tbsp	
Basil, dried, crumbled	½ oz (½ cup)	
Black pepper	1 Tbsp	
Garlic powder	1 tsp	
Salt	1 oz (1½ Tbsp)	
Bay leaves	2	
Tomato juice	five 46-oz cans	Add tomato juice and paste to vegetables. Heat to boiling.
Tomato paste	1 lb 12 oz	Reduce heat and simmer uncovered for 15–20 minutes. Remove bay leaves.
Zucchini squash, sliced	2 lb	Add zucchini and mushrooms just before serving. Cook only
Mushrooms, sliced	1 lb	until zucchini is tender. Keep hot, 180°F.
Pasta	5 lb	Cook pasta according to directions on p. 507.
Water, boiling	5 gal	Serve 6 oz sauce over 4 oz pasta.
Salt	5 oz	
Vegetable oil (optional)	3 Tbsp	

Approximate nutritive values per portion

Calories	Carbohydrate	Protein	Fat	Cholesterol	Sodium	Fiber	Iron
263 kcal	44 g	9 g	7 g	43 mg	1030 mg	4 g	5 mg

Notes

- Potentially hazardous food. *Food Safety Standards:* Hold food for service at an internal temperature of 135°F or above. Do not mix old product with new. Cool leftover product quickly following time standards and cooling procedures on p. 167. Reheat leftover product quickly (within 2 hours) to 165°F or above. Reheat product only once; discard if not used.
- 2 cups finely chopped fresh basil may be substituted for dried basil.
- 4 oz (2 cups) dehydrated onions, rehydrated in 3 cups water, may be substituted for fresh onions.

Variations

- **Italian Sausage Pasta.** Delete olive oil, salt, and zucchini. Brown 5 lb bulk Italian sausage in steam-jacketed kettle. Drain. Add onions to sausage and continue to cook until onions are tender. Add spices, tomato juice, and tomato paste. Simmer for 15–20 minutes. Add meat sauce to 6 lb 8 oz cooked pasta (approximately 3 lb AP) and mix gently. Be careful not to overcook pasta. Scale 12 lb per 12 × 20 × 2-inch pan. Sprinkle 1 lb shredded mozzarella cheese over each pan and place in low oven until cheese is melted. Suggested pasta combination: 1 lb (AP) rotini, 1 lb (AP) bow ties, 1 lb (AP) rigatoni.
- **Pizza Sauce.** Reduce olive oil to 4 oz. Delete zucchini and mushrooms. Increase tomato paste to 5 lb 8 oz and decrease tomato juice to 5¼ qt. Add 1 tsp fennel seed, 2 Tbsp sugar, 1 tsp paprika, and ¼ tsp cayenne. Spread 1 qt sauce on top of 18 × 26-inch pizza dough before adding toppings.
- **Sandwich Tomato Sauce.** Delete salt, zucchini, and mushrooms. Add 1 Tbsp sugar. Reduce olive oil to 1 Tbsp, onions to ½ cup, oregano to 1 tsp, basil to 1 Tbsp, black pepper to ½ tsp, garlic powder to ½ tsp, bay leaf to 1 leaf, tomato juice to 1½ qt, and tomato paste to 1½ cups. Yield: 50 1-oz servings.

VEGETABLE LO MEIN

Yield: 50 porions   *Portion:* 6 oz + 4 oz fettuccine

Ingredient	Amount	Procedure
Sugar, granulated	1 oz	Combine sugar, cornstarch, and seasonings in a steam-jacketed kettle. Using a wire whip, blend well.
Cornstarch	11 oz	
White pepper	1 tsp	
Ginger, ground	4½ tsp	
Garlic powder	¾ tsp	
Ground red pepper	few grains	
Water	6½ qt	Stir water, soy sauce, and vegetable base into sugar-spice mixture. Cook until thickened and clear, stirring constantly with a wire whip.
Soy sauce	8 oz	
Vegetable base	5 oz	
Bamboo shoots, canned, drained and rinsed	1 lb EP	Add drained and rinsed bamboo shoots and water chestnuts to sauce.
Sliced water chestnuts, canned, drained	1 lb EP	
Broccoli florets	2 lb	Add vegetables to sauce. Heat to 180–190°F. Transfer into 12 × 10 × 4-inch pans. Cover and keep hot.
Carrots, small julienne cut	12 oz EP	
Green onions, sliced into 1-inch pieces	10 oz EP	
Bell peppers, strips (green, red, and yellow)	1 lb 4 oz EP	
Fettuccine	5 lbs	Cook pasta according to directions on p. 507. Drain.
Water	5 gal	Keep hot.
Salt	5 oz	Portion 6 oz of sauce over 4 oz pasta.

Approximate nutritive values per portion

Calories	Carbohydrate	Protein	Fat	Cholesterol	Sodium	Fiber	Iron
230 kcal	47 g	7.7 g	1.2 g	0 mg	1655 mg	2.8 g	2 mg

Note

- Potentially hazardous food. *Food Safety Standards:* Hold food for service at an internal temperature of 135°F or above. Do not mix old product with new. Cool leftover product quickly following time standards and cooling procedures on p. 167. Reheat leftover product quickly (within 2 hours) to 165°F or above. Reheat product only once; discard if not used.

PASTA WHEELS AND VEGETABLES

Yield: 50 portions   *Portion:* 4 oz

Ingredient	Amount	Procedure
Pasta wheels	5 lb	Cook according to directions on p. 507. Drain. (Should yield 10 lb cooked pasta.)
Water	5 gal	
Salt	5 oz	Scale into three 12 × 10 × 4-inch counter pans, 3 lb 5 oz each.
Vegetable oil	3 Tbsp	
Margarine, melted	1 lb	Combine margarine and basil. Ladle 5 oz over each pan of pasta.
Basil, dried, crumbled	3 Tbsp	Toss to coat. Keep hot.
Broccoli florets	1 lb	Steam vegetables separately until tender-crisp.
Red bell pepper strips	1 lb	To each pan of pasta, add 5 oz broccoli, 5 oz peppers, and 2 oz carrots.
Carrot sticks, matchstick	6 oz	Toss. Keep warm, 160° F.

Approximate nutritive values per portion

Calories	Carbohydrate	Protein	Fat	Cholesterol	Sodium	Fiber	Iron
247 kcal	35 g	6 g	9 g	0 mg	1202 mg	0.2 g	2 mg

Notes

- Potentially hazardous food. *Food Safety Standards:* Hold food for service at an internal temperature of 135°F or above. Do not mix old product with new. Cool leftover product quickly following time standards and cooling procedures on p. 167. Reheat leftover product quickly (within 2 hours) to 165°F or above. Reheat product only once; discard if not used.
- Other vegetables and pasta may be substituted. Suggested vegetables: zucchini, summer squash, asparagus, bell peppers (green, yellow, or red). Suggested pasta: shells, mostaccioli, bow ties.
- May be served as a side dish with poultry or pork or as an entrée sprinkled with Parmesan or Romano cheese.

Variations

- **Fettuccine with Herbed Butter Sauce.** Substitute fettuccine for pasta wheels. Omit vegetables. To the melted margarine, add 3 Tbsp dried basil leaves, 1 Tbsp dried thyme leaves, 1 cup snipped parsley, and ½ cup chopped chives. Toss pasta in margarine sauce. Serve hot.
- **Fettuccine with Pesto Sauce.** Cook and drain fettuccine. Toss with pesto sauce (2 oz pesto to 6 oz cooked pasta). If necessary, thin sauce with small amount of pasta water. Serve at once. May sprinkle with freshly grated Parmesan or Romano cheese and black pepper.

FRESH TOMATO LINGUINE WITH RAW TOMATO SAUCE

Yield: 50 portions   *Portion:* 4 oz

Ingredient	Amount	Procedure
Olive oil (see Note)	4 oz	Mix oil, tomatoes, basil, vinegar, and seasonings in baker's bowl.
Fresh tomatoes, diced	5 lb 4 oz EP	Cover and let stand at room temperature for 1–2 hours.
Fresh basil, chopped	1 oz	
Red wine vinegar	4 oz	
Salt	2½ tsp	
Black pepper	1 tsp	
Linguine	2 lb 10 oz	Cook according to directions on p. 507.
Water	2 gal	Drain. (Yield: 6 lb 12 oz cooked pasta.)
Salt	2 oz	
Parmesan cheese, grated	1 lb	Toss tomato mixture with hot pasta. Scale into pans and sprinkle with Parmesan cheese. Serve soon after mixing.

Approximate nutritive values per portion

Calories	Carbohydrate	Protein	Fat	Cholesterol	Sodium	Fiber	Iron
150 kcal	13.6 g	6 g	8 g	30 mg	660 mg	1 g	2 mg

Notes

- Potentially hazardous food. *Food Safety Standards:* Hold food for service at an internal temperature of 135°F or above. Do not mix old product with new. Cool leftover product quickly following time standards and cooling procedures on p. 167. Reheat leftover product quickly (within 2 hours) to 165°F or above. Reheat product only once; discard if not used.
- Basil oil can be substituted for olive oil. Basil oil can be purchased or made by combining ½ cup olive oil, 1 cup vegetable oil, and ½ tsp dried basil leaves, crumbled. Store covered in refrigerator for 24 hours before using.
- 2 Tbsp dried basil can be substituted for fresh basil.
- Double the recipe for an 8-oz entrée-size portion.

Variation

- **Tomato Linguine.** Substitute canned diced tomatoes for fresh tomatoes. Heat tomatoes with other ingredients to 170°F before mixing with pasta.

CREOLE SPAGHETTI

Yield: 50 portions or 2 pans, 12 × 20 × 2 inches   *Portion:* 8 oz
Oven: 325°F   *Bake:* 25–30 minutes

Ingredient	Amount	Procedure
Ground beef	7 lb AP (4 lb 10 oz EP)	Cook beef in steam-jacketed or other kettle until meat reaches 155°F. Drain off fat.
Onion, chopped Green bell pepper, chopped	8 oz 5 oz	Add onion and pepper to meat. Cook until vegetables are tender.
Water Diced tomatoes, canned Tomato purée Tomato paste	2 qt 2 qt 2 qt 1 qt	Add water and tomato products to meat.
Salt Sugar, granulated Cayenne pepper Garlic cloves, minced Worcestershire sauce Bay leaves Thyme, ground Oregano, dried, crumbled	2 Tbsp 1 Tbsp 1 tsp 2 ¼ cup 4 1 tsp 1 Tbsp	Add seasonings to meat mixture. Stir to blend. Simmer for 15 minutes. Remove bay leaves.
Spaghetti Water, boiling Salt Vegetable oil (optional)	2 lb AP (6 lb cooked) 3 gal 3 oz 2 Tbsp	Cook spaghetti according to directions on p. 507. Do not overcook.
Cheddar cheese, shredded	1 lb 4 oz	Combine hot sauce and hot cooked spaghetti. Pour into two 12 × 20 × 2-inch baking pans, 13 lb 12 oz per pan. Sprinkle cheese over top. Bake at 325°F for 20–30 minutes, 180°F internal temperature.

Approximate nutritive values per portion

Calories	Carbohydrate	Protein	Fat	Cholesterol	Sodium	Fiber	Iron
273 kcal	23 g	18 g	12 g	53 mg	767 mg	3 g	3 mg

Notes

- Potentially hazardous food. *Food Safety Standards:* Hold food for service at an internal temperature of 135°F or above. Do not mix old product with new. Cool leftover product quickly following time standards and cooling procedures on p. 167. Reheat leftover product quickly (within 2 hours) to 165°F or above. Reheat product only once; discard if not used.
- 1 oz (½ cup) dehydrated onions, rehydrated in ¾ cup water, may be substituted for fresh onions.

VEGETABLE PAD THAI

Yield: 50 portions   *Portion:* 8 oz

Ingredient	Amount	Procedure
Water	3 gal	Bring water to a boil in steam-jacketed or other large kettle.
Rice stick noodles	2 lb 12 oz	Add rice stick noodles to boiling water. Stir to keep noodles separated. Boil for 2 minutes. Drain noodles and rinse well under cold running water. Drain well. Spread in a thin layer on tea towel lined baking pan to dry. Let dry for at least 20 minutes. Reserve for later step.
Salad oil	⅔ cup	Heat oil in tilting fry pan. Add garlic, shallots, and hot chile sauce. Cook for about 30 seconds.
Garlic, minced	2 Tbsp	
Shallots, finely chopped	12 oz	
Hot chile sauce (see Note)	2 Tbsp	
Catsup	3 cups	Add catsup, sugar, soy sauce, salt, and water to garlic-shallot mixture. Reduce heat to low and cook for about 5 minutes, stirring frequently. Stir in reserved rice stick noodles, stirring gently to separate. Toss until all the sauce is absorbed, 5–7 minutes. Turn off heat.
Sugar, granulated	10 oz	
Soy sauce	5½ Tbsp	
Salt	2¼ tsp	
Water	3¾ cups	
Fresh bean sprouts	1 lb 12 oz	Fold bean sprouts into noodles.
Green onions, thinly sliced	3 oz	Scale 6 lb of noodles into 12 × 10 × 2-inch pans. Sprinkle green onions over the top. Hold sauced noodles hot for assembly.
Asian vegetables, frozen blend (see Note)	10 lb	Steam vegetables until tender-crisp. Drain. Hold vegetables for assembly.
Asian Dipping Sauce (p. 701)	1½ qt	Assembly: 1. Portion 4 oz noodles on plate. 2. Portion 3 oz vegetables over noodles. 3. Ladle 1 oz sauce over vegetables. 4. Sprinkle with toasted peanuts. 5. Place a lemon wedge on the side of plate.
Peanuts, toasted (see Note)	12 oz	
Lemon wedges	50	

Approximate nutritive values per portion

Calories	Carbohydrate	Protein	Fat	Cholesterol	Sodium	Fiber	Iron
249 kcal	45 g	4 g	7 g	0 mg	899 mg	3.4 g	1.6 mg

Notes

- Potentially hazardous food. *Food Safety Standards:* Hold food for service at an internal temperature of 135°F or above. Do not mix old product with new. Cool leftover product quickly following time standards and cooling procedures on p. 167. Reheat leftover product quickly (within 2 hours) to 165°F or above. Reheat product only once; discard if not used.
- Recipe tested using Sriracha hot chile sauce. Sriracha is available through most broadline foodservice distributors and in stores that carry Asian foods.
- Fresh steamed vegetables can be substituted for Asian blend. The frozen Asian vegetable blend used in testing included broccoli, green beans, mushrooms, red peppers, and onions.
- Toast peanuts by spreading in a shallow pan in a thin layer. Heat in a 250°F oven, stirring occasionally, until nuts are slightly browned.

VEGETARIAN SPAGHETTI

Yield: 50 portions or 1 pan, 12 × 20 × 4 inches   *Portion:* 8 oz

Ingredient	Amount	Procedure
Margarine, melted Flour, all-purpose	1 lb 12 oz	Combine margarine and flour in steam-jacketed kettle. Cook and stir until smooth. Cook for 5 minutes, stirring frequently.
Milk	1 gal	Add milk gradually. Cook over low heat until thickened, stirring constantly. Turn off heat.
Salt American cheese, shredded	1 Tbsp 1 lb 6 oz	Add salt and cheese to sauce. Stir until cheese melts.
Carrots, sliced Green bell peppers, chopped Celery, chopped Broccoli, cut	1 lb 12 oz 8 oz 1 lb 1 lb	Steam vegetables until tender. Drain. Combine with cheese sauce.
Mushrooms, pieces and stems, canned	3 lb	Add mushrooms to sauce. Keep hot, 180°F.
Spaghetti Water, boiling Salt Vegetable oil	2 lb 12 oz 2¾ gal 3 oz 2 Tbsp	Cook spaghetti according to directions on p. 507. Drain. Combine cooked spaghetti gently with cheese sauce.

Approximate nutritive values per portion

Calories	Carbohydrate	Protein	Fat	Cholesterol	Sodium	Fiber	Iron
296 kcal	32 g	10 g	15 g	22 mg	684 mg	3 g	2 mg

Note

- Potentially hazardous food. *Food Safety Standards:* Hold food for service at an internal temperature of 135°F or above. Do not mix old product with new. Cool leftover product quickly following time standards and cooling procedures on p. 167. Reheat leftover product quickly (within 2 hours) to 165°F or above. Reheat product only once; discard if not used.

Variations

- **Garden Pasta.** Substitute 3 lb rotini for spaghetti. Omit bell peppers and salt. Reduce mushrooms to 2 lb. Increase milk to 1¼ gal and cheese to 2 lb. Add 4 oz chicken base. Add 1 lb 8 oz cauliflower florets, steamed only until tender-crisp.
- **Spaghetti with Vegetarian Sauce.** Ladle 4 oz of sauce over 4 oz cooked spaghetti. Increase spaghetti to 5 lb AP for 50 servings.

SPAGHETTI WITH CHICKEN SAUCE

Yield: 50 portions   *Portion:* 6 oz sauce + 4 oz spaghetti

Ingredient	Amount	Procedure
Celery, chopped	1 lb 8 oz	Sauté vegetables in margarine until tender-crisp.
Onions, chopped	1 lb 8 oz	
Green bell peppers, chopped	2 oz	
Margarine	7 oz	
Flour, all-purpose	10 oz	Stir in flour. Cook over low heat for 10 minutes.
Chicken stock (p. 738)	4¾ qt	Add stock to vegetable mixture, stirring constantly. Cook until thickened.
Salt	2 tsp	Season with salt and pepper.
White pepper	1 tsp	
Cooked chicken, cubed	7 lb	Fold in chicken and pimento.
Pimento, chopped	2 oz	Keep hot, 180°F.
Spaghetti	5 lb	Cook spaghetti according to directions on p. 507.
Water, boiling	5 gal	Serve 6 oz sauce over 4 oz spaghetti.
Salt	5 oz	
Vegetable oil (optional)	3 Tbsp	

Approximate nutritive values per portion

Calories	Carbohydrate	Protein	Fat	Cholesterol	Sodium	Fiber	Iron
366 kcal	40 g	27 g	10 g	54 mg	709 mg	2 g	4 mg

Notes

- Potentially hazardous food. *Food Safety Standards:* Hold food for service at an internal temperature of 135°F or above. Do not mix old product with new. Cool leftover product quickly following time standards and cooling procedures on p. 167. Reheat leftover product quickly (within 2 hours) to 165°F or above. Reheat product only once; discard if not used.
- Sauce may be combined with spaghetti and served as a casserole.
- 3 oz (1½ cups) dehydrated onions, rehydrated in 2¼ cups water, may be substituted for fresh onions.

SPAGHETTI WITH MEAT SAUCE

Yield: 50 portions   *Portion:* 6 oz sauce + 4 oz spaghetti

Ingredient	Amount	Procedure
Ground beef	8 lb AP	Brown beef until internal temperature reaches 155°F. Drain off fat.
Tomato purée (or tomatoes)	5 qt	Add remaining sauce ingredients to cooked beef.
Water	1 qt	Cook slowly, stirring frequently, until thickened, approximately
Tomato sauce	1¾ qt	½ hour.
Onions, chopped	1 lb	Remove bay leaves before serving.
Bay leaves	2	Keep hot, 190°F.
Thyme, ground	1 tsp	
Garlic clove, minced	1	
Oregano, dried, crumbled	1 Tbsp	
Basil, dried, crumbled	1 Tbsp	
Sugar, granulated	1 oz (2 Tbsp)	
Worcestershire sauce	¼ cup	
Cayenne pepper	1 tsp	
Salt	1 oz (1½ Tbsp)	
Spaghetti	5 lb	Cook spaghetti according to directions on p. 507.
Water, boiling	5 gal	Serve 6 oz sauce over 4 oz spaghetti.
Salt	5 oz	
Vegetable oil	3 Tbsp	

Approximate nutritive values per portion

Calories	Carbohydrate	Protein	Fat	Cholesterol	Sodium	Fiber	Iron
371 kcal	48 g	21 g	11 g	47 mg	1090 mg	4 g	6 mg

Notes

- Potentially hazardous food. *Food Safety Standards:* Hold food for service at an internal temperature of 135°F or above. Do not mix old product with new. Cool leftover product quickly following time standards and cooling procedures on p. 167. Reheat leftover product quickly (within 2 hours) to 165°F or above. Reheat product only once; discard if not used.
- Grated Parmesan cheese may be sprinkled over top of each serving.
- 2 oz (1 cup) dehydrated onions, rehydrated in 1½ cups water, may be substituted for fresh onions.

SPAGHETTI WITH MEATBALLS

Yield: 50 portions   *Portion:* three 2-oz or two 3-oz meatballs + 4 oz spaghetti
Oven: 400°F, 350°F   *Bake:* 15–20 minutes, 30 minutes

Ingredient	Amount	Procedure
MEATBALLS		
Ground beef	15 lb (AP)	Mix meat, bread crumbs, eggs, milk, and seasonings on low speed. Do not overmix.
Bread crumbs, dry	8 oz	
Eggs	16 (1 lb 10 oz)	Portion meat with No. 20 dipper onto baking sheets for 150 2-oz balls; use No. 12 dipper for 100 3-oz balls.
Milk	3¾ cups	
Salt	3 oz	Brown in 400°F oven for 15–20 minutes, or until internal temperature reaches 155°F.
Black pepper	4 tsp	Remove to 12 × 20 × 4-inch counter pan or roasting pan.
Basil, dried, crumbled	4 Tbsp	
Garlic cloves, minced	6	
Fresh parsley, chopped (optional)	3 cups	
SAUCE		
Italian Tomato Sauce, p. 691	2 gal (1 recipe)	Make sauce according to directions. Pour over browned meatballs. Cover and cook in 350°F oven for about 30 minutes.
PASTA		
Spaghetti	5 lb	Cook spaghetti according to directions on p. 507.
Water, boiling	5 gal	Serve 2 or 3 meatballs and 5 oz sauce over 4 oz spaghetti.
Salt	5 oz	
Vegetable oil	3 Tbsp	

Approximate nutritive values per portion

Calories	Carbohydrate	Protein	Fat	Cholesterol	Sodium	Fiber	Iron
550 kcal	50 g	33 g	24 g	148 mg	1962 mg	4 g	8 mg

Notes

- Potentially hazardous food. *Food Safety Standards:* Hold food for service at an internal temperature of 135°F or above. Do not mix old product with new. Cool leftover product quickly following time standards and cooling procedures on p. 167. Reheat leftover product quickly (within 2 hours) to 165°F or above. Reheat product only once; discard if not used.
- If desired, mix the cooked spaghetti with the tomato sauce. Place in two counter pans, arrange meatballs over top, and bake at 375°F for 20–30 minutes.

HUNGARIAN GOULASH

Yield: 50 portions   *Portion:* 6 oz goulash + 4 oz noodles

Ingredient	Amount	Procedure
Beef, cubed	10 lb AP	Brown beef and vegetables in shortening in steam-jacketed
Onions, chopped	1 lb 8 oz	kettle or tilting fry pan.
Garlic clove, finely chopped	1	
Shortening	8 oz	
Sugar, brown	5 oz	Combine sugar, seasonings, and liquid ingredients.
Dry mustard	1 Tbsp	Add to browned meat.
Paprika	1 oz (¼ cup)	Cover container and simmer for 1–2 hours or until meat is tender.
Cayenne pepper	⅛ tsp	
Salt	2½ oz	
Worcestershire sauce	1½ cups	
Vinegar, cider	2 Tbsp	
Catsup	1 qt	
Water	3 qt	
Flour, all-purpose	1 lb 4 oz	Mix flour and water until smooth.
Water, cold	1 qt	Add gradually to hot mixture and cook until thickened.
		Keep hot, 190°F.
Noodles	4 lb 8 oz	Cook noodles according to directions on p. 507.
Water, boiling	4½ gal	Serve 6 oz goulash over 4 oz noodles.
Salt	2 oz	
Vegetable oil	3 Tbsp	

Approximate nutritive values per portion

Calories	Carbohydrate	Protein	Fat	Cholesterol	Sodium	Fiber	Iron
390 kcal	48 g	24 g	11 g	90 mg	1093 mg	2 g	6 mg

Notes

- Potentially hazardous food. *Food Safety Standards:* Hold food for service at an internal temperature of 135°F or above. Do not mix old product with new. Cool leftover product quickly following time standards and cooling procedures on p. 167. Reheat leftover product quickly (within 2 hours) to 165°F or above. Reheat product only once; discard if not used.
- Beef may be browned in a roasting pan in 450°F oven.
- 3 lb 8 oz dry rice, cooked, may be substitued for the noodles. See p. 542 for directions for cooking.
- 3 oz (1½ cups) dehydrated onions, rehydrated in 2¼ cups water, may be substituted for fresh onions.

Variation

- **Neapolitan Noodles.** Brown 7 lb 12 oz ground beef until it reaches 165°F. Drain off fat. Add 8 oz chopped onions and 1 Tbsp minced garlic. Cook until onions are tender. Add 3 qt canned diced tomatoes, 1 qt tomato purée, 6 oz chopped green olives, 1 Tbsp salt, and 3 Tbsp dried oregano. Simmer for 40 minutes. Stir in 2½ Tbsp Worcestershire sauce and 2 lb 4 oz shredded processed cheese. Cook until cheese is melted. Stir in 8 lb 4 oz cooked noodles (prepared from cooking 3 lb noodles per cooking directions on p. 507).

CHICKEN TETRAZZINI

Yield: 50 portions or 2 pans, 12 × 20 × 2 inches   *Portion:* 8 oz
Oven: 350°F   *Bake:* 30–40 minutes

Ingredient	Amount	Procedure
Cooked chicken	6 lb	Dice chicken.
Pimento, chopped	4 oz	Add pimento and parsley.
Fresh parsley, chopped	2 Tbsp	
Spaghetti	3 lb AP (9 lb cooked)	Cook spaghetti according to directions on p. 507. Drain.
Water, boiling	3 gal	
Salt	1 oz (1½ Tbsp)	
Vegetable oil (optional)	2 Tbsp	
Onions, finely chopped	1 lb	Sauté vegetables in margarine.
Green bell peppers, chopped	4 oz	
Mushrooms, sliced	1 lb 8 oz	
Margarine	6 oz	
Flour, all-purpose	9 oz	Blend flour and seasonings into sautéed vegetables.
Salt	1 tsp	Stir in chicken base. Cook for 5 minutes.
Black pepper	1 tsp	
Chicken base	3 oz	
Water	1 gal	Add water, stirring constantly. Cook until thickened. Combine cooked spaghetti, chicken, and sauce. Scale into two greased 12 × 20 × 2-inch baking pans, 10 lb per pan.
Processed cheese, shredded	1 lb	Sprinkle 8 oz cheese over top of each pan. Bake at 350°F for 30–40 minutes or until internal temperature reaches 180°F and cheese is bubbly.

Approximate nutritive values per portion

Calories	Carbohydrate	Protein	Fat	Cholesterol	Sodium	Fiber	Iron
284 kcal	25 g	22 g	10 g	54 mg	500 mg	2 g	2 mg

Notes

- Potentially hazardous food. *Food Safety Standards:* Hold food for service at an internal temperature of 135°F or above. Do not mix old product with new. Cool leftover product quickly following time standards and cooling procedures on p. 167. Reheat leftover product quickly (within 2 hours) to 165°F or above. Reheat product only once; discard if not used.
- 2 oz (1 cup) dehydrated onions, rehydrated in 1½ cups water, may be substituted for fresh onions.

Variations

- **Tuna Tetrazzini.** Substitute tuna for chicken.
- **Turkey Tetrazzini.** Substitute turkey for chicken.

PASTA, BEEF, AND TOMATO CASSEROLE

Yield: 50 portions   *Portion:* 8 oz

Ingredient	Amount	Procedure
Ground beef	10 lb AP (7 lb EP)	Cook meat in kettle until internal temperature reaches 155°F. Stir often to prevent lumps from forming. Drain off fat.
Onions, chopped Celery, chopped	6 oz 3 oz	Add onions and celery to meat. Cook until tender.
Diced tomatoes, canned Tomato purée Chile sauce Salt Black pepper Sugar, granulated	1½ gal 2 cups 3 cups 2 oz (3 Tbsp) 1½ tsp 2 Tbsp	Add tomato products and seasonings to meat mixture. Simmer for 45–60 minutes.
Macaroni, elbow Water, boiling Salt Vegetable oil	2 lb 8 oz 2½ gal 2 oz 2 Tbsp	Cook macaroni according to directions on p. 507. Fold into tomato-meat mixture. Keep hot, 180°F.

Approximate nutritive values per portion

Calories	Carbohydrate	Protein	Fat	Cholesterol	Sodium	Fiber	Iron
313 kcal	27 g	22 g	13 g	62 mg	982 mg	1 g	4 mg

Notes

- Potentially hazardous food. *Food Safety Standards:* Hold food for service at an internal temperature of 135°F or above. Do not mix old product with new. Cool leftover product quickly following time standards and cooling procedures on p. 167. Reheat leftover product quickly (within 2 hours) to 165°F or above. Reheat product only once; discard if not used.
- Other pasta shapes may be substituted for macaroni.
- ¾ oz (⅓ cup) dehydrated onions, rehydrated in ¾ cup water, may be substituted for fresh onions.

BEEF, PORK, AND NOODLE CASSEROLE

Yield: 50 portions or 2 pans, 12 × 20 × 2 inches   *Portion:* 6 oz
Oven: 325°F   *Bake:* 30 minutes

Ingredient	Amount	Procedure
Ground beef	4 lb AP	Brown meat and onions until internal temperature reaches 155°F.
Ground pork	4 lb AP	Drain off fat.
Onions, finely chopped	1 lb	
Tomato soup	1½ qt	Mix soup, water, and seasonings. Add to meat and simmer for 10 minutes.
Water	1½ qt	
Salt	1 Tbsp	
Black pepper	1 tsp	
Noodles	1 lb 12 oz	Cook noodles according to directions on p. 507. Drain.
Water, boiling	1¼ gal	
Salt	2 Tbsp	
Vegetable oil (optional)	1 Tbsp	
Cheddar cheese, grated or ground	2 lb	Combine noodles, meat mixture, and cheese. Scale into two 12 × 20 × 2-inch pans, 8 lb 4 oz per pan.
Bread crumbs	1 lb 2 oz	Combine crumbs and margarine.
Margarine, melted	5 oz	Sprinkle over meat and noodle mixture, 10 oz per pan. Bake at 325°F for 30 minutes. Keep hot, 180°F.

Approximate nutritive values per portion

Calories	Carbohydrate	Protein	Fat	Cholesterol	Sodium	Fiber	Iron
332 kcal	21 g	20 g	18 g	77 mg	581 mg	1 g	3 mg

Notes

- Potentially hazardous food. *Food Safety Standards:* Hold food for service at an internal temperature of 135°F or above. Do not mix old product with new. Cool leftover product quickly following time standards and cooling procedures on p. 167. Reheat leftover product quickly (within 2 hours) to 165°F or above. Reheat product only once; discard if not used.
- 2 oz (1 cup) dehydrated onions, rehydrated in 1½ cups water, may be substituted for fresh onions.

BEEF ON NOODLES

Yield: 50 portions   *Portion:* 6 oz meat and sauce + 4 oz noodles

Ingredient	Amount	Procedure
Beef, cubed	15 lb AP (10 lb EP)	Brown beef in steam-jacketed or other kettle.
Onions, chopped Celery, chopped	2 lb 8 oz 1 lb 8 oz	Add onions and celery to meat. Sauté until vegetables are tender.
Water Black pepper Worcestershire sauce	2 qt 1 Tbsp ½ cup	Add water and seasonings to meat-vegetable mixture. Simmer until beef is tender.
Flour, all-purpose Water Beef base	12 oz 1½ qt 5 oz	Make a smooth paste of flour, water, and beef base. Add to meat mixture to make a gravy. Cook until thickened. Keep hot, 180°F.
Noodles Water, boiling Salt Vegetable oil	4 lb AP (12 lb cooked) 4 gal 4 oz 2 Tbsp	Cook noodles according to directions on p. 507. Drain. Serve 6 oz beef and sauce over 4 oz cooked noodles.

Approximate nutritive values per portion

Calories	Carbohydrate	Protein	Fat	Cholesterol	Sodium	Fiber	Iron
381 kcal	34 g	35 g	11 g	122 mg	237 mg	2 g	6 mg

Notes

- Potentially hazardous food. *Food Safety Standards:* Hold food for service at an internal temperature of 135°F or above. Do not mix old product with new. Cool leftover product quickly following time standards and cooling procedures on p. 167. Reheat leftover product quickly (within 2 hours) to 165°F or above. Reheat product only once; discard if not used.
- 5 oz (2½ cups) dehydrated onions, rehydrated in 3¼ cups water, may be substituted for fresh onions.

Rice Recipes

COOKING RICE

Yield: 50 portions   *Portion:* 4 oz

Ingredient	Amount	Procedure
Rice, converted	3 lb 8 oz	Cook in steamer, oven, or a stockpot or steam-jacketed
Salt	2 Tbsp	kettle, according to directions that follow.
Margarine or vegetable oil	2 Tbsp	
Water, hot	4¼ qt	

STEAMER

Weigh rice into a 12 × 20 × 2-inch counter pan. Add salt and margarine.
Pour boiling water over rice. Stir.
Steam uncovered for 30–40 minutes.
Fluff with fork.

OVEN

Weigh rice into a 12 × 20 × 2-inch counter pan. Add salt and margarine.
Pour boiling water over rice. Stir.
Cover pans tightly with aluminum foil.
Bake at 350°F for 1 hour.
Remove from oven and let stand covered for 5 minutes.
Fluff with fork.

STOCKPOT OR STEAM-JACKETED KETTLE (BOILED RICE)

Bring water to a boil in steam-jacketed kettle or other large kettle.
Add salt, rice, and margarine. Stir. Cover tightly.
Cook on low heat until rice is tender and all water is absorbed, about 15–20 minutes.
Remove from heat and let stand covered for 5–10 minutes.
Fluff with fork.

Approximate nutritive values per portion

Calories	Carbohydrate	Protein	Fat	Cholesterol	Sodium	Fiber	Iron
118 kcal	25 g	2 g	1 g	0 mg	265 mg	0 g	1 mg

Notes

- If using regular white rice in place of converted rice, the cooking time may need to be reduced.
- For brown rice, increase cooking time to 50–60 minutes for steamed rice, to 1½ hours for baked rice, and to 40–50 minutes for boiled rice.
- For buttered rice, add 5 oz butter or margarine. Add to dry rice in counter pan. Add salt and hot water.
- 1 lb uncooked rice yields 2 qt cooked rice.
- Suggested spices to use with rice: allspice, basil, coriander, curry powder, ginger, marjoram, mint, oregano, rosemary, tarragon, thyme.

Variation

- **Sticky Rice.** In each 12 × 10 × 4-inch pan, place 2 lb uncooked Asian sticky rice. Sprinkle 1 Tbsp salt over rice. Pour 1 qt water over rice and stir to mix. Let stand for 30 minutes to allow rice to begin absorbing water. Steam uncovered for 20 minutes. Cover and let stand for 15 minutes. Fluff with a fork before serving.

GINGER RICE

Yield: 50 portions   *Portion:* 4 oz
Oven: 350°F   *Bake:* 45 minutes

Ingredient	Amount	Procedure
Margarine	½ cup	Sauté vegetables and cinnamon in oil until vegetables
Onions, diced	1 lb EP	begin to soften, 10–15 minutes.
Garlic, minced	4 oz EP	
Fresh ginger, peeled and minced	4 oz EP	
Carrots, peeled and diced	8 oz EP	
Cinnamon, ground	1 tsp	
Oil	½ cup	
Rice, converted	3 lb	Add uncooked rice to vegetables and stir over heat until completely coated with margarine and oil.
Salt	1 tsp	Place rice-vegetable mixture in a 12 × 20 × 4-inch counter pan.
Black pepper	¼ tsp	Add seasonings and chicken stock. Stir to combine. Cover tightly with aluminum foil.
Chicken stock (p. 738)	1 gal	
		Bake at 350°F for 45 minutes, or steam uncovered for 30 minutes. Stir before serving.

Approximate nutritive values per portion

Calories	Carbohydrate	Protein	Fat	Cholesterol	Sodium	Fiber	Iron
160 kcal	24.5 g	3.8 g	4.7 g	0 mg	320 mg	0.8 g	1 mg

Note

- Potentially hazardous food. *Food Safety Standards:* Hold food for service at an internal temperature of 135°F or above. Do not mix old product with new. Cool leftover product quickly following time standards and cooling procedures on p. 167. Reheat leftover product quickly (within 2 hours) to 165°F or above. Reheat product only once; discard if not used.

GINGER RICE STIR-FRY

Yield: 50 portions   *Portion:* 3 oz
Griddle: 300°F

Ingredient	Amount	Procedure

Rice, converted
Water
	3 lb 4 oz
	3⅓ cups
		Place 1 lb 10 oz rice and 1⅔ cups water in each of two
		    12 × 4 × 10-inch pans.
		Steam uncovered for 15 minutes or until all of the liquid has been
		    absorbed. Rice will be firm.

Soy sauce Sugar, granulated Garlic powder White pepper Ginger, ground	1 cup 1 Tbsp 1 tsp 1 tsp 1 tsp	Mix together soy sauce and seasonings. Set aside.

Eggs
Green onions,
    chopped
	1 lb 12 oz
	1 lb 8 oz
		Grease griddle lightly with cooking oil. Preheat to 300°F.
		Place eggs on griddle. Spread thin, scramble, and chop into small pieces.
		Add chopped onions and continue to cook for 3–4 minutes
		    until onions are tender.
		Add steamed rice and blend well.
		Drizzle soy sauce mixture over rice.
		Cook, turning frequently until mixture reaches 160°F.
		Place in 12 × 10 × 4-inch pan. Serve 3 oz with No. 12 dipper.

Approximate nutritive values per portion

Calories	Carbohydrate	Protein	Fat	Cholesterol	Sodium	Fiber	Iron
141 kcal	26 g	4 g	2 g	68 mg	353 mg	1 g	1 mg

Notes

- Potentially hazardous food. *Food Safety Standards:* Hold food for service at an internal temperature of 135°F or above. Do not mix old product with new. Cool leftover product quickly following time standards and cooling procedures on p. 167. Reheat leftover product quickly (within 2 hours) to 165°F or above. Reheat product only once; discard if not used.
- If griddle is small, prepare in two batches. Use ½ cup soy sauce, 14 oz eggs, and 12 oz green onions for each pan of cooked rice.

FRIED RICE

Yield: 50 portions   *Portion:* 3 oz

Ingredient	Amount	Procedure
Rice	2 lb 8 oz	Cook rice according to directions on p. 542.
Water	3 qt	Do not overcook. Let cool.
Salt	2 tsp	
Peas, frozen	1 lb 8 oz	Cook peas and drain. Set aside.
Eggs	6 (11 oz)	Break eggs into bowl and stir until yolks and whites are
Salt	2 tsp	mixed. Add salt.
Vegetable oil	2 Tbsp	Cook eggs in oil, stirring to break into small pieces. Set aside.
Onions, chopped	1 lb	Sauté onions and carrots in oil until tender.
Carrots, shredded	8 oz	Add rice and cook until heated.
Vegetable oil	¾ cup	
Soy sauce	1 cup	Add soy sauce to rice mixture, stirring to mix evenly.
		Stir in peas and eggs. Serve at once.

Approximate nutritive values per portion

Calories	Carbohydrate	Protein	Fat	Cholesterol	Sodium	Fiber	Iron
147 kcal	22 g	3 g	5 g	27 mg	513 mg	1 g	1 mg

Note

- Potentially hazardous food. *Food Safety Standards:* Hold food for service at an internal temperature of 135°F or above. Do not mix old product with new. Cool leftover product quickly following time standards and cooling procedures on p. 167. Reheat leftover product quickly (within 2 hours) to 165°F or above. Reheat product only once; discard if not used.

Variations

- **Confetti Rice.** Delete peas, eggs, carrots, and soy sauce. Cook rice until almost done. Heat oil in fry pan. Sauté for 2 minutes 12 oz sliced green bell peppers, 12 oz sliced mushrooms, and 4 oz chopped scallions. Stir vegetables into cooked rice. Add 8 oz chopped pimentos.
- **Fried Rice with Almonds.** Cook 3 lb rice according to directions on p. 542. Sauté 4 oz chopped onions and 4 oz chopped green bell peppers in 1 cup vegetable oil. Add cooked rice, 1 Tbsp black pepper, 1 tsp garlic salt, ½ cup soy sauce, and 2 lb slivered almonds. Add salt if needed. Bake until heated.
- **Fried Rice with Ham.** Delete peas. Reduce chopped onions to 4 oz. Increase carrots to 12 oz. Add 4 oz sliced green onions, 12 oz sliced celery, and 1 lb chopped ham.
- **Plain Fried Rice.** Heat a small amount of vegetable oil in tilting fry pan. Sauté 12 oz sliced celery and 4 oz onion until tender-crisp. Stir 10 lb cooked, cold rice into vegetables. Reduce heat and cover. Cook for 15–20 minutes. Pour 1 cup eggs over surface of hot rice, stir to mix. Cover and cook for 5 minutes. Stir in 1 cup soy sauce, 12 oz finely shredded carrots, and 6 oz thinly sliced green onion. Cover for 5 minutes. Transfer to serving pans. Recipe portion: 4 oz.
- **Pork Fried Rice.** Delete peas. Add 4 lb cubed, cooked pork. Fry 1 lb bacon. Use bacon fat for sautéing vegetables and rice. Crumble bacon and add.
- **Rice and Black-Eyed Peas.** Cook 1 lb rice according to directions on p. 542. Cook 3 lb 8 oz frozen black-eyed peas according to directions on p. 770. Sauté 8 oz onion in ¼ cup vegetable oil. Add hot rice and black-eyed peas. Stir to combine. Add 1 tsp ground allspice, 1 Tbsp dried whole thyme, and 2 tsp coarse ground black pepper. Heat until very hot. Stir in 4 lb fresh tomatoes (peeled, seeded, and diced), 2 cups chopped fresh parsley, and 1 lb shredded cheddar cheese.
- **Shrimp Fried Rice.** Add 1 lb 8 oz cooked shrimp.

ASIAN FRIED RICE

Yield: 50 portions   *Portion:* 4 oz

Ingredient	Amount	Procedure
Jasmine rice	3 lb 8 oz	Cook rice according to directions on p. 542.
Water	4¼ qt	Chill rice and reserve for later step.
Margarine	2 Tbsp	
Salt	2 Tbsp	
Butter, un-salted	4 oz	Heat butter in tilting fry pan.
Sweet onion, chopped	8 oz	Add onion, ginger, garlic, and cumin.
		Sauté until fragrant, about 4 minutes.
Fresh ginger, minced	2½ oz	
Garlic, minced	2 Tbsp	
Whole cumin, toasted, then ground (see Note)	1½ Tbsp	
Catsup	½ cup	Add catsup, fish sauce, sugar, and salt to sautéed vegetables.
Fish sauce	2 Tbsp	Simmer until the sauce is slightly thickened, about 5 minutes.
Sugar, granulated	2 tsp	Add rice reserved from earlier step. Stir-fry rice until thoroughly
Salt, kosher	1½ tsp	mixed and hot.
Green onions, thinly sliced	4 oz	Stir in green onions and mix well. Transfer to 12 × 10 × 4-inch pans.

Approximate nutritive values per portion

Calories	Carbohydrate	Protein	Fat	Cholesterol	Sodium	Fiber	Iron
135 kcal	26.5 g	1.9 g	2.6 g	4.7 mg	410 mg	0.2 g	1 mg

Notes

- Potentially hazardous food. *Food Safety Standards:* Hold food for service at an internal temperature of 135°F or above. Do not mix old product with new. Cool leftover product quickly following time standards and cooling procedures on p. 167. Reheat leftover product quickly (within 2 hours) to 165°F or above. Reheat product only once; discard if not used.
- See p. 731 for spice toasting instructions.

HOPPING JOHN

Yield: 50 portions   *Portion:* 4 oz

Ingredient	Amount	Procedure
Rice, converted	1 lb	Cook rice according to directions on p. 542. Rice should yield 3 lb cooked rice. Save cooked rice for later step.
Vegetable oil Onions, chopped Garlic, minced	¼ cup 1 lb 6 oz EP 2 oz EP	Heat oil in steam-jacketed kettle. Add onions and garlic and cook until transparent.
Black-eyed peas, frozen or fresh Water Salt Vegetable base Parsley, dried Thyme, dried Liquid smoke Black pepper Red pepper sauce	4 lb 5½ qt 1 Tbsp 1½ oz 3 Tbsp 1 tsp ½ tsp ½ tsp ¼ tsp	Add peas, water, and seasonings to vegetables. Bring to a boil, reduce heat, and simmer until peas are tender, 40–50 minutes. If peas become dry, add a small amount of water. Most of the water should be evaporated when peas are done.
Red wine vinegar Green onions, sliced	¾ cup 1 oz EP	Stir vinegar and rice into black-eyed peas. Transfer to 12 × 10 × 4-inch pan. Garnish with sliced green onions.

Approximate nutritive values per portion

Calories	Carbohydrate	Protein	Fat	Cholesterol	Sodium	Fiber	Iron
100 kcal	18 g	4 g	1.8 g	0 mg	264 mg	2.2 g	1 mg

Note

- Potentially hazardous food. *Food Safety Standards:* Hold food for service at an internal temperature of 135°F or above. Do not mix old product with new. Cool leftover product quickly following time standards and cooling procedures on p. 167. Reheat leftover product quickly (within 2 hours) to 165°F or above. Reheat product only once; discard if not used.

ARROZ DE COCO

Yield: 50 portions   *Portion:* 4 oz

Ingredient	Amount	Procedure
Olive oil	4 oz	Heat oil in a tilting fry pan. Sauté onions and peppers until soft but not brown, about 5 minutes.
Onions, chopped	1 lb	
Green bell peppers, chopped	12 oz	
White rice	2 lb	Add rice to skillet. Stir and cook 2–3 minutes, until the grains are evenly coated and beginning to brown.
Coconut milk	7½ cups	Add coconut milk, water, tomatoes, salt, and hot sauce. Bring to a simmer. Cover and simmer until all the liquid is absorbed and rice is tender, about 20 minutes.
Water, boiling	1½ qt	
Chopped tomatoes, canned	1 lb 4 oz	
Salt	1½ Tbsp	
Hot sauce (see Note)	3 Tbsp	

Approximate nutritive values per portion

Calories	Carbohydrate	Protein	Fat	Cholesterol	Sodium	Fiber	Iron
168 kcal	19 g	2 g	10 g	0 mg	271 mg	0.5 g	1.8 mg

Notes

- Potentially hazardous food. *Food Safety Standards:* Hold food for service at an internal temperature of 135°F or above. Do not mix old product with new. Cool leftover product quickly following time standards and cooling procedures on p. 167. Reheat leftover product quickly (within 2 hours) to 165°F or above. Reheat product only once; discard if not used.
- Recipe was tested using green Tabasco hot sauce.

JALAPEÑO RICE

Yield: 50 portions   *Portion:* 4 oz
Oven: 275°F   *Bake:* 1 hour

Ingredient	Amount	Procedure
Rice, converted	1 lb 12 oz	Cook rice according to directions on p. 542. Chill and reserve for later step.
Water	1¾ qt	Should yield 5 lb 10 oz cooked rice.
Salt	1 Tbsp	
Sliced jalapeño peppers, canned, drained	3 oz	Put peppers, chiles, sour cream, milk, chives, salt, and Monterey Jack cheese into mixer bowl.
Diced green chiles, canned, drained	4 oz	Add 5 lb 10 oz cooked rice reserved from earlier step.
Sour cream	3 lb 4 oz	Mix on low speed only until combined.
Milk	3 cups	
Chives, dried	1 Tbsp	
Salt	¼ tsp	
Monterey Jack cheese, shredded	2 lb	
American cheese, shredded	8 oz	Scale 3 lb into 12 × 10 × 2-inch pans. Sprinkle 2 oz cheese over each pan. Bake uncovered at 275°F until rice mixture reaches 180°F, approximately 1 hour. Cover loosely with foil if browning too quickly.

Approximate nutritive values per portion

Calories	Carbohydrate	Protein	Fat	Cholesterol	Sodium	Fiber	Iron
219 kcal	16 g	8 g	14 g	35 mg	476 mg	0 g	0.7 mg

Note

- Potentially hazardous food. *Food Safety Standards:* Hold food for service at an internal temperature of 135°F or above. Do not mix old product with new. Cool leftover product quickly following time standards and cooling procedures on p. 167. Reheat leftover product quickly (within 2 hours) to 165°F or above. Reheat product only once; discard if not used.

SOPA DE ARROZ

Yield: 50 portions   *Portion:* 4 oz

Ingredient	Amount	Procedure
Salad oil	9 oz	Heat oil to 350°F in tilting or other large fry pan.
Rice, converted	2 lb 10 oz	Stir rice, onions, and garlic into oil. Stir and cook until rice is a light
Onions, minced	10 oz	golden brown.
Garlic, minced	1 oz	
Fresh diced tomatoes	1 lb 12 oz	Add tomatoes and cilantro. Heat through.
Cilantro, dried	1½ Tbsp	
Vegetable base (see Note)	2½ oz	Mix vegetable base and concentrates with water. Add to rice. Stir.
Ancho flavor concentrate (see Note)	1 oz	Cover and simmer for 20–30 minutes, until rice is tender and liquids absorbed.
Chipotle flavor concentrate (see Note)	¼ oz	
Water	3¼ qt	

Approximate nutritive values per serving

Calories	Carbohydrate	Protein	Fat	Cholesterol	Sodium	Fiber	Iron
144 kcal	22 g	2 g	6 g	0 mg	172 mg	0.4 g	1 mg

Notes

- Potentially hazardous food. *Food Safety Standards:* Hold food for service at an internal temperature of 135°F or above. Do not mix old product with new. Cool leftover product quickly following time standards and cooling procedures on p. 167. Reheat leftover product quickly (within 2 hours) to 165°F or above. Reheat product only once; discard if not used.
- Chicken base can be substituted for vegetable base. Minor's Ancho Flavor Concentrate (made from ancho peppers and sautéed onions) and Minor's Chipotle Flavor Concentrate (a blend of red, chipotle, and jalapeño peppers with onion, garlic, and spice) are available from most broadline foodservice distributors.

RISOTTO

Yield: 50 portions   *Portion:* 4 oz

Ingredient	Amount	Procedure
Vegetable base (see Note)	2 oz	Mix vegetable base and water in a steam-jacketed kettle. Bring to a boil, then reduce heat to low.
Water	1 gal	Cover and keep hot. Reserve broth for later step.
Olive oil	3 oz	Heat oil to 350°F in fry pan.
Onions, finely chopped	12 oz EP	Sauté onions and garlic in oil until translucent, about 4 minutes.
Garlic, minced	1 oz	
Arborio rice	2 lb 4 oz	Add rice to onion. Stir and cook for 3 minutes.
Water	1½ cups	Add water and cook until water evaporates. Reduce temperature and add broth slowly, 2 cups at a time (broth reserved from earlier step). Stir very often but not constantly. Do not let the pan become dry before adding more broth. Cook and stir rice until rice is *al dente* and mixture is creamy (about 20 minutes). Turn off heat.
Butter	12 oz	Add butter and Parmesan cheese. Stir until incorporated.
Parmesan cheese, freshly shredded	12 oz	
		Transfer risotto to 12 × 10 × 2-inch pans. Cover. Hold for service above 140°F. Prepare close to serving time.

Approximate nutritive values per portion

Calories	Carbohydrate	Protein	Fat	Cholesterol	Sodium	Fiber	Iron
190 kcal	22 g	4 g	9 g	21 mg	190 mg	0.6 g	0.5 mg

Notes

- Potentially hazardous food. *Food Safety Standards:* Hold food for service at an internal temperature of 135°F or above. Do not mix old product with new. Cool leftover product quickly following time standards and cooling procedures on p. 167. Reheat leftover product quickly (within 2 hours) to 165°F or above. Reheat product only once; discard if not used.
- When extending recipe, add broth to rice at a rate of 1 cup per pound of rice.
- Parmesan cheese can be stirred into the rice after it has been put in a pan. Add Parmesan cheese in a ratio of 1 oz cheese to 1 lb rice mixture.
- Risotto should be soft and creamy, but not runny. The product will stiffen during holding and may require additional small amounts of hot broth.
- Chicken base may be substituted for vegetable base. Adjust salt as necessary.

TOMATO CILANTRO RICE

Yield: 50 portions   *Portion:* 4 oz

Ingredient	Amount	Procedure
Vegetable oil	½ cup	Heat oil to 350°F in tilting or other large fry pan.
Rice, converted Garlic, minced Onions, chopped	3 lb 2 Tbsp 1 lb (EP)	Add rice and vegetables to hot oil. Stir and cook until rice is slightly browned.
Diced tomatoes, canned Vegetable base (see Note) Water	2 lb 5 oz 3 qt	Add tomatoes, vegetable base, and water to rice mixture. Bring to a boil. Reduce heat to low. Cover and simmer until rice is tender and liquids are absorbed, 25–30 minutes.
Fresh cilantro, minced	1 oz	Fold cilantro into rice mixture. Transfer to serving pans.

Approximate nutritive values per portion

Calories	Carbohydrate	Protein	Fat	Cholesterol	Sodium	Fiber	Iron
135 kcal	25 g	2 g	2.5 g	0 mg	220 mg	0.7 g	0.5 mg

Notes

- Potentially hazardous food. *Food Safety Standards:* Hold food for service at an internal temperature of 135°F or above. Do not mix old product with new. Cool leftover product quickly following time standards and cooling procedures on p. 167. Reheat leftover product quickly (within 2 hours) to 165°F or above. Reheat product only once; discard if not used.
- Chicken base can be substituted for vegetable base. Adjust salt if necessary.

Variation

- **Rice and Vegetables.** Heat 3 oz olive oil in tilting fry pan. Sauté 1 lb chopped onions, 2 Tbsp minced garlic, and 2 lb rice until onion is fragrant and softened. Stir in 1½ tsp salt, ¼ tsp ground red pepper, 2 oz vegetable or chicken base, and 4 lb 12 oz water. Cover and simmer for 20 minutes or until liquid is absorbed. Add 12 oz matchstick carrots, 1 lb 4 oz (frozen) green peas, and 2 lb 4 oz diced fresh tomatoes. Heat to 175°F.

VEGETABLE PAELLA

Yield: 50 portions   *Portion:* 8 oz

Ingredient	Amount	Procedure
Vegetable oil	½ cup	Lightly coat bottom of fry pan with oil. Heat to 375°F.
Onions, diced (½ inch)	1 lb 12 oz	Add onions and garlic. Sauté 3 minutes or until garlic is fragrant.
Garlic, fresh, minced	1 oz	
Water	3½ qt	Add water and vegetable base. Bring to a boil.
Vegetable base (see Note)	4 oz	
Rice	3 lb	Stir in rice and spices. Cover. Reduce heat and simmer for 15 minutes.
Salt	3½ tsp	
Paprika	1 Tbsp	
Turmeric	1 Tbsp	
Black pepper	4 tsp	
Red bell peppers, cut in strips	1 lb 8 oz	Add peppers and vegetables. Cover and cook for 10 minutes or until liquid is absorbed and endpoint temperature is 170°F.
Yellow bell peppers, cut in strips	1 lb 8 oz	Scale into 12 × 10 × 4-inch pans.
Green peas, frozen	1 lb 12 oz	
Artichoke quarters, canned, drained	4 lb	
Kidney beans, canned, drained	2 lb	
Baby corn, frozen	2 lb	

Approximate nutritive values per portion

Calories	Carbohydrate	Protein	Fat	Cholesterol	Sodium	Fiber	Iron
202 kcal	202 g	5 g	5 g	0 mg	341 mg	4 g	2 mg

Notes

- Potentially hazardous food. *Food Safety Standards:* Hold food for service at an internal temperature of 135°F or above. Do not mix old product with new. Cool leftover product quickly following time standards and cooling procedures on p. 167. Reheat leftover product quickly (within 2 hours) to 165°F or above. Reheat product only once; discard if not used.
- Recipe is calculated for an entrée portion. For 50 4-oz side dish portions, reduce the amount of ingredients by ½.
- Chicken base may be substituted for the vegetable base. Adjust salt if base is highly salted.

RICE PILAF

Yield: 50 portions or 1 pan, 12 × 20 × 4 inches   *Portion:* 4 oz
Oven: 350°F   *Bake:* 45 minutes

Ingredient	Amount	Procedure
Onions, finely chopped	1 lb 8 oz	Sauté onions in margarine until they begin to soften. Do not brown.
Margarine, melted	8 oz	
Rice, converted	3 lb	Add uncooked rice to onions and stir over heat until completely coated with the margarine.
Salt	1 tsp	Place rice in a 12 × 20 × 4-inch counter pan.
White pepper	¼ tsp	Add seasonings and Chicken Stock.
Bay leaf	1	Stir to combine.
Chicken Stock (p. 738)	1 gal	Cover tightly with aluminum foil.
		Bake at 350°F for 45 minutes, or steam uncovered for 30 minutes.
		Stir before serving.

Approximate nutritive values per portion

Calories	Carbohydrate	Protein	Fat	Cholesterol	Sodium	Fiber	Iron
151 kcal	24 g	4 g	4 g	0 mg	336 mg	1 g	1 mg

Notes

- Potentially hazardous food. *Food Safety Standards:* Hold food for service at an internal temperature of 135°F or above. Do not mix old product with new. Cool leftover product quickly following time standards and cooling procedures on p. 167. Reheat leftover product quickly (within 2 hours) to 165°F or above. Reheat product only once; discard if not used.
- Suggested additions for variety: chopped green bell pepper, pimento, tomato, or nuts; sliced mushrooms or water chestnuts; ground or diced ham.
- 3 oz (1½ cups) dehydrated onions, rehydrated in 2¼ cups water, may be substituted for fresh onions.

Variations

- **Curried Rice.** Add 3 Tbsp curry powder.
- **Mexican Rice.** Sauté 14 oz chopped onions, 10 oz chopped green bell pepper, and 3 oz chopped celery in ⅓ cup vegetable oil. Add uncooked rice and stir for 2–3 minutes until grains are coated with oil. Stir in 3 Tbsp salt, 2 oz chile powder, and 1 tsp garlic powder. Place in a 12 × 20 × 4-inch counter pan. Pour a mixture of 2½ qt tomato juice and 1¾ qt Beef Stock (p. 738) over rice. Steam for 25–35 minutes. Stir before serving.
- **Mushroom Rice Pilaf.** Reduce rice to 1 lb 12 oz and Chicken Stock to 2½ qt. Delete bay leaf and add 1½ tsp thyme. Add 2 lb mushroom pieces and stems and 1 lb 8 oz chopped celery.
- **Toasted Herb Rice.** Measure uncooked rice into 12 × 2 × 4-inch pan. Bake at 325°F for 20 minutes or until rice is toasted and golden. Proceed as for Rice Pilaf. Add 2 Tbsp crumbled dried basil or tarragon.
- **Caribbean Rice**. Heat 4 oz olive oil in tilting fry pan. Add 1 lb 10 oz cubed sweet potatoes, 2 oz minced ginger, and 1 oz minced garlic. Sauté until soft. Add 4 lb 6 oz cooked rice (made from 1 lb 7 oz raw rice, 4 tsp salt, and 2 lb 14 oz water and cooked following directions on p. 542, 2 lb canned, drained, and rinsed black beans, ¼ cup canned diced jalapeño peppers, 2 Tbsp curry powder, and 1¾ tsp ground allspice. Stir lightly to combine. Stir in 12 oz diced fresh or frozen mangos and 1 lb chopped green bell pepper. Bring temperature to 165°F.

BASMATI RICE AND LENTIL PILAF

Yield: 50 portions   *Portion*: 4 oz

Ingredient	Amount	Procedure
Lentils, dried	10 oz	Combine lentils and water in a steam-jacketed kettle.
Water	3 qt	Bring to a boil, then reduce heat and simmer for 25–30 minutes until just tender.
		Drain and save for later step.
Margarine	10 oz	Heat margarine in tilting fry pan.
Onions, chopped	1 lb EP	Sauté onions and rice until onions are fragrant and rice begins to turn brown.
Basmati rice	3 lb	Stir often.
Water	1½ qt	Add water, vegetable base, spices, and juice to rice mixture. Stir to blend.
Vegetable base (see Note)	2 oz	Bring to a boil. Reduce heat, cover, and simmer for 10 minutes.
Salt (see Note)	4 tsp	Add cooked lentils reserved from earlier step. Continue cooking until rice
Black pepper	½ tsp	is tender and water is absorbed, approximately 10–15 minutes.
Cumin, ground	2½ Tbsp	Scale into 12 × 10 × 2-inch pans, 6 lb per pan.
Turmeric	1 tsp	
Fresh lemon juice	2½ Tbsp	

Approximate nutritive values per portion

Calories	Carbohydrate	Protein	Fat	Cholesterol	Sodium	Fiber	Iron
165 kcal	2.5 g	3.8 g	5.7 g	0 mg	350 mg	3.2 g	1 mg

Notes

- Potentially hazardous food. *Food Safety Standards:* Hold food for service at an internal temperature of 135°F or above. Do not mix old product with new. Cool leftover product quickly following time standards and cooling procedures on p. 167. Reheat leftover product quickly (within 2 hours) to 165°F or above. Reheat product only once; discard if not used.
- Double the recipe for an 8-oz entrée-size portion.
- Chicken base can be substituted for vegetable base. Taste before adding salt. Salt concentration varies among brands of bases.

SICILIAN RICE AND VEGETABLES

Yield: 48 portions   *Portion:* 8 oz
Oven: 325°F   *Bake:* 10–15 minutes

Ingredient	Amount	Procedure
Brown rice	1 lb 4 oz	Cook rice according to directions on p. 542. Should yield 4 lb 8 oz
Water	1½ qt	cooked rice. Save for later step.
Salt	1 Tbsp	
Onions, sliced	1 lb	Sauté onions and garlic in oil until tender.
Garlic cloves, minced	4	
Olive oil	½ cup	
Oregano, dried, crumbled	2 Tbsp	Add seasonings and brown sugar to onions. Mix well.
Sweet basil, dried, crumbled	3 Tbsp	
Salt	2 Tbsp (3 oz)	
Black pepper	1 tsp	
Bay leaves	4	
Fresh parsley, chopped	2 cups	
Sugar, brown	¼ cup (1½ oz)	
Tomato juice	3 qt (two 46-oz cans)	Combine tomato products with spices and onion. Reduce heat and simmer uncovered for 15–20 minutes.
Tomato paste	12 oz	Remove bay leaves.
Diced tomatoes, canned	1½ qt	Add cooked rice from first step.
Broccoli stalks, sliced	2 lb	Add broccoli, carrots, and mushrooms to sauce and cook for 5 minutes.
Carrots, julienne cut	1 lb	
Fresh mushrooms, sliced	1 lb 8 oz	
Yellow summer squash	3 lb	Quarter squash lengthwise, then slice ½ inch thick. Carefully stir squash into sauce. Cook for 5 minutes.
Zucchini squash	3 lb	Scale into four 12 × 10 × 2-inch pans, 6 lb per pan.
Mozzarella cheese, shredded	2 lb	Sprinkle 8 oz cheese over each pan. Place in 325°F oven 10–15 minutes to melt cheese.

Approximate nutritive values per portion

Calories	Carbohydrate	Protein	Fat	Cholesterol	Sodium	Fiber	Iron
170 kcal	22 g	7 g	7 g	15 mg	808 mg	2 g	2 mg

Notes

- Potentially hazardous food. *Food Safety Standards:* Hold food for service at an internal temperature of 135°F or above. Do not mix old product with new. Cool Leftover product quickly following time standards and cooling procedures on p. 167. Reheat leftover product quickly (within 2 hours) to 165°F or above. Reheat product only once; discard if not used.
- Mixture may be scaled into pan after the raw vegetables are added, then baked at 350°F for approximately 30 minutes. Sprinkle with cheese the last 2–3 minutes of baking.
- Other vegetables may be substituted, or the ratio of vegetables changed, for those listed in the recipe. Use a total of 10 lb 8 oz vegetables for 50 servings. Suggested substitutes: eggplant, Japanese eggplant, celery, onion, frozen green beans, peas.

RICE PRIMAVERA

Yield: 50 portions   *Portion:* 4 oz

Ingredient	Amount	Procedure
Rice, converted	2 lb	Cook rice according to directions on p. 542. Save for later step. (Should yield 6 lb 8 oz cooked rice.)
Water	2½ qt	
Salt	2 Tbsp	
Yogurt, plain	1½ cups	Combine in steam-jacketed kettle.
Milk, skim	2½ cups	Heat over low heat.
Parmesan cheese	6 oz	Add rice. Toss to coat.
Salt	1 oz (1½ Tbsp)	
White pepper	1 tsp	
Garlic powder	¼ tsp	
Broccoli florets	12 oz	Cook vegetables until tender-crisp (p. 770). Drain.
Zucchini squash, sliced	1 lb 8 oz	Add to rice mixture. Toss to coat.
Fresh mushrooms, sliced	8 oz	Heat.
Carrots, julienne	1 lb	
Fresh parsley, minced	1¼ cups	Stir in. Put in 12 × 10 × 4-inch pans. Cover and keep hot.

Approximate nutritive values per portion

Calories	Carbohydrate	Protein	Fat	Cholesterol	Sodium	Fiber	Iron
101 kcal	18 g	4 g	1 g	4 mg	531 mg	0.3 g	1 mg

Note

- Potentially hazardous food. *Food Safety Standards:* Hold food for service at an internal temperature of 135°F or above. Do not mix old product with new. Cool leftover product quickly following time standards and cooling procedures on p. 167. Reheat leftover product quickly (within 2 hours) to 165°F or above. Reheat product only once; discard if not used.

BROCCOLI RICE AU GRATIN

Yield: 50 portions   *Portion:* 4 oz

Ingredient	Amount	Procedure
Rice, converted Water Salt	1 lb 4 oz 1½ qt 1 Tbsp	Cook rice according to directions on p. 542. Reserve for later step. Should yield 4 lb 4 oz cooked rice.
Onions, minced Margarine, melted	3 oz 5 oz	Sauté onions in margarine in steam-jacketed kettle until transparent. Do not brown.
Flour, all-purpose Seasoned salt White pepper	8 oz 2 tsp ½ tsp	Add flour and seasonings to onions. Stir with a wire whip. Cook for 15–20 minutes to make a roux. Stir often.
Milk	2 qt	Add milk to roux gradually, blending with a wire whip. Cook until thickened, 10–20 minutes.

American cheese,
  shredded
Cheddar cheese,
  shredded
	12 oz
	
	12 oz
		Add cheeses and cooked rice.
		Heat until cheese melts.

Broccoli cuts, frozen	3 lb	Steam broccoli (p. 770) until tender-crisp. Do not drain. Add to sauce. Stir gently. Put in 12 × 10 × 4-inch pans. Keep hot.

Approximate nutritive values per portion

Calories	Carbohydrate	Protein	Fat	Cholesterol	Sodium	Fiber	Iron
163 kcal	16 g	6 g	8 g	19 mg	321 mg	0.4 g	1 mg

Note

- Potentially hazardous food. *Food Safety Standards:* Hold food for service at an internal temperature of 135°F or above. Do not mix old product with new. Cool leftover product quickly following time standards and cooling procedures on p. 167. Reheat leftover product quickly (within 2 hours) to 165°F or above. Reheat product only once; discard if not used.

Variations

- **Broccoli Rice Casserole.** Combine in steam-jacketed kettle 4 lb 6 oz cut broccoli, 8 lb canned cream of mushroom soup, 8 oz chopped onion, 2 cups water, 1 Tbsp vegetable base, ½ tsp black pepper, 3 lb shredded mild cheddar cheese, and 10 lb cooked white rice (cooked from 3 lb 5 oz raw rice). Scale into 12 × 20 × 2-inch pans, 6 lb per pan. Sprinkle 8 oz shredded mild cheddar cheese over the top of each pan. Portion size: 8 oz.
- **Cauliflower Rice au Gratin.** Substitute cauliflower for broccoli. Sprinkle each pan with chopped fresh parsley.
- **Golden Rice Bake.** Steam 4 lb 8 oz finely chopped carrots until just hot. Drain and set aside. In steam-jacketed kettle combine 5 lb 8 oz canned cream of mushroom soup, 1½ qt milk, 12 oz margarine, ¼ tsp salt, 1 tsp black pepper, 3 Tbsp dried chives, and 9 lb 12 oz cooked rice (cooked from 3 lb 4 oz raw rice). Heat to very hot, 190°F. Stir in 2 lb 12 oz shredded cheddar cheese until melted. Scale into 12 × 20 × 2-inch pans, 6 lb per pan. Sprinkle 4 oz shredded mild cheddar cheese over the top of each pan. Portion size: 8 oz.
- **Green Rice.** To 2 lb rice, cooked, add 4 lb finely chopped raw or frozen spinach, 2 Tbsp chopped onion, and 1¼ qt medium White Sauce (p. 603). Place in one 12 × 20 × 2-inch counter pan. Bake at 325°F for 30–40 minutes.

LENTILS AND RICE WITH OLIVES & TOMATOES

Yield: 50 portions   *Portion:* 4 oz

Ingredient	Amount	Procedure
Water	3½ qt	Bring water and salt to a rolling boil in steam-jacketed or other large kettle. Stir in lentils. Reduce heat and simmer until tender but not soft, 15–20 minutes. Drain. Expected yield 3 lb 4 oz cooked lentils. Reserve lentils for later step.
Salt	1¼ tsp	
Lentils, dried	1 lb 2 oz	
Water	3¾ cups	Cook rice per directions on p. 542. Expected yield 2 lb 8 oz cooked rice. Reserve rice for later step.
Salt	2½ tsp	
Rice, white	1 lb	
Olive oil	3 Tbsp	Heat oil in tilting fry pan or other heavy bottomed pan. Sauté onions, peppers, and garlic.
Onions, chopped	1 lb	
Green bell peppers, diced	8 oz	
Garlic, minced	3 oz	
Cumin, ground	2½ Tbsp	Add cumin and peppers. Cook for 1 minute.
Chopped jalapeño peppers, canned, drained	3 Tbsp	
Ripe olives, sliced	1 lb	Carefully stir in 3 lb 4 oz cooked lentils and 2 lb 8 oz cooked rice reserved from earlier steps. Heat to 170°F.
Garbanzo beans, drained	2 lb 12 oz	
Fresh diced tomatoes	1 lb 4 oz	Carefully stir in tomatoes, herbs, and lime juice. Transfer to 12 × 10 × 2-inch pans. Serve hot.
Flat leaf parsley, chopped	½ oz	
Cilantro, chopped	½ oz	
Fresh lime juice	2 Tbsp	

Approximate nutritive values per portion

Calories	Carbohydrate	Protein	Fat	Cholesterol	Sodium	Fiber	Iron
102 kcal	17 g	3 g	2 g	0 mg	313 mg	3 g	1.5 mg

Notes

- Potentially hazardous food. *Food Safety Standards:* Hold food for service at an internal temperature of 135°F or above. Do not mix old product with new. Cool leftover product quickly following time standards and cooling procedures on p. 167. Reheat leftover product quickly (within 2 hours) to 165°F or above. Reheat product only once; discard if not used.
- 2 lb 8 oz cooked brown rice or cooked barley may be substituted for the white rice.

RICE AND LENTILS WITH BALSAMIC GLAZED CARROTS

Yield: 50 portions   *Portion:* 4 oz
Oven: 400°F

Ingredient	Amount	Procedure
Balsamic Vinegar Marinade (p. 724)	2¾ cups	Prepare Balsamic Vinegar Marinade recipe. Reserve for later step.
Carrots, baby cut	3 lb 8 oz EP	Steam carrots until bright in color and just beginning to soften, 1–3 minutes. Pour marinade (reserved from earlier step) over carrots. Stir to coat. Drain carrots. Reserve marinade. Place carrots in a single layer on a baking pan. Roast carrots at 400°F until tender and browned. Reserve carrots for later step.
Water Lentils, dried	3 cups 8 oz	Combine water and lentils in steam-jacketed or other kettle. Bring to a boil. Reduce heat and simmer until lentils are beginning to soften, 15–20 minutes. Drain lentils. Reserve lentils for later step.
Olive oil Onions, finely chopped Garlic, minced Rosemary, dried Oregano, dried Salt Black pepper	2 oz 1 lb EP 1 oz EP 2½ Tbsp 1 Tbsp 1 Tbsp 2 tsp	Heat oil to 300°F in tilting fry pan. Add onions, garlic, herbs, and spices to hot oil. Sauté until onions are just beginning to soften, about 5 minutes.
Water Vegetable base (see Note) Rice, converted	1¾ qt 1 oz 1 lb 4 oz	Add water, vegetable base, and rice to onions. Add cooked and drained lentils, reserved from earlier step. Bring mixture to a boil. Reduce heat, cover, and simmer until rice is almost tender, about 15 minutes. Stir in carrots and marinade, reserved from earlier steps. Cook until rice is tender, liquid is absorbed, and carrots are hot. Transfer to two 12 × 20 × 2-inch pans, approximately 6 lb per pan.
Fresh parsley, coarsely chopped	¼ cup	Sprinkle 2 Tbsp over each pan.

Approximate nutritive values per portion

Calories	Carbohydrate	Protein	Fat	Cholesterol	Sodium	Fiber	Iron
160 kcal	16 g	2.3 g	10 g	0 mg	259 mg	2.7 g	1 mg

Notes

- Potentially hazardous food. *Food Safety Standards:* Hold food for service at an internal temperature of 135°F or above. Do not mix old product with new. Cool leftover product quickly following time standards and cooling procedures on p. 167. Reheat leftover product quickly (within 2 hours) to 165°F or above. Reheat product only once; discard if not used.
- To shorten the assembly time, carrots and lentils may be cooked ahead and refrigerated.
- Chicken base may be substituted for vegetable base. Adjust salt as necessary.

CURRIED RICE, BEANS, AND VEGETABLE PILAF

Yield: 50 entrées or 100 accompaniment portions   *Portion:* 8 oz (entrée) or 4 oz (accompaniment)

Ingredient	Amount	Procedure
Frozen greens, thawed and drained (see Note)	2 lb 8 oz EP	Weigh greens after thawing and draining well in a colander (may thaw overnight). Discard liquid drained from greens. Coarsely chop greens using a sharp knife. Reserve for later step.
Orange marmalade Vegetable base Water Crushed red pepper	1 lb 3 oz 1 gal ½ tsp	Blend marmalade, vegetable base, water, and pepper. Reserve for a later step.
Olive oil	3 oz	Heat oil to 350°F in tilting or other large fry pan.
Red bell peppers, cut in 1-inch-long strips Yellow bell peppers, cut in 1-inch-long strips Garlic, minced	1 lb EP 1 lb EP 8 oz EP	Sauté peppers and garlic in hot oil for 3 minutes.
Rice, converted Curry powder	3 lb 1½ oz	Add rice and curry powder to fry pan with peppers. Stir and cook for 1 minute.
Sweet potatoes, peeled, ½-inch dice Kidney beans, canned, drained Raisins	2 lb 4 oz EP 5 lb 4 oz EP 1 lb	Add sweet potatoes, beans, and raisins to peppers and rice.
		Stir in chopped greens and marmalade mixtures reserved from earlier steps. Bring to a boil. Reduce heat to low. Cover and simmer until rice and vegetables are tender and liquids are absorbed, about 25 minutes. Turn off heat and let stand covered for 10 minutes.

Approximate nutritive values per portion (Entrée Portion)

Calories	Carbohydrate	Protein	Fat	Cholesterol	Sodium	Fiber	Iron
250 kcal	52 g	6 g	2 g	0 mg	268 mg	6 g	2 mg

Notes

- Potentially hazardous food. *Food Safety Standards:* Hold food for service at an internal temperature of 135°F or above. Do not mix old product with new. Cool leftover product quickly following time standards and cooling procedures on p. 167. Reheat leftover product quickly (within 2 hours) to 165°F or above. Reheat product only once; discard if not used.
- Frozen collard or spinach greens can be used.
- A frozen pepper blend can be substituted for the red and yellow bell peppers.

SUSHI-STYLE RICE

Yield: 50 portions   *Portion:* 4 oz

Ingredient	Amount	Procedure
Sticky rice	3 lb 10 oz	Cook rice according to rice cooking directions on p. 542.
Water	3¾ qt	Place cooked rice in baker's bowl. Cool to 70°F.
Salt	2 Tbsp	
Rice wine vinegar	2¾ cups	Combine liquid ingredients and seasonings to make a dressing.
Salad oil	⅓ cup	Pour dressing over cooled rice. Stir with a rubber spatula until all of the
Toasted sesame oil	⅓ cup	rice is coated with dressing.
Soy sauce	⅓ cup	Cool quickly and use for wraps; rice bowls.
Fresh ginger, minced	2 Tbsp	Use within 48 hours.
Garlic, minced	2¾ Tbsp	
Wasabi paste (see Note)	1 Tbsp	

Approximate nutritive values per portion

Calories	Carbohydrate	Protein	Fat	Cholesterol	Sodium	Fiber	Iron
137 kcal	25 g	2 g	2.7 g	0 mg	359 mg	0 g	0.5 mg

Notes

- Potentially hazardous food. *Food Safety Standards:* Hold food for service at an internal temperature of 135°F or above. Do not mix old product with new. Cool leftover product quickly following time standards and cooling procedures on p. 167. Reheat leftover product quickly (within 2 hours) to 165°F or above. Reheat product only once; discard if not used.
- Horseradish can be substituted for wasabi paste.

Cereal and Grain Recipes

COOKED BREAKFAST CEREALS

Yield: 50 portions   *Portion:* 6 oz

Ingredient	Amount	Procedure
Water	2–2¼ gal	Measure water into steam-jacketed kettle or heavy stockpot.
Salt	2 oz (3 Tbsp)	Add salt and bring to a rolling boil.
Cereal, granular or flaked (cream of wheat, oatmeal)	2 lb	Stir dry cereal gradually into boiling water, using a wire whip. Stir until some thickening is apparent. Reduce heat and cook until cereal reaches desired consistency and raw starch taste has disappeared. Cereal should be thick and creamy but not sticky.

Approximate nutritive values per portion

Calories	Carbohydrate	Protein	Fat	Cholesterol	Sodium	Fiber	Iron
73 kcal	13 g	3 g	1 g	0 mg	406 mg	1 g	1 mg

Notes

- Potentially hazardous food. *Food Safety Standards:* Hold food for service at an internal temperature of 135°F or above. Do not mix old product with new. Cool leftover product quickly following time standards and cooling procedures on p. 167. Reheat leftover product quickly (within 2 hours) to 165°F or above. Reheat product only once; discard if not used.
- Granular cereals may be mixed with cold water to separate particles and prevent formation of lumps.
- Do not stir excessively; overstirring or overcooking produces a sticky, gummy product.
- 1 lb raisins may be added to cereal the last 2 minutes of cooking.

Variation

- **Rice and Raisins.** Cook 8 oz rice (2 lb cooked) according to directions on p. 542. Heat 1 gal milk. Add cooked rice, 8 oz softened raisins, 12 oz granulated sugar, and 2 Tbsp cinnamon.

DRIED FRUIT AND NUT GRANOLA

Yield: 50 servings   *Portion:* 1 cup
Oven: 350°F

Ingredient	Amount	Procedure
Rolled oats	4 lb 8 oz	Spread oats on baking pan. Toast in 350°F oven for 10–15 minutes. Shake pan once during baking to ensure even browning. Transfer to mixing bowl.
Coconut, shredded	1 lb	Spread coconut, almonds, and pecans on baking pan. Toast in oven until lightly browned, 6–8 minutes. Shake pan once during cooking to ensure even browning.
Almonds, sliced	1 lb	
Pecan pieces	1 lb	Add nut mixture to toasted oats.
Unprocessed bran	6 cups	Add to oat-nut mixture. Mix lightly until all ingredients are evenly distributed.
Raisins	2 lb	Cool.
Dried apricots, coarsely chopped	1 lb	Store in airtight container.
Sugar, brown	8 oz	
Cinnamon, ground	1 Tbsp	

Approximate nutritive values per portion

Calories	Carbohydrate	Protein	Fat	Cholesterol	Sodium	Fiber	Iron
400 kcal	64 g	9 g	16 g	0 mg	8.2 mg	7 g	4 mg

Notes

- Serve as a cereal, on ice cream, or on yogurt.
- Substitute any dried fruit for raisins and apricots. Sunflower seeds may be substituted for part of the nuts.

BAKED CHEESE GRITS

Yield: 48 portions or 3 pans, 12 × 10 × 2 inches   *Portion:* 6 oz
Oven: 350°F   *Bake:* 30–40 minutes

Ingredient	Amount	Procedure
Water	1¾ gal	Bring water to a brisk boil in steam-jacketed kettle.
Grits, quick	2 lb 4 oz	Stir in grits and salt quickly with a wire whip. Reduce heat to medium.
Salt	2 tsp	Cook for 5–7 minutes or until thickened.
Eggs	9 (1 lb)	Stir a small amount of cooked grits into eggs. Add to remainder of grits in kettle, stirring constantly.
Cheddar cheese, shredded	2 lb 4 oz	Add to grits. Cook over low heat until cheese is melted.
Margarine	8 oz	Scale into three greased 12 × 10 × 2-inch pans, 6 lb per pan.
Garlic powder	1 tsp	
Worcestershire sauce	⅓ cup	
Paprika	½ tsp	Sprinkle lightly over grits. Bake at 350°F for 30–40 minutes or until top is set and slightly puffed. Let stand for 5 minutes before serving. To serve, cut 4 × 4.

Approximate nutritive values per portion

Calories	Carbohydrate	Protein	Fat	Cholesterol	Sodium	Fiber	Iron
203 kcal	17 g	8 g	12 g	61 mg	473 mg	1 g	6 mg

Note

- Potentially hazardous food. *Food Safety Standards:* Hold food for service at an internal temperature of 135°F or above. Do not mix old product with new. Cool leftover product quickly following time standards and cooling procedures on p. 167. Reheat leftover product quickly (within 2 hours) to 165°F or above. Reheat product only once; discard if not used.

BARLEY CASSEROLE

Yield: 50 portions or 1 pan, 12 × 20 × 2 inches   *Portion:* 4 oz
Oven: 350°F   *Bake:* 1½ hours

Ingredient	Amount	Procedure
Pearl barley	2 lb 6 oz	Sauté barley and vegetables in margarine.
Onions, chopped	1 lb 4 oz	
Mushroom pieces and stems, canned	1 lb 11 oz	
Margarine	6 oz	
Chicken Stock (p. 738)	3½ qt	Add Chicken Stock to barley mixture. Pour into a 12 × 20 × 2-inch counter pan. Bake at 350°F for 1½ hours. Serve with No. 10 dipper.

Approximate nutritive values per portion

Calories	Carbohydrate	Protein	Fat	Cholesterol	Sodium	Fiber	Iron
119 kcal	19 g	4 g	3 g	0 mg	317 mg	4 g	1 mg

Notes

- Potentially hazardous food. *Food Safety Standards:* Hold food for service at an internal temperature of 135°F or above. Do not mix old product with new. Cool leftover product quickly following time standards and cooling procedures on p. 167. Reheat leftover product quickly (within 2 hours) to 165°F or above. Reheat product only once; discard if not used.
- $2\frac{1}{2}$ oz ($1\frac{1}{4}$ cups) dehydrated onions, rehydrated in 2 cups water, may be substituted for fresh onions.

Variations

- **Chicken Barley Casserole.** Increase chicken stock to 1 gal. Stir in 6 lb cooked cubed chicken. Turkey may be substituted for chicken.
- **Mediterranean Barley Pilaf.** Add 1 lb 8 oz golden raisins, 1 lb chopped pecans, and 1 tsp dried thyme.

BARLEY AND VEGETABLE MEDLEY

Yield: 50 portions   *Portion:* 4 oz

Ingredient	Amount	Procedure
Olive oil	3 oz	Heat oil to 350°F in tilting fry pan or steam-jacketed kettle.
Onions, sliced into thin half-rings	1 lb 8 oz EP	Sauté onions, garlic, and barley in hot oil until onions and barley are golden brown, about 5 minutes.
Garlic, minced	1 Tbsp	
Barley	1 lb	
Vegetable base (see Note)	1 oz	Mix vegetable base with part of the water. Add water and vegetable base to vegetable-barley mixture.
Water	$1\frac{1}{4}$ qt	Heat to boiling. Reduce heat and simmer until barley is almost tender, about 30 minutes. Stir occasionally.
Carrots, peeled, sliced	1 lb 6 oz EP	Add carrots, cauliflower, broccoli, herbs, and spices to barley mixture. Cover and simmer for 12–15 minutes.
Cauliflower, small florets	10 oz EP	
Broccoli, small florets	8 oz EP	
Basil, dried	1 Tbsp	
Thyme, dried	1 Tbsp	
Salt	2 tsp	
Black pepper	$\frac{1}{2}$ tsp	
Diced tomatoes, fresh	2 lb EP	Add tomatoes, squash, peppers, and peas to barley mixture. Cook for 5–10 minutes until vegetables are tender.
Zucchini squash, sliced	1 lb EP	
Green bell peppers, diced	10 oz EP	
Peas, frozen	1 lb 8 oz	

Approximate nutritive values per portion

Calories	Carbohydrate	Protein	Fat	Cholesterol	Sodium	Fiber	Iron
80 kcal	13 g	2.6 g	2 g	0 mg	198 mg	3.4 g	1 mg

Notes

- Potentially hazardous food. *Food Safety Standards:* Hold food for service at an internal temperature of 135°F or above. Do not mix old product with new. Cool leftover product quickly following time standards and cooling procedures on p. 167. Reheat leftover product quickly (within 2 hours) to 165°F or above. Reheat product only once; discard if not used.
- Chicken base can be substituted for the vegetable base. Adjust salt if necessary.

Variation

- **Barley and Stir-Fried Vegetables.** In a tilting fry pan stir 1 oz ancho flavor concentrate and 1 tsp chipotle flavor concentrate (see note) into 12 oz olive oil. Heat oil, add 12 oz pecan halves, and cook until nuts are golden brown and fragrant. Add 1 lb carrot coins, 1 lb bell pepper strips (combination of green, red, yellow), 1 lb sliced celery, and 2 oz minced garlic. Sauté until vegetables are tender-crisp. Stir in 2 lb 8 oz canned black beans, drained and rinsed, 4 lb 10 oz cooked barley, 4 tsp salt, 2 tsp black pepper, and 3 Tbsp dried mint leaves. Heat to 170°F. Serve hot. (Note: 1 lb 12 oz uncooked barley cooked in $1\frac{1}{4}$ gal water and 2 oz salt will yield, after draining, 4 lb 10 oz cooked barley. Minor's Ancho Flavor Concentrate and Minor's Chipotle Flavor Concentrate are available from most broadline foodservice distibutors.)

SOUTHWEST BARLEY RISOTTO

Yield: 50 portions   *Portion:* 4 oz

Ingredient	Amount	Procedure
Margarine	4 oz	Heat margarine in steam-jacketed or other heavy-bottomed kettle. Sauté onions and garlic until barely tender.
Onions, chopped Garlic, minced	12 oz 3 Tbsp	
Pearl barley	2 lb	Add barley. Cool for 2–3 minutes until barley is coated with fat and lightly toasted.
Water	2½ cups	Add water. Slowly cook uncovered until water is absorbed.
Chicken base (see Note) Water Fresh lime juice	6 oz 1¾ gal ⅓ cup	Mix chicken base with water and lime juice to make a stock. Heat stock and keep hot. Add stock (1 qt at a time) to barley mixture while cooking over medium heat. Add additional stock only after liquid from previous addition is absorbed. Barley will become tender and have a creamy consistency. Stir very often, but not continuously, throughout the liquid-adding step.
Whipping cream Fresh diced tomatoes Sliced jalapeño peppers, canned Parmesan cheese, shredded	2 cups 3 lb 12 oz 3 oz 10 oz	Stir in cream, tomatoes, peppers, and cheese. Stir until cheese melts.
Green onions, thinly sliced Fresh cilantro, chopped	8 oz 1½ oz	Stir green onions and cilantro into barley mixture.

Approximate nutritive values per portion

Calories	Carbohydrate	Protein	Fat	Cholesterol	Sodium	Fiber	Iron
166 kcal	19 g	5 g	8 g	20 mg	474 mg	4 g	1 mg

Notes

- Potentially hazardous food. *Food Safety Standards:* Hold food for service at an internal temperature of 135°F or above. Do not mix old product with new. Cool leftover product quickly following time standards and cooling procedures on p. 167. Reheat leftover product quickly (within 2 hours) to 165°F or above. Reheat product only once; discard if not used.
- Substitute vegetable base for chicken base for vegetarian risotto.

Variation

- **Barley Tomato Risotto.** Omit lime juice and jalapeño peppers. Substitute chopped flat leaf parsley for cilantro.

GINGER VEGETABLES AND BARLEY

Yield: 50 entrée portions   *Portion*: 8 oz (for 4-oz side portions, decrease recipe by ½)

Ingredient	Amount	Procedure
Water	3¾ gal	Bring water to boil in steam-jacketed kettle.
Salt	5 oz (7½ Tbsp)	Stir barley and salt into boiling water. Cook for about 50 minutes or until
Barley	5 lb	tender. Stir occasionally.
		Drain and save for later step. (Yield: 13 lb 12 oz cooked barley.)
Olive oil	6 oz	Heat oil to 325°F in tilting fry pan.
Fresh ginger, minced	4 oz EP	Add ginger and carrots to oil. Sauté until fragrant, approximately 1 minute.
Carrots, ½-inch dice	3 lb 6 oz EP	
Red bell peppers, ½-inch dice	1 lb EP	Add peppers. Sauté to heat through, approximately 1 minute.
Yellow bell peppers, ½-inch dice	1 lb EP	
Green bell peppers, ½-inch dice	12 oz EP	
Corn, whole kernel, frozen, defrosted	2 lb 12 oz	Add corn, peas, and seasonings. Sauté for 1 minute. Add 13 lb 12 oz cooked barley (reserved from earlier step) to pepper mixture.
Peas, frozen, defrosted	3 lb	Heat through to 165–170°F.
Salt	2¼ oz (3½ Tbsp)	
Black pepper	2 tsp	
Green onions, sliced	1 lb 5 oz	Stir in onions and mint.
Mint leaves, finely chopped (see Note)	3 oz	Transfer to 12 × 10 × 2-inch pans. Cover.

Approximate nutritive values per portion

Calories	Carbohydrate	Protein	Fat	Cholesterol	Sodium	Fiber	Iron
250 kcal	48 g	7.6 g	4.4 g	0 mg	1620 mg	10 g	2 mg

Notes
- Potentially hazardous food. *Food Safety Standards:* Hold food for service at an internal temperature of 135°F or above. Do not mix old product with new. Cool leftover product quickly following time standards and cooling procedures on p. 167. Reheat leftover product quickly (within 2 hours) to 165°F or above. Reheat product only once; discard if not used.
- 1 oz dried crushed mint leaves may be substituted for fresh mint.

SPICY BARLEY WITH CONFETTI VEGETABLES

Yield: 50 entrée portions   *Portions:* 8 oz (for 4-oz side portions, decrease recipe by ½)

Ingredient	Amount	Procedure
Water	3¾ gal	Bring water to a boil in steam-jacketed kettle.
Salt	5 oz (7½ Tbsp)	Stir barley and salt into boiling water. Cook for about 50 minutes or until tender. Stir occasionally.
Barley	5 lb	Drain and save for later step. (Yield: 13 lb 12 oz cooked barley.)
Olive oil	1 lb 4 oz	Heat oil and vegetable base to 350°F in a tilting fry pan.
Vegetable base (see Note)	2 oz	
Carrots, fine julienne cut	2 lb 4 oz EP	Add carrots to oil and sauté 1 minute.
Roasted red bell peppers, chopped (p. 796)	4 lb 4 oz	Add roasted peppers and seasonings to carrots. Sauté just until peppers are soft.
Salt (see Note)	1½ oz	Add 13 lb 12 oz cooked barley reserved from earlier step.
Black pepper	1 Tbsp	Heat through, 165–170°F.
Crushed red pepper	1 tsp	
Green onions, sliced	3 lb 4 oz EP	Add onions, peas, and thyme.
Peas, frozen, thawed	3 lb	Mix gently to distribute.
Thyme, dried	1 Tbsp	Transfer to 12 × 10 × 2-inch pans. Cover.

Approximate nutritive values per portion

Calories	Carbohydrate	Protein	Fat	Cholesterol	Sodium	Fiber	Iron
228 kcal	38 g	4 g	12 g	0 mg	1026 mg	8 g	2 mg

Notes

- Potentially hazardous food. *Food Safety Standards:* Hold food for service at an internal temperature of 135°F or above. Do not mix old product with new. Cool leftover product quickly following time standards and cooling procedures on p. 167. Reheat leftover product quickly (within 2 hours) to 165°F or above. Reheat product only once; discard if not used.
- Chicken base can be substituted for vegetable base. Taste before adding salt. Salt concentration varies among brands of bases.

BARLEY AND VEGETABLES

Yield: 50 entrée portions   *Portion:* 8 oz (for 4-oz side portions, decrease recipe by ½)

Ingredient	Amount	Procedure
Water	2½ gal	Bring water to a boil in steam-jacketed kettle.
Salt	3 oz (4⅔ Tbsp)	Stir barley and salt into boiling water. Cook for about 50 minutes or until
Barley	3 lb 6 oz	tender. Stir occasionally.
		Drain and save for later step. (Yield: 9 lb 6 oz cooked barley.)
Olive oil	2¾ cup	Heat oil and vegetable base to 350°F in a tilting fry pan.
Vegetable base	2 oz	
Pecan halves	1 lb 5 oz	Add pecans to hot oil and cook until golden brown.
Fresh carrot coins	2 lb EP	Add vegetables and seasoning to pecans and sauté until
Red bell peppers, ½-inch dice	2 lb EP	tender-crisp, approximately 5 minutes.
Yellow bell peppers, ½-inch dice	2 lb EP	
Green bell peppers, ½-inch dice	2 lb EP	
Celery, ¼-inch slices	2 lb EP	
Salt	1½ oz (2⅓ Tbsp)	
Black pepper	1 Tbsp	
Garlic, minced	4 oz EP	Add garlic, beans, and 9 lb 6 oz cooked barley reserved from earlier step.
Black beans, canned, drained, rinsed	5 lb 4 oz EP	Heat until hot, 165–170°F.
Fresh mint, finely chopped	1 oz	Add mint and toss lightly to distribute. Transfer to 12 × 10 × 2-inch pans. Cover.

Approximate nutritive values per portion

Calories	Carbohydrate	Protein	Fat	Cholesterol	Sodium	Fiber	Iron
350 kcal	38 g	8 g	20 g	0 mg	1150 mg	9.4 g	2 mg

Notes

- Potentially hazardous food. *Food Safety Standards:* Hold food for service at an internal temperature of 135°F or above. Do not mix old product with new. Cool leftover product quickly following time standards and cooling procedures on p. 167. Reheat leftover product quickly (within 2 hours) to 165°F or above. Reheat product only once; discard if not used.

Variation

- **Red Beans and Barley.** Cook 1 lb 8 oz pearl barley in 1 gal water and 2 Tbsp salt as for Barley and Vegetables. Reserve cooked barley for later step. Sauté vegetables until tender using 6 oz margarine: 1 lb 8 oz chopped onions, 12 oz chopped celery, and 3 Tbsp minced garlic. Stir in 2 Tbsp chopped canned jalapeño peppers and 2 Tbsp Cajun seasoning. Stir in barley reserved from earlier step. Add 1½ qt water, 1 Tbsp vegetable soup base, 1 lb 12 oz canned, drained red beans, 1 lb canned chopped tomatoes, 12 oz small julienne cut carrots, 8 oz diced green bell pepper, and 1½ Tbsp salt (if needed). Heat to 170°F. Yield: 50 4-oz portions.

BULGUR-STUFFED SWEET DUMPLING SQUASH

Yield: 50 portions   *Portion:* 1 stuffed squash
Oven: 350°F   *Bake:* 30–45 minutes

Ingredient	Amount	Procedure
Sweet dumpling squash (approximately 1 lb each) (see Note)	50	Cut tops off squash and remove seeds and strings from the inside. Bake at 350°F until tender, 30–45 minutes. Prepare bulgur stuffing while squash is baking.
Margarine Leeks, sliced	14 oz 3 lb	Melt margarine over medium heat in steam-jacketed or other large kettle. Sauté leeks until tender, 5–10 minutes.
Vegetable base Water	10 oz 1½ gal	Blend vegetable base with water. Add to leeks and bring to a boil.
Coarse bulgur Cranberries, dried Salt Black pepper	5 lb 3 oz 1 lb 2 oz 2 Tbsp	Stir bulgur, cranberries, and seasonings into boiling water mixture. Cover and reduce heat to simmer. Cook until bulgur is tender and broth has been absorbed, 20–30 minutes.
Toasted slivered almonds (see Note)	1 lb 8 oz	Mix almonds into bulgur mixture. Portion 8 oz of bulgur stuffing inside each cooked squash.

Approximate nutritive values per portion

Calories	Carbohydrate	Protein	Fat	Cholesterol	Sodium	Fiber	Iron
665 kcal	118 g	15 g	22 g	0 mg	1623 mg	18 g	7 mg

Notes

- Potentially hazardous food. *Food Safety Standards:* Hold food for service at an internal temperature of 135°F or above. Do not mix old product with new. Cool leftover product quickly following time standards and cooling procedures on p. 167. Reheat leftover product quickly (within 2 hours) to 165°F or above. Reheat product only once; discard if not used.
- If squash are larger than approximately 1 lb, cut in half or quarters.
- Chicken base can be substituted for vegetable base. Taste before adding salt. Salt concentration varies among brands of bases.
- To toast almonds, spread in a single layer on a baking pan. Toast at 300°F until nuts are golden and become fragrant, about 15 minutes. Stir two or three times during toasting. Cool completely and cover tightly if prepared in advance.

Variations

- **Acorn Squash Stuffed with Bulgur, Leeks, Cranberries, and Almonds.** Substitute small acorn squash for sweet dumpling squash.
- **Bulgur, Leek, and Cranberry–Stuffed Portabella.** Prepare half of the bulgur stuffing as for Bulgur-Stuffed Sweet Dumpling Squash. Clean 50 portabella mushroom caps by removing stems and gills. Pat dry after rinsing. Dip mushroom caps in a mixture of 1 qt salad oil, 1¼ tsp dried thyme, 1 tsp salt, and ½ tsp black pepper. Roast mushrooms at 325°F until tender, about 10 minutes. Portion 4 oz bulgur mixture onto each mushroom cap.
- **Bulgur with Cranberries and Toasted Almonds.** Prepare half of the bulgur stuffing. Serve 4 oz as a side dish.

BULGUR PILAF WITH ROASTED TOMATOES AND CHICKPEAS

Yield: 50 portions   *Portion:* 4 oz
Oven: 400°F   *Bake:* 30 minutes

Ingredient	Amount	Procedure
Bulgur, coarse Water, warm	1 lb 4 oz 1½ qt	Combine bulgur and water in baker's bowl. Let stand for 1 hour or longer. Drain by pressing out any excess liquid. Reserve for later step.
Fresh diced tomatoes Onion wedges Salt Black pepper Olive oil	6 lb lb 4 oz 2 tsp 2 tsp 3 oz	Place tomatoes and onions on shallow baking sheets without crowding. Sprinkle with salt and pepper and drizzle with olive oil. Roast at 400°F for 30 minutes, stirring occasionally, until beginning to brown.
Garbanzo beans, canned, drained	2 lb 12 oz	Add garbanzo beans to roasted vegetables. Continue roasting until beans are golden brown. Reserve for later step.
Olive oil Garlic, minced	4 oz 2 oz	Heat olive oil in tilting fry pan. Sauté garlic until fragrant. Add rehydrated bulgur reserved from earlier step and sauté until golden brown. Add roasted vegetables reserved from earlier step. Continue to sauté until vegetables are hot and all ingredients are combined.
Flat leaf parsley, minced Dill weed, dried Fresh lemon juice	½ cup 2 Tbsp 2½ Tbsp	Stir parsley, dill weed, and juice into bulgur mixture.
Flat leaf parsley, chopped	1 oz	Garnish each pan with chopped parsley.

Approximate nutritive values per portion

Calories	Carbohydrate	Protein	Fat	Cholesterol	Sodium	Fiber	Iron
90 kcal	12 g	2 g	4 g	0 mg	109 mg	2 g	0.75 mg

Note

- Potentially hazardous food. *Food Safety Standards:* Hold food for service at an internal temperature of 135°F or above. Do not mix old product with new. Cool leftover product quickly following time standards and cooling procedures on p. 167. Reheat leftover product quickly (within 2 hours) to 165°F or above. Reheat product only once; discard if not used.

Variation

- **Israeli Couscous with Roasted Tomatoes and Chickpeas.** Substitute 3 lb 4 oz cooked Israeli couscous for the bulgur. (Note: 1 lb uncooked Israeli couscous boiled in 1 gal water with 1 oz salt will yield, after draining, 3 lb 4 oz cooked couscous.)

GRAINS AND LENTILS AU GRATIN

Yield: 50 portions   *Portion:* 4 oz

Ingredient	Amount	Procedure
Carrots, finely chopped	1 lb	Steam carrots for 1 minute. Do not drain. Reserve for later step.
Water	1 gal	Bring water, salt, and margarine to boil in steam-jacketed or other large kettle.
Salt	1½ Tbsp	
Margarine	4 tsp	
Pearl barley	8 oz	Add barley to boiling water. Reduce heat and simmer for 10 minutes.
Lentils, dried, rinsed	4 oz	Add lentils to kettle with barley. Stir and simmer for 5 minutes.
Rice, brown	8 oz	Add brown rice to kettle. Stir and simmer for 10 minutes.
Rice, white	8 oz	Add white rice to kettle. Stir and simmer for 20 minutes.
Cream of mushroom soup, canned	2 lb 8 oz	Add soup, milk, margarine, and seasonings to grains.
Milk	3 cups	Add carrots reserved from earlier step.
Margarine	6 oz	Stir well to blend. Heat to 180°F, stirring often.
Black pepper	½ tsp	
Chives, dried	2½ Tbsp	
Crushed red pepper	¼ tsp	
Salt	¼ tsp	
Mushroom pieces, canned, drained	8 oz	Stir in mushrooms and shredded cheese.
Cheddar cheese, shredded	1 lb 4 oz	Scale into 12 × 20 × 2-inch pans, 6 lb per pan.

Approximate nutritive values per portion

Calories	Carbohydrate	Protein	Fat	Cholesterol	Sodium	Fiber	Iron
161 kcal	16 g	5 g	9 g	12 mg	484 mg	2 g	1 mg

Note

- Potentially hazardous food. *Food Safety Standards:* Hold food for service at an internal temperature of 135°F or above. Do not mix old product with new. Cool leftover product quickly following time standards and cooling procedures on p. 167. Reheat leftover product quickly (within 2 hours) to 165°F or above. Reheat product only once; discard if not used.

ISRAELI COUSCOUS WITH OLIVES AND ROASTED TOMATOES

Yield: 50 portions   *Portion:* 8 oz
Oven: conventional, 250°F; convection, 200°F

Ingredient	Amount	Procedure
Cherry tomatoes	10 lb 8 oz	Place tomatoes in single layer on silicone-paper-lined 18 × 26 × 1-inch pans. Roast at 250°F (conventional oven) or 200°F (convection oven) for about 1 hour or until slightly shriveled. Hold warm to combine with cooked couscous in a later step.
Garlic cloves	4 oz	Mix garlic with oil and stir to coat.
Olive oil	1½ Tbsp	Place tomatoes and garlic on silicone-paper-lined pans.
Cherry tomatoes	2 lb	Roast tomatoes and garlic at 250°F (conventional oven) or 200°F (convection oven) for about 1 hour or until slightly shriveled. Cool slightly before processing into a tomato-garlic dressing in the next step.
Olive oil	2 cups	Make tomato-garlic dressing by putting cooled tomatoes and garlic, oil, liquids, and seasonings in a food processor.
Water, warm	2 cups	Process until smooth. (Process in batches if using a small food processor.)
Fresh lemon juice	3 Tbsp	Save tomato-garlic dressing for later step.
Salt	2½ Tbsp	
Black pepper	1 Tbsp	
Vegetable base (see Note)	4 oz	
Water	3½ gal	Bring water and salt to a rolling boil in steam-jacketed or other kettle.
Salt	1 oz (1½ Tbsp)	Add couscous while stirring.
Middle Eastern couscous (see Note)	4 lb 6 oz	Return water to a boil. Reduce heat and simmer for 10–12 minutes until couscous is *al dente.* Stir occasionally. Drain and hold warm. (Yield: 13 lb cooked couscous.)
Olive oil	4 oz	To 13 lb cooked couscous add oil, olive pesto, herbs, and seasonings.
Kalamata Olive Pesto (see Note)	10 oz	Add tomato-garlic dressing reserved from earlier step. Add roasted tomatoes reserved from earlier step.
Fresh parsley, minced	2½ oz EP	Toss gently to distribute ingredients.
Thyme, dried	1 Tbsp	Transfer to 12 × 10 × 2-inch pans. Serve warm.
Salt	2 tsp	
Black pepper	1 Tbsp	

Approximate nutritive values per portion

Calories	Carbohydrate	Protein	Fat	Cholesterol	Sodium	Fiber	Iron
260 kcal	33.8 g	6 g	11.7 g	1.2 mg	817 mg	3.2 g	1 mg

Notes

- Potentially hazardous food. *Food Safety Standards:* Hold food for service at an internal temperature of 135°F or above. Do not mix old product with new. Cool leftover product quickly following time standards and cooling procedures on p. 167. Reheat leftover product quickly (within 2 hours) to 165°F or above. Reheat product only once; discard if not used.
- Kalamata Olive Pesto is a Minor's product manufactured by Nestle and available through most distributors. If unavailable, substitute sliced or puréed Kalamata olives. The amount of salt may need to be adjusted when substituting Kalamata olives for the pesto.
- The salt concentration of vegetable bases varies by brand. Add less salt if a highly salted base is used.

ISRAELI COUSCOUS WITH LEEKS, CORN, AND OLIVES

Yield: 50 portions   *Portion:* 4 oz

Ingredient	Amount	Procedure
Water	5½ gal	Bring water and salt to a rolling boil. Add couscous and return to a boil. Reduce heat and simmer for 10–12 minutes until *al dente*. Drain. Reserve for later step.
Salt	2 tsp	
Israeli couscous	1 lb 12 oz	
Olive oil	8 oz	Heat oil over medium heat. Add leeks and corn. Sauté until tender, 5–8 minutes.
Leeks, sliced	2 lb 12 oz	
Corn kernels, fresh or frozen	1 lb 5 oz	
White cooking wine	1¼ qt	Add cooking wine and thyme to leeks and corn. Bring to a boil. Stir in 5 lb 4 oz cooked Israeli couscous reserved from earlier step.
Thyme, dried	2½ tsp	
Kalamata Olive Pesto (see Note)	3 oz	Stir olive pesto, juice, and seasonings into couscous mixture.
Fresh lemon juice	1 cup	
Salt	2½ tsp	
Black pepper	1¼ tsp	

Approximate nutritive values per portion

Calories	Carbohydrate	Protein	Fat	Cholesterol	Sodium	Fiber	Iron
145 kcal	19 g	3 g	5 g	0 mg	270 mg	1.6 g	1 mg

Notes

- Potentially hazardous food. *Food Safety Standards:* Hold food for service at an internal temperature of 135°F or above. Do not mix old product with new. Cool leftover product quickly following time standards and cooling procedures on p. 167. Reheat leftover product quickly (within 2 hours) to 165°F or above. Reheat product only once; discard if not used.
- Kalamata Olive Pesto is a Minor's product manufactured by Nestle and available through most broadline foodservice distributors. If unavailable, substitute sliced or puréed Kalamata olives or Black Olive Tapenade, p. 197. The amount of salt may need to be adjusted when substituting Kalamata olives for the pesto.

Variation

- **Israeli Couscous with Carrots and Thyme.** Heat 12 oz olive oil in steam-jacketed or large kettle. Sauté 1 lb 8 oz small julienne cut carrots (matchstick size), 4 oz onion, and 2 minced garlic cloves until softened but not brown. Add 3 oz fresh lemon juice, 1 Tbsp sugar, 1 cup water, 1 Tbsp dried thyme, and 4 tsp salt. Stir in 9 lb 4 oz cooked Israeli couscous and 2½ oz chopped fresh flat leaf parsley. (Note: 3 lb uncooked Israeli couscous, cooked in 2½ gal water and 2 Tbsp salt, drained, will yield 9 lb 4 oz cooked couscous.)

MOROCCAN COUSCOUS AND VEGETABLES

Yield: 50 portions   *Portion:* 4 oz

Ingredient	Amount	Procedure
Water Allspice, ground	1¾ qt ¼ tsp	Bring water and allspice to a boil in steam-jacketed or other large kettle.
Couscous Fresh diced tomatoes	1 lb 4 oz 4 oz	Add couscous to boiling water. Stir. Cover tightly. Turn off heat and let set for 5 minutes. Fluff with fork. Transfer to 12 × 10 × 2-inch pans. Cover and hold hot. Reserve for later step.
Roasted red peppers (see Note)	1 lb 4 oz	Chop coarsely and reserve for later step.
Olive oil	3 oz	Heat olive oil over medium-high heat in tilting fry pan.
Onions, ½-inch dice Garlic, minced Carrot coins Leeks, sliced Sugar snap peas Quartered red radishes (without tops)	10 oz 3 oz 8 oz 1 lb 8 oz 1 lb 1 lb	Sauté vegetables until tender-crisp.
Sugar, granulated Salt Garbanzo beans, drained	2 tsp 1½ tsp 3 lb 12 oz	Add peppers reserved from ealier step, sugar, salt, and beans. Cook until beans are hot, about 5 minutes.
Spinach leaves, without stems Flat leaf parsley, chopped Harissa sauce (see Note)	4 oz 1½ oz 1 cup	Stir in spinach, parsley, and harissa sauce. Cover and hold hot. Portion 2 oz couscous on plate. Portion 3 oz vegetables over couscous.

Approximate nutritive values per portion

Calories	Carbohydrate	Protein	Fat	Cholesterol	Sodium	Fiber	Iron
132 kcal	23 g	4 g	3 g	0 mg	242 mg	4 g	2 mg

Notes

- Potentially hazardous food. *Food Safety Standards:* Hold food for service at an internal temperature of 135°F or above. Do not mix old product with new. Cool leftover product quickly following time standards and cooling procedures on p. 167. Reheat leftover product quickly (within 2 hours) to 165°F or above. Reheat product only once; discard if not used.
- See p. 796 for instructions for roasting peppers. Frozen roasted red peppers are available from most broadline foodservice distributors. If fresh bell peppers are substituted, sauté along with other vegetables.
- Harissa sauce (a hot chile condiment) is available from most broadline foodservice distributors or specialty food stores. To make 8 oz **Harissa Sauce**, process the following ingredients in a food processor until finely chopped: 4½ tsp caraway seed, 1¼ tsp ground coriander, 1 tsp ground cumin, 2 tsp crushed red pepper, 1½ tsp black pepper, 1½ Tbsp minced garlic, and 5 Tbsp sliced jalapeño peppers, drained. Add 3 oz red wine vinegar and 3 Tbsp olive oil to spices and process until smooth.

Variation

- **Vegetable Couscous.** Heat 8 oz margarine in steam-jacketed or other large kettle and sauté 1 lb 12 oz julienne cut zucchini, 12 oz julienne cut carrots, and 4 oz sliced green onions. Mix 3 oz chicken soup base with 3 qt water. Add to vegetables. Bring to a rolling boil. Stir in 3 lb couscous. Cover. Turn off heat and let stand for 5 minutes. Stir to fluff. Placed in 12 × 10 × 4-inch pans. Cover tightly and keep hot. For vegetarian couscous, substitute vegetable base for chicken base. Bases vary in the amount of salt. Check for salt and adjust if necessary.

RED PEPPER COUSCOUS

Yield: 50 portions   *Portion:* 4 oz

Ingredient	Amount	Procedure
Green onion, sliced	1 lb	Sauté vegetables in oil in a steam-jacketed kettle or stockpot until tender-crisp.
Red bell pepper, julienne	6 oz	
Garlic, minced	2 Tbsp	
Olive oil	½ cup	
Paprika	2 Tbsp	Add paprika and cook for 1 minute.
Water	3 qt	Add water, juice, tomato paste, pimento, and seasonings to sautéed vegetable mixture.
Fresh lemon juice	¼ cup	
Tomato paste	8 oz	Bring to a rolling boil.
Pimento, chopped	8 oz	
Crushed red pepper	½ tsp	
Salt	1 Tbsp	
Couscous, quick cooking	3 lb	Add couscous to mixture and stir. Cover, turn off heat. Let stand for 5 minutes. Stir to fluff.

Approximate nutritive values per portion

Calories	Carbohydrate	Protein	Fat	Cholesterol	Sodium	Fiber	Iron
141 kcal	26 g	4 g	3 g	0 mg	141 mg	5 g	1 mg

Note

- Potentially hazardous food. *Food Safety Standards:* Hold food for service at an internal temperature of 135°F or above. Do not mix old product with new. Cool leftover product quickly following time standards and cooling procedures on p. 167. Reheat leftover product quickly (within 2 hours) to 165°F or above. Reheat product only once; discard if not used.

QUINOA PILAF

Yield: 50 portions   *Portion:* 4 oz

Ingredient	Amount	Procedure
Green onions, sliced	1 lb 8 oz	Sauté vegetables in olive oil until tender-crisp.
Celery	1 lb	
Fresh mushrooms, sliced	1 lb 8 oz	
Garlic, minced	1 Tbsp	
Olive oil	1 cup	
Chicken base	3 oz	Mix chicken base with water. Add to vegetables. Bring to a rolling boil.
Water	3½ qt	
Quinoa, rinsed and drained	3 lb 8 oz	Add quinoa to vegetables and stir. Cover and reduce heat to low. Simmer until all liquid is absorbed and the grains are translucent, 10–15 minutes.

Approximate nutritive values per portion

Calories	Carbohydrate	Protein	Fat	Cholesterol	Sodium	Fiber	Iron
166 kcal	24 g	5 g	6 g	0 mg	18 mg	2 g	3 mg

Notes

- Potentially hazardous food. *Food Safety Standards:* Hold food for service at an internal temperature of 135°F or above. Do not mix old product with new. Cool leftover product quickly following time standards and cooling procedures on p. 167. Reheat leftover product quickly (within 2 hours) to 165°F or above. Reheat product only once; discard if not used.
- Vegetable base may be substituted for the chicken base. If vegetable base is lightly salted or unsalted, add salt.
- Quinoa must be rinsed to remove the bitter coating on the grain.
- Quinoa may be toasted prior to cooking. Toast as for a dry spice, p. 731.

SOFT POLENTA

Yield: 50 portions   *Portion:* 4 oz

Ingredient	Amount	Procedure
Oil	5 oz	Heat oil in steam-jacketed kettle.
Onions, chopped	12 oz	Sauté onions and garlic until fragrant.
Garlic, minced	1 Tbsp	
Water	4½ qt	Add water and vegetable base to sautéed onions and garlic. Stir to dissolve base.
Vegetable base (see Note)	4 oz	Bring water mixture to a boil. Turn off heat.
Cornmeal	1 lb 12 oz	Pour cornmeal in a very slow stream into water. Stir constantly with a wire whip while pouring to prevent lumping. Turn heat on medium low and simmer until mixture thickens (becomes the consistency of thick pudding).
Milk (see Note)	2 qt	Stir in milk, chives, salt, and pepper.
Chives, dried	3 Tbsp	Transfer to 12 × 10 × 4-inch pans.
Salt	1½ tsp	Cover. Serve hot.
Black pepper	1 tsp	If polenta thickens during service, stir in warm milk to adjust consistency.

Approximate nutritive values per portion

Calories	Carbohydrate	Protein	Fat	Cholesterol	Sodium	Fiber	Iron
105 kcal	4.5 g	2.7 g	4.2 g	5 mg	268 mg	1.2 g	0.5 mg

Notes

- Potentially hazardous food. *Food Safety Standards:* Hold food for service at an internal temperature of 135°F or above. Do not mix old product with new. Cool leftover product quickly following time standards and cooling procedures on p. 167. Reheat leftover product quickly (within 2 hours) to 165°F or above. Reheat product only once; discard if not used.
- Serve as an accompaniment or under meat or grilled/roasted vegetable entrées.
- Chicken base can be substituted for vegetable base. Taste before adding salt. Salt concentration varies among brands of bases.
- For a vegan polenta, substitute soy milk for cow's milk.

Variation

- **Polenta with Bean Pico de Gallo and Tomato Pesto.** Prepare ½ recipe (6 lb) Soft Polenta (p. 577), ⅔ recipe (6 lb) Black Bean Pico de Gallo (p. 706), and ¼ recipe (1 lb 12 oz) Tomato Pesto (p. 706). Serve 2 oz Soft Polenta with 2 oz Black Bean Pico de Gallo and then 1 Tbsp Tomato Pesto on top.

PARMESAN POLENTA

Yield: 48 portions   *Portion:* 2 triangles

Ingredient	Amount	Procedure
Onions, finely chopped Garlic, minced Butter	2 lb 10 oz EP 2 oz EP 1 lb	Sauté onions and garlic in butter, using stockpot or steam-jacketed kettle, until fragrant.
Water Vegetable base (see Note)	3½ gal 12 oz	Add water and vegetable base to onion mixture. Bring to a boil and turn off heat.
Cornmeal	5 lb 8 oz	Stir into water very quickly, blending with a wire whisk. Turn heat on medium low and simmer for 10 minutes, stirring often to prevent sticking and burning. Turn off heat.
Parmesan cheese, shredded Milk Chives, freeze dried Salt Black pepper	1 lb 2 cups ¼ oz 1 oz 1 Tbsp	Stir cheese, milk, chives, and seasonings into cornmeal mixture. Scale into four 12 × 20 × 2-inch pans (7 lb 3 oz per pan) that have been oiled or sprayed with a food release spray. Chill at or below 40°F until polenta sets up, at least 6 hours.
		Cut 4 × 3. Cut each square in half diagonally to make two triangles.
Vegetable oil	1 cup	Lightly coat grill with oil. Heat to 325–350°F. Cook polenta until lightly browned on both sides, approximately 180°F. Turn only once during cooking.

Approximate nutritive values per portion

Calories	Carbohydrate	Protein	Fat	Cholesterol	Sodium	Fiber	Iron
365 kcal	46 g	8.3 g	16 g	31 mg	785 mg	4 g	2 mg

Notes

- Potentially hazardous food. *Food Safety Standards:* Hold food for service at an internal temerature of 41°F or below. Do not mix old product with new. Keep leftover product chilled at 41°F or below. See p. 167 for cooling procedures.
- Chicken base may be substituted for vegetable base. Adjust salt as necessary.

Variation

- **Polenta Cups with Marinara Sauce.** Mix 1 lb 13 oz yellow cornmeal with 5¼ qt water in steam-jacketed kettle. Cook, stirring constantly, until mixture thickens and boils. Reduce heat, cover, and simmer, stirring occasionally, for about 10 minutes. Turn off heat and stir in 1 lb 8 oz Parmesan cheese. Portion 3 oz (use No. 12 dipper) into greased muffin tins. Bake at 375°F until brown and crusty (approximately 1 hour). Cool in pans. Remove carefully after loosening sides with a sharp-pointed knife. Reheat in low oven to 165°F. Serve one per serving with marinara sauce.

Bean and Tofu Recipes

BEAN RAGOUT OVER GRILLED PARMESAN POLENTA

Yield: 50 portions   *Portion:* 4 oz ragout + 2 polenta triangles

Ingredient	Amount	Procedure
Onions, chopped	1 lb 12 oz EP	Sauté onions and garlic in oil, using stockpot or steam-jacketed kettle.
Garlic, minced	2 oz EP	
Vegetable oil	⅓ cup	
Diced green chiles, canned	6 oz	Add chiles and peppers to sautéed vegetables. Cook for 1–2 minutes.
Red bell peppers, ¼-inch dice	1 lb 4 oz EP	
Chile powder	2 oz	Add seasonings and continue to cook for 1–2 minutes.
Cumin, ground	2 Tbsp	
Oregano, dried	2 tsp	
Black pepper	1 tsp	
Diced tomatoes, canned	4 lb 12 oz	Add vegetables and beans to sautéed mixture. Bring to a boil.
Zucchini squash, coarsely chopped	1 lb 12 oz EP	Reduce heat and simmer until zucchini is tender-crisp.
Pinto beans, canned, drained and rinsed	2 lb 12 oz EP	
Black beans, canned, drained and rinsed	2 lb 12 oz EP	
Parmesan Polenta (p. 578)		Serve 4 oz ragout over two polenta triangles. Garnish with fresh shredded Parmesan cheese if desired.

Approximate nutritive values per portion of Bean Ragout

Calories	Carbohydrate	Protein	Fat	Cholesterol	Sodium	Fiber	Iron
80 kcal	12 g	3.6 g	2 g	0 mg	348 mg	4 g	1 mg

Note

- Potentially hazardous food. *Food Safety Standards:* Hold food for service at an internal temperature of 135°F or above. Do not mix old product with new. Cool leftover product quickly following time standards and cooling procedures on p. 167. Reheat leftover product quickly (within 2 hours) to 165°F or above. Reheat product only once; discard if not used.

Variation

- **Bean Ragout on Pasta.** Cook 5–6 lb pasta according to directions on p. 507. Prepare 1½ recipes of Bean Ragout. Serve 6 oz Bean Ragout over 4 oz pasta.

BLACK BEANS AND COUSCOUS

Yield: 50 entrées or 100 accompaniment portions   *Portion:* 8 oz (entrée) or 4 oz (accompaniment)

Ingredient	Amount	Procedure
Green onions, cut lengths	12 oz EP	Sauté onions and peppers in margarine just until soft, using
Red bell peppers, ¼-inch dice	3 lb 8 oz EP	a stockpot or steam-jacketed kettle.
Margarine	1 lb	
Black beans, canned, drained and rinsed	5 lb 8 oz EP	Stir beans, water, vegetable base, and juice into sautéed vegetables.
Water	4¾ qt	Bring to a rolling boil.
Vegetable base (see Note)	5 oz	
Fresh lime juice	1½ cups	
Instant couscous	5 lb	Add couscous to liquid and stir. Turn off heat. Cover and let stand for 5 minutes. Stir to fluff.
Fresh parsley, chopped	1 oz	Sprinkle parsley over each pan or stir into couscous.

Approximate nutritive values per portion (Entrée Portion)

Calories	Carbohydrate	Protein	Fat	Cholesterol	Sodium	Fiber	Iron
295 kcal	45 g	9 g	8 g	0 mg	393 mg	5.8 g	2 mg

Notes

- Potentially hazardous food. *Food Safety Standards:* Hold food for service at an internal temperature of 135°F or above. Do not mix old product with new. Cool leftover product quickly following time standards and cooling procedures on p. 167. Reheat leftover product quickly (within 2 hours) to 165°F or above. Reheat product only once; discard if not used.
- Chicken base can be substituted for vegetable base. Depending on the base used, salt may need to be added.

CUBAN BLACK BEANS AND RICE

Yield: 50 entrées or 100 accompaniment portions   *Portion:* 8 oz (entrée) or 4 oz (accompaniment)

Ingredient	Amount	Procedure
Black beans, canned	6 lb 4 oz	Drain beans and reserve juice. Save both beans and juice for later step.
Vegetable oil	6 oz	Heat oil to 350°F in tilting or other large fry pan.
Onions, chopped Garlic, minced Rice, converted	1 lb 8 oz EP 1 oz EP 4 lb	Add vegetables and rice to hot oil. Stir and cook until rice is browned.
Black bean juice plus water	4¾ qt	Measure bean juice reserved from earlier step. Add enough water to equal the required volume. Pour juice-water mixture over the rice.

Chipotle flavor concentrate (see Note)
Vegetable base
  (see Note)
Oregano, dried
Cumin, ground
Cilantro, dried
	4 oz
	4 oz
	
	1 tsp
	1 Tbsp
	1 Tbsp
		Stir chipotle concentrate, vegetable base, and seasonings
		  into rice mixture.
		Reduce heat and simmer covered for 15 minutes.

Green bell peppers, cut in
  1-inch-long thin strips
Red bell peppers, cut in
  1-inch-long thin strips
Yellow bell peppers, cut in
  1-inch-long thin strips
	1 lb EP
	
	12 oz EP
	
	12 oz EP
		Stir peppers and beans reserved from earlier step into the rice mixture.
		Cover and simmer for 10–15 minutes or until liquid is absorbed
		  and rice is tender.
		Transfer to 12 × 10 × 2-inch pans. Cover.

Approximate nutritive values per portion (Entrée Portion)

Calories	Carbohydrate	Protein	Fat	Cholesterol	Sodium	Fiber	Iron
235 kcal	41 g	6.3 g	4.5 g	0 mg	603 mg	4 g	2 mg

Notes

- Potentially hazardous food. *Food Safety Standards:* Hold food for service at an internal temperature of 135°F or above. Do not mix old product with new. Cool leftover product quickly following time standards and cooling procedures on p. 167. Reheat leftover product quickly (within 2 hours) to 165°F or above. Reheat product only once; discard if not used.
- A frozen pepper blend can be substituted for the bell peppers.
- Chipotles are dried jalapeño peppers that have been slow roasted to give them a smoky flavor. To use dried chipotles, cover with boiling water and let set for 30 minutes. Remove from the water and drain. Using a sharp knife, split chipotles open and remove seeds before chopping. If using canned chipotles, drain and chop.
- Chicken base can be substituted for the vegetable base. Adjust salt as required.
- Minor's Chipotle Flavor Concentrate (a blend of red, chipotle, and jalapeño peppers with onion, garlic, and spice) is available from most broadline foodservice distributors.

BLACK BEANS AND HAM ON RICE

Yield: 50 portions   *Portion:* 6 oz ham and beans + 4 oz rice

Ingredient	Amount	Procedure
Black turtle beans	3 lb	Rinse beans with cold running water.
Water	1¼ gal	Discard any stones and other foreign material or shriveled beans.
		Add water and bring to a boil. Boil for 2 minutes.
		Cover. Turn off heat and allow to stand for 1 hour.
Cumin, ground	1 Tbsp	Add seasonings to beans. Simmer until almost tender, about 45 minutes.
Hot pepper sauce	1½ tsp	If beans become too thick, add some tomato juice from the diced tomatoes
Black pepper	1 tsp	used in a later step.
Thyme, dried, crumbled	1 Tbsp	
Oregano, dried, crumbled	1 Tbsp	
Onions, chopped	12 oz	Add to beans. Simmer until beans are tender, about 30 minutes.
Garlic cloves, minced	3	Add tomato juice from later step or a small amount of water if necessary to keep
Salt	1½ oz	beans from becoming too thick.
Ham, diced	2 lb 8 oz	
Diced tomatoes, canned	3 lb 8 oz	Add tomatoes with juice and peppers.
Green bell peppers, ¾-inch chunks	12 oz	Simmer for 15 minutes.
Rice, converted	3 lb 8 oz	Cook rice according to directions on p. 542.
Water, boiling	4½ qt	
Salt	2 Tbsp	
Vegetable oil	2 Tbsp	
Fresh parsley, chopped	4 oz	Serve 6 oz ham and beans over 4 oz cooked rice. Garnish plate by sprinkling with 1 Tbsp chopped parsley.

Approximate nutritive values per portion

Calories	Carbohydrate	Protein	Fat	Cholesterol	Sodium	Fiber	Iron
212 kcal	35 g	10 g	3 g	13 mg	987 mg	2 g	3 mg

Notes

- Potentially hazardous food. *Food Safety Standards:* Hold food for service at an internal temperature of 135°F or above. Do not mix old product with new. Cool leftover product quickly following time standards and cooling procedures on p. 167. Reheat leftover product quickly (within 2 hours) to 165°F or above. Reheat product only once; discard if not used.
- Anaheim chiles may be substituted for green bell peppers.
- 6 lb 8 oz canned black beans, rinsed, may be substituted for dried beans and water. Add beans toward the end of the cooking period. Serving temperature 180–190°F.

Variations

- **Black Beans and Andouille Sausage over Rice.** Reduce hot sauce to ½ tsp. Omit ham. Add 3 lb cooked andouille sausage cut diagonally into ¾-inch pieces.
- **Black Beans over Rice.** Delete ham. Increase salt to 2 oz. Chicken broth may be substituted for the water to enhance flavor.
- **Black Bean Soup.** Follow recipe for Black Beans and Ham on Rice but make the following changes: Increase beans to 4 lb, water to 2¼ gal, onions to 1 lb, and salt to 2 oz. Decrease ham to 2 lb, tomatoes to 2 lb, and green bell peppers to 6 oz. Delete rice.

BLACK BEAN AND TORTILLA CASSEROLE

Yield: 48 portions   *Portion:* 8 oz

Ingredient	Amount	Procedure
Onions, chopped	2 lb 10 oz	Combine onions, peppers, tomatoes, picante sauce, and seasonings in steam-jacketed kettle.
Green bell peppers, chopped	2 lb 4 oz	
Diced tomatoes, canned	2¼ qt	Bring to a boil. Reduce heat and simmer uncovered for 15–20 minutes.
Picante sauce	1 qt	
Garlic cloves, minced	6	
Cumin, ground	3 Tbsp	
Black beans, canned, drained and rinsed	10 lb	Stir beans into tomato mixture. Turn off heat. Spread 2 lb 6 oz of bean mixture into four 12 × 10 × 2-inch pans.
Tortillas, corn, 6 inch	64	Top bean mixture with 8 corn tortillas, overlapping as necessary.
Monterey Jack cheese, shredded	3 lb	Sprinkle 6 oz cheese over tortillas. Spread 2 lb 6 oz bean mixture over cheese. Top with 8 corn tortillas, overlapping as necessary. Sprinkle 6 oz cheese over tortillas. Cover and bake at 350°F for 30–35 minutes or to 165°F. Cut each pan 4 × 3.
Fresh tomatoes finely diced	1 lb	Sprinkle 4 oz tomatoes and 1 Tbsp sliced onions over each pan. Keep hot (above 140°F).
Green onions, thinly sliced	2 oz	
Picante sauce	6 lb	Serve immediately with picante sauce as a condiment.

Approximate nutritive values per portion

Calories	Carbohydrate	Protein	Fat	Cholesterol	Sodium	Fiber	Iron
379 kcal	54 g	20 g	12 g	25 mg	1261 mg	6 g	4 mg

Note

- Potentially hazardous food. *Food Safety Standards:* Hold food for service at an internal temperature of 135°F or above. Do not mix old product with new. Cool leftover product quickly following time standards and cooling procedures on p. 167. Reheat leftover product quickly (within 2 hours) to 165°F or above. Reheat product only once; discard if not used.

GRAINS AND BEANS

Yield: 50 entrées or 100 accompaniment portions   *Portion:* 8 oz (entrée) or 4 oz (accompaniment)

Ingredient	Amount	Procedure
Cracked bulgur	1 lb 6 oz	Combine bulgur, barley, and water in a stockpot or steam-jacketed kettle.
Barley	2 lb	Bring to a boil. Reduce heat. Cover and simmer for 40–50 minutes or
Water	7 qt	until grains are tender.
		Drain excess liquid from grains. Save grains for a later step.
Vegetable oil	8 oz	Heat oil to 350°F in a fry pan. Add corn and stir-fry corn for 5 minutes.
Baby corn, frozen (small, Asian style)	2 lb 12 oz	
Green onions, sliced into thin rings	8 oz EP	Add onions and peppers to pan. Stir-fry for 1–2 minutes, until softened slightly.
Red bell peppers, ¼-inch dice	1 lb 12 oz EP	
Garbanzo beans, canned, drained and rinsed	3 lb 12 oz EP	Add beans, pimento, and seasonings to vegetables.
Black beans, canned, drained and rinsed	5 lb EP	Add cooked grains from previous step. Bring temperature to 180°F, stirring often to prevent sticking.
Pimento, chopped	8 oz	
Hot pepper sauce	3 Tbsp	
Cumin, ground	3 Tbsp	
Cilantro, dried	3 Tbsp	
Salt	2 oz	

Approximate nutritive values per portion (Entrée Portion)

Calories	Carbohydrate	Protein	Fat	Cholesterol	Sodium	Fiber	Iron
250 kcal	39 g	9 g	6 g	0 mg	783 mg	11 g	3 mg

Notes

- Potentially hazardous food. *Food Safety Standards:* Hold food for service at an internal temperature of 135°F or above. Do not mix old product with new. Cool leftover product quickly following time standards and cooling procedures on p. 167. Reheat leftover product quickly (within 2 hours) to 165°F or above. Reheat product only once; discard if not used.
- Grains and Beans may thicken during holding. Add vegetable stock as needed.

Variation

- **Green Pepper Stuffed with Grains and Beans.** Prepare Grains and Beans, above, and Marinara Sauce, p. 690. Smooth 8 oz marinara sauce into the bottom of 12 × 10 × 2-inch pans. Cut off the tops of the peppers and removes seeds. Fill each pepper with grain-bean mixture and stand up in prepared pan. Portion 1–2 Tbsp marinara sauce over the top of each stuffed pepper. Bake at 350°F for 20–30 minutes, or until peppers are tender-crisp and filling is 160°F.

SPANISH RICE AND BLACK BEANS

Yield: 50 portions   *Portion:* 8 oz

Ingredient	Amount	Procedure
Vegetable oil	12 oz	Heat oil in a tilting fry pan.
Garlic, minced	2 oz EP	Add garlic, onions, and rice. Cook until vegetables are fragrant and rice
Onions, chopped	1 lb 3 oz EP	becomes translucent and begins to brown.
Rice, white	4 lb 8 oz	
Water	2 qt	Add liquids and seasonings to rice mixture. Stir to blend.
Tomato juice	4½ qt	Bring to a boil. Reduce heat, cover, and simmer for about 20 minutes.
Chipotle flavor concentrate (see Note)	2 oz	
Cumin, ground	1 Tbsp	
Crushed red pepper	1¼ tsp	
Oregano, dried	2½ tsp	
Black beans, canned, drained and rinsed	2 lb EP	Add beans, corn, and peppers to rice mixture. Stir to blend.
Corn, whole kernel, frozen	1 lb	Cook for 10–15 minutes or until rice is tender and liquid is absorbed.
Red bell peppers, ½-inch dice	1 lb EP	Scale into 12 × 10 × 2-inch pans, 6 lb per pan.
Yellow bell peppers, ½-inch dice	12 oz EP	
Green bell peppers, ½-inch dice	12 oz EP	

Approximate nutritive values per portion

Calories	Carbohydrate	Protein	Fat	Cholesterol	Sodium	Fiber	Iron
270 kcal	43 g	5.3 g	8.6 g	0 mg	635 mg	2.6 g	2 mg

Notes

- Potentially hazardous food. *Food Safety Standards:* Hold food for service at an internal temperature of 135°F or above. Do not mix old product with new. Cool leftover product quickly following time standards and cooling procedures on p. 167. Reheat leftover product quickly (within 2 hours) to 165°F or above. Reheat product only once; discard if not used.
- Minor's Chipotle Flavor Concentrate (a blend of red, chipotle, and jalapeño peppers with onion, garlic, and spice) is available from most broadline foodservice distributors.

Variation

- **Latin-Style Black Beans and Rice.** In a tilting fry pan heat 4 oz olive oil. Sauté 2 lb diced onions until translucent. Add 3 oz garlic, 1 lb red bell pepper strips, 2 Tbsp cumin, and 2 Tbsp black pepper. Stir occasionally and cook for 2 minutes. Add 3 lb rice and cook, stirring, for 1 minute. Dissolve 2 oz vegetable or chicken base and 4 tsp salt in 2¾ qt water. Add liquid to rice mixture. Cover and cook until water is absorbed and rice is tender, about 15 minutes. Stir in 5 lb 12 oz black beans, drained and rinsed. Stir gently to mix. Heat to 170°F. Stir in 1½ cups chopped cilantro just before service.

RED BEANS AND RICE

Yield: 50 portions   *Portion:* 6 oz red beans + 4 oz rice

Ingredient	Amount	Procedure
Celery, chopped	2 lb EP	Sauté vegetables in oil in steam-jacketed or large kettle until softened.
Onions, chopped	2 lb EP	
Green bell peppers, chopped	1 lb 6 oz EP	
Garlic, finely chopped	1 oz EP	
Vegetable oil	4 oz	
Red beans, canned, undrained	14 lb	Add beans, water, and seasonings to vegetables. Bring to a boil. Reduce heat.
Water	1 qt	Cover and simmer for approximately 1 hour, until bean mixture is thickened slightly. Stir often.
Liquid smoke	2 tsp	
Red pepper sauce	2 Tbsp	
Salt	1 tsp	
Black pepper	1 tsp	
Ground red pepper	2 tsp	
Thyme, dried	1 tsp	
Oregano, dried	2 tsp	
Bay leaves, dried	5	
Rice, converted	3 lb 8 oz	Cook rice according to directions on p. 542.
Water, boiling	4½ qt	Serve 6 oz red beans over 4 oz cooked rice.
Salt	2 Tbsp	
Vegetable oil	2 Tbsp	

Approximate nutritive values per portion

Calories	Carbohydrate	Protein	Fat	Cholesterol	Sodium	Fiber	Iron
265 kcal	49 g	10 g	3.5 g	0 mg	784 mg	10 g	3 mg

Note

- Potentially hazardous food. *Food Safety Standards:* Hold food for service at an internal temperature of 135°F or above. Do not mix old product with new. Cool leftover product quickly following time standards and cooling procedures on p. 167. Reheat leftover product quickly (within 2 hours) to 165°F or above. Reheat product only once; discard if not used.

Variation

- **Chile Black Beans on Rice.** Heat olive oil in steam-jacketed or large kettle. Add 1 lb 8 oz chopped bell peppers (combination of green, red, and yellow), 2 lb chopped onions, and 4 oz minced garlic. Sauté until onions and peppers are softened. Add 2 oz chile powder, 2 Tbsp dried oregano, 1⅓ Tbsp cumin, and 3 Tbsp chipotle flavor concentrate. Mix well and cook for 5 minutes. Add 8 lb 8 oz canned black beans, drained and rinsed, 2 qt canned chopped tomatoes, and 2 qt water. Bring to a boil, stirring occasionally. Reduce heat to medium low and simmer until flavors blend and chili thickens, 30–60 minutes. Add salt and pepper as needed. Serve on steamed rice as for Red Beans and Rice.

PINTO BEANS WITH ANDOUILLE SAUSAGE

Yield: 50 portions   *Portion:* 8 oz

Ingredient	Amount	Procedure
Pinto beans, canned, drained and rinsed	9 lb EP	Combine beans, ham base, water, vegetables, and seasonings in a steam-jacketed or other large kettle. Bring to a boil.
Ham base (see Note)	1 oz	
Water	1 gal	
Onions, chopped	1 lb 10 oz	
Diced green chiles, canned	1 lb 4 oz	
Cumin, ground	5½ Tbsp	
Black pepper	4 tsp	
Chile powder	2 oz	
Andouille pork sausage, sliced	7 lb 6 oz	Add sausage to beans. Simmer for 30–45 min. Optional: Serve with Corn Bread, p. 244, or Jalapeño Cheese Muffins, p. 244, or over rice.

Approximate nutritive values per portion

Calories	Carbohydrate	Protein	Fat	Cholesterol	Sodium	Fiber	Iron
270 kcal	18 g	13 g	16 g	39 mg	1114 mg	5 g	2.5 mg

Notes

- Potentially hazardous food. *Food Safety Standards:* Hold food for service at an internal temperature of 135°F or above. Do not mix old product with new. Cool leftover product quickly following time standards and cooling procedures on p. 167. Reheat leftover product quickly (within 2 hours) to 165°F or above. Reheat product only once; discard if not used.
- Ham base and andouille sausage vary in amounts of salt. Taste for seasoning before serving and adjust salt if needed.

Variation

- **San Antonio Beans.** Heat ¼ cup oil in steam-jacketed or other large kettle. Sauté 10 oz chopped bell peppers (combination of green and red) and 8 oz chopped onions until fragrant and softened. Stir in 3 lb 12 oz canned pinto beans, drained and rinsed, 3 lb 4 oz canned kidney beans, drained and rinsed, 2 qt picante sauce, 4 Tbsp Dijon style mustard, 1 Tbsp liquid smoke, and 1 cup water. Bring to a boil. Reduce heat and simmer for 10–20 minutes.

SWEET AND SOUR TOFU

Yield: 50 portions   *Portion:* 6 oz tofu + 4 oz rice
Oven: 350°F   *Bake:* 30 minutes

Ingredient	Amount	Procedure
Tofu	5 lb	Drain tofu and dice into ½-inch cubes.
Water	1 cup	Mix water, garlic powder, and soy sauce.
Garlic powder	2 tsp	Dip cubed tofu in liquid, then roll in bread crumbs.
Soy sauce	¼ cup	Place breaded tofu on silicone-paper-lined or lightly greased baking sheet.
Dry bread crumbs	1 lb	Bake tofu until brown and crisp, approximately 30 min. Hold for later step at above 140°F.
Pineapple chunks, canned, drained (reserve juice)	2 lb 4 oz	Reserve drained pineapple tidbits for later step. Mix pineapple juice with cornstarch and water.
Pineapple juice (reserved juice from draining pineapple plus water to make up the difference)	2 qt	In steam-jacketed or other large kettle, mix pineapple juice–cornstarch mixture with tomato purée, vinegar, soy sauce, brown sugar, and granulated sugar, using a wire whip. Bring to a boil. Boil until mixture thickens.
Cornstarch	2 oz	
Tomato purée	1 qt	
Vinegar, cider	1½ cups	
Soy sauce	1½ cups	
Sugar, brown	4 oz	
Sugar, granulated	10 oz	
Onions, ½-inch dice	1 lb EP	Stir pineapple reserved from earlier step, onions, mushrooms, and peppers into thickened mixture. Return to a boil.
Fresh mushrooms, quartered	8 oz EP	Just prior to serving, gently stir in baked tofu reserved from earlier step.
Green bell peppers, ½-inch dice	1 lb EP	
Rice, converted	3 lb 8 oz	Cook rice according to directions on p. 542.
Water, boiling	4½ qt	Serve 6 oz sweet and sour tofu on 4 oz rice.
Salt	2 Tbsp	
Vegetable oil	2 Tbsp	

Approximate nutritive values per portion

Calories	Carbohydrate	Protein	Fat	Cholesterol	Sodium	Fiber	Iron
395 kcal	80 g	10 g	3.6 g	0 mg	976 mg	2.5 g	3 mg

Note

- Potentially hazardous food. *Food Safety Standards:* Hold food for service at an internal temperature of 135°F or above. Do not mix old product with new. Cool leftover product quickly following time standards and cooling procedures on p. 167. Reheat leftover product quickly (within 2 hours) to 165°F or above. Reheat product only once; discard if not used.

GRILLED TOFU CANTONESE OVER RICE

Yield: 50 portions   *Portion:* 4 oz rice, 3 oz tofu, 2 oz sauce

Ingredient	Amount	Procedure
Olive oil	3 oz	Heat oil to 350°F in a steam-jacketed or other kettle.
Onion, finely chopped	4 oz	Sauté onion, garlic, and ginger for 2 minutes until fragrant.
Garlic, minced	2 Tbsp	
Fresh ginger, minced	1½ Tbsp	
Bell pepper strips (combination of red, green, and yellow)	1 lb 12 oz	Add peppers and cook for 1–2 minutes, until only beginning to soften.
Soy sauce	2 cups	Whisk liquids and Clear Jel together in baker's bowl.
Rice wine vinegar	2½ cups	Add to sautéed vegetables and cook until sauce thickens and is clear.
Water	4½ cups	
Clear Jel (see Note)	3½ oz	
Sesame oil	5½ tsp	Blend sesame oil and toasted sesame seeds into sauce. Reserve sauce for later step.
Toasted sesame seeds (see Note)	2½ Tbsp	
Firm tofu	10 lb	Cut tofu into approximately 1-oz squares.
Soy sauce	2 cups	Coat grill with oil and heat to 300°F. Cover surface of grill lightly with soy sauce. Grill tofu on both sides, being careful to not break up. Transfer to 12 × 10 × 2-inch pans and keep hot.
Rice, converted	3 lb 8 oz	Cook rice according to directions on p. 542.
Water, boiling	4½ qt	Serve 4 oz rice with 3 oz tofu on top and 2 oz sauce ladled over the top.
Salt	2 Tbsp	
Vegetable oil	2 Tbsp	

Approximate nutritive values per portion

Calories	Carbohydrate	Protein	Fat	Cholesterol	Sodium	Fiber	Iron
272 kcal	47 g	11 g	6 g	0 mg	1665 mg	1 g	3 mg

Notes

- Potentially hazardous food. *Food Safety Standards:* Hold food for service at an internal temperature of 135°F or above. Do not mix old product with new. Cool leftover product quickly following time standards and cooling procedures on p. 167. Reheat leftover product quickly (within 2 hours) to 165°F or above. Reheat product only once; discard if not used.
- To toast sesame seeds: Spread seeds in a thin even layer in a dry skillet. Heat over medium-high heat until fragrant, 2–3 minutes. Shake pan throughout cooking to prevent burning.
- Alternatively, substitute ⅓ less cornstarch for Clear Jel.

TOFU AND BROCCOLI SZECHWAN

Yield: 50 portions   *Portion:* 6 oz tofu and broccoli + 4 oz rice
Oven: 300°F   *Bake:* 30 minutes

Ingredient	Amount	Procedure
Tofu	5 lb	Drain tofu and dice into ½-inch cubes.
Vegetable oil	½ cup	Place tofu on silicone-paper-lined or lightly greased baking sheet. Drizzle with vegetable oil.
		Bake at 300°F for 30 minutes. Hold for later step at above 140°F.
Vegetable oil	¼ cup	Heat oil in steam-jacketed kettle.
Onions, diced	1 lb 12 oz EP	Sauté onions until barely tender. Add broccoli and peppers. Stir-fry until tender-crisp.
Broccoli florets	2 lb 12 oz EP	
Red bell peppers, ½-inch dice	1 lb EP	Remove vegetables from kettle. Save for later step.
Soy sauce	2 cups	Add soy sauce and cornstarch to tilting fry pan. Mix until smooth.
Cornstarch	2½ oz	Stir in water, sherry, sugar, ginger, and pepper.
Water	1¾ qt	Boil until mixture thickens, about 5 minutes.
Cooking sherry	1 cup	Stir in reserved vegetables and tofu. Transfer to 12 × 20 × 4-inch counter pans.
Sugar, granulated	1¾ oz	Garnish with mandarin oranges.
Fresh ginger, finely minced	2 oz	Hold for service at 165°F.
Cayenne pepper	1 tsp	
Mandarin oranges, canned, drained	2 lb	
Rice, converted	3 lb 8 oz	Cook rice according to directions on p. 542.
Water, boiling	4½ qt	Serve 6 oz tofu and broccoli over 4 oz rice.
Salt	2 Tbsp	
Vegetable oil	2 Tbsp	

Approximate nutritive values per portion

Calories	Carbohydrate	Protein	Fat	Cholesterol	Sodium	Fiber	Iron
335 kcal	36 g	7 g	6 g	0 mg	981 mg	2 g	2 mg

Notes

- Potentially hazardous food. *Food Safety Standards:* Hold food for service at an internal temperature of 135°F or above. Do not mix old product with new. Cool leftover product quickly following time standards and cooling procedures on p. 167. Reheat leftover product quickly (within 2 hours) to 165°F or above. Reheat product only once; discard if not used.
- 1 lb cashews may be sautéed with the onions and broccoli.

VEGETABLE AND TOFU JAMBALAYA

Yield: 50 portions   *Portion:* 8 oz

Ingredient	Amount	Procedure
Olive oil	2 cups	Heat oil to 350°F in the bottom of tilting or other large fry pan.
Onions, chopped Garlic, minced Celery, chopped Green bell peppers, chopped	6 lb EP 2 oz EP 1 lb 4 oz EP 12 oz EP	Sauté vegetables in hot oil for 10 minutes. Stir often enough to keep vegetables from sticking.
Cajun seasoning Salt Rice, converted	2 oz 2 tsp 3 lb 14 oz	Add seasonings and rice to vegetable mixture. Stir and cook for 10 minutes. Add more oil if rice begins to stick.
Vegetable base Water Red pepper sauce	2½ oz 3 qt 2 tsp	Dissolve vegetable base in some of the water. Add water-base mixture, remaining water, and red pepper sauce to the rice. Stir to mix. Reduce heat to low. Cover and simmer until rice is tender and liquids are absorbed, 25–30 minutes.
Tofu, firm, ½-inch cubes	2 lb	Gently fold tofu into rice mixture.
Sugar snap peas, fresh or frozen Carrots, cut into ¼-inch slices Red bell peppers, ½-inch dice Yellow bell peppers, ½-inch dice Green bell peppers, ½-inch dice Green onions, cut in 1-inch lengths	1 lb 10 oz EP 1 lb 10 oz EP 4 oz EP 4 oz EP 4 oz EP 8 oz EP	Steam peas, carrots, and peppers separately until tender-crisp. Drain vegetables. Fold steamed vegetables and green onions into rice mixture. Scale into 12 × 10 × 2-inch pans, 6 lb per pan.
Red onions, coarsely chopped Fresh parsley, minced	4 oz EP 6 oz EP	Sprinkle 1 oz onions and 1½ oz parsley on top of each pan of jambalaya.

Approximate nutritive values per portion

Calories	Carbohydrate	Protein	Fat	Cholesterol	Sodium	Fiber	Iron
250 kcal	36 g	4.7 g	9.8 g	0 mg	280 mg	2 g	1 mg

Notes

- Potentially hazardous food. *Food Safety Standards:* Hold food for service at an internal temperature of 135°F or above. Do not mix old product with new. Cool leftover product quickly following time standards and cooling procedures on p. 167. Reheat leftover product quickly (within 2 hours) to 165°F or above. Reheat product only once; discard if not used.
- A frozen pepper blend can be substituted for the green, red, and yellow bell peppers.

Variation

- **Garden Vegetable Jambalaya.** Delete tofu. Add along with other vegetables 2 lb edamame, steamed until tender-crisp.

Salads and Salad Dressings

Salads

Salads are popular menu items, versatile enough to be served in a variety of ways. Appetizer salads are served as a first course and play an important role in stimulating the appetite and creating a sense of anticipation for the remainder of the meal. Visual appearance as well as taste and flavor combinations must be considered.

Accompaniment salads are considered side dishes to the entrée. These salads should be selected carefully so that the flavor and food group characteristics will be in harmony. Many accompaniment salads have traditional significance: turkey and cranberries, pork and applesauce, sandwiches and pasta or potato salad, and fish and coleslaw.

Entrée salads offer an upscale approach to dining, particularly at the noon meal and among the health-conscious patrons. Other than bread or crackers and a beverage, the salad is generally the only menu item, making the ingredient selections especially important. Entrée salads should be substantial in the amount of food provided, and they may include at least one ingredient that is a source of protein. The salad should be fresh in appearance and attractive in design.

A salad course is occasionally offered after the entrée. The objective is to "cleanse the palate" in preparation for dessert. The salad served as a separate course should be light and refreshing. Fruit salads or lightly dressed greens are appropriate choices.

With the exception of separate course salads, which are always served, the presentation of salads may be either individually placed at each place setting or self-service from a buffet line or salad bar. The choice of method will depend on the clientele's expectations and objectives of the foodservice.

Arranged Salads

Arranged salads may be served to patrons either after they have been seated, on the table as for some banquets and catered functions, or à la carte from a cafeteria counter. Regardless of

the serving method, the principles of placed salad construction are the same:

- Select plates or bowls that are appropriately sized and will add to the salad's attractiveness.
- Place salad green underliners on the dish. The curly edge should be at the back and top of the salad and should not extend over the edge of the plate. Tossed green salads may not include an underliner but are decorated with an attractive garnish.
- To gain height, place chopped lettuce on the underliner and under salad ingredients.
- Place the main salad ingredients neatly on the plate. They should be prepared and arranged attractively with careful consideration given to color and balance.
- Garnish appropriately to give accent in color and flavor.
- Keep salad chilled and sprinkle with dressing just before serving or pass dressings for individual service.

Salad Bars

Salad bars have expanded the selection of items available and are very popular in many types of foodservices. For a salad bar to be successful, enough variety must be offered so patrons will enjoy creating their own salad. See Table 17.1 for components of a basic salad bar and Figure 17.1 for a suggested salad bar arrangement. Basic rules for salad bars are as follows:

- The salad bar should be equipped with a sneeze guard, and standards of good sanitation should be maintained. A clean plate should be used each time a patron visits the salad bar. Serving utensils should facilitate sanitary service.
- A salad bar should look well supplied throughout the serving period. This can be accomplished by selecting appropriate-size containers and resupplying them when one-half to two-thirds empty. Avoid arranging too few food items on plates that will look empty after only a few servings are taken.
- Spills, drips, and misplaced food items should be cleaned up regularly. Arranging food containers so spills are reduced is

TABLE 17.1   Basic salad bar components

TABLE 17.1   **Basic salad bar components**

Item	Number of choices	Ideas for choices
Greens	1 bowl	Combine 2–3 different greens. See p. 121 for types of greens.
Fresh vegetables	3–5 containers	Alfalfa sprouts, broccoli, cabbage (red or green), carrots, cauliflower, celery, cucumber, green onions, mushrooms, bell peppers (red, green, yellow), radishes, snow peas, tomatoes, zucchini
Toppings	2–3 containers	Bacon bits, garbanzo beans, croutons, pickles, olives, peanuts, raisins, sesame seeds, sunflower seeds
Gelatin	1–2 molds	Fruit or vegetable gelatin salads
Fruit, pasta, and vegetable salads	2–3 containers	Rice salad, potato salad, pasta salad, ambrosia, applesauce, other fruit or marinated vegetable salads
Protein	2–3 containers	Chopped hard-cooked eggs, egg salad, meat salad, cottage cheese, shredded cheese, beans, bean salad, tofu
Crackers and bread	1 basket	Variety crackers, warm breads
Dressings	3–4 containers	Blue cheese, buttermilk, French, Italian, oil and vinegar, Thousand Island

Notes • More choices are appropriate if the salad bar or buffet serving area can accommodate the variety.
 • Select salads that will retain quality during the serving period.

FIGURE 17.1   Suggested salad bar arrangement: (1) plates and bowls; (2) greens; (3) fresh vegetables; (4) toppings; (5) gelatins; (6) fruit, pasta, and vegetable salads; (7) protein salads; (8) crackers and breads; (9) dressings.

important, and items that could become unsightly should be placed where they will be easy to reach without spilling onto other food. Correct serving utensils will help eliminate untidiness.

• The selections should be varied and creative enough to appeal to many different people. The variety of items offered should be changed periodically when serving repeat customers.

• Potentially hazardous food should be kept at 41°F or below, and temperatures should be monitored throughout the serving period.

Salad Ingredients

Many salad ingredients may be purchased with some or all of the preliminary preparation completed. Torn salad greens, prepared grapefruit sections, and diced or chopped vegetables

are examples. In many foodservices, however, salad ingredients are prepared on the premises. Information about the most commonly used salad ingredients and their preparation is provided in Chapter 5.

The following describes preparation methods for other salad ingredients that are commonly used on arranged salads and salad bars.

Almonds, Blanched—To blanch almonds, cover with boiling water and let stand until skins will slip. Drain. Cover with cold water and rub off skins. Place skinned almonds between dry clean towels to remove water.

Almonds, Toasted—Spread blanched almonds in a shallow pan in a thin layer. Heat in oven at 250°F, stirring occasionally until nuts are light brown in color.

Cheese—Grate, shred, or cut in tiny cubes; or soften and put through a pastry tube.

Chicken or Turkey—Cook and remove skin, gristle, and bone. Cut into $\frac{1}{3}$-inch cubes. Marinate if desired. Mix with dressing and other ingredients just before serving.

Eggs—Hard-cook (p. 384). Use whole, halved, sliced, or sectioned. Slice or mince whites. Force yolks through ricer.

Fish—Cook and remove skin and bones. Flake. Marinate if desired. Mix with dressing just before serving. See pp. 401 and 402 for preparation of crab, lobster, and shrimp.

Flowers—Edible flowers are commonly used for garnish. See Table 5.19 on p. 131 for color information.

Meat—Cut cooked meat into $\frac{1}{3}$-inch cubes. Marinate with French or Italian dressing. Mix just before serving.

Nuts—Heat in hot oven to freshen if desired. Use whole, shredded, or chopped.

Salad Dressings

A salad dressing's function is to "dress" or accent the salad; it should not mask the flavor of the other ingredients. Care should be taken to choose an appropriate dressing to match the salad.

The basic ingredients of a salad dressing are oil combined with vinegar or another acid liquid such as lemon juice. Cooking oils such as canola, corn, safflower, soybean, and sesame seed are often used for salad dressing. Other oils that are commonly used include avocado, nut, olive, and oils infused with herbs, peppers, or other seasonings. Variation in the vinegar will change the salad dressing flavor. Types of vinegars that may be used for making salad dressings are described on p. 132.

Salad dressings should be stored in glass, plastic, or stainless steel containers with tight-fitting lids at 41°F.

Vegetable and Pasta Salad Recipes

BASIC MIXED GREEN SALAD

Yield: 50 portions or 10 lb   *Portion:* 3 oz

Ingredient	Amount	Procedure
Head lettuce (iceberg)	7 lb	Cut or tear lettuce and other greens into bite-size pieces. (Use sharp steel-bladed knife if greens are cut.)
Leaf lettuce, Bibb, or romaine	3 lb	
French dressing, oil and vinegar, or Italian dressing	$1\frac{1}{4}$ qt	Just before serving, toss lightly with dressing, or portion greens into individual salad bowls, 3 oz per bowl, and serve with choice of dressings.

Approximate nutritive values per portion

Calories	Carbohydrate	Protein	Fat	Cholesterol	Sodium	Fiber	Iron
125 kcal	3 g	1 g	13 g	0 mg	8 mg	1 g	0.5 mg

Notes

- Any combination of salad greens may be used. For contrast, mix dark greens with light, crisp with tender, and smooth leaves with curly. With pale iceberg lettuce, use dark green spinach, romaine, curly endive, or red-tipped leaf lettuce. See p. 121 for major types of salad greens.
- If serving on a salad bar, place greens in a large bowl and offer choice of dressing and garnishes (see p. 593).

Variations

- **Hawaiian Tossed Salad.** To 7 lb mixed greens, add sections from 8 grapefruits, 8 oranges, 4 avocados, and 1 fresh pineapple, cubed. Serve with Honey French Dressing (p. 645).
- **Salad Greens with Grapefruit.** Place 3 oz greens in each bowl. Garnish each with 3 sections of pink grapefruit. Serve with Poppy Seed Dressing (p. 650) or French Dressing (p. 644).
- **Spinach Mushroom Salad.** Use 10 lb fresh spinach (may be part lettuce), 4 lb fresh mushrooms, sliced, and 2 bunches green onions, sliced. Toss lightly with French Dressing (p. 644) just before serving. Sprinkle with cooked crumbled bacon if desired.
- **Spinach Salad.** Use 4 lb lettuce and 6 lb fresh spinach, 2 bunches green onions, sliced, and 12 eggs, hard-cooked and sliced. To serve, toss lightly with French Dressing (p. 644) or Dijon Mustard Vinaigrette Dressing (p. 647) and portion into bowls. Sprinkle with 1 lb bacon that has been diced, cooked until crisp, and drained.

TOSSED VEGETABLE SALAD

Yield: 50 portions or 10 lb   *Portion:* 3 oz

Ingredient	Amount	Procedure
Salad greens (see Note)	7 lb	Wash greens thoroughly and drain. Tear into bite-size pieces.
Salad ingredients (see Note)	3 lb	Add salad ingredients to greens. Toss lightly. Portion into individual salad bowls or plates, 3 oz per portion.
Garnish (see Note)	as needed	Garnish salads if desired.
Salad dressing (see Note)	1¼ qt	Serve with choice of dressings. If preferred, French, Italian, or oil-and-vinegar dressing may be added to the salad just before serving.

Notes

- **Salad Greens.** Select one or more: iceberg, leaf, Bibb, Boston, or romaine lettuce; endive; spinach; escarole; celery cabbage; watercress. See p. 121 for types of salad greens.
- **Salad Ingredients.** Select one or more: diagonally sliced asparagus, sliced Jerusalem artichokes, artichoke hearts, sliced avocado, bean sprouts, garbanzo beans, broccoli florets or sliced broccoli stems, chopped or shredded red cabbage, shredded or thinly sliced carrots, sliced cauliflower florets, sliced or diced celery, sliced or diced cucumbers, sliced green onions or scallions, diced green peppers, sliced fresh mushrooms, cooked green peas, sliced radishes, halved cherry tomatoes, fresh tomato wedges, sliced water chestnuts, sliced zucchini.
- **Garnishes.** Alfalfa sprouts, crumbled crisp-cooked bacon, crumbled blue cheese, shredded cheddar cheese, cheese strips or cubes, seasoned croutons, sliced or quartered hard-cooked eggs, sliced olives, onion rings (fresh or French-fried), parsley sprig, green bell pepper rings or strips, sunflower seeds, cherry tomatoes, tomato wedges, toasted wheat germ.
- **Salad Dressings.** French, Italian, oil and vinegar, Roquefort, Thousand Island, buttermilk, Horseradish Cream, Green Peppercorn Cream, Sour Cream Basil.

TENDER GREENS AND FRUIT SALAD

Yield: 50 portions   *Portion:* 3 oz greens + 1 oz fruit

Ingredient	Amount	Procedure
Tender greens (see Note)	10 lb	Toss greens with fruit. Sprinkle garnish on top.
Fruit (see Note)	4 lb	Serve with dressing to the side.
Cheese/nuts (see Note)	1 lb–1 lb 8 oz	
Salad dressing (see Note)	1¾ qt	

Approximate nutritive values per portion

Calories	Carbohydrate	Protein	Fat	Cholesterol	Sodium	Fiber	Iron
276 kcal	22 g	5 g	20 g	10 mg	413 mg	3 g	1 mg

Notes

- **Greens:** Bibb, Boston, leaf (red and green), mesclun mix, romaine, spinach.
- **Fruit:** Fresh—apples, apricots, blueberries, cantaloupe, grapes, grapefruit, honeydew, oranges, peaches, raspberries, strawberries. Dried—apricots, cherries, cranberries.
- **Cheese/Nuts:** Select one or more: asiago, bleu, Brie, cotija, beta, fontina, goat, cheese, manchego, parmesan. Choose nuts from the following: almonds, cashews, hazelnuts, pecans, pepitas, pine nuts, pistachios, walnuts.
- **Dressing:** Sweet Sesame Vinaigrette (p. 648), Golden Fruit Dressing (p. 650), Lemon Vinaigrette (p. 646) other vinaigrette dressing.

CARRIFRUIT SALAD

Yield: 50 portions or 4½ qt   *Portion:* ⅓ cup (3 oz)

Ingredient	Amount	Procedure
Carrots, shredded	4 lb 8 oz	Combine ingredients. Mix lightly.
Pineapple tidbits, canned, drained	2 lb 12 oz	
Flaked coconut	8 oz	
Marshmallows, miniature	9 oz	
Mayonnaise	2¼ cups	Mix mayonnaise and half-and-half.
Half-and-half	¾ cup	Add to salad ingredients. Mix carefully. Serve with No. 12 dipper.

Approximate nutritive values per portion

Calories	Carbohydrate	Protein	Fat	Cholesterol	Sodium	Fiber	Iron
143 kcal	14 g	1 g	10 g	7 mg	75 mg	1 g	0.5 mg

Notes

- 8 oz raisins may be added.
- Best when served the same day it is prepared.

CARROT RAISIN SALAD

Yield: 50 portions or 4¼ qt   *Portion:* ⅓ cup (2½ oz)

Ingredient	Amount	Procedure
Raisins	8 oz	Soften raisins in steamer or simmer in a small amount of water for about 3 minutes.
Carrots, raw	7 lb AP	Peel carrots. Shred or grind coarsely. Combine with raisins.
Mayonnaise	2 cups	Mix mayonnaise, salad dressing, and salt.
Salad dressing	2 cups	Add to carrot-raisin mixture. Mix lightly.
Salt	1 Tbsp	Serve with No. 12 dipper.

Approximate nutritive values per portion

Calories	Carbohydrate	Protein	Fat	Cholesterol	Sodium	Fiber	Iron
141 kcal	13 g	1 g	10 g	8 mg	267 mg	2 g	0.5 mg

Variations

- **Carrot-Apple-Celery Salad.** Substitute 3 lb diced apples for 2 lb carrots.
- **Carrot-Celery-Cucumber Salad.** Use 4 lb 8 oz shredded carrots, 1 lb 8 oz chopped celery, and 1 lb 8 oz chopped cucumber.
- **Carrot-Celery Salad.** Omit raisins. Use 5 lb ground carrots. Add 2 lb chopped celery and 2 oz sugar.
- **Carrot-Coconut Salad.** Substitute 1 lb toasted coconut for raisins.

TRIPLE BEAN SALAD

Yield: 50 portions or 6 qt   *Portion:* ½ cup (4 oz)

Ingredient	Amount	Procedure
Green beans, French style or cut, canned	3 lb 8 oz (1 No.10 can)	Drain green and wax beans thoroughly.
Wax beans, cut, canned	2 lb 8 oz	
Kidney beans, canned	3 lb	Rinse kidney beans. Drain.
Onions, thinly sliced	1 lb 8 oz	Add onions, pepper, and seasonings to beans.
Green bell pepper, diced	6 oz	Cover. Marinate overnight in the refrigerator.
Vinegar, cider	3 cups	
Sugar, granulated	1 lb 8 oz	
Salt	1 Tbsp	
Black pepper	1 Tbsp	
Celery seed	1 Tbsp	
Salad oil	1 cup	Just before serving, drain vegetables well. Add oil and toss lightly. Serve with No. 12 dipper.

Approximate nutritive values per portion

Calories	Carbohydrate	Protein	Fat	Cholesterol	Sodium	Fiber	Iron
168 kcal	29 g	4 g	5 g	0 mg	277 mg	5 g	1 mg

Variations

- **Cauliflower Bean Salad.** Delete kidney beans and add 3 lb cauliflower florets, slightly cooked.
- **Oriental Bean Salad.** Delete kidney beans. Add 1 lb 8 oz cooked red beans, drained and rinsed, and 1 lb 8 oz bean sprouts.

BROWN BEAN SALAD

Yield: 50 portions or 6 qt   *Portion:* ½ cup (4 oz)

Ingredient	Amount	Procedure
Eggs, hard cooked (p. 384)	12	Peel and dice eggs.
Brown or kidney beans	1½ No. 10 cans	Rinse beans with cold water. Drain.
Celery, diced	12 oz	Combine with beans. Add eggs.
Green bell pepper, chopped	3 oz	
Onion, minced	3 oz	
Pickle relish	10 oz	
Salad dressing or mayonnaise	3 cups	Combine and add to bean mixture.
Salt	2 Tbsp	Mix lightly.
Vinegar, cider	¾ cup	

Approximate nutritive values per portion

Calories	Carbohydrate	Protein	Fat	Cholesterol	Sodium	Fiber	Iron
197 kcal	17 g	7 g	12 g	59 mg	665 mg	4 g	2 mg

Notes

- Potentially hazardous food. *Food Safety Standards:* Hold food for service at an internal temperature of 41°F or below. Do not mix old product with new. Keep leftover product chilled at 41°F or below. See p. 167 for cooling procedures.
- 4 lb dried beans, cooked according to directions on p. 505, may be substituted for canned beans.
- Great northern or pinto beans may be substituted for half of the kidney beans.

GARBANZO BEAN SALAD

Yield: 50 portions or 4½ qt   *Portion:* ⅓ cup (3 oz)

Ingredient	Amount	Procedure
Garbanzo beans, canned	2 lb 8 oz	Rinse beans with cold water. Drain.
Red beans, canned	1 lb 8 oz	
Pinto beans, canned	2 lb	
Celery, sliced	1 lb	Combine with beans.
Cucumbers, peeled and sliced	12 oz	
Green onions, sliced	5 oz	
Radishes, sliced	8 oz	
Black olives, sliced	4 oz	
French Dressing (p. 644)	1 cup	Pour dressing over bean mixture. Toss lightly. Marinate for 2 hours.

Approximate nutritive values per portion

Calories	Carbohydrate	Protein	Fat	Cholesterol	Sodium	Fiber	Iron
80 kcal	10 g	3 g	4 g	0 mg	260 mg	2 g	1 mg

Notes

- Potentially hazardous food. *Food Safety Standards:* Hold food for service at an internal temperature of 41°F or below. Do not mix old product with new. Keep leftover product chilled at 41°F or below. See p. 167 for cooling procedures.
- Cooked great northern beans may be substituted for garbanzo beans.
- Vegetable Marinade (p. 722) may be substituted for French Dressing.

Variation

- **Garbanzo Pasta Salad.** Delete pinto beans. Cook 8 oz shell macaroni to the *al dente* stage. Combine with other ingredients.

BARLEY AND BLACK BEAN SALAD

Yield: 50 portions   *Portion:* 4 oz

Ingredient	Amount	Procedure
Water	1¼ gal	Bring water and salt to boil in steam-jacketed kettle.
Salt	1½ oz (2⅓ Tbsp)	Stir barley into boiling water. Cook for about 50 minutes or until tender. Stir occasionally.
Barley	1 lb 10 oz	Drain, cool, and save for later step. (Yield: 4 lb 8 oz cooked barley)
Black beans, canned, drained and rinsed	2 lb 12 oz EP	Add beans, vinegar, and pepper to 4 lb 8 oz cooked and cooled barley reserved from earlier step.
Vinegar, red wine	3 oz	
Black pepper	¾ tsp	
Corn, whole kernel, frozen, defrosted	2 lb 5 oz	Add vegetables and cilantro. Toss to combine.
Green bell peppers, chopped	1 lb 3 oz EP	
Red jalapeño peppers, canned, chopped	4 oz	
Fresh cilantro, chopped	1½ oz (2½ cups)	
Fresh lime juice	6 oz	Whisk juice and spices together in a bowl.
Salt	5 tsp	
Cumin, ground	3½ Tbsp	
Ancho chile powder	4 Tbsp	
Olive oil	12 oz	Whisk oil into juice while pouring in a slow stream. Drizzle dressing over salad and toss to combine.

Approximate nutritive values per portion

Calories	Carbohydrate	Protein	Fat	Cholesterol	Sodium	Fiber	Iron
150 kcal	17 g	4 g	7.4 g	0 mg	652 mg	4.5 g	1 mg

Note

- Potentially hazardous food. *Food Safety Standards:* Hold food for service at an internal temperature of 41°F or below. Do not mix old product with new. Keep leftover product chilled at 41°F or below. See p. 167 for cooling procedures.

ROASTED CORN AND BLACK BEAN SLAW

Yield: 50 garnish-size portions   *Portion:* 2 oz

Ingredient	Amount	Procedure
Pineapple, crushed	2 Tbsp	Place in a mesh sieve and drain until all liquid is gone, pressing with spatula if needed. Place in baker's bowl.
Corn, whole kernel, fresh or frozen	5 oz	Roast corn in an oven until just beginning to char. Cool.
Black beans, canned, rinsed	5 oz EP	Add corn and black beans to pineapple.
Shallots, finely chopped	2 oz	Add shallots, mayonnaise, and seasonings to pineapple mixture. Mix until blended.
Mayonnaise	1 qt	
Garlic cloves, minced	4	
Fresh lemon juice	¼ cup	
Hot pepper sauce	2 Tbsp	
Tarragon, dried	1 Tbsp	
Parsley, dried (see Note)	1½ Tbsp	
Black pepper	½ tsp	
Salt	¼ tsp	
Green cabbage, shredded	3 lb 12 oz	Place shredded cabbage in baker's bowl. Pour mayonnaise mixture over cabbage and toss lightly to coat.

Approximate nutritive values per portion

Calories	Carbohydrate	Protein	Fat	Cholesterol	Sodium	Fiber	Iron
144 kcal	4 g	1 g	14 g	7 mg	118 mg	1 g	0.44 mg

Notes

- Potentially hazardous food. *Food Safety Standards:* Hold food for service at an internal temperature of 41°F or below. Do not mix old product with new. Keep leftover product chilled at 41°F or below. See p. 167 for cooling procedures.
- Use as a garnish for fish tacos and pulled pork sandwiches.
- May substitute ⅓ cup chopped fresh parsley for dried parsley.

COLESLAW

Yield: 50 portions or 4½ qt   *Portion:* ⅓ cup (2½ oz)

Ingredient	Amount	Procedure
Cabbage	7 lb EP (9 lb AP)	Shred or chop cabbage.
Vinegar, cider	3 cups	Combine vinegar, sugar, and seasonings.
Sugar, granulated	1 lb 8 oz	Add to cabbage. Mix lightly.
Salt	1 oz (1½ Tbsp)	
Celery seed	1 Tbsp	

Approximate nutritive values per portion

Calories	Carbohydrate	Protein	Fat	Cholesterol	Sodium	Fiber	Iron
68 kcal	18 g	1 g	0 g	0 mg	204 mg	1 g	0.5 mg

Note

- Red cabbage may be substituted for part or all of green cabbage.

Variations

- **Cauliflower Broccoli Salad.** Substitute 3 lb 8 oz EP each of cauliflower and broccoli florets for the cabbage. Add 3 oz chopped onion. Serve soon after preparing.
- **Green Pepper Slaw.** Add 4 oz chopped green bell pepper, 2 oz chopped onion, and 4 Tbsp celery seed.
- **Asian Coleslaw.** Substitute $\frac{1}{3}$ recipe Sesame Seed Dressing (p. 645) for dressing given in recipe.

CREAMY COLESLAW

Yield: 50 portions or 4¼ qt   *Portion:* $\frac{1}{3}$ cup (2½ oz)

Ingredient	Amount	Procedure
Cabbage	7 lb EP (9 lb AP)	Shred or chop cabbage.
Mayonnaise or salad dressing	2 cups	Combine and add to cabbage. Mix lightly.
Half-and-half	2 cups	Serve with No. 12 dipper.
Vinegar, cider	½ cup	
Sugar, granulated	4 oz	
Salt	1 oz (1½ Tbsp)	
White pepper	½ tsp	

Approximate nutritive values per portion

Calories	Carbohydrate	Protein	Fat	Cholesterol	Sodium	Fiber	Iron
100 kcal	7 g	1 g	8 g	9 mg	258 mg	1 g	0.5 mg

Note

- Potentially hazardous food. *Food Safety Standards:* Hold food for service at an internal temperature of 41°F or below. Do not mix old product with new. Keep leftover product chilled at 41°F or below. See p. 167 for cooling procedures.

Variations

- **Apple Cabbage Salad.** See p. 617.
- **Cabbage-Carrot Slaw.** Reduce cabbage to 5 lb. Add 1 lb shredded or chopped carrots, 8 oz chopped green bell pepper, and 4 oz chopped onion.
- **Cabbage-Pineapple-Marshmallow Salad.** To 4 lb shredded or chopped cabbage, add 2 lb canned pineapple tidbits, drained, 1 lb miniature marshmallows, and a dressing made of 2 cups mayonnaise or salad dressing and 2 cups whipped cream.
- **Creamy Cauliflower-Broccoli Salad.** Substitute 3 lb 8 oz EP each of cauliflower and broccoli for the cabbage. Add 3 oz chopped green onion. Garnish with cherry tomatoes.

SLICED CUCUMBER AND ONION IN SOUR CREAM

Yield: 50 portions or 4¼ qt   *Portion:* ⅓ cup (2½ oz)

Ingredient	Amount	Procedure
Cucumbers	6 lb	Cut cucumbers and onions in thin slices.
Onions	6 oz	
Sour cream	2 cups	Blend rest of ingredients to form a thin cream dressing.
Mayonnaise	2 cups	Pour over cucumbers and onions. Mix lightly.
Salt	1½ tsp	Garnish with a sprig of curly parsley.
Sugar, granulated	2 Tbsp	
Vinegar, cider	½ cup	

Approximate nutritive values per portion

Calories	Carbohydrate	Protein	Fat	Cholesterol	Sodium	Fiber	Iron
135 kcal	4 g	1 g	14 g	14 mg	148 mg	0 g	0.5 mg

Notes

- Potentially hazardous food. *Food Safety Standards:* Hold food for service at an internal temperature of 41°F or below. Do not mix old product with new. Keep leftover product chilled at 41°F or below. See p. 167 for cooling procedures.
- This cream dressing may be used as a dressing for lettuce.

Variation

- **German Cucumbers.** Reduce onions to 4 oz. Delete cream dressing. Pour mixture of 1 cup apple cider vinegar, 1 cup water, 1 Tbsp salt, and 8 oz sugar over cucumbers and onions. Marinate for at least 1 hour.

MARINATED MUSHROOMS

Yield: 50 portions   *Portion:* 2¾ oz

Ingredient	Amount	Procedure
Fresh mushrooms, small	6 lb	Clean mushrooms and trim ends. Leave whole.
Water	1 qt	Combine water and juice.
Fresh lemon juice	½ cup	Bring to a boil. Add mushrooms and blanch for 1–3 minutes. Drain and immerse in cold water. Drain.
Vegetable Marinade (p. 722)	1½ qt	Pour marinade over mushrooms. Refrigerate for 2–3 hours. Drain off most of the marinade before serving.

Approximate nutritive values per portion

Calories	Carbohydrate	Protein	Fat	Cholesterol	Sodium	Fiber	Iron
37 kcal	3 g	1 g	3 g	0 mg	110 mg	1 g	1 mg

Note

- Before serving, mushrooms may be tossed with fresh minced parsley or other fresh herb.

Variations

- **Marinated Asparagus.** Blanch fresh asparagus spears (see instructions for mushrooms). Marinate. To serve, drain and arrange 3–5 spears on plate with Bibb lettuce liner. Garnish with lemon twist or pimento strip.
- **Marinated Green Beans.** Cover whole green beans with marinade. If fresh green beans are used, cook until tender-crisp.
- **Vegetable Collage.** Pour 3 cups Italian Dressing (p. 645) or Vegetable Marinade (p. 722) over 2 lb broccoli florets, 2 lb cauliflower florets, 12 oz sliced celery, 1 lb 8 oz cherry tomatoes cut in half, 2 lb sliced zucchini, 1 lb sliced green onions, 6 oz sliced carrots, and 1 lb 8 oz sliced black olives. Marinate in refrigerator for 4 hours, but if salad is to be held longer than 4 hours, add broccoli shortly before serving. Add 1 lb cooked crumbled bacon and toss.

TOMATO BASIL SALAD

Yield: 50 portions   *Portion:* ½ cup

Ingredient	Amount	Procedure
Tomatoes	15 lb AP	Peel and seed tomatoes (see Notes). Cut tomatoes into bite-size pieces. Put in baker's bowl.
Fresh basil leaves	2 oz	Cut or tear basil into small pieces. Gently stir into tomatoes.
Vinegar, red wine Sugar, granulated Salt Black pepper	2 cups 1½ cups 2 tsp ½ tsp	Mix vinegar, sugar, and spices. Pour over tomatoes. Let stand for 30 minutes.
		Serve tomatoes in a bowl with some of the vinegar dressing. Garnish with fresh basil leaves.

Approximate nutritive values per portion

Calories	Carbohydrate	Protein	Fat	Cholesterol	Sodium	Fiber	Iron
50 kcal	12 g	1 g	0.4 g	0 mg	104 mg	1.4 g	0.5 mg

Notes

- Use very ripe, bright red tomatoes.
- Procedure for seeding tomatoes: Cut the tomato in half horizontally. Gently squeeze each half of the tomato to push out the seeds.

Variation

- **Tomato Basil and Romaine Salad.** Cut or tear 10 lb romaine lettuce into bite-size pieces. Portion 3 oz lettuce onto individual salad plates. Using a No. 12 dipper, portion tomatoes on top of greens (being careful not to use too much vinegar dressing). Sprinkle 1 tsp freshly grated Parmesan cheese on top of each salad. Drizzle a small amount of the vinegar on top, if desired. Garnish with whole basil leaves. May substitute slices of fresh mozzarella cheese for the Parmesan cheese.

MARINATED TOMATOES

Yield: 50 portions   *Portion:* 2 slices

Ingredient	Amount	Procedure
Fresh tomatoes, peeled	6 lb	Cut peeled tomatoes into ½-inch slices. Place in bottom of 12 × 20 × 2-inch pan.
Onion, chopped	¾ cup	Combine. Pour over tomato slices.
Garlic cloves, minced	3	Cover tightly. Refrigerate if storing for later use.
Fresh parsley, chopped	⅓ cup	
Basil, dried, crumbled	1 Tbsp	
Sugar, granulated	1 Tbsp	
Salt	2 tsp	
Black pepper	1½ tsp	
Olive oil	2 cups	
Vinegar, red wine or balsamic	1½ cups	

Approximate nutritive values per portion

Calories	Carbohydrate	Protein	Fat	Cholesterol	Sodium	Fiber	Iron
99 kcal	4 g	1 g	9 g	0 mg	203 mg	1 g	0.5 mg

Notes

- ⅓ cup fresh basil may be substituted for dried.
- Salad oil may be substituted for olive oil.
- Refrigerator storage causes tomatoes to lose some flavor.

Variation

- **Fresh Tomato Relish.** Cut peeled tomatoes in half and gently squeeze out most of the seeds. Chop coarsely and stir into the marinade.

FRESH SLICED TOMATOES AND CUCUMBERS

Yield: 50 portions   *Portion:* 2 tomato and 2 cucumber slices

Ingredient	Amount	Procedure
Tomatoes	8 lb	Slice tomatoes and cucumbers ¼ inch thick.
Cucumbers	5 lb	Alternate tomatoes and cucumbers, slightly overlapping, on a serving platter.
Fresh basil chopped	½ cup	Sprinkle basil and parsley over tomatoes and cucumbers.
Fresh parsley, chopped	½ cup	
Italian salad dressing	2½ cups	Drizzle salad dressing evenly over tomatoes and cucumbers.
Fresh basil leaves	for garnish	Garnish with fresh basil leaves and serve immediately.

Approximate nutritive values per portion

Calories	Carbohydrate	Protein	Fat	Cholesterol	Sodium	Fiber	Iron
79 kcal	5 g	1 g	6 g	0 mg	249 mg	1 g	0.5 mg

Note

- Cucumbers may be scored with tines of a fork before slicing. Cucumbers may be peeled or unpeeled.

Variation

- **Sliced Tomato and Mozzarella Salad.** Substitute 4 lb low-fat mozzarella cheese slices for cucumbers.

MARINATED CARROTS

Yield: 50 portions   *Portion:* ⅓ cup (3 oz)

Ingredient	Amount	Procedure
Fresh carrots, cut in ¼-inch slices	5 lb	Cook carrots until tender-crisp. Drain.
Tomato soup	2 cups	Combine and heat to boiling point.
Sugar, granulated	1 lb	Pour over warm carrots.
Salad oil	½ cup	Marinate for at least 4 hours.
Vinegar, cider	1½ cups	
Salt	2 tsp	
Black pepper	1 tsp	
Prepared mustard	1 Tbsp	
Worcestershire sauce	1 Tbsp	
Onions, chopped	12 oz	
Green bell pepper, chopped	3 oz	

Approximate nutritive values per portion

Calories	Carbohydrate	Protein	Fat	Cholesterol	Sodium	Fiber	Iron
81 kcal	16 g	1 g	2 g	0 mg	143 mg	1 g	0.5 mg

Notes

- Frozen crinkle-sliced carrots, cooked until tender-crisp, may be substituted for fresh carrots.
- Marinated carrots will keep in the refrigerator for a week.

MARINATED GARDEN SALAD

Yield: 50 portions or 8 lb   *Portion:* ⅓ cup (2½ oz)

Ingredient	Amount	Procedure
Carrots, sliced	1 lb EP	Steam carrots just until tender-crisp. Drain.
Fresh cauliflower	2 lb EP	Cut cauliflower into florets.
Broccoli spears	2 lb EP	Cut broccoli into florets and slice stems.
Fresh mushrooms	1 lb	Clean mushrooms. Cut large mushrooms in half. Combine all vegetables.
French Dressing (p. 644)	1½ qt	Combine dressing and seasonings.
Dill weed	¼ oz	Pour over vegetables.
Basil, dried, crumbled	1 Tbsp	Marinate for at least 2 hours.
Oregano, dried, crumbled	1 tsp	

Approximate nutritive values per portion

Calories	Carbohydrate	Protein	Fat	Cholesterol	Sodium	Fiber	Iron
145 kcal	9 g	1 g	12 g	4 mg	463 mg	1 g	1 mg

Note

- Peel broccoli stems before slicing if they appear tough.

SPINACH CHEESE SALAD

Yield: 50 portions   *Portion:* 3 oz

Ingredient	Amount	Procedure
Spinach, chopped, frozen	3 lb	Thaw spinach. Squeeze out excess moisture and drain.
Eggs, hard cooked (p. 384)	10	Peel eggs and chop coarsely.
Onion, chopped Celery, chopped Cheddar cheese, shredded	6 oz 8 oz 1 lb	Add onion, celery, cheese, and eggs to spinach. Mix lightly.
Mayonnaise or salad dressing Vinegar, cider Salt Hot pepper sauce Horseradish	1¼ qt 2 Tbsp 2 tsp 2 tsp ⅔ cup	Combine mayonnaise, vinegar, and seasonings. Pour over spinach mixture. Mix lightly. Refrigerate for 2 hours. Serve with No. 12 dipper.

Approximate nutritive values per portion

Calories	Carbohydrate	Protein	Fat	Cholesterol	Sodium	Fiber	Iron
221 kcal	3 g	5 g	22 g	65 mg	343 mg	1 g	3 mg

Note

- Potentially hazardous food. *Food Safety Standards:* Hold food for service at an internal temperature of 41°F or below. Do not mix old product with new. Keep leftover product chilled at 41°F or below. See p. 167 for cooling procedures.

BASIC PASTA SALAD

Yield: 50 portions   *Portion:* 4 oz

Ingredient	Amount	Procedure
Pasta Water, boiling Salt Vegetable oil	3 lb 8 oz AP 3½ gal 3 oz 2 Tbsp	Cook pasta according to directions on p. 507. Do not overcook. Pasta should be *al dente*. There should be approximately 9 lb cooked pasta. Information on cooked weights of pasta is given on p. 507.
Dressing	1½–1¾ qt	Add dressing and toss gently to mix.
Vegetables and/or other ingredients	1 lb 8 oz–2 lb	Fold in other ingredients. Chill.

Suggested Ingredients

- **Pasta:** Rotini, rigatoni, shell macaroni, elbow macaroni, radiatore, wheels. See Figure 5.2 for other pasta choices.
- **Dressing:** Vinaigrette and variations (p. 647), Lemon Basil (p. 647), Lime Salad Dressing (p. 647), Green Peppercorn Cream (p. 641), Thousand Island (p. 641), Italian (p. 645), Sour Cream Basil (p. 641).
- **Vegetables (cooked until tender-crisp):** Asparagus cuts, broccoli florets, carrot coins, Italian green beans, snow peas, sugar snap peas.
- **Vegetables (raw):** Avocado slices or chunks, broccoli, cauliflower, chives, cucumbers, green bell peppers, red onion rings, parsley, radishes, summer squash slices, tomatoes, water chestnuts, zucchini slices or strips.
- **Other:** Chicken strips, beef strips, pepperoni slices, ham, crabmeat, scallops, shrimp, turkey, olives, pickles, cheese.

Note

- Yield for this recipe may vary, depending on the shape of the pasta used and the amount of vegetables and other ingredients added.

MACARONI SALAD

Yield: 50 portions or 6 qt   *Portion:* ½ cup (4 oz)

Ingredient	Amount	Procedure
Elbow macaroni	2 lb 8 oz	Cook macaroni according to directions on p. 507.
Water, boiling	2½ gal	Rinse in cold water. Drain well after rinsing.
Salt	2 Tbsp	(Should be 6 lb 10 oz cooked macaroni.)
Vegetable oil	1 Tbsp	
French Dressing (p. 644)	2 cups	Combine. Pour over macaroni and let marinate overnight.
Salt	¾ tsp	
Vinegar, cider	½ cup	
Eggs, hard cooked (p. 384)	12	Peel eggs and chop coarsely.
Green bell peppers, chopped	6 oz	Add vegetables, cheese, and eggs to marinated macaroni.
Celery, chopped	1 lb 4 oz	
Onions, chopped	6 oz	
Pimento, chopped and drained	3 oz	
Cheddar cheese, diced or shredded	1 lb	
Salad dressing	1 lb	Combine dressing and relish.
Sweet pickle relish, drained	10 oz	Pour over macaroni mixture. Mix carefully to combine. Serve with No. 10 dipper.

Approximate nutritive values per portion

Calories	Carbohydrate	Protein	Fat	Cholesterol	Sodium	Fiber	Iron
260 kcal	22 g	7 g	16 g	67 mg	610 mg	0.3 g	1 mg

Notes

- Potentially hazardous food. *Food Safety Standards:* Hold food for service at an internal temperature of 41°F or below. Do not mix old product with new. Keep leftover product chilled at 41°F or below. See p. 167 for cooling procedures.
- Other types of pasta may be substituted for elbow macaroni. (See Figure 5.2.)

Variations

- **Chicken and Pasta Salad.** Delete cheese, pickle relish, and eggs. Cook 2 lb 8 oz fettuccine or other type of pasta according to directions on p. 507. Add 3 lb cooked chicken, diced.
- **Ham and Pasta Salad.** Delete eggs. Add 2 lb cooked ham, diced.

ISRAELI COUSCOUS SALAD

Yield: 50 portions   *Portion:* 4 oz

Ingredient	Amount	Procedure
Water	2 gal	Bring water and salt to a rolling boil in steam-jacketed or other kettle.
Salt	2 tsp	
Middle Eastern couscous (see Note)	2 lb 6 oz	Add couscous while stirring. Return water to boil. Reduce heat and simmer for 10–12 minutes until couscous is *al dente*. Stir occasionally. Drain, cool, and save for later step. (Yield: 7 lb 3 oz cooked couscous)
Cucumbers, diced, unpeeled	1 lb 12 oz EP	Add vegetables, oil, vinegar, juice, and seasonings to cooled couscous reserved from earlier step.
Red onions, chopped	1 lb	Toss well to distribute ingredients.
Olive oil	1½ cups	
Vinegar, red wine	2 cups	
Fresh lemon juice	2 oz (¼ cup)	
Fresh parsley, minced	2¾ oz EP	
Fresh mint, finely chopped	6 Tbsp	
Salt	1¼ oz (2 Tbsp)	
Black pepper	2 Tbsp	

Approximate nutritive values per portion

Calories	Carbohydrate	Protein	Fat	Cholesterol	Sodium	Fiber	Iron
145 kcal	17.5 g	3 g	6.8 g	0 mg	693 mg	0.9 g	1 mg

Notes

- Potentially hazardous food. *Food Safety Standards:* Hold food for service at an internal temperature of 41°F or below. Do not mix old product wih new. Keep leftover product chilled at 41°F or below. See p. 167 for cooling procedures.
- Middle Eastern or Israeli couscous is the size of a small pea and resembles pearl tapioca.

CITRUS COUSCOUS SALAD

Yield: 50 portion   *Portion:* 4 oz

Ingredient	Amount	Procedure
Water	1 ¾ gal	Bring water and salt to a rolling boil in steam-jacketed kettle or other kettle.
Salt	2 tsp	Add couscous while stirring. Return water to boil. Reduce heat and simmer
Middle Eastern couscous	2 lb 2 oz	for 10–12 minutes until couscous is *al dente*. Stir occasionally.
(Israeli couscous)		Drain, cool, and save for later step. (Yield: 6 lb 6 oz cooked couscous)
Olive oil	¾ cup	Combine liquids, vegetables, raisins, nuts, and spices in baker's bowl. Mix.
Fresh lemon juice	¾ cup	Add cooked and cooled couscous reserved from earlier step.
Orange juice, frozen, reconstituted	1½ cups	Toss to mix. Cool quickly to 41°F or below.
Garlic, minced	4 Tbsp	
Green onions, thinly sliced	8 oz	
Fresh ginger, minced	2 Tbsp	
Raisins	8 oz	
Toasted slivered almonds (see Note)	8 oz	
Salt	1¼ tsp	
Black pepper	1½ tsp	
Mandarin oranges	3 lb	Gently stir in mandarin oranges.

Approximate nutritive values per portion

Calories	Carbohydrate	Protein	Fat	Cholesterol	Sodium	Fiber	Iron
156 kcal	15 g	2 g	5 g	0 mg	76 mg	1 g	0.7 mg

Notes

- Potentially hazardous food. *Food Safety Standards:* Hold food for service at an internal temperature of 41°F or below. Do not mix old product with new. Keep leftover product chilled at 41°F or below. See p. 167 for cooling procedures.

- To toast almonds: Spread nuts in a thin even layer in a dry skillet. Heat over medium-high heat until golden brown and fragrant, 2–3 minutes, or in the oven at 300°F for 10–15 minutes. Shake pan throughout cooking to prevent burning. Cool on baking sheet.

ITALIAN PASTA SALAD

Yield: 50 portions   *Portion:* ½ cup (4 oz)

Ingredient	Amount	Procedure
Rotini or other pasta	2 lb 8 oz	Cook pasta according to directions on p. 507.
Water, boiling	2½ gal	Rinse in cold water. Drain.
Salt	2 Tbsp	
Vegetable oil	1 Tbsp	
Thousand Island Dressing (p. 641)	1¾ qt	Combine dressing and seasonings.
Basil, dried, crumbled	1 Tbsp	Pour over pasta. Mix gently.
Salt	1 Tbsp	Chill.
Garbanzo beans, canned	8 oz	Drain and rinse beans.
		Add to pasta mixture.
Fresh tomatoes, cut in wedges	1 lb 8 oz	Add vegetables and olives to pasta mixture.
Cucumbers, peeled and sliced	1 lb	Toss gently. Refrigerate until served.
Fresh cauliflower, sliced	8 oz	
Black olives, large, pitted	4 oz	

Approximate nutritive values per portion

Calories	Carbohydrate	Protein	Fat	Cholesterol	Sodium	Fiber	Iron
229 kcal	24 g	3 g	13 g	11 mg	484 mg	2 g	2 mg

Notes

- Potentially hazardous food. *Food Safety Standards:* Hold food for service at an internal temperature of 41°F or below. Do not mix old product wih new. Keep leftover product chilled at 41°F or below. See p. 167 for cooling procedures.
- An oil-based dressing may be substituted for Thousand Island Dressing.

CHILLED FETTUCCINE VINAIGRETTE

Yield: 50 portions   *Portion:* 5 oz

Ingredient	Amount	Procedure
Fettuccine	3 lb 6 oz	Cook fettuccine according to directions on p. 507. Drain.
Water	3½ gal	There should be 10 lb cooked fettuccine.
Salt	2 Tbsp	
Vegetable oil	2 Tbsp	
Yogurt, plain, nonfat	2 lb	Blend yogurt and vinaigrette well.
Vinaigrette Dressing (p. 647)	2 qt	Pour over hot fettuccine. Toss, using tongs, until all pasta is coated with dressing. Cover and chill until service.

Approximate nutritive values per portion

Calories	Carbohydrate	Protein	Fat	Cholesterol	Sodium	Fiber	Iron
331 kcal	25 g	5 g	24 g	0 mg	610 mg	0 g	1 mg

Notes

- Potentially hazardous food. *Food Safety Standards:* Hold food for service at an internal temperature of 41°F or below. Do not mix old product with new. Keep leftover product chilled at 41°F or below. See p. 167 for cooling procedures.
- Serve Fettuccine Vinaigrette as an accompaniment to a chilled poultry breast. Add a colorful fruit garnish.
- Bottled Italian salad dressing may be substituted for Vinaigrette Dressing.

Variation

- **Marinated Fettuccine.** Prepare as for Chilled Fettuccine Vinaigrette. After the yogurt and dressing are added, heat in oven. Serve hot.

POTATO SALAD

Yield: 50 portions or 7 qt   *Portion:* ½ cup (4 oz)

Ingredient	Amount	Procedure
Potatoes, peeled	10 lb EP (12 lb AP)	Cook potatoes until tender. Dice while warm.
Salad oil	½ cup	Make a marinade of oil, vinegar, juice, and seasonings.
Vinegar, cider	½ cup	Add to warm potatoes and mix gently.
Fresh lemon juice	1 Tbsp	Marinate until cold.
Prepared mustard	2 Tbsp	
Sugar, granulated	3 oz	
Salt	1 Tbsp	
Hot pepper sauce	few drops	
Eggs, hard cooked (p. 384), diced	12	Add eggs, celery, onion, and pepper to marinated potatoes.
Celery, diced	1 lb	Mix lightly.
Onion, finely chopped	8 oz	
Black pepper	½ tsp	
Mayonnaise	2 cups	Add mayonnaise. Mix carefully to blend. Chill for at least 1 hour before serving. Serve with No. 10 dipper.

Approximate nutritive values per portion

Calories	Carbohydrate	Protein	Fat	Cholesterol	Sodium	Fiber	Iron
190 kcal	21 g	3 g	11 g	56 mg	214 mg	1 g	0.5 mg

Notes

- Potentially hazardous food. *Food Safety Standards:* Hold food for service at an internal temperature of 41°F or below. Do not mix old product with new. Keep leftover product chilled at 41°F or below. See p. 167 for cooling procedures.
- 2 cups French Dressing may be substituted for the marinade given in the recipe.
- Sour cream or yogurt may be substituted for half of the mayonnaise.
- Potatoes may be cooked with skins on, then peeled. Use 12 lb AP.
- 4 oz pickle relish, chopped pimento, or chopped green bell pepper may be added.

Variation

- **Sour Cream Potato Salad.** Reduce eggs to 8 and mayonnaise to 1 cup. Add 2 cups sour cream, 1 tsp celery seed, and 12 oz peeled, sliced cucumbers.

HOT POTATO SALAD

Yield: 50 portions   *Portion:* ⅔ cup (6 oz)

Ingredient	Amount	Procedure
Potatoes	12 lb EP (15 lb AP)	Wash potatoes and trim as necessary. Steam until just tender, about 30 minutes. Peel and slice.
Bacon	1 lb	Dice bacon, cook until crisp. Drain. Reserve fat.
Onion, chopped	8 oz	Sauté onion in bacon fat.
Flour, all-purpose	4 oz	Add flour to onion and stir until well mixed. Cook for 5 minutes.
Sugar, granulated Salt Black pepper Celery seed Vinegar, cider Water	1 lb 2½ oz 2 tsp 1 Tbsp 3 cups 1 qt	Mix sugar, spices, vinegar, and water. Boil for 1 minute. Add to fat-flour mixture gradually while stirring. Cook until slightly thickened.
		Add hot dressing to warm potatoes and bacon. Mix lightly. Serve hot.

Approximate nutritive values per portion

Calories	Carbohydrate	Protein	Fat	Cholesterol	Sodium	Fiber	Iron
205 kcal	34 g	3 g	7 g	8 mg	597 mg	2 g	0.5 mg

Notes

- Potentially hazardous food. *Food Safety Standards:* Hold food for service at an internal temperature of 135°F or above. Do not mix old product with new. Cool leftover product quickly following time standards and cooling procedures on p. 167. Reheat leftover product quickly (within 2 hours) to 165°F or above. Reheat product only once; discard if not used.
- 12 hard-cooked eggs, sliced or diced, may be added.
- Mayonnaise or a combination of mayonnaise and salad dressing may be used in place of the hot vinegar dressing. Add to potato mixture and heat to serving temperature.

CURRIED ORZO AND VEGETABLE SALAD

Yield: 50 portions   *Portion:* 3 oz

Ingredient	Amount	Procedure
Orzo, dry	1 lb 10 oz	Cook orzo *al dente* according to directions on p. 507. Drain well. Reserve for later step. (Yield: 4 lb cooked orzo)
Water	1½ gal	
Salt	1 Tbsp	
Edamame	2 lb 4 oz	Steam or boil edamame until tender-crisp. Reserve for later step.
Mayonnaise	1⅓ cups	Blend mayonnaise, juice, and seasonings in baker's bowl.
Fresh lime juice	½ cup	
Curry powder	1 Tbsp	
Salt	1 Tbsp	
Cayenne pepper	¼ tsp	
Fresh cilantro, chopped	1 cup	
Roasted red peppers (p. 796)	12 oz	Coarsely chop peppers. Mix with celery and onion.
Sliced celery	4 oz	Stir orzo, edamame, peppers, celery, and onion into mayonnaise mixture.
Chopped onion	6oz	Chill thoroughly.
Cherry tomatoes	1 lb 4 oz	Cut tomatoes in half. Toss gently with orzo mixture just before serving.

Approximate nutritive values per portion

Calories	Carbohydrate	Protein	Fat	Cholesterol	Sodium	Fiber	Iron
141 kcal	15 g	5 g	7 g	2 mg	351 mg	2 g	0 mg

Note

- Potentially hazardous food. *Food Safety Standards:* Hold food for service at an internal temperature of 41°F or below. Do not mix old product with new. Keep leftover product chilled at 41°F or below. See p. 167 for cooling procedures.

Gelatin Salad Recipes

FRUIT GELATIN SALAD

Yield: 40 or 48 portions or 1 pan, 12 × 20 × 2 inches   *Portion:* $2\frac{1}{4}$ × $2\frac{1}{2}$ inches or 2 × $2\frac{1}{2}$ inches

Ingredient	Amount	Procedure
Water, boiling	2 qt	Pour boiling water over gelatin.
Gelatin, flavored	1 lb 8 oz	Stir until dissolved.
Fruit juice or water, cold	2 qt	Add to hot liquid. Chill.
Fruit, drained	4 lb	Place fruit in counter pan.
		When gelatin begins to congeal, pour over fruit.
		Place in refrigerator to congeal.
		Cut 5 × 8 for 40 portions.
		Cut 6 × 8 for 48 portions.

Approximate nutritive values per portion (cut 48)

Calories	Carbohydrate	Protein	Fat	Cholesterol	Sodium	Fiber	Iron
91 kcal	10 g	13 g	0 g	0 mg	20 mg	1 g	1 mg

Notes

- For quick preparation, dissolve 1 lb 8 oz flavored gelatin in $1\frac{1}{2}$ qt boiling water. Measure $2\frac{1}{2}$ qt chipped or finely crushed ice, then add enough cold water or fruit juice to cover ice. Add to gelatin and stir constantly until ice is melted. Gelatin will begin to congeal at once. Speed of congealing depends on proportion of ice to water and size of ice particles.
- One or more canned, frozen, or fresh fruits, cut into desired shapes and sizes, may be used. Fresh or frozen pineapple must be cooked before adding to gelatin salad.
- Fruit juice may be used for part or all of the liquid. Not more than 50 percent of heavy syrup, however, should be substituted for water.
- If unflavored granulated gelatin is used, sprinkle $2\frac{1}{2}$ oz over 2 cups cold water and let stand for 10 minutes. Add $3\frac{1}{2}$ qt boiling fruit juice and 1 lb sugar.

Variations

- **Apple Cinnamon Swirl.** Heat $1\frac{1}{4}$ qt water to boiling. Add 1 lb lemon gelatin and 10 oz cinnamon candies (red hots). Stir until dissolved. Stir in 3 lb ($1\frac{1}{2}$ qt) applesauce, $\frac{1}{4}$ cup lemon juice, and 1 Tbsp salt. Pour into a 12 × 20 × 2-inch pan and chill until partially set. Fold in 8 oz coarsely chopped walnuts. Beat 10 oz cream cheese, $\frac{1}{2}$ cup milk, $\frac{1}{4}$ cup mayonnaise until smooth. Spoon mixture (2 cups) on top of gelatin. Swirl through gelatin with rubber spatula to marble.

- **Applesauce Gelatin Salad.** Heat 6 lb 10 oz (1 No. 10 can) applesauce, 8 oz granulated sugar, 1 Tbsp ground cinnamon, and 2 tsp ground nutmeg, stirring frequently. Add 1 lb 8 oz strawberry gelatin and stir until dissolved. Add 2 qt cold water and $\frac{1}{3}$ cup lemon juice.

- **Arabian Peach Salad.** Drain 1 No. 10 can sliced peaches, saving juice. Combine peach juice, $1\frac{1}{2}$ cups white vinegar, 1 lb 12 oz granulated sugar, 1 oz stick cinnamon, and 2 tsp whole cloves. Simmer for 10 minutes. Strain and add enough hot water to make 1 gal liquid. Add to 1 lb 8 oz orange gelatin and stir until dissolved. When slightly thickened, add peaches. Apricot halves may be substituted for peaches.

- **Autumn Salad.** Dissolve 1 lb 8 oz orange gelatin in 2 qt boiling water. Add 2 qt cold liquid, 2 lb 8 oz sliced fresh peaches, and 3 lb 8 oz fresh pears.

- **Blueberry Gelatin Salad.** Make in two layers. First layer: Drain 1 No. 10 can blueberries. Add water to juice if necessary to make 1 qt and heat to boiling. Add 12 oz raspberry gelatin and stir until dissolved. Pour into 12 × 20 × 2-inch pan and chill. Second layer: Drain 1 No. 10 can crushed pineapple. Add water if necessary to make 1 qt liquid. Heat to boiling and add 12 oz lemon gelatin. Stir until dissolved. Stir in the crushed pineapple and 1 qt sour cream. Cool. Pour over first layer and chill.

- **Boysenberry Mold.** Thaw 2 lb 12 oz frozen boysenberries in a colander. Reserve juice. Heat juice plus water if needed to make 2 qt. Add 1 lb 8 oz raspberry gelatin and stir until dissolved. Stir in $1\frac{1}{2}$ cups cold water. Chill until gelatin is the consistency of egg whites. Whip $1\frac{1}{4}$ qt whipped topping until soft peaks form. Fold in the thickened gelatin mixture and boysenberries. Pour into molds and refrigerate until firm.

- **Cranberry Apple Salad.** Dissolve 1 lb 8 oz cherry or raspberry gelatin in 2 qt boiling water. Add 3 lb fresh or frozen cranberry relish, 1 lb chopped, unpeeled apples, and 1 lb crushed pineapple. One No. 10 can whole cranberry sauce and 4 oranges, ground, may be used in place of the relish. Delete pineapple.

- **Cranberry Mold.** Drain $3\frac{1}{2}$ cups crushed pineapple ($2\frac{1}{2}$ cups drained). Heat juice, plus enough water to make $3\frac{1}{4}$ cups, to boiling. Add 1 lb raspberry gelatin and stir until dissolved. Stir in $1\frac{1}{2}$ qt cranberry relish. Chill until consistency of unbeaten egg whites. Fold in 3 cups mandarin oranges, drained and chopped, and $3\frac{1}{4}$ cups whipped topping whipped until stiff ($6\frac{1}{2}$ cups whipped). Spread in oiled gelatin molds.

- **Cucumber Soufflé Salad.** Dissolve 1 lb 8 oz lime or lemon gelatin in $1\frac{1}{2}$ qt boiling water. Add 2 qt ice and cold water. Chill until partially set. Whip until fluffy. Add 3 cups mayonnaise and $\frac{1}{3}$ cup lemon juice. Fold in 5 lb chopped cucumbers.

- **Frosted Cherry Salad.** Dissolve 1 lb 8 oz cherry gelatin in 2 qt boiling water. Add 2 qt cold fruit juice, 2 lb drained, pitted red cherries, and 2 lb crushed pineapple. When congealed, frost with whipped cream cheese and chopped toasted almonds.

- **Frosted Lime Salad.** Dissolve 1 lb 8 oz lime gelatin in 2 qt boiling water. Add 2 qt cold fruit juice and, when mixture begins to congeal, add 4 lb crushed pineapple, drained, 2 lb 8 oz cottage cheese, 8 oz diced celery, 4 oz chopped pimento, and 4 oz chopped nuts. When congealed, frost with mixture of 4 lb cream cheese blended with $\frac{1}{2}$ cup mayonnaise.

- **Jellied Waldorf Salad.** Dissolve 1 lb 8 oz raspberry or cherry gelatin in 2 qt boiling water. Add 1 cup red cinnamon candies (red hots) and stir until dissolved. Add 2 qt cold water or fruit juice. When mixture begins to congeal, add 2 lb diced apple, 12 oz finely diced celery, and 8 oz chopped pecans or walnuts.

- **Lemon Cream Mold.** Dissolve 1 lb 8 oz lemon gelatin in 1 qt boiling water. Stir in 1 qt cold water, $\frac{3}{4}$ cup vinegar, and $\frac{1}{4}$ tsp salt. Cool to room temperature. Add to 3 lb 12 oz sour cream and mix until smooth. Garnish with very thin slices of lemon and cucumber.

- **Molded Pineapple Cheese Salad.** Dissolve 1 lb 8 oz lemon gelatin in 2 qt boiling water. Add 2 qt cold fruit juice, 1 lb grated cheddar cheese, 3 lb drained crushed pineapple, 3 oz chopped green bell pepper or pimento, and 4 oz finely chopped celery.

- **Ribbon Gelatin Salad.** Dissolve 1 lb 8 oz raspberry gelatin in 1 gal boiling water. Divide into three equal parts. Pour one-third into one 12 × 20 × 2-inch pan and chill. Add 1 lb cream cheese to another third and whip to blend; pour on the first part when it is congealed. Return it to the refrigerator until it, too, is congealed, then top with remaining portion.

- **Sunshine Salad.** Dissolve 1 lb 8 oz lemon gelatin in 2 qt boiling water. Add 2 qt cold fruit juice, 3 lb drained crushed pineapple, and 8 oz grated raw carrot.

- **Swedish Green-Top Salad.** Dissolve 12 oz lime gelatin in 2 qt boiling water. Pour into a 12 × 10 × 2-inch pan. Dissolve 12 oz orange gelatin in 2 qt boiling water. While still hot, add 1 lb 8 oz marshmallows and stir until melted. When cool, add 12 oz cream cheese, $1\frac{1}{2}$ cups mayonnaise, and $\frac{1}{2}$ tsp salt, blended together. Fold in 1 pt cream, whipped. Pour over congealed lime gelatin and return to the refrigerator to chill. To serve, invert so that green portion is on top.

- **Under-the-Sea Salad.** Dissolve 1 lb 8 oz lime gelatin in 1 gal boiling water. Divide into two parts. Pour one part into a 12 × 20 × 2-inch pan and chill. When it begins to congeal, add 12 oz drained crushed pineapple or sliced pears. To the remaining gelatin mixture, add 1 lb cream cheese and whip until smooth. Pour over first portion.

PERFECTION SALAD

Yield: 40 or 48 portions or 1 pan, 12 × 20 × 2 inches   *Portion:* 2¼ × 2½ or 2 × 2½ inches

Ingredient	Amount	Procedure
Gelatin, unflavored	3 oz	Sprinkle gelatin over cold water.
Water, cold	2 cups	Let stand for 10 minutes.
Water, boiling	3 qt	Add boiling water to gelatin. Stir until gelatin is dissolved.
Vinegar, cider	1 cup	Add to gelatin mixture. Stir until sugar is dissolved.
Fresh lemon juice	1 cup	Chill.
Salt	1 oz (1½ Tbsp)	
Sugar, granulated	1 lb	
Cabbage, chopped	1 lb 8 oz	When liquid begins to congeal, add vegetables.
Celery, chopped	10 oz	Pour into a 12 × 20 × 2-inch counter pan. Place in the refrigerator to congeal.
Pimento, chopped	4 oz	Cut 5 × 8 for 40 portions. Cut 6 × 8 for 48 portions.
Green bell pepper, chopped	4 oz	
Paprika	1 Tbsp	

Approximate nutritive values per portion (cut 48)

Calories	Carbohydrate	Protein	Fat	Cholesterol	Sodium	Fiber	Iron
50 kcal	11 g	2 g	0 g	0 mg	213 mg	0.4 g	0.5 mg

TOMATO ASPIC

Yield: 40 or 48 portions or 1 pan, 12 × 20 × 2 inches   *Portion:* 2¼ × 2½ or 2 × 2½ inches

Ingredient	Amount	Procedure
Gelatin, unflavored	4 oz	Sprinkle gelatin over cold water.
Water, cold	1 qt	Let stand for 10 minutes.
Tomato juice	1 gal	Combine tomato juice and seasonings.
Onions, small, sliced	2	Boil for 5 minutes. Strain.
Bay leaf	1	Add gelatin mixture. Stir until dissolved.
Celery stalks	4	
Cloves, whole	8	
Dry mustard	2 tsp	
Sugar, granulated	14 oz	
Salt	1 Tbsp	
Vinegar or lemon juice	2 cups	Add vinegar or lemon juice.
		Pour into a 12 × 20 × 2-inch counter pan.
		Place in refrigerator to congeal.
		Cut 5 × 8 for 40 portions. Cut 6 × 8 for 48 portions.

Approximate nutritive values per portion (cut 48)

Calories	Carbohydrate	Protein	Fat	Cholesterol	Sodium	Fiber	Iron
58 kcal	13 g	3 g	0 g	0 mg	435 mg	1 g	0.5 mg

Fruit Salad Recipes

WALDORF SALAD

Yield: 50 portions or 6 qt   *Portion:* ⅓ cup (3 oz)

Ingredient	Amount	Procedure
Whipping cream (optional) Mayonnaise or salad dressing	½ cup 2 cups	Whip cream. Combine with mayonnaise.
Apples, tart, peeled or unpeeled Fruit juice	8 lb EP (see Note)	Dice apples into fruit juice to prevent apples from turning dark. Drain and stir fruit into salad dressing.
Celery, chopped Salt Sugar, granulated (optional) Walnuts, coarsely chopped	2 lb EP 1 oz (1½ Tbsp) 6 oz 8 oz	Add celery, seasonings, and nuts to apples. Mix lightly until all ingredients are coated with dressing. Serve with No. 12 dipper.

Approximate nutritive values per portion

Calories	Carbohydrate	Protein	Fat	Cholesterol	Sodium	Fiber	Iron
158 kcal	16 g	1 g	11 g	8 mg	260 mg	2 g	0.5 mg

Notes

- Add walnuts only to salad that will be used immediately, as nuts will cause the salad to become gray.
- Fruit Salad Dressing (p. 650) may be substituted for mayonnaise.
- Use acetic fruit juice such as diluted lemon, orange, or pineapple. Use only enough juice to moisten the cut surface of apples.

Variations

- **Apple Cabbage Salad.** Use 6 lb diced apples and 4 lb crisp shredded cabbage. Omit celery. Sour cream or plain yogurt may be substituted for half the mayonnaise.
- **Apple Carrot Salad.** Use 6 lb diced apples, 3 lb shredded carrots, and only 1 lb chopped celery.
- **Apple Celery Salad.** Delete walnuts. Add 8 oz marshmallows.
- **Apple Date Salad.** Substitute 2 lb cut dates for celery.
- **Apple Fruit Salad.** Substitute 4 lb fresh fruit in season for half the apples.

APPLE PEAR SALAD

Yield: 50 plated salads

Ingredient	Amount	Procedure
Apples, Red Delicious	8–10 lb	Core and section fruit according to directions on pp. 117 and 120.
Pears, Anjou	8–10 lb	Section each pear and apple into 6–8 slices. Dip in diluted lemon juice to reduce discoloration.
Leaf lettuce leaves	50	Line salad plate with lettuce leaf.
Blue cheese, crumbled	3 lb	Alternate 3–4 sections of each fruit in a pinwheel-like arrangement on top of lettuce leaf.
Apple Cider Dressing (p. 649)	1 qt	Sprinkle with 1 oz blue cheese. Drizzle with 1–2 Tbsp Apple Cider Dressing.

Approximate nutritive values per portion

Calories	Carbohydrate	Protein	Fat	Cholesterol	Sodium	Fiber	Iron
250 kcal	35 g	6.6 g	11 g	20 mg	407 mg	4 g	1 mg

ACINI DE PEPE FRUIT SALAD

Yield: 50 portions   *Portion:* 4 oz

Ingredient	Amount	Procedure
Acini de pepe (see Note) Water, boiling Salt	2 lb 6 oz AP 2 gal 1 oz (1½ Tbsp)	Cook pasta according to directions on p. 507. Drain and cool slightly. There should be 7 lb 8 oz cooked product. Save for later step.
Sugar, granulated Flour, all-purpose Salt	7 oz 2 Tbsp 1 tsp	Combine sugar, flour, and salt in steam-jacketed kettle.
Pineapple juice, drained from pineapple in later step	1½ cups	Pour juice slowly into mixture while stirring with a wire whip. Cook over moderate heat, stirring until slightly thickened.
Eggs, beaten	2 (3 oz)	Stir a small amount of the hot mixture into eggs, then stir eggs into the hot mixture. Cook and stir until thickened, 190°F.
Fresh lemon juice	1 Tbsp	Add juice. Cool to room temperature. Combine with cooked pasta. Mix lightly. Chill.

Mandarin oranges, canned,
  drained
Crushed pineapple, canned,
  drained
Pineapple tidbits, canned,
  drained
	1 lb
	
	1 lb 12 oz
	
	1 lb 12 oz
		Add fruit to pasta mixture.
		Mix lightly but thoroughly.

Whipped topping	1¼ cups	Whip topping to stiff peaks. There should be 2½ cups whipped. Fold into salad. Chill until served. Serve with No. 8 dipper.

Approximate nutritive values per portion

Calories	Carbohydrate	Protein	Fat	Cholesterol	Sodium	Fiber	Iron
144 kcal	28 g	3 g	2 g	14 mg	246 mg	0.4 g	1 mg

Note

- Acini de pepe is a small round pasta resembling BB shot (p. 108).

AMBROSIA FRUIT SALAD

Yield: 50 portions   *Portion:* 2½ oz

Ingredient	Amount	Procedure
Mandarin oranges, canned, drained	3 lb	Combine fruits, marshmallows, and coconut.
Pineapple tidbits, canned, drained	3 lb 8 oz	Add sour cream to fruit. Toss lightly to combine.
Marshmallows, miniature	12 oz	Serve with No. 12 dipper.
Coconut, shredded	6 oz	
Sour cream	12 oz	

Approximate nutritive values per portion

Calories	Carbohydrate	Protein	Fat	Cholesterol	Sodium	Fiber	Iron
82 kcal	15 g	1 g	3 g	3 mg	17 mg	1 g	0.5 mg

Notes

- Salad does not hold well and is best when served soon after mixing.
- Plain unflavored yogurt may be substituted for sour cream.

GRAPEFRUIT ORANGE SALAD

Yield: 50 portions   *Portion:* 2 orange sections, 3 grapefruit sections

Ingredient	Amount	Procedure
Grapefruit, medium	16	Peel and section fruit according to directions on p. 119
Oranges, large	17	For each salad, arrange 3 grapefruit sections and 2 orange sections, alternately on lettuce or other salad greens. Serve with Celery Seed Fruit Dressing (p. 650) or Honey French Dressing (p. 645).

Approximate nutritive values per portion

Calories	Carbohydrate	Protein	Fat	Cholesterol	Sodium	Fiber	Iron
45 kcal	11 g	1 g	0 g	0 mg	0 mg	2 g	0 mg

Variations

- **Citrus Pomegranate Salad.** Arrange grapefruit and orange sections on curly endive. Sprinkle pomegranate seeds over fruit. Serve with Celery Seed Dressing (pp. 644 and 650).
- **Fresh Fruit Salad Bowl.** Place chopped lettuce or other salad greens in individual salad bowls, 2 oz per bowl. Arrange wedges of cantaloupe, honeydew melon, and avocado, and sections of orange or grapefruit on the lettuce. Garnish with green grapes, bing cherries, or fresh strawberries. Fresh pineapple, peaches, or apricots also are good in this salad. Serve with Celery Seed Fruit Dressing (p. 650) or Honey French Dressing (p. 645).
- **Grapefruit Apple Salad.** Substitute wedges of unpeeled red apples for oranges.
- **Grapefruit-Orange-Avocado Salad.** Place avocado wedges between grapefruit and orange sections. Garnish with fresh strawberries.
- **Grapefruit-Orange-Pear Salad.** Alternate slices of fresh pear with grapefruit and orange sections.

SPICED APPLE SALAD

Yield: 50 portions   *Portion:* 1 apple

Ingredient	Amount	Procedure
Sugar, granulated	6 lb	Combine sugar, water, flavorings, and coloring.
Water	2 qt	Boil for about 5 minutes to form a thin syrup.
Vinegar, cider	1 cup	Set aside for next step.
Red food coloring	½ tsp	
Cloves, whole	1 oz	
Cinnamon sticks	1 oz	
Fresh apples	50	Core and peel apples. Leave apples whole unless they are large; then cut in half crosswise. Place apples in a flat pan. Pour syrup over apples. Cook on top of range or in oven until tender. Turn while cooking. Cool.
Celery, chopped	8 oz	Combine celery and nuts.
Nuts, chopped	4 oz	Add mayonnaise and salt.
Mayonnaise	¾ cup	Fill centers of cooked apples with this mixture.
Salt	½ tsp	

Approximate nutritive values per portion

Calories	Carbohydrate	Protein	Fat	Cholesterol	Sodium	Fiber	Iron
165 kcal	34 g	1 g	4 g	0 mg	61 mg	2 g	0.5 mg

Notes

- Select apples that will hold their shape when cooked, such as Jonathan, Rome Beauty, or Winesap. Approximately 12 lb will be needed.
- 8 oz softened cream cheese may be substituted for mayonnaise.

FROZEN FRUIT SALAD

Yield: 48 portions or 1 pan, 12 × 20 × 2 inches   *Portion:* 4 oz

Ingredient	Amount	Procedure
Gelatin, unflavored	1 oz	Sprinkle gelatin over cold water.
Water, cold	½ cup	Let stand for 10 minutes.
Orange juice	1¾ cups	Combine juices and heat to boiling point.
Pineapple juice	1¾ cups	Add gelatin mixture and stir to dissolve.
		Cool until slightly congealed.
Whipping cream	2 cups	Whip cream. Combine with mayonnaise.
Mayonnaise	1 cup	Fold into the slightly congealed gelatin mixture.
Pineapple chunks, canned, drained	1 lb 12 oz	Fold fruit into gelatin mixture.
Orange sections, cut in halves	1 lb 8 oz	Pour into a 12 × 20 × 2-inch counter pan or into molds.
Sliced peaches, canned, drained	1 lb 8 oz	Freeze.
Bananas, diced	2 lb	Cut 6 × 8.
Pecans, chopped	12 oz	
Maraschino cherries	8 oz	
Marshmallows, miniature	8 oz	

Approximate nutritive values per portion

Calories	Carbohydrate	Protein	Fat	Cholesterol	Sodium	Fiber	Iron
178 kcal	19 g	2 g	12 g	14 mg	33 mg	2 g	0.5 mg

Notes

- Whipped topping may be used in place of whipped cream.
- Other combinations of fruit (a total of 8 lb) may be used.

Entrée Salad Recipes

CHEF'S SALAD BOWL

Yield: 50 portions   *Portion:* 7 oz

Ingredient	Amount	Procedure
Head lettuce or mixed greens	12 lb	Cut or tear lettuce into bite-size pieces. Portion into individual salad bowls, 4 oz per bowl.
Cooked turkey	6 lb	Cut meat and cheese into thin strips.
Cooked ham	3 lb	Arrange on top of lettuce: 2 oz turkey, 1 oz ham, 1 oz cheese per bowl.
Cheddar or Swiss cheese	3 lb	
Green bell pepper rings	50 (8 lb AP)	Garnish with 1 pepper ring, 2 tomato wedges, and 2 egg quarters.
Tomatoes, cut into wedges	6 lb AP	
Eggs, hard cooked, quartered (p. 384)	25	
Salad dressing (see Note)	1½–2 qt	Serve salad with choice of dressings.

Approximate nutritive values per portion

Calories	Carbohydrate	Protein	Fat	Cholesterol	Sodium	Fiber	Iron
457 kcal	15 g	35 g	29 g	200 mg	987 mg	4 g	3 mg

Notes

- Potentially hazardous food. *Food Safety Standards:* Hold food for service at an internal temperature of 41°F or below. Do not mix old product with new. Keep leftover product chilled at 41°F or below. See p. 167 for cooling procedures.
- Suggested salad dressings: mayonnaise, Thousand Island, Roquefort, creamy French, or ranch.

Variations

- **Chicken and Bacon Salad.** Delete ham and turkey. Cut 6 lb cooked chicken into strips or cubes and mix with salad greens. Sprinkle 4 lb chopped, crisply cooked bacon over tops of salads, 1 oz per salad.
- **Seafood Chef Salad.** Delete turkey and ham. Substitute 1 oz salmon, drained and broken into small chunks, 1 oz shrimp pieces, or 2 whole shrimp for each salad.
- **Taco Salad.** Fry 50 10-inch flour tortillas by forming in basket shape around a large dipper or can. Submerge tortillas in hot fat, while still formed around dipper or can, for 20–30 seconds. Remove from fat and drain on paper towel. Prepare ground beef mixture (p. 464). Chill. Prepare lettuce mixture (p. 454). In bottom of shell basket, place 2½ oz lettuce mixture, then 4 oz cold ground beef mixture on top of lettuce. Sprinkle with sliced black olives and cheddar cheese. Serve with Salsa (p. 702).

CHICKEN SALAD

Yield: 50 portions or 6¼ qt   *Portion:* ½ cup (4 oz)

Ingredient	Amount	Procedure
Cooked chicken	8 lb	Cut chicken into ½-inch cubes.
Eggs, hard cooked (p. 384)	12	Peel and dice eggs.
Celery, diced	3 lb	Combine all ingredients. Mix lightly. Chill quickly to below 41°F.
Onion, minced	2 Tbsp	Serve with No. 8 dipper.
Salt	2 Tbsp	
White pepper	1 tsp	
Mayonnaise	1 qt	
Fresh lemon juice	4 tsp	

Approximate nutritive values per portion

Calories	Carbohydrate	Protein	Fat	Cholesterol	Sodium	Fiber	Iron
227 kcal	2 g	23 g	21 g	122 mg	446 mg	0.4 g	1 mg

Notes

- Potentially hazardous food. *Food Safety Standards:* Hold food for service at an internal temperature of 41°F or below. Do not mix old product with new. Keep leftover product chilled at 41°F or below. See p. 167 for cooling procedures.
- Chilling the ingredients before combining shortens the amount of time product is in the temperature danger zone (above 41°F). 24–25 lb AP chicken will yield approximately 8 lb cooked meat.
- Cubed chicken may be marinated for 2 hours in ⅔ cup French Dressing (p. 644).

Variations

- **Chicken-Avocado-Orange Salad.** Delete eggs. Gently stir into chicken mixture 1 qt diced orange segments, drained, 12 oz broken or slivered toasted almonds, and 6 oz chopped pimento. Just before serving, add 6 diced avocados.
- **Crunchy Chicken Salad.** Add 8 oz sliced water chestnuts or toasted slivered almonds or walnuts.
- **Curried Chicken Salad.** Add 1 Tbsp curry powder to mayonnaise.
- **Fruited Chicken Salad.** Just before serving, add 2 lb 8 oz seedless grapes or pineapple chunks, drained, and 8 oz sunflower seeds.
- **Mandarin Chicken Salad.** Delete eggs and pepper. Reduce mayonnaise to 2 cups. Add 2 cups sour cream. Substitute 2 Tbsp lime juice for lemon juice. Gently fold in 1 No. 10 can mandarin oranges and 1 No. 10 can pineapple tidbits, well drained.
- **Turkey Salad.** Substitute turkey for chicken.

MARINATED CHICKEN AND FRESH FRUIT SALAD

Yield: 50 portions   *Portion:* 3 oz chicken + 3 oz greens + 3 oz fruit + 2 oz dressing

Ingredient	Amount	Procedure
Chicken breasts, 3 oz	50	Prepare and grill chicken as for Tarragon Chicken, p. 502. Chill quickly to below 41°F.
Head lettuce (iceberg) Leaf lettuce, Bibb or romaine	7 lb 3 lb	Cut or tear lettuce into bite-size pieces.
Fresh fruit in season (see Note)	10–12 lb	Prepare fruit. Peel if necessary and cut into wedges, medium-size chunks, or clusters.
Leaf lettuce	2 lb	
Golden Fruit Dressing (p. 650)	3 qt	

TO ASSEMBLE:

1. Line 50 9-inch luncheon plates with leaf lettuce.
2. Arrange 3 oz cut or torn greens on each plate.
3. Place 3 oz grilled chicken strips in center of plate.
4. Arrange 3 oz fruit around the chicken.
5. In a side dish, serve Golden Fruit Dressing.

Approximate nutritive values per portion

Calories	Carbohydrate	Protein	Fat	Cholesterol	Sodium	Fiber	Iron
462 kcal	34 g	16 g	31 g	39 mg	431 mg	2 g	2 mg

Notes

- Potentially hazardous food. *Food Safety Standards:* Hold food for service at an internal temperature of 41°F or below. Do not mix old product with new. Keep leftover product chilled at 41°F or below. See p. 167 for cooling procedures.
- Choose at least three kinds of fruit that complement each other. Suggested fruits: cantaloupe wedges, watermelon chunks, fresh pineapple spears or chunks, whole fresh strawberries, papaya pieces, mango slices, green or red grapes.

Variation

- **Blackened Chicken Salad.** Season 25 chicken breasts with Cajun Seasoning (p. 727). Cook as for Grilled Chicken Breast. Increase lettuce to 13 lb. Arrange 4 oz lettuce on plate and top with one-half sliced chicken breast. Garnish with chopped tomato and yellow bell pepper. Dress as desired.

CHICKEN AND PASTA SALAD PLATE

Yield: 50 portions   *Portion:* 7 oz

Ingredient	Amount	Procedure
Rotini	1 lb 2 oz AP (2 lb 8 oz cooked)	Cook according to directions on p. 507. Drain.
Water, boiling	1 gal	
Salt	1 Tbsp	
Vinegar, cider	2¾ cups	Combine in mixing bowl.
Fresh lemon juice	⅓ cup	
Prepared mustard	3 Tbsp	
Garlic cloves, minced	3	
Salt	2 Tbsp	
Oregano, dried, crumbled	1 tsp	
Black pepper	2 tsp	
Sugar, granulated	2 tsp	
Salad oil	3½ cups	Add oil very gradually while mixing on medium speed with a wire whip attachment.
Cooked chicken, cut in 1-inch pieces	8 lb 8 oz	Add chicken to dressing. Toss to coat well. Add cooked rotini and mix well. Chill quickly to 41°F.
Broccoli florets	1 lb 4 oz	Steam broccoli until tender-crisp. Add to marinated mixture shortly before serving.
Cherry tomatoes, cut in half	3 lb	Add to marinated mixture shortly before serving.
Fresh zucchini squash, cut in julienne strips	2 lb 4 oz	
Carrots, shredded	10 oz	
Green onions, chopped	8 oz	
Leaf lettuce	2 lb	Cover plate with leaf lettuce.
Hard rolls	50	Portion 7 oz salad onto lettuce. Place one hard roll on each salad plate shortly before service.

Approximate nutritive values per portion

Calories	Carbohydrate	Protein	Fat	Cholesterol	Sodium	Fiber	Iron
498 kcal	43 g	29 g	23 g	64 mg	837 mg	1 g	4 mg

Notes

- Potentially hazardous food. *Food Safety Standards:* Hold food for service at an internal temperature of 41°F or below. Do not mix old product with new. Keep leftover product chilled at 41°F or below. See p. 167 for cooling procedures.
- Chilling ingredients before combining shortens the time product is in the temperature danger zone (above 40°F).
- Salad may be served in a bowl or on a plate with a bed of shredded lettuce.

SHRIMP TORTELLINI SALAD PLATE

Yield: 50 portions   *Portion:* 6 oz salad mixture

Ingredient	Amount	Procedure
Spinach tortellini, cheese-stuffed, frozen	4 lb AP (6 lb cooked)	Cook tortellini in boiling water for 3–5 minutes. Drain. Place in bowl.
Italian Dressing (p. 645)	2¼ qt	Pour dressing over pasta and toss gently to coat. Chill quickly to 41°F or less.
Salad shrimp, cooked, frozen	5 lb	Thaw shrimp under cold running water. Drain well and add to cold pasta.
Celery, thinly sliced	1 lb 10 oz	Add to pasta mixture. Toss well.
Carrots, cut into ¾-inch-long thin julienne strips	12 oz	Cover. Refrigerate until chilled to 41°F or less.
Green onions, thinly sliced	10 oz	
Sliced water chestnuts, canned, drained	1 lb 6 oz	
Leaf lettuce	2 lb 12 oz	Cover plate with leaf lettuce. Portion 6 oz salad onto lettuce.
Black olives	1 lb	Garnish plate with 3 black olives and 1 cherry tomato.
Cherry tomatoes	1 lb	Serve with 2 bread sticks.
Bread sticks	100	

Approximate nutritive values per portion

Calories	Carbohydrate	Protein	Fat	Cholesterol	Sodium	Fiber	Iron
704 kcal	88 g	24 g	28 g	89 mg	2465 mg	3 g	5 mg

Notes

- Potentially hazardous food. *Food Safety Standards:* Hold food for service at an internal temperature of 41°F or below. Do not mix old product with new. Keep leftover product chilled at 41°F or below. See p. 167 for cooling procedures.
- Chilling ingredients before combining shortens the time product is in the temperature danger zone (above 41°F).

POACHED SALMON ON FIELD GREENS

Yield: 50 portions   *Portion:* 4 oz salmon fillet +4 oz greens +1–2 oz dressing

Ingredient	Amount	Procedure
Salmon fillets, poached (4 oz)	50	Poach salmon according to directions on p. 411.
Lettuce assortment (see Note)	12 lb 8 oz	Place 4 oz lettuce on plate. Drizzle with ½–1 oz Vinaigrette Dressing. Carefully place salmon fillet on top of greens.
Vinaigrette Dressing (p. 647)	2 qt	Drizzle with ½–1 oz Vinaigrette Dressing. Garnish with fresh herbs or edible flowers. (See p. 128 for suggestions.)

Notes

- Potentially hazardous food. *Food Safety Standards:* Hold food for service at an internal temperature of 41°F or below. Do not mix old product with new. Keep leftover product chilled at 41°F or below. See p. 167 for cooling procedures.
- One of several commercial lettuce assortments may be used or an assortment made using several different salad greens (p. 121).
- Horseradish Caper Sauce (p. 694) may be ladled over salmon fillet in place of Vinaigrette Dressing.

CRAB SALAD

Yield: 50 portions or 6 qt   *Portion:* ½ cup (4 oz)

Ingredient	Amount	Procedure
Eggs, hard cooked (p. 384)	30	Peel eggs and chop coarsely.
Almonds, blanched, slivered (optional)	1 lb	Add eggs and other ingredients to crabmeat. Mix lightly. Chill quickly to below 41°F.
Black olives, sliced	1 lb	Serve with No. 10 dipper.
Fresh lemon juice	⅓ cup	
Mayonnaise	1 qt	
Crabmeat, flaked	5 lb	

Approximate nutritive values per portion

Calories	Carbohydrate	Protein	Fat	Cholesterol	Sodium	Fiber	Iron
281 kcal	4 g	14 g	24 g	183 mg	445 mg	1 g	1 mg

Notes

- Potentially hazardous food. *Food Safety Standards:* Hold food for service at an internal temperature of 41°F or below. Do not mix old product with new. Keep leftover product chilled at 41°F or below. See p. 167 for cooling procedures.
- Chilling ingredients before combining shortens the time product is in the temperature danger zone (above 41°F).
- Olives may be deleted and 1 lb diced cucumbers added.
- If desired, omit mayonnaise and marinate with French Dressing (p. 644).

Variation

- **Lobster Salad.** Substitute lobster for crabmeat.

PASTA AND CRAB SALAD

Yield: 50 portions   *Portion:* 2½ oz

Ingredient	Amount	Procedure
Radiatore Water Salt	1 lb 8 oz 1½ gal 1 oz (1½ Tbsp)	Cook pasta according to directions on p. 507. Drain. Yield should be 3 lb cooked radiatore.
Lemon Basil Dressing (p. 647)	3¾ cups	Add dressing. Toss to coat pasta. Chill to below 41°F.
Green onions, finely chopped Snow peas, thawed, uncooked	2 oz 1 lb 4 oz	Add onions and snow peas. Toss.
Crabmeat, diced	2 lb	Add crabmeat. Toss. Keep chilled below 41°F.

Approximate nutritive values per portion

Calories	Carbohydrate	Protein	Fat	Cholesterol	Sodium	Fiber	Iron
139 kcal	14 g	5 g	7 g	18 mg	416 mg	0.3 g	1 mg

Notes

- Potentially hazardous food. *Food Safety Standards:* Hold food for service at an internal temperature of 41°F or below. Do not mix old product with new. Keep leftover product chilled at 41°F or below. See p. 167 for cooling procedures.
- Chilling ingredients before combining shortens the time product is in the temperature danger zone (above 41°F).
- Cooked shrimp, cooked scallops, or lobster may be substituted for crabmeat.

SHRIMP SALAD

Yield: 50 portions or 6¼ qt   *Portion:* ½ cup (4 oz)

Ingredient	Amount	Procedure
Cooked shrimp (see Note)	6 lb	Cut shrimp into ½-inch pieces. Place in bowl.
Celery, diced	2 lb	Add vegetables to shrimp.
Cucumber, diced	1 lb	
Lettuce, chopped (optional)	1 head	
Mayonnaise	1 qt	Combine mayonnaise and seasonings.
Fresh lemon juice	2 Tbsp	Add to shrimp mixture. Mix lightly. Chill quickly to below 41°F.
Salt	2 tsp	Serve with No. 10 dipper.
Paprika	1 tsp	
Prepared mustard	2 tsp	

Approximate nutritive values per portion

Calories	Carbohydrate	Protein	Fat	Cholesterol	Sodium	Fiber	Iron
187 kcal	2 g	12 g	15 g	117 mg	327 mg	0.4 g	2 mg

Notes

- Potentially hazardous food. *Food Safety Standards:* Hold food for service at an internal temperature of 41°F or below. Do not mix old product with new. Keep leftover product chilled at 41°F or below. See p. 167 for cooling procedures.
- Chilling ingredients before combining shortens the time product is in the temperature danger zone (above 41°F).
- 12 lb raw shrimp in shell or 10 lb raw, peeled, and deveined shrimp will yield the 6 lb cooked shrimp needed. Cook according to directions on p. 401.
- 1 dozen hard-cooked eggs (p. 384), coarsely chopped, may be added. Reduce shrimp to 5 lb.
- Salad may be garnished with tomato wedges or served in a tomato cup.

SHRIMP RICE SALAD

Yield: 50 portions   *Portion:* ½ cup (4 oz)

Ingredient	Amount	Procedure
Rice, converted	1 lb	Cook rice according to directions on p. 542.
Water	1¼ qt	Chill.
Salt	1 Tbsp	
Margarine or vegetable oil	1 Tbsp	
Celery	1 lb 8 oz	Cut celery in thin slices crosswise.
Green bell peppers	1 lb	Slice peppers in thin strips.
Cooked shrimp, chilled	5 lb	Combine shrimp, rice, and vegetables.
Vinegar, cider	1 cup	Combine and pour over shrimp-rice mixture.
Salad oil	½ cup	Marinate in refrigerator for at least 3 hours.
Worcestershire sauce	2 Tbsp	
Sugar, granulated	2 Tbsp	
Salt	1 Tbsp	
Curry powder	2 tsp	
Ginger, ground	¾ tsp	
Black pepper	½ tsp	
Pineapple chunks, canned or frozen, drained	3 lb	Just before serving, add pineapple. Serve with No. 8 dipper.

Approximate nutritive values per portion

Calories	Carbohydrate	Protein	Fat	Cholesterol	Sodium	Fiber	Iron
122 kcal	13 g	10 g	3 g	89 mg	377 mg	1 g	2 mg

Notes

- Potentially hazardous food. *Food Safety Standards:* Hold food for service at an internal temperature of 41°F or below. Do not mix old product with new. Keep leftover product chilled at 41°F or below. See p. 167 for cooling procedures.
- Chilling ingredients before combining shortens time the product is in the temperature danger zone (above 41°F).

TUNA PASTA SALAD PLATE

Yield: 50 portions   *Portion:* 3½ oz salad mixture

Ingredient	Amount	Procedure
Shell macaroni	2 lb AP (6 lb cooked)	Cook macaroni according to directions on p. 507. Drain. Place in bowl.
Water, boiling	2 gal	
Salt	2 oz	
Vegetable oil	2 Tbsp	
Italian Dressing (p. 645)	1 qt	Pour dressing over cooked macaroni. Stir to coat evenly. Cover and refrigerate for 6–8 hours.
Canned tuna	2 lb	Drain tuna. Carefully fold into macaroni.
Green bell peppers	1 lb 6 oz	Cut peppers into strips approximately 1 inch long. Add to macaroni mixture.
Stuffed green olives, chopped	4 oz	Add chopped olives to macaroni mixture.
Lettuce leaves	1 lb 8 oz	Place 1 lettuce leaf off center on dinner plate. Place 3½ oz (¾ cup) salad on lettuce.
Eggs, hard cooked (p. 384)	25	Place half an egg on one side of macaroni salad.
Fresh tomatoes	6 lb	Cut each tomato into 8 wedges. Place 2 wedges on other side of salad. Place one hard roll on plate shortly before serving.
Hard rolls	50	

Approximate nutritive values per portion

Calories	Carbohydrate	Protein	Fat	Cholesterol	Sodium	Fiber	Iron
402 kcal	50 g	17 g	15 g	112 mg	651 mg	1 g	4 mg

Notes

- Potentially hazardous food. *Food Safety Standards:* Hold food for service at an internal temperature of 41°F or below. Do not mix old product with new. Keep leftover product chilled at 41°F or below. See p. 167 for cooling procedures.
- Chilling ingredients before combining shortens time product is in the temperature danger zone (above 41°F).

TUNA SALAD

Yield: 50 portions or 6¼ qt   *Portion:* ½ cup (4 oz)

Ingredient	Amount	Procedure
Eggs, hard cooked (p. 384)	12	Peel and dice eggs.
Celery, chopped	1 lb	Add vegetables, relish, and eggs to tuna. Mix lightly.
Cucumbers, diced	1 lb	
Onion, minced	2 oz	
Pickle relish, drained	8 oz	
Tuna, flaked	7 lb	
Mayonnaise	1 qt	Add mayonnaise to tuna mixture. Mix lightly to blend. Chill quickly to below 41°F. Serve with No. 8 dipper.

Approximate nutritive values per portion

Calories	Carbohydrate	Protein	Fat	Cholesterol	Sodium	Fiber	Iron
228 kcal	3 g	18 g	16 g	80 mg	374 mg	0.2 g	1 mg

Notes

- Potentially hazardous food. *Food Safety Standards:* Hold food for service at an internal temperature of 41°F or below. Do not mix old product with new. Keep leftover product chilled at 41°F or below. See p. 167 for cooling procedures.
- Chilling ingredients before combining shortens time product is in the temperature danger zone (above 41°F).

Variations

- **Salmon Salad.** Substitute salmon for tuna.
- **Tuna Apple Salad.** Substitute tart, diced apples for cucumbers. Omit pickle relish.
- **Tuna Pea Salad.** Delete eggs and minced onion. Substitute 5 cups sour cream mixed with ½ cup lemon juice for the mayonnaise. Add 2 lb frozen green peas, thawed, 8 oz green bell pepper, and 8 oz sliced green onions.

STUFFED TOMATO SALAD

Yield: 50 portions   *Portion:* 1 tomato

Ingredient	Amount	Procedure
Tomatoes, medium size	50	Place tomatoes in a wire basket and dip in boiling water. Let stand for 1 minute. Dip in cold water. Remove skins.
Chicken, crab, shrimp, tuna, or egg salad (chilled)	10 lb	Turn tomato stem end down. Cut, not quite through, into fourths. Fill with No. 12 dipper of salad.

Approximate nutritive values per portion

Calories	Carbohydrate	Protein	Fat	Cholesterol	Sodium	Fiber	Iron
248 kcal	13 g	13 g	16 g	30 mg	628 mg	3 g	2 mg

Notes

- Potentially hazardous food. *Food Safety Standards:* Hold food for service at an internal temperature of 41°F or below. Do not mix old product with new. Keep leftover product chilled at 41°F or below. See p. 167 for cooling procedures.
- 50 medium-size tomatoes will weigh approximately 12 lb.

Variations

- **Tomato Cabbage Salad.** Combine 1 lb cabbage and 1 lb celery, finely chopped, 1 Tbsp salt, and 1 cup mayonnaise for salad mixture. Fill tomato cups, using No. 40 dipper.
- **Tomato Cottage Cheese Salad.** Substitute 6 lb cottage cheese for salad mixture. Fill tomato cups, using No. 20 dipper.

COTTAGE CHEESE SALAD

Yield: 50 portions or 6 qt   *Portion:* ½ cup (4 oz)

Ingredient	Amount	Procedure
Fresh tomatoes, peeled and diced	3 lb	Prepare vegetables.
Green bell peppers, chopped	4 oz	
Celery, diced	1 lb	
Cucumber, diced	1 lb	
Radishes, sliced	8 oz	
Cottage cheese, dry curd (see Note)	6 lb	Just before serving, add vegetables and mix all ingredients gently.
Salt	1 oz (1½ Tbsp)	
Mayonnaise	3 cups	

Approximate nutritive values per portion

Calories	Carbohydrate	Protein	Fat	Cholesterol	Sodium	Fiber	Iron
150 kcal	3 g	10 g	11 g	11 mg	328 mg	0.4 g	0.5 mg

Notes

- Potentially hazardous food. *Food Safety Standards:* Hold food for service at an internal temperature of 41°F or below. Do not mix old product with new. Keep leftover product chilled at 41°F or below. See p. 167 for cooling procedures.
- Chilling ingredients before combining shortens time product is in the temperature danger zone (above 41° F).
- If creamed cottage cheese is used, reduce mayonnaise to 1 cup and omit salt.

DELI PLATE

Yield: 50 portions   *Portion:* 2½ oz salad + 2 oz meat and cheese

Ingredient	Amount	Procedure
Pasta Salad (p. 606) or Potato Salad (p. 611) or Macaroni Salad (p. 607)	9 lb	Prepare salad.
Pastrami, corned beef, or other cold cuts	3 lb	Wafer-slice meat.
Lettuce leaves	1 lb 8 oz	Place lettuce leaf on dinner plate.
Swiss cheese, 1-oz slices	3 lb	Place one 1-oz cheese slice on lettuce.
		Portion 1 oz pastrami on cheese.
		Place No. 16 dipper pasta, potato, or macaroni salad on plate.
Tomatoes, sliced	6 lb 8 oz EP	Arrange on plate:
Dill pickle spears, drained	1 lb 8 oz	2 tomato slices
Black olives	6 oz	1 dill pickle spear
		1 black olive
Rye bread	100 slices	Place alongside meat on plates.

Note

- Potentially hazardous food. *Food Safety Standards:* Hold food for service at an internal temperature of 41°F or below. Do not mix old product with new. Keep leftover product chilled at 41°F or below. See p. 167 for cooling procedures.

Variation

- Ham rolls or slices, sliced turkey, deviled or hard-cooked eggs, green bell pepper rings, green onions, cucumber slices, onion slices, cherry tomatoes, or marinated mushrooms may be used.

TURKEY CROISSANT SALAD PLATE

Yield: 50 portions   *Portion:* 2½ oz turkey

Ingredient	Amount	Procedure
Fresh spinach, raw	2 lb EP	Prepare vegetables and fruits.
Fresh tomatoes, sliced	7 lb	
Fresh navel oranges, unpeeled, sliced	3 lb 3 oz	
Grapes, red seedless	6 lb	
Alfalfa sprouts	2 oz	
Smoked turkey, wafer-sliced	8 lb	
Croissants	50 (2½-oz size)	Assemble plates according to the following directions.

TO ASSEMBLE TURKEY CROISSANT PLATES:

1. Line ¾ of plate with ¾ oz spinach.
2. Place 2 tomato slices on spinach leaves.
3. Cut orange slices in half. Place beside tomato slices.
4. Place 2½ oz turkey beside orange slices.
5. Place 1 Tbsp alfalfa sprouts beside turkey.
6. Place a 2-oz cluster of grapes beside sprouts.
7. Place 1 croissant on plate.

Approximate nutritive values per portion

Calories	Carbohydrate	Protein	Fat	Cholesterol	Sodium	Fiber	Iron
304 kcal	31 g	17 g	14 g	88 mg	885 mg	3 g	3 mg

Notes

- Potentially hazardous food. *Food Safety Standards:* Hold food for service at an internal temperature of 41°F or below. Do not mix old product with new. Keep leftover product chilled at 41°F or below. See p. 167 for cooling procedures.
- Chicken salad, crab salad, shrimp salad, or other wafer-sliced deli meats may be substituted for smoked turkey. If substituting salad meat for solid meat, omit tomato slices and add another fruit (e.g., apples or plums).

FRUIT SALAD PLATE

Yield: 50 portions   *Portion:* 6 oz fruit + 4 oz salad or sherbet

Ingredient	Amount	Procedure
Fruit in season (3–4 selections from fruits listed in Note)	20 lb EP	Prepare fruit.
Cottage cheese, Chicken Salad (p. 624), or sherbet	12 lb	Prepare salad according to recipe, if using.
Nut bread sandwiches or muffins	50–100	
Lettuce	1 lb 8 oz	Prepare lettuce. Place lettuce leaf on dinner plate. Arrange fruit, salad, and bread on lettuce.

Note

• Choose a combination that offers contrast in shape, color, and flavor from the following lists:

Fruit suggestions

Apple wedges
Avocado wedges, slices, or halves
Bananas, cut in strips or chunks,
   rolled in chopped nuts
Cherries, sweet
Grape clusters, red or green
Grapefruit sections
Kiwi fruit
Mangoes
Melon: cantaloupe, honeydew,
   watermelon; cut in wedges,
   rings, or balls
Orange slices, half slices, sections
Papayas
Peach halves or slices: cream
   cheese filling, cranberry sauce,
   or cottage cheese in halves
Pear halves, filled, or slices
Pineapple chunks, spears, rings
Plums
Strawberries

Salad suggestions

Cheese strips or slices
Cottage cheese
Chicken salad
Sliced chicken or turkey
Ham roll

Bread suggestions

Hard roll
Muffin
Finger sandwich: chicken, tuna
Nut bread sandwich
Raisin bread–cream cheese sandwich

Garnishes (See p. 829 for additional garnish suggestions.)

Coconut
Lemon or lime wedge
Pomegranate seeds
Stuffed prune

Relish Recipes

BUTTERED APPLES

Yield: 50 portions or 7 qt   *Portion:* ½ cup (4 oz)

Ingredient	Amount	Procedure
Fresh apples	13 lb EP (16 lb AP)	Wash apples and cut into sections. Remove cores. Arrange in pan.
Margarine, melted Water, hot Sugar, granulated Salt	8 oz 2 cups 1 lb 8 oz 1 Tbsp	Mix remaining ingredients and pour over apples. Cover and simmer until apples are tender, approximately 1 hour.

Approximate nutritive values per portion

Calories	Carbohydrate	Protein	Fat	Cholesterol	Sodium	Fiber	Iron
155 kcal	32 g	0 g	4 g	0 mg	171 mg	3 g	0.5 mg

Notes

- Select apples that will hold their shape when cooked, such as Jonathan, Rome Beauty, or Winesap.
- Apple sections may be arranged in a counter pan and steamed until tender. Sprinkle margarine and sugar over the top and bake for 15–20 minutes.
- Hot buttered apples often are served in place of a vegetable.
- Frozen or canned apples may be used.

Variations

- **Apple Rings.** Cut rings of unpared apples and steam until tender. Add sugar and margarine and bake for 15 minutes.
- **Cinnamon Apples.** Cut pared apples into rings. Add cinnamon drops (red hots) for flavor and color. Proceed as for Buttered Apples, but reduce sugar to 12 oz.
- **Fried Apples.** Melt 1 lb margarine or butter in frying pan. Add sliced apples. Add 8 oz brown sugar, 1 tsp salt, and 1 tsp cinnamon. Cook apples, turning occasionally, until apples are lightly browned and just tender. Frozen apple slices, thawed and drained, may be used.

CRANBERRY RELISH (RAW)

Yield: 50 portions or 5 qt   *Portion:* ⅓ cup (3 oz)

Ingredient	Amount	Procedure
Oranges, unpeeled Apples, cored Cranberries, raw	3 (size 72) 5 lb 3 lb	Wash and quarter oranges and apples. Sort and wash cranberries. Put fruit through chopper or grinder.
Sugar, granulated	2 lb 4 oz	Add sugar to fruit and blend. Chill for 24 hours. Serve with No. 16 dipper as a relish or salad.

Approximate nutritive values per portion

Calories	Carbohydrate	Protein	Fat	Cholesterol	Sodium	Fiber	Iron
123 kcal	32 g	0 g	0 g	0 mg	0 mg	2 g	0 mg

Variation

- **Cranberry Orange Relish.** Delete apples. Increase oranges to 6 and sugar to 3 lb. Add ¼ cup lemon juice.

CRANBERRY SAUCE

Yield: 50 portions or 5 qt *Portion:* 1/3 cup

Ingredient	Amount	Procedure
Cranberries	4 lb AP	Wash cranberries. Discard soft berries.
Sugar, granulated	2 lb	Combine sugar and water. Bring to a boil.
Water	1¼ qt	Add cranberries and boil gently until skins burst. Do not overcook. Chill.

Approximate nutritive values per portion

Calories	Carbohydrate	Protein	Fat	Cholesterol	Sodium	Fiber	Iron
158 kcal	41 g	0 g	0 g	0 mg	0 mg	2 g	0 mg

Notes

- Make sauce at least 24 hours before using.
- Serve sauce chilled.
- Reduce water to 1 qt for a slightly thicker sauce.
- Substitute dark brown sugar for some or all of the granulated sugar for a darker sauce with a light molasses-like flavor.

Variations

- **Baked Cranberry Relish.** Wash and drain 4 lb cranberries. Stir in 2 lb 12 oz granulated sugar, 1/3 cup water, and 1 tsp cinnamon. Place berries in glass chafing dishes or other baking pan suitable for serving. Mix together 2½ cups chopped pecans, ½ cup grated fresh lemon rind, and 4 cups orange marmalade. Spread on top of berries. Bake at 350°F for 45 minutes. Serve warm.
- **Gingered Cranberry Sauce.** Substitute 2 cups orange juice for 2 cups of the water. Add ¼ cup finely chopped ginger and ¼ cup finely grated orange peel. Cook as for Cranberry Sauce.
- **Puréed Cranberry Sauce.** Add water to cranberries and cook until skins burst. Purée cranberries and add sugar. Cook until sugar is dissolved.
- **Royal Cranberry Sauce.** Make half of cranberry sauce recipe. When cool, add 3 chopped oranges, 1 lb chopped apples, 1 lb seeded white grapes, 1 lb diced pineapple, and 4 oz coarsely chopped pecans. Serve with No. 24 dipper as a relish. Yield: 1 gal.

CORN RELISH

Yield: 50 portions *Portion:* 3 oz

Ingredient	Amount	Procedure
Sugar, granulated	1 lb	Mix sugar, flour, and salt in steam-jacketed kettle or stockpot until well blended.
Flour, all-purpose	2 oz (½ cup)	
Salt	1 oz	
Water	1½ cups	Add to dry ingredients in kettle. Stir until smooth.
Vinegar, cider	1⅔ cups	Cook until thickened, stirring constantly.
Prepared mustard	6 Tbsp	
Corn, whole kernel, frozen, defrosted	6 lb	Place vegetables and seasonings in baker's bowl.
Fresh onion, finely chopped	2 oz	Pour hot dressing over corn and mix lightly.
Green bell pepper, chopped	3 oz	Serve chilled.
Celery seed	1½ tsp	
Pimento, chopped, drained	3 oz	

Approximate nutritive values per portion

Calories	Carbohydrate	Protein	Fat	Cholesterol	Sodium	Fiber	Iron
84 kcal	21 g	2 g	0 g	0 mg	247 mg	0 g	0.5 mg

Variation

- **Black Bean and Corn Relish.** Substitute 2 lb cooked black beans for 2 lb corn.

SAUERKRAUT RELISH

Yield: 50 portions   *Portion:* ⅓ cup (3 oz)

Ingredient	Amount	Procedure
Sauerkraut	1 No. 10 can	Combine all ingredients.
Carrots, shredded	1 lb	Refrigerate for at least 12 hours.
Celery, chopped	12 oz	
Onion, chopped	8 oz	
Green bell pepper, chopped	1 lb	
Sugar, granulated	1 lb 8 oz	

Approximate nutritive values per portion

Calories	Carbohydrate	Protein	Fat	Cholesterol	Sodium	Fiber	Iron
73 kcal	18 g	1 g	0 g	0 mg	399 mg	2 g	1 mg

Note

- Sauerkraut may be chopped before combining with other ingredients.

PICKLED BEETS

Yield: 50 portions or 2 gal   *Portion:* 3 oz

Ingredient	Amount	Procedure
Beets, canned, sliced or whole	2 No. 10 cans	Drain beets. Reserve 1 cup juice for next step.
Vinegar, cider	2 qt	Mix vinegar, sugars, spices, and liquid from beets.
Sugar, brown	1 lb	Heat to boiling point. Boil for 5 minutes.
Sugar, granulated	8 oz	Pour hot mixture over beets.
Salt	1 tsp	Chill for 24 hours before serving.
Black pepper	½ tsp	
Cinnamon sticks	2	
Cloves, whole	1 tsp	
Allspice, whole	1 tsp	

Approximate nutritive values per portion

Calories	Carbohydrate	Protein	Fat	Cholesterol	Sodium	Fiber	Iron
74 kcal	21 g	1 g	0 g	0 mg	246 mg	1 g	2 mg

Notes

- If using fresh beets, cook 14 lb AP according to directions on p. 770. Peel and slice, then proceed as in the recipe. Substitute 1 cup water for beet juice.
- Sliced onions, separated into rings, may be added.
- Granulated sugar may be substituted for brown sugar.

Variation

- **Pickled Red Onions.** Cut 3 lb red onions into ¼-inch-thick half rings. Place onions in a perforated pan or colander over sink. Pour 1½ gal boiling water over onions. Drain well. Put onions in baker's bowl and reserve for later step. Stir together 1 qt rice wine vinegar, 1 qt cold water, 1 Tbsp black pepper, 1 tsp salt, 3 Tbsp sugar, 2 tsp crushed red pepper (or less for less spicy onions), 6 bay leaves, and 12 sprigs fresh thyme. Stir onions into liquid mixture. Weigh down onions with a plate to keep them submerged. Cover with plastic film and refrigerate for 8–12 hours. Remove bay leaves. Serve cold. May hold for 7 days, but onions will lose crispness.

MINTED TABOULI

Yield: 50 portions   *Portion:* 2 oz

Ingredient	Amount	Procedure
Bulgur	8 oz	Combine bulgur and water in large mixing bowl. Let stand for
Water	1¼ qt	at least 2 hours.
		Drain well.
Fresh tomatoes, seeded and diced	1 lb	Add to bulgur.
Cucumbers, peeled and chopped	6 oz	
Red onions, finely chopped	6 oz	
Fresh parsley, chopped	2 oz	
Fresh mint leaves, coarsely chopped	½ oz	
Fresh lemon juice	1¼ cups	Blend juice, oil, and seasonings.
Olive oil	½ cup	Pour over bulgur mixture. Toss to blend. Cover.
Salt	2¼ tsp	Refrigerate for at least 12 hours before serving. Keeps well.
Black pepper	1 tsp	
Sugar, granulated	1½ tsp	

Approximate nutritive values per portion

Calories	Carbohydrate	Protein	Fat	Cholesterol	Sodium	Fiber	Iron
41 kcal	5 g	1 g	2 g	0 mg	100 mg	1 g	0.5 mg

Note

- Salad oil may be substituted for olive oil. Mint leaves may be omitted for plain tabouli.

Salad Dressing Recipes

MAYONNAISE

Yield: 1 gal

Ingredient	Amount	Procedure
Egg yolks (see Note)	8 (5 oz)	Place egg yolks and seasonings in mixer bowl.
Salt	2 oz (3 Tbsp)	Mix thoroughly, using a wire whip.
Paprika	2 tsp	
Dry mustard	2 Tbsp	
Vinegar, cider	¼ cup	Add vinegar and blend.
Salad oil	2 qt	Add oil very slowly, beating steadily on high speed until an emulsion is formed. Oil may then be added, ½ cup at a time and later 1 cup at a time, beating well after each addition.
Vinegar, cider	¼ cup	Add vinegar. Beat well.
Salad oil	2 qt	Continue beating and adding oil until all oil has been added and emulsified.

Approximate nutritive values per ounce

Calories	Carbohydrate	Protein	Fat	Cholesterol	Sodium	Fiber	Iron
246 kcal	0 g	0 g	28 g	14 mg	150 mg	0 g	0 mg

Notes

- Potentially hazardous food. *Food Safety Standards:* Hold food for service at an internal temperature of 41°F or below. Do not mix old product with new. Keep leftover product chilled at 41°F or below. See p. 167 for cooling procedures.
- For safety reasons, the use of pasteurized frozen egg yolks is recommended.
- The addition of oil too rapidly or insufficient beating may cause the oil to separate from the other ingredients, resulting in a curdled appearance. Curdled or broken mayonnaise may be re-formed by adding it (a small amount at a time) to 2 well-beaten egg yolks or eggs and beating well after each addition. It also may be re-formed by adding it to a small portion of uncurdled mayonnaise.

Variations

To make approximately 2 qt dressing:

- **Buttermilk Dressing.** To 1 qt mayonnaise, add 1 qt buttermilk, 2 tsp basil, $\frac{1}{2}$ tsp oregano, 1 Tbsp finely chopped fresh parsley, 1 minced garlic clove, 2 tsp black pepper, 2 oz chopped onion, and 1 tsp tarragon.
- **Campus Dressing.** To 2 qt mayonnaise, add $\frac{1}{3}$ cup fresh parsley, $\frac{1}{4}$ cup chopped green bell pepper, and $\frac{1}{2}$ cup finely chopped celery.
- **Chantilly Dressing.** To 1$\frac{1}{2}$ qt mayonnaise, fold in 1$\frac{1}{2}$ cups cream, whipped.
- **Creamy Blue Cheese Dressing.** To 1 qt mayonnaise, add 2 cups (1 lb) sour cream, $\frac{1}{4}$ cup lemon juice, 1 Tbsp grated onion, 1 tsp salt, and 8 oz finely crumbled blue cheese.
- **Dilly Dressing.** To 1$\frac{1}{2}$ qt mayonnaise, add 2 cups evaporated milk or buttermilk, 1 Tbsp seasoned salt, 1 tsp garlic powder, and $\frac{1}{4}$ cup chopped dill weed.
- **Egg and Green Pepper Dressing.** To 1$\frac{3}{4}$ qt mayonnaise, add 12 chopped hard-cooked eggs, $\frac{1}{4}$ cup finely chopped green bell pepper, 2 Tbsp onion juice, and a few grains cayenne pepper.
- **Garden Dressing.** Combine 3 cups mayonnaise and 1$\frac{1}{2}$ qt (3 lb) sour cream. Add 3 oz granulated sugar, 2 tsp salt, and 1 tsp black pepper. Fold in 12 oz thinly sliced green onions, 8 oz thinly sliced radishes, 8 oz chopped cucumbers, and 8 oz minced green bell pepper. This may be used for a vegetable dip also.
- **Green Peppercorn Cream Dressing.** To 1 cup mayonnaise, add 1$\frac{1}{4}$ qt (2 lb 8 oz) sour cream, 1 cup Dijon-style mustard, $\frac{1}{3}$ cup finely crushed and drained green peppercorns, $\frac{1}{4}$ cup white wine vinegar, and $\frac{2}{3}$ cup chopped parsley (optional).
- **Honey Cream Dressing.** Blend together 4 oz cream cheese, 1$\frac{1}{3}$ cups honey, 1 cup lemon or pineapple juice, and $\frac{1}{4}$ tsp salt; then fold into 1$\frac{1}{2}$ qt mayonnaise.
- **Honey Yogurt Dressing.** To 1 cup mayonnaise, add 1$\frac{1}{2}$ qt unflavored yogurt, $\frac{1}{3}$ cup honey, $\frac{1}{4}$ cup raspberry vinegar, 2 Tbsp lemon juice, and 1 Tbsp grated fresh orange peel.
- **Horseradish Cream Dressing.** To 1 cup mayonnaise, add 1$\frac{1}{2}$ qt (3 lb) sour cream, 2 Tbsp lemon juice, 2 tsp curry powder, 5 oz horseradish, 1 tsp salt, and 1 tsp paprika.
- **Roquefort Dressing.** To 1$\frac{1}{2}$ qt mayonnaise, add 2 cups French dressing, 8 oz crumbled Roquefort cheese, and 2 tsp Worcestershire sauce.
- **Russian Dressing.** To 2 qt mayonnaise, add 2 cups chile sauce, 2 Tbsp Worcestershire sauce, 2 tsp onion juice, and a few grains cayenne pepper.
- **Sour Cream Basil Dressing.** To 1 cup mayonnaise, add $\frac{3}{4}$ cup vinegar, 1$\frac{1}{2}$ qt (3 lb) sour cream, 1 oz granulated sugar, 1$\frac{1}{2}$ oz salt, 1$\frac{1}{2}$ Tbsp celery seed, and 2 Tbsp basil leaves.
- **Thousand Island Dressing.** To 1$\frac{1}{2}$ qt mayonnaise, add 1$\frac{1}{2}$ oz minced onion, 3 oz chopped pimento, 1 cup chile sauce, 8 chopped hard-cooked eggs, 1 tsp salt, $\frac{1}{4}$ cup pickle relish, and a few grains cayenne pepper.

COOKED SALAD DRESSING

Yield: 3 gal

Ingredient	Amount	Procedure
Sugar, granulated	3 lb	Combine dry ingredients in steam-jacketed kettle or stockpot.
Flour, all-purpose	1 lb 8 oz	
Salt	6 oz	
Dry mustard	3 oz	
Water, cold	1 qt	Add water to dry ingredients and stir with a wire whip until a smooth paste is formed.
Milk, hot	1 gal	Add hot milk and water, stirring continuously while adding.
Water, hot	2 qt	Cook for 20 minutes, or until thickened.
Margarine	1 lb	Stir in margarine and vinegar.
Vinegar, cider, hot	3 qt	
Egg yolks, beaten (see Note)	50 (2 lb)	Add cooked mixture slowly to egg yolks, stirring briskly. Cook for 7–10 minutes. Remove from heat and cool quickly to below 41°F.

Approximate nutritive values per ounce

Calories	Carbohydrate	Protein	Fat	Cholesterol	Sodium	Fiber	Iron
44 kcal	6 g	1 g	2 g	32 mg	189 mg	0 g	0.5 mg

Notes

- Potentially hazardous food. *Food Safety Standards:* Hold food for service at an internal temperature of 41°F or below. Do not mix old product with new. Keep leftover product chilled at 41°F or below. See p. 167 for cooling procedures.
- 25 whole eggs may be substituted for egg yolks; hot water may be substituted for hot milk.

Variation

- **Combination Dressing.** Combine 1 qt Cooked Salad Dressing and 1 qt mayonnaise.

CHILEAN DRESSING

Yield: 1½ qt

Ingredient	Amount	Procedure
Salad oil	2 cups	Combine all ingredients.
Vinegar, cider	1 cup	Beat on low speed until well blended.
Sugar, granulated	4 oz	Store in covered container.
Salt	2 tsp	Shake or beat well before serving.
Onion, finely chopped	2 oz	
Chile sauce	2 cups	
Catsup	1 cup	

Approximate nutritive values per ounce

Calories	Carbohydrate	Protein	Fat	Cholesterol	Sodium	Fiber	Iron
106 kcal	7 g	0 g	9 g	0 mg	275 mg	0 g	0 mg

BACON DRESSING

Yield: 2 qt

Ingredient	Amount	Procedure
Bacon, sliced, cut into 1-inch pieces	12 oz	Fry bacon until crisp. Remove from fat.
Onion, finely chopped	4 oz	Sauté onion in bacon fat.
Sugar, granulated Vinegar, cider Water	8 oz ¼ cup 1½ cups	Add sugar, vinegar, and water to sautéed onions. Bring to boiling point. Cool.
Mayonnaise (p. 640)	3 cups	Place Mayonnaise in mixer bowl. Add cooled onion-vinegar mixture slowly, beating on low speed until smooth. Stir in bacon pieces. Serve with tossed green salad.

Approximate nutritive values per ounce

Calories	Carbohydrate	Protein	Fat	Cholesterol	Sodium	Fiber	Iron
97 kcal	4 g	1 g	9 g	7 mg	83 mg	0 g	0 mg

Note

- Potentially hazardous food. *Food Safety Standards:* Hold food for service at an internal temperature of 41°F or below. Do not mix old product with new. Keep leftover product chilled at 41°F or below. See p. 167 for cooling procedures.

SOUR CREAM DRESSING

Yield: 3 qt

Ingredient	Amount	Procedure
Eggs, beaten Sour cream	16 (1 lb 12 oz) 1 qt	Mix eggs and sour cream.
Sugar, granulated Flour, all-purpose Water, cold	2 lb 1½ oz 1 cup	Combine sugar and flour. Add water and mix only until smooth. Add to the cream-and-egg mixture.
Vinegar, cider	2 cups	Add vinegar and cook until thick. Stir as necessary. Chill quickly to below 41°F.

Approximate nutritive values per portion

Calories	Carbohydrate	Protein	Fat	Cholesterol	Sodium	Fiber	Iron
107 kcal	16 g	2 g	4 g	59 mg	24 mg	0 g	0.5 mg

Notes

- Potentially hazardous food. *Food Safety Standards:* Hold food for service at an internal temperature of 41°F or below. Do not mix old product with new. Keep leftover product chilled at 41°F or below. See p. 167 for cooling procedures.
- 2 cups whipped cream may be added before serving.

FRENCH DRESSING (THICK)

Yield: 2 qts

Ingredient	Amount	Procedure
Sugar, granulated	2 lb	Combine sugar and seasonings in mixer bowl, using a wire whip.
Paprika	2 Tbsp	
Dry mustard	4 tsp	
Salt	2 Tbsp	
Onion juice	1½ tsp	
Vinegar, cider	1½ cups	Add vinegar. Mix well.
Salad oil	1 qt	Add oil gradually in small amounts. Beat well after each addition.

Approximate nutritive values per ounce

Calories	Carbohydrate	Protein	Fat	Cholesterol	Sodium	Fiber	Iron
235 kcal	20 g	0 g	18 g	0 mg	267 mg	0 g	0 mg

Note

- If a French dressing of usual consistency is desired, use only 8 oz of sugar.

Variations

- **Celery Seed Dressing.** Add 2 oz celery seed.
- **Poppy Seed Dressing.** Add 1 oz poppy seed.

FRENCH DRESSING

Yield: 3 qt

Ingredient	Amount	Procedure
Salt	2 oz (3 Tbsp)	Combine dry ingredients in mixer bowl.
Dry mustard	2 Tbsp	
Paprika	2 Tbsp	
Black pepper	1 Tbsp	
Vinegar, cider	1 qt	Add vinegar and onion juice to dry ingredients.
Onion juice	4 tsp	Add salad oil slowly. Beat on high speed until thick and blended.
Salad oil	2 qt	This is a temporary emulsion that separates rapidly. Beat well or pour into a jar and shake vigorously just before serving.

Approximate nutritive values per ounce

Calories	Carbohydrate	Protein	Fat	Cholesterol	Sodium	Fiber	Iron
161 kcal	0 g	0 g	18 g	0 mg	204 mg	0 g	0 mg

Variations

Prepare by adding the following to 3 qt (1 recipe) French Dressing:

- **Chiffonade Dressing.** Add ⅓ cup chopped fresh parsley, 4 oz chopped onion, 6 oz chopped green bell pepper, 4 oz chopped red pepper or pimento, and 16 chopped hard-cooked eggs.
- **Italian Dressing.** Delete paprika. Add 2 tsp oregano, ¼ tsp garlic powder, and 1 Tbsp dried basil.
- **Mexican Dressing.** Add 3 cups chile sauce, 10 oz chopped green bell pepper, 2 oz chopped onion, and 1 Tbsp dried cilantro or 3 Tbsp chopped fresh.
- **Oil and Vinegar.** Delete mustard, paprika, and onion juice.
- **Roquefort Cheese Dressing.** Add French Dressing slowly, while whipping, to 1 lb finely crumbled Roquefort cheese. 1 qt cream may be mixed with cheese before it is added to the dressing.
- **Sesame Seed Dressing.** Delete salt, paprika, pepper, and onion juice. Increase mustard to ¼ cup and vinegar to 5½ cups. Add 3½ cups granulated sugar, 1¼ cups soy sauce, and ½ cup toasted sesame seeds.
- **Tarragon Dressing.** Use tarragon vinegar in place of cider vinegar.
- **Tomato Dressing.** Add 1 lb granulated sugar, 1½ qt tomato soup, and ¼ cup celery or poppy seeds. Increase onion juice to 2 Tbsp.

HONEY FRENCH DRESSING

Yield: 2 qt

Ingredient	Amount	Procedure
Dry mustard	4 tsp	Mix mustard, salt, and celery seed in large mixing bowl.
Salt	1 tsp	
Celery seed or poppy seed	4 tsp	
Honey	2 cups	While mixing, add remaining ingredients in order listed.
Vinegar, cider	1¼ cups	
Fresh lemon juice	¼ cup	
Onion, grated	1 Tbsp	
Salad oil	1 qt	

Approximate nutritive values per ounce

Calories	Carbohydrate	Protein	Fat	Cholesterol	Sodium	Fiber	Iron
155 kcal	9 g	0 g	14 g	0 mg	34 mg	0 g	0 mg

HONEY LIME DRESSING

Yield: 3 qt

Ingredient	Amount	Procedure
Mayonnaise, low-fat	1 qt	Measure all ingredients into mixer bowl. Blend together, using a wire whip.
Yogurt, plain	1 qt	Cover and refrigerate. Store below 41°F.
Honey	2 cups	
Fresh lime juice	2 cups	
Celery seed	1 Tbsp	

Approximate nutritive values per ounce

Calories	Carbohydrate	Protein	Fat	Cholesterol	Sodium	Fiber	Iron
45 kcal	10 g	0.6 g	0.8 g	0.6 mg	100 mg	0 g	0 mg

Note

- Potentially hazardous food. *Food Safety Standards:* Hold food for service at an internal temperature of 41°F or below. Do not mix old product with new. Keep leftover product chilled at 41°F or below. See p. 167 for cooling procedures.

LEMON VINAIGRETTE

Yield: 1¼ qt

Ingredient	Amount	Procedure
Shallot, minced	2 oz	Whisk together shallot, garlic, lemon peel, vinegars, sugar, salt, and pepper.
Garlic cloves, minced	2	
Lemon peel, grated	1 Tbsp	
Fresh lemon juice	¾ cup	
Vinegar, red wine	½ cup	
Vinegar, balsamic	½ cup	
Sugar, granulated	1 tsp	
Salt	1 oz	
Black pepper	¼ tsp	
Extra virgin olive oil	3 cups	Slowly whisk oil into vinegar mixture until emulsified.

Approximate nutritive values per ounce

Calories	Carbohydrate	Protein	Fat	Cholesterol	Sodium	Fiber	Iron
17 kcal	1 g	0 g	10 g	0 mg	163 mg	0 g	0 mg

BASIL VINAIGRETTE DRESSING

Yield: 1½ qt

Ingredient	Amount	Procedure
Vinegar, cider	2 cups	Combine in mixer bowl, using a wire whip.
Water	¾ cup	
Sugar, granulated	2 oz	
Garlic, minced	1½ Tbsp	
Salt	2 oz	
Basil, dried, crumbled	⅔ cup	
Salad oil	2 cups	Add oil very gradually while mixing.
Olive oil	½ cup	Store covered in the refrigerator.
		Stir before serving.

Approximate nutritive values per ounce

Calories	Carbohydrate	Protein	Fat	Cholesterol	Sodium	Fiber	Iron
108 kcal	2 g	0 g	12 g	0 mg	468 mg	0 g	0 mg

VINAIGRETTE DRESSING

Yield: 2 qt

Ingredient	Amount	Procedure
Vinegar, cider	2 cups	Combine in mixer bowl.
Salt	1½ oz	
White pepper	2 tsp	
Cayenne pepper	¼ tsp	
Salad oil	2½ cups	Combine oils. Add very slowly to vinegar mixture, mixing on low speed
Olive oil	2¾ cups	until oil is blended in.
Fresh parsley, chopped	½ cup	Add to dressing. Mix.
Garlic cloves, minced	5	Store in refrigerator.
Chives, frozen	½ cup	Stir or shake before serving.
Capers	4 oz	

Approximate nutritive values per ounce

Calories	Carbohydrate	Protein	Fat	Cholesterol	Sodium	Fiber	Iron
158 kcal	0 g	0 g	18 g	0 mg	258 mg	0 g	0 mg

Variations

- **Dijon Mustard Vinaigrette.** Combine 2½ cups red wine vinegar, ¾ oz chopped chives, ¾ cup Dijon mustard, and 1 oz (1½ Tbsp) salt in mixer bowl. Slowly add 4¾ cups salad oil while mixing on medium speed, using a wire whip. Mix until oil is blended in. Makes approximately 2 qt.
- **Lemon Basil Dressing.** Combine 2 cups cider vinegar, 1½ cups lemon juice, 6 oz granulated sugar, 2½ oz salt, and 4½ Tbsp dried basil leaves. Gradually add 3 cups salad oil.
- **Lime Salad Dressing.** Combine in mixer bowl 2½ cups frozen reconstituted lime juice, 1¼ cups sugar, 2 oz salt, 1 tsp white pepper, ¾ tsp ground red pepper, and 1½ tsp celery salt. Add 4½ cups salad oil very slowly, mixing on medium speed until oil is blended in. Makes approximately 2 qt dressing.
- **Pimento Vinaigrette Dressing.** Substitute 4 oz diced pimento for capers.

SWEET SESAME VINAIGRETTE DRESSING

Yield: 2 qt

Ingredient	Amount	Procedure
Sugar, granulated	1 lb 10 oz	Combine in mixer bowl.
Sesame seed	4 oz	
Poppy seed	2 oz	
Paprika	1½ tsp	
Onion, minced	3 Tbsp	
Worcestershire sauce	1½ tsp	
Salad oil	3 cups	Using a wire whip, add vinegar and oil in a slow stream.
Vinegar, cider	1⅔ cups	Whip for at least 1 minute and make sure sugar is dissolved.

Approximate nutritive values per ounce

Calories	Carbohydrate	Protein	Fat	Cholesterol	Sodium	Fiber	Iron
113 kcal	10 g	0 g	9 g	0 mg	0 mg	0.3 g	0.5 mg

Note

- Serve over fresh greens and fruit.

CREAMY VINAIGRETTE

Yield: 3 qt

Ingredient	Amount	Procedure
Vinegar, rice wine	1 qt	Blend in mixer bowl, using a flat beater.
Red wine	3 cups	
Yogurt, plain	3 cups	
Whole-grain mustard	1 cup	
Dijon mustard	1 cup	
Garlic, minced	1 oz EP	Mix garlic, onions, and seasonings into yogurt mixture.
Red onions, finely diced	6 oz EP	Store covered in refrigerator for up to 1 week.
Green onions, sliced into thin rings	8 oz EP	Shake before serving.
Fresh basil, finely chopped	¼ cup	
Mustard seed, whole	2 tsp	
Tarragon, dried	1 tsp	
Oregano, dried	2 tsp	
Black pepper	2 tsp	

Approximate nutritive values per ounce

Calories	Carbohydrate	Protein	Fat	Cholesterol	Sodium	Fiber	Iron
25 kcal	4 g	0.8 g	0.5 g	0.5 mg	148 mg	0.2 g	0.5 mg

Note

- Potentially hazardous food. *Food Safety Standards:* Hold food for service at an internal temperature of 41°F or below. Do not mix old product with new. Keep leftover product chilled at 41°F or below. See p. 167 for cooling procedures.

Variation

- **Creamy Raspberry Vinaigrette.** Delete oregano. Add 8 oz puréed fresh raspberries.

HOT VINAIGRETTE (FOR SALAD GREENS)

Yield: 50 portions (1¾ qt)   *Portion:* 2 Tbsp (1 oz)

Ingredient	Amount	Procedure
Vinegar, balsamic	1½ qt	Combine vinegar, honey, and mustard in steam-jacketed kettle or saucepan. Using a wire whip, mix until blended.
Honey	½ cup	
Dijon mustard	¼ cup	
Green onions, sliced into thin rings	2 oz EP	Add onions, garlic, and seasonings to vinegar mixture. Heat over medium heat to 200°F.
Garlic, minced	1 oz EP	
Tarragon, dried	2 Tbsp	
Black pepper, coarsely ground	1 tsp	
Salt	½ tsp	
		Spoon 2 Tbsp over single servings of bitter greens or fresh spinach leaves.

Approximate nutritive values per ounce

Calories	Carbohydrate	Protein	Fat	Cholesterol	Sodium	Fiber	Iron
55 kcal	12 g	0 g	0 g	0 mg	36 mg	0 g	0.5 mg

APPLE CIDER DRESSING

Yield: 1 qt

Ingredient	Amount	Procedure
Apple cider	1 gal	In steam-jacketed kettle, slowly boil apple cider with cinnamon sticks and cloves until reduced by ¾ and slightly thickened. Discard cinnamon sticks and cloves.
Cinnamon sticks	4	
Cloves, whole	1 tsp	
Mustard, stone ground	⅓ cup	Using a wire whip, mix mustard, oil, pepper, and poppy seed. Serve at room temperature. Shake or mix before serving.
Olive oil	½ cup	
Black pepper, coarsely ground	¼ tsp	
Poppy seed	1 tsp	

Approximate nutritive values per ounce

Calories	Carbohydrate	Protein	Fat	Cholesterol	Sodium	Fiber	Iron
95 kcal	17 g	0.3 g	4 g	0 mg	38 mg	0.2 g	1 mg

CELERY SEED FRUIT DRESSING

Yield: 2 qt

Ingredient	Amount	Procedure
Sugar, granulated	1 lb 8 oz	Mix dry ingredients in kettle.
Cornstarch	⅓ cup	
Dry mustard	2 Tbsp	
Salt	2 Tbsp	
Paprika	2 Tbsp	
Vinegar, cider	2 cups	Add vinegar to dry ingredients. Stir and cook until thickened and clear.
Onion juice	1 tsp	Add onion juice. Cool to room temperature.
Salad oil	1 qt	Add oil slowly to cooked mixture while beating on high speed.
Celery seed	2 Tbsp	Add celery seed. Serve with any fruit salad combination.

Approximate nutritive values per ounce

Calories	Carbohydrate	Protein	Fat	Cholesterol	Sodium	Fiber	Iron
167 kcal	12 g	0 g	14 g	0 mg	201 mg	0 g	0.5 mg

Variations

- **Golden Fruit Dressing.** Add 1½–2 Tbsp prepared mustard after mixture has cooked.
- **Poppy Seed Fruit Dressing.** Substitute poppy seed for celery seed.

FRUIT SALAD DRESSING

Yield: 4 qt

Ingredient	Amount	Procedure
Pineapple juice	1 qt	Combine juices. Heat to boiling point.
Orange juice	3 cups	
Lemon juice	2 cups	
Sugar, granulated	2 lb	Mix sugar and cornstarch.
Cornstarch	5 oz	Add to hot mixture while stirring with a wire whip.
Eggs, beaten	16 (1 lb 12 oz)	Add eggs to hot mixture while stirring. Cook until thickened. Chill quickly (within 4 hours) to below 41°F.
Whipping cream	2 cups	Whip cream and fold into dressing just before serving. Serve with fruit salads.

Approximate nutritive values per ounce

Calories	Carbohydrate	Protein	Fat	Cholesterol	Sodium	Fiber	Iron
53 kcal	9 g	1 g	2 g	27 mg	9 mg	0 g	0 mg

Note

- Potentially hazardous food. *Food Safety Standards:* Hold food for service at an internal temperature of 41°F or below. Do not mix old product with new. Keep leftover product chilled at 41°F or below. See p. 167 for cooling procedures.

YOGURT HERB DRESSING

Yield: 3½ qt

Ingredient	Amount	Procedure
Yogurt, plain	6 lb	Blend in mixer bowl, using a flat beater.
Salad dressing	1 lb	
Prepared horseradish	4 oz	
Basil, dried, crumbled	1 Tbsp	Add seasonings. Blend well.
Tarragon, dried, crumbled	1 Tbsp	Store in refrigerator in covered containers.
Thyme, ground	½ tsp	
Celery seed	1 Tbsp	
Black pepper, cracked	1 Tbsp	

Approximate nutritive values per ounce

Calories	Carbohydrate	Protein	Fat	Cholesterol	Sodium	Fiber	Iron
30 kcal	2 g	1 g	2 g	4 mg	49 mg	0 g	0 mg

Notes

- Potentially hazardous food. *Food Safety Standards:* Hold food for service at an internal temperature of 41°F or below. Do not mix old product with new. Keep leftover product chilled at 41°F or below. See p. 167 for cooling procedures.
- May be used as a dip for fresh vegetables.

YOGURT ORANGE DRESSING

Yield: 3½ qt

Ingredient	Amount	Procedure
Yogurt, plain	6 lb	Measure all ingredients into mixer bowl. Blend together, using a wire whip.
Honey	1¼ cups	Refrigerate covered until chilled.
Orange juice concentrate, frozen, thawed	6 oz	Serve over fruit.
Cinnamon, ground	1⅓ tsp	
Nutmeg, ground	1 tsp	

Approximate nutritive values per ounce

Calories	Carbohydrate	Protein	Fat	Cholesterol	Sodium	Fiber	Iron
29 kcal	5 g	1 g	1 g	3 mg	11 mg	0 g	0 mg

Notes

- Potentially hazardous food. *Food Safety Standards:* Hold food for service at an internal temperature of 41°F or below. Do not mix old product with new. Keep leftover product chilled at 41°F or below. See p. 167 for cooling procedures.
- May be used as a dip for fresh fruit.

CUCUMBER YOGURT DRESSING

Yield: 2½ qt

Ingredient	Amount	Procedure
Salad dressing	2 cups	Combine in mixer bowl.
Sour cream	12 oz	
Garlic, minced	1 Tbsp	
Chives, frozen	½ cup	
Salt	1½ tsp	
Black pepper	⅛ tsp	
Fresh cucumbers	1 lb 8 oz AP	Peel and seed cucumbers. Chop finely. Add to sour cream mixture.
Yogurt, plain	3½ cups	Fold in. Chill.

Approximate nutritive values per ounce

Calories	Carbohydrate	Protein	Fat	Cholesterol	Sodium	Fiber	Iron
39 kcal	2 g	1 g	3 g	5 mg	88 mg	0 g	0 mg

Note

- Potentially hazardous food. *Food Safety Standards:* Hold food for service at an internal temperature of 41°F or below. Do not mix old product with new. Keep leftover product chilled at 41°F or below. See p. 167 for cooling procedures.

GARLIC HERB DRESSING

Yield: 1½ qt

Ingredient	Amount	Procedure
Nonfat cream cheese, softened	1 lb 12 oz	Beat cream cheese until smooth and creamy.
Skim milk	1¼ cups	Add milk and vinegar, beating until smooth.
Vinegar, tarragon	¼ cup	
Garlic cloves, minced	6	Stir in garlic, onion, and spices.
Onion, minced	6 oz	Chill quickly (within 4 hours) to below 41°F.
Tarragon, dried	1 tsp	
Parsley, dried	1 Tbsp	
Celery seed	½ tsp	
Black pepper	¾ tsp	
Salt	¾ tsp	

Approximate nutritive values per ounce

Calories	Carbohydrate	Protein	Fat	Cholesterol	Sodium	Fiber	Iron
19 kcal	1 g	3 g	0 g	0 mg	136 mg	0 g	0 mg

Notes

- Potentially hazardous food. *Food Safety Standards:* Hold food for service at an internal temperature of 41°F or below. Do not mix old product with new. Keep leftover product chilled at 41°F or below. See p. 167 for cooling procedures.
- Serve as a dip for vegetables or dressing for salad greens.

Sandwiches

Sandwiches continue to be favorite choices for the noon and evening meals. They have become popular, too, at breakfast or any meal throughout the day where a fast, flavorful meal is desired. Sandwiches are also popular as hors d'oeuvres or buffet foods. Sandwiches may be closed or open faced and may be served hot or cold. Nutritional requirements are easily satisfied by choosing breads and fillings that are high in fiber, low in fat, and low in cholesterol.

Preparation of Ingredients

Sandwich ingredients include bread, spread, filling, and vegetable accompaniments. Many ingredient variations are possible, but the basic procedures for preparing ingredients are the same.

BREADS

Different breads and rolls add variety in flavor, texture, size, and shape. In addition to the traditional loaves, foccacia, pita, tortillas, quick breads, and flavored speciality breads may be used for sandwiches.

Bread should be kept fresh during and after preparation. Keep bread tightly wrapped until used. French bread or other crusty breads, however, should not be wrapped because the crust will soften. They should be used the day they are baked. Bread should not be refrigerated, because it will become stale faster than if kept at room temperature. If bread must be kept longer than 1–2 days, it may be frozen. Defrost frozen bread without unwrapping.

SPREADS

Bread for sandwiches is first spread with plain or seasoned margarine or butter, mayonnaise, flavored mayonnaise (p. 732), mustard, olive paste, pesto, chutney, or a Sandwich Spread (p. 655). Covering bread evenly with a spread helps keep the sandwich from becoming soggy. Margarine or butter may be softened by letting it stand at room temperature, or it may be whipped for easy spreading (see p. 655). Allow 1 tsp spread per slice of bread.

FILLINGS

Slice meat and cheese into even slices. Tender meats may be sliced thicker than less tender ones. A serving of thinly sliced or wafer-sliced meats usually appears larger than an equal weight of thicker slices. Because sliced meats and cheese dry out quickly, they should be sliced only as needed and kept covered. Mixed fillings should be prepared the day they are served and kept chilled. Nonmeat fillings in addition to cheese may include salads and grilled or fresh vegetables.

VEGETABLE ACCOMPANIMENTS

Prepare greens, tomato and onion slices, and pickles or other vegetable accompaniments. Ingredients should be fresh, crisp, and attractive. See pp. 120–127 for preparing vegetable accompaniments.

Preparation of Sandwiches

CLOSED SANDWICHES

1. Prepare filling and spread.
2. Arrange fresh bread in rows on a baking sheet or a worktable. Four rows of 10 slices each is a manageable number.
3. Spread all bread slices to the edges with softened margarine or butter or other spread.
4. Portion filling with dipper or spoon on alternate rows of bread and spread to the edges, or arrange sliced filling to fit the sandwich.
5. If lettuce or other vegetable accompaniment is used, arrange on filling. If sandwiches are to be held for some time, vegetable accompaniments should be omitted.
6. Place plain buttered (or spread) slices of bread on the filled slices.
7. If the sandwiches are to be cut in half or in fourths, stack two or three together and cut with a sharp knife, being careful not to mash bread.

8. To keep sandwiches fresh, place in sandwich bags or plastic wrap. Avoid stacking sandwiches more than three high, because stacking insulates the filling and prevents it from reaching the desired temperature as quickly as it should.

9. Refrigerate until served. If freezing sandwiches for later use, see precautions on pp. 654–655.

10. Handle bread and fillings as little as possible during preparation. Use plastic gloves or tongs when picking up food.

GRILLED AND TOASTED SANDWICHES

1. For a grilled sandwich, place filling between two slices of bread. Fillings may be sliced cheese, meat, or poultry; chopped fillings as in salads; or a combination of fillings as in a Reuben Sandwich (p. 677).

2. Brush the outside with melted margarine or butter. For large quantities, a brush or roller dipped in the melted spread may be used. The steps for this method are as follows: (a) Place parchment paper in bottom of baking sheet. (b) Place bread slices directly on coated paper. Add filling to all slices in pan. (c) Top with slices of bread.

3. Brown sandwich on a griddle, in a hot oven, or under a broiler.

4. For a toasted sandwich, toast the bread before filling.

OPEN-FACED HOT SANDWICHES

1. Place buttered or unbuttered bread on a serving plate.

2. Cover with hot meat or other filling.

3. Top with gravy, sauce, or other topping.

4. For a hot sandwich that is to be broiled, arrange slices of bread on a baking sheet. Cover with slices of cheese or other topping. Broil just before serving.

CANAPÉS

1. Remove crusts from bread.

2. Cut into desired shapes.

3. Spread with softened margarine or butter.

4. Cover with filling.

5. Decorate with parsley, sliced olives, sliced radishes, pimento pieces, chopped hard-cooked eggs, or other garnish.

RIBBON SANDWICHES

1. Remove crusts from two kinds of bread, being careful to have all slices the same size.

2. Spread one or more fillings on slices of bread.

3. Make stacks of five slices of bread, alternating kinds of bread.

4. Press together firmly.

5. Arrange stacks in shallow pan; cover with plastic wrap, plastic bag, or waxed paper.

6. Chill for several hours.

7. To serve, cut each slice into thirds, halves, or triangles.

CHECKERBOARD SANDWICHES

1. Spread slices of white and whole-wheat bread with desired filling.

2. Make stacks of ribbon sandwiches by alternating two slices of white and two slices of whole-wheat bread. Trim and cut each stack into ½-inch slices.

3. Using butter or smooth spread as a filling, stack three slices together so that white and whole-wheat squares alternate to give a checkerboard effect.

4. Chill for several hours.

5. Remove from refrigerator and, with sharp knife, slice into checkerboard slices, ½ inch thick.

ROLLED SANDWICHES

1. Remove crusts from three sides of a loaf of unsliced bread.

2. With crust at left, cut loaf into lengthwise slices ⅛–¼ inch thick.

3. Run rolling pin the length of each slice to make it easier to handle.

4. Spread with softened margarine or butter.

5. Spread with desired smooth filling.

6. Place olives, watercress, or other foods across the end.

7. Starting at end with garnish, roll tightly, being careful to keep sides straight. Tight rolling makes for easier slicing.

8. Wrap rolls individually in waxed paper or aluminum foil, twisting ends securely.

9. Chill several hours or overnight. Rolls may be made ahead of time, then wrapped and frozen. Let thaw for about 45 minutes before slicing.

10. Cut chilled rolls into ¼–⅓ inch slices.

Freezing Sandwiches

When making sandwiches to be frozen for later use, certain precautions should be taken.

1. Spread bread with margarine or butter instead of mayonnaise or salad dressing.

2. Do not use fillings containing mayonnaise, egg white, or some vegetables such as tomatoes and parsley. Chicken, meat, fish, cheese, and peanut butter freeze well.

3. Place large closed sandwiches individually in a sandwich bag or wrap individually in plastic wrap.

4. Pack tea-sized closed sandwiches in layers, separated by waxed paper or plastic wrap, in freezer boxes; or place in any suitable box and overwrap with moistureproof material.

5. Place open-faced sandwiches on trays; wrap as for closed sandwiches.

6. Wrap ribbon, closed, or other loaf sandwiches uncut.

7. Allow 1–2 hours for sandwiches to defrost. Do not remove outer wrapping until sandwiches are partly thawed.

8. If sandwiches are not served immediately after thawing, refrigerate until serving time.

Sandwich Recipes

WHIPPED MARGARINE OR BUTTER

Yield: spread for 50 sandwiches   *Portion:* 1 tsp per slice

Ingredient	Amount	Procedure
Margarine or butter	1 lb	Place in mixer bowl. Let stand at room temperature until soft enough to mix.
Milk or boiling water (optional)	½ cup	Add milk or water while whipping. Mix on low speed, gradually increasing to high speed. Whip until fluffy.

Variations

- **Honey Butter.** Cream 1 lb butter or margarine until light and fluffy. Add 8 oz honey gradually, beating on medium speed until mixture is light. Serve with hot biscuits or other hot bread.
- **Savory Spread.** Add minced cucumber, onion, or pimento; chopped chives or parsley; horseradish; or prepared mustard to whipped butter or margarine.

SANDWICH SPREAD

Yield: spread for 100 sandwiches   *Portion:* 1 tsp per slice

Ingredient	Amount	Procedure
Margarine or butter	8 oz	Whip margarine on high speed until light and fluffy.
Half-and-half	¼ cup	Add half-and-half and mix.
Prepared mustard	1½ tsp	Fold in remaining ingredients.
Mayonnaise	3 cups	Use as a spread for meat or cheese sandwiches.
Pickle relish	½ cup	

CHEESE SALAD SANDWICH

Yield: 50 sandwiches

Ingredient	Amount	Procedure
Cheddar cheese	3 lb 8 oz	Grind or shred cheese.
Salad dressing or cream	2 cups	Combine with cheese. Refrigerate and remove small amounts of filling as necessary for production.
Salt	2 tsp	
Cayenne pepper	few grains	
Margarine, softened	4 oz	
Bread	100 slices	Assemble filling and bread (p. 653). Portion filling with No. 20 dipper.

Approximate nutritive values per portion

Calories	Carbohydrate	Protein	Fat	Cholesterol	Sodium	Fiber	Iron
318 kcal	28 g	13 g	18 g	36 mg	726 mg	6 g	2 mg

Note

- Potentially hazardous food. *Food Safety Standards:* Hold food for service at an internal temperature of 41°F or below. Do not mix old product with new. Keep leftover product chilled at 41°F or below. See p. 167 for cooling procedures.

Variation

- **Pimento Cheese Sandwich.** Add 6 oz chopped pimento.

EGG SALAD SANDWICH

Yield: 50 sandwiches   *Portion:* 2 oz filling

Ingredient	Amount	Procedure
Eggs, hard-cooked (p. 384)	36	Peel eggs and chop coarsely.
Mayonnaise or salad dressing	2½ cups	· Combine and add to eggs. Mix lightly.
Pickle relish	1 cup	Refrigerate and remove small amounts of filling as necessary
Salt	2 tsp	for production.
White pepper	¼ tsp	
Onion juice	1 tsp	
Pimento, chopped	4 oz	
Bread	100 slices	Assemble filling, bread, and lettuce (p. 653).
Lettuce, iceberg or leaf	2–3 heads	Portion filling with No. 20 dipper.

Approximate nutritive values per portion

Calories	Carbohydrate	Protein	Fat	Cholesterol	Sodium	Fiber	Iron
248 kcal	31 g	10 g	10 g	157 mg	611 mg	7 g	3 mg

Notes

- Potentially hazardous food. *Food Safety Standards:* Hold food for service at an internal temperature of 41°F or below. Do not mix old product with new. Keep leftover product chilled at 41°F or below. See p. 167 for cooling procedures.
- Chilling ingredients before combining shortens the time product is in the temperature danger zone (above 41°F).
- 1 lb chopped celery may be substituted for pickle relish.
- 2 Tbsp prepared mustard may be added.

Variations

- **Deli Egg Salad.** In baker's bowl, dice 8 lb 8 oz peeled hard-cooked eggs. Stir in 2 lb chopped celery, 1 lb 8 oz pickle relish, and 3 Tbsp chopped pimento. In a seperate bowl, blend 1 lb 8 oz mayonnaise, 2 Tbsp Grey Poupon mustard, 2 tsp salt, 2 oz fresh lemon juice, and 2 tsp white pepper. Pour dressing mixture over egg mixture. Mix lightly until well blended. Makes 50 sandwiches. Portion: 4 oz.
- **Quick Egg Salad Sandwich.** In baker's bowl, dice 6 lb 8 oz peeled hard-cooked eggs. Mix in 1 lb 6 oz chopped celery. In a seperate bowl blend 12 oz salad dressing or mayonnaise, 3 oz pickle relish, and 3¾ tsp salt. Pour dressing mixture over eggs and celery. Mix lightly until well blended. Makes 50 sandwiches. Portion: 4 oz.

HAM SALAD SANDWICH

Yield: 50 sandwiches   *Portion:* 2 oz filling

Ingredient	Amount	Procedure
Cooked ham	4 lb	Grind ham coarsely.
Eggs, hard-cooked (p. 384)	6	Peel eggs and chop coarsely.
Onion, finely chopped	4 oz	Combine all ingredients. Mix lightly.
Pickle relish	8 oz	Refrigerate and remove small amounts of filling as necessary for
Mayonnaise or salad dressing	2–2½ cups	production.
Bread	100 slices	Assemble filling, bread, and lettuce (p. 653).
Lettuce, iceberg or leaf	2–3 heads	Portion filling with No. 20 dipper.

Approximate nutritive values per portion

Calories	Carbohydrate	Protein	Fat	Cholesterol	Sodium	Fiber	Iron
257 kcal	30 g	15 g	10 g	50 mg	1013 mg	7 g	3 mg

Notes

- Potentially hazardous food. *Food Safety Standards:* Hold food for service at an internal temperature of 41°F or below. Do not mix old product with new. Keep leftover product chilled at 41°F or below. See p. 167 for cooling procedures.
- Chilling ingredients before combining shortens the time product is in the temperature danger zone (above 41°F).

Variations

- **Deli Ham Salad.** Coarsely chop 9 lb ham. Add 2 lb 4 oz chopped celery, 8 oz finely chopped onion, and 1 lb 3 oz pickle relish to ham and mix lightly. In a separate bowl combine 2 lb 3 oz mayonnaise, 1 Tbsp dry mustard, and 1¼ tsp black pepper. Pour dressing mixture over ham mixture. Mix lightly until well blended. Makes 50 sandwiches. Portion: 4 oz.
- **Ham and Cheese Sandwich.** Delete eggs. Reduce ham to 3 lb. Add 1 lb 8 oz cheddar or Swiss cheese, ground.
- **Meat Salad Sandwich.** Substitute ground cooked beef or pork for ham. Add 4 oz finely chopped celery. Check for seasoning and add salt and pepper if needed.

CHICKEN SALAD SANDWICH

Yield: 50 sandwiches   *Portion:* 2 oz filling

Ingredient	Amount	Procedure
Cooked chicken	5 lb	Chop chicken coarsely.
Salt	2 tsp	Add remaining ingredients. Mix to blend.
White pepper	½ tsp	Refrigerate and remove small amounts of filling as necessary for production.
Celery, finely chopped	8 oz	
Fresh lemon juice or cider vinegar	¼ cup	
Mayonnaise or salad dressing	2–2½ cups	
Bread	100 slices	Assemble filling, bread, and lettuce (p. 653).
Lettuce, iceberg or leaf	2–3 heads	Portion filling with No. 20 dipper.

Approximate nutritive values per portion

Calories	Carbohydrate	Protein	Fat	Cholesterol	Sodium	Fiber	Iron
258 kcal	28 g	18 g	9 g	40 mg	546 mg	7 g	3 mg

Notes

- Potentially hazardous food. *Food Safety Standards:* Hold food for service at an internal temperature of 41°F or below. Do not mix old product with new. Keep leftover product chilled at 41°F or below. See p. 167 for cooling procedures.
- Chilling ingredients before combining shortens the time product is in the temperature danger zone (above 41°F).
- 4 oz chopped, toasted almonds may be added.
- Alfalfa sprouts may be placed on top of filling for variety.

Variation

- **Deli Chicken Salad.** Coarsely chop 5 lb cooked chicken breasts. Add 1 lb 12 oz peeled hard-cooked eggs and 3 lb 6 oz chopped celery. Mix lightly. In a separate bowl blend 1 lb 6 oz mayonnaise, 4 oz pickle relish, 3 Tbsp sweet pickle juice, 1½ tsp salt, and ½ tsp black pepper. Mix lightly until well blended. Makes 50 sandwiches. Portion: 4 oz.

TUNA SALAD SANDWICH

Yield: 50 sandwiches   *Portion:* 2 oz filling

Ingredient	Amount	Procedure
Eggs, hard-cooked (p. 384)	7	Peel eggs and chop coarsely.
Tuna, flaked	4 lb	Combine all filling ingredients.
Celery, chopped	4 oz	Refrigerate and remove small amounts of filling as necessary for production.
Fresh lemon juice	¼ cup	
Onion juice	1 tsp	
Mayonnaise or salad dressing	1½ cups	
Bread	100 slices	Assemble filling, bread, and lettuce (p. 653).
Lettuce, iceberg or leaf	2–3 heads	Portion filling with No. 20 dipper.

Approximate nutritive values per portion

Calories	Carbohydrate	Protein	Fat	Cholesterol	Sodium	Fiber	Iron
251 kcal	28 g	17 g	9 g	38 mg	547 mg	7 g	3 mg

Notes

- Potentially hazardous food. *Food Safety Standards:* Hold food for service at an internal temperature of 41°F or below. Do not mix old product with new. Keep leftover product chilled at 41°F or below. See p. 167 for cooling procedures.
- Chilling ingredients before combining shortens the time product is in the temperature danger zone (above 41°F).
- 1 cup pickle relish may be substituted for celery.

Variations

- **Deli Tuna Salad.** Refrigerate canned tuna overnight. Put 7 lb 8 oz drained tuna in baker's bowl. Add 1 lb 8 oz diced hard-cooked eggs, 1 lb 4 oz chopped celery, 4 Tbsp chopped pimento, 3 lb 4 oz mayonnaise, 1 lb drained pickle relish, 1¾ tsp celery seed, ½ tsp onion powder, and 1 tsp salt. Mix lightly until well blended. Makes 50 sandwiches. Portion: 4 oz.
- **Grilled Tuna Salad Sandwich.** Brush both sides of sandwiches with melted margarine or butter. Grill until golden brown.
- **Salmon Salad Sandwich.** Substitute salmon for tuna.

BACON, LETTUCE, AND TOMATO SANDWICH

Yield: 50 sandwiches

Ingredient	Amount	Procedure
Fresh tomatoes	7 lb	Wash tomatoes. Peel, if desired, and cut into thin slices.
Lettuce, iceberg or leaf	2–3 heads or 2 lb leaf	Wash lettuce and separate leaves. Drain.
Bacon	150 slices (7 lb)	Cook bacon according to directions on p. 470. Drain.
Bread, white or whole-wheat	100 slices	Spread 50 slices of bread with mayonnaise. Place 3 cooked bacon slices, 2 tomato slices, and a lettuce leaf on each.
Mayonnaise	1 cup	Top with remaining 50 slices of bread that have been spread with Whipped
Whipped Margarine or Butter (p. 655)	8 oz	Margarine or Butter.

Approximate nutritive values per portion

Calories	Carbohydrate	Protein	Fat	Cholesterol	Sodium	Fiber	Iron
287 kcal	29 g	12 g	15 g	18 mg	770 mg	7 g	3 mg

Variations

- **Club Sandwich.** Use 150 thin slices white bread, toasted. Spread with mayonnaise. Place on first slice 1 lettuce leaf, 2 tomato slices, and 2 strips of bacon. Place second slice of toast on top, spread side down. Spread top with mayonnaise, then add 2 oz thinly sliced turkey or chicken breast and lettuce leaf. Top with third slice of toast, spread side down. Secure with 4 picks. Cut into quarters to serve.
- **Sliced Ham and Cheese Sandwiches.** Substitute 6 lb 8 oz wafer-sliced ham and 3 lb 2 oz (1 oz slices) cheese for bacon.
- **Turkey Club Hoagie.** Reduce bacon to 2 lb. Substitute 7-inch hoagie buns for sliced bread. Use 6 lb 8 oz cooked turkey breast (approximately 10 lb AP), wafer sliced. Each sandwich includes choice of sandwich spread, 2 oz sliced turkey, 1 bacon slice, 1 lettuce leaf, and 2 tomato slices. Garnish plate with dill pickle spear.

CHICKEN POCKET SANDWICH

Yield: 50 sandwiches   *Portion:* 1 sandwich

Ingredient	Amount	Procedure
Pita pockets, 6 inch	50	Open pita pockets carefully.
Leaf lettuce leaves	2 lb	Just before service fill each pocket in the following order:
Tomato slices	3 lb	1 leaf lettuce
Alfalfa sprouts	1 lb 8 oz	2 tomato slices
Chicken Salad (p. 658)	1 recipe	3 oz Chicken Salad
		½ oz alfalfa sprouts
		Serve soon after filling.

Approximate nutritive values per portion

Calories	Carbohydrate	Protein	Fat	Cholesterol	Sodium	Fiber	Iron
480 kcal	29 g	19 g	32 g	95 mg	990 mg	2 g	3 mg

Note

- Potentially hazardous food. *Food Safety Standards:* Hold food for service at an internal temperature of 41°F or below. Do not mix old product with new. Keep leftover product chilled at 41°F or below. See p. 167 for cooling procedures.

Variation

- **Vegetarian Pocket.** Delete Chicken Salad. In addition to the lettuce, tomato, and alfalfa sprouts, stuff each pita pocket with 1 oz cucumber slices, ½-oz slices Swiss cheese, and 1 oz avocado slices. Drizzle sandwich with ½ oz Italian salad dressing.

SPICY PORK LOIN SANDWICH WITH SOUTHWEST PEACH SALSA

Yield: 50 sandwiches   *Portion:* 1 sandwich (4 oz meat, 2 oz salsa, 1 bun)

Ingredient	Amount	Procedure
Garlic and Peppercorn Pork Loin (p. 462)	20 lb EP	Prepare pork loin according to recipe. Chill. Slice thinly.
Southwest Peach Salsa (p. 704)	1 recipe	
Kaiser bun	50	To serve, place open bun on plate. Portion on bottom half of bun, 4 oz thinly sliced pork garnished on top with 2 oz salsa.

Approximate nutritive values per portion

Calories	Carbohydrate	Protein	Fat	Cholesterol	Sodium	Fiber	Iron
512 kcal	41 g	59 g	11 g	125 mg	474 mg	2 g	2 mg

Note

- Potentially hazardous food. *Food Safety Standards:* Hold food for service at an internal temperature of 41°F or below. Do not mix old product with new. Keep leftover product chilled at 41°F or below. See p. 167 for cooling procedures.

PULLED PORK SANDWICH

Yield: 50 portions   *Portion:* 1 sandwich (4 oz meat mixture, 1 bun)
Oven: 300°F   *Bake:* 5–6 hours

Ingredient	Amount	Procedure
Salt	3 Tbsp	Blend salt, sugar, chipotle concentrate, sage, and garlic in baker's bowl. Press 1 oz of mixture over the entire surface of each 4–5 lb roast. Cover and refrigerate seasoned pork for 24 hours before cooking.
Sugar, brown	¼ cup	
Chipotle flavor concentrate (see Note)	1 Tbsp	
Rubbed sage	2½ Tbsp	
Garlic powder	1¾ Tbsp	
Boneless pork butt roast, thawed	22 lb	
		To cook pork, tent pans loosely with aluminum foil, leaving ends open. Roast at 300°F in a conventional oven until internal temperature reaches 180°F, 5–6 hours. Remove from oven and cover tightly with foil and let rest for 30–45 minutes. Cut roasts into 2-inch-thick slices. Shred slices and discard fat. Save for later step.
Salt	1 Tbsp	While meat is resting, make vinegar sauce. Combine ingredients and bring to a boil over medium heat. Reduce heat and simmer for 10 minutes. Strain to remove jalapeños. Save for later step.
Sugar, brown	6 oz	
Chipotle flavor concentrate (see Note)	1 tsp	
Rubbed sage	2 tsp	
Garlic powder	2 tsp	
Vinegar, cider	1¼ qt	
Sliced jalapeños, canned, drained	10 oz	
		Place pork in 12 × 10 × 4-inch pans, 5 lb per pan. Scale 1½ cups (12 oz) vinegar sauce over each pan. Toss to coat pork with sauce. Heat to 165°F.
Seeded hamburger-style buns	50	Portion 4 oz pork mixture on bun.

Approximate nutritive values per sandwich

Calories	Carbohydrate	Protein	Fat	Cholesterol	Sodium	Fiber	Iron
426 kcal	33 g	31 g	18 g	90 mg	1058 mg	1 g	4 mg

Notes

- Potentially hazardous food. *Food Safety Standards:* Hold food for service at an internal temperature of 135°F or above. Do not mix old product with new. Cool leftover product quickly following time standards and cooling procedures on p. 167. Reheat leftover product quickly (within 2 hours) to 165°F or above. Reheat product only once; discard if not used.
- Minor's Chipotle Flavor Concentrate (a blend of red, chipotle, and jalapeño peppers with onion, garlic, and spice) is available from most broadline foodservice distributors. May substitute canned chipotles.

Variation

- **Home-Roasted Pulled Pork.** Substitute the following rub for the rub in the Pulled Pork Sandwich: 3 Tbsp salt; ½ cup ancho chile powder, ⅔ cup cumin, ⅔ cup garlic powder, 3 Tbsp black pepper. Follow cooking procedures for pork in Pulled Pork Sandwich.

SUBMARINE SANDWICH

Yield: 50 sandwiches   *Portion:* 3 oz meat + 1 oz cheese

Ingredient	Amount	Procedure
Buns, submarine or hoagie, 4–5 inches	50	Slice buns in half lengthwise.
Sandwich Spread (p. 655)	½ recipe	Spread both sides of bun with Sandwich Spread.
Salami, 1-oz slices	3 lb 2 oz	Cut slices of meat and cheese in half.
Luncheon meat, 1-oz slices	3 lb 2 oz	Arrange 1 oz of each kind of meat and 1 oz cheese on bottom half of each bun.
Ham, pullman, 1-oz slices	3 lb 2 oz	Alternate meat and cheese and arrange so that full length of each bun is covered.
Cheese, processed, American or Swiss, 1-oz slices	3 lb 2 oz	
Fresh tomatoes, sliced	24	Place 2 slices tomato, ½ oz shredded lettuce, and 2 dill pickle slices on each sandwich.
Shredded head lettuce	1 lb 9 oz	
Dill pickle slices, well drained (optional)	1 qt	Cover with top half of bun.
		To serve, cut each sandwich in half.

Approximate nutritive values per portion

Calories	Carbohydrate	Protein	Fat	Cholesterol	Sodium	Fiber	Iron
789 kcal	81 g	32 g	37 g	80 mg	2557 mg	5 g	5 mg

Notes

- Potentially hazardous food. *Food Safety Standards:* Hold food for service at an internal temperature of 41°F or below. Do not mix old product with new. Keep leftover product chilled at 41°F or below. See p. 167 for cooling procedures.
- Other meats such as turkey, corned beef, pastrami, or roast beef may be used.
- Shredded red or green cabbage, alfalfa sprouts, or leaf lettuce may be substituted for shredded head lettuce.
- Mayonnaise or Italian dressing may be substituted for sandwich spread.

Variations

- **Buffet Submarine.** Use 12 long, thin buns, approximately 18 inches. Arrange 4 oz each of meats and cheese on each bun. Garnish with 2 tomatoes, sliced, ⅓ cup pickle slices, and 1–2 oz shredded lettuce. Secure with long picks. Portion as served into 4–5-inch sections.
- **Ring Submarine.** Use bread shaped in a ring. See p. 262 for Sandwich Ring recipe.

DELI WRAP

Yield: 50 portions   *Portion:* 1 wrap (2 halves)

Ingredient	Amount	Procedure
Wraps, 10-inch	50	If frozen, thaw under refrigeration.
Spread selection (see pp. 732–736)	2 lb 8 oz	Place wraps flat on baking sheet or tray. Spread 1½ Tbsp spread over each wrap.
Deli meat, wafer sliced	6½ lb	Portion 2 oz meat over wrap.
Salsa (see pp. 703, 704, 708) or	3 qt	Portion 2 oz salsa or 2 tomato slices over meat.
Sliced tomatoes	5 lb	
Shredded or leaf lettuce	2 lb 8 oz	Portion ¾ oz lettuce over meat and salsa/tomato.
Shredded or sliced cheese (see Variations)	1 lb 8 oz	Portion ½ oz cheese over lettuce and meat. To roll sandwich: 1. Fold two sides of wrap 2 inches over filling. 2. Roll tightly as for jelly roll, starting to roll from side that is not over filling. Cut wrap in half diagonally. One portion is two halves. Keep cold, below 41°F. See Variations.

Note

- Potentially hazardous food. *Food Safety Standards:* Hold food for service at an internal temperature of 41°F or below. Do not mix old product with new. Keep leftover product chilled at 41°F or below. See p. 167 for cooling procedures.

Variations

- **Southwestern Steak Wrap.** Brown 5 lb seasoned fajita meat in hot oil. Add 3 lb 8 oz sliced mushrooms and sauté until tender. In a separate bowl, combine 2 lb 8 oz diced tomatoes, 1 lb 4 oz chopped red onion, 3 oz chopped fresh cilantro. Mix together in a separate bowl 3 lb 4 oz shredded cheddar cheese and 2 lb 8 oz shredded Monterey Jack cheese. Place 12-inch wrap on plate. Portion 2 oz mixed cheeses onto center of wrap, leaving 1-inch border. Sprinkle 1 oz tomato mixture over cheese. Portion 2 oz of beef-mushroom mixture over vegetables. Fold two sides over filling and roll, beginning on a side that is not covering the meat.
- **Turkey, Tomato, and Guacamole Wrap.** Meat selection: sliced turkey. Spread selection: garlic-thyme mayonnaise. Add: 2 oz guacamole (p. 202) per sandwich.

ASIAN ORANGE GINGER BEEF WRAP

Yield: 50 portions   *Portion:* 1 wrap

Ingredient	Amount	Procedure
Sushi-Style Rice (p. 562)	12 lb 8 oz	Prepare rice according to directions on p. 542. Reserve for later step.
Ginger Orange Beef (p. 433)	12 lb	Prepare ginger beef according to directions on p. 433. Reserve for later step.
Asian Sesame Sauce (p. 688)	3½ cups	Prepare sauce according to directions on p. 688. Reserve for later step.
Wraps, 12-inch Lettuce leaves	50 2 lb 12 oz	*Wrapping Procedure* 1. Place one wrap on flat surface. 2. Place lettuce leaf on half of the wrap extending to the edge of the wrap. 3. Portion 4 oz Sushi-Style Rice on wrap. Distribute rice on the side of the wrap opposite the lettuce leaf in approximately a 3 × 8-inch shape from the top of the wrap to the bottom. Stop 1½ inches on the wrap's edge. 4. Portion 4 oz Ginger Orange Beef over rice. 5. Pour 1 Tbsp Asian Sesame Sauce over beef. 6. Fold border edge of wrap (1½ inch without filling) over fillings. Roll wrap tightly. Cut in half diagonally and serve with Asian Sesame Sauce.

Note

- Potentially hazardous food. *Food Safety Standards:* Hold food for service at an internal temperature of 41°F or below. Do not mix old product with new. Keep leftover product chilled at 41°F or below. See p. 167 for cooling procedures.

PACK-A-PITA PLATE

Yield: 50 portions   *Portion:* one plate = 3 oz filling, 2 pita halves

Ingredient	Amount	Procedure
Leaf lettuce	1 lb 8 oz EP	Place one large leaf on dinner plate, leaving room for the pita bread.
Pita filling (see Note)	9 lb 8 oz	Place 3 oz filling on top of lettuce leaf.
Tomatoes, thinly sliced	12 lb EP	Place 4 tomato slices beside filling.
Alfalfa sprouts (see Note)	8 oz	Place a small amount of sprouts on top of tomatoes.
Sweet pickles, sliced Olives, black	4 lb 8 oz	Garnish plate with 6 pickle slices and 2 black olives.
Pita bread rounds	50	Just before service, place 2 pita halves on plate.

Notes

- Potentially hazardous food. *Food Safety Standards:* Hold food for service at an internal temperature of 41°F or below. Do not mix old product with new. Keep leftover product chilled at 41°F or below. See p. 167 for cooling procedures.
- Alfalfa sprouts may be potentially hazardous. Purchase sprouts from a reputable source and follow carefully all food safety standards.
- Filling choices may include egg salad, tuna salad, ham salad, sliced meats, sliced cheese, or chilled grilled vegetables. Small, thin portions of cooked and chilled solid meats may be used; for example, chicken breast, baked salmon.

Variation

- **Ratatouille Wrap.** Place 12-inch wrap on plate and portion 5–6 oz Summer Ratatouille (without eggplant) (p. 820) onto center, leaving a 2-inch border. Drizzle 1 Tbsp Balsamic Vinegar Marinade for vegetables (p. 724) over filling. Starting with an open side, roll wrap tightly, jelly-roll fashion. Cut in half diagonally to serve. Needed: 50 12-inch wraps, 18 lb ratatouille, and 3 cups marinade.

MARINATED VEGETABLE PITA

Yield: 50 portions   *Portion:* one-half pita, 2 oz vegetables, 1 oz cheese

Ingredient	Amount	Procedure
Herb and Garlic Marinade (p. 725)	1 qt	Prepare marinade.
Eggplant, ½-inch dice	1 lb 4 oz EP	Pour marinade over vegetables. Toss to coat.
Summer squash, ½-inch dice	1 lb EP	Let stand for 30 minutes; drain well. Heat fry pan. Stir-fry vegetables 8–10 minutes, until vegetables
Zucchini squash, ½-inch dice	1 lb EP	are tender-crisp.
Red bell pepper, ¼ × 1-inch strips	8 oz EP	
Green bell pepper, ¼ × 1-inch strips	8 oz EP	
Onion, sliced (rings separated)	8 oz EP	
Mushrooms, sliced	1 lb 12 oz EP	
Pita bread rounds (see Note)	25	Cut pita bread into halves.
Mozzarella cheese, shredded	3 lb	Open pita and stuff with 2 oz vegetables. Sprinkle 1 oz cheese over filling.

Approximate nutritive values per portion

Calories	Carbohydrate	Protein	Fat	Cholesterol	Sodium	Fiber	Iron
300 kcal	20 g	9 g	21 g	21 mg	412 mg	1.6 g	1 mg

Notes

- Potentially hazardous food. *Food Safety Standards:* Hold food for service at an internal temperature of 135°F or above. Do not mix old product with new. Cool leftover product quickly following time standards and cooling procedures on p. 167. Reheat leftover product quickly (within 2 hours) to 165°F or above. Reheat product only once; discard if not used.
- Gyro bread may be substituted for the pita bread. Serve by placing one warmed gyro-style bread on a plate. Portion 2 oz filling onto center of bread. Sprinkle with 1 oz cheese. Fold over and serve immediately.

Variation

- **Marinated Vegetable Fajita.** Substitute flour tortillas for pita bread. Serve with Mexican condiments.

GRILLED SANDWICHES

Yield: 50 portions   *Portion:* 1 sandwich
Grill: 350°F

Ingredient	Amount	Procedure
Bread, white, whole-wheat, or rye	100 slices	See following procedures for preparing sandwiches.
Meat and/or cheese	6 lb 4 oz	
Margarine	1 lb	Grill sandwiches at 350°F on griddle until both sides are delicately brown.

PROCEDURE NO. 1

1. Melt margarine. Pour into 2-inch counter pan.
2. Pick up two slices of bread, one in each hand. Dip one side of one slice in melted margarine. Press dipped slice against second slice.
3. Place buttered side of one slice on 18 × 26-inch baking sheet lined with parchment or waxed paper. Place 24 slices 4 × 6.
4. Top each slice with 2 oz meat and/or cheese.
5. Top meat and/or cheese with buttered bread (from Step 2), buttered side up.
6. Cover layer with parchment or waxed paper.
7. Repeat for a second layer or use another baking sheet. Cover tightly with plastic wrap if the sandwiches are not to be grilled immediately.

PROCEDURE NO. 2

1. Place meat and/or cheese between two slices of bread.
2. Brush sandwiches with melted margarine; or in large quantities, use a roller dipped in melted margarine.
3. Place sandwiches on baking sheet and cover with plastic wrap until grilled.

Note

- Potentially hazardous food. *Food Safety Standards:* Hold food for service at an internal temperature of 135°F or above. Do not mix old product with new. Cool leftover product quickly following time standards and cooling procedures on p. 167. Reheat leftover product quickly (within 2 hours) to 165°F or above. Reheat product only once; discard if not used.

Variations

- **Grilled Cheese.** Use processed American cheese, two 1-oz slices per sandwich.
- **Grilled Corned Beef and Swiss on Rye.** Substitute corned beef for ham in Grilled Ham and Cheese. Use Swiss cheese and rye bread.
- **Grilled Ham and Cheese.** Use 1½ oz ham and 1 oz cheese per sandwich; 4 lb 12 oz wafer-sliced ham and 3 lb 2 oz (1-oz slices) will be needed.
- **Grilled Turkey and Swiss on Whole Wheat.** Use 1½ oz turkey and 1 oz Swiss cheese per sandwich; 4 lb 12 oz wafer-sliced turkey and 3 lb 2 oz cheese (1-oz slices) will be needed.
- **Hot Tuna Grill.** Use No. 10 dipper Tuna Salad Sandwich filling (pp. 658, 659) for each sandwich. Other salad sandwich fillings may be used.

GRILLED FLATBREAD SANDWICH

Yield: 50 portions   *Portion:* 1 sandwich
Griddle: 300°F

Ingredient	Amount	Procedure
Flatbread rounds, 7-inch	50	Brush flatbread generously on both sides with oil.
Olive oil	3 cups	Place on a preheated 300°F griddle and cook until golden on both sides. Should be very pliable.
Romaine leaves	50	Remove flatbread from griddle.
Filling (see Note)	50 servings	Lay romaine leaves in center of bread.
		Place filling on romaine and fold in half. Serve soon after filling while flatbread is warm and pliable.

Approximate nutritive values per grilled flatbread (no filling calculated)

Calories	Carbohydrate	Protein	Fat	Cholesterol	Sodium	Fiber	Iron
282 kcal	46 g	8 g	8 g	0 mg	669 mg	4 g	2 mg

Notes

- Potentially hazardous food. *Food Safety Standards:* Hold food for service at an internal temperature of 135°F or above. Do not mix old product with new. Cool leftover product quickly following time standards and cooling procedures on p. 167. Reheat leftover product quickly (within 2 hours) to 165°F or above. Reheat product only once; discard if not used.
- Filling suggestions: chicken tenders, Chicken Salad (p. 658), Poached Salmon (p. 411), fish and coleslaw.
- Flatbread may be called gyro bread or pita bread.

Variations

- **Avocado Salad Flatbread.** Fill with sliced avocado, diced tomatoes, red onion rings, and shredded cheese. Serve Italian salad dressing as a condiment.
- **Baja Fish Flatbread.** See Fish Tacos (p. 404). Serve fresh Anaheim Salsa Rojo (p. 708) as a condiment.
- **Chicken Caesar Flatbread.** Brush flatbread with Caesar dressing after grilling. Place 2 cooked chicken tenders in flatbread and sprinkle with ½ oz grated Parmesan cheese. Serve Caesar salad dressing as a condiment.
- **Grilled Vegetable and Mozzarella Pita.** See p. 664. Serve topped with shredded mozzarella cheese and red onion rings.

ROASTED PORTABELLA GYRO

Yield: 50 portions   *Portion:* 1 gyro
Oven: 375°F; impinger, 490°F   *Bake:* 10 minutes; impinger, 4–5 minutes

Ingredient	Amount	Procedure
Portabella mushroom caps	8 lb	Remove gills and stems. Reserve stems for another use such as soup or stock. Discard gills. Slice mushroom caps into ½-inch slices.
Balsamic Vinegar Marinade for Vegetables (p. 724)	1 qt	Put marinade into a deep narrow pan. Dip mushrooms into marinade. Let drain briefly. Place mushrooms on a shallow baking pan. Roast in conventional oven for 10 minutes at 375°F, or conveyor oven for approximately 4–5 minutes at 490°F. Hold warm.
Grilled flatbread, 7-inch (p. 666)	50	Prepare per recipe. Hold warm for service.
Tomatoes, diced Cucumbers, diced unpeeled Red onions, large dice Lettuce, shredded Ripe olives, sliced Feta cheese, crumbled	3 lb 1 lb 1 lb 1 lb 12 oz 12 oz 1 lb	Mix vegetables and cheese together just before service. Mix in batches if mixture will be held for longer than 30 minutes.
Tzatziki sauce (see Note)	3 lb 4 oz	To serve, portion the following onto the center of each grilled flatbread in the order listed (taco style): 1. 1 oz mushroom strips 2. 1 oz tzatziki sauce (serve additional sauce as a condiment) 3. 2½ oz raw vegetable-cheese mixture.

Approximate nutritive values per sandwich

Calories	Carbohydrate	Protein	Fat	Cholesterol	Sodium	Fiber	Iron
429 kcal	59 g	13 g	17 g	10 mg	1021 mg	6 g	3.6 mg

Notes

- Potentially hazardous food. *Food Safety Standards:* Hold food for service at an internal temperature of 135°F or above. Do not mix old product with new. Cool leftover product quickly following time standards and cooling procedures on p. 167. Reheat leftover product quickly (within 2 hours) to 165°F or above. Reheat product only once; discard if not used.
- Tzatziki sauce can be purchased from most broadline distributors. **Tzatziki Sauce** may be prepared using the following recipe: Drain 4 lb plain (not sweetened) yogurt by placing in a fine mesh sieve, in the refrigerator (covered), while suspended over a bowl for 8 hours or longer. Discard the liquid that accumulates. To the drained yogurt add 2 lb 12 oz peeled, seeded, and finely chopped cucumber, ¾ tsp salt, ¼ cup finely minced garlic, ¼ cup olive oil, 3 Tbsp red wine vinegar, and 1 oz very finely chopped mint leaves. Store refrigerated for up to 5 days. Yield: 6 cups.

Variation

- **Roasted Portabella on Focaccia.** Prepare mushroom caps as for Roasted Portabello Gyro. Do not slice. Prepare Sun-Dried Tomato Pesto (p. 706). Assemble sandwich using made (p. 268) or purchased focaccia rolls (or wedges) in the following order: Spread 1 oz Sun-Dried Tomato Pesto on bottom portion of bread. Place roasted mushroom cap over pesto. Place 2 tomato slices on top of mushroom. Place lettuce leaf on top of tomato. Close sandwich with top portion of bun.

BIEROCKS

Yield: 50 sandwiches
Oven: 400°F   *Bake:* 25–30 minutes, 5 minutes

Ingredient	Amount	Procedure
DOUGH		
Yeast, active dry	1¼ oz	Sprinkle yeast over water. Let stand for 5 minutes.
Water, warm (110°F)	2 qt	
Sugar, granulated	14 oz	Add sugar, salt, and flour to yeast.
Salt	1 oz (1½ Tbsp)	Mix on medium speed, until mixture is smooth, using a dough arm or
Flour, all-purpose	2 lb 6 oz	flat beater.
Eggs	8 (14 oz)	Add eggs and shortening. Continue beating.
Shortening, melted	5 oz	
Flour, all-purpose	5 lb 8 oz	Add flour on low speed to make a soft dough. Knead for 5 minutes.
		Cover and let rise until double in bulk.
		When dough has doubled, punch down and divide into four or five portions.
		Roll dough ¼ inch thick.
		Cut into 4 × 6-inch rectangles.
		Place on each piece of dough a No. 8 dipper of filling (recipe follows).
		Fold lengthwise and pinch edges of dough securely to seal.
		Place on baking sheets with sealed edges down.
		Bake at 400°F for 25–30 minutes.
Egg yolk	1	Brush with egg and water mixture.
Water	2 Tbsp	Return to oven for 5 minutes.
FILLING		
Ground beef	10 lb AP (7 lb EP)	Cook beef to an internal temperature of 155°F. Drain.
Cabbage, chopped	2 lb 8 oz	Steam cabbage and onions until slightly underdone.
Onions, chopped	3 lb	
Worcestershire sauce	⅓ cup	Add seasonings and vegetables to beef.
Salt	2½ oz	If not used immediately, cool quickly to below 41°F. See p. 167
Black pepper	1½ tsp	for cooling procedures.
Savory, ground	1 tsp	
Chile powder	1½ tsp	

Approximate nutritive values per portion

Calories	Carbohydrate	Protein	Fat	Cholesterol	Sodium	Fiber	Iron
530 kcal	67 g	27 g	17 g	100 mg	834 mg	3 g	6 mg

Note
- Potentially hazardous food. *Food Safety Standards:* Hold food for service at an internal temperature of 135°F or above. Do not mix old product with new. Cool leftover product quickly following time standards and cooling procedures on p. 167. Reheat leftover product quickly (within 2 hours) to 165°F or above. Reheat product only once; discard if not used.

Variation
- **Bierock Pockets.** Scale 3 lb dough onto 18 × 26 × 1-inch greased pans. Cut dough in half lengthwise. Spread 2 lb beef mixture evenly onto each strip of dough. Roll jelly-roll fashion and seal tightly. Place seam side down on greased 18 × 26 × 1-inch pan. Bake at 350°F for 30–35 minutes or until done. Cut each roll into 8 portions, 16 per pan.

HOT MEAT AND CHEESE SANDWICH

Yield: 50 sandwiches   *Portion:* 2½ oz meat + 1½ oz sauce

Ingredient	Amount	Procedure
Ham, roast beef, or corned beef	8 lb	Wafer-slice meat into 12 × 10 × 2-inch pans. Cover and heat to 165°F.
Hamburger buns	50	To serve, place open bun on plate. Portion 2½ oz meat on bottom half of bun.
Cheese Sandwich Sauce, American or Cheddar (p. 683) or Swiss (p. 683)	3 qt	Ladle 1½ oz (No. 30 dipper) sauce over meat.

Approximate nutritive values per portion

Calories	Carbohydrate	Protein	Fat	Cholesterol	Sodium	Fiber	Iron
458 kcal	29 g	30 g	24 g	80 mg	1740 mg	0 g	3 mg

Note

- Potentially hazardous food. *Food Safety Standards:* Hold food for service at an internal temperature of 135°F or above. Do not mix old product with new. Cool leftover product quickly following time standards and cooling procedures on p. 167. Reheat leftover product quickly (within 2 hours) to 165°F or above. Reheat product only once; discard if not used.

HOT ROAST BEEF SANDWICH

Yield: 50 sandwiches   *Portion:* 3 oz meat + ¼ cup gravy

Ingredient	Amount	Procedure
Beef roast	10 lb EP (15 lb AP)	Roast beef according to directions on pp. 147 and 422. Slice into 3-oz portions. Place in two 12 × 20 × 2-inch counter pans.
Beef Stock (p. 738)	1½ qt	Heat stock to 190°F. Pour over meat. Cover with aluminum foil and place in oven to keep warm.
Bread	50 slices	Place 3 oz meat on each slice of bread.
Mashed Potatoes (p. 798) Pan Gravy (p. 685)	12 lb 8 oz 1 gal	Serve No. 12 dipper of Mashed Potatoes on the plate beside the bread. Cover meat and potato with Pan Gravy, using 2-oz ladle.

Approximate nutritive values per portion

Calories	Carbohydrate	Protein	Fat	Cholesterol	Sodium	Fiber	Iron
417 kcal	35 g	32 g	17 g	84 mg	1025 mg	5 g	4 mg

Notes

- Potentially hazardous food. *Food Safety Standards:* Hold food for service at an internal temperature of 135°F or above. Do not mix old product with new. Cool leftover product quickly following time standards and cooling procedures on p. 167. Reheat leftover product quickly (within 2 hours) to 165°F or above. Reheat product only once; discard if not used.
- A tender cut of meat should be used.
- Meat may be covered with additional slice of bread if desired. Omit mashed potatoes. Cover entire sandwich with gravy.

Variations

- **Barbecued Beef Sandwich.** Place thinly sliced beef roast in two counter pans and keep warm. Heat 1½ qt Barbecue Sauce (p. 688) and pour 3 cups over each pan of meat. Toss together until sauce is evenly distributed. Serve in warm hamburger buns.
- **French Dip Sandwich.** Slice roast beef wafer thin. Place in 12 × 20 × 2-inch counter pan. Pour 1 cup Beef Stock (p. 738) over meat. Cover with aluminum foil and keep warm. To serve, place 3 oz beef on hard roll. Serve with side cup of hot seasoned broth for dipping.
- **Hot Roast Pork Sandwich.** Substitute roast pork for beef.
- **Hot Turkey Dip.**   Follow directions for French Dip Sandwich, but substitute wafer-sliced turkey for beef and chicken broth for beef broth. Season chicken stock with poultry seasoning.
- **Hot Turkey Sandwich.** Substitute roast turkey or turkey roll for beef. Use Chicken Stock (p. 738) in place of Beef Stock.
- **Meat Loaf Sandwich.** Prepare Meat Loaf (p. 440). Substitute Meat Loaf for roast beef.

BROCCOLI AND RICOTTA CALZONE

Yield: 50 portions   *Portion:* 1 calzone
Oven: 350°F   *Bake:* 18–25 minutes

Ingredient	Amount	Procedure
Broccoli cuts, frozen	6 lb AP	Thaw broccoli cuts in a colander or perforated pan. Drained EP yield should equal 5 lb 8 oz. Save drained broccoli for later step.
Pizza dough	50 dough balls (5 oz)	If using frozen dough balls, cover and let thaw to 65°F, 2–3 hours. Working with a small number of dough balls at a time, flatten into rounds.
Ricotta cheese	6 lb 6 oz	Blend cheeses and seasonings together.
Parmesan cheese, shredded	10 oz	Portion 2 oz (No. 16 dipper) of cheese mixture onto half of flattened dough ball. Smooth filling slightly, leaving ½-inch border.
Black pepper	1 Tbsp	Distribute ½ cup (1¾ oz) of thawed broccoli (reserved from earlier step)
Garlic powder	½ tsp	over cheese.
Mozzarella cheese, shredded	2 lb	Sprinkle ¾ oz cheese over broccoli. Brush edges of dough with water. Fold dough over filling and crimp edges to seal tightly.
Eggs	2 oz	Mix eggs and water. Brush over tops of calzones.
Water	3 oz	Sprinkle with herbs.
Italian herbs	3 Tbsp	Bake at 350°F for 18–25 minutes in a conventional oven until the calzone registers 185°F. Follow the manufacturer's directions when using a conveyor-type pizza oven.
Marinara sauce	3¼ qt	Serve 2 oz warm marinara sauce ladled on top of calzone.
Parmesan cheese, shredded	1 lb	Serve with Parmesan cheese.

Approximate nutritive values per portion

Calories	Carbohydrate	Protein	Fat	Cholesterol	Sodium	Fiber	Iron
587 kcal	79 g	28 g	17 g	36 mg	1273 mg	5 g	4.5 mg

Note

- Potentially hazardous food. *Food Safety Standards:* Hold food for service at an internal temperature of 135°F or above. Do not mix old product with new. Cool leftover product quickly following time standards and cooling procedures on p. 167. Reheat leftover product quickly (within 2 hours) to 165°F or above. Reheat product only once; discard if not used.

Variations

- **Ham and Swiss Florentine Calzone.** Steam 2 lb fresh spinach for 1 minute. Drain well and reserve for later step. Blend together 6 lb 6 oz ricotta cheese, 10 oz freshly grated Parmesan cheese, and 1 Tbsp black pepper. Portion 2 oz cheese mixture and ¾ oz (No. 30 dipper) drained spinach on dough. Portion ¾ oz of wafer-sliced ham over spinach. Follow makeup and service procedures as for Broccoli and Ricotta Calzone.
- **Pepperoni Calzone.** Omit broccoli from Broccoli and Ricotta Calzone. Use 1 lb 4 oz thinly sliced pepperoni and 2 lb shredded mozzarella cheese. Place 6 slices pepperoni on filling and ¾ oz shredded mozzarella over pepperoni before folding and sealing.
- **Roasted Vegetable and Ricotta Calzone.** Substitute the following mixture for the broccoli and ricotta cheese mixture: Blend in baker's bowl 6 lb 6 oz ricotta cheese, 10 oz shredded Parmesan cheese, ½ cup dried parsley, ¼ cup dried basil, 1½ Tbsp black pepper, ¼ tsp crushed red pepper, 10 oz chopped bell peppers (green, red, yellow frozen blend), 1 lb fresh sliced mushrooms, 6 oz chopped onion, and 4 oz sliced ripe olives. Sprinkle vegetable mixture with ¾ oz shredded mozzarella cheese. Assemble as for Broccoli and Ricotta Calzone.
- **Spinach and Roasted Red Pepper Calzone.** Blend in baker's bowl 6 lb 6 oz ricotta cheese, 10 oz grated Parmesan cheese, and 2½ tsp black pepper. Steam 3 lb fresh spinach for 1 minute. Drain well. Portion 2 oz cheese mixture, No. 30 dipper spinach, and 1 Tbsp coarsely chopped roasted red peppers onto dough. Substitute shredded Swiss cheese for mozzarella cheese. Assemble as for Broccoli and Ricotta Calzone.

GRILLED CORN AND ROASTED PEPPER QUESADILLAS

Yield: 50 portions   *Portion:* 2 quesadillas

Ingredient	Amount	Procedure
Vegetable oil	4 oz	Mix oil and chipotle base. Heat in a tilting fry pan or on a
Chipotle flavor concentrate (see Note)	2 oz	griddle.
Corn, frozen (see Note)	5 lb 4 oz	Sauté corn and onions in flavored oil until onions are translucent and corn is slightly browned.
Onions, chopped	2 lb EP	
Roasted Red Bell Peppers, diced (p. 796) (see Note)	3 lb 4 oz	Add roasted peppers and crushed red pepper. Heat through.
Crushed red pepper	¾ tsp	Save for later step.
Flour tortillas, 6-inch	100	Place tortillas flat on 18 × 26 × 1-inch pans.
Cojack cheese, shredded	6 lb 4 oz	Distribute 1 oz shredded cheese on half of tortilla, leaving a ½-inch border without cheese.
		Distribute 1¾ oz corn-pepper blend over cheese (reserved from earlier step).
		Place open tortilla on oiled 300°F griddle.
		Cook until cheese begins to melt and tortilla is soft.
		Fold empty half of tortilla over filled half, pressing slightly with a spatula. Turn and grill until slightly brown.
		Serve immediately. May serve with salsa, guacamole, and sour cream.

Approximate nutritive values per portion

Calories	Carbohydrate	Protein	Fat	Cholesterol	Sodium	Fiber	Iron
525 kcal	50 g	20 g	27 g	51 mg	847 mg	4 g	3 mg

Notes

- Potentially hazardous food. *Food Safety Standards:* Hold food for service at an internal temperature of 135°F or above. Do not mix old product with new. Cool leftover product quickly following time standards and cooling procedures on p. 167. Reheat leftover product quickly (within 2 hours) to 165°F or above. Reheat product only once; discard if not used.
- Minor's Chipotle Flavor Concentrate (a blend of red, chipotle, and jalapeño peppers with onion, garlic, and spice) is available from most broadline foodservice distributors.
- Roasted corn and roasted peppers may be purchased frozen and substituted for the corn and peppers in the recipe. When using frozen roasted peppers, place in a single layer on a baking sheet and heat in a 375°F oven until heated through (discard liquid that accumulates).

Variations

- **Cheese Quesadillas.** Mix together 6 lb shredded Monterey Jack cheese, 6 lb shredded cheddar cheese, 3 lb 8 oz canned diced green chiles, drained, and 4 Tbsp dried cilantro. Scale 2½ oz cheese mixture on half of each 8-inch tortilla, leaving a ½-inch border on the filled side. Proceed as for Grilled Corn and Roasted Pepper Quesadillas. Yield: 100 8-inch quesadillas.
- **Chicken Quesadillas.** Mix together 5 lb 6 oz chicken strips, 3 lb canned diced green chile, 1 lb 10 oz chopped red onion, and ½ cup chopped fresh cilantro. On each 8-inch flour tortilla, distribute 1½ oz shredded Monterey Jack cheese, leaving a ½-inch border. Distribute 1½ oz chicken mixture over the cheese on only half of the tortilla. Proceed as for Grilled Corn and Roasted Pepper Quesadillas. Yield: 100 8-inch quesadillas.
- **Grilled Vegetable and Mozzarella Pitas.** Follow recipe for Grilled Vegetable and Mozzarella Quesadillas. Serve grilled vegetable mixture folded inside a warmed 7-inch round flatbread. See p. 666 for flatbread grilling directions.
- **Grilled Vegetable and Mozzarella Quesadillas.** Prepare vegetable marinade using red wine vinegar in place of balsamic vinegar (p. 724) and put in baker's bowl. To the marinade, add 1 lb 12 oz chopped bell peppers (green, red, and yellow combination), 2 lb sliced fresh mushrooms, 1 lb 4 oz eggplant rounds, sliced ¼ inch thick and quartered, 1 lb 4 oz sliced yellow summer squash, and 1 lb sliced zucchini squash. Stir vegetables to coat with marinade and let stand for 30 minutes. Drain well. Heat tilting fry pan to 375°F. Sauté vegetables until tender-crisp, 8–10 min. Substitute sautéed vegetables for the vegetable mixture in Grilled Corn and Roasted Pepper Quesadillas. Substitute 4 lb 8 oz shredded mozzarella cheese for shredded cojack cheese. Proceed as for Grilled Corn and Roasted Pepper Quesadillas. Yield: 50 8-inch quesadillas.

- Cheese and filling suggestions:

Cheese suggestions			Filling suggestions		
Asiago	Gruyère	Swiss	**Produce**	**Canned**	**Other**
Bleu	Havarti	Goat cheese	Baby greens	Rinsed beans	Cooked seafood
Colby	Manchego	Feta	Mushrooms	Sun-dried tomatoes	Crushed red pepper
Cheddar	Monterey Jack	Fromage blanc	Diced tomato	Roasted peppers	Scallions
Fontina	Mozzarella		Leeks	Sliced olives	Smoked paprika
Gouda	Provolone		Onions		
			Shallots	**Meat**	
				Bacon	
				Pancetta	

CHICKEN FAJITAS

Yield: 50 fajitas   *Portion:* 4 oz meat mixture (two 6-inch fajitas or one 10-inch fajita)

Ingredient	Amount	Procedure
Vegetable oil	¼ cup	Heat oil to 350°F in tilting or large fry pan.
Chicken white meat, cut into strips	10 lb EP	Add chicken and garlic. Stir-fry until chicken begins to brown.
Garlic, minced	3 oz EP	
Fresh lime juice	1 qt	Add liquids, herbs, and spices to chicken. Cook until liquid evaporates and chicken is done, above 165°F.
Water	2 cups	
Chicken base	2 oz	
Fresh cilantro, finely chopped (see Note)	¾ oz	
Black pepper	1 Tbsp	
Crushed red pepper	1 tsp	
Salt	1½ Tbsp	
Onions, sliced	2 lb 6 oz EP	Add onions and peppers. Stir-fry until tender-crisp.
Green bell peppers, cut in 1-inch-long strips	12 oz EP	
Red bell peppers, cut in 1-inch-long strips	8 oz EP	
Yellow bell peppers, cut in1-inch-long strips	8 oz EP	
Flour tortillas	50 10-inch or 100 6-inch	Heat tortillas to soften. Keep covered. Do not allow to dry out. Serve 4 oz meat mixture on one 10-inch or two 6-inch tortillas. Serve with condiments: Guacamole (p. 202), shredded Monterey Jack cheese, shredded lettuce, sour cream, Salsa (p. 702), sliced black olives, sliced jalapeños.

Approximate nutritive values per portion

Calories	Carbohydrate	Protein	Fat	Cholesterol	Sodium	Fiber	Iron
350 kcal	41 g	27 g	7 g	53 mg	733 mg	3 g	3 mg

Notes

- Potentially hazardous food. *Food Safety Standards:* Hold food for service at an internal temperature of 135°F or above. Do not mix old product with new. Cool leftover product quickly following time standards and cooling procedures on p. 167. Reheat leftover product quickly (within 2 hours) to 165°F or above. Reheat product only once; discard if not used.
- 3 Tbsp dried cilantro can be substituted for fresh cilantro.
- Ranchero base (commercial product) can be substituted for chicken base. Adjust seasonings as necessary.

BEEF FAJITAS

Yield: 50 fajitas   *Portion:* 1 fajita, 2 oz meat + 2 oz vegetable

Ingredient	Amount	Procedure
Puréed jalapeño peppers, with juice	4 oz	Combine in bowl to make a marinade.
Fresh lemon juice	1½ cups	
Fresh pineapple juice	1½ cups	
Salt	1 Tbsp	
Black pepper	2 Tbsp	
Meat tenderizer	2 oz	
Water	3 cups	
Beef, round or flank steak	10 lb AP	Cut beef into 1 × 5-inch strips, ¼ inch thick (see Note). Pour marinade over meat. Stir to coat meat. Cover and marinate for 24 hours.
		Drain meat in colander. Discard marinade. Stir-fry in frying pan with a small amount of oil until cooked.
Onions, sliced, separated in rings	2 lb 8 oz	Add onions and peppers to meat. Stir-fry until tender-crisp.
Green bell pepper strips	1 lb 8 oz	Transfer to 12 × 10 × 4-inch pan.
Fresh tomatoes	2 lb 8 oz	Cut tomatoes into thin wedges. Combine carefully with beef. Gently lift beef and vegetables from juice into 12 × 20 × 2-inch counter pan.
Flour tortillas, 10-inch	50	Heat tortillas to soften. Keep covered. Do not allow to dry out. Serve 1 tortilla on plate and 4 oz beef and vegetables in center of tortilla. Tortilla may be rolled or folded in half.
		Serve with condiments: Guacamole (p. 202), shredded Monterey Jack cheese, shredded lettuce, sour cream, Salsa (p. 702), sliced black olives, sliced jalapeños.

Approximate nutritive values per portion

Calories	Carbohydrate	Protein	Fat	Cholesterol	Sodium	Fiber	Iron
246 kcal	25 g	21 g	7 g	51 mg	360 mg	1 g	3 mg

Notes

- Potentially hazardous food. *Food Safety Standards:* Hold food for service at an internal temperature of 135°F or above. Do not mix old product with new. Cool leftover product quickly following time standards and cooling procedures on p. 167. Reheat leftover product quickly (within 2 hours) to 165°F or above. Reheat product only once; discard if not used.
- Meat will slice more easily if it is partially frozen.
- Fajita meat can be made spicier by substituting additional puréed jalapeños for equal parts water. More water in proportion to less jalapeños may be used for a less spicy fajita.
- Beef strips may be purchased frozen, seasoned, or unseasoned.
- Commercial fajita marinade mix may be substituted for marinade in the recipe.
- May serve beef separate from onions, peppers, and tomatoes.

Variation

- **Chicken Fajitas.** Delete meat tenderizer. Increase salt to 2 Tbsp. Substitute chicken breasts for beef.

WESTERN SANDWICH

Yield: 50 sandwiches   *Portion:* 3 oz

Ingredient	Amount	Procedure
Ground beef	10 lb AP	Brown beef and onions until internal temperature reaches 155°F. Drain off fat.
Onions, chopped	1 lb	
Tomato purée	3 cups	Add remaining filling ingredients to meat.
Catsup	3 cups	Simmer for 15–20 minutes.
Water	1 cup	
Salt	1 Tbsp	
Paprika	2 tsp	
Dry mustard	2 tsp	
Worcestershire sauce	2 Tbsp	
Chile powder	1 Tbsp	
Hamburger buns	50	Serve with No. 12 dipper of filling on buns.

Approximate nutritive values per portion

Calories	Carbohydrate	Protein	Fat	Cholesterol	Sodium	Fiber	Iron
330 kcal	28 g	21 g	14 g	62 mg	646 mg	1 g	3 mg

Notes

- Potentially hazardous food. *Food Safety Standards:* Hold food for service at an internal temperature of 135°F or above. Do not mix old product with new. Cool leftover product quickly following time standards and cooling procedures on p. 167. Reheat leftover product quickly (within 2 hours) to 165°F or above. Reheat product only once; discard if not used.
- If mixture becomes dry, add a small amount of water.
- 2 oz (1 cup) dehydrated onions, rehydrated in 1½ cups water, may be substituted for fresh onions.

Variations

- **Beanie Joe.** Drain and rinse enough canned red beans to equal 6 lb. Lightly coat bottom of fry pan with vegetable oil. Sauté 2½ Tbsp minced garlic, 1 lb chopped onions, and 1 lb 5 oz chopped green bell peppers until fragrant. Add rinsed and drained beans to vegetables and mix. Heat while stirring and lightly breaking up the beans. In baker's bowl, combine 1½ qt tomato paste, 4¼ cups water, 1 cup catsup, 1 Tbsp soy sauce, 4 tsp honey, 3 tsp dried oregano, 1 tsp ground red pepper, 2 tsp salt (see Note), and 6 Tbsp Southwest seasoning blend. Mix liquids and spices with bean mixture. Heat to 180–190°F. Serve 4 oz bean mixture on a hamburger bun. (Note: Use any Southwest seasoning blend with paprika, cumin, and garlic. Seasoning blends vary in the amount of salt. Taste product before adding additional salt.)
- **Pizzaburger.** Delete paprika and chile powder. Add 1 Tbsp oregano, 1½ tsp basil, and 8 oz sliced mushrooms. Serve meat on bun and sprinkle with 1 lb 8 oz grated mozzarella cheese, ½ oz per serving.
- **Sloppy Joe.** Reduce ground beef to 8 lb. Sauté 2 lb chopped onions, 1 lb chopped celery, and 1 lb chopped green bell peppers with ground beef. Add 1½ oz flour to beef-vegetable mixture; mix to combine. Cook for 10 minutes. Add 2¾ cups tomato purée, 2¾ cups catsup, ⅓ cup water, ⅔ cup Worcestershire sauce, 1 Tbsp red pepper sauce, 1 Tbsp dry mustard, 2 Tbsp paprika, 3 Tbsp chile powder, 3 Tbsp sugar, and ¾ oz beef base. Stir to mix. Cover and simmer for 15–20 minutes. Stir occasionally.

TACOS

Yield: 50 tacos   *Portion:* 2 tacos

Ingredient	Amount	Procedure
Ground beef, round	13 lb AP (9 lb EP)	Brown beef in steam-jacketed or other kettle until internal temperature reaches 155°F. Drain off fat.
Onions, chopped	1 lb	Add onions and cook until softened.
Cornstarch	3 Tbsp	Combine cornstarch and seasonings in a bowl.
Chile powder	½ cup	Add to ground beef and onions. Mix well.
Garlic powder	1¾ Tbsp	
Salt	3 Tbsp	
Oregano, leaf, dried	1 Tbsp	
Cumin, ground	2 Tbsp	
Cayenne pepper	1 Tbsp	
Water	1½ qt	Add water to meat mixture. Mix. Simmer for 45 minutes, stirring frequently.
Taco shells	100	Place shells in counter pans. Heat in oven until warm and crisp. To serve, fill each taco shell with No. 24 dipper of meat mixture, 1½ oz each.

TOPPING

Head lettuce, chopped	4 lb EP	Cover meat mixture with lettuce, then tomato, and then shredded cheese. Serve with Salsa (p. 702) to spoon on top.
Fresh tomatoes, diced	3 lb EP	
Processed cheese, shredded	2 lb	

Approximate nutritive values per portion

Calories	Carbohydrate	Protein	Fat	Cholesterol	Sodium	Fiber	Iron
447 kcal	29 g	24 g	26 g	64 mg	1171 mg	4 g	3 mg

Notes

- Potentially hazardous food. *Food Safety Standards:* Hold food for service at an internal temperature of 135°F or above. Do not mix old product with new. Cool leftover product quickly following time standards and cooling procedures on p. 167. Reheat leftover product quickly (within 2 hours) to 165°F or above. Reheat product only once; discard if not used.
- Commercial salsa may be substituted for Salsa recipe.
- Commercial taco seasoning mix may be substituted for spices. Follow manufacturer's directions for amount to use.
- 2 oz (1 cup) dehydrated onions, rehydrated in 1½ cups water, may be substituted for fresh onions.

Variations

- **Nacho Tostados.** Place ¾ oz (about 6 large) round unsalted nacho chips on serving plate. Place No. 12 dipper (3 oz) taco meat on top of chips. Ladle 2 oz Nacho Sauce (p. 203) over meat. Place approximately 1½ oz shredded head lettuce and ¾ oz diced fresh tomatoes on top of meat. Serve with condiments: Guacamole (p. 202), sour cream, and Salsa (p. 702).
- **Tostados.** Fry 50 10-inch flour or corn tortillas in hot oil, 20–30 seconds on each side, until crisp and golden brown. Drain on paper towel. Keep warm. To serve, spread each tortilla with No. 20 dipper Refried Beans (p. 779), then No. 12 dipper of meat (3 oz). Top with 1½ oz chopped head lettuce, ¾ oz chopped fresh tomatoes, and 1 oz shredded cheese. Serve with condiments: Guacamole (p. 202), sour cream, Salsa (p. 702), chopped green onions, chopped green chiles, and sliced ripe olives.
- **Turkey Tacos.** Substitute ground turkey for ground beef.

REUBEN SANDWICH

Yield: 50 sandwiches   *Portion:* 3 oz
Grill: 325°F

Ingredient	Amount	Procedure
Cooked corned beef	4 lb 8 oz	Cut corned beef into very thin slices.
Rye bread	100 slices	Spread No. 100 dipper (scant 2 tsp) dressing on bread.
Mayonnaise or Sandwich Spread (p. 655)	2 cups	
Sauerkraut, well drained	1½ qt	Place filling on bread, in order given:
Swiss cheese, 1-oz slices	3 lb 2 oz	1½ oz corned beef 2 Tbsp sauerkraut 1 oz cheese Cover with top slice of bread.
Margarine, melted	1 lb	Brush sandwiches with melted margarine. Preheat grill to 325°F. Grill sandwiches on both sides until delicately browned.

Approximate nutritive values per portion

Calories	Carbohydrate	Protein	Fat	Cholesterol	Sodium	Fiber	Iron
447 kcal	29 g	24 g	26 g	64 mg	1171 mg	4 g	3 mg

Note

- Potentially hazardous food. *Food Safety Standards:* Hold food for service at an internal temperature of 135°F or above. Do not mix old product with new. Cool leftover product quickly following time standards and cooling procedures on p. 167. Reheat leftover product quickly (within 2 hours) to 165°F or above. Reheat product only once; discard if not used.

Variation

- **Reuben Sandwich with Reuben Filling.** Omit mayonnaise and sauerkraut from Reuben Sandwich. Drain 3 lb 4 oz sauerkraut until well drained (overnight). Chop sauerkraut finely and place in baker's bowl. Add to sauerkraut mixture 12 oz drained and chopped dill pickles, 6 oz yellow mustard, and 1 lb 8 oz mayonnaise or salad dressing. Mix well. Spread No. 24 dipper (2 oz) over corned beef. Proceed as for Reuben Sandwich. Makes 50 sandwiches.

CHIMICHANGA

Yield: 50 portions   *Portion:* 4 oz
Deep-fat fryer: 350°F

Ingredient	Amount	Procedure
Ground beef	10 lb 12 oz AP	Brown meat in steam-jacketed kettle until internal temperature reaches 155°F. Drain.
Onions, chopped	1 lb 10 oz	Add onions and chile peppers to meat.
Green chile peppers, chopped	8 oz	Cook until tender.
Flour, all-purpose	4 oz	Stir flour and seasonings into meat mixture.
Garlic powder	½ tsp	
Cumin, ground	2 tsp	
Chile powder	1 Tbsp	
Salsa (see Note)	1 lb 14 oz	Add salsa, beef base, and water. Cook for 15–20 minutes or until very thick.
Beef base	¾ oz	The filling may be prepared the day before and refrigerated.
Water	1 qt	
Flour tortillas, 10-inch	5 lb 8 oz	Separate tortillas and place slightly overlapping in counter pans. Cover tightly and heat a few at a time for about 5 minutes or just until soft.
Water, cold	2¼ cups	Mix water and cornstarch.
Cornstarch	2 oz	

To Assemble:

1. Brush edges of tortillas with water-cornstarch mixture.
2. Place No. 12 dipper or 4 oz meat mixture slightly below center of each tortilla.
3. Fold bottom edge over filling.
4. Fold sides in, then roll into a cylinder. If necessary, brush on more water-cornstarch mixture to help seal edges.
5. Place seam side down on baking sheets until ready to fry. Cover.
6. Fry at 350°F until golden brown and crisp. Internal temperature should be 165°F.
7. Place in counter pans with liners. Do not cover.
8. Serve with topping (recipe follows).

Topping

Lettuce, shredded	3 lb 8 oz	Serve each Chimichanga with 1 oz each shredded lettuce, chopped onion, Guacamole, sour cream, and olives; and 2 oz Salsa. See Note.
Tomato, chopped	3 lb 8 oz	
Guacamole (p. 202)	3 lb 8 oz	
Sour cream	3 lb 8 oz	
Black olives, chopped	3 lb 8 oz	
Salsa (p. 702) or Spanish Sauce (p. 692)	3 qt	

Approximate nutritive values per portion

Calories	Carbohydrate	Protein	Fat	Cholesterol	Sodium	Fiber	Iron
581 kcal	46 g	27 g	36 g	76 mg	1148 mg	2 g	5 mg

Notes

- Potentially hazardous food. *Food Safety Standards:* Hold food for service at an internal temperature of 135°F or above. Do not mix old product with new. Cool leftover product quickly following time standards and cooling procedures on p. 167. Reheat leftover product quickly (within 2 hours) to 165°F or above. Reheat product only once; discard if not used.
- Salsa (p. 702) or commercial salsa may be used.
- 7 lb shredded cooked beef may be substituted for ground beef. Omit browning the beef and sauté onions and peppers in a little shortening.
- 3 oz (1½ cups) dehydrated onions, rehydrated in 2½ cups water, may be substituted for fresh onions.

Variation

- **Shredded Beef Chimichanga.** See p. 455.

CROISSANT WITH SAUTÉED GARDEN VEGETABLES

Yield: 50 portions   *Portion:* 1 sandwich
Oven: 350°F   *Bake:* 5–10 minutes

Ingredient	Amount	Procedure
Green bell peppers, sliced	2 lb 6 oz	Toss together.
Onions, sliced	2 lb 6 oz	
Fresh mushrooms, sliced	2 lb 6 oz	
Margarine	14 oz	Melt margarine in steam-jacketed kettle. Add vegetables. Sauté until tender-crisp. Drain.
Croissants, cut in half lengthwise	50 (2½-oz size)	Assemble sandwiches in 12 × 20 × 2-inch pans:
Swiss cheese, ⅔-oz slices	4 lb 3 oz (100 slices)	1. Bottom of croissant 2. ⅔-oz Swiss cheese slice 3. 2 oz sautéed vegetables
Sliced ripe olives, canned, drained	1 lb 6 oz	4. ½ oz sliced olives 5. 2 tomato slices
Tomatoes, sliced	2 lb	6. ⅔-oz Swiss cheese slice 7. Top of croissant Heat at 350°F just long enough to melt cheese, 5–10 minutes. Do not hold more than 15 minutes before serving.

Approximate nutritive values per portion

Calories	Carbohydrate	Protein	Fat	Cholesterol	Sodium	Fiber	Iron
346 kcal	18 g	14 g	24 g	64 mg	544 mg	2 g	2 mg

FALAFEL IN PITA BREAD

Yield: 50 portions   *Portion:* 1 sandwich
Deep-fat fryer: 350°F

Ingredient	Amount	Procedure
Garbanzo beans, canned, drained	4 lb 10 oz	Cook garbanzo beans in steamer or with a little water in steam-jacketed kettle until soft enough to mash with a fork. Drain well. Put in mixer bowl and mash with a flat paddle until paste-like.
Eggs	10 oz	Combine eggs, tahini paste, vegetables, cornflake crumbs, and seasonings with mashed beans.
Tahini paste	14 oz	Mix well.
Garlic, minced	¼ cup EP	Portion with a No. 40 dipper into balls.
Celery, finely chopped	10 oz EP	Flatten slightly into a 1¾ × ¾-inch disk shape.
Green onions, finely chopped	14 oz EP	Deep-fry at 350°F until golden brown, 2–3 minutes.
Cornflake crumbs	1 lb 8 oz	
Cumin, ground	1 Tbsp	
Turmeric	1 Tbsp	
Ground red pepper	2 tsp	
Black pepper	½ tsp	
Salt	4½ tsp	
Pita bread pieces, warmed	50	Assemble sandwich by placing three falafel disks in center of warm pita bread.
Leaf lettuce	1 lb 8 oz EP	Garnish with leaf lettuce.
Tahini and Yogurt Sauce (p. 701)	50 portions	Serve with Tahini and Yogurt Sauce.

Approximate nutritive values per portion

Calories	Carbohydrate	Protein	Fat	Cholesterol	Sodium	Fiber	Iron
485 kcal	68 g	16 g	18 g	41 mg	933 mg	6 g	1 mg

Note

- Potentially hazardous food. *Food Safety Standards:* Hold food for service at an internal temperature of 135°F or above. Do not mix old product with new. Cool leftover product quickly following time standards and cooling procedures on p. 167. Reheat leftover product quickly (within 2 hours) to 165°F or above. Reheat product only once; discard if not used.

Sauces, Salsas, Marinades, Rubs, and Seasonings

A sauce complements an entrée, vegetable, or dessert. It may be used as a binding agent to hold foods together or as a topping. Sauces add richness, moistness, color, and form to foods and may enhance or offer contrast in flavor or color to foods they accompany. Marinades, rubs, and seasoning blends add flavor to entrées and vegetables. They may be used also to tenderize.

Entrée and Vegetable Sauces

Basic to many sauces is a roux, which is a cooked mixture of fat and flour, usually equal parts by weight. A roux may range from white, in which the fat and flour are cooked only for a short time, to brown, cooked until it is light brown in color and has a nutty aroma. The amount of browning will influence both the flavor and color characteristics of the sauce. Calories may be lowered by eliminating the fat and making the sauce with a starch thickener, such as flour or cornstarch, mixed with a cold liquid (stock or milk).

Other starch thickening agents commonly used in sauces are arrowroot, cornstarch, pregelatinized or instant starch, and waxy maize. Waxy maize is preferred for sauces that will be frozen because it will not break and separate as easily as other starches. When reheated, products containing waxy maize are smoother than those with cornstarch. Egg yolks have a slight thickening power and are used for some sauces. When egg yolks are cooked to too high a temperature, or held too long, the egg protein will coagulate and cause a curdled effect.

Most meat and vegetable sauces are modifications of the basic recipes: white sauce, blond sauce, brown sauce, red sauce, and butter sauces.

- **White sauce** (p. 683), made with a roux of fat and flour and with milk as the liquid, has many uses in quantity food preparation, as a sauce with vegetables, eggs, and fish and as an ingredient in many casseroles. A White Sauce Mix (p. 682), combining flour, fat, and nonfat dry milk, may be made and stored in the refrigerator until needed. Water and seasonings are added when the mixture is to be used. Béchamel Sauce (p. 684) is a white sauce that uses milk and chicken stock as the liquid and, with its variations, usually is served with poultry, seafood, eggs, or vegetables.

- **Blond sauce** is made from a roux that is cooked a little longer than the white sauce, just until the roux begins to brown. Velouté Sauce (p. 684) is a blond sauce that uses chicken, veal, or fish broth as its liquid.

- **Brown sauce** (p. 686) is made with a well-browned roux, and beef stock as the liquid. Brown sauce is used with meat.

- **Red sauces** (pp. 688–692) include tomato as a primary ingredient. These sauces are generally used with meat and pasta.

- **Butter sauces** (pp. 700, 720, 721) are used with vegetables, fish, meats, and egg dishes.

Some sauces use chicken, beef, or vegetable stock as part or all of the liquid. Recipes for stocks are on pp. 738–740. A broth made with a high-quality commercial stock base can be substituted for the chicken or beef stock called for in sauces, but the salt in the recipe may need to be adjusted if the base is highly seasoned.

Sauces made from concentrated canned soups are time-saving and may be used effectively in many items. Undiluted canned cream soups such as chicken, mushroom, celery, cheese, or tomato soup may be used alone or in combination. If the soup is too thick, a small amount of milk or chicken or meat stock may be added. Two soups may be combined for a special flavor effect, or pimento, green bell pepper, almonds, curry powder, or other ingredients may be added for variety.

Dessert Sauces

Dessert sauces serve as both a garnish and a basic ingredient for many desserts. The choice of sauce should complement the dessert in both color and flavor. Most dessert sauces are added shortly before serving.

Salsa-Style Accompaniments

Salsa-style condiments are often used to make food more interesting, flavorful, and visually appealing. They also can be used to add ethnic flavors to menus. The accompaniments should complement the foods they are served with. Recipes for entrée accompaniments begin on p. 702. See Chapter 17, p. 637, for additional accompaniments.

Marinades, Rubs, and Seasonings

Marinades are used to flavor and tenderize meats, poultry, and fish and to flavor raw or cooked vegetables. The less tender cuts of meat should be marinated for at least 2 hours. Pork, chicken, and the more tender cuts of beef often are basted before and during cooking; however, they do not need to stand in the marinade. Rubs and other seasonings add flavor and can be used to provide an ethnic or regional flavor profile to foods. See pp. 134–138 for suggestions for using herbs and spices.

Entrée and Vegetable Sauce Recipes

WHITE SAUCE MIX

Yield: 13 lb 8 oz mix

Ingredient	Amount	Procedure
Flour, all-purpose	3 lb	Blend flour and milk in 60-qt mixer bowl.
Nonfat dry milk	6 lb	
Shortening	2 lb 4 oz	Using a pastry knife or flat beater, blend fats with dry ingredients until mixture is crumbly, scraping sides of bowl occasionally.
Margarine	2 lb 4 oz	Store in covered containers in the refrigerator.

To Prepare 1 Gallon of White Sauce:

Water	3¼ qt	Heat water and salt to boiling point.
Salt	1 oz (1½ Tbsp)	
White sauce mix		Add mix for sauce of desired thickness. Stirring with a wire whip, continue cooking until thickened.
Thin	1 lb 12 oz	
Medium	2 lb 4 oz	
Thick	2 lb 14 oz	

WHITE SAUCE

Yield: 1 gal

Ingredients

Consistency	Milk	Flour, all-purpose	Margarine or butter	Salt	Uses
Thin	4 qt	6 oz	6 oz	1 oz	Cream soups
Medium	4 qt	8 oz	8 oz	1 oz	Creamed foods, gravy
Thick	4 qt	12 oz	12 oz	1 oz	Soufflés

Notes

- Potentially hazardous food. *Food Safety Standards:* Hold food for service at an internal temperature of 135°F or above. Do not mix old product with new. Cool leftover product quickly following time standards and cooling procedures on p. 167. Reheat leftover product quickly (within 2 hours) to 165°F or above. Reheat product only once; discard if not used.
- 1 lb nonfat dry milk and 3¾ qt cool water may be substituted for fluid milk. Combine dry milk and water and whip until smooth. Heat to scalding (185°F). Add, while stirring, roux made of margarine and flour. Cook on low heat, stirring as necessary, until thickened.
- 1 oz salt equals 1½ Tbsp.
- **Method 1.** Melt margarine, remove from heat. Add flour and salt. Stir until smooth. Cook for 5–10 minutes. Add milk gradually, stirring constantly with a wire whip. Cook and stir as necessary until smooth and thick, about 15 minutes.
- **Method 2.** This method is used for making quantities larger than 4 qt. Make a roux by melting margarine, adding flour, and cooking and stirring until smooth. Add one-fourth of the milk and beat with a wire whip until smooth. Gradually add remaining milk while stirring. Cook until smooth and thickened, about 15 minutes.
- **Method 3.** Combine flour with one-fourth of the milk. Heat remaining milk. Add milk-flour paste, using a wire whip. Cook to desired consistency, then add margarine and salt.
- **Method 4.** This method uses a steamer. Make a paste of flour and margarine. Add cold milk until mixture is the consistency of cream. Heat remaining milk. Add flour and margarine mixture, stirring constantly with a wire whip. Place in steamer until flour is cooked; if necessary, stir once during cooking.

Variations

To be used with 1 gal medium white sauce:

- **À la King Sauce.** Add 12 oz chopped green bell pepper, 12 oz sliced mushrooms, sautéed, and 1 lb chopped pimento. Combine with cubed chicken, meats, seafood, vegetables, or hard-cooked eggs.
- **Bacon Sauce.** Add 1 lb 8 oz cooked chopped bacon. Use bacon fat in making the sauce. Combine with eggs or vegetables in scalloped dishes.
- **Cheese Broccoli Sauce.** Steam 2 lb 8 oz broccoli florets until tender-crisp. Carefully stir into Cheese Sauce (see below). Serve 4 oz sauce ladled over baked potato.
- **Cheese Sandwich Sauce (American or Cheddar).** Prepare 2 qt (½ recipe) Thick White Sauce. Add ¼ cup dry mustard and 1 tsp white pepper with the flour. When sauce has thickened, stir in 2 lb shredded sharp cheese and ½ tsp hot pepper sauce. Ladle 1½ oz sauce over meat in sandwich.
- **Cheese Sandwich Sauce (Swiss).** Prepare 2 qt (½ recipe) Medium White Sauce. Reduce margarine to 6 oz. After sauce has thickened, add 2 lb shredded Swiss cheese and stir until melted. Serve 1½ oz sauce ladled over meat in sandwich.
- **Cheese Sauce.** Add 3 lb sharp cheddar cheese, shredded or ground, 2 Tbsp Worcestershire sauce, and a few grains cayenne pepper. Serve on fish, egg dishes, soufflés, and vegetables. Worcestershire sauce and cayenne pepper may be omitted for a milder sauce.
- **Egg Sauce.** Add 20 chopped hard-cooked eggs and 2 Tbsp prepared mustard. Serve over salmon or other fish loaf.
- **Golden Sauce.** Add 2 cups slightly beaten egg yolks. Serve on fish, chicken, or vegetables.
- **Mushroom Sauce.** Add 1 lb 8 oz sliced mushrooms and 4 oz minced onion, sautéed in 4 oz margarine or butter. Serve over egg, meat, or poultry dishes or over vegetables.
- **Parsley Sauce.** Add 1 oz chopped fresh parsley.
- **Pimento Sauce.** Add 1 lb 4 oz finely chopped pimento and 2 cups finely chopped parsley. Serve with poached fish, croquettes, or egg dishes.
- **Shrimp Sauce.** Add 4 lb cooked shrimp, 2 Tbsp prepared mustard, and 2 Tbsp Worcestershire sauce. Serve with fish, eggs, or cheese soufflé.
- **Swiss Cheese and Mushroom Sauce.** Sauté 4 oz chopped onion, 2 oz chopped green bell pepper, and 8 oz sliced mushrooms in 4 oz margarine. Stir in 4 oz flour. Cook for 10–15 minutes. Add 2 qt milk slowly, while stirring, and heat to 170°F. Add 2 lb 8 oz shredded Swiss cheese and stir until melted.

BÉCHAMEL SAUCE

Yield: 2 qt   *Portion:* 3 Tbsp (1½ oz)

Ingredient	Amount	Procedure
Chicken Stock (p. 738)	1½ qt	Simmer stock, vegetables, and seasonings together for 20 minutes. Strain.
Onion slices	4	Save liquid for preparation of sauce. There should be 1 qt liquid.
Carrots, chopped	3 oz	
Black peppercorns	2 Tbsp	
Bay leaf	1	
Margarine	8 oz	Melt margarine. Add flour and stir until smooth. Cook
Flour, all-purpose	4 oz	for 5–10 minutes.
Seasoned stock (prepared in previous step)	1 qt	Add liquids gradually, stirring constantly with a wire whip. Cook until smooth and thickened.
Milk, hot	1 qt	Add seasonings.
Salt	½ tsp	Serve with scant 2-oz ladle on chicken or meat entrées.
White pepper	½ tsp	
Cayenne pepper	few grains	

Approximate nutritive values per ounce

Calories	Carbohydrate	Protein	Fat	Cholesterol	Sodium	Fiber	Iron
38 kcal	2 g	1 g	3 g	2 mg	90 mg	0 g	0 mg

Note

- Potentially hazardous food. *Food Safety Standards:* Hold food for service at an internal temperature of 135°F or above. Do not mix old product with new. Cool leftover product quickly following time standards and cooling procedures on p. 167. Reheat leftover product quickly (within 2 hours) to 165°F or above. Reheat product only once; discard if not used.

Variations

- **Mornay Sauce.** Add gradually to hot Béchamel Sauce 4 oz each of grated Parmesan and Swiss cheese. Let sauce remain over heat until cheese is melted, then remove and gradually beat in 8 oz margarine or butter. Serve with fish or egg entrées.
- **Velouté Sauce.** Cook the margarine and flour (roux) until slightly brown in color. Substitute Chicken Stock for milk. Serve on chicken entrées. For Fish Velouté, substitute fish stock for milk. Serve on fish.

PAN GRAVY

Yield: 1 gal   *Portion:* ⅓ cup (2½ oz)

Ingredient	Amount	Procedure
Flour, all-purpose	8 oz	Add flour to fat and blend.
Fat, hot (meat drippings)	8 oz	
Salt	1 Tbsp	
Black pepper	1 tsp	Stir in salt and pepper. Cook for 5 minutes.
Chicken or Meat Stock (p. 738)	1 gal	Add stock gradually. Cook, stirring constantly with a wire whip. Cook until smooth and thickened.

Approximate nutritive values per ounce

Calories	Carbohydrate	Protein	Fat	Cholesterol	Sodium	Fiber	Iron
25 kcal	0 g	1 g	2 g	2 mg	148 mg	0 g	0 mg

Notes

- Potentially hazardous food. *Food Safety Standards:* Hold food for service at an internal temperature of 135°F or above. Do not mix old product with new. Cool leftover product quickly following time standards and cooling procedures on p. 167. Reheat leftover product quickly (within 2 hours) to 165°F or above. Reheat product only once; discard if not used.
- If beef or chicken base is used for stock, delete or reduce salt.

Variations

- **Brown Gravy.** Use 10 oz flour and brown in the fat.
- **Chicken Gravy.** Use chicken drippings for fat and chicken stock for liquid.
- **Chicken or Turkey Gravy (using base).** In steam-jacketed kettle melt 12 oz margarine. Using a wire whip, stir in 14 oz flour. Cook for 30 minutes, stirring often. Add 3½ qt water and 3 oz chicken base. Cook until thickened and no starchy flavor remains, 190°F. Add 1 tsp black pepper, ½ tsp poultry seasoning, and 1 tsp caramel coloring (Kitchen Bouquet)(optional). Makes 1 gal. Salt may need to be adjusted depending on the amount of salt in the chicken base.
- **Cream Gravy.** Substitute milk for water or stock.
- **Giblet Gravy.** Use chicken drippings for fat and chicken stock for liquid. Add 1 qt cooked giblets, chopped.
- **Onion Gravy.** Lightly brown 1 lb thinly sliced onions in fat before adding flour.
- **Vegetable Gravy.** Add 1 lb diced carrots, 4 oz chopped celery, and 12 oz chopped onion, cooked in water or meat or vegetable stock.

BROWN SAUCE

Yield: 2 qt   *Portion:* 3 Tbsp (1½ oz)

Ingredient	Amount	Procedure
Onion, thinly sliced	4 oz	Add onion and seasonings to beef stock. If base has been used to make stock, taste before adding salt.
Salt	2 tsp	Simmer for about 10 minutes.
Black pepper	¼ tsp	Strain.
Beef Stock (p. 738)	2 qt	
Shortening	8 oz	Heat shortening and blend with flour. Cook for about 10 minutes until it becomes uniformly brown in color.
Flour, all-purpose	5 oz	Add hot stock while stirring with a wire whip. Cook until thickened.

Approximate nutritive values per ounce

Calories	Carbohydrate	Protein	Fat	Cholesterol	Sodium	Fiber	Iron
39 kcal	2 g	1 g	3 g	0 mg	150 mg	0 g	0 mg

Note

- Potentially hazardous food. *Food Safety Standards:* Hold food for service at an internal temperature of 135°F or above. Do not mix old product with new. Cool leftover product quickly following time standards and cooling procedures on p. 167. Reheat leftover product quickly (within 2 hours) to 165°F or above. Reheat product only once; discard if not used.

Variations

- **Jelly Sauce.** Add 2 cups currant jelly, beaten until soft, 2 Tbsp tarragon vinegar, and 4 oz sautéed minced onions. Serve with lamb or game.
- **Mushroom Sauce.** Add 1 lb sliced mushrooms and 2 oz minced onions, sautéed. Serve with steak.
- **Olive Sauce.** Add 6 oz chopped stuffed olives. Serve with meat or duck.
- **Piquant Sauce.** Add 2 oz minced onion, 2 oz capers, ½ cup vinegar, 4 oz sugar, ¼ tsp salt, ¼ tsp paprika, and ½ cup chile sauce or chopped sweet pickle. Serve with meats.
- **Savory Mustard Sauce.** Add ½ cup prepared mustard and ½ cup horseradish. Serve with meats.

CHIPOTLE SAUCE

Yield: 1¼ gal   *Portion:* 3 oz

Ingredient	Amount	Procedure
Margarine	1 lb	Melt margarine in steam-jacketed or other heavy-bottomed kettle.
Onion, minced	3 oz	Add onion and garlic and sauté until fragrant.
Garlic, minced	1 oz	
Flour, all-purpose	14 oz	Add flour. Blend with a wire whip. Cook for 30 minutes, stirring often. Turn off heat.
Ancho chile powder	3 Tbsp	Add seasonings and blend with a wire whip.
Garlic powder	2 Tbsp	
Chipotle flavor concentrate (see Note)	3 Tbsp	
Salt	1 Tbsp	
Water	4¼ qt	Add water gradually, stirring constantly with a wire whip. Cook until thickened and no starchy flavor remains.

Approximate nutritive values per portion

Calories	Carbohydrate	Protein	Fat	Cholesterol	Sodium	Fiber	Iron
62 kcal	5 g	0.7 g	5 g	0 mg	127 mg	0.3 g	0.3 mg

Notes

- Potentially hazardous food. *Food Safety Standards:* Hold food for service at an internal temperature of 135°F or above. Do not mix old product with new. Cool leftover product quickly following time standards and cooling procedures on p. 167. Reheat leftover product quickly (within 2 hours) to 165°F or above. Reheat product only once; discard if not used.
- Minor's Chipotle Flavor Concentrate (a blend of red, chipotle, and jalapeño peppers with onion, garlic, and spice) is available from most broadline foodservice distributors. Canned chipotles may be substituted for the chipotle flavor concentrate. Adjust the amount per taste.
- Serve as a savory for meats, such as meatballs or grilled sirloin steak.

FRESH MUSHROOM SAUCE

Yield: 1 gal   *Portion:* 2½ oz

Ingredient	Amount	Procedure
Fresh mushrooms	4 lb	Clean, trim, and slice mushrooms.
Margarine Onion, minced	8 oz 2 oz	Melt margarine. Sauté onion and mushrooms.
Flour, all-purpose	4 oz	Add flour and blend. Cook for 5 minutes.
Chicken Stock, hot (p. 738) Milk or cream Salt	2 qt 2 cups to taste	Add stock and milk while stirring with a wire whip. Cook until thickened. Taste for seasoning. Add salt if needed.

Approximate nutritive values per ounce

Calories	Carbohydrate	Protein	Fat	Cholesterol	Sodium	Fiber	Iron
21 kcal	0 g	1 g	1 g	0 mg	58 mg	0.2 g	0.5 mg

Notes

- Potentially hazardous food. *Food Safety Standards:* Hold food for service at an internal temperature of 135°F or above. Do not mix old product with new. Cool leftover product quickly following time standards and cooling procedures on p. 167. Reheat leftover product quickly (within 2 hours) to 165°F or above. Reheat product only once; discard if not used.
- Canned, drained mushrooms may be substituted for fresh mushrooms. Stir into prepared sauce.

Variations

- **Mushroom and Almond Sauce.** Add 1 lb slivered almonds. Serve over rice as an entrée.
- **Mushroom and Cheese Sauce.** Add 1 lb shredded cheese. Serve over asparagus or broccoli.

ASIAN SESAME SAUCE

Yield: 2 qt   *Portion:* 1 oz

Ingredient	Amount	Procedure
Soy sauce	2¼ cups	Combine all ingredients in baker's bowl.
Sugar, brown	12 oz	Mix with a wire whip until sugar is dissolved.
Catsup	5 oz	Put mixture in a squeeze bottle and shake before use.
Toasted sesame oil	2½ oz	
Mirin (cooking sake)	3½ cups	

Approximate nutritive values per ounce

Calories	Carbohydrate	Protein	Fat	Cholesterol	Sodium	Fiber	Iron
49 kcal	6 g	1 g	1 g	0 mg	471 mg	0 g	0 mg

Variation

- **Asian Sesame Sauce with Carrots and Onions.** To Asian Sesame Sauce, add 12 oz fine julienne cut carrots (matchstick) and 8 oz thinly sliced green onions.

BARBECUE SAUCE (COOKED)

Yield: 1½ gal

Ingredient	Amount	Procedure
Catsup	1 No. 10 can	Combine all ingredients.
Water	3 qt	Simmer for 10 minutes.
Vinegar, cider	2 cups	Baste chicken or meat with sauce during cooking.
Salt	2 Tbsp	
Black pepper	1 tsp	
Sugar, granulated	4 oz	
Chile powder	1 tsp	
Worcestershire sauce	¼ cup	
Hot pepper sauce	1 Tbsp	
Onion, grated	4 oz	

Approximate nutritive values per ounce

Calories	Carbohydrate	Protein	Fat	Cholesterol	Sodium	Fiber	Iron
17 kcal	5 g	0 g	0 g	0 mg	211 mg	0.2 g	0 mg

Note

- ½ oz (¼ cup) dehydrated onion may be substituted for the fresh onion.

BARBECUE SAUCE (UNCOOKED)

Yield: 1 gal

Ingredient	Amount	Procedure
Catsup	1 No. 10 can	Mix all ingredients.
Vinegar, cider	3 cups	Pour over meat or chicken.
Sugar, granulated	12 oz	Follow cooking directions for meat or poultry.
Salt	4 oz	
Onion, grated	4 oz	

Approximate nutritive values per ounce

Calories	Carbohydrate	Protein	Fat	Cholesterol	Sodium	Fiber	Iron
34 kcal	9 g	0 g	0 g	0 mg	583 mg	0.4 g	0.5 mg

Note

- ½ oz (¼ cup) dehydrated onion may be substituted for the fresh onion.

MARINARA SAUCE

Yield: 2 gal   *Portion:* 4 oz

Ingredient	Amount	Procedure
Onion, chopped	1 lb	Sauté onion and garlic in oil until tender and golden in color.
Garlic cloves, minced	8	
Olive oil	¾ cup	
Plum tomatoes, canned, undrained	20 lb (2½ gal)	Add tomatoes to onion-garlic mixture. Break tomatoes into small pieces.
Fresh parsley, chopped	3 oz	Stir in parsley, salt, and pepper. Cover and simmer for 2 hours, stirring occasionally. Cook until sauce reaches desired consistency.
Salt	2 Tbsp	
Black pepper	1½ tsp	Stir in basil in the last 30 minutes.
Basil, dried, crumbled	3 Tbsp	

Approximate nutritive values per ounce

Calories	Carbohydrate	Protein	Fat	Cholesterol	Sodium	Fiber	Iron
14 kcal	2 g	0 g	1 g	0 mg	108 mg	0.3 g	0.5 mg

Notes

- Potentially hazardous food. *Food Safety Standards:* Hold food for service at an internal temperature of 135°F or above. Do not mix old product with new. Cool leftover product quickly following time standards and cooling procedures on p. 167. Reheat leftover product quickly (within 2 hours) to 165°F or above. Reheat product only once; discard if not used.
- Serve over pasta, meats, or poultry. Sprinkle with Parmesan cheese.
- 3 Tbsp brown sugar may be added for a sweeter sauce.
- Vegetable oil may be substituted for olive oil.
- 2 oz finely chopped sweet red bell pepper may be added along with parsley and spices.
- Diced tomatoes may be substituted for plum tomatoes. Drain some of the juice before adding or cook longer until the liquid evaporates and sauce thickens.
- To make a thicker sauce requiring less cooking time, substitute 6 lb tomato purée for 6 lb tomatoes.

Variations

- **Garden Fresh Marinara.** Heat 3 oz olive oil in steam-jacketed or other large kettle. Sauté 8 oz chopped onion and 6 minced garlic cloves until soft and fragrant but not browned. Stir in 12 lb diced fresh tomatoes, ¼ cup sugar, and 3 Tbsp salt. Continue to cook for 2 minutes until tomatoes are heated through but not cooked. Turn off heat. Stir in ¾ cup red wine vinegar, 2 tsp black pepper, ¼ tsp crushed red pepper, 1 cup chopped flat leaf parsley, and ½ cup chopped fresh basil. Yield: approximately 50 4-oz portions.
- **Marinara Sauce with Olives.** Add to sauce 2 lb 8 oz sliced black olives, drained, 2 Tbsp dried oregano, and 2 tsp crushed red pepper. Small whole olives may be substituted for sliced olives. 8 oz capers may be added.
- **Tomato Zucchini Sauce.** Follow recipe for Marinara Sauce with Olives. Add 3 lb sliced zucchini squash just before serving and heat to serving temperature. Serve with grated Romano or Parmesan cheese.

ITALIAN TOMATO SAUCE

Yield: 1½ gal   *Portion:* 4 oz

Ingredient	Amount	Procedure
Onions, finely chopped	1 lb 6 oz EP	In steam-jacketed kettle or large pan, sauté onions, garlic, and peppers in oil until onions are transparent.
Garlic, minced	2 oz EP	
Green bell peppers, finely chopped	6 oz EP	
Olive oil	3 oz	
Tomato juice	2½ qt	Add liquids and seasonings. Stir well to combine.
Tomato purée	3 cups	Heat to boiling. Reduce heat and simmer for 20–30 minutes. For a thicker sauce, increase cooking time.
Tomato paste	3½ cups	Remove bay leaves before serving.
Water	2 qt	
Oregano, dried	1 Tbsp	
Thyme, dried	1 tsp	
Basil, dried	¼ cup	
Crushed red pepper	1 tsp	
Parsley, dried	¼ cup	
Bay leaves	4	
Black pepper	1 Tbsp	
Salt	1 oz	
Sugar, granulated (see Note)	2 Tbsp	

Approximate nutritive values per portion

Calories	Carbohydrate	Protein	Fat	Cholesterol	Sodium	Fiber	Iron
60 kcal	10 g	1.6 g	2 g	0 mg	472 mg	2 g	1 mg

Notes

- Potentially hazardous food. *Food Safety Standards:* Hold food for service at an internal temperature of 135°F or above. Do not mix old product with new. Cool leftover product quickly following time standards and cooling procedures on p. 167. Reheat leftover product quickly (within 2 hours) to 165°F or above. Reheat product only once; discard if not used.
- For a less sweet sauce, omit sugar. For a sweeter sauce, increase sugar to 3 Tbsp.
- Serve over pasta or as a base for Italian sauces with meat or shellfish.
- The names Marinara and Italian Tomato Sauce may be used interchangeably.

MILANO SAUCE

Yield: 2 qt   *Portion:* 2 oz

Ingredient	Amount	Procedure
Onion, chopped	8 oz	Sauté onion and garlic in margarine until tender.
Garlic cloves, minced	3	
Margarine	¼ cup	
Tomato juice	1¾ qt	Add tomato products and seasonings to onion mixture. Bring to a boil: Reduce heat and simmer for 15–20 minutes.
Tomato paste	8 oz	
Oregano, dried	1 tsp	
Basil, dried	2 Tbsp	
Black pepper	½ tsp	
Crushed red pepper	⅛ tsp	

Approximate nutritive values per portion

Calories	Carbohydrate	Protein	Fat	Cholesterol	Sodium	Fiber	Iron
30 kcal	4 g	1 g	1 g	0 mg	23 mg	0 g	1 mg

Note

- Potentially hazardous food. *Food Safety Standards:* Hold food for service at an internal temperature of 135°F or above. Do not mix old product with new. Cool leftover product quickly following time standards and cooling procedures on p. 167. Reheat leftover product quickly (within 2 hours) to 165°F or above. Reheat product only once; discard if not used.

SPANISH TOMATO SAUCE

Yield: 3 qt   *Portion:* 3 Tbsp (2 oz)

Ingredient	Amount	Procedure
Onion, chopped	4 oz	Sauté onion in oil.
Olive oil	4 oz	
Diced tomatoes, canned	2 qt	Add remaining ingredients.
Celery, diced	1 lb	Simmer until vegetables are tender.
Green bell pepper, chopped	8 oz	
Pimento, chopped	6 oz	
Salt	1 Tbsp	
Black pepper	½ tsp	
Cayenne pepper	few grains	

Approximate nutritive values per ounce

Calories	Carbohydrate	Protein	Fat	Cholesterol	Sodium	Fiber	Iron
17 kcal	1 g	0 g	1 g	0 mg	104 mg	0.3 g	0.5 mg

Notes

- Potentially hazardous food. *Food Safety Standards:* Hold food for service at an internal temperature of 135°F or above. Do not mix old product with new. Cool leftover product quickly following time standards and cooling procedures on p. 167. Reheat leftover product quickly (within 2 hours) to 165°F or above. Reheat product only once; discard if not used.
- Serve with meat, fish, cheese, or Mexican entrées.
- ½ oz (¼ cup) dehydrated onion, rehydrated in ½ cup water, may be substituted for fresh onion.
- 1 tsp dried or 1 Tbsp chopped fresh cilantro may be added.

POMEGRANATE PORT WINE SAUCE

Yield: 1¼ qt

Ingredient	Amount	Procedure
Butter, unsalted	2⅓ Tbsp	Melt butter in a heavy-bottomed pan over low heat.
Onion, chopped	1 lb 12 oz	Add onion, garlic and pepper. Sauté until onion is tender, about 5 minutes.
Garlic, minced	1⅔ Tbsp	
Black pepper	1 Tbsp	
Port wine	3 cups	While stirring, add the port and cook until most of it has evaporated.
Chicken stock	1 gal	Add chicken stock, pomegranate juice, molasses, and brown sugar to the port wine mixture.
Pomegranate juice	6¼ cups	
Pomegranate molasses	½ cup	Raise heat to medium high and reduce slowly to a saucy consistency. Will reduce by approximately 80 percent.
Sugar, brown	2 oz	Serve as a finishing sauce with meats, poultry, or fish.

Approximate nutritive values per 1½ Tbsp

Calories	Carbohydrate	Protein	Fat	Cholesterol	Sodium	Fiber	Iron
42 kcal	8 g	2 g	1 g	1 mg	179 mg	0 g	0 mg

Note

- Potentially hazardous food. *Food Safety Standards:* Hold food for service at an internal temperature of 135°F or above. Do not mix old product with new. Cool leftover product quickly following time standards and cooling procedures on p. 167. Reheat leftover product quickly (within 2 hours) to 165°F or above. Reheat product only once; discard if not used.

HORSERADISH SAUCE

Yield: 5 cups   *Portion:* 1½ Tbsp (½ oz)

Ingredient	Amount	Procedure
Horseradish, drained	8 oz	Combine.
Prepared mustard	2 Tbsp	
Salt	½ tsp	
Paprika	¼ tsp	
Cayenne pepper	⅛ tsp	
Vinegar, cider	⅓ cup	
Whipping cream	2 cups	Whip cream. Fold in horseradish mixture. Chill.

Approximate nutritive values per ounce

Calories	Carbohydrate	Protein	Fat	Cholesterol	Sodium	Fiber	Iron
54 kcal	1 g	1 g	5 g	19 mg	61 mg	0.4 g	0 mg

Notes

- Potentially hazardous food. *Food Safety Standards:* Hold food for service at an internal temperature of 41°F or below. Do not mix old product with new. Keep leftover product chilled at 41°F or below. See p. 167 for cooling procedures.
- Serve with ham or roast beef.

COCKTAIL SAUCE

Yield: 2 qt   *Portion:* 2½ Tbsp (1½ oz)

Ingredient	Amount	Procedure
Chile sauce	1 qt	Mix all ingredients. Chill.
Catsup	2 cups	
Fresh lemon juice	1 cup	
Onion juice	2 Tbsp	
Celery, finely chopped	10 oz	
Worcestershire sauce	5 tsp	
Horseradish	3 oz	
Hot pepper sauce	few drops	

Approximate nutritive values per ounce

Calories	Carbohydrate	Protein	Fat	Cholesterol	Sodium	Fiber	Iron
26 kcal	6 g	0 g	0 g	0 mg	288 mg	0.3 g	0.5 mg

Note

- Serve as a condiment for clam, crab, lobster, oyster, or shrimp.

HORSERADISH CAPER SAUCE

Yield: 50 portions   *Portion:* 1 oz

Ingredient	Amount	Procedure
Nonfat sour cream	3 cups	Combine all ingredients in mixer bowl. Mix until combined.
Buttermilk	2 cups	Chill quickly (within 4 hours) to below 41°F.
Fresh chives, minced	¾ cup	
Capers, small	½ cup	
Horseradish	⅓ cup	
Black pepper	¼ tsp	

Approximate nutritive values per portion

Calories	Carbohydrate	Protein	Fat	Cholesterol	Sodium	Fiber	Iron
13 kcal	2 g	1 g	0 g	0 mg	21 mg	0 g	0 mg

Notes

- Potentially hazardous food. *Food Safety Standards:* Hold food for service at an internal temperature of 41°F or below. Do not mix old product with new. Keep leftover product chilled at 41°F or below. See p. 167 for cooling procedures.
- Serve with fish.

Variation

- **Horseradish–Dill Sauce.** Delete capers. Add ⅓ cup fresh dill weed.

MUSTARD SAUCE (COLD)

Yield: 3 cups   *Portion:* 1 Tbsp

Ingredient	Amount	Procedure
Sugar, granulated	2 Tbsp	Mix dry ingredients.
Salt	½ tsp	
Dry mustard	2 tsp	
Water	2 Tbsp	Add water, vinegar, and eggs to dry ingredients.
Vinegar, cider	¼ cup	Cook until thick.
Eggs, beaten	2 (3 oz)	
Margarine	1 oz	Add margarine. Stir until melted. Cool quickly to below 41°F.
Whipping cream	2 cups	Whip cream and fold into cooked mixture.

Approximate nutritive values per ounce

Calories	Carbohydrate	Protein	Fat	Cholesterol	Sodium	Fiber	Iron
77 kcal	2 g	1 g	7 g	37 mg	72mg	0 g	0 mg

Notes

- Potentially hazardous food. *Food Safety Standards:* Hold food for service at an internal temperature of 41°F or below. Do not mix old product wih new. Keep leftover product chilled at 41°F or below. See p. 167 for cooling procedures.
- Serve cold with ham, pork, or beef roast.

Variation

- **Hot Chinese Mustard.** Combine 8 oz dry mustard, ⅓ cup salad oil, and 1 oz (1½ Tbsp) salt. Add 2 cups boiling water. Stir until smooth. Serve with egg rolls.

MUSTARD SAUCE (HOT)

Yield: 2 qt   *Portion:* 2 Tbsp (1 oz)

Ingredient	Amount	Procedure
Beef Stock (p. 738)	2 qt	Heat stock to boiling point.
Cornstarch	5 oz	Blend dry ingredients with cold water.
Sugar, granulated	2 Tbsp	Add gradually to hot stock. Cook and stir until thickened.
Salt	2 tsp	
White pepper	½ tsp	
Water, cold	½ cup	
Prepared mustard	2 oz	Add remaining ingredients.
Horseradish	4 oz	Stir until blended.
Vinegar, cider	2 Tbsp	
Margarine	1 oz	

Approximate nutritive values per ounce

Calories	Carbohydrate	Protein	Fat	Cholesterol	Sodium	Fiber	Iron
14 kcal	2 g	0 g	0 g	0 mg	155 mg	0 g	0 mg

Notes

- Potentially hazardous food. *Food Safety Standards:* Hold food for service at an internal temperature of 135°F or above. Do not mix old product with new. Cool leftover product quickly following time standards and cooling procedures on p. 167. Reheat leftover product quickly (within 2 hours) to 165°F or above. Reheat product only once; discard if not used.
- Serve hot with fresh or cured ham or fish.

SWEET-SOUR SAUCE

Yield: 1¼ qt   *Portion:* 1½ Tbsp

Ingredient	Amount	Procedure
Sugar, granulated	10 oz	Combine sugar and cornstarch in kettle.
Cornstarch	¼ cup	
Vinegar, cider	1 cup	Add vinegar, water, and soy sauce to dry ingredients and stir until smooth.
Water	2½ cups	
Soy sauce	¼ cup	
Catsup	¾ cup	Stir catsup into mixture in kettle.
		Cook until translucent, stirring constantly.
		Serve as a condiment with egg rolls or chicken nuggets.

Approximate nutritive values per ounce

Calories	Carbohydrate	Protein	Fat	Cholesterol	Sodium	Fiber	Iron
24 kcal	7 g	0 g	0 g	0 mg	106 mg	0 g	0 mg

RAISIN SAUCE

Yield: 1½ qt   *Portion:* 2 Tbsp

Ingredient	Amount	Procedure
Raisins, seedless	1 lb	Steam raisins or simmer in small amount of water for 3–5 minutes.
Sugar, granulated	4 oz	Mix sugar and water and heat to boiling point.
Water	2 cups	
Currant jelly	1 lb	Add cooked raisins and remaining ingredients.
Vinegar, cider	⅓ cup	Simmer for 5 minutes or until jelly is melted.
Margarine	2 oz	
Worcestershire sauce	1 Tbsp	
Salt	1 tsp	
White pepper	¼ tsp	
Cloves, ground	½ tsp	
Mace	⅛ tsp	
Red food coloring (optional)	few drops	

Approximate nutritive values per ounce

Calories	Carbohydrate	Protein	Fat	Cholesterol	Sodium	Fiber	Iron
66 kcal	15 g	0 g	1 g	0 mg	56 mg	0.4 g	0.5 mg

Note

- Serve with baked ham.

CUCUMBER SAUCE

Yield: 3 cups   *Portion:* 1 Tbsp (½ oz)

Ingredient	Amount	Procedure
Cucumbers	1 lb	Peel cucumbers; remove seeds. Grate or chop finely.
Sour cream	1 cup	Combine remaining ingredients and add to cucumber. Chill.
Onion, grated	1 Tbsp	
Vinegar, cider	1 Tbsp	
Fresh lemon juice	1½ Tbsp	
Salt	½ tsp	
Cayenne pepper	few grains	

Approximate nutritive values per ounce

Calories	Carbohydrate	Protein	Fat	Cholesterol	Sodium	Fiber	Iron
23 kcal	0 g	0 g	2 g	4 mg	50 mg	0 g	0 mg

Notes

- Potentially hazardous food. *Food Safety Standards:* Hold food for service at an internal temperature of 41°F or below. Do not mix old product with new. Keep leftover product chilled at 41°F or below. See p. 167 for cooling procedures.
- Serve with fish.

TARTAR SAUCE

Yield: 1¾ qt   *Portion:* 2 Tbsp (1 oz)

Ingredient	Amount	Procedure
Mayonnaise	1 qt	Mix all ingredients.
Pickle relish	6 oz	
Green bell pepper, chopped	¼ cup	
Fresh parsley, chopped	¼ cup	
Green olives, chopped	6 oz	
Onion, minced	1 Tbsp	
Pimento, chopped	2 oz	
Vinegar or lemon juice	½ cup	
Worcestershire sauce	few drops	
Hot pepper sauce	few drops	

Approximate nutritive values per ounce

Calories	Carbohydrate	Protein	Fat	Cholesterol	Sodium	Fiber	Iron
135 kcal	2 g	0 g	15 g	10 mg	198 mg	0 g	0.5 mg

Note

- Serve with fish.

HOLLANDAISE SAUCE

Yield: 12 portions   *Portion:* 1½ Tbsp (¾ oz)

Ingredient	Amount	Procedure
Butter	2 oz	Place butter, juice, and egg yolks over hot (not boiling) water.
Fresh lemon juice	1½ Tbsp	Cook slowly, beating constantly.
Egg yolks (see Note)	3 (2 oz)	
Butter	2 oz	When first portion of butter is melted, add second portion and beat until mixture thickens.
Butter	2 oz	Add third portion of butter and seasonings.
Salt	few grains	Beat until thickened.
Cayenne pepper	few grains	Serve immediately. Discard any unused sauce.

Approximate nutritive values per ounce

Calories	Carbohydrate	Protein	Fat	Cholesterol	Sodium	Fiber	Iron
176 kcal	0 g	1 g	19 g	127 mg	180 mg	0 g	0.5 mg

Notes

- Potentially hazardous food. Serve immediately or hold for a short period of time at an internal temperature of 135ºF or above.
- Serve with fish or green vegetables such as asparagus or broccoli.
- If sauce tends to curdle, add hot water, a teaspoon at a time, stirring vigorously.
- For safety and quality reasons, it is recommended that this sauce be made only in small quantities.
- Pasteurized eggs are recommended.

MOCK HOLLANDAISE SAUCE

Yield: 2 qt   *Portion:* 2½ Tbsp (1½ oz)

Ingredient	Amount	Procedure
Butter or margarine	6 oz	Melt butter. Add flour and stir until smooth.
Flour, all-purpose	3 oz	Cook for 3–5 minutes.
Milk	1½ qt	Add milk gradually, stirring constantly with a wire whip. Cook until smooth and thickened.
Salt	1 tsp	Add seasonings.
White pepper	½ tsp	
Cayenne pepper	few grains	
Egg yolks, unbeaten (see Note)	12 (8 oz)	Add a little egg yolk at a time, a little butter, and a little lemon juice until all are added.
Butter, cut in pieces	1 lb	Beat well.
Fresh lemon juice	½ cup	Serve immediately. Discard any unused sauce.

Approximate nutritive values per ounce

Calories	Carbohydrate	Protein	Fat	Cholesterol	Sodium	Fiber	Iron
82 kcal	2 g	1 g	8 g	51 mg	104 mg	0 g	0 mg

Notes

- Potentially hazardous food. Serve immediately or hold for a short period of time at an internal temperature of 135ºF or above.
- Pasteurized eggs are recommended.

MEUNIÈRE SAUCE

Yield: 3 cups

Ingredient	Amount	Procedure
Margarine	1 lb 4 oz	Heat margarine until lightly browned.
Onion, minced	2 oz	Add onion and brown slightly.
Fresh lemon juice	½ cup	Add juice and seasonings.
Worcestershire sauce	1 Tbsp	Serve hot over broccoli, Brussels sprouts, green beans, spinach, or cabbage.
Lemon peel, grated	1 Tbsp	
Salt	1 tsp	

Approximate nutritive values per ounce

Calories	Carbohydrate	Protein	Fat	Cholesterol	Sodium	Fiber	Iron
180 kcal	0 g	0 g	20 g	0 mg	333 mg	0 g	0 mg

Note

- 3 oz toasted sliced almonds may be sprinkled over top of vegetable.

HOT BACON SAUCE

Yield: 2½ qt

Ingredient	Amount	Procedure
Bacon	1 lb	Dice bacon. Fry until crisp.
Flour, all-purpose	4 oz	Add flour and stir until smooth.
Sugar, granulated	1 lb 4 oz	Mix sugar, salt, vinegar, and water. Boil for 1 minute.
Salt	¼ cup	Add to fat-flour mixture gradually while stirring.
Vinegar, cider	3 cups	Cook until slightly thickened.
Water	3 cups	

Approximate nutritive values per ounce

Calories	Carbohydrate	Protein	Fat	Cholesterol	Sodium	Fiber	Iron
65 kcal	9 g	2 g	3 g	5 mg	411 mg	0 g	0.5 mg

Note

- Use to wilt lettuce or spinach, or with hot potato salad or shredded cabbage.

DRAWN BUTTER SAUCE

Yield: 2 qt   *Portion:* 3 Tbsp (1½ oz)

Ingredient	Amount	Procedure
Butter	2 oz	Melt butter. Add flour and blend.
Flour, all-purpose	4 oz	
Water, hot	2 qt	Gradually add hot water, while stirring with wire whip. Cook for 5 minutes until thickened.
Salt	1 tsp	When ready to serve, add salt and butter. Beat until blended.
Butter, cut into pieces	6 oz	

Approximate nutritive values per ounce

Calories	Carbohydrate	Protein	Fat	Cholesterol	Sodium	Fiber	Iron
29 kcal	1 g	0 g	3 g	7 mg	58 mg	0 g	0 mg

Note

- Serve with green vegetables, fried or broiled fish, or egg dishes.

Variations

- **Almond Butter Sauce.** Add ¼ cup lemon juice and 6 oz toasted slivered almonds just before serving.
- **Lemon Butter Sauce.** Add 1 Tbsp grated lemon peel and ¼ cup lemon juice just before serving. Serve with fish, new potatoes, broccoli, or asparagus.
- **Maître d'Hôtel Sauce.** Add ¼ cup lemon juice, ¼ cup chopped fresh parsley, and 6 oz pasteurized egg yolks, well beaten.
- **Parsley Butter Sauce.** Add 1½ cups minced fresh parsley just before serving. Serve with fish, potatoes, or other vegetables.

CHILE CILANTRO SAUCE

Yield: 1 gal   *Portion:* 3 oz

Ingredient	Amount	Procedure
Granulated sugar	1 lb 8 oz	Put in the bowl of a food processor.
Fresh ginger, chopped	10 oz EP	Process until finely chopped.
Fresh cilantro	2 oz	
Garlic cloves	4 oz	
Small hot chiles, seeded and chopped	½ oz EP (see Note)	
Vinegar, rice wine	2⅔ cups	Add vinegar and process until smooth.
Fish sauce	4 cups	Put processed mixture in a nonreactive container. Stir in fish sauce, water, juice, and soy sauce.
Water	3 cups	Cover tightly and refrigerate until ready to serve.
Fresh lime juice	3 cups	Serve as a dipping sauce or condiment for rice.
Soy sauce	1⅓ cups	

Approximate nutritive values per ounce

Calories	Carbohydrate	Protein	Fat	Cholesterol	Sodium	Fiber	Iron
70 kcal	16.2 g	1.9 g	0.1 g	0 mg	1977 mg	0.3 g	0.5 mg

Notes

- Potentially hazardous food. *Food Safety Standards:* Hold food for service at an internal temperature of 41°F or below. Do not mix old product wih new. Keep leftover product chilled at 41°F or below. See p. 167 for cooling procedures.
- Use 12–20 hot chiles depending on the degree of hotness desired. The hotness of chile peppers varies among varieties. Thai bird chile peppers are suggested.

ASIAN DIPPING SAUCE

Yield: $1\frac{1}{2}$ qt

Ingredient	Amount	Procedure
Garlic, minced	$1\frac{1}{2}$ oz	Blend into a paste using a mortar and pestle or food processor.
Hot chile sauce (see Note)	$3\frac{1}{2}$ Tbsp	
Fresh ginger, minced	3 oz	
Fresh cilantro, finely chopped	$3\frac{1}{2}$ oz	Add remaining ingredients to the garlic mixture. Mix well until sugar is dissolved.
Sugar, granulated	7 oz	
Soy sauce	2 cups	
Fresh lime juice	1 cup	
Water	$1\frac{1}{2}$ cups	

Approximate nutritive values per ounce

Calories	Carbohydrate	Protein	Fat	Cholesterol	Sodium	Fiber	Iron
24 kcal	6 g	1 g	0 g	0 mg	509 mg	0 g	0 mg

Notes

- Recipe tested using Sriracha hot chile sauce. Sriracha is available through most broadline foodservice distributors and in stores that carry Asian food products.
- To make sauce more spicy, add additional hot chile sauce.

TAHINI AND YOGURT SAUCE

Yield: 50 portions   *Portion:* $1\frac{1}{2}$ oz

Ingredient	Amount	Procedure
Garlic, minced	1 oz	Blend garlic and tahini together in a bowl.
Tahini	12 oz	
Yogurt unflavored	3 lb 4 oz	Add yogurt, lemon juice, and seasonings to garlic-tahini mixture and mix well.
Fresh lemon juice	1 cup	
Paprika	1 tsp	
Salt	1 tsp	

Approximate nutritive values per portion

Calories	Carbohydrate	Protein	Fat	Cholesterol	Sodium	Fiber	Iron
58 kcal	4 g	3 g	4 g	2 mg	59 mg	0 g	0 mg

Note

- Potentially hazardous food. *Food Safety Standards:* Hold food for service at an internal temperature of 41°F or below. Do not mix old product with new. Keep leftover product chilled at 41°F or below. See p. 167 for cooling procedures.

Salsa-Style Accompaniment Recipes

SALSA

Yield: 1 gal

Ingredient	Amount	Procedure
Crushed tomatoes, canned	3 lb 10 oz	Combine all ingredients in stainless steel or glass container.
Tomato juice	3 lb 6 oz	Mix well.
Green bell pepper, dried, chopped	1 oz	Store covered in refrigerator.
Onion, chopped	8 oz	May be heated before service.
Garlic powder	¼ tsp	
Green chiles	8 oz	
Jalapeño peppers, canned, chopped	10 oz	
Vinegar, cider	¾ cup	
Salt	2 tsp	
Sugar, granulated	1 Tbsp	
Hot pepper sauce	1 Tbsp	
Oregano, dried, crumbled	½ tsp	
Cayenne pepper	¾ tsp	
Cumin, ground	¾ tsp	

Approximate nutritive values per ounce

Calories	Carbohydrate	Protein	Fat	Cholesterol	Sodium	Fiber	Iron
6 kcal	0 g	0 g	0 g	0 mg	134 mg	0.3 g	0.5 mg

Note

- May be served as a condiment with tacos, tostadas, chimichangas, or other Mexican entrées.

SUMMER CUCUMBER AND MELON SALSA

Yield: 50 portions   *Portion:* 4 oz

Ingredient	Amount	Procedure
Cucumber, peeled, ¼-inch dice	4 lb EP	Gently mix all ingredients, being careful not to mash fruit and vegetables.
Red bell pepper, chopped	1 lb 8 oz EP	Cover and refrigerate up to 6 hours.
Red onion, finely chopped	1 lb 8 oz EP	
Fresh cilantro, chopped	4 oz	
Cantaloupe, peeled, ½-inch dice	4 lb 8 oz EP	
Olive oil	¾ cup	
Fresh lime juice	¾ cup	
Vinegar, red wine	¾ cup	
Sugar, granulated	2 tsp	
Salt	½ tsp	
Black pepper	⅛ tsp	

Serve as a side accompaniment with chicken or fish.
Keep cold, below 41°F.

Approximate nutritive values per portion

Calories	Carbohydrate	Protein	Fat	Cholesterol	Sodium	Fiber	Iron
55 kcal	7 g	0.9 g	3.4 g	0 mg	34 mg	1 g	0.5 mg

BLACK EYED PEA AND CORN SALSA

Yield: 50 portions   *Portion:* 3 oz

Ingredient	Amount	Procedure
Tomatoes, ¼-inch dice	2 lb 10 oz EP	Combine in stainless steel bowl, being careful to not mash tomatoes.
Roasted red bell peppers, ¼-inch dice (p. 796)	10 oz	
Seasoned Black Eyed Peas (p. 794)	2 lb 4 oz	Drain well and add to tomato-and-pepper mixture.
Green onions, thinly sliced	7 oz EP	Add vegetables and seasonings. Stir lightly, being careful not to overmix.
Garlic, finely chopped	2 Tbsp EP	Cover and refrigerate for 6–8 hours, stirring occasionally.
Corn, whole kernel, frozen, thawed	2 lb 4 oz	
Picante sauce	1 qt	
Fresh cilantro, chopped	1 oz EP (1½ cups)	
Fresh lime juice	¼ cup	
Salt	2 tsp	

Approximate nutritive values per ounce

Calories	Carbohydrate	Protein	Fat	Cholesterol	Sodium	Fiber	Iron
50 kcal	10 g	1.8 g	4 g	0 mg	295 mg	1.2 g	0.5 mg

Note

• Serve with nacho chips or as a plate garnish for Southwest seasoned pork or chicken.

FRUIT SALSA

Yield: 50 portions   *Portion:* 2 oz

Ingredient	Amount	Procedure
Fresh fruit (see suggestions below)	3 lb 12 oz EP	Prepare fruit as required (peel, seed, etc.). Slice or cut into ¼-inch cubes.
Red bell peppers Anaheim chile peppers Jalapeño peppers	1 lb 4 oz EP 6 oz EP 6 oz EP	Remove stem end and seed pod from peppers. Dice bell peppers into ¼-inch cubes. Slice Anaheim and jalapeño peppers into thin slices. Stir carefully into fruit.
Red onions	6 oz	Dice onions into ¼-inch cubes. Stir carefully into fruit.
Crushed red pepper Fresh lime juice Fresh cilantro, chopped	1 tsp 1 cup 1 oz (¾ cup)	Stir carefully into fruit mixture. Cover and chill.

Fruit suggestions
Tropical fruit: papaya or papaya and mango
Sunburst: papaya and orange
Southwest peach: fresh peaches
Fruit and cucumber: papaya and cucumber
Hawaiian Isle: pineapple and 1 Tbsp lime zest

Approximate nutritive values per portion

Calories	Carbohydrate	Protein	Fat	Cholesterol	Sodium	Fiber	Iron
65 kcal	16 g	2 g	0 g	0 mg	62 mg	2 g	1 mg

Notes

- Canned jalapeño peppers, drained and chopped, can be substituted for fresh jalapeño peppers.
- Reconstituted frozen lime juice may be substituted for fresh lime juice.

WHITE BEAN AND TOMATO SAUCE

Yield: 50 portions   *Portion:* 3 oz
Oven: 425°F   *Bake:* 15–20 minutes plus 15 minutes

Ingredient	Amount	Procedure
Diced tomatoes, canned Onions, chopped coarsely Garlic, minced Olive oil	3 lb 12 oz 1 lb 8 oz 3 oz 1 cup	Combine tomatoes, onions, garlic, and oil. Put mixture into one 12 × 20 × 4-inch pan and bake at 425°F until most of the tomato liquid evaporates and onions are tender, approximately 20 minutes.
White beans, canned Vinegar, red wine Fresh flat leaf parsley, chopped Fresh basil, chopped Fresh thyme, chopped Black pepper Salt	9 lb ⅓ cup 2 cups ¼ cup 2 Tbsp 1 Tbsp 1½ tsp	Carefully combine undrained beans (see Note), vinegar, herbs, and seasonings with tomato mixture. Cover and bake until heated to 165°F, approximately 15 minutes. Remove from oven and keep warm, above 135°F. Serve as a base under fish or poultry.

Approximate nutritive values per portion

Calories	Carbohydrate	Protein	Fat	Cholesterol	Sodium	Fiber	Iron
122 kcal	16 g	5 g	5 g	0 mg	489 mg	1 g	2 mg

Notes

- Potentially hazardous food. *Food Safety Standards:* Hold food for service at an internal temperature of 135°F or above. Do not mix old product with new. Cool leftover product quickly following time standards and cooling procedures on p. 167. Reheat leftover product quickly (within 2 hours) to 165°F or above. Reheat product only once; discard if not used.
- If canned beans have a large amount of liquid, partially drain and carefully stir in reserved liquid until the desired consistency is achieved.
- Fresh tomatoes may be substituted for canned. Peel and remove seeds before coarsely chopping.
- ¼ cup fresh cilantro may be substituted for the parsley.

Variation

- **Black Bean and Tomato Sauce.** Substitute canned black beans for the white beans.

WARM WHITE BEAN SALSA

Yield: 50 portions   *Portion:* 4 oz

Ingredient	Amount	Procedure
Great northern beans, canned, drained and rinsed	4 lb EP	Place beans, liquids, and seasonings in steam-jacketed or other large kettle. Heat to 160°F. (See Variation.)
Olive oil	12 oz	
Fresh lemon juice	8 oz	
Salt	1½ Tbsp	
Black pepper	1 tsp	
Sugar, granulated	1 Tbsp	
Fresh tomatoes, diced	8 lb	Gently stir in tomatoes, green onions, basil, and cilantro. Heat to 135°F. (See Variation.)
Green onions, sliced	8 oz	Serve 4 oz salsa over 4 oz pasta or as an accompaniment served under fish or chicken.
Fresh basil, chopped	½ oz	
Fresh cilantro, chopped (see Note)	½ oz	

Approximate nutritive values per portion

Calories	Carbohydrate	Protein	Fat	Cholesterol	Sodium	Fiber	Iron
83 kcal	5 g	1 g	7 g	0 mg	327 mg	2 g	1 mg

Notes

- Potentially hazardous food. *Food Safety Standards:* Hold food for service at an internal temperature of 135°F or above. Do not mix old product with new. Cool leftover product quickly following time standards and cooling procedures on p. 167. Reheat leftover product quickly (within 2 hours) to 165°F or above. Reheat product only once; discard if not used.
- Flat leaf parsley can be substituted for some or all of the cilantro. Increase parsley to 1 cup.

Variation

- **White Bean Salsa.** Prepare as for Warm White Bean Salsa but do not heat. Flat leaf parsley can be substituted for some or all of the cilantro. Serve as a dip with tortilla chips, as a salad bar item, or as an accompaniment to a chilled salmon entrée.

TOMATO PESTO

Yield: 50 portions   *Portion:* 2 oz

Ingredient	Amount	Procedure
Sun-dried tomatoes Water, hot	10 oz 2 qt	In baker's bowl, cover tomatoes with hot water. Let stand for 1 hour to rehydrate. Drain well. Discard liquid. Purée tomatoes in a food processor.
Olive oil	1 cup	Add oil to tomatoes in a slow stream while processor is running. Transfer to a bowl and reserve for later step.
Chopped tomatoes, canned	4 lb	Drain tomatoes. Reserve juice for later step. Purée tomatoes in food processor. Add puréed tomatoes to sun-dried tomato–and–oil mixture reserved from earlier step. Stir in enough of the reserved tomato juice to make mixture spreading consistency.
Garlic, minced Salt Black pepper Sugar, granulated Parmesan cheese, grated	3 Tbsp 1¾ tsp 1 tsp 2 oz 4½ oz	Whisk in garlic, salt, pepper, sugar, and Parmesan cheese.

Approximate nutritive values per portion

Calories	Carbohydrate	Protein	Fat	Cholesterol	Sodium	Fiber	Iron
119 kcal	7 g	2 g	10 g	2 mg	334 mg	1 g	1 mg

BLACK BEAN PICO DE GALLO

Yield: 50 portions   *Portion:* 3 oz

Ingredient	Amount	Procedure
Fresh tomatoes, diced Green onions, sliced Olive oil Fresh lemon juice Salt Black pepper Sugar, granulated	6 lb 6 oz 1¼ cups 7 oz 4 tsp ½ tsp 2 tsp	In baker's bowl, combine tomatoes, onions, liquids, and seasonings.
Black beans, canned, drained Fresh basil, chopped Flat leaf parsley, chopped	3 lb EP ¾ cup 1½ cups	Rinse beans. Drain well. Add beans and herbs to vegetables just before serving.

Approximate nutritive values per portion

Calories	Carbohydrate	Protein	Fat	Cholesterol	Sodium	Fiber	Iron
85 kcal	7 g	2 g	6 g	0 mg	299 mg	3 g	1 mg

Notes

- Potentially hazardous food. *Food Safety Standards:* Hold food for service at an internal temperature of 41°F or below. Do not mix old product with new. Keep leftover product chilled at 41°F or below. See p. 167 for cooling procedures.
- Cilantro can be substituted for some or all of the basil.

Variation

- **Mango Pico de Gallo.** Substitute diced fresh or frozen mango cubes for some or all of the black beans. Substitute cilantro for basil. Substitute sliced red onions for green onions.

WARM TOMATO OLIVE AND FENNEL RAGOUT

Yield: 50 portions   *Portion:* 1 oz

Ingredient	Amount	Procedure
Olive oil	1½ Tbsp	Heat oil in a tilting fry pan or other heavy-bottomed pan.
Onions, chopped	12 oz	Sauté onions until fragrant and beginning to soften.
Garlic, minced	2 Tbsp	Add garlic, pepper, and fennel seed to the onions and sauté for 5 minutes.
Crushed red pepper	1 tsp	
Fennel seed, dried	1 tsp	
Fennel bulb, coarsely chopped	6 oz	Add fennel bulb and sauté for 5 minutes.
Chopped tomatoes, canned	2 lb 12 oz	Add tomatoes and olives. Bring to a boil.
Sliced ripe olives	3 oz	Reduce heat and simmer until onions are tender, juices evaporate, and sauce thickens, stirring occasionally, 20–30 minutes.
Fresh basil, chopped	2 Tbsp	Stir in herbs and butter.
Flat leaf parsley, chopped	1 Tbsp	Serve as a condiment with beef or lamb.
Butter, unsalted	½ Tbsp	

Approximate nutritive values per ounce

Calories	Carbohydrate	Protein	Fat	Cholesterol	Sodium	Fiber	Iron
20 kcal	3 g	0 g	1 g	1 mg	67 mg	1 g	1 mg

Note

- Potentially hazardous food. *Food Safety Standards:* Hold food for service at an internal temperature of 135°F or above. Do not mix old product with new. Cool leftover product quickly following time standards and cooling procedures on p. 167. Reheat leftover product quickly (within 2 hours) to 165°F or above. Reheat product only once; discard if not used.

FRESH TOMATILLO-SERRANO SALSA

Yield: 6 cups   *Portion:* 2 Tbsp

Ingredient	Amount	Procedure
Tomatillos	3 lb 4 oz AP	Remove tomatillo husks and rinse under warm water to remove stickiness. Cut into quarters. (Yield: about 2.5 lb)
Red onion, quartered	8 oz	In a food processor, combine tomatillos with onion, garlic, chiles, and cilantro.
Garlic cloves	4	Pulse until mixture is coarsely chopped.
Serrano chiles, stemmed	1 oz (6–8 medium chiles)	
Fresh cilantro, chopped	2 oz	
Honey	3 Tbsp	Add honey, juice, and seasonings. Pulse only until combined with tomatillo mixture.
Fresh lime juice	½ cup	
Kosher salt	1 Tbsp	
Black pepper	¼ tsp	

Approximate nutritive values per portion

Calories	Carbohydrate	Protein	Fat	Cholesterol	Sodium	Fiber	Iron
25 kcal	6 g	0.6 g	0.5 g	0 mg	5 mg	1 g	0.4 mg

Note

- Alternatively, finely dice all ingredients and mix by mashing with a fork or hand potato masher.

Variations

- **Classic Tomatillo Salsa.** Omit honey. Substitute white onion for red onion.
- **Tomatillo-Cucumber Salsa.** Add 1 lb seeded cucumber along with onions and garlic.
- **Tomatillo Mint Salsa.** Substitute fresh mint for half of the cilantro. Serve with lamb.
- **Tomatillo Salsa Verde.** Delete onion, garlic, and honey.
- **Tomato-Serrano Salsa.** Delete honey. Substitute fresh tomatoes for tomatillos. Hand-chop onions, garlic, chiles, and cilantro. Cut tomatoes in half and gently squeeze out some of the seeds. Finely dice tomatoes. Stir together all ingredients by hand.

FRESH ANAHEIM SALSA ROJO

Yield: 1½ qt   *Portion:* 1 Tbsp

Ingredient	Amount	Procedure
Anaheim chile peppers	4 oz	Remove seeds and veins from chiles. Dice into ¼-inch pieces. Place in bowl.
Tomatoes, ¼-inch dice	2 lb 8 oz	Stir tomatoes, onion, and garlic into chiles.
Red onion, chopped	6 oz	
Garlic cloves, minced	4	
Sugar, brown	1 tsp	Mix together sugar, vinegar, Tabasco sauce, and salt until sugar dissolves.
Vinegar, red wine	1 tsp	Stir vinegar mixture and cilantro into diced tomato mixture.
Green Tabasco sauce	1 tsp	
Salt	½ tsp	
Fresh cilantro, chopped	⅓ cup	

Approximate nutritive values per teaspoon

Calories	Carbohydrate	Protein	Fat	Cholesterol	Sodium	Fiber	Iron
14 kcal	3 g	0.6 g	0.1 g	0 mg	73 mg	1 g	0.21 mg

Note

- Use as a condiment for fish tacos.

ROASTED TOMATILLO-SERRANO SALSA

Yield: 6 cups   *Portion:* 2 Tbsp
Oven: 500°F

Ingredient	Amount	Procedure
Tomatillos	3 lb 4 oz AP	Remove tomatillo husks and rinse under warm water to remove stickiness. Roast in a 500°F convection oven, turning occasionally until they begin to blister and blacken and release juices. (See Note.) Cool. Reserve tomatillos and released juice for later step.
Serrano chiles, stemmed Garlic cloves, unpeeled	2 oz (12–16 medium chiles) 4	Using a dry cast iron or other heavy pan, sauté chiles and garlic over medium-high heat until softened and beginning to blacken. (See Note.) Peel garlic and discard peel. Coarsely chop chiles and peeled garlic. Place in food processor along with cooled tomatillos with their juice. Pulse until coarsely puréed. Transfer to baker's bowl.
Red onion, chopped Fresh cilantro, minced Sugar, granulated Salt	6 oz 2 oz 2 tsp 1 Tbsp	Briefly rinse onion in cold water. Blot dry using a paper towel. Stir onion, cilantro, sugar, and salt into tomatillo mixture.
Water (see procedure)	⅔ cup	Add water if not enough juice is released to make a spoonable salsa. The amount of juices released will increase when the salsa is made 3–5 hours before service.

Approximate nutritive values per tablespoon

Calories	Carbohydrate	Protein	Fat	Cholesterol	Sodium	Fiber	Iron
5 kcal	1 g	0 g	0 g	0 mg	71 mg	0.3 g	0.1 mg

Note

- Alternatively, heat tomatillos, chiles, and garlic on a foil-lined griddle or under a broiler about 4 inches from heat source until they begin to blacken.

Variations

- **Roasted Tomatillo Mint Salsa.** Substitute fresh mint for half or all of the cilantro. Serve with lamb.
- **Roasted Tomato Salsa.** Delete sugar and water. Substitute halved and seeded plum tomatoes for tomatillos. Substitute jalapeño peppers for serrano chiles. To char the tomatoes, place them skin side up in the oven or skin side down on a griddle. Add 2 Tbsp lemon juice.
- **Tomatillo Mint Chutney.** Heat ¼ cup olive oil in a heavy-bottomed pan. When the oil is very hot, add 3 lb tomatillos (husks removed, rinsed under warm water, and quartered), 6 oz chopped onion, 3 minced serrano chiles, 1½ oz minced garlic, 1 Tbsp salt, and ½ tsp black pepper. Sauté while stirring frequently until the vegetables are softened. Add 1½ oz minced fresh mint and 3 Tbsp sugar. Cook until sugar is dissolved. Serve warm with lamb.

CHIMICHURRI SAUCE

Yield: 6 cups   *Portion:* 2 Tbsp

Ingredient	Amount	Procedure
Carrots, finely grated	2 oz	Combine vegetables in baker's bowl.
Onions, finely diced	12 oz	
Garlic cloves, minced	6	
Red bell pepper, finely diced	8 oz	
Oregano, dried	3 Tbsp	Stir seasonings into vegetables.
Smoked paprika	3 Tbsp	
Cumin, ground	1 tsp	
Crushed red pepper	1½ tsp	
Black pepper	2 tsp	
Kosher salt	1 Tbsp	
Vinegar, red wine	½ cup	Stir vinegar, juice, and water into vegetable-spice mixture. Let stand at room
Fresh lime juice	¼ cup	temperature for 30 minutes.
Water	½ cup	
Flat leaf parsley, finely chopped	2½ oz	Stir in parsley and olive oil. Let stand for 1 hour before serving. Stir before
Olive oil	1½ cups	serving.

Approximate nutritive values per tablespoon

Calories	Carbohydrate	Protein	Fat	Cholesterol	Sodium	Fiber	Iron
69 kcal	2 g	0 g	7 g	0 mg	149 mg	0.6 g	0.5 mg

Note

- Spoon on steaks, roasts, chops, and poultry or use as a marinade.

Variation

- **Green Chimichurri Sauce.** Combine 4 Tbsp minced garlic, 2 minced jalapeño peppers, ⅓ cup fresh lime juice, and 4 tsp kosher salt. Whisk in ¾ cup red wine vinegar, and 2 cups olive oil. Stir in 2 cups finely chopped flat leaf parsley and 2 cups finely chopped fresh cilantro.

MOROCCAN CHARMOULA

Yield: 3½ cups

Ingredient	Amount	Procedure
Fresh cilantro, coarsely chopped	2 cups	Combine in a food processor.
Flat leaf parsley, coarsely chopped	2 cups	
Garlic cloves	3 oz	
Fresh lemon juice	1 cup	
Lemon peel, grated	2 Tbsp	
Spanish paprika	3 Tbsp	
Cumin, ground	2 Tbsp	
Coriander, ground	1 tsp	
Cayenne pepper	1 tsp	
Salt	2 tsp	
Black pepper	½ tsp	
Olive oil	2 cups	With motor running, add oil in a slow stream until incorporated.

Approximate nutritive values per tablespoon

Calories	Carbohydrate	Protein	Fat	Cholesterol	Sodium	Fiber	Iron
74 kcal	1 g	0 g	8 g	0 mg	88 mg	0.4 g	0.5 mg

Notes

- Thin with a little additional oil when used as a marinade or to baste.
- Use as a finishing sauce for lamb, fish, poultry, and grilled vegetables.

GREMOLATA

Yield: approximately 2 cups   *Portion:* 1–2 tsp

Ingredient	Amount	Procedure
Flat leaf parsley	2 oz	Wash and dry parsley. Finely chop.
Garlic cloves, finely chopped	3 oz	Stir together parsley, garlic, lemon zest, and seasonings.
Lemon zest	5 Tbsp	
Salt	¼ tsp	
Black pepper	¼ tsp	

Approximate nutritive values per teaspoon

Calories	Carbohydrate	Protein	Fat	Cholesterol	Sodium	Fiber	Iron
2 kcal	0 g	0 g	0 g	0 mg	7 mg	0 g	0 mg

Note

- Sprinkle over roasted, braised, or grilled meats; pasta; and vegetables.

Variations

- **Basil Gremolata.** Substitute 1 oz finely chopped fresh basil for 1 oz parsley.
- **Lime Cilantro Gremolata.** Substitute 1 oz finely chopped fresh cilantro for 1 oz parsley. Substitute lime zest for lemon zest.
- **Orange Gremolata.** Substitute orange zest for lemon zest.
- **Orange Gremolata Dressing or Condiment.** Mix ¾ cup chopped red onion with ¾ cup balsamic vinegar and let stand for 10 minutes. Into onion mixture, whisk 1 cup chopped flat leaf parsley, ⅓ cup olive oil, 6 finely chopped garlic cloves, 1 Tbsp brown sugar, 1 Tbsp grated orange zest, 1 tsp salt, and ¼ tsp crushed red pepper.
- **Persillade.** Proceed as for Gremolata. Omit lemon zest. Add 2 Tbsp chopped shallots (optional). Use for meats, especially lamb, and vegetables.
- **Salsa Verde.** Combine in a food processor 2 oz fresh basil, 2 oz flat leaf parsley, 1 tsp crushed red pepper, 4 Tbsp chopped garlic, 1½ Tbsp drained capers, ½ cup roasted red bell peppers, ¼ cup chopped onion, 2 Tbsp grated lemon zest, ½ cup lemon juice, and 2 tsp salt. Slowly add 1¼ cups extra virgin olive oil and puree until smooth. Serve as a sauce or condiment for meat or pasta. For lamb, substitute mint for basil. Hold for a short time because the lemon juice will cause the herbs to turn brown.
- **Spicy Gremolata for Vegetables.** Mix together 2 oz (2 cups) finely chopped flat leaf parsley, 1 cup extra virgin olive oil, 1 cup fresh lemon juice, 6 Tbsp finely grated lemon zest, 2 Tbsp finely minced garlic, 2 tsp crushed red pepper, and ¼ tsp salt. Lightly toss with cooked broccoli or cauliflower. Mix vegetables and gremolata just before serving.

SWEET AND SAVORY GOOSEBERRY SAUCE

Yield: 50 portions   *Portion:* 1½ oz

Ingredient	Amount	Procedure
Gooseberries, IQF, thawed	4 oz	Place gooseberries in steam-jacketed kettle or other pan. Crush gooseberries.
Sugar, granulated Clear Jel (see Note) Salt Nutmeg, ground Ginger, ground	2 lb 4 oz 1 oz 1 tsp ¼ tsp 1 tsp	Blend sugar, Clear Jel, and seasonings. Add to gooseberries.
Orange juice, reconstituted	4 oz	Add orange juice to gooseberry mixture. Cook over medium heat until mixture boils.
Frozen gooseberries, IQF Orange zest (optional) (see Note)	2 lb 4 oz 2 Tbsp	Add gooseberries and orange zest, if using, to thickened mixture. Cook for 3–5 minutes until gooseberries become soft and have broken up. Serve warm with pork loin roast, lamb, or other meat.

Approximate nutritive values per portion

Calories	Carbohydrate	Protein	Fat	Cholesterol	Sodium	Fiber	Iron
95 kcal	24 g	0 g	0 g	0 mg	63 mg	1 g	0 mg

Notes
- Alternatively, substitute ⅓ less cornstarch for Clear Jel. Clear Jel is available from most broadline foodservice distributors.
- Finely cut strips of orange zest provide a decorative appearance to the sauce. See Exhibit 7 for making citrus strips.

Dessert Sauce Recipes

BUTTERSCOTCH SAUCE

Yield: 1¼ qt   *Portion:* 1½ Tbsp (1 oz)

Ingredient	Amount	Procedure
Sugar, brown Corn syrup, light Water	1 lb 1⅓ cups ⅔ cup	Combine and cook to soft-ball stage (240°F). Remove from heat.
Margarine Marshmallows	6 oz 2 oz	Add margarine and marshmallows. Stir until melted. Cool.
Evaporated milk	1⅓ cups	When cool, add milk.

Approximate nutritive values per ounce

Calories	Carbohydrate	Protein	Fat	Cholesterol	Sodium	Fiber	Iron
97 kcal	17 g	1 g	3 g	2 mg	50 mg	0 g	0.5 mg

CARAMEL SAUCE

Yield: 2 qt   *Portion:* 2½ Tbsp (1½ oz)

Ingredient	Amount	Procedure
Sugar, brown	1 lb	Mix sugars and flour. Stir in water.
Sugar, granulated	1 lb	Boil until thickened.
Flour, all-purpose	2 oz	
Water	1 qt	
Margarine	8 oz	Stir in margarine and vanilla.
Vanilla	1 Tbsp	

Approximate nutritive values per ounce

Calories	Carbohydrate	Protein	Fat	Cholesterol	Sodium	Fiber	Iron
82 kcal	15 g	0 g	3 g	0 mg	36 mg	0 g	0.5 mg

Note

• Serve warm or cold over ice cream or apple desserts.

CHOCOLATE SAUCE

Yield: 1½ qt   *Portion:* 2 Tbsp (1 oz)

Ingredient	Amount	Procedure
Sugar, granulated	12 oz	Mix dry ingredients.
Cornstarch	2 oz	
Salt	1 tsp	
Cocoa	3 oz	
Water, cold	1 cup	Add cold water gradually to form a smooth paste.
Water, boiling	3½ cups	Add boiling water slowly while stirring. Boil for 5 minutes or until thickened. Remove from heat.
Margarine	6 oz	Add margarine and vanilla. Stir to blend.
Vanilla	1 tsp	

Approximate nutritive values per ounce

Calories	Carbohydrate	Protein	Fat	Cholesterol	Sodium	Fiber	Iron
59 kcal	9 g	0 g	3 g	0 mg	77 mg	0 g	0.5 mg

Note

• Serve warm or cold on puddings, cake, cream puffs, or ice cream.

HOT FUDGE SAUCE

Yield: 1½ qt   *Portion:* 2 Tbsp (1 oz)

Ingredient	Amount	Procedure
Margarine, soft	8 oz	Combine margarine, sugar, and milk over hot water.
Sugar, powdered	1 lb 8 oz	Stir and cook slowly for 30 minutes.
Evaporated milk	one 13-oz can	
Unsweetened chocolate, chipped or melted	8 oz	Add chocolate and stir until blended.

Approximate nutritive values per ounce

Calories	Carbohydrate	Protein	Fat	Cholesterol	Sodium	Fiber	Iron
133 kcal	18 g	1 g	8 g	2 mg	58 mg	0.3 g	0.5 mg

Notes

- Serve hot over ice cream.
- This sauce may be stored in the refrigerator. Heat over hot water before serving. If too thick or grainy, add evaporated milk before heating.

CUSTARD SAUCE

Yield: 1 gal   *Portion:* ⅓ cup (2½ oz)

Ingredient	Amount	Procedure
Sugar, granulated	14 oz	Mix dry ingredients.
Cornstarch	2 oz	
Salt	½ tsp	
Milk, cold	2 cups	Add cold milk and mix until smooth.
Milk, hot	3 qt	Add cold mixture to hot milk gradually while stirring.
Egg yolks, beaten	10 (6 oz)	Stir in egg yolks gradually. Cook over hot water until thickened, about 5 minutes.
Vanilla	2 Tbsp	Remove from heat and add vanilla. Cool.

Approximate nutritive values per ounce

Calories	Carbohydrate	Protein	Fat	Cholesterol	Sodium	Fiber	Iron
35 kcal	5 g	1 g	1 g	21 mg	22 mg	0 g	0 mg

Notes

- Potentially hazardous food. *Food Safety Standards:* Hold food for service at an internal temperature of 41°F or below. Do not mix old product with new. Keep leftover product chilled at 41°F or below. See p. 167 for cooling procedures.
- Serve over cake-type puddings.

FLUFFY ORANGE SAUCE

Yield: 3 qt   *Portion:* 3 Tbsp (1½ oz)

Ingredient	Amount	Procedure
Butter or margarine	1 lb 5 oz	Melt butter or margarine. Gradually add sugar.
Sugar, powdered	2 lb 2 oz	Beat with a wire whip until it resembles whipped cream.
Eggs, beaten	10 (1 lb 2 oz)	Add eggs slowly, beating constantly.
Fresh orange juice	1¾ cup	Slowly blend in orange juice and peel. Heat for 10–15 minutes on low heat until thickened.
Orange peel, grated	1½ Tbsp	Beat again.

Approximate nutritive values per ounce

Calories	Carbohydrate	Protein	Fat	Cholesterol	Sodium	Fiber	Iron
109 kcal	12 g	1 g	6 g	27 mg	77 mg	0 g	0 mg

LEMON SAUCE

Yield: 3 qt   *Portion:* 3 Tbsp (2 oz)

Ingredient	Amount	Procedure
Sugar, granulated	2 lb	Mix dry ingredients.
Cornstarch	3 oz	
Salt	½ tsp	
Water, boiling	2 qt	Add boiling water. Cook until clear.
Fresh lemon juice	⅔ cup	Add juice and margarine.
Margarine	1 oz (2 Tbsp)	

Approximate nutritive values per ounce

Calories	Carbohydrate	Protein	Fat	Cholesterol	Sodium	Fiber	Iron
48 kcal	12 g	0 g	0 g	0 mg	17 mg	0 g	0 mg

Note

- Serve hot with Christmas Pudding (p. 372), Bread Pudding (p. 370), or Rice Custard (p. 370).

Variations

- **Nutmeg Sauce.** Omit lemon juice. Add 1 tsp nutmeg. Increase margarine to 4 oz.
- **Orange Sauce.** Substitute orange juice for lemon juice. Add 1 tsp freshly grated orange peel.
- **Vanilla Sauce.** Omit lemon juice and reduce sugar to 1 lb 4 oz. Add 2 Tbsp vanilla.

HARD SAUCE

Yield: 3⅓ cups   *Portion:* 1 Tbsp (½ oz)

Ingredient	Amount	Procedure
Butter	8 oz	Cream butter on medium speed until soft and fluffy.
Water, boiling	2 Tbsp	Add water and continue to cream until very light.
Sugar, powdered Fresh lemon juice	1 lb 3 oz ½ tsp	Add sugar gradually. Continue creaming. Add juice. Place in refrigerator to harden.

Approximate nutritive values per ounce

Calories	Carbohydrate	Protein	Fat	Cholesterol	Sodium	Fiber	Iron
143 kcal	21 g	0 g	7 g	19 mg	73 mg	0 g	0 mg

Note

- Serve with Christmas Pudding (p. 372), Baked Apples (p. 375), or Peach Cobbler (p. 378).

Variations

- **Cherry Hard Sauce.** Add ½ cup chopped maraschino cherries.
- **Strawberry Hard Sauce.** Omit lemon juice and water. Add ¾ cup fresh or frozen strawberries, chopped.

BROWN SUGAR HARD SAUCE

Yield: 1 qt   *Portion:* 1 Tbsp (½ oz)

Ingredient	Amount	Procedure
Butter	12 oz	Cream butter on medium speed until light.
Sugar, light brown Vanilla	1 lb 4 oz 2 tsp	Add sugar gradually while creaming. Add vanilla. Cream until fluffy.
Whipping cream	¾ cup	Whip cream. Fold into sugar mixture. Chill.

Approximate nutritive values per ounce

Calories	Carbohydrate	Protein	Fat	Cholesterol	Sodium	Fiber	Iron
160 kcal	18 g	0 g	10 g	30 mg	97 mg	0 g	0.5 mg

Note

- Serve with Christmas Pudding (p. 372).

PEANUT BUTTER SAUCE

Yield: 2 qt   *Portion:* 2½ Tbsp (1½ oz)

Ingredient	Amount	Procedure
Sugar, granulated	12 oz	Combine sugar, syrup, and water.
Corn syrup, light	1⅓ cups	Cook to 228°F and turn off heat or remove from burner.
Water, hot	¾ cup	
Margarine	6 oz	Add margarine and marshmallows.
Marshmallows, miniature	3 oz	Stir until melted. Cool. Place in mixer bowl.
Evaporated milk	12 oz	Add milk and peanut butter.
Peanut butter, creamy	8 oz	Beat until well blended. Refrigerate.

Approximate nutritive values per ounce

Calories	Carbohydrate	Protein	Fat	Cholesterol	Sodium	Fiber	Iron
109 kcal	15 g	2 g	5 g	2 mg	59 mg	0.3 g	0 mg

Note

- Serve over ice cream.

RASPBERRY SAUCE

Yield: 3 qt   *Portion:* 3 Tbsp (2 oz)

Ingredient	Amount	Procedure
Red raspberries, frozen	5 lb	Defrost berries. Do not drain.
Sugar, granulated	2 oz	Combine sugar and cornstarch and add to berries.
Cornstarch	1 oz	Cook until clear.
Currant jelly	1 lb 8 oz	Add jelly. Stir until melted. Cool.

Approximate nutritive values per ounce

Calories	Carbohydrate	Protein	Fat	Cholesterol	Sodium	Fiber	Iron
47 kcal	12 g	0 g	0 g	0 mg	0 mg	1 g	0.5 mg

Notes

- Serve over vanilla ice cream or raspberry, lemon, or lime sherbet.
- Raspberries may be strained before thickening.

Variations

- **Fresh Strawberry Sauce.** Substitute 5 lb fresh strawberries, cleaned and hulled, for raspberries. Mash berries, add 2½ cups water, and strain to remove seeds. Combine 1¼ cups sugar and ⅓ cup cornstarch with juice. Heat to boiling, stirring constantly. Cook until thickened and clear. Chill. Serve over ice cream or other desserts.
- **Peach Melba.** Pour 3 Tbsp Raspberry Sauce over a scoop of vanilla ice cream placed in the center of a canned, fresh, or frozen peach half.

BROWN SUGAR SYRUP

Yield: 2 gal

Ingredient	Amount	Procedure
Sugar, brown	5 lb	Combine all ingredients.
Sugar, granulated	5 lb 8 oz	Stir and heat until sugar is dissolved.
Corn syrup	1 cup	
Water	2½ qt	
Margarine	4 oz	

Approximate nutritive values per ounce

Calories	Carbohydrate	Protein	Fat	Cholesterol	Sodium	Fiber	Iron
80 kcal	20 g	0 g	0 g	0 mg	9 mg	0 g	0.5 mg

Notes

- Serve warm or cold on pancakes, fritters, or waffles.
- ½ tsp maple flavoring may be added.

Variation

- **Blueberry Syrup.** Combine 1½ qt water, 12 oz granulated sugar, 1 tsp salt, and ⅓ cup lemon juice. Heat to boiling. Mix 4 oz waxy maize starch and 1½ cups cold water to make a paste. Add slowly to sugar mixture, stirring constantly. Cook until thickened and clear. Fold in 3 lb 8 oz individually quick-frozen (IQF) blueberries. Serve warm over pancakes, French toast, or ice cream.

Marinade, Rub, and Seasoning Recipes

COMPOUND BUTTERS

Yield: 2 lb

Ingredient	Amount	Procedure
Butter, unsalted, softened	2 lb	Mix flavoring with softened butter.
Flavoring	see Variations	Form into ¾-inch-diameter logs or cube.
		Refrigerate until firm enough to slice.
		Use for meats, pasta, rice, vegetables, and breads. A ¼-inch slice equals 1 tsp; a ¾-inch slice equals 1 Tbsp.

Note

- Compound butter may be tightly wrapped in foil and frozen. Freeze for no more than 1 month.

Variations

- **Basil Butter.** Add 4 cups fresh basil leaves, 3 minced garlic cloves, and ¼ cup lemon juice.
- **Chipotle Butter**. Add 10–15 canned chipotle chiles in adobo that have been stemmed, seeded, and minced, ½ cup fresh lime juice, 2 Tbsp ground cumin, and 1 Tbsp kosher salt.
- **Dill Butter.** Add 2 cups minced dill or ½ cup dried dill weed and ¼ cup lemon juice. Use on potatoes and other cooked vegetables, rice, and fish.
- **Fresh Peach Butter.** Add 2 cups diced fresh peaches and 1 cup brown sugar. Serve with pancakes or waffles.
- **Garlic Butter.** Add 16 crushed garlic cloves. Use on potatoes and other cooked vegetables, pasta, and pasta sauce.
- **Garlic and Parsley Butter.** Add 2 cups packed chopped flat leaf parsley, 6 finely minced garlic cloves, and 1 tsp salt.
- **Herb Butter.** Add 1 cup finely chopped chives, 1 cup finely chopped fresh parsley, ¼ cup fresh tarragon, and 1 tsp lemon juice.
- **Lemon Butter.** Add 1 cup lemon juice, 2 tsp grated lemon zest, and ¼ cup Dijon-style mustard (optional).
- **Lime Cumin Butter.** Add ½ cup fresh lime juice, ½ cup (packed) finely chopped flat leaf parsley, ⅓ cup toasted and cooled cumin seeds, 2 tsp salt, and 2 tsp black pepper.
- **Mustard Butter.** Add 10 oz minced scallions, 8 oz whole-grain mustard, 1 oz chopped fresh parsley, ¼ cup lemon juice, and ½ tsp ground red pepper.
- **Mustard Caper Butter.** Add 1½ cups coarsely chopped capers, drained, 1 cup chopped fresh dill, ½ cup whole-grain mustard, 2 Tbsp grated lemon zest, and ½ tsp black pepper.
- **Orange Marmalade Butter.** Add 4 cups orange marmalade and ½ tsp kosher salt.
- **Parsley Butter.** Add 2 cups finely chopped fresh parsley. Use on potatoes and other vegetables, rice, fish, soups, and sauces.
- **Parsley Lemon Butter.** Add 2 cups finely chopped fresh parsley and ¾ cup lemon juice.
- **Red Pepper Butter.** Add 1 cup finely chopped sweet red pepper, 1 cup finely chopped yellow onion, and 8 finely minced garlic cloves.
- **Rosemary Garlic Butter.** Add 12 crushed garlic cloves and 1 cup finely minced fresh rosemary.
- **Strawberry Honey Butter.** Add 2 ½ cups hulled minced strawberries, ½ cup honey, 4 Tbsp lemon juice, and 1 tsp grated orange zest. Serve with pancakes or waffles.

HERB BUTTER SEASONING

Yield: 1 qt

Ingredient	Amount	Procedure
Butter	2 lb	Place butter in mixer bowl. Let stand at room temperature until soft enough to mix.
Fresh lemon juice	2 tsp	Add juice and seasonings to butter. Mix on low speed, using a flat beater, until all ingredients are mixed thoroughly.
Seasonings	See next step	
For vegetables:		
Basil leaves, dried, crushed	1 Tbsp	
Marjoram, ground	2 tsp	
Savory leaves, dried, crushed	1 Tbsp	
For meats:		
Marjoram, ground	2 tsp	
Dry mustard	4 tsp	
Tarragon leaves, dried, crushed	1 Tbsp	
Rosemary leaves, dried, crushed	1 Tbsp	

Notes

- Other spices and herbs may be substituted for those listed in the recipe. See pp. 133–138 for use of herbs and spices in cooking.
- White, cider, or wine vinegar may be substituted for part or all of the lemon juice.
- Unsalted butter may be substituted for salted butter.
- See Compound Butters, p. 720.

Variations

- **Curry Butter.** Omit seasonings. Add 1 Tbsp curry powder.
- **Dill Butter.** Omit seasonings. Add 1 Tbsp dill weed.
- **Lemon Butter.** Omit seasonings. Increase lemon juice to 1 cup and add 3 Tbsp freshly grated lemon peel.
- **Onion Butter.** Omit seasonings and lemon juice. Blend in 2 oz onion soup mix.
- **Tarragon Butter.** Omit seasonings. Add 4 Tbsp dried tarragon.

MEAT OR POULTRY MARINADE

Yield: for 20 pounds of meat or poultry

Ingredient	Amount	Procedure
Spice Blend (p. 730)	4 oz (1 cup)	Mix spices with onions, garlic, oil, and juice. May be prepared in food processor.
Onions, very finely chopped	1 lb	Rub over meat or poultry. Marinate for several hours or overnight in the refrigerator.
Garlic cloves, minced	2 oz	Grill or roast meat or poultry as per recipe instructions.
Vegetable oil	½ cup	
Fresh lemon juice	½ cup	

MEAT MARINADE

Yield: 2 qt

Ingredient	Amount	Procedure
Salad oil	1 qt	Combine ingredients, mixing well.
Worcestershire sauce	¼ cup	Pour over meat. Marinate in the refrigerator for 6 hours or longer.
Liquid smoke	¼ cup	
Soy sauce	2 cups	
Vinegar, cider	¼ cup	
Garlic cloves, minced	4	
Celery salt	¼ cup	
Dry mustard	¼ cup	
Ginger, ground	¼ cup	
Sugar, brown	1 cup	

Note

• Pour over pork or beef.

FISH MARINADE

Yield: 2½ qt

Ingredient	Amount	Procedure
Vegetable oil	1 qt	Combine ingredients, mixing well.
Olive oil	3 cups	Place fish in marinade.
Fresh lemon juice	3 cups	Refrigerate for 3 hours. Remove fish from marinade and grill or broil.
Oregano, dried, crumbled	¼ cup	
Parsley, dried	¼ cup	
Basil, dried, crumbled	¼ cup	
Garlic powder	1 Tbsp	
Salt	1 Tbsp	
Black pepper	1 tsp	

VEGETABLE MARINADE

Yield: 1½ qt

Ingredient	Amount	Procedure
Fresh lemon juice	2½ Tbsp	Combine.
Vinegar, white	⅓ cup	
Salad oil	1 cup	
Worcestershire sauce	1 Tbsp	
Water	⅓ cup	
Onion, finely chopped	3 oz	Add and mix.
Garlic cloves, crushed	2	
Pimento, chopped	¼ cup	
Fresh parsley, finely chopped	¼ cup	
Salt	1½ Tbsp	Blend in and mix.
Sugar, granulated	1 Tbsp	Pour over fresh vegetables and marinate for 6 hours or longer.
Black pepper	⅛ tsp	
Tarragon, dried	1 Tbsp	

Note

• Pour over fresh mushrooms or other fresh vegetables or pasta.

ASIAN MARINADE

Yield: 2 qt

Ingredient	Amount	Procedure
Soy sauce	3 cups	Combine all ingredients in stainless steel container. Mix well.
Sugar, granulated	11 oz	
Toasted sesame oil	1¼ cups	
White pepper	5 tsp	
Green onions, finely chopped	1 lb EP	
Garlic, minced	5 oz EP	
Sesame seeds	2 Tbsp	Toast sesame seeds: • Spread in a thin, even layer in a dry skillet or baking pan. • Cook over medium heat (375°F) until seeds become golden brown and just begin to smoke (3–5 minutes). Shake pan once or twice and watch carefully so seeds do not burn. Add seeds to soy sauce mixture. Stir to distribute.

Note

• Use to marinate ribs, poultry, and pork loin or chops.

Variations

• **Teriyaki Citrus Marinade.** Stir together 2 cups soy sauce, 2 cups orange juice, ½ cup granulated sugar, ½ cup vegetable oil, 3 Tbsp grated fresh ginger, 8 minced garlic cloves, and ½ tsp black pepper. Use to marinate poultry.
• **Teriyaki Marinade.** Stir together 2 cups soy sauce, 1¼ cups brown sugar, 1¼ cups water, 1 cup rice wine vinegar, 1½ tsp garlic powder, and 1 Tbsp ground ginger. Use to marinate beef, chicken, and pork.

GRILLED VEGETABLE MARINADE

Yield: 3½ cups

Ingredient	Amount	Procedure
Olive oil	1 lb 5 oz	Combine ingredients. Use as a vegetable marinade.
Vinegar, balsamic	8 oz	
Garlic, minced	1½ Tbsp	
Thyme, dried	½ tsp	
Basil, dried	1 tsp	
Parsley, dried	1 Tbsp	
Crushed red pepper	½ tsp	
Black pepper	½ tsp	
Salt	1 Tbsp	

Note

• Red wine vinegar may be substituted for balsamic vinegar.

BALSAMIC VINEGAR MARINADE FOR VEGETABLES

Yield: 1¼ qt

Ingredient	Amount	Procedure
Vinegar, balsamic	¾ cup	Mix vinegars, onion, garlic, and seasonings using a wire whip.
Vinegar, sherry wine	¼ cup	
Onion, finely minced	3 oz	
Garlic cloves, finely minced	3	
Salt	½ tsp	
Black pepper	½ tsp	
Vegetable oil	1½ cups	Whisk in oils.
Olive oil	2 cups	Store in a covered container in refrigerator for up to 1 week. Stir before using.

HONEY-BALSAMIC MARINADE

Yield: 5½ cups

Ingredient	Amount	Procedure
Honey	2 cups	Mix all ingredients.
Olive oil	2 Tbsp	Brush on fish or chicken before grilling or baking.
Dijon mustard	2 cups	
Vinegar, balsamic	1¼ cups	
Black pepper, coarsely ground	1 Tbsp	
Garlic salt	1 Tbsp	

HERB MARINADE FOR POULTRY OR FISH

Yield: For approximately 50 portions of poultry or fish

Ingredient	Amount	Procedure
White wine	¾ cup	Combine all ingredients.
Fresh lemon juice	1½ cups	Rub on both sides of chicken or fish portions.
Garlic cloves, minced	2 oz EP	Marinate in refrigerator for 30 minutes.
Fresh parsley, minced	2 oz	Follow recipe instructions for grilling, broiling, or roasting.
Dijon mustard	¼ cup	
Crushed red pepper	2 Tbsp	
Fennel seed, crushed	1 Tbsp	
Tarragon, dried	1 Tbsp	
Salt	1 tsp	

Variation

- **Lime Cilantro Marinade for Poultry or Fish.** Stir together 4 Tbsp grated lime zest, 2 cups fresh lime juice, 2 cups olive oil, 1 cup packed fresh cilantro, 4 tsp granulated sugar, 4 tsp salt, 8 small, finely chopped jalapeno peppers, and 8 finely minced garlic cloves. Fresh flat leaf parsley can be substituted for the cilantro.

HERB AND GARLIC MARINADE FOR VEGETABLES

Yield: 1½ qt

Ingredient	Amount	Procedure
Olive oil	1¼ qt	Combine all ingredients and stir to combine.
Vinegar, red wine	1 cup	Stir before using.
Garlic, minced	2 oz EP	
Salt	1 oz	
Black pepper	1½ tsp	
Thyme, dried	1 tsp	
Basil, dried	1 tsp	
Parsley, dried	1 tsp	
Crushed red pepper	2 tsp	

VINAIGRETTE MARINADE

Yield: 3 qt

Ingredient	Amount	Procedure
Vegetable oil	1 qt	Using a wire whip, whisk together all ingredients.
Olive oil	1 qt	Use to marinate vegetables before roasting or to season steamed
Vinegar, cider	2½ cups	vegetables.
Fresh lemon juice	1¼ cups	
Soy sauce	¼ cup	
Garlic, finely minced	4 oz EP	
Tarragon, dried	2 oz	
Dijon mustard	⅓ cup	
Salt	2 tsp	
Black pepper	1 tsp	

Note

• Use marinade within 1 week. Keep refrigerated.

Seasonings and Rubs

Yield: All approximately 2 cups (unless otherwise noted)   *Portion:* See Table 19.1

ADOBO SEASONING BLEND

Yield: ½ cup

Ingredient	Amount	Procedure	Use
Garlic powder	4 tsp	Mix spices. Store in airtight container in a cool dry place.	For seasoning pork or poultry.
Dehydrated minced onions	2 Tbsp		
Black pepper	1½ tsp		
Ground red pepper	2 tsp		
Oregano, dried	2 Tbsp		
Cumin, ground	2 ½ tsp		

ANCHO CHILE RUB

Yield: 1 cup

Ingredient	Amount	Procedure	Use
Ancho chile powder	½ cup	Mix all ingredients together thoroughly.	For seasoning meats.
Cumin, ground	5 tsp	Store covered.	
Oregano, dried	1 Tbsp		
Garlic powder	4 tsp		
Coriander, ground	4 tsp		
Black pepper	1½ tsp		
Kosher salt	1 Tbsp		
Paprika	5 tsp		

ASIAN SPICE BLEND

Ingredient	Amount	Procedure	Use
Chinese five spice	1 cup	Mix spices. Store in airtight container in a cool dry place.	Rub on beef, pork, or poultry.
Dehydrated minced garlic	½ cup		
Crushed red pepper	¼ cup		
Kosher salt	⅓ cup		

BARBECUE RUB

Ingredient	Amount	Procedure	Use
Paprika	¾ cup	Mix spices. Store in airtight container in a cool dry place.	Rub on beef, pork, or poultry.
Garlic powder	2 Tbsp		
Onion powder	2 Tbsp		
Salt	5 Tbsp		
Black pepper	2 Tbsp		

BLACKENING SEASONING

Ingredient	Amount	Procedure	Use
Paprika	2 oz	Mix spices. Store in airtight container in a cool dry place.	Use to season pork, poultry, and fish.
Garlic powder	2 oz		For blackened chicken or fish, rub with seasoning before browning in a heavy pan.
Onion powder	1 oz		
Marjoram, dried	¼ cup		
Thyme, dried	¼ cup		
Ground red pepper	3 Tbsp		
Black pepper	¼ cup		
Salt	¼ cup		

CAJUN RUB

Ingredient	Amount	Procedure	Use
Garlic powder	6 Tbsp	Mix spices. Store in airtight container in a cool dry place.	Use to season pork and poultry.
Thyme, dried	4 Tbsp		
Oregano, dried	4 Tbsp		
Cumin, ground	1 Tbsp		
Nutmeg, ground	1 tsp		
Paprika	1 cup		
Black pepper	1 Tbsp		
Ground red pepper	1 Tbsp		
Salt	l Tbsp		

CHILE SPICE RUB (WET)

Ingredient	Amount	Procedure	Use
Fresh lime juice	1 cup	Mix juice, oil, and seasonings.	Rub on beef, pork, or poultry or use as a marinade.
Olive oil	¼ cup		
Chile powder	¼ cup		
Garlic cloves, minced	8		
Cumin, ground	3 Tbsp		
Cinnamon, ground	1 Tbsp		
Hot pepper sauce	2 tsp		
Kosher salt	1 tsp		

CITRUS MUSTARD RUB (WET)

Ingredient	Amount	Procedure	Use
Lemons	8	Finely shred lemon peel. Spread on baking pan. Dry in 350°F oven for about 10 minutes. Cool. Mix dried lemon peel with other ingredients. Use at once or store covered in refrigerator for up to 1 week. Use lemon juice for other recipes.	Rub on pork, beef, or lamb before roasting. ½ cup freshly dried orange peel may be substituted for lemon peel.
Dijon-style mustard	2 cups		
Fresh parsley, minced	1 cup		
Rosemary, dried	½ cup		
Black pepper	¼ cup		

CURRY SEASONING

Ingredient	Amount	Procedure	Use
Curry powder	1 cup	Mix all ingredients together thoroughly. Store in airtight container in a cool dry place.	Use to season beef, pork, and chicken.
Ginger, ground	6 Tbsp		
Garlic powder	½ cup		
Black pepper	½ cup		
Ground red pepper	2 Tbsp		
Salt	½ cup		

ESPRESSO SPICE

Ingredient	Amount	Procedure	Use
Cumin seed[a]	½ cup	Spread cumin seeds in a thin even layer in a dry skillet. Heat over medium-high heat until fragrant, 2–3 minutes. Shake pan throughout cooking to prevent burning. Cool and grind in a spice grinder.	Use to season beef and pork.
Sugar, brown	⅔ cup		
Cinnamon, ground	2 Tbsp		
Ground red pepper	¼ cup		
Cracked black pepper	2 Tbsp		
Ground coffee (espresso grind)	4 tsp	Mix all ingredients together thoroughly. Store in airtight container in a cool dry place.	
Kosher salt	3 Tbsp		

FIERY PEPPER BLEND

Ingredient	Amount	Procedure	Use
White pepper	¼ cup	Mix spices. Store in airtight container in a cool dry place.	General spice blend for meat. Use sparingly.
Black pepper	¼ cup		
Ground red pepper	¼ cup		
Paprika	¾ cup		
Salt	¼ cup		
Thyme, ground	¾ cup		
Onion powder	¼ cup		
Garlic powder	¼ cup		

LEMON HERBS

Ingredient	Amount	Procedure	Use
Lemons	8	Finely shred lemon peel. Spread on baking pan. Dry in 350°F oven for about 10 minutes. Cool. Crush herbs. Mix with dried lemon peel. Store in airtight container in a cool dry place.	Use to season soups, stews, fish, poultry, lamb, and vegetables. May substitute herbs with celery flakes, cilantro, dill weed, oregano, rosemary, tarragon.
Basil, dried[b]	5 Tbsp		
Marjoram, dried	5 Tbsp		
Rubbed sage	2 Tbsp		
Savory, dried	5 Tbsp		
Parsley, dried	¼ cup		
Thyme, dried	5 Tbsp		

HERB BOUQUET

Ingredient	Amount	Procedure	Use
Rosemary, dried	¼ cup	Mix spices. Store in airtight container in a cool dry place.	Sprinkle over beef, lamb, or chicken.
Thyme, dried	½ cup		
Oregano, dried	½ cup		
Basil, dried	¼ cup		
Dry mustard	¼ cup		
Black pepper, coarsely ground	3 Tbsp		

JAMAICAN JERK

Ingredient	Amount	Procedure	Use
Dehydrated minced garlic	¼ cup	Mix spices. Store in airtight container in a cool dry place.	Use to season beef, pork, and chicken.
Dehydrated granulated onion	¼ cup		
Ginger, ground	½ cup		
Cloves, ground	2 tsp		
Allspice, ground	3 Tbsp		
Nutmeg, ground	1 tsp		
Ground red pepper	1 Tbsp		
Thyme, dried	½ cup		
Black pepper, coarsely ground	1 Tbsp		
Kosher salt	¼ cup		

JAMAICAN SPICE RUB (WET)

Ingredient	Amount	Procedure	Use
Extra virgin olive oil	1 cup	Process into a paste.	Rub on pork and chicken before baking.
Fresh lime juice	1 cup		
Fresh ginger, peeled	4 oz		
Allspice, ground	2 Tbsp		
Coriander, ground	2 Tbsp		
Black pepper	2 Tbsp		
Kosher salt	3 Tbsp		

RIB-STYLE SEASONING

Ingredient	Amount	Procedure	Use
Chile powder	¾ cup	Mix spices. Store in airtight container in a cool dry place.	Rub on ribs before cooking.
Hungarian paprika	6 Tbsp		
Ground red pepper	3 Tbsp		
Black pepper	6 Tbsp		
Garlic salt	6 Tbsp		

SALT-FREE HERB SEASONING

Ingredient	Amount	Procedure	Use
Dehydrated minced onion	½ cup	Mix spices. Store in airtight container in a cool dry place.	Use for fish or chicken.
Garlic powder	2 Tbsp		
Celery seed	2 Tbsp		
Tarragon, dried	¼ cup		
Dill weed, dried	⅔ cup		
Oregano, dried	¼ cup		
Lemon pepper	2 Tbsp		
Crushed red pepper	2 Tbsp		

SEASONED SALT

Ingredient	Amount	Procedure	Use
Salt	1 lb	Mix all ingredients together thoroughly. Store covered.	For seasoning meats, salads, and vegetables.
Celery salt	2 oz		
Onion powder	2 oz		
Garlic powder	1 oz		
Paprika	1 Tbsp		
Chile powder	¼ cup		

SPICE BLEND

Ingredient	Amount	Procedure	Use
Salt	2 oz	Mix spices. Store in airtight container in a cool dry place.	General spice blend for meat and poultry.
Black pepper	1 Tbsp		
Paprika	¼ cup		
Oregano, dried	1 oz		
Thyme, dried	2 oz		
Cumin, ground	2 Tbsp		

SOUTHWEST BLEND

Ingredient	Amount	Procedure	Use
Kosher salt	2 Tbsp	Mix spices. Store in airtight container in a cool dry place.	General spice blend for meat and poultry.
Black pepper	2 tsp		
Cumin, ground	½ cup		
Cilantro, dried	½ cup		
Garlic powder	½ cup		

SOUTHWEST STEAK RUB (WET)

Ingredient	Amount	Procedure	Use
Chile powder	¾ cup	Mix all ingredients together. Store unused rub in the refrigerator. Use within 7 days.	Rub on steaks before cooking.
Sugar, brown	¾ cup		
Cumin, ground	⅓ cup		
Ground red pepper	1½ tsp		
Paprika	½ tsp		
Fresh garlic, minced	¼ cup		
Vinegar, cider	¼ cup		
Worcestershire sauce	2 Tbsp		

SWEET SPICES (FOR ROOT VEGETABLES)

Yield: 1 cup

Ingredient	Amount	Procedure	Use
Sugar, light brown	½ cup	Mix spices. Store in airtight container in a cool dry place.	Spices for roasted root vegetables (carrots), popcorn, baked sweet potatoes, winter squash.
Cinnamon, ground	½ cup		
Ginger, ground	5 tsp		
Nutmeg, ground	1 Tbsp		
Cloves, ground	1½ tsp		
Cardamom, ground	2 tsp		
White pepper	¼ tsp		

TOASTED SPICE BLEND

Ingredient	Amount	Procedure	Use
Allspice, ground	2 Tbsp	Combine spices. Spread in a thin even layer in a dry skillet (stove top, medium heat) or baking pan (oven 375°F). Heat until fragrant and just beginning to smoke, 1–2 minutes. Shake skillet throughout cooking to prevent burning. Oven shake once. Cool. Store in airtight container in a cool dry place for up to 2 weeks.	Use sparingly to season soups, stews, and meats. The flavor profile complements Moroccan and African dishes.
Cardamom, ground	4 tsp		
Cinnamon, ground	2 Tbsp		
Cumin, ground	¼ cup		
Ginger, ground	½ cup		
Mace, ground	2 tsp		
Dry mustard	¼ cup		
Turmeric, ground	¼ cup		
Black pepper, coarsely ground	2 Tbsp		
Cayenne pepper	¼ cup		

WARM CHILE SPICE BLEND

Ingredient	Amount	Procedure	Use
Fennel seed[a]	1 Tbsp	Spread seeds in a thin even layer in a dry skillet. Heat over medium-high heat until fragrant, 2–3 minutes. Shake pan throughout cooking to prevent burning. Cool and grind in batches using a spice grinder.	General spice blend for meat and poultry.
Anise seed[a]	1 Tbsp		
Coriander seed[a]	1 Tbsp		
Kosher salt	1 tsp		
Black pepper	2 tsp		
Paprika	1 Tbsp		
Chile powder	1 cup		
Thyme, dried	¼ cup	Mix ground seeds with other spices. Store in airtight container in a cool dry place.	
Oregano, dried	¼ cup		
Cumin, ground	1 Tbsp		

WEST INDIES SPICE (POUDRE DE COLOMBO BLEND)

Ingredient	Amount	Procedure	Use
Cumin seed[a]	½ cup	Spread seeds in a thin even layer in a dry skillet. Heat over medium-high heat until fragrant, 2–3 minutes. Shake pan throughout cooking to prevent burning. Cool and grind in batches using a spice grinder.	General spice rub blend for meat and poultry. Flavoring for stews and soups.
Coriander seed[a]	½ cup		
Mustard seed[a]	3 Tbsp		
Fenugreek seed[a]	3 Tbsp		
Black peppercorns	3 Tbsp		
Cloves, whole	2 Tbsp		
Turmeric, ground	½ cup	Toast turmeric over medium-high heat until fragrant and lightly browned, 1–2 minutes. Cool. Mix pepper and turmeric with other spices. Store in airtight container in a cool dry place.	
Ground red pepper	½ tsp		

ZATAR BLEND

Ingredient	Amount	Procedure	Use
Toasted sesame seed[a]	1 cup	Grind sesame seed in a spice grinder. Mix with other spices. Store in airtight container in the refrigerator.	Mix with extra virgin olive oil and serve with warm pita bread. Sprinkle on vegetables before roasting.
Sumac, ground	½ cup		
Thyme, ground	¼ cup		
Kosher salt	1 tsp		

[a] When toasting whole spices (seed), cover loosely with a lid to prevent seeds from popping out of the pan. Toast whole seeds for 2–3 minutes or until seeds begin to pop and are fragrant. Cool before grinding. Toast ground spices for 1–2 minutes.

[b] To substitute fresh herbs for dried herbs, use a ratio of 3 fresh to 1 dry. If using ground dried herbs in place of dried leaves, use one-fourth as much ground as dried leaves.

Mayonnaise (based) Sauces and Spreads (for sandwiches)

Yield: All approximately 1 quart

BLUE CHEESE MAYO

Ingredient	Amount	Procedure
Mayonnaise	1 qt	Mix all ingredients. Hold for service at or below 40°F.
Crumbled blue cheese	2 cups	
Fresh parsley, finely chopped	1 cup	
Garlic, puréed	½ cup	

CHIPOTLE MAYO

Ingredient	Amount	Procedure
Mayonnaise	1 qt	Mix until smooth.
Chopped chipotle chiles in adobo, canned	4 oz	Hold for service at or below 40°F.
Lime zest	3 Tbsp	
Fresh lime juice	2 Tbsp	
Honey	2 Tbsp	

CURRIED MAYO

Ingredient	Amount	Procedure
Curry powder	3½ Tbsp	Heat curry powder in a dry skillet over medium-low heat until fragrant, about
Mayonnaise	1 qt	2 minutes. Set aside to cool.
Fresh lemon juice	5 Tbsp	Mix curry powder with mayonnaise and juice until combined.
		Hold for service at or below 40°F.

GARLIC-THYME MAYO

Ingredient	Amount	Procedure
Garlic cloves, peeled	3 oz	Toss garlic cloves with oil to completely coat. Place garlic in a single layer and
Olive oil	1 Tbsp	roast until golden brown in a 350°F oven. When soft, mash with a fork or
Thyme, dried	1 Tbsp	side of a French knife until paste consistency.
Mayonnaise	1 qt	Mix thyme and mayonnaise with garlic. Hold for service at or below 40°F.

HONEY MUSTARD MAYO

Ingredient	Amount	Procedure
Mayonnaise	1 qt	Mix until combined.
Honey mustard	1 lb 4 oz	Hold for service at or below 40°F.

HORSERADISH AND PEPPERCORN MAYO

Ingredient	Amount	Procedure
Mayonnaise	1 qt	Mix all ingredients.
Prepared horseradish	½ cup	Hold for service at or below 40°F.
Cracked black peppercorns	4 tsp	

LEMON-LIME MAYO

Ingredient	Amount	Procedure
Mayonnaise	3 cups	Mix all ingredients.
Fresh orange juice	¼ cup	Hold for service at or below 40°F.
Orange zest	1 Tbsp	
Fresh lemon juice	2 Tbsp	
Lemon zest	1 tsp	
Garlic cloves, puréed	4	
Black pepper	1 tsp	

LIME CILANTRO MAYO

Ingredient	Amount	Procedure
Mayonnaise	1 qt	Mix until combined.
Fresh lime juice	¼ cup	Hold for service at or below 40°F.
Fresh cilantro, finely chopped	¼ cup	

PARMESAN MAYO

Ingredient	Amount	Procedure
Mayonnaise	3 cups	Mix until combined.
Garlic, minced	3 Tbsp	Hold for service at or below 40°F.
Salt	¼ tsp	
Fresh lemon juice	3 oz	
Brown mustard	3 tsp	
Worcestershire sauce	3 tsp	
Parmesan cheese, grated	4 oz	

RED CHILE MAYO

Ingredient	Amount	Procedure
Mayonnaise	2 cups	Mix until smooth.
Hot chile sauce (Sriracha)	5 oz	Hold for service at or below 40°F.
Fresh lemon juice	5 Tbsp	

RED PEPPER MAYO

Ingredient	Amount	Procedure
Mayonnaise	3 cups	Purée all ingredients in a food processor or blender until smooth.
Roasted red bell pepper	1 lb	Hold for service at or below 40°F.
Garlic, minced	1 Tbsp	
Sweet curry powder	1 Tbsp	
Salt	¼ tsp	
Black pepper	½ tsp	

REMOULADE SAUCE

Ingredient	Amount	Procedure
Mayonnaise	2 cups	Mix mayonnaise, oil, and lemon juice in baker's bowl using a wire whip.
Salad oil	¼ cup	Stir in remaining ingredients and mix well to evenly distribute.
Fresh lemon juice	¼ cup	Hold for service at or below 40°F.
Onion, coarsely chopped	4 oz	
Green onions, thinly sliced	3 oz	
Celery, chopped	2 oz	
Parsley, chopped	3 Tbsp	
Horseradish	3 Tbsp	
Brown mustard	1 tsp	
Dijon-style mustard	2 Tbsp	
Salt	¼ tsp	
Hot sauce	2 Tbsp	
Tarragon, dried	1½ tsp	

ROSEMARY LEMON MAYO

Ingredient	Amount	Procedure
Mayonnaise	1 qt	Mix all ingredients.
Fresh rosemary, minced	¼ cup	Hold for service at or below 40°F.
Lemon zest	¼ cup	

SMOKED PAPRIKA MAYO

Ingredient	Amount	Procedure
Mayonnaise	1 qt	Mix all ingredients.
Smoked paprika	4 tsp	Hold for service at or below 40°F.
Cumin, ground	2 tsp	
Sun-dried tomatoes, finely chopped	2 tsp	

WASABI MAYO

Ingredient	Amount	Procedure
Mayonnaise	1 qt	Whisk together until sugar is dissolved.
Soy sauce	3 oz	Hold for service at or below 40°F.
Sugar, granulated	3 oz	
Fresh lemon juice	3 Tbsp	
Wasabi powder	2 oz	

TABLE 19.1 Guide for using spice mixtures and marinades

Meat	Quantity	Rub amount	Marinade amount
BEEF			
Flat brisket	3–5 lb	¼ cup	1 cup
Whole brisket	8–12 lb	1 cup	3 cups
Standing rib roast	10–15 lb	¾ cup	Not recommended
Strip loin roast	12–15 lb	1 cup	Not recommended
Sirloin steak	12 lb (24 steaks)	2–4 Tbsp	2 cups
FISH			
Fillets/steaks	12 lb (24 steaks)	1 cup	3 cups
LAMB			
Leg of lamb	6–8 lb	¼ cup	1 cup
PORK			
Loin	3–5 lb	¼ cup	1 cup
Tenderloin	1–2 lb	2 Tbsp	½ cup
Ribs	4–5 lb	¼ cup	2 cups
Shoulder or butt	3–5 lb	¼ cup	1 cup
POULTRY			
Whole chicken	3–4 lb	¼ cup	1 cup
Whole turkey	12 lb	½ cup	Not recommended

Soups

Homemade soups are popular and versatile menu items that may be served as an appetizer or as a center-of-the-plate entrée. The type of soup served should complement the other menu items or be hearty enough for the entrée. Hot soups should be heated to 180°F, and cold soups should be served below 41°F.

Types of Soups

Soups may be clear and thin or thick and hearty. Stock or broth, the basic ingredient of many soups, is made by simmering meat and/or meat, fish, or poultry bones, and/or vegetables in water to extract their flavor. The most frequently used stocks are brown (made from beef that has been browned before simmering) and white or light (made from veal and/or chicken). See pp. 738–740 for stock recipes.

Mirepoix, a mixture of chopped vegetables—usually in the proportion of 50 percent onions, 25 percent carrots, and 25 percent celery—is used in flavoring soup stock. Flavorings commonly used are bay leaves, peppercorns, whole cloves, and parsley stems.

For a clear soup, the stock should be clarified. Clarifying removes flecks that are too small to be strained out with cheesecloth, but that will cloud a soup's appearance. Stock is highly perishable. If it is not to be used immediately, it may be reduced in volume by boiling to one-half or one-fourth its volume and frozen for later use. Recipes for beef, chicken, and vegetable stocks and directions for clarifying stock are given on pp. 738–740.

Clear soups are made from a clear, seasoned stock or broth and include the following:

- **Bouillon,** made from beef broth that may or may not be clarified.
- **Consommé,** a strong, concentrated stock or broth.
- **Vegetable soup,** a clear seasoned stock or broth, with vegetables and sometimes meat or poultry products added.

Thick soups are opaque rather than transparent. They are thickened by either a roux, which is a mixture of melted fat and flour slightly browned, or a purée of one of the ingredients. Examples are as follows:

- **Cream soups,** made with a thin or medium white sauce combined with either mashed, strained, or finely chopped vegetables or meat, chicken, or fish. Chicken stock may be used to replace part of the milk in the sauce to enhance the flavor. If a stock base is used, it may be added to the margarine-flour roux or may be added to water and used as part of the liquid.
- **Chowders,** unstrained, chunky, hearty soups prepared from meat, poultry, seafood, and/or vegetables. Most chowders contain potatoes and milk or cream.
- **Purées,** thick soups made by pressing cooked vegetables or fish through a sieve into their own stock.

Commercial Soup Bases

Because preparation of soups, especially those made from stock, is time-consuming, commercial food or soup bases are often used. The amount of meat concentrate in commercial soup bases varies, so the choice of base should be made carefully to ensure a desirable, full-flavored stock. A high-quality base is a concentrate of cooked meat, poultry, seafood, or vegetables that includes the concentrated cooking juices and seasonings. It has a purée or pastelike consistency and may require refrigeration. One pound of base produces an average of 5 gal ready-to-use stock. Most granulated bases and many paste products are highly salted. When using these products, the salt listed in the recipe should be deleted or reduced. Bases also can be used to prepare sauces, gravies, and stuffings.

Serving and Holding Soups

Hot soup cools off quickly in serving bowls. It is important that soup be very hot when served. Using a heated bowl helps hot soups retain their heat. Soups should be prepared in batches small enough for ingredients to retain their texture throughout the serving period. Cream soups will curdle if kept at too high a temperature or held for too long a time. For this reason, the milk may be added just before serving and the mixture reheated to serving temperature (180°F). Cold soups should be served in chilled bowls at 41°F.

Stock Soup Recipes

CHICKEN STOCK

Yield: 3 gal

Ingredient	Amount	Procedure
Chicken bones	24 lb	Rinse chicken bones and place in steam-jacketed kettle or large stockpot.
Water, cold	5 gal	Add water. Simmer for 3–4 hours. Skim as necessary.
Onions, quartered	1 lb 8 oz	Add vegetables and seasonings. Bring to boiling point. Reduce heat and
Celery, with leaves, chopped	12 oz	simmer for 1 hour longer.
Carrots, chopped	12 oz	
Salt	3 oz	
Peppercorns, cracked	1 Tbsp	
Bay leaves	4	
Thyme, dried	2 tsp	
		Remove bones from broth.
		Strain and refrigerate.
		When broth is cold, fat will congeal on top; skim off.

Notes

- Potentially hazardous food. *Food Safety Standards:* Hold food for service at an internal temperature of 135°F or above. Do not mix old product with new. Cool leftover product quickly following time standards and cooling procedures on p. 167. Reheat leftover product quickly (within 2 hours) to 165°F or above. Reheat product only once; discard if not used.
- If a clear broth is desired, clarify by adding egg shells and whites to broth. Bring stock to boiling point and simmer for 15 minutes. Strain through a fine strainer.

Variations

- **Chicken Stock with Base.** Add 8 oz concentrated chicken base to 2½ gal water. Exact proportion of base and water may vary among manufacturers. Chicken base is often highly salted. When using chicken base for making stock, taste recipes before adding salt. The flavor of chicken stock made with base can be enhanced by simmering 12 oz clean vegetable trimmings (or vegetables listed above) with 2½ gal stock for approximately 15 minutes. Strain before using.
- **White Stock.** Substitute knuckle of veal for part of chicken bones.

BEEF STOCK

Yield: 3 gal

Ingredient	Amount	Procedure
Beef shank, lean	20 lb	Pour water over beef shanks in steam-jacketed kettle or large stockpot.
Water, cold	5 gal	Bring water to boiling point. Reduce heat and simmer until meat leaves bone, about 3 hours.
Onions, quartered	1 lb 8 oz	Add vegetables and seasonings. Simmer for 1 hour.
Celery, with leaves, chopped	12 oz	Remove meat and strain broth.
Carrots, chopped	12 oz	Refrigerate for several hours.
Peppercorns, cracked	1 Tbsp	Skim congealed fat off top.
Bay leaves	2	
Salt	3 oz	

Note

- Potentially hazardous food. *Food Safety Standards:* Hold food for service at an internal temperature of 135°F or above. Do not mix old product with new. Cool leftover product quickly following time standards and cooling procedures on p. 167. Reheat leftover product quickly (within 2 hours) to 165°F or above. Reheat product only once; discard if not used.

Variations

- **Beef Stock with Base.** Add 8 oz concentrated beef base to 2½ gal water. Exact proportions may vary with different manufacturers. Beef base is often highly salted. When using beef base for making stock, taste recipes before adding salt. The flavor of beef stock made with base can be enhanced by simmering 12 oz clean vegetable trimmings (or the vegetables listed above) with 2½ gal stock for approximately 15 minutes. Strain before using.
- **Brown Stock.** Roast beef bones in hot oven until they are a rich brown color. Brown or caramelize vegetables before adding to the water. Proceed as for Beef Stock.

BOUILLON

Yield: 3 gal

Ingredient	Amount	Procedure
Beef, lean	8 lb	Sear beef. Add bone and water.
Beef bone, cracked	4 lb	Simmer for 3–4 hours. Replace water as necessary.
Water, cold	4 gal	
Carrots, diced	8 oz	Add vegetables and seasonings.
Celery, chopped	8 oz	Cook for 1 hour. Strain.
Onions, quartered	8 oz	Chill overnight.
Bay leaves	4	Remove congealed fat from broth.
Peppercorns	1 Tbsp	
Salt	¼ cup	
To clarify:		Add egg shells and whites to clarify the broth.
Egg shells, washed and crushed	3	Bring slowly to boiling point, stirring constantly. Boil for 15–20 minutes without stirring.
Egg whites, beaten	3	Strain through a fine strainer.

Note

- Potentially hazardous food. *Food Safety Standards:* Hold food for service at an internal temperature of 135°F or above. Do not mix old product with new. Cool leftover product quickly following time standards and cooling procedures on p. 167. Reheat leftover product quickly (within 2 hours) to 165°F or above. Reheat product only once; discard if not used.

Variations

- **Chicken Bouillon.** Substitute 20 lb chicken, cut up, for the beef and bone. Do not sear chicken.
- **Tomato Bouillon.** To 1½ gal bouillon, add four 46-oz cans tomato juice, 2 oz chopped onion, 2 oz sugar, 2 oz salt (amount will vary), ½ tsp black pepper, and 2 bay leaves.

VEGETABLE STOCK

Yield: 3 gal

Ingredient	Amount	Procedure
Vegetable oil	6 oz	Heat oil in steam-jacketed kettle or large stockpot.
Green cabbage, coarsely chopped	12 oz	Add vegetables to oil. Cover and cook until softened and moisture is released, 3–5 minutes.
Carrots, coarsely chopped	1 lb 8 oz	
Celery, coarsely chopped	1 lb 8 oz	
Celery leaves, coarsely chopped	1 lb	
Garlic cloves, crushed	8	
Onions, quartered	2 lb 8 oz	
Parsley stems, chopped	3 oz	
Parsnips, peeled	1 lb	
Tomatoes, chopped	1 lb	
Turnips, chopped	12 oz	
Water	5 gal	Add water and seasonings.
Salt	3 oz	Simmer for 40–50 minutes.
Peppercorns, cracked	1 Tbsp	Strain stock and cool.
Bay leaves	6	
Thyme, dried	2 tsp	

Notes

- Potentially hazardous food. *Food Safety Standards:* Hold food for service at an internal temperature of 135°F or above. Do not mix old product with new. Cool leftover product quickly following time standards and cooling procedures on p. 167. Reheat leftover product quickly (within 2 hours) to 165°F or above. Reheat product only once; discard if not used.
- Clean vegetable trimmings may be substituted for part of the vegetables specified.

Variation

- **Vegetable Stock with Base.** Exact proportions of base and water differ among brands. Follow manufacturers' directions. Vegetable base is often highly salted. When using vegetable base for making stock, taste recipes before adding salt. The flavor of vegetable stock made with base can be enhanced by simmering 2 lb clean vegetable trimmings (or the soft or leafy vegetables listed in the recipe) with 3 gal stock for approximately 15 minutes. Strain before using.

BEEF BARLEY SOUP

Yield: 50 portions or 3 gal   *Portion:* 1 cup (8 oz)

Ingredient	Amount	Procedure
Beef, cubed	3 lb	Brown beef cubes in kettle. Drain off fat.
Celery, chopped	1 lb 6 oz	Add celery and onions. Sauté until tender.
Onions, chopped	1 lb 6 oz	
Beef Stock (p. 738)	3 gal	Add remaining ingredients. Bring to a boil.
Black pepper	1 tsp	Lower heat and simmer for 1 hour.
Salt	1 tsp	Taste for seasoning and add salt if needed.
Bay leaf	1	
Carrots, diced	1 lb 6 oz	
Pearl barley	10 oz	

Approximate nutritive values per portion

Calories	Carbohydrate	Protein	Fat	Cholesterol	Sodium	Fiber	Iron
81 kcal	7 g	9 g	2 g	15 mg	818 mg	2 g	1 mg

Notes

- Potentially hazardous food. *Food Safety Standards:* Hold food for service at an internal temperature of 135°F or above. Do not mix old product with new. Cool leftover product quickly following time standards and cooling procedures on p. 167. Reheat leftover product quickly (within 2 hours) to 165°F or above. Reheat product only once; discard if not used.
- 2¾ oz (1⅓ cups) dehydrated onions may be substituted for fresh onions.

VEGETABLE BEEF SOUP

Yield: 50 portions or 3 gal   *Portion:* 1 cup (8 oz)

Ingredient	Amount	Procedure
Beef Stock (p. 738)	2 gal	Heat stock in kettle.
Carrots, cubed	8 oz	Add vegetables and seasonings.
Celery, chopped	1 lb	Cover and simmer for about 1 hour. Replace water as necessary.
Onions, chopped	1 lb 8 oz	Taste for seasoning. Add additional salt if needed.
Potatoes, cubed	1 lb	
Diced tomatoes, canned	1 No. 10 can	
Salt	1 Tbsp	
Black pepper	1 tsp	
Cooked beef, chopped	2 lb	Add chopped beef. Heat to serving temperature, 180°F.

Approximate nutritive values per portion

Calories	Carbohydrate	Protein	Fat	Cholesterol	Sodium	Fiber	Iron
80 kcal	6 g	9 g	2 g	18 mg	748 mg	0.4 g	1 mg

Notes

- Potentially hazardous food. *Food Safety Standards:* Hold food for service at an internal temperature of 135°F or above. Do not mix old product with new. Cool leftover product quickly following time standards and cooling procedures on p. 167. Reheat leftover product quickly (within 2 hours) to 165°F or above. Reheat product only once; discard if not used.
- 8 oz uncooked rice or 4 oz dry noodles may be substituted for the potatoes.
- Browned beef cubes may be substituted for cooked beef. Brown in kettle before stock is added.
- 3 oz (1½ cups) dehydrated onions may be substituted for fresh onions.

Variations

- **Julienne Soup.** Cut carrots, celery, and potatoes in long, thin strips.
- **Mexican Beef Soup.** Omit carrots and celery. Add 12 oz whole-kernel corn, 4 oz chopped green bell peppers, 1 lb 8 oz sliced zucchini, and 3 Tbsp ground cumin.
- **Vegetable Soup.** Delete beef. Increase carrots and celery to 1 lb 8 oz each.

HEARTY BEEF VEGETABLE SOUP

Yield: 50 portions or 3 gal   *Portion:* 1 cup (8 oz)

Ingredient	Amount	Procedure
Ground beef	8 lb AP	Brown meat. Drain off fat.
Onions, chopped	1 lb	Add onions to meat and cook until tender.
Margarine Flour, all-purpose	9 oz 9 oz	Melt margarine and stir in flour. Cook for 5 minutes.
Beef Stock (p. 738) Salt Black pepper	1¼ gal 1 Tbsp ½ tsp	Add stock and seasonings, stirring constantly. Cook until mixture boils and has thickened. Add browned meat and onions.
Fresh carrots, diced Celery, sliced	12 oz 10 oz	Cook vegetables until barely tender. Drain. (Vegetables should be crunchy.)
Mixed vegetables, frozen	4 lb	Cook mixed vegetables until partially done. Add, with other vegetables, to the soup. Stir carefully to blend.
Diced tomatoes, canned	2 lb 8 oz	Add tomatoes. Heat to serving temperature, 180°F.

Approximate nutritive values per portion

Calories	Carbohydrate	Protein	Fat	Cholesterol	Sodium	Fiber	Iron
228 kcal	11 g	15 g	14 g	48 mg	281 mg	2 g	2 mg

Notes

- Potentially hazardous food. *Food Safety Standards:* Hold food for service at an internal temperature of 135°F or above. Do not mix old product with new. Cool leftover product quickly following time standards and cooling procedures on p. 167. Reheat leftover product quickly (within 2 hours) to 165°F or above. Reheat product only once; discard if not used.
- 2 oz (1 cup) dehydrated onions may be substituted for fresh onions.

BEEF NOODLE SOUP

Yield: 50 portions or 3 gal   *Portion:* 1 cup (8 oz)

Ingredient	Amount	Procedure
Vegetable oil Fresh beef, cubed Salt Black pepper	½ cup 2 lb 2 tsp ½ tsp	Heat oil in kettle. Add beef cubes and seasonings and cook until lightly browned. Drain off fat.
Onions, chopped Celery, chopped	8 oz 12 oz	Add onions and celery and sauté.
Beef Stock (p. 738)	2¾ gal	Add stock. Simmer for 1 hour.
Noodles	12 oz	Add noodles and simmer until tender, 5–10 minutes. Add salt if needed.

Approximate nutritive values per portion

Calories	Carbohydrate	Protein	Fat	Cholesterol	Sodium	Fiber	Iron
85 kcal	6 g	7 g	4 g	17 mg	786 mg	0 g	1 mg

Notes

- Potentially hazardous food. *Food Safety Standards:* Hold food for service at an internal temperature of 135°F or above. Do not mix old product with new. Cool leftover product quickly following time standards and cooling procedures on p. 167. Reheat leftover product quickly (within 2 hours) to 165°F or above. Reheat product only once; discard if not used.
- 1 oz (½ cup) dehydrated onions may be substituted for fresh onions.

Variations

- **Alphabet Soup.** Use alphabet noodles.
- **Beef Rice Soup.** Substitute 1 lb 8 oz rice for noodles.
- **Creole Soup.** Reduce Beef Stock to 2¼ gal. Add 1 No. 10 can tomatoes, 8 oz shredded green bell peppers, 1 lb sliced okra, and 4 bay leaves. Substitute rice for noodles.

CHICKEN NOODLE SOUP

Yield: 50 portions or 3 gal   *Portion:* 1 cup (8 oz)

Ingredient	Amount	Procedure
Chicken Stock (p. 738)	3 gal	Bring stock to a boil.
Onion, chopped	8 oz	Add onion and celery. Cook until tender.
Celery, chopped	8 oz	
Noodles	1 lb	Add noodles. Cook for about 15 minutes or until noodles are tender.
Margarine, melted	8 oz	Blend margarine and flour.
Flour, all-purpose	4 oz	Add to soup, stirring until slightly thickened.
Salt	1 tsp	Add seasonings.
White pepper	½ tsp	
Cooked chicken, diced	1 lb 8 oz	Add chicken and simmer for 5 minutes.

Approximate nutritive values per portion

Calories	Carbohydrate	Protein	Fat	Cholesterol	Sodium	Fiber	Iron
140 kcal	10 g	10 g	6 g	21 mg	846 mg	0 g	1 mg

Notes

- Potentially hazardous food. *Food Safety Standards:* Hold food for service at an internal temperature of 135°F or above. Do not mix old product with new. Cool leftover product quickly following time standards and cooling procedures on p. 167. Reheat leftover product quickly (within 2 hours) to 165°F or above. Reheat product only once; discard if not used.
- 1 oz (½ cup) dehydrated onions may be substituted for fresh onions.

Variation

- **Chicken Rice Soup.** Substitute 12 oz rice for the noodles.

TURKEY VEGETABLE SOUP

Yield: 50 portions   *Portion:* 1 cup (8 oz)

Ingredient	Amount	Procedure
Fresh carrots	1 lb	Cut carrots into thin julienne strips.
Red potatoes	2 lb	Do not peel potatoes. Dice into ½-inch cubes.
Onions, minced	12 oz	Combine in steam-jacketed kettle.
Celery, chopped	10 oz	Add carrots and potatoes.
Mushrooms, sliced	8 oz	Simmer for 20 minutes or until vegetables are tender.
Chicken Stock (p. 738)	2½ gal	
Rubbed sage	⅛ tsp	Add seasonings to soup.
Thyme, ground	¼ tsp	
Black pepper	¼ tsp	
Cooked turkey, chopped	2 lb	Add turkey and parsley. Heat to 180°F.
Fresh parsley, chopped	2 oz	

Approximate nutritive values per portion

Calories	Carbohydrate	Protein	Fat	Cholesterol	Sodium	Fiber	Iron
87 kcal	6 g	10 g	2 g	15 mg	645 mg	0 g	1 mg

Notes

- Potentially hazardous food. *Food Safety Standards:* Hold food for service at an internal temperature of 135°F or above. Do not mix old product with new. Cool leftover product quickly following time standards and cooling procedures on p. 167. Reheat leftover product quickly (within 2 hours) to 165°F or above. Reheat product only once; discard if not used.
- 1½ oz (¾ cup) dehydrated onions may be substituted for fresh onions.

CHILI CON CARNE

Yield: 3 gal   *Portion:* 1 cup (8 oz)

Ingredient	Amount	Procedure
Ground beef	10 lb AP	Cook beef, onions, and garlic in steam-jacketed kettle until meat
Onions, chopped	8 oz	loses pink color.
Garlic clove, minced	1	
Diced tomatoes, canned	2½ qt	Mix tomato products, water, and seasonings.
Tomato purée	2 qt	Add to beef. Cook until blended.
Water	1 qt	
Chile powder	3 oz	
Cumin, ground	1½ Tbsp	
Salt	1 oz (1½ Tbsp)	
Black pepper	½ tsp	
Sugar, granulated	2 oz	
Beans, pinto, kidney, or red, canned	9 lb 8 oz	Add beans to meat mixture. Cover and simmer for 1 hour. Add water if chili becomes too thick.

Approximate nutritive values per portion

Calories	Carbohydrate	Protein	Fat	Cholesterol	Sodium	Fiber	Iron
293 kcal	23 g	22 g	13 g	51 mg	791 mg	2 g	4 mg

Notes

- Potentially hazardous food. *Food Safety Standards:* Hold food for service at an internal temperature of 135°F or above. Do not mix old product with new. Cool leftover product quickly following time standards and cooling procedures on p. 167. Reheat leftover product quickly (within 2 hours) to 165°F or above. Reheat product only once; discard if not used.
- If dried beans are used, substitute 3 lb for canned beans. Wash and prepare according to directions on p. 505.
- If desired, thicken chili by mixing 5 oz flour and 2 cups cold water. Add to chili mixture and heat until flour is cooked.
- 1 oz (½ cup) dehydrated onions, rehydrated in ¾ cup water, may be substituted for fresh onions.

Variations

- **Chili and Cheese.** Sprinkle grated cheddar or Monterey Jack cheese over chili, 1 Tbsp per bowl.
- **Chili Buffet.** Serve chili with accompaniments: chopped onions, tomatoes, and green bell peppers; sliced black olives; shredded cheese; and sliced jalapeño peppers.
- **Chili Spaghetti.** Use only 7 lb ground beef. Cook 1 lb 8 oz spaghetti according to directions on p. 507. Add to chili mixture just before serving. Macaroni or other pasta shapes may be used also.
- **Turkey Chili.** Substitute 8 lb ground turkey for ground beef.

GARDEN CHILI

Yield: 50 portions   *Portion:* 8 oz

Ingredient	Amount	Procedure
Vegetable oil	¾ cup	Heat oil. Add onions and garlic and sauté until transparent.
Onions, chopped	3 lb 12 oz	
Garlic, minced	1½ Tbsp	
Celery, chopped	2 lb 4 oz	Add celery, carrots, and seasonings to onions.
Carrots, chopped finely	1 lb	Cook until tender-crisp.
Oregano, dried, crumbled	2 tsp	
Cumin, ground	2 Tbsp	
Chile powder	2 Tbsp	
Salt	1 oz (1½ Tbsp)	
Black pepper	1 Tbsp	
Green bell peppers, chopped	1 lb	Add to onion mixture.
Zucchini squash, chopped	2 lb	Heat to 180°F.
Mushrooms and stems, canned	1 lb 8 oz	
Diced tomatoes, canned	5 lb 6 oz	
Water	1 qt	
Red beans, canned	5 lb 6 oz	
Lemon juice, frozen, reconstituted	⅓ cup	
Chipotle flavor concentrate (see Note)	1 oz	
Cheddar cheese, shredded	1 lb 8 oz	To serve, ladle chili into soup bowls. Sprinkle ½ oz cheese over each portion.

Approximate nutritive values per portion

Calories	Carbohydrate	Protein	Fat	Cholesterol	Sodium	Fiber	Iron
169 kcal	17 g	8 g	8 g	14 mg	600 mg	5 g	2 mg

Notes

- Potentially hazardous food. *Food Safety Standards:* Hold food for service at an internal temperature of 135°F or above. Do not mix old product with new. Cool leftover product quickly following time standards and cooling procedures on p. 167. Reheat leftover product quickly (within 2 hours) to 165°F or above. Reheat product only once; discard if not used.
- Chipotle base is a Minor's product available through most broadline foodservice distributors. Canned chipotles can be substituted for base.

WHITE CHILI

Yield: 50 portions   *Portion:* 8 oz

Ingredient	Amount	Procedure
Great northern beans	3 lb	Sort and wash beans. Cover with water to 2 inches above beans. Let soak overnight.
		Drain beans. Place in steam-jacketed kettle.
Water	2 gal	Add to beans. Bring to a boil. Cover.
Chicken soup base	6 oz	Reduce heat and simmer for 2 hours, stirring occasionally.
Onions, chopped	2 lb	
Garlic, minced	1 oz	
Salt	1½ tsp	
Chicken or turkey, white meat, diced	3 lb	Add to beans. Cover and simmer for 30 minutes.
Diced green chiles, canned	1 lb 8 oz	
Cumin, ground	2 Tbsp	
Oregano, dried, crumbled	1½ Tbsp	
Cayenne pepper	1½ tsp	
Cloves, ground	½ tsp	
Cilantro, dried, crumbled	1 Tbsp	
Monterey Jack cheese, shredded (optional)	1 lb 12 oz	Sprinkle ½ oz cheese over each portion as it is served.

Approximate nutritive values per portion

Calories	Carbohydrate	Protein	Fat	Cholesterol	Sodium	Fiber	Iron
210 kcal	20 g	18 g	7 g	35 mg	859 mg	0.4 g	2 mg

Notes

- Potentially hazardous food. *Food Safety Standards:* Hold food for service at an internal temperature of 135°F or above. Do not mix old product with new. Cool leftover product quickly following time standards and cooling procedures on p. 167. Reheat leftover product quickly (within 2 hours) to 165°F or above. Reheat product only once; discard if not used.
- If a highly salted chicken base is used, check for seasoning before adding salt.

BLACK BEAN CHILI WITH SCALLION CORN CAKES

Yield: 50 portions   *Portion:* 6 oz chili + 1 corn cake

Ingredient	Amount	Procedure
Oil	8 oz	Heat oil in a steam-jacketed or other large kettle.
Green bell peppers, chopped	6 oz	Sauté peppers, onions, and garlic until golden brown.
Red bell peppers, chopped	6 oz	Stir in cumin.
Yellow bell peppers, chopped	6 oz	
Onions, chopped	2 lb 8 oz	
Garlic, minced	1 oz	
Cumin, ground	4 Tbsp	
Chipotle flavor concentrate	1 oz	Stir flavorings and water into vegetables.
Ancho flavor concentrate	1 oz	
Vegetarian base	1 Tbsp	
Water	2 qt	
Black beans, canned, drained and rinsed	7 lb	Add beans and tomatoes. Bring to a boil. Reduce heat and simmer uncovered for 30–45 minutes.
Chopped tomatoes, canned, with juice	6 lb 4 oz	
Scallion Corn Cakes (p. 245)	50	Portion a 6-oz ladle of chili into soup bowl. Place 1 corn cake on top of chili.

Approximate nutritive values per portion

Calories	Carbohydrate	Protein	Fat	Cholesterol	Sodium	Fiber	Iron
362 kcal	37 g	12 g	19 g	33 mg	1026 mg	7 g	3 mg

Notes

- Potentially hazardous food. *Food Safety Standards:* Hold food for service at an internal temperature of 135°F or above. Do not mix old product with new. Cool leftover product quickly following time standards and cooling procedures on p. 167. Reheat leftover product quickly (within 2 hours) to 165°F or above. Reheat product only once; discard if not used.
- Minor's Ancho Flavor Concentrate (made from ancho peppers and sautéed onions) and Minor's Chipotle Flavor Concentrate (a blend of red, chipotle, and jalapeño peppers with onion, garlic, and spice) are available from most broadline foodservice distributors.

MINESTRONE SOUP

Yield: 50 portions or 3 gal   *Portion:* 1 cup (8 oz)

Ingredient	Amount	Procedure
Bacon, diced	1 lb	Fry bacon until crisp. Drain.
Onions, chopped	12 oz	Sauté onions and garlic in a little bacon fat until tender.
Garlic cloves, minced	2	Place, with bacon, in a large kettle.
Beef Stock (p. 738)	2 gal	Add stock and seasonings. Heat to boiling.
Bay leaves	2	
Black pepper	1 tsp	
Cabbage, chopped	12 oz	Add vegetables and spaghetti. Simmer for 45 minutes.
Fresh carrots, diced	12 oz	
Potatoes, raw, chopped	12 oz	
Celery, chopped	12 oz	
Fresh spinach, chopped	3 oz	
Green beans, cut, canned	12 oz	
Diced tomatoes, canned	2 lb	
Red beans, canned	1 lb 12 oz	
Spaghetti, long	2 oz	
Flour, all-purpose	3 oz	Make a smooth paste of the flour and water.
Water, cold	1 cup	Stir into soup. Cook for 10 minutes longer.
Fresh parsley, chopped	¼ cup	Add parsley just before serving.

Approximate nutritive values per portion

Calories	Carbohydrate	Protein	Fat	Cholesterol	Sodium	Fiber	Iron
69 kcal	9 g	4 g	2 g	2 mg	634 mg	2 g	1 mg

Notes

- Potentially hazardous food. *Food Safety Standards:* Hold food for service at an internal temperature of 135°F or above. Do not mix old product with new. Cool leftover product quickly following time standards and cooling procedures on p. 167. Reheat leftover product quickly (within 2 hours) to 165°F or above. Reheat product only once; discard if not used.
- 1½ oz (¾ cup) dehydrated onions may be substituted for fresh onions.

PASTA e FAGIOLI SOUP

Yield: 50 portions   *Portion:* 8 oz

Ingredient	Amount	Procedure
Olive oil	1 Tbsp	Heat oil in steam-jacketed or other heavy-bottomed kettle. Add onions and celery and cook until softened, 5–10 minutes. Stir occasionally.
Onions, chopped	1 lb 5 oz	
Celery, chopped	10 oz	
Garlic, minced	5½ Tbsp	Add garlic and seasonings to onion-celery mixture. Cook, stirring constantly, until fragrant.
Italian seasoning	2½ Tbsp	
Crushed red pepper	¾ tsp	
Diced tomatoes, canned	3½ qt	Add tomatoes, beans, water, vegetable base, and seasonings to steam-jacketed kettle.
Great northern beans, canned, drained and rinsed	5 lb 10 oz	Bring to a boil. Reduce heat and simmer for 10 minutes. Remove bay leaves.
Water	5½ qt	
Vegetable or chicken base	4 oz	
Bay leaves	5	
Salt (see Note)	1 Tbsp	
Black pepper	2 tsp	
Elbow macaroni	1 lb 8 oz	Add macaroni and cook until pasta is al dente, 8–10 minutes.
Flat leaf parsley, chopped	1 oz	Stir parsley into soup just before serving.
Parmesan cheese, shredded	6 oz	Optional: Garnish each bowl with Parmesan cheese and a drizzle of olive oil.
Extra virgin olive oil	8 oz	

Approximate nutritive values per portion

Calories	Carbohydrate	Protein	Fat	Cholesterol	Sodium	Fiber	Iron
167 kcal	20 g	5 g	8 g	4 mg	767 mg	3 g	1 mg

Notes

- Potentially hazardous food. *Food Safety Standards:* Hold food for service at an internal temperature of 135°F or above. Do not mix old product with new. Cool leftover product quickly following time standards and cooling procedures on p. 167. Reheat leftover product quickly (within 2 hours) to 165°F or above. Reheat product only once; discard if not used.
- Salt amount varies between brands of bases. Taste for salt before adding additional salt.

Variation

- **Pasta e Fagioli Soup (with Bacon or Pancetta).** Cut 1 lb 12 oz bacon or pancetta into pieces and cook until barely crisp. Drain well. Add to the soup when adding tomatoes. Substitute chicken base for vegetable base.

LENTIL AND BLACK BEAN SOUP

Yield: 50 portions   *Portion:* 1 cup (8 oz)

Ingredient	Amount	Procedure
Onions, chopped	3 lb	In a steam-jacketed or other large kettle, sauté onions, garlic, and carrots
Garlic cloves, minced	2	in oil until just tender.
Carrots, chopped	1 lb 12 oz	
Vegetable oil	1 cup	
Water	1½ gal	Add water and rinsed lentils to vegetables. Bring to a boil and simmer
Lentils, dried, rinsed	2 lb 8 oz	for 25 minutes.
Black beans, canned, drained	4 lb	Add beans, tomatoes, and seasonings. Cover and simmer until lentils are tender, but not mushy, approximately 20–30 minutes.
Diced tomatoes, canned	3 qt	Serve hot, 180°F.
Thyme, dried	2 tsp	
Marjoram, dried	1½ tsp	
Fresh parsley	1 oz	
Salt	1 oz	
Black pepper	1 Tbsp	
Cumin, ground	½ tsp	
Tortillas, 6-inch	50	Serve garnished with a warm, rolled tortilla on the side of the plate.

Approximate nutritive values per portion

Calories	Carbohydrate	Protein	Fat	Cholesterol	Sodium	Fiber	Iron
233 kcal	38 g	9 g	5 g	0 mg	547 mg	5 g	3 mg

Notes

- Potentially hazardous food. *Food Safety Standards:* Hold food for service at an internal temperature of 135°F or above. Do not mix old product with new. Cool leftover product quickly following time standards and cooling procedures on p. 167. Reheat leftover product quickly (within 2 hours) to 165°F or above. Reheat product only once; discard if not used.
- If soup becomes too thick, add hot water to bring to desired consistency.
- Chicken broth may be substituted for water. Reduce salt if a salted chicken base is used.

Variation

- **Split Pea and Black Bean Soup.** Substitute dried split peas for lentils.

BRAZILIAN BLACK BEAN SOUP

Yield: 50 portions   *Portion:* 8 oz

Ingredient	Amount	Procedure
Water	4 qt	Combine water, beans, vegetables, and seasonings in a steam-jacketed or other large kettle. Bring to a boil.
Black beans, canned, drained	9 lb 8 oz	
Onions, chopped	3 lb 10 oz	Reduce heat to a simmer and cook until vegetables are tender-crisp, 30–45 minutes.
Garlic, minced	6 oz	
Carrot coins	1 lb	Remove bay leaves.
Celery, chopped	6 oz	
Cumin, ground	3 Tbsp	
Bay leaves	4	
Salt (see Note)	1 Tbsp	
Chopped bell peppers (combination of green, red, yellow)	1 lb 8 oz	Add to bean mixture. Simmer for 15 minutes.
Fresh cilantro, chopped	1 oz	
Fresh orange juice	1 qt	
Black pepper	2 tsp	
Ground red pepper	½ tsp	
Hot sauce (see Note)	1½ tsp	
Vegetable base (see Note)	1 oz	
Water, cold	1 cup	Mix water and flour to make a smooth paste. Whisk flour-water paste into soup. Cook just until thickened.
Flour	1¼ oz	Optional: Serve each bowl garnished with 1 tsp sour cream, a sprig of cilantro, and an orange section.

Approximate nutritive values per portion

Calories	Carbohydrate	Protein	Fat	Cholesterol	Sodium	Fiber	Iron
120 kcal	24 g	7 g	0 g	0 mg	590 mg	7 g	2 mg

Notes

- Potentially hazardous food. *Food Safety Standards:* Hold food for service at an internal temperature of 135°F or above. Do not mix old product with new. Cool leftover product quickly following time standards and cooling procedures on p. 167. Reheat leftover product quickly (within 2 hours) to 165°F or above. Reheat product only once; discard if not used.
- Recipe was tested using green Tabasco hot sauce.
- Chicken base can be substituted for vegetable base.
- Salt varies between brands of vegetable or chicken base. Taste for salt and adjust if necessary.

NAVY BEAN SOUP

Yield: 50 portions or 3 gal   *Portion:* 1 cup (8 oz)

Ingredient	Amount	Procedure
Navy beans, dried	4 lb	Wash beans. Add boiling water. Cover and let stand for 1 hour or longer.
Water, boiling	3 gal	Simmer beans for about 1 hour.
Ham cubes	3 lb	Add ham, vegetables, and pepper to beans.
Onions, chopped	12 oz	Cook until beans are tender, 1–1½ hours.
Celery, diced	8 oz	Add water to make volume of 3¼ gal.
Black pepper	1 Tbsp	Check seasoning. Add salt if needed. Heat to 180°F.
Water	see Procedure	

Approximate nutritive values per portion

Calories	Carbohydrate	Protein	Fat	Cholesterol	Sodium	Fiber	Iron
93 kcal	8 g	9 g	3 g	16 mg	582 mg	0.2 g	1 mg

Notes

- Potentially hazardous food. *Food Safety Standards:* Hold food for service at an internal temperature of 135°F or above. Do not mix old product with new. Cool leftover product quickly following time standards and cooling procedures on p. 167. Reheat leftover product quickly (within 2 hours) to 165°F or above. Reheat product only once; discard if not used.
- Great northern beans may be substituted for navy beans.
- Ham base may be added for additional flavor.
- 1½ oz (¾ cup) dehydrated onions may be substituted for fresh onions.

Variation

- **Ham and Beans with Cornbread.** Prepare cornbread recipe, p. 244. Pick over, wash, and drain 6 lb dried great northern beans. Measure 1½ gal water into steam-jacketed or other large kettle. Add beans and bring to a boil. Add 8 oz chopped onion, 1 lb chopped celery, and 1 Tbsp black pepper. Simmer covered until beans are almost done (1½–2 hours). Add more water if needed. Cut 7 lb 8 oz ham into ½-inch cubes and add to beans. Add 4 oz ham base. Simmer for 30 minutes longer. Check for seasoning. Add salt if needed. Serve with cornbread.

SPLIT PEA SOUP

Yield: 50 portions or 3 gal   *Portion:* 1 cup (8 oz)

Ingredient	Amount	Procedure
Split peas	3 lb	Wash peas. Add water and bring to a boil.
Water	2 gal	Boil for 2 minutes, then turn off heat.
		Cover and let stand for 1 hour.
Ham cubes	2 lb	Add ham, onions, carrots, and potatoes.
Onions, chopped	1 lb	Cook for 1 hour or until peas are soft.
Fresh carrots, chopped	1 lb 8 oz	
Potatoes, raw, chopped	2 lb	
Margarine	4 oz	Melt margarine and add flour. Stir until smooth. Cook for 5 minutes.
Flour, all-purpose	2 oz	Add stock, while stirring, and cook until thickened.
Chicken Stock (p. 738)	2 qt	Add to peas.
Black pepper	1 tsp	Taste for seasoning. Add pepper. Add salt to taste.

Approximate nutritive values per portion

Calories	Carbohydrate	Protein	Fat	Cholesterol	Sodium	Fiber	Iron
175 kcal	23 g	12 g	4 g	11 mg	432 mg	2 g	2 mg

Notes

- Potentially hazardous food. *Food Safety Standards:* Hold food for service at an internal temperature of 135°F or above. Do not mix old product with new. Cool leftover product quickly following time standards and cooling procedures on p. 167. Reheat leftover product quickly (within 2 hours) to 165°F or above. Reheat product only once; discard if not used.
- If soup becomes too thick, add hot water to bring to desired consistency. If a smoother soup is desired, cook and purée peas before adding ham and vegetables.
- 1 lb chopped celery may be substituted for 1 lb potatoes.
- 3 lb sliced Polish sausage may be added to soup before serving. Reduce ham to 1 lb.
- 2 oz (1 cup) dehydrated onions may be substituted for fresh onions.

Variations

- **Lentil Soup.** Substitute lentils for split peas.
- **Yellow Split Pea Soup.** Substitute yellow split peas for green split peas.

TOMATO RICE SOUP

Yield: 50 portions or 3 gal   *Portion:* 1 cup (8 oz)

Ingredient	Amount	Procedure
Chicken or Beef Stock (p. 738)	2 gal	Heat stock and purée to boiling point.
Tomato purée	1 gal	
Onion, chopped	2 oz	Add vegetables and rice. Cook until rice is tender.
Green bell pepper, chopped	4 oz	
Rice, converted	8 oz	
Margarine	6 oz	Melt margarine and add flour. Mix until smooth.
Flour, all-purpose	3 oz	Add to soup while stirring. Add salt to taste.

Approximate nutritive values per portion

Calories	Carbohydrate	Protein	Fat	Cholesterol	Sodium	Fiber	Iron
92 kcal	13 g	4 g	3 g	0 mg	852 mg	2 g	1 mg

Notes

- Potentially hazardous food. *Food Safety Standards:* Hold food for service at an internal temperature of 135°F or above. Do not mix old product with new. Cool leftover product quickly following time standards and cooling procedures on p. 167. Reheat leftover product quickly (within 2 hours) to 165°F or above. Reheat product only once; discard if not used.
- ¼ oz (2 Tbsp) dehydrated onions may be substituted for fresh onions.

Variation

- **Tomato Barley Soup.** Add 1 lb barley in place of rice.

PEPPER POT SOUP

Yield: 50 portions or 3 gal   *Portion:* 1 cup (8 oz)

Ingredient	Amount	Procedure
Onion, finely chopped	8 oz	Sauté vegetables in margarine until lightly browned, about 15 minutes.
Green bell peppers, finely chopped	8 oz	
Celery, thinly sliced	6 oz	
Potatoes, diced	3 lb 8 oz	
Margarine	12 oz	
Flour, all-purpose	5 oz	Add flour to vegetables and stir until well blended.
Chicken or Beef Stock (p. 738)	2¼ gal	Combine stock and milk. Add to vegetable mixture, while stirring.
Milk, hot	1 qt	If soup base is used for the stock, taste before adding salt.
Salt	1 oz (1½ Tbsp)	
Pimento, chopped	2 Tbsp	Add pimento. Keep just below boiling point for 30 minutes, stirring frequently.

Approximate nutritive values per portion

Calories	Carbohydrate	Protein	Fat	Cholesterol	Sodium	Fiber	Iron
115 kcal	11 g	4 g	7 g	3 mg	834 mg	1 g	0.5 mg

Notes

- Potentially hazardous food. *Food Safety Standards:* Hold food for service at an internal temperature of 135°F or above. Do not mix old product with new. Cool leftover product quickly following time standards and cooling procedures on p. 167. Reheat leftover product quickly (within 2 hours) to 165°F or above. Reheat product only once; discard if not used.
- This soup is good served with Spaetzle (p. 258). Prepare 1 recipe for 50 servings.
- 1 oz (½ cup) dehydrated onions may be substituted for fresh onions.

FRENCH ONION SOUP

Yield: 50 portions or 3 gal   *Portion:* 1 cup (8 oz)

Ingredient	Amount	Procedure
Onions	8 lb	Cut onions in thin slices.
Margarine or shortening	12 oz	Sauté in margarine in large kettle.
Flour, all-purpose	3 oz	Add flour and pepper. Cook for 10 minutes.
Black pepper	1 tsp	
Beef Stock (p. 738)	3 gal	Add stock and Worcestershire sauce.
Worcestershire sauce	3 Tbsp	Cook until onions are tender and temperature is 190°F.
Salt	1 tsp (if needed)	Add salt to taste.
Croutons	12 oz	To serve, ladle soup over croutons or toasted bread.
Parmesan cheese, grated, or Swiss cheese, shredded	2 oz	Sprinkle with cheese.

Approximate nutritive values per portion

Calories	Carbohydrate	Protein	Fat	Cholesterol	Sodium	Fiber	Iron
128 kcal	12 g	5 g	6 g	0 mg	974 mg	2 g	1 mg

Note

- Potentially hazardous food. *Food Safety Standards:* Hold food for service at an internal temperature of 135°F or above. Do not mix old product with new. Cool leftover product quickly following time standards and cooling procedures on p. 167. Reheat leftover product quickly (within 2 hours) to 165°F or above. Reheat product only once; discard if not used.

TOMATO SHRIMP AND CLAM SOUP

Yield: 50 portions   *Portion:* 6 oz

Ingredient	Amount	Procedure
Chopped clams, canned	2 lb	Drain clams, reserving juice and clams for later steps.
Onions, chopped Garlic, minced Green bell peppers, chopped Oil	1 lb 12 oz 2 Tbsp 1 lb ⅓ cup	In a steam-jacketed or other large kettle, sauté onions, garlic, and peppers in oil until soft.
Clam juice and water	2¾ qt	Measure clam juice reserved from earlier step and add enough water to make 2¾ qt. Add clam juice–water mixture to sautéed vegetables.
Diced tomatoes, canned Shrimp base (see Note) Fresh lemon juice Bay leaves, dried whole Basil, dried Oregano, dried Italian seasoning Crushed red pepper	9 lb 4 oz 7 oz 4 1 Tbsp 1 tsp 2 tsp 1 tsp	Add tomatoes, shrimp base, lemon juice, and seasonings to vegetable mixture. Bring to a boil.
Shrimp, small Flat leaf parsley, minced	1 lb 12 oz 1½ cups	Stir shrimp and parsley into soup. Cook only until shrimp are pink, 2–3 minutes. Stir in reserved clams. Heat through. Remove and discard bay leaves before serving.

Approximate nutritive values per portion

Calories	Carbohydrate	Protein	Fat	Cholesterol	Sodium	Fiber	Iron
92 kcal	9 g	9 g	2 g	42 mg	552 mg	2 g	6 mg

Notes

- Potentially hazardous food. *Food Safety Standards:* Hold food for service at an internal temperature of 135°F or above. Do not mix old product with new. Cool leftover product quickly following time standards and cooling procedures on p. 167. Reheat leftover product quickly (within 2 hours) to 165°F or above. Reheat product only once; discard if not used.
- Minor's shrimp base is available from most broadline foodservice distributors.
- Other fish or shellfish can be substituted for the clams and shrimp.

Cream Soup Recipes

BASIC SAUCE FOR CREAM SOUP

Yield: 2½ gal basic sauce

Ingredient	Amount	Procedure
Margarine	8 oz	Melt margarine. Add onion and sauté until tender.
Onion, finely chopped	2 oz	
Flour, all-purpose	12 oz	Add flour, chicken base, and pepper to onion. Stir until blended. Cook for 5 minutes.
Chicken base	3 oz	
White pepper	½ tsp	
Water	2 qt	Add water and stir until mixture thickens. Add vegetables and seasonings as suggested in Variations to make a variety of cream soups.
Milk, hot	2 gal	Stir in milk. Heat to 180°F.

Notes

- Potentially hazardous food. *Food Safety Standards:* Hold food for service at an internal temperature of 135°F or above. Do not mix old product with new. Cool leftover product quickly following time standards and cooling procedures on p. 167. Reheat leftover product quickly (within 2 hours) to 165°F or above. Reheat product only once; discard if not used.
- Chicken base may be omitted. Omit the water and use 2½ gal milk. Add 2 oz salt.
- ¼ oz (2 Tbsp) dehydrated onions, rehydrated in ¼ cup water, may be substituted for fresh onions.
- A reduced-fat milk may be substituted for whole milk. Reduced-fat milk is less stable (curdles more easily) than whole milk.

Variations

- To make 3 gal soup (50–60 1-cup, 8-oz portions), use 1 recipe Basic Sauce for Cream Soup plus suggested additions that follow.
- **Cream of Asparagus Soup.** Add 6 lb cooked, chopped (or puréed) asparagus.
- **Cream of Broccoli Soup.** Add 6 lb cooked, chopped broccoli.
- **Cream of Cauliflower Soup.** Increase onion to 1 lb 8 oz and water to 1 gal. Reduce milk to 1½ gal. Add 6 lb cauliflower, cut into small florets, and 1 Tbsp Worcestershire sauce. Stir in 1 lb 8 oz processed American cheese, shredded. Stir until melted. Sprinkle with chopped chives.
- **Cream of Celery Soup.** Increase onion to 8 oz. Add 2 lb 8 oz cooked chopped celery and 1 lb cooked diced carrots.
- **Cream of Mushroom Soup.** Increase onion to 8 oz. Add 3 lb mushrooms, sliced or chopped, sautéed with the onion in margarine.
- **Cream of Potato Soup.** Increase onion to 12 oz. Add 8 lb cooked diced potatoes and 1 lb cooked chopped celery. Increase chicken base to 5 oz. Potatoes may be mashed or puréed if desired.
- **Cream of Spinach Soup.** Increase onion to 8 oz. Add 3 lb chopped spinach, cooked.
- **Cream of Vegetable Soup.** Increase onion to 1 lb. Add 1 lb cooked chopped celery, 1 lb 8 oz cooked diced carrots, and 2 lb cooked diced potatoes.
- **Mushroom Barley Soup.** Reduce milk to 3 qt and increase water to 1¾ gal. Increase margarine to 1 lb, onion to 1 lb, and chicken base to 8 oz. Add 3 lb sliced mushrooms, ½ tsp garlic powder, and 1 lb barley after water has been added. Simmer for about 30 minutes, then add milk slowly and heat to 180°F. Sprinkle with chopped parsley.

CREAM OF CHICKEN SOUP

Yield: 50 portions or 3 gal   *Portion:* 1 cup (8 oz)

Ingredient	Amount	Procedure
Margarine	8 oz	Melt margarine. Sauté celery until tender.
Celery, chopped	1 lb	
Flour, all-purpose	8 oz	Add flour and salt. Stir until blended.
Salt	1 oz (1½ Tbsp)	Cook for 5 minutes.
Chicken Stock (p. 738)	2 gal	Add stock and seasonings. Cook over low heat until it has the
Celery salt	2 tsp	consistency of thin white sauce. If chicken base is used for
White pepper	½ tsp	stock, taste before adding celery salt.
Milk	1 gal	Add milk while stirring.
Cooked chicken, chopped	3 lb	Add chicken. Heat to 180°F.

Approximate nutritive values per portion

Calories	Carbohydrate	Protein	Fat	Cholesterol	Sodium	Fiber	Iron
172 kcal	8 g	14 g	9 g	34 mg	839 mg	0.3 g	1 mg

Notes

- Potentially hazardous food. *Food Safety Standards:* Hold food for service at an internal temperature of 135°F or above. Do not mix old product with new. Cool leftover product quickly following time standards and cooling procedures on p. 167. Reheat leftover product quickly (within 2 hours) to 165°F or above. Reheat product only once; discard if not used.
- 1 lb cooked rice or noodles may be added. Reduce margarine and flour to 4 oz each.

Variation

- **Chicken Velvet Soup.** Substitute 2 qt half-and-half for 2 qt milk. Increase flour to 12 oz.

CHEESE SOUP

Yield: 50 portions or 3 gal   *Portion:* 1 cup (8 oz)

Ingredient	Amount	Procedure
Onions, chopped	8 oz	Sauté onions in margarine until lightly browned.
Margarine	8 oz	
Flour, all-purpose	4 oz	Add flour and cornstarch. Blend.
Cornstarch	2 oz	Cook for 5 minutes.
Paprika	1 tsp	Add seasonings and blend.
Salt	2 Tbsp	Add milk and stock slowly, while stirring.
White pepper	1 tsp	Cook until thickened.
Milk	1 gal	
Chicken Stock (p. 738)	1½ gal	
Carrots, finely diced	1 lb	Cook carrots and celery until tender but slightly crisp. Add to soup.
Celery, finely diced	12 oz	
Cheddar cheese, sharp, shredded	1 lb	Add cheese and stir until melted.
Fresh parsley, chopped	½ cup	Garnish with chopped parsley.

Approximate nutritive values per portion

Calories	Carbohydrate	Protein	Fat	Cholesterol	Sodium	Fiber	Iron
156 kcal	9 g	8 g	10 g	21 mg	776 mg	0.5 g	0.5 mg

Notes

- Potentially hazardous food. *Food Safety Standards:* Hold food for service at an internal temperature of 135°F or above. Do not mix old product with new. Cool leftover product quickly following time standards and cooling procedures on p. 167. Reheat leftover product quickly (within 2 hours) to 165°F or above. Reheat product only once; discard if not used.
- 1 oz (½ cup) dehydrated onions, rehydrated in ¾ cup water, may be substituted for fresh onions.
- Vegetable base and water may be substituted for Chicken Stock.

BROCCOLI AND CHEESE SOUP

Yield: 50 portions or 3 gal   *Portion:* 1 cup (8 oz)

Ingredient	Amount	Procedure
Margarine	10 oz	Melt margarine in steam-jacketed or other large kettle.
Onions, finely chopped	10 oz	Add onions and sauté until tender.
Flour, all-purpose	12 oz	Add flour and seasonings. Stir until blended.
Salt	1 Tbsp	Cook for 5 minutes, stirring often.
Black pepper	1 tsp	
Chicken base	3 oz	Stir in chicken base, then add water and milk, stirring constantly.
Water	3 qt	Reduce heat and cook until thickened, stirring often.
Milk	1½ gal	
Processed cheese, coarsely shredded	2 lb 8 oz	Add cheese and stir until melted.
Broccoli cuts, frozen	4 lb	Steam broccoli until just tender. Chop, if necessary. Add to cheese mixture and heat to 180°F.

Approximate nutritive values per portion

Calories	Carbohydrate	Protein	Fat	Cholesterol	Sodium	Fiber	Iron
239 kcal	14 g	11 g	16 g	38 mg	890 mg	2 g	1 mg

Notes

- Potentially hazardous food. *Food Safety Standards:* Hold food for service at an internal temperature of 135°F or above. Do not mix old product with new. Cool leftover product quickly following time standards and cooling procedures on p. 167. Reheat leftover product quickly (within 2 hours) to 165°F or above. Reheat product only once; discard if not used.
- 1¼ oz (⅔ cup) dehydrated onions, rehydrated in 1 cup water, may be substituted for fresh onions.
- Vegetable base may be substituted for chicken base.

Variation

- **Broccoli Swiss Soup.** In a steam-jacketed kettle, combine 1 lb chopped onions, 10 oz chopped celery, and 10 oz margarine. Sauté vegetables until tender. Stir in 10 oz flour, 1 tsp white pepper, and 2 tsp salt. Cook for 5–10 minutes, stirring often. Using a wire whip, gradually stir in 1½ gal milk, 1¾ qt water, and 4 oz vegetable or chicken base. Reduce heat and cook until thickened, stirring constantly. Add 2 lb 12 oz shredded processed Swiss cheese. Stir until cheese melts. Add 5 lb 8 oz frozen broccoli cuts that have been steamed only until beginning to soften. Heat to 180°F. Makes 3 gal. Salt may need to be adjusted depending on the amount of salt in the vegetable or chicken base.

BAKED POTATO SOUP

Yield: 50 portions   *Portion:* 1 cup (8 oz)

Ingredient	Amount	Procedure
Baking potatoes	11 lb 10 oz	Bake and cool potatoes before dicing. Follow cooling procedures on p. 167. After potatoes cool, dice into ½-inch cubes. Do not peel. Reserve for later step.
Margarine Green onions, finely chopped	4 oz 16 oz EP	Heat margarine in steam-jacketed kettle. Add onions. Sauté until fragrant.
Flour	2 oz	Stir flour into margarine and onions. Stir and cook for 10–15 minutes to make roux.
Chicken Stock (p. 738) (see Note)	5 qt	Add stock to roux, stirring constantly with a wire whip. Bring to a boil. Reduce heat and simmer for 15–20 minutes. Add diced potatoes reserved from earlier step.
Milk Cooked bacon, crumbled	1¾ qt 6 oz	Add milk and bacon. Bring to 180–190°F.
Cheddar cheese, shredded Green onions, sliced thin Black pepper	12 oz 4 oz EP 3½ tsp	Add cheese, onions, and pepper. Stir until cheese is melted. Taste for salt and adjust as needed.

Approximate nutritive values per portion

Calories	Carbohydrate	Protein	Fat	Cholesterol	Sodium	Fiber	Iron
180 kcal	25 g	6.2 g	6.3 g	11.1 mg	347 mg	2.5 g	1 mg

Notes

- Potentially hazardous food. *Food Safety Standards:* Hold food for service at an internal temperature of 135°F or above. Do not mix old product with new. Cool leftover product quickly following time standards and cooling procedures on p. 167. Reheat leftover product quickly (within 2 hours) to 165°F or above. Reheat product only once; discard if not used.
- 4 oz of chicken base and 4¾ qt water can be substituted for the Chicken Stock.

Chowder Recipes

CORN CHOWDER

Yield: 50 portions or 3 gal　　*Portion:* 1 cup (8 oz)

Ingredient	Amount	Procedure
Potatoes, diced	2 lb	Cook potatoes. Drain. Save for later step.
Onion, finely chopped Celery, chopped Margarine, melted	4 oz 6 oz 8 oz	Sauté onion and celery in margarine until tender.
Flour, all-purpose White pepper Chicken base	12 oz 1 tsp 3 oz	Add flour, pepper, and chicken base to onions. Stir until well blended. Cook for 5 minutes.
Water	1½ gal	Add water, stirring constantly. Cook until mixture thickens.
Corn, cream style Chives, frozen	1 No. 10 can 1 cup	Add corn, chives, and potatoes. Heat until hot.
Milk	2½ qt	Stir milk into soup. Heat to 180°F.

Approximate nutritive values per portion

Calories	Carbohydrate	Protein	Fat	Cholesterol	Sodium	Fiber	Iron
153 kcal	23 g	4 g	6 g	7 mg	392 mg	1 g	0.5 mg

Notes

- Potentially hazardous food. *Food Safety Standards:* Hold food for service at an internal temperature of 135°F or above. Do not mix old product with new. Cool leftover product quickly following time standards and cooling procedures on p. 167. Reheat leftover product quickly (within 2 hours) to 165°F or above. Reheat product only once; discard if not used.
- Vegetable base may be substituted for chicken base.
- ½ oz (¼ cup) dehydrated onions, rehydrated in ½ cup water, may be substituted for fresh onions.
- 1 lb bacon, diced and cooked until crisp, may be added before serving.

Variations

- **Potato Chowder.** Omit corn and increase potatoes to 8 lb.
- **Vegetable Chowder.** Substitute 3 lb whole-kernel corn for cream-style corn. Add 4 oz chopped green bell pepper and 1 lb cooked, diced carrots.
- **Chipotle Corn Chowder.** Steam 2 lb diced red potatoes until tender. Drain and reserve for later step. Combine 8 oz margarine, 12 oz flour, and ½ tsp ground white pepper in steam-jacketed kettle. Cook roux until light brown, stirring often. Turn off heat. Measure into roux 5½ qt water, 6 oz vegetable base, and 2 oz chipotle base. Stir with a wire whip until mixed. Cook and stir until mixture boils and thickens. Stir in cooked potatoes, 7 oz chopped celery, and 3 oz finely chopped onion. Stir in 5 lb 5 oz cream-style corn and 3 oz chopped roasted red peppers. Stir in 2⅓ qt whole milk. Heat to 180°F. Check for salt and add if needed. Portion: 8 oz.

NEW ENGLAND CLAM CHOWDER

Yield: 50 portions or 3 gal   *Portion:* 1 cup (8 oz)

Ingredient	Amount	Procedure
Potatoes, cubed	6 lb	Cook potatoes until tender. Drain.
Water	1 qt	Reserve potatoes to add in last step.
Salt	1 Tbsp	
Bacon, finely diced	4 oz	Sauté bacon, onion, and celery in steam-jacketed or other large kettle for
Onion, chopped	8 oz	5 minutes, or until lightly browned.
Celery, chopped	12 oz	
Margarine	8 oz	Add margarine to onion and stir until melted.
Flour, all-purpose	8 oz	Add flour, pepper, and chicken base. Stir until blended.
White pepper	1 tsp	Cook for 5 minutes.
Chicken base (see Note)	4 oz	
Milk	2 gal	Add milk gradually while stirring. Cook until thickened.
Minced clams, canned, undrained	4 lb	Add clams and potatoes. Heat to 180°F.

Approximate nutritive values per portion

Calories	Carbohydrate	Protein	Fat	Cholesterol	Sodium	Fiber	Iron
235 kcal	25 g	12 g	10 g	34 mg	709 mg	2 g	1 mg

Notes

- Potentially hazardous food. *Food Safety Standards:* Hold food for service at an internal temperature of 135°F or above. Do not mix old product with new. Cool leftover product quickly following time standards and cooling procedures on p. 167. Reheat leftover product quickly (within 2 hours) to 165°F or above. Reheat product only once; discard if not used.
- 1 gal fresh clams may be used. Clean and steam until tender. Drain and chop. Save juice.
- Garnish with fresh or frozen chives, chopped.
- 1 oz (½ cup) dehydrated onion, rehydrated in ¾ cup water, may be substituted for fresh onion.
- Clam base may be substituted for chicken base.

Variation

- **Fish Chowder.** Delete clams. Add 1 tsp thyme, 1 tsp crushed rosemary, 2 tsp Worcestershire sauce, ½ tsp hot pepper sauce, and 3 lb flaked white fish, or 1 lb shrimp and 2 lb minced clams.

POTATO AND ROASTED RED PEPPER SOUP

Yield: 50 portions   *Portion:* 8 oz

Ingredient	Amount	Procedure
Potatoes, medium dice	6 lb 4 oz	Using a steamer or other steam equipment, steam potatoes until tender. Hold for later step.
Onions, finely chopped Celery, chopped Margarine	1 lb EP 1 lb EP 8 oz	In a steam-jacketed kettle or large stockpot, sauté vegetables in margarine until tender.
Flour	10 oz	Add flour to vegetables. Stir with a wire whip to combine. Cook for 5–10 minutes. Turn off heat.
Water Chicken base White pepper Salt	2 qt 4 oz 1 tsp 1½ oz	Add water, chicken base, and seasonings to roux, stirring constantly. Cook until mixture thickens.
Roasted red peppers, cut into ¼ × ½-inch strips (p. 796)	1 lb	Add steamed potatoes and Roasted Red Peppers to vegetable mixture. Heat to 185°F.
Milk	5 qt	Add milk slowly to potato mixture. Stir constantly to combine. Heat to 180°F.

Approximate nutritive values per portion

Calories	Carbohydrate	Protein	Fat	Cholesterol	Sodium	Fiber	Iron
170 kcal	20 g	5.8 g	7.5 g	13 mg	739 mg	1.7 g	1 mg

Notes

- Potentially hazardous food. *Food Safety Standards:* Hold food for service at an internal temperature of 135°F or above. Do not mix old product with new. Cool leftover product quickly following time standards and cooling procedures on p. 167. Reheat leftover product quickly (within 2 hours) to 165°F or above. Reheat product only once; discard if not used.
- A frozen roasted pepper blend can be substituted for the Roasted Red Peppers. When using frozen roasted vegetables, place in a single layer on a baking sheet and heat in a 375°F oven until heated through (discard liquid that accumulates).
- Green, orange, or yellow bell peppers can be substituted for some or all of the red bell peppers.
- Vegetable base can be substituted for the chicken base. Adjust salt as required.

HEARTY POTATO HAM CHOWDER

Yield: 50 portions or 3 gal   *Portion:* 1 cup (8 oz)

Ingredient	Amount	Procedure
Margarine	3 oz	Melt margarine in steam-jacketed or other large kettle.
Green onions, finely chopped	8 oz	Add onions and peppers and sauté until tender.
Green bell peppers, chopped	12 oz	
Flour, all-purpose	3 oz	Add flour and seasonings. Stir until blended.
White pepper	½ tsp	Cook for 5 minutes, stirring often.
Paprika	1 tsp	
Chicken Stock (p. 738)	3 qt	Add stock and stir until smooth. Cook until mixture begins to thicken.
Ham, coarsely chopped	2 lb 8 oz	Add ham, potatoes, and corn. Heat to 180°F.
Potatoes, cooked, cubed	5 lb 8 oz	
Corn, whole kernel	3 lb 12 oz	
Milk	2¾ qt	Add milk and mix well. Heat to 180°F.
Fresh parsley, chopped	½ cup	Sprinkle parsley over chowder before serving.

Approximate nutritive values per portion

Calories	Carbohydrate	Protein	Fat	Cholesterol	Sodium	Fiber	Iron
276 kcal	41 g	13 g	7 g	21 mg	584 mg	5 g	2 mg

Notes

- Potentially hazardous food. *Food Safety Standards:* Hold food for service at an internal temperature of 135°F or above. Do not mix old product with new. Cool leftover product quickly following time standards and cooling procedures on p. 167. Reheat leftover product quickly (within 2 hours) to 165°F or above. Reheat product only once; discard if not used.
- 1 oz (½ cup) dehydrated onions, rehydrated in ¾ cup water, may be substituted for fresh onions.

OYSTER STEW

Yield: 50 portions or 3 gal   *Portion:* 1 cup (8 oz)

Ingredient	Amount	Procedure
Milk	2½ gal	Scald milk by heating to point just below boiling.
Oysters, undrained Butter or margarine	2½ qt 8 oz	Heat oysters and butter only until edges of oysters begin to curl.
Salt Black pepper	2 oz (3 Tbsp) ½ tsp	About 10 minutes before serving, add hot oysters, with the oyster liquid, and seasonings to scalded milk. Serve immediately to avoid curdling.

Approximate nutritive values per portion

Calories	Carbohydrate	Protein	Fat	Cholesterol	Sodium	Fiber	Iron
203 kcal	12 g	12 g	12 g	76 mg	599 mg	0 g	3 mg

Note

- Potentially hazardous food. *Food Safety Standards:* Hold food for service at an internal temperature of 135°F or above. Do not mix old product with new. Cool leftover product quickly following time standards and cooling procedures on p. 167. Reheat leftover product quickly (within 2 hours) to 165°F or above. Reheat product only once; discard if not used.

MANHATTAN FISH OR CLAM CHOWDER

Yield: 50 portions or 3 gal   *Portion:* 1 cup (8 oz)

Ingredient	Amount	Procedure
Bacon, diced	1 lb	Cook bacon until crisp. Drain off excess fat.
Onions, chopped	1 lb 6 oz	Add onion and sauté until tender. Place onion and bacon in large kettle.
Water Diced tomatoes, canned Potatoes, chopped Carrots, diced Celery, chopped Catsup Worcestershire sauce Salt Black pepper Bay leaves Thyme, ground	3 qt 1 No. 10 can 3 lb 1 lb 4 oz 1 lb 4 oz 2 cups ⅓ cup 2 Tbsp 1 tsp 2 1 tsp	Add water, vegetables, and seasonings. Bring to a boil. Reduce heat. Simmer for 40–45 minutes or until vegetables are tender. Remove bay leaves before serving.
Fish, boneless, cooked and flaked, or minced clams	3 lb 8 oz	Add fish. Cover and simmer for 5–10 minutes.
Fresh parsley, chopped	¼ cup	Sprinkle parsley over soup before serving.

Approximate nutritive values per portion

Calories	Carbohydrate	Protein	Fat	Cholesterol	Sodium	Fiber	Iron
98 kcal	15 g	6 g	2 g	13 mg	543 mg	2 g	3 mg

Notes

- Potentially hazardous food. *Food Safety Standards:* Hold food for service at an internal temperature of 135°F or above. Do not mix old product with new. Cool leftover product quickly following time standards and cooling procedures on p. 167. Reheat leftover product quickly (within 2 hours) to 165°F or above. Reheat product only once; discard if not used.
- 2¾ oz (1½ cups) dehydrated onions, rehydrated in 2¼ cups water, may be substituted for fresh onions.

Chilled Soup Recipes

GAZPACHO (SPANISH CHILLED SOUP)

Yield: 50 portions or 1¾ gal   *Portion:* ½ cup (4 oz)

Ingredient	Amount	Procedure
Fresh mushrooms, chopped	4 oz	Sauté mushrooms in oil until light brown.
Olive oil	½ cup	
Garlic cloves	3	Crush garlic in salt.
Salt	2 Tbsp	
Fresh tomatoes, finely chopped	3 lb	Combine remaining ingredients in a stainless steel or glass container.
Green bell peppers, finely chopped	1 lb 4 oz	Add mushrooms and garlic.
Celery, finely chopped	12 oz	If too thick, add more tomato juice.
Cucumbers, finely chopped	1 lb	Cover and chill quickly to below 41°F.
Onions, finely chopped	1 lb 8 oz	
Fresh chives, chopped	2 Tbsp	
Fresh parsley, chopped	3 Tbsp	
Black pepper	1 Tbsp	
Worcestershire sauce	1 Tbsp	
Vinegar, tarragon	1½ cups	
Hot pepper sauce	1 tsp	
Tomato juice	2½ qt	

Approximate nutritive values per portion

Calories	Carbohydrate	Protein	Fat	Cholesterol	Sodium	Fiber	Iron
45 kcal	6 g	1 g	2 g	0 mg	487 mg	1 g	1 mg

Note
- Potentially hazardous food. *Food Safety Standards:* Hold food for service at an internal temperature of 41°F or below. Do not mix old product with new. Keep leftover product chilled at 41°F or below. See p. 167 for cooling procedures.

Variation
- **Summer Gazpacho.** Combine 6¼ qt tomato juice, 1 lb 12 oz diced fresh tomatoes, 1 lb 12 oz chopped celery, 1 lb 8 oz chopped green bell peppers, 10 oz chopped green onions, 1¼ cups cider vinegar, ½ cup chopped flat leaf parsley, 1 oz minced garlic, 1½ Tbsp salt, 2 tsp black pepper, and 2 Tbsp Worcestershire sauce. Serve chilled. Portion: 6 oz.

VICHYSSOISE (CHILLED POTATO SOUP)

Yield: 50 portions or 3 gal   *Portion:* 1 cup (8 oz)

Ingredient	Amount	Procedure
Chicken Stock (p. 738) Onions, chopped	1 gal 3 lb	Combine stock and onions. Cook until onions are tender. Strain.
Potatoes, diced	6 lb	Steam potatoes until tender. Mash.
Salt Celery salt Garlic salt White pepper	1 Tbsp 2 tsp 1 tsp $\frac{1}{2}$ tsp	Add seasonings and chicken stock to potatoes. If soup base is used in stock, salt may need to be reduced.
Half-and-half	$1\frac{1}{4}$ gal	Add half-and-half and mix well. Chill quickly to below 41°F.
Fresh parsley, chives, or green onion tops, chopped	$\frac{1}{3}$ cup	Garnish chilled soup with chopped parsley, chives, or green onion tops.

Approximate nutritive values per portion

Calories	Carbohydrate	Protein	Fat	Cholesterol	Sodium	Fiber	Iron
200 kcal	19 g	6 g	12 g	36 mg	546 mg	2 g	0.5 mg

Note

- Potentially hazardous food. *Food Safety Standards:* Hold food for service at an internal temperature of 41°F or below. Do not mix old product with new. Keep leftover product chilled at 41°F or below. See p. 167 for cooling procedures.

With the increased interest in nutrition, the place of the vegetable in today's foodservice menu has assumed new importance. A wide array of fresh vegetables is available year-round, as is a variety of frozen and canned vegetables. Proper preparation and cooking are essential to preserving the nutritive value, color, and palatability of fresh vegetables. The addition of herbs and spices enhances the vegetables without adding salt and fat.

Frozen and canned vegetables require less labor to prepare than fresh vegetables and have more predictable yields, but fresh vegetables, especially those that are not too time-consuming to prepare, should be considered when they are in season.

The quantity of vegetables to buy depends on the portion size and the method of preparation. One No. 10 can or 5 lb of most frozen vegetables will yield 25 3-oz portions. For fresh vegetables, the loss in preparation must be considered in determining the amount to purchase. Table 4.1 suggests amounts to buy, and Table 4.3 gives the approximate yield in the preparation of fresh vegetables.

Fresh and Frozen Vegetables

Fresh or frozen vegetables may be cooked by boiling, steaming, baking, or frying. The method used depends largely on the type of product, the amount to be cooked, and the equipment available. Fresh vegetables should be washed, trimmed, peeled if necessary, and cut into even-size pieces for cooking. Detailed instructions are given for individual recipes in this section. (Salad vegetables and their preparation are discussed in Chapter 6.) Preparing fresh vegetables too far in advance causes them to discolor. Covering prepared vegetables with cold water helps retain color but reduces their nutritive value if they are held too long.

A small steam-jacketed kettle is satisfactory for cooking both fresh and frozen vegetables. It should be large enough to prevent crowding and to allow the water to return to the boiling point quickly after vegetables are added. A tilting fry pan also may be used successfully.

Vegetables may be cooked in a steamer in small quantities and arranged in thin layers in shallow pans. The time and temperature must be controlled carefully. Cooking in a high-pressure or zero-pressure steamer is especially successful. One advantage of steam cooking is that vegetables may be weighed and placed in serving pans, then cooked and served from the same pans.

When steam equipment is not available, top-of-range cooking may be used. Vegetables should be cooked in as small an amount of water as is practicable and as quickly as possible.

Whatever the method used, vegetables should be cooked only until tender. *Do not overcook.* Vegetables should be cooked in as small a quantity at one time as is feasible for the type of service. The needs of most food services can be met by continuous cooking of vegetables in small quantities (batch cooking). Vegetables should be served as soon as possible after cooking for optimum quality and should be handled carefully to prevent breaking or mashing. Vegetables that have been cooked and held for any period of time should not be combined with freshly prepared batches. Appearance is most important to customer acceptance of vegetables, as is the seasoning. Individual recipes recommend the amount of salt for 50 portions and suggest seasonings appropriate to that vegetable.

DIRECTIONS FOR BOILING

1. Prepare vegetables. See pp. 120–127 for directions for preparing fresh vegetables. Frozen vegetables should not be thawed before cooking except for solid-pack frozen vegetables, which should be thawed only long enough to break apart easily.

2. Add prepared vegetables to boiling salted water in steam-jacketed kettle or stockpot. Cook in lots no larger than 10 lb. Use 1 oz (1½ Tbsp) salt to the amount of water specified in Table 21.1, except for corn. Add salt and/or sugar after cooking to prevent toughening and discoloring of corn kernels.

The amount of water used in cooking all vegetables is important for retention of nutrients. The less water used, the more nutrients retained. Addition of baking soda to the water also causes loss of vitamins. Mature root vegetables that need longer cooking require more

TABLE 21.1 Timetable for boiling or steaming fresh and frozen vegetables

	Boiling—approximate cooking time[a,b] (minutes)	Steaming—approximate cooking time[c,d] for 1–3 pans (minutes)		
		5–6 psi[e]	12–15 psi[e]	Zero pressure
Asparagus, fresh, frozen	10–12	10–12	4–8	6–13
Beans, black-eyed beans or peas, frozen	30–45	20–25	10–20	25–35
Beans, green or wax, fresh	15–25	15–20	4–10	10–15
Beans, green or wax, frozen	10–12	10–12	7–11	6–13
Beans, lima, frozen	10–15	10–12	6–10	6–13
Beets, whole, fresh	40–50	40–50	25–35	40–50
Broccoli, cuts or spears, fresh, frozen	10–12	10–15	4–8	5–10
Brussels sprouts, fresh, frozen	10–15	10–12	6–10	9–14
Cabbage, cored, cut	10–12	14–16	7–14	14–18
Carrots, fresh	10–20	18–20	6–15	18–20
Carrots, frozen	10–20	9–10	5–9	7–12
Cauliflower, fresh, frozen	10–12	10–15	5–10	7–15
Celery, fresh	10–12	10–15	5–10	10–15
Corn, whole kernel, frozen	6–8	9–10	5–9	5–10
Corn on the cob, fresh, frozen	5–15	10–12	5–10	8–12
Eggplant, fresh	15–20	10–15	4–8	5–15
Greens, collard, fresh	25–35	10–15	8–10	12–15
Kale, fresh	15–20	10–15	8–10	12–15
Okra, fresh, frozen	8–15	10–12	6–10	10–12
Onions, fresh	20–30	15–20	5–10	10–15
Parsnips, fresh	20–40	15–20	6–15	18–20
Peas, green, fresh, frozen	8–12	8–10	3–4	5–6
Potatoes, fresh, whole, small	25–40	20–25	13–25	35–40
Rutabagas, fresh	20–35	25–30	10–20	25–30
Spinach, fresh	3–5	3–5	1–3	3–5
Spinach, frozen, thawed	3–5	8–10	4–8	8–10
Squash, summer, fresh, frozen	5–10	8–12	5–8	7–10
Squash, winter, fresh, diced	30–40	15–20	7–9	15–20
Sweet potatoes, fresh	30–40	20–30	13–25	30–40
Turnips, fresh	20–40	25–30	10–20	25–30
Vegetables, mixed, frozen	10–15	10	5–9	5–10

[a]Cook vegetables at a slow boil.

[b]Figures calculated for boiling 10—12 lb of vegetables in 1–3 qt water. Greens do not require the addition of extra water; the water clinging to their leaves is sufficient.

[c]Figures calculated for steaming 5–6 lb vegetables per batch. A steamer filled to less than capacity will need the cooking time reduced slightly. An overloaded steamer may require a longer cooking time.

[d]When posssible, use 2½-inch-deep perforated steamer pans. For best results, break up frozen vegetables to speed cooking.

[e]Pounds per square inch.

Note: Canned vegetables require the following cooking times: 5 psi, 3–5 minutes; 15 psi, 3–4 minutes; 0 psi, 5–10 minutes.

water than young, tender vegetables. Spinach and other greens need only the water clinging to their leaves from washing.

3. Cover and bring water quickly back to the boiling point. Green vegetables retain their color better if the lid is removed just before boiling begins; strong-flavored vegetables, such as cabbage, cauliflower, and brussels sprouts, should be cooked uncovered to prevent development of unpleasant flavors.

4. Start timing when water returns to the boiling point. Use Table 21.1 as a guide. Stir greens occasionally while boiling.

5. Drain cooked vegetables and place in serving pans. Add 4–8 oz melted margarine or butter to each 50 portions.

6. Adjust seasonings.

DIRECTIONS FOR STEAMING

1. Place prepared vegetables not more than 3–4 inches deep in stainless steel inset pans. Perforated pans provide the best circulation, but if cooking liquid needs to be retained, use solid pans. When cooking winter squash or sweet potatoes, cover with a lid or aluminum foil to prevent water from accumulating in the pan.

2. Steam, using Table 21.1 as a guide. Begin timing when steamer reaches proper cooking pressure.

3. Add 2–4 oz melted margarine or butter and 2 tsp salt to each 5 lb drained vegetables.

DIRECTIONS FOR STIR-FRYING

1. Select vegetables for color, texture, shape, and flavor.

2. Cut or dice diagonally into small uniform pieces (see p. 174–175 for dicing instructions.)

3. Heat a small amount of oil or seasoned oil in a pan, steam-jacketed kettle, or tilting fry pan. Prepare seasoned oil for stir-frying by adding $\frac{1}{2}$ oz sliced fresh ginger and $\frac{1}{2}$ oz fresh peeled garlic to 2 cups salad oil. Refrigerate for 8 hours. For safety reasons, use within 24 hours. Strain before using (see p. 520 for Basil Oil recipe).

4. Stir in vegetables, starting with those that take longer to cook (carrots, onions, turnips). Continue to stir for 1 minute until vegetables are coated with oil.

5. Add liquid (water or broth) and seasonings to vegetables. Cover and steam for 3 minutes or until vegetables are tender-crisp.

6. Add cornstarch mixed with a small amount of cold water. (See recipe on p. 818.) Cook and stir just until the sauce thickens and vegetables are glazed.

Canned Vegetables

Heating of canned vegetables should be scheduled so they will be served soon after heating. Prepare one or two No. 10 cans at a time, with approximately 25 portions in each can.

DIRECTIONS FOR HEATING

Stockpot or Steam-Jacketed Kettle

1. Drain off half the liquid; use for soups, gravies, and sauces.

2. Heat vegetables and remaining liquid in a stockpot or steam-jacketed kettle. Heat only long enough to bring to 160°F.

3. Drain vegetables and place in counter pans. Add 4–8 oz melted margarine or butter.

Steamer or Oven

1. Drain off half the liquid; use for soups, gravies, and sauces.

2. Transfer vegetables and remaining liquid to steamer pans and cover. A 12 × 20 × 2-inch pan will hold contents of two No. 10 cans, or 50 portions of most vegetables.

3. Heat in steamer at 5–6 lb pressure for 1 minute, or in a 350°F oven until 160°F is reached.

4. Drain vegetables and add 4–8 oz melted margarine or butter for each lot of vegetables.

Dried Vegetables

Among the many kinds of dried legumes available today are dried peas (whole green or split green, yellow split, and black-eyed); beans (navy, black, fava, red kidney, brown, pinto, butter beans, and garbanzo, also known as chickpeas); and lentils (brown and red). High in protein and fiber, legumes are an important factor in meatless dishes and health-conscious menus.

DIRECTIONS FOR COOKING

1. Sort, discarding any stones or other foreign material and shriveled vegetables. Rinse with cold water.

2. Heat water to boiling in steam-jacketed or other kettle.

3. Add vegetables and boil for 3 minutes.

4. Turn off steam and allow to stand for 1 hour.

5. Add salt and cook slowly until vegetables are tender, 1–1$\frac{1}{2}$ hours. Add more water if needed.

6. Alternatively, vegetables may be covered with cold water and soaked overnight, drained, fresh water added, then cooked.

Vegetable Recipes

SEASONED FRESH ASPARAGUS

Yield: 50 portions   *Portion:* 3 oz

Ingredient	Amount	Procedure
Fresh asparagus	18–20 lb AP (10 lb EP)	Break or cut off tough stems. Wash and thoroughly clean remaining portions. Arrange spears in steamer pans with tips in one direction. Sprinkle with salt. Steam (p. 770). Asparagus may be cut into 1-inch pieces and steamed or placed in a kettle and boiled (p. 770).
Margarine, melted	4 oz	Pour margarine over cooked asparagus.
Salt	1 oz (1½ Tbsp)	If boiling asparagus, add salt to cooking water.

Approximate nutritive values per portion

Calories	Carbohydrate	Protein	Fat	Cholesterol	Sodium	Fiber	Iron
59 kcal	8 g	4 g	2 g	0 mg	220 mg	3 g	1 mg

Notes

- For frozen asparagus, use 10 lb. See p. 770 for cooking instructions.
- Seasonings for asparagus: sesame seeds, lemon juice, browned butter, crumb butter, basil, chives, tarragon.

Variations

- **Asparagus with Cheese Sauce.** Serve 5–6 stalks of cooked asparagus with 2 Tbsp Cheese Sauce (p. 683). Make 2 qt sauce.
- **Asparagus Vinaigrette.** Blanch asparagus (see p. 150). Marinate in 1½ qt Vinaigrette Dressing (p. 647) or Vegetable Marinade (pp. 722–724).
- **Creamed Asparagus.** Add 1 gal Medium White Sauce (p. 683) to 10 lb asparagus cut in 2-inch lengths and cooked.
- **Fresh Asparagus with Hollandaise Sauce.** Serve 1 Tbsp Hollandaise Sauce (p. 698) over cooked asparagus spears.

SEASONED FRESH GREEN OR WAX BEANS

Yield: 50 portions   *Portion:* 3 oz

Ingredient	Amount	Procedure
Fresh green or wax beans	11–12 lb AP (10 lb EP)	Wash beans. Trim ends. Cut or break into 1-inch pieces. Steam or boil (p. 770).
Margarine, melted Salt	4 oz 1 oz (1½ Tbsp)	Pour margarine over cooked beans and sprinkle with salt. If boiling the beans, add salt to cooking water.

Approximate nutritive values per portion

Calories	Carbohydrate	Protein	Fat	Cholesterol	Sodium	Fiber	Iron
51 kcal	8 g	2 g	2 g	0 mg	216 mg	2 g	1 mg

Notes

- For frozen beans, use 10 lb. See p. 770 for cooking.
- For canned beans, use 2 No. 10 cans. See p. 771 for heating.
- Seasonings for green beans: basil, dill, marjoram, oregano, rosemary, savory, tarragon, thyme, onion, chives, mushrooms, bacon.

Variations

- **French Green Beans.** Cook 10 lb frozen French cut green beans. Drain and season with 1 cup mayonnaise, ¾ cup sour cream, 2 Tbsp vinegar, 2 oz chopped onion sautéed in 2 oz margarine, and salt and pepper to taste.
- **Green Beans Amandine.** Add 8 oz slivered almonds lightly browned in 8 oz margarine.
- **Green Beans and Mushrooms.** Add 2 lb sliced mushrooms that have been sautéed in 8 oz margarine.
- **Green Beans Provincial.** Season green beans with 8 oz Onion Butter (p. 721), 2 minced garlic cloves, 3 Tbsp chopped fresh parsley, and 2 tsp crumbled dried thyme.
- **Herbed Green Beans.** Season 10 lb frozen green beans, cooked, or 2 No. 10 cans green beans with 1 lb chopped onions, 8 oz chopped celery, and 1 tsp minced garlic sautéed in 8 oz margarine, 2 tsp crumbled dried basil, and 2 tsp dried rosemary.
- **Southern-Style Green Beans.** Cut 1 lb 8 oz bacon into small pieces. Add 6 oz chopped onion and sauté until onion is lightly browned. Add to hot, drained green beans. Good served with ham and Corn Bread (p. 224).

GREEN BEAN CASSEROLE

Yield: 50 portions or 1 pan, 12 × 20 × 2 inches   *Portion:* 4 oz
Oven: 350°F   *Bake:* 30–40 minutes

Ingredient	Amount	Procedure
Green beans, frozen, French cut or cut	7 lb 8 oz	Cook green beans (p. 770). Drain.
Fresh mushrooms	10 oz	Clean mushrooms and slice.
Margarine, melted	3 oz	Sauté in margarine.
Cream of mushroom soup, undiluted	1 qt	Blend soup, milk, and seasonings.
Milk	1 cup	
Black pepper	½ tsp	
Onion powder	1 tsp	
Soy sauce	1 Tbsp	
Sliced water chestnuts, canned, drained	1 lb	Combine soup mixture, mushrooms, and water chestnuts. Add to green beans. Mix lightly. Pour into one 12 × 20 × 2-inch pan.
Swiss cheese, shredded	8 oz	Sprinkle cheese over beans. Bake at 350°F for 25 minutes.
Bread crumbs	4 oz	Combine crumbs and margarine and sprinkle over bean mixture.
Margarine, melted	4 oz	Bake for 5–10 minutes.

Approximate nutritive values per portion

Calories	Carbohydrate	Protein	Fat	Cholesterol	Sodium	Fiber	Iron
107 kcal	10 g	3 g	6 g	5 mg	262 mg	1 g	1 mg

Notes

- Two No. 10 cans cut green beans may be substituted for frozen beans. Drain before using.
- 8 oz crumbled canned French-fried onion rings may be sprinkled over the top during the last 10 minutes of baking.

SPANISH GREEN BEANS

Yield: 50 portions   *Portion:* 3 oz

Ingredient	Amount	Procedure
Bacon, diced	8 oz	Sauté bacon, onion, and pepper until lightly browned.
Onion, chopped	6 oz	
Green bell pepper, chopped	4 oz	
Flour, all-purpose	4 oz	Add flour and stir until smooth.
Tomatoes, canned	2 qt	Chop tomatoes and heat. Add salt.
Salt	1 Tbsp	Add gradually to bacon-vegetable mixture. Stir and cook until thickened.
Green beans, drained	2 No. 10 cans	Gently stir tomato sauce into the green beans. Simmer for 15–20 minutes or until beans are heated to 160°F.

Approximate nutritive values per portion

Calories	Carbohydrate	Protein	Fat	Cholesterol	Sodium	Fiber	Iron
48 kcal	9 g	2 g	1 g	0 mg	213 mg	3 g	1 mg

Note

- 8 lb fresh or frozen green beans may be substituted for canned beans. Cook before combining with tomato sauce.

Variations

- **Creole Green Beans.** Omit bacon. Sauté onion, green bell pepper, and 8 oz chopped celery in 2 oz margarine. Add 2 oz sugar to tomatoes.
- **Green Beans with Dill.** Delete bacon and onion. Sauté the green bell pepper in 5 oz margarine. Add 1 tsp pepper and 1 Tbsp dill seed. Simmer slowly for 10–15 minutes. Tomatoes may be increased to 1 No. 10 can.
- **Hacienda Green Beans.** Add 1 oz sugar, 1½ Tbsp chile powder, and ½ tsp garlic powder.

SEASONED LIMA BEANS

Yield: 50 portions   *Portion:* 3 oz

Ingredient	Amount	Procedure
Lima beans, baby or fordhook, frozen	10 lb	Steam or boil beans (p. 770).
Margarine, melted Salt	4 oz 1 oz (1½ Tbsp)	Pour margarine over beans and sprinkle with salt. If boiling the beans, add salt to cooking water.

Approximate nutritive values per portion

Calories	Carbohydrate	Protein	Fat	Cholesterol	Sodium	Fiber	Iron
130 kcal	21 g	7 g	2 g	0 mg	216 mg	6 g	2 mg

Note

- Seasonings for lima beans: basil, chives, dill, marjoram, oregano, sage, savory, tarragon, thyme, pimento, mushrooms, onion butter, sour cream.

Variations

- **Baked Lima Beans and Peas.** Thaw 5 lb frozen baby lima beans and 5 lb frozen peas. Combine with 2 Tbsp dried basil, 1 oz (1½ Tbsp) salt, ½ tsp black pepper, and 16 sliced green onions. Place in baking pan. Sprinkle with 1 cup water and dot with 4–6 oz margarine. Cover and bake at 325°F for 45 minutes. Stir occasionally.
- **Succotash.** Use 5 lb lima beans and 5 lb frozen or canned whole-kernel corn. Season with 4 oz margarine.

BAKED LIMA BEANS

Yield: 50 portions or 2 pans, 12 × 20 × 2 inches   *Portion:* 5 oz
Oven: 350°F   *Bake:* 1 hour

Ingredient	Amount	Procedure
Lima beans, dried, large	6 lb AP	Wash beans (p. 771). Add boiling water. Cover. Let stand for 1 hour or longer.
Water, boiling	1 gal	Cook beans in the same water until tender, about 1 hour.
Pimento, chopped Salt Molasses	4 oz 1 oz (1½ Tbsp) 1 cup	Add seasonings to beans. Scale into two 12 × 20 × 2-inch pans, 8 lb 6 oz per pan.
Bacon, sliced	1 lb 8 oz	Place bacon on top of beans. Bake at 350°F until top is brown, about 1 hour.

Approximate nutritive values per portion

Calories	Carbohydrate	Protein	Fat	Cholesterol	Sodium	Fiber	Iron
80 kcal	12 g	4 g	2 g	3 mg	444 mg	0 g	2 mg

Variations

- **Baked Lima Beans and Sausage.** Omit bacon. Place 6 lb link sausages on top of beans.
- **Boiled Lima Beans and Ham.** Omit bacon and seasonings. Add 5 lb diced ham to beans and simmer until tender.

RANCH-STYLE BEANS

Yield: 50 portions or 1 pan, 12 × 20 × 4 inches   *Portion:* 5 oz
Oven: 300°F   *Bake:* 3–4 hours

Ingredient	Amount	Procedure
Beans, red or pinto, dried	5 lb	Wash beans (p. 771). Add boiling water.
Water, boiling	1½ gal	Cover and let stand for 1 hour or longer.
Bacon, 1-inch cubes	2 lb 8 oz	Add bacon to beans.
Water, cold	to cover	Add water to cover. Cook slowly until tender, about 1 hour.
Chile peppers	3–4 pods	Soak chile peppers in warm water. Remove and discard seeds. Add pods to beans.
Tomatoes, canned	2 qt	Add tomatoes, onions, and seasonings.
Onions, sliced	8 oz	Cook slowly in kettle for an additional 2 hours, or pour into a
Garlic cloves, chopped	2	12 × 20 × 4-inch baking pan and bake at 300°F for
Salt	1 oz (1½ Tbsp)	2–3 hours.
Black pepper	1 Tbsp	
Cayenne pepper	few grains	

Approximate nutritive values per portion

Calories	Carbohydrate	Protein	Fat	Cholesterol	Sodium	Fiber	Iron
200 kcal	31 g	12 g	4 g	5 mg	364 mg	0.4 g	3 mg

Notes

- If chile peppers are not available, 1 oz chile powder may be substituted.
- Two No. 10 cans red beans may be substituted for dry beans. Reduce baking time to 1–2 hours.

BAKED BEANS

Yield: 50 portions or 1 pan, 12 × 20 × 4 inches   *Portion:* 5 oz
Oven: 350°F   *Bake:* 3–4 hours

Ingredient	Amount	Procedure
Beans, navy or great northern, dried	5 lb AP	Wash beans (p. 771). Add boiling water and let stand 1 hour.
Water, boiling	1½ gal	Cook in same water until tender, about 1 hour. Add more water as necessary.
Salt	4 oz	Add remaining ingredients to beans.
Sugar, brown	6 oz	Pour into one 12 × 20 × 4-inch baking pan.
Dry mustard	1 tsp	Cover and bake at 350°F for 3–4 hours. Add more water if needed during baking.
Vinegar, cider	2 Tbsp	
Molasses	1 cup	Uncover during last 30 minutes of baking.
Catsup	2½ cups	
Bacon, cubed	1 lb	
Onion, chopped	3 oz	

Approximate nutritive values per portion

Calories	Carbohydrate	Protein	Fat	Cholesterol	Sodium	Fiber	Iron
108 kcal	20 g	4 g	1 g	2 mg	1059 mg	2 g	2 mg

Variations

- **Baked Pork and Beans.** Use 2 No. 10 cans pork and beans. Fry 1 lb diced bacon until partially cooked. Add 4 oz chopped onion and cook until onion is tender. Pour off fat. Add bacon and onion to pork and beans. Stir in 1 cup catsup, ¼ cup vinegar, 4 oz brown sugar, and 1 Tbsp prepared mustard. Bake at 350°F for 1–2 hours.
- **Boston Baked Beans.** Omit catsup.
- **Trio Baked Beans.** Fry 2 lb diced bacon until partially cooked. Drain. Steam 1 lb 12 oz frozen lima beans. Add to bacon. Add 8 oz chopped onion, 2 lb 8 oz canned red beans, 2 lb 12 oz pork and beans, ½ cup molasses, 6 oz brown sugar, 3 cups catsup, ¼ cup vinegar, and 1 Tbsp liquid smoke. Mix to blend. Scale into two 12 × 10 × 2-inch counter pans. Bake at 225°F for 3½ hours.

REFRIED BEANS

Yield: 50 portions　　　*Portion:* 4 oz

Ingredient	Amount	Procedure
Pinto beans, dried	5 lb	Wash beans. Add boiling water. Cover and let stand for 1 hour or longer.
Water, boiling	1 gal	Cook beans in the same water until tender, about 1 hour. Add more water if necessary.
		When beans are done, drain, reserving liquid for later step.
		Place cooked beans in mixer bowl and mash thoroughly.
Vegetable oil	1½ cups	Heat oil in frying pan.
Onion, chopped	6 oz	Add chopped onion. Cook until tender.
Chile powder	2 Tbsp	Add seasonings to onion and mix thoroughly.
Garlic powder	1 tsp	Add beef stock and mix well.
Salt	2 tsp	Add mashed beans, mixing until well blended. Turn mixture constantly to keep from burning.
Hot pepper sauce	few drops	Bean liquid in small amounts may be added if mixture becomes too thick.
Beef Stock (p. 738)	1 qt	Cook bean mixture for 45–60 minutes or until dry.

Approximate nutritive values per portion

Calories	Carbohydrate	Protein	Fat	Cholesterol	Sodium	Fiber	Iron
132 kcal	14 g	4 g	7 g	0 mg	528 mg	0.2 g	1 mg

Notes

- Potentially hazardous food. *Food Safety Standards:* Hold food for service at an internal temperature of 135°F or above. Do not mix old product with new. Cool leftover product quickly following time standards and cooling procedures on p. 167. Reheat leftover product quickly (within 2 hours) to 165°F or above. Reheat product only once; discard if not used.
- 10 lb canned pinto beans may be substituted for dried beans. Drain beans and reserve liquid.

Variation

- **Spicy Black Beans.** Use 3 lb dried black beans. Combine 1½ lb beans and 1½ qt water in each of two 12 × 10 × 4-inch pans. Into each pan measure 1 Tbsp cumin, 1 tsp garlic powder, 1 tsp salt, and 1½ Tbsp chile powder. Stir into the beans. Steam for 50–60 minutes or until beans are tender but not mushy. Beans may also be cooked with seasonings in steam-jacketed kettle.

SEASONED FRESH BEETS

Yield: 50 portions   *Portion:* 3 oz

Ingredient	Amount	Procedure
Fresh beets	14 lb AP (11 lb EP)	Cut off all but 2 inches of the beet tops. Wash beets and leave whole, with root ends attached. Boil or steam until tender (p. 770). Drain. Run cold water over beets. Slip off skins and remove root ends. Slice, dice, or cut into shoestring pieces.
Margarine, melted Salt	4 oz 1 oz (1½ Tbsp)	Pour margarine over cooked beets and sprinkle with salt. Heat to serving temperature.

Approximate nutritive values per portion

Calories	Carbohydrate	Protein	Fat	Cholesterol	Sodium	Fiber	Iron
61 kcal	0 g	2 g	2 g	0 mg	290 mg	0 g	1 mg

Notes

- For canned beets, use 2 No. 10 cans. See p. 771 for heating directions.
- Seasonings for beets: allspice, bay leaves, caraway seed, cloves, dill, ginger, mint, marjoram, mustard seed, basil, nutmeg, onion, orange, sour cream, vinegar.

Variations

- **Beets in Sour Cream.** Grate fresh cooked beets and season with a mixture of 1½ cups lemon juice, 1½ Tbsp onion juice, 2 tsp salt, and 10 oz sugar. Toss lightly. Serve with a spoonful of sour cream on each portion.
- **Julienne Beets.** Cut 8 lb cooked beets into julienne strips. Season with a mixture of 4 oz margarine, 4 oz sugar, 4 tsp salt, and 1 cup lemon juice.
- **Pickled Beets.** See p. 639.
- **Roasted Beets.** Choose small beets. Preheat oven to 400°F. Trim off beet tops, leaving 1 inch of stem. Scrub beets to remove dirt. Put beets in a baking pan in a single layer. Roast until tender, approximately 1 hour. Remove beets from oven. Cool for 30 minutes. Cut off top and root end. Peel. Heat before serving. Season with plain or flavored butter.

HARVARD BEETS

Yield: 50 portions   *Portion:* 3 oz

Ingredient	Amount	Procedure
Beets, sliced or diced	2 No. 10 cans	Drain beets. Reserve juice for sauce.
Bay leaf Cloves, whole Beet juice	1 1 tsp 1½ qt	Add bay leaf and cloves to beet juice. Heat to boiling point. Remove bay leaf.
Sugar, granulated Salt Cornstarch	12 oz 1 oz (1½ Tbsp) 6 oz	Combine dry ingredients. Add to beet juice while stirring briskly. Cook until thickened and clear.
Margarine Vinegar, cider	4 oz 2 cups	Add margarine and vinegar. Stir until mixed and margarine is melted. Heat beets. Add sauce.

Approximate nutritive values per portion

Calories	Carbohydrate	Protein	Fat	Cholesterol	Sodium	Fiber	Iron
92 kcal	19 g	1 g	2 g	0 mg	272 mg	2 g	1 mg

Note

- For fresh beets, use 10 lb EP (13 lb AP). See p. 770 for cooking procedure.

Variations

- **Beets with Orange Sauce.** Omit bay leaf, cloves, and vinegar. Add 2 cups orange juice and ½ cup lemon juice.
- **Hot Spiced Beets.** Drain juice from 2 No. 10 cans sliced beets and add 1 Tbsp whole cloves, 1½ Tbsp salt, ½ tsp cinnamon, 1 lb brown sugar, 8 oz granulated sugar, and 1 qt cider vinegar. Cook for 10 minutes. Pour sauce over beets and heat to serving temperature.

SEASONED BROCCOLI

Yield: 50 portions   *Portion:* 3 oz

Ingredient	Amount	Procedure
Fresh broccoli	16–20 lb AP (10 lb EP)	Wash broccoli and remove outer leaves and tough part of stalks. Cut broccoli stalks lengthwise into uniform spears, following branching lines. Steam or boil broccoli spears (p. 770).
Margarine, melted Salt	4 oz 1 oz (1½ Tbsp)	Pour margarine over cooked broccoli and sprinkle with salt. If boiling the broccoli, add salt to cooking water.

Approximate nutritive values per portion

Calories	Carbohydrate	Protein	Fat	Cholesterol	Sodium	Fiber	Iron
42 kcal	5 g	3 g	2 g	0 mg	238 mg	3 g	1 mg

Notes

- For frozen broccoli, use 12 lb spears or 10 lb chopped.
- Seasonings for broccoli: caraway, dill, mustard seed, tarragon, lemon, almond, oregano, pimento, onion butter.

Variations

- **Almond Buttered Broccoli.** Brown slivered almonds in margarine and pour over cooked, drained broccoli.
- **Broccoli with Cheese Sauce.** Prepare 2 qt Cheese Sauce (p. 683). Serve 2 Tbsp (1 oz) sauce over each portion of cooked broccoli.
- **Broccoli with Hollandaise Sauce or Lemon Butter.** Serve cooked spears or chopped broccoli with 1 Tbsp Hollandaise Sauce (p. 698) or 1 tsp Lemon Butter (p. 720).

SEASONED BRUSSELS SPROUTS

Yield: 50 portions   *Portion:* 3 oz

Ingredient	Amount	Procedure
Fresh Brussels sprouts	14 lb AP (11 lb EP)	Trim stem end of brussels sprouts. Discard wilted outside leaves. Steam or boil (p. 770) until just tender.
Margarine, melted Salt	4 oz 1 oz (1½ Tbsp)	Pour margarine over brussels sprouts and sprinkle with salt. If boiling the vegetable, add salt to the cooking water.

Approximate nutritive values per portion

Calories	Carbohydrate	Protein	Fat	Cholesterol	Sodium	Fiber	Iron
55 kcal	9 g	3 g	2 g	0 mg	234 mg	4 g	1 mg

Note

- Seasonings for brussels sprouts: dill, celery seed, fennel, lemon.

SEASONED CABBAGE

Yield: 50 portions   *Portion:* 3 oz

Ingredient	Amount	Procedure
Fresh cabbage	14 lb AP (12 lb EP)	Remove wilted outer leaves and wash cabbage. Crisp in cold water if wilted. Cut into wedges and remove center core, or shred coarsely. Steam or boil (p. 770). Drain.
Margarine, melted Salt	4 oz 1 oz (1½ Tbsp)	Pour margarine over cabbage and sprinkle with salt. If boiling cabbage, add salt to the cooking water.

Approximate nutritive values per portion

Calories	Carbohydrate	Protein	Fat	Cholesterol	Sodium	Fiber	Iron
42 kcal	6 g	1 g	2 g	0 mg	233 mg	2 g	0.5 mg

Note

- Seasonings for cabbage: basil, caraway seed, celery seed, curry powder, dill, nutmeg.

Variations

- **Cabbage au Gratin.** Reduce cabbage to 7 lb. Alternate layers of cooked coarsely shredded cabbage, white sauce, and grated sharp cheese in a 12 × 20 × 2-inch baking pan. (Use 2½ qt white sauce and 1 lb cheddar cheese.) Combine 6 oz bread crumbs and 3 oz melted margarine and sprinkle on top. Bake at 350°F for about 25 minutes.
- **Cabbage Polonaise.** Arrange cabbage wedges, partially cooked, in baking pans. Cover with 3 qt medium white sauce. Sprinkle with buttered bread crumbs. Bake at 350°F for about 25 minutes.
- **Creamed Cabbage.** Omit margarine. Pour 2 qt medium white sauce over shredded, cooked, drained cabbage.
- **Scalloped Cabbage.** Omit margarine or butter. Pour 2 qt medium white sauce over chopped, cooked, drained cabbage. Cover with buttered crumbs. Bake at 400°F for 15–20 minutes. Shredded cheese may be added.
- **Stir-Fried Cabbage.** Melt 6 oz margarine in frying pan. Add 6 lb EP (7 lb AP) shredded cabbage, 12 oz sliced onions, and 12 oz diagonally sliced celery. Stir gently while cooking for 6–10 minutes. Just before serving, add 4 lb fresh tomatoes, diced in ½-inch cubes.

HOT CABBAGE SLAW

Yield: 50 portions or 1¼ gal   *Portion:* 3 oz

Ingredient	Amount	Procedure
Fresh cabbage	7 lb 8 oz AP (6 lb EP)	Remove outside leaves and wash cabbage. Shred coarsely.
Sugar, granulated Salt Flour, all-purpose Dry mustard	12 oz 2 tsp 3 oz 1 tsp	Mix dry ingredients in a saucepan or kettle.
Milk, hot Water, hot	2½ cups 3 cups	Add milk and water while stirring. Cook until thickened.
Eggs, beaten Vinegar, cider, hot	5 (9 oz) 1½ cups	Add eggs gradually while stirring briskly. Cook for 2–3 minutes. Add vinegar.
Celery seed	2½ tsp	Pour hot sauce over cabbage just before serving. Add celery seed and mix lightly.

Approximate nutritive values per portion

Calories	Carbohydrate	Protein	Fat	Cholesterol	Sodium	Fiber	Iron
61 kcal	12 g	2 g	1 g	23 mg	110 mg	1 g	0.5 mg

PARSLEY BUTTERED CARROTS

Yield: 50 portions   *Portion:* 3 oz

Ingredient	Amount	Procedure
Fresh carrots	14 lb AP (10 lb EP)	Wash, trim, and peel carrots. Cut into desired shapes (slices, strips, cubes, or quarters). Steam or boil until just tender (p. 770).
Margarine, melted Salt Fresh parsley, chopped	4 oz 1 oz (1½ Tbsp) 1 oz	Pour margarine over carrots and sprinkle with salt and parsley. If boiling carrots, add salt to the cooking water.

Approximate nutritive values per portion

Calories	Carbohydrate	Protein	Fat	Cholesterol	Sodium	Fiber	Iron
56 kcal	9 g	1 g	2 g	0 mg	245 mg	2 g	0.5 mg

Note

- Seasonings for carrots: allspice, basil, caraway seed, cloves, cumin, curry powder, dill, fennel, ginger, mace, marjoram, mint, nutmeg, thyme, parsley.

Variations

- **Candied Carrots.** Cut carrots into 1-inch pieces. Cook until tender but not soft. Melt 8 oz margarine. Add 8 oz sugar and 1½ tsp salt. Add to carrots. Bake at 400°F for 15–20 minutes. Turn frequently. Carrots may be prepared using a skillet instead of the oven. Melt butter, sugar, and salt in a skillet. Add carrots and cook until slightly browned and glazed.
- **Candied Carrots and Parsnips.** Use half carrots and half parsnips. Cook as for Candied Carrots. Season lightly with ground ginger.
- **Glazed Parsnips.** Peel parsnips. If parsnip cores are hard and woody, remove the core. Cut in strips and proceed as for Candied Carrots.
- **Lyonnaise Carrots.** Arrange cooked carrot strips in baking pan. Add 3 lb chopped onion that has been cooked until tender in 4 oz margarine. Bake at 350°F for 10–15 minutes or until vegetables are lightly browned. Just before serving, sprinkle with chopped parsley.
- **Marinated Carrots.** See p. 605.
- **Mint-Glazed Carrots.** Cut carrots into quarters lengthwise. Cook until almost tender. Drain. Melt 8 oz margarine, 8 oz sugar, 1½ tsp salt, and 1 cup mint jelly. Blend. Add carrots and simmer for 5–10 minutes.
- **Savory Carrots.** Cook carrots in beef or chicken stock. When done, season with 4 oz melted margarine, salt and pepper, and ¼ cup lemon juice. Sprinkle with chopped parsley.
- **Sweet-Sour Carrots.** Add to cooked carrots a sauce made of 1½ qt vinegar, 2 lb 4 oz sugar, 2 Tbsp salt, and 12 oz melted margarine. Bake at 350°F for 15–20 minutes, or simmer until carrots and sauce are thoroughly heated.

CAULIFLOWER AND POTATO CURRY

Yield: 50 portions   *Portion:* 4 oz

Ingredient	Amount	Procedure
Salad oil	½ cup	Heat oil in steam-jacketed or other kettle.
Yukon gold potatoes, peeled, 1½-inch dice	5 lb 6 oz EP	Add potatoes to kettle. Stir to coat with oil. Cook for 5–10 minutes, stirring frequently, until potatoes just begin to soften.
Water	3½ cups	Add water. Cover and cook for 3 minutes. Turn off heat. Reserve for later step.
Salad oil	¼ cup	Over medium-high heat in a separate pan, heat oil.
Anise seed	¼ tsp	Add seasonings and cook for 1 minute.
Cloves, ground	⅛ tsp	
Cardamom, ground	½ tsp	
Cinnamon sticks, broken into 1-inch lengths	12 inches	
Bay leaves	4	
Onions, finely chopped	1 lb	Add onions to spice mixture. Cook for 1–2 minutes.
Diced tomatoes, canned	1 lb	Add tomatoes, garlic, ginger, sugar, and salt to onions. Cook until onions are translucent.
Garlic, minced	2½ Tbsp	
Fresh ginger, minced	5 Tbsp	
Sugar, granulated	¼ cup	
Salt	2 Tbsp	
Water	2½ cups	Add onion to seasoning-oil mixture. Cook for 1–2 minutes.
Ground red pepper	4 tsp	Add pepper and turmeric to tomato-onion mixture. Stir to blend. Cook for 3 minutes.
Turmeric, ground	¼ tsp	Add tomato-onion mixture and potatoes reserved from earlier step to kettle.
Cauliflower florets	4 lb 6 oz	Add cauliflower and water. Bring to a boil. Cook uncovered for approximately 15 minutes, until liquid is reduced and cauliflower and potatoes are tender. Stir frequently, being careful to not break up the potatoes and cauliflower. Remove cinnamon sticks and bay leaves before serving.
Water	3 cups	

Approximate nutritive values per portion

Calories	Carbohydrate	Protein	Fat	Cholesterol	Sodium	Fiber	Iron
135 kcal	28 g	3 g	4 g	0 mg	258 mg	13 g	7 mg

Notes

- Potentially hazardous food. *Food Safety Standards:* Hold food for service at an internal temperature of 135°F or above. Do not mix old product with new. Cool leftover product quickly following time standards and cooling procedures on p. 167. Reheat leftover product quickly (within 2 hours) to 165°F or above. Reheat product only once; discard if not used.
- 12 inches of cinnamon sticks is equal to approximately ¾ oz.

Variation

- **Cauliflower and Potato Curry on Rice.** Serve 4 oz Cauliflower and Potato Curry on or alongside 4 oz cooked rice.

CELERY AND CARROTS AMANDINE

Yield: 50 portions   *Portion:* 3 oz

Ingredient	Amount	Procedure
Celery	7 lb AP (5 lb EP)	Wash and trim celery. Cut into diagonal slices. Steam or boil (p. 770). Sprinkle with salt. If boiling the celery, add salt to cooking water.
Salt	2 tsp	
Fresh carrots	7 lb AP (5 lb EP)	Wash and peel carrots. Cut into strips. Steam or boil until tender-crisp. Drain. Sprinkle with salt. If boiling the carrots, add salt to the cooking water.
Salt	2 tsp	
Margarine	8 oz	Heat margarine in frying pan.
Almonds, blanched, slivered	8 oz	Add almonds and brown lightly.
Fresh lemon juice	⅓ cup	Remove almonds from heat. Add juice. Combine vegetables. Pour almond mixture over and stir carefully to mix seasoning with vegetables.

Approximate nutritive values per portion

Calories	Carbohydrate	Protein	Fat	Cholesterol	Sodium	Fiber	Iron
86 kcal	7 g	2 g	6 g	0 mg	269 mg	2 g	0.5 mg

Note

- Seasonings for celery: fresh basil, parsley, thyme.

Variation

- **Creole Celery.** Cook 5 lb diced celery until partially done. Add 1 lb chopped onion and 4 oz chopped green bell pepper that have been sautéed in 6 oz margarine. Add 2 No. 10 cans tomatoes and 1½ tsp salt. Cook until tender.

SEASONED CAULIFLOWER

Yield: 50 portions   *Portion:* 3 oz

Ingredient	Amount	Procedure
Fresh cauliflower	16 lb AP (10 lb EP)	Wash cauliflower. Remove outer leaves and woody stem. Break into florets. Steam or boil cauliflower (p. 770).
Margarine, melted	4 oz	Pour margarine over cooked cauliflower and sprinkle with salt. If boiling the cauliflower, add salt to the cooking water.
Salt	1 oz (1½ Tbsp)	

Approximate nutritive values per portion

Calories	Carbohydrate	Protein	Fat	Cholesterol	Sodium	Fiber	Iron
49 kcal	6 g	3 g	2 g	0 mg	239 mg	0 g	0.5 mg

Note

- Seasonings for cauliflower: caraway seed, celery salt, dill, mace, tarragon, buttered crumbs, cheese, lemon juice.

Variations

- **Cauliflower with Almond Butter.** Season freshly cooked cauliflower with 12 oz slivered almonds that have been browned in 8 oz margarine.
- **Cauliflower with Cheese Sauce.** Pour 3 qt Cheese Sauce (p. 683) over cooked fresh cauliflower.
- **Cauliflower with Peas.** Combine 6 lb freshly cooked cauliflower with 4 lb cooked frozen peas. Season with 4 oz melted margarine.
- **Creamed Cauliflower.** Pour 3 qt white sauce over cooked cauliflower.
- **French-Fried Cauliflower.** See p. 794.

SEASONED WHOLE KERNEL CORN

Yield: 50 portions   *Portion:* 3 oz

Ingredient	Amount	Procedure
Corn, whole kernel, frozen	10 lb	Steam or boil corn (p. 770). Do not add salt until after cooking to prevent toughening and discoloring of corn kernels.
Margarine, melted Salt	4 oz 1 oz (1½ Tbsp)	Pour margarine over corn. Stir in salt.

Approximate nutritive values per portion

Calories	Carbohydrate	Protein	Fat	Cholesterol	Sodium	Fiber	Iron
90 kcal	19 g	3 g	2 g	0 mg	218 mg	2 g	0.5 mg

Notes

- Seasonings for corn: cilantro, curry, green pepper, rosemary, savory, thyme.
- For canned corn, use 2 No. 10 cans. See p. 771 for heating instructions.

Variations

- **Corn in Cream.** Add 1¼ qt half-and-half, 6 oz margarine or butter, 1½ Tbsp salt, and 1 Tbsp white pepper to cooked corn. Bring just to boiling point and serve immediately.
- **Corn O'Brien.** Add 1 lb chopped bacon, 12 oz chopped green bell pepper, and 12 oz chopped onion that have been cooked together. Just before serving, add 3 oz chopped pimento, salt, and pepper.
- **Creamed Whole-Kernel Corn.** Combine 2 cups whipping cream, 2 oz granulated sugar, and 1 oz (1½ Tbsp) salt. Bring to a boil. Add 1 cup whipping cream and 1½ oz cornstarch that have been mixed with a wire whip until smooth. Stir and cook until thick and bubbly. Cook for 2 minutes longer. Stir into 10 lb cooked frozen whole-kernel corn.

SCALLOPED CORN

Yield: 50 portions or 2 pans, 12 × 20 × 2 inches   *Portion:* 4 oz
Oven: 350°F   *Bake:* 35–40 minutes

Ingredient	Amount	Procedure
Corn, cream style Milk Salt Black pepper	2 No. 10 cans 1 qt 1 Tbsp ½ tsp	Mix corn, milk, and seasonings.
Cracker crumbs Margarine, melted	14 oz 12 oz	Combine crumbs and margarine. Place alternate layers of buttered crumbs and corn mixture in two 12 × 20 × 2-inch baking pans. Bake at 350°F for 35–40 minutes.

Approximate nutritive values per portion

Calories	Carbohydrate	Protein	Fat	Cholesterol	Sodium	Fiber	Iron
180 kcal	28 g	4 g	8 g	3 mg	641 mg	1 g	1 mg

Note

- 6 oz chopped green bell pepper and 6 oz chopped pimento may be added.

CORN PUDDING

Yield: 50 portions or 2 pans, 12 × 20 × 2 inches   *Portion:* 5 oz
Oven: 325°F   *Bake:* 40–45 minutes

Ingredient	Amount	Procedure
Corn, whole kernel, frozen	9 lb	Thaw corn.
Egg yolks, beaten	24 (1 lb)	Combine corn and all ingredients except egg whites.
Milk	3 qt	
Margarine, melted	6 oz	
Salt	2 Tbsp	
White pepper	1 tsp	
Egg whites	24 (1 lb 10 oz)	Beat egg whites until stiff but not dry. Fold into corn mixture. Pour into two 12 × 20 × 2-inch baking pans. Place in pans of hot water. Bake at 325°F for approximately 40–45 minutes or until internal temperature reaches 180°F.

Approximate nutritive values per portion

Calories	Carbohydrate	Protein	Fat	Cholesterol	Sodium	Fiber	Iron
398 kcal	64 g	13 g	11 g	124 mg	373 mg	9 g	3 mg

Note

- Potentially hazardous food. *Food Safety Standards:* Hold food for service at an internal temperature of 135°F or above. Do not mix old product with new. Cool leftover product quickly following time standards and cooling procedures on p. 167. Reheat leftover product quickly (within 2 hours) to 165°F or above. Reheat product only once; discard if not used.

BAKED EGGPLANT

Yield: 50 portions   *Portion:* 3 oz
Oven: 375°F   *Bake:* 30 minutes

Ingredient	Amount	Procedure
Eggplant	12 lb AP (10 lb EP)	Peel eggplant and cut into ½-inch slices. Sprinkle with salt and let stand for 30 minutes. Rinse, drain, and pat dry with paper towels.
Eggs, beaten Milk	6 (10 oz) 2 cups	Combine beaten eggs and milk.
Flour, all-purpose Bread crumbs	1 lb 1 lb 8 oz	Dip eggplant slices in flour, then in egg mixture. Roll in crumbs.
Margarine, melted	8 oz	Place on greased baking sheets. Sprinkle with melted margarine. Bake at 375°F for 30 minutes.

Approximate nutritive values per portion

Calories	Carbohydrate	Protein	Fat	Cholesterol	Sodium	Fiber	Iron
157 kcal	23 g	4 g	6 g	25 mg	158 mg	1 g	1 mg

Note

- Seasonings for eggplant: basil, garlic, marjoram, onion, oregano, cheese, tomato, parsley.

Variations

- **Eggplant Parmesan.** Prepare Italian Tomato Sauce (p. 691). Prepare 10 lb AP eggplant (yield: 8 lb EP) and cook as directed for Baked Eggplant. (Frozen eggplant cutlets may be substituted for fresh eggplant.) Cheeses needed: 5 lb shredded mozzarella and 1 lb 4 oz grated Parmesan. Layer eggplant, sauce, and cheeses as follows into each of four 12 × 10 × 2-inch baking pans:
  1½ cups sauce
  1 lb cooked eggplant cutlets
  8 oz shredded mozzarella cheese
  2 oz Parmesan cheese
  2½ cups sauce
  1 lb cooked eggplant cutlets
  8 oz shredded mozzarella cheese
  3 oz Parmesan cheese
  2½ cups sauce
  4 oz shredded mozzarella cheese
  Bake at 350°F for 25–30 minutes or until heated through. To serve, cut 4 × 3.
- **Sautéed Eggplant.** Prepare eggplant as in recipe. Sauté in margarine until tender.

GRILLED EGGPLANT PEPERONATA ON GARLIC BASIL FUSILLI

Yield: 50 portions   *Portion:* 2 slices eggplant + 6 oz pasta

Ingredient	Amount	Procedure
Peperonata (p. 796)	50 portions	Prepare peperonata according to recipe on p. 796. Reserve for later step.
Salt	1 Tbsp	Sprinkle salt and pepper on each side of eggplant slices.
Black pepper	2 tsp	Lightly grease tilting or other fry pan. (See Note for Seasoned Oil.)
Eggplant, peeled or unpeeled, sliced ¾ inch thick	14 lb EP	Heat fry pan and place eggplant slices in single layer into pan. Cook for 8–10 minutes until tender but not mushy. Turn once during cooking. Add more oil as needed. Place eggplant in a single layer in a lightly oiled 12 × 20 × 2-inch pan. Portion 1–2 oz peperonata (reserved from earlier step) onto each eggplant slice. Cover and keep warm.
Fusilli	5 lb	Cook pasta according to directions on p. 507. Drain.
Water	5 gal	Pan in 10 × 12 × 4-inch counter pans (6 lb/pan).
Salt	5 oz	
Olive oil	¾ cup	Mix oil, garlic, and basil.
Garlic, minced	1 tsp	Drizzle pasta lightly with seasoned oil, 2 oz per pan. Toss lightly to coat. Keep hot.
Fresh basil, minced	2 tsp	
Parmesan cheese, freshly grated	2 lb	Serve 4 oz pasta on plate with two slices of eggplant on top. When serving eggplant, take care to keep peperonata topping on top of eggplant. Serve eggplant topped with grated cheese.

Approximate nutritive values per portion

Calories	Carbohydrate	Protein	Fat	Cholesterol	Sodium	Fiber	Iron
355 kcal	28 g	19 g	19 g	33 mg	1182 mg	7 g	2 mg

Notes

- Potentially hazardous food. *Food Safety Standards:* Hold food for service at an internal temperature of 135°F or above. Do not mix old product with new. Cool leftover product quickly following time standards and cooling procedures on p. 167. Reheat leftover product quickly (within 2 hours) to 165°F or above. Reheat product only once; discard if not used.
- **Seasoned Oil.** Mix equal parts of Garlic Oil, Olive Oil, and Salad Oil. Add a small amount of dried basil leaves if desired.

Variations

- **Grilled Eggplant Parmesan on Fusilli.** Substitute 12 lb 8 oz cooked fusilli (6 lb 4 oz EP) for soft polenta in Grilled Eggplant Paramesan on Soft Polenta recipe, which follows. Cook fusilli according to directions on p. 507.
- **Grilled Eggplant Parmesan on Soft Polenta.** Coat the bottom of a heavy pan with oil. Sauté 1 lb thinly sliced red onion and 1 oz minced garlic until fragrant and onion begins to soften. Reserve for later step. Cut 14 lb eggplant into ¾ inch rounds. Sprinkle with salt and let stand for 30 minutes. Rinse, drain, and pat dry. Lightly sprinkle pepper on eggplant. Place in a single layer in fry pan or on grill. Sauté for 8–10 minutes until tender but not mushy, turning once. Add oil as needed. Place eggplant in a single layer on oiled pan. Assemble 2 lb shredded mozzarella, 1 qt marinara sauce, and 4 oz shredded Parmesan cheese. Portion a small amount of onion-garlic mixture on top of each slice of eggplant. Sprinkle shredded mozzarella over onion and spoon 1 Tbsp marinara sauce on top. Finish with shredded Parmesan cheese sprinkled on top. Heat in oven just until cheese begins to melt and sauce is hot. To serve, put 4 oz soft polenta on plate, ladle 4 oz sauce on polenta, and place 2 slices of eggplant on top.

CREOLE EGGPLANT

Yield: 50 portions or 2 pans, 12 × 20 × 2 inches   *Portion:* 3 oz
Oven: 350°F   *Bake:* 30 minutes

Ingredient	Amount	Procedure
Eggplant	10 lb AP (8 lb EP)	Peel eggplant and cut into 1-inch cubes. Sprinkle with salt and let stand for 30 minutes.
Salt	2 Tbsp	Rinse and drain.
Water, boiling	1½ gal	Steam or boil (p. 770).
Onion, chopped	1 lb 8 oz	Cook onion, pepper, and celery in margarine until tender.
Green bell pepper, coarsely chopped	12 oz	
Celery, coarsely chopped	1 lb	
Margarine, melted	1 lb	
Diced tomatoes, canned	1 No. 10 can	Combine tomatoes and seasonings with eggplant and other ingredients.
Salt	2 Tbsp	Pour into two 12 × 20 × 2-inch baking pans.
Black pepper	2 tsp	
Sugar, granulated	2 Tbsp	
Bread crumbs	12 oz	Top with buttered crumbs.
Margarine, melted	8 oz	Bake at 350°F for 30 minutes.

Approximate nutritive values per portion

Calories	Carbohydrate	Protein	Fat	Cholesterol	Sodium	Fiber	Iron
166 kcal	15 g	2 g	12 g	0 mg	800 mg	1 g	1 mg

Variation

- **Eggplant Tomato Bake.** Peel eggplant and slice 1 inch thick. Steam or parboil until fork-tender. Place on baking sheets in a single layer. Sprinkle with salt and pepper. Cook 1 lb 8 oz chopped onion and 3 minced garlic cloves in 1½ cups vegetable oil and 12 oz margarine. Add to 5 lb peeled chopped fresh tomatoes, 1 cup chopped fresh parsley, ¼ tsp dried oregano, ½ tsp dried thyme, 1 tsp dried basil, and 1 lb bread crumbs. Pile mixture on individual slices of eggplant. Sprinkle 2 lb grated Swiss cheese over top. Bake at 350°F until eggplant is hot and cheese is melted.

ROASTED PORTABELLA MUSHROOMS

Yield: 50 portions   *Portion:* 1 mushroom
Oven: 375°F   *Bake:* 10–12 minutes

Ingredient	Amount	Procedure
Portabella mushrooms (see Note)	50 (approx. 18 lb)	Clean mushrooms. Dry well. Brush both sides of mushrooms with Balsamic Vinegar Marinade.
Balsamic Vinegar Marinade (p. 724)	1 qt	Place mushrooms gill side down on lightly oiled baking pan. Roast for 10–12 minutes, until tender. After baking, brush mushrooms with marinade.

Notes

- Potentially hazardous food. *Food Safety Standards:* Hold food for service at an internal temperature of 135°F or above. Do not mix old product with new. Cool leftover product quickly following time standards and cooling procedures on p. 167. Reheat leftover product quickly (within 2 hours) to 165°F or above. Reheat product only once; discard if not used.
- The gills from the underside of the mushroom cap may be removed before baking.

Variation

- **Portabella Peperonata on Orzo Pilaf.** Prepare Orzo Pilaf (p. 508) (delete mushrooms). Prepare Peperonata (p. 796). Serve one portabella mushroom on a bed of Orzo Pilaf topped with 2 oz peperonata.

BAKED ONIONS

Yield: 50 portions   *Portion:* one 4-oz onion
Oven: 400°F   *Bake:* 20–30 minutes

Ingredient	Amount	Procedure
Onions, Bermuda or Spanish, 4 oz	50 (15 lb AP)	Peel onions and steam (p. 770) until tender. Place in greased baking pans.
Salt	1 Tbsp	Sprinkle salt and buttered crumbs on onions.
Bread crumbs	8 oz	
Margarine, melted	8 oz	
Chicken or Beef Stock (p. 738)	1 qt	Pour stock around onions. Bake at 400°F for 20–30 minutes.

Approximate nutritive values per portion

Calories	Carbohydrate	Protein	Fat	Cholesterol	Sodium	Fiber	Iron
103 kcal	15 g	2 g	4 g	0 mg	271 mg	2 g	0.5 mg

Notes

- Potentially hazardous food. *Food Safety Standards:* Hold food for service at an internal temperature of 135°F or above. Do not mix old product with new. Cool leftover product quickly following time standards and cooling procedures on p. 167. Reheat leftover product quickly (within 2 hours) to 165°F or above. Reheat product only once; discard if not used.
- Onions may be cut into thick slices.
- Seasonings for onions: basil, caraway seed, marjoram, oregano, rosemary, sage, thyme.

Variations

- **Creamed Pearl Onions.** Cook 12 lb 8 oz small unpeeled white onions (p. 770), then peel. Add 2 qt Medium White Sauce (p. 683) to which 4 oz additional margarine has been added. Garnish with paprika.
- **Glazed Onions.** Mix 1 lb 12 oz brown sugar, 2 cups water, 8 oz margarine, and ½ tsp salt. Pour over cooked onions and bake.
- **Onion Casserole.** Cook 10 lb small pearl onions (p. 770). Combine with 10 oz chopped walnuts, 8 oz pimento strips, and eight 10½-oz cans cream of mushroom or cream of chicken soup. Cover with 6 oz shredded cheddar or Swiss cheese. Bake at 400°F for approximately 30 minutes.

PORTABELLA PEPPER STEAK OVER SOFT POLENTA

Yield: 50 portions   *Portion:* 5 oz mushrooms + 4 oz soft polenta

Ingredient	Amount	Procedure
Portabella mushrooms, stems trimmed (see Note)	3 lb 8 oz	Slice mushrooms into ⅓-inch-thick slices and set aside for a later step.
Olive oil	5 oz	Heat oil to 350°F in a tilting fry pan.
Onions, ½-inch dice	4 lb 5 oz EP	Sauté onions for approximately 2 minutes until translucent.
Green bell peppers, 1-inch squares	3 lb EP	Add peppers and garlic. Sauté for 3–5 minutes or until peppers just begin to soften.
Garlic, minced	8 oz EP	
Soy sauce	10 oz	Add sauces, black pepper, vinegar, tomatoes, and roasted peppers. Mix and heat to 170°F.
Hot pepper sauce	4½ tsp	Add mushrooms reserved from earlier step. Heat to 170°F.
Black pepper	2¾ tsp	Transfer to 12 × 10 × 4-inch pans.
Vinegar, balsamic	4 Tbsp	
Fresh roma tomatoes, chopped	3 lb EP	
Roasted red Peppers (p. 796)	2 lb	
Soft polenta	Recipe p. 577	Serve mushroom mixture over soft polenta. (See Note.)

Approximate nutritive values per portion

Calories	Carbohydrate	Protein	Fat	Cholesterol	Sodium	Fiber	Iron
170 kcal	21.5 g	5 g	7.9 g	0 mg	535 mg	3.7 g	1 mg

Notes

- Potentially hazardous food. *Food Safety Standards:* Hold food for service at an internal temperature of 135°F or above. Do not mix old product with new. Cool leftover product quickly following time standards and cooling procedures on p. 167. Reheat leftover product quickly (within 2 hours) to 165°F or above. Reheat product only once; discard if not used.
- Increase mushrooms to 4 lb if brown gills are removed.
- May be served over a string pasta, rice, or grilled/baked polenta.

Variation

- **Portabella and Peppers over Rice.** Remove the stems and gills from 4 lb portabella mushrooms. Cut mushroom caps into ⅓-inch-thick slices. Heat 5 oz olive oil in tilting fry pan. Sauté 8 oz minced garlic and 4 lb 4 oz diced onion until translucent (about 2 minutes). Add 3 lb bell peppers (combination of green, red, yellow) and cook for 3–5 minutes, until peppers begin to soften. Add 1¼ cup soy sauce, 4 tsp hot pepper sauce (Tabasco), 2 tsp black pepper, 3 lb canned chopped tomatoes, 2 lb roasted red peppers, and 2 oz balsamic vinegar. Serve 4 oz mushrooms over 4 oz rice.

FRENCH-FRIED ONION RINGS

Yield: 50 portions   *Portion:* 3 oz
Deep-fat fryer: 350°F   *Fry:* 3–4 minutes

Ingredient	Amount	Procedure
Onions, large round	10 lb AP (8 lb EP)	Peel onions and cut crosswise into ¼-inch slices. Separate into rings.
Eggs, beaten Milk	6 (10 oz) 2 cups	Combine eggs and milk.
Flour, all-purpose Baking powder Salt	12 oz 2 tsp 1½ tsp	Combine dry ingredients. Add to egg-milk mixture to make a batter. Dip onion rings in batter and fry in deep fat for 3–4 minutes. Drain.

Approximate nutritive values per portion plus frying oil

Calories	Carbohydrate	Protein	Fat	Cholesterol	Sodium	Fiber	Iron
67 kcal	12 g	3 g	1 g	25 mg	90 mg	1 g	0.5 mg

Variations

- **Deep-Fat Fried Bananas.** Cut peeled bananas crosswise into 2-inch pieces. Sprinkle with lemon juice and powdered sugar. Let stand for 30 minutes. Dip in batter and fry at 370°F for 1–3 minutes.
- **French-Fried Cauliflower.** Dip 10 lb cold cooked cauliflower into batter and fry at 370°F for 3–4 minutes.
- **French-Fried Eggplant.** Peel and cut 13 lb AP eggplant as for French-Fried Potatoes (p. 799). Dip in batter and fry at 370°F for 5–7 minutes. Eggplant may be dipped in egg-and-crumb mixture (p. 156) and fried. Eggplant discolors quickly, so it should be placed in cold water if not breaded immediately.
- **French-Fried Mushrooms.** Clean small, uniform-size mushrooms by brushing or rinsing. Do not soak. Dip in batter and fry at 370°F for 4–6 minutes.
- **French-Fried Zucchini Sticks.** Cut unpeeled zucchini squash lengthwise into strips about ½ inch thick. Dip in batter and fry at 370°F for 4–6 minutes.

SEASONED BLACK-EYED PEAS

Yield: 50 portions   *Portion:* 4 oz

Ingredient	Amount	Procedure
Bacon	12 oz	Cut bacon into 1-inch pieces. Cook in a steam-jacketed kettle until crisp.
Onion, chopped Garlic, minced Fresh parsley, chopped Bay leaves Salt Black pepper	5 oz 1 tsp 1 cup 4 1⅓ Tbsp ½ tsp	Add vegetables and seasonings to bacon. Sauté until onion and garlic are fragrant.
Black-eyed peas, frozen	12 lb	Add peas to vegetable mixture.
Water	3½ qt	Add water to barely cover peas. Simmer peas until tender, 45–50 minutes, adding water as necessary. Remove bay leaves before serving.

Approximate nutritive values per portion

Calories	Carbohydrate	Protein	Fat	Cholesterol	Sodium	Fiber	Iron
135 kcal	20.4 g	3.8 g	4.2 g	4.4 mg	232 mg	5.4 g	1 mg

Note

- Potentially hazardous food. *Food Safety Standards:* Hold food for service at an internal temperature of 135°F or above. Do not mix old product with new. Cool leftover product quickly following time standards and cooling procedures on p. 167. Reheat leftover product quickly (within 2 hours) to 165°F or above. Reheat product only once; discard if not used.

SEASONED PEAS

Yield: 50 portions   *Portion:* 3 oz

Ingredient	Amount	Procedure
Peas, frozen	10 lb	Steam or boil peas (p. 770).
Margarine, melted Salt	4 oz 1 oz (1½ Tbsp)	Pour margarine over cooked peas and sprinkle with salt. If boiling the peas, add salt to the cooking water.

Approximate nutritive values per portion

Calories	Carbohydrate	Protein	Fat	Cholesterol	Sodium	Fiber	Iron
87 kcal	13 g	5 g	2 g	0 mg	292 mg	3 g	1 mg

Notes

- If using canned peas, heat 2 No. 10 cans. See p. 771.
- For fresh peas, use 25 lb AP. Shell and rinse. Steam or boil (p. 770).
- Seasonings for peas: basil, dill, marjoram, mint, oregano, rosemary, sage, savory, mushrooms, water chestnuts, onions.

Variations

- **Creamed Peas with New Potatoes.** Combine 7 lb freshly cooked new potatoes and 5 lb cooked frozen peas with 3 qt Medium White Sauce (p. 683).
- **Green Peas and Sliced New Turnips.** Combine 5 lb cooked frozen peas with 3 lb new turnips, sliced and cooked. Add 4 oz melted margarine and salt to taste.
- **Green Peas with Lemon-Mint Butter.** Cream 1 lb butter or margarine, ¼ cup lemon juice, and 1 tsp grated lemon peel. Add ½ cup finely chopped fresh mint. The lemon-mint butter can be made ahead and stored in the refrigerator. When ready to use, melt and pour over hot peas.
- **Green Peas with Mushrooms.** Add 2 lb fresh mushrooms, sliced and sautéed in 8 oz margarine, to 10 lb cooked frozen peas.
- **Green Peas with Pearl Onions.** Combine 7 lb 8 oz cooked frozen peas and 3 lb cooked pearl onions. Add 4 oz melted margarine for buttered or 2 qt Medium White Sauce (p. 683) for creamed.

ROASTED BELL PEPPERS

Yield: 1 lb

Ingredient	Amount	Procedure
Bell peppers, large (see Note)	4	Stem peppers and remove seeds and ribs. Cut in half lengthwise. Flatten peppers slightly. Lay peppers skin side up on foil-lined baking sheet. Broil 4 inches from heat until skins are charred black, 12–15 minutes. Place peppers in a bowl and cover tightly with plastic wrap. Let steam for 15–20 minutes. Peel off charred skin.
Olive oil (optional)	2 Tbsp	Drizzle oil and lemon juice over peppers, if using.
Fresh lemon juice (optional)	2 tsp	Use immediately or refrigerate.
		Serve on sandwiches, in sauces, as a topping for focaccia, and so on.

Notes

- All colors of bell peppers may be roasted. Red, yellow, and orange are often specified in recipes because they remain colorful after roasting.
- Roasted peppers may be kept frozen, and thawed as needed.

PEPERONATA

Yield: 50 portions   *Portion:* 2 oz

Ingredient	Amount	Procedure
Olive oil	8 oz	Heat olive oil in fry pan or steam-jacketed kettle.
Onions, sliced	1 lb EP	Sauté onions until golden and translucent.
Garlic cloves, minced	4	Add garlic and cook until tender, about 3 minutes.
Red bell peppers, julienne strips	1 lb 12 oz EP	Add peppers and cook until just beginning to soften.
Yellow bell peppers, julienne strips	1 lb 12 oz EP	
Chopped tomatoes, canned	1 lb 8 oz	Add tomatoes, vinegar, spices, and parsley.
Vinegar, red wine	½ cup	Cook only until juices evaporate, to 150–160°F. (Note: Peppers should be tender-crisp and brightly colored.)
Salt	1 tsp	Serve as an accompaniment to sandwiches, with pasta, or as a garnish.
Black pepper	1 Tbsp	
Crushed red pepper	¼ tsp	
Fresh parsley, coarsely chopped	1 oz	

Approximate nutritive values per portion

Calories	Carbohydrate	Protein	Fat	Cholesterol	Sodium	Fiber	Iron
55 kcal	3.5 g	0.7 g	5 g	0 mg	76 mg	0.8 g	0.5 mg

Note

- Potentially hazardous food. *Food Safety Standards:* Hold food for service at an internal temperature of 135°F or above. Do not mix old product with new. Cool leftover product quickly following time standards and cooling procedures on p. 167. Reheat leftover product quickly (within 2 hours) to 165°F or above. Reheat product only once; discard if not used.

Variation

- **Caramelized Onions.** Using a covered pan, fry 6 lb fresh sliced onions in 1 cup olive oil on low 200°F heat until reduced in bulk. Uncover and continue cooking on very low heat until onions are browned and dry. Approximate yield 2 lb.

BAKED POTATOES

Yield: 50 portions   *Portion:* 1 potato
Oven: 400°F   *Bake:* 1–1½ hours

Ingredient	Amount	Procedure
Baking potatoes, uniform size	50	Scrub potatoes and remove blemishes.
Shortening	4 oz	Rub or brush lightly with shortening. Place on baking sheets. Bake at 400°F for 1–1½ hours or until tender.

Approximate nutritive values per portion

Calories	Carbohydrate	Protein	Fat	Cholesterol	Sodium	Fiber	Iron
165 kcal	34 g	3 g	2 g	0 mg	8 mg	4 g	0.5 mg

Notes

- Potentially hazardous food. *Food Safety Standards:* Hold food for service at an internal temperature of 135°F or above. Do not mix old product with new. Cool leftover product quickly following time standards and cooling procedures on p. 167. Reheat leftover product quickly (within 2 hours) to 165°F or above. Reheat product only once; discard if not used.
- Select a long, mealy-type potato, such as russet.

Variations

- **Baked Potato with Toppings.** Prepare potatoes and bake (see recipe). Serve with one of the following toppings and one or more of the accompaniments: *Toppings* include Cheese Sauce (p. 683), 3 oz; Chili con Carne (p. 744), 3 oz; Creamed Chicken (p. 491), Ham (p. 470) or Sausage (p. 473), 3 oz; Nacho Sauce (p. 203), 3 oz; sour cream, 1 oz. *Accompaniments* include Guacamole (p. 202), chopped broccoli, shredded cheese, sliced mushrooms, chopped green onions, chopped chives, sliced black olives, chopped ham or chicken, chopped lettuce, chopped tomatoes, crumbled cooked bacon, slivered almonds.
- **Broccoli Cheese-Topped Potato.** See p. 683 for Cheese Broccoli Sauce. Serve over baked potato.
- **Cheese-Topped Potato.** Whip 1 lb softened margarine. Add 2 lb sour cream and mix thoroughly. Fold in 1 lb finely shredded American cheese and 6 oz finely chopped green onions. Serve over baked potato.
- **Stuffed Baked Potato.** Cut hot baked potatoes into halves lengthwise. If potatoes are small, cut a slice from one side. Scoop out contents. Mash and season with 2 Tbsp salt, 1 tsp white pepper, 8 oz melted margarine, and 3–4 cups hot milk. Beat until light and fluffy. Pile lightly into shells, leaving tops rough. Sprinkle with paprika or Parmesan cheese, if desired. Bake at 425°F until potatoes are hot and lightly browned, about 30 minutes.

MASHED POTATOES

Yield: 50 portions   *Portion:* 5 oz

Ingredient	Amount	Procedure
Potatoes	15 lb AP (12 lb EP)	Peel potatoes and remove eyes. Cut into uniform-size pieces. Steam or boil (p. 770). When done, drain and place in mixer bowl. Mash, using the wire whip attachment, on low speed until there are no lumps. Whip on high speed for about 2 minutes.
Milk, hot Margarine Salt	2–2½ qt 8 oz 2 oz (3 Tbsp)	Add hot milk, margarine, and salt. Whip on high speed until light and creamy.

Approximate nutritive values per portion

Calories	Carbohydrate	Protein	Fat	Cholesterol	Sodium	Fiber	Iron
158 kcal	25 g	3 g	5 g	5 mg	451 mg	3 g	0.5 mg

Notes

- Potentially hazardous food. *Food Safety Standards:* Hold food for service at an internal temperature of 135°F or above. Do not mix old product with new. Cool leftover product quickly following time standards and cooling procedures on p. 167. Reheat leftover product quickly (within 2 hours) to 165°F or above. Reheat product only once; discard if not used.
- A low-moisture white potato must be used to produce a fluffy product.
- Potato water may be substituted for part of the milk.
- 8 oz nonfat dry milk and 2–2½ qt water may be substituted for the liquid milk. Sprinkle dry milk over potatoes before mashing.
- Dehydrated potatoes (2–2½ lb) may be substituted for the raw potatoes. Follow processor's instructions for preparation.
- Seasonings for mashed potatoes: chives, dill, garlic, ground horseradish, nutmeg.

Variations

- **Duchess Potatoes.** Add 18 eggs (2 lb), beaten, to mashed potatoes. Add additional milk if necessary. Pile lightly into baking pans. Bake at 350°F for 20–30 minutes, or until set.
- **Mashed Potato Casserole.** Add ½ cup chopped chives; ½ cup crisp, cooked, crumbled bacon; 12 oz cream cheese; 1 tsp white pepper; and ¼ tsp garlic powder. Mix until blended. Place in baking pans. Sprinkle lightly with grated Parmesan cheese and paprika. Brush lightly with melted margarine. Bake at 375°F for 30 minutes or until light brown.
- **Potato Croquettes.** Add 18 egg yolks, well beaten. Shape into croquettes and dip in egg-milk mixture and crumbs (p. 156). Chill. Fry in deep fat at 360°F for 5–8 minutes.
- **Potato Rosettes.** Force Mashed Potatoes through a pastry tube, forming rosettes. Bake at 350°F until lightly browned. Use as a garnish for planked steak.
- **Roasted Garlic Mashed Potatoes.** Add 8 oz roasted garlic (pp. 798, 823) along with the milk and margarine. **Roasted Garlic:** Preheat oven to 350°F. Remove the loose outside skins of the garlic heads by rolling them back and forth on cutting board, being careful not to loosen the cloves. Place garlic heads on a baking sheet. Drizzle ½ tsp olive oil over each head to coat. Roast until tender, about 1 hour. Cool. Cut garlic head horizontally, exposing the soft flesh. Using a table knife, press the softened cloves out of their skins. Drizzle baked garlic pulp with olive oil. Store covered in refrigerator. Use within 48 hours.
- **Whipped Rutabagas and Potatoes.** Peel 10 lb AP rutabagas and 5 lb potatoes. Cut into uniform-size pieces and steam or boil (p. 770). Mash and season as for potatoes. 1 tsp nutmeg may be added.

FRENCH-FRIED POTATOES

Yield: 50 portions *Portion:* 3 oz
Deep-fat fryer: 365°F *Fry:* 6–8 minutes

Ingredient	Amount	Procedure
Potatoes, white	18 lb AP (15 lb EP)	Peel potatoes and cut into uniform strips ¼–⅜ inch thick. Cover with cold water to keep potatoes from darkening.
		Just before frying, drain potatoes and dry with paper towels. Fill fryer basket about one-third full of potatoes. Fry according to Method 1 or 2.

METHOD 1

Half-fill fryer with fat. Preheat to 365°F. Fry potatoes for 6–8 minutes. Drain. Sprinkle with salt. Serve immediately.

METHOD 2

Blanching: Heat fat to 360°F. Place drained potato strips in hot fat, using an 8-to-1 ratio of fat to potatoes, by weight, as a guide for filling fryer basket. Fry for 3–5 minutes depending on thickness of potato. (The potatoes should not brown.) Drain. Turn out on sheet pans. Refrigerate for later browning.

Browning: Reheat fat to 375°F. Place about twice as many potato strips in the kettle as for first-stage frying. Fry for 2–3 minutes or until golden brown. Drain. Sprinkle with salt if desired. Serve immediately.

Approximate nutritive values per portion

Calories	Carbohydrate	Protein	Fat	Cholesterol	Sodium	Fiber	Iron
269 kcal	34 g	3 g	14 g	0 mg	184 mg	0 g	0.5 mg

Notes

- Select a long, mealy potato, such as a russet.
- To cook frozen French-Fried Potatoes, use 12 lb for 50 3-oz portions. Fry at 375°F for 3–5 minutes or until golden brown.

Variations

- **Deep-Fat Browned Potatoes.** Partially cook peeled whole or half potatoes. Fry in deep fat at 365°F for 5–7 minutes. Transfer to serving pan. Sprinkle with salt.
- **Lattice Potatoes.** Cut potatoes with lattice slicer. Fry at 365°F for 3–6 minutes. Transfer to serving pan. Sprinkle with salt.
- **Potato Chips.** Cut potatoes into very thin slices. Fry at 365°F for 3–6 minutes. Transfer to serving pan. Sprinkle with salt.
- **Shoestring Potatoes.** Cut potatoes into ⅛-inch-thick strips. Fry at 365°F for 3–6 minutes. Transfer to serving pan. Sprinkle with salt.

PARSLEY BUTTERED NEW POTATOES

Yield: 50 portions   *Portion:* 3 oz

Ingredient	Amount	Procedure
New potatoes	15 lb AP (10 lb EP)	Wash and peel potatoes and remove eyes (see Note).
Salt	1 oz (1½ Tbsp)	Cut potatoes into 1½-inch cubes or leave whole. If whole potatoes, cut as necessary to be of uniform size. Sprinkle with salt. If boiling the potatoes, add salt to the cooking water. Steam or boil (p. 770) until tender.
Margarine, melted	8 oz	Distribute margarine uniformly over cooked potatoes.
Fresh parsley, chopped	1 oz	Sprinkle with parsley.

Approximate nutritive values per portion

Calories	Carbohydrate	Protein	Fat	Cholesterol	Sodium	Fiber	Iron
104 kcal	17 g	1 g	4 g	0 mg	239 mg	0 g	0.5 mg

Note

- New potatoes may be peeled after cooking. If skins are thin they may be served unpeeled.

Variations

- **Creamed New Potatoes.** Add 3 qt Medium White Sauce (p. 683) to cooked potatoes.
- **Creamed New Potatoes and Peas.** See p. 795.
- **Lemon-Seasoned New Potatoes.** Peel and cook uniform, small new potatoes. Pour a mixture of ¼ cup lemon juice and 8 oz melted margarine over them, then roll in minced parsley.
- **New Potatoes in Mustard.** Add ¾ cup Dijon mustard and 2 Tbsp dried chervil to the melted margarine.
- **New Potatoes Parmesan.** Scrub small uniform-size new potatoes. Remove 1 inch of peel from around the center of each potato. Steam or boil (p. 770) until just done. Roll potatoes in melted butter or margarine. Place in baking pans. Sprinkle with Parmesan cheese. Bake at 350°F for 20–25 minutes. Canned small whole potatoes may be substituted for fresh potatoes.
- **Paprika-Seasoned New Potatoes.** Delete parsley. Sprinkle potatoes with 1 Tbsp paprika. Stir lightly to mix seasoning.

ROASTED RED-SKINNED POTATOES

Yield: 50 portions   *Portion:* 5 oz
Oven: 400°F   *Bake:* 30–35 minutes

Ingredient	Amount	Procedure
Red-skinned potatoes, unpeeled, cut into irregular 2-inch chunks, or left whole if small	17 lb EP	Place potatoes in large bowl.
Olive oil	1 lb 8 oz	Pour olive oil over potatoes. Stir to coat. Drain excess oil from potatoes.
Salt Black pepper Garlic, minced (optional)	2 oz 1 Tbsp 1 oz EP	Sprinkle salt, pepper, and garlic, if using, over potatoes. Stir to coat. Spread potatoes in a single layer on oiled baking sheets. Roast potatoes at 400°F until tender and golden brown, 30–35 minutes.

Approximate nutritive values per portion

Calories	Carbohydrate	Protein	Fat	Cholesterol	Sodium	Fiber	Iron
230 kcal	28 g	1.9 g	14 g	0 mg	495 mg	1.9 g	0 mg

Notes

- Potentially hazardous food. *Food Safety Standards:* Hold food for service at an internal temperature of 135°F or above. Do not mix old product with new. Cool leftover product quickly following time standards and cooling procedures on p. 167. Reheat leftover product quickly (within 2 hours) to 165°F or above. Reheat product only once; discard if not used.
- Sliced potatoes (³⁄₈ inch-thick) may be used. Reduce cooking time to 20–25 minutes.

Variations

- **Oven-Roasted Sweet Potatoes with Soy Sauce.** Substitute peanut oil for olive oil and sweet potatoes for red potatoes. Delete garlic. Take sweet potatoes out of the oven after 30 minutes and drizzle with ¹⁄₃ cup soy sauce. Roast for an additional 5 minutes or until tender. Serve sprinkled with 8 oz toasted almonds and 1 oz coarsely chopped fresh parsley.
- **Roasted New Potatoes.** Substitute whole new potatoes for red-skinned potatoes.
- **Rosemary Roasted Potatoes.** Delete garlic if desired. Sprinkle ¹⁄₂ oz finely minced fresh rosemary on potatoes along with the salt and pepper. Garnish with fresh sprigs of rosemary. May substitute Yukon Gold or other yellow potato.

AU GRATIN POTATOES

Yield: 50 portions or 2 pans, 12 × 10 × 2 inches   *Portion:* 5 oz
Oven: 350°F   *Bake:* 25–30 minutes

Ingredient	Amount	Procedure
Potatoes	10 lb AP (8 lb EP)	Peel and dice potatoes.
Salt	1 Tbsp	Steam or boil (p. 770) until just tender.
		Sprinkle with salt. If boiling the potatoes, add salt to the cooking water.
Margarine	12 oz	Melt margarine. Add flour and salt.
Flour, all-purpose	6 oz	Stir until smooth. Cook for 5–10 minutes.
Salt	1 Tbsp	
Milk	3 qt	Add milk gradually while stirring.
		Cook until thickened.
Cheddar cheese, shredded	1 lb 8 oz	Add cheese to sauce and stir until cheese is melted.
		Pour over potatoes.
		Scale into two 12 × 20 × 2-inch baking pans, 8 lb per pan.
Bread crumbs	12 oz	Combine crumbs and margarine.
Margarine, melted	8 oz	Sprinkle over top of potatoes, 10 oz per pan.
		Bake at 350°F for 25–30 minutes.

Approximate nutritive values per portion

Calories	Carbohydrate	Protein	Fat	Cholesterol	Sodium	Fiber	Iron
279 kcal	26 g	8 g	16 g	22 mg	530 mg	2 g	1 mg

Notes

- Potentially hazardous food. *Food Safety Standards:* Hold food for service at an internal temperature of 135°F or above. Do not mix old product with new. Cool leftover product quickly following time standards and cooling procedures on p. 167. Reheat leftover product quickly (within 2 hours) to 165°F or above. Reheat product only once; discard if not used.
- 1 lb 10 oz sliced dehydrated potatoes, reconstituted in 5 qt boiling water, and 1½ oz salt may be substituted for fresh potatoes.

COTTAGE FRIED POTATOES

Yield: 50 portions   *Portion:* 4 oz

Ingredient	Amount	Procedure
Potatoes	18 lb AP (15 lb EP)	Peel potatoes. Steam or boil until tender (p. 770).
Fat, hot Salt Black pepper	as needed 1 oz (1½ Tbsp) 1 tsp	Slice cooked potatoes. Add to hot fat in frying pan. Add salt and pepper. Turn potatoes as needed and fry until browned.

Approximate nutritive values per portion

Calories	Carbohydrate	Protein	Fat	Cholesterol	Sodium	Fiber	Iron
192 kcal	29 g	3 g	7 g	0 mg	285 mg	3 g	0.5 mg

Variations

- **American Fried Potatoes.** Add raw sliced potatoes to hot fat. Fry until potatoes are brown and tender. Add additional fat as needed.
- **Hashed Brown Potatoes.** Add finely chopped boiled potatoes to hot fat in frying pan. Add salt and pepper. Stir occasionally and fry until browned.
- **Lyonnaise Potatoes.** Cook 2 lb chopped onion slowly in fat without browning. Add seasoned cut, boiled potatoes and cook until browned.
- **O'Brien Potatoes.** Cook cubed potatoes in a small amount of fat with chopped onion and pimento.
- **Oven-Fried Potatoes.** Prepare potatoes as for French-Fried Potatoes. Place in greased shallow pans in a thin layer and brush with melted fat, turning to cover all sides. Bake at 450°F for 20–30 minutes, or until browned, turning occasionally. Drain on absorbent paper and sprinkle with salt.

POTATO PANCAKES

Yield: 50 portions or 100 cakes   *Portion:* two 2-oz cakes

Ingredient	Amount	Procedure
Potatoes Onions	15 lb AP (12 lb EP) 1 lb 8 oz	Peel potatoes and onions. Grind. Drain.
Eggs, beaten Flour, all-purpose Salt Baking powder Milk	8 (14 oz) 8 oz 2 oz (3 Tbsp) 1 tsp ¾ cup	Combine and add to potatoes and onions. Refrigerate batter, removing small quantities as needed for production.
		Drop potato mixture with No. 20 dipper on hot greased griddle. Fry, turning once, until golden brown on both sides. Serve with warm applesauce.

Approximate nutritive values per portion

Calories	Carbohydrate	Protein	Fat	Cholesterol	Sodium	Fiber	Iron
121 kcal	25 g	3 g	1 g	34 mg	407 mg	0.4 g	0.5 mg

SCALLOPED POTATOES

Yield: 50 portions or 2 pans, 12 × 20 × 2 inches   *Portion:* 6 oz
Oven: 350°F   *Bake:* 1½–2 hours

Ingredient	Amount	Procedure
Potatoes	15 lb AP (12 lb EP)	Peel potatoes and remove eyes. Slice and place in two greased 12 × 20 × 2-inch baking pans, 6 lb per pan.
Salt	2 oz (3 Tbsp)	Sprinkle with salt.
Margarine	8 oz	Melt margarine. Add flour and salt.
Flour, all-purpose	4 oz	Stir until smooth. Cook for 5 minutes.
Salt	1 oz (1½ Tbsp)	
Milk	1 gal	Add milk gradually, stirring with a wire whip. Cook until thickened. Pour over potatoes.
Bread crumbs	6 oz	Combine crumbs and margarine.
Margarine, melted	2 oz	Sprinkle over potatoes. Bake at 350°F for 1½–2 hours.

Approximate nutritive values per portion

Calories	Carbohydrate	Protein	Fat	Cholesterol	Sodium	Fiber	Iron
212 kcal	31 g	5 g	7 g	11 mg	698 mg	3 g	0.5 mg

Notes

- Potentially hazardous food. *Food Safety Standards:* Hold food for service at an internal temperature of 135°F or above. Do not mix old product with new. Cool leftover product quickly following time standards and cooling procedures on p. 167. Reheat leftover product quickly (within 2 hours) to 165°F or above. Reheat product only once; discard if not used.
- Potatoes may be partially cooked and hot White Sauce (p. 683) added to shorten baking time.
- Dehydrated sliced potatoes may be substituted for fresh. Reconstitute according to package directions.

Variations

- **Scalloped Potatoes with Ham.** Add 5 lb cubed ham to White Sauce (p. 683). Reduce salt to 1 Tbsp.
- **Scalloped Potatoes with Onions.** Before baking, cover potatoes with onion rings. About 5 minutes before removing from oven, cover potatoes with shredded cheese.

SOUR CREAM POTATOES

Yield: 50 portions or 3 pans, 12 × 10 × 2 inches   *Portion:* 5 oz
Oven: 350°F   *Bake:* 35–45 minutes

Ingredient	Amount	Procedure
Hashed brown potatoes, frozen	10 lb	Thaw potatoes. Steam for 10–15 minutes. Hold for later step.
Margarine	4 oz	Melt margarine in steam-jacketed or other kettle.
Onions, chopped	1 lb	Add onions and sauté until transparent.
Sour cream	2 lb 12 oz	Add to onions and mix well.
Salt (see Note)	1 oz	
Black pepper	1 Tbsp	
Eggs, beaten slightly	6 (10 oz)	
Chicken base	1 Tbsp	
Water	2 cups	
		Add potatoes to onion mixture. Mix lightly. Scale into three greased 12 × 10 × 2-inch pans, 5 lb 5 oz per pan.
Cornflake crumbs	3 oz	Combine crumbs and margarine in mixer bowl, using a flat paddle.
Margarine, melted	⅓ cup	Mix until crumbly. Sprinkle 2 oz over each pan of potatoes. Bake at 350°F for 35–45 minutes. To serve, spoon into 50 5-oz portions or cut each pan 4 × 4 for 48 servings.

Approximate nutritive values per portion

Calories	Carbohydrate	Protein	Fat	Cholesterol	Sodium	Fiber	Iron
297 kcal	29 g	5 g	19 g	35 mg	381 mg	1 g	2 mg

Notes

- Potentially hazardous food. *Food Safety Standards:* Hold food for service at an internal temperature of 135°F or above. Do not mix old product with new. Cool leftover product quickly following time standards and cooling procedures on p. 167. Reheat leftover product quickly (within 2 hours) to 165°F or above. Reheat product only once; discard if not used.
- Undiluted cream of mushroom, cream of celery, or cream of chicken soup may be substituted for sour cream. Delete salt and chicken base.
- If a highly salted chicken base is used, delete or reduce salt.
- 2 oz (1 cup) dehydrated onions, rehydrated in 1½ cups water, may be substituted for fresh onions.

POTATOES ROMANOFF

Yield: 60 portions or 2 pans, 12 × 20 × 2 inches   *Portion:* 6 oz
Oven: 350°F   *Bake:* 35–45 minutes

Ingredient	Amount	Procedure
Hashed brown potatoes, frozen	16 lb	Thaw potatoes. Steam for 15 minutes.
Sour cream	4 lb 4 oz	Combine in mixer bowl and blend on low speed.
Green onions, sliced	6 oz	
Salt	1½ oz	
Black pepper	1 Tbsp	
Cheddar cheese, shredded	12 oz	
Paprika	½ tsp	Add cooked potatoes to sour cream mixture. Mix well. Scale into two greased 12 × 20 × 2-inch pans, 10 lb per pan. Sprinkle lightly with paprika. Bake uncovered at 350°F for 35–45 minutes. Cut 6 × 5.

Approximate nutritive values per portion

Calories	Carbohydrate	Protein	Fat	Cholesterol	Sodium	Fiber	Iron
356 kcal	36 g	6 g	23 g	20 mg	369 mg	1 g	2 mg

Note

- Potentially hazardous food. *Food Safety Standards:* Hold food for service at an internal temperature of 135°F or above. Do not mix old product with new. Cool leftover product quickly following time standards and cooling procedures on p. 167. Reheat leftover product quickly (within 2 hours) to 165°F or above. Reheat product only once; discard if not used.

OVEN-BROWNED OR RISSOLÉ POTATOES

Yield: 50 portions   *Portion:* 1 potato
Oven: 450°F   *Bake:* 1 hour

Ingredient	Amount	Procedure
Potatoes, baking variety	50	Peel potatoes and partially cook by boiling or steaming, about 10 minutes.
Margarine, melted	1 lb	Place potatoes on well-greased baking sheets.
Salt	1 oz (1½ Tbsp)	Pour margarine over potatoes. Sprinkle with salt. Bake at 450°F for 1 hour or until tender. Baste every 15 minutes with margarine from pan. Turn potatoes once during baking to ensure uniform browning.

Approximate nutritive values per portion

Calories	Carbohydrate	Protein	Fat	Cholesterol	Sodium	Fiber	Iron
210 kcal	34 g	3 g	7 g	0 mg	286 mg	4 g	0.5 mg

Variations

- **Franconia Potatoes.** Cook peeled uniform-size potatoes for approximately 15 minutes. Drain and place in pan in which meat is roasting. Bake approximately 40 minutes or until tender and lightly browned, basting with drippings in pan or turning occasionally to brown all sides. Serve with roast.
- **French Baked Potatoes.** Select small, uniform-size potatoes and peel. Roll potatoes in melted margarine or shortening, then in cracker crumbs or crushed cornflakes. Place in shallow pans and bake.
- **Herbed Potato Bake.** Peel baking potatoes and cut into ½-inch-thick slices. Place in greased baking pans. Combine 1½ cups melted margarine, 3½ oz dehydrated onion soup mix, and 2 Tbsp rosemary. Sprinkle over potatoes and toss lightly. Bake at 325°F for 1½ hours or until potatoes are tender.

GLAZED OR CANDIED SWEET POTATOES

Yield: 50 portions   *Portion:* 4 oz
Oven: 400°F   *Bake:* 20–30 minutes

Ingredient	Amount	Procedure
Sweet potatoes	16 lb AP (13 lb EP)	Scrub potatoes. Steam or boil in skins until tender (p. 770). When potatoes are cool enough to handle, peel and cut into halves lengthwise. Arrange in shallow pans.
Sugar, brown Water Margarine Salt	1 lb 12 oz 2 cups 8 oz ½ tsp	Mix sugar, water, margarine, and salt. Heat to boiling point. Pour over potatoes. Bake at 400°F for 20–30 minutes.

Approximate nutritive values per portion

Calories	Carbohydrate	Protein	Fat	Cholesterol	Sodium	Fiber	Iron
213 kcal	44 g	2 g	4 g	0 mg	82 mg	4 g	1 mg

Notes

- Three No. 10 cans of sweet potatoes may be substituted for fresh sweet potatoes.
- Seasonings for sweet potatoes: allspice, cardamom, cinnamon, cloves, nutmeg.

Variations

- **Baked Sweet Potatoes.** Select small even-size sweet potatoes. Scrub. Bake at 425°F for 40–50 minutes, or until tender.
- **Candied Sweet Potatoes with Almonds.** Proceed as for Glazed Sweet Potatoes. Increase margarine to 12 oz and reduce brown sugar to 1 lb 8 oz. Add 1 cup dark corn syrup and 2 tsp mace. When partially glazed, sprinkle tops with chopped almonds and continue cooking until almonds are toasted.
- **Glazed Sweet Potatoes with Orange Slices.** Add ¼ cup grated orange peel to syrup. Cut 5 oranges into thin slices; add to sweet potatoes when syrup is added.
- **Sweet Potatoes and Apples.** Reduce sweet potatoes to 9 lb, cooked, peeled, and sliced. Peel and slice 5 lb tart apples. Place alternate layers of sweet potatoes and apples in baking pans. Pour hot syrup (see recipe for Glazed Sweet Potatoes) over potatoes and apples. Bake at 350°F for 45 minutes.

WHIPPED SPICED SWEET POTATOES

Yield: 50 portions   *Portion:* 4 oz

Ingredient	Amount	Procedure
Sweet potatoes, peeled and cubed	10 lb EP	Steam or boil sweet potatoes until fork-tender. Drain. Place in mixer bowl. Using a flat paddle, mix until smooth.
Whipping cream Whole milk Butter	½ cup ½ cup 6 oz	Heat cream, milk, and butter. Add to whipped sweet potatoes.
Fresh lime juice Sugar, brown Salt Cinnamon, ground	½ cup 8 oz 1½ tsp 1 Tbsp	Add juice, sugar, and seasonings to sweet potatoes. Mix until combined.

Approximate nutritive values per portion

Calories	Carbohydrate	Protein	Fat	Cholesterol	Sodium	Fiber	Iron
180 kcal	36 g	2 g	4 g	11 mg	163 mg	4 g	1 mg

Notes

- Potentially hazardous food. *Food Safety Standards:* Hold food for service at an internal temperature of 135°F or above. Do not mix old product with new. Cool leftover product quickly following time standards and cooling procedures on p. 167. Reheat leftover product quickly (within 2 hours) to 165°F or above. Reheat product only once; discard if not used.
- Frozen sweet potatoes can be substituted for fresh sweet potatoes.

Variations

- **Chipotle Mashed Sweet Potatoes.** Increase brown sugar to 1 lb. Mince 3 oz chipotle chiles in adobo sauce until well puréed. Mix chipotle chiles into potato mixture. Use fewer adobo chiles for a less spicy sweet potato.
- **Whipped Sweet Potatoes.** Increase milk to 1–2 cups. Omit lime juice and cinnamon. Add 1 tsp nutmeg (optional).

SWEET POTATO SOUFFLÉ

Yield: 50 portions or 1 pan, 12 × 20 × 2 inches   *Portion:* 4 oz
Oven: 375°F   *Bake:* 30 minutes

Ingredient	Amount	Procedure
Frozen sweet potatoes	8 lb	Steam potatoes for 25 minutes. Place in mixer bowl and whip on low, medium, and high speeds for 1 minute each, or until smooth.
Margarine, melted Sugar, brown Cinnamon, ground Mace, ground Ginger, ground Cloves, ground Milk Eggs	12 oz 1 lb 8 oz 1 Tbsp 1 Tbsp 1 tsp ¼ tsp 1 cup 9 (1 lb)	Add to sweet potatoes. Mix until thoroughly blended. Begin on low speed and progress to high speed for a total of approximately 5 minutes or until mixture is fluffy.
Marshmallows, miniature	6 oz	Fold marshmallows into potato mixture. Scale into greased 12 × 20 × 2-inch pan. Bake at 375°F for 30 minutes or until hot.
Marshmallows, miniature	4 oz	Sprinkle marshmallows over sweet potatoes. Return to oven long enough for marshmallows to puff and brown slightly.

Approximate nutritive values per portion

Calories	Carbohydrate	Protein	Fat	Cholesterol	Sodium	Fiber	Iron
212 kcal	36 g	3 g	7 g	39 mg	95 mg	2 g	1 mg

Notes

- Potentially hazardous food. *Food Safety Standards:* Hold food for service at an internal temperature of 135°F or above. Do not mix old product with new. Cool leftover product quickly following time standards and cooling procedures on p. 167. Reheat leftover product quickly (within 2 hours) to 165°F or above. Reheat product only once; discard if not used.
- Fresh boiled or steamed sweet potatoes may be substituted for frozen sweet potatoes.

SEASONED FRESH SPINACH AND OTHER GREENS

Yield: 50 portions   *Portion:* 3 oz

Ingredient	Amount	Procedure
Fresh spinach or other greens	12 lb AP (10 lb EP)	Sort and trim greens. Remove veins, coarse stems, and roots. Wash leaves thoroughly, lifting out of water after each washing. Steam or boil (p. 770).
Margarine, melted Salt	4 oz 1 oz (1½ Tbsp)	Pour margarine over greens and sprinkle with salt. If boiling the greens, add salt to the cooking water.

Approximate nutritive values per portion

Calories	Carbohydrate	Protein	Fat	Cholesterol	Sodium	Fiber	Iron
36 kcal	3 g	3 g	2 g	0 mg	285 mg	2 g	2 mg

Notes

- Beet greens, chard, collards, kale, mustard greens, or turnip greens may be used. For kale, strip leaves from coarse stems.
- For frozen spinach, use 10 lb. See p. 770 for cooking.
- Greens may be garnished with 12 hard-cooked eggs, chopped, and 1 lb 8 oz crisp-cooked bacon, crumbled.
- Seasonings for spinach: basil, garlic, mace, marjoram, nutmeg, oregano, mushrooms, bacon, cheese, hard-cooked eggs, vinegar.

Variations

- **Creamed Spinach.** Cook spinach. Drain. Chop coarsely. Add 2 qt White Sauce (p. 683). Season with salt, pepper, and nutmeg.
- **Wilted Spinach or Lettuce.** To 10 lb chopped raw spinach or lettuce, or a combination of the two, add 2 qt Hot Bacon Sauce (p. 699) just before serving.

HOT ASIAN SPINACH

Yield: 50 portions   *Portion:* 2½ oz

Ingredient	Amount	Procedure
Soy sauce Sesame oil Garlic cloves, minced Green onions, chopped Ground red pepper White pepper Sugar, granulated	1½ cups ¼ cup 10 3 oz 1 Tbsp 1 Tbsp ½ cup	Mix soy sauce, oil, garlic, onions, spices, and sugar in baker's bowl.
Sesame seeds	2 oz	Spread sesame seeds in a thin even layer in a dry skillet. Heat over medium-high heat until fragrant, 2–3 minutes. Shake pan throughout cooking to prevent burning. Add toasted seeds to soy sauce mixture. Save for later step.
Fresh spinach	7 lb	Scale spinach into two 12 × 10 × 4-inch perforated pans, 3 lb 8 oz each. Steam for 4 minutes in compartment steamer until just cooked and still bright green. Drain. Transfer to two 12 × 10 × 4-inch pans. Stir half of the soy sauce mixture (about 7 oz) into each pan of cooked spinach.

Approximate nutritive values per portion

Calories	Carbohydrate	Protein	Fat	Cholesterol	Sodium	Fiber	Iron
47 kcal	6 g	3 g	2 g	0 mg	374 mg	2 g	2 mg

Notes

- Potentially hazardous food. *Food Safety Standards:* Hold food for service at an internal temperature of 135°F or above. Do not mix old product with new. Cool leftover product quickly following time standards and cooling procedures on p. 167. Reheat leftover product quickly (within 2 hours) to 165°F above. Reheat product only once; discard if not used.
- To substitute frozen spinach, thaw spinach and cut block into 8 cubes.

SPINACH SOUFFLÉ

Yield: 48 portions or 2 pans, 12 × 20 × 2 inches   *Portion:* 4 oz
Oven: 350°F   *Bake:* 40 minutes

Ingredient	Amount	Procedure
Margarine	1 lb 4 oz	Melt margarine. Add flour and salt.
Flour, all-purpose	8 oz	Stir until smooth and cook for 5 minutes.
Salt	2½ Tbsp	
Milk	1¼ qt	Add milk and sour cream. Blend over low heat until smooth, stirring constantly.
Sour cream	1¼ qt	Remove from heat.
Chopped spinach, frozen	6 lb	Thaw spinach. Drain.
Onion, finely chopped	8 oz	Add spinach, onion, nutmeg, and egg yolks to sauce. Mix.
Nutmeg	1½ Tbsp	
Egg yolks, beaten	18 (12 oz)	
Egg whites	18 (1 lb 5 oz)	Beat egg whites until stiff.
		Fold into spinach mixture.
		Lightly grease two 12 × 20 × 2-inch counter pans on the bottom only.
		Scale 7 lb 8 oz of the mixture into each pan.
		Set in pans of hot water.
		Bake at 350°F for 40 minutes or until soufflé is set. Cut 4 × 6.

Approximate nutritive values per portion

Calories	Carbohydrate	Protein	Fat	Cholesterol	Sodium	Fiber	Iron
219 kcal	10 g	7 g	18 g	105 mg	542 mg	2 g	1 mg

Notes

- Potentially hazardous food. *Food Safety Standards:* Hold food for service at an internal temperature of 135°F or above. Do not mix old product with new. Cool leftover product quickly following time standards and cooling procedures on p. 167. Reheat leftover product quickly (within 2 hours) to 165°F or above. Reheat product only once; discard if not used.
- 1 oz (½ cup) dehydrated onion, rehydrated in 1½ cups water, may be substituted for fresh onion.

BAKED ACORN SQUASH

Yield: 50 portions   *Portion:* ½ squash
Oven: 350°F   *Bake:* 30–40 minutes

Ingredient	Amount	Procedure
Acorn squash	25	Wash squash and cut in half lengthwise. Scrape out seeds. Place cut side down in shallow pans with a small amount of water. Bake at 350°F for 20–25 minutes, or until just tender. (Squash may be steamed for 20 minutes.)
Margarine, melted	8 oz	Place squash hollow side up.
Salt	1 oz (1½ Tbsp)	Sprinkle cavities with margarine, salt, and brown sugar.
Sugar, brown	12 oz	Bake until sugar is melted, about 10–15 minutes.

Approximate nutritive values per portion

Calories	Carbohydrate	Protein	Fat	Cholesterol	Sodium	Fiber	Iron
115 kcal	21 g	1 g	4 g	0 mg	242 mg	2 g	1 mg

Variations

- **Acorn Squash with Sausage.** Place 4-oz sausage patty or 2 link sausages, partially cooked, in each cooked squash half. Continue baking until meat is done.
- **Cajun Spiced Acorn Squash.** Cut acorn squash into crescents or butternut squash into approximately 4-inch pieces. Rub inside with oil and sprinkle with Cajun seasoning (p. 727). Bake as for Baked Acorn Squash recipe. Serve with 2 oz Peperonata (p. 796) or Caramelized Onions (p. 796) placed on the squash. Sprinkle each portion with Cajun seasoning and a drizzle of balsamic vinegar (optional).
- **Cinnamon Maple Baked Squash.** Substitute maple syrup for brown sugar. Sprinkle with cinnamon before baking.
- **Stuffed Acorn Squash.** Fill cooked squash with No. 12 dipper of the following mixture: 5 qt cooked rice, 4 lb chopped cooked meat, and 4 oz minced onion, sautéed in margarine and moistened with meat stock.

SPAGHETTI SQUASH

Yield: 50 portions   *Portion:* 6 oz
Oven: 350°F   *Bake:* 45–60 minutes

Ingredient	Amount	Procedure
Spaghetti squash	15 (approximately 3 lb each)	Wash squash and cut in half lengthwise. Scrape out seeds. Place cut side down in shallow pans with ½ inch water. Bake at 350°F for 45–60 minutes, or until squash is just tender when pricked with a fork. Remove squash from water and cool slightly. With a fork, scrape the soft flesh (lengthwise) into pastalike strands. Serve with melted butter or margarine or top with sauce.

Approximate nutritive values per portion

Calories	Carbohydrate	Protein	Fat	Cholesterol	Sodium	Fiber	Iron
91 kcal	24 g	2 g	0 g	0 mg	9 mg	4 g	1 mg

Note

- Potentially hazardous food. *Food Safety Standards:* Hold food for service at an internal temperature of 135°F or above. Do not mix old product with new. Cool leftover product quickly following time standards and cooling procedures on p. 167. Reheat leftover product quickly (within 2 hours) to 165°F or above. Reheat product only once; discard if not used.

Variations

- **Indian Spiced Spaghetti Squash.** Prepare spaghetti squash as for Spaghetti Squash. In a heavy-bottomed pan over medium heat, toast 2 Tbsp brown mustard seed and 1 Tbsp cumin seed. (Cover seeds to keep them from popping out of pan.) Heat 8 oz olive oil in a tilting fry pan. Add toasted spices, 1 lb chopped onions, 3 Tbsp minced ginger, 3 Tbsp minced garlic, 1 Tbsp ground coriander, 1 Tbsp kosher salt, and ½ tsp crushed red pepper. Sauté until onions are translucent. Add 1 lb 4 oz seeded chopped tomatoes and 1 oz minced serrano chiles (approximately 5 small chiles). Continue to cook until tomatoes begin to soften and serrano chiles are fragrant. Gently toss spaghetti squash strands with vegetable-spice mixture and heat through. Toss with 2 oz coarsely chopped cilantro (approximately 2 cups) just before serving.
- **Spaghetti Squash with Clam Sauce.** Prepare Clam Sauce (p. 513) and serve over squash.
- **Spaghetti Squash with Vegetable Sauce.** Prepare Vegetable Sauce (p. 527) and serve over squash.

MASHED WINTER SQUASH

Yield: 50 portions   *Portion:* 3 oz

Ingredient	Amount	Procedure
Winter squash	15 lb AP (10 lb EP)	Peel squash and cut into pieces. Steam or boil until tender (p. 770).
Milk, hot Margarine, melted Salt Sugar, brown	1½ qt 8 oz 2 Tbsp 8 oz	Mash squash. Add milk, margarine, and seasonings. Whip until light. May be garnished with toasted slivered almonds.

Approximate nutritive values per portion

Calories	Carbohydrate	Protein	Fat	Cholesterol	Sodium	Fiber	Iron
103 kcal	14 g	2 g	5 g	4 mg	316 mg	3 g	0.5 mg

Notes

- Potentially hazardous food. *Food Safety Standards:* Hold food for service at an internal temperature of 135°F or above. Do not mix old product with new. Cool leftover product quickly following time standards and cooling procedures on p. 167. Reheat leftover product quickly (within 2 hours) to 165°F or above. Reheat product only once; discard if not used.
- Acorn, buttercup, butternut, hubbard, turbin, or another winter squash variety may be used.
- Seasonings for winter squash: allspice, basil, cinnamon, cloves, fennel, ginger, marjoram, nutmeg, oregano, rosemary, savory.

Variations

- **Baked Whipped Squash.** Mix cooked squash until smooth. Add 12 oz margarine, melted; 1 lb brown sugar; 1 Tbsp ground cinnamon; 1 tsp ground allspice; ½ tsp ground cloves; and 1 oz (1½ Tbsp) salt. Mix thoroughly. Scale into 12 × 20 × 2-inch pan. Bake in 350°F oven for 1 hour or until heated through. Cover with 12 oz miniature marshmallows and heat until marshmallows have browned slightly.
- **Butternut Squash–Apple Casserole.** Cook 8 lb peeled, cored, and sliced apples, 12 oz margarine or butter, and 12 oz sugar until apples are barely tender. Arrange in baking pans. Cover with 10 lb mashed butternut squash. Top with mixture of crushed cornflakes, chopped pecans, melted margarine, and brown sugar. Bake at 350°F for 30–40 minutes.

SEASONED ZUCCHINI OR SUMMER SQUASH

Yield: 50 portions   *Portion:* 3 oz

Ingredient	Amount	Procedure
Zucchini or other summer squash	11–12 lb AP (10 lb EP)	Wash squash and remove ends. Do not pare. Cut into slices or spears. Steam or simmer until tender (p. 770).
Margarine, melted Salt White pepper	4 oz 1 Tbsp 1 tsp	Pour margarine over squash and sprinkle with salt and pepper.

Approximate nutritive values per portion

Calories	Carbohydrate	Protein	Fat	Cholesterol	Sodium	Fiber	Iron
29 kcal	3 g	1 g	2 g	0 mg	152 mg	1 g	0.5 mg

Notes

- 1 tsp garlic or onion salt may be substituted for part of salt.
- ½ cup Parmesan cheese may be sprinkled over zucchini before serving.
- Seasonings for summer squash: basil, chives, coriander, dill, garlic, ginger, marjoram, oregano, rosemary, savory, tarragon.

Variations

- **French-Fried Zucchini.** See p. 794.
- **Zucchini Casserole.** Steam or parboil 8 lb sliced zucchini squash until tender-crisp. Drain. Combine one 46-oz can cream of chicken soup, 3 cups sour cream, 1 cup chopped green onions, and 1 oz shredded carrots. Combine with zucchini. Mix 1 lb 12 oz herb-seasoned bread crumbs and 8 oz melted margarine and spread half in a 12 × 20 × 2-inch counter pan. Pour zucchini mixture over crumbs. Top with remaining crumbs. Bake at 350°F for 30–40 minutes or until heated through. Other vegetables such as broccoli, asparagus, cauliflower, or French-cut green beans may be used in this casserole.
- **Zucchini and Summer Squash.** Wash and slice 5 lb zucchini squash and 5 lb yellow summer squash. Cook until just tender. Season with 8 oz melted margarine; add salt and pepper to taste. Add 2 lb cherry tomatoes just before serving.
- **Zucchini and Tomato Casserole.** In 12 × 20 × 2-inch counter pan, layer 7 lb zucchini squash; 3 lb fresh tomatoes, peeled and chopped; and 1 lb chopped onions. Season lightly with salt and pepper. Sprinkle 1 lb grated cheddar cheese and 1 lb bacon, cooked and crumbled, over top. Cover with buttered bread crumbs. Bake covered at 400°F for about 1 hour, uncovered for the last 20 minutes.

BAKED TOMATOES

Yield: 50 portions   *Portion:* ½ tomato
Oven: 400°F   *Bake:* 15–20 minutes

Ingredient	Amount	Procedure
Fresh tomatoes, 5 oz	25	Wash tomatoes. Cut in halves.
Salt	1 tsp	Sprinkle each tomato with salt and pepper or seasoned salt.
Black pepper	1 tsp	
Margarine, melted	6 oz	Combine margarine, bread crumbs, and onion.
Bread crumbs	2 oz	Place 2 tsp mixture on each tomato half.
Onion, finely chopped	6 oz	Bake at 400°F for 15–20 minutes, until heated through.

Approximate nutritive values per portion

Calories	Carbohydrate	Protein	Fat	Cholesterol	Sodium	Fiber	Iron
45 kcal	4 g	1 g	3 g	0 mg	90 mg	1 g	0.5 mg

Note

- Seasonings for tomatoes: basil, bay leaf, chile powder, garlic, marjoram, oregano, rosemary, tarragon, thyme.

Variations

- **Broiled Tomato Slices.** Cut tomatoes in ½-inch-thick slices. Salt, dot with margarine, and broil.
- **Mushroom-Stuffed Tomatoes.** Add 2 lb sautéed mushrooms, sliced or chopped, to crumb mixture.
- **Spinach-Stuffed Tomatoes.** Wash medium-size fresh tomatoes. Remove core and part of the tomato pulp. Fill center with 2 oz Spinach Soufflé (p. 811). Sprinkle with buttered crumbs and Parmesan cheese. Bake at 350°F for about 1 hour.
- **Stewed Tomatoes.** In a steam-jacketed kettle or other deep pan, melt 4 oz butter or olive oil and sauté 4 oz finely chopped onion and 2 oz finely chopped green bell pepper until vegetables are fragrant. Add 12 lb canned diced tomatoes, ½ tsp black pepper, and 6 oz granulated sugar. Simmer until hot. Serve with croutons if desired. Yield: 50 ½-cup servings.

HERB-ROASTED TOMATOES

Yield: 50 portions *Portion:* 3 halves
Oven: 350°F *Bake:* 50–60 minutes

Ingredient	Amount	Procedure
Plum tomatoes, halved lengthwise (stem and blossom blemish removed)	14 lb	Place tomatoes cut side up in a 12 × 20 × 2-inch pan. Brush with olive oil.
Olive oil	8 oz	
Salt	1 Tbsp	Sprinkle tomatoes lightly with salt and pepper.
Black pepper	1½ tsp	
Fresh parsley, chopped	8 Tbsp (½ cup)	Mix herbs. Sprinkle half of herb mixture over tomatoes. Save remainder of herb mixture for garnish.
Fresh basil, chopped	8 Tbsp (½ cup)	
Fresh rosemary, finely chopped	4 Tbsp (¼ cup)	
Fresh thyme, chopped	4 Tbsp (¼ cup)	
		Bake tomatoes at 350°F until tender and slightly browned around the edges, 50–60 minutes.
Parmesan cheese, freshly grated (optional)	1 cup	Garnish tomatoes with remaining herbs and parmesan cheese.

Approximate nutritive values per portion

Calories	Carbohydrate	Protein	Fat	Cholesterol	Sodium	Fiber	Iron
77 kcal	6 g	2 g	5.6 g	1.6 mg	189 mg	1.5 g	1 mg

Notes

- Other herbs may be substituted for those in the recipe.
- A vegetable marinade may be substituted for the olive oil.
- If substituting dried herbs, reduce amount by two-thirds.
- ½ tsp balsamic vinegar per tomato may be substituted or used along with olive oil.

BAKED ITALIAN TOMATOES AND ZUCCHINI

Yield: 50 portions   *Portion:* 4 oz
Oven: 325°F   *Bake:* 40–50 minutes

Ingredient	Amount	Procedure
Plum tomatoes, small	3 lb 12 oz AP	Submerge tomatoes in boiling water for a few seconds to loosen skins. Peel tomatoes and core. Cut tomatoes in half, from stem to flower end (long way). Save for layering step.
Marinara Sauce (p. 690)	2 qt	Layer ingredients in the following order in each of two 12 × 10 × 2-inch pans: 1. Marinara Sauce, 2 cups
Zucchini squash, ½-inch dice	3 lb EP	2. Diced zucchini, 12 oz 3. Tomato halves, 12 oz
Mozzarella cheese, shredded	3 lb	4. Mozzarella cheese, 1 lb 5. Parmesan cheese, 2 oz
Parmesan cheese, freshly shredded	8 oz	Repeat steps 1, 2, and 3. Bake at 325°F, covered, for 30–40 minutes or until mixture reaches 165°F.
Fresh parsley, chopped (see Note)	1 oz	Remove from oven and uncover. Top each pan with 8 oz mozzarella cheese and 2 oz Parmesan cheese.
Fresh basil, chopped	1 oz	Sprinkle ½ oz parsley and ½ oz basil on each pan. Bake uncovered for 10 minutes, until cheese is melted and lightly browned.

Approximate nutritive values per portion

Calories	Carbohydrate	Protein	Fat	Cholesterol	Sodium	Fiber	Iron
128 kcal	6.3 g	8 g	8 g	2.5 mg	319 mg	1.4 g	1 mg

Notes

- Potentially hazardous food. *Food Safety Standards:* Hold food for service at an internal temperature of 135°F or above. Do not mix old product with new. Cool leftover product quickly following time standards and cooling procedures on p. 167. Reheat leftover product quickly (within 2 hours) to 165°F or above. Reheat product only once; discard if not used.
- Dried basil and dried parsley may be substituted for fresh. Use 2 Tbsp parsley and 1 Tbsp basil.
- Serve as a vegetable or with pasta for a nonmeat entrée.
- 1 lb mushrooms (small whole or quartered) may be substituted for 1 lb of the zucchini.

STIR-FRIED VEGETABLES

Yield: 50 portions   *Portion:* 3 oz

Ingredient	Amount	Procedure
Cornstarch	2 oz	Combine cornstarch and water. Set aside for last step.
Water	1 cup	
Assorted vegetables (see Notes for suggestions)	5 lb 8 oz (EP)	Cut vegetables into uniform-size thin slices, strips, or diagonal slices to ensure quick cooking. Pat dry before frying.
Cooking oil	1 cup	Combine oil, garlic, and ginger in frying pan.
Garlic cloves, minced	2	Heat to 350°F and cook slightly.
Fresh ginger, sliced	½ tsp	Remove ginger and discard.
Sliced water chestnuts, canned, drained	8 oz	Add water chestnuts and prepared vegetables to heated oil. Stir with long spatula in a folding motion. Cook until vegetables are tender-crisp.
Chicken Stock (p. 738)	3 cups	Combine stock and soy sauce.
Soy sauce	½ cup	Mix quickly into vegetables. Reduce heat. Pour cornstarch mixture over vegetables. Cook and stir just until sauce thickens and vegetables are glazed.

Approximate nutritive values per portion

Calories	Carbohydrate	Protein	Fat	Cholesterol	Sodium	Fiber	Iron
63 kcal	5 g	2 g	5 g	0 mg	238 mg	0 g	0.5 mg

Notes

- Select vegetables for contrast in color, shape, texture, and flavor. At least three vegetables should be selected. Cut vegetables into small enough pieces to cook quickly. Frozen vegetables should be thawed before stir-frying.
- Suggested vegetables: asparagus cut diagonally, broccoli or cauliflower florets, green beans, carrot strips or diagonal slices, celery slices, sliced fresh mushrooms, snow peas, onion rings, bell pepper strips (red, green, or yellow), zucchini or summer squash slices or sticks.
- Suggested combinations (total of 5 lb 8 oz): 1 lb 8 oz sliced carrots, 1 lb 8 oz broccoli florets, 1 lb 8 oz celery sticks, 8 oz mushroom slices, and 8 oz sliced onion; 1 lb 8 oz asparagus cut diagonally, 1 lb 8 oz zucchini slices, 1 lb 8 oz cauliflower florets, 8 oz sliced onions, and 8 oz fresh mushrooms; 1 lb 8 oz sliced celery, 1 lb 8 oz pea pods, 1 lb 8 oz julienne carrots, 8 oz green bell pepper strips, and 8 oz sliced fresh mushrooms.

RATATOUILLE

Yield: 50 portions   *Portion:* 4 oz
Oven: 300°F   *Heat:* 5 minutes

Ingredient	Amount	Procedure
Olive oil	⅓ cup	Heat oil in tilting fry pan.
Onion, cut in wedges	8 oz	Add onion and garlic. Cook until tender-crisp.
Garlic clove, minced	1	
Eggplant, peeled, 1-inch cubes	2 lb 8 oz	Add eggplant. Sauté 2 minutes.
Zucchini squash, ½-inch slices	2 lb	Add zucchini and peppers. Sauté for 5 minutes or until vegetables are still crisp and brightly colored.
Green bell peppers, 1½-inch strips	2 lb	
Diced tomatoes, canned	6 lb	Add to vegetable mixture. Simmer for 5 minutes.
Salt	2½ tsp	Scale into two 12 × 10 × 2-inch pans, 6 lb per pan.
Black pepper	1½ tsp	
Basil, dried, crumbled	1 tsp	
Oregano, dried, crumbled	1 tsp	
Monterey Jack cheese, shredded	1 lb	Sprinkle 8 oz cheese over each pan. Heat in 300°F oven for 5 minutes to melt the cheese. Do not cover. Serve with a spoon.

Approximate nutritive values per portion

Calories	Carbohydrate	Protein	Fat	Cholesterol	Sodium	Fiber	Iron
73 kcal	6 g	3 g	4 g	8 mg	246 mg	1 g	0.5 mg

Notes

- Sliced Japanese eggplant may be substituted for all or part of the cubed eggplant.
- Yellow summer squash may be substituted for some or all of the zucchini.

SUMMER RATATOUILLE

Yield: 50 portions   *Portion:* 4 oz
Oven: 350°F   *Bake:* 20 minutes

Ingredient	Amount	Procedure
Eggplant, unpeeled, 1-inch cubes	3 lb 10 oz EP	Put eggplant in colander. Sprinkle with salt and let set for 30 minutes. Rinse eggplant and drain thoroughly. Use eggplant in following step.
Salt	1 oz	
Olive oil	5 oz	Heat oil in large fry pan or steam-jacketed kettle.
Onions, ¼-inch slices	1 lb 12 oz EP	Sauté onions, garlic, and eggplant until tender, 10–12 minutes.
Garlic, minced	3 oz EP	
Zucchini squash, ½-inch slices	2 lb EP	Add squash to onion-garlic-eggplant mixture.
Yellow summer squash, ½-inch slices	1 lb 8 oz EP	Sauté squash and peppers until heated through and most of the liquid is absorbed.
Red bell peppers, cut in 1-inch square pieces	8 oz EP	
Green bell peppers, cut in 1½-inch strips	12 oz EP	
Fresh tomatoes, quartered	2 lb EP	Add tomatoes and seasonings. Stir to combine.
Salt	1 Tbsp	Transfer to two 12 × 10 × 2-inch pans. Bake at 350°F, uncovered, for 20 minutes.
Black pepper	1 tsp	
Crushed red pepper	¼ tsp	
Fresh basil, coarsely chopped	1 oz	
Oregano, dried	1½ tsp	

Approximate nutritive values per portion

Calories	Carbohydrate	Protein	Fat	Cholesterol	Sodium	Fiber	Iron
55 kcal	7 g	1 g	3 g	0 mg	367 mg	2 g	0.5 mg

Note

- Potentially hazardous food. *Food Safety Standards:* Hold food for service at an internal temperature of 135°F or above. Do not mix old product with new. Cool leftover product quickly following time standards and cooling procedures on p. 167. Reheat leftover product quickly (within 2 hours) to 165°F or above. Reheat product only once; discard if not used.

Variation

- **Summer Ratatouille [without eggplant].** Cover lightly the bottom of tilting or other heavy-bottomed fry pan with olive oil. Heat. Add 12 oz onion wedges (½ inch) and 2 tsp minced garlic. Cook until fragrant. Add 3 lb 4 oz 1-inch green bell pepper cubes, 3 lb 8 oz sliced yellow squash (¼ inch), 3 lb 8 oz sliced zucchini (¼ inch), 1 Tbsp black pepper, 1 Tbsp dried oregano (or 3 Tbsp fresh), 2 Tbsp dried basil (or ⅓ cup chopped fresh), and 2 tsp salt. Sauté for 3–4 min until vegetables just begin to soften but are still crisp and brightly colored. Add 8 lb 12 oz tomato wedges. Heat through. Scale 6 lb into three 12 × 10 × 2-inch pans. Sprinkle 8 oz shredded Monterey Jack cheese on each pan. Recipe yield: 18 lbs, fifty 6 oz portions.

VEGETABLE TIMBALE

Yield: 40 portions or 1 pan, 12 × 20 × 2 inches   *Portion:* 3 oz
Oven: 300°F   *Bake:* 2 hours

Ingredient	Amount	Procedure
Eggs	16 (1 lb 9 oz)	Beat eggs.
Salt Margarine, melted Milk	2 Tbsp 5 oz 1½ qt	Add salt, margarine, and milk.
Chopped spinach, frozen	3 lb	Cook spinach (p. 770). Drain well. Add to egg mixture. Mix until well blended.
		Pour into greased 12 × 20 × 2-inch pan. Set into another pan with 3 cups hot water in it. Bake at 300°F for 2 hours. Test with a silver knife as for custard. Cut 5 × 8. Serve with 1 oz Cheese Sauce (p. 683).

Approximate nutritive values per portion

Calories	Carbohydrate	Protein	Fat	Cholesterol	Sodium	Fiber	Iron
44 kcal	5 g	1 g	2.4 g	0 mg	367 mg	1.6 g	0.5 mg

Notes

- Potentially hazardous food. *Food Safety Standards:* Hold food for service at an internal temperature of 135°F or above. Do not mix old product with new. Cool leftover product quickly following time standards and cooling procedures on p. 167. Reheat leftover product quickly (within 2 hours) to 165°F or above. Reheat product only once; discard if not used.
- Spinach, broccoli, brussels sprouts, asparagus, or any combination of these vegetables may be used.

Variation

- **Chicken Timbale.** Use 32 eggs (3 lb 8 oz), 1 oz salt, 1 lb melted margarine, 1 tsp white pepper, 12 oz bread crumbs, and 6 lb chopped cooked chicken. Mix margarine, bread crumbs, and milk. Cook for 5 minutes. Add beaten eggs, seasonings, and chicken. Bake as for Vegetable Timbale. Cut 6 × 8. Serve with Béchamel Sauce (p. 684).

GRILLED OR ROASTED MARINATED VEGETABLES

Yield: 50 portions   *Portion:* 3 oz
Oven: 400–500°F

Ingredient	Amount	Procedure
Vegetables (see suggestions listed in Table 21.2)	12 lb EP	Prepare vegetables per instructions in Table 21.2.
Marinade: Vegetable Marinade (pp. 722, 723) Balsamic Vinegar Marinade (p. 724) Vinaigrette Marinade (p. 725) Herb and Garlic Marinade (p. 725)	3 qt	Marinate vegetables for 10–15 minutes. Drain marinade from vegetables before grilling or roasting. **Save marinade.** Baste vegetables once or twice with marinade while grilling or roasting. Reserved marinade may be heated to 165°F and drizzled on vegetables when served. (See grilling and oven roasting instructions that follow.)

GRILLING INSTRUCTIONS

1. Clean grill grids thoroughly. Clean as often as necessary to keep vegetables from sticking.
2. Preheat grill grids until very hot. Place drained vegetables on grill. Turn often. Brush marinade on vegetables after each turn.
3. Grill vegetables until they reach the desired doneness. Serve warm or at room temperature.

OVEN ROASTING INSTRUCTIONS

1. Preheat oven according to Table 21.2. Oven must be hot enough to caramelize the vegetables but not so hot as to dry them out.
2. Place vegetables on a lightly greased sheet pan in a single layer. Do not overcrowd or they will steam rather than roast. For large quantities of vegetables, roast separately and combine before service. For smaller quantities, put the slower-cooking, hard vegetables to the outside of the roasting pan (vegetables will cook faster on the outside of the pan).
3. Turn vegetables often during roasting. If cooking different kinds of vegetables on the same pan, remove the vegetables as they become tender. Brush marinade on vegetables after each turn.
4. Roast vegetables until they reach the desired doneness. Serve warm or at room temperature.

Notes

- Potentially hazardous food. *Food Safety Standards:* Hold food for service at an internal temperature of 135°F or above. Do not mix old product with new. Cool leftover product quickly following time standards and cooling procedures on p. 167. Reheat leftover product quickly (within 2 hours) to 165°F or above. Reheat product only once; discard if not used.
- Vegetables may be roasted without first marinating. Use the following ratio: 1 lb vegetables, 1–2 oz olive oil, ½–1 tsp kosher salt, 1 Tbsp finely chopped fresh herbs (oregano, rosemary, sage, thyme). Combine vegetables, salt, and herbs in a bowl. Toss to coat. Follow roasting instructions.

Variations

- **Garlic and Fennel Seed Roasted Vegetables.** Do not use a marinade. Mix and set aside 3 Tbsp olive oil with 2 Tbsp crushed fresh garlic and 2 Tbsp toasted fennel seed (see p. 731 for instructions for toasting spices). Toss vegetables in ½ cup olive oil, 1 oz salt, and 1 tsp black pepper. Roast vegetables according to instructions. When vegetables are *al dente,* remove from oven and toss with oil, garlic, and fennel seed mixture. Roast for 10 minutes longer. Remove from oven and toss with 1 oz chopped fresh parsley and ¼ cup balsamic vinegar.
- **Mashed Potatoes and Roasted Vegetables.** Serve 5 oz Mashed Potatoes or Roasted Garlic Mashed Potatoes (p. 798) surrounded by 3–6 oz roasted vegetables (not potatoes, unless sweet potatoes). Serve garnished with chopped fresh parsley. Drizzle Mashed Potatoes with olive or nut oil if desired. Serve for a nonmeat entrée.
- **Sesame Roasted Vegetables.** Do not use a marinade. Mix and set aside 2 Tbsp sesame oil, 2 Tbsp crushed garlic, 2 Tbsp crushed ginger, and ⅓ cup soy sauce. Toss vegetables in ⅓ cup sesame oil, 1 oz salt, and 1 tsp black pepper. Roast vegetables according to instructions. When vegetables are al dente, remove from oven and toss with oil, garlic, ginger, and soy sauce mixture. Roast for 10 minutes longer. Remove from oven and toss with 2 Tbsp toasted sesame seeds and ¼ cup rice vinegar (see pp. 731–732 for instructions for toasting seeds).
- **Sherry Roasted Root Vegetables.** Select root vegetables from Table 21.2. Use the following ratio: 1 lb vegetables, 2 oz olive oil, 3 oz dry sherry, 1 tsp kosher salt, 1 Tbsp finely chopped fresh thyme. Combine vegetables, salt, and thyme in a bowl. Toss to coat. Follow roasting instruction.

TABLE 21.2 Timetable for roasting vegetables

Vegetable	Preparation instructions[a–c]	Temperature	Time[d,e]
Asparagus	Leave whole.	450°F	15 minutes
Green or wax beans	Leave whole.	450–500°F	15 minutes
Beets	(A) Do not peel or coat with oil. Wrap in foil. Peel after cooking while warm.	350°F	45–60 minutes (baby)
	(B) Peel, coat with oil. Roast unwrapped.		60–75 minutes (medium)
			1½–2 hours (large)
Belgian endive	Slice in half lengthwise.	450°F	25 minutes
Brussels sprouts	Remove outer leaves and trim base. Cut in half if large.	450°F	15 minutes
Carrots	Slice into ¼–½ inch slices or 1–2 inch sections, or split in half lengthwise.	425°F	20–40 minutes (depending on size)
Cauliflower	Cut into florets.	450°F	20 minutes
Celery root	Cut away thick skin. Cut bulb in half or cube.	425°F	30–40 minutes
Corn on the cob	To roast in husks, roll back husks and remove silks.	500°F	20–30 minutes (in husks)
	Fold husk back against corn ear. May remove husk entirely and coat with oil.		15 minutes (husks removed)
Eggplant	Peel globe eggplant if desired. Slice ½ inch thick (round or lengthwise). When roasting whole, prick with fork before roasting. For Japanese eggplant, split lengthwise.	400°F	20–25 minutes (slices) / 40–60 minutes (whole)
Fennel	Trim base and core. Cut into wedges.	425°F	20 minutes
Garlic	Slice off top of entire head. Drizzle with oil. Cover tightly.	425°F	45 minutes
Kohlrabi	Peel; cut into matchsticks or cubes.	425°F	15 minutes
Leeks	Split in half lengthwise.	450°F	20 minutes
Mushrooms	Leave whole, cut into thick slices, or quarter. (Watch carefully so as not to overcook.)	450°F	20–30 minutes
Okra	Leave whole.	450°F	15 minutes
Onions	Leave whole, cut in half, or slice.	450°F	20–30 minutes (slices)
			20–30 minutes (whole pearl)
			30–40 minutes (whole mature)
Parsnips	Peel and slice into ¼–½ inch slices or 1–2 inch sections, or split in half lengthwise.	425°F	25–30 minutes
Peppers, bell	Char pepper skin under a broiler or over an open flame. Turn to roast evenly. Remove charred skin after first placing in a closed paper or plastic bag for 10 minutes to loosen skin. Peel, seed, and slice.	Open flame or broiler	15 minutes
Potatoes, baking	Peeled or unpeeled. Cut into wedges.[e]	425°F	20 minutes
Potatoes, new	Cut in half.	425°F	20–40 minutes depending on size
Rutabagas	Quarter or slice into ½–1 inch pieces.	450°F	25–30 minutes
Squash, summer/ zucchini	Slice small squash lengthwise in half. Larger squash may be cut into 1-inch-thick slices.	450°F	15 minutes (small halves and slices)
Squash, winter	Peel and dice, or cut into wedges or ½-inch slices.[e]	350–375°F	20–30 minutes
Sweet potatoes	Peel if desired. Cut into wedges.[e]	500°F	15–20 minutes
Tomatillos	Peel off papery skin. Rinse and let dry.	425°F	15 minutes
Tomatoes	Cut in half.	425°F	30–45 minutes (as a side dish)
			75–90 minutes (for sauce)
Tomatoes, cherry	Leave whole.	425°F	20 minutes
Turnips	Quarter or slice into ½-inch-thick slices or wedges.	425°F	25 minutes

[a] Unless noted otherwise, all vegetables are coated lightly with oil, butter, or a marinade and arranged in a single layer on a sheet pan.
[b] Time can be reduced by blanching the larger vegetables until slightly tender.
[c] Before roasting, clean vegetables following preparation guidelines for vegetables, p. 120–127.
[d] Roasting time will vary depending on the size of the vegetables, how many are in the pan, and whether they are blanched. For best results, do not crowd vegetables in the pan.
[e] Turn larger vegetables once during baking, about halfway through.
Note: Season with salt and pepper.

TABLE 21.2 Timetable for roasting vegetables

Appendix A

SUGGESTED MENU ITEMS AND GARNISHES

Appetizers

See p. 818.

Entrées

Meat

Beef

Roast
  Chuck
  Corned beef
  Pot roast
  Rib eye
  Standing rib
  Sauerbraten
  Smoked beef brisket
Steak
  Broiled or grilled
    Club
    Filet mignon
    Sirloin
    Sirloin steak Milano
    T-bone
    Tanpico
  Chicken-fried steak
  Country-fried steak
  Pepper steak
  Spanish steak
  Steak teriyaki
Ground beef
  Bacon-wrapped beef
  Cheeseburger pie
  Chuck wagon steak
  Salisbury steak
  Meat loaf
  Meatballs
    Italian
    Swedish
    Spanish
    With spaghetti
    With chipotle sauce
Beef with pasta or rice
  Beef on noodles
  Beef, pork, and noodle
    casserole
  Beef stroganoff on noodles
  Chipped beef and noodles
  Chop suey on rice
  Creole spaghetti

Hungarian goulash
Pasta, beef, and tomato
    casserole
Spaghetti and meatballs
Spanish rice
Other beef entrées
  Beef birds
  Beef liver, braised
    Grilled with onions
    With bacon
  Beef Lo Mein
  Beef pot pie
  Beef stew
    With vegetables
    With biscuits
    Beef wrap
  Chile con carne
  Creamed beef on biscuits
    or baked potato
  Creamed chipped beef on
    toast or baked potato
  Fajitas
  Green chile stew
  Kebobs
  Korean BBQ
  Lasagna
  Pizza
  Stir-fried beef
    With broccoli
    With sugar snap peas
  Stuffed peppers
  Taco salad casserole

Veal

Veal birds
Veal cacciatore
Breaded veal cutlets
Veal New Orleans
Veal Parmesan
Veal piccata
Veal scallopine

Lamb

Roast leg of lamb
Broiled lamb chops
Lamb stew
Curried lamb with rice
Grilled lamb chops
Back of lamb
Lamb patties

Pork

Pork chops
  Breaded
  Baked
  Barbecued
  Chile seasoned
  Deviled
  With dressing
  Stuffed
Pork cutlets, breaded
Rack of pork
Pork roast, loin
  Garlic and peppercorn
  Herbed
  Honey cumin
  Jeweled
  Rosemary
  Southwest
  Teriyaki glazed
  With dressing
Pork roast, fresh ham
Spareribs
  Barbecued
  Sweet-sour
  With dressing
  With sauerkraut
Other pork entrées
  Stir-fried pork
  Sweet and sour pork
  Pork and noodle casserole
Pork (cured)
  Bacon
  Frankfurters
    Barbecued
    Cheese-stuffed
  Ham
    Baked glazed
    Grilled slices
    Ham balls
    Ham loaf
    Ham patties
      With cranberries
      With pineapple
    Creamed ham on
      spoonbread or
      biscuits
    Plantation shortcake
    Black beans and ham
      on rice

Ham and cheese quiche
    Scalloped potatoes and ham
Sausage
  Gravy on biscuits
  Patties or links
  With acorn squash
  And egg bake
  Rolls
Breakfast polenta
Pinto beans and sausage

Poultry

Chicken (quarters, pieces, whole)

Barbecued
Cantonese
Cacciatore
Cornish game hens, orange
    glazed
Fricassee
Fried
  Deep-fat fried
  Oven-fried
  Pan-fried
Herb baked
Italian baked
Parmesan
Poached
Stewed
  With dumplings
Tahitian

Chicken Breast (grilled or broiled)

Cheese-stuffed
  With tomato basil sauce
Chicken Breast Parmesan
Curried
Dijon
Herb marinated
Sesame mustard
Tarragon
With tomato sauce

Chicken (using diced meat)

Brunswick stew
Chicken à la king or creamed
  On biscuits
  On chow mein noodles
  On potatoes

On spoonbread
In patty shell
Chicken crepes
Chicken pot pie
Chow mein
Chicken and noodles
Chicken rice casserole
Chicken and snow peas on rice
Chicken tetrazzini
Chicken and vegetable stir-fry
Hot chicken salad
Scalloped chicken
Singapore curry
Spaghetti with chicken sauce
Sweet-sour chicken
Szechwan chicken

Turkey

Whole turkey
Roast, with dressing
Steaks, grilled
  Lime tarragon
Scalloped turkey
Turkey à la king
Turkey with dumplings
Turkey tetrazzini

Fish and Shellfish

Fin Fish

Baja fish taco
Fillets
  Baked
  Breaded
  Deep-fat fried
  Grilled
  Lemon baked
  Poached
Fillet of sole amandine
Fajita trout
Herb marinated fish steak
Halibut
Lemon rice-stuffed cod
Salmon
  Baked (whole)
  Loaf
  Poached
  Scalloped
Scallops
Tuna
  À la king
  And noodles
  Broiled
  Scalloped

Shellfish

Deviled crab
Scalloped oysters

Caribbean shrimp
Creole shrimp
Oriental shrimp and pasta
Pasta with clam sauce
Pasta with shrimp sauce
Seafood quiche
Shrimp fried rice
Shrimp peel
See also Entrée Salads

Meatless Entrées

Vegetable

Black beans and couscous
Cuban rice and tortilla
Broccoli and cheese
  casserole
Broccoli and rice au gratin
Cheese and broccoli strata
Cheese pizza
Eggplant Parmesan
Falafel
Hummus
Golden rice bake
Grilled eggplant
Mushroom soufflé
Portabella pepper steak
Quiche
  Leek and roasted pepper
  Mushroom
  Spinach
  Vegetable
Sicilian rice and vegetables
Spinach cheese crepes
Spinach lasagna
  Lasagna florentine
Spinach soufflé
Stuffed peppers
Tofu, broccoli Szechwan and
  vegetables jambalaya
  stir-fry
  sweet-and-sour
  Grilled tofu
Vegetable chow mein
Vegetable fajita
Vegetable lo mein
Vegetable paella
Vegetable pot pie
Vegetable pad thai
Vegetable timbale
Zucchini corn cakes

Pasta, Rice, and Grains

Baked ziti with four cheeses
Barley and vegetable medley
Black beans and rice
Bulgur-stuffed squash

Curried cauliflower and
  potatoes
Curried rice, beans, and
  vegetable pilaf
Couscous
Garden pasta
Ginger rice
Ginger vegetables and barley
Grains and beans
Jalapeño rice
Macaroni and cheese
Orzo pilaf
Pasta primavera
Pasta with vegetable sauce
Pepper and garlic shells
Polenta
Quesadillas
Red beans and rice
Roasted portabella mushroom
  on orzo pilaf
Spanish rice and black beans
Roasted vegetables
Spicy barley
Southwest ziti
Tomato linguine

Cheese and Eggs

Asian omelets
Cheese balls on pineapple slice
Cheese and broccoli strata
Cheese soufflé
  With cheese sauce
  With mushroom sauce
Eggs à la king
Frittata
Goldenrod eggs
Hot stuffed eggs
Nachos
Omelet
  Baked
  Chinese
  Mushroom and cheese
  Spanish
Quesadillas
Quiche
Risotto
Scotch woodcock
Swiss broccoli pasta
Tomato cilantro rice
Vegetarian spaghetti

Sandwich Entrées

Cold Sandwiches

Bacon, lettuce, tomato
Cheese salad
Chicken pocket
Chicken salad

Club sandwich
Egg salad
Ham
  With cheese
Ham salad
Pork loin
Sliced turkey
Submarine
Tuna salad
Turkey club hoagie

Hot Sandwiches

Bacon and tomato on bun
  With cheese sauce
Beef
  Barbecued
  French dip
  Roast beef
Bierocks
Chicken cutlet
Chile dog
Chimichangas
Crab salad
Croissant with sautéed garden
  vegetables
Fajitas
Grilled sandwiches
  Cheese
  Corned beef and Swiss
    on rye
  Flatbread and variations
Ham and cheese
Hamburgers
  Barbecued
  With cheese
Hot meat and cheese
Hot tuna grill
Meat loaf
Nacho dog
Patty melt
Pulled pork
Quesadillas
Roasted Portabello Gyro
Roast pork
Shredded beef burro
Tacos
Tuna melt
Turkey, hot
  And Swiss on whole wheat
Western

Salad Entrées

Chef's salad bowl
  Seafood chef salad
Chicken or turkey salad
  Crunchy
  Curried

Fruited
    Mandarin
    And bacon
    With orange-avocado
Chicken and pasta salad
Cottage cheese salad
Crab salad
Pasta salad
    Italian pasta salad
Pasta and crab salad
Salad plates
    Chicken and pasta salad
        plate
    Deli plate
    Fruit salad plate
    Marinated chicken and
        fresh fruit
    Salmon, poached
    Shrimp tortellini
        salad plate
    Tuna pasta salad plate
Shrimp salad
    Rice
    Tortellini
Stuffed tomato salad
Taco salad
Tomato cottage cheese salad
Tuna salad

Entrée Accompaniments

Pasta, Rice, and Cereals

Arroz de coco
Baked cheese grits
Barley casserole
Broccoli and cheese
    casserole
Broccoli rice au gratin
Bulgur
Bulgur pilaf
Caribbean rice
Couscous
Grains and lentils au gratin
Fettuccine
    With pesto sauce
    Grilled vinaigrette
    Herbed
Noodles
    Buttered
    Romanoff
Orzo
    Lemon
    Pilaf
Pasta wheels with vegetables
Penne with garlic
Polenta

Quinoa pilaf
Rice
Southwest barley risotto
Basmati pilaf
    With black-eyed peas
    Buttered
    Curried
    Fried
        With almonds
        Asian
    Ginger rice stir-fry
    Green
    Mexican
    Pilaf
    Primavera
    Risotto
    Sicilian with vegetables
    Toasted herb
    Tomato
See also Meatless Entrées

Potatoes

White Potatoes

Au gratin
Baked
    With toppings
    French
    Herbed
    Lyonnaise
    Stuffed
Creamed
Croquettes
Duchess
Fried
French fried
Hashed brown
Lyonnaise
Mashed
New potatoes
    Buttered
    Creamed
    Creamed with peas
    Lemon seasoned
    In mustard
    Paprika seasoned
    Parmesan
    Roasted
O'Brien
Oven-browned
Potato pancakes
    With applesauce
Potato salad, hot or cold
Rissole
Romanoff
Rosettes
Scalloped
    With onion

Shoestring
Sour cream

Sweet Potatoes

Baked
Candied or glazed
    With almonds
    With apples
Mashed
Soufflé

Starchy Vegetables

Corn

On the cob
Creamed
O'Brien
Pudding
Scalloped
Succotash

Beans

Baked beans
Barley and black bean
Bean ragout
Black beans and couscous
Black-eyed pea salsa
Grains and beans
Lima beans
    Baked
    Seasoned
Ranch style beans
Red beans and rice
Spicy black beans

Squash

Baked acorn
Mashed butternut or
    hubbard
    With apples
Seasoned spaghetti squash

Vegetables

Green Vegetables

Asparagus

Seasoned
Creamed
With cheese or hollandaise
    sauce
Vinaigrette

Broccoli

Seasoned
    With almonds
    With crumb butter
    With lemon butter
With cheese sauce
With hollandaise sauce

Brussels Sprouts

Seasoned

Cabbage

Seasoned
Au gratin
Hot slaw
Polonaise
Scalloped

Celery

Seasoned
Creamed with almonds
Creole
With carrots amandine

Green Beans

Seasoned
    With almonds
    With dill
    With mushrooms
Casserole
Creole
Herbed
Southern style
Spanish

Peas

Seasoned
    With almonds
    With lemon-mint butter
    With mushrooms
With carrots
With cauliflower
With new potatoes
With pearl onions
With turnips

Spinach

Seasoned
    With egg or bacon
    Asian (hot)
Creamed
Soufflé
Wilted

Zucchini

Seasoned
Casserole
    With tomato

Other Vegetables

Beets

Seasoned
    Julienne
Harvard
Hot spiced
With orange sauce
In sour cream
Pickled

Carrots

Seasoned
  With parsley
Candied or glazed
Mint glazed
Lyonnaise
Marinated
Savory
Sweet-sour
With celery
With peas

Cauliflower

Seasoned
  With almonds
Creamed
French fried
With cheese sauce
With peas

Eggplant

Baked
Creole
French fried
Parmesan
Ratatouille
Sautéed
Tomato bake

Mushrooms

Broiled
French fried
Marinated
Sautéed

Onions

Seasoned
Au gratin
Baked
Casserole
Creamed
French fried

Parsnips

Seasoned
Browned
Glazed
  With carrots

Rutabagas

Seasoned
Mashed
  With potatoes

Summer Squash

Seasoned
With zucchini

Tomatoes

Baked

Broiled
Herb roasted
Stewed
Stuffed
  With mushrooms
  With spinach

Turnips

Seasoned
Mashed
With peas
See p. 818 for suggested
  combinations for stir-
  fried vegetables.

Salads and Relishes

Vegetable Salads

Salad bar
Mixed green
Tossed vegetable
Tossed greens and fruit
Hawaiian tossed
Marinated garden salad
Vegetable collage

Asparagus

Marinated

Beans

Brown bean
Garbanzo bean
  With pasta
Triple bean
Roasted corn and black bean
  slaw
Cauliflower bean
Oriental bean

Cabbage

Cole slaw
Creamy cole slaw
Green pepper slaw

Carrots

Carrifruit
Carrot celery
Carrot raisin
Marinated carrots

Cauliflower

Cauliflower-broccoli
Creamy cauliflower

Cucumbers

Sliced cucumbers and onions
Sliced cucumbers and
  tomatoes
German cucumbers

Green Beans

Marinated green beans

Potatoes

Potato salad
Sour cream potato salad
Hot potato salad

Spinach

Spinach-cheese
Spinach-mushroom

Tomatoes

Marinated
Sliced
Sliced with cucumbers
Tomato basil

Fruit Salads

Acini de pepe
Ambrosia fruit
Waldorf
Apple-cabbage
Apple-carrot
Spiced apple
Grapefruit-orange
  With apple
  With avocado
Frozen fruit
Tossed greens with fruit

Gelatin Salads

Perfection
Tomato aspic
Applesauce
Apple cinnamon swirl
Arabian peach
Autumn salad
Blueberry
Boysenberry mold
Cranberry apple
Cranberry mold
Cucumber soufflé
Frosted cherry
Frosted lime
Jellied Waldorf
Lemon cream
Pineapple cheese
Ribbon gelatin
Sunshine
Swedish green top
Under-the-sea

Pasta and Rice Salads

Citrus couscous
Garbanzo and pasta
Dilled rice
Macaroni

Italian pasta
See also Salad Entrées

Relishes

Fruit

Buttered apples
Cantaloupe or watermelon
  chunks
Cranberry relish
Cranberry sauce
  Baked
Grapes, green or red
Israeli couscous
Pineapple, broiled
  Spears
Salsa
Tomato-serrano salsa
Spiced fruit
  Apples
  Crabapples
  Pears
  Peaches
  Tomatillo salsa verde

Vegetables

Broccoli florets
Carrot curls or sticks
Marinated carrots
Cauliflower florets
Celery sticks
Stuffed celery
Cherry tomatoes
Green bell pepper rings
  or sticks
Marinated mushrooms
Radishes
Tomato slices or wedges
Turnip sticks or slices
Zucchini sticks or slices

Miscellaneous

Cucumber and melon salsa
Olives, green, ripe, stuffed
Pickles
  Beet
  Corn relish
  Dill
  Sweet
  Watermelon

Soups

Stock soups

Beef alphabet
Beef barley
Beef noodle
Beef rice
Creole beef

French onion
Hearty beef vegetable
Mexican beef
Minestrone
Vegetable beef
 Julienne
Vegetable
Brunswick stew
Chicken bouillon
Chicken gumbo
Chicken noodle
Chicken rice
Chicken with spaetzle
Pepper pot
Turkey vegetable
Tomato barley
Tomato bouillon
Tomato rice
Manhattan clam or fish
  chowder
Tomato, shrimp, and crab

Cream Soups
Broccoli cheese soup
Cheese soup
Chicken velvet
Chipotle corn chowder
Cream of:
 Asparagus
 Broccoli
 Cauliflower
 Celery
 Chicken
 Mushroom
 Mushroom barley
 Potato
 Potato baked
 Potato and roasted pepper
 Spinach
 Tomato
 Vegetable

Chowders
Clam (New England)
Corn
Fish
Potato
Vegetable
Oyster stew

Bean and Lentil Soups
Black bean
Black bean chile
Brazilian black bean
Ham and bean
Navy bean
Chile con carne
 Chile spaghetti

Garden chile
 Pasta fagioli soup
 White chile
Lentil soup
Lentil and black bean
Split pea soup

Chilled Soups
Gazpacho
Vichyssoise

Desserts
Cakes
Angel food
 Chocolate
 Frozen filled
 Yellow
Chiffon
 Cocoa
 Orange
 Walnut
Cupcakes
White, with variations
Yellow, with variations
Applesauce
Banana
Boston cream pie
Burnt sugar
Carrot
Chocolate
Coconut lime
Dutch apple
Fruit cake
Fudge
German chocolate
Lady Baltimore
Lazy daisy
Marble
Pineapple cashew
Pineapple upside-down
Poppy seed
Pound cake
Praline
Pumpkin
Jelly roll
Chocolate roll
Ice cream roll
Pumpkin cake roll
Gingerbread

Cookies
Drop Cookies

Butterscotch
Butterscotch pecan
Chocolate
Coconut macaroons
Chocolate chip

Fruitcake
Gingersnaps
Jumbo chunk chocolate
Molasses
Oatmeal
Peanut butter
Peanut butter chocolate chip
Peanut
Snickerdoodles
Sugar
Whole-wheat sugar

Bar Cookies

Brownies
Butterscotch squares
Coconut pecan bars
Date bars
Dreamland bars
Oatmeal date bars
Marshmallow krispie
  squares

Pressed, Molded, and Rolled Cookies
Butterscotch refrigerator
  cookies
Butter tea cookies
Chocolate tea cookies
Christmas wreath cookies
Coconut cookies
Crisp ginger cookies
Filled cookies
Frosty date balls
Oatmeal crispies
Pinwheel cookies
Rolled sugar cookies
Sandies
Thimble cookies

Pies
Fruit Pies

Apple
 Crumb
 Sour cream
Apricot
Berry
Cherry
Cranberry raspberry
Gooseberry
Peach
Pineapple
Raisin
Rhubarb
 Custard

Soft Pies

Chiffon
 Chocolate

Lemon
Strawberry
Cream
 Banana
 Butterscotch
 Chocolate
 Coconut
 Date
 Fruit-glazed
 Nut cream
 Pineapple
Custard
 Coconut
Frozen mocha almond
Ice cream
Lemon
Pumpkin
 Praline
 Pecan
  Cream cheese

Frozen Desserts
Sundaes and Parfaits

Caramel sundae
Hot fudge sundae
Peanut butter sundae
Strawberry sundae
Chocolate parfait
Strawberry parfait

Ice Cream

Butter brickle
Chocolate
Chocolate chip
Chocolate almond
Coffee
Lemon custard
Peach
Pecan
Peppermint
Pistachio
Strawberry
Toffee
Vanilla
Frozen yogurt

Sherbet

Cranberry
Lemon
Lime
Orange
Pineapple
Raspberry

Puddings and Other Desserts
Cream puddings
 Banana

Butterscotch
Chocolate
Coconut
Pineapple
Tapioca
Vanilla
Custard, baked
 Caramel
 Rice
 Bread pudding
 Floating island
Baked date pudding
Lemon cake pudding
Christmas pudding
 (steamed)
Cream puffs
Eclairs
Ice cream puff
Orange cream puffs with
 chocolate filling
Baked apples
Apple dumplings
Apple crisp
Fruit crisp
Fruit cobbler
 Apple
 Apricot
 Cherry
 Peach
 Plum
Fruit and cheese
Strawberry shortcake
Bavarian creams
 Apricot
 Pineapple
 Strawberry
Russian cream
Cheese cake
 With fruit glaze

Garnishes

Yellow-Orange

Cheese and Eggs

Cheese, grated, strips
Egg, hard-cooked or sections
Deviled egg halves
Riced egg yolk

Fruit

Apricot halves
Cantaloupe balls
Lemon wedges, slices
Orange section, slices
Peach slices
Peach halves with jelly
Spiced peaches

Vegetables

Carrots, rings, shredded, strips
Banana peppers

Sweets

Peanut brittle, crushed
Sugar, yellow or orange

Miscellaneous

Coconut, tinted

Flowers

Carnations
Daisies
Dandelions
Day lilies
Marigolds
Nasturtiums
Pansies
Rose petals
Snapdragons
Squash blossoms

Red/Pink

Fruit

Cherries
Cinnamon apples
Cranberries
Plums
Pomegranate seeds
Red raspberries
Maraschino cherries
Strawberries
Watermelon cubes, balls

Vegetables

Beets, pickled, julienne
Beet relish
Red cabbage
Red peppers, rings, strips,
 shredded
Pimento, chopped, strips
Red radishes, sliced, roses
Cherry tomatoes
Tomato wedges, slices, broiled

Sweets

Red jelly: currant, cherry,
 loganberry, raspberry
Red sugar

Miscellaneous

Paprika
Tinted coconut
Stuffed olives
Cinnamon drops (red hots)

Flowers

Carnations, mini
Geraniums

Rose petals
Nasturtiums

Green

Fruit

Avocados
Frosted grapes
Green plums
Honeydew melon
Kiwifruit
Lime slices or wedges
Maraschino cherries
Mint jelly

Vegetables

Broccoli florets
Celery
Endive
Green bell pepper strips,
 chopped
Green onions
Lettuce cups
Lettuce, shredded
Mint leaves
Nasturtium leaves
Parsley, sprig, chopped
Spinach leaves
Watercress
Zucchini sticks, slices

Miscellaneous

Capers
Coconut, tinted
Olives
Pickles, burr gherkins, strips,
 fans, rings
Sunflower seeds
Pistachios

White

Fruit

Apple rings
Grapefruit sections

Vegetables

Cauliflower florets
Celery cabbage
Celery curls, hearts, strips
Cucumber rings, strips,
 wedges, cups
Mashed potato rosettes
Onion rings
Onions, pickled
White radishes

Miscellaneous

Almonds
Popcorn
Sliced hard-cooked egg white

Parmesan cheese
Shredded coconut
Marshmallows
Powdered sugar
Whipped cream

Flowers

Carnations
Daisies
Geraniums
Lilacs
Pansies
Rose petals
Snapdragons
Violets

Brown/Tan

Breads

Croustades
Croutons

Miscellaneous

Chocolate, shredded or
 shaved
Cinnamon
Dates
French-fried cauliflower
Mushrooms
Nutmeats
Nut-covered cheese balls
Potato chips
Toasted coconut

Flowers

Pansies

Black

Caviar
Prunes
Spiced prunes
Raisins, currants
Ripe olives
Rye croutons
Truffles

Blue/Purple

Bachelor buttons
Chive flowers
Chrysanthemums
Geraniums
Pansies
Lavender
Lilacs
Violets

Appendix B

RESOURCES WITH IDEAS FOR NAMING, PLATING, AND GARNISHING FOOD

Trade and Professional Magazines

Food Management	www.food-management.com
FoodService Director	www.fsdmag.com
Plate	www.plateonline.com
Restaurants & Institutions	www.rimag.com
Santé	www.isantemagazine.com

Popular Magazines

Bon Appétit
Cooking Light
Cooks Illustrated
Cuisine at Home
Eating Well
Every Day with Rachael Ray
Fine Cooking
Food & Wine
Saveur
Southern Living
Sunset
Taste of Home
Vegetarian Times

Trade Associations

American Lamb Board
Australian Lamb
National Cattlemen's Beef Association
National Pork Producers

Other

www.epicurious.com
www.foodnetwork.com

Appendix C

COMMON PRICING METHODS

Factor Method	Example
Selling price = Food cost × Pricing factor	Food cost = $1.00
(Pricing factor = 100% ÷ Desired food cost percentage of the selling price)	Desired food cost percentage = 40%
	Pricing factor = 100 ÷ 40 = 2.5
	Selling price = $1.00 × 2.5 = $2.50

The **factor method** for pricing is simple to use, but because it is based on food cost alone it may result in a selling price too low for labor-intensive, low-food-cost menu items and too high for low-labor, high-food-cost items. The selling price calculated by using the factor method is intended to include labor, supplies, and profit margin. The goals and objectives of the foodservice will determine the desired food cost percentage. Commercial restaurants generally assign a lower food cost percentage than onsite or not-for-profit operations. A food cost percentage ranging between 25 and 45 percent is typical.

Ratio Price	Example
Selling price = Food cost ÷ Pricing ratio	Food cost = $40,000
(Pricing ratio = Food cost for a specific period of time ÷ Sales for same period of time)	Sales = $100,000
	Pricing ratio = $40,000 ÷ $100,000 = 0.4
	Menu item food cost = $1.00
	Selling price = $1.00 ÷ 0.4 = $2.50

The **ratio price method** of pricing compares sales for a specific period of time to food cost for the same period. This method does not consider labor and may result in menu items being priced to high or low.

Prime Cost	Example
Selling price = Prime cost × Pricing factor	Food cost = $1.00
(Prime Cost = Food cost ÷ Direct labor cost)	Direct labor cost = $0.45
(Pricing factor = 100 ÷ [target food cost percentage + target labor cost percentage])	Target food cost percentage = 40%
	Target labor cost percentage = 25%
	Pricing factor = 100 ÷ (40 + 25) = 1.54
	Selling price = (1.00 + 0.45) × 1.54 = $2.23

The **prime cost method** for pricing considers labor costs separate from food cost. A disadvantage of this pricing method is that it is time-consuming to determine the amount of direct labor required to produce a menu item. To simplify direct labor cost calculations, some foodservices establish a labor factor based on how labor-intensive products are to prepare. An advantage is that this method of pricing more accurately reflects the direct labor cost on a per-item basis.

Percentage Markup	Example
Selling price = Menu item food cost ÷ Target food cost	Food cost = $1.00
	Target food cost = 40%
	Selling price = 1.00 ÷ 0.4 = $2.50

The **percentage markup method** for pricing is based on an established food cost percentage. It has the advantage of being easy to apply and the disadvantage of not considering labor cost, and thus pricing may be too high or too low.

Note: For all pricing methods, the calculated selling price should be considered as a guide. It may be necessary to round the selling price to a number that makes transactions simpler or a number that has more positive customer appeal. For example a calculated selling price of $2.03 that is rounded to $1.99 would make transactions easier and would likely evoke a more positive customer response.

Appendix D

BASIC FORMULAS FOR CALCULATING YIELDS AND PURCHASING FOOD

Scenario 1

A recipe calls for 10 lb raw potatoes (AP). Peeled potatoes (EP) are on hand. How many of the peeled potatoes should be used?

Data:

Potato yield = 80% (Table 4.3, p. 85)

Formula:

Yield $\times$ AP need = EP need

Calculation:

0.8×10 lb = 8 lb of the on-hand peeled potatoes are needed for the recipe.

Scenario 2

A recipe calls for 10 lb peeled quartered potatoes (EP). How many AP potatoes should be purchased?

Data:

Potato yield = 80% (Table 4.3, p. 85)

Formula:

EP need $\div$ Yield = AP need

Calculation:

10 lb $\div$ 0.8 = 12.5 lb = 12 lb 8 oz of potatoes should be purchased (for conversion, see p. 91).

Scenario 3

A recent delivery of 50 lb beef roast yielded 37 lb EP product. Is the purveyor's product meeting the specifications within a 4 percent variance?

Data:

Beef yield = 70% (Table 4.1, p. 65)

Formula:

EP $\div$ AP = Yield percentage

Calculation:

37 lb $\div$ 50 lb = 74% yield. Yes, specifications are met.

Scenario 4

A catering order for a served banquet with 100 guests specifies fresh green beans. A 3-oz portion will be served. How many fresh green beans are needed for the banquet?

Data:

Green bean yield = 88% (Table 4.3, p. 82)

Formula:

Step 1 Ounces per guest $\times$ Number of guests = EP ounces needed $\div$ 16 = EP pounds needed

Step 2 EP need $\div$ Yield = AP need

Calculation:

Step 1 3 oz $\times$ 100 = 300 oz $\div$ 16 = 18 lb 12 oz = 18.75 lb (for conversion, see p. 91)

Step 2 18.75 lb $\div$ 0.88 = 21.3 lb (round order up to 22 lb)

Scenario 5

How much dry spaghetti is needed to serve 100 3-oz portions of cooked pasta?

Data:

1 lb dry spaghetti = 2 lb 8 oz cooked spaghetti (p. 507)

Formula:

Step 1 EP ÷ AP = Yield percentage

Step 2 Ounces per portion × Number of portions = EP ounces needed ÷ 16 = EP pounds needed

Step 3 EP need ÷ Yield= AP need

Calculation:

Step 1 2.5 ÷ 1 = 250%

Step 2 3 oz × 100 = 300 oz ÷ 16 = 18 lb 12 oz = 18.75 lb (for conversion, see p. 91)

Step 3 18.75 lb ÷ 2.5 = 7.5 lb = 7 lb 8 oz

Scenario 6

A 20-lb watermelon (AP) costs $5.00. What would a 4-oz serving (EP) cost?

Data:

Watermelon yield = 57% (Table 4.3, p. 86)

Formula:

Step 1 AP cost ÷ AP lb = Cost/lb (AP)

Step 2 AP cost/lb ÷ Yield = Cost per lb (EP)

Step 3 EP cost/lb ÷ Servings/lb = Cost per serving (EP)

Calculation:

Step 1 $5.00 ÷ 20 lb = 0.25 cost/lb (AP)

Step 2 0.25 ÷ 0.57 = 0.44 cost/lb (EP)

Step 3 0.44 ÷ 4 = 0.11 cost/serving (EP)

Glossary of Menu and Cooking Terms

à la (ah lah) French. In the manner of.

à la carte (ah lah cart′) French. On the menu, but not part of a meal, usually prepared as ordered and individually priced.

à la king French. Served in cream sauce containing green bell pepper, pimento, and mushrooms.

à la mode (ah lah mohd′) French. When applied to desserts, means with ice cream. *À la mode boeuf* is a well-larded piece of beef cooked slowly in water with vegetables, similar to braised beef.

al dente (al den′ tay) Italian. The point in cooking pasta at which it is still fairly firm to the bite. The term is sometimes used interchangeably with *tender-crisp* when referring to vegetables.

allemande (ahl mahnd′) French. A smooth yellow sauce consisting of white sauce with the addition of cream, egg yolk, and lemon juice.

allumette A small matchstick cut, $\frac{1}{8} \times \frac{1}{8} \times 1$–2 inches.

amandine Served with almonds.

amaranth Small grain about the size of a poppy seed. High in protein. Doubles when cooked in liquid.

antipasto (ahn tee pahs′ toe) Italian. Appetizer; a course consisting of relishes, vegetables, fish, or cold cuts.

AP As purchased weight. The weight of an item before trimming or other preparation (as opposed to edible portion weight, or EP).

appetizer A small portion of hot or cold food usually served as a first course.

aromatics Herbs and spices used to enhance the flavor and fragrance of food.

arroz (ah ros′) The Spanish-American word for rice.

aspic A jellied meat juice or liquid held together with gelatin.

au gratin (oh grah′ ton) French. Made with crumbs, scalloped. Often refers to dishes made with cheese sauce.

au jus (oh zhu′) French. Meat served in its natural juices or gravy.

au lait (oh lay) French. Served or prepared with milk. Often with beverages, as in *café au lait*.

au naturel French. Served in its natural state without cooking.

bake To cook in the oven by dry heat.

barbecue To cook on a grill or spit over hot coals, or in an oven, basting intermittently with a highly seasoned sauce.

bar-le-duc (bahr luh dük′) French. A preserve made of currants and honey. It frequently forms a part of the cheese course.

barley Grain low in gluten and high in protein. Quadruples when cooked in liquid.

baron Double sirloin of beef.

baste To moisten meat while roasting to add flavor and to prevent drying of the surface. Melted fat or meat drippings may be used for basting.

batch cooking Dividing the estimated amount needed into smaller quantities and cooking as required to meet the demand.

baton/batonnet A small stick cut, $\frac{1}{4} \times \frac{1}{4} \times 2$–$2\frac{1}{2}$ inches.

batter Flour and liquid mixture, usually combined with other ingredients, thin enough to pour or drop from a spoon.

béarnaise (bay ar nayz′) French. Sauce of clarified butter, egg yolks, vinegar or white wine, onion, and spices.

beat To mix ingredients with a rotating motion, using a spoon, wire whip, or the paddle attachment of a mixer.

béchamel (bay sha mel′) French. A cream sauce made with equal parts of chicken stock and cream or milk.

beurre (buhr) French. Butter.

beurre blanc (buhr blanhk) French. A light-colored butter sauce made from butter, shallots, and white wine. May be finished with fresh herbs or other seasonings. Often called *white butter*.

beurre composé (burr kom-poz-ay) Softened butter with flavorings added. Also known as *compound butter*.

beurre manié (burr man-yay) A well-blended mixture of 50 percent softened butter and 50 percent flour (by weight). Used to thicken and give added sheen and flavor to soups and sauces.

beurre noir (burr nwor) Butter browned in a pan until dark, sometimes flavored with vinegar. Often called *black butter*.

beurre noisette (burr nwah-zett) Butter heated in a pan until lightly browned hazelnut color. Often called *hazelnut butter* or *brown butter*.

beurre rouge (burr rooge) A reddish-colored butter sauce made from butter, shallots, and red wine.

bisque (bisk) French. A thick soup usually made from fish or shellfish. Also a frozen dessert. Sometimes defined as ice cream to which finely chopped nuts are added.

bitters Liquid used to flavor cocktails. A distillation of aromatic herbs, flowers, seeds, plant roots, and the like.

blackened A cooking technique that cooks food that has been coated with a seasoning (often Cajun) in a very hot skillet (usually cast iron). Blackened foods have a dark crispy crust that results from the hot pan and seasoning rub.

blanch To dip briefly in boiling water, then into cold water to stop the cooking.

blanquette (blang ket′) French. A white stew usually made with veal, lamb, or chicken.

blend To thoroughly mix two or more ingredients.

bleu (bluh) French. Blue.

boeuf (buff) French. Beef. *Boeuf à la jardinière* (buff a lah zhar de nyoyr) is braised beef with vegetables; *boeuf roti* (buff rotee) is roast beef.

boil To cook foods in water or a liquid in which the bubbles are breaking on the surface and steam is given off.

bombe (bahm) French. A frozen dessert made of a combination of two or more frozen mixtures packed in a round or melon-shaped mold.

bordelaise (bor d′layz′) French. Of Bordeaux. *Sauce bordelaise* is a sauce with Bordeaux wine as its foundation, with various seasonings added.

borscht (borsht) Russian. A soup made with beets and served with thick sour cream.

bouillabaisse (boo yah bes') French. A highly seasoned fish soup made with two or more kinds of fish.

bouillon (boo yon') French. Clear stock made by cooking vegetables, poultry, meat or fish in water.

bouquet (boo kay') Volatile oils that give aroma.

bouquet garni (boo kay' gar nee') French. Herbs and spices tied in a cloth bag, used for flavoring soups, stews, and sauces, then removed after cooking is completed. Classic herbs: parsley, thyme, and bay leaf.

bourguignon (bohr ghee n'yang') French. In the Burgundy style, especially a beef stew made with red wine (for which burgundy is noted).

braise (brays) French. To brown in a small amount of fat, cover, add a small amount of liquid, and cook slowly.

bran The high-fiber outer layer of a cereal grain.

bread To coat food with an egg-milk mixture and then bread crumbs before frying.

brew To cook in liquid to extract flavor, as with beverages.

brine A mixture of salt, water, and seasonings used to preserve food.

brioche (bree ohsh') French. A slightly sweetened rich bread used for rolls or babas.

brochette, à la (bro shet') French. Food arranged on a skewer and broiled.

broil To cook over or under direct heat, as in a broiler or over live coals.

broth A flavorful liquid obtained from the simmering of meats and/or vegetables.

brulé (broo-lay) French. Meaning burned, as in crème brulée.

brunoise (broo-nwah) Foods cut into cubes, $\frac{1}{8} \times \frac{1}{8} \times \frac{1}{8}$ inch. Foods are garnished with brunoise-size cut vegetables.

brush Cooking term meaning to apply a liquid with a pastry brush to the surface of food.

buckwheat Seed of a plant related to rhubarb. Marketed as buckwheat flour and kasha (roasted buckwheat groats).

buffet (boo fay') French. A table displaying a variety of food.

bulgur Wheat that is parched, steamed, and dried before being ground.

butterfly cut Boneless meat, fish, or shrimp cut nearly in half lengthwise and spread open like the wings of a butterfly to increase surface area and shorten cooking time.

cacciatore (ca chi a tor' ee) Italian. Stewed with tomatoes, onion, and garlic.

café au lait (ca fay' oh lay') French. Coffee with hot milk.

café noir (ca fay' nwar) French. Black coffee, after-dinner coffee.

canapé (can ah pay') French. An appetizer of meat, fish, egg, or cheese arranged on a bread base.

candy To preserve or cook with heavy syrup.

caper (kay' per) Small pickled bud from wild caper bush; used in salads and sauces.

capsaicin Compound in chiles that gives them their heat.

caramelize To heat sugar until a brown color and a characteristic flavor develops.

carte au jour (kart o zhur') French. Bill of fare or menu for the day.

caviar (cav ee ar') French. Salted roe of sturgeon or other large fish. May be black or red.

chantilly (shang te' ye) French. Foods containing whipped cream.

charlotte (shar' lot) French. Dessert with gelatin, whipped cream, fruit, or other flavoring, in a mold, garnished with ladyfingers.

chayote Also known as *mirliton* in Louisiana. Gourdlike fruit prepared in ways suitable for summer squash.

chiffonade (shee' fahn ahd) French. With thin strips or shreds of vegetables. Used raw in salad dressings or to garnish.

chill To refrigerate until thoroughly cold.

chop To cut food into fairly fine pieces with a knife or other chopping device.

choux paste (shoo paste) French. Cream puff batter.

chowder A thick soup of fish or vegetables and milk.

chutney (chut' ni) A sweet and sour condiment made of fruits and/or vegetables cooked with sugar, spices, and usually vinegar.

cilantro The pungent leaf of the coriander plant, also known as *Chinese parsley*. Used to season Asian and Mexican foods.

clarified butter Melted butter from which the milk and water have been removed, leaving pure butterfat. Clarification raises the smoke point of butter. Also called *drawn butter* and *ghee* when highly clarified.

clarify To make clear by skimming or adding egg white and straining.

cloche (klosh) French. Bell, dish cover. *Sous cloche* (soo klosh) means under cover.

coat To cover the entire surface with flour, fine crumbs, sauce, batter, or other food as required.

cocktail An appetizer, either a beverage or a light, highly seasoned food, served before a meal.

coddle To simmer gently in liquid for a short time.

compote (kom' poht) French. Mixed fruit, either raw or stewed in syrup; a stemmed serving dish.

compound butter Butter combined with herbs or other seasonings and used to sauce vegetables and grilled or broiled meats. Also known as *beurre composé* (French).

condiment An aromatic mixture, such as pickles, chutney, and some sauces and relishes, that accompanies food.

consommé (kon so may') French. A clear meat or fish broth that has been clarified.

convection A method of heat transfer in which heat is transmitted through the circulation of air.

converted (parboiled) rice A specially processed long-grain rice that has been partially cooked under steam pressure, redried, then milled and polished.

core The center of a fruit. May be seeds as in an apple or pear or woody as in a pineapple.

cornichon French. Crisp tart pickles made from tiny cucumbers (gherkins).

coulis (koo-lees) A sauce made from a purée of vegetables or fruit.

court bouillon (cor boo yon') French. Water simmered with seasonings, vegetables, and vinegar or wine. Used for poaching vegetables, fish, and shellfish.

couscous Granular semolina usually cooked by steaming.

cream To mix fat and sugar until soft, smooth, and "creamy."

crème French. A word for cream.

crème anglaise (crem ahn-glas) Vanilla custard sauce. Also called *stirred custard*.

crème chantilly (crem chan-tee) Whipped heavy cream flavored with sugar and vanilla.

crème de French. Means *cream of.* Often used to describe a sweet liqueur, as in *crème de cacao* (chocolate), *crème de cassis* (black currant), and *crème de menthe* (mint).

crème fraiche (crem fresh) Very heavy cream (35 percent butterfat), cultured to give it a thick consistency and a slightly tangy flavor; similar to sour cream but not as acidic.

creole (kre′ ohl) French. Foods containing meat or vegetables with tomatoes, celery, peppers, onions, and other seasonings.

crepe (krayp) French. Thin, delicate pancake, often rolled and stuffed, served as appetizer, entrée, or dessert. *Crepe suzette* is a small, very thin and crisp pancake served for tea or as dessert.

crisp To make foods firm and brittle, as in chilling vegetables or heating cereals or crackers in the oven to remove excessive moisture.

critical control point A step during the processing of food when a mishandling or temperature mistake can result in the transmission, growth, or survival of pathogenic bacteria.

croissant (krwa sang′) French. Crescent; applied to rolls and confectionery of crescent shape.

croquette (crow ket′) Mixture of chopped, cooked meat, poultry, fish, or vegetables bound with thick cream sauce, shaped, breaded, and fried.

croustade (krus tad′) A toasted case or shell of bread.

croute, en (awn croot) A food encased in a bread or pastry crust.

croutons (kroo tons) Bread cubes, toasted, for use in garnishing soups and salads.

crudités (croo dee tay′) French. Raw vegetables.

cube To cut into $\frac{1}{2}$-inch squares.

cuisine French. Term referring to a specific style of cooking (as in *Asian cuisine*). *Haute cuisine* refers to food prepared in an elaborate, special, or gourmet manner.

curry (kur′ ee) Highly spiced condiment from India; a stew seasoned with curry.

cut in To cut a solid fat into flour with knives or mixer until fat particles are of desired size.

cutlet Thin slice of meat, usually breaded, for frying; also croquette mixture made in a flat shape.

deep fry To cook in fat deep enough for food to float.

deglaze To dilute and wash down pan juices and browned pieces by adding liquid.

de la maison (de lah may zon′) French. Specialty of the house.

demitasse (deh mee tahss′) French. Small cup of black coffee served after dinner.

dice To cut into $\frac{1}{4}$-inch cubes.

dot To scatter small bits of butter or margarine over surface of food.

dough A mixture of flour, liquid, and other ingredients, thick enough to roll or knead.

drawn butter Melted butter.

dredge To thoroughly coat a food with flour or other fine substance.

drippings Fat and liquid residue from frying or roasting meat or poultry.

drizzle To pour a liquid in a very thin stream over food.

du jour (doo zhoor′) French. Of the day, such as *soup of the day.*

dust To sprinkle lightly with flour.

eau (oh) French. Water.

eclair (ay klair′) French. Finger-shaped cream puff pastry filled with whipped cream or custard.

edamame (eh-dah-mah-meh) Green soybean.

egg and crumb To dip a food into diluted, slightly beaten egg and dredge with crumbs. This treatment is used to prevent soaking of the food with fat or to form a surface easily browned.

egg wash A mixture of beaten eggs (whites, whole eggs, yolks) and liquid (milk or water), used to coat bread dough prior to baking, to add sheen.

emulsion A mixture of two or more liquids, of which one is a fat or oil and the other is water-based, so that tiny globules of one are suspended in the other. Emulsions may be temporary, permanent, or semipermanent.

enchilada (en chee lah′ dah) Mexican. Tortillas filled and rolled, served with sauce.

en cocotte (ahn ko cot′) French. An individual casserole.

entrée (ahn′ tray) French. The main course of a meal or a single dish served before the main course of an elaborate meal.

EP Edible portion. The weight of an item after trimming and preparation (as opposed to AP weight, or as purchased weight). Edible portion may not all be edible, as in the case of a bone-in chicken.

espagnole (ays pah nyol′) French. Brown sauce.

farci (far′ see) French. Stuffed.

fermentation The breakdown of carbohydrates into carbon dioxide gas and alcohol, usually through the action of yeast on sugar.

filé (fee-lay) A seasoning and thickening agent made from dried, ground sassafras leaves. Used primarily in gumbos.

filet or fillet (fee lay′) French. A boneless cut of meat, fish, or poultry.

fines herbes (fen zerb′) French. A mixture of herbs, classically chervil, chives, parsley, and tarragon.

flake To break into small, dry, flat, flakelike pieces, usually with a fork.

flambé (flam bay′) French. To flame, using alcohol as the burning agent.

flan In France, a filled pastry; in Spain, a custard.

florentine A food containing or placed upon spinach.

fold in To blend an ingredient into a batter by cutting vertically through the mixture, and turning over and over by sliding the implement across the bottom of the mixing bowl with each turn.

fond French. A French name for stock, as in *fond blanc* (white stock), *fond brun* (brown stock), and *fond de vegetal* (vegetable stock).

fork tender A test for doneness. When foods are fork tender, they should be easily pierced or cut by a fork.

frappé (fra pay′) French. Mixture of fruit juices frozen to a mush.

French fry To cook in a deep-fryer.

fricassee (frik a see′) To cook by browning in a small amount of fat, then stewing or steaming; most often applied to fowl or veal cut into pieces.

frijoles (free hol′ ays) Mexican. Beans cooked with fat and seasonings.

frittata (free-tah-ta) An open-faced omelet.

fritter A deep-fat fried batter containing meat, vegetables, or fruit.

frizzle To pan fry in a small amount of fat until edges curl.

froid (frwä) French. Cold.

frothy A cooking term referring to mixtures that are foamy with tiny light bubbles.

fry To cook in hot fat. The food may be cooked in a small amount of fat (also called *sauté* or *pan-fry*), or in a deep layer of fat (also called *deep-fat fry*).

garam masala A spice blend made from roasted and ground spices. Used often in East Indian dishes.

garde-manger (garhd e mah zha′) French. Pantry chef/station. Responsible for cold food preparation.

garni (gar nee′) French. Garnish. An edible decoration or accompaniment to a food item.

gelatinization A phase in the process of thickening a liquid with starch in which starch molecules swell to form a network that traps water molecules.

ghee Butter that has been clarified, then simmered until all of the moisture evaporates and the milk solids begin to brown. Nutty, caramel-like flavor and aroma. Has a smoke point higher than regular clarified butter (375 °F) and can be used for light sautéing.

glacé (glah say′) French. Iced, frozen, or coated with sugar syrup.

glaze To make a shiny surface. In meat preparation, a jellied broth applied to the meat surface; in breads and pastries, a wash of egg or syrup; for doughnuts and cakes, a coating with a sugar preparation.

gluten An elastic protein formed when hard wheat flour is moistened and agitated. Gluten gives yeast doughs their elasticity.

goulash (goo′ lash) Hungarian. Thick beef or veal stew with vegetables, seasoned with paprika.

grand sauce One of several basic sauces that are used in the preparation of many other small sauces. The grand sauces are demi-glace, veloute, béchamel, hollandaise, and tomato. Also called *mother sauce*.

gratinée (grah teen ay′) French. To brown a food sprinkled with cheese or bread crumbs; or a food covered with a sauce that turns brown under a broiler flame or over intense heat.

grate To rub food against a coarse serrated surface (grater) to form small particles or shreds.

grease To rub lightly with fat.

griddle A heavy metal surface, which may be either built into a stove or heated by its own gas or electric elements. Cooking is done directly on the griddle.

grill To cook by direct heat. May be on an open grid over a heat source or on a flat cooking surface such as a griddle.

grind To change a food to small particles by putting through a grinder or food chopper.

grits Coarsely ground corn, served either boiled, or boiled and then fried.

gumbo A rich, thick Creole soup containing okra or filé.

HACCP (Hazard Analysis Critical Control Points) An established plan and monitoring system used to minimize or prevent a safety risk or hazard as food moves through a foodservice facility. Requires establishing standards and controls for time and temperature and safe handling practices.

harissa A fiery-hot condiment made with hot chiles, garlic, and spices. Traditional accompaniment for couscous.

herbs Aromatic plants used for seasoning and garnishing of foods.

herbs de Provence (ehrb duh proh vawns) A seasoning mixture of herbs commonly used to season meat, poultry, and vegetables in southern France. Mixture classically includes lavender, marjoram, rosemary, sage, summer savory, and thyme.

hollandaise (hol′ ahn days) French, of Dutch origin. Sauce of eggs, butter, lemon juice, and seasonings; served hot with fish or vegetables.

hors d'oeuvre (oh durv′) French. Small portions of food served as appetizers.

induction cooking A cooking technology that uses magnetic energy to heat the cooking vessel.

infusion To steep an aromatic or other item in liquid to extract the flavor.

IQF Individually quick-frozen.

Italienne (e tal yen′) French. Italian style.

jalapeño A hot pepper used for seasoning Mexican food.

jardinière (zhar de nyayr′) French. Mixed vegetables in a savory sauce or soup.

jicama Tuberous root used in salads.

julienne (zhu lee en′) French. Food cut into small stick-shape pieces, approximately $\frac{1}{8} \times \frac{1}{8} \times 1$–2 inches.

jus (zhoo) French. Juice or gravy.

jus lié (zhew lee-ay) An arrowroot- or cornstarch-thickened brown sauce often used as a demi-glace.

kasha Roasted buckwheat groats (the hulled crushed seed).

kebobs Marinated meat and vegetables cooked on skewers.

kippers Lightly salted and smoked fish.

knead To work dough with a pressing motion accompanied by folding and stretching.

kolache (ko′ lahch) Bohemian. Fruit-filled bun.

kosher (ko′ sher) Food handled in accordance with Jewish religious customs.

kuchen (koo′ ken) German. Cake, not necessarily sweet.

lait (lay) French. Milk.

lard To insert small strips of fat into or on top of uncooked lean meat or fish to give flavor or prevent dryness.

lebkuchen (lab koo′ ckhen) German. Famous German cake; sweet cake or honey cake.

leek Seasoning vegetable resembling a large spring onion with wide leaves, always cooked.

legumes The seeds of certain plants, including beans and peas, which are eaten for their earthy flavor and high nutritional value.

limpa Swedish rye bread.

liqueur Sweet and syrupy alcoholic beverage made by mixing or re-distilling liquor with fruits, flowers, spices, or other flavorings. Also known as a cordial.

liquor An alcoholic beverage made by distilling grains or other foods.

lox Yiddish. Smoked salmon.

lyonnaise (lee′ oh nayz) French. Seasoned with onions and parsley, as in lyonnaise potatoes.

macédoine (mah say dwan′) French. Mixture or medley of cut vegetables or fruits cut in uniform pieces.

maitre d'hôtel (mai tre doh tel′) French. Steward. *Maître d'hôtel butter* is a well-seasoned mixture of butter, minced parsley, and lemon juice.

marinade (mah ree nahd′) French. Mixture of oil, acid, and seasonings used to flavor and tenderize meats and vegetables; French dressings often used as marinades.

marinate To steep a food in a marinade long enough to modify its flavor.

marzipan (mahr′ zi pan) Powdered sugar and almond paste colored and formed into fruit and vegetable shapes.

mask To coat a food with a thick sauce before it is served. Cold foods may be masked with a mayonnaise mixture or white sauce, which gels after chilling.

medallion A small, round piece of meat or fish.

melt To liquefy by the application of heat.

meringue (mah rang′) Stiffly beaten egg white and sugar mixture used as a topping for pies or other desserts, or formed into small cakes or cases and browned in the oven.

merunière, à la (meh nyair′) French. Floured, sautéed in butter and served with butter sauce and lemon and sprinkled with chopped parsley; usually refers to fish.

Milanaise (me lan ayz′) French. Food cooked in a style developed in Milan, Italy. Implies the use of pasta and cheese with a suitable sauce, often béchamel.

mince To chop food into very small pieces—not so fine and regular as grinding, yet finer than those produced by chopping.

minestrone (mee ne stroh′ nay) Italian. Thick vegetable soup with beans and pasta.

mirepoix (meer′ pwa) French. Mixture of chopped vegetables used in flavoring soup stock, usually 25 percent carrots, 50 percent onions, and 25 percent celery.

mirliton Also known as chayote. Gourdlike fruit prepared in ways suitable for summer squash.

mise en place (meez oh plahss′) French. The preparation, organization, and setup before production. Means *everything in place*.

mix To combine two or more ingredients by stirring.

mocha (moh′ ka) Coffee flavor or combination of coffee and chocolate.

mollusks Shellfish with a soft body and no internal skeleton and a hard outer shell.

monosodium glutamate (MSG) White crystalline material made from vegetable protein, used to enhance flavor of food.

Mornay (mohr nay′) French. Sauce of thick cream, eggs, cheese, and seasonings.

mother of vinegar Slimy substance made up of bacteria that forms in vinegar. Not harmful. Should be discarded.

mousse (moose) French. Frozen dessert with fruit or other flavors, whipped cream and sugar; also a cold dish of puréed chicken or fish with egg whites, gelatin, and unsweetened whipped cream.

mulligatawny (mul i ga taw′ ni) A highly seasoned thick soup, of Indian origin, flavored with curry powder and other spices.

napoleons Puff pastry kept together in layers with a custard filling, cut into portion-size rectangles, and iced.

Neopolitan (also *harlequin* and *panachée*) Molded dessert of two to four kinds of ice cream or ices arranged in layers.

Nesselrode pudding Frozen dessert with a custard foundation to which chestnut purée, fruit, and cream have been added.

Newburg, à la Creamed dish with egg yolk added, flavored with sherry; most often applied to lobster, but may be used with other foods.

noisette (nooa zet′) French. Nut-brown color; may imply nut-shaped. A small round piece of lean meat. *Potatoes noisette* are potatoes cut into the shape and size of hazelnuts and browned in fat.

nouvelle cuisine French. "New cooking." A culinary movement emphasizing freshness, lightness, and innovative combinations of foods.

oeuf (oof) French. Egg.

oven spring The rapid initial rise of yeast dough when placed in a hot oven. Heat accelerates the growth of yeast, which produces more carbon dioxide gas and also causes this gas to expand.

paella (pä ay′ yah) Spanish. Dish with rice, seafood, chicken, and vegetables, usually served in a wide shallow pan in which it is cooked.

pan-broil To cook, uncovered, on hot metal, such as a fry pan, pouring off the fat as it accumulates. Liquid is never added.

pan-fry To cook in a skillet in a small amount of fat.

panko Flaky breadcrumbs used in Japanese cooking for coating fried foods.

papillote (pah pe yote′) French. A cooking method in which food is wrapped in paper and heated to a high enough temperature so that steam is produced and the food cooks in its own steam.

parboil To boil until partially cooked, the cooking being completed by another method.

parch To cook in dry heat until slightly browned.

parchment Heat-resistant paper used in cooking for lining baking pans.

parcooking Partially cooking a food.

pare To cut off the outside covering, usually with a knife.

parfait (par fay′) French. A mixture containing whipped cream, egg, and syrup that is frozen without stirring. May be ice cream layered with fruit or syrup in parfait glasses.

parmigiana (par mee zhan′ ah) Italian. Parma style, particularly veal, chicken, or eggplant covered with tomato sauce, mozzarella cheese, and Parmesan cheese and browned under the broiler or in the oven.

pasta Italian. Any of a large family of flour paste products, such as macaroni, spaghetti, and noodles.

paste Soft, smooth mixture of a dry ingredient and a liquid.

pastrami (pahs tram′ ee) Yiddish. Boneless meat cured with spices and smoked.

pâté (pah tay′) French. Paste, dough; highly seasoned meat paste used as an appetizer.

pâté de foie gras (pah tay d′fwah grah′) French. Paste of fat goose livers.

patty shell Shell or case of pastry or puff paste used for individual portions of creamed mixtures.

peel To strip off the outside covering.

persillade (payr se yad′) French. Served with or containing parsley.

pesto Italian. A thick puréed mixture of an herb, usually basil, and oil used as a sauce for pasta. May also contain pine nuts, grated cheese, garlic, and other seasonings.

petit pois (puh tee pooá) French. A fine grade of very small peas with a delicate flavor.

petits fours (pe teet foor′) French. Small fancy cakes frosted and decorated.

phyllo dough Greek. Extremely thin pastry dough that produces a flaky pastry.

picante A highly spiced tomato sauce used as a condiment with Mexican foods.

pilaf or pilau (′pih lahf or pih low) Turkish. Dish of rice cooked with meat, fish, or poultry, and seasoned with spices. A technique for cooking grains, in which the grain is sautéed briefly in butter, then simmered in stock or water with various seasonings.

piquant (pee kahnt′) French. Sharp, highly seasoned.

pizza (peet′ zah) Italian. Flat yeast bread covered with tomato, cheese, and meat, or other toppings.

plank Hardwood board used for cooking and serving broiled meat or fish. *Planked steak* is a broiled steak served on a plank and garnished with a border of suitable vegetables.

poach To cook gently in a hot liquid, held just below the boiling point, the original shape of the food being retained.

polanaise (po lo nays′) French. Dishes prepared with bread crumbs, chopped eggs, browned butter, and chopped parsley.

polenta (poh lent′ ah) Italian. Thick cornmeal mush; cheese is usually added before serving.

pollo (po′ yo) Italian. Italian and Spanish-American term for chicken.

pomme de terre (pom de tare′) French. Potato; literally, *apple of the earth.*

potage (po tazh′) French. Soup, usually of a thick type.

pot-au-feu (poh toh fu′) French. Meat and vegetables boiled together in broth.

pot roast To cook large cuts of meat by braising.

prawn Large shrimp.

prix fixe (prefix) Multicourse meal with a fixed price. May offer choice within a menu category.

preheat To heat oven or other cooking equipment to the desired temperature before putting in the food.

proof To allow yeast dough to rise.

prosciutto (pro shoot′ toh) Italian. Ham, usually thinly sliced and served as an appetizer or as a component in veal dishes.

puff paste Rich dough, made flaky by repeated folding and rolling.

pulse The edible seeds of various leguminous crops (peas, beans, lentils).

purée (pu ray′) French. Foods rubbed through a sieve; also a nutritious vegetable soup in which milk or cream is seldom used.

quiche (keesh) Custard, cheese, and seasonings baked in a pie shell and served warm.

quinoa Grain high in protein. Grown primarily in South America.

ragout (ra goo′) French. A thick, well-seasoned, rich stew.

ramekin (ram′ e kin) Small baking dish for individual portions.

rarebit Mixture of white sauce, cheese, and seasonings.

ravioli (rav vee oh′ lee) Italian. Bite-size cases of pasta dough filled with finely ground meat, cheese, and spinach; served with a highly seasoned tomato sauce.

reconstitute To restore concentrated foods to their normal state, usually by adding water, as in fruit juice and milk.

reduce To boil down, evaporating liquid from a cooked dish.

refritos Twice-cooked Mexican beans that are boiled once and fried once. Also called *refried beans.*

rehydrate To cook or soak dehydrated foods or restore water lost during drying.

remoulade (ray moo lad′) French. Pungent sauce made of hard-cooked eggs, mustard, oil, vinegar, and seasonings. Served with cold dishes.

risotto (ri sot′ toh) Italian. Rice that has been sautéed with onion and other aromatics and then combined with stock. Adding stock slowly while stirring produces a creamy texture with the rice grains still *al dente.*

rissolé (ree saw lay′) French. Savory meat mixture encased in rich pastry and fried in deep fat.

roast To cook uncovered in oven by dry heat, usually meat or poultry.

roe Eggs of fish.

rosette (roh zet′) French. Thin, rich batter made into fancy shapes with special irons and fried in deep fat.

roulade (roo lahd′) French. Rolled thin piece of meat, usually stuffed and roasted or braised.

roux (roo) French. A browned mixture of equal parts flour and fat (by weight) used as a thickener for sauces, soups, and stews.

sabayon (sa by on′) French. Custard sauce with wine added.

sachet d'epices or sachet (sah-shay day-pea-say) French. Aromatic ingredients (herbs and spices) tied in a cheesecloth bag and used to flavor stocks and other liquids.

salsa A highly spiced tomato sauce used as a condiment with Mexican foods.

sauerbraten (sour brah′ ten) German. Beef marinated in spiced vinegar, pot-roasted, and served with gingersnap gravy.

sauté (soh tay′) French. To cook in a small amount of fat.

savory Spiced or seasoned foods, as opposed to sweet foods. Also a family of herbs.

scald To heat a liquid to a point just below boiling; to pour boiling water over or dip food briefly into boiling water.

scallion An onion that has not developed a bulb.

scallop To bake food cut into pieces and covered with a liquid or sauce and crumbs. The food and sauce may be mixed together or arranged in alternate layers in a baking dish, with or without crumbs. *Escalloped* is a synonymous term. A thin boneless slice of meat. A shellfish (mollusk).

scallopine (skol a pee′ nee) Italian. Small flat pieces of meat, usually veal, sautéed and served in a sauce.

scone (scahn) Scottish quick bread containing currants.

score To make shallow lengthwise and crosswise slits on the surface of meat.

sear To brown the surface of meat quickly at high temperatures.

semolina Coarsely milled hard wheat endosperm used for gnocchi, some pasta, and couscous.

set Allow to stand until congealed, as in gelatin and puddings.

shallot Small onion having a stronger but more mellow flavor than the common variety.

shirr To break eggs into a dish, cover with cream and crumbs, and bake.

shortening Fat suitable for baking or frying.

simmer To cook in a liquid in which bubbles form slowly and break just below the surface.

skewer Pin of metal or wood used for fastening meat or poultry while cooking; or long pins used for holding bits of food for broiling or roasting.

skim To remove surface fat or foam from liquid mixture.

sliver To cut into long, slender pieces, as in slivered almonds.

smorgasbord (smor gas bohrd′) Swedish. Arrangement of appetizers and other foods on a table in an attractive assortment.

sorbet (sor bay′) French. Sherbet made of several kinds of fruits.

soubise (soo′ bees) French. White sauce containing onion and sometimes parsley.

soufflé (soo flay′) French. A light, fluffy baked dish with beaten egg whites; may be sweet or savory.

soy sauce Chinese sauce made from fermented soybeans.

spaetzle (spet′ zel) Austrian. Fine noodles made by pressing batter through a colander into boiling water or broth.

spoon bread Southern corn bread baked in a casserole and served with a spoon.

springerle (spring′ er le) German. A Christmas cookie. The dough is rolled into a sheet and pressed with a springerle mold before baking.

spumoni (spoo moh′ nee) Italian. Rich ice cream made in different layers, usually containing fruit and nuts.

stabilizer An ingredient added to an emulsion to prevent it from separating.

steam To cook in steam with or without pressure. Steam may be applied directly to the food, as in a steamer, or to the vessel, as in a double boiler.

steam-jacketed kettle A kettle with double-layered walls, between which steam circulates, providing even heat for cooking stocks, soups, and sauces.

steep To cover with boiling water and let stand to extract flavors and colors.

stew To simmer in a small amount of liquid.

stir To mix food materials with a circular motion.

stir-fry To cook quickly in a small amount of oil over high heat, using a light tossing and stirring motion to preserve shape of food.

stock Liquid in which meat, fish, poultry, or vegetables have been cooked.

stroganoff (stro′ gan off) Russian. Sautéed beef in sauce of sour cream, with mushrooms and onions.

strudel (stroo′ dl) German. Pastry of flaky, paper-thin dough filled with fruit.

sweating Cooking vegetables (usually) in a covered pan with a small amount of fat over low heat, without browning, until the food softens and releases moisture.

table d'hôte (tabl doht′) French. Meal at a fixed price.

tacos (tah′ cos) Mexican. Rolled sandwiches of tortillas filled with meat, onions, lettuce, and hot sauce.

tamale (ta mah′ lee) Mexican. Highly seasoned meat mixture rolled in cornmeal mush, wrapped in corn husks, and steamed.

tart Small pie or pastry.

tartar sauce Mayonnaise to which chopped pickles, onions, and other seasonings have been added; usually served with fish.

tender-crisp The point in cooking vegetables at which they are firm and slightly crisp.

terrine (tay reen′) French. Tureen, an earthenware pot resembling a casserole. *Chicken en terrine* is chicken cooked and served in a tureen.

timbale Thin fried case for holding creamed mixtures; or unsweetened baked custard with meat, poultry, or vegetables.

toast To apply direct heat until the surface of the food is browned.

tofu Bean curd.

torte (tor′ te) German. Rich cake made from crumbs, eggs, and nuts; or meringue in the form of a cake.

tortilla (tohr tee′ yah) Mexican. A round thin unleavened flour or cornmeal cake baked on a griddle.

toss To mix ingredients lightly without crushing.

tournedos (tur ne′ doe) Spanish. A small round filet of beef. French, a small cut from the tenderloin of beef.

trifle English. Dessert made with sponge cake soaked in fruit juice and wine and layered with jam, custard, almonds, and whipped cream.

truffle A dark mushroomlike fungus, found chiefly in France. Used mainly for garnishing and flavor.

truss To tie or skewer poultry or meat so that it will hold its shape while cooking.

turnover Food encased in pastry and baked.

tutti frutti Mixed fruit.

value added Raw or preprocessed foods whose value has been increased through the addition of ingredients or processes that make them more attractive to the buyer and/or more readily usable by the consumer.

velouté (ve loo tay′) French. A rich white sauce, usually made of chicken or veal broth.

vinaigrette (vin nay greht) French. A temporary emulsion of 3 parts oil and 1 part vinegar and often seasoned with herbs and spices. Wine or lemon juice is often substituted for some of the vinegar.

whip To beat rapidly and increase volume by the incorporation of air.

Wiener schnitzel (ve′ ner schnit sel) German. Breaded cutlets, frequently served with tomato sauce or lemon.

wonton Stuffed dumplings cooked in chicken broth.

Yorkshire pudding English. Accompaniment for roast beef, a popoverlike mixture baked in drippings of the roast.

zest Colored peel of citrus fruits, such as orange or lemon, which contains aromatic oil.

zwieback (tsvee′ bahk) German. Toasted bread, crisp and slightly sweet.

Index

Note: Pages with recipes are in bold type.
Pages containing tables are followed by "t."